Lithuanian Grammar

Lietuvių kalbos gramatika

Vytautas Ambrazas, Emma Geniušienė,
Aleksas Girdenis, Nijolė Sližienė, Dalija Tekorienė,
Adelė Valeckienė, Elena Valiulytė

Lithuanian Grammar

Edited by Vytautas Ambrazas

baltos lankos

INSTITUTE OF THE LITHUANIAN LANGUAGE

Supported by the Lithuanian Government,
the Lithuanian National Science Foundation,
the State Commission of the Lithuanian Language,
and the Soros Foundation

Designer Vida Kuraitė

© Vytautas Ambrazas, author and editor, 1997
© Emma Geniušienė, author, translator, 1997
© Aleksas Girdenis, author, 1997
© Nijolė Sližienė, author, 1997
© Adelė Valeckienė, author, 1997
© Elena Valiulytė, author, 1997
© Dalija Tekorienė, author, translator, 1997
© Lionginas Pažūsis, translator, 1997
© Institute of the Lithuanian Language, 1997
© Baltos lankos, 1997

Rinko ir maketavo BALTOS LANKOS
Printed in Lithuania
ISBN 9986-813-22-0

PREFACE

This book is the first comprehensive description of the grammatical structure of Lithuanian, including phonology, morphonology, morphology and syntax, to be published in English. The aim of this volume is to make the Lithuanian language more accessible to the international linguistic community and to all those who are interested in Lithuanian.

The Lithuanian language belongs to the Baltic branch of the Indo-European language family, Latvian being the other surviving Baltic language. Lithuanian is the official language of the independent state of Lithuania. It is spoken by about 3.5 million people, its usage covering all spheres of social, cultural, and scientific communication. A remarkable feature of Lithuanian is dialect diversity, the main dialect areas being High Lithuanian (*aukštaičių tarmė̃*) and Low Lithuanian, or Samogitian (*žemaičių tarmė̃*). Standard Lithuanian is based on the West High Lithuanian dialect spoken in the southern part of the area.

This volume is essentially a description of the grammatical system of present-day Standard Lithuanian. Dialectal and historical data are dealt with insofar as they have a bearing on grammatical variation current in the standard language.

Lithuanian is the most conservative of the living Indo-European languages: it has best preserved many archaic features which can be directly observed and investigated in their present-day usage. Antoine Meillet wrote: "He who wants to know how our forefathers spoke should go and listen to how a Lithuanian peasant talks". From the typological viewpoint, Lithuanian is particularly important because of many unique features, including its rich inflection, a distinctive synthesis of tonic and dynamic accent and an extremely variable word order which reflects the complicated relations between the communicative and the syntactic levels of discourse. All this accounts for the importance of Lithuanian for both diachronic and synchronic linguistics.

The earliest grammars of Lithuanian, by Daniel Klein (1653, 1654) and Sapūnas-Schultz (1673), appeared more than a century after Mažvydas' Catechism (1547), the first printed Lithuanian book. These grammars served as a basis for most of the grammars of Lithuanian written in the 18th–19th centuries. The *Litauische*

Grammatik by August Schleicher (1856) firmly established Lithuanian in comparative Indo-European linguistics, and the *Grammatik der littauischen Sprache* by Friedrich Kurschat (1876) laid the foundation for Lithuanian accentology. The grammars of Jonas Jablonskis (1901, 1911, 1922) played a major role in the development and codification of Standard Lithuanian. Among grammars of the subsequent period, the works of Jan Otrębski (1958–1966) and Alfred Senn (1966) deserve special mention. The most comprehensive so far is the three-volume Academy grammar (*Lietuvių kalbos gramatika*, ed. Kazys Ulvydas, 1965–1976). It contains a wealth of data from Standard Lithuanian as well as from dialects, folklore and old texts. The latest one-volume grammars (1985, 1994) and the present grammar have drawn heavily on the materials assembled in it.

Most Lithuanian grammars and most of the specialist literature are written in Lithuanian. So far, only a few introductions to Lithuanian or text-books for learners have been published in English[*]. Therefore, the present *Grammar* aims to fill the conspicuous gap in linguistic literature.

This *Grammar* comprises four parts: *Phonology*, *Morphonology*, *Morphology* and *Syntax*. *Phonology* deals with phonemes – the smallest linear linguistic units, while *Morphology* deals with word forms, their grammatical meanings and functions, and also with classes of words. Some derivational peculiarities are briefly treated here insofar as they are relevant for the characterization of word classes and their morphological categories. The rules of phonemic change considered in *Morphonology* are essential for the description of inflectional paradigms. In *Syntax*, the units of sentence structure (word groups, parts of the sentence) are distinguished and defined by the types of syntactic relations (interdependence, subordination and coordination) among word forms; they are further interpreted in terms of their semantic functions. Simple sentence patterns are distinguished according to the obligatory constituents whose number and form are determined by the valence properties of the predicate.

The present *Grammar* follows the long-established tradition in such important issues as classification of words into parts of speech, morphological categories, parts of the sentence and sentence types. But in many cases the traditional terms and inventories are modified with the aim of more distinct differentiation between the formal and the semantic levels of analysis. The basic principles of description employed here are outlined in the introductory sections of each part of the *Grammar*.

---

[*] L. Dambrauskas, A. Klimas, W.R. Schmalstieg. *Introduction to Modern Lithuanian*. New York, 1966; D. Tekorienė. *Lithuanian: Basic Grammar and Conversation*. Kaunas, 1990; A. Paulauskienė, L. Valeika. *Modern Lithuanian: A Textbook for Foreign Students*. Vilnius, 1994.

For the convenience of the reader, a list of the more important grammars of Lithuanian and other works on grammar (excepting literature on general theoretical issues) is provided at the end of the book, and references to literature in the body of this *Grammar* are dispensed with. For reasons of economy of presentation, many illustrative examples from authentic sources are abridged or adapted and their number is limited to the essential minimum. Stress is marked according to the Standard Lithuanian norm. The reader can find more information on certain issues and references to sources in the Academy grammars of 1965–1976, 1985 and 1994.

The present volume was produced by a group of linguists of the Institute of the Lithuanian Language and Vilnius University. Phonology and Morphonology were written by Aleksas Girdenis and translated by Lionginas Pažūsis; Morphology and Syntax were written by Vytautas Ambrazas, Nijolė Sližienė, Adelė Valeckienė and Elena Valiulytė in collaboration with Emma Geniušienė and Dalija Tekorienė. Some of the sections are based on the respective chapters of the earlier Academy grammars written by Adelė Laigonaitė (The Noun), Pranas Kniūkšta (The Numeral), Kazys Ulvydas (The Adverb), etc. The subject index was compiled by Artūras Judžentis. The preparation and publication of this book has been supported by grants from the Lithuanian Government, the Lithuanian National Science Foundation and the Soros Foundation.

The authors and the editor express their deep appreciation and gratitude to Prof. William R. Schmalstieg for checking through the English text of this volume and for valuable suggestions and criticism. Of course, we assume responsibility for all the shortcomings and possible errors.

Contents

I/ PHONOLOGY (1.1–6.10) 11
1. Spelling and transcription (1.1–5) 13
2. Theoretical preliminaries (2.1–5) 20
3. Vowels, diphthongs and semidiphthongs (3.1–7) 24
4. Consonants (4.1–14) 35
5. Syllable (5.1–4) 50
6. Prosodic (suprasegmental) features (6.1–10) 53

II/ MORPHONOLOGY (1.1–2.8) 59
1. Alternations of phonemes (1.1–24) 61
2. Accentuation (2.1–8) 77

III/ MORPHOLOGY (0.1–11.15) 85
   General remarks (0.1–7) 89
1. Noun (1.1–38) 93
2. Adjective (2.1–42) 134
3. Numeral (3.1–15) 165
4. Pronoun (4.1–43) 180
5. Verb (5.1–156) 220
6. Adverb (6.1–28) 377
7. Particles (7.1–15) 395
8. Prepositions (8.1–33) 404
9. Conjunctions (9.1–7) 424
10. Interjections (10.1–9) 432
11. Onomatopoeic words (11.1–15) 440

IV / SYNTAX (1.1–6.21) 449

1 Sentence and its structure (1.1–41) *453*
2 Word groups (2.1–156) *497*
3 The simple sentence (3.1–125) *599*
4 Extended sentences (4.1–24) *674*
5 Word order (5.1–31) *690*
6 The communicative types of sentences (6.1–22) *707*
7 The composite sentence (7.1–129) *717*

Selected bibliography 783
Subject index 787

I/Phonology

1 Spelling and transcription (1.1–5) 13
2 Theoretical preliminaries (2.1–5) 20
3 Vowels, diphthongs and semidiphthongs (3.1–7) 24
4 Consonants (4.1–14) 35
5 Syllable (5.1–4) 50
6 Prosodic (suprasegmental) features (6.1–10) 53
    Stress (6.1–5) 53
    Tonemes, or syllable accents (6.6–10) 55

1 SPELLING AND TRANSCRIPTION
Rašýba ir transkrìpcija

1.1 The Lithuanian alphabet has developed from the Latin alphabet under the influence of the writing systems of such languages as Polish, German, and Czech. The earliest manuscripts date from the early 16th century, and the first printed book, a catechism by Martynas Mažvydas, was published in 1547. The imperfections of spelling in early publications have led to numerous changes which took place in less remote periods: *ą, ę, į* and *ų* (with a diacritic mark attached below) were introduced to represent the nasalized vowels [ã:], [æ̃:], [ĩ:], and [ũ:] respectively which lost their nasal resonance later and coincided with the respective long vowels; *ė* came to stand for [e:], the digraphs *sz* and *cz* which had represented [š] and [č] respectively were replaced by the Czech letters *š* and *č*; the letters *w* and *ł* fell out of use and were replaced by *v* and *l* respectively, etc. The present-day Lithuanian alphabet took shape by the early 20th century.

Today the Lithuanian alphabet consists of 32 letters (each may be small or capital). Some sounds (not to mention biphonemic diphthongs) are represented by digraphs: *ch* = [x], *dz* = [ʣ], *dž* = [ʤ]; also *ie* and *uo*, representing monophonemic diphthongs [iɛ] and [uɔ]. Digraphs or sometimes trigraphs are also used to represent palatalized consonants before back vowels (see 1.3).

To indicate certain sounds in writing, auxiliary marks are added above or below some letters: *č* = [tʃ], *š* = [ʃ], *ž* = [ʒ], *ą* = [ɑ:], *ę* = [æ:], *į* = [i:], *ų* and *ū* = [u:], *ė* = [e:].

In scholarly and teaching texts (but not in common texts) diacritics are used to indicate word stress and syllable tonemes (the latter are sometimes called syllable accents or intonations, Lith. *príegaidės*). A grave accent (`) placed over a vowel shows short stressed syllables, e.g., *vìsas* ['vɪsas] 'whole'. Long stressed syllables may have one of the two syllable tonemes: an acute accent (´) indicates a sharp falling toneme, and a circumflex (~) is used to indicate a smooth rising toneme, cf.: *stóras* ['sto:ras] 'thick' and *dõras* ['do:ras] 'honest', *káulas* [`kɑ·ołas] 'bone' and *draũgas* ['drɑʊ·gas] 'friend', *kárštas* [`kɑ·rʃtas] 'hot' and *kaȓštis* ['kaȓʃtɪs] 'heat'. The falling toneme is also indicated by the grave accent (`) which is placed over the sequences of letters *ui* and *u, i + l, m, n, r* (also *o, e + i, l, m, n, r* in international words), e. g.: *gùiti* [`gʊɪtɪ] 'to drive', *pìlnas* [`pɪɫnas] 'full', *kùrmis* [`kʊɾmɪs] 'mole', *spòrtas* [ˈspɔrtas] 'sports'. The mark of the falling toneme is always placed over the first letter of a sequence representing a diphthong or a semidiphthong, whereas the circumflex is always placed over the second one (cf.: *gùiti* 'to drive' and *draũgas* 'friend', *kárštas* 'hot' and *karŝtis* 'heat').

In the chapters on phonology and morphonology in the present grammar, the international phonetic transcription is used (instead of the traditional Lithuanian phonetic transcription usually applied in the works on dialectology, phonology, and phonetics in Lithuania, see Table 1). Slants (/ /) enclose phonemic transcription, square brackets ([ ]) enclose phonetic transcription; peripheral sounds, which occur only in borrowings and onomatopoeic words, are given in angle brackets (<>).

1.2 **Vowels** are represented in writing by 12 letters: *a* [a, aː], *ą* [aː], *e* [ɛ, æː], *ė* [eː], *i* [ɪ], *y* and *į* [iː], *o* [oː, ɔ], *u* [o], *ū* and *ų* [uː]; monophonemic diphthongs [iɛ] and [uɔ] are represented by the above-mentioned digraphs *ie* and *uo* respectively.

The two pairs of letters – *y* and *į*, *ū* and *ų* – represent the same vowel phonemes, /iː/ and /uː/ respectively. The letters *a* and *ą*, *e* and *ę* mark different phonemes only in unstressed and final positions, cf.: *gražù* [graˈʒo] '(it's) nice' and *grąžà* [graːˈʒa] 'change', *nešì* [ɲɛˈʃɪ] '(you) carry' and *tęsì* [tæːˈsɪ] '(you) continue', *tà* [ˈta] 'that (NOM. SG. FEM)' and *tą* [ˈtaː] 'that (ACC. SG)'. In stressed non-final positions, they represent long vowels /aː/ and /æː/. The difference in representing these vowels in writing was determined by historical and morphological reasons. In the 16th and 17th centuries, the letters *ą, ę, į, ų* represented long nasalized vowels [ãː], [æ̃ː], [ĩː], [ũː] derived from the sequences [a, ɛ, ɪ, o] + [n]. Now the diacritic below a letter in most cases indicates an alternation of a vowel with the sequences [a, ɛ, ɪ, o] + [n] (cf.: *kąsti* 'to bite' and *kanda* '(he) bites', *siųsti* 'to send' and *siunčia* '(he) sends') or performs the role of a mark differentiating one grammatical form from the other, cf.: *klėtį* 'storehouse (ACC. SG)' and *klėty* 'storehouse (LOC. SG)'.

The letters *ą, ę, ė, į, y, ų, ū* and *o* (in native morphs) represent long (tense) vowels, whereas the letters *i* and *u* represent only short (lax) vowels. In stressed non-final syllable, the letters *a* and *e*, as a rule, correspond to long (in acuted diphthongs and diphthongal combinations also half-long) sounds, whereas in stressed final and unstressed syllables they correspond to short sounds (cf.: *ráktas* [ˈraːktas] 'key', *mẽdis* [ˈmæːdɪs] 'tree', *kárštas* [ˈkaːrʃtas] 'hot', *vérda* [ˈyæːrda] '(it) boils', but *galvà* [gaɫˈva] 'head', *miškè* [mʲɪˈʃkɛ] 'in the forest', *raktẽlis* [rakˈtæːlɪs] 'small key', *vežìmas* [vɛˈʒɪmas] 'cart'). In exceptional cases, the letters *a* and *e* may be used to represent the short vowels [a] and [ɛ] respectively in stressed non-final position, e.g.: *kàsti* [ˈkastɪ] 'to dig', *mèsiu* [ˈmɛsʲo] '(I) will throw' (see II.1.4); in international words, the letter *e* may facultatively correspond to a short closer (narrower) vowel sound, e.g. *poètas* = [pɔˈɛtas] or [pɔˈetas].

1.3 **Consonants** are represented in writing by 20 letters: *b, c, č, d, f, g, h, j, k, l, m, n, p, r, s, š, t, v, z, ž;* for three consonants the digraphs *ch, dz, dž* are used. These graphic signs (the only exception being *j*) represent non-palatalized (hard, velarised) consonants. The functional palatalization before back vowels is indicated by the letter *i* inserted between a consonant and a vowel, e. g.: *liáutis* [ˈlʲæˑoʈs] 'to cease', *džiùs* [ˈdʑʲos] '(it) will dry'. Before front vowels (represented by the letters *e, ę, ė, i, y, į*) and palatalized consonants, all consonants are also more or less palatalized (see 4.4), but in such positions their palatalization is not indicated in writing.

In some cases the Lithuanian [j] is not represented in writing either, e.g.: *ievà* [jiɛˈva] 'bird-cherry', *pāieškos* [ˈpaːjiɛʃkoːs] 'searching', *biològija* [bʲɪjɔˈɫɔɡʲɪjɛ] 'biology'. The graphemes *f, ch* and *h* are used to represent peripheral consonants which occur only in recent loanwords.

1.4 Lithuanian orthography (standardised spelling) is essentially morphonological (or morphological): the spelling of a word (or its form) is determined by its phonological structure and the effort to maintain the graphic form of a morph unchanged. Only in comparatively rare cases the historical (or traditional) principle is applied (the usage of the above-mentioned so-called 'nasal' vowel letters *ą, ę, į, ų* to represent long vowels derived from nasal vowels, the irregular representation of [j]). The phonological principle is paramount in cases when it does not contradict the morphonological principle or when a morphonological spelling differs too much from the representation of a real pronunciation. The standardised spelling reflects the phonological changes occurring at the morphological boundary between the root and suffixes (dissimilation, metathesis, degemination, etc.), cf.: *mèsti < mèt-ti* 'to throw', *vèsti < vèd-ti* 'to lead' and *mēta* '(he) throws', *vēda* '(he) leads'; *láuk < láuk-k* 'wait!', *dèk < dèg-k* 'burn, light!' and *láukia* '(he) waits', *dēga* '(it) burns, (he) lights'; *nèšiu < nèš-siu* '(I) will carry', *vèšiu < vèž-siu* '(I) will drive' and *nēša* '(he) carries', *vēža* '(he) drives'.

The representation of consonants in writing is basically morphonological: it ignores the neutralization of the opposition between voiced and voiceless consonants (and some other oppositions) before plosive or fricative consonants and sometimes in word-final position. For instance, *grąžtas* 'drill', *nèšdamas* 'carrying', *kàsčiau* '(I) would dig', *daũg* 'many, much' (cf.: *grę̃žia* '(he) drills', *nēša* '(he) carries', *kāsa* '(he) digs', *daũgelis* 'many'), but not **grą̃štas, *nèždamas, *kàščiau, *daũk*. Spelling also ignores the alternation of the stressed short vowels [a] and [ɛ] and their long correspondents [aː, æː], e.g.: *kàsti* [ˈkaʂʈɪ] 'to dig' : *kāsa* [ˈkaːsa] '(he) digs', *nèšti* [ˈnʲɛʃʈɪ] 'to carry' : *nēša* [ˈnʲæːʃa] '(he) carries'.

1.5 In dictionaries and other lists of words arranged in alphabetical order, *a* and *ą, e, ę* and *ė, i, y* and *į, u, ū* and *ų* are treated as if they were identical letters, even though they represent different sounds. Therefore the following alphabetical order is customary: *aržùs – ąsà – asambléja, ẽsti – ěsti – èstiškas, įkélti – ìkrai – ýla – ìlgas*.

The full set of letters in customary alphabetical order, their names and letter-sound correspondences in Standard Lithuanian are shown in Table 1. Names of the letters are important to know, because they are used to pronounce acronyms: *JTO* [jɔtʲtʲeːˈoː] 'UNO', *JAV* [jɔtaːˈjeː] 'USA' (but *NATO* [ˈnaːtɔ] 'NATO').

Table 1. **Letter-sound correspondence in Standard Lithuanian**

Letters and digraphs	Their names	Sounds		Examples		
		IPA transcription	Traditional Lithuanian transcription	Spelling	IPA transcription	Traditional Lithuanian transcription
A a	[ˈaː]	[a]	[a]	dariaũ	[daˈrʲæoˑ]	[darʲæũ]
		[aː]	[aˑ]	dãro	[ˈdaːroː]	[dãˑroˑ]
Ą ą	[ˈaː] nósinė	[aː]	[aˑ]	ką́sti	[ˈkaːsʲtʲɪ]	[ką́ˑsʲtʲi]
B b	[beː]	[b]	[b]	bárti	[ˈbarʲtʲɪ]	[bárʲtʲi]
		[bʲ]	[bʲ]	bim̃bia	[ˈbʲɪmʲˑbʲɛ]	[bim̃ʲbʲæ]
C c	[ˈtseː]	[ts]	[ts]	cùkrus	[ˈtsokros]	[tsùkrus]
		[tsʲ]	[tsʲ]	cỹpti	[ˈtsʲiːpʲtʲɪ]	[tsʲĩːpʲtʲi]
Ch ch	[ˈxaː]	[x]	[x]	chòras	[ˈxɔras]	[xɔ̀ras]
		[xʲ]	[xʲ]	chèmija	[ˈxʲɛmʲɪjɛ]	[xʲèmʲijæ]
Č č	[ˈtʲʃeː]	[tʃ]	[tš]	bačkà	[batʃˈka]	[batškà]
		[tʃʲ]	[tšʲ]	čiulpti	[ˈtʃʲolʲpʲtʲɪ]	[čʲulʲpʲti]
D d	[ˈdeː]	[d]	[d]	dúoti	[ˈduɔtʲɪ]	[dúoʲti]
		[dʲ]	[dʲ]	děti	[ˈdʲeːtʲɪ]	[dʲę́ʲti]
Dz dz	[ˈdzeː]	[dz]	[dz]	dzūkas	[ˈdzuːkas]	[dzū́kas]
		[dzʲ]	[dzʲ]	dzingsėti	[dzʲɪŋkˈsʲeːtʲɪ]	[dzʲiŋksę́ʲti]
Dž dž	[ˈdʒeː]	[dʒ]	[dž]	džáulis	[ˈdʒaˑolʲɪs]	[džáulʲis]
		[dʒʲ]	[džʲ]	vedžiaũ	[vʲɛˈdʒʲæoˑ]	[vʲedžʲæũ]
E e	[ˈæː]	[ɛ]	[e]	vèžti	[ˈvʲɛʒʲtʲɪ]	[vʲèšʲti]
		[æː]	[eˑ]/[æˑ]	vėžė	[ˈvʲæːʒʲeː]	[vʲę̃·žʲęˑ]
Ę ę	[ˈæː] nósinė	[æː]	[eˑ]/[æˑ]	gėlę	[ˈɡʲeːlʲæː]	[gʲę́ˑlʲę]
Ė ė	[ˈeː]	[eː]	[ęˑ]	ėsti	[ˈeːsʲtʲɪ]	[ę́ˑsʲti]
F f	[ˈɛf]	[f]	[f]	fābrikas	[ˈfaːbrʲɪkas]	[fā́brʲikas]
		[fʲ]	[fʲ]	fìlmas	[ˈfʲɪɫmas]	[fìlmas]
G g	[ˈɡeː]	[ɡ]	[ɡ]	gāras	[ˈɡaːras]	[gā́ras]
		[ɡʲ]/[ɟ]	[ɡʲ]	gẽras	[ˈɡʲæːras]	[gʲæ̃ˑras]
H h	[ˈɣaː]	[ɣ]	[h]	harmònija	[ɣarˈmɔnʲɪjɛ]	[harmɔ̀nʲijæ]
		[ɣʲ]	[hʲ]	hìmnas	[ˈɣʲɪmnas]	[hʲìmnas]
I i	[ˈɪ] trumpóji	[ɪ]	[i]	bìjo	[ˈbʲɪjoː]	[bʲìjoˑ]

SPELLING AND TRANSCRIPTION

Letters and digraphs	Their names	Sounds		Examples		
		IPA transcription	Traditional Lithuanian transcription	Spelling	IPA transcription	Traditional Lithuanian transcription
Į į	[′i:] nósinė	[i:]	[i·]	gaĩdį	[′gai:dį:]	[gaĩ·dį·]
Y y	[′i:] ilgóji	[i:]	[i·]	mýli	[`mi:lı]	[mí·l̂i]
J j	[jɔt], [′jɔtas]	[j]	[j]	jáunas	[′jæ·onas]	[jǽ·unas]
K k	[′ka:]	[k]	[k]	kálti	[′ka·lt̬ı]	[ká·l̂t̂i]
		[k̬]/[c]	[k̂]	kélti	[`kæ:lt̬ı]	[ké·l̂t̂i]
L l	[′ɛɫ·]	[ɫ]	[l]	laĩkas	[′ɫaı·kas]	[ɫaĩ·kas]
		[l]	[l̂]	lýti	[`li:t̬ı]	[lí·t̂i]
M m	[′ɛm·]	[m]	[m]	mamà	[ma′ma]	[mamà]
		[m̥]	[m̂]	mèsti	[′m̥ɛst̬ı]	[m̂èŝt̂i]
N n	[′ɛn·]	[n]	[n]	nãmas	[′na:mas]	[nã·mas]
		[ŋ]	[n̂]	nèšti	[′ŋɛʃt̬ı]	[n̂èŝ̂t̂i]
O o	[′o:]	[o:]	[o·]	óras	[′o:ras]	[ó·ras]
		[ɔ]	[ɔ]	baliònas	[ba′lɔnas]	[baliɔ̀nas]
P p	[′p̬e:]	[p]	[p]	plaũkti	[′pɫåo·kt̬ı]	[pɫåũ·k̂t̂i]
		[p̥]	[p̂]	pinigaĩ	[pı̬nı′gaı·]	[p̂iñigaĩ·]
R r	[′ɛr·]	[r]	[r]	rankà	[raŋ′ka]	[raŋkà]
		[r̬]	[r̂]	riñkti	[′r̬ıŋ·kt̬ı]	[r̂iñ·k̂t̂i]
S s	[′ɛs]	[s]	[s]	sáu	[`sa:o]	[sá·u]
		[s̬]	[ŝ]	silpnas	[′s̬ıɫ·pnas]	[ŝiɫ̂·pnas]
Š š	[′ɛʃ]	[ʃ]	[š]	šáuti	[′ʃa·ot̬ı]	[šá·ut̂i]
		[ʃ̬]	[š̂]	šim̃tas	[′ʃ̬ım̃·tas]	[š̂im̃·tas]
T t	[′t̬e:]	[t]	[t]	tàs	[′tas]	[tàs]
		[t̬]	[t̂]	tìkti	[′t̬ıkt̬ı]	[t̂ìk̂t̂i]
U u	[′o] trumpóji	[o]	[u]	bùvo	[′bovo:]	[bùvo·]
Ų ų	[′u:] nósinė	[u:]	[u·]	vaikų̃	[vaı′ku:]	[vaıkũ·]
Ū ū	[′u:] ilgóji	[u:]	[u·]	búti	[`bu:t̬ı]	[bú·t̂i]
V v	[′ve:]	[v]/[β]	[v]/[β]	gãvo	[′ga:vo:]	[gã·vo·]
		[v̬]	[v̂]	víenas	[`vienas]	[v̂íenas]
Z z	[′z̞e:]	[z]	[z]	zuĩkis	[′zoı·kı̬s]	[zuĩ·k̂is]
		[z̬]	[ẑ]	zir̃zti	[′z̬ır·ʂt̬ı]	[ẑir̃·ŝt̂i]
Ž ž	[′ʒe:]	[ʒ]	[ž]	žaĩsti	[′ʒaı·st̬ı]	[žaĩ·ŝt̂i]
		[ʒ̬]	[ž̂]	žẽmė	[′ʒ̬æ:me:]	[ž̂ẽ·m̂e·]

Notes: In foreign names (especially personal names), some more letters may be used: Q q, W w, X x (and sometimes Ä ä, Ö ö, Ü ü).

The following letters have special names in mathematics and special literature: H h – [′γaʃ], Y y – [′i:grɛkas], Z z – [′zɛt] (|| [ʒɛt]).

Only 'true' Latin letters of the alphabet are used for enumeration (i.e. ą, č, ę, ė, etc. are omitted).

The correspondence between the Lithuanian letters and the similar sounds of English is shown in Table 2.

Table 2. The approximate pronunciation of the Lithuanian letters

Lithuanian letter	Pronounced somewhat like the English (AmE or BrE)
A a	*a* in *father* (if long), *u* in *mud* (if short)
Ą ą	always long, like *a* in *father*
B b	*b* in *baby*, *boss*
C c	*ts* in *ants*, *bets* (in Lithuanian may occur initially, e.g., *cukrus* ['tsokros] 'sugar')
Č č	*ch* in *child*, *chip*
D d	true dental (not aspirated), close to *d* in *indeed*
E e	*a* in *bad*, *man* (if long), but wider; *e* in *debt* (if short but more open)
Ę ę	always long, like long E, e above
Ė ė	narrow, close front vowel, like *e* in German *geh*, or *a* in *rate* without the off-glide; always long
F f	*f* in *fool*, *fit*
G g	always like *g* in *goose*, *guilty* (never like *g* in *manager*)
H h	*h* in *behind* (voiced)
I i	*i* in *it*, *pit*; in *ia,ią, io, iu, ių* the *i* is not pronounced (except in international words); it only shows that the preceding consonant is soft (palatalized)
Į į	always long, like *ee* in *deed*, but without any off-glide
Y y	exactly like the Į, į above; always long
J j	always like *y* in *yes* (never like *j* in *joke*)
K k	*c* in *cool*, *k* in *key* (not aspirated)
L l	hard like *l* in *belt*, soft like *l* in (BrE) *least*
M m	*m* in *mother*, *meet*
N n	*n* in *nose*, *neat*
O o	*oo* in *door* (but more closed and rounded, like *o* in German *rot*; always long in native Lithuanian words); *o* in (BrE) *got* (in international words)
P p	*p* in *sport*, *spit* (not aspirated)
R r	apical trill, like in Italian and Scots
S s	*s* in *so*, *sit*
Š š	*sh* in *sharp*, *sheep*
T t	true dental, not aspirated, like *t* in *stood*, *steep*
U u	always short, like *u* in *butcher*, *put*
Ų ų	always long, like *oo* in *school*, *pool*, but without any off-glide
Ū ū	always long, exactly like Ų, ų above
V v	*v* in *voice*, *vain*
Z z	*z* in *zoo*, *zeal*
Ž ž	*s* in *measure*, *treasure* (may occur initially)

Digraphs	Pronounced somewhat like the English (AmE or BrE)
Ch ch	*ch* in German *acht, echt*
Dz dz	*ds* in *demands, mends* (may occur initially)
Dž dž	*j* in *joke, jet*

Diphthongs	Pronounced somewhat like the English (AmE or BrE)
ai	*ai* in *aisle*, *i* in *bite*; *ay* in *way* (if preceded by the letter *i*)
au	*ow* in *cow*, *ou* in *out*; *o* in *vogue* (if preceded by the letter *i*)
ei	*ei* in *weight*, *ay* in *way*
ie	*eo* in *peony*
ui	*ooey* in *phooey* (when pronounced rapidly)
uo	*o a* in *do a* (pronounced like the *o* in *do* and the *a* in the article *a* in rapid succession)

Notes: 1. All the consonants are soft (palatalized) before front (or fronted back) vowels and soft (palatalized) consonants and [j].

2. All the voiced consonants are more sonorous than their counterparts in English.

3. The long vowels are not diphthongized, therefore they differ sharply from the corresponding English sounds.

4. These diphthongs may also be pronounced in two contrastive ways: with more emphasis on the first component or with more emphasis on the second component.

5. Some other diphthongs (*eu, oi, ou*) occur only in international words where they are pronounced as sequences of the short vowels described above.

2 THEORETICAL PRELIMINARIES

2.1 The description of the Lithuanian phonology in this section is based on the following theoretical principles.

Pure phonetics is the study of all possible speech sounds and their properties from a physical (acoustic phonetics) or a physiological (articulatory phonetics) point of view. Phonology is concerned only with those speech sounds or, to be exact, those features of speech sounds which have a distinctive function in differentiating words and their forms. For instance, the difference between the Lithuanian voiceless [t] and its voiced counterpart [d] is phonological, because it distinguishes, for example, the word *dãrė* '(he) did' from the word *tãrė* '(he) said', *bãdas* 'famine' from *bãtas* 'shoe'; whereas the difference between the prenasalized [ⁿd] and the simple [d] which is possible in initial position is interesting only to pure phonetics, because, e.g. the words [ⁿdɒ] and [ˈdɒ] 'two', [ˈⁿduːɾeː] and [ˈduːɾeː] '(he)pricked' do not differ in meaning – in this case the two sounds are phonologically identical.

2.2 Phonology is mainly concerned with **phonemes** and **prosodic (suprasegmental) elements,** or prosodemes.

If continuous speech is segmented into smaller stretches of speech, it turns out that it consists of one or more phonological sentences (phrases); each sentence contains one or more phonological words and an intonation pattern; each word has one or several syllables and a stress pattern (extra prominence in the articulation of one syllable compared with another); each syllable is a sequence of phonemes (or a single phoneme) which in certain cases may have an additional feature, the so-called syllable toneme.

Words, syllables and phonemes are linear linguistic elements, because the order in which they occur may perform a distinctive function (cf.: *Karštà vãsara* 'a hot summer' and *Vãsara karštà* 'summer is hot', *sùka* '(he) turns' and *kasù* '(I) dig', *takùs* Acc. Pl. 'paths' and *atkùs* '(he) will recover'). They are distinguished from intonation, stress and syllable tonemes, i.e. from the so-called prosodic suprasegmental elements which occur along with the linear elements as certain additional features. The analysis of the latter elements is the domain of that part of phonology which is known as **prosody**.

Phonemes are seen as the shortest linear segments of phonological analysis. On the other hand, each phoneme is a particular set of phonetic (articulatory or acoustic) **distinctive features** which cause changes in the meaning of a word and its forms. For instance, the feature of voice which is present in voiced consonants but lacking in voiceless consonants in Lithuanian, cf.: *bùvo* '(he) was' and *pùvo* '(it) rotted', *dãrė* '(he) did' and *tãrė* '(he) said', *gãras* 'steam' and *kãras* 'war', etc.; that the length (tenseness) of vowels is also a distinctive feature becomes clear when we contrast the words *lìs* '(it) will rain' and *lį̃s* '(he) will crawl', *kàsti* 'to dig' and *ką́sti* 'to bite', etc. The prosodic elements are distinguished from the distinctive features of phonemes, because they extend over stretches of utterance larger than a single phoneme: intonation affects sentences, stress affects words, and syllable tonemes affect syllables or at least certain combinations of phonemes. Distinctive features are always assignable to a certain **single** phoneme.

Thus, all the phonetic features are primarily divided into phonologically **irrelevant** and phonologically **relevant**. The latter are said to have a distinctive function. Some of them combine and their simultaneous combinations make up phonemes, some other extend over combinations of phonemes and larger segments to form prosodic elements. A speech sound (which is the domain of pure phonetics) has a fairly direct correspondence with a phoneme, but it definitely differs from it, because a speech sound has a number of phonologically irrelevant features, whereas a phoneme involves analysis only in terms of **distinctive features**. Besides, the transition from one phoneme to another is always rather categorical, while the boundaries between speech sounds are not clear-cut. Discreet phonetic units can be identified in the stream of speech only because we know or perceive combinations of phonemes they correspond to.

2.3   Phonemes may have a number of **allophones**, i.e. positional variants conditioned by their environment. For instance, the velar [ŋ] and the dental [n] are allophones of the Lithuanian phoneme /n/: the first one occurs before [k] and [g], the second one in other positions where [ŋ] is impossible (cf.: *ba*[ŋ]*gà* 'wave', *ra*[ŋ]*kà* 'hand' and [n]*ãmas* 'house', *ba*[n]*dà* 'herd'). Allophones are distinguished from **free variants**. These may be differently articulated sounds, but they occur in the same position and represent one and the same phoneme. Examples are the apico-alveolar [r] or the uvular [R] in German: their articulation is different, but they do not affect the meaning of words. The choice of one free variant rather than another may be made on sociological grounds or for the purpose of expressing a person's feelings. In other words, free variants may perform an **expressive function**. They refer to the substitutability of one sound for another in a given environment, with no consequent change in the word's meaning.

2.4 **Neutralization** (a term used in Prague School phonology) refers to a regular loss of the distinction between some phonemes as a result of which their allophones come to be physically indistinguishable in certain environments. For instance, in Standard Lithuanian, soft (palatalized) and hard (non-palatalized) consonants before back vowels (/o/, /o:/, etc.) perform a distinctive function (see 4.2, 3, 5), i.e. they are separate phonemes (cf.: *kiùro* '(it) got holes' ≠ *kùro* 'fuel (GEN. SG)', *siùsti* 'to grow angry' ≠ *sùsti* 'to grow scabby'); but this contrast is lost, or neutralized, elsewhere: soft (palatalized) consonants do not occur in the final position and before hard (non-palatalized) consonants (cf. *švil̃pti* [ˈʃyu̯lʲ·pʲtʲɪ] 'to whistle', but *švil̃pt* [ˈʃyu̯ɫ·pt] '(a clipped form) to whistle'), while hard (non-palatalized) consonants do not occur before soft consonants and front vowels (cf. *báltas* [ˈbɑ·ɫtas] 'white', but *baltèsnis* [balʲˈtʲɛsʲnʲɪs] 'whiter'). Members of a phonemic opposition which occur in a neutralisable position and do not depend on adjacent phonemes (in this case, hard consonants in the final position) are said to be **unmarked**, while members of the same opposition which never occur in such a position (in this case, soft consonants) are said to be **marked**. In connected speech, unmarked members are usually more frequent and have more allophones.

The opposition existing between marked and unmarked members is called **correlation**, and a phonemic feature which distinguishes them is referred to as a **mark of correlation** (in our example, palatalization is the mark of correlation).

2.5 Phonology is also concerned with the specific arrangements of phonemes (and partly of other phonological elements) in sequences which occur in a language and can be stated in terms of rules. This is a preoccupation of **phonotactics**.

Besides pure phonetics, there is one more branch of linguistics closely connected with phonology. It is **morphonology** (or morphophonology), i.e. a term referring to the analysis and classification of phonological factors which affect the appearance of morphemes, or, correspondingly, the grammatical factors which affect the appearance of phonemes. It covers the differences in phonemic structure between allomorphs of the same morpheme. In contrast to phonological phenomena, morphonological phenomena lack **regularity** (morphophonemic rules may have numerous exceptions) and are often phonetically not justified. For example, in Lithuanian, the velar allophone [ŋ] of the phoneme /n/ appears whenever this phoneme occurs before /k/ and /g/; the consonant /l/ is inevitably palatalized before a soft consonant, etc. These are phonological phenomena. In contrast, such an undoubtedly morphonological phenomenon as metatony (an alternation of syllable tonemes) is far from being regular (cf.: *kója* 'foot' → *pakõjė* 'footboard', *kálnas* 'hill' → *pakal̃nė* 'hillside', but *lángas* 'window' → *palángė* 'window-sill', *tìltas* 'bridge' → *patìltė* 'place under a bridge'); suffixed verbs usually undergo the vowel change *e* → *a* (cf.: *sèkti* 'to narrate' → *sakýti* 'to say', *bèsti* 'to pierce' → *badýti* 'to prick'), but this rule has many exceptions (cf.: *dègti* 'to light' → *degióti* 'to light often', *vèsti* 'to lead' → *vedžióti* 'to lead often'). Even in the identical environment, morphonological alternations may occur in some forms and may not occur in others (cf.: *tu mýli* 'you (SG) love' → *mýlie-si* 'you (SG) love each other', but *jie mýli* 'they love' → *mýli-si* 'they love each other'; the alternation of vowels occurs only in the second person singular form, though the phonetic environment here is the same as in the third person plural form).

Morphonology is seen as a separate level of linguistic structure intermediate between morphology and phonology. Strictly speaking, it is not part of phonology, but a part of grammar.

3 VOWELS, DIPHTHONGS, AND SEMIDIPHTHONGS

Balsiai, dvìbalsiai, dvìgarsiai

3.1 The following are 10 types of simple vowels (or monophthongs) – 6 long vowels and 4 short vowels – distinguished in Standard Lithuanian:

long (tense)

```
        [i:                      u:
            e:            o:
                æ:
                      ɑ:]
```

short (lax)

```
        [ɪ                       ɔ
            ɛ
                      a]
```

Besides, two more short vowels [e] and [ɔ] sometimes occur in recent loanwords, or international words, cf.: *mètras* = ['metras] / ['mɛtras] 'metre', *spòrtas* [`spɔrtas] 'sports'. Due to its low frequency of occurence [ɔ] remains on the periphery of the system, whereas the vowel [e], which is used only by some speakers of Standard Lithuanian, is an optional phonological element.

The phonemic status of the Lithuanian monophthongs can be determined by the following minimal pairs:

(1) qualitative contrasts

(a) according to the horizontal movement of the tongue (front *vs.* back), cf.:

lỹdi '(he) accompanies'	: *liũdi* '(he) is sad'
brólį 'brother (ACC. SG)'	: *brólių* (GEN.PL)
ėda '(it) eats'	: *óda* 'leather'
sẽnė 'old woman'	: *sẽnio* 'old man (GEN. SG)'
eĩsi '(you) will go'	: *eĩsiu* '(I) will go'
kìšti 'to push (into)'	: *kiùžti* 'to break'

(b) according to the vertical movement of the tongue (high *vs.* mid *vs.* low):

rýžtis 'to make up one's mind' : rėžtis 'to get deep' : rę́žtis 'to strain oneself'
dìdelį 'large (ACC. SG. MASC)' : dìdelė (NOM. SG. FEM) : dìdelę (ACC. SG. FEM)
šū́kių 'slogan (GEN. PL)' : šõkių 'dance (GEN. PL)' : šãkių 'forks (GEN. PL)'
lãpų 'leaf (GEN. PL)' : lãpo (GEN. SG) : lãpą (ACC. SG)

(2) quantitative contrasts (based on a difference in length and tension):

dýdis 'size' : dìdis 'great'
klė́tys 'storehouses' : klė̃tis 'storehouse'
trę́šti 'to fertilize' : trè̃šti 'to rot'
sẽnę 'old woman (ACC. SG)' : sẽne (VOC. SG)
tólis 'distance' : tòlis 'tar paper'
pū́sti 'to blow' : pùsti 'to swell'
výrų 'husband (GEN. PL)' : výru (INSTR. SG)
ką́s '(he) will bite' : kàs '(he) will dig'
vãsarą 'summer (ACC. SG)' : vãsara (NOM. SG)

Pairs of long and short vowels differ not so much in quantity (length) as in quality, i.e. in the amount of muscular tension required to produce them. The difference in quality (tense *vs.* lax) is more important in producing high vowels, whereas the difference in quantity (long *vs.* short) is more important in producing low vowels.

Each of the above-mentioned Lithuanian long and short vowels is a separate phoneme. Long vowels cannot be treated as biphonemic combinations of two short vowels ([ɑ:]=/a+a/) or as combinations of short qualitatively 'neutral' vowels and the prosodeme of length ([ɑ:]=/a/+/:/), because native words in standard Lithuanian have no short vowels corresponding to the long vowels [e:] and [o:].

3.2 According to their function in the syllable, **diphthongs** and **semidiphthongs** (i.e. tautosyllabic clusters 'vowel + sonorant') are those units which are equivalent to long vowels. The syllables containing them are long and form the basis for the distinction in syllable tonemes (see 6.7).

In Lithuanian, there are two types of pure (or vocalic) diphthongs: gliding (merging) diphthongs (or polyphthongs, Lith. *sutaptìniai dvìbalsiai*) [iɛ] (≈ [ⁱɛₐ]) and [uɔ] (≈ [ᵘɔₐ]), which have no distinct components, e.g. *dienà* 'day', *dúona* 'bread', and compound diphthongs (Lith. *sudėtìniai dvìbalsiai*) [ai], [ao], [ɛi], [oi] ([ɛo], [ɔi], [ɔo]), in which we can easily distinguish an initial and final component, e.g.: *vaĩkas* 'child', *veĩkti* 'to do', *daũg* 'many, much', *smuĩkas* 'violin', *neutralùs* 'neutral', *boikòtas* 'boycott', *klòunas* 'clown'.

Semidiphthongs (Lith. *mišríeji dvìgarsiai*) consist of the vowels + /l/, /r/, /m/, /n/:

/ɪ/ +
(<e>) +   } /l, r, m, n/
/ɛ/ +

/o/ +
<ɔ> +   } /l, r, m, n/, cf.:
/a/ +

šìlti 'to grow warm'   *kùlti* 'to thrash'
kir̃pti 'to cut'   *kùrti* 'to create'
im̃ti 'to take'   *stùmti* 'to push'
riñkti 'to gather'   *sunkùs* 'heavy'
vélnias 'devil'   *kálti* 'to hammer'
ver̃kti 'to weep'   *spar̃nas* 'wing'
tem̃pti 'to pull'   *skambė́ti* 'to sound'
leñkti 'to bend'   *krañtas* 'shore' (*studeñtas* 'student',
                              fòrtas 'fort')

Combinations of long vowels with any following sonorant or non-syllabic [ɪ], [w] may also be regarded as diphthong-like sequences:

pirmỹn 'forward(s)'
jū́rligė 'seasickness'
kodė̃l 'why'
ropõm 'on all fours'
rytój [rɪ:'to:ɪ] 'tomorrow'

Likewise, the gliding diphthongs [iɛ] and [uɔ] combine with sonorants and non-syllabic [ɪ] and [w] to form triphthong-like sequences:

diẽnraštis 'daily paper'
dúonriekis 'bread knife'
sudiẽu 'good-bye'
tuõj ['tuɔɪ] 'soon'

Semidiphthongs are undoubtedly **biphonemic** sound complexes, as they occur only before consonants and a juncture (the position $[-^C{}_\#]$), whereas before vowels they are broken up into two syllables:

šìl-ti 'to grow warm'   : *šì-lo* '(it) grew warm'
kùr-ti 'to create'   : *kù-ria* '(he) creates'
kál-ti 'to hammer'   : *ka-lù* '(I) hammer'
teñ 'there' (clipped form) : *te-naĩ* 'there'
gál 'maybe'   : *gã-li* '(he) may'

Therefore combinations of vowels and sonorants should be treated as follows:

[ɪl ($^C{}_\#$)] = /ɪ/+/l/, [ɔr ($^C{}_\#$)] = /o/+/r/, [ɛn ($^C{}_\#$)] = /ɛ/+/n/, [am ($^C{}_\#$)] = /a/+/m/, and so on.

3.3   **Compound diphthongs** also occur only before consonants and a juncture, whereas before vowels they are broken up into a vowel and /j/ or /v/. In other words, compound diphthongs and non-diphthongal sequences *vowel* + /j/ or /v/ are in complementary distribution, cf.:

gùi-ti 'to drive'	: *gu-jù* '(I) drive'
saĩ-tas 'tie'	: *są́sa-ja* 'linkage'
kariáu-ti 'to fight'	: *kariã-vo* '(he) fought'
gáu-ti 'to receive'	: *gã-vo* '(he) received'
táu 'you (DAT. SG)'	: *ta-vè* (ACC. SG)
dangùj [daŋˊgoʟ.] 'in the sky' (clipped form)	: *dan-gu-jè* 'in the sky'

Both the elements of compound diphthongs can be easily replaced with other sounds (commutation test):

laĩkas 'time'	: *laũkas* 'field'
áibė 'multitude'	: *éibė* 'harm'
kaĩsti 'to grow hot'	: *kuĩsti* 'to rummage'
sēniui 'old man (DAT. SG)'	: *sēnei* 'old woman (DAT. SG)'
kuĩnas 'worn-out horse'	: *kulnas* 'heel'
veĩsti 'to breed'	: *veřsti* 'to turn'
šáuti 'to shoot'	: *šálti* 'to grow cold'

Consequently, compound diphthongs should be treated as biphonemic combinations and their second elements – non-syllabic [ɪ] and [w] – should be regarded as the allophones of the consonants /j/ and /v/ (or the allophones of the vowels /ɪ/ and /o/ respectively).

Gliding diphthongs (polyphthongs) [iɛ] and [uɔ] are interpreted as monophonemic entities. The following are some of the minimal pairs illustrating single phonological oppositions between the gliding diphthongs and other vowel phonemes:

líeti 'to water'	: *lýti* 'to rain'
riēkti 'to slice (bread)'	: *rēkti* 'to shout'
púodas 'pot'	: *pū́das* 'pood'
kuõpti 'to clean'	: *kõpti* 'to take honey combs out of a hive'

Unlike compound diphthongs, [iɛ] and [uɔ] do not depend on the phonetic position and cannot alternate with distinct sound sequences. Their syllabic accents are very much the same as those of long vowels. It is also important to mention that [iɛ] and [uɔ], like long vowels, participate in the same morphonological alternations (see 3.1).

Thus, the following 14 vowel phonemes are distinguished in Standard Lithuanian (one of them, i.e. <e>, is optional):

/i: u: /ɪ   ɔ
 iɛ   uɔ
 e: o: (<e>)   <ɔ>
 æ: ɑ:/   ɛ   a/

Their phonetic and phonological features are summarized in Table 3.

Table 3. Distinctive features of vowel phonemes

(A plus indicates the presence of a prime feature, a minus indicates the presence of its opposite, and a zero means the absence of the feature or its irrelevance; indications enclosed in parentheses are relevant if the system includes optional phonemes.)

Articulatory features	i:	ɪ	iɛ	e:	<e>	æ:	ɛ	ɑ:	a	o:	<ɔ>	uɔ	u:	ɔ	Acoustic features
(1) long (short)	+	−	+	+	(−)	+	−	+	−	+	(−)	+	+	−	tense (lax)
(2) front (non-front)	+	+	+	+	(+)	+	+	−	−	−	(−)	−	−	−	acute (grave)
(3) low (non-low)	−	−	−	−	(−)	+	+	+	+	−	(−)	−	−	−	compact (non-compact)
(4) high (non-high)	+	(+)	−	−	(−)	0	0	0	0	−	(−)	−	+	(+)	diffuse (non-diffuse)
(5) gliding (pure)	0	0	+	−	(0)	0	0	0	0	−	(0)	+	0	0	shifting (constant)

3.4 The allophonic variation of the Lithuanian vowel phonemes mostly depends on soft consonants, stress and syllabic tonemes.

(1) After soft (palatalized) consonants (i.e. in the position [Ĉ–]) and /j/, all the back vowels are realized by their fronted (advanced) variants [u:₊], [o₊], [o:₊], <ɔ₊>, cf.:

žmonų̃ [ʒmoˈːnuː] 'wife (GEN. PL)'   : žmonių̃ [ʒmoˈːŋuː₊] 'people (GEN PL)'
kùrti [ˈkorʲtɪ] 'to create'   : kiùrti [ˈkʲo₊rʲtɪ] 'to get holes'
žalúosius [ʒaˈɫuɔʂo₊s] 'red-haired   : žaliúosius [ʒaˈlʲuɔ₊ɕo₊s] 'green
(ACC. PL. MASC) (about bulls   (ACC. PL. MASC)'
or cows)'
žalóji [ʒaˈɫoːjɪ] 'red-haired   : žalióji [ʒaˈlʲoː₊jɪ] 'green (NOM. SG. FEM)'
(NOM. SG. FEM) (cow)'
kòksas [ˈkɔksas] 'coke'   : kiòskas [ˈkʲɔ₊skas] 'kiosk'

The vowels /ɑ:/ and /a/ in this position usually (except in artificial spelling pronunciation) coincide with /æ:/ and /ɛ/ respectively, cf.:

gìlią 'deep (ACC. SG. FEM)'   = gìlę 'acorn (ACC. SG. FEM)'

giliàs 'deep (ACC. PL. FEM)' = *gilès* 'acorn (ACC. PL)'
sēnei 'old woman (DAT. SG)' = *sēniai* 'old men (NOM. PL)'

(2) Before hard (non-palatalized) consonants, the vowel /æ:/ is more open (as [æ:] ≈ ['æₐ:]), e.g.: *nẽša* ['ŋᵆa:₊ʃa] '(he) carries', *grę̃žtų* ['gʳᵆa:₊ʃtu:] '(he) would drill', whereas before soft (palatalized) consonants it is articulated as a somewhat closer sound, e.g. *nẽšė* ['ŋᵉæ:ʃe:] '(he) carried', *grę̃žė* ['gʳᵉæ:ʒe:] '(he) drilled'; both articulations are quite often, by way of a generalization, pronounced as [æ:].

(3) The timbre (or tone-colour) of all the vowels (especially back ones) before soft consonants is usually higher and sometimes slightly diphthongoid-like.

(4) The vowels /ɛ/ and /a/ in acuted (falling) diphthongal combinations (i.e. in the positions [´–R$^C_\#$] and [–w($^C_\#$), –ι($^C_\#$)] are half long (or, optionally, even long), e.g.:

véidas [`yæ·ιdas] 'face'
káulas [`ka·ołas] 'bone'
kálnas [`ka·ɫnas] 'hill, mountain'
pérnai [`pæ·rnaι] 'last year'

It is recommended that the vowels [ι] and [ɑ] (also <ɔ>) in the same position (i.e. when marked with the grave accent `) were pronounced as short (at least not tense) vowels, but as this pronunciation norm is established on a very narrow dialectal basis they are often lengthened, cf.:

dìrbti [`dιrpṭι]      / [`di·rpṭι] 'to work'
pùlti [`poɫṭι]       / [`pu·ɫṭι] 'to attack'
giùiti [`goιṭι]       / [`gu·ιṭι] 'to drive'
(also *spòrtas* [`spɔrtas] / [`spɔ·rtas] 'sports')

(5) The vowels /ɛ/ and /a/ in circumflexed (rising) diphthongal combinations are slightly reduced, their articulation is nearer to that of the second element, i.e. /ɛ/ → [e] and /a/ → [å], [ə], e.g.:

peĩlis [´peι·ḷιs] 'knife'
laũkas [´ɫåo·kas] 'field'
laĩkas [´ɫəι·kas] 'time'

The same is true about the vowels /ɛ/ and /a/ in unstressed diphthongal combinations, e.g.:

peĩliai [´peι·ḷeι] 'knives'
laikaĩ [ɫəι´kəι·] 'times'
taupaũ [tåo´påo·] '(I) save'

The vowel /a/ is also slightly reduced in unstressed non-diphthongal syllables, especially in the final position, e.g., *vaĩkas* [´vəι·kəs] 'child'.

(6) The gliding diphthongs /iɛ/ and /uɔ/ show an exceptionally wide range of allophonic variation. The quality of the final element may vary from [e] and [o] (as a rule, before soft consonants) to [æ] ([a]) and [ɑ] (quite often before hard consonants and an open juncture in slow speech), e.g.: *tiẽ* [ˈtʲiᵃ] 'those', *šuõ* [ˈʃuᵃ] 'dog'.

The contrast between long (tense) and short (lax) vowels is normally maintained both in stressed and unstressed positions, cf.:

rūdą [ˈruːdɑː] 'ore (ACC. SG)'   ≠ *rùdą* [ˈrodɑː] 'brown (ACC. SG)'
rūdõs [ruːˈdoːs] 'ore (GEN. SG)'   ≠ *rudõs* [roˈdoːs] 'brown (GEN. SG. FEM)'
dúoną [ˋduɔnɑː] 'bread (ACC. SG)'   ≠ *dúona* [ˋduɔna] (NOM. SG)'
výrų [ˋyiːruː] 'men (GEN. PL)'   ≠ *výru* [ˋyiːro] 'man (INSTR. SG)'

Nevertheless unstressed vowels in Standard Lithuanian show a tendency to be shortened and turn into half-long (sometimes even relatively short) **tense** vowels. These changes do not harm the phonological system: the contrast is not lost, but only modified. The occasional complete neutralization of the quantity of unstressed vowels can be explained only as a phenomenon of some other (mainly dialectal or sociolectal) phonological system.

3.5   Clusters of vowel phonemes are not common in Lithuanian; in roots they occur only in the international words, e.g.:

aòrta 'aorta'
teãtras 'theatre'
teòrija 'theory'
duètas 'duet'
poètas 'poet'
oãzė 'oasis'

The sequences /ɩ+V/ and /V+ɩ/ are usually pronounced with /j/ inserted medially, e.g.:

bi[j]*ònika* 'bionics'
hi[j]*acìntas* 'hyacinth'
ši[j]*ìtas* 'Shiite'
hero[j]*ìzmas* 'heroism'
bedu[j]*ìnas* 'bedouin'

The epenthetic /j/ is not represented graphically.

In native words, sequences of vowel phonemes occur at the morphological boundary of compound words and prefixed derivatives:

/a+V/
juodaãkis 'black-eyed'   *paĕsti* 'to eat'
paežerẽ 'lakeside'   *pàima* '(he) takes'

juodaõdis 'black man'
paupỹs 'riverside'

aukštaũgis 'tall'
šilauogė 'pine-forest berry'

/ɛ+V/
neapkę̃sti 'to hate'
neeilìnis 'unusual'
nèėmė '(he) didn't take'

neilgaĩ 'for a short time'
neįmãnomas 'impossible'
neũkiškas 'uneconomical'

/ɪ+V/ or /iː+V/
priartė́ti 'to approach'
apýaklis 'half-blind'
prieĩti 'to come up (to)'
apýerdvis 'spacious enough'
priėmìmas 'reception'
įėjìmas 'entrance'
pasìima '(he) takes (for himself)'

apýilgis 'long enough'
prisiýrė '(he) rowed to'
nusiobliúoti 'to plane off (for oneself)'
išsiugdýti 'to develop (for oneself)'
į̃ūžti 'to get into noisily'
prisiúostyti 'to sniff enough'

/iɛ+V/
príeangis 'porch'
príeupis 'tributary'

/oː+V/
próanūkis 'great-grandchild'
póelgis 'deed'

póilsis 'rest'
póodis 'dermis'

/ɒ+V/
tarpùakis 'bridge of the nose'
nùėmė '(he) took off'
suirùtė 'turmoil'
suỹra '(it) falls apart'

suõšti 'to rustle'
suur̃gzti 'to growl'
nuũžti 'to fly away noisily'
suúosti 'to smell out'

/uɔ+V/
núoalpis 'swoon'

Such sequences of vowels are also often contracted, e.g.:

neyrà → *nėrà* 'isn't, aren't'
neė̃jo → *nė̃jo* '(he) didn't go'
neesù → *nesù* 'am not'
juodaãkis → *juodãkis* 'black-eyed'

In dialects, they are eliminated by the insertion of the epenthetic consonants /j/ or /v/, e.g.: *į̃[j]eĩti* 'to enter', *nu[v]eĩti* 'to go (away)'. The sequences /V+iɛ/ are excluded, because they are pronounced as [Vjiɛ]: *pa[j]ieškà* 'search', *ne[j]íeško* '(he) doesn't look for', *su[j]ieškóti* 'to find'. The consonant /j/ in these cases is part of the root, as it always occurs before the initial /iɛ/, e.g. [j]íeško '(he) looks for', [j]íena 'thill', [j]íetis 'spear', [j]ievà 'bird-cherry', though the letter *j* represents it only in the words *jiẽ* 'they', *jiẽdu* 'they both', and some place-names, e.g. *Jiesià*, *Jiẽznas*.

3.6 The following are some other features characteristic of the phonotactics (syntagmatic relations) of the Lithuanian vowels:

(1) Unlike the short vowels /ɩ/, (<e>), /ɛ/, /a/, <ɔ>, /o/, the long vowels /i:/, /iɛ/, /e:/, /æ:/, /o:/, /uɔ/, /u:/ are equivalent to VR combinations (semidiphthongs). In semidiphthongs, long vowels are usually replaced by variants of short vowels, cf.:

devynì 'nine'   : *deviñtas* 'ninth'
aštuonì 'eight'   : *aštuñtas* 'eighth'

Long vowels in this position are possible only at an open juncture and in some other rare cases, e.g.:

mólduobė 'loam-pit'
tólsta '(he) moves away'
žemỹn 'downwards'
morkà 'carrot'
šélti 'to rage' (see II.1.5)

(2) According to their relations with hard and soft (palatalized) consonants, the vowels may be classified into two types:

(a) V^u = /u:/, /o/, /uɔ/, /o:/, <ɔ>, /a:/, /a/, i.e. vowel phonemes which occur after both soft and hard consonants;

(b) V^i = /i:/, /ɩ/, /iɛ/, /e:/, (<e>), /æ:/, /ɛ/, i.e. vowel phonemes which occur only after soft consonants and /j/.

In other words, the opposition between soft and hard consonants exists only before V^u vowels, whereas before V^i vowels it is neutralized (see 2.16). Consequently, the V^i type is marked, and the V^u type is unmarked.

(3) In many dialects and especially in Standard Lithuanian, the oppositions /a:/ : /æ:/ and /a/ : /ɛ/ are neutralized after all consonants: in the position [Ĉ–] /a:/ and /a/ are usually pronounced as [æ:] and [ɛ] respectively, whereas combinations of non-palatalized consonants and [æ:] or [ɛ] are impossible. These oppositions exist in the absolute word initial position (cf.: *áibė* 'multitude' : *éibė* 'harm') and after /t/ and /d/ (if the palatalized [ț] and [d̦] are treated as allophones of /t/ and /d/: *tāko* gen. sing. 'path' : *tẽko* '(I) had to', *darinỹs* 'composition' : *derinỹs* 'cluster'). In other cases, [a:] or [a] occur after hard consonants, and [æ:] or [ɛ] occur after soft consonants (which are separate phonemes):

pāną ['pɑːnaː] 'young girl (ACC. SG)' : *pē̜ną* ['pæːnaː] 'food (ACC. SG)'
bādė ['baːdʲeː] '(he) pricked' : *bēdė* ['bʲæːdʲeː] '(he) thrust (into)'
gė̃lą ['ɡʲeːɫaː] 'pain (ACC. SG)' : *gė̃lę* ['ɡʲeːlʲæː] 'flower (ACC. SG)'
senàs [sʲɛˈnas] 'old (ACC. PL. FEM)' : *senès* [sʲɛˈnʲɛs] 'old women (ACC. PL)'

The same relation is also maintained in almost all dialects in which *Ce* type combinations are depalatalized (cf.: *lė̃das* ['lʲæːdas] 'ice' in Standard Lithuanian and *lãdas* ['ɫaˑdəs] 'ice' in the eastern dialects).

Besides, the vowels [a] and [ɛ] vary in duration: in non-final stressed syllables they are almost regularly lengthened (see 6.7).

(4) The vowels /iː/ and /ɪ/, /uː/ and /ʊ/ are definitely contrastive in length and tenseness:

trỹs ['tʲrʲiːs] 'three (NOM)' : *trìs* ['tʲrʲɪs] (ACC)'
pūsti ['puːsʲtʲɪ] 'to blow' : *pùsti* ['pʊsʲtʲɪ] 'to swell'

The long vowels /eː/ and /oː/ can be contrasted only with the short vowels (<e>) and <ɔ> which belong to the periphery of the system; /iɛ/ and /uɔ/ have no short counterparts (they may occur only in some dialects).

3.7 The above-mentioned syntagmatic properties of vowels correlate with the following **paradigmatic relations** and distinctive features.

(1) The vowels equivalent to *VR* combinations (semidiphthongs) phonologically contrast with other vowels as long vowels with short vowels (acoustically as tense vowels with lax vowels).

(2) The marked phonemes which occur only after soft consonants are front vowels, whereas the members of the opposite type (V^u) are non-front vowels. Labialization which is common to all non-front vowels (except /ɑː/ and /a/) is an additional important feature noticeably distinguishing them from front vowels, e.g.: /ɪ/ from /ʊ/, /eː/ from /oː/, etc. (it is very important in the position [$\hat{C}$–] where the V^u type vowels are fronted). Acoustically, front vowels are acute, and non-front vowels are grave.

(3) The members of the neutralisable oppositions /ɑː/ : /æː/ = /a/ : /ɛ/ in contrast to all other vowels are low, though phonetically [æː, ɛ] are evidently intermediate between low and mid vowels. The articulatory distinctive features 'low *vs.* non-low' correspond to the acoustic features 'compact *vs.* non-compact'.

(4) The 'paired' /iː, ɪ/ and /uː, ʊ/ are seen as diametrically opposed to low vowels. They contrast with the rest of non-low vowels as 'high *vs.* non-high'. Acoustically they are diffuse as apposed to the non-diffuse vowels /iɛ, eː, (<e>)/ and /uɔ, oː, <ɔ>/.

(5) The vowel oppositions /iɛ/ : /eː/ and /uɔ/ : /oː/ are differentiated by the features 'gliding *vs.* pure'. The formants of [iɛ, uɔ] detected on spectrograms move from diffuse to non-diffuse (even compact) values. Other vowels (especially [eː, oː]) do not noticeably change in quality.

The classification of Standard Lithuanian vowel phonemes is presented in Table 3. A tree diagram shows their paradigmatic relations.

Tree diagram of vowel phonemes

(Numbers above branching lines correspond to the distinctive features in Table 3.)

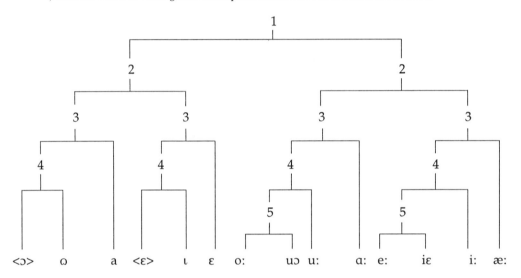

4 CONSONANTS
Príebalsiai

4.1 The following types of consonants are distinguished in Standard Lithuanian (and practically in all dialects):

```
[p    b    t    d              k    g
          ts   dz   tʃ   dʒ
<f>       s    z    ʃ    ʒ     <x   ɣ>
     v                    j
     m         n                    (ŋ)
               l         r]
```

The consonants <f x ɣ> can only occur in recent loanwords and certain interjections. The velar [ŋ] is a positional variant of /n/ (see 4.8a).

4.2 All the consonants, except the palatal (mediolingual) [j], can contrast by being either soft (palatalized) or hard (non-palatalized, velar or velarised), cf.:

trapùs (NOM. SG. MASC)   : *trapiùs* (ACC. PL. MASC) 'fragile'
gabùs (NOM. SG. MASC)   : *gabiùs* (ACC. PL. MASC) 'capable'
puikùs (NOM. SG. MASC)   : *puikiùs* (ACC. PL. MASC) 'nice'
pigùs (NOM. SG. MASC)   : *pigiùs* (ACC. PL. MASC) 'cheap'
baisùs (NOM. SG. MASC)   : *baisiùs* (ACC. PL. MASC) 'awful'
irzùs (NOM. SG. MASC)   : *irziùs* (ACC. PL. MASC) 'irritable'
našùs (NOM. SG. MASC)   : *našiùs* (ACC. PL. MASC) 'productive'
gražùs (NOM. SG. MASC)   : *gražiùs* (ACC. PL. MASC) 'beautiful'
žavùs (NOM. SG. MASC)   : *žaviùs* (ACC. PL. MASC) 'charming'
ramùs (NOM. SG. MASC)   : *ramiùs* (ACC. PL. MASC) 'quiet'
sumanùs (NOM. SG. MASC)   : *sumaniùs* (ACC. PL. MASC) 'clever'
žvalùs (NOM. SG. MASC)   : *žvaliùs* (ACC. PL. MASC) 'cheerful'
švarùs (NOM. SG. MASC)   : *švariùs* (ACC. PL. MASC) 'clean'

The soft <f, x, ɣ> are very rare, cf.:

fotogrāfų (GEN. PL. MASC) : *fotogrāfių* (GEN. PL. FEM) 'photographer'
kazãchų (GEN. PL. MASC)   : *kazãchių* (GEN. PL. FEM) 'Kazakh'
hùnai 'Huns'   : *Hiùstonas* 'Houston'

In the production of soft consonants the non-front articulatory focus moves towards the middle part of the tongue (in the cases of [kʲ, gʲ], <xʲ ɣʲ>, [ŋʲ]) or the front (middle) of the tongue is additionally raised towards the hard palate (in all other cases). The hard (non-palatalized) consonants (especially [ɫ ʃ ʒ]) are characterized not only by the absence of palatalization, but also by velarisation, i.e. by raising of the back part of the tongue towards the soft palate (velum). Besides, the hard [ʃ ʒ] are slightly labialized.

The affricates [ts dz tʃ dʒ] are composite sounds, merging sequences of plosive [t d] and fricative [s z ʃ ʒ] elements: they are contrasted by being soft or hard as well, cf.:

cùkrus 'sugar'	: *cŷpti* 'to squeal'
dzū̃kas 'southeastern Lithuanian'	: *Rādzio* (a surname, GEN. SG)'
giñčas 'argument'	: *čiùpti* 'to snatch'
Džònas 'John'	: *džiū̃gauti* 'to rejoice'

4.3   All the above-mentioned consonants perform the distinctive function and therefore should be considered as separate phonemes. Their main oppositions are seen in the following minimal pairs or sets:

(a) modal oppositions (based on a difference in the manner of articulation):

pãsas 'passport'	: *fãsas* 'face side'
takaĩ 'paths'	: *sakaĩ* 'resin'
kalvà 'hill'	: *chalvà* 'halvah'
dujóti 'to be foggy'	: *zujóti* 'to run about'
gaidùkas 'cock'	: *haidùkas* 'Haiduk'
bãdą 'hunger (ACC. SG)'	: *vãdą* 'commander (ACC. SG)' : *mãdą* 'fashion (ACC.SG)'
dãmą 'lady (ACC. SG)'	: *nãmą* 'house (ACC. SG)' : *lãmą* 'lama (ACC.SG)'
zujóti 'to run about'	: *nujóti* 'to ride off' : *rujóti* 'to rut'
rankà 'hand'	: *lankà* 'meadow'
žeñgti 'to step'	: *reñgti* 'to dress'
žiáunos 'jaws'	: *jáunos* 'young (NOM. PL. FEM)'
valdýti 'to govern'	: *maldýti* 'to quiet'
niáutis 'to squabble'	: *liáutis* 'to cease'
nagaĩ 'nails'	: *ragaĩ* 'horns'
lė̃kti 'to fly'	: *rė̃kti* 'to shout'
gijaũ '(I) recovered'	: *gimiaũ* '(I) was born' : *giliaũ* 'deeper'

(b) local oppositions (based on a difference in the place of articulation):

pìlti 'to pour' : *t̃ìlti* 'to grow silent' : *kìlti* 'to rise'
bùrti 'to tell fortunes' : *dùrti* 'to pierce' : *gùrti* 'to get weaker'
fėja 'fairy' : *sėja* '(he/she) sows'
svarùs 'weighty' : *švarùs* 'clean'
zìlinti 'to cut with a dull tool' : *žìlinti* 'to make grey'
šãšas 'scab' : *šāchas* 'shah'
žãdas 'faculty of speech' : *Hãdas* 'Hades'
mȳkti 'to low' : *nȳkti* 'to disappear'

(c) the voicing correlation (voiceless *vs.* voiced):

pãdas 'sole (of the foot)' : *bãdas* 'hunger'
tù 'thou' : *dù* 'two'
kalvà 'hill' : *galvà* 'head'
tausà 'saving' : *tauzà* 'nonsense'
šìlas 'pine forest' : *žìlas* 'grey'
chòras 'choir' : *Hòras* 'Horus'

(d) the timbre correlation (hard *vs.* soft):

kùrti 'to create' : *kiùrti* 'to get holes'
sùsti 'to grow scabby' : *siùsti* 'to grow mad'
šuõ 'dog' : *šiuõ* 'this (INSTR. SG. MASC)'

(for more examples see 3.4, 4.2).

4.4 The soft (palatalized) consonants occur in the following positions:

(a) [–Vⁱ] – before front vowels, e.g.:
gulì [gɔ'lʲɪ] '(you) lie (SG)'
neši [ɲɛ'ʃʲɪ] '(you) carry (SG)'
strėlẽ [sʲtʲrʲeː'lʲeː] 'arrow'

(b) [–Vⁱⁱ] – before fronted back vowels (see the examples in 4.2), e.g.:
guliù [gɔ'lʲɔ₊] '(I) lie'
nèšiu ['ɲɛʃʲɔ₊] '(I) will carry'
žaviùs [ʒa'vʲɔ₊s] 'charming (ACC. PL. MASC)'

(c) [–(Ĉ)Ĉ] – before palatalized or palatal consonants and [j], e.g.:
gu[lʲ]*siu* '(I) will lie (down)'
nè[ʃʲ]*ti* 'to carry'
[bʲ]*jaurùs* 'ugly'

The consonants [k g] before soft consonants are usually not palatalized, but they are 'transparent' for further palatalization, e.g. [ˈalˑksɲɪs] 'alder', [ˈvɪrɡdʲeː] '(he) made one weep' (but cf.: [ˈʒɛŋˑkʲtʲɪ] 'to step', [aŋgˈlʲɪs] 'coal' : [ˈʒɛŋˈgʲɔ] '(I) step',

38   PHONOLOGY

[`mæ·n̪ke:] 'cod'). In some idiolects, the palatalization of [p b m] in the same position is hardly noticeable either, e.g. [´ʃɫapt̪ɪ] / [´ʃɫapt̪ɪ] 'to get wet', [´sta:bde:] / [´sta:bde:] '(he) tried to stop', [`stomde:] / [`stomde:] '(he) pushed (about)'.

Only hard (non-palatalized) consonants occur in all other positions:

(a) [–Vⁿ] – before non-fronted back vowels, e.g.:

gulù '(I) lie (down)'
nešù '(I) carry'
žavùs 'charming';

(b) [–(C)C], e.g.:

gulˆtų '(he) would lie (down)'
nèštų '(he) would carry';

(c) [–#], e.g.:

gulˆt 'to lie (down)'
nèšt 'to carry' (clipped infinitives)
(but [´gol·t̪ɪ], [´n̪ɛʃt̪ɪ] – full infinitive forms)

The only exception to this general rule is the consonant [ļ]: in some professional terms (borrowings) it is sometimes pronounced before hard consonants or a pause, e.g.: *pùlsas* [`poɫsas] / [`poļsas] 'pulse', *sálto mortãle* [´sa·]ɫtɔ mɔr´ta:]ɛ] 'somersault', *sòl* [`sɔļ] 'the fifth note in the musical octave'. In dialects, especially in eastern dialects, such cases are more frequent, because after dropping a final front vowel the palatalization of the consonant is often retained, e.g.: [`ga·ļ] < *gàli 'maybe, perhaps', [sɔ´ʃɫapt̪] < *suslàpti 'to get wet', [`ma·n̪] < *màni 'for me'.

4.5 The fronted back vowels [u₊: o₊ o₊:] and the non-fronted back vowels [u: o o:] often occur in the same morphemes (especially in endings):

galiù '(I) can'   : *gulù* '(I) lie (down)'
kārio 'warrior (GEN. SG)'   : *kāro* 'war (GEN. SG)'

Since from the grammatical point of view -[u:] / -[u₊:] = {-u:}, -[o] / -[o₊] = {-o}, -[o:] / -[o₊:] = {-o:}, there is no doubt that [u₊: o₊ o₊:] are variants of /u: o o:/. Consequently, hard and soft consonants contrast before back vowels and should be considered as separate phonemes.

Theoretically, palatalization may also be considered as: (a) a suprasegmental element (long component) distinguishing whole *(Ĉ)ĈVⁿ* sequences (*galiù* [ga´]o₊] = /ga´l̂o/ where ˆ is a suprasegmental sign to represent palatalization), (b) an allophonic feature adopted by consonants from front and fronted vowel phonemes (*galiù* = /ga'lü/), (c) the realization of *Cj* type sequences (*galiù* = /ga'ljo/). The application of the grammatical criterion, however, supports the traditional interpretation (*galiù* = /ga'ļo/).

In native words the soft [tʲ dʲ] occur only in the positions [–Vⁱ] or [–Ĉ] in which their hard counterparts are excluded. Therefore in the main phonemic inventory [tʲ dʲ] are treated as the allophones of /t d/, though in loan words and onomatopoeic words they are sometimes used as separate (or secondary) phonemes, e.g. *bordiū́ras* 'edge, border', *tiùlis* 'tulle'.

4.6 The most frequent affricates are [tʃ dʒ]. Before front vowels they are almost always replaced by [tʲ dʲ], cf.:

mẽdis (NOM. SG)	: *mẽdžių* (GEN. PL) 'tree'
svetỹs (NOM. SG)	: *svečių̃* (GEN. PL) 'guest'
sáváitė (NOM. SG)	: *saváičių* (GEN. PL) 'week'
(cf.: *brólis* (NOM. SG)	: *brólių* (GEN. PL) 'brother'
ùpė (NOM. SG)	: *ùpių* (GEN. PL) 'river')

In this position they occur only in loan words and onomatopoeic words, e.g. *čìrkšt* 'chirp', *džìnas* 'gin' (but cf. *atsikėlė* [atʃʲɪˋkʲeːlʲeː] '(he) rose'). Some native words may also contain hard affricates, e.g. *giñčas* 'argument', *kivìrčas* 'quarrel'. In comparison with <f x ɣ>, affricates occupy a firmer position in the consonant system, because they are closely related to such phonemes as /s z ʃ ʒ/: [tʃ dʒ] are related to [tʃ dʒ] as /ʃ ʒ/ to /ʃʲ ʒʲ/, while the relationships between [tsʲ dzʲ] and [ts dz] on the one hand are the same as those between /sʲ zʲ/ and /s z/ on the other hand. This relationship and especially the position of affricates in consonant clusters (it is the same as that of plosives, cf.: *ščiūti* 'to become quiet', *čmìkis* 'a blow with a whip', *nèščiau* '(I) would carry') show that they should be regarded not as sequences of phonemes, but as single functional units.

4.7 Thus the consonant system of Standard Lithuanian consists of 45 phonemes, 8 of which (<tʲ dʲ f fʲ x xʲ ɣ ɣʲ>) are peripheral:

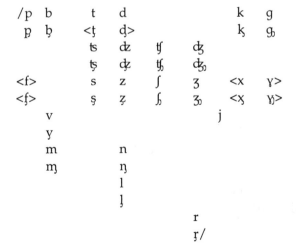

40   PHONOLOGY

4.8   The following are some of the major allophonic variations of consonant phonemes in Standard Lithuanian:

(a) velarization of /n/ before backlingual consonants:
bangà [baŋ'ga] 'wave'
lankà [laŋ'ka] 'meadow'

(b) vocalization of /j v/, i.e. their systematic change into non-syllabic [ι w] at the end of a word and before consonants, cf.:

žolėjè : žolė̃j [ʒo:'ʲe:ι] 'in the grass'
sváičioti 'to talk nonsense' (← svajóti 'to dream of')
sudiẽu 'goodbye' (← su Dievù 'with God')

also (as a facultative variation) in the intervocalic position:

vijìmas = [yι'jιmas] / [yι'ι̯ιmas] 'chasing'
bùvo   = ['bɒvo:] / ['bɒwo:] '(he) was'

(c) lengthening of sonorants in stressed circumflexed diphthongal combinations:

balnas   [`baɫ·nas] 'saddle'
tem̃pti   [`tɛm̰·(p)tι] 'to drag'
peñktas   [`pɛŋ·ktas] 'fifth'
pir̃štas   [`pιr·ʃtas] 'finger'

(d) labialization of all consonants before the rounded vowels [u: o o:]:

tū̃ris   ['t_wu:rιs] 'volume'
kùlti   [`k_wɔlʲtι] 'to thresh'
ródo   [`r_wo:d_wo:] '(he) shows'
skuñdo   [`s_wk_wɔn_w·d_wo:] 'complaint (GEN. SG)'

(e) aspiration of the word final [t k] (sometimes also [p]) before a pause:

kasmẽt   [kaş'mæ:tʰ] 'annually'
bė́k   [`bʲe:kʰ] 'run!'
kaĩp   ['kaι·p⁽ʰ⁾] 'how'

(f) the change of /m mʲ/ into labio-dentals [ɱ ɱʲ] before /v vʲ/ and <f fʲ>:

žemvaldỹs [ʒʲɛɱvaʎ'dʲi:s] 'landowner'
simfònija [şιɱ'fɔnʲιjæ] 'symphony'

(g) the change of /p b t d/ into nasal (faucal) and lateral plosives before /m n l/:

apmáuti   [ap̚'mɑ·ɒtʲι] 'to cheat'
stabmeldỹs [stab̰mɛʎ'dʲi:s] 'idolater'
pùtnagas   ['pɒt̚nagas] 'quartz'
liũdnas   ['ʎu:d̚nas] 'sad'

putlùs [pɔˈtlˠɔs] 'soft'
vedlỹs [vʲɛˈdʲlʲiːs] 'guide'

(h) the change of /t d/ into alveolars [t̪ d̪ t̺ d̺] before /r r̺/:

tráukti [ˈt̺rɑˑokt̺ɪ] 'to pull'
dróbė [ˈd̺robʲeː] 'linen cloth'
trỹs [ˈt̺r̺iːs] 'three'

4.9 **Word-initial clusters** (i.e. sequences of adjacent consonants) contain two or three phonemes.

Three-consonant clusters fit the pattern *STR-* (in which *S* is a sibilant, *T* is a plosive, and *R* is a resonant, except, in this particular case, a nasal sonorant):

sklaidýti 'to scatter'
skraidýti 'to fly'
skvarbùs 'penetrating'
spjáuti 'to spit'
sprãgilas 'flail'
stráipsnis 'article'
stvérti 'to seize'

(in dialectal words also *spl-, škr-, škl-, špr-, štr-, zdr-, zgr-*)

Two-consonant clusters preserve the same order of positions, though not all positions have to be filled:

ST-:
skabýti 'to pluck'
spalvà 'colour'
stãlas 'table'
špagà 'foil'
štaĩ 'here'
ščiūti 'to become quiet'

(in dialectal and international words also *šk-, zg-, zb-, zd-*)

TR-:

bjaurùs 'ugly'	*gražùs* 'beautiful'
blãkė 'bedbug'	*gvaldýti* 'to shell'
brangùs 'dear'	*klaidà* 'mistake'
draũgas 'friend'	*kmỹnai* 'caraway'
dvãras 'manor'	*knar̃kti* 'to snore'
glamonėti 'to fondle'	*kraũjas* 'blood'
gnáibyti 'to nip'	*kvãpas* 'smell'

pjáuti 'to cut'
platùs 'wide'
pradžià 'beginning'

SR-:
slãptas 'secret'
smagùs 'cheerful'
snãpas 'beak'
sráigė 'snail'
svarbùs 'important'
šlãpias 'wet'
šmėkla 'ghost'
šnỹpšti 'to hiss'

trą̃šos 'fertilizer'
tvãnas 'flood'

švarùs 'clean'
zliaũkti 'to flow incessantly'
zmèkti 'to get hard'
zvim̃bti 'to whiz'
žlium̃bti 'to whine'
žmogùs 'man'
žnýbti 'to pinch'
žvãkė 'candle'

This last group of two-consonant clusters also contains nasals /m n/ in the position of *R*.

4.10 According to their position in two- and three-member clusters, all consonants can be divided into two classes: (**1**) *R* class consisting of /j l m n r v/ which occur only directly before a vowel, (**2**) *O* class consisting of /b d g k p s ʃ t z ʒ/ which do not occur exclusively only directly before a vowel. *O* class can be further subdivided into: (**a**) *S* subclass containing /s ʃ z ʒ/ which occur only at the very beginning of a word (i.e. in the initial position), (**b**) *T* subclass consonants /b d g k t p/ can go in the first and second position. The following is a graphic representation of this syntagmatic classification of consonants (in which *C* stands for any consonant, *R* for a sonorant, *O* for an obstruent, *T* for a plosive, *S* for a sibilant):

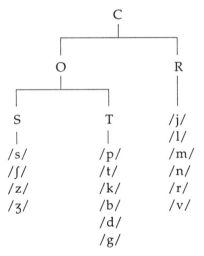

4.11 **Final clusters** in most cases are the reverse of those discussed above. Thus an initial *STR(V)* turns into a final *(V)RTS*, *SR(V)* into *(V)RS*, *TR(V)* into *(V)RT*, *ST(V)* into *(V)TS* (the asterisked clusters occur only in proper names and loanwords):

(1) *STR(V) → (V)RTS*
  skl- : -lks (*vil̃ks* '(he) will drag')
  skr- : -rks (*ver̃ks* '(he) will weep')
  spr- : -rps (*ver̃ps* '(he) will spin')
 *spl- : -lps (*al̃ps* '(he) will faint')
 *škr- : -rkš (*čir̃kš* '(he) will chirp')
 *špr- : -rpš (*šnir̃pš* '(he) will breathe heavily')

In final position, there are, however, (V)RTS type clusters which in reversed order do not occur initially, e.g. -mps (*tem̃ps* '(he) will pull'), -nks (*liñks* '(he) will bend'), -nkš (*kreñkš* '(he) will cough').

(2) *SR(V) → (V)RS*
  sl- : -ls (*bal̃s* '(he) will grow white')
  sm- : -ms (*viśíems* 'for all')
  sn- : -ns (*skiñs* '(he) will pluck')
  sr- : -rs (*patar̃s* '(he) will advise')
  šl- : -lš (*mel̃š* '(he) will milk')
  šm- : -mš (*kim̃š* '(he) will stuff')
 *šr- : -rš (*nir̃š* '(he) will be enraged')

For historic reasons *šn-* has no reversed counterpart (cf. dial. *greñš* and Stand. *grę̃š* '(he) will drill').

(3) *TR(V) → (V)RT*
  kl- : -lk (*pìlk* 'pour!')
  kn- : -nk (*augìnk* 'grow!')
  kr- : -rk (*pir̃k* 'buy!')
 *km- : -mk (*stùmk* 'push!')
  pr- : -rp (*tar̃p* 'between')
  tr- : -rt (*vìrt* 'to boil')

There are, however, some sequences of consonants which are impossible as initial clusters: -mt (*im̃t* 'to take'), -nt (*sént* 'to get old', *añt* 'on').

(4) *ST(V) → (V)TS*
  sk- : -ks (*tóks* 'such')
  sp- : -ps (*kõps* '(he) will climb')
  st- : -ts (*pàts* 'himself')
 *šk- : -kš (*trõkš* '(he) will be thirsty')
  šp- : -pš (*šnỹpš* '(he) will hiss')

Sometimes these clusters are extended by adding structurally unmotivated /k t/, e.g.:

čirkš-k 'chirp!',   cf. *čirkš-t* 'to chirp'
mè[k]s-k 'knit!',   cf. *mè[k]s-t* 'to knit'

šnỹpš-k 'hiss!', cf. *šnỹpš-t* 'to hiss'
veȓp-k 'spin!', cf. *veȓp-t* 'to spin'
(also cf.: *lìp-k* 'climb!', *vès-k* 'lead!')

4.12 The largest **medial** (intervocalic) **clusters** which can occur in morphologically simple (non-compound and unprefixed) words are four-consonant groups. Their structural pattern (with very rare exceptions: *irštvà* 'bear's den', *žiegždrà* 'gravel') can be described by the formula -RTS_R^T-, e.g.:

álksta '(he) suffers hunger'	*alĩksnis* 'alder'
liñksta '(he) bends'	*veȓksmas* 'weeping'
gaȓgždas 'grit'	*vìnkšna* 'elm'

Three-consonant and two-consonant groups are derivable from four-consonant clusters by leaving one or two positions vacant but maintaining the sequence of phonemes unchanged, cf.:

álksta '(he) suffers hunger' – *vilĩktas* 'dragged', *kalĩstas* 'stake', *nìkstas* 'sprain', *vilĩksi* '(you) will drag (2. SG)';

rąstas 'log', *káltas* 'chisel', *vilĩkas* 'wolf', *skalsà* 'slowness of consumption', *úoksas* 'hollow of a tree', *ráktas* 'key'.

If a larger cluster is found, we should expect simpler groups to conform to the pattern: -RTS_R^T- ⊃ -TS_R^T- ⊃ -S_R^T-, etc. (⊃ here indicates material implication, i.e. a logical relation "if ... then"). Cf.:

(a)-*lkst*-(a)   }   : (ni)-*kst*-(as) }
(li)-*nkst*-(a) }   } : (rą)-*st*-(as)
(a)-*lpst*-(a) }   : (sla)-*pst*-(o) }
(si)-*rpst*-(a) }

Using the symbol *x* to mark groups -*ST*-, -*SR*- and (very rare!) -*STR*-, or separate consonants -*S*-, -*T*-, we get a simpler formula -*RTx*- ⊃ -*Tx*- & -*Rx*-, e.g.:

(mu)-*rks*-(o) '(it) purrs with closed eyes' / (li)-*nks*-(i) '(he) nods' : (stū)-*ks*-(o) '(he) looms' : (vi)-*s*-(as) 'whole';

(vi)-*lkt*-(i) 'to drag' / (pe)-*nkt*-(as) 'fifth' : (ra)-*kt*-(as) 'key' : (ra)-*t*-(as) 'wheel'.

4.13 The following oppositions of consonants are neutralized in Standard Lithuanian:

(a) voiced obstruents *vs.* voiceless obstruents before all obstruents and at the end of a word:

dìrba '(he) works'	: *dìr*[p]*ti* 'to work'
keȓpa '(he) cuts'	: *kiȓ*[b]*davo* '(he) used to cut'

vėža '(he) transports'	: *vè*[ʃ]*ti* 'to transport'
nėša '(he) carries'	: *nè*[ʒ]*davo* '(he) used to carry'
daũgelis 'great number	: *daũ*[k] 'many'
mãžas 'small'	: *bemà*[ʃ] 'almost'

Resonants are neither devoiced, nor cause voicing of other consonants, e.g.: *sleñkstis* 'threshold', *tvarkà* 'order';

(**b**) hard (non-palatalized) *vs.* soft (palatalized) consonants at the end of a word, before consonants and front vowels (see 4.8): [ˈŋɛʃʲkʲɪ] : [ˈŋɛʃk] (full and clipped forms) 'carry! (2. SG. IMPERAT)'

[ˈγɛrʲʃʲtʲɪ]	: [γɛrʃt] (full and clipped forms) 'to tighten'
[ˈɪlʲʂtʲɪ] 'to grow tired'	: [ˈɪlˑsta] '(he) grows tired'

(**c**) dental sibilants *vs.* alveolar sibilants (/s ş z ʐ/ *vs.* /ʃ ʂ ʒ ʐ/) before affricates /ʧ ʤ/:

[ˈkɑːsa] '(he) digs'	: [ˈkaʃʧæo] '(I) would dig'
[ˈʐiːʐæ] '(he) whines'	: [ˈʐiːʃʧæo] '(I) would whine'
[ˈpoʂeː] 'half'	: [ˈpoʒʤuːyɪs] 'half dry'

(**d**) labial nasals *vs.* non-labial nasals before labials:

sán-dėlis 'warehouse', but *sám-brūzdis* 'commotion'
kri-ñ-ta '(he) falls' (cf. *krìto* '(he) fell'), but *ki-m̃-ba* '(it) sticks to' (cf. *kìbo* '(it) stuck to').

Vacillation is possible in compound words, e.g. *sé*[n]*bernis* and *sé*[m]*bernis* '(old) bachelor'.

The unmarked members of these oppositions (correlations) are voiceless, hard, dental and non-labial consonants respectively.

All contrasts of consonants are possible before back vowels:

sùs '(he) will grow scabby' : *siùs* '(he) will grow angry' : *šùs* '(he) will swelter' : *žùs* '(he) will perish' : *pùs* '(it) will rot' : *bùs* '(he) will be' : *tùs* '(it) will get sticky' : *dùs* '(he) will be short of breath' : *kùs* '(he) will get stronger' : *kiùs* '(it) will disintegrate' : *gùs* '(he) will get used' : *čiùs* '(it) will get quiet' : *džiùs* '(it) will dry' : *mùs* 'us' : *rùs* '(it) will become brown' : *jùs* 'you (ACC. PL)'.

Voiceless and voiced consonants also contrast before front vowels and sonorant consonants, cf.:

kélti 'to lift'	: *gélti* 'to sting'
prastà 'bad (NOM. SG. FEM)'	: *brastà* 'ford'
klóstyti 'to spread'	: *glóstyti* 'to caress'

Lithuanian also provides us with grounds to speak about a sort of **zero neutralization**, i.e. the deletion of a phoneme before an identical or similar consonant, cf.: *pùsseserė* = ['pɔşɛşɛɾeː] '(female) cousin', *užsùkti* = [ɔ'sɔkʲtʲɪ] 'to turn off'. This phenomenon, however, is partly conditioned by its morphonological position (cf.: *už+siùto* = [ɔ'şɔtoː] '(he) became angry' and *vèž-siu* = ['ɣɛʃʲɔ] '(I) will transport') and therefore is ascribable to morphonology. It is only appropriate to mention here that the geminates and clusters /gk, dt, kg, td, ʒs, sʒ, sʃ/ are not used (for /ʃs/ see II.1.22).

4.14 Taking into consideration their syntagmatic relations and the cases of neutralization, all the consonant phonemes can be described by the following hierarchically arranged sets of distinctive features (see Table 5):

(1) sonorant *vs.* non-sonorant: this set of features distinguishes R class consonants from all the other consonants (/j/, /v/ and /ɣ/ also belong to R class);

(2) nasal *vs.* oral distinguishes /m/, /mʲ/, /n/, /ŋ/ (which do not occur in initial three-consonant clusters) from the other sonorants;

Table 5. **Lithuanian consonant matrix**

Features	/p/	/pʲ/	/b/	/bʲ/	/t/	/d/	<tʲ>	<dʲ>	/k/	/kʲ/	/g/	/gʲ/	/ʦ/	/ʂ/	/ʒ/	/ʒʲ/	/ʧ/	/ʧʲ/	/ʤ/	/ʤʲ/
(1) sonorant (non-sonorant)	–	–	–	–	–	–	–	–	–	–	–	–	–	–	–	–	–	–	–	–
(2) nasal (non-nasal)	0	0	0	0	0	0	0	0	0	0	0	0	0	0	0	0	0	0	0	0
(3) fricative (non-fricative)	–	–	–	–	–	–	–	–	–	–	–	–	–	–	–	–	–	–	–	–
(4) affricate (non-affricate)	–	–	–	–	–	–	–	–	–	–	–	–	+	+	+	+	+	+	+	+
(5) labial (non-labial)	+	+	+	+	–	–	–	–	–	–	–	–	0	0	0	0	0	0	0	0
(6) backlingual (non-backlingual)	0	0	0	0	–	–	–	–	+	+	+	+	0	0	0	0	0	0	0	0
(7) alveolar (non-alveolar)	0	0	0	0	0	0	0	0	0	0	0	0	–	–	–	–	+	+	+	+
(8) voiced (voiceless)	–	–	+	+	–	+	–	+	–	–	+	+	–	–	+	+	–	–	+	+
(9) palatalized (non-palatalized)	–	+	–	+	–	–	+	+	–	+	–	+	–	+	–	+	–	+	–	+

(3) fricative *vs.* non-fricative enables to contrast S and T syntagmatic classes of obstruents, also /j/, /v/, /y/ and other non-nasal sonorants;

(4) affricate *vs.* non-affricate differentiates the composite /ʧ/, /ʨ/, /ʤ/, /ʥ/ from 'simple' T class consonants;

(5) labial *vs.* non-labial distinguishes between the marked phonemes of the type /p/, <f>, /m/, /v/ and the unmarked phonemes of the type /t/, /k/, <x>, /s/, /ʃ/, /n/, /j/;

(6) backlingual *vs.* non-backlingual (cf.: <x> : /s/, /k/ : /t/ – the choice of this set of features is syntagmatically irrelevant);

(7) alveolar *vs.* non-alveolar distinguishes the marked consonants of the type /ʧ/, /ʃ/ from the unmarked consonants of the type /ʦ/, /s/, also the trilled /r/, /ɽ/ from the lateral /l/, /ʎ/;

(8) voiced *vs.* voiceless serves as a contrast between marked and unmarked members of the neutralisable oppositions of obstruents;

<f>	<f̑>	<x>	<x̑>	<γ>	<γ̑>	/s/	/ş/	/z/	/ʐ/	/ʃ/	/ʃ̑/	/ʒ/	/ʒ̑/	/l/	/ʎ/	/r/	/ɽ/	/v/	/y/	/j/	/m/	/m̨/	/n/	/ŋ/
–	–	–	–	–	–	–	–	–	–	–	–	–	–	+	+	+	+	+	+	+	+	+	+	+
0	0	0	0	0	0	0	0	0	0	0	0	0	0	–	–	–	–	–	–	–	–	+	+	+
+	+	+	+	+	+	+	+	+	+	+	+	+	+	–	–	–	–	+	+	+	0	0	0	0
0	0	0	0	0	0	0	0	0	0	0	0	0	0	0	0	0	0	0	0	0	0	0	0	0
+	+	–	–	–	–	–	–	–	–	–	–	–	–	–	–	–	–	+	+	–	+	+	–	–
0	0	+	+	+	+	–	–	–	–	–	–	–	–	0	0	0	0	0	0	0	0	0	0	0
0	0	0	0	0	0	–	–	–	–	+	+	+	+	–	–	+	+	0	0	0	0	0	0	0
0	0	–	–	+	+	–	–	+	+	–	–	+	+	0	0	0	0	0	0	0	0	0	0	0
–	+	–	+	–	+	–	+	–	+	–	+	–	+	–	+	–	+	0	–	+	–	+

(9) palatalized *vs.* non-palatalized distinguishes one set of consonants (Ĉ) from another (C) which contrast only before non-front vowels.

The frequency of the consonants and other phonemes in Standard Lithuanian is shown in Table 6.

Table 6. **Phoneme frequency**
(processed on the corpus of texts containing 100,001 phonemes)

No.	Phoneme	N of occurrences	%	No.	Phoneme	N of occurrences	%
1	/a/	10,455	10.46	29	/æː/	1,244	1.24
2	/ɪ/	7,175	7.18	30	/iɛ/	1,212	1.21
3	/s/	5,883	5.88	31	/m̹/	1,208	1.21
4	/oː/	5,010	5.01	32	/p̹/	1,175	1.18
5	/j/	4,811	4.81	33	<d>	1,059	1.06
6	/ɛ/	4,542	4.54	34	/ɕ/	989	0.99
7	/k/	4,066	4.07	35	/ʃ/	911	0.91
8	/ɔ/	3,713	3.71	36	/b/	837	0.84
9	/t/	2,850	2.85	37	/ʣ/	742	0.74
10	/v/	2,777	2.78	38	/g̹/	734	0.73
11	/r/	2,763	2.76	39	/b̹/	663	0.66
12	/eː/	2,613	2.61	40	/uɔ/	614	0.61
13	/ʀ/	2,583	2.58	41	/ʨ/	527	0.53
14	/n/	2,513	2.51	42	/ʒ/	472	0.47
15	<t>	2,494	2.49	43	/ʤ/	199	0.20
16	/ŋ/	2,395	2.40	44	/ʦ/	145	0.15
17	/ʂ/	2,242	2.24	45	<ɔ>	124	0.12
18	/ḷ/	2,155	2.16	46	/z/	122	0.12
19	/p/	2,003	2.00	47	/ʐ/	92	0.09
20	/iː/	1,939	1.94	48	/ʦ/	21	0.02
21	/m/	1,689	1.69	49	<f>	18	0.01
22	/aː/	1,621	1.62	50	/ʥ/	11	0.01
23	/d/	1,549	1.55	51	/ʧ/	8	0.01
24	/ɣ/	1,520	1.52	52	<f̹>	8	0.01
25	/uː/	1,472	1.47	53	<ɣ̹>	3	0.00
26	/k̹/	1,355	1.36	54	<x>	2	0.00
27	/l/	1,355	1.36	55	<x̹>	1	0.00
28	/g/	1,317	1.32	56	<ɣ>	0	0.00

Tree diagram of consonant phonemes
(numbers above branching lines correspond to the distinctive features in Table 5)

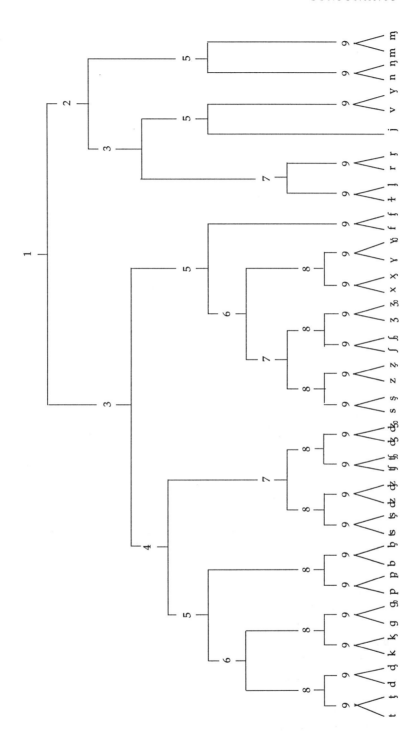

5 SYLLABLE
Skiemuõ

5.1 A vowel phoneme – alone or together with consonants attached to it – forms a phonological syllable whose phonetic realization is perceived as the smallest articulatory unit. E.g.: *a-kìs* 'eye', *į-ė̃-jo* '(he) entered', *skry-bė-lẽ* 'hat'. A vowel always constitutes the **nucleus** of a syllable, because in certain cases a single vowel by itself makes a syllable and performs its functions. For prosodic reasons (see 5.3), biphonemic diphthongs and semidiphthongs are also treated as the **extended nucleus** of a syllable, e.g.: *áu-gau* '(I) grew', *dìr-bam* '(we) work'. Some interjections can be identified as exceptional syllables in which the nucleus is the sonorant /r/ or the sibilants /s/ or /ʃ/, e.g.: [ˈtr̩ː] 'a command to halt horses', [ˈtsː] 'pst!'.

The minimum syllable consists of a single vowel (e.g.: *a-vìs* 'sheep', *o-ā-zė* 'oasis'), and the maximum syllable contains a vowel and two three-consonant clusters, e.g., in the word *springs* /ˈṣpr̩ɪnks/ '(he) will become choked' /ɪ/ is the nucleus of the syllable, /ṣpr̩-/ is an initial clusters of consonants, and /-nks/ is a final clusters of consonants. Analysed into immediate constituents, this syllable would be divided into the initial cluster /ṣpr̩-/ and the rhyme /-ɪnks/; then the rhyme would be broken down further into the nucleus /-ɪ-/ and the final cluster /-nks/.

5.2 The boundary between adjacent phonological syllables falls before the largest part of the medial cluster of consonants which structurally coincides with a possible initial cluster, e.g.:

liñk-sta '(it) bends'
nȳk-sta '(it) disappears'
rą́-stas 'log' (cf. *stãčias* 'steep')
veřk-smas 'weeping'
klȳk-smas 'scream'
põ-smas 'stanza' (cf. *smagùs* 'cheerful')
gařg-ždas 'grit'
kreg-ždẽ 'swallow'
kù-žda '(he) whispers'

(/ʒd-/ and /zd-/ are of the ST- type, cf. *štaĩ* 'here!')
ir-štvà 'bear's den'
žieg-ždrà 'gravel'
žì-zdras 'coarse sand'
(/ʃtv-/, /ʒdr-/, /zdr-/ are of STR- type, cf. *strakséti* 'to leap')

As there are no initial clusters of *R(T)S-, *R(T)T-, *TS-, *TT- types, the following words are to be divided thus:

mur̃k-so '(it) purrs with closed eyes'
stū̃k-so '(it) looms'
gar̃-sas 'sound'
peñk-tas 'fifth'
rãk-tas 'key'
plén-tas 'highway'

Consequently, even a single intervocalic consonant phonologically is always assigned not to the preceding syllable, but to the following ('right-hand') one, e.g., *ne-be-su-si-ti-ki-nĕ-da-vo-me* '(we) used not to meet each other'.

The boundary of a phonetic syllable apparently does not always coincide with the boundary of a phonological syllable. Open syllables are very common in Lithuanian (see Table 7), therefore in connected speech the medial -TT- or even -TSTR- clusters can wholly be assigned to the following syllable: *rã-ktas* 'key', *sla-ptaĩ* 'secretly', *ra-kštìs* 'splinter'.

5.3 From the prosodic point of view syllables in Lithuanian are classified into **short** and **long**. Short syllables are those whose nucleus is a short (lax) vowel which is not part of a diphthong or a semidiphthong, e.g. *buk-štùs* 'timid', *pa-ki-lì-mas* 'rise'. In long syllables, the nucleus (simple or extended) is formed by a long (tense) vowel or a diphthong, or a semidiphthong (i.e. a tautosyllabic VR-type group), e.g. *grą̃-žtą* 'drill (ACC. SG)', *gy-vý-bė* 'life', *plau-kaĩ* 'hair', *pil-nám* 'full (DAT. SG. MASC)', *var-daĩ* 'names'. If a syllable contains a long semidiphthong or a triphthong, its long quantity has a double justification, e.g.: *tõl-sta* '(he) moves away', *žē-mèn* 'to the ground', *su-diẽu* 'goodbye'.

5.4 The difference between open and closed syllables is not crucial in Lithuanian. As mentioned before (5.2), phonologically established closed (i.e. ending in a consonant) syllables phonetically can be realized as open (i.e. ending in a vowel) syllables, cf.: *rãktas* = /ˈraːk-tas/ → [ˈraː-ktas] 'key'. Only semidiphthongal and final syllables generally remain checked, but in rapid speech even final syllables are established according to the common rules of syllable division: *tas tur̃tas* 'that wealth' – [taˈstorː-tas], *jis vãkar atėjo* 'he came yesterday' [jɪˈsvaː-ka-ra-ˈʈeː-joː].

Table 7. Types of syllables and their frequency in texts

(V = vowel, C = consonant, V^w = pure compound diphthong; the corpus of texts contained 41,734 syllables)

Type of syllable	N of syllables	%
CV	22,813	54.663
CVC	7,346	17.602
CV^w	2,682	6.426
CCV	2,661	6.376
VC	2,026	4.855
V	1,434	3.436
CCVC	780	1.869
CV^wC	573	1.373
CCV^w	494	1.184
CVCC	405	0.970
VCC	138	0.331
V^w	120	0.288
V^wC	60	0.144
CCV^wC	59	0.141
CCVCC	46	0.110
CCCV	34	0.081
CCCVC	28	0.067
$CCCV^w$	20	0.048
CV^wCC	6	0.014
CVCCC	4	0.010
CCCVCC	2	0.005
CCV^wCC	2	0.005
CCVCCC	1	0.002

6 PROSODIC (SUPRASEGMENTAL) FEATURES

Prozòdiniai põžymiai

Stress

Kir̃tis

6.1 Each word consisting of more than one syllable has an additional prosodic feature which is referred to as stress. It is a contrast between stressed and unstressed syllables, the former being more prominent (higher in pitch, louder and sometimes longer) than the latter, e.g., *nèši* /ˈnɛ-ʃɪ/ '(you) will carry (SING)', *nešì* /nɛ-ˈʃɪ/ '(you) carry (SING)'. The more prominent syllable is said to be stressed (accented), or, in other words, it has a special phonological feature, the stress.

Since monosyllabic words performing various functions in the sentence are similar to stressed syllables, it is possible to assume that the stressed syllable forms the phonological nucleus of a word (cf. the similar role of a vowel in a syllable), whereas unstressed syllables constitute the margins of the word. If the number of syllables preceding or following the nucleus is determined by simple phonological rules, we have **fixed** (non-distinctive) stress; when such rules don't exist, the word stress is **free** and therefore capable of performing a distinctive function.

Indisputably, Lithuanian has a free word stress; it performs at least two functions. Its constitutive function manifests itself in distinguishing a word from a combination of words, cf.:

dù jõs 'two of her' ≠ *dùjos* 'gas'
ką̃ ràs 'what (he) will find' ≠ *kãras* 'war'

The second function of word stress, or, to be more precise, of its position, is the distinctive function which distinguishes otherwise identical words by the place where the stress falls, e.g.:

gìria '(he) praises' ≠ *girià* 'forest'
nuskùsti 'to shave (off)' ≠ *nuskustì* 'shaven'
šìrdis 'heart (ACC. PL)' ≠ *širdìs* (NOM. SG)

All Lithuanian dialects also have free stress, though in some of them this 'freedom' is somewhat restricted.

The position of the stress in Lithuanian depends on the stress pattern (or accentual paradigm) of the word and its morphological structure (see II.2.1–8).

6.2 In contrast with **orthotonic** words, which are usually stressed, there are also the so-called **clitics** (proclitics and enclitics), which include monosyllabic particles, prepositions, conjunctions, certain pronouns and other unstressed words regularly attached to the beginning or the end of an orthotonic word, e.g., *ir‿atẽ-jome prie‿to‿nãmo* 'and (we) came to that house' (proclitics), *tėvas‿gi seniaĩ sugrį̃žo* 'but Father returned long ago' (an enclitic). All enclitics in modern Lithuanian can also occur as proclitics, but some proclitics (e.g., prepositions and conjunctions) never form a unit with an orthotonic word preceding it.

6.3 A lower degree of word stress (i.e. **secondary stress**) may also occur in Lithuanian (especially in its western dialects). It most often falls on the second posttonic syllable (mainly the penultimate one) of a longer word, e.g., *mókyˌtojas* 'teacher', *pùskeˌpalis* 'half a loaf'. A phonological secondary stress is also possible, and it is noticeable in some rural dialects as well as idiolects of Standard Lithuanian, cf.: (tu) *mýˌli* '(you) love (SG)' ≠ (jis) *mýli* '(he) loves', *dróˌbės* 'linen cloth (GEN. SG)' ≠ *dróbės* 'linen cloth (NOM. PL)'.

6.4 Stress in Standard Lithuanian is a complex of sound properties. Increases in loudness and pitch, partly an increase in length of the nucleus of the stressed syllable may contribute to the overall impression of prominence. Under otherwise identical conditions, the stressed syllable is stronger (louder) and higher in pitch, often it is of longer duration and more precise timbre (or tonal quality).

All these are complementary features: which one prevails depends on specific phonetic conditions. Therefore the word stress in Lithuanian can be characterized neither as a dynamic stress, nor as a pitch stress. It is of a mixed type.

6.5 Statistically, there is an evident interdependence between the stress and the quantity of syllables. Most stressed syllables in connected standard speech are **long** (they outnumber short syllables in the ratio 2.3 to 1). This tendency is also proved by the fairly systematic lengthening of the non-final stressed /a/ and /ɛ/ (see II.1.4) and by lengthening of the first or second component of stressed diphthongs and semidiphthongs (see 6.7). More of such phenomena occur in dialects (especially in north-west dialects), and they are related to the shortening of unstressed long vowels, the reduction of the first component of diphthongs or semidiphthongs and other similar phenomena.

In Standard Lithuanian unstressed syllables are phonologically unreduced: both in stressed and unstressed syllables we have the same inventory of vowel phonemes. Typologically it is a peculiar feature, because free word stress usually does not coexist with the free quantity of vowels.

Tonemes, or syllable accents
Príegaidės

6.6 Lithuanian is a language in which long stressed syllables may prosodically contrast in tonemes or syllable accents, cf.:

šáuk 'shoot!'	≠ šaũk 'shout!'
gìnti 'to defend'	≠ giñti 'to drive (off)'
klóstė '(he) spread out'	≠ klõstė 'frill'
týrė '(he) explored'	≠ tỹrė 'mush'
rú[k]ti 'to turn sour'	≠ rũkti 'to smoke'

In identical phonetic conditions two contrastive tonemes are distinguished: the sharp falling (or acute) accent (Lith. *tvirtaprādė príegaidė*) and the smooth rising (or circumflex) accent (Lith. *tvirtagālė príegaidė*). The diacritic mark ´, or ` (for semi-diphthongs whose first element is one of the lax vowels /ɪ/, /o/, <ɔ>, (<e>)) is used to indicate the falling accent, and the diacritic mark ˜ is used to indicate the rising accent (cf. 1.1).

In earlier times, some linguists also recognized the 'short' toneme supposedly characteristic of short stressed syllables. Now it is rejected, because phonologically short syllables have no additional contrastive prosodic feature (e.g., *skùsi* '(you) will shave' and *skųsi* '(you) will complain' contrast not in tonemes, but in the duration and tenseness of the stressed vowel). Therefore the diacritic mark ` (grave accent) placed over a vowel in a short syllable indicates stress, but not toneme.

Tonemes (or syllable accents) are separate prosodic elements, but not distinctive features of phonemes: they characterize not only syllables containing long vowels, but also syllables whose expanded nucleus is a biphonemic diphthong or a semi-diphthong, i.e. a *VR* combination of phonemes, cf.:

láuk 'wait!'	: laũk 'get out!'
išvìrsi '(you) will boil'	: išvir̃si '(you) will fall out'

6.7 In Standard Lithuanian, a clear distinction is made between diphthongal and monophthongal allotones of syllable accents.

A diphthongal circumflexed (rising) allotone is produced by emphasizing and lengthening the second element of a biphonemic diphthong or a semi-diphthong and by reducing its first element, e.g.:

gaĩla [ˈgɑʊ·ɫa] 'it's a pity'   *kur̃pė* [ˈkorˑpeː] '(he) made carelessly'
šaũk [ˈʃɑ̀uːk] 'shout!'   *kaĩtas* [ˈkaɫ·tas] 'guilty'
giñti [ˈɡʲɪn·tʲɪ] 'to drive off'   *ver̃kti* [ˈvɛrˑkʲtʲɪ] 'to weep'

In acuted (rising) allotones, more prominence is given to the first element: [a] and [ɛ] become tense and half-long or even long, e.g.:

šáuk [ˋʃaˑok['shoot!'
káltas [ˋkaˑɫtas] 'chisel'
pavérgti [paˋyæˑrkʲtʲɪ] 'to enslave'

[ɪ], [o], <ɔ> (<e>) tend to remain lax, e.g.:

gìnti [ˋɡʲɪnʲtʲɪ] 'to defend'
kùrpė [ˋkorpeː] '(wooden) shoe'
spòrtas [ˋspɔrtas] 'sport'

Monophthongal falling and rising tonemes are smoother than diphthongal ones: in their production, the contrast between the beginning and the end of a syllable is not so clear-cut. This (and also the tempo of speech) apparently accounts for a levelling tendency which is evident in eastern and southern dialects, also in the speech of townspeople. The distinction between tonemes is most clear-cut in the western part of Lithuania, especially in Northern Žemaitian dialects, where the main acuted toneme is realized by the so-called broken (glottalized) allotone.

6.8 Tonemes are phonetic phenomena of composite nature, their specific properties to a considerable extent depend on the syllable nucleus.

According to the latest experimental studies, monophthongal falling and rising allotones are distinguished mainly by fundamental frequency, certain qualitative (timbre) features, relative duration, and partly by intensity. The pitch of acuted long vowels abruptly changes, their timbre (especially at the beginning) is prominent, the articulation is precise and very tense, the duration is shorter than that of rising (circumflexed) vowels. The tone of rising (circumflexed) vowels is almost level or slightly rising, their articulation is not so tense, and their duration is slightly longer. The main distinctive features of diphthongal allotones are the above-mentioned (see 3.4) quantitative and qualitative properties of the first component of a diphthong.

6.9 In unstressed syllables, the oppositions of tonemes, or syllable accents, are neutralized, cf.:

várpą 'ear (of a cereal) (ACC. SG)' ≠ var̃pą 'bell (ACC. SG)'
varpẽlių 'small ear (of a cereal) (GEN. PL)' = varpẽlių 'bell (GEN. PL)'

Unstressed syllables in Standard Lithuanian are perceived as rising (circumflexed), especially this is true for diphthongs occurring before a stressed syllable.

The tendency of neutralization of syllable accents, or tonemes, is evident in the final syllables, cf.:

sugáuti 'to catch' → sugaũs '(he) will catch'
and
sugaũsti 'to sound' → sugaũs '(it) will sound'
pavérgti 'to enslave' → paver̃gs '(he) will enslave'
and
paver̃kti 'to weep (for a while)' → paver̃ks '(he) will weep (for a while)'

There are also exceptions to this rule: the dative forms with -m(s) (tám 'that (DAT. SG. MASC)', gerám 'good (DAT. SG. MASC)', laukáms 'field (DAT. PL)', jauníems 'young (DAT. PL. MASC)', visóms 'all (DAT. PL. FEM)'), certain adverbs (pusiáu 'half', visái 'completely', velnióp 'to hell'), pronouns (jóks 'none', tóks 'such') and interjections.

Consequently, in Standard Lithuanian the rising (circumflexed) accent is the **unmarked** member of the syllable accent opposition, and the falling (acuted) accent is its marked member. The evidence from frequency of occurrence supports this view: circumflexed syllables are 1.5 times more frequent than acuted ones.

6.10 A schematic representation of the relationship of all prosodic elements of a word and a syllable is given below (S – syllable, L – long, Sh – short, St – stressed, Un – unstressed, C – circumflexed, A – acuted):

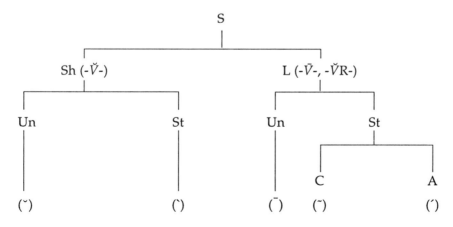

A system of two tonemes exists in all Lithuanian dialects, even in those which are said to have broken (glottalized), level or other tonemes (they are only allotones of the main types of tonemes). But the relationship of these prosodemes and the position of their maximum contrast may be essentially different. For example, in northern (Samogitian) dialects, acuted syllables occur in the final and even posttonic position (*sakâ·* ~ *sakái* '(you) say' ≠ *sakā·* / *sàkā·* ~ *sakaĩ* 'resin'), and the sharp (acute) accent is the **unmarked** member of the opposition.

II/Morphonology

1 Alternations of phonemes (1.1–24) 12
   Alternation of vowels in endings (1.1–3) 23
   Automatic quantitative changes of vowels (1.4–8) 45
   Loss of tautosyllabic /n/ and compensatory lengthening
   of vowels (1.9–11) 65
   Apophony (1.12–21) 67
   Alternations of consonants (1.22–24) 54

2 Accentuation (2.1–8) 34

1 ALTERNATIONS OF PHONEMES
Fonèmų kaĩtos

Alternation of vowels in endings
Balsių kaĩtos galūnėse

1.1 Short vowels in most endings before the enclitic affixes of reflexive verbs and definite nominals regularly change into long vowels (-V̆ → -V̄/{– encl.}).

The following alternations are possible:

(1)
(a) -/a/ → -/oː/
gerà (INDEF) : geró-ji (DEF) 'good (NOM. SG. FEM)'

(b) -/a/ → -/ɑː/ (-ą)
gerà (INDEF) : gerą́-ja (DEF) 'good (INSTR. SG. FEM)'
geràs (INDEF) : gerą́s-ias (DEF) 'good (ACC. PL. FEM)'

(2) -/ɛ/ → -/eː/ (-ė)
nẽšame '(we) carry' : nẽšamė-s '(we) carry for ourselves'
nẽšate '(you) carry' : nẽšatė-s '(you) carry for yourselves'

(3)
(a) -/ɪ/ → /iɛ/
nešì '(you) carry' : nešíe-s(i) '(you) carry for yourself'
gerì (INDEF) : geríe-ji (DEF) 'good (NOM. PL. MASC)'

(b) -/ɪ/ → -/iː/ (-y)
dìdis (INDEF) : didỹs-is (DEF) 'great (NOM. SG. MASC)'
paskutìnis (INDEF) : paskutinỹs-is (DEF) 'last (NOM. SG. MASC)'

(4) -/ʊ/ → -/uɔ/
nešù '(I) carry' : nešúo-si '(I) carry for myself'
gerù (INDEF) : gerúo-ju (DEF) 'good (INSTR. SG. MASC)'
gerùs (INDEF) : gerúos-ius (DEF) 'good (ACC. PL. MASC)'

Alternative endings may have stress shifted from the penultimate short or circumflexed syllable (see 2.4, 3); their long stressed variants, which occur in the afore-mentioned cases instead of short ones, are almost always acuted (but cf. *didỹs-is* 'great').

1.2 Some endings remain short even before the enclitic affixes, cf.:

nẽša '(he) carries' : *nẽša-s(i)* '(he) carries for himself'
gẽras (INDEF) : *geràs-is* (DEF) 'good (NOM. SG. MASC)'
gražùs (INDEF) : *gražùs-is* (DEF) 'nice (NOM. SG. MASC)'

Consequently, in endings we can distinguish changeable and unchangeable vowel morphonemes. The former ones can be marked as -*à* (*ô*), -*ã* (*ã̂*), -*e* (*ê*), -*ì* (*íe*), -*ì* (*î*), -*ù* (*úo*), and the latter are -*a*, -*a* (*à*), -*i* and -*u* (with appropriate marks indicating possible stress and syllable tonemes if in stressed position).

1.3 The insertion of *i* between the reflexive affix and a consonant of the preceding part of a word can also be considered a morphonological change, e.g.:

kàs '(he) will dig' : *kàs-i-s* '(he) will dig for himself'
nèš '(he) will carry' : *nèš-i-s* '(he) will carry for himself'
mókant 'while teaching' : *mókant-i-s* 'while teaching oneself, learning'
mókymas 'teaching' : *mókymas-i-s* 'learning'
slė̃pęs 'having hidden' : *slė̃pęs-i-s* 'having hidden himself'

They may be treated as cases of metathesis conditioned by a morphonological (phono-morphonological) position: -*si* → -*is* / {C-}.

Automatic quantitative changes of vowels

Automātinės kiekýbinės baĩsių kaĩtos

1.4 The vowels /ɛ/ and /a/ are lengthened in non-final stressed syllables, cf.:

nešù '(I) carry' : *nẽša* '(he) carries'
vakaraĩ 'evenings' : *vakāris* 'westerly wind'

In Standard Lithuanian, this rule of positional lengthening has a lot of exceptions. The vowels /ɛ/ and /a/ remain short in non-final syllables of the following types of words and their forms:

(1) verbal prefixes, e.g.: *àt-neša* '(he) brings', *nè-neša* '(he) doesn't carry', *tè-neša* 'may (he) carry', *pà-mečiau* '(I) lost', *tebè-guli* '(he) still lies' (but cf. *pāsakojau* '(I) told' ← *pāsaka* 'tale');

(2) disyllabic (excluding prefixes) infinitives and forms derived from them:

(a) infinitives: *nèšti* 'to carry', *dègti* 'to burn', *kàsti* 'to dig', *šlàpti* 'to get wet';

(b) forms of the frequentative past tense: *nèšdavau* '(I) used to carry', *dègdavau* '(I) used to burn', *kàsdavote* '(you) used to dig', *šlàpdavo* '(he) used to get wet';

(c) forms of the future tense: *nèšiu* '(I) will carry', *dègsi* '(you) will burn', *kàsime* '(we) will dig', *šlàpsite* '(you) will get wet';

(d) forms of the subjunctive mood: *nèščiau* '(I) would carry', *dègtum(ei)* '(you) would burn', *kàstumėte* '(you all) would dig', *šlàptų* '(he) would get wet';

(e) imperative forms: *nèškime* 'let's carry', *dèkime* 'let's burn', *kàskite* 'dig!', *šlàpki* 'get wet!';

(f) participles (and half-participles): *nèšdamas* 'carrying', *nèšiąs* 'which will carry';

(3) verbs formed from interjections: *krèstelėti* 'to give a jolt', *bràkštel(ė)ti* 'to crack';

(4) the comparative degree suffix of adjectives: *aukštèsnis* masc. 'higher', *jaunèsnė* fem. 'younger', *gerėlèsnis* masc. 'slightly better', *ilgėlèsnė* fem. 'slightly longer';

(5) the nominative singular masculine endings of definite adjectives and other adjectival words: *geràsis* 'good', *pirmàsis* 'the first one', *užmirštàsis* 'the forgotten one';

(6) the possessive genitive singular forms of personal pronouns *màno* 'my', *tàvo* 'your', *sàvo* 'one's own';

(7) compound adverb and prepositions: *anàpus* 'on the other side', *šiàpus* 'on this side'.

Besides, /ɛ/ (or optional <e>) remains short in international words, e.g.: *poèzija* 'poetry', *tèkstas* 'text'.

In word final position and monosyllabic words, the stressed /ɛ/ and /a/ are usually short, e.g.:

tà 'that (FEM)'
tàs 'that (MASC)'
nè 'no'
šakàs 'branches (ACC. PL)'
akmeninès 'stony (ACC. PL. FEM)'

They are lengthened only in the pronoun *mẽs* 'we' (cf. *mès* '(he) will throw') and the adverbs *kasmẽt* 'annually', *kasnãkt* 'nightly', *pernãkt* 'all night long'.

1.5 Long vowels (including /iɛ/ and /uɔ/) are systematically shortened, if they become the first element of diphthongs and semi-diphthongs (/iː/ → /ɪ/, /uː/ and /uɔ/ → /ʊ/, /eː/ → /ɛ/, /oː/ → /a/, i.e. V̄R → V̆R / -C). E.g.:

(a) *septynì* '(he) seven' : *septỹn-tas* → *septiñtas* 'seventh'
púolė '(he) attacked' : *púol-ti* → *pùlti* 'to attack'

(b) *dū̃rė* '(he) pricked' : *dū̃r-ti* → *dùrti* 'to prick'
bė̃rė '(he) poured (dry substances)' : *bė̃r-ti* → *beŕti* 'to pour'
kórė '(he) hanged' : *kór-ti* → *kárti* 'to hang'
(cf.: *pū̃tė* '(he) blew' : *pūsti* 'to blow', *plė̃tė* '(he) widened' : *plė̃sti* 'to widen', *võgė* '(he) stole' : *võgti* 'to steal')

(c) *rãšo* '(he) writes' : *rãšo-nt-ys* → *rãšantys* 'who write'
vaĩko '(he) chases' : *vaĩko-nt-ys* → *vaĩkantys* 'who chase'
(cf.: *kaĨba* '(he) speaks' : *kaĨbantys* 'who speak', *mýli* '(he) loves' : *mýlintys* 'who love')

Group (b) also includes the change of {o:v} into [aʊ] = /av/ in such cases as:

grióvė '(he) demolished' : *grióv-ti* → *griáuti* 'to demolish'
lióvėsi '(it) ceased' : *lióv-ti-s* → *liáutis* 'to cease'
šóvė '(he) shot' : *šóv-ti* → *šáuti* 'to shoot'

There are some exceptional cases when long vowels before tautosyllabic /r, l, n, m/ remain long:

(a) in word final position: *artỹn* 'nearer', *kasdiẽn* 'daily', *visóm(s)* 'all (DAT. PL. FEM)', *paskubõm* 'in a hurry';

(b) before an internal open juncture in compound words: *dúon-milčiai* 'flour for bread', *žvyr-duobė* 'gravel-pit';

(c) in verbs whose present tense is formed with the suffix *-sta*: *mė̃lti* 'to turn blue' : *mė̃lsta* '(it) turns blue', *tõlti* 'to move away' : *tõlsta* '(he) moves away';

(d) in some old borrowings: *kortà* [koːrˈta] 'card', *morkà* [moːrˈka] 'carrot', *Mortà* [moːrˈta] 'Martha'.

1.6 A special case of automatic quantitative changes is the alternation of the type /ɩ-j/ (/ [-V]) : /iː/ (/ [-C]) and /ʊ-v/ (/ [-V]) : /uː/ (/ [-C]), e.g.:

gìjo '(he) got well' : *gìj-ti* → *gýti* 'to get well'
rìjo '(he) swallowed' : *rìj-ti* → *rýti* 'to swallow'
bùvo '(he) was' : *bùv-ti* → *bū́ti* 'to be'
žùvo '(he) perished' : *žùv-ti* → *žū́ti* 'to perish'

1.7 In third person future tense forms related to dissylabic (excluding prefixes) infinitives whose acuted long vowel occurs directly before the suffix *-ti* (e.g.: *lýti* 'to rain', *griū́-ti* 'to fall down'), the long vowels /iː/ and /uː/ are shortened, cf.:

lýti 'to rain' : *lìs* '(it) will rain'
džiúti 'to dry' : *džiùs* '(it) will dry'
žúti 'to perish' : *žùs* '(he) will perish'

Exceptions: *výti* 'to chase' : *vỹs* '(he) will chase', *siúti* 'to sew' : *siũs* '(he) will sew'.

This rule is prescriptive – besides, it was established not long ago. Therefore in some previously printed texts it is often not observed (e.g., *trùks plìš* instead of *trũks plỹš* 'by hook or by crook').

In polysyllabic forms, the length of a vowel is retained, e.g.:

laiký-ti 'to keep' : *laikỹs* '(he) will keep'
taisý-ti 'to repair' : *taisỹs* '(he) will repair'

1.8 The vowel /i:/ is also shortened in the nominative and vocative singular endings of *-(i)ia*-stem nouns. This change occurs only in unstressed position, cf.:

gaidỹs 'cock', *žaltỹs* 'grass-snake' and *brólis* 'brother', *mẽdis* 'tree'
gaidỹ 'oh cock', *žaltỹ* 'oh grass-snake' and *bróli* 'oh brother', *mẽdi* 'oh tree'

Otherwise /i:/ is also possible in unstressed endings, e.g.:

ãkys ['ɑ:ki̯:s] 'eyes'
dañtys ['danti̯:s] 'teeth'

Loss of tautosyllabic /n/ and compensatory lengthening of vowels

1.9 In most morphemes, *Vn*-type semidiphthongs lose the nasal element and turn into long vowels before sonorant and fricative consonants. In other words, in this position /n/ disappears, lengthening the vowel which stands before it: $Vn \rightarrow \bar{V} / [-R]$. E.g.:

(a) *sán-kaba* 'clutch', but *są́-statas* 'composition', *są́-junga* 'union', *są́-lytis* 'contact', *są́-rašas* 'list';

(b) *kándo* '(he) bit' : (*kánd-snis* → *kánsnis* →) *ką́snis* 'bit'
skleñdė '(door) bolt' : (*sklend-ti* → *skleñsti* →) *sklę́sti* 'to bolt'
liñdo '(he) went into' : (*lind-ti* → *liñsti* →) *lį́sti* 'to go into'
siuñtė '(he) sent' : (*siunt-ti* → *siuñsti* →) *sių́sti* 'to send'

(c) *šãlo* '(he) got chilled'   : (*ša-ñ-la* →) *šą̃la* '(he) gets chilled'
klẽro '(he) became loose'   : (*kle-ñ-ra* →) *klę̃ra* '(he) becomes loose, shaky'
cf.: *rãdo* '(he) found' : *ra-ñ-da* '(he) finds', *gẽdo* '(it) decayed' : *ge-ñ-da* '(it) decays'.

In the latter (c) case, the expected *-į-* and *-ų-* are traditionally substituted by *-y-* and *-ū-* respectively in writing, cf.:

kìlo '(he) rose'   : (*ki-ñ-la* →) *kỹla* '(he) rises'
spùro '(it) frayed out'   : (*spu-ñ-ra* →) *spū̃ra* '(it) frays out'

but

švìto '(it) grew light'   : *švi-ñ-ta* '(it) grows light'
bùdo '(he) awoke'   : *bu-ñ-da* '(he) awakes'

1.10 Exceptions to the aforementioned rule of denasalization:

(a) tense forms derived from the infinitives in which /n/ stands directly before the suffix *-ti*, e.g.:

gyvén-ti 'to live'   : *gyveñs* '(he) will live'
sén-ti 'to grow old'   : *señs* '(he) will grow old'
tìn-ti 'to swell'   : *tìnsta* '(he) swells', *tiñs* '(he) will swell'

(b) loan words, e.g.: *benzìnas* 'petrol, gasoline', *tránsas* 'trance';

(c) junctures of compound words, e.g.: *skán-skoniai* 'titbits', *šùn-snukis* 'scoundrel';

(d) *-ns* combination occurring in the genitive singular endings of some nouns, e.g.: *akmeñs* 'of a stone', *šuñs* 'of a dog'.

1.11 In the history of Lithuanian, *Vn*-type semidiphthongs were also denasalized at the end of a word, e.g.:

ãkį [ˈaːki̯ː] 'eye (ACC. SG)'   < **àkin*
žẽmę [ˈʒæːmæː] 'land, earth (ACC. SG)'   < **žèmen*
výrą [ˋyːrɑː] 'husband, man (ACC. SG)'   < **vĩran*
sū́nų [ˋsuːnuː] 'son (ACC. SG)'   < **sū́nun*

However, in Modern Lithuanian we simply have here long vowels represented in writing by special letters (*ą, ę, į, ų*) to perform a phonological (cf.: *várną* 'crow (ACC. SG)' : *várna* (NOM. SG), *sẽnę* 'old woman (ACC. SG)' : *sẽne* (VOC. SG)) or even a purely morphological (cf.: *smẽlį* 'sand (ACC. SG)' : *smẽly* (LOC. SG)) function.

Apophony
Apofònija, bal̃sių kaità

1.12 In derivation and the inflexional forms of a verb, **apophony** (non-automatic alternation of vowels and diphthongs) is possible, cf.:

platùs 'wide' : plõtis 'width'
nẽša '(he) carries' : nãščiai 'yoke'
skrìdo '(he) flew' : skraĩdė '(he) flew about'
stvẽria '(he) seizes' : stvérė '(he) seized'
riẽčia '(he) bends' : raĩto '(he) rolls'
leñda '(he) crawls' : liñdo '(he) crawled'
liẽka '(he) remains' : lìko '(he) remained'

Apophony is an additional means of marking different functions of a word by varying the vowel sound in its stem, cf.:

{plat-} + {-is} → {plàtis} → plõtis
{stver-} + {-ė} → {stvèrė} → stvérė

Therefore apophony in Lithuanian is defined as covering the differences between allomorphs of the same morpheme, but not as an internal inflexion.

1.13 With certain reservations, apophony may include the alternation of long vowels -ė-, -a- and short stressed vowels -e-, -a- in the aforementioned (1.4) forms of the verb (kãsa '(he) digs' : kàsti 'to dig', nẽša '(he) carries' : nèšiu '(I) will carry').

Apophony only indirectly is related to the aforementioned alternations au : ov, ū : uv, y : ij (1.5, 6), an : ą, en : ę, in : į (y), un : ų (ū) (see 1.9) and especially au : av, ui : uj (see I.3.3). In all these cases they can be described as positionally conditioned alternants and practically can be seen as allophones of the same phonemes (see 1.3).

Apophony excludes the alternations of vowels in onomatopoeic words, because the distinctive features of their vowels function as direct (iconic) signs (cf.: tìkšt : týkšt 'dash!' where the long vowel marks a more intensive sound or action).

1.14 Lithuanian (and Baltic) linguistics traditionally distinguishes between quantitative and qualitative apophony (or vowel gradation).

Quantitative apophony is best illustrated by the alternations $i : y$ and $u : ū$ (sometimes also by $i : ai, u : au$, etc.), e.g.:

pìla '(he) pours' : pýlė '(he) poured'

mùša '(he) beats' : mū́šis 'battle'
mìsti 'to feed on' : maĩstas 'food'
jùkti 'to break up in disorder' : jaũkti 'to put into disorder'

Besides, functionally the alternations e : ė and a : o can also be ascribed to quantitative apophony, because they are parallel to such alternations as i : y, and u : ū, cf.:

gìria '(he) praises' : gýrė '(he) praised'
dùria '(he) pricks' : dū́rė '(he) pricked'
gẽria '(he) drinks' : gė́rė '(he) drank'
kãria '(he) hangs' : kórė '(he) hanged'

Qualitative apophony includes all other possible vowel alternations among which e : a, e (R)[1] : i (R), ie (ei) : ai, ie : y, au : ū, uo : au (= /a/+/v/) are most typical, e.g.:

sẽka '(he) tells (a tale)' : pãsaka 'tale'
sleñka '(he) slides' : sliñko '(he) slid'
viẽši '(he) stays as a guest' : váišės 'treat'
keĩsti 'to change' : kaità 'change'
žíedas 'blossom' : žydė́ti 'to blossom'
láužti 'to break' : lū́žti 'to break' (intransitive)
dúoda '(he) gives' : dãvė '(he) gave'

Some alternations are rare or even unique, such as y (i) : ei, a : i, ie : ei, ai : ui, ė : o, ė : uo, o : ū, o : uo, o : ui, e (R) : u (R), e.g.:

plýšti 'to burst' : pléišėti 'to crack'
málti 'to grind' : mìltai 'flour'
Diẽvas 'God' : deĩvė 'goddess'
klaĩkti 'to become foolish' : klùika 'fool'
sėdė́ti 'to sit' : sodìnti 'to seat'
brė́žti 'to draw' : brúožas 'stroke'
smõgti 'to strike a blow' : smū́gis 'blow'
šókti 'to jump' : šúokoti 'to hop'
lóti 'to bark' : sulùiti 'to begin to bark'
srẽbia '(he) sips' : sriubà 'soup'

Some other vowel alternations are of a mixed (quantitative-qualitative) type, e.g.: i : ė, ė : i, e.g.:

ìma '(he) takes' : ė̃mė '(he) took'
rė̃kia '(he) shouts' : surìko '(he) cried out'

[1] The letter R indicates that an alternation usually occurs before sonorants, e.g. vérda '(it) boils' : vìrė '(it) boiled', gẽria '(he) drinks' : girà 'weak beer'.

1.15 All direct relationships which exist between apophonic alternants are **privative** and **binary**. The underlying stem has an unmarked alternant, and the derived stem has a marked alternant (in the examples given above unmarked members of alternations come first), cf.:

platùs 'wide'	→ *plõtis* 'width'
nẽša '(he) carries'	→ *nãščiai* 'yoke'
pìla '(he) pours'	→ *pýlė* '(he) poured'
sleñka '(he) slides'	→ *sliñko* '(he) slid'
viẽši '(he) stays as a guest'	→ *váišės* 'treat'

Series of vocalic alternations can almost always be split into binary parts whose members have a direct derivational or grammatical relationship, e.g.:

svẽria '(he) weighs' : *svė̃rė* '(he) weighed' : *svìro* '(he) swayed' : *svýroja* '(it) hangs' : *svarùs* 'weighty' : *svõris* 'weight' =

svẽria	: *svė̃rė*
svẽria	: *svìro*
svìro	: *svýroja*
svẽria	: *svarùs*
svarùs	: *svõris*

sniẽgas 'snow' : *snaĩgė* 'snow-flake' : *snìgo* '(it) snowed' : *snỹguriuoja* '(it) snows lightly' : *snéigėja* '(it) snows slightly' =

sniẽgas	: *snaĩgė*
sniẽgas	: *snìgo*
snìgo	: *snỹguriavo*
snìgti	: *snéigėti*

džiaũgtis 'to rejoice' : *(prasi)džiùgti* 'to become cheerful' : *džiū́gauti* 'to exult' =

džiaũgtis	: *(prasi)džiùgti*
(prasi)džiùgti	: *džiū́gauti*

1.16 Apophonic alternations, as a rule, take place within certain microsystems, i.e. in the so-called apophonic series. Three series are distinguished in Standard Lithuanian:

(1) *a (e)* series including alternations with the underlying alternants *e, a* and occasionally *ė, o*;

(2) *i (ie)* series including alternations with the underlying alternants *ie, ei* (= *e+j*), *i* and occasionally *ai, y*;

(3) *u (au)* series represented by the alternants *au* (= *a+v*, sometimes *o+v*), *u, ū* and *uo*.

Besides, there are some apophonic alternations of a mixed type comprising alternants belonging to different series (see 1.14).

1.17 The microsystem of the *a (e)* series can be presented in the following diagram[2]:

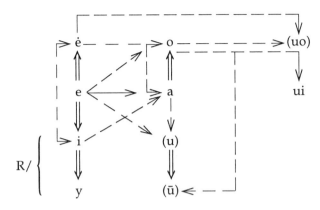

The unmarked member of the microsystem in all respects is *ě*, e.g.:

plěčia '(he) widens' : *plětė* '(he) widened' : *plìto* '(it) spread' : *plỹti* '(it) expands' : *platùs* 'wide' : *plōtis* 'width' =

plěčia : *plětė*
plěčia : *plìto*
plìto   : *plỹti*
plěčia : *platùs*
platùs : *plōtis*

By the way, all these examples show all the regular and productive alternations of the series. The other alternations (see 1.14), except *u : ū* which would be ascribed rather to the *u (au)* series, are unproductive, cf.:

ė	: *o* (*bėga* '(he) runs')	: *bogìnti* 'to carry quickly'
o	: *a* (*skōbti* 'to pluck')	: *skabýti* 'to pluck repeatedly'
ė	: *uo* (*rėžia* '(he) cuts')	: *rúožas* 'tract of land'
a	: *u* (*slánkioja* '(he) idles about')	: *sluñkius* 'idler'
o	: *ū* (*šókti* 'to jump')	: *šúksnis* 'jump'
ě	: *o* (*plěpa* '(he) chatters')	: *pliópa* 'chatterbox', etc.

The alternants *i, y* (also *u, ū*) in this series usually occur only in the environment of sonorant consonants (see 1.14), but exceptions are also possible, e.g.:

---

[2] The arrows in the diagram are directed to marked alternants. The arrow ⇒ indicates the most productive alternations which exist both in word formation and in oppositions of verbal forms; the arrow → shows productive alternations which occur only in word formation; the arrow --> shows peripheral or less productive alternations. Completely unproductive alternants which occur in words whose derivational character is established only diachronically are given in brackets.

tėškia '(he) splashes' : *tiško* '(it) splashed'
stìpti 'to die' : *stapìnti* 'to let sb. die (of hunger)'

1.18 The apophonic series *i (ie)* includes the following alternants:

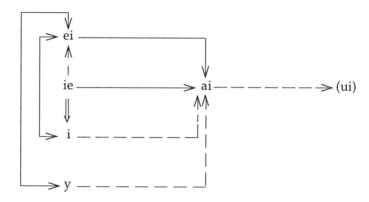

The main unmarked member of this microsystem is *ie*, e.g.:

šviẽčia '(it) shines' : *švìto* '(it) grew light' : *švyturỹs* 'light-house' : *šveĩčia* '(he) rubs until bright' : *švaĩsto* '(he) holds a light for somebody' =

šviẽčia : *švìto*
šviẽčia : *šveĩčia*
šveĩčia : *švaĩsto*
švìto : *švyturỹs*

liẽka '(he) remains' : *lìko* '(he) remained' : *lỹkija* '(he) makes it remain' : *palaikaĩ* '(human) remains' =

liẽka : *lìko*
liẽka : *palaikaĩ*
lìko : *lỹkija*

(but cf. *lìpti* 'to climb' : *liẽptas* 'foot-bridge', where *ie* is marked).

Only rarely does the diphthong *ei* appear in this role, cf.: *skleĩdžia* '(it) spreads' : *sklìdo* '(it) spread' and *skleĩdžia* : *sklaidà* 'dispersion'. It seldom alternates with *ie*, but it can become the marked alternant compared with *y* and *i* (see 1.15).

The diphthong *ai* is unmarked only in the alternation *ai* : *ui* which occurs in dialectal words, e.g.: *raĩnas* 'streaky' : *Ruĩnis* 'name of a streaky cat', *ráišas* 'lame' : *rùišis* 'lame man'.

To the same series we can evidently ascribe also the alternations *i* : *y* which have no diphthongal alternants and cannot be derived from the underlying *e*, cf.:

skìria '(he) distinguishes' : *skýrė* '(he) distinguished'
šìlo '(it) grew warmer' : *atóšylis* 'thaw'

1.19 The last apophonic microsystem, i.e. the *u* (*au*) series, may be presented in the following way:

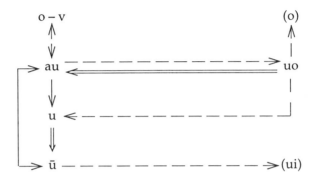

In this series, only the alternations *au* : *u* : *ū* and *au* : *u*, *au* : *ū* are completely regular, cf.:

daũžia '(he) breaks' : *dùžo* '(it) broke' : *dũžis* 'blow, stroke'
šiáušia '(he) ruffles' : *šiùša* '(he) rustles'
stáugia '(he) howls' : *stúgauja* '(he) makes howls'

The alternant *o–v* is included only with certain reservations, e.g. *sraũtas* 'flow' : *srovẽ* 'stream' : *srùvo* '(it) oozed' (*srùtos* 'dung water'), because *o–v* in tautosyllabic position is not possible.

The alternant *uo* is quite regular in verbs where it alternates with the heterosyllabic variant *a–v*, cf.:

melúoja '(he) lies' : *melãvo* '(he) lied'
šlúoja '(he) sweeps' : *šlãvė* '(he) swept'

Otherwise it is rare, e.g.:

juõkas 'laughter' : *jùkinti* 'to make one laugh'
daubà 'hollow' : *dùbti* 'to grow hollow' : *įdūbis* 'hollow space' : *duobẽ* 'pit'
gùli '(he) lies' : *guõlis* 'resting-place'

The alternations *uo* : *o* (*dúoti* 'to give' : *dosnùs* 'generous') and *ū* : *ui* (*bū́ti* 'to be' : *buitìs* 'everyday life') are irregular.

To the same series we can probably ascribe also the alternations *u* : *ū* (without *au* and *uo*), e.g.:

mùša '(he) beats'	: mū̃šis 'battle'
sùka '(he) turns'	: pósūkis 'turning'
stùmia '(he) pushes'	: stū́mė '(he) pushed'

1.20 The diagrams presented in 1.18–20 show that some different apophonic series have common alternants: *i* and *y* occur both in the *a* (*e*) and *i* (*ie*) series, *u*, *ū* and *uo* occur both in the *a* (*e*) and *u* (*au*) series. The common alternants cause the so-called **analogous apophony**, i.e. the occurrence of morpheme alternants belonging to different series, cf.:

krẽčia '(he) shakes' : krė̃tė '(he) shook' : krìto '(he) fell' : ãtkrytis 'relapse' (*a* (*e*) series) and kráičioja '(he) frequently falls' (*i* (*ie*) series),

breñda '(he) wades' : brìdo '(he) waded' : brastà 'ford' (*a* (*e*) series) and braĩdo '(he) wades about' (*i* (*ie*) series),

brė́žti 'to draw, to scratch' : brìžės 'harrow' : brỹžis 'line, scratch' : brúožas 'streak, feature' (*a* (*e*) series) and braižýti 'to draw, to scratch' (*i* (*ie*) series) : brū̃žinti 'to scrub' (*u* (*au*) series).

1.21 Finally, it is worth mentioning that Modern Lithuanian shows a strong tendency to level apophonic alternations, especially in the most productive and regular suffixing derivation, cf.:

pèšti 'to pull, to pluck'	: pašióti 'to pull, to pluck (repeatedly)'	→ pešióti
vèsti 'to lead'	: vadžióti 'to lead (repeatedly)'	→ vedžióti
mer̃kti 'to soak'	: markýti 'to soak thoroughly'	→ mirkýti
juõktis 'to laugh'	: jùkinti 'to make laugh'	→ juõkinti
výsti 'to wither'	: vaitìnti 'to cause withering'	→ výtinti

When such morphological doublets occur, the item which contains no vocalic alternation (i.e. no marked alternant) is more recent.

Alternations of consonants

Príebalsių kaĩtos

1.22 At the end of morphemes preceding the root, the correlations of palatalization and voice are neutralized, and the opposition between sibilants and shibilants is also neutralized before affricates. The sequences *t*, *d* + *s*, *z*, *š*, *ž* undergo these changes and are usually retained in this position in *lento* forms, e.g.: *at-sùkti* 'to turn back', *at-šáuti* 'to reply sharply', *púo*[t]-*šakės* 'long-handled fork for lifting and moving pots in an oven', *a*[d̦]-*žygiúoti* 'to come marching'; in *allegro* forms, they become affricates: a[ts]ùkti, a[tʃ]áuti, púo[tʃ]akės, a[dʒ]ygiúoti. Affricates are **always** pronounced at the boundary between a prefix and the reflexive affix, e.g.: atsisakýti [aʦɪsaˋkʲiːtʲɪ] 'to refuse', atsitráukti [aʦɪˋtrɑˑoktʲɪ] 'to draw back'.

A sequence of two identical adjacent consonants in the aforementioned position usually undergoes **degemination,** and only the second one is being pronounced, e.g.:

pùsseserė ['pɔʂɛʂɛɾeː] '(female) cousin'   užsùkti [ɔˈsoktʲɪ] 'to turn off'
iššókti [ɪˋʃoːktʲɪ] 'to jump out'   užšálti [ɔˋʃɑˑlʲtʲɪ] 'to freeze over'
užžélti [ɔˋʒʲæːlʲtʲɪ] 'to overgrow (with)'   pùsžalis ['pɔʒalʲɪs] 'underdone'

In carefully articulated speech, however, the longer duration of the consonant or even the sequence [ʃs] may be retained, e.g.:

ùžsienis 'foreign country' = ['oʂiɛɲɪs] ‖ ['osˑiɛɲɪs] ‖ ['oʃʂiɛɲɪs]

Especially frequent and regular is the geminate [r̝ː] (and [rː]) in such cases, cf.:

parìtinti [paˈr̝ɪtʲɪɲtʲɪ] 'to roll a little' ≠ parrìtinti [paˈr̝ˑɪtʲɪɲtʲɪ] 'to roll back'

1.23 Consonants at the boundary between the root and suffixes are subject to more intricate morphonological processes. Along with the neutralizations, the following are of the greatest importance:

(1) **Dissimilation** of the adjacent t and d, i.e. t, d → s /– t and d, t → z /– d, e.g.:

met- + -ti (mēta '(he) throws')   → mèsti 'to throw'
ved- + -ti (vēda '(he) leads')   → vèsti 'to lead'
ved- + -damas   → vè[z]damas 'while leading'
met- + -damas → med-damas   → mè[z]damas 'while throwing'
kand- + -ti (kánda '(he) bites')   → kánt-ti → kánsti → ką́sti 'to bite' (see 1.9)
žaid- + -da (žeĩdė '(he) wounded')   → žaizdà 'wound'

The second person singular imperative forms, such as mèsk 'throw!' and vèsk 'lead!', are made from the infinitive root variant which had undergone a dissimilative change in the infinitive.

(2) **Contraction** of adjacent sibilants, i.e. š, ž + s → š, e.g.:

rìš- + -siu (rìša '(he) ties')   → rìšiu '(I) will tie'
mėž- + -slas (mėžia '(he) manures')   → mė́šlas 'manure'

(3) **Elision** (omission) of t and d before s, i.e. t, d → ∅ /– s, e.g.:

mèt- + -s (mēta '(he) throws')   → mès '(he) will throw'
júod- + -svas (júodas 'black')   → júosvas 'blackish'
prat- + -smẽ (supràto '(he) understood', prõtas 'mind, sense') → prasmẽ 'sense, meaning'
kánd- + -snis (kánda '(he) bites')   → kánsnis → ką́snis 'bit'

The sequences *t, d + š*, however, simply change into affricates, e.g.:

gùd- + -šas (*gudrùs* 'clever', *ìgudęs* 'skilful') → *gùčas* 'crafty man'
snùd- + -šas (*snáudė* '(he) drowsed') → *snùčas* 'sleepy person'

Some other omissions of consonants are also possible, but they are less regular (cf. *smárd- + -vė → smárvė* 'stink' and *smardìnti* 'to give a stink').

(4) Metathesis (exchange of positions of consonants) such as *SK + C → KSC* (*K* – backlingual plosive, *S* – sibilant, *C* – any consonant), e.g.:

drė̃sk- + -ti (*drė̃skė* '(he) tore') → *drė̃ksti* 'to tear'
tìšk- + -ti (*tìško* '(it) splashed') → *tìkšti* 'to splash'
mèzg- + -damas (*mēzga* '(he) knits') → *mègzdamas* 'while knitting'
čiršk- + -lys (*čiřškia* '(he) chirps') → *čirkšlys̃* 'chirper'
trýšk- + -sta (*trýško* '(it) spouted') → *trýkš-sta → trýkšta* '(it) spouts'

1.24 The only nonautomatic alternations of consonants (functionally resembling apophony) are **palatalization** and, less frequently, **depalatalization**, cf.:

geraĩ 'well' : *geriaũ* 'better'
vėlaĩ 'late' : *vėliaũ* 'later'
blogaĩ 'badly' : *blogiaũ* 'worse'
žãlias 'green' : *žalùmas* 'greenness'

Affrication such as {t̪, d̪} → [t͡ɕ, d͡ʑ] is only a particular ("external") case of palatalization, e.g.:

aukštaĩ 'high' : *aukščiaũ* (← *aukš{t̪}aũ*) 'higher' = *juodaĩ* 'black' : *juodžiaũ* (← *juo{d̪}aũ*) 'blacker'

Morphonological palatalization is changing of a stem final non-palatalized consonant into a corresponding palatalized one before certain "palatalising" affixes beginning with a non-front vowel, e.g.:

laisv- + -ʹau (*laisvaĩ* 'freely') → *laisviaũ* 'more freely'
maž- + -ʹukas (*mãžas* 'small') → *mažiùkas* 'very small'

Depalatalization is changing of a stem final palatalized consonant into a corresponding non-palatalized one before "depalatalising" affixes, e.g.:

tuš{t̪}- + -okas (*tùščias* 'empty') → *tuštókas* 'somewhat empty'
ža{l̪}- + -umas (*žãlias* 'green') → *žalùmas* 'greenness'

Palatalization regularly occurs, for instance, before the superlative suffix, cf.:

gēras 'good' → *geriáusias* 'best'
tiřštas 'thick' → *tirščiáusias* (= *tirš{t̪}ausias*) 'thickest'

Depalatalization is regular in the formation of nouns from adjectives with the suffix *-ùmas*, e.g.:

dìdis 'great' (Gen. Sg. *dìdžio*) → *didùmas* 'greatness'
plókščias (= *plokš{ţ}as*) 'flat' → *plokštùmas* 'flatness'

Palatalization and depalatalization are to be considered as an additional feature of a suffix (or a derivational ending, cf.: *kùbilas* 'tub, barrel' : *kubìlius* 'cooper'), but not that of an underlying stem. Therefore palatalising suffixes (and endings) need to be marked, for instance, {-´av}, {-´avşas}, {-´ɑkas} (in the standard orthography *-iau*, *-iausias*, *-iukas* respectively), to indicate that a consonant preceding these affixes is always palatalized. The absence of ´ (or of the letter *i* in spelling) shows that an affix does not possess this feature. Suffixes which have both palatalising and depalatalising allomorphs might be indicated in the following way: {-(´)ɑkas}, {-(´)ɑķe:} (*-(i)ukas*, *-(i)ukė* respectively), cf.:

krãštas 'edge' : *kraščiùkas* (← *kraš{ţ}ùkas*) 'small edge'
šlúota 'broom' : *šluočiùkė* (← *šluo{ţ}ùkė*) 'small broom'
but: *lãpas* 'leaf' : *lapùkas* 'small leaf'
širdìs (Gen. Pl. *širdžių̃*) 'heart' : *širdùkė* 'little heart'

2 ACCENTUATION

Kirčiāvimas

2.1 As it has been mentioned before (I.6.1), the Lithuanian language has a free (or distinctive) word stress: it means that words and their forms can be distinguished by stress contrast (cf.: *lìkime* 'let's stay' ≠ *likìme* 'oh fate' ≠ *likimè* '(in the) fate'). The position of the stress is determined not by the phonetic properties of syllables or their distance in relation to the word boundary, but by the accentual properties of morphemes a word is composed of, i.e. by their relative **accentual value**. Besides, in certain cases the stress pattern of a word can be modified by the quantity of morphemes and their toneme (or syllable accent). This influence, however, depends on morphonological factors.

The essential principles of Lithuanian accentuation can be clearly and simply expounded by using examples of dissyllabic noun declension.

2.2 According to their accentual value, all stems of dissyllabic nouns (i.e. all monosyllabic stems) can be classified into two types:

(1) **strong** stems (*A*), i.e. stems receiving stress before any ending(*e*, *E*), e.g.: Acc. Sg. *píev-(-ą)* 'meadow', *viẽt-(-ą)* 'place', *vìšt-(-ą)* 'hen';

(2) **weak** stems (*a*), i.e. stems receiving stress only before a weak ending (*e*), e.g.: Acc. Sg. *skíedr-(-ą)* 'chip', *diẽn-(-ą)* 'day', *mìgl-(-ą)* 'mist'.

Besides, each type can be subdivided into **acuted** stems (*Á*, e.g., Acc. Sg. *píev-[-ą]*; *á*, e.g., *skíedr-[-ą]*) and **non-acuted** (i.e. short or circumflexed) stems (*Ã*, e.g., Acc. Sg. *vìšt-[-ą]*, *viẽt-[-ą]*; *ã*, e.g., *mìgl-[-ą]*, *diẽn-[-ą]*).

The accentual value of stems is usually determined according to the position of the stress in the dative or genitive plural: in these forms **strong** stems are always **stressed**, while **weak** stems are **unstressed**, cf.: *pievóms* '(to the) meadows', *pievų̃* '(of the) meadows' or *viẽt-oms* '(to the) places', *viẽt-ų* '(of the) places' (strong stems; *A*) and *skiedr-óms* '(to the) chips', *skiedr-ų̃* '(of the) chips' or *dien-óms* '(to the) days', *dien-ų̃* '(of the) days' (weak stems; *a*). The toneme (or syllable accent) of a long stem is usually determined through the accusative singular form, cf.: *píev-ą* (*Á*) : *viẽt-ą* (*Ã*) : *skíedr-ą* (*á*) : *diẽn-ą* (*ã*), or (for instance, in cases of *pluralia*

78   MORPHONOLOGY

tantum) through any other form containing a stressed stem, cf.: Nom. Pl. *žirklės* 'scissors' (*Á*) : *kar̃čiai* 'mane' (*Ã*) : *rùngčios* 'competition' (*à*) : *kriaũnos* 'handle' (*ã*).

2.3   The inflexional endings can be classified into the same types as stems (the stressed morpheme is indicated in bold type):

(1) **strong** endings (*E*), i.e. endings receiving stress if the stem is weak (*aE* → *aE*), but remaining unstressed in a combination with a strong stem (*AE* → *AE*), cf.: Gen. Pl. (*migl-*)-*ų̃* '(of the) mists' : (*višt-*)-*ų* '(of the) hens', Dat. Pl. (*migl-*)-*óms* '(to the) mists' : (*višt-*)-*oms*, Loc. Pl. (*migl-*)-*osè*[3] : (*višt-*)-*ose* '(in the) hens';

(2) **weak** endings (*e*) remain unstressed following both strong and weak stems (*Ae* → *Ae*, *ae* → *ae*), e.g.: Dat. Sg. (*višt-*)-*ai* '(to the) hen', (*mìgl-*)-*ai* '(to the) mist', Acc. Sg. (*mìgl-*)-*ą* 'mist', (*višt-*)-*ą* 'hen'.

Each type has special **attractive** endings (*È, è*), i.e. endings always attracting stress onto themselves from the preceding **non-acuted** syllable in compliance with the so-called penultimate-syllable rule (or de Saussure and Fortunatov's synchronic law), e.g.: Nom. Sg. (*višt-*)-*à* (*È*), Instr. Sg. (*višt-*)-*à*, Acc. Pl. (*višt-*)-*às* (*è*), but Voc. Sg. (*vìšt-*)-*a* (*e*, i.e. a non-attractive ending). In combination with acuted stems they behave like simple endings of corresponding accentual value (see 2.4).

Note: Short attractive endings in most cases have long acuted allomorphs before enclitic affixes (cf.: *višt-à* 'hen' : *ger-ó-ji* 'good', see 1.1).

2.4   (1) If the ending is non-attractive, the position of the stress in dissyllabic forms is determined by applying the following rules:

(a) the stress falls on any strong stem (or simply on the first strong morph):

Ae → *Ae*:	Dat. Sg.	PÍEV-*ai*	→ *píevai* '(to the) meadow'
		VIẼT-*ai*	→ *viẽtai* '(to the) place'
	Acc. Sg.	PÍEV-*ą*	→ *píevą*, VIẼT-*ą* → *viẽtą*;
	Nom. Pl.	PÍEV-*os*	→ *píevos* 'meadows'
		VIẼT-*os*	→ *viẽtos* 'places'
		VÌŠT-*os*	→ *vìštos* 'hens'
AE → *AE*:	Gen. Pl.	PÍEV-*Ų*	→ *píevų*
		VIẼT-*Ų*	→ *viẽtų*
	Dat. Pl.	PÍEV-OMS	→ *píevoms*
		VIẼT-OMS	→ *viẽtoms*
	Loc. Pl.	PÍEV-OSE	→ *píevose*
		VIẼT-OSE	→ *viẽtose*

[3] In stressed dissyllabic inflexional endings, the stress always falls on the last syllable.

(b) the stress falls on strong endings following weak stems:

aE → aE: Gen. Pl. skíedr-Ų̃   → skiedrų̃ '(of the) chips'
                    dien-Ų̃   → dienų̃ '(of the) days'
          Dat. Pl. skíedr-ÓMS   → skiedróms
                    díēn-ÓMS   → dienóms
          Loc. Pl. skíedr-OSÈ   → skiedrosè
                    dien-OSÈ   → dienosè

(c) the stress falls on weak stems preceding weak endings:

ae → **a**e: Dat. Sg. skíedr-ai → skíedrai
                        dien-ai   → diēnai;
              Acc. Sg. skíedr-ą   → skíedrą
                        dien-ą   → diēną

(2) Attractive endings in combination with acuted stems are stressed or unstressed according to the general rules:

(a) Áè → **Á**e: Instr. Sg. PÍEV-à   → píeva
                  Acc. Pl.   PÍEV-às → píevas
ÁÈ → **Á**E: Nom. Sg.   PÍEV-à   → píeva
(b) áÈ → aÈ: Nom. Sg.   skíedr-À → skiedrà
(c) áè → **á**e: Instr. Sg. skíedr-à → skíedra
                  Acc. Pl.   skíedr-às → skíedras

(3) Attractive endings following **non-acuted** (i.e. short or long circumflected) stems are always stressed (de Saussure and Fortunatov's law), e.g.:

Ãè → Aè: Instr. Sg. VIẼT-à   → vietà
                        VÌŠT-à   → vištà
            Acc. Pl.   VIẼT-às → vietàs
                        VÌŠT-às → vištàs
ÃÈ → AÈ: Nom. Sg.   VIẼT-À   → vietà
                        VÌŠT-À   → vištà
ãè → aè: Instr. Sg. dien-à   → dienà
                        mìgl-à   → miglà
            Acc. Pl.   dien-às → dienàs
                        mìgl-às → miglàs

(cf. also ãÈ → aÈ: Nom. Sg. dien-À → dienà, mìgl-À → miglà, when the ending must receive the doubly motivated stress according to the general rule as well, see 2.3, 1).

2.5 The accentuation rules stated above can be demonstrated by means of the declension and accentuation paradigms of the nouns *várpa* 'ear (of a cereal plant)', *rankà* 'hand', *galvà* 'head' and *kalvà* 'hill':

Singular

Nom.	várpa	(ÁÈ)	rankà	(ÃÈ → AÈ)	
Gen.	várpos	(ÁE)	rañkos	(ÃE)	
Dat.	várpai	(ÁE)	rañkai	(Ãe)	
Acc.	várpą	(Áe)	rañką	(Ãe)	
Instr.	várpa	(Áè)	rankà	(Ãè → Aè)	
Loc.	várpoje	(ÁE)	rañkoje	(ÃE)	
Voc.	várpa	(Áe)	rañka	(Ãe)	
Nom.	galvà	(áÈ)	kalvà	(ãE)	
Gen.	galvõs	(áE)	kalvõs	(ãE)	
Dat.	gálvai	(áe)	kálvai	(ãe)	
Acc.	gálvą	(áe)	kálvą	(ãe)	
Instr.	gálva	(áè)	kalvà	(ãè → aè)	
Loc.	galvojè	(áE)	kalvojè	(ãE)	
Voc.	gálva	(áe)	kálva	(ãe)	

Plural

Nom./Voc.	várpos	(Áe)	rañkos	(Ãe)	
Gen.	várpų	(ÁE)	rañkų	(ÃE)	
Dat.	várpoms	(ÁE)	rañkoms	(ÃE)	
Acc.	várpas	(Áè)	rankàs	(Ãè → Aè)	
Instr.	várpomis	(ÁE)	rañkomis	(ÃE)	
Loc.	várpose	(ÁE)	rañkose	(ÃE)	
Nom./Voc.	gálvos	(áe)	kálvos	(ãe)	
Gen.	galvų̃	(áE)	kalvų̃	(ãE)	
Dat.	galvóms	(áE)	kalvóms	(ãE)	
Acc.	gálvas	(áè)	kálvas	(ãè → aè)	
Instr.	galvomìs	(áE)	kalvomìs	(ãE)	
Loc.	galvosè	(áE)	kalvosè	(ãE)	

Each of the examples used above represents one of the four accentuation paradigms. Paradigm 1 refers to dissyllabic nouns with a strong acuted stem (their dative and accusative plural endings are unstressed: *várpoms, várpas*), Paradigm 2 to nouns with a strong non-acuted stem (their dative plural ending is unstressed, and the accusative plural ending is stressed: *rañkoms*, but *rankàs*), Paradigm 3 to nouns with a weak acuted stem (in the dative plural the stress occurs in the ending, while in the accusative plural it occurs in the stem: *galvóms*, but gálvas), and Paradigm 4 to nouns with a weak non-acuted stem (the ending is stressed both in the dative and accusative plural: kalvóms, kalvàs). In dictionaries, the numbers of accentuation paradigms are usually provided for nouns and other declinable words, e.g.: píeva (1), várpa (1), vištà (2), vietà (2), rankà (2), skiedrà (3), galvà (3), miglà (4), dienà (4), kalvà (4) (for more detail see III.1.34–38).

2.6 From the standpoint of accentuation, polysyllabic nouns with a stressed stem-final syllable do not differ from dissyllabic ones, but only very few of them belong to accentuation Paradigm 4 (except such place names as Garliavà (4): Gen. Garliavõs, Acc. Garliãvą).

Stems with at least one **intermediate** syllable between the stressed syllable and the ending function the same way as monosyllabic acuted stems, even if the stressed syllable is short or circumflected. In such cases the intermediate syllable prevents the application of de Saussure and Fortunatov's law, cf.:

Nom. Sg. šỹpsena (1) 'smile' : píeva (1) 'meadow', gilumà (3)[4] 'depth' : skiedrà (3) 'chip'
Instr. Sg. šỹpsena : píeva, gìluma : skíedra
Acc. Pl. šỹpsenas : píevas, gìlumas : skíedras

Therefore words of this type can be ascribed only to accentuation Paradigms 1 or 3.

2.7 The accentuation of derivatives is also mainly based on the accentual value of morphemes. According to their effect on underlying stems, for instance, most nominal suffixes can be classified into two types:

(1) strengthening suffixes (S), i.e. those which convert weak stems into strong ones (a1 + S → A2), e.g.: (a) žolė̃ (4) 'grass' → žolýnas (1) 'grass-plot', (b) žmónės 'people', Gen. Pl. žmonių̃ (3) → žmóniškas (1) 'humane', (c) dárbas 'work', Gen. Pl. darbų̃ (3) → darbiniñkas (2) 'worker', skolà 'debt', Gen. Sg. skolõs (4) → skoliniñkas (2) 'debtor' (cf.: mókslas (1) 'science' → mókslininkas (1) 'scientist', kopà 'dune', Nom. Pl. kõpos (2) → kõpininkas (1) 'inhabitant of the sand-dune area';

(2) weakening suffixes (s), i.e. those which convert strong stems into weak ones (A1+s → a2), e.g.: ámžius 'century', Gen. Pl. ámžių (1) → ámžinas (3a) 'eternal', stìrna (1) 'doe' → stirnenà (3a) 'doeskin', lãpė (2) 'fox' → lapenà (3b) 'fox-fur'.

Among strengthening suffixes we can also distinguish:

(a) strong suffixes (S), i.e. those which always attract the stress onto themselves

---

[4] 3ᵇ to be more exact. In such cases de Saussure and Fortunatov's law does not apply, the stress falls on the ending according to the general rule aE → aE (see 2.4).

($A+S \rightarrow AS$), cf.: úoga (1) 'berry' → uogienė (2) '(berry) jam', vaĩkas (4) 'child' → vaikẽlis (2) 'little child';

(b) **weak** suffixes ($\bar{X}$), i.e. those before which the underlying stem maintains or receives the stress ($A+\bar{X} \rightarrow A\bar{X}$, $a+\bar{X} \rightarrow a\bar{X}$), cf.: výras (1) 'man, male' → výriškas (1) 'manly, masculine', vaĩkas (4) 'child' → vaĩkiškas (1) 'childish';

(c) **neutral** suffixes (S), i.e. those which attract the stress from weak underlying stems, but do not shift it away from strong stems ($a+S \rightarrow aS$, $A+S \rightarrow AS$), cf.: šakà 'branch', Gen. Sg. šakõs (4) → šakìnis (2) 'made of branches', galvà 'head', Gen. Sg. galvõs (3) → galvìnis (2) '(belonging to the) head', but úoga (1) 'berry' → úoginis (1) 'made of berries', druskà 'salt', Gen. Sg. drùskos (2) → drùskinė (1) 'salt-box'.

2.8 Composition and derivation do not obey the accentuation rules so consistently as inflection.

First, additional phonological and morphological factors sometimes complicate these rules. For instance, in the derivational system of the verb an important role belongs to de Saussure and Fortunatov's law: the stress shifts from a non-acuted final (or single) syllable of the underlying stem to a weak attractive (acuted) suffix ($\bar{A}\acute{s} \rightarrow A\acute{s}$, cf.: laĩko '(he) keeps' : laĩk-ýti → laikýti 'to keep', but sváido '(he) throws' : sváid-ý-ti → sváidyti 'to throw'. Some suffixes and most derivational endings cause a shift of the stress to the final syllable of the underlying stem or an alternation of tonemes (i.e. the so-called metatony), cf.:

(a) geležìs 'iron', Acc. Sg. gēležį̃ → gelẽžtė 'blade (of the knife)',

(b) kùbilas 'tub' → kubìlius 'cooper', piemuõ 'shepherd', Acc. Sg. píemenį → piemẽnė 'shepherdess' (a change in the position of the stress), púodas 'pot' → puodžius 'potter', stóras 'thick' → stõris 'thickness' (circumflex metatony),

(c) plaũkti 'to swim' → pláukioti 'to swim to and fro', padraĩko '(he) scatters' → padráikos 'litter' (acute metatony).

Functionally, these phenomena do not differ from apophony (cf. 1.14).

Secondly, the accentuation of derivatives and compounds is subject to the influence of semantic factors and many other phenomena which all together produce morphonological **idiomaticness**.

The influence of a semantic factor is evident even in the accentuation of derivatives with an exceptionally productive suffix -inis: on the whole, this suffix belongs to the type of neutral strengthening morphemes (see 2.7), but in words denoting material it becomes a strong morpheme, e.g.:

bùlvė (1) 'potato' → bulvìnis 'made of potatoes'
mólis (1) 'clay' → molìnis 'made of clay'
mẽdis (2) 'tree' → medìnis 'wooden'

The semantic influence is especially conspicuous in the accentuation of compound words, cf.:

daugiãsienis 'polyhedron' : daugiasiẽnis 'polyhedral'
dvìratis 'bicycle' : dvirãtis 'with two wheels'
trìkampis 'triangle' : trikam̃pis 'triangular'

Morphonological idiomaticness is a peculiarity of the phonological 'shape' of certain derivatives and compounds which occurs not as result of the properties of their components. For instance, the suffix *-iena* in words denoting flesh of animals and birds belongs to the type of strong strengthening suffixes (cf.: ántis (1) 'duck' → antíena (1) 'meat of duck', kiaũlė (2) 'pig' → kiaulíena (1) 'pork'), but in the word *jáutiena* 'beef' it behaves as a weak suffix. A high degree of idiomaticness is especially characteristic of the derivatives with the suffix *-tuvė* (cf. vélti 'to full' : veltùvė 'fulling-mill', málti 'to grind' : maltuvẽ 'room for a quern', kráuti 'to load' : kráutuvė 'shop, store') and the prefix *pa-* (cf.: tìltas (1) 'bridge' : patìltė (1) 'place under the bridge', júosta (1) 'girdle' : pajuõstė (2) 'place under the girdle', kálnas (3) 'hill' : pakalnė (2) 'hillside', krañtas (4) 'bank, shore' : pakrántė (1) 'riverside, seaside', kẽlias (4) 'road' : pakelẽ (3b) 'roadside'), numerous compounds, and, lastly, place names and proper names. The accentuation of such words (like the meaning of idiomatic expressions) should be memorized as a whole. The same is true about the accentual value of simple stems (or the accentuation paradigm of a corresponding word).

III/Morphology

    General remarks (0.1–7) 89

1 Noun (1.1–38) 93
    Proper nouns (1.2, 3) 93
    Common nouns (1.4, 5) 95
    Morphological categories of the noun (1.6–15) 96
    Gender (1.6–10) 96
    Number (1.11–14) 101
    Case (1.15) 106
    Declension of nouns (16–33) 107
    Accentuation of nouns (1.34–38) 126

2 Adjective (2.1–42) 134
    Morphological categories of the adjective (2.2–24) 134
    Gender, number and case (2.2–6) 134
    Comparison (2.7–16) 138
    Definiteness (2.17–24) 142
    Declension of simple adjectives (2.25–33) 147
    Declension of definite adjectives (2.34, 35) 156
    Accentuation of adjectives (2.36–42) 159

3 Numeral (3.1–15) 165
    Cardinal numerals (3.3–6) 166
    Plain cardinal numerals (3.3, 4) 166
    Cardinal plural numerals (3.5, 6) 168
    Collective Cardinal Numerals (3.6) 168
    Ordinal numerals (3.7, 8) 169
    Fractions (3.9, 10) 172
    Declension and accentuation (3.11–15) 174

4 Pronoun (4.1–43) *180*
Morphological categories of pronouns (4.2–7) *181*
Gender (4.2–4) *181*
Number (4.5–6) *184*
Case (4.7) *186*
Semantic subclasses of pronouns (4.8–30) *187*
Personal pronouns (4.9–17) *187*
Demonstrative pronouns (4.18–22) *195*
Interrogative and relative pronouns (4.23–25) *198*
Indefinite pronouns (4.26–30) *200*
Declension and accentuation of pronouns (4.31–43) *207*

5 Verb (5.1–156) *220*
Transitive and intransitive verbs (5.6–11) *223*
Reflexive verbs (5.12–17) *227*
Aspectual differences (518–20) *234*
Morphological categories of the verb (5.21–78) *237*
Tense (5.21–40) *237*
  SIMPLE TENSES (5.27–34) *243*
  COMPOUND TENSES (5.35–40) *248*
Mood (5.41–54) *254*
  INDICATIVE MOOD (5.44–46) *256*
  SUBJUNCTIVE MOOD (5.47, 48) *258*
  IMPERATIVE MOOD (5.49, 50) *261*
  OBLIQUE MOOD (5.51–54) *262*
Person (5.55–62) *266*
Number (5.63) *272*
Voice (5.64–78) *273*
Finite forms of the verb (5.79–111) *284*
  VERBAL STEMS AND THEMATIC VOWELS (5.80–85) *285*
  ENDINGS INDICATING PERSON AND NUMBER (5.86–88) *296*
Conjugations (5.89–96) *298*
Conjugation and accentuation of simple finite verbs (5.97–107) *307*
Non-finite forms of the verb (5.112–156) *326*
Participles (5.112–153) *326*
  ACTIVE PARTICIPLES (5.114–120) *329*
  PASSIVE PARTICIPLES (5.121–123) *340*
  NEUTER PARTICIPLES (5.124) *346*

       Reflexive participles (5.125–128) *347*
       Definite participles (5.129, 130) *350*
       Meaning and usage of participles (5.131–153) *352*
         Attributive usage (5.132–140) *353*
         Semi-predicative usage (5.141–151) *360*
         Predicative usage (5.152, 153) *370*
      The infinitive (5.154–156) *372*
         Formal properties (5.154) *372*
         Meaning and usage (5.155, 156) *373*

6 Adverb (6.1–28) *377*
   Formal properties (6.2–15) *378*
   Degrees of comparison (6.16–22) *375*
   Semantic types of adverbs (6.23–28) *389*

7 Particles (7.1–15) *395*

8 Prepositions (8.1–33) *404*
   Prepositions with the genitive case (8.7–18) *407*
   Prepositions with the accusative case (5.19–27) *414*
   Prepositions with the instrumental case (8.28–31) *419*
   Prepositions with two and more case forms (8.32, 33) *420*

9 Conjunctions (9.1–7) *424*
   Coordinating conjunctions (9.5) *427*
   Subordinating conjunctions (9.6, 7) *429*

10 Interjections (10.1–9) *432*
   Meaning and usage of interjections (10.6) *436*
   Vocative interjections (10.7–9) *437*

11 Onomatopoeic words (11.1–15) *440*
   Formal properties (11.4–13) *441*
   Meanings and usage (**11.14, 15**) *447*

General remarks

0.1 This section concerns the forms of words belonging to various word classes (parts of speech) and their grammatical meanings. The derivational properties of words are dealt with in so far as they are relevant for inflection and help to characterize the word classes and their categories.

In Lithuanian, which is an inflectional language, the majority of word forms are made with affixes, viz. endings and inflectional suffixes. The endings are the principal means of marking the syntagmatic relations between words in a sentence and/or the relations between word forms in a paradigm.

0.2 **Endings** mostly are fusional, i.e. an ending encodes two or more grammatical meanings and thus a word form enters into the same number of morphological categories. For instance, the ending -*a* in the word form *dain-à* 'song' denotes the nominative case, singular number and feminine gender; the ending -*ais* in *vaik-aĩs* 'with children' indicates the instrumental case, plural number and masculine gender.

On the other hand, one and the same cluster of grammatical meanings can be marked by various endings. Thus the nominative singular of feminine nouns is also encoded by the endings -*i*, -*ė*, -*is* (cf. respectively: *mart-ì* 'daughter-in-law', *žol-ė̃* 'grass', *nakt-ìs* 'night'), the instrumental plural of masculine nouns is marked by the endings -*ais* and -*umis* (cf. *vaik-aĩs* 'with children', *sūn-umìs* 'with sons'). The choice of an ending is determined by the difference in the selective features of nouns which belong to different declension paradigms.

Inflectional endings may be homonymous. For instance, apart from marking the nominative singular of the feminine gender, the ending -*a* in the cited form *dain-à* 'song' also marks the instrumental singular form of the same noun, as in *sù dainà* 'with a song'. In such cases the broader context resolves homonymy.

0.3 **Suffixes** are also widely used in Lithuanian to make up word forms. They mainly indicate paradigmatic relations between word forms rather than syntagmatic relations. Inflectional suffixes are used to mark the degrees of comparison in adjectives and many adverbs, some tense and mood forms in verbs, and also the non-finite verb forms: the infinitive, participles (including gerunds) and verbal adverbs *(būdinỹs)*.

An inflectional suffix may be the only grammatical marker of a word form, containing no ending. Thus, the suffix *-ti* indicates an infinitive (*bĕg-ti* 'to run', *gáu-ti* 'to receive'), the suffix *-nt* is a marker of the present tense gerund (*bĕga-nt* 'running'), *gáuna-nt* 'receiving'), the suffix *-us* marks the past gerund (*bĕg-us* 'having run', *gāv-us* 'having received'). In most cases, however, inflectional suffixes are supplemented by endings, in other words, in a word form, some grammatical meaning(s) may be expressed by a suffix, and some by an ending. Thus, the suffix *-s(i)* marks the future tense and the endings indicate person and number in the verb forms *bĕg-si-u* 'I'll run', *bĕg-si-me* 'we will run', *bĕg-si-te* 'you will run', *bẽgs* 'he/they will run' (the 3rd person ending has a zero form, i.e. the absence of an overt ending is grammatically meaningful and indicates the 3rd person). The above mentioned suffixes *-nt* and *-us* denote voice and tense in participles, while endins indicate gender, number and case, e.g.: *bĕga-nt-is (žmogùs)* 'running (man) (PRES. ACT. PART. MASC. NOM. SG)', *bĕg-us-ią (mergáitę)* 'running (girl) (PAST. ACT. PART. FEM. ACC. SG)'.

0.4 In word forms, affixation is often (especially in the verbal paradigm) conjoined with changes in the root: it may be vowel alternation (cf. *keliù* '(I) raise' – *kėliau* '(I) raised', *dúodu* '(I) give' – *daviaũ* '(I) gave)', consonant alternation (cf. *jáut-is* 'bull (NOM)' – *jáuči-o* (GEN), *draũs-ti* 'forbid' – *draũdži-a* 'forbids' – *draũd-ė* 'forbade') or changes in stress and tone, cf. *ein-ù* '(I) go' – *eĩn-a* '(he) goes', *kél-ti* 'raise' – *kėlia* '(he) raises' – *kėlė* 'he raised' – *kels* '(he) will raise'. In these cases we find different root variants determined by general morphonological processes.

Sometimes, word forms are made up by means of suppletion, i.e. the forms of a word have different stems whose relationship cannot be accounted for by any morphonological rules. The common examples are the case forms of personal pronouns (e.g. *àš* 'I (NOM)' – *manè* 'me (ACC)'; *mẽs* 'we (NOM)' – *mū́sų* 'us (GEN)') and the various forms of the verb *bū́ti* 'be' (*esù* '(I) am' – *yrà* '(he) is, (they) are' – *bū̃na* '(it) happens to be').

0.5 Alongside simple (synthetic) word forms, made with affixes, a paradigm may contain **periphrastic (analytical) word forms** comprised of the main word and an auxiliary. Lithuanian employs periphrasis to make up some verbal tense and mood and voice forms, e.g. *esù bùvęs* 'I have been' (lit. 'I-am been'), *buvaũ rãšęs* 'I had written' (lit. 'I-was written'), *esù mùšamas* 'I am beaten' (lit. 'I-am being-beaten'), *buvaū nėštas* 'I was carried', *bū́čiau atė̃jęs* 'I would have come'. Periphrastic forms enter into an opposition with the synthetic forms of the same main word within a morphological category. Therefore they are also included in the system of morphological devices of Lithuanian.

0.6 A morphological category of a word class is structured as an opposition of inflectional word forms contrasted with respect to their distinctive feature which can have a syntactic or semantic character. Distinctive syntactic features (signaling grammatical relations between words in the sentence) motivate the formal oppositions of case in all the classes of declinable words, oppositions of voice, person, and number in verbs and also of gender and number in adjectives. Distinctive semantic features motivate number in nouns, definiteness in adjectives, comparison in adjectives and adverbs, and tense and mood in verbs. The category of gender in nouns has a partly derivational character but it is interrelated with their inflectional paradigms and therefore it is treated along with the categories of number and case.

0.7 According to the shared morphological, syntactic and semantic properties, words are classified into grammatical classes traditionally termed parts of speech. In Lithuanian, 11 parts of speech are distinguished: the noun, adjective, numeral, pronoun, verb, adverb, particle, preposition, conjunction, interjection and onomatopoeic words.

With respect to their function, the parts of speech are divided into notional, structural (functional) and expressive.

The notional parts of speech are the noun, adjective, numeral, pronoun, verb and adverb. They perform syntactic functions in a sentence and can constitute word groups. The words belonging to the notional parts of speech are mostly variable (except for most adverbs) and thus have morphological categories.

The structural parts of speech are the particle, preposition and conjunction. They have no autonomous syntactic function in a sentence and do not constitute word groups, instead, they serve to link (prepositions and conjunctions) or specify (particles) notional words. The structural parts of speech are invariable and thus have no morphological categories.

The expressive parts of speech are the interjection and onomatopoeic words. They are usually attached to other words or clauses to add emphasis or colour. They are invariable, like the structural parts of speech, but some of them can acquire a syntactic function as verb substitutes.

1 NOUN
Daiktāvardis

1.1 Nouns constitute a class of inflected words having independent morphological categories of gender, number and case. In a sentence a noun is mostly used as the subject or object.

Most typically, nouns refer to animate and inanimate things, human beings, substances, natural and social phenomena:

akmuõ 'stone' *ùpė* 'river'
brólis 'brother' *žuvìs* 'fish'
žiemà 'winter' *šveñtė* 'holiday'

Nouns may also refer to actions, states or qualities:

kvėpãvimas 'breathing' *grõžis* 'beauty'
lenktỹnės 'race' *lygýbė* 'equality'
liūdesỹs 'sadness' *gerùmas* 'kindness'

Morphological categories and syntactic functions of the latter nouns are identical with those of the nouns denoting things.

Nouns can be divided into two big groups – proper nouns and common nouns.

PROPER NOUNS
Tikriniai daiktāvardžiai

1.2 Proper nouns are names of individual phenomena singled out from a class.

All proper nouns are written with an initial capital letter. If a common noun is used as the name of a publication, institution or product, it becomes a proper noun (usually placed in quotation marks), e.g.:

"*Aušrà*" 'Dawn' (the name of a journal)
"*Snaĩgė*" 'Snowflake' (the brand name of a refrigerator)

Semantically proper nouns can be divided into two groups: those denoting living beings, and those denoting inanimate things.

The first group includes:

(1) personal names, surnames, aliases: *Ãgnė, Kęstùtis* (names); *Mačeŕnis, Vaĩšnoras* (surnames); *Mairónis, Žemaĩtė* (aliases of Lithuanian writers);

(2) names of animals: *Bėris, Sākalas* (names of horses), *Dañgė, Žãlė* (names of cows), *Brìsius, Saŕgis* (names of dogs);

(3) names of mythological beings: *Perkūnas* 'God of thunder', *Žemýna* (Goddess of the Earth).

The second group of proper nouns, which denotes inanimate things, includes:

(1) place-names, i.e. the names of settlements, lakes, rivers, mountains, forests, etc.: *Lietuvà* 'Lithuania', *Krãžiai, Dùsetos* (names of towns), *Medvėgalis* (name of a hill), *Nėmunas, Šventóji* (names of rivers);

(2) names of celestial bodies: *Aušrìnė* 'Morning Star', *Mėnùlis* 'Moon', *Satùrnas* 'Saturn';

(3) titles of books, periodical publications, art objects: *"Fonològija", "Aušrà", "Šaulỹs"*;

(4) names of associations, enterprises, organizations, institutions: *"Sántara"* (party association), *"Žálgiris"* (a factory);

(5) names of epochs, historic events, holidays: *Renesánsas* 'Renaisance', *Kalėdos* 'Christmas', *Velýkos* 'Easter';

(6) names of various products and their brands: *"Taũras"* (the brand name of a television set), *"Karvùtė"* (a candy brand name).

Semantically, the nouns of the last group are slightly different from those of the previous groups in that they are names of a particular group of things rather than names of individual things.

1.3 Proper nouns differ from common nouns in some of their morphological properties: generally, they are not inflected for number and are used either in the singular (*Kaũnas, Nerìs*), or in the plural: *Príenai, Zarasaĩ* (names of towns). But a proper noun which is usually used in the singular can also be used in the plural when it refers to several things bearing the same name, e.g.,

Šventóji   (the name of a river)
Šveñtosios (two rivers bearing the same name)
Birùtė   (a feminine name)
Birùtės (referring, for example, to two girls with the same name in a group)
Kaĺnius (a masculine surname)
Kalniaĩ (husband and wife, or two brothers)

COMMON NOUNS
Bendriniai daiktāvardžiai

1.4 Common nouns refer to any member of a class of similar things.

According to the properties of things they refer to, common nouns can be divided into two groups – concrete and abstract nouns.

Concrete nouns refer to concrete things, living beings, various phenomena. Most of such things are countables, therefore, the nouns used to refer to them are inflected for number:

nãmas – namaĩ 'house'
gėlė̃ – gė̃lės 'flower'
pavãsaris – pavãsariai 'spring'

Among the nouns which refer to countables there is a small group which have only the plural form (*pluralia tantum*, see 1.14). In this case the plural is used to refer both to one and more things, e.g.: *žìrklės* 'scissors', *marškiniaĩ* 'shirt'.

To indicate a definite number of their referents a special form of cardinal numerals, termed cardinal plural numerals, is used with plural nouns:

dvejì marškiniaĩ 'two shirts' cf. *dù výrai* 'two men'
peñkerios žìrklės 'five scissors' cf. *penkì paũkščiai* 'five birds'

Another group of concrete nouns consists of uncountables. This group includes mass nouns and collective nouns.

Mass nouns refer to substances which can be measured but cannot be counted. Therefore mass nouns are not inflected for number. Some of them are used only in the singular:

píenas 'milk'   *pliẽnas* 'steel'
grietìnė 'cream'   *giñtaras* 'amber'
áuksas 'gold'   *smė̃lis* 'sand'

Others are used only in the plural:

mìltai 'flour'   *dùjos* 'gas'
taukaĩ 'fat'   *klijaĩ* 'glue'

Mass nouns are not used with cardinal numbers, except in idioms, e.g.: *Gardù kaip devynì mẽdūs* lit.: 'Delicious like nine honeys.'

But mass nouns very often go together with words denoting measure units. Then they are used in the genitive (singular or plural):

lìtras píeno 'a liter of milk'   maĩšas mìltų 'a bag of flour'
kilogrãmas svíesto 'a kilo of butter'   bùtelis klijų̃ 'a bottle of glue'

Collective nouns refer to a group of similar things or persons as one indivisible whole:

aukštúomenė 'the higher walks of life'   profesūrà 'professorial staff'
jaunìmas 'youth'   žmonijà 'mankind'
moksleivijà 'school children'   senìmas 'the elderly'
studentijà 'students'

Collective nouns are not inflected for number. They possess only the singular and are never used with cardinal numerals. But they can be used with the adverbs *daũg* 'a lot of', *mažaĩ* 'little, few' and words denoting parts or proportions, e.g.:

Susirìnko daũg/mažaĩ jaunìmo.   'A lot of young people came.'
Pùsė žmonìjos.   'One half of mankind.'

1.5 **Abstract nouns** refer to abstract concepts, and also to generic actions, states and qualities. Abstract nouns are not inflected for number. The majority of them are used only in the singular:

esmẽ 'essence'   bū́klė 'state, condition'
drąsà 'courage'   šaĨtis 'the cold'
ramýbė 'quietude'   skubėjimas 'hurry'

There is also a small group of abstract nouns which are used only in the plural:

atóstogos 'holiday, leave'   vedýbos 'marriage'
láidotuvės 'funeral'   muštỹnės 'fight, brawl'

With indefinite or definite specific reference abstract nouns can sometimes be used in the singular as well as in the plural:

džiaũgsmas – džiaugsmaĩ 'joy'
rū́pestis – rū́pesčiai 'worry'
skaũsmas – skausmaĩ 'pain'

Morphological categories of the noun
GENDER
Giminẽ

1.6 Gender for nouns is a classificational category based on the opposition between the masculine and the feminine. That means that every Lithuanian noun is either masculine (*arklỹs* 'horse', *lángas* 'window', *sūnùs* 'son') or feminine (*aušrà* 'dawn', *bìtė* 'bee', *nósis* 'nose', *sesuõ* 'sister'), but one and the same noun is not inflected for both genders.

The gender of the noun determines the gender of all the other words – adjectives, participles, some numerals and some pronouns – which can be inflected for gender and which stand in agreement with the noun in a sentence:

dìdelis laũkas 'a big field' *šìtas studeñtas* 'this student'
dìdelė píeva 'a big meadow' *šità studeñtė* 'this student'

dù stalaĩ 'two tables' *pavar̃gęs výras* 'a tired man'
dvì kė̃dės 'two chairs' *pavar̃gusi móteris* 'a tired woman'

pirmàsis sūnùs 'the first son'
pirmóji duktė̃ 'the first daughter'

In many nouns gender distinctions are determined by the natural sex distinctions of their referents. A close connection between the biological category 'sex' and the grammatical category 'gender' can be observed in personal nouns and nouns denoting animals that man has a close connection with. Usually such nouns make pairs of different gender and their gender distinctions are most often (1) marked by affixes – inflexions (in the so called *substantiva mobilia* and sometimes (2) by suffixes, the root remaining the same:

(1) *darbiniñkas* *darbiniñkė* 'worker'
gýdytojas *gýdytoja* 'doctor'
vadõvas *vadõvė* 'guide'

(2) *ántis* 'duck' *añtinas* 'drake'
avìs 'ewe' *ãvinas* 'ram'
žąsìs 'goose' *žą̃sinas* 'gander'

Only a small group of nouns mark their gender distinctions both by different roots and inflections:

výras 'man' *móteris* 'woman'
výras 'husband' *žmonà* 'wife'
tė́vas 'father' *mótina* 'mother'
sūnùs 'son' *duktė̃* 'daughter'
brólis 'brother' *sesuõ* 'sister'
dė̃dė 'uncle' *tetà* 'aunt'
berniùkas 'boy' *mergáitė* 'girl'
arklỹs 'horse' *kumẽlė* 'mare'
jáutis 'bull' *kárvė* 'cow'
šuõ 'dog' *kalė̃* 'bitch'
gaidỹs 'cock' *vištà* 'hen'

When sex distinctions of animals are irrelevant and they are referred to generically, the noun is either masculine, which is a more frequent case, or feminine, e.g.:

Dúok, motùt, geriaũ katėms (fem.). 'You had better give it to the cats, mother.'

Tvártai šiamè kiemè didelì, pilnì galvìjų (masc.) ir kiaũlių (fem.), avių̃ (fem.), arklių̃ (masc.). 'The barns on this farm are large, full of cattle and pigs, sheep, horses.'

Both sexes of lower animals or animals that man does not have a very close connection with are referred to by one and the same noun, which is either masculine (a) or feminine (b):

(a) *bangìnis* 'whale'
ežỹs 'hedgehog'
erẽlis 'eagle'
varnėnas 'starling'
žvìrblis 'sparrow'
úodas 'gnat'
žaltỹs 'grass-snake'

(b) *pelė̃* 'mouse'
beždžiõnė 'monkey'
gegùtė 'cockoo'
lakštiñgala 'nightingale'
zýlė 'titmouse'
lydekà 'pike'
varlė̃ 'frog'

The young of animals or birds are referred to by masculine nouns:

ėriùkas 'lamb'
kačiùkas 'kitten'
kumeliùkas 'colt'
paršiùkas 'piglet'

šuniùkas 'puppy'
ančiùkas 'duckling'
viščiùkas 'chicken'
žąsiùkas 'gosling'

Thus, the semantic motivation of the gender of nouns denoting living beings is rather irregular: it is more transparent for nouns denoting human beings, less transparent or not transparent at all for nouns denoting animals.

The gender of nouns denoting inanimate things and phenomena, also names of actions and qualities do not have any semantic motivation whatever. Their gender is determined exclusively by their stems, case endings and modifiers.

1.7 Nouns possessing the following endings belong to the masculine gender:

(1) Nom. Sg. *-(i)as, -is, -ys*
Gen. Sg. *-(i)o*

dárbas 'work'
jaunìmas 'youth'
kẽlias 'road'
vėjas 'wind'

lietùvis 'Lithuanian'
kìškis 'hare'
arklỹs 'horse'
gaidỹs 'cock'

This group is the largest among masculine nouns.

(2) Nom. Sg. *-(i)us*
Gen. Sg. *-(i)aus*

dangùs 'sky' *skaĩčius* 'number'
lietùs 'rain' *vaĩsius* 'fruit'
medùs 'honey' *vasarójus* 'spring corn'

(3) Nom. Sg. *-uo*
Gen. Sg. *-s* (after the stem in *-n-*)

akmuõ – akmeñs 'stone' *piemuõ – piemeñs* 'shepherd'
dubuõ – dubeñs 'bowl' *šuõ – šuñs* 'dog'
liemuõ – liemeñs 'waist'

Here belongs also *mėnuo – mėnesio* 'month' (with the Gen. Sg. *-io*).

Groups (1)–(3) account for the majority of masculine nouns. The following groups are not numerous:

(4) Nom. Sg. *-is*
Gen. Sg. *-ies*
Dat. Sg. *-iui*

dantìs – dantiẽs – dañčiui 'tooth' *debesìs – debesiẽs – dēbesiui* 'cloud'
vagìs – vagiẽs – vãgiui 'thief' *viẽšpat(i)s – viẽšpaties – viẽšpačiui* 'Lord'
žvėrìs – žvėriẽs – žvėriui 'beast'

(5) Nom. Sg. *-a*
Gen. Sg. *-os*

These are typical feminine endings. Only a few nouns with them are masculine because they refer to male persons:

barzdylà 'bearded man'
vaidilà 'heathen priest'
viršilà 'warrant officer'

Here belong some masculine surnames:

Daukšà *Noreikà* *Dirgėla*
Póška *Daugėla* *Skirgáila*
Jogáila *Šniukštà* *Laučkà*

(6) Similar, but even more rare, are masculine nouns ending in:

Nom. Sg. *-ė*
Gen. Sg. *-ės*

                 Surnames:
dailìdė 'carpenter' *Breĩvė*
dėdė 'uncle' *Krėvė̃*
tėtė̃ 'father'

1.8 Nouns possessing the following endings belong to the feminine gender:

(1) Nom. Sg. *-(i)a*
Gen. Sg. *-(i)os*

algà 'salary'
dainà 'song'
galvà 'head'
žiemà 'winter'

girià 'wood'
galià 'might'
kirpėja 'hair-dresser'
valià 'will'

Here belong also:

Nom. *martì* – Gen. *marčiõs* 'daughter-in-law'
      patì –   *pačiõs* 'wife'

(2) Nom. Sg. *-ė*
Gen. Sg. *-ės*

bìtė 'bee'
dùlkė 'dust'
ẽglė 'fir'

mergáitė 'girl'
sáulė 'sun'
žolẽ 'grass'

Groups (1) and (2) account for the majority of feminine nouns. The other groups are less numerous.

(3) Nom. Sg. *-is*
Gen. Sg. *-ies*
Dat. Sg. *-iai*

ánkštis – ánkšties – ánkščiai 'pod'
akìs – akiẽs – ãkiai 'eye'
ausìs – ausiẽs – aũsiai 'ear'
avìs – aviẽs – ãviai 'sheep'
dalìs – daliẽs – dãliai 'part'

mintìs – mintiẽs – miñčiai 'thought'
pušìs – pušiẽs – pùšiai 'pine'
šalìs – šaliẽs – šãliai 'country'
žąsìs – žąsiẽs – žą̃siai 'goose'

(4) two nouns, ending in the nominative singular in *-uo* and in the other cases possessing the stem in *-n-*:

sesuõ – seseřs 'sister'
duktẽ – dukteřs 'daughter'

1.9 Indeclinable nouns of foreign origin are also treated as being either masculine or feminine. This is manifested in the endings of the words which are usually governed by the noun.

Indeclinable nouns of foreign origin ending in *-o, -u, -i* are usually treated as masculine:

nesuprañtamas argò 'incomprehensible argot'
polìtinis krèdo 'political credo'

geltónas taksì 'yellow taxi'
svarbùs interviù 'important interview'

Exceptions are nouns which refer to female persons:

gražì lèdi 'beautiful lady'

Indeclinable nouns of foreign origin ending in *-ė* are treated as feminine:

dìdelė fojė̃ 'big foyer'
pirmà kupė̃ 'the first compartment'
gerà ateljė̃ 'good atelier'

Exceptions are nouns which refer to male persons:

karìnis atašė̃ 'military attaché'

1.10 There is a sizable group of nouns which can be used in reference both to male and female persons without changing their endings. When these nouns refer to male persons, they are treated as being masculine. When they refer to female persons, they are treated as being feminine. In each case the gender of these nouns is manifested in the morphological forms of their modifiers:

Jìs bùvo tìkras nepasėda, nenúorama.	'He was such a fidget.'
Jì bùvo tikrà nepasėda, nenúorama.	'She was such a fidget.'
Nùslėpiau vìską nuo tõ kváišos Vinc̀ùlio.	'I concealed everything from that fool, Vinculis.'

Such nouns are said to be of **common gender**. The majority of them end in *-a*, which is a typical feminine ending. From the point of view of their semantics they form a fairly uniform group in that most of them refer to persons by pointing out their prominent negative quality, e.g.:

akìplėša 'impudent person'	*naktìbalda* 'night-owl'
dabità 'dandy'	*nekláužada* 'disobedient person'
ìšgama 'degenerate'	*pikčiùrna* 'spitfire'
kerėpla 'awkward, clumsy person'	*válkata* 'tramp'
kū́tvela 'dishevelled person'	

Some words ending in *-ė, -as* can be occasionally used in reference both to male and female persons, e.g.: *pliauškỹnė* 'chatterbox', *taũškalas* 'windbag, chatterbox'.

NUMBER
Skaĩčius

1.11 The Lithuanian number system consists of two groups of morphological forms – singular forms, which denote 'one', and plural forms, which denote 'more than one'. These meanings of singularity and plurality find expression in the case endings:

vaĩkas – vaikaĩ 'child, children'	sūnùs – sū́nūs 'son, sons'
pušìs – pùšys 'pine, pines'	duktė̃ – dùkterys 'daughter, daughters'
rankà – rañkos 'hand, hands'	akmuõ – ãkmenys 'stone, stones'

Some Lithuanian dialects have retained dual forms, mostly in the nominative and the accusative, which are used in reference to two and always go together with the numerals dù, dvì 'two' or the pronouns abù, abì, abùdu, abìdvi 'both'.

Gerbė ir mylėjo jìs abùdu Butkiù.	'He esteemed and loved both Butkuses.'
O dvì martì, melždamì kárves gretimuosè kiemuosè, plū́do vienà añtrą.	'While milking cows in the adjacent yards, the two daughters-in-law cursed each other.'

Such relics of the dual are inherited from Old Lithuanian which possessed a three-member number system, based on the opposition of 'one – two – more than two'.

From the point of view of their number nouns fall into two big groups: (1) variable nouns which can be inflected for number, i.e. nouns that can occur with either singular or plural number; (2) nouns which cannot change their number but are either singular or plural.

Nouns variable for number

1.12 Variable nouns are always count nouns which can occur with either singular or plural number, e.g.:

ą́žuolas – ąžuolaĩ 'oak'	mė́nuo – mė́nesiai 'month'
gãtvė – gãtvės 'street'	mintìs – miñtys 'thought'
mergáitė – mergáitės 'girl'	

The singular forms of count nouns can be used generically, i.e. they can refer to the class of things. When this is the case, the distinctions of number are neutralized, e.g.:

Šiaĩp jau lū́šis tokià pàt bailė̃, kaĩp ir kiáunė.	'Normally, the lynx is as timid as the marten.'
Neáuga mū́sų pušìs tokiojè žẽmėje.	'Our pine does not grow in soil like this.'

Some variable nouns are much more often used in the plural than in the singular. They include:

(1) nouns which refer to things consisting of two equal parts:

bãtai 'shoes'
kójinės 'stockings'
šlepėtės 'slippers'
langìnės 'shutters'
ūsai 'moustache'
pir̃štinės 'gloves'

(2) nouns the plural of which denotes an accummulation of things rather than a certain number of discrete things:

ãvižos 'oats'
javaĩ 'crops'
kviečiaĩ 'wheat'
rugiaĩ 'rye'
gárbanos 'curls'
mezginiaĩ 'lace'
pinigaĩ 'money'
plaukaĩ 'hair'

Nouns invariable for number

Nouns invariable for number are either singular (*singularia tantum*) or plural (*pluralia tantum*).

1.13 **Singularia tantum** include:

(1) abstract mass nouns:

kantrýbė 'patience'
kūrýba 'creation'
drąsà 'courage'
méilė 'love'
esmẽ 'essence'
grõžis 'beauty'
išdidùmas 'pride'
są́žinė 'conscience'

(2) collective nouns:

liáudis 'people'
aukštúomenė 'nobility'
profesūrà 'professors'
inteligentijà 'intellectuals'
jaunìmas 'youth'
vargúomenė 'the poor'

(3) concrete mass nouns (names of substances):

píenas 'milk'
áuksas 'gold'
sidãbras 'silver'
betònas 'concrete'
cùkrus 'sugar'
šokolãdas 'chocolate'
mólis 'clay'
varškẽ 'curds'

(4) many proper nouns:

Lietuvà Kaũnas Klaĩpėda Vaĩžgantas

Many of the nouns in the above groups can sometimes admit a plural form. Reclassification of mass nouns as count nouns is always connected with a shift in their meaning. For example, an abstract mass noun used in the plural refers to cases of concrete manifestation of a certain quality or action, e.g.:

Kaimiẽčiai nebùvo priprãtę prie švelnùmų.	'The village people were not used to amiabilities.'
Ir vẽl jái ùžima skausmaĩ žãdą.	'The pains take her breath again.'

The plural of names of substances usually refers to different kinds or products of the substance:

minerãliniai vándenys	'mineral waters'
įvaĩrios drùskos	'various salts'
gintaraĩ	'amber jewelry'

The plural of concrete or abstract mass nouns can sometimes be used to indicate a great amount or a great intensity of something, e.g.:

Devynì prakaitaĩ *išpýlė, kõl parnẽšiau.*	lit.'I was covered with nine sweats while bringing it.'
Griñdys bùvo kraujaĩs *paplū́dusios.*	'The floor was covered with bloods (i.e. a lot of blood).'

1.14 **Pluralia tantum** include:

(1) concrete nouns which refer to things consisting of two or more (equal) parts:

akė́čios 'harrow'	*marškiniaĩ* 'shirt'
akiniaĩ 'glasses'	*neštùvai* 'stretcher'
griñdys 'floor'	*rṍgės* 'sledge'
kailiniaĩ 'fur coat'	*var̃tai* 'gate'
kélnės 'trousers'	*žìrklės* 'scissors'

(2) nouns which refer to an accumulation or an amassment of certain things:

bùrtai 'magic'	*pãjamos* 'revenue'
išlaidos 'expenses'	*rãštai* 'writings'
lė́šos 'funds'	*sántaupos* 'savings'

(3) nouns denoting certain substances, dishes, waste or remnants:

bar̃ščiai 'beet soup'	*ãtsijos* 'siftings'
sakaĩ 'resin'	*dùjos* 'gas'
dažaĩ 'paint'	*išrūgos* 'whey'
mìltai 'flour'	*núosėdos* 'sediment'
pelenaĩ 'ashes'	*pãsukos* 'butter milk'
riebalaĩ 'fat'	*pjùvenos* 'sawdust'

(4) nouns referring to actions, processes and states performed or experienced by several (or many) persons:

derýbos 'talks'	*ríetenos* 'squabble'
eitỹnės 'procession'	*riáušės* 'riot'
imtỹnės 'wrestling'	*rinkìmai* 'election'
įkurtùvės 'house warming'	*skyrýbos* 'divorce'
kautỹnės 'fight, battle'	*vedýbos* 'marriage'
láidotuvės 'funeral'	*vestùvės* 'wedding'

(5) nouns denoting a time span, names of festivals, rites and celebrations:

atóstogos 'vacation'	*Kalė̃dos* 'Christmas'
išvakarės 'eve'	*Kū̃čios* 'Christmas Eve'
mẽtai 'year'	*Sekmìnės* 'Whitsunday'
príešpiečiai 'forenoon'	*Velýkos* 'Easter'

(6) names of some diseases:

niežaĩ 'scabies'	*tymaĩ* 'measles'
raupaĩ 'smallpox'	*vėjaraupiai* 'chicken-pox'

(7) names of the cardinal points:

Piẽtūs 'the South'	*Vakaraĩ* 'the West'
Rytaĩ 'the East'	

(8) some proper nouns:

Kybártai   *Šakiaĩ*   *Šiauliaĩ*   *Zarasaĩ*

Some of the above groups of plural nouns denote countable things (*kélnės* 'trousers', *žìrklės* 'scissors', *atóstogos* 'vacation', *vestùvės* 'wedding'), others denote uncountable things (*klijaĩ* 'glue', *mìltai* 'flour').

Plural nouns which denote countable things can be used in reference to

(a) one thing:

Padúok mán žìrkles.	'Give me the scissors.'
Jaũ mẽtai, kaĩ čià atvažiavaũ.	'It has been a year since I came here.'

(b) more than one thing:

Nusipirkaũ dvejàs žìrkles.	'I've bought two pairs of scissors.'
Daũg mẽtų nebuvaũ gimtãjame káime.	'I haven't visited my native village for many years.'

Note should be taken here of the special form of cardinal numerals which are used with plural nouns (see 3.5, 3.12).

Plural nouns which refer to uncountable things are incompatible with the meaning of number.

CASE
Liñksnis

1.15 The case indicates the syntactic and semantic relations of the noun in a sentence and is marked by the variations in its morphological form.

Each case is characterized by a specific range of functions and meanings; e.g. the nominative is primarily the case of the grammatical subject of the sentence, the accusative is primarily the case of the direct object, the genitive refers to such notions as possession, origin and so on.

In Standard Lithuanian there are six cases expressing the relations of nouns: nominative, genitive, dative, accusative, instrumental, locative. Traditionally, the vocative is considered to be the 7th case, although it does not indicate the syntactic function of a noun in a sentence. It merely refers to a person or thing addressed by the speaker. In the plural the vocative coincides with the nominative.

Some Lithuanian dialects possess still more cases. For example, the Eastern High Lithuanian dialect possesses two cases with a locative meaning:

(1) the inessive, which is encountered in Standard Lithuanian, denoting position or location within:

miškè 'in the forest' *miškuosè* 'in the forests'
píevoje 'in the meadow' *píevose* 'in the meadows'

(2) the illative, denoting motion into something:

miškañ 'into the forest' *miškúosna* 'into the forests'
píevon 'into the meadow' *píevosna* 'into the meadows'

Pockets of Lithuanian speakers in Belorus have preserved two more ancient Lithuanian cases with a locative meaning:

(3) the adessive, denoting presence at (or near) a place:

miškíep(i) 'at the forest'
miškúosemp(i) 'at the forests'

(4) the allative, denoting movement toward, in the direction of:

miškóp(i) 'toward the forest'
miškumˆp(i) 'toward the forests'

Declension of nouns

1.16 Declensional endings of nouns indicate not only the case, but also the number and (usually) the gender of the noun. For example, in the noun *mìškas* 'forest' the ending *-as* carries three meanings: (1) nominative, (2) singular, (3) masculine.

Differences in the inflectional forms of the same case are determined by the inflectional stem of the noun, or rather, by the final vowel of the stem. In the course of time the final stem vowels merged with the endings and, although they continue to exert a major influence upon the type of the inflectional form, they are, in the majority of cases, no longer clearly distinguishable from the endings. The easiest way to distinguish the inflectional stem is to look at the vowel before the final consonants *-ms* in the dative plural. For example, *dárbas* 'work', *výras* 'man' have the *a*-stem because in the dative plural they have the vowel *a* before *-ms*: *darbá-ms*, *výra-ms*. More examples:

ia-stem nouns:

| Nom. Sg.: | *svẽčias* 'guest', | *dal̃gis* 'scythe', | *gaidỹs* 'cock' |
| Dat. Pl.: | *svečiá-ms* | *dal̃gia-ms* | *gaidžiá-ms* |

u-stem nouns:

| Nom. Sg.: | *sūnùs* 'son' | *viršùs* 'top' |
| Dat. Pl.: | *sūnù-ms* | *viršù-ms* |

o-stem nouns:

| Nom. Sg.: | *galvà* 'head' | *jū́ra* 'sea' |
| Dat. Pl.: | *galvó-ms* | *jū́ro-ms* |

io-stem nouns:

| Nom. Sg.: | *valdžià* 'authority' | *martì* 'daughter-in-law' |
| Dat. Pl.: | *valdžió-ms* | *marčió-ms* |

ė-stem nouns:

| Nom. Sg.: | *draũgė* 'girlfriend' | *gėlė̃* 'flower' |
| Dat. Pl.: | *draũgė-ms* | *gėlė́-ms* |

i-stem nouns:

| Nom. Sg.: | *ausìs* 'ear' | *dantìs* 'tooth' |
| Dat. Pl.: | *ausì-ms* | *dantì-ms* |

Nouns with the final stem vowel *a* or *o* after the consonant *j*, which is always palatalized, are considered to have the *ia*- or *io*-stem, for example:

Nom. Sg.:   *vėjas* 'wind'   *kója* 'foot, leg'
Dat. Pl.:   *vėja-ms*   *kójo-ms*

iu-stem nouns, which in the nominative singular have the ending *-ius* (or *-us* after the consonant *j*), can no longer be determined by their dative plural endings because they have come to coincide with the endings of the *ia*-stem nouns: *vaĩsius* 'fruit' – *vaĩsiams*, *sõdžius* 'village' – *sõdžiams*, *pavõjus* 'danger' – *pavõjams*.

One cannot distinguish the old consonantal stems ending in *r* or *n* from the dative plural either. These consonantal stems have been retained only in the genitive singular. In all the other cases, except the nominative singular, consonant stem nouns are now inflected like *i*-stem nouns:

Nom. Sg.:   *akmuõ* 'stone'   *šuõ* 'dog'   *duktė̃* 'daughter'
Gen. Sg.:   *akmeñ-s*   *šuñ-s*   *dukter̃-s*
Dat. Pl.:   *akmenì-ms*   *šunì-ms*   *dukterì-ms*

Although differences between the declensional classes of present-day Lithuanian nouns are determined by their inflectional stems, these stems have merged with the case endings, such that the ending is considered an integral unitary morpheme containing both stem and case specification. For example, in the following way:

Nom. Sg.: *svẽč-ias, dal̃g-is, gaid-ỹs; sūn-ùs, virš-ùs; galv-à, jū́r-a; valdž-ià, mart-ì; draũg-ė, gèl-ė̃; aus-ìs, dant-ìs; vėj-as, kój-a;*

Dat. Pl.: *sveč-iáms, dal̃g-iams, gaidž-iáms; sūn-ùms, virš-ùms; galv-óms, jū́r-oms; valdž-ióms, marč-ióms; draũg-ėms, gel-ė̃ms; aus-ìms, dant-ìms; vėj-ams, kój-oms.*

1.17 In Modern Lithuanian there are five declensions, i.e. five classes of nouns having the same type of inflectional forms determined by the inflectional stem: *(i)a-, (i)u-, (i)o-, ė-* and *i-* declensions. The easiest way to define which declension a noun belongs to is by their endings in the nominative singular and the dative plural. Within each declension (except the *ė*-declension) it is possible to distinguish two or more slightly different paradigms, the total number of which is twelve (see Table 1).

The description of the five declensions here by reference to their inflectional stems does not introduce any radical changes in the grouping of Lithuanian declensions traditionally referred to by numbers, but it is more convenient in that it captures their interrelations, distribution according to gender, and, which is most important of all, it is applicable to the other declinable parts of speech (adjectives, numerals and pronouns).

1.18 Each case has more than one grammatical meaning, which becomes apparent in phrases. For example, the grammatical meaning of the instrumental case varies with the change of its lexical collocates and is different in each of the following phrases:

(1) *domĕtis mùzika*   'take interest in music'
(2) *pjáuti peiliù*   'cut with a knife'
(3) *važiúoti keliù*   'to drive along a road'
(4) *dìrbti vakaraĩs*   'to work evenings'
(5) *sùktis ratù*   'turn in a circle'

The meanings of grammatical cases are described in Syntax under "Subordinative word groups".

Table 1. **Noun declensions and paradigms**

Ending of Nom. Sg.	Ending of Dat. Pl.	Paradigm	Declension
-as	-ams	1	(i)a
-ias	-iams	2	"
-is, -ys	-iams	3	"
-us	-ums	4	(i)u
-ius	-iams	5	"
-a	-oms	6	(i)o
-ia, -i	-ioms	7	"
-ė	-ėms	8	ė
-is	-ims	9	i
-is	-ims	10	"
-uo	-ims	11	"
-uo, -ė	-ims	12	"

The *(i)a*-declension

1.19 The *(i)a*-declension comprises nouns of masculine gender with the following endings:

Nom. Sg.: *-as, -ias, -is, -ys*
Dat. Pl.: *-ams (-iams)*

Within this declension it is possible to distinguish three paradigms.

Paradigm 1:

Nom. Sg.: *-as* after a hard consonant: *výras* 'man', *pirštas* 'finger', *lángas* 'window', *mìškas* 'forest'

Dat. Pl.: *-ams* after a hard consonant: *výrams, pirštams, langáms, miškáms*
Acc. Sg.: *-ą* after a hard consonant: *výrą, piřštą, lángą, mìšką*

Paradigm 2:

Nom. Sg.: *-as* after a palatalized consonant, spelled as *-ias/-j-as*: *élnias* 'deer', *kẽlias* 'road', *vẽjas* 'wind', *galvìjas* 'head of cattle'
Dat. Pl.: *-ams* after a palatalized consonant, spelled as *-iams/-j-ams*: *élniams, keliáms, vẽjams, galvìjams*
Acc. Sg.: *-ą* after a palatalized consonant, spelled as *-ią/-j-ą*: *élnią, kẽlią, vẽją, galvìją*

Paradigm 3:

Nom. Sg.: non-accentuated *-is*, accentuated *-ys*: *brólis* 'brother', *peĩlis* 'knife', *arklỹs* 'horse', *būrỹs* 'detachment'
Dat. Pl.: *-ams* after a palatalized consonant, spelled as *-iams/-j-ams*: *bróliams, peĩliams, arkliáms, būriáms*
Acc. Sg.: *-į* : *brólį, peĩlį, árklį, bū̃rį*

DECLENSION PATTERNS

Paradigm 1

výras 'man', *piřštas* 'finger', *lángas* 'window', *mìškas* 'forest'

Singular

Nom.	výras	piřštas	lángas	mìškas
Gen.	výro	piřšto	lángo	mìško
Dat.	výrui	piřštui	lángui	mìškui
Acc.	výrą	piřštą	lángą	mìšką
Instr.	výru	pirštù	lángu	miškù
Loc.	výre	piřštè	langè	miškè
Voc.	výre	piřšte	lánge	mìške

Plural

Nom.,Voc.	výrai	piřštai	langaĩ	miškaĩ
Gen.	výrų	piřštų	langų̃	miškų̃
Dat.	výrams	piřštams	langáms	miškáms
Acc.	výrus	pirštùs	lángus	mìškùs
Instr.	výrais	piřštais	langaĩs	miškaĩs
Loc.	výruose	piřštuose	languosè	miškuosè

Paradigm 2

élnias 'deer', *kẽlias* 'way', *vėjas* 'wind', *galvìjas* 'cattle'

Singular

Nom.	élnias	kẽlias	vėjas	galvìjas
Gen.	élnio	kẽlio	vėjo	galvìjo
Dat.	élniui	kẽliui	vėjui	galvìjui
Acc.	élnią	kẽlią	vėją	galvìją
Instr.	élniu	keliù	vėju	galvijù
Loc.	élnyje	kelyjè	vėjuje/vėjyje	galvìjuje
Voc.	élni	kelỹ	vėjau	galvìjau

Plural

Nom., Voc.	élniai	keliaĩ	vėjai	galvìjai
Gen.	élnių	kelių̃	vėjų	galvìjų
Dat.	élniams	keliáms	vėjams	galvìjams
Acc.	élnius	keliùs	vėjus	galvijùs
Instr.	élniais	keliaĩs	vėjais	galvìjais
Loc.	élniuose	keliuosè	vėjuose	galvìjuose

Paradigm 3

brólis 'brother', *peĩlis* 'knife', *arklỹs* 'horse', *būrỹs* 'detachment'

Singular

Nom.	brólis	peĩlis	arklỹs	būrỹs
Gen.	brólio	peĩlio	árklio	bū̃rio
Dat.	bróliui	peĩliui	árkliui	bū̃riui
Acc.	brólį	peĩlį	árklį	bū̃rį
Instr.	bróliu	peiliù	árkliu	būriù
Loc.	brólyje	peĩlyje	arklyjè	būryjè
Voc.	bróli	peĩli	arklỹ	bū̃rỹ

Plural

Nom., Voc.	bróliai	peĩliai	arkliaĩ	būriaĩ
Gen.	brólių	peĩlių	arklių̃	būrių̃
Dat.	bróliams	peĩliams	arkliáms	būriáms
Acc.	brólius	peiliùs	árklius	būriùs
Instr.	bróliais	peĩliais	arkliaĩs	būriaĩs
Loc.	bróliuose	peĩliuose	arkliuosè	būriuosè

1.20 There is a certain degree of variation in the inflectional forms of the vocative singular of nouns attributable to the *(i)a*-declension.

(1) The vocative of personal names, declined according to Paradigm 1, has the ending *-ai*: *Jõnai! Juõzai! Antãnai! Daũnorai!* In colloquial Lithuanian this ending sometimes occurs in the vocative of common nouns as well, which is due to dialectal influence: *vãbalai!* (instead of *vabale!*) 'bug', *žéntai!* (cf. *žénte!*) 'son-in-law', *tėvai!* (cf. *tėve!*) 'father'. In colloquial Lithuanian the vocative of some personal names of this declension can also be formed without any ending: *Adõm! Póvil! Mýkol!*

(2) The vocative of diminutive nouns with the suffix *-(i)ukas* has two alternative morphological forms: (a) the form without any ending (most frequent): *Antanùk! broliùk!* 'little brother', *tėveliùk!* 'daddy'; and (b) the form with the ending *-ai*, which is less frequent and slightly dialectal: *Antanùkai! broliùkai! tėveliùkai!*

(3) The vocative of diminutive nouns with the suffixes *-elis*, *-ėlis* also has two alternative forms: (a) the standard form with the ending *-i* (see Paradigm 2): *vaikėli!* 'kid', *kunigėli!* 'Father (used to address a priest)', *bernužėli!* 'laddie'; and (b) the form without any ending, which is colloquial: *vaikėl! kunigėl! bernužėl!*

(4) The vocative of nouns, ending in *-jas* and declined according to Paradigm 2, has the ending *-au*, which is typical of *(i)u*-stem nouns: *mókytojau!* 'teacher', *kepėjau!* 'baker', *vėjau!* 'wind'.

(5) The vocative of two nouns, *brólis* 'brother', *Dievùlis* 'God', has two alternative forms ending in *-i* and *-au*: *bróli/brolaũ! Dievùli/Dievùliau!*

1.21 Simple non-derived nouns of Paradigm 2 with *-jas* in the nominative singular have two alternative locative singular endings, viz. *-uje* and *-yje*: Nom. *vėjas* 'wind', *kraũjas* 'blood'; Loc. *vėjyje/vėjuje, kraujyjè/kraujujè*. Nouns with a suffix ending in *-jas* have only one locative form ending in *-uje*: *mókytojas* 'teacher' – *mókytojuje, kepėjas* 'baker' – *kepėjuje*.

In the plural, verbal reflexive nouns without a prefix are used only in two cases – nominative: *veržìmaisi* 'invasions', *keitìmaisi* 'changes', and genitive: *veržìmųsi, keitìmųsi*.

The *(i)u*-declension

1.22 The *(i)u*-declension comprises nouns of the masculine gender with the following endings:

Nom. Sg.: *-us, -ius*
Dat. Pl.: *-ums, -iams*

Within this declension it is possible to distinguish two paradigms (Paradigm 4 and Paradigm 5).

Paradigm 4:

Nom. Sg.: *-us* after a hard consonant: *tuȓgus* 'market', *sūnùs* 'son', *dangùs* 'sky'
Dat. Pl.: *-ums*: *tuȓgums, sūnùms, dangùms*

Paradigm 5:

Nom. Sg.: *-ius/-jus*: *vaĩsius* 'fruit', *korìdorius* 'corridor', *sõdžius* 'village', *pavõjus* 'danger'
Dat. Pl.: *-iams/-jams*: *vaĩsiams, korìdoriams, sõdžiams, pavõjams*

DECLENSION PATTERNS

Paradigm 4

tuȓgus 'market', *sūnùs* 'son', *dangùs* 'sky'

Singular

Nom.	*tuȓgus*	*sūnùs*	*dangùs*
Gen.	*tuȓgaus*	*sūnaũs*	*dangaũs*
Dat.	*tuȓgui*	*sū́nui*	*dañgui*
Acc.	*tuȓgų*	*sū́nų*	*dañgų*
Instr.	*tuȓgumi*	*sūnumì*	*dangumì*
Loc.	*tuȓguje*	*sūnujè*	*dangujè*
Voc.	*tuȓgau*	*sūnaũ*	*dangaũ*

Plural

Nom., Voc.	*tuȓgūs*	*sū́nūs*	*dañgūs*
Gen.	*tuȓgų*	*sūnų̃*	*dangų̃*
Dat.	*tuȓgums*	*sūnùms*	*dangùms*
Acc.	*turgùs*	*sūnùs*	*dangùs*
Instr.	*tuȓgumis*	*sūnumìs*	*dangumìs*
Loc.	*tuȓguose*	*sūnuosè*	*danguosè*

Paradigm 5

korìdorius 'corridor', *sõdžius* 'village', *pavõjus* 'danger'

Singular

Nom.	korìdorius	sõdžius	pavõjus
Gen.	korìdoriaus	sõdžiaus	pavõjaus
Dat.	korìdoriui	sõdžiui	pavõjui
Acc.	korìdorių	sõdžių	pavõjų
Instr.	korìdoriumi	sõdžiumi	pavõjumi
Loc.	korìdoriuje	sõdžiuje	pavõjuje
Voc.	korìdoriau	sõdžiau	pavõjau

Plural

Nom., Voc.	korìdoriai	sõdžiai	pavõjai
Gen.	korìdorių	sõdžių	pavõjų
Dat.	korìdoriams	sõdžiams	pavõjams
Acc.	korìdorius	sodžiùs	pavojùs
Instr.	korìdoriais	sõdžiais	pavõjais
Loc.	korìdoriuose	sõdžiuose	pavõjuose

1.23 *(i)u*-stem nouns are not very numerous. In dialects they tend to acquire *(i)a*-stem inflectional forms, which sometimes penetrate into colloquial speech, e.g.:

Nom. Sg.: sū́nūs/sū́naĩ tuȓgūs/tuȓgai
Dat. Pl.: sūnùms/sūnáms tuȓgums/tuȓgams

Forms typical of *(i)a*-stems have become the norm in the nominative and dative plural of Paradigm 5: *sõdžiai, vaĩsiai, pavõjai; sõdžiams, vaĩsiams, pavõjams*; their ancient (now obsolete) forms were: *sõdžiūs, vaĩsiūs; sõdžiums, vaĩsiums*).

On the other hand, *ia*-stem nouns of Paradigm 2 have acquired *iu*-stem forms of Paradigm 5 in the locative and vocative singular (see 1.20–21).

1.24 Note should be taken of the inflectional forms of the noun *žmogùs* 'man': in the singular it is inflected according to Paradigm 4 of the *(i)u*-declension; in the plural it has *ė*-stem with a different final consonant (the consonant *n*) and it is inflected according to Paradigm 8 of *ė*-declension:

	Singular	Plural
Nom.	žmogùs	žmónės
Gen.	žmogaũs	žmonių̃
Dat.	žmógui	žmonėms
Acc.	žmógų	žmónes
Instr.	žmogumì	žmonėmìs
Loc.	žmogujè	žmonėsè
Voc.	žmogaũ	žmónės

The *(i)o*-declension

1.25 The *(i)o*-declension comprises nouns with the following endings:

Nom. Sg.: *-a*, *-ia*, *-i*
Dat. Pl.: *-oms*, *-ioms/-j-oms*

Those are:

mostly nouns of the feminine gender, e.g.: *jū́ra* 'sea', *rankà* 'hand', *galvà* 'head', *aušrà* 'dawn'; *sáuja* 'handful', *vyšnià* 'cherry', *žinià* 'news', and two nouns with the ending *-i*: *martì* 'daughter-in-law', *patì* 'wife';

a few nouns referring to male persons which are masculine, e.g.: *vaidilà* 'high heathen priest', *Veñclova* (a masculine surname), *Stùndžia* (a masculine surname); most of the nouns of the "common gender", e.g.: *vėpla* 'gawk', *drìmba* 'hulky person'.

There are two paradigms of this declension.

Paradigm 6: with endings after a hard consonant (*o*-stem nouns)

Paradigm 7: with endings after a palatalized consonant (*io*-stem nouns)

DECLENSION PATTERNS

Paradigm 6

jū́ra 'sea', *rankà* 'hand', *galvà* 'head', *aušrà* 'dawn'

Singular

Nom.	jū́ra	rankà	galvà	aušrà
Gen.	jū́ros	rañkos	galvõs	aušrõs
Dat.	jū́rai	rañkai	gálvai	aũšrai

Acc.	júrą	rañką	gálvą	aũšrą
Instr.	júra	rankà	galvà	aušrà
Loc.	júroje	rañkoje	galvojè	aušrojè
Voc.	júra	rañka	gálva	aũšra

Plural

Nom., Voc.	júros	rañkos	gálvos	aũšros
Gen.	júrų	rañkų	galvų̃	aušrų̃
Dat.	júroms	rañkoms	galvóms	aušróms
Acc.	júras	rankàs	gálvas	aušràs
Instr.	júromis	rañkomis	galvomìs	aušromìs
Loc.	júrose	rañkose	galvosè	aušrosè

Paradigm 7

sáuja 'cupped hand', *vyšnià* 'cherry-tree', *žinià* 'piece of news', *martì* 'daughter-in-law'

Singular

Nom.	sáuja	vyšnià	žinià	martì
Gen.	sáujos	vỹšnios	žiniõs	marčiõs
Dat.	sáujai	vỹšniai	žìniai	mar̃čiai
Acc.	sáują	vỹšnią	žìnią	mar̃čią
Instr.	sáuja	vyšnià	žinià	marčià
Loc.	sáujoje	vỹšnioje	žiniojè	marčiojè
Voc.	sáuja	vỹšnia	žìnia	martì

Plural

Nom., Voc.	sáujos	vỹšnios	žìnios	mar̃čios
Gen.	sáujų	vỹšnių	žinių̃	marčių̃
Dat.	sáujoms	vỹšnioms	žinióms	marčióms
Acc.	sáujas	vyšniàs	žinià̀s	marčiàs
Instr.	sáujomis	vỹšniomis	žiniomìs	marčiomìs
Loc.	sáujose	vỹšniose	žiniosè	marčiosè

The ė-declension

1.26 The ė-declension comprises nouns with the following endings:

Nom. Sg.: *-ė*
Dat. Pl.: *-ėms*

Except for a few nouns which are masculine, e.g. *dėdė* 'uncle', *Krėvė* (a masculine surname) and a few which are of the "common gender", e.g.: *mėmė* 'foolish/sluggish person', *spirgėlė* 'fussy person', all ė-stem nouns are feminine.

DECLENSION PATTERNS
Paradigm 8

gérvė 'crane', *bìtė* 'bee', *aikštė̃* 'square', *žolė̃* 'grass'

Singular

Nom.	gérvė	bìtė	aikštė̃	žolė̃
Gen.	gérvės	bìtės	aikštė̃s	žolė̃s
Dat.	gérvei	bìtei	áikštei	žõlei
Acc.	gérvę	bìtę	áikštę	žõlę
Instr.	gérve	bitè	áikšte	žolè
Loc.	gérvėje	bìtėje	aikštėjè	žolėjè
Voc.	gérve	bìte	áikšte	žõle

Plural

Nom., Voc.	gérvės	bìtės	áikštės	žõlės
Gen.	gérvių	bìčių	aikščių̃	žolių̃
Dat.	gérvėms	bìtėms	aikštė́ms	žolė́ms
Acc.	gérves	bìtes	áikštes	žolès
Instr.	gérvėmis	bìtėmis	aikštėmìs	žolėmìs
Loc.	gérvėse	bìtėse	aikštėsè	žolėsè

1.27 The inflectional forms of the ė-declension have retained their old stem best of all: we can observe here only the alternation of the long *ė* and its shortened variant *e*.

In colloquial Lithuanian the vocative singular of some polysyllabic nouns (mostly diminutives) is formed without any ending at all, e.g. *mergėl!* 'lassie!', *martėl!* 'daughter-in- law!', *sesùt!* 'sister!', *Elenùt!* (a female name), *mamýt!* 'mummy!' (cf. the vocative *mótin!* 'mother!' of the *o*-declension, see 1.20).

The *i*-declension

1.28 The *i*-declension comprises nouns with the following endings:

Nom. Sg.: -*is* (the most frequent ending for nouns declined according to this pattern)
-*uo* (which is traced back to the vowel of the old stem)
-*ė* (this ending appears only in one noun, *duktė̃* 'daughter', declined according to this pattern.)
Dat. Pl.: -*ims*

The *i*-declension has four paradigms. The number of the paradigms and the variety of endings in the nominative singular of the *i*-declension can be explained historically: the majority of nouns declined according to the *i*-declension can be traced back to the old *i*-stems, but there is also a number of nouns declined according to this declension that can be traced back to the old consonantal stems.

DECLENSION PATTERNS

Paradigm 9

Paradigm 9 is typical of feminine nouns ending in -*is* in nominative singular, e.g. *krósnis* 'stove', *širdìs* 'heart', *žuvìs* 'fish'. In the dative singular the ending is -*iai*, which accounts for the difference between Paradigms 9 and 10 (see Paradigm 10). In the genitive plural some nouns of this paradigm have the ending -*ų* after a hard consonant (*žuv-ų̃*), whereas others have this ending after a palatalized consonant (*krósn-ių*). This can also be explained historically: the former nouns are traced back to the consonantal stems, the latter to the *i*-stems (cf. the same variation in genitive plural in Paradigm 10).

krósnis 'stove', *širdìs* 'heart', *žuvìs* 'fish'

Singular

Nom.	krósnis	širdìs	žuvìs
Gen.	krósnies	širdiẽs	žuviẽs
Dat.	krósniai	šìrdžiai	žùviai
Acc.	krósnį	šìrdį	žùvį

Instr.	*krósnimi*	*širdimì*	*žuvimì*
Loc.	*krósnyje*	*širdyjè*	*žuvyjè*
Voc.	*krósnie*	*širdiẽ*	*žuviẽ*

Plural

Nom., Voc.	*krõsnys*	*šìrdys*	*žùvys*
Gen.	*krósnių*	*širdžių̃*	*žuvų̃*
Dat.	*krósnims*	*širdìms*	*žuvìms*
Acc.	*krósnis*	*šìrdis*	*žuvìs*
Instr.	*krósnimis*	*širdimìs*	*žuvimìs*
Loc.	*krósnyse*	*širdysè*	*žuvysè*

Paradigm 10

Paradigm 10 is typical of masculine nouns which have the nominative singular ending *-is*, e.g. *žvėrìs* 'beast', *dantìs* 'tooth', *debesìs* 'cloud'. Differently from feminine nouns, in the dative singular the ending is *-iui* (cf. Paradigm 9). Variation in the endings of genitive plural (*žvėr-ių̃*, *dant-ų̃*) is the same in nature and origin as in Paradigm 9.

žvėrìs 'beast', *dantìs* 'tooth', *debesìs* 'cloud'

Singular

Nom.	*žvėrìs*	*dantìs*	*debesìs*
Gen.	*žvėriẽs*	*dantiẽs*	*debesiẽs*
Dat.	*žvėriui*	*dañčiui*	*dėbesiui*
Acc.	*žvė́rį*	*dañtį*	*dė́besį*
Instr.	*žvėrimì*	*dantimì*	*debesimì*
Loc.	*žvėryjè*	*dantyjè*	*debesyjè*
Voc.	*žvėriẽ*	*dantiẽ*	*debesiẽ*

Plural

Nom., Voc.	*žvėrys*	*dañtys*	*dė́besys*
Gen.	*žvėrių̃*	*dantų̃*	*debesų̃*
Dat.	*žvėrìms*	*dantìms*	*debesìms*
Acc.	*žvė́ris*	*dantìs*	*dė́besis*
Instr.	*žvėrimìs*	*dantimìs*	*debesimìs*
Loc.	*žvėrysè*	*dantysè*	*debesysè*

Paradigm 11

Paradigm 11 comprises a small number of masculine nouns which in the nominative singular end in *-uo*.

akmuõ 'stone', *vanduõ* 'water', *šuõ* 'dog'

Singular

Nom.	akmuõ	vanduõ	šuõ
Gen.	akmeñs	vandeñs	šuñs
Dat.	ãkmeniui	vándeniui	šùniui
Acc.	ãkmenį	vándenį	šùnį
Instr.	ãkmeniu	vándeniu	šunimì/šuniù
Loc.	akmenyjè	vandenyjè	šunyjè
Voc.	akmeniẽ	vandeniẽ	šuniẽ

Plural

Nom., Voc.	ãkmenys	vándenys	šùnys
Gen.	akmenų̃	vandenų̃	šunų̃
Dat.	akmenìms	vandenìms	šunìms
Acc.	ãkmenis	vándenis	šunìs
Instr.	akmenimìs	vandenimìs	šunimìs
Loc.	akmenysè	vandenysè	šunysè

In the nominative singular the noun *šuõ* has an alternative form *šuvà* and in the genitive singular – *šuniẽs*.

Paradigm 12

There are only two nouns of the feminine gender, which are declined according to this pattern.

sesuõ 'sister', *duktė̃* 'daughter'

Singular

Nom.	sesuõ	duktė̃
Gen.	seseřs	dukteřs
Dat.	sẽseriai	dùkteriai
Acc.	sẽserį	dùkterį

Instr.	*seserimì/sẽseria*	*dukterimì/dùkteria*
Loc.	*seseryjè*	*dukteryjè*
Voc.	*seseriẽ*	*dukteriẽ*

Plural

Nom., Voc.	*sẽserys*	*dùkterys*
Gen.	*seserų̃*	*dukterų̃*
Dat.	*seserìms*	*dukterìms*
Acc.	*sẽseris*	*dùkteris*
Instr.	*seserimìs*	*dukterimìs*
Loc.	*seserysè*	*dukterysè*

Note: On the basis of the ancient differences in some case forms Paradigms 11 and 12 are assigned to a separate declension in many Lithuanian grammars.

1.29 In dialects and colloquial Lithuanian there is a strong tendency for masculine nouns of the *i*-declension to acquire endings typical of the *(i)a*-declension. Therefore in certain cases some of these nouns have alternative inflectional forms, e.g.:

Nom. Sg.	*debesìs/debesỹs* 'cloud'
Gen. Sg.	*dantiẽs/dañčio* 'tooth'
	debesiẽs/dẽbesio 'cloud'
	žvėriẽs/žvė̃rio 'beast'
	piemeñs/píemenio 'shepherd'
	rudeñs/rùdenio 'autumn'
Instr. Sg.	*žvėrimì/žvė̃riu* 'beast'
	dantimì/dančiù 'tooth'
	debesimì/dẽbesiu 'cloud'

The nouns *deguõnis* 'oxygen', *grobuõnis* 'predatory animal', *veliónis* 'the deceased' can be declined either according to *(i)a*-declension or the *i*-declension.

	Singular	Plural
Nom.	*grobuõnis*	*grobuõnys/grobuõniai*
Gen.	*grobuõnies/grobuõnio*	*grobuõnių*
Dat.	*grobuõniui*	*grobuõnims/grobuõniams*
Acc.	*grobuõnį*	*grobuoniùs*
Instr.	*grobuõnimi/grobuoniù*	*grobuõnimis/grobuõniais*
Loc.	*grobuõnyje*	*grobuõnyse/grobuõniuose*
Voc.	*grobuõni/grobuoniẽ*	*grobuõnys*

Table 2. **Noun case endings**

Cases	Singular				
	(i)a-declension			(i)u-declension	
	Par. 1	Par. 2	Par. 3	Par. 4	Par. 5
Nom.	-as	-ias	-is, -ys	-us	-ius
Gen.	-o	-io	-io	-aus	-iaus
Dat.	-ui	-iui	-iui	-ui	-iui
Acc.	-ą	-ią	-į	-ų	-ių
Instr.	-u	-iu	-iu	-umi	-iumi
Loc.	-e	-yje, -uje	-yje	-uje	-iuje
Voc.	-e	-i, -y, -(i)au	-i, -y	-au	-iau

	Plural				
Nom., Voc.	-ai	-iai		-ūs	-iai
Gen.	-ų	-ių		-ų	-ių
Dat.	-ams	-iams		-ums	-iams
Acc.	-us	-ius		-us	-ius
Instr.	-ais	-iais		-umis	-iais
Loc.	-uose	-iuose		-uose	-iuose

Some nouns of the *i*-declension have permanently replaced one, two or even more of their older inflectional forms with those of the *(i)a*-declension so that their paradigms are now a mixture from two sets of inflectional forms – the *i*- and *(i)a*-declensions. For example, in the instrumental singular the nouns *akmuõ* 'stone', *vanduõ* 'water', *piemuõ* 'shepherd' are *ãkmeniu, vándeniu, píemeniu* instead of the older forms *akmenimì, vandenimì, piemenimì*. The paradigms of the nouns *petỹs* 'shoulder' (the older form is *petìs*), *viẽšpats* 'lord' contain only two forms typical of the *i*-declension – the genitive singular *petiẽs, viẽšpaties* and the instrumental singular *petimì, viẽšpatimi*, which are often replaced by *pečiù, viẽšpačiu*. All their other forms coincide with those of the *(i)a*-declension:

	Singular		Plural	
Nom.	petỹs	viẽšpats	pečiaĩ	viẽšpačiai / viẽšpatys
Gen.	petiẽs	viẽšpaties	pečių̃	viẽšpačių
Dat.	pēčiui	viẽšpačiui	pečiáms	viẽšpačiams
Acc.	pētį	viẽšpatį	pečiùs	viẽšpačius
Instr.	petimì / pečiù	viẽšpačiu / viẽšpatimi	pečiaĩs	viẽšpačiais
Loc.	petyjè	viẽšpatyje	pečiuosè	viẽšpačiuose
Voc.	petỹ	viẽšpatie	pečiaĩ	viẽšpačiai / viẽšpatys

	Singular						
(i)o-declension		ė-declension	i-declension				
Par. 6	Par. 7	Par. 8	Par. 9	Par. 10	Par. 11	Par. 12
-a	-ia, -i	-ė	-is	-is	-uo	-uo, -ė
-os	-ios	-ės	-ies	-ies	-s	-s
-ai	-iai	-ei	-iai	-iui	-iui	-iai
-ą	-ią	-ę	-į	-į	-į	-į
-a	-ia	-e	-imi	-imi	-iu, -imi	-imi, -ia
-oje	-ioje	-ėje	-yje	-yje	-yje	-yje
-a	-ia/i	-e	-ie	-ie	-ie	-ie

	Plural				
-os	-ios	-ės	-ys		-ys
-ų	-ių	-ių	-i(ų)		-ų
-oms	-ioms	-ėms	-ims		-ims
-as	-ias	-es	-is		-is
-omis	-iomis	-ėmis	-imis		-imis
-ose	-iose	-ėse	-yse		-yse

In spite of its ending -*uo* in the nominative singular the noun *mėnuo* 'month' is declined according to the *(i)a*-declension:

	Singular	Plural
Nom.	mėnuo	mėnesiai
Gen.	mėnesio	mėnesių
Dat.	mėnesiui	mėnesiams
Acc.	mėnesį	mėnesius
Instr.	mėnesiu	mėnesiais
Loc.	mėnesyje	mėnesiuose
Voc.	mėnesi	mėnesiai

1.30 In Standard Lithuanian the inflectional forms of the feminine nouns of the *i*-declension exhibit more stability than those of the masculine nouns, except for:

(1) *sesuõ* 'sister', *duktė̃*, 'daughter', which in the instrumental singular have two alternative forms – one typical of the *i*-declension, the other typical of the *(i)o*-declension – *seserimì / sẽseria, dukterimì / dùkteria*; and

(2) *móteris* 'woman', *obelìs* 'apple tree', which in the genitive singular have two alternative forms – *móters*, *obelìs* (the older forms of the consonantal stem) and *móteries*, *obeliẽs* (the newer forms of the *i*-stem).

In dialects, however, there is more variability among the inflectional forms of the feminine nouns, for example, *širdìs* 'heart', *ugnìs* 'fire', *žuvìs* 'fish', *móteris* 'woman', *obelìs* 'apple tree' may have two alternative forms in the instrumental singular – one of the *i*-declension: *širdimì*, *ugnimì*, *žuvimì*, *móterimi*, *obelimì*, the other of the *(i)o*-declension *šìrdžia*, *ugnià*, *žuvià*, *móteria*, *óbele* (in the latter word the ending is of the *ė*-declension).

General comments on the declension of nouns

1.31 Modern Lithuanian tends to make a clear differentiation between the declension of feminine and masculine nouns: masculine nouns are mostly declined according to the *(i)a*- and *(i)u*-declensions, while feminine nouns are mostly declined according to the *(i)o*- and *ė*-declensions (except for a few masculine nouns which refer to persons). Though the *i*-declension is the only mixed declension, it is still dominated by the feminine gender (except for Paradigm 11, which comprises masculine nouns of the old consonantal stems).

The majority of Lithuanian nouns are declined according to the *(i)a*-, *(i)o*- and *ė*- declensions. Nouns which in the nominative singular end in -*(i)as*, -*ys*, -*(i)us* are masculine. In the dative singular all masculine nouns have the ending -*(i)ui*, while all feminine nouns have the endings -*(i)ai* or -*ei*.

Modern Lithuanian, its dialects in particular, exhibit a definite tendency to unify the inflection of nouns: less frequent inflectional forms are very often replaced by the more commonly used ones. The process is facilitated and spurred on by the existence of identical inflectional forms in different declensions. Thus, in the plural (Paradigm 5) the *iu*-stem nouns have acquired the endings typical of the *ia*-stem nouns of Paradigms 2 and 3; *i*-stem masculine nouns are often declined according to the *(i)a*-declension; similarly, *i*-stem feminine nouns are often declined according to the *(i)o*-declension. In this way the declensional system of Modern Lithuanian is becoming simpler.

1.32 A tendency to shorten certain inflectional forms can be observed in almost all Lithuanian dialects. The most frequently shortened forms are the following ones:

the locative singular (except for the *a*-stem nouns), e.g.: *kelỹ*, *būrỹ*, *tuřguj*, *júroj*, *aikštėj, širdỹ, vandenỹ* instead of *kelyjè, būryjè, tur̃guje, jū́roje, aikštėjè, vandenyjè* (but only *výre, pirštè, langè, miškè*);

the locative plural, particularly of the *a*-stem nouns, e.g.: *languõs, miškuõs* instead of *languosè, miškuosè*;

the instrumental singular of the *i*- and *(i)u*-stem nouns with the ending *-mi*, e.g., *sūnum̃, dangum̃, širdim̃, dantim̃, seserim̃* instead of *sūnumì, dangumì, širdimì, dantimì, seserimì*;

the instrumental plural of the *(i)o*-, *ė*-, *i*-, *u*- and consonant-stem nouns with the ending *-mis*, e.g.: *rañkom, galvõm, sáujom, bìtėm, žolė̃m, žvėrim̃, širdim̃, dantim̃, akmenim̃, dukterim̃, sūnum̃* instead of *rañkomis, galvõmis, sáujomis, bìtėmis, žolė̃mis, žvėrimìs, širdimìs, dantimìs, akmenimìs, dukterimìs, sūnumìs*;

the dative plural ending often drops its final *-s*, except in the Low Lithuanian (Žemaitian) dialect, e.g.: *káimam, namám, rañkom, ausìm, sūnùm, piemenìm* instead of *káimams, namáms, rañkoms, ausìms, sūnùms, piemenìms*.

From dialects the shortened forms are penetrating into Standard colloquial Lithuanian, which phenomenon is reflected in fiction, e.g.:

Sukinėjosi, trỹpė šlapiõj āsloj, mìndamas dár didèsnį pùrvą.	'He kept turning and stamping on the wet floor, making it still muddier.'
Jõ kišẽnėj dár yrà kẽletas skatìkų.	'In his pocket there are still a few coins.'
Kar̃tą pavìjom ją eĩnančią viẽškeliu jaunìmo būrỹ.	'Once we overtook her walking on the road in a group of young people.'
Miglótuos gyvẽnimo vìngiuos kiek kar̃tų manè apgavaĩ.	'In the hazy convolutions of life how many times have you deceived me.'
Ką par̃neši bróliam artójam?	'What are you bringing to your brother ploughmen?'

Indeclinable nouns

1.33 Indeclinable words are mostly borrowings of the following kinds:

(1) nouns ending in stressed *-ė, -i, -o, -u*, e.g.:

ateljẽ 'atelier'	*dominò* 'domino'
fojẽ 'foyer'	*taksì* 'taxi'
ragù 'ragout'	*tabù* 'taboo'

(2) a few nouns ending in unstressed *-i, -o, -u*, e.g.:

lèdi 'lady'	*maèstro* 'maestro'
spagèti 'spaghetti'	*zèbu* 'zebu'

Accentuation of nouns

1.34 There are nouns which have a constant stress, i.e. in all their grammatical cases the stress falls on one and the same syllable:

síena 'wall', *ãšara* 'tear'

	Singular		Plural	
Nom.	síena	ãšara	síenos	ãšaros
Gen.	síenos	ãšaros	síenų	ãšarų
Dat.	síenai	ãšarai	síenoms	ãšaroms
Acc.	síeną	ãšarą	síenas	ãšaras
Instr.	síena	ãšara	síenomis	ãšaromis
Loc.	síenoje	ãšaroje	síenose	ãšarose

But in the majority of nouns the stress is not constant, i.e. throughout the noun's paradigm the stress alternates between the ending and the stem. According to the pattern of the stress alternation all nouns can be broken down into four accentuation classes. The principal criterion for the attribution of a noun to one or another accentuation class is its stress pattern in the dative and the accusative plural.

Accentuation class 1

1.35 The first accentuation class comprises nouns which in the dative and the accusative plural always have their stress on one and the same syllable of their stem, i.e. their stress is constant.

When the stress in those nouns falls on the second syllable from the end, it always carries the acute toneme, for example:

Nom. Sg.:	*saváitė* 'week'	*pušýnas* 'pine forest'	*šokėjas* 'dancer'
Dat. Pl.:	*saváitėms*	*pušýnams*	*šokėjams*
Acc. Pl.:	*saváites*	*pušýnus*	*šokėjus*

(See also the accentuation of the following words given to exemplify the declension patterns in 1.19, 25, 26, 28: *výras* 'man', *élnias* 'deer', *vėjas* 'wind', *brólis* 'brother', *jūra* 'sea', *sáuja* 'handful', *gérvė* 'crane', *krósnis* 'stove'.)

When the stress falls on the third or fourth syllable from the end, it may have either the acute or the circumflex toneme, or it may be short, for example:

Nom. Sg.:	tė́viškė 'native land'	vãsara 'summer'	gìrininkas 'forester'
Dat. Pl.:	tė́viškėms	vãsaroms	gìrininkams
Acc. Pl.:	tė́viškes	vãsaras	gìrininkus

Beside simple, non-derived, nouns the first accentuation class comprises derived nouns with the following derivational affixes:

(1) nouns with a stressed suffix having the acute toneme:

-áila: sapáila 'nonsense talker', strapáila 'fidget';

-áitis, -ė: gimináitis 'relative', našláitis 'orphan', vaikáitis 'grandchild'; egláitė 'little fir', kumeláitė 'young mare', mergáitė 'girl'; but aukštaĩtis 'High Lithuanian (Aukštaitian)', žemaĩtis 'Low Lithuanian (Žemaitian)' are exceptions, they have the circumflex toneme and belong to the second accentuation class;

-ė́jas, -a: kirpė́jas 'barber', kirpė́ja 'hairdresser', pjovė́ja 'cutter (FEM)', siuvė́jas 'tailor', siuvė́ja 'dressmaker (FEM)';

-ė́nas, -ė: anykštė́nas, anykštė́nė 'inhabitant of Anykščiai', kupiškė́nas, kupiškė́nė 'inhabitant of Kupiškis';

-íena: kvietíena 'wheat stubble', rugíena 'rye stubble', naujíena 'news', avíena 'mutton', kiaulíena 'pork' (but: jáutiena);

-íenė: Budríenė, Kruopíenė, Žemaitíenė (female surnames), karalíenė 'queen';

-ýba, -ýbos: mitýba 'nutrition', sargýba 'guard', žvejýba 'fishing', dalýbos 'sharing', lažýbos 'wager', piršlýbos 'matchmaking';

-ýbė: aukštýbė 'height', didýbė 'grandeur', gyvýbė 'life', tuštýbė 'vanity';

-ýnas: ąžuolýnas 'oak grove', beržýnas 'birch grove', knygýnas 'book shop';

-ýna: lentýna 'shelf', šeimýna 'family';

-ýtis, -ė: brolýtis 'little brother', paukštýtis 'birdie', šunýtis 'puppy', akýtė 'eyelet', mergýtė 'girlie', sesýtė 'little sister';

-ójas: sienójas 'log', šilójas 'heather';

-ójus: vasarójus 'summer crops', rytójus 'tomorrow';

-ónis, -ė: ligónis 'he-patient', ligónė 'she-patient';

-óvė: bendróvė 'company', daržóvė 'vegetable', draugóvė 'brigade';

-(i)úkštis, -ė: varliúkštis 'naughty child', velniúkštis 'little imp', mergiúkštė 'derog. little girl';

-úomenė: kariúomenė 'army', visúomenė 'society';

(2) nouns with a stressed root or a stressed suffix of the derivational base (having the stress on the third, forth or further syllable from the end):

-ana: liẽkana 'remainder', ū́kana 'mist';

-atis: jáunatis 'young moon', pìlnatis 'full moon' (parallel with jaunatìs, pilnatìs 3ª)

-iava: *baũdžiava* 'serfdom', *gãniava* 'pasturage', *páiniava* 'confusion';

-estis: *gaĩlestis* 'pity', *lūkestis* 'expectation', *mókestis* 'tax', *rūpestis* 'worry';

-ėlis, -ė: *apkiaũtėlis, -ė* 'degraded person', *atsiskýrėlis, -ė* 'hermit', *išdýkėlis, -ė* 'mischievous child' (personal nouns derived from prefixed verbs);

-ininkas, -ė: *dùrininkas, -ė* 'doorman', *júrininkas, -ė* 'sailor', *mókslininkas, -ė* 'scientist' (nouns derived from nouns of the first and second accentuation class);

-ymas: *ardymas* 'disassembling', *mìnkymas* 'kneading', *tárdymas* 'interrogation', *válgymas* 'eating';

-liava: *rāšliava* 'scribble', *riñkliava* 'levy';

-sena: *eĩsena* 'gait', *galvósena* 'mentality', *rašýsena* 'handwriting', *vartósena* 'usage';

-tojas, -a: *gýdytojas, -a* 'physician', *mókytojas, -a* 'teacher', *rašýtojas, -a* 'writer';

-(i)uvienė: *keřdžiuvienė* 'wife of a herdsman', *Señkuvienė* 'a married woman's surname, wife of Senkus';

(3) nouns with following stressed prefixes, derived from nouns:

añt-: *añtkaklis* 'collar', *añtkapis* 'tombstone', *añtpetis* 'shoulder strap';

apý-: *apýkaklė* 'collar', *apýrankė* 'bracelet', *apýaušris* 'pre-dawn';

āt-, ató-: *ātgarsis* 'echo', *ātspalvis* 'hue', *atósmūgis* 'recoil', *atóveiksmis* 'counteraction';

į́-: *į́brolis* 'stepbrother', *į́sūnis* 'stepson', *į́rankis* 'tool';

ìš-: *ìšvakarės* 'eve', *ìšduktėrė* 'foster-daughter';

núo-: *núokalnė* 'slope', *núošimtis* 'percent';

pó-: *pógrindis* 'underground', *pózemis* 'underground', *póklasis* 'subclass';

príe-: *príeangis* 'porch', *príebalsis* 'consonant', *príegalvis* 'pillow', *príeskonis* 'spice';

príeš-: *príešaušris* 'pre-dawn', *príeškambaris* 'anteroom', *príešnuodis* 'antidote';

pró-: *prókalbė* 'parent language', *prótėvis* 'ancestor', *prótarpis* 'interval';

ùž-, užúo-: *ùžjūris* 'overseas countries', *ùžkrosnis* 'area behind the stove', *ùžkulnis* 'counter', *užúovėja* 'lee'.

(4) nouns derived from prefixed verbs by means of derivative flexions, with the stress on the prefix: *į́našas* 'contribution', *į́vadas* 'introduction', *į́žanga* 'preamble', *póbūvis* 'party', *sájunga* 'union', *sá̧žinė* 'conscience', *sándara* 'structure', *užúolaida* 'curtain'.

The first accentuation class also comprises the following compound nouns:

(1) compound nouns with the long stressed linking vowels *-ė̃-, -ý-, -ó-, -ū̃-*, carrying the acute toneme: *eilė̃raštis* 'poem', *saulė̃grą̌ža* 'sun flower', *darbýmetis* 'busy

season', *prekýstalis* 'counter', *dirvóžemis* 'soil', *galvósūkis* 'puzzle', *galvúgalis* 'head of the bed', *kojúgalis* 'foot of the bed';

(2) compound nouns with the stressed linking vowel -(i)a-, carrying the circumflex toneme: *bendrãbutis* 'hostel', *daiktãvardis* 'noun', *keliãlapis* 'voucher', *ugniãvietė* 'fireplace';

(3) compound nouns with the stressed short linking vowels -i-, -u-: *akìmirka* 'moment', *akìplėša* 'impudent person', *galùlaukė* 'the end of a field', *vidùdienis* 'noon';

(4) compounds carrying the stress on their first syllable: *bãdmetis* 'famine', *brángakmenis* 'precious stone', *brólvaikis* 'nephew', *rañkraštis* 'manuscript', *saváitgalis* 'weekend', *malūnsparnis* 'helicopter', *žíedlapis* 'petal'.

Accentuation class 2

1.36 The second accentuation class comprises nouns which in the dative plural have their stress on the stem (the second syllable from the end, which carries either the circumflex toneme or is short), while in the accusative plural they are stressed on the ending, e.g.:

Nom. Sg.:	*pir̃štas*	*galvìjas*	*peĩlis*	*tur̃gus*	*rankà*	*bìtė*
	'finger'	'neat'	'knife'	'market'	'hand'	'bee'
Dat. Pl.:	*pir̃štams*	*galvìjams*	*peĩliams*	*tur̃gums*	*rañkoms*	*bìtėms*
Acc. Pl.:	*pirštùs*	*galvijùs*	*peiliùs*	*turgùs*	*rankàs*	*bitès*

(See the full paradigms in 1.19, 22, 25, 26.)

Beside simple (underived) nouns, the second accentuation class comprises derived nouns with the following derivational affixes:

(1) nouns with the following suffixes:

-*aĩnis*, -*ė*: *riestaĩnis* 'ring-shaped cracknel', *saldaĩnis* 'candy', *cukraĩnė* 'confectionery shop', *mišraĩnė* 'salad';

-*ãlius*, -*ė*: *snaudãlius*, -*ė* 'sleepy-head', *tauškãlius*, -*ė* 'gasbag';

-*ãtvė*: *jaunãtvė* 'youth', *senãtvė* 'old age';

-*ė̃lis*, -*ė*: *bernė̃lis* 'laddie', *kalnė̃lis* 'little hill', *lovė̃lė* 'little bed', *mergė̃lė* 'lassie';

-*ė̃lis*, -*ė*: *dobilė̃lis* 'little clover', *vainikė̃lis* 'little wreath', *valandė̃lė* 'moment';

-*ė̃sis*: *degė̃sis* 'charred log', *džiuvė̃sis* 'piece of dry bread', *griuvė̃siai* 'ruins';

-*iẽnė*: *bulviẽnė* 'potato soup', *kiaušiniẽnė* 'fried eggs', *uogiẽnė* 'jam', *vakariẽnė* 'supper';

-*iẽtis*, -*ė*: *kauniẽtis*, -*ė* 'inhabitant of Kaunas', *miestiẽtis*, -*ė* 'town dweller', *pietiẽtis*, -*ė* 'southerner';

-ìkas, -ė: *liejìkas* 'smelter', *lupìkas, -ė* 'usurer';

-iniñkas, -ė: *daininiñkas, -ė* 'singer', *darbiniñkas, -ė* 'worker', *kalbiniñkas, -ė* 'linguist' (derivatives made from nouns of the third and fourth accentuation class);

-yklà: *čiuožyklà* 'skating-rink', *dažyklà* 'dye-house', *mokyklà* 'school', *valgyklà* 'canteen';

-ỹklė: *rodỹklė* 'pointer, arrow', *taupỹklė* 'money-box', *svarstỹklės* 'scales';

-ỹnė: *kankỹnė* 'anguish', *sėdỹnė* 'seat', *tėvỹnė* 'homeland', *vaikštỹnės* 'outdoor fete';

-ỹstė: *draugỹstė* 'friendship', *jaunỹstė* 'youth';

-(i)õkas, -(i)õkė: *berniõkas* 'chap', *naujõkas,-ė* 'novice', *pirmõkas,-ė* 'first-former';

-(i)õklis, -ė: *klajõklis, -ė* 'wanderer', *vijõklis* 'climbing plant', *medžiõklė* 'hunt';

-õnė: *abejõnė* 'doubt', *svajõnė* 'dream';

-õtis: *ąsõtis* 'pitcher', *gyslõtis* 'plantain', *šakõtis* 'branchy cake';

-õvas, -ė: *ieškõvas, -ė* 'plaintiff', *valdõvas, -ė* 'ruler', *žinõvas, -ė* 'connoisseur';

-uõklis, -uõklė: *girtuõklis, -ė* 'drunkard', *švytuõklė* 'pendulum';

-uõlis, -ė: *gražuõlis, -ė* 'handsome man/woman', *jaunuõlis,-ė* 'a youth';

-ùtis,-ė: *kiškùtis* 'little hare', *langùtis* 'little window', *motùtė* 'mummy';

-ùžis, -ė: *bernùžis* 'lad', *brolùžis* 'dear brother', *draugùžis* 'dear friend';

-tỹnės: *eitỹnės* 'parade', *imtỹnės* 'wrestling', *kautỹnės* 'battle', *rungtỹnės* 'match';

-tùvas: *droztùvas* 'plane', *kastùvas* 'spade', *lėktùvas* 'airplane', *žadintùvas* 'alarm clock';

(2) nouns with the following prefixes:

be-: *bedar̃bis, -ė* 'unemployed', *belaĩsvis, -ė* 'prisoner', *beprõtis, -ė* 'madman, mad woman', *berãštis, -ė* 'illiterate person' (but: *begė́dis, -ė* 'shameless person', *besótis, -ė* 'insatiable person' belong to the first accentuation class);

(3) compound nouns with the stress on the root (in some cases, on the suffix) of the second component:

ančiasnãpis 'duck-bill', *bendradar̃bis* 'co-worker', *šimtakõjis* 'centipede', *skeltanãgis* 'cloven-hoofed animal', *bendrakeleĩvis* 'fellow passenger', *ilgaliežùvis* 'gossiper'.

Accentuation class 3

1.37 The third accentuation class comprises nouns which in the dative plural have their stress on the ending while in the accusative plural the stress may fall on any syllable of their stem. When the stress falls on the penultimate syllable, it is always acute, when the stress falls on any other syllable of the stem before penultima it may be acute, circumflex or the syllable may be short.

According to the place of the stress and the toneme of the stressed syllable in the accusative plural, nouns of the third accentuation class are broken into five groups, which dictionaries indicate as 3, 3ª, 3ᵇ, 3⁴ᵃ and 3⁴ᵇ.

Nouns indicated as 3 have the acute toneme in the accusative plural on the penultimate syllable:

Nom. Sg.:	lángas	arklỹs	sūnùs	galvà	aikštė̃	širdìs
	'window'	'horse'	'son'	'head'	'square'	'heart'
Dat. Pl.:	langáms	arkliáms	sūnùms	galvóms	aikštė́ms	širdìms
Acc. Pl.:	lángus	árklius	sū́nus	gálvas	áikštes	šìrdis

(See the full paradigms in 1.19, 22, 25, 26, 28.)

Nouns indicated as 3ª have the acute toneme in the accusative plural on the third syllable from the end:

Nom. Sg.:	áudeklas	lygumà	dóbilas
	'cloth'	'plain'	'clover'
Dat. Pl.:	audekláms	lygumóms	dobiláms
Acc. Pl.:	áudeklus	lýgumas	dóbilus

Nouns indicated as 3ᵇ have the short stressed vowel or circumflex in the accusative plural on the third syllable from the end:

Nom. Sg.:	rašinỹs	kẽpalas	duburỹs
	'composition'	'loaf'	'pit'
Dat. Pl.:	rašiniáms	kepaláms	duburiáms
Acc. Pl.:	rãšinius	kẽpalus	dùburius

Nouns indicated as 3⁴ᵃ have the acute toneme on the fourth syllable from the end:

Nom. Sg.:	laiškanešỹs	nuožulnumà
	'postman'	'declivity'
Dat. Pl.:	laiškanešiáms	nuožulnumóms
Acc. Pl.:	láiškanešius	núožulnumas

Nouns indicated as 3⁴ᵇ have the short stressed vowel or circumflex toneme on the fourth syllable from the end:

Nom. Sg.:	āpmušalas	tētervinas	uždavinỹs
	'upholstery'	'black grouse'	'task'
Dat. Pl.:	apmušaláms	tetervináms	uždaviniáms
Acc. Pl.:	āpmušalus	tētervinus	ùždavinius

Beside simple nouns the third accentuation class includes derived nouns with the following suffixes:

-alas: *barškalas* 'rattle', *gaĩvalas* 'element', *tiřpalas* 'solution' (3ᵇ);

-atìs: *bjauratìs* 'nastiness', *gaišatìs* 'delay', *kamšatìs* 'squash', *maišatìs* 'confusion' (3ᵇ);

-enà: *arklenà* 'horse hide', *ožkenà* 'goatskin' (3ᵃ), *kiškenà* 'hare-skin', *meškenà* 'bear-skin' (3ᵇ);

-esỹs: *barškesỹs* 'clatter', *blizgesỹs* 'glitter', *čiulbesỹs* 'warble', *liūdesỹs* 'sadness' (3ᵇ);

-inas: *ãvinas* 'ram', *kãtinas* 'tomcat', *lãpinas* 'he-fox', *žą̃sinas* 'gander' (3ᵇ);

-inỹs: *audinỹs* 'fabric', *brėžinỹs* 'drawing', *leidinỹs* 'publication', *traukinỹs* 'train' (3ᵃ), *mezginỹs* 'knitting', *sukinỹs* 'pirouette' (3ᵇ);

-ulas: *burbulas* 'bubble', *gniùtulas* 'lump', *gniùžulas* 'tuft' (3ᵇ);

-ulỹs: *čiaudulỹs* 'sneeze', *kosulỹs* 'cough' (3ᵃ), *nuobodulỹs* 'boredom' (3⁴ᵃ), *šleikštulỹs* 'nausea' (3ᵇ), *iškyšulỹs* 'cape' (3⁴ᵇ);

-umà: *aukštumà* 'height', *storumà* 'thickness', *tolumà* 'distance' (3ᵃ), *ankštumà* 'tightness', *dykumà* 'desert' (3ᵇ), *iškilumà* 'prominence' (3⁴ᵇ);

-uras: *bum̃buras* 'bulge', *pum̃puras* 'bud' (3ᵇ);

-urỹs: *duburỹs* 'pit', *sūkurỹs* 'vortex', *švyturỹs* 'lighthouse', *žiburỹs* 'light' (3ᵇ).

The third accentuation class also includes compounds which in the nominative singular have the stressed endings *-ỹs, -ė̃*:

brolžudỹs, -ė̃ 'fratricide', *chorvedỹs, -ė̃* 'choir master', *darbdavỹs, -ė̃* 'employer' (3ᵃ), *batsiuvỹs* 'shoemaker', *šienpjovỹs* 'haymaker' (3ᵇ), *jaunavedỹs* 'bridegroom' (3⁴ᵃ, 3ᵇ), *angliakasỹs* 'coal miner' (3⁴ᵇ, 3ᵇ).

Accentuation class 4

1.38 The fourth accentuation class comprises nouns which in the dative and accusative plural have their stress on the ending. Throughout their paradigm, however, the stress alternates between the ending and the penultimate syllable, which is either short or has the circumflex toneme:

Nom. Sg.: *mìškas* 'forest', *kẽlias* 'way', *būrỹs* 'detachment', *dangùs* 'sky', *aušrà* 'dawn', *žinià* 'piece of news', *žolė̃* 'grass', *dantìs* 'tooth'
Dat. Pl.: *miškáms, keliáms, būriáms, dangùms, aušróms, žinióms, žolė́ms, dantìms*
Acc. Pl.: *miškùs, keliùs, būriùs, dangùs, aušràs, žinià̀s, žolès, dantìs*

(See the full paradigms in 1.19, 22, 25, 26, 28.)

Nouns of the fourth accentuation class are mostly simple two-syllable nouns, except for several derived placenames (*Alytùs, Ašvijà, Sasnavà, Virvyčià*) and a few derivatives with the prefix *ne-*: *nedarnà* 'disharmony', *nedrąsà* 'timidity', *negarbė̃* 'dishonour', *nedalià* 'ill luck', *netiesà* 'untruth', *nešvarà* 'dirtiness'.

2 ADJECTIVE
Būdvardis

2.1 Adjectives constitute a class of words which identify qualities and are inflected for gender, number and case.

Adjectives can identify qualities directly by their lexical meaning, e.g. *áukštas* (MASC), *aukštà* (FEM) 'tall', *saldùs* (MASC), *saldì* (FEM) 'sweet', or through their relation to a basic word, e.g. *medìnis* (MASC), *medìnė* (FEM) 'wooden' (cf. *mẽdis* 'wood').

Morphological categories of the adjective
GENDER, NUMBER AND CASE
Giminẽ, skaĩčius, liñksnis

2.2 Adjectives agree in gender, number and case with words they are related to in a sentence.

There are three gender forms of adjectives in Lithuanian: masculine, feminine and neuter. All adjectives can have masculine forms (with the endings Nom. Sg. -(*i*)*as*, -*us*, -*is*) and the respective feminine forms (with the endings -(*i*)*a*, -*i*, -*ė*). The neuter forms ending in -(*i*)*a* can be derived from adjectives in -(*i*)*as* (MASC), -(*i*)*a* (FEM), and the neuter forms ending in -*u* – from adjectives in -*us* (MASC), -*i* (FEM), e.g.:

Masc.	Fem.	Neuter	
gẽras	*gerà*	*gẽra*	'good'
kárštas	*karštà*	*kársta*	'hot'
žãlias	*žalià*	*žãlia*	'green'
gražùs	*gražì*	*gražù*	'beautiful'
kartùs	*kartì*	*kartù*	'bitter'
puikùs	*puikì*	*puikù*	'fine'

Adjectives, which end in -is, -ė (e.g. *auksìnis, auksìnė* 'golden', *mažýtis, mažýtė* 'tiny'), do not have neuter forms.

2.3 As attributes, adjectives can be used only with nouns. Therefore the grammatical meanings and forms of gender, number and case of attributive adjectives depend upon the respective meanings and forms of nouns they modify, e.g. *gẽras tẽvas* (MASC) 'good father', *gerà mótina* (FEM) 'good mother':

	Singular		Plural	
Nom.	gẽras tẽvas	gerà mótina	gerì tėvaĩ	gẽros mótinos
Gen.	gẽro tẽvo	gerõs mótinos	gerų̃ tėvų̃	gerų̃ mótinų
Dat.	gerám tẽvui	gẽrai mótinai	gelíems tėváms	geróms mótinoms
Acc.	gẽrą tẽvą	gẽrą mótiną	gerùs tẽvus	geràs mótinas
Instr.	gerù tėvù	gerà mótina	geraĩs tėvaĩs	geromìs mótinomis
Loc.	geramè tėvè	gerojè mótinoje	geruosè tėvuosè	gerosè mótinose

Like nouns which can be either masculine or feminine, attributive adjectives can also be either masculine or feminine.

Predicative adjectives are syntactically related to the subject of the sentence. This means that the grammatical meaning (and the grammatical form) of the adjective depends on the grammatical meaning of the words used as the subject of the sentence.

When the subject is expressed by a noun or pronoun, which is either masculine or feminine, the predicative adjective is also either masculine or feminine.

Jìs malonùs.	'He is kind.'
Jì malonì.	'She is kind.'
Tẽvas bùvo pìktas.	'Father was angry.'
Jì sėdėjo liūdnà.	'She was sitting (and feeling) sad.'

2.4 When the subject of the sentence is expressed by a word possessing the generalized meaning e.g. such pronouns as *vìskas, taĩ, vìsa taĩ*, the predicative adjective is used in the neuter form, e.g.:

Vìskas pigù.	'Everything is inexpensive.'
Taĩ absuřdiška.	'It is absurd.'
Vìsa taĩ pasiródė jám keĩsta.	'All this seemed strange to him.'

Some other uses of the neuter adjectival forms:

(1) Neuter adjectives are often used as predicatives in impersonal sentences, e.g.:

| *Kambaryjè bùvo tamsù.* | 'It was dark in the room.' |
| *Taĩp giẽdra iř liñksma!* | 'It's so clear and joyful!' |

(2) One of the two neuter adjectival forms in the sentence can be used as the subject, the other as the predicative:

Saldù – gardù.	'Sweet is delicious.'
Raudóna – gražù.	'Red is beautiful.'

(3) Neuter forms can sometimes be used as the predicatives of masculine or feminine nouns, in which case there is no agreement between the gender of the subject of the sentence and the predicative:

Siūloma prēkė nebrangù.	'An offered commodity is not expensive.'
Pernýkštės bùlvės neskanù.	'Last year's potatoes don't taste good.'

The neuter forms in such sentences can be replaced by masculine or feminine forms, cf.:

Siūloma prēkė nebrangì.
Pernýkštės bùlvės neskānios.

(4) Neuter adjectival forms with a generalized meaning are used to perform the function of a noun in the nominative, accusative and sometimes genitive or instrumental:

Gēra eĩna tolì, blōga dár toliaũ.	'Good goes far, evil goes still farther.'
Esù jaũ iř šìlta, iř šálta mãtęs.	'I've seen both warm and hot.'
Buvaũ mãžas iř negalėjau atskìrti gēra nuõ pìkta.	'I was a small child and couldn't tell good from evil.'
Nejuokáuk iš tō, kã laikaũ šveñta.	'Don't mock what I consider to be sacred.'

Masculine adjectives in the singular case form can also be sometimes used in a similar way, cf.:

Pìkto/Pìkta nepatýręs, gēro/gēra nepažìnsi.	'Having experienced no evil, you can not recognize good.'

(5) Neuter adjectives in the nominal function very often go together with the pronoun *kàs* and its combinations with other pronouns:

Su motulè atsitìko kažin kàs baisù.	'Something terrible happened to mother.'
Gál jaũčia kã pìkta?	'Perhaps he feels some evil.'

2.5 To sum up: masculine and feminine adjectives refer to a quality which is attributed to a thing:

Pirkià tamsì.	'The house is dark.'
Šiañdien šáltas óras.	'Today the weather is cold.'

Neuter adjectives refer to a quality in general. They are never attributes to a noun, and the quality they refer to is never an attribute to a concrete thing:

Pirkiojè tamsù. 'It is dark in the house.'
Šiañdien šálta. 'It's cold today.'

Even when the neuter adjectives are correlated with the other neuter adjectives or pronouns (*Saldù – gardù* 'Sweet is delicious.' *Vìsa taĩ gražù* 'All this is beautiful.') or when they are used as predicatives with subjects expressed by nouns, they always retain the meaning of a generalized quality.

The relation between the masculine, feminine and neuter adjectives could be represented graphically in the following way:

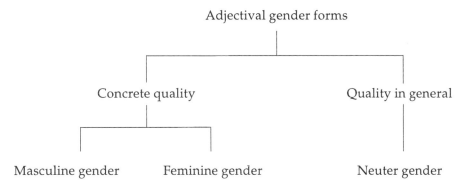

2.6 Masculine and feminine adjectives have two numbers – singular and plural.

Singular		Plural	
áukštas stãlas	'a high table'	aukštì stalaĩ	'high tables'
aukštà kėdė̃	'a high chair'	áukštos kė̃dės	'high chairs'
jìs gražùs	'he's handsome'	jiẽ grãžūs	'they're handsome'
jì gražì	'she's beautiful'	jõs grãžios	'they're beautiful'

Neuter adjectives haven't different forms for number or case. They can be used as predicatives with nouns both in the singular and plural.

Medùs skanù. 'Honey is delicious.'
Ilgì sijõnai negražù. 'Long skirts are not beautiful.'

Masculine and feminine forms have six cases: nominative, genitive, dative, accusative, instrumental and locative. Differently from the noun, most adjectives (except for the masculine adjectives of the *medìnis* kind, see 2.27) have no vocative. The function of the vocative is performed by their nominative case, e.g. *gẽras tėve!* 'good father!'

COMPARISON
Láipsnis

2.7 The comparison of adjectives is based on the semantic opposition between the positive adjectival forms, which do not refer to any difference in the degree of a quality (e.g. *gēras* 'good'), and the adjectival forms, which do indicate differences in the degree of a quality, i.e. the comparative and superlative adjectival forms (e.g. *gerèsnis* 'better', *geriáusias* 'best'). Thus, the positive adjectival forms are the unmarked member of the opposition while the comparative and superlative forms constitute the marked member.

2.8 Masculine and feminine comparative forms are formed with the suffix *-esn-(is/ė)*:

gēras, gerà – *gerèsnis, gerèsnė* 'better'
gražùs, gražì – *gražèsnis, gražèsnė* 'more beautiful'

Another, less frequent, form of the comparative degree is built with the suffix *-ėlesn-(is/ė)*, which is, in fact, a blend of the diminutive suffix *-ėl-* and the comparative suffix *-esn-*:

gēras, gerà – *gerėlèsnis, gerėlèsnė* 'a little bit better'
gražùs, gražì – *gražėlèsnis, gražėlèsnė* 'a little bit more beautiful'

These forms are considered to be diminutive comparative forms since they indicate a slightly lesser degree of a quality than the basic comparative forms.

2.9 Masculine and feminine superlative forms are built with the suffix *-iaus-(ias/ia)*:

gēras, gerà – *geriáusias, geriáusia* 'best'
gražùs, gražì – *gražiáusias, gražiáusia* 'most beautiful'

Some grammars distinguish the so called intensified superlative degree, which is, in fact, a combination of a superlative adjective with the pronoun *pàts/patì* or with the plural genitive form of the pronoun *vìsas*:

pàts geriáusias   patì geriáusia   'the very best'
visų̃ geriáusias   visų̃ geriáusia   'the best of all'

The meaning of the intensified superlative degree can also be expressed by a combination of a definite adjective (in the positive degree) with the same pronouns *pàts, patì* and *visų̃*:

pàts geràsis   patì geróji
visų̃ geràsis   visų̃ geróji

2.10 There are some comparative and superlative adjectives which do not possess the positive degree. They are most probably derived from nouns.

vyrèsnis vyrèsnė 'older, senior' (cf. *výras* 'man')
vyriáusiasvyriáusia 'oldest, chief'

viršèsnis viršèsnė 'superior' (cf. *viršùs* 'top')
viršiáusias viršiáusia 'chief, supreme'

galiáusias galiáusia 'last' (cf. *gãlas* 'end')

2.11 The comparative degree of neuter adjectives is formed with the derivational morpheme *-iau*:

gẽra 'good' *geriaũ* 'better'
gražù 'beautiful' *gražiaũ* 'more beautiful'

The diminutive comparative degree of neuter adjectives has the form-building element *-ėliaũ*:

gẽra gerėliaũ 'a little bit better'
gražù gražėliaũ 'a little bit more beautiful'

The superlative degree of neuter adjectives is formed with the form-building element *-iausia*:

gẽra geriáusia 'the best'
gražù gražiáusia 'the most beautiful'

To express the meaning of intensified (or emphatic) superlative, the superlative forms of neuter adjectives can be combined only with the pronoun *visų*:

visų geriáusia 'best of all'
visų gražiáusia 'most beautiful of all'

2.12 Comparative adjectives usually indicate that something has more of a quality than something else. The other thing involved in the comparison is specified by the preposition *ùž* followed by a noun in the accusative, or by the conjunctions *kaĩp, nekaĩp, negù, neĩ* followed by a noun in the nominative.

Teisýbė už áuksą brangèsnė.	'The truth is dearer than gold.'
Gerèsnis *tėvas, kàd iř žiaurùs, nekaĩp/negù/neĩ patėvis.*	'A father is better, although cruel, than a stepfather.'

Comparative adjectives may also indicate that something has more of a quality at one time than at another time or under other circumstances.

Po tárdymo Pečiūrà pasidãrė ramèsnis.	'After the interrogation Pečiūra became quieter.'
Dabař jìs gerèsnis *negù anksčiaũ.*	'Now he is better than before.'

The other thing involved in the comparison may not even possess the quality compared. E.g. *Tėvas* gerèsnis *už mótiną* 'Father is better than mother' does not mean at all that father is good.

The difference in the degree of the quality compared may sometimes be quantified, which is usually expressed by a combination of numerals and nouns in the instrumental case; sometimes, by the preposition *peř* and a noun in the accusative.

Augustìnas tìk penkeriaĩs mētais bùvo už manè vyrèsnis.	'Augustinas was only five years older than I was.'
Sūnùs per vìsą sprìndį *yrà jaũ* aukštèsnis *už tėvą*.	'The son is taller than his father by the whole span of a hand.'

2.13 The superlative degree indicates that something has more of a quality than anything else of its kind.

Superlative adjectives may be used without indicating the point of comparison, but if the speaker wants to refer to the point of the comparison, he uses a qualifying phrase which consists of:

(1) the prepositions *ìš, tařp* with the plural accusative or genitive which may be modified by the pronoun *vìsas, visì* 'all':

aukščiáusias iš visų brólių	'the tallest of all the brothers'
aukščiáusias tarp visų brólių	

(2) a noun and the pronoun *visì* 'all' in the plural genitive:

visų brólių gražiáusias	'the handsomest of the brothers'
visų kalnų aukščiáusias	'the highest of the mountains'

(3) adverbs *užvìs, pervìs* 'of all':

užvìs/pervìs didžiáusias	'the biggest of all'

More rarely, superlative adjectives indicate that something has more of a quality at a certain time or under certain circumstances than at any other time or under any other circumstances.

Užvìs brangiáusias *laĩkas pavāsarį*.	'Time is dearest in the spring.'

When used with the prepositional phrase *ùž* + Acc., the meaning of the superlative degree may also be expressed by a comparative adjective, e.g.:

Sveikatà už vìską/užvìs meilèsnė.	'Health is dearest of all.'
Pranùkas už visùs kaltèsnis.	'Pranukas is to be blamed most of all.'

2.14 Adjectives with the comparative or superlative suffixes are not always true comparatives or superlatives in their meaning.

Sometimes, adjectives with the superlative suffix simply indicate an extremely high degree of quality without any reference to comparison. In this meaning, they are used only as attributes, with or without intensifiers (*kuõ, kõ*, the plural genitive of the same adjective in the positive degree), and they are never accompanied by the qualifying phrases mentioned in 2.13.

Danguje̋ nẽ mažiáusio debesẽlio.	'There is not a smallest single cloud in the sky.'
Įdíekit, mótinos, vaikáms Tėvỹnės méilę kuõ didžiáusią.	'Mothers, try to instill in your children love as great as possible for their homeland.'
Jái vaidẽnosi baisių̃ baisiáusi vaizdaĩ.	'In her mind's eye she saw most horrible sights.'

In such a non-comparative meaning, adjectives with the superlative suffix can sometimes be replaced by definite adjectives.

Tėvẽli màno brangiáusias/ brangùsis, kuõ àš táu taĩp nusidėjau?!	'My dearest father, what sin have I committed against you?!'

Adjectives with the comparative suffix *-esn-* may also be used in the non-comparative meaning, which sometimes becomes very similar to that of adjectives with the prefixes *apy-, po-* and the suffix *-ok-(as/a)* denoting a pretty small degree of a quality, e.g.

Staklỹs ė̃mė lankýtis pàs Mõrtą, kadà tìk bū́davo laisvèsnis/apýlaisvis/laisvókas/ pólaisvis malūnè.	'Staklys began to visit Morta whenever he had some free time in the mill.'

2.15 Superlative and comparative adjectives may have definite forms:

Jų̃ vaikaĩ bùvo pérėję į̇̃ aukštesnią́sias klasès.	'Their children had been transferred to senior forms.'
Màno tėvas laĩko sàvo geriáusiąjį vỹną molìniuose ìnduose.	'My father keeps his best wine in clay vessels.'

2.16 The following adjectives have no comparative or superlative forms:

(1) Adjectives with the ending *-is, -ė,* e.g.:

apýgeris vaĩkas	'not a bad child'
medìnis nãmas	'a wooden house'
kvietìnė dúona	'wheat bread'
mažýtė mergáitė	'a very small girl'

(*dìdis, -ė, dìdelis, -ė* 'big' and adjectives with the suffix *-utinis* are an exception, e.g. *kraštutiniáusios príemonės* 'the most extreme measures');

(2) adjectives with the suffix *-okas*, and diminutive adjectives because the meaning of a reduced degree of a quality is already built into their derivation:

mažókas, -a	'somewhat too small'
mažiùkas, -ė	'very small'

(3) adjectives with the suffix *-iškas*, which classify objects into different kinds:

píeniška sriubà	'milk soup'
výriški marškiniaĩ	'men's shirt'

(4) adjectives which are derived from nouns and describe objects as being covered with something:

pur̃vinas	'muddy'
miltúotas	'covered with flour'

(5) a large number of adjectives which refer to qualities the degree of which does not usually change:

bãsas	'barefoot'
išvirkščias	'inside out'
pė́sčias	'on foot'
raĩtas	'mounted'
príešingas	'opposite'
pãskiras	'individual'

DEFINITENESS

Apibrėžtùmas

2.17 The category of definiteness in the adjective is based on the opposition of definite adjectival forms, which in addition to their lexical meaning of a quality contribute definite status to the noun they determine, and simple, or indefinite, adjectival forms, which lack the meaning of definiteness. Thus, definite adjectives are considered to be the marked members of the opposition, whereas simple forms are the unmarked members of the opposition.

Historically, definite forms derived from the blend of adjectival endings with the pronoun *jìs, jì* (see 2.34):

gẽras + jis = geràs-is   *gerà + ji = ger-óji*
gražùs + jis = gražùs-is   *gražì + ji = graž-ióji*

2.18 Definite adjectives contribute to the definite status of the noun they determine by: (1) making reference to a quality which helps the users of the language to identify the object referred to (situational reference); and (2) by referring back to what has already been said (linguistic reference).

(1) Situational reference. Definite adjectives help the users of language to understand the reference of the noun they modify:

(a) by pointing to the referent's quality which has a higher degree of intensity than the same quality of any other object in a group of similar objects:

Prìėmė jį̃ kunigáikštis didžiõjoje *pilie͂s mẽnėje.*	'The Duke received him in the big hall of the castle.'
Sekmãdienį jìs reñgdavosi geraĩsiais *drabùžiais.*	'On Sundays he always put on his best clothes.'

(b) by pointing to the referent's quality which is opposite to the quality of other similar objects:

Nè tìk upẽlis, bèt iȓ didžióji *ùpė jaũ bùvo apsitráukusi ledù.*	'Ice had covered not only the brook but also the big river.'
Jìs bijójo senų̃jų *dievų̃ keȓšto iȓ nepasitikėjo* naujų̃jų *galýbe.*	'He was afraid of the vengeance of the old gods and didn't trust the powers of the new ones.'
Sẽnis geriaũ girdėjo dešiniája *ausimì.*	'The old man heard better with his right ear.'

(c) by pointing to the referent's quality which makes it unique in a group of similar things because the other things do not have that quality:

Nepraėjo iȓ valandėlė, kaĩp jìs taȓp krùtančiųjų skarėlių pamãtė mėlynąją *iȓ tuojaũ ją̃ pažìno iȓ ìšskyrė ìš visų̃ tokių̃ aȓ beñt panãšių̃.*	'It wasn't long before he noticed the blue kerchief among other moving kerchiefs and recognized and distinguished it immediately among all such or similar ones.'

Because they refer to qualities which make things easily identifiable, definite adjectives are used:

(a) to form proper names:

Didžióji gãtvė	'Great Street'
Didỹsis kãras	'The Great War'
Mažóji Lietuvà	'Lithuania Minor'
Žemóji pilìs	'The Lower Castle'
Juodóji jū́ra	'The Black Sea'
Žaliàsis tìltas	'The Green Bridge'

(b) to indicate species and to form various terms:

ankstývosios bùlvės	'the early potatoes'
juodàsis gañdras	'the black stork'
saldíeji pipìrai	'the sweet pepper'
lengvóji prãmonė	'the light industry'
juodíeji serbeñtai	'the black currants'
dėmė́toji šiltinė	'spotted fever'
trumpíeji balsiai	'the short vowels'

(2) **Linguistic reference**. Definite adjectives also function as anaphoric determiners in that they help the users to identify the referent of the noun they modify by referring back to an earlier mention of the quality of the referent.

Ant áukšto stataũs kálno pasiródė stebuklìngas žiburỹs... Bèt nè vienì jaũ mẽtai aukų̃ iř pasišventìmo praė̃jo, õ dar nè víenas iš lìpančiųjų nepasilytė́jo stebuklìngojo žiburio.	'A miraculous light appeared on a high steep mountain... More than a few years of casualties and utmost devotion have passed, but not a single climber has ever touched the miraculous light.'

As anaphoric determiners definite adjectives are often used with the demonstrative pronouns *tàs, tà* 'that', *šìs, šì, šìtas, šìta, šità* 'this'.

Iř štaĩ iš tankių̃ mẽdžių pasiródė trỹs puĩkios, báltos gulbės. Ančiùkas pažìno tuõs nuostabiúosius paũkščiùs.	'Suddenly three wonderful white swans appeared from behind the thick trees. The duckling recognized those wonderful birds.'

2.19 The distinction between definite and simple adjectives is often neutralized.

On the one hand, definite adjectival forms are sometimes used:

(1) to refer to indefinite representatives of two groups of things which are opposed to each other:

Paskutìniai spinduliaĩ švelniai glóstė aukštesniųjų/aukštesnių̃ egláičių iř pušáičių viršū́nes.	'The last sunrays caressed softly the tops of the taller pines and fir-trees.'
Jiẽ sàvo bylàs pavèsdavo krìviams iř seníesiems/seníems výrams.	'They would refer their cases to priests and the older men.'

(2) in various generalizations, e.g. proverbs:

Tylióji/Tylì kiaũlė gìlią šãknį knìsa.	'The quiet pig always roots up a deeper root' (i.e. Still waters run deep).

On the other hand, in the context of definite reference simple adjectival forms are often used to replace definite adjectives, for example:

(1) when preceded by an anaphoric demonstrative pronoun:

Taĩ bùvo nepàprastas kirvùkas. Su tuõ stebuklìngu/stebuklìnguoju kirvukù iř pagýdė Viñcę.	'It was not a simple axe. With that wonderful axe Vincė was cured.'

(2) in some terminological phrases:

juodà iř baltà dúona	'brown and white bread'
saldùs iř rūgštùs píenas	'sweet and sour milk'
cf.:	
saldíeji iř kartíeji pipìrai	'sweet and bitter pepper'

In terminological phrases definite adjectives sometimes may be replaced by derivative adjectives with -is, -ė:

drýžosios kélnės	dryžìnės kélnės	'striped trousers'
jaunàsis brólis	jaũnis brólis	'youngest brother'

(3) simple, rather than definite adjectives, are often used in the superlative degree to refer to a thing identified by the greatest degree of the quality possessed: vyriáusias sūnùs 'the eldest son' is often used instead of vyriáusiasis sūnùs even when the speaker uses it to distinguish from the other sons. The same can also be observed in terminological phrases: cf. vyriáusias redãktorius, inžiniẽrius 'chief editor, engineer' instead of vyriáusiasis redãktorius, inžiniẽrius.

2.20 Definite adjectives can also be used for emphasis. In this case they are used to emphasize the quality of a thing rather than to identify that thing by the quality referred to.

Čià giliųjų ežerėlių iř tyliųjų miško upėlių pakrántėse áugo klestėjo įvairių įvairiáusių mẽdžių.	'Here on the banks of the deep lakes and the quiet forest streams grew and flourished a great variety of trees.'

Definite adjectives are often used in folklore and fiction as standard traditional epithets to refer to one of the most characteristic qualities of a thing:

Áuga tàvo mergužėlė pas senúosius tėvužėliùs. Pas senúosius tėvužėliùs tarp jaunųjų brolužėlių.	'Your girl is growing up at her old parents. At her old parents' among her young brothers.'

As traditional epithets definite adjectives also go together with proper nouns:

Pagaliaũ pamãtėme sẽnąjį Vìlnių.	'At last we saw the old Vilnius.'

2.21 As evidenced by the above examples, definite adjectives are used mostly as prepositive attributes. They are very rarely used as predicatives (e.g. *Tàs kẽlias tikràsis* 'This road is the right one').

Another syntactical peculiarity of definite adjectives is absence of complementation, c.f.: *labaĩ gẽras* 'very good' but **labaĩ geràsis*.

2.22 The following adjectives have no definite forms:

(1) Adjectives with the ending *-is, -ė*, including those with the suffix *-inis, -ė*, e.g.:

auksìnis, auksìnė	'golden'
geraširdis, geraširdė	'kind-hearted'

Adjectives with the suffix *-utinis, -ė* form an exception, e.g.:

paskutìnis, paskutìnė	'last'	*paskutinỹsis, paskutinióji*	'the last'
vidutìnis, vidutìnė	'medium'	*vidutinỹsis, vidutinióji*	'the medium'

(2) Adjectives with suffixes or prefixes indicating the degree of a quality, e.g.:

didókas, didóka	'rather big'
mažiùkas, mažiùkė	'tiny'

2.23 In the southern dialects definite adjectives are used only for emphatic purposes whereas in the limiting function they are replaced either by diminutive adjectives or by simple adjectives (which are sometimes used with the demonstrative pronoun *tàs, tà, tasaĩ, tóji*).

greitàsis traukinỹs	→	*greitùkas traukinỹs*	'express train'
didỹsis pir̃štas	→	*didžiùlis pir̃štas*	'the middle finger'
jaunóji mókytoja	→	*tóji jaunà mókytoja*	'the young tacher'

2.24 Definite adjectives can be used as substantives in the function of subject or object of the sentence. The following cases are to be noted:

(1) the plural forms of masculine definite adjectives denoting a group of people:

Krā̃štą val̃dė nè galìngieji, bèt žmonių̃ išrinktíeji.	'The country was governed not by the powerful, but by the elected.'
Jõs nemė́go neĩ savíeji, neĩ svetimíeji.	'She was disliked both by her own people and by the strangers.'

(2) masculine singular definite adjectives with generic reference:

Akylàsis bū́tų seniaĩ vìską suprãtęs.	'A more observant man would have understood everything long ago.'
Ir̃ gùdriojo ne visadà teisýbė.	'Even the clever man does not always have the truth.'

Masculine simple adjectives can also be used as nouns with generic reference:

Pirmiaũ jìs pas svẽtimus/sveti- 'Before that he used to work
múosius dìrbdavo. for others.'

(3) masculine or feminine definite adjectives used to avoid the taboo nouns or nouns with undesirable connotations such as those referring to diseases, the devil, a snake, etc.

geltonóji	'the yellow one'	meaning	'yellow fever'
piktóji	'the evil one'	"	'a snake'
kruvinóji	'the bloody one'	"	'dysentery'
šaltóji	'the cold one'	"	'a prison'
nelabàsis	'the wicked one'	"	'the devil'

(4) feminine definite adjectives with abstract reference similar to that of neuter adjectives.

Jaũ jám atẽjo paskutinióji.   'He has already been visited by the last one (i.e. 'death').'

Declension of simple adjectives

2.25 Just as in the case of nouns, differences in the inflectional forms of adjectives are determined by their stems, or rather, by the final vowel of the stem, which in the course of time merged with the case endings (cf. 1.16). The declension of masculine and feminine adjectives is quite different. Masculine adjectives possess the endings of the *(i)a-* and *(i)u-*stems, whereas feminine adjectives have the *(i)o-* and *ė-*stem forms. Within the *(i)a-*declension it is possible to distinguish 4 slightly different paradigms, the *(i)o-*declension has 3 paradigms (see Table 3). Masculine adjectives have adopted some of the endings of the gender pronouns, whereas feminine adjectives follow the declension of the respective noun stems more faithfully.

DECLENSION OF MASCULINE ADJECTIVES

2.26 Masculine adjectives are declined according to two declensions: *(i)a-* and *(i)u-*declension. Thus, their declension is similar to that of nouns of the respective stems except for certain cases (marked out in following) where the endings of masculine adjectives are similar to those of pronouns, cf.:

| | Adjective | | Noun | | Pronoun |
| | a-stem | u-stem | a-stem | u-stem | a-stem |

Table 3. **Adjective declensions and paradigms**

Gender	Ending of Nom. Sg.	Ending of Nom. Pl.	Paradigm	Declension
Masculine	-as	-i	1	(i)a
	-ias	-i	2	
	-is, -ys	-i	3	
	-is	-iai	4	
	-us	-ūs	5	u
Feminine	-a	-os	6	(i)o
	-ia	-ios	7	
	-i	-ios	8	
	-ė	-ės	9	ė

Singular

Nom.	gẽras	gražùs	výras	tuřgus	kìtas
Gen.	gẽro	gražaũs	výro	tuřgaus	kìto
Dat.	gerám	gražiám	výrui	tuřgui	kitám
Acc.	gẽrą	grãžų	výrą	tuřgų	kìtą
Instr.	gerù	gražiù	výru	tuřgumi	kitù
Loc.	geramè	gražiamè	výre	tuřguje	kitamè

Plural

Nom.	gerì	grãžūs	výrai	tuřgūs	kitì
Gen.	gerų̃	gražių̃	výrų	tuřgų	kitų̃
Dat.	geríems	gražíems	výrams	tuřgums	kitíems
Acc.	gerùs	gražiùs	výrus	turgùs	kitùs
Instr.	geraĩs	gražiaĩs	výrais	tuřgumis	kitaĩs
Loc.	geruosè	gražiuosè	výruose	tuřguose	kituosè

The (i)a-declension

2.27 This declension comprises masculine adjectives which in the nominative singular end in -(i)as, -is, -ys. Within this declension it is possible to distinguish four paradigms. Differences among the paradigms can be traced in the following cases:

Paradigm 1

Nom. Sg. -*as* after a hard consonant (*a*-stem):

	gẽras 'good',	*jáunas* 'young',	*laimìngas* 'happy',	*ãpskritas* 'round'
Acc. Sg	*gẽrą*	*jáuną*	*laimìngą*	*ãpskritą*
Nom. Pl.	*gerì*	*jaunì*	*laimìngi*	*apskritì*
Dat. Pl.	*geríems*	*jauníems*	*laimìngiems*	*apskritíems*

Paradigm 2

Nom. Sg. -*ias* after a palatalized consonant or -*as* after *j* (*ia*-stem): *žãlias* 'green', *naũjas* 'new'. All adjectives of the superlative degree are declined according to this paradigm, e.g. *geriáusias* 'the best'

Acc. Sg.	*žãlią*	*naũją*	*geriáusią*
Nom. Pl.	*žalì*	*naujì*	*geriáusi*
Dat. Pl.	*žalíems*	*naujíems*	*geriáusiems*

Paradigm 3

Nom. Sg. -*is* (rare -*ys*) (*ia*-stem): *dìdelis* 'big', *kairỹs* 'left', and all the adjectives of the comparative degree, which end in -*esnis*: *gerèsnis* 'better', *didèsnis* 'bigger'

Acc. Sg.	*dìdelį*	*kaĩrį*	*gerèsnį*
Nom. Pl.	*dideli*	*kairì*	*geresnì*
Dat. Pl.	*dideliems*	*kairíems*	*geresníems*

Paradigm 4

Nom. Sg. -*is* (*ia*-stem). These are derivative adjectives with suffixes and prefixes *apy*-, *po*-: *medìnis* 'wooden', *mažýtis* 'little', *apýmažis* 'rather small', *póžalis* 'fairly raw', and compound adjectives: *geraširdis* 'good-hearted'

Acc. Sg.	*medìnį*	*mažýtį*	*póžalį*
Nom. Pl.	*medìniai*	*mažýčiai*	*póžaliai*
Dat. Pl.	*medìniams*	*mažýčiams*	*póžaliams*

DECLENSION PATTERNS

Paradigm 1

áukštas 'tall, high', *gẽras* 'good', *laimìngas* 'happy', *ãpskritas* 'round'

Singular

Nom.	*áukštas*	*gẽras*	*laimìngas*	*ãpskritas*
Gen.	*áukšto*	*gẽro*	*laimìngo*	*ãpskrito*
Dat.	*aukštám*	*gerám*	*laimìngam*	*apskritám*

Acc.	áukštą	gẽrą	laimìngą	ãpskritą
Instr.	áukštu	gerù	laimìngu	ãpskritu
Loc.	aukštamè	geramè	laimìngame	apskritamè

Plural

Nom.	aukštì	gerì	laimìngi	apskritì
Gen.	aukštų̃	gerų̃	laimìngų	apskritų̃
Dat.	aukštíems	geríems	laimìngiems	apskritíems
Acc.	áukštus	gerùs	laimìngus	ãpskritus
Instr.	aukštaĩs	geraĩs	laimìngais	apskritaĩs
Loc.	aukštuosè	geruosè	laimìnguose	apskrituosè

Paradigm 2

žãlias 'green', *naũjas* 'new', *geriáusias* 'the best'

Singular

Nom.	žãlias	naũjas	geriáusias
Gen.	žãlio	naũjo	geriáusio
Dat.	žaliám	naujám	geriáusiam
Acc.	žãlią	naũją	geriáusią
Instr.	žaliù	naujù	geriáusiu
Loc.	žaliamè	naujamè	geriáusiame

Plural

Nom.	žalì	naujì	geriáusi
Gen.	žalių̃	naujų̃	geriáusių
Dat.	žalíems	naujíems	geriáusiems
Acc.	žaliùs	naujùs	geriáusius
Instr.	žaliaĩs	naujaĩs	geriáusiais
Loc.	žaliuosè	naujuosè	geriáusiuose

Paradigm 3

dìdelis 'big', *kairỹs* 'left', *gerèsnis* 'better'

Singular

Nom.	dìdelis	kairỹs	gerèsnis
Gen.	dìdelio	kaĩrio	gerèsnio

Dat.	dideliám	kairiám	geresniám
Acc.	dìdelį	kaĩrį	gerèsnį
Instr.	dìdeliu	kairiù	geresniù
Loc.	dideliamè	kairiamè	geresniamè

Plural

Nom.	dìdelì	kairì	geresnì
Gen.	didelių̃	kairių̃	geresnių̃
Dat.	didelíems	kairíems	geresníems
Acc.	dìdelius	kairiùs	geresniùs
Instr.	dideliaĩs	kairiaĩs	geresniaĩs
Loc.	dideliuosè	kairiuosè	geresniuosè

Paradigm 4

medìnis 'wooden', *apýmažis* 'rather small', *geraširdis* 'kind-hearted'

Singular

Nom.	medìnis	apýmažis	geraširdis
Gen.	medìnio	apýmažio	geraširdžio
Dat.	medìniam	apýmažiam	geraširdžiam
Acc.	medìnį	apýmažį	geraširdį
Instr.	medìniù	apýmažiu	geraširdžiù
Loc.	medìniame	apýmažiame	geraširdžiame
Voc.	medìni	apýmaži	geraširdi

Plural

Nom.	medìniai	apýmažiai	geraširdžiai
Gen.	medìnių	apýmažių	geraširdžių
Dat.	medìniams	apýmažiams	geraširdžiams
Acc.	medìniùs	apýmažius	geraširdžiùs
Instr.	medìniais	apýmažiais	geraširdžiais
Loc.	medìniuose	apýmažiuose	geraširdžiuose

2.28 Differently from the other paradigms, Paradigm 4 has the vocative case in the singular, e.g. *medìni* (cf. *bróli!* 'brother').

Compound adjectives the second component of which is an adjectival stem may have in the dative plural either the ending *-iams*, as all the other compound adjectives, or the ending *-iems*, e.g. *pùsžalis* 'not quite ripe' – *pùsžaliams / pùsžaliems*.

2.29 Diminutive adjectives with the suffix *-(i)ukas* (*baltùkas* 'white', *mažiùkas* 'little') are declined exactly like *a*-stem nouns, i.e. in the dative and locative singular, and nominative and dative plural, differently from all the other adjectives, their endings coincide with those of *a*-stem nouns, but not with those of pronouns.

Dat. Sg.:	*baltùkui*	*mažiùkui*
Loc. Sg.:	*baltukè*	*mažiukè*
Nom. Pl.:	*baltùkai*	*mažiùkai*
Dat. Pl.:	*baltùkams*	*mažiùkams*

The *(i)u*-declension

2.30 The *(i)u*-declension comprises adjectives which have the ending *-us* in the nominative singular, e.g. *gražùs* 'beautiful', *lýgus* 'smooth, equal', *mandagùs* 'polite', *panašùs* 'similar'. This ending is very typical of prefixed adjectives, e.g. *nuolaidùs* 'submissive, compliant', *apsukrùs* 'clever, bright', *nuokalnùs* 'slanting'.

DECLENSION PATTERNS

Paradigm 5

gražùs 'beautiful', *lýgus* 'smooth, equal', *mandagùs* 'polite', *panašùs* 'similar'

Singular

Nom.	*gražùs*	*lýgus*	*mandagùs*	*panašùs*
Gen.	*gražaũs*	*lygaũs*	*mandagaũs*	*panašaũs*
Dat.	*gražiám*	*lygiám*	*mandagiám*	*panašiám*
Acc.	*grãžų*	*lýgų*	*mandãgų*	*panãšų*
Instr.	*gražiù*	*lýgiu*	*mandagiù*	*panašiù*
Loc.	*gražiamè*	*lygiamè*	*mandagiamè*	*panašiamè*

Plural

Nom.	*grãžūs*	*lýgūs*	*mandãgūs*	*panãšūs*
Gen.	*gražių̃*	*lygių̃*	*mandagių̃*	*panašių̃*
Dat.	*gražíems*	*lygíems*	*mandagíems*	*panašíems*
Acc.	*gražiùs*	*lýgius*	*mandagiùs*	*panašiùs*
Instr.	*gražiaĩs*	*lygiaĩs*	*mandagiaĩs*	*panašiaĩs*
Loc.	*gražiuosè*	*lygiuosè*	*mandagiuosè*	*panašiuosè*

DECLENSION OF FEMININE ADJECTIVES

Feminine adjectives are declined according to the *(i)o-* and *ė-*declensions.

The *(i)o-*declension

2.31 This declension comprises feminine adjectives which have the endings *-a*, *-ia*, and *-i* in the nominative singular. Accordingly, three paradigms can be distinguished within this adjectival declension:

Paradigm 6

Nom. Sg. the ending *-a* (*o-*stem adjectives), e.g. *aukštà* 'high', *gerà* 'good', *laimìnga* 'happy', *apskrità* 'round', which are declined like feminine nouns of the *o-*stem, cf. *síena* 'wall', *lentà* 'board'.

Paradigm 7

Nom. Sg. the ending *-ia* (*io-*stem adjectives), e.g. *žalià* 'green', *naujà* 'new', *geriáusia* 'the best', which are declined like feminine nouns of the *io-*stem, cf. *girià* 'wood', *valdžià* 'authority'.

Paradigm 8

Nom. Sg. the ending *-i* (*io-*stem adjectives), e.g. *gražì* 'beautiful', *lýgi* 'smooth, equal', *mandagì* 'polite', *panašì* 'similar', which are declined like feminine nouns of the *io-*stem, cf. *martì* 'daughter-in-law', see 1.25.

Paradigm 6

aukštà 'high', *gerà* 'good', *laimìnga* 'happy', *apskrità* 'round'

Singular

Nom.	aukštà	gerà	laimìnga	apskrità
Gen.	aukštõs	gerõs	laimìngos	apskritõs
Dat.	áukštai	gẽrai	laimìngai	ãpskritai
Acc.	áukštą	gẽrą	laimìngą	ãpskritą
Instr.	áukšta	gerà	laimìnga	ãpskrita
Loc.	aukštojè	gerojè	laimìngoje	apskritojè

Plural

Nom.	áukštos	gẽros	laimìngos	ãpskritos
Gen.	aukštų̃	gerų̃	laimìngų	apskritų̃
Dat.	aukštóms	geróms	laimìngoms	apskritóms
Acc.	áukštas	geràs	laimìngas	ãpskritas
Instr.	aukštomìs	geromìs	laimìngomis	apskritomìs
Loc.	aukštosè	gerosè	laimìngose	apskritosè

Paradigm 7

žalià 'green', *naujà* 'new', *geriáusia* 'the best'

Singular

Nom.	žalià	naujà	geriáusia
Gen.	žaliõs	naujõs	geriáusios
Dat.	žãliai	naũjai	geriáusiai
Acc.	žãlią	naũją	geriáusią
Instr.	žalià	naujà	geriáusia
Loc.	žaliojè	naujojè	geriáusioje

Plural

Nom.	žãlios	naũjos	geriáusios
Gen.	žalių̃	naujų̃	geriáusių
Dat.	žalióms	naujóms	geriáusioms
Acc.	žaliàs	naujàs	geriáusias
Instr.	žaliomìs	naujomìs	geriáusiomis
Loc.	žaliosè	naujosè	geriáusiose

Paradigm 8

gražì 'beautiful', *lýgi* 'smooth, egual', *mandagì* 'polite', *panašì* 'similar'

Singular

Nom.	gražì	lýgi	mandagì	panašì
Gen.	gražiõs	lygiõs	mandagiõs	panašiõs
Dat.	grãžiai	lýgiai	mandãgiai	panãšiai
Acc.	grãžią	lýgią	mandãgią	panãšią
Instr.	gražià	lýgia	mandagià	panašià
Loc.	gražiojè	lygiojè	mandagiojè	panašiojè

Plural

Nom.	grãžios	lýgios	mandãgios	panãšios
Gen.	gražių̃	lygių̃	mandagių̃	panašių̃
Dat.	gražióms	lygióms	mandagióms	panašióms
Acc.	gražiàs	lýgias	mandagiàs	panašiàs
Instr.	gražiomìs	lygiomìs	mandagiomìs	panašiomìs
Loc.	gražiosè	lygiosè	mandagiosè	panašiosè

It is obvious from Patterns 6, 7, and 8 that the declension of feminine adjectives is more uniform than that of masculine adjectives. Paradigms 7 and 8, for example, differ only in the nominative singular.

The ė-declension

2.32 This declension comprises feminine adjectives which in the nominative singular end in -ė (ė-stem adjectives), e.g. *medìnė* 'wooden', *kairė̃* 'left', *gerèsnė* 'better', *apýmažė* 'rather small', *geraširdė̃* 'good-hearted'. These adjectives are declined like the ė-stem feminine nouns, e.g. *žolė̃* 'grass', *bìtė* 'bee', see 1.27.

Paradigm 9

medìnė 'wooden', *gerèsnė* 'better', *apýmažė* 'rather small', *geraširdė̃* 'kind-hearted'

Singular

Nom.	medìnė	dìdelė	gerèsnė	apýmažė	geraširdė̃
Gen.	medìnės	didelė̃s	geresnė̃s	apýmažės	geraširdė̃s
Dat.	medìnei	dìdelei	gerèsnei	apýmažei	geraširdei
Acc.	medìnę	dìdelę	gerèsnę	apýmažę	geraširdę
Instr.	medìnė	dìdele	geresnè	apýmaže	geraširdè
Loc.	medìnėje	didelėjè	gerèsnėje	apýmažėje	geraširdė̃je

Plural

Nom.	medìnės	dìdelės	gerèsnės	apýmažės	geraširdė̃s
Gen.	medìnių	didelių̃	geresnių̃	apýmažių	geraširdžių̃
Dat.	medìnėms	didelė́ms	geresnė́ms	apýmažėms	geraširdė̃ms
Acc.	medìnes	dìdeles	gerèsnes	apýmažes	geraširdès
Instr.	medìnėmis	didelėmìs	geresnėmìs	apýmažėmis	geraširdė̃mis
Loc.	medìnėse	didelėsè	geresnėsè	apýmažėse	geraširdė̃se

Table 4. **Correlation of masculine and feminine gender forms of adjectives**

Masculine		Nom. Sg. Masc.	Nom. Sg. Fem	Feminine	
(i)a-declension	Par. 1	-as	-a	Par. 6	(i)o-declension
	Par. 2	-ias	-ia	Par. 7	
	Par. 3–4	-is, -ys	-ė	Par. 8	io-declension
(i)u-declension	Par. 5	-us	-i	Par. 9	ė-declension

Examples: *gĕras – gerà* 'good'; *žãlias – žalià* 'green'; *gerèsnis – gerèsnė* 'better'; *kairỹs, -ẽ* 'left-handed'; *medìnis – medìnė* 'wooden'; *gražùs – gražì* 'beautiful.'

The shorter case endings

2.33 Certain case endings of both masculine and feminine adjectives have shorter variants widely used in colloquial speech and fiction. The tendency to use shorter forms is observed in the following cases:

Masculine adjectives   Feminine adjectives

Loc. Sg.: *geramè – geram̃*   Loc. Sg.: *gerojè – gerõj*
          gražiamè – gražiam̃   *gražiojè – gražiõj*
Dat. Pl.: *geríems – geríem*   Dat. Pl.: *geróms – geróm*
          gražíems – gražíem   *gražióms – gražióm*
Loc. Pl.: *geruosè – geruõs*   Instr. Pl.: *geromìs – gerõm*
          gražiuosè – gražiuõs   *gražiomìs – gražiõm*

The shortened endings always attract the stress and, with the exception of the dative plural, bear the circumflex toneme.

Declension of definite adjectives

2.34 All definite adjectives of the feminine gender, no matter what the declension of their corresponding simple adjectives may be, are declined in the same way.

Differences in the case endings of masculine definite adjectives can be observed only in the nominative and accusative singular, cf.:

Nom.	geràsis	žaliàsis	geresnỹsis	gražùsis
Acc.	gẽrąjį	žãliąjį	gerèsnįjį	grãžųjį

Definite forms cannot be formed from simple adjectives declined according to Paradigm 4 (e.g., medìnis, pómažis, gerašir̃dis), but they can be formed from comparative adjectives, e.g. gerèsnis – geresnỹsis.

DECLENSION PATTERNS

Masculine gender

geràsis 'the good', *žaliàsis* 'the green', *geresnỹsis* 'the better', *gražùsis* 'the beautiful'

Singular

Nom.	geràsis	žaliàsis	geresnỹsis	gražùsis
Gen.	gẽrojo	žãliojo	gerèsniojo	grãžiojo
Dat.	gerájam	žaliájam	geresniájam	gražiájam
Acc.	gẽrąjį	žãliąjį	gerèsnįjį	grãžųjį
Instr.	gerúoju	žaliúoju	geresniúoju	gražiúoju
Loc.	gerãjame	žaliãjame	geresniãjame	gražiãjame

Plural

Nom.	geríeji	žalíeji	geresníeji	gražíeji
Gen.	gerū́jų	žalių̃jų	geresniū̃jų	gražių̃jų
Dat.	geríesiems	žalíesiems	geresníesiems	gražíesiems
Acc.	gerúosius	žaliúosius	geresniúosius	gražiúosius
Instr.	geraĩsiais	žaliaĩsiais	geresniaĩsiais	gražiaĩsiais
Loc.	geruõsiuose	žaliuõsiuose	geresniuõsiuose	gražiuõsiuose

Feminine gender
Singular

Nom.	geróji	žalióji	geresnióji	gražióji
Gen.	gerõsios	žaliõsios	geresniõsios	gražiõsios
Dat.	gẽrajai	žãliajai	gerèsniajai	grãžiajai
Acc.	gẽrąją	žãliąją	gerèsniąją	grãžiąją
Instr.	gerája	žalią́ja	geresnią́ja	gražią́ja
Loc.	gerõjoje	žaliõjoje	geresniõjoje	gražiõjoje

Plural

Nom.	*gėrosios*	*žãliosios*	*gerèsniosios*	*grãžiosios*
Gen.	*gerų̃jų*	*žalių̃jų*	*geresnių̃jų*	*gražių̃jų*
Dat.	*gerósioms*	*žaliósioms*	*geresniósioms*	*gražiósioms*
Acc.	*gerą́sias*	*žalią́sias*	*geresnią́sias*	*gražią́sias*
Instr.	*gerõsiomis*	*žaliõsiomis*	*geresniõsiomis*	*gražiõsiomis*
Loc.	*gerõsiose*	*žaliõsiose*	*geresniõsiose*	*gražiõsiose*

As can easily be seen from the declension patterns, the case endings of definite adjectives are a blend of the case endings of simple adjectives and the pronouns *jìs, jì*; e.g.:

Masculine **Feminine**

Singular

Nom.	*geràsis*	< *gẽras + (j)is*	*geróji*	< *geró + ji*
Gen.	*gẽrojo*	< *gẽro + jo*	*gerõsios*	< *gerõs + jos*
Dat.	*gerájam*	< *gerá(m) + jam*	*gẽrajai*	< *gẽra(i) + jai*
Acc.	*gẽrąjį*	< *gẽrą + jį*	*gẽrąją*	< *gẽrą + ją*
Instr.	*gerúoju*	< *gerúo + ju(o)*	*gerája*	< *gerá + ja*
Loc.	*gerãjame*	< *gera(mè) + jame*	*gerõjoje*	< *gero(jè) + joje*

Plural

Nom.	*geríeji*	< *geríe(e) + ji(e)*	*gẽrosios*	< *gẽros + jos*
Gen.	*gerų̃jų*	< *gerų̃ + jų*	*gerų̃jų*	< *gerų̃ + jų*
Dat.	*geríesiems*	< *geríe(m)s + (j)iems*	*gerósioms*	< *geró(m)s + joms*
Acc.	*gerúosius*	< *gerúos + ju(o)s*	*gerą́sias*	< *gerą́s + jas*
Instr.	*geraĩsiais*	< *geraĩs + jais*	*gerõsiomis*	< *gero(mì)s + jomis*
Loc.	*geruõsiuose*	< *geruos(è) + juose*	*gerõsiose*	< *geros(è) + jose*

The shorter case endings of definite adjectives

2.35 Just as simple adjectives, definite adjectives are also used with the shorter endings in the following cases:

Masculine gender   **Feminine gender**

Loc. Sg.   *gerãjame – gerãjam*   Loc. Sg.   *gerõjoje – gerõjoj*

Dat. Pl.   *geríesiems – geríesiem*   Dat. Pl.   *gerósioms – gerósiom*
Loc. Pl.   *geruõsiuose – geruõsiuos*   Instr. Pl.   *gerõsiomis – gerõsiom*

Accentuation of adjectives

SIMPLE TWO-SYLLABLE ADJECTIVES

2.36 Two-syllable adjectives are stressed like two-syllable nouns of the 3rd and 4th accentuation class (cf. 1.37, 38). Differences can only be observed in the dative singular of masculine adjectives, which bear the stress on the ending while nouns bear it on the root, cf.:

Dat. Sg. *gerám, gražiám – stãlui* 'table', *sū́nui* 'son'

Adjectives with the ending *-us, -i* in the nominative singular usually bear the stress on the ending (*gražùs, gražì* 'handsome', *gardùs, gardì* 'delicious'; see 2.30). Exceptions are: *áiškus* 'clear', *lýgus* 'smooth', *ráiškus* 'distinct', *smùlkus* 'fine', *sódrus* 'lush', *sótus* 'satiated', *švánkus* 'decent', *tánkus* 'dense', *váiskus* 'bright', *véikus* 'quick', which bear the stress on the root. In all the other cases, however, the latter adjectives follow the regular pattern of accentuation class 3 (see 1.37, 2.30).

SIMPLE POLYSYLLABIC ADJECTIVES

According to their accentuation patterns polysyllabic adjectives fall into the same accentuation classes as nouns.

Accentuation class 1

2.37 The adjectives belonging to this class have a constant stress. (Accentuation patterns are those of *laimìngas, laimìnga, geriáusias, geriáusia, apýmažis, apýmažė* – given in 2.27, 31, 32).

Accentuation class 1 includes polysyllabic adjectives with the following suffixes:

-áitis, -ė: *girtutėláitis* 'absolutely drunk', *karštutėláitis* 'absolutely hot';
-ė́tas, -a: *dulkė́tas* 'dusty', *gėlė́tas* 'flowery', *pūslė́tas* 'blistered';
-ė́tinas, -a: *pusė́tinas* 'middling', *ganė́tinas* 'sufficient';

-iáusias, -ia: (superlative degree): *aukščiáusias* 'highest', *geriáusias* 'best', *mokyčiáusias* 'best educated';

-ýkštis, -ė: *vakarýkštis* 'yesterday's', *pernýkštis* 'from last year';

-ýkščias, -ia: *vakarýkščias* 'yesterday's';

-ýlas, -a: *akýlas* 'sharp-sighted', *ausýlas* 'having a keen ear';

-ìngas, -a: *laimìngas* 'happy', *išmintìngas* 'wise', *akmenìngas* 'stony';

-iñtelis, -ė: *vieniñtelis* '(the) only', *pilniñtelis* 'absolutely full';

-iškas, -a: (these adjectives have the same stress as the accusative singular of the nouns they are derived from): *móteriškas* 'feminine' (cf. *móterį* 'woman'), *vaīkiškas* 'childlike' (cf. *vaīką*), *senóviškas* 'old-fashioned' (cf. *senóvę*);

-ýtas, -a: *akýtas* 'porous', *dantýtas* 'toothed';

-ýtis, -ė: *mažýtis* 'very little';

-ývas, -a: *ankstývas* 'early', *vėlývas* 'late';

-ódas, -a: *vienódas* 'uniform';

-ókas, -a: *mažókas* 'rather small';

-(i)ópas, -a: *dvejópas* 'of two kinds', *šimteriópas* 'hundredfold';

-ótas, -a: *galvótas* 'intelligent', *gyslótas* 'sinewy';

-ùistas, -a: *ligùistas* 'sickly', *miegùistas* 'sleepy';

-ùitas, -a: *medùitas* 'smeared with honey', *pienùitas* 'spattered with milk';

-(i)úotas, -a: *kalnúotas* 'mountainous', *akiniúotas* 'bespectacled';

-úotinis, -ė: *visúotinis* 'universal'.

Colour adjectives with the unstressed suffix *-ynas, -a* and *-onas, -a* can follow two accentuation patterns:

that of Class 1:

Nom. Sg.	*mélynas*	*mélyna*	*raudónas*	*raudóna*
Dat. Sg.	*mélynam*	*mélynai*	*raudónam*	*raudónai*
Dat. Pl.	*mélyniems*	*mélynoms*	*raudóniems*	*raudónoms*

and Class 3:

Nom. Sg.	*mélynas*	*mėlynà*	*raudónas*	*raudonà*
Dat. Sg.	*mėlynám*	*mélynai*	*raudonám*	*raudónai*
Dat. Pl.	*mėlyníems*	*mėlynóms*	*raudoníems*	*raudonóms*

Accentuation class 1 also includes:

(**1**) adjectives with the suffix *-inis, -ė* formed from:

(**a**) nouns which in the dative plural are stressed on the penultimate syllable (these adjectives retain the same stress as the nouns they are formed from):

kójinis, -ė 'pedal' (cf. *kójoms*), *rañkinis* 'manual' (*rañkoms*), *viẽtinis* 'local' (*viẽtoms*), *aplinkýbinis* 'adverbial' (*aplinkýbėms*), *medžióklinis* 'hunting' (*medžióklėms*), *valstýbinis* 'state' (*valstýbėms*). Exception: adjectives referring to materials (e.g. *medìnis* 'wooden', *auksìnis* 'golden') and a number of polysyllabic a.o. adjectives (e.g. *išorìnis* 'external').

(b) polysyllabic nouns with foreign roots stressed on the pre-penultimate syllable (these adjectives also retain the same stress as the nouns they are formed from):

ãkcinis, -ė 'stock' (ãkcija), *archeològinis, -ė* 'archeological' (*archeològija*), *analòginis, -ė* 'analogous' (*analògija*), *istòrinis, -ė* 'historical' (*istòrija*);

(2) adjectives with the following prefixes:

apý-:	*apýgeris* 'fairly good', *apýmažis* 'fairly small';
põ-:	*põmažis* 'a little too small', *põžalis* 'a little too green';
príe-:	*príekurtis* 'hard of hearing', *príekvailis* 'a little silly';

(3) compound adjectives which bear the stress on the first component or on the linking vowel: *vasaródrungis, -ė* 'luke-warm'; all other compound adjectives follow the stress patterns of Class 2 and 4.

Accentuation class 2

2.38 The accentuation pattern is that of *medìnis, medìnė, geraširdis, geraširdė* presented in 2.27, 32.

Accentuation class 2 includes adjectives with the following stressed suffixes:

-aĩnis, -ė:	*dešimtaĩnis* 'decimal', *ketvirtaĩnis* 'quandrangular';
-ė̃lis, -ė:	*jaunė̃lis* 'youngest', *mažė̃lis* 'smallest';
-iẽnis, -ė:	*avižiẽnis* 'oat(meal)', *miežiẽnis* 'barley';
-ìklis, -ė:	*jaunìklis* (young);
-ỹlis, -ė:	*jaunỹlis* 'youngest', *mažỹlis* 'little (one)';
-ìnis, -ė:	(excluding those indicated in 2.37) *vakarìnis* 'evening', *rytìnis* 'morning', *laukìnis* 'wild';
-ìškis, -ė:	*kalnìškis* 'living in the mountains', *kaunìškis* 'living in, pertaining to Kaunas';
-ỹvis, -ė:	*ankstỹvis* 'early', *vėlỹvis* 'late';
-õnis, -ė:	*vilnõnis* 'woolen', *marškõnis* 'cotton';
-õtis, -ė:	*šakõtis* 'branchy';
-(i)ùkas, -ė:	*juodùkas* 'black', *mažiùkas* 'little';
-(i)ùlis, -ė:	*didžiùlis* 'huge', *mažiùlis* 'tiny';
-utìnis, -ė:	*kraštutìnis* 'extreme', *paviršutìnis* 'superficial', *žemutìnis* 'bottom';
-ùtis, -ė:	*baltùtis* 'very white, clean', *silpnùtis* 'feeble', *mažùtis* 'tiny'.

Accentuation class 2 also includes:

(1) compound adjectives which bear the stress on the second component: *antraeĩlis, -ė* 'of minor importance', *lygiagretis, -ė* 'parallel'. Adjectives which differ in their toneme and meaning are exceptions:

Accentuation class 1:

ilgakártis 'with long poles'
daugiavárpis 'with many ears'

Accentuation class 2:

ilgakartis 'with a long mane'
daugiavarpis 'with many bells'

(2) adjectives with the prefix *-be*: *bevar̃dis* 'nameless', *beginklis* 'defenceless', *bevertis* 'worthless';

(3) derived adjectives with the ending *-is*: *kasdiēnis* 'ordinary', *vasāris* 'summer', *palaĩkis* 'threadbare'.

Accentuation class 3

2.39 Accentuation patterns are those of *dìdelis, dìdelė, ãpskritas, apskrità*, see 2.27, 31, 32.

This class includes:

(1) adjectives with the suffixes:

-anas, -à: *álkanas* 'hungry', *rúškanas* 'gloomy', *var̃ganas* 'poor';
-imas, -à: *ar̃timas* 'near, intimate', *grẽtimas* 'adjacent', *svẽtimas* 'somebody else's';
-inas, -à: *ámžinas* 'eternal', *kùpinas* 'full', *sklìdinas* 'brimful';
-išas, -à: *víenišas* 'lonely';
-itas, -à: *sãvitas* 'distinctive';
-zganas, -à: *bal̃zganas* 'whitish', *juõzganas* 'blackish';

(2) prefixed adjectives with the endings *-(i)as, -(i)a*: *ãpskritas* 'round', *ãtlapas* 'wide open', *atãtupstas* 'moving backwards', *ìšdrikas* 'incoherent', *ìštisas* 'entire', *núosavas* 'one's own', *pãdrikas* 'scattered', *paĩlgas* 'elongated', *pãprastas* 'simple', *prãviras* 'ajar', *ùždaras* 'closed';

(3) some other adjectives, e.g. *dìdelis* 'big', *dešinỹs* 'right', *žãbalas* 'blind'.

Accentuation class 4

2.40 Accentuation patterns are those of *gerèsnis, gerèsnė, mandagùs, mandagì, panašùs, panašì*, presented in 2.27, 30, 31, 32.

Accentuation class 4 includes:

(**1**) adjectives with the ending *-us, -i*: *įdomùs* 'interesting', *mandagùs* 'polite', *nuobodùs* 'boring', *padorùs* 'decent', *pravartùs* 'handy', *sumanùs* 'clever', *atkaklùs* 'persistent', *objektyvùs* 'objective';

(**2**) comparative adjectives with the suffixes *-esnis, -ė, -ėlesnis, -ė*: *gerèsnis, mažèsnis, gerėlèsnis*;

(**3**) adjectives with the suffix *-ainas, -a*: *apvalaĩnas* 'round'.

DEFINITE ADJECTIVES

2.41 According to the peculiarities of their accentuation, definite adjectives fall into two groups:

(**1**) Adjectives which have a constant stress (i.e. the stress falls on the same syllable in all the cases and the stressed syllable has the same toneme. Such adjectives are formed from simple adjectives which belong to accentuation class 1, e.g.:

laimìngasis	*laimìngoji*	'the happy'
geriáusiasis	*geriáusioji*	'the best'
draũgiškasis	*draũgiškoji*	'the friendly'

(**2**) In all the other definite adjectives the stress alternates between the penultimate and pre-penultimate syllable, e.g.

geràsis	*geróji*	'the good'
geresnỹsis	*geresnióji*	'the better'
pažangùsis	*pažangióji*	'the progressive'

NEUTER ADJECTIVES

2.42 Neuter adjectives with the ending *-(i)a* retain the stress and the toneme of the respective masculine adjectives in Acc. Sg., e.g.:

gẽra	cf. *gẽrą*	'good'
liñksma	*liñksmą*	'merry'
žãlia	*žãlią*	'green'
aiškiáusia	*aiškiáusią*	'clearest'

Neuter adjectives with the ending *-u* bear the stress on the ending: *gražù* 'beautiful', *malonù* 'nice', *saugù* 'safe'.

Exceptions:

áišku	cf. Acc. Sg. Masc.	*áiškų*	'clear'
lýgu		*lýgų*	'smooth, equal'
smùlku		*smùlkų*	'fine'
sótu		*sótų*	'satiated'
tánku		*tánkų*	'dense'

3 NUMERAL
Skaĩtvardis

3.1 Numerals constitute a class of words which are inflected for case, partly for gender and number, and which denote numbers, the exact quantity or the order of countable things.

In their grammatical properties some numerals are similar to nouns (*dešimtìs* 'ten', cf. *akìs* 'eye'), others to adjectives (*víenas, vienà* 'one', cf. *báltas, baltà* 'white'). Certain numerals are similar to adverbs, e.g., *dẽšimt* 'ten', *dvìdešimt* 'twenty', cf., *daũg* 'many, much.'

Two main groups of numerals are distinguished: cardinal and ordinal numerals.

Cardinal numerals denote an abstract number or an exact quantity of things. They are subdivided into several groups: plain cardinal numerals (*víenas, dù, trỹs*...), plural numerals which are used with nouns that have only the plural form (*pluralia tantum*) (*dvejì, trejì*...), collective numerals (*dvẽjetas, trẽjetas*...) and fractions (*vienà antróji, trỹs dešim̃tosios*...).

Ordinal numerals indicate a specified order in a countable series (*pìrmas, pirmà* 'the first', *añtras, antrà* 'the second', *vienúoliktas, vienúolikta* 'the eleventh').

3.2 According to their morphemic structure numerals are simple, derived, compound or composite (multiword) numerals.

Derived numerals contain one of the following suffixes:

-eji, -ejos: *dvì : dvejì, dvẽjos*
-eri, -erios: *penkì : penkerì, peñkerios*
-etas: *dvì : dvẽjetas, penkì : peñketas*
-tas: *ketverì : kẽtvertas*
-tas, -ta: *penkì : peñktas, penktà*.

Compound numerals contain two roots. Both roots may be those of numerals (*dvìdešimt* 'twenty', cf. *dvì dẽšimtys* 'two tens'), or one of the roots may belong to a word of another part of speech (*trẽčdalis* 'one third', cf. *trečià dalìs*).

Composite (multiword) numerals may consist of several simple numerals (*šim̃tas penkì* 'a hundred and five', *tū́kstantis šim̃tas keturì* 'a thousand one hundred four') and a group of simple derived and compound numerals (*dù šim̃taĩ aštúoniasdešimt añtras* 'two hundred eighty second', *trỹs ketviȓtosios* 'three fourths').

Cardinal Numerals

Kiẽkiniai skaĩtvardžiai

PLAIN CARDINAL NUMERALS

Pagrindìniai skaĩtvardžiai

3.3 Numerals denoting numbers from one to ten are simple numerals:

Masc.	Fem.		Masc.	Fem.	
víenas	vienà	'one'	šešì	šẽšios	'six'
dù	dvì	'two'	septynì	septýnios	'seven'
	trỹs	'three'	aštuonì	aštúonios	'eight'
keturì	kẽturios	'four'	devynì	devýnios	'nine'
penkì	peñkios	'five'		dẽšimt/dešimtìs	'ten'

Numbers from eleven to nineteen are denoted by compound numerals which are built by adding *-lika* (derived historically from the verb *lìkti* 'remain') to simple numerals from one to nine. They are not inflected for gender:

vienúolika 'eleven'
dvýlika 'twelve'
trýlika 'thirteen'
keturiólika 'fourteen'
penkiólika 'fifteen'

šešiólika 'sixteen'
septyniólika 'seventeen'
aštuoniólika 'eighteen'
devyniólika 'nineteen'

Tens are indicated by compound numerals the first constituent of which coincides with the accusative form of simple feminine numerals (*dvi-, tris-, keturias-*) and the second constituent is the stem *dešimt*:

dvìdešimt 'twenty'
trìsdešimt 'thirty'
kẽturiasdešimt 'fourty'
peñkiasdešimt 'fifty'

šẽšiasdešimt 'sixty'
septýniasdešimt 'seventy'
aštúoniasdešimt 'eighty'
devýniasdešimt 'ninety'

A hundred and a thousand are indicated by the numerals *šim̃tas* and *tū́kstantis* respectively, which are simple underived words.

Million, billion and higher numbers are indicated by numerals of non-Lithuanian origin – *milijõnas, milijárdas*, etc.

All the other numbers are designated by composite (multiword) numerals, which are in fact clusters of the numerals described above:

dvìdešimt víenas, dvìdešimt vienà	21
dvìdešimt dù, dvìdešimt dvì	22
dvìdešimt devynì, dvìdešimt devýnios	29
trìsdešimt víenas, trìsdešimt vienà	31
devýniasdešimt devynì, devýniasdešimt devýnios	99
šim̃tas víenas, šim̃tas vienà	101
šim̃tas dẽšimt	110
šim̃tas dvìdešimt	120
šim̃tas dvìdešimt víenas, šim̃tas dvìdešimt vienà	121
šim̃tas devýniasdešimt víenas, šim̃tas devýniasdešimt vienà	191
dù šimtaĩ víenas, dù šimtaĩ vienà	201
devynì šimtaĩ devýniasdešimt devynì	999
devynì šimtaĩ devýniasdešimt devýnios	999
dẽšimt tū́kstančių dù šimtaĩ dvìdešimt víenas	10221
dẽšimt tū́kstančių dù šimtaĩ dvìdešimt vienà	10221

Multiword numerals designating tens can be replaced by groups consisting of a numeral and the respective noun, e.g.: *dvìdešimt – dvì dẽšimtys, trìsdešimt – trỹs dẽšimtys*, etc.

3.4 Numerals from 1 to 9 are used as adjectives and agree with quantified nouns in gender, case and number, e.g.:

víenas berniùkas	'one boy'
vienà mergáitė	'one girl'
septynì stalaĩ	'seven tables'
devýnios kė̃dės	'nine chairs'

Numerals from 10 to 19, numerals indicating tens (20–90), also *šim̃tas, tū́kstantis, milijõnas, milijárdas, bilijõnas* (and higher) are used as nouns and they require the genitive plural of any quantified noun, e.g.:

dẽšimt/dvìdešimt vaikų̃	'ten/twenty children'
dvýlika kėdžių̃	'twelve chairs'
šim̃tas/tū́kstantis keleĩvių	'hundred/thousand of passengers'

Composite numerals are used as nouns or adjectives depending on the last word, cf.:

šim̃tas dvìdešimt vaikų̃	'one hundred and twenty children'
šim̃tas dvìdešimt penkì vaikaĩ	'one hundred and twenty five children'

CARDINAL PLURAL NUMERALS

Daugìniai skaĩtvardžiai

3.5 Traditionally there have always been eight numerals which are used with *pluralia tantum*:

dvejì, dvẽjos 'two'	*šešerì, šẽšerios* 'six'
trejì, trẽjos 'three'	*septynerì, septýnerios* 'seven'
ketverì, kẽtverios 'four'	*aštuonerì, aštúonerios* 'eight'
penkerì, peñkerios 'five'	*devynerì, devýnerios* 'nine'

The numeral *vienerì, víenerios* 'one' is a comparatively recent addition in Standard Lithuanian. Dialects continue to use the plural forms of the cardinal numeral *víenas, vienà* instead of it. In Standard Lithuanian *vienì – vienerì, víenos – víenerios* are considered to be equivalent, e.g.:

víenos/víenerios dùrys	'one door'
vienì/vienerì mẽtai	'one year'

Numerals of this group are formed by adding the suffixes *-eji, -ejos* or *-eri, -erios* to a simple cardinal numeral: *dvejì, dvẽjos; penkerì, peñkerios*. The numeral *ketverì, kẽtverios* is the only numeral which has a stem slightly different from that of the respective cardinal numeral.

Numerals of this group are used as adjectives:

(1) with nouns which have only the plural form:

dvejì mẽtai	'two years'
trẽjos žìrklės	'three pairs of scissors'
ketverì marškiniaĩ	'four shirts'

(2) sometimes – with the plural form of nouns indicating objects which come in pairs:

dvejì langaĩ	'two windows'
dvẽjos pir̃štinės	'two pairs of gloves'
dvejì bãtai	'two pairs of shoes'

COLLECTIVE CARDINAL NUMERALS

Kúopiniai skaĩtvardžiai

3.6 There are eight collective numerals:

dvẽjetas	*šẽšetas*
trẽjetas	*septýnetas*

kėtvertas *aštúonetas*
peñketas *devýnetas*

They are formed on the plain cardinal numerals (2–3) or on the cardinal plural numerals (5–9) with the help of the suffix *-etas*. The collective numeral *kėtvertas* has the suffix *-tas* and a slightly modified stem.

Collective numerals are used as nouns indicating objects as one single group. They require the genitive plural of the quantified noun, e.g.:

Jìs laĩko peñketą arklių̃. 'He keeps five horses.'
Prisiar̃tino dár dvėjetas výrų. 'Two more men approached.'

They can also indicate an approximate number:

Lìko trėjetas kilomètrų kẽlio. 'There are three more kilometres left to go.'

Ordinal Numerals

Keliñtiniai skaĩtvardžiai

3.7 Ordinal numerals are created by adding the suffix *-tas*, *-ta* to the roots of cardinal numerals, except for the ordinal numerals *pìrmas, pirmà* 'first', *añtras, antrà* 'second' and *trẽčias, trečià* 'third' the formation of which differs from that of all the other ordinal numerals. The stem of the ordinal numerals *ketvir̃tas, ketvirtà* 'fourth'; *septiñtas, septintà* 'seventh'; *aštuñtas, aštuntà* 'eighth'; *deviñtas, devintà* 'ninth' is also slightly different from that of its cardinal counterpart:

pìrmas, pirmà	(1)	*vienúoliktas, vienúolikta*	(11)
añtras, antrà	(2)	*dvýliktas, dvýlikta*	(12)
trẽčias, trečià	(3)	*trýliktas, trýlikta*	(13)
ketvir̃tas, ketvirtà	(4)	*keturióliktas, keturiólikta*	(14)
peñktas, penktà	(5)	*penkióliktas, penkiólikta*	(15)
šẽštas, šeštà	(6)	*šešióliktas, šešiólikta*	(16)
septiñtas, septintà	(7)	*septynióliktas, septyniólikta*	(17)
aštuñtas, aštuntà	(8)	*aštuonióliktas, aštuoniólikta*	(18)
deviñtas, devintà	(9)	*devynióliktas, devyniólikta*	(19)
dešiñtas, dešimtà	(10)	*dvidešiñtas, dvidešimtà*	(20)
		trisdešiñtas, trisdešimtà	(30)
		keturiasdešiñtas, keturiasdešimtà	(40)
		penkiasdešiñtas, penkiasdešimtà	(50)
		šešiasdešiñtas, šešiasdešimtà	(60)
		septyniasdešiñtas, septyniasdešimtà	(70)

aštuoniasdešimtas, aštuoniasdešimtà	(80)
devyniasdešimtas, devyniasdešimtà	(90)
šimtas, šimtà	(100)
tūkstantas, tūkstanta	(1000)

If the stem of a cardinal numeral ends in -*t*, this final consonant merges with the ordinal suffix -*tas*, -*ta*:

dẽšimt + -tas – dešimtas
dvìdešimt + -tas – dvidešimtas
tūkstant-(is) + -tas – tūkstantas

Ordinal numerals *milijónas, -à* 'million' and *šimtas, -à* 'hundred' coincide with their cardinal counterparts (they do not contain the ordinal suffix -*tas*, -*ta*), the only difference between them being the existence of two gender – masculine and feminine – ordinal forms. However, these ordinal numerals are mostly used in their definite forms; *milijonàsis, milijonóji; šimtàsis, šimtóji*

The following ordinal numerals are also mostly used in their definite forms:

Simple ordinal numerals		Definite ordinal numerals
dušimtas, dušimtà	(200)	dušimtàsis, dušimtóji
trišimtas, trišimtà	(300)	trišimtàsis, trišimtóji
keturiašimtas, -à	(400)	keturiašimtàsis, -óji
penkiašimtas, -à	(500)	penkiašimtàsis, -óji
šešiašimtas, -à	(600)	šešiašimtàsis, -óji
septyniašimtas, -à	(700)	septyniašimtàsis, -óji
aštuoniašimtas, -à	(800)	aštuoniašimtàsis, -óji
devyniašimtas, -à	(900)	devyniašimtàsis, -óji
dutūkstantas, -à	(2000)	dutūkstantàsis, -óji
tritūkstantas, -à	(3000)	tritūkstantàsis, -óji
keturiatūkstantas, -à	(4000)	keturiatūkstantàsis, -óji
penkiatūkstantas, -à	(5000)	penkiatūkstantàsis, -óji
šešiatūkstantas, -à	(6000)	šešiatūkstantàsis, -óji
septyniatūkstantas, -à	(7000)	septyniatūkstantàsis, -óji
aštuoniatūkstantas, -à	(8000)	aštuoniatūkstantàsis, -óji
devyniatūkstantas, -à	(9000)	devyniatūkstantàsis, -óji

In the composite (multiword) numerals it is only the last numeral which acquires the ordinal declinable form, while all the others retain their cardinal form, e.g.:

dvìdešimt pìrmas, dvìdešimt pirmà (21)
dvìdešimt añtras, dvìdešimt antrà (22)
trìsdešimt ketvìrtas, trìsdešimt ketvirtà (34)

kėturiasdešimt šėštas, kėturiasdešimt šeštà (46)
šim̃tas deviñtas, šim̃tas devintà (109)
dù šimtaĩ vienúoliktas, dù šimtaĩ vienúolikta (211)
trỹs šimtaĩ dvideši̇̀m̃tas, trỹs šimtaĩ dvìdešim̃tà (320)
aštuonì šimtaĩ dvìdešimt trẽčias, ... trečià (823)
tū́kstantis pìrmas, tū́kstantis pirmà (1001)
tū́kstantis devynì šimtaĩ dvìdešimt septiñtas, ... septintà (1927)
dù tū́kstančiai septynì šimtaĩ trìsdešimt añtras, ... antrà (2732)
trỹs milijõnai penkì šimtaĩ trìsdešimt tū́kstančių septýniasdešimt ketvir̃tas, ... ketvirtà (3,530,074)

3.8 Ordinal numerals are inflected for gender, number and case and, like adjectives, agree with the nouns they modify, e.g.:

Nom. *añtras pùslapis*   *pirmóji knygà*
Gen. *añtro pùslapio*   *pirmõsios knỹgos*
Dat. *antrám pùslapiui*   *pìrmajai knỹgai*, etc.

In multiword numerals it is only the last word which is inflected and stands in agreement with the noun, e.g.:

dù šimtaĩ dvìdešimt añtras pùslapis   'two hundred twenty second page'
šim̃tas kėturiasdešimt penktà eilùtė   'one hundred forty fifth line'

Beside masculine and feminine forms ordinal numerals also have a neuter form, e.g., *pìrma, añtra, trẽčia, ketvir̃ta, peñkta... dešim̃ta, vienúolikta*, etc., which is mostly used in enumerations:

Pìrma, reĩkia sudarýti dárbo   'First, it is necessary to draw up a working
plãną, añtra, pažymė́ti ter̃minus.   schedule, second, to mark the terms.'

Ordinal numerals possess definite forms the usage of which is similar to that of definite adjectives:

pirmàsis, pirmóji (1)
antràsis, antróji (2)
dešimtàsis, dešimtóji (10)
vienúoliktasis, vienúoliktoji (11)
dvidešimtàsis, dvidešimtóji (20)
šimtàsis, šimtóji (100)
dvìdešimt ketvirtàsis, dvìdešimt ketvirtóji (24)
šim̃tas trìsdešimt penktàsis, šim̃tas trìsdešimt penktóji (135)
dù tū́kstančiai trỹs šimtaĩ dvìdešimt pirmàsis (2321)
dù tū́kstančiai trỹs šimtaĩ dvìdešimt pirmóji (2321)

Definite ordinal numerals are used to designate dates:

Taĩ įvỹko tū́kstantis septynì šimtaĩ 'It happened in 1722.'
dvìdešimt antraĩsiais mẽtais.

Prasidė́jo tū́kstantis devynì šimtaĩ 'The year 1995 has started.'
devýniasdešimt penktíeji mẽtai.

Definite ordinal numerals are also used in designating fractions (see 3.9).

The ordinal numeral *pìrmas, pirmà* has two degrees of comparison:

Comparative degree: *pirmèsnis, pirmèsnė*
Superlative degree: *pirmiáusias, pirmiáusia*

The neuter form *pìrma* has only the superlative degree *pirmiáusia*.

These forms have developed certain adjectival meanings. Thus *pirmèsnis* means not only 'being ahead of something', but also 'earlier'; *pirmiáusias* is often used in the meaning 'most important.'

Fractions

Trupmenìniai skaĩtvardžiai

3.9   The first component of fractions – the numerator – is usually a feminine cardinal numeral, while the second component – the denominator – is a feminine ordinal numeral in the definite form. When the numerator is a numeral from 1 to 9 (alone or as the last component of a multiword numeral), the denominator agrees with the numerator in gender, number and case, e.g.:

vienà antróji (1/2)
vienà trečióji (1/3)
dvì trečiosios (2/3)
vienà ketvirtóji (1/4)
dvì ketvir̃tosios (2/4)
trỹs ketvir̃tosios (3/4)
vienà penktóji (1/5)
dvìdešimt vienà šeštóji (21/6)
trỹs šimtaĩ peñkios šē̃štosios (305/6)
dù šimtaĩ trìsdešimt devýnios dešim̃tosios (239/10)
devynióms dešimtósioms (DAT) (9/10)
dù šimtaĩ penkiàs dešimtą́sias (ACC) 205/10)
peñkiasdešimt devyniomìs dešimtõsiomis (INSTR) (59/10)

The feminine form of fractions is determined by agreement with the implied noun *dalìs* 'part', which is a feminine noun, e.g.:

vienà antróji (dalìs) 'one second (part)'
dvì trēčiosios (dãlys) 'two third (parts)'

When the numerator is any other numeral except a numeral from 1 to 9, the denominator is always in the genitive plural, e.g.:

dēšimt dvýliktųjų (10/12)
vienúolika šimtų̃jų (11/100)
trìsdešimt penkióliktųjų (30/15)
dù šimtaĩ dvýlika šim̃tas penktų̃jų (212/105)

3.10 Fractions *vienà antróji* 'one second (= one half)' and *vienà ketvirtóji* 'one fourth' are often replaced by the feminine noun *pùsė* 'half' and the masculine noun *ketvir̃tis* 'quarter' respectively. Parts of things are most often indicated by a compound numeral, the first component of which is the root of an ordinal numeral, and the second component of which is the noun *dalìs* 'part', e.g.:

trēčdalis (1/3)	*septintãdalis* (1/7)
ketvirtãdalis (1/4)	*aštuntãdalis* (1/8)
penktãdalis (1/5)	*devintãdalis* (1/9)
šeštãdalis (1/6)	*dešimtãdalis* (1/10)

These compound fractions are sometimes replaced by corresponding phrases, e.g.:

trēčdalis = trečióji dalìs	*penktãdalis = penktóji dalìs*
ketvirtãdalis = ketvirtóji dalis	*šeštãdalis = šeštóji dalìs*, etc.

Numbers including 'a half' can be indicated by compound indeclinable numerals the first component of which is the root of the noun *pùsė* and the second component of which is an ordinal numeral in the genitive, e.g.:

pusañtro (1 1/2)	*pusseptiñto* (6 1/2)
pustrēčio (2 1/2)	*pusaštuñto* (7 1/2)
pusketvir̃to (3 1/2)	*pusdeviñto* (8 1/2)
puspeñkto (4 1/2)	*pusdešim̃to* (9 1/2)
pusšēšto (5 1/2)	*pusvienúolikto* (10 1/2)

These numerals are used with a noun in the genitive singular and agree with the latter in gender, e.g.:

Mótina àtnešė pusañtro kilogrãmo dúonos.	'Mother brought one and a half kilos of bread.'
Jìs pakélė pustrečiõs tònos króvinį.	'He lifted a load of two and a half tons.'

When used with *pluralia tantum*, the compound fraction numeral acquires the form of the genitive plural, e.g.:

mergáitė pustrečių mẽtų   'a two and a half year old girl'

Declension and accentuation
CARDINAL NUMERALS

3.11 The masculine numeral *víenas* and the feminine numeral *vienà* are declined like adjectives of the *(i)a-* and *(i)o-* declensions respectively (cf. *báltas, baltà* 'white'). These numerals are accented according to accentuation class 3.

	Singular	Plural
Nom.	*víenas, vienà*	*vienì, víenos*
Gen.	*víeno, vienõs*	*vienų̃, vienų̃*
Dat.	*vienám, víenai*	*vieníems, vienóms*
Acc.	*víeną, víeną*	*víenus, víenas*
Instr.	*víenu, víena*	*vienaĩs, vienomìs*
Loc.	*vienamè, vienojè*	*vienuosè, vienosè*

The numeral *dù, dvì* is declined in the following way:

Nom.	*dù*	*dvì*
Gen.	*dviejų̃*	*dviejų̃*
Dat.	*dvíem*	*dvíem*
Acc.	*dù*	*dvì*
Instr.	*dviẽm*	*dviẽm*
Loc.	*dviejuosè*	*dviejosè*

Although in all the cases, except the genitive and the locative, this numeral has retained the forms of the dual number, it has grammatical agreement with nouns in the plural, e.g.:

Dat. Sg.   *dvíem akìms* 'for two eyes'
               dvíem vaikáms 'for two children'
Instr. Pl.   *dviẽm akimìs* 'with two eys'
               dviẽm vaikaĩs 'with two children'

The numeral *trỹs* is declined like an *i*-declension noun (cf. *ausìs*), except the locative, which has the *(i)a*-stem (masculine) and *(i)o*-stem (feminine) adjectival endings. In all the other cases the masculine and feminine forms coincide:

Nom.	trỹs
Gen.	trijũ
Dat.	trìms
Acc.	trìs
Instr.	trimìs
Loc.	trijuosè, trijosè

Numerals from *keturì, kēturios* 'four' to *devynì, devýnios* 'nine' are declined like the adjectives of *(i)a-* (masculine) and *(i)o-* (feminine) declensions, except that the masculine form in the accusative ends in *-is*:

Nom.	keturì, kēturios	septynì, septýnios
Gen.	keturiũ, keturiũ	septyniũ, septyniũ
Dat.	keturíems, keturióms	septyníems, septynióms
Acc.	kēturis, kēturias	septýnis, septýnias
Instr.	keturiaĩs, keturiomìs	septyniaĩs, septyniomìs
Loc.	keturiuosè, keturiosè	septyniuosè, septyniosè

Aštuonì, aštúonios are accented like *septynì, septýnios*, whereas *penkì, peñkios* and *šešì, šẽšios* are accented according to accentuation class 4 (i.e., like the adjective *žalì, žãlios* 'green').

Dẽšimt/dešimtìs is declined like an *i*-declension feminine noun (cf. *žuvìs* 'fish', see 1.28). In the nominative and accusative singular this numeral is mostly used in its short inflexionless form. It is accented according to accentuation class 3:

	Singular	Plural
Nom.	dẽšimt/dešimtìs	dẽšimtys
Gen.	dešimtiẽs	dešimčiũ
Dat.	dẽšimčiai	dešimtìms
Acc.	dẽšimt/dẽšimtį	dẽšimtis
Instr.	dešimtimì/dẽšimčia	dešimtimìs
Loc.	dešimtyjè	dešimtysè

The numerals *dvìdešimt* (20), *trìsdešimt* (30)... *devýniasdešimt* (90) are declined like *dẽšimt* in the singular. However, the inflected forms of these numerals are most often replaced by their uninflected short forms, e.g.:

Mùms pritrūko dẽšimt/dvìdešimt lìtų. 'We were short by ten/twenty litas.'
Sù dẽšimt/dvìdešimt lìtų neišsiveřsi. 'You cannot make do with ten/twenty litas.'

The numerals *vienúolika, dvýlika ... devyniólika* are declined like *o*-declension feminine nouns (cf. *jūra* 'sea' in 1.25), except that in the accusative they have a short ending *-a*, which coincides with that of the nominative. The stress falls on the same syllable in all the cases:

Nom.	*vienúolika*	*dvýlika*
Gen.	*vienúolikos*	*dvýlikos*
Dat.	*vienúolikai*	*dvýlikai*
Acc.	*vienúolika*	*dvýlika*
Instr.	*vienúolika*	*dvýlika*
Loc.	*vienúolikoje*	*dvýlikoje*

The numerals *šim̃tas, milijõnas, milijárdas* are declined like *(i)a*-declension nouns of paradigm 1 (cf. *mìškas* 'wood' in 1.19). *Túkstantis* is declined like an *(i)a*-declension noun of paradigm 3 (cf. *brólis* 'brother').

Šim̃tas and *milijõnas* are accented according to accentuation class 4 and 2 respectively. *Túkstantis* and *milijárdas* always retain the stress on the same syllable.

In declining multiword cardinal numerals we decline all the components except for the inflexionless ones, e.g.:

Nom.	*šim̃tas dvìdešimt keturì* (124)
Gen.	*šim̃to dvìdešimt keturių̃*
Dat.	*šim̃tui dvìdešimt keturíems*
Acc.	*šim̃tą dvìdešimt kẽturis*
Instr.	*šimtù dvìdešimt keturiaĩs*
Loc.	*šimtè dvìdešimt keturiuosè*

Nom.	*trỹs túkstančiai dù šimtaĩ penkì* (3,205)
Gen.	*trijų̃ túkstančių dviejų̃ šimtų̃ penkių̃*
Dat.	*trìms túkstančiams dvíem šimtáms penkíems*
Acc.	*trìs túkstančius dù šimtùs penkìs*
Instr.	*trimìs túkstančiais dviẽm šimtaĩs penkiaĩs*
Loc.	*trijuosè túkstančiuose dviejuosè šimtuosè penkiuosè*

In colloquial speech, however, only the last component is often declined, e.g.:

Gen.	*šim̃tas dvìdešimt keturių̃*	*trỹs túkstančiai dù šimtaĩ penkių̃*
Dat.	*šim̃tas dvìdešimt keturíems*	*trỹs túkstančiai dù šimtaĩ penkíems*

Cardinal plural numerals

3.12   Numerals of this group are declined like the adjectives of *(i)a*- (masculine) and *(i)o*- (feminine) declensions (cf. *žãlias, žalià* 'green').

Nom.	*dvejì, dvẽjos* 'two'	*ketverì, kẽtverios* 'four'
Gen.	*dvejų̃, dvejų̃*	*ketverių̃, ketverių̃*

Dat.	*dvejíems, dvejóms*	*ketveríems, ketveri̇́oms*	
Acc.	*dvejùs, dvejàs*	*kẽtverius, kẽtverias*	
Instr.	*dvejaĩs, dvejomìs*	*ketveriaĩs, ketveriomìs*	
Loc.	*dvejuosè, dvejosè*	*ketveriuosè, ketveriosè*	

In the accusative masculine these numerals have the ending *-ius*, which makes them different from the respective cardinal numerals, the accusative form of which ends in *-is*, cf. accusative plural:

trejùs/peñkerius/šẽšerius/septýnerius metùs (cardinal plural)
trìs/penkìs/šešìs/septýnis mė́nesius (plain cardinal).

The numerals *dvejì, dvẽjos* and *trejì, trẽjos* are accented according to accentuation class 4, whereas all the other cardinal plural numerals are accented according to accentuation class 3.

Collective cardinal numerals

3.13 Collective numerals are declined like *(i)a*-declension masculine nouns and possess a stable accent which falls on the same syllable in all the case forms:

Nom.	*dvė́jetas*	*devýnetas*
Gen.	*dvė́jeto*	*devýneto*
Dat.	*dvė́jetui*	*devýnetui*, etc.

ORDINAL NUMERALS

3.14 Ordinal numerals are declined like the adjectives of *(i)a-* (masculine) and *(i)o-* (feminine) declension:

	Masculine		Feminine	
		Singular		
Nom.	*pìrmas* 'first'	*trẽčias* 'third'	*pirmà*	*trečià*
Gen.	*pìrmo*	*trẽčio*	*pirmõs*	*trečiõs*
Dat.	*pirmám*	*trečiám*	*pìrmai*	*trẽčiai*
Acc.	*pìrmą*	*trẽčią*	*pìrmą*	*trẽčią*
Instr.	*pìrmu*	*trečiù*	*pirmà*	*trečià*
Loc.	*pirmamè*	*trečiamè*	*pirmojè*	*trečiojè*

Plural

Nom.	pirmì	tretì	pìrmos	trẽčios
Gen.	pirmų̃	trečių̃	pirmų̃	trečių̃
Dat.	pirmíems	tretíems	pirmóms	trečióms
Acc.	pìrmus	trečiùs	pìrmas	trečiàs
Instr.	pirmaĩs	trečiaĩs	pirmomìs	trečiomìs
Loc.	pirmuosè	trečiuosè	pirmosè	trečiosè

The following ordinal numerals possess a stable accent (i.e., an accent which always falls on the same syllable):

(a) *vienúoliktas, vienúolikta... devynióliktas, devyniólikta;*

(b) *tū́kstantas, tū́kstanta;*

(c) compound numerals including the second component *-tū́kstantas, -a* (e.g.: *dutū́kstantas, dutū́kstanta*).

Pìrmas, pirmà is accented according to accentuation class 3, whereas all the other ordinal numerals are accented according to accentuation class 4.

All the compound ordinal numerals including the component *-šim̃tas, -šimtà*, are accented like the numeral *šim̃tas, šimtà*, e.g. *dušim̃tas, dušimtà, keturiašim̃tas, keturiašimtà*.

Definite ordinal numerals are declined and accented exactly like definite adjectives (see 2.34, 41), e.g.:

Nom.	*pirmàsis, pirmóji*
Gen.	*pìrmojo, pirmõsios*
Dat.	*pirmájam, pìrmajai*, etc.

If the simple ordinal numeral has a fixed accent, the definite form has the same fixed accent, e.g.:

vienúoliktas – vienúoliktasis, vienúoliktoji
tū́kstantas – tū́kstantasis, tū́kstantoji

When declining multiword ordinal numerals, we decline only the last numeral, e.g.:

Nom.	*trỹs šimtaĩ septýniasdešimt ketvir̃tas/ketvirtà*
Gen.	*trỹs šimtaĩ septýniasdešimt ketvir̃to/ketvirtõs*
Dat.	*trỹs šimtaĩ septýniasdešimt ketvirtám/ketvir̃tai*
Acc.	*trỹs šimtaĩ septýniasdešimt ketvir̃tą/ketvir̃tą*, etc.

FRACTIONS

3.15 When the numerator of the fraction is a numeral from 1 to 9 (alone, or as the last component of a multiword numeral), both the numerator and the denominator are declined and are in grammatical agreement with each other. The numerator is declined like the respective cardinal numeral, while the denominator is declined like the respective ordinal numeral, e.g.:

Nom.	vienà antróji (1/2)	peñkios šim̃tosios (5/100)
Gen.	vienõs antrõsios	penkių̃ šimtų̃jų
Dat.	víenai añtrajai	penkióms šimtósioms
Acc.	víeną añtrąją	penkiàs šimtą́sias
Instr.	víena antrą́ja	penkiomìs šimtósiomis
Loc.	vienojè antrõjoje	penkiosè šimtõsiose

Cf. also: *dvìdešimt keturių̃ šimtų̃jų* (GEN, 24/100)
dù šimtaĩ trìsdešimt keturióms tū́kstantosioms (DAT, 234/1000).

When the numerator of the fraction is expressed by any other numeral except a numeral from 1 to 9, the denominator always retains the form of the genitive case, e.g.:

Nom.	trýlika šimtų̃jų (13/100)
Gen.	trýlikos šimtų̃jų
Dat.	trýlikai šimtų̃jų
Acc.	trýlika šimtų̃jų
Instr.	trýlika šimtų̃jų
Loc.	trýlikoje šimtų̃jų

Cf. also: Nom. *dù šimtaĩ penkiólika tū́kstantųjų* (215/1000)

Gen. *dviejų̃ šimtų̃ penkiólikos tū́kstantųjų*, etc.

Components of fractions are accented like the respective cardinal and ordinal numerals.

Compound fractions containing the component *-dalis* are declined like nouns of (i)a- declension and always have a fixed accent, e.g.:

Nom.	ketvirtãdalis (quarter)
Gen.	ketvirtãdalio
Dat.	ketvirtãdaliui, etc.

Compound fractions containing the component *pus-* are accented like the respective ordinal numeral *añtras, antrà* in the genitive: *pusañtro, pusantrõs, pusantrų̃*.

4 PRONOUN
Įvardis

4.1 Pronouns constitute a closed class of words which refer to things or qualities without naming them. Pronouns possess the categories of gender, number and case having specific properties.

From the syntactical point of view pronouns fall into three major classes:

(1) nominal pronouns, which fill nominal syntactic functions, e.g.:

àš 'I (NOM. SG)', *mẽs* 'we (NOM. PL)', *tù* 'you (NOM. SG)', *jū̃s* 'you (NOM. PL)', *jìs* 'he', *jì* 'she', *támsta* 'you', *savę̃s* 'oneself', *kàs* 'what, who', *kažkàs* 'something, somebody', *niẽkas* 'nothing, nobody', *ābejetas* 'both', *kẽletas* 'how many, some (between 3 and 9)', *keliólika* 'how many, some (between 11 and 19)', *šìs tàs* 'something';

(2) adjectival pronouns, which have adjectival syntactic functions, e.g.:

tóks, tokià 'of this kind', *šióks, šiokià* 'of this kind', *mãnas, manà, manàsis, manóji, manìškis, manìškė* 'my, mine', *abejì, ābejos* 'both', *pàts tàs, patì tà* 'just the kind', *tam tìkras, tam tikrà* 'certain';

(3) pronouns that can have both nominal and adjectival functions, e.g.:

tàs, tà 'this, that', *šìs, šì* 'this', *kurìs, kurì, katràs, katrà* 'which, whichever', *nė víenas, nė vienà* 'not a single one, nobody', *kìtas, kità* 'other, some' (see table 5).

Nominal pronouns can replace nouns and noun groups. Adjectival pronouns can replace adjectives. However, there is no one-to-one correspondence between the nominal syntactic function of pronouns and their ability to replace nouns, for

(a) there are nominal pronouns, e.g. *àš* 'I', *tù* 'you', which cannot replace any noun, although they fill the syntactical functions of a noun;

(b) there are nominal forms of pronouns, e.g. *taĩ* 'this, that', which usually replace sentences and clauses.

Syntactically, nominal pronouns differ from nouns in that they do not occur with premodification (**didelis jis* 'big he'); adjectival pronouns differ from adjectives in that they do not occur with adverbs (**labai toks* 'very such').

PRONOUN 181

Table 5. **Syntactic subclasses of pronouns**

Nominal	Adjectival	Nominal-Adjectival
ābejetas 'both', *àš* 'I', *mẽs* 'we', *bet kàs* 'whoever, anyone', *daug kàs* 'quite a few', *jìs* 'he', *jì* 'she', *kai kàs* 'someone, some', *kàs* 'what, who, someone, something', *kàs ne kàs* 'a few', *kas nórs* 'someone, something', *kaži(n) kàs* 'someone, somebody, something', *kažkàs* 'someone, somebody, something', *kẽletas* 'how many, a few, some (implying a number between 3 and 9)', *keliólika* 'how many, some (between 11 and 19)', *niẽkas* 'nobody, nothing', *savẽs* 'oneself', *šìs tàs* 'something', *támsta* 'you (polite form)', *tù, jū̃s* 'you'	*abejì, -os* 'both', *anóks, -ia* 'of that kind', *bet kóks, -ià* 'of any kind', *jóks, -ià* 'no one, none, of no kind', *jūsàsis, -óji, jūsìškis, -ė̃* 'your', *kai kóks, -ià* 'of one kind or another', *kaži(n) kóks, -ià, kažkóks, -ià* 'of some kind', *kitóks, -ia* 'of another kind', *kóks, -ià* 'what kind of, some kind of', *koks, -ia nórs* 'some kind of', *mãnas, -à, manàsis, -óji, manìškis, -ė̃* 'my', *mū̃sasis, -óji, mūsìškis, -ė̃* 'our', *nė̃ kóks, -ià* 'of no kind, none, no one', *pàts tàs, patì tà* 'just the kind', *sãvas, -à, savàsis, -óji, savìškis, -ė̃* 'one's own', *šióks, -ià* 'of this kind', *šióks tóks, šiokià tokià* 'something of', *šìtoks, -ia* 'of this kind', *tam tìkras, -à* 'certain', *tãvas, -à, tavàsis, -óji, tavìškis, -ė̃* 'your', *tóks, -ià* 'of this kind', *vienóks, -ia* 'of one kind', *visóks, -ia* 'of all kinds'	*abù, abì, abùdu, abìdvi* 'both', *aliái víenas, -à* 'absolutely all', *anàs, -à* 'that', *bet katràs -à, bet kurìs, -ì* 'any', *kai katràs, -à, kai kurìs, -ì* 'some', *katràs, -à* 'which, whichever, whoever (of two)', *katras, -a nórs* 'some, anyone', *kaži(n) katràs, -à, kažkatràs, -à* 'whichever (unknown)', *kaži(n) kurìs, -ì, kažkurìs, -ì* 'whichever (unknown)', *kelerì, -ios, kelì, -ios* 'how many, some', *keliñtas, -à* 'which, whichever in a series, some', *kiekvíenas, -à* 'every', *kìtas, -à* 'other, some', *kurìs, -ì* 'which, whichever, whoever', *kurìs ne kurìs, kurì ne kurì* 'very few', *kuris, -i nórs* 'some, anyone', *nė̃ víenas, -à* 'not a single one, nobody', *pàts, -ì* 'oneself', *šìs, šì, šìtas, šità* 'this', *tàs, tà* 'this, that', *tas pàts, ta patì* 'the same', *tū́las, -à* 'quite a few', *víenas, -à* 'one, a certain (no matter which one)', *víenas kìtas, vienà kità* 'a few', *vìsas, -à, vìsi, -os* 'all, the whole'

Morphological categories of pronouns
GENDER
Giminẽ

4.2 All adjectival pronouns and the nominal pronoun *jìs, jì* 'he, she' are inflected for masculine and feminine gender. In a sentence they always agree with the respective noun.

The adjectival pronouns agree in gender, number and case with the head noun they modify in a sentence as syntactic attributes:

tóks žmogùs 'such a man'   *tokià móteris* 'such a woman'
tókio žmogaũs 'of such a man'   *tokiõs moteř̃s* 'of such a woman'
tokiẽ žmónės 'such people'   *tókios móterys* 'such women'

The nominal pronoun *jìs, jì* agree in gender and number (but not necessarily in case) with the antecedent noun:

Tėvo nebùvo namiẽ. Jìs bùvo darbè.	'Father was not at home. He was at work.'
Mótinos nebùvo namiẽ. Jì bùvo darbè.	'Mother was not at home. She was at work.'

Pronouns which can fill both adjectival and nominal functions are also inflected for masculine and feminine gender: *šitas, šita/šità* 'this', *tàs, tà* 'this, that', *anàs, anà* 'that'. When they are used as adjectives, they agree with their head noun in gender, number and case:

tàs výras 'that man'   *tà móteris* 'that woman'
tõ výro 'of that man'   *tõs móter̃s* 'of that woman'
tiẽ výrai 'those men'   *tõs móterys* 'those women'

When they are used as nouns, they agree in gender and number (but not necessarily in case) with the antecedent noun:

Jì žiū̃ri į̃ tė́vą. Tàs niẽko nesãko.	'She looks at her father. He does not say anything.'
Àš jõ seserim̃ pasìtikiu. Ta taĩp nepadarỹs.	'I trust his sister. She won't do it.'

There are several forms of nominal pronouns which are classed as neuters: *taĩ* 'it, this', *šita(i)* 'this', *víena* 'one', *kìta* 'another', *vìsa, vìsa taĩ* 'everything'.

They are classed as neuters because of their formal, syntactic and semantic properties.

Syntactic properties:

(1) these forms agree with neuter adjectives:

Taĩ gražù. Vìsa kìta nesvarbù.	'That's beautiful. Everything else is not important.'

(2) Their antecedent is usually a phrase, a sentence, an entire utterance, or even a longer piece of the text, but not a concrete noun:

Jìs kalbė́jo sù manim̃ kaĩp sù suáugusiu. Taĩ mán patìko.	'He spoke with me as with a grown-up person. I liked it.'

Jám dãvė pasiriñkti víena　　　'He was given two choices – to
iš dviejų̃: mir̃ti arbà　　　die or to sniff the powder.'
paúostyti miltẽlių.

Semantically these pronouns can be characterized as words of generalized reference – their referents are usually situations or groups of non-specified things or phenomena in general.

Vìsa taĩ geriaũ negù tù galvóji.　　　'Everything is better than you think.'
Víena reĩkia galvóti, kìta kalbė́ti.　　　'You have to think one way and speak another.'

Having a generalized meaning these pronouns are not inflected either for number or case. They are used in the syntactic position of nominative or accusative. In the position of other cases they are replaced by the respective masculine forms, c.f.:

Jìs taĩ mãtė.　　　'He saw it (NOM. ACC. NEUTR).'
Jìs tõ nemãtė.　　　'He didn't see it (GEN. SG. MASC).'
　　　(see 4.21).

4.3　　The pronoun *vìskas* is declined like a masculine pronoun, but in all other respects it functions like a neuter pronoun: it has no plural, in a sentence it agrees with neuter adjectives and its meaning is always that of general reference.

Mán čià vìskas gražù.　　　'To me everything is beautiful here.'

The nominal pronoun *kàs* 'what, who' and other compound and composite pronouns formed with *kàs* (*kažkàs* 'somebody, something', *niẽkas* 'nobody, nothing', *kai kàs* 'something, somebody', *bet kàs* 'anything, anybody', *kas nórs* 'somebody, something') should be addressed separately. These pronouns are declined like masculine pronouns but they are used both in the meaning of general and concrete reference (even in reference to persons). Syntactically, they may agree with masculine, feminine or neuter adjectives, depending on their reference.

Kàs gražùs?　　　Who/what is handsome (MASC)?
Kàs gražì?　　　Who/what is handsome (FEM)?
Kàs gražù?　　　What is beautiful?

4.4　　The personal pronouns *àš* 'I', *mẽs* 'we', *tù* 'you', *jū̃s* 'you', *támsta* 'you' and the reflexive *savę̃s* 'oneself' are not inflected for gender, but in a sentence they can be used either with masculine or feminine adjectives depending on whether they refer to male or female persons.

àš, tù, támsta liñksmas/linksmà　　　'I, you am/are merry'

mēs, jū̃s, tāmstos linksmì/liñksmos   'we, you are merry'
àš nemataũ savę̃s patiẽs/pačiõs   'I don't see myself'

The other personal pronouns are inflected for gender:

Masc.   Fem.

mùdu	*mùdvi*	'we two'
jùdu	*jùdvi*	'you two'
jìs	*jì*	'he, she'
jiẽ	*jõs*	'they'
juõdu	*jiẽdvi*	'they two'

The nominal pronouns *ābejetas* 'both', *kēletas, keliólika* 'how many, some', *kēliasdešimt* 'some (between 30 and 90)' are not inflected for gender. Syntactically, they require complementation, but not agreement in gender with other words, e.g. *kēletas výrų* 'some men (GEN. PL)', *kēletas móterų* 'some women (GEN. PL)'.

NUMBER

Skaĩčius

4.5   The majority of nominal and adjectival pronouns have two numbers – the singular and the plural:

tàs, tà	–	*tiẽ, tõs*	'that, those'
kurìs, kurì	–	*kuriẽ, kuriõs*	'which'
kìtas, kità	–	*kitì, kìtos*	'another, others'

There are, however, some pronouns which have a third number, the dual. They include:

personal pronouns:

mùdu, mùdvi 'we two'
jùdu, jùdvi 'you two'
juõdu (jiẽdu), jiẽdvi 'they two'

demonstrative pronouns (used much more rarely):

tuõdu (tiẽdu), tiẽdvi 'those two'
šiuõdu, šiẽdvi 'these two'
anuõdu, aniẽdvi 'those two'
šìtuodu, šìtiedvi 'these two'

interrogative pronouns, which are also rarely used:

katruõdu, katriẽdvi 'which two'
kuriuõdu, kuriẽdvi 'which two'

The pronouns *abù (abùdu), abì (abìdvi)* 'both' possess only the dual meaning which can be defined as 'the one as well as the other'.

As the dual number of other classes of words has disappeared almost entirely, dual pronominal forms are used with the plural forms of nouns, adjectives and verbs.

Mùdu *verčiaũ paklausýkim(e).*	'We two had better listen.'
Koncertù abù juõdu *bùvo labaĩ paténkinti.*	'Both of them were very much pleased with the concert.'

Distribution and oppositions of pronominal number forms

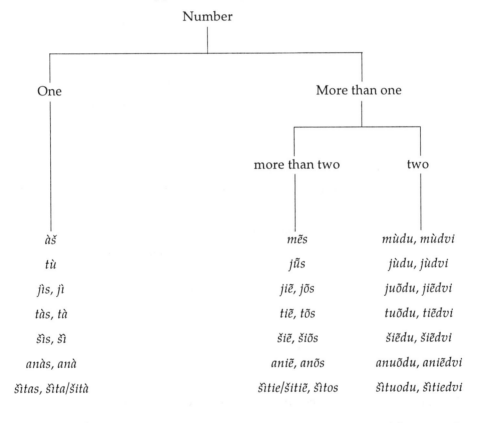

One	more than two	two
àš	mẽs	mùdu, mùdvi
tù	jũs	jùdu, jùdvi
jìs, jì	jiẽ, jõs	juõdu, jiẽdvi
tàs, tà	tiẽ, tõs	tuõdu, tiẽdvi
šìs, šì	šiẽ, šiõs	šiẽdu, šiẽdvi
anàs, anà	aniẽ, anõs	anuõdu, aniẽdvi
šìtas, šìta/šità	šìtie/šitiẽ, šìtos	šìtuodu, šìtiedvi

However, in present-day Lithuanian the use of dual pronominal forms is also very much on the decline and they are usually replaced by plural forms. Thus, the semantic opposition 'two referents : more than two referents' is disappearing, and the grammatical category of number rests now mainly on the binary opposition 'one : more than one'.

4.6 Although the pronouns *savęs* 'oneself', *kàs* 'what, who', *niēkas* 'nothing, nobody', *kažkàs* 'somebody, something', *kas nórs* 'somebody, something' have only singular forms, in a sentence they can be used both with the singular and plural forms of other words:

Jìs savęs patiẽs nekeñčia.	'He hates himself.'
Jiē savęs pačių nekeñčia.	'They hate themselves.'
Kàs tù esì?	'Who are you (NOM. SG)?'
Kàs jũs ēsate?	'Who are you (NOM. PL)?'
Kàs jìs *per víenas*?	'Who is he after all?'
Kàs jiē *per vienì*?	'Who are they after all?'

The plural forms of the pronouns *kiekvíenas, -à* 'each, every', *aliái víenas, -à* 'absolutely all', *nè víenas, -à* 'not a single one' are used only with invariable plural nouns (*pluralia tantum*):

kiekvíenos dùrys	'every door'
kiekvienì mētai	'every year'
nė víenos žìrklės	'not a single pair of scissors'
nė vienì mētai	'not a single year'

There are some other pronouns which have no plural, e.g.:

nominal pronouns referring to a group: *ābejetas* 'both', *kēletas* 'a few, some (between 3 and 9)', *keliólika* 'some (between 11 and 19)'; the indefinite pronoun *šìs tàs* 'something (insignificant)'.

The following pronominal quantifiers have no singular:

kelì, kēlios	'some, how many'
kelerì, kēlerios	'some'
abejì, ābejos	'both'

CASE
Liñksnis

4.7 Pronouns are declined similary to nouns or adjectives.

Pronouns have no vocative case because they are not used to address people.

Pronouns *àš, tù, savęs, kàs* (and its derivatives, e.g. *kažkàs, niēkas,* etc.) have two genitive case forms which differ in their meaning: the possessive genitive *màno, tàvo, sàvo, kienõ, kažkienõ, niēkieno* and the non-possessive genitive *manęs, tavęs, savęs, kõ, kažkõ, niēko* (see 4.15).

Semantic subclasses of pronouns

4.8 According to the type of reference to things or properties pronouns fall into four major semantic groups:

(1) personal,

(2) demonstrative,

(3) interrogative and relative,

(4) indefinite.

Some pronouns have more than one meaning and therefore belong to more than one semantic group (see Table 6).

PERSONAL PRONOUNS

4.9 Personal proper pronouns refer to persons according to their involvement in the speech act.

The core of this group of pronouns includes the pronouns *àš* 'I', *tù* 'you (2. SG)', *jū̃s* 'you (2. PL)', *mẽs* 'we', *jìs* 'he', *jì* 'she'.

The 1st person pronoun *àš* refers to the speaker/writer of the message. The reference of the plural *mẽs* includes the speaker/writer of the message together with some other person or persons.

The 2nd person pronouns *tù*, *támsta* (the polite 'you') refers to the addressee of the message. The reference of the plural *jū̃s*, *támstos* includes the addressee(s), but excludes the speaker(s)/writer(s). The plural *jū̃s* is also used as the polite form in reference to a single addressee (see 4.13).

The reference of the 3rd person pronouns *jìs* (plural *jiẽ*), *jì* (plural *jõs*) excludes both the speaker(s) and the addressee(s).

Thus, the 1st and 2nd person pronouns refer to the participants of the speech act, whereas the 3rd person pronouns refer to persons or things not directly involved in the speech act.

Distinctions of person are also typical of pronouns having a possessive meaning (4.15) and the reflexive *savę̃s*.

The pronoun *tù* can function generically with reference to people in general. In such cases it is often used together with the noun *žmogùs* 'man':

Table 6. Semantic subclasses of pronouns

Personal	Proper	àš 'I', mēs 'we', tù, jũs 'you', jìs 'he', jì 'she', támsta 'you', pàts, -ì 'you'
	Reflexive	savę̃s 'oneself'
	Possessive	manàsis, -ója 'my', tavàsis, -ója 'your', savàsis, -ója 'one's own', mūsàsis, -ója 'our', jūsàsis, -ója 'your'; mānas, -à 'my', tãvas, -à 'your', sãvas, -à 'one's own'; manìškis, -ė̃ 'my', tavìškis, -ė̃ 'your', savìškis, -ė̃ 'one's own', mūsìškis, -ė̃ 'our', jūsìškis, -ė̃ 'your'
	Demonstrative	tàs, tà 'this, that', šìs, šì, šìtas, šìtà 'this', anàs, -à 'that'; tóks, -ià 'of this kind', šióks, -ià, šìtoks, -ia 'of this kind', anóks, -ia 'of that kind'; tas pàts, ta patì 'the same', pàts tàs, patì tà 'just the kind, just this'
	Interrogative-Relative	kàs 'who, what', kóks, -ià 'what kind of', kurìs, -ì, katràs, -à 'which', kelì, -ios, kelerì, -ios 'how many', keliñtas, -à 'which', keliólika 'how many', kēletas 'how many'
Indefinite	Proper	kàs 'someone, something', kóks, -ià 'some kind of', kurìs, -ì, katràs, -à 'whichever, whoever', kelì, -ios, kelerì, -ios 'a few, some', keliñtas, -à 'some', kēletas 'a few, some (between 3 and 9)', keliólika 'some (between 11 and 19)'; kažkàs, kaži(n) kàs 'someone, somebody, something', kažkóks, -ià, kaži(n) kóks, -ià 'of some kind', kažkurìs, -ì, kaži(n) kurìs, -ì, kažkatràs, -à, kaži(n) katràs, -à 'which ever (unknown)', kas nórs 'someone, something', koks, -ia nórs 'some kind of', kuris, -i nórs, katras, -a nórs 'some, anyone', bet kàs 'anyone, anything', bet kóks, -ià 'of any kind', bet kurìs, -ì, bet katràs, -à 'any', kai kàs 'someone, some', kai kóks, -ià 'of one kind or another', kai kurìs, -ì, kai katràs, -à 'some', kàs ne kàs 'a few, not many', kurìs ne kurìs, kurì ne kurì 'very few', víenas, -à 'one, no matter which one', víenas kìtas, vienà kità 'a few', kìtas, -à 'some', tóks, -ià 'of some kind', šìs tàs 'something insignificant', šióks tóks, šiokià tokià 'something of'
	Differentiating	víenas, -à 'one', kìtas, -à 'another', vienóks, -ia 'of one kind', kitóks, -ia 'of another kind', tam tìkras, -à 'certain'
	Generalizing — Positive	vìsas, -à 'the whole', visì, -os 'all', visóks, -ia 'of all kinds', ābejetas, abù (abùdu), abì (abìdvi), abejì, -os 'both', kiekvíenas, -à 'every', kàs 'every', aliái víenas, -à 'absolutely all', tū́las, -à 'quite a few', daug kàs 'quite a few'
	Generalizing — Negative	niẽkas 'nobody, nothing, no one', nè víenas, -à 'not a single one', jóks, -ià, nè kóks, -ià 'no one, none, of no kind'
	Emphatic	pàts, -ì 'oneself, the very, just one'

Keliáuk dabař̃ tù žmogùs *pė́sčias tókį kẽlią.*	'Imagine covering (lit. 'Cover you man') now this distance on foot.'

Personal pronouns *àš* (*mẽs*), *tù* (*jū̃s*) may refer to things or animals when the latter are personified for stylistic purposes.

Tù, *paukštẽli míels, ne põniškai prisiválgai.*	'You, my dear birdie, do not have lordly meals.'
Piliẽ! Tù *tíek ámžių praléidai garsiaĩ!*	'Oh castle! You have had so many glorious centuries!'

In the sentence personal pronouns agree with the finite verb in person and number. In this way the meaning of person and number (i.e. reference to person(s)) may be expressed twice: by the personal pronoun and by the ending of the finite verb.

(*Àš*) *einù namõ.*	'I am going home.'
(*Tù*) *einì namõ.*	'You are going home.'
(*Jìs*) *eĩna namõ.*	'He is going home.'
(*Mẽs*) *eĩname namõ.*	'We are going home.'
(*Jū̃s*) *eĩnate namõ.*	'You are going home.'

However, the 1st person pronouns in such sentences have an optional character; they are needed mainly for contrast of person or for emphasis.

The classification of the Lithuanian pronouns *jìs, jì, jiẽ, jõs* as personal pronouns is, to a certain extent, relative because they are used to refer not only to persons, but also to inanimate objects and animals. They are functionally similar to demonstrative pronouns in that they are used in reference to the antecedent noun(s), e.g.:

Pẽtras nẽšė baĩną į klė́tį, bet rãdo ją *užrakìntą.*	'Petras took the saddle to the barn, but found it locked.'

It may also be noted that etymologically the pronoun *jìs, jì* is also related to demonstrative pronouns.

4.10 The semantic relation between the singular *àš* and the plural *mẽs* is different from that which exists between a noun in the singular and in the plural in that *mẽs* does not mean 'two or more *àš*' as is the case with nouns.

The 1st person plural pronoun *mẽs* may be used inclusively or exclusively depending on whether it includes reference to the addressee(s) or not.

The exclusive *mẽs* may refer to:

(1) the speakers/writers of the message:

Mẽs, žemiaũ pasirãšiusieji	'We, the undersigned'

(2) the speaker(s)/writer(s) + a third party:

Nórs ir vaikáms, ir mán koncer̃tas labaĩ patìko, mẽs turė́jome išeĩti jám nepasibaĩgus.	'Although the children and I enjoyed the concert very much, we had to leave before it ended.'

The inclusive *mẽs* may refer to:

(1) the speaker(s)/writer(s) + the addressee(s):

Mẽs, *Jonùk, negãlim pỹktis.*	'We can't quarrel, Jonukas, (Johny).'

(2) the speaker(s)/writer(s) + the addressee(s) + a third party:

Tavè, Onùtę ir manè kviẽčia dirèktorius. Mẽs tùrime tuõj pàt eĩti.	'The director wants to see you, Onutė and me. We have to go immediately.'

The reference of the pronoun *mẽs* is very often explicated by the preposition *sù* and a noun (or pronoun) in the Instrumental case.

Mẽs *su tavim̃ šìto nesupràsim.*	'You and me (lit. 'We with you') won't understand it.'
Mẽs *su tėvu šìto nesupràsim.*	'Father and I (lit. 'Father with me') won't understand it.'

In formal (especially scientific) writing the use of *mẽs* 'we' (the so called editorial we) is sometimes prompted by a desire to avoid I, which may be felt to be somewhat egotistical, e.g.:

Síekinio viẽtoje rãštuose paprastaĩ, kaip jaũ mū́sų pažymė́ta, beñdratį dabar̃ sãkome.	'In writing, instead of a supine, now we usually use, as we have already noted, the infinitive.'

4.11 The plural *jū̃s* 'you' refers to more than one addressee or the addressee and a third party:

Laurỹnai, brolaũ! Brólienè! Jùs *mýliu ir į̃ vestuvès prašaũ.*	'Laurynas, my brother! My sister-in-law! I love you and ask you to come to my wedding.'
Tù ir Jõnas lìksite namiẽ. Jũs *niẽkur neĩsite.*	'You and Jonas will stay at home. You won't go anywhere.'

The reference of the pronoun *jū̃s* is sometimes explicated by adding the prepositional phrase with the preposition *sù*:

Jūs su Jõnu *niekur neĩsite*.	'You and Jonas (John) (lit. 'You with John') won't go anywhere.'

4.12 Personal pronouns also include dual pronouns which refer to two persons (see 4.5), e.g.:

Pavėlãvom mùdu.	'We two are late.'
Jùdu *gerì draugaĩ*.	'You two are good friends.'
Jiẽdvi *abì dìrba daržè*.	'They both are working in the garden.'

In present-day Lithuanian, however, the distinction between reference to two and more than two persons is not always maintained so that more often than not plural pronouns are used instead of dual forms.

4.13 Polite reference to the addressee is expressed by the pronouns *jūs, támsta, pàts, patì*. *Jūs* is used in polite reference both to one and more than one addressee. *Támsta, pàts, patì* have plural forms, therefore the singular is used in reference to one addressee and the plural is used in reference to more than one addressee.

When *jūs* is used in polite reference to one addressee, it agrees with the plural form of the finite verb, but with the singular form of the appositive noun and of the nominal or adjectival predicative.

Kaĩp jūs, *tóks rim̃tas žmogùs, niekaĩs užsìimate?*	'How can you, such a serious man, concern yourself with nonsense?'
Ar̃ jūs *dabar̃ laimìngas, senẽli?*	'Are you happy now, grandad?'

As a means of polite reference, *támsta* is nowadays used much more rarely than *jūs*, mostly by the older generation. In reference to one addressee, it is used in the singular and usually agrees with the singular form of the finite verb, appositive and predicative noun or adjective:

Támsta *bauginì manè, pónia Liùcija.* Támsta *nelaimingèsnė negù àš buvaũ mãnęs.*	'You scare me, Mrs. Liucija. You are unhappier than I thought.'

In reference to more than one addressee it is used in the plural in agreement with the plural form of the finite verb, appositive and predicative noun or adjective:

Bū́kite támstos *tokiẽ gerì, ateĩkite.*	'Please be so good and come.'

Pàts, patì are not as formal as *jūs* or *támsta*. They are usually used speaking to one's equals when *tù* is felt to be too rude, while *jūs* and *támsta* are too cold or respectful. The use and grammatical concord of the singular *pàts, patì* and the plural *pātys, pãčios* is like that of *támsta (támstos)*:

Kaĩp pàts *laikaĩs?*	'How's life with you?'
Ar pàts *ne iš čià kìlęs?*	'You come from these places, don't you?'
Ar pãtys *niẽko nežinójote?*	'Didn't you know anything?'

4.14 **The reflexive** *savę̃s* indicates the relation of all the three persons – the speaker/writer, the addressee and a third party – to himself/herself. As this pronoun has no nominative case and no plural, it has only five case forms:

Gen. *savę̃s*
Dat. *sáu*
Acc. *savè*
Instr. *savimì*
Loc. *savyjè*

These forms are used both in the singular and plural meaning.

Rètkarčiais àš ir sáu *kai ką̃ perkù.*	'Sometimes I buy something for myself as well.'
Rẽtkarčiais jiẽ ir sáu *kai ką̃ peřka.*	'Sometimes they buy something for themselves (DAT. SG) as well.'
Jìs nekeñčia savę̃s.	'He hates himself (GEN. SG).'
Jiẽ abùdu susìtarė tarp savę̃s.	'They both agreed between themselves (GEN. SG).'

4.15 **Possessive forms** of pronouns are classified as personal pronouns. They indicate that an object belongs to some person(s). This possessive meaning is usually expressed by the genitive form of pronouns. Personal pronouns *àš, tù,* and the reflexive pronoun have separate possessive genitive singular forms *màno, tàvo, sàvo* which differ from the genitive singular *manę̃s, tavę̃s, savę̃s* used in other functions, cf.:

Pérskaityk màno *láišką.*	'Read my (POSS. GEN. SG) letter.'
Draugaĩ manę̃s *láukė.*	'The friends waited for me (GEN. SG).'
Tàvo tėvų̃ neradaũ namuosè.	'I didn't find your (POSS. GEN. SG) parents at home.'
Tavę̃s neradaũ namuosè.	'I didn't find you (GEN. SG) at home.'
Pasakýk sàvo *tėváms.*	'Tell it to your (POSS. GEN. SG) parents.'
Jìs nežiū̃ri savę̃s.	'He doesn't care for himself (GEN. SG).'

The possessive genitive *sàvo* refers to the subject of sentence regardless of its person and number, e.g.:

Àš nètikiu sàvo *ausimìs.*	'I don't believe my ears.'
Tù nètiki sàvo *ausimìs.*	'You don't believe your ears.'

Jìs/Jì nètiki sàvo ausimìs.	'He/She doesn't believe his/her ears.'
Mēs nètikime sàvo ausimìs.	'We don't believe our ears.'
Jūs nètikite sàvo ausimìs.	'You don't believe your ears.'
Jiẽ/Jõs nètiki sàvo ausimìs.	'They don't believe their ears.'

The possessive genitive forms màno, tàvo can also express the semantic subject in a passive construction (see 5.66), e.g.:

Láiškas bùvo màno/tàvo pàliktas.	'The letter was left by me/you (POSS. GEN. SG).'

Pronouns kàs 'who', kažkàs (kažin kàs) 'somebody, something', niẽkas 'nobody, nothing' have the separate possessive genitive singular forms as well: kienõ, kažkienõ (kažin kienõ), niẽkieno, e.g.:

Kienõ tà knygà?	'Whose book is it?'
Čià niẽkieno žẽmė.	'It is no man's (lit. 'nobody's') land.'

Cf. the non-possessive genitive singular forms kõ, niẽko in other functions:

Kõ tù nóri?	'What do you want?'
Àš niẽko nenóriu.	'I don't want anything.'

4.16 Beside the possessive genitive forms mentioned the special declined pronouns mãnas, -à 'my', tãvas, -à 'your', sãvas, -à are rarely used. More frequent in present day Lithuanian are the definite forms manàsis, manóji; tavàsis, tavóji; savàsis, savóji (mostly with emphatic colour), e.g.:

Čià tėviškė manà/manóji.	'Here is my homeland.'
Tavóji síela neramì.	'Your heart is troubled.'
Pašaũk savùs/savúosius vaikùs.	'Call your children.'

Possessive pronouns with the suffix -iškis, -iškė: manìškis, -ė, tavìškis, -ė, also mūsìškis, -ė 'our', jūsìškis, -ė 'your' are used with the corresponding meaning, e.g.:

Manìškis/Tavìškis výras gẽras.	'My/Your husband is good.'
Mūsìškis/Jūsìškis dirèktorius išvažiãvęs.	'Our/Your director has left.'

The substantivized plural forms manìškiai, tavìškiai, savìškiai are also used to indicate relatives or friends of the respective person, e.g.:

Manìškiai sugrĩš vakarè.	'My relatives (My family) will return in the evening.'
Eĩk pas savìškius.	'Go to your relatives (your friends).'

4.17 The plural pronouns *mẽs, jū̃s* and the pronouns *jìs, jì* in singular and plural have only one genitive form *mū́sų, jū́sų; jõ, jõs; jų̃* which is used both in possessive as in other functions, cf.:

Mū́sų/Jū́sų píevos jaũ sužaliãvo.	'Our/Your (GEN. PL) meadows are already green.'
Mū́sų/Jū́sų niẽkas neláukė.	'Nobody expected us/you (GEN. PL).'
Čià jõ/jõs namaĩ.	'This is his/her (GEN. SG) home.'
Jõ/Jõs neradaũ namiẽ.	'I didn't find him/her (GEN. SG) at home.'
Jų̃ sõdas bùvo labaĩ dìdelis.	'Their (GEN. PL) garden was very large.'
Vaikaĩ jų̃ nemė́go.	'The children didn't like them (GEN. PL).'

Table 7. **The relations of possessive pronominal forms to the participants of the speech act and third parties**

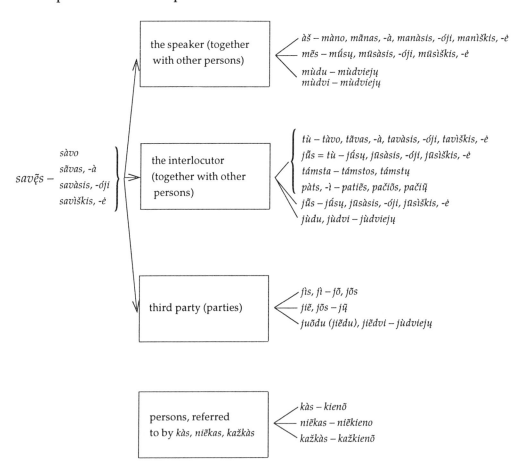

DEMONSTRATIVE PRONOUNS

4.18 Demonstrative pronouns usually refer to:

(1) a definite thing (person, phenomenon): *tàs, tà* 'this', 'that', *šìs, šì, šìtas, šìta/šità* 'this (one here)', *anàs, anà* 'that (one)', *tas pàts, ta patì* 'the same';

(2) a definite property of a thing (of a person or phenomenon): *tóks, tokià* 'of this kind', *šióks, šiokià, šìtoks, šìtokia* 'of this kind', *anóks, anókia* 'of that kind', *pàts tàs, patì tà* 'just the kind';

(3) a situation: *taĩ* 'it', *šìta(i)* 'it', *tas pàt(s)* 'the same'.

4.19 Demonstrative pronouns also have a contrast between 'near' (*šìs, šì, šìtas, šìta/šità, šìtai, šìtoks, šìtokia, šióks, šiokià*) and 'distant' (*anàs, anà, anóks, anókia*) reference. *Tàs, tà, tóks, tokià* are the neutral members of the near-distant opposition: they can be contrasted both to *šìs, šì, šìtas, šìta/šità* and *anàs, anà*. They are also used when no contrast between near and distant reference is implied.

Ar dár tebė̃r tà trobà, kuř seniaũ gyvẽnom?	'Does the house where we lived earlier still exist?'
Geriaũ pirkim šìtą pavéikslą, anàs mán nepatiñka.	'Let's better buy this picture, I don't like that one.'
Šiojè pùsėje pasistãtė Vilkas, õ anõj pùsėj Stãgaras.	'Vilkas built on this side while Stagaras built on the other.'

4.20 Demonstrative pronouns can be used both in the nominal and adjectival positions.

When *šìs, šì, šìtas, šìta/šità, tàs, tà, anàs, anà, tas pàts, ta patì* are used in the adjectival position, i.e. before a noun, they contribute definite status to that noun.

In the adjectival position pronouns *tàs, tà*, however, sometimes lose their demonstrative meaning altogether.

Sunkù, kad tiẽ *arkliaĩ vìs užimtì.*	'It's difficult because those horses are always busy.'
Tiẽ *daržaĩ vìs nebaigtì ravė́ti.*	'The weeding of those gardens is never finished.'

The same is true of *šìtas, šìta/šità*, although to a much lesser degree.

Nebèrà ramýbės nuo šìtų *vaikų̃.*	'There's no peace because of these children.'

Pronouns *tas pàts, ta patì* 'the same' indicate the identity of things:

Žiūri ir žiūri, vìs į̃ tą pačią vietą.	'You look and look, all the time at the same spot.'
Jõ drabùžiai visuomèt tie pātys, juodì, apdìlę.	'His clothes are always the same: dirty, shabby.'
Tą pačią dieną vė̃l suláukė visì dìdelio džiaũgsmo.	'The same day great joy came to everybody again.'

When *tàs, tà, šìs, šì, šìtas, šìta/šità, anàs, anà, tas pàts, ta patì* are used in nominal positions, they usually have anaphoric reference to an antecedent noun, although the latter function is more characteristic of the personal pronouns *jìs, jì* (see 4.9). By the frequence of their use as nominal demonstratives with anaphoric reference demonstratives could be arranged in the following sequence: *tàs, tà* (most frequent), *šìs, šì, šìtas, šìta/šità* (less frequent), *anàs, anà* (rare), *tas pàts, ta patì* (retaining the meaning of identity), e.g.:

Iš tėvo jìs gãvo šíek tíek pinigų̃, tiẽ jám labaĩ pràvertė.	'He got some money from his father, it came in very handy to him.'
Mótina kálbina sū́nų, šìs tuõ tárpu niẽko neatsãko.	'Mother speaks to her son, the latter doesn't say anything so far.'
Víeną sū́nų teturiù, tą pãtį būtinaĩ nóri numarìnti.	'I have only one son left, but they do everything to kill him.'

4.21 Pronominal forms which refer to a situation (situational demonstratives) *taĩ (tataĩ)*, rarely – *šìta(i) (šìtatai)* are used with anaphoric reference to a 'sentential antecedent', i.e. to a noun phrase, a clause, sentence, sequence of sentences, or a larger segment of discourse. These pronouns occur only in nominal positions, and never in adjectival positions:

Su klãsės draugaĩs jìs bendrãvo tik tíek, kíek taĩ/šìtai *bùvo bū́tina.*	'With his school friends he communicated only as much as it was necessary.'
Ar jìs susir̃gs, ar liū̃dnas bùs, ar nelaimìngas – niẽkam niẽko nerū̃pės, niẽkas apie taĩ/tataĩ *nepagalvõs.*	'Whether he falls ill, or is sad, or unhappy – nobody will care, nobody will think about it.'
Nežinaũ, ar gãli žmogùs sàvo láimę atspė́ti. Negalvójau apie taĩ.	'I don't know if a person can guess his lot. I haven't thought about it.'

As can be seen from the examples, situational demonstratives are most often used in nominal positions of the nominative and accusative cases:

Taĩ labaĩ gražù.	'That's very beautiful.'
Nežiūrĕk į taĩ.	'Don't look at it.'

In the nominal position of the genitive case situational demonstratives are used more rarely. Here, as well as in the nominal positions of all the other cases, they are most often replaced by the respective singular case forms of masculine demonstrative tàs, šìtas.

Nėrà tõ pasáuly, kõ neišdrį́stų Āras.	'There's nothing in the world that Aras wouldn't dare to do.'
Jùk šeimininkė namuosè tám ir yrà, kad viskuõ rūpintųsi.	'The housewife is at home exactly for the purpose of taking care of everything.'
Prisipažį́stu, esù išdidùs ir šìtuo/tuõ džiaugiúosi.	'I admit I'm proud and I'm glad I am.'

Masculine demonstratives tàs, šìtas are sometimes used to replace taĩ, šìtai even in the positions of the nominative and accusative cases.

Spalvos nublùko, bèt niẽkas negalėjo pasakýti, aȓ tàs/taĩ atsitìko keliõnės metù, aȓ iš síelvarto.	'The colours faded out, but nobody could say whether this happened during the journey or due to heartbreak.'
Tã/taĩ numãnė iȓ Pètras.	'Petras also understood that.'
Visì sténgėsi pralõbti, bèt mán mažaĩ šìtas/šìtai rūpėjo.	'Everybody tried to get rich, but I didn't think much about it.'

Situational and anaphoric sentential reference of identity is indicated by the singular forms of the masculine demonstrative tas pàts.

Visì miȓsime, visų̃ tas pàts láukia.	'All of us are going to die, the same is awaiting everybody.'
Vìlius Karãlius smaũkia nuo piȓšto žiẽdą, Grẽtė dãro tą pātį.	'Vilius Karalius is slipping his ring from his finger, Grėtė is doing the same.'

Situational demonstratives taĩ, šìta(i) are in concord with neuter adjectives.

Taĩ nuostabù!	'That's wonderful!'
Šìtai nelengva.	'That's not easy.'

4.22 Contrast between 'near' and 'distant' reference is also characteristic of demonstratives which refer to qualities: šìtoks, šìtokia are used for near reference, anóks, anókia for distant reference, tóks, tokià being the neutral member of the near – distant opposition.

Jéigu jaũ àš šìtoks patinkù mókytai põniai, taĩ dár labiaũ patìksiu su gùrgždančiais bãtais.	'If an educated lady likes me like this, she will like me more with new crisp boots on.'
Anóks mán nepatiñka, tóks taĩ kas kìta.	'I don't like that kind, this one is quite another matter.'
Dienà išaũšo apsiniáukusi, darganóta. Tókią diẽną jóks dárbas nesìseka.	'The day broke overcast and rainy. Nothing goes well on a day like this.'

Pronouns *šìtoks, šìtokia, tóks, tokià* can also be used before adjectives as intensifiers.

Jì bùvo dár visái visái jaunùtė, bet tokià sudžiúvusi!	'She was very, very young, but so skinny!'
Šìtoks ilgas kelias!	'Such a long way!'
Paskaità bùvo tokià nuobodì, kad àš užmigaũ.	'The lecture was so boring that I fell asleep.'

Used as intensifiers before nouns these pronouns sometimes convey the meaning of approval or disapproval, which depends upon the intonation.

Šìtoks tuŕtas!	'Such fortune!'
Tóks iŕ paũkštis, kàd sàvo lìzdą teŕšia.	'The bird is not much good if it fouls its nest.'

The pronoun *anóks, anókia* can function as an intensifier only before a noun and in this function it always conveys the meaning of disapproval.

Anóks čia tuŕtas.	'Not very much of a fortune.'

INTERROGATIVE AND RELATIVE PRONOUNS

4.23 All interrogative and relative pronouns begin with the consonant *k*: *kàs* 'what, who', *kóks, kokià* 'what kind of', *kurìs, kurì* 'which', *katràs, katrà* 'which of two', *kelì, kẽlios* 'how many', *kelerì, kẽlerios* 'how many (used with *pluralia tantum*)', *keliñtas, kelintà* 'which (asking about the order or position in a series)', *keliólika* 'how many (implying a number between 11 and 19).

When these pronouns introduce a direct question, they are used in the interrogative function and are considered to be **interrogative pronouns**.

Kàs teñ šlãma?	'What is rustling there?'
Kokiõs knỹgos táu reĩkia?	'What book do you need?'

Kurìs tàvo rãktas?	'Which is your key?'
Katràs iš jų̃dviejų mán padė́site?	'Which of you two will help me?'
Kelì jū̃s čià bū́sit rytõj?	'How many of you will be here tomorrow?'
Kelerì mẽtai prabė́go nuo tõ laĩko, kaĩ mē̃s paskutìnį kar̃tą mãtėmės?	'How many years have passed since we last saw each other?'
Keliñtas tàvo bùtas?	'Which is your flat?'
Keliólika jų̃ teñ bùvo?	'How many of them were there?'

Pronoun *kàs* can refer to a human being as well as to an animate or inanimate thing, but its possessive genitive *kienõ* 'whose' can refer only to human beings.

Kàs teñ?	'Who's there?'
Ką̃ mán àtnešei válgyti?	'What have you brought me to eat?'
Kienõ čià knygà?	'Whose book is it?'

Sometimes, particularly in fossilized phrases, *kàs* is used to replace the pronoun *kóks*.

Kàs per̃ vė́jas (= kóks vė́jas) vãkar pū̃tė?	'Which wind was blowing yesterday?'
Kuõ vardù tàvo sūnùs?	'What is your son's name?'

Interrogative *kóks, kokià* is equivalent to the English phrase 'what kind of' (or 'what' used in the adjectival position).

Interrogative *kurìs, kurì* is used when asking somebody to specify one or more people or things from a group of two or any limited number.

Kurìs iš berniùkų aukščiáusias?	'Which of the boys is tallest?'

Interrogative *katràs, katrà* is mostly used when asking somebody to specify a person or thing from a group of two.

Katràs aukštèsnis, tù ar̃ Jõnas?	'Which of you is taller, you or Jonas?'

4.24 Used to introduce subordinate clauses, all the above pronouns function as **relative pronouns**.

Relative pronouns fall into two groups: those that are used only to introduce explicative (mostly object) clauses, and those that can introduce both explicative and attributive clauses.

The first group includes pronouns with quantitative meaning: *kelì, kẽlios; keleri, kẽlerios; keliñtas, kelintà; keliólika*. These pronouns never have an antecedent in the principal clause:

Pasakýk, kelì jū̃s čià bū́sit rytōj.	'Tell me how many of you wil be here l tomorrow.'
Užmiršaũ, keliñtas tàvo bùtas.	'I don't remember the number of your flat.'
À̃š nesuprataũ, keliólika jų̃ teñ bùvo.	'I didn't understand how many of them were there.'

The second group of relative pronouns includes *kàs; kóks, kokià; kurìs, kurì; katràs, katrà*. They can introduce both a completive (1) and a relative clause (2):

(1) *Užmiršaũ, kóks tàvo ãdresas.*	'I forgot your address.'
Nežinaũ, kurį̃ pasiriñkti.	'I don't know which to choose.'
Jìs kláusia, ką̃ darýti.	'He is asking what he is to do.'
Kàs nóri, tàs rañda.	'He who wants can find it.'
Kõ ieškójo, tą̃ iř rãdo.	'He found what he was looking for.'
Taĩ, ką̃ tù sakaĩ, netiesà.	'What you are saying is not true.'
(2) *Jiẽ vẽl atsìmena senẽlį tókį, kóks jìs dár bùvo gývas.*	'They remember grandad again as he was alive.'
Tuõs, kuriẽ lìps, baidỹs visų̃ bjauriáusios šmė̃klos.	'Those who will try to climb it will be beset by the most horrible spectres.'

Relative pronouns introducing an attributive clause and the pronoun *kàs* often have pronominal antecedents in the principal clause.

4.25 The pronouns *kàs, kóks, kokià, kurìs, kurì* can also have an emphatic meaning.

Kóks tù esì mókytas, Vincèli!	'How well educated you are, Vincelis!'
Kàs tõ vaĩko gabùmas!	'What talent this boy has!'
Užtàt kókio džiaũgsmo bùvo išjójus tėvui akė́ti!	'But what joy it was when father went to harrow the fields!'

INDEFINITE PRONOUNS

4.26 Indefinite pronouns lack the element of definiteness which is present in demonstrative pronouns. They do not refer to any definite thing, person or quality.

From the semantic point of view indefinite pronouns can be divided into three classes: indefinite proper, differentiating and generalizing. The latter fall into two groups – positive and negative.

From the syntactic poit of view indefinite pronouns also fall into three groups:

(1) those that can be used only in nominal positions;

(2) those that can be used only in adjectival positions;

(3) and those that can be used both in nominal and adjectival positions.

From the morphological point of view indefinite pronouns are simple, compound and composite.

4.27 **Indefinite proper pronouns.** Here is a list of indefinite proper pronouns, which are mostly identical in form to the corresponding interrogative or to some other pronouns:

kàs 'someone, somebody, something'
kóks, kokià 'whatever, some kind of; some'
kurìs, kurì 'whichever, whoever, some'
katràs, katrà 'whichever, whoever (of two)'
kelì, kẽlios 'some'
keliñtas, kelintà 'whichever in a series, some'
kẽletas 'a few, some (between 3 and 9)'
keliólika 'some (between 11 and 19)
kẽliasdešimt 'some (between 30 and 90)'
kelerì, kẽlerios 'a few, some (used with *pluralia tantum*)'
víenas, vienà 'one, no matter which one'
kìtas, kità 'some'
tóks, tokià 'of some kind', cf.:

Gál kóks paũkštis teñ skreñda.	'May be some (kind of) bird flies there.'
Lýg veřkia, lýg vaitója kàs.	'Somebody seems to be crying and moaning.'
Labaĩ seniaĩ gyvẽno tóks pirklỹs.	'Long ago there lived a certain merchant.'
Jìs mókėsi tik kẽlerius metùs.	'He studied some years only.'
Manè aplañkė kẽletas/keliólika draugų̃.	'Some friends visited me.'

Compound indefinite pronouns are formed by adding *kaž-, kaži(n)-* : *kažkàs, kažkurìs, kažkatràs, kažkóks, kažkeliñtas*. All these pronouns share a common semantic element meaning 'uncertain, someone not known, what, which, what kind of, which one in a series'. The same meaning is shared by the corresponding composite pronouns with the first component *kaži(n)*, e.g.: *kaži(n) kàs, kaži(n) kurìs, kaži(n) katràs, kaži(n) kóks*:

Jám vaidẽnasi, kàd piřkios vidurỹ kažkàs/kažin kàs stóvi.	'He imagines there is somebody standing in the middle of the room.'
Antãnas ùžčiuopė kažkókį kíetą dáiktą.	'Antanas touched something hard.'
Staigà pasigiřdo kažkóks/kažin kóks cypìmas.	'Suddenly there was some kind of squeaking.'

A majority of other composite indefinite (proper) pronouns include one of the following elements: *nórs, bèt, kaĩ, nè*:

(a) *kas nórs; koks nórs, kokia nórs; kuris nórs, kuri nórs; katras nórs, katra nórs*. Their meaning is 'someone, somebody, anybody, something, some kind of', e.g.:

Ar kas nórs *béldžiasi į durìs?*	'Is anybody knocking at the door?'
Norė́jau, kad beñt kas nórs *taĩ galė́tų suprásti.*	'I wished that at least somebody (no matter who) could understand it.'
Pakviẽsk kurį̃ nórs *iš vaikų̃.*	'Call someone (no matter which) of the children.'
Grą̃žinsiu skõlą katrai nórs *iš tàvo seserų̃.*	'I'll return my debt to one of your (two) sisters.'

(b) *bet kàs; bet kóks, bet kokià; bet kurìs, bet kurì; bet katràs, bet katrà* share the common semantic element 'any', e.g.:

Čià bet kàs *táu kẽlią paródys.*	'Here anyone will show you the way.'
Padúok mán bet kókį *pãgalį.*	'Give me any kind of stick.'
Dìrbsiu su bet kuriuõ *iš jū́sų.*	'I'll work with anyone of you.'

(c) *kai kàs; kai kóks, kai kokià; kai kurìs, kai kurì*; their common semantic element is 'part of the whole number, not every', e.g.:

Kai kàs *dár tìkisi sugrį̃žti.*	'Somebody still trust to return.'
Kai ką̃ *sužinójau iš vežė́jo.*	'I learnt something from the driver.'
Kai kuriẽ *namaĩ jaũ be stogų̃.*	'Some homes no longer have roofs.'

(d) *kàs ne kàs, kurìs ne kurìs* 'some, not many, very few', e.g.:

Kám ne kám, *o mùms taĩ bùs bėdà.*	'Whoever suffers it's us.'

The composite pronoun *víenas kìtas, vienà kità* 'very few', *šìs tàs* 'something (not very significant)', *šióks tóks, šiokià tokià* 'of an insignificant kind' have the indefinite proper meaning as well, e.g.:

Tik víenas kìtas *sugrį̃žo iš kãro.*	'Very few returned from the war.'
Rẽtkarčiais iř mùms šìs tàs *kliū́davo.*	'Sometimes something (insignificant) would come our way as well.'
Gál iš tõ bùs šiokiõs tokiõs *naudõs.*	'Perhaps there will be some insignificant gain in that.'

4.28 **Differentiating pronouns** refer to a certain portion of indefinite things, persons or qualities clearly setting them apart from the others: *víenas, vienà* 'one'; *kìtas, kità* 'other, another'; *vienóks, vienókia* 'of one kind'; *kitóks, kitókia* 'of another kind'; *tam tìkras, tam tikrà* 'certain'.

The pronouns *víenas, vienà, kìtas kità* can be used both in nominal and adjectival positions; *víenas, vienà* refer to an indefinite thing meaning 'only this one without the others'; *kìtas, kità* refer to the second one of two contrasted things. Because of their meaning these pronouns are very often combined with each other, some other pronouns or ordinal numerals.

Móterys víenos *dar daĩrėsi aplink krósnį,* kìtos *jau sėdėjo ant súolo ir veřpė.*	'Some of the women were still looking around the stove, the others were a ready sitting on a bench spinning.'
Ar tàs, ar kìtas *méistras siũs, vìs tas pàts.*	'It makes no difference if this or that tailor makes it.'
Ant kìto *šãpą pamãto, o ant savęs – nė vežìmo.*	'He sees a mote in another person's eye, but cannot see a cartload in his own.'
Bepigù sakýti kitíems, *bet nedarýti patíems.*	'It's easy to order others about, and not to do a thing oneself.'
Jì pàėmė puodėlį rū́gusio píeno, mẽs kitùs *reĩkiamus dáiktus.*	'She took a cup of milk, we took other necessary things.'

These two pronouns also have a neuter form to refer to phenomena in general.

Kaĩp galėjai manýti, kad mą̃stėme víena, *o sãkėme* kìta?	'How could you think that we had in mind one thing and said another?'
Víena *tik negẽra: nèrà grỹbų.*	'There's one thing which is not good: there are no mushrooms.'

Neuter forms are used in nominative, accusative, rarely genitive, positions. In other nominal positions they are replaced by masculine singular forms, wich are sometimes used to refer to phenomena in general and replace the neuter forms in nominative, accusative and genitive positions as well:

Víeno (= *víena*) *betróško: kokiu nórs bū́dù sàvo výrą pamatýti.*	'She longed only for one thing: to see her husband in one way or another.'

The fusions of the neuter form *kìta* with the pronoun *kàs – kas kìta, kìta kas, kìtkas* 'another matter, other things' – are also used to refer to phenomena in general:

Mótinai skaũda šìrdį dėl kìta ko.	'The mother's heart aches for another reason.'
Pamiřšęs sàvo ankstèsnę miñtį, jìs jaũ kalbėjo apie ką kìta.	'Having forgotten his former trend of thought, he was already speaking about another thing.'

Vienóks, vienókia 'of one kind', *kitóks, kitókia* 'of another kind', *tam tìkras* 'certain' are adjectival pronouns:

Ne visų vienókios ãkys.	'Not everybody has eyes of the same kind.'
Šiañdien óras vienóks, *o ry-tõj* kitóks.	'Today the weather is of one kind, tomorrow of another kind.'
Ūkininkai dãlį grūdų̃ dár iš rudeñs supìldavo į tam tikràs klė́tis.	'The farmers would pour some part of their grain into certain grain barns in autumn.'

In some contexts certain interrogative and demonstrative pronouns when coupled together acquire indefinite differentiating meaning as well, e.g.:

Kálvėje pìlna žmonių̃. Kàs *su reikalaĩs,* kàs *su tauškalaĩs.*	'The smithery is full of people. Some come on business, some with idle talk.'
Kar̃tais šį̃ *ar* tã̃ (= vieną̃ *ar kitą̃*) *reikė́davo gárbint.*	'Sometimes respects had to be paid to this or that (one or another).'

4.29 **Generalizing pronouns** fall into two groups: positive and negative.

Positive generalizing pronouns refer to indefinite things, persons or qualities which constitute one complete or almost complete whole: *vìsas, visà* 'the whole'; *visì, vìsos* 'all'; *visóks, visókia* 'of all kinds'; *abù, abì* 'both'; *abejì, ābejos* 'both (used with *pluralia tantum*)'; *ābejetas* 'both'; *kiekvíenas, kiekvienà* 'every'; *aliái víenas, aliái vienà* 'absolutely all'; *tū́las, tūlà, daug kàs* 'quite a few'.

The meaning of the singular and plural forms of the pronoun *vìsas, visà* (plural: *visì, vìsos*) is rather different. The singular forms are used only in adjectival positions and they indicate that a quality (action or state) is attributed to the whole thing (person) or to the whole set of things or persons:

Vakarè vìsas káimas susiriñko prie ẽžero.	'In the evening all the village came to the lake.'
Dabar̃ jaũ vìsą šim̃tą turė́siu.	'Now I'll have a complete hundred.'

The plural forms *visì, vìsos* are used both in nominal and adjectival positions and they indicate the entire number of things or persons:

Àš išdainavaũ visàs daineles.	'I have sung all my songs.'
Tylùs tylùs bùvo Mykoliùkas, o visíems mãtės, jog jìs šnẽka.	'Mykoliukas would be absolutely silent, but everybody thought he was talking.'

When used with *pluralia tantum*, the plural forms *visì, vìsos* possess both meanings: they may indicate that a quality, state or action is attributed to the whole thing (i) or to the complete set of things (ii):

(i) *Visùs metùs ištarnavaũ.*	'I served the whole year.'

(ii) *Visùs sàvo gyvēnimo metùs*   'I served all the years of my
ištarnavaũ.   life.'

The neuter form *vìsa* as well as *vìskas, visa kàs* refer to all things and phenomena in general.

Vìsa prapúolė.   'Everything has disappeared.'

Išmintìngas nuolatõs mókosi,   'A wise man is learning all the
o kvaĩlas dìngos vìsa žìnąs.   time, a stupid one thinks he
    knows everything.'

Tą̃ stebuklìngąją nāktį vìskas   'That miraculous night everything
yrà stebùklas.   is a miracle.'

Visa kõ aslojè pristatýta.   'There's everything on the floor.'

Visóks, visókia is used in adjectival positions only and means 'of all kinds':

Lū́žo teñ arúodai nuo visókio   'The grain bins overflowed with
javo.   all kinds of grain there.'

The generalizing pronouns *kiekvíenas, -à* 'every, each' (picking out the members of a set), *aliái víenas, -à* 'absolutely all', *tū́las, -à* 'quite a few', *abù, abì* 'both', *abejì, -os* 'both' (only *pluralia tantum*) are used both in nominal and adjectival positions, e.g.:

Susė́dę visì ė̃mė mẽdų válgyti   'All sat down and started eating
ir kiekvíenas bitelès gárbinti.   the honey, each praising the bees.'

Kaimýnai aliái víenas išvažiãvo   'Every single family of the
į miestẽlį.   neighbours left for town.'

Tū́las atsigrę̃ždamas žvìlgčiojo   'Not a single one turned back and cast
į papíevius.   glances at the edge of the meadow.'

Abù sēniai susirū́pinę galvójo.   'Both old people worried and thought.'

Máukis abejomìs pir̃štinėmis,   'Put on both pairs of gloves,
vienomìs bùs šálta.   you'll be cold with only one pair on.'

Pronouns *daug kàs* 'quite a few' *ābejetas* 'both (as a whole)' are used only in nominal positions, e.g.:

Iki trečiãdienio daug kàs   'Quite a few people expected to finish
tikėjos pabaĩgti mė̃šlą vèžti.   taking the manure to the fields
    by Wednesday .'

When used in adjectival positions the pronoun *kàs* can also have generalizing meaning similar to that of *kiekvíenas, -à* 'every', indicating the sequence of each thing or person referred to.

Kàs *välandą dãrėsi tamsiaũ*.	'Every hour it was getting darker and darker.'
Dabar̃ kàs *žiñgsnis atsìveria nematýti vaizdaĩ*.	'At every step new views unfold before our eyes.'

Negative generalizing pronouns (usually used in negative sentences) indicate that there are no things, persons or qualities which would possess a certain property or would be in a certain state, or would perform a certain action: *niēkas* 'nothing, nobody', *nė víenas, nė vienà* 'not a single one', *jóks, jokià* 'of no kind, none, no one', *nė kóks, nė kokià* 'of no kind, none, no one.'

Niēkas tíek nežinójo pãsakų, kíek senàsis Lãpinas.	'Nobody knew as many fairy tales as old Lapinas.'
Mẽs nè víenas netikėjom, kad ligónis mir̃tų.	'Nobody of us believed that the patient would die.'
Dangùs bùvo giēdras, be jókio debesėlio.	'The sky was blue, without a single cloud.'
Nė kokiõs/jokiõs žymės nėr̃, kur̃ pérėjau rugiùs.	'There's no trace left where I crossed the rye.'

In their meaning negative pronouns are opposed to positive generalizing pronouns:

niēkas is opposed to *visì, vìsos, vìsa, vìskas, daug kàs*:

Niēkas nežìno.	'Nobody knows.'
Visì/daug kàs žìno.	'Everybody knows/quite a few know.'
Niēkas jám nerūpi.	'Nothing worries him.'
Vìsa/vìskas/daug kàs jám rūpi.	'Everything/quite a lot worries him.'

Nė víenas, nė vienà is opposed to *kiekvíenas, kiekvienà, aliái víenas, aliái vienà, visì, vìsos*:

Nė víenas taĩp nepadarỹs	'Not a single man can do it.'
Kiekvíenas/aliái víenas/ visì taĩp padarỹs	'Everyone, every single man, all can do it.'

Jóks, jokià, nė kóks, nė kokià are opposed to *visóks, visókia, visì, vìsos*:

Jokių/nė kokių dainų nemokėjau.	'I didn't know any songs.'
Visókių dainų mokėjau.	'I knew all kinds of songs.'
Jokių/nė kokių dainų nedainavaũ.	'I didn't sing any/any sort of songs.'
Išdainavaũ visàs dainàs.	'I sang all the songs (I knew).'

4.30 *Pàts, patì* is considered to be an indefinite **emphatic pronoun**. It indicates that a person performs an action by himself without anybody's help.

| Šiañdien (àš) patì vakariẽnę gaminaũ. | 'Today I myself (FEM) cooked the supper.' |

When used in adjectival positions, pàts, patì can have only an emphatic meaning.

| Saulẽlė stovẽjo pačiamè dangaũs viduryjè. | 'The sun stood in the very middle of the sky.' |

Note: In some investigations on the Lithuanian pronouns the words šióks tóks, šiokià tokià 'of an insignificant kind', tam tìkras, tam tikrà 'certain', túlas, tūlà 'quite a few', vìsas, visà 'the whole', visóks, visókia 'of all kinds', pàts tàs, patì tà 'just the kind' are classed as adjectives rather than as indefinite pronouns.

Declension and accentuation of pronouns

PRONOUNS NOT INFLECTED FOR GENDER

4.31 The singular and plural forms of personal pronouns have different roots. The pronoun savę̃s has no nominative and no plural.

Singular

Nom.	àš	tù	–
Gen.	manę̃s/màno	tavę̃s/tàvo	savę̃s/sàvo
Dat.	mán	táu	sáu
Acc.	manè	tavè	savè
Instr.	manimì	tavimì	savimì
Loc.	manyjè	tavyjè	savyjè

Plural

Nom.	mẽs	jū̃s
Gen.	mū́sų	jū́sų
Dat.	mùms	jùms
Acc.	mùs	jùs
Instr.	mumìs	jumìs
Loc.	mumysè	jumysè

As is obvious from the paradigm, some case forms of the personal pronouns resemble those of nouns:

i-declension:	Singular Instr.	*manimì*	(cf. *vagimì* 'thief')
	Singular Loc.	*manyjè*	(cf. *vagyjè*)
	Plural Loc.	*mumysè*	(cf. *vagysè*)
u-declension:	Plural Dat.	*mùms*	(cf. *sūnùms* 'son')
	Plural Acc.	*mùs*	(cf. *sūnùs*)
	Plural Instr.	*mumìs*	(cf. *sūnumìs*)

Differently from nouns, personal pronouns have a short ending in the accusative singular: *manè, tavè, savè* (although in some dialects this ending is long: *manę̃, tavę̃, savę̃*, cf. *pẽlę*).

The genitive singular ending *-ęs* is etymologically derived from the accusative ending *ę* plus *s*, which has been added by analogy with nouns (cf. *pelẽs, vagiẽs, sūnaũs*).

Personal pronouns have two genitive forms – possessive and non-possessive (see 4.15).

Note should be taken of the change in the stressed syllable tone in the nominative and genitive plural: *mẽs – mū́sų, jū̃s – jū́sų*.

The pronoun *támsta* is declined and accented like the *o*-stem feminine noun *jū́ra* (see 1.25).

The pronouns *jìs* 'he', *jì* 'she' have different gender forms and are declined according to paradigms 4 and 8 of pronouns inflected for gender (see 4.33, 4.35).

PRONOUNS INFLECTED FOR GENDER

Masculine pronouns

4.32 Masculine pronouns inflected for gender are declined similarly to those adjectives which took over the following pronominal endings:

Masc.	Dat. Sg.	-ám	(kitám – gerám)
"	Loc. Sg.	-amè	(kitamè – geramè)
"	Nom. Pl.	-ì	(kitì – gerì)
"	Dat. Pl.	-íems	(kitíems – geríems)

Masculine pronouns have two declension patterns: *(i)a* declension and *i* declension.

Although *kàs* is not inflected for gender, it is declined like a masculine pronoun.

The (i)a-declension

4.33 In this declension there are four paradigms, which differ according to the following patterns:

	Par. 1	Par. 2	Par. 3	Par. 4
Sg. Nom.	-as	-as	-s	-is
" Gen.	-o	-o	-io	-io
" Acc.	-ą	-ą	-į	-į
" Instr.	-uo	-u	-iu	-iuo
Pl. Nom.	-ie	-i	-ie	-ie
" Acc.	-uos	-us	-ius	-iuos

Paradigm 1

tàs, šìtas, anàs, katràs, kàs

Singular

Nom.	tàs	šìtas	anàs	katràs	kàs
Gen.	tõ	šìto	anõ	katrõ	kõ
Dat.	tám	šitám	anám	katrám	kám
Acc.	tą̃	šìtą	aną̃	katrą̃	ką̃
Instr.	tuõ	šituõ	anuõ	katruõ	kuõ
Loc.	tamè	šitamè	anamè	katramè	kamè

Plural

Nom.	tiẽ	šitiẽ	aniẽ	katriẽ
Gen.	tų̃	šitų̃	anų̃	katrų̃
Dat.	tíems	šitíems	aníems	katríems
Acc.	tuõs	šituõs	anuõs	katruõs
Instr.	taĩs	šitaĩs	anaĩs	katraĩs
Loc.	tuosè	šituosè	anuosè	katruosè

Paradigm 2

kìtas, vìsas, víenas, kiekvíenas, tū́las, tam tìkras, mãnas, tãvas, sãvas

Singular

Nom.	kìtas	vìsas	víenas	tū́las	sãvas
Gen.	kìto	vìso	víeno	tū́lo	sãvo

Dat.	kitám	visám	vienám	tūlám	savám
Acc.	kìtą	vìsą	víeną	tū́lą	sãvą
Instr.	kitù	visù	víenu	tū́lu	savù
Loc.	kitamè	visamè	vienamè	tūlamè	savamè

Plural

Nom.	kitì	visì	vienì	tūlì	savì
Gen.	kitų̃	visų̃	vienų̃	tūlų̃	savų̃
Dat.	kitíems	visíems	vieníems	tūlíems	savíems
Acc.	kitùs	visùs	víenus	tū́lus	savùs
Instr.	kitaĩs	visaĩs	vienaĩs	tūlaĩs	savaĩs
Loc.	kituosè	visuosè	vienuosè	tūluosè	savuosè

Paradigm 3

tóks, šióks, šìtoks, anóks, kóks, jóks, visóks, vienóks, kitóks, kažkóks, kai kóks, etc.

Singular

Nom.	tóks	jóks	visóks	kitóks
Gen.	tókio	jókio	visókio	kitókio
Dat.	tokiám	jokiám	visókiam	kitókiam
Acc.	tókį	jókį	visókį	kitókį
Instr.	tókiu	jókiu	visókiu	kitókiu
Loc.	tokiamè	jokiamè	visókiame	kitókiame

Plural

Nom.	tokiẽ	jokiẽ	visókie	kitókie
Gen.	tokių̃	jokių̃	visókių	kitókių
Dat.	tokíems	jokíems	visókiems	kitókiems
Acc.	tókius	jókius	visókius	kitókius
Instr.	tokiaĩs	jokiaĩs	visókiais	kitókiais
Loc.	tokiuosè	jokiuosè	visókiuose	kitókiuose

Paradigm 4

jìs, šìs, kurìs

Singular

Nom.	jìs	šìs	kurìs
Gen.	jõ	šiõ	kuriõ

Dat.	*jám*	*šiám*	*kuriám*
Acc.	*jį̃*	*šį̃*	*kurį̃*
Instr.	*juõ*	*šiuõ*	*kuriuõ*
Loc.	*jamè*	*šiamè*	*kuriamè*

Plural

Nom.	*jiẽ*	*šiẽ*	*kuriẽ*
Gen.	*jų̃*	*šių̃*	*kurių̃*
Dat.	*jíems*	*šíems*	*kuríems*
Acc.	*juõs*	*šiuõs*	*kuriuõs*
Instr.	*jaĩs*	*šiaĩs*	*kuriaĩs*
Loc.	*juosè*	*šiuosè*	*kuriuosè*

The *i*-declension

4.34 The pronoun *pàts* is the only pronoun which is declined according to this declension.

Paradigm 5

	Singular	Plural
Nom.	*pàts*	*pãtys*
Gen.	*patiẽs/pãčio*	*pačių̃*
Dat.	*pačiám*	*patíems*
Acc.	*pãtį*	*pačiùs*
Instr.	*pačiù/patim̃(i)*	*pačiaĩs*
Loc.	*pačiamè*	*pačiuosè*

This pronoun has more case forms which coincide with those of nouns than any other pronoun. Many of its case forms are of *ia* declension: Instr. Sg. *pačiù* (cf. *tókiu*), Acc. Pl. *pačiùs* (cf. *tókius*), Instr. Pl. *pačiaĩs* (cf. *tokiaĩs*), Loc. Pl. *pačiuosè* (cf. *tokiuosè*).

In genitive singular and instrumental singular *pàts* alternative forms of *i* and *ia* declensions are used.

Feminine pronouns

The *(i)o*-declension

4.35 Feminine pronouns are declined like nouns of *(i)o*-declension. There are three paradigms in this declension:

Paradigm 1: *tà, šita/šità, kità*, a.o. (declined like *aušrà* 'dawn')
Paradigm 2: *tokià, kokià, visókia*, a.o. (declined like *žinià* 'piece of news')
Paradigm 3: *jì, šì, kurì, patì* (declined like *martì* 'daughter-in-law').

Paradigm 6

tà, šita/šità, kità, visà, anà, katrà, vienà, kiekvienà, manà, tavà, savà etc.

Singular

Nom.	*tà*	*šita/šità*	*kità*	*visà*
Gen.	*tõs*	*šitos/šitõs*	*kitõs*	*visõs*
Dat.	*tái*	*šitai/šitái*	*kìtai*	*vìsai*
Acc.	*tą̃*	*šìtą*	*kìtą*	*vìsą*
Instr.	*tà*	*šita/šità*	*kità*	*visà*
Loc.	*tojè*	*šitoje/šitojè*	*kitojè*	*visojè*

Plural

Nom.	*tõs*	*šìtos*	*kìtos*	*vìsos*
Gen.	*tų̃*	*šitų/šitų̃*	*kitų̃*	*visų̃*
Dat.	*tóms*	*šìtoms/šitóms*	*kitóms*	*visóms*
Acc.	*tàs*	*šitas/šitàs*	*kitàs*	*visàs*
Instr.	*tomìs*	*šitomis/šitomìs*	*kitomìs*	*visomìs*
Loc.	*tosè*	*šitose/šitosè*	*kitosè*	*visosè*

Paradigm 7

tokià, kokià, visókia, šiókia, šìtokia, anókia, vienókia, kitókia, kažkókia, jókia, etc.

Singular

Nom.	*tokià*	*kokià*	*visókia*
Gen.	*tokiõs*	*kokiõs*	*visókios*
Dat.	*tókiai*	*kókiai*	*visókiai*
Acc.	*tókią*	*kókią*	*visókią*
Instr.	*tókia*	*kókia*	*visókia*
Loc.	*tokiojè*	*kokiojè*	*visókioje*

Plural

Nom.	*tókios*	*kókios*	*visókios*
Gen.	*tokių̃*	*kokių̃*	*visókių*

Dat.	tokióms	kokióms	visókioms
Acc.	tókias	kókias	visókias
Instr.	tokiomìs	kokiomìs	visókiomis
Loc.	tokiosè	kokiosè	visókiose

Paradigm 8

jì, šì, patì, kurì, kažkurì

Singular

Nom.	jì	šì	patì	kurì
Gen.	jõs	šiõs	pačiõs	kuriõs
Dat.	jái	šiái	pāčiai	kuriái
Acc.	ją̃	šią̃	pą́čią	kurią̃
Instr.	jà	šià	pačià	kurià
Loc.	jojè	šiojè	pačiojè	kuriojè

Plural

Nom.	jõs	šiõs	pãčios	kuriõs
Gen.	jų̃	šių̃	pačių̃	kurių̃
Dat.	jóms	šióms	pačióms	kurióms
Acc.	jàs	šiàs	pačiàs	kuriàs
Instr.	jomìs	šiomìs	pačiomìs	kuriomìs
Loc.	josè	šiosè	pačiosè	kuriosè

Table 8. **Correspondence between the grammatical forms of feminine and masculine pronouns**

Masculine forms		Feminine forms	
Paradigm	Nom. Sg.	Paradigm	Nom. Sg.
1, 2	-as	6	-a
3	-s	7	-ia
4, 5	-is, -s	8	-i

4.36 If we compare the declension of masculine and feminine pronouns, we will see that the declension of feminine pronouns is much more uniform than that of masculine pronouns, e.g. jìs, šìs are declined according to Paradigm 4, pàts is declined according to Paradigm 5. The feminine forms of the same pronouns *jì, šì, patì* are all declined according to Paradigm 8. Similarly, *tàs, šìtas* are declined according to Paradigm 1, *kìtas, vìsas* – according to Paradigm 2. The feminine forms of all these pronouns – *tà, šità, kità, visà* – are declined according to Paradigm 6.

Pronouns with the nominal suffix *-iškis, -ė* (*manìškis, -ė* 'my', *tavìškis, -ė* 'your', *savìškis, -ė* 'one's', *mūsìškis, -ė* 'our', *jūsìškis, -ė* 'your') are declined and accented like the noun *namìškis, namìškė* 'a member of the same household'.

Pronouns with quantitative meaning are declined and accented like corresponding numerals: *kelì, kėlios* are declined and accented like *šešì, šėšios*; *keliñtas, kelintà* like *peñktas, penktà*; *kėletas* like *kėtvertas*; *kelerì, kėlerios* like *ketverì, kėtverios*; *keliólika* like *keturiólika*; *ābejetas* like *dvėjetas*; *abejì, ābejos* like *dvejì, dvėjos*.

4.37 **Composite pronouns** fall into two declensional groups:

(1) those that consist of one declinable and one indeclinable component: *kažin kàs* (declined like *kàs*), *koks nórs* (declined like *kóks*), *kokia nórs* (declined like *kokià*); *tam tìkras* (declined like the adjective *tìkras*), etc., e.g.:

Nom. *kažin kàs, koks nórs*
Gen. *kažin kienõ, kokio nórs*
Dat. *kažin kám, kokiam nórs*, etc.

(2) those that consist of two declinable components:

Nom. *kàs ne kàs, šióks tóks*
Gen. *kõ ne kõ, šiókio tókio*
Dat. *kám ne kám, šiokiám tokiám*, etc.

ACCENTUATION OF GENDER PRONOUNS

4.38 There are following accentuation patterns for gendered pronouns:

Pattern 1. Like adjectival accentuation pattern 1. The stress falls on the same syllable throughout the whole paradigm: *anóks, anókia; kitóks, kitókia; šìtoks, šìtokia; vienóks, vienókia; visóks, visókia*. Pronoun *šìtas, šìta/šità* is accented according to two patterns: 1 and 5 (see Paradigm 6 in 4.35).

Pattern 2. Like nominal accentuation pattern 2: *niēkas* like *pir̃štas*.

Pattern 3. Like adjectival accentuation pattern 3: *jóks, jokià; kóks, kokià; šióks, šiokià; tóks, tokià; víenas, vienà; túlas, tūlà; kažkóks, kažkokià; kiekvíenas, kiekvienà*.

Pattern 4. Like adjectival accentuation pattern 4: *kìtas, kità; pàts, patì; vìsas, visà; šìtas, šità; mānas, manà; tāvas, tavà; sāvas, savà.*

Pattern 5. This pattern is specific to gendered pronouns. It includes one syllable pronouns *jìs, jì; šìs, šì; tàs, tà; kàs* and the pronouns *anàs, anà; katràs, katrà; kurìs, kurì; kažkàs; kažkurìs, kažkurì* bearing the stress consistently on the last syllable (cf. also *kienõ; jamè, jojè; jomìs, juosè, josè*).

4.39 The majority of composite pronouns consisting of two words bear the stress on the second component, which is accented throughout the paradigm like the corresponding one-word pronoun, e.g. *bet kàs; bet kóks, bet kokià; bet kurìs, bet kurì; bet katràs, bet katrà; kai kàs; kai kóks, kai kokià; kai kurìs, kai kurì; kai katràs, kai katrà; kas nórs; koks nórs, kokia nórs; kuris nórs, kuri nórs; katras nórs, katra nórs; kažin kàs; kažin kóks, kažin kokià; kažin kurìs, kažin kurì; kažin katràs, kažin katrà; nè kóks, nè kokià; nè víenas, nè vienà; tam tìkras, tam tikrà; tas pàts, ta patì; tóks pat, tokià pat(i)*. The pronoun *daug kas* can bear the stress on the first or on the second component: *daũg kas, daũg ko, daũg kam...* or *daug kàs, daug kõ, daug kám...* Some composite pronouns can be stressed on both components, e.g.: *aliái víenas, aliái vienà; šióks tóks, šiokià tokià; víenas kìtas, vienà kità; kàs ne kàs; kurìs ne kurìs, kurì ne kurì*.

DUAL NUMBER

4.40 Pronominal dual forms are derived from the corresponding pronominal root and the numeral *dù, dvì*. They are declined according to two patterns.

Pattern 1

mùdu, mùdvi, jùdu jùdvi, abù (abùdu), abì (abìdvi)

Masculine gender

Nom.	mùdu	jùdu	abù (abùdu)
Gen.	mùdviejų	jùdviejų	abiejų̃
Dat.	mùdviem	jùdviem	abíem
Instr.	mùdviem	jùdviem	abiẽm
Loc.	mùdviejuose	jùdviejuose	abiejuosè

Feminine gender

Nom.	mùdvi	jùdvi	abì (abìdvi)
Gen.	mùdviejų	jùdviejų	abiejų̃

Dat.	*mùdviem*	*jùdviem*	*abíem*
Acc.	*mùdvi*	*jùdvi*	*abì (abìdvi)*
Instr.	*mùdviem*	*jùdviem*	*abiẽm*
Loc.	*mùdviejose*	*jùdviejose*	*abiejosè*

Pattern 2

juõdu (jíedu), jíedvi, tuõdu, tíedvi, šiuõdu, šíedvi, anuõdu, aníedvi, šituõdu, šitíedvi, katruõdu, katríedvi, kuriuõdu, kuríedvi

Masculine gender

Nom.	*juõdu (jíedu)*	*tuõdu*	*šiuõdu*
Gen.	*jų́dviejų*	*tų́dviejų*	*šių́dviejų*
Dat.	*jié(m)dviem*	*tié(m)dviem*	*šié(m)dviem*
Acc.	*juõdu (jíedu)*	*tuõdu*	*šiuõdu*
Instr.	*jié(m)dviem*	*tié(m)dviem*	*šié(m)dviem*

Feminine gender

Nom.	*jíedvi*	*tíedvi*	*šíedvi*
Gen.	*jų́dviejų*	*tų́dviejų*	*šių́dviejų*
Dat.	*jó(m)dviem*	*tó(m)dviem*	*šió(m)dviem*
Acc.	*jíedvi*	*tíedvi*	*šíedvi*
Instr.	*jõ(m)dviem*	*tõ(m)dviem*	*šiõ(m)dviem*

Shortening of pronominal endings

4.41 In Modern Lithuanian there is a tendency to shorten certain case endings of pronouns, similarly to those of adjectives. Most often shortened endings occur in the following case forms:

instrumental singular:

manim̃, tavim̃, savim̃ instead of: *manimì, tavimì, savimì;*

locative singular:

manỹ, tavỹ, savỹ instead of: *manyjè, tavyjè, savyjè*
tam̃, kitam̃, jam̃ instead of: *tamè, kitamè, jamè*
tõj, kitõj, jõj instead of: *tojè, kitojè, jojè;*

dative plural:

tíem, kitíem, jíem instead of: *tíems, kitíems, jíems*
tóm, kitóm, jóm instead of: *tóms, kitóms, jóms;*

locative plural:

tuõs, kituõs, juõs instead of: *tuosè, kituosè, juosè*.

DECLENSION AND ACCENTUATION OF DEFINITE PRONOUNS

4.42 The following pronouns have definite forms:

tàs, tà – tasaĩ, tóji
šìs, šì – šisaĩ, šióji
anàs, anà – anasaĩ, anóji
jìs, jì – jisaĩ, jóji
mãnas, manà – manàsis, manóji
tãvas, tavà – tavàsis, tavóji
sãvas, savà – savàsis, savóji

Masculine gender

Singular

Nom.	tasaĩ	jisaĩ	manàsis
Gen.	tõjo	jõjo	mãnojo
Dat.	tájam	jájam	manájam
Acc.	tą̃jį	jį̃jį	mãnąjį
Instr.	túoju	júoju	manúoju
Loc.	tãjame	jãjame	manãjame

Plural

Nom.	tíeji	jíeji	maníeji
Gen.	tų̃jų	jų̃jų	manų̃jų
Dat.	tíesiems	jíesiems	maníesiems
Acc.	túosius	júosius	manúosius
Instr.	taĩsiais	jaĩsiais	manaĩsiais
Loc.	tuõsiuose	juõsiuose	manuõsiuose

Feminine gender

Singular

Nom.	tóji	jóji	manóji
Gen.	tõsios	jõsios	manõsios
Dat.	tájai	jájai	mãnajai
Acc.	tą̃ją	ją̃ją	mãną́ją
Instr.	tą́ja	ją́ja	maną́ja
Loc.	tõjoje	jõjoje	manõjoje

Plural

Nom.	tõsios	jõsios	mãnosios
Gen.	tū̃jų	jū̃jų	manū̃jų
Dat.	tósioms	jósioms	manósioms
Acc.	tą́sias	ją́sias	maną́sias
Instr.	tõsiomis	jõsiomis	manõsiomis
Loc.	tõsiose	jõsiose	manõsiose

4.43   In the nominative singular, masculine definite pronouns (except for definite possessive pronouns with the ending -*asis*) have the ending -*ai*, etymologically derived from the emphatic particle (this makes them different from definite adjectives, cf. 2.17ff.).

The emphatic particle -*ai* is also to be found in the nominative singular of some other pronouns which are not definite:

toksaĩ cf.	tóks	'of this kind'
koksaĩ	kóks	'what kind of; some kind of'
šioksaĩ	šióks	'of this kind'
šìtoksai	šìtoks	'of this kind'
anoksaĩ	anóks	'of that kind'
joksaĩ	jóks	'of no kind'
visoksaĩ	visóks	'of all kinds'
vienoksaĩ	vienóks	'of one kind'
kitoksaĩ	kitóks	'of another kind'
patsaĩ	pàts	'oneself'

The stressed syllable in the dative singular of definite pronouns bears the acute toneme: *tájam* (< *támjam*), *tájai* (< *táijai*).

The endings of the first component, protected by the second component, have retained the long vowel or the diphthong and the acute toneme:

Instr. Sg.	túoju	cf. tuõ
	tája	tà
Acc. Pl.	túosius	tuõs
	tą́sias	tàs

5 VERB

Veiksmãžodis

5.1 Verbs are a class of words denoting actions, processes and states and possessing the morphological categories of tense, mood, person, number and voice.

Finite and non-finite verb forms are distinguished. Finite verb forms are inflected for person, number, tense and mood, and they are used exclusively as predicates in a sentence. Non-finite verb forms cannot be inflected for person: here belong participles (including half-participles and gerunds) and infinitive.

The morphological categories of the verb comprise the following sets of forms:

3 persons of which the 1st and 2nd persons have specific endings: 1st person singular -*u* and plural -*me*, 2nd person singular -*i* and plural -*te*, e.g. *ein-ù* 'I go', *eĩname* 'we go', *ein-ì* 'you (SG) go', *eĩna-te* 'you (PL) go'. The 3rd person form coincides with the stem and thus has no special ending.

2 numbers: singular and plural, which are distinguished in the 1st and 2nd person only. In the 3rd person, number is not distinguished, e.g.: *jis/ji/jie eĩna, ẽjo, eĩs, eĩtų* 'he/she/they go, went, will go, would go'.

4 tenses: present, past, past frequentative and future. Each tense is represented by simple (synthetic) forms and also by compound (periphrastic) forms. The latter are expressed by a present or past participle (active or passive) of the notional verb with the finite form of the auxiliary *bū́ti* 'be'.

4 moods: the indicative, subjunctive, imperative (represented by finite verb forms) and oblique mood *(modus relativus)*, expressed by participles in predicate position.

2 voices: active and passive, the opposition of which is marked mainly by participles. Compound (periphrastic) passive forms with present and past passive participles enter into voice opposition to both compound verb forms containing active participles and simple finite verb forms representing the active voice.

5.2 To mark morphological categories in the verb, Lithuanian employs endings and inflectional suffixes.

Endings are used to mark the 1st and 2nd person singular and plural forms and case, number and gender in participles. The endings are attached either to the verbal stem or to the suffix. An ending may have zero form (e.g., in the 3rd person finite forms).

Inflectional suffixes are employed to mark the past tenses, the future tense and all the non-finite verb forms. Some inflectional suffixes (e.g. *-ė-ti, -y-ti, -o-ti, -uo-ti*) coincide with derivational suffixes, cf. the inflexional suffix in *gul-ě-ti* 'to lie', *gùli* (PRES), *gul-ě-jo* (PAST) and derivational suffix in *áukl-ė-ti* 'to educate', *áukl-ė-ja* (PRES), *áukl-ė-jo* (PAST).

Aspect, transitivity, reflexivity and a number of other semantic and syntactic properties of the verb are not morphologized in Lithuanian. They are expressed mostly by various derivational means (suffixes, prefixes, reflexive formants, etc.)

5.3 From the semantic point of view, actional, processual and stative verbs can be distinguished.

Actional verbs typically denote: (1) physical actions which may be objectless (e.g. *eĩti* 'go, walk', *bė́gti* 'run', *dìrbti* 'work') or directed at an object (e.g. *nèšti (vaĩką)* 'carry (a child)', *statýti (namùs)* 'build (a house)', *válgyti (košę̃)* 'eat (porridge)'), and (2) social and mental activities (e.g. *pir̃kti* 'buy', *susitìkti* 'meet', *skaitýti* 'read', *galvóti* 'think (about)').

Stative verbs denote (1) physical states of things and persons (*gulě́ti* 'lie', *blizgě́ti* 'glitter', *sir̃gti* 'be ill', *žiojě́ti* 'be wide open'), (2) mental states and perceptions (*mylě́ti* 'love', *tikě́ti* 'believe', *žinóti* 'know', *jaũsti* 'feel', *girdě́ti* 'hear'), and (3) relations (*turě́ti* 'have, possess', *priklausýti* 'belong (to), depend (on)', *tìkti* 'fit, match', *atródyti* 'seem', etc.).

Processual verbs denote a change of state (*áugti* 'grow', *sénti* 'grow old(er)', *kìsti* 'change', *susir̃gti* 'fall ill', *rū́gti* 'turn/grow sour', *nókti* 'ripen'), including spontaneous natural phenomena (*lýti* 'rain', *snìgti* 'snow', *témti* 'grow dark', *šálti* 'freeze').

Some verbs may have dual class membership. For instance, a verb may denote an action and a process in different contexts, cf. respectively: *vérdu sriùbą* 'I am cooking soup' – *sriubà vérda* 'the soup is cooking'. But more commonly the differences in meaning are marked by means of derivational suffixes, prefixes and the reflexive formant.

Note: In cases when the subcategorization of verbs into actional, processual and stative verbs is irrelevant the term action is used in a wider meaning including processes and states as well.

5.4 **Derivational suffixes** are used to derive verbs from nouns, adjectives, other verbs and onomatopoeic words. Verbs are derived by means of the following suffixes: *-(i)au-ti, -en-ti, -ė-ti, -inė-ti, -in-ti, -y-ti, -(i)o-ti, -(i)uo-ti, -tel(ė)-ti/-ter(ė)-ti*.

Verbs with the same suffix may have different meanings, depending on the grammatical class and semantic type of the underlying word, e.g.: *grỹbas* 'mushroom': *gryb-áuti* 'pick mushrooms', *našlỹs/našlẽ* 'widower/widow': *našl-áuti* 'be a widower/widow', *šaũkti* 'shout': *šū́k-auti* 'shout frequently'. Verbs with causative, iterative, semelfactive and other meanings are often derived by means of suffixes (see below). A derivational suffix (unlike an inflectional suffix) is retained in all the grammatical forms of the verb.

Verbal prefixes (unlike suffixes) are used to derive verbs from other verbs only. Prefixes may change the aspectual character of a verb (see 5.18–20), modify the verbal meaning in a variety of ways and transitivize some intransitive verbs (see 5.10). Most of the prefixes have corresponding prepositions either quite identical in form (cf. *į- – į̃* 'in', *iš- – ìš* 'from', *pér- – peř* 'over, across', *su- – sù* 'with', *už- – ùž* 'over; for; by') or with apophonic vowel alternation, cf. *ap(i)- – apiẽ* 'round; about', *pa- – põ* 'under; after', *nu- – nuõ* 'from', *pri- – priẽ* 'at, by'. The prefixes *at-* and *par-* alone have no counterparts among prepositions in Standard Lithuanian (in Eastern dialects, however, the preposition *par̃* is attested, cf. *par-eĩti* 'come back', and *par mumì* 'in our surroundings'). The affixes *ne-* and *be-* are also prefixed to verbs, but they differ from the above prefixes in function: *ne-* expresses negation and *be-* is sometimes used to emphasize the duration.

Most of the prefixes retain the spatial meanings of direction, especially with verbs of motion, e.g.: *eĩti* 'go' – *ap-eĩti* 'go round', *at-eĩti* 'come, arrive at/in', *iš-eĩti* 'go out', *nu-eĩti* 'go down/away', *už-eĩti* 'go round, behind', *pér-eĩti* 'go over, through', *pra-eĩti* 'go past/by', *pri-eĩti*, 'go up to', *par-eĩti* 'come back, return home', *su-eĩti* 'come together'. Prefixes may change the mode of action by rendering such meanings as completeness or end of an action (e.g. *su-dègti* 'burn out') or its beginning (*su-gaũsti* 'begin to drone'), a small degree (*ap-gýdyti* 'cure a little', *į-leñkti* 'bend somewhat, a little'), ability to perform an action (*iš-dainúoti* 'be able to sing', *pa-nèšti* 'be able to carry'), limited duration (*pa-dainúoti* 'sing a while'), etc.

5.5 **Reflexive marker** *-si/-s is* also widely used as a derivational affix with a broad range of semantic functions. In Standard Lithuanian it occupies the final position (after the ending) in unprefixed verbs and the middle position between prefix and root in prefixed verbs, cf.: *keliúo-si* 'I get up' – *at-si-kė́liau* 'I got up'.

The full allomorph *-si-* is used in final position in most of the finite verb forms, e.g.: *kẽlia-si* 'he (they) get(s) up', *kė́lėsi* 'he (they) got up', *kéldavo-si* 'he (they) used to get up'; it is also used in the plural forms of participles (including half-participles) of unprefixed verbs, e.g.: *kelią̃-si*, *kēliančio(s)-si* 'getting up'; *kė́lę-si*, *kė́lusio(s)-si* 'having got up'; *kéldamie-si*, *kéldamo(s)-si* '(while) getting up', also in feminine of the half-participle, e.g.: *kéldama-si* '(while) getting up'. In medial position, the full allomorph *-si-* alone can be used: *at-si-kė́liau* 'I got up'.

The shortened allomorph -s is used in final position: in the 1st and 2nd person plural indicative, subjunctive and imperative, 2nd person singular imperative and in the infinitive, e.g.: *kėliamė-s* 'we get up', *kėliatė-s* 'you get up', *kéltumė-s* 'we would get up', *kélkimė-s* 'let's get up' etc. If the reflexive marker is preceded by a consonant, the vowel marker -i- is inserted before the short allomorph in final position, as in the 3rd person future tense form: *kel̃s-is* 'he will get up', in the nominative singular masculine of active participles: *keliąs-is, kėlęs-is, kel̃siąs-is, kéldamas-is* and gerunds: *kėliant-is, kėlus-is, kéldavus-is, kélsiant-is*.

In many dialects, the short variant of the reflexive marker alone is employed in the final position. Under their influence the shortened reflexive forms of finite verbs are often used in colloquial speech as well, e.g.: *keliúo-s* 'I get up', *kelíe-s* 'you (SG) get up', *kėliau-s* 'I got up', etc.

TRANSITIVE AND INTRANSITIVE VERBS

5.6   Transitive and intransitive verbs constitute two major syntactic classes the members of which are also characterized by semantic and derivational properties. Transitive verbs are used with a direct object in the accusative case (e.g. *darýti klaidàs* 'make mistakes', *skaitýti knỹgą* 'read a book') or by the genitive (*láukti draũgo* 'wait for a friend', *norėti óbuolio* 'want an apple'). Intransitive verbs take no direct object, e.g. *miegóti* sleep', *váikščioti* 'walk', *bė́gti* 'run'.

Some verbs can be used as intransitives or transitives with a difference in their meaning (i.e. with or without relation to an object), cf.:

Sẽnis dár māto geraĩ.   'The old man sees well yet' (intransitive).
Mataũ mìšką.   'I see a forest' (transitive).

However, many transitive verbs have intransitive counterparts related to them by various formal and derivational means. Here belong:

(1) pairs of verbs with apophonic vowel alternation in the root, such as *kìlti* 'rise' – *kélti* 'raise';

(2) pairs comprised of an intransitive verb and its transitive derivative with the causative suffixes *-(d)in-ti; -(d)y-ti*, cf. *pỹkti* 'be angry' – *pýkdyti* 'make angry';

(3) pairs with a prefixed transitive derivative, cf. *ver̃kti* 'cry' – *praver̃kti akis* 'cry one's eyes out';

(4) pairs comprising a transitive verb and its reflexive derivative, cf. *keĩsti* 'change, make different' (tr.) – *keĩstis* 'change' (intr.).

The first two formal oppositions express the semantic causative opposition. In the case of prefixation, the lexical meaning is usually changed.

Verbs with vowel alternation

5.7 The oldest core of the transitive : intransitive opposition in Lithuanian is represented by primary verbs with the apophonic vowel alternation in the root marking causative relationship:

drìksti 'tear, become torn'– drė́ksti 'tear, make torn'
kìsti 'change, become different' – keĩsti 'change, make different'
liñkti 'bend, become bent' – leñkti 'bend, make bent'
lúžti 'break, become broken' – láužti 'break, make broken'
tį̃sti 'become longer, stretch'– tę̃sti 'make longer, pull, stretch'
vir̃sti 'overturn, be overturned' – ver̃sti 'overturn (something)'
žìrti 'spill, be spilled' – žer̃ti/žér̃ti 'spill (something)'

The intransitive members of the oppositions usually denote process, i.e. a change of state, and their transitive counterparts denote causation of the same state. The intransitive verb typically takes an inanimate subject which becomes a direct object of the transitive verb which acquires an animate (typically human), sometimes inanimate subject, e.g.:

Šakà paliñko.	'The branch bent.'
Vaĩkas/Vėjas pàlenkė šãką.	'The boy/the wind bent the branch.'

This means of derivation is unproductive in Modern Lithuanian.

A few verbs, namely dègti 'burn', kèpti 'bake, fry' and vìrti 'boil, cook', are grammatical indeterminates: they are used both transitively as causatives and intransitively without any change of form:

Dúona kẽpa.	'The bread is baking.'
Mamà kẽpa dúoną.	'Mother is baking bread.'

Semantically, they are identical with the lúžti – láužti type of verbs in that they express the causative opposition.

Verbs with causative suffixes

5.8 The causative suffixes -(d)in-ti and -(d)y-ti which add the causative sense to non-causative verbs also have transitivizing force. They are a productive means of derivation in the verbal system of Lithuanian. The following principal subtypes of this derivational pattern can be distinguished:

(1) The suffix is added to the root of primary verbs some of which have the infix -n- or -st- in the present tense form; cf.:

(a) verbs without an infix:

áugti 'grow' (intr.)	: augìnti 'grow' (trans.)
àuga	augìna
dègti 'burn' (intr.)	: dẽginti 'burn, fry' (trans.)
dẽga	dẽgina

(b) verbs with an infix -n- or -st- in the present:

blùkti 'fade, lose colour'	: blùkinti 'bleach' (trans.)
bluñka	blùkina
smilkti 'smoulder, fume'	: smilkýti 'fumigate'
smilksta	: smilko

(2) The suffix is added in conjunction with vowel alternation in the root which usually has an infix in the present tense, cf.:

dýgti 'sprout, begin to grow'	: daigìnti 'cause to grow'
dýgsta	daigìna
gèsti 'spoil, go bad'	: gadìnti 'spoil (sth)'
geñda	gadìna

(3) The causative suffix alternates with the suffix -ė-ti of an intransitive verb, cf.:

kabéti 'be hanging'	: kabìnti 'make hang'
kalėti 'be imprisoned'	: kālinti 'keep in prison'
klūpėti 'kneel'	: klupdýti 'make kneel'
varvėti 'drip, fall in drops'	: vařvinti 'drip, let fall in drops'

The suffixes -(d)in-ti, -(d)y-ti are also used to derive causative verbs from a few transitives:

válgyti 'eat'	: valgydìnti 'feed, give to eat'
gérti 'drink'	: gìrdyti 'give (sb) to drink water (animals)'
lèsti 'peck'	: lėsinti 'feed (birds, poultry)'

The object of the underlying verb is usually deleted in the causative construction, the subject being demoted to direct object:

Vaĩkas válgė kõšę.	'The child ate gruel.'
Áuklė valgydìno vaĩką.	'The nurse fed the child.'

5.9 Among transitive verbs, a small group of so-called **curative verbs** (*parūpinamíeji veiksmãžodžiai*) is distinguished which are close in meaning to causative verbs. They are derived from transitive verbs by means of the suffix *-dinti* and have the meaning 'make somebody to perform the action', as in the following oppositions:

statýti nãmą	'build a house'
statýdinti nãmą	'build a house by inviting builders to do the actual work'
kálti monetàs	'mint coins'
káldinti monetàs	'mint coins by ordering the mint to make them'
siúti sijõną	'make (lit. sew) a skirt'
siúdinti sijõną	'have a skirt made by a dress-maker'

Prefixation

5.10 Derivation by prefixation sometimes involves transitivization of intransitive verbs without ever involving semantic causativization, cf.:

skrìsti 'fly'	: *apskrìsti namùs* 'fly round the house'
veřkti 'cry'	: *praveřkti akìs* 'cry one's eyes out'
áugti 'grow'	: *išáugti švařką* 'grow out of (one's) coat'

The direct object of a transitive derivative usually has specifying or limiting force. Most regularly, prefixes transitivize verbs of motion, in which case they retain their spatial meaning of direction and the verbs acquire an object with a spatial or contiguous meaning, cf.:

eĩti 'go'	: *péreiti gãtvę* 'cross (go across) the street'
keliáuti 'travel'	: *apkeliáuti pasáulį* 'travel round the world'
važiúoti 'go (by car), drive'	: *pérvažiuoti káimą* 'go (drive) through a village'

Sometimes the derivative verb requires a tautological (dummy) object:

gyvénti 'live'	: *pragyvénti gyvẽnimą* 'live (through) one's life'

Prefixed derivative verbs retain the subject of the underlying intransitive verb and their semantic relationship with it.

Reflexivization

5.11 A great number of reflexive verbs are opposed to their non-reflexive counterparts with respect to transitivity: the non-reflexive verb is transitive and the corresponding reflexive verb is intransitive, cf.:

reñgti 'dress (smb), prepare (sth)'	: *reñgtis* 'dress oneself, prepare for (oneself)'
gìnti 'defend, protect'	: *gìntis* 'defend oneself, protect oneself'
mókyti 'teach'	: *mókytis* 'learn, study'
maitìnti 'feed, nourish'	: *maitìntis* 'feed on, take food'

The semantic relationship between a reflexive derivative and its underlying verb varies within broad limits, due to the polysemy of the reflexive marker. Reflexive verbs constitute a wide set of semantic and syntactic classes described in the following chapter.

REFLEXIVE VERBS

5.12 Verbs derived from verbal stems by means of the reflexive marker alone constitute the major class of reflexive verbs in Lithuanian. The reflexive marker may change the verbal meaning in a variety of ways, it is also a valence-changing derivational affix. Therefore, reflexive verbs are heterogeneous with respect to their semantic relations with the underlying verbs and, correspondingly, to changes in their syntactic properties. A number of regular syntactic and semantic types of reflexive verbs can be distinguished.

Reflexive verbs can be divided into the following principal types:

(1) Subjective reflexives termed so because they retain the subject of the underlying verb; the direct object of the latter is most frequently deleted, e.g.:

Àprengiau vaĩką.	'I dressed the child.'
– Apsìrengiau.	'I dressed myself.'

In some verbs, the direct object is demoted to an oblique object:

Vaikaĩ sváido ãkmenis.	'The children throw stones (ACC).'
– Vaikaĩ sváidosi akmenimìs.	'The children throw stones (INSTR).'

These reflexives are rather heterogenuous lexically, and they do not make up any distinct semantic types.

(2) Objective reflexives in which the direct object of the underlying verb becomes subject, while the original subject is deleted, as in:

Jiē viską pàkeitė.	'They changed everything.'
– Vìskas pasìkeitė.	'Everything (NOM) changed.'

or it is demoted to an oblique object:

Visùs žãvi vaikaĩ. 'The children (NOM) charm everybody (ACC).'
– *Visì žãvisi vaikaĩs.* 'Everybody (NOM) admires the children (INSTR).'

Both subjective and objective reflexives are derived from transitive verbs and undergo intransitivization, but their intransitivity is a result of different syntactic processes.

(3) **Transitive reflexives** which retain both the subject and direct object of the underlying verb: the reflexive affix marks deletion of the indirect object in the dative case:

Nupirkaũ sū́nui kepùrę. 'I bought (my) son a cap.'
– *Nusipirkaũ kepùrę.* 'I bought myself a cap.'

Transitive reflexives with the dative reflexive meaning 'for oneself' are as numerous as subjective and objective reflexives.

(4) Opposed to the above syntactic types are rather numerous reflexive verbs which retain the syntactic properties of the underlying verb. They are derived from some transitive and intransitive verbs. These verbs either retain their meaning or they aquire some additional sense; e.g.:

bijóti	*bijótis*	'be afraid'
įkvė̃pti	*įsikvė̃pti (óro)*	'inhale (some air)'
pakláusti	*pasikláusti*	'ask'
užtarnáuti	*užsitarnáuti*	'deserve, earn for oneself'
apžer̃gti	*apsižer̃gti*	'straddle'
sė́sti	*sė́stis*	'sit down'

5.13 The overwhelming majority of reflexive verbs, which are extremely numerous in Lithuanian, are derived from non-reflexive verbs by adding the clitic *s(i)* alone, as is described above. A considerable number of reflexives are derived by adding a prefix and the reflexive affix to an unprefixed verb, e.g.:

draugáuti 'be friends' : *susidraugáuti* 'become friends'
liepsnóti 'flame, blaze' : *užsiliepsnóti* 'flame up, flare up'
lýti 'rain' : *įsilýti* 'rain incessantly'

There are also reflexive verbs derived from nouns and adjectives by means of both a verb-forming suffix and the reflexive affix, e.g.:

svẽčias 'guest' : *svečiúotis* 'be a guest'
dárbas 'work' : *darbúotis* 'work, be engaged in work'
šakà 'branch' : *šakótis* 'branch out'
kuklùs 'modest' : *kùklintis* 'be over-modest'
bjaurùs 'nasty' : *bjaurė́tis* 'loath (regard as nasty)'
skaidrùs 'clear' : *skaĩdrytis* 'clear up/away'

A number of reflexive verbs are unrelated to any underlying verbs (or other words), i.e. **reflexiva tantum**, e.g.:

juõktis 'laugh'	*dairýtis* 'look around'
elĝtis 'behave'	*sténgtis* 'try, strive'
bastýtis 'wander, roam'	*teiráutis* 'inquire'

5.14 **Subjective reflexives with deleted object** fall into the following principal semantic groups:

(1) **Semantic reflexives** (or **reflexives proper**), i.e. reflexive verbs with the affix meaning 'oneself', e.g.:

mazgótis 'wash oneself'	*ginklúotis* 'arm oneself'
aukótis 'sacrifice oneself'	*gìntis* 'defend oneself'

In these verbs the reflexive affix denotes coreference of the semantic subject (Agent) and semantic object (Patient). They derive from verbs taking a human object.

(2) **Partitive-reflexive verbs** termed so because the reflexive affix denotes coreference of a partitive semantic object (usually a body-part or some possession or property of the Agent) with the semantic subject (the whole). These reflexives are derived from verbs taking a partitive object, cf.:

skùstis barzdą 'shave one's beard'	: *skùstis* 'shave oneself'
užmérkti akìs 'close one's eyes'	: *užsimérkti* 'close one's eyes'
išžeřgti kójas 'spread one's legs'	: *išsižeřgti* 'spread one's legs'
valdýti jausmùs 'control one's feelings'	: *valdýtis* 'control oneself'
užsègti márškinius 'button up one's shirt'	: *užsisègti* 'button up one's clothes'

A number of reflexives allow two interpretations, either as semantic reflexives or as partitive-reflexive verbs, e.g.:

praũstis 'wash oneself/one's face'
susižeĩsti 'hurt oneself/a body part'

(3) **'Absolute' reflexives**, in which the reflexive clitic marks deletion of the direct object without denoting any coreference; they often develop the modal-potential meaning and come to denote a habitual activity or permanent characteristic of the subject referent, as in:

vaĩkas mùšasi 'the boy fights (is pugnacious)'
arklỹs spárdosi 'the horse kicks (is in the habit of kicking)'

Here belong:

kéiktis 'swear'	*kìbintis* 'pester'
bártis 'curse'	*stùmdytis* 'jostle, push'
mėgdžiotis 'tease'	*badýtis* 'butt (of horned animals)' etc.

(4) **Self-moving, or autocausative reflexives** mostly denoting motion or change of posture of the semantic subject:

kéltis 'rise, get up' (cf. *kélti* 'raise (sth.)')
leñktis 'bend (down)'
spráustis 'squeeze oneself (into)'
sùktis 'whirl, turn'
artintis 'approach, come nearer'
veřstis 'turn (from side to side), roll down'
mèstis 'throw oneself'
slė̃ptis 'hide (oneself)'
išsitiẽsti 'draw oneself up, stretch oneself' etc.

These reflexives are intransitivized both syntactically and semantically, and they are similar in meaning to intransitive verbs of motion like *judė́ti* 'move', *bė́gti* 'run', *šókti* 'jump'.

(5) **Reciprocal reflexives**, with the derivational meaning 'each other':

bučiúotis 'kiss each other'	*apsikabìnti* 'embrace each other'
svéikintis 'greet each other'	*mùštis* 'fight, beat each other'
bártis 'quarrel'	*spárdytis* 'kick each other'

Some of the verbs double as reciprocals, when used with a plural subject, and absolute reflexives, when used with a singular subject, e.g.:

Vaikaĩ mùšasi.	'The boys are fighting.'
– *Vaĩkas mùšasi.*	'The boy is pugnacious.'
Mẽs visadà svéikinamės.	'We always say hello to each other.'
– *Jìs visadà svéikinasi.*	'He always says hello (is polite).'

5.15 **Objective reflexives with deleted subject** also fall into a number of semantic types of which the most numerous and semantically prominent are decausative reflexives, and also quasi-passive reflexives.

(1) **Decausative reflexives** are termed so because they lose the causative sense of the underlying verb, the reflexive affix serving as an anticausative marker. Decausative reflexives enter into the causative semantic opposition with the underlying verbs in the same way as primary intransitive verbs with their causative derivatives (e.g. *áugti* 'grow' : *augìnti* 'grow (sth)') and verbs with apophonic vowel alternation (e.g. *lū́žti* 'break' : *láužti* 'break (sth)'), cf.:

Ùždegiau šviẽsą.	'I turned on the lights.'
– *Šviesà užsìdegė.*	'The lights came on.'

Here the transitive verb *uždègti* 'cause to start burning' is the causative counterpart of the reflexive *užsidègti* 'start burning'.

Decausative reflexive verbs may denote states, processes (both spontaneous and induced), and actions.

The following verbs illustrate the lexical range of this semantic type of reflexives:

atsidarýti 'open (intr.)'	*baidýtis* 'get frightened'
kartótis 'repeat itself'	*jáudintis* 'worry'
keĩstis 'change'	*įsižeĩsti* 'be offended'
kūréntis 'burn (of a stove)'	*rūstintis* 'be angry'
líetis 'pour, flow'	*nusivìlti* 'be disappointed'
pìldytis 'come true'	*ramìntis* 'calm down'
plė̃stis 'dilate, spread'	*užsigáuti* 'take offence'
taisýtis 'improve'	*kankìntis* 'suffer'
kaũptis 'accumulate'	*nusivarýti* 'get tired out'
výstytis 'develop'	*rikiúotis* 'line up'
rìstis 'roll'	*riñktis* 'come together'
sklaidýtis 'clear away, lift (of fog, etc.)'	*jùngtis* 'unite'
tę̃stis 'continue, last'	*spiẽstis* 'gather, come together'
sùktis 'rotate, turn'	*skìrstytis* 'disperse', etc.

Quite a number of reflexive decausatives enter into triads like *kìsti* 'change' (intr.) – *keĩsti* 'change' (tr.) – *keĩstis* 'change' (intr.), *liñkti* 'bend' (intr.) – *leñkti* 'bend' (tr.) – *leñktis* 'bend' (intr.), *mažė́ti* 'become small(er)' – *mãžinti* 'make smaller' – *mãžintis* 'become smaller'.

In these triads both intransitives enter into a causative opposition with the transitive verbs, while between themselves they may differ in lexical meaning and combinability to a greater or lesser degree (cf. *plìsti* 'spread' – *plė̃stis* 'expand'). The intransitive verbs with apophonic alternation in the root mostly denote spontaneous changes in the non-animate subjects whereas the corresponding reflexive verbs express the changes induced through the effort of animate (usually human) subjects, cf.:

Mẽdžiai liñko nuo sniẽgo.	'The trees bent under the snow.'
– Lenkiúosi jùms ligi žẽmės.	'I bow low before you.'
Jaũ kỹla rū̃kas.	'A mist is rising already.'
– Duktė̃ dár tik kẽliasi.	'My daughter is getting up yet.'

However, sometimes the reflexive verbs are very similar in meaning to their non-reflexive intransitive counterparts, e.g.:

Vìskas kiñta / keĩčiasi.	'Everything changes.'

(2) **Quasi-passive reflexives** enter into specific semantic relations with the underlying verbs:

(a) *Užrakìnk durìs!*   'Lock the door!'
– *Dùrys lengvaĩ rakìnasi.*   'The door locks easily.'

(b) *Išeikvójau daũg pinigų̃.*   'I (have) spent much money.'
– *Daũg pinigų̃ išsieikvójo.*   'Much money got spent.'

These reflexives are termed quasi-passive because they always imply a human agent (though it may be unexpressed) and sometimes they can be paraphrased by a passive construction, e.g.:

Vìsos kráutuvės užsidãrė/bùvo uždarýtos.   'All shops were closed.'

In cases like (a) quasi-passive reflexives acquire the modal potential meaning and characterize the subject referent; they occur, as a rule, with qualitative adverbials (*geraĩ* 'well', *lengvaĩ* 'easily', *suñkiai* 'with difficulty', etc.) or with negation. In cases like (b) they acquire the modal sense 'unexpectedly', 'by chance'. In the latter case the verb occurs in the past tense with the perfect meaning. The following sentences also illustrate the use of quasi-passive reflexives:

Nósinės greĩtai tẽpasi.   'Handkerchiefs get dirty fast.'

Peřkelis geraĩ dẽvisi.   'Cotton wears well (i.e. lasts a long time without showing damage).'

Tà vielà nesilañksto.   'This wire does not bend (is not flexible).'

Muĩlas greĩt susimuĩlijo.   'The soap got used up fast.'

Bãtai nusiavėjo.   'The shoes got worn out.'

5.16 **Objective reflexives with demoted subject** comprise two important, though not numerous semantic types of verbs:

(1) **Converse reflexives**, in which the reflexive affix marks lexical converseness, e.g.:

Ẽžeras atspiñdi dañgų.   'The lake (NOM) reflects the sky (ACC).'
– *Dangùs atsispiñdi ežerè.*   'The sky (NOM) is reflected in the lake (LOC).'
Girdžiù mùziką.   'I (NOM) hear music (ACC).'
– *Man gir̃disi/girdė́ti mùzika.*   'I (DAT) can hear music (NOM).'

Converse reflexives are rather heterogeneous lexically; here also belong:

vainikúotis 'be crowned with (fig.)'
sapnúotis 'appear in a dream'
nusivìlti 'be disappointed'
susivilióti 'be tempted'
žavĕtis 'be charmed'

(2) Reflexive-causative verbs are related to the underlying verb in the following way:

Sēnis samdė darbininkùs.	'The old man (NOM) hired labourers (ACC).'
– *Darbiniñkai pasisamdė pas sēnį.*	'Labourers (NOM) hired themselves out to a farmer (Prep – ACC).'
Kirpėja manè apkir̃po.	'The barber (NOM) gave me (ACC) a haircut.'
– *Aš apsikirpaũ pas kirpėją.* '	I (NOM) had my hair cut at the barber's (Prep – ACC).'

Reflexive-causative verbs are derived from verbs of professional activities and they acquire the causative meaning of initiating the action named by the underlying verb. Here belong:

skùstis 'get a shave'
gýdytis 'undergo treatment'
registrúotis 'register oneself'
fotografúotis 'have one's photo taken'

5.17 **Transitive reflexives** with indirect object deletion acquire the dative-reflexive meaning 'for oneself' (cf. 5.12(3)). This meaning signifies coreference of the subject and dative object: *nusipir̃kti* = *nupir̃kti sáu* 'buy (for) oneself'. Dative transitive reflexives are extremely numerous and widely used.

The following subtypes can be distinguished:

(1) reflexives of dressing derived from verbs with an obligatory dative object according to the pattern *uždėti vaĩkui kepùrę* lit. 'put on a cap (ACC) to the child (DAT)':

užsivil̃kti páltą 'put on a coat'
aũtis 'put on (shoes)'
nusiaũti 'take off (shoes)'
nusivil̃kti 'take off (a coat and the like)'
užsimáuti 'put on (gloves, etc.)'
nusimáuti 'take off (gloves, etc.)'

(2) reflexive-possessive verbs like:

praũstis véidą	'wash one's face'
valýtis dantìs	'clean one's teeth'
susitèpti rankàs	'dirty one's hands'
įsipjáuti pir̃štą	'cut one's finger', etc.

(in this case the possessive relationship between subject and object is obligatorily marked);

(3) reflexive-benefactive verbs derived from verbs with an optional dative object:

nusipir̃kti 'buy for oneself'
pasidarýti 'make for oneself'
statýtis 'build for oneself'
užsirašýti 'write down (for oneself, one's own sake)'
mègztis 'knit for oneself'
prašýtis 'beg for oneself'

This subset is particularly numerous and varied with respect to the range of lexical meanings.

ASPECTUAL DIFFERENCES

5.18 Aspect is a semantic category of the Lithuanian verb expressed by derivational means, mainly by prefixation. Two aspectual meanings are distinguished: perfective and imperfective. The perfective aspect (*įvykio véikslas*) comprises the notion of completed action with an implication of its limit or achieved result. The imperfective aspect (*eigõs véikslas*) lacks this meaning; it views an action in its continuation.

5.19 **The perfective meaning** is mainly characteristic of prefixed verbs. Many prefixed verbs, especially in the past and future tense forms, carry the meaning of a completed action and in this respect they are contrasted with the unprefixed verbs, cf.:

rašiaũ 'I was writing'   : *parašiaũ* 'I wrote/have written'
stačiaũ 'I was building'   : *pastačiaũ* 'I built/have built'
baudžiaũ 'I was punishing'   : *nùbaudžiau* 'I punished'
gélbėjau 'I was rescuing'   : *išgélbėjau* 'I rescued/have rescued'
výkdžiau 'I was accomplishing' : *įvýkdžiau* 'I accomplished/have accomplished'

The prefix *pa-* is the most common perfectivizing prefix. Other prefixes also often add to the verb a meaning of limit or result of action, cf.: *láužti* 'break' : *atláužti* 'break off', *dègti* 'burn (intr.)' : *sudègti* 'burn up' etc. In the case of intransitive process verbs the unprefixed verb usually denotes a process in its progress while the prefixed derivative denotes the completed process, e.g.:

bálti 'be growing white'   : *išbálti* 'become white'
nókti 'be ripening'   : *prinókti* 'become ripe'

skę̃sti 'be drowning' : *nuskę̃sti / paskę̃sti* 'be drowned'
mažė́ti 'be growing small(er)' : *sumažė́ti* 'become small'

However, there are few 'purely' perfective-imperfective pairs of prefixed vs. unprefixed verbs in Lithuanian like *darýti* : *padarýti* 'make'. The perfectivizing prefixes usually modify the lexical meaning of the verb in a variety of ways. The prefixed verbs can denote the beginning of an action (cf.: *dainúoti* 'sing' : *uždainúoti* 'begin to sing', *sir̃gti* 'be ill' : *susir̃gti* 'fall ill'), the single event (*bučiúoti* 'kiss' : *pabučiúoti* 'give a kiss', *žvel̃gti* 'look' : *pažvel̃gti* 'cast a glance'), the renewing (repeating) of an action (*kùrti* 'create' : *atkùrti* 'recreate, renew'; *rašýti* 'write' : *pérrašyti* 'rewrite'), etc.

An unprefixed verb may have a number of prefixed derivatives each having a perfective sense together with other different meanings, cf.:

dìrbti 'work' : *nudìrbti* 'accomplish some work'
                             išdìrbti 'spend some time working'
                             sudìrbti 'spoil, discredit'

rū́gti 'grow sour' : *išrū́gti* 'turn sour, finish fermenting'
                             parū́gti 'become somewhat (a little) sour, ferment (for some time)'
                             pérrūgti 'turn sour (all through, entirely)'
                             surū́gti 'become sour'

The perfective-imperfective contrast is often expressed by the opposition of tense forms. Many verbs with prefixes denoting the direction or modifying the verbal meaning in some other way, have a perfective meaning in past and future tense forms but they are imperfective in the present, cf.:

ateinù 'I am coming'	*atė́jau* 'I came)'	*ateĩsiu* 'I will come'
įnešù 'I am bringing in'	*įnẽšiau* 'I brought in'	*įnèšiu* 'I will bring in'
apžiūriù 'I am inspecting'	*apžiūrė́jau* 'I inspected'	*apžiūrė́siu* 'I will inspect'
uždaraũ 'I am closing'	*uždariaũ* 'I closed'	*uždarýsiu* 'I will close'

There is also a group of unprefixed verbs of dual aspectual character, e.g. *mir̃ti* 'die', *gìmti* 'be born', *dùrti* 'thrust, prick', *ràsti* 'find', *laimė́ti* 'win', *baĩgti* 'finish'. The aspectual meaning of these verbs also depends on the tense form and context: their present tense form is imperfective and the simple past and future tense forms are either perfective (mostly) or imperfective according to context, e.g.:

Jìs mìršta.	'He dies, is dying (IMPF).'
Mergáitė mìrė vãkar.	'The girl died (PF) yesterday.'
Žmónės mìrė kasdiẽn.	'People died (IMPF) every day.'

5.20 **The imperfective meaning** is most characteristic of unprefixed verbs, e.g.: *árti* 'plough', *dìrbti* 'work', *lýti* 'rain', *láukti* 'wait', *nèšti* 'carry', *pìlti* 'pour', *pìnti* 'weave', *tráukti* 'pull', *švìlpti* 'whistle', *vèžti* 'carry, drive', *žiūrėti* 'look', *žaĩsti* 'play', and a host of others. All tense forms of such verbs are imperfective.

The verbs derived by means of suffixes are usually imperfective, because the suffixes (except *-el(ė)-ti/-er(ė)-ti*) have imperfectivizing force, e.g.:

braukýti 'wipe, brush away (repeatedly)'	(: *braũkti* 'wipe, brush away')
nešióti 'carry (repeatedly), wear'	(: *nèšti* 'carry, bear')
švilpáuti 'whistle (repeatedly, slightly)'	(: *švil̃pti* 'whistle')
šū́kauti 'shout (repeatedly, for some time)'	(: *šaũkti* 'shout')
mė́tyti 'throw, fling (repeatedly)'	(: *mèsti* 'throw (once)')
sūpúoti 'rock (gently; for some time)'	(: *sùpti* 'rock, swing')
šokinė́ti 'jump (repeatedly), hop'	(: *šókti* 'jump, leap (once or repeatedly)')
žvilgčioti 'glance (repeatedly), look (from time to time)'	(: *žvel̃gti* 'glance, cast a glance')
lū́kuriuoti 'wait patiently, tarry'	(: *láukti* 'wait')

As we see, in most cases the suffixed verbs acquire the imperfective meanings of iterativity, or duration, or state. The only perfectivizing suffix is *-er(ė)ti/-el(ė)ti* with momentary meaning, e.g.:

šū́ktelėti	'utter a cry'
trìnktelėti	'bang, slam (once)'
žvìlgterėti	'cast a glance'

Among prefixed verbs, the imperfective aspect is characteristic of those which do not occur without a prefix (e.g.: *pāsakoti* 'tell (about), narrate', *prieštaráuti* 'object', *užgaulióti* 'offend, insult', *uždarbiáuti* 'earn a living') or whose lexical meaning is quite different from that of the unprefixed counterpart, e.g.:

padė́ti 'help'	(: *dė́ti* 'put, place')
priklausýti 'depend'	(: *klausýti* 'listen')
apsieĩti 'manage (without)'	(: *eĩti* 'walk, go')
atsidúoti 'smell (of)'	(: *dúoti* 'give')
užjaũsti 'sympathize (with)'	(: *jaũsti* 'feel')
sutar̃ti 'get on (with smb)'	(cf. *tar̃ti* 'say')

The prefixed verbs denoting the ability to perform the action are imperfective in all the tense forms, e.g.:

paeĩti	'be able to walk'
paskaitýti	'be able to read'
nusėdė́ti	'be able to keep one's seat', etc.

Verbs with the suffix *-inė-ti* derived from prefixed verbs are also imperfective. Due to its iterative meaning this suffix is often used as means of secondary imperfectivization: it ascribes the imperfective meaning to the prefixed verbs, which are usually perfective in the past and future tense forms, e.g.:

atidavinėti 'give back, return repeatedly'	(: *atidúoti* 'give back, return')
atleidinėti 'dismiss repeatedly'	(: *atléisti* 'dismiss')
pažeidinėti 'violate repeatedly'	(: *pažeĩsti* 'violate')
supirkinėti 'buy up repeatedly'	(: *supir̃kti* 'buy up')
užpuldinėti 'attack repeatedly'	(: *užpùlti* 'attack')

Morphological categories of the verb
TENSE
Laĩkas

5.21 The category of tense finds expression in sets of verbal forms marking the different time relation of the action, process or state to the moment of speech or to another point or period of time indicated in the sentence. Accordingly, there are three main tense groups in Lithuanian: present, past and future.

Depending on whether the tense forms are formed with the help of endings or with the help of auxiliaries, Lithuanian tenses are said to be simple or compound. Simple tenses are four in number:

Present:	*dìrba* 'works'
Past:	*dìrbo* 'worked'
Past frequentative:	*dìrbdavo* 'used to work'
Future:	*dir̃bs* 'will work'

All the simple tenses belong to the active voice. Compound tenses can be found both in the active and in the passive voice. In the active two groups of compound tenses can be distinguished:

(**1**) the perfect tenses:

Present perfect:	*yrà dìrbęs, dìrbusi* 'has worked'
Past perfect:	*bùvo dìrbęs, dìrbusi* 'had worked'
Past perfect frequentative:	*bū́davo dìrbęs, dìrbusi* 'used to have worked'
Future perfect:	*bùs dìrbęs, dìrbusi* 'will have worked'

(**2**) the continuative tenses:

Past continuative:	*bùvo bedìrbąs, bedìrbanti* 'had been working'

238   MORPHOLOGY

Past continuative frequentative: *bū́davo bedìrbąs, bedìrbanti* 'used to have been working'

Future continuative: *bùs bedìrbąs, bedìrbanti* 'will have been working'

The compound passive tenses are also divided into two groups:

(1) the imperfect tenses:

Present imperfect: *yrà dãromas, dãroma* 'is (being) done'
Past imperfect: *bùvo dãromas, dãroma* 'was (being) done'
Past imperfect frequentative: *bū́davo dãromas, dãroma* 'used to be done'
Future imperfect: *bùs dãromas, dãroma* 'will be done'

(2) the perfect tenses:

Present perfect: *yrà padarýtas, padarýta* 'is done', 'has been done'
Past perfect: *bùvo padarýtas, padarýta* 'was done', 'had been done'
Past perfect frequentative: *bū́davo padarýtas, padarýta* 'used to be done', 'used to have been done'
Future perfect: *bùs padarýtas, padarýta* 'will be done', 'will have been done'

Tense forms can be found both in the indicative mood and in the oblique mood. The participles and gerunds have tense forms as well.

The participles and gerunds of the verb *dìrbti* 'work':

Tense forms of active participles:

Present: *dìrbąs* (m), *dìrbanti* (f); *dìrbdamas* (m), *dirbdamà* (f)
Past: *dìrbęs* (m), *dìrbusi* (f)
Past frequentative: *dìrbdavęs* (m), *dìrbdavusi* (f)
Future: *dìrbsiąs* (m), *dìrbsianti* (f)

Tense forms of passive participles:

Present: *dìrbamas, dirbamà*
Past: *dìrbtas, dirbtà*

Tense forms of gerunds:

Present: *dìrbant*
Past: *dìrbus*
Past frequentative: *dìrbdavus*
Future: *dìrbsiant*

5.22 All verbal tense forms are grouped according to their basic meaning. The past and past frequentative forms indicate a state of affairs or an event which existed or took place prior to the moment of speech. They are clearly opposed to the present and future forms which do not possess this meaning. Thus, the past tense forms are considered to be the marked members while the present and future tense forms the unmarked members of the basic tense opposition.

The present and future tense forms, in their turn, are opposed to each other in that the future forms denote an action following the moment of speech whereas the present tense does not possess this meaning, being the absolute unmarked member of all tense oppositions. It is most often used to denote an existing state of affairs, although sometimes it can also be used with future or past tense reference.

The opposition between the past and the past frequentative tenses is based on their aspectual rather than temporal differences: the frequentative forms (containing the suffix -*dav*-) indicate a repetitive (or frequentative) action in the past while the past – the unmarked member of the opposition – can be used to denote either a single or a (sometimes) repetitive event.

Relationships in the system of the simple tense forms are shown in the Figure below.

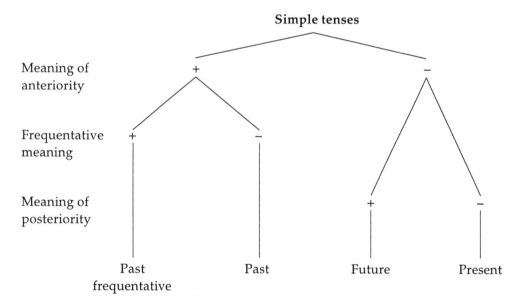

5.23 In each tense we can find both simple and compound forms.

Compound tense forms of the active voice refer the event to present, past or future time with respect to the main time of the context rather than to the moment of speech. Thus, compound perfect tenses indicate a state which, having resulted from a previous event, is simultaneous with the main time of the context. Compound continuative tenses indicate an event which is simultaneous with the main time of the context, but is of a longer duration since it started earlier.

Simple tense forms constitute the unmarked member of the opposition. They can indicate a period of time in relation to the moment of speech or to the main time reference of the context. Certain simple tense forms (the past forms in particular) tend to supersede their respective compound tenses, driving them little by little out of use.

The differences in the meaning of simple and compound tense forms are shown in the Figure below.

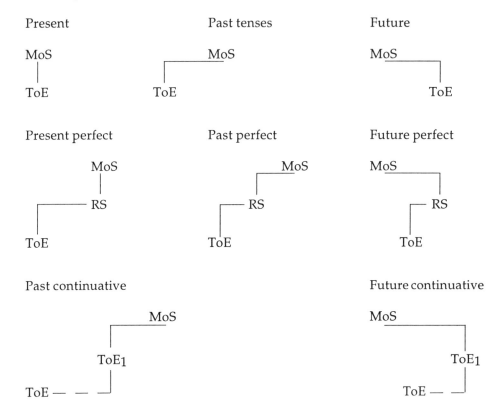

MoS – moment of speech; ToE – time of the event; RS – resulting state coincident with the main time of the context; ToE$_1$ – time of the event coincident with the main time of the context.

The compound present perfect holds a unique place among Lithuanian tense forms. It indicates a period of time stretching backwards from the moment of speech, but like all the other perfect tenses the present perfect tense also denotes a state which has resulted from some previous event and is simultaneous with the main time of the context or the moment of speech. The present perfect tense is usually used in the context of the simple present tense forms.

The compound tenses of the passive voice constitute an opposition to the simple tenses of the active voice. In their meanings passive tense forms correspond to the respective simple and compound tense forms of the active voice.

5.24 Tense meanings defined in relation to the moment of speech are known as absolute tense meanings, whereas those defined in relation to another event in the context are known as relative tense meanings.

Simple tense forms usually possess absolute tense meanings.

Išnýksiu kaip dū́mas, neblā̃škomas vė́jo, ir niẽkas manę̃s neminė̃s.	'I'll vanish like smoke without being scattered by the wind, and nobody will ever mention me again.'
Tíek tū́kstančių ámžiais gyvẽno, kentė́jo, o kàs jų̃ bent var̃dą atspė̃s?	'So many thousand have lived and suffered through ages, whoever can guess as much as their names?'
Kaip bañgos ant mãrių, kaip miñtys žmogaũs, taip maĩnos pasáulio darbaĩ!	'The deeds of the world change like waves on the sea, like human thoughts!'

A relative meaning is characteristic of simple tenses when they are used in subordinate clauses (or in corresponding asyndetic clauses). The present tense with the relative meaning indicates coincidence with the time denoted in the principal clause:

Vakarè sužinójau, kad atvažiúoja nekviestì svečiaĩ.	'In the evening I learnt that uninvited guests were coming.'
Rytój pamatýsi, kad jaũ lỹja.	'The next day you'll see it is raining.'

The past tense with the relative meaning indicates a time which precedes the time denoted in the principal clause:

Tik tadà mán paaiškė́jo, kodė̃l jìs taĩp el̃gėsi.	'Only then did it become clear to me why he had behaved like that.'
Mótina niekadà nekláusdavo, kur̃ jìs bùvo.	'Mother never asked where he had been.'

The future tense with the relative meaning indicates a time following that which is denoted in the principal clause:

Niekadà netikė́jau, kad tù manè išdúosi.	'I never believed you were going to betray me.'

| *Kar̃tais mán atródydavo, kad niẽko iš tõ nebùs.* | 'Sometimes I thought nothing would ever come of it.' |

5.25 The meaning of the compound tenses is always relative, although in a slightly different way (cf. 5.36–37) since it is related to the meaning of the respective simple tenses. Compound perfect tenses indicate anteriority with respect to the time denoted by a simple tense form.

Jìs válgo, ką̃ yrà atsinẽšęs iš namų̃.	'He eats what he has brought from home.'
Jìs válgė, ką̃ bùvo atsinẽšęs iš namų̃.	'He ate what he had brought from home.'
Jìs válgydavo, ką̃ bū́davo atsinẽšęs iš namų̃.	'He used to eat what he had brought from home.'
Jìs válgys, ką̃ bùs atsinẽšęs iš namų̃.	'He will eat what he will have brought from home.'

Compound perfect tenses (the present perfect tense in particular) can also denote the relation of the state resulting from an earlier action to the action denoted by a simple tense form.

| *Àš žinójau, kad jìs yrà jaũ pasireñgęs važiúoti.* | 'I knew he was ready to go.' |
| *Kai kareĩviai apsùpo namùs, jìs jaũ bùvo išvažiãvęs.* | 'By the time the soldiers surrounded the house, he had already gone.' |

Compound continuative tenses indicate an action concurrent with the action denoted by a simple tense form, except that it is of a longer duration since it starts earlier:

| *Kai mẽs atẽjome, jìs bùvo ùž stãlo besė́dįs.* | 'When we came he had already been sitting at the table.' |

5.26 For stylistic purposes tenses can be used with time reference which is not typical of them. Thus, for example, the simple present tense can be used with past time reference (historical present) to make a story seem more vivid:

| *Ilgaĩ ėjaũ pāmiškė. Staigà žiūriù – tùpi kìškis ant kélmo ir daĩrosi.* | 'For a long time I was following the edge of the forest. Suddenly I see a hare sitting on a tree stump, looking around.' |

The simple future tense can be used to indicate a repetitive (frequentative) action (1) in the present, or (2) in the past:

(1) *Keistì dabař žmónės: nepasi-* 'People are strange nowadays:
kalbės, nepasitařs su kìts kitù, they will not talk or discuss
kaip prìdera. things with each other as they should.'

(2) *Sēnis Lãpinas klaũsė ir juõ-* 'Old Lapinas listened and smiled to
kėsi sáu po ũsais. Klausỹs, klau- himself under his moustache. He would
sỹs ir pridẽs sàvo žodėlį. listen and listen and add a word of his
  own.'

The past frequentative tense is never used to replace other tenses with different time reference.

Compound tenses are very rarely used with time reference which is not typical of them. If they are, they usually go together with simple tenses:

Jìs kasdiēn sẽdi sàvo kambarỹ. 'Every day he sits in his room.
Sėdẽs taĩp nuo pat rýto, rašỹs, He will sit since morning like
o iki vãkaro vìs bùs ką̃ parãšęs. this, write and by the evening he will
  have written something.'

Simple tenses
Vientisìniai laikaĩ

PRESENT
Esamàsis laĩkas

5.27 There are two main uses of the present tense: the generalized present and the concrete present.

The concrete present indicates a particular, individual event the relation of which to the moment of speech can be different.

(1) Most often the present tense indicates a state of affairs or an action which includes the moment of speech but has started before it and may continue for some time in the near future (this meaning is characteristic of the imperfective verbs only):

Ar tù sergì, kad taĩp dejúoji? 'Are you ill that you are moaning like this?'

(2) The present tense signifies an event which is taking place only at the moment of speech while in the process of (a) saying or writing the verb, (b) performing the action here and now:

(a) *Tè, dovanóju táu ir áukso* 'Here, I give you a gold and
bei sidãbro kir̃vį. silver axe as a present.'

(b) *Užsìimu ausìs, mataĩ!*   'I am blocking my ears, look!'

(3) The present tense indicates an action or process which is not happening right at the moment of speech because:

(a) a short break has been made:

Àš tik trumpám. Kol árklius pamainỹs. Mataĩ, pas gìmines Rygõn važiúoju.	'I'm here for a sec. While they change horses. See, I'm travelling to visit my relations in Riga.'

(b) the action has just ended:

Kaĩp čià patekaĩ? – Tė́vo sių̃stas ateinù... Nešù iš jõ láišką.	'How did you find your way here? – I'm coming on my father's mission... I'm bringing a letter from him.'

(c) the action has not started yet:

Už savái̇̃tės àš ìšteku...   'In a week's time I'm getting married...'

When referring to a future happening the 1st and 2nd person plural forms of the present tense acquire a meaning similar to that of the imperative mood, except that the order, instruction or advice to act is expressed in this case even more strongly than by the imperative form proper.

Lēkiam, lēkiam greičiaũ, mielóji!	'Let's dash, dear, quick!'
Atsiminkite: šiąnakt jū̃s bùdite.	'Remember: tonight you're on duty.'

Third person forms of the present tense may indicate a wished for event, but only in certain set expressions.

Ìma jį̃ gãlas!   'Let it (him) perish!'

But when the third person forms of the present tense are used with the prefix *te-* or the particle *tegu(l)*, they always carry the meaning of a wished for event.

Tepasidžiaũgia sūneliù patì!	'Let her enjoy her sonny!'
Tegù jìs nemãno, kad mẽs nusiléisime.	'Let him never think we are going to give in.'

(4) The present tense is used in descriptions to make them more vivid, e.g.:

O po kójų žemaĩ stebuklìngai gražì žýdi rõžėmis Álpių šalìs.	'Down below our feet the wonderfully beautiful Alpine land is covered with roses.'

For the sake of vividness the present tense can also be used to describe past events. It is usually used while discussing what happens in a book, picture, play or film.

Pavéiksle jaunà móteris žvel̃gia   'From the picture a young woman is
į mùs didelėmìs, liūdnomìs akimìs.   looking at us with her big sad eyes.
Ant jōs rañkų miẽga kūdikis.   A baby is sleeping in her arms.'

5.28 The generalized present tense usually indicates:

(**1**) universal time statements:

Vėliaũ mókslininkai įródė, kad iš   'Later scientists proved that the Earth
tikrųjų Žẽmė sùkasi apie sàvo ãšį   really rotates round its axis and at
ir kartù skríeja aplink Sáulę.   the same time it flies round the Sun.'

(**2**) habitual time statements:

Antanùkas ir miẽga su senelè vienõj   'Antanukas also sleeps with his granny
lóvoj. Kadà jì gùla ir kẽliasi,   in the same bed. Antanukas rarely feels,
Antanùkas retaĩ tejuñta.   when she goes to bed or gets up.'

PAST

Būtàsis kartìnis laĩkas

5.29 The past tense is used to describe both single (1) and regularly repeated (2) events:

(**1**) *Móterims besìkalbant, kiemè*   'While the women were talking, they
pasigir̃do žiñgsniai, prasivér̃ė   heard the sound of footsteps in the yard,
dùrys ir ant sleñksčio pasiródė   the door opened and a neighbour
kaimýnas.   appeared on the threshold.'

(**2**) *Iš atliẽkamo píeno móterys*   'From surplus milk women churned
sùko svíestą, spáudė sūrį ir vėžė   butter, pressed cheese and
į miẽstą pardúoti.   took (those goods) to town to sell.'

The past tense can also indicate limitless events or states:

Píevas ir ežerẽlį sùpo aukštì   'Steep banks surrounded the
krantaĩ.   meadows and the little lake.'

5.30 The past tense usually denotes:

(1) an action which was taking place for some time in the past (forms of the imperfective verbs):

Bùvo vėjúotas rudeñs vãkaras.   'It was a windy autumnal evening. All the
Visà šeimýna triūsėsi pir̃kioje.   family were busy inside the house.'

(2) an action which was completed at a certain moment in the past (forms of the perfective verbs):

Staigà kiemè sulójo šuõ, ir į piřkią įsìveržė kēletas výrų.	'Suddenly the dog barked in the yard and several men burst into the house.'

5.31 Sometimes the past tense (especially of verbs in the perfective aspect) becomes similar in its meaning to (1) compound present perfect or (2) past perfect tenses (cf. 5.36).

(1) *Màno gerklē visái išdžiúvo* (cf. *yrà išdžiūvusi*), *dúokite gérti.*	'My throat is absolutely dry (cf. has become dry), give me something to drink.'
(2) *Šeštādienio vãkarą jìs rãdo netikėtą svečią: atvažiãvo* (cf. *bùvo atvažiãvęs*) *brólis.*	'On Saturday evening he found an unexpected visitor: his brother had arrived.'

The past tense (mostly the 1st and 2nd person forms) can also have certain modal shades of meaning, being related then to the attitudes of the speaker rather than to time. Thus, it can imply uncertainty, doubt, timidity, politeness associated with the present state of affairs:

Valandėlę norėjau támstą sutrukdýti.	lit. 'I wanted to bother you a little' (i.e. 'I wondered if I could bother you a little.')

PAST FREQUENTATIVE
Būtàsis dažnìnis laĩkas

5.32 The past frequentative tense indicates a repeated action in the past. The longer the period in which the repeated action took place the more general is the meaning of the past frequentative tense.

Visaĩp atsitìkdavo Kaukāzo kalnuosè: kariáudavo kaimýninės taũtos, susipèšdavo gìminės.	'All kinds of things used to happen in the Caucasian mountains: neighbouring nations would war, related families would quarrel.'
Kasdiēn eĩdavau tavęs pasitìkti, láukdavau ìlgas vãlandas.	'Every day I went to meet you, waited for you long hours.'

If the sentence contains the indication of at least an approximately limited number of times the action was repeated, the past rather than the past frequentative should be used:

| *Trìs/kelìs kartùs jau veřkė jì* | 'She has already cried three/ |
| (not *veřkdavo), *būdamà vienà.* | several times while alone.' |

Sometimes the past frequentative tense is used to talk about habitual actions (processes, states) in the past:

| *O senóvėje, kaip pāsakoja mū́sų* | 'In the past, as our parents |
| *tėvaĩ, dár geriaũ bū́davo.* | say, it used to be even better.' |

In certain contexts the simple past frequentative tense becomes similar in its meaning to the past perfect frequentative tense.

Motùtė sutìkdavo sakýti tą̃ pãsaką	'Mummy would agree to tell me
tik tadà, kadà àš prisižadė́davau (cf.	this fairy-tale only after I
bū́davau prisižadė́jęs) *neraudóti.*	had promised not to cry.'

FUTURE
Būsimàsis laĩkas

5.33 The future tense is used to denote both (1) a concrete action which will take place at some specific time in the future, and (2) a generalized action in the future.

(1) *Netrùkus ateĩs pavãsaris, su-*	'Spring will come soon, the
žaliuõs mẽdžiai, o tavę̃s nebùs.	trees will become green, but you will
	not be here any more.'

| (2) *Pasáulis platùs – viẽtos už-* | 'The world is large, there'll be |
| *tèks visíems.* | plenty of room for everybody.' |

In certain contexts the simple future tense becomes similar in meaning to the compound future perfect tense.

Nãmą pradė́siu statýti už mė́nesio,	'I'll begin to build the house
kai leidìmą gáusiu (cf. *bū́siu*	in a month after I have
gãvęs).	received the permission.'

5.34 The future tense is apt to acquire a variety of modal meanings. It can be used to express certainty or prediction that the action is going to take place; determination, threat or promise to perform an action; necessity that it shoud happen; a possibility that it may happen, etc. Sometimes the future tense becomes similar in meaning to the imperative (1) or the subjunctive (2):

| (1) *Pérduosi* (cf. *pérduok*) | 'To the insurgents you will |
| *sukilė́liams šìtokį įsãkymą.* | pass the following order.' |

(2) *Kad šìrdį paródyčiau, ir taĩ sakýsi* (cf. *sakýtum*), *kad mėsõs gãbalas.*   'Even if I showed you my heart, you'll say it is a piece of flesh.'

The future tense can also be used to express:

(a) the uncertainty or doubt about a present action or state:

Nuo tõ laĩko jau bùs kẽturios dẽšimtys mẽtų su viršum̃.   'Since then over two score years must have passed.'

(b) the speaker's displeasure at the action, his wish that it should be terminated:

Tai tù čià ilgaĩ sėdėsi be dárbo?   'Are you going to sit here long without work?'

Compound tenses
Sudėtìniai laikaĩ

ACTIVE VOICE
Veikiamóji rū́šis

The compound perfect tenses
Sudėtìniai atliktìniai laikaĩ

5.35 There are four compound perfect tenses:

present perfect,
past perfect,
past perfect frequentative,
future perfect.

Both the perfective and imperfective verbs have the compound tense forms.

Compound perfect tenses denote a state resulting from a previous action which is relevant at a certain moment in the present, past or future. In their meaning Lithuanian compound perfect tenses are similar to the perfect tenses in some other languages (e.g., Latin).

In different contexts the meaning of the perfect tenses may range from (1) concrete to (2) broadly general.

(1) *Kažkàs namiẽ yrà nakvójęs – lóva nepaklotà.*   'Somebody must have slept at home, the bed has not been made.'

(2) *Esù apkeliãvęs vìsą pasáulį*   'I have travelled all over the
ir daũg kraštų mãtęs.   world and have seen many countries.'

The general meaning is mostly characteristic of the imperfective verbs.

5.36 The meaning of the perfect tenses can be described as both resultative and relative. While denoting a state resulting from a previous action, they also indicate the relation of the state to its cause – the previous action. The relative meaning of the perfect tenses becomes clear in the context of the simple tenses, since their action always precedes that expressed by a simple tense (it is only the resultative state which is concurrent with the action of the simple tenses). Therefore the compound perfect tenses are often used together with the simple tenses to indicate the relation between two or more actions in a compound or complex sentence.

The past perfect tense is different from the other perfect tenses in that under certain circumstances it may denote a resultative state which lasted for some time in the past and then was discontinued.

Buvaũ pamiřšęs, brólis prāšė táu   'I forgot (lit. 'had forgotten'), my brother
pérduoti šį láišką.   has asked me to give you this letter.'

Sometimes the meaning of a resultative state fades out and then the past perfect tense denotes a past action which was superseded by another explicit or implicit action.

Buvaũ mãnęs táu niẽko nesa-   'I had intended not to tell you anything,
kýti, bet dabař pasakýsiu.   but now I'm going to tell you.'

Ar buvaĩ užė́jęs pas Jõną?   'Have you called (lit. 'Had you called')
    on John?'

The future perfect tense very often has a modal meaning: it expresses supposition and then it is used instead of the present perfect tense.

Juk bū́si (cf. *esì*) *girdė́jusi,*   'You must (lit. will) have heard
kad jìs tuōs namùs nusipiřkęs.   that he has bought that house.'

Ar nebùs tik vaikaĩ lángo išmùšę?   'It looks as if the children have (lit. 'would
    have') broken the window.'

Sometimes the future perfect tense is used to indicate a state which is taking place at the moment of speech, but the speaker attributes it to the future.

– *Dabař bū́siu ir vil̃ką mãtęs, –*   'Now I will have seen a wolf
tārė Jõnas, eĩdamas iš žvėrýno.   as well, – said John leaving the zoo.'

Simple tenses (the past in particular) can also possess the meaning typical of the compound perfect tenses (see 5.31–33), but the expression of this meaning is not the principal function of the simple tenses and it depends entirely upon the context.

A permanently existing state, however, is denoted exclusively by the compound tenses.

Visà atòmo mãsė bevéik ištisaĩ yrà susitel̃kusi (not **susìtelkė*) *branduolyjè.*	'Almost the entire mass of the atom is concentrated in its nucleus.'

The compound continuative tenses
Sudėtìniai pradėtìniai laikaĩ

5.37 The system of compound continuative tenses includes three forms: the past continuative, the past continuative frequentative and the future continuative tense, but it is only the past continuative tense which has a wider use in present-day Lithuanian, the others being found almost exclusively in the Low Lithuanian (Samogitian) dialect.

The compound continuative tenses indicate an action which started some time before another action and is still continuing at the time when that other action starts or is taking place. The longer duration of the action is emphasized by the prefix *be-*:

Kai įėjo šeiminiñkas, visì jau bùvo besėdį̃ už stãlo.	'When the master came in, everybody was already sitting at the table.'
Matýsi, àš bū́siu bemíegąs, kai ateĩsi manę̃s guldýti.	'You'll see, I'll be sleeping, when you come to put me to bed.'

The past continuative tense most often indicates an action which was begun or intended but not finished.

Jùras jau bùvo beatkelią̃s atvỹkstantiems vartùs, bet vė̃l juõs privė́rė.	'Juras was about to open the gate for the visitors, but closed it again.'
Bùvo jaũ ir blynùs bèkepanti, tik staigà ją̃ išmùšė prãkaitas ir pasidãrė taĩp negẽra.	'She was on the point of making pancakes when suddenly she broke into sweat and felt so faint.'

The future continuative tense is most often used in a modal meaning: it indicates an action which is supposed to have taken place (1) in the future, (2) sometimes in present:

(1) *Kaminè kažìn kàs vaitója. – Užsižiẽbk tik žìburį, bùs beįsibráunąs į vìdų, –*	'Somebody is moaning in the chimney. – Just put on the light and

mą̃sto sau vaikaĩ.   he will break into the house,–
the children think to themselves.'

(2) *Jìs jau trẽčią pãčią bùs beturį̃s.*   '(I think) he has a third wife already.'

PASSIVE VOICE
Neveikiamóji rū́šis

5.38   Only compound tenses are found in the passive voice. They can be divided into two groups: tense forms with the present passive participle (the so-called imperfect tenses) and tense forms with the past passive participle (perfect tenses).

The compound imperfect passive tenses

5.39   The compound imperfect passive tenses correspond to the simple active tenses, cf.:

yrà rāšomas 'is (being) written'   –   *rãšo* 'writes'
bùvo rāšomas 'was (being) written'   –   *rãšė* 'wrote'
bū́davo rāšomas 'used to be written'   –   *rašýdavo* 'used to write'
bùs rāšomas 'will be written'   –   *rašỹs* 'will write'

The tense forms of the imperfective aspect verbs are used both in the (1) concrete and (2) generalized meaning. Only the generalized meaning is characteristic of the past frequentative tense forms.

Present imperfect:

(1) *Laukuosè dabař̃ (yrà) kāsamos bùlvės.*   'Potatoes are being dug in the fields now.'

(2) *Jìs yrà visų̃ mýlimas.*   'He is loved by everyone.'

Laĩkraščiai mán (yrà) pristãtomi kiekvíeną díeną.   'The newspapers are delivered to me every day.'

Past imperfect:

(1) *Tamè pósėdyje bùvo spréndžiamas į́monės likìmas.*   'The fate of the enterprise was being discussed at the meeting.'

(2) *Sąskaitos bùvo tìkrinamos kiekvíeną mė́nesį.*   'The accounts were (being) checked every month.'

Past imperfect frequentative:

Į̃ vóką bū́davo į̃dedamas tùščias põpieriaus lãpas.   'A blank sheet of paper used to be enclosed in the envelope.'

Future imperfect:

(1) *Vestùvės bùs šveñčiamos linksmaĩ.* — 'The wedding will be celebrated merrily.'

(2) *Tù visadà bū́si kviẽčiamas į̃ Vyriausýbės pósėdžius.* — 'You will be always invited to the meetings of the Government.'

The compound perfect passive tenses

5.40 The compound perfect passive tenses have two main meanings: (1) the meaning of the state resulting from a previous action and (2) the meaning of the past or future action. The present perfect is devoid of the 2nd meaning; the past action, however, can be expressed by the passive past participle alone.

(1) In the first case the meaning of the perfect passive tenses corresponds to that of the perfect active tenses, cf.:

yrà parašýtas 'is written, has been written' – *yrà parãšęs* 'has written'
bùvo parašýtas 'was written, had been written' – *bùvo parãšęs* 'had written', etc.

Present perfect:

Ant vóko (yrà) užrašýta tàvo pavardė̃. — 'Your name is written on the envelope.'

Àš ne kar̃tą esù tė́vo išbártas. — 'I have been scolded by father more than once.'

Past perfect:

Síenos jau bùvo uždarýtos ir mẽs negalė́jome išvýkti į̃ užsíenį. — 'The frontiers were closed already and we could not go abroad.'

Àš nusipirkaũ knýgą, kurì bùvo išleistà priẽš kãrą. — 'I bought a book which had been published before the war.'

Past perfect frequentative:

Kalnų̃ gyvéntojai per žiẽmą bū́davo atskirtì nuo vìso pasáulio. — 'In winter the mountain dwellers used to be separated from the whole world.'

Future perfect:

Kaĩp tù įeĩsi, jéigu dùrys bùs užrakìntos? — 'How will you get in if the door is locked (lit. 'will be locked').'

(2) The second meaning of the perfect passive tenses corresponds to the meaning of simple active tenses, cf.:

bùvo parašýtas 'was written' — *parãšė* 'wrote'
bùs parašýtas 'will be written' — *parašỹs* 'will write', etc.

Past perfect:

Kìtą diēną nusikaĨtėlis bùvo sùimtas ir pasodìntas į kalė́jimą. 'The following day the criminal was arrested and put into prison.'

Past perfect frequentative:

Jì siū́davo tõl, kõl drabùžis bū́davo pasiū́tas. 'She used to sew until the garment was made (lit. 'used to be made').'

Future perfect:

Rytój bùs paródytas naũjas filmas. 'A new film will be shown tomorrow.'

The second meaning is usually characteristic of the perfective aspect verbs. They generally denote a particular single action, as in (a), and differ from the corresponding imperfect passive forms which, as a rule, indicate repeated, customary actions, as in (b), cf.:

(a) *Nãkčiai lóva bùvo atitrauktà nuo síenos.* 'For (this) night the bed was moved away from the wall.'

(b) *Kiekvíeną nãktį lóva bùvo atitraukiamà nuo síenos.* 'Every night the bed was moved away from the wall.'

Compound tenses of the passive voice

| Perfect passive tenses of verbs in the imperfective aspect (*bùvo výtas* 'has been chased') | Perfect passive tenses of verbs in the perfective aspect (*bùvo pavýtas* 'has been chased', 'was chased') | Imperfect passive tenses of verbs in the imperfective aspect (*bùvo vėjamas* 'was (being) chased') | Imperfect passive tenses of verbs in the perfective aspect (*bùvo pàvejamas* 'was (being) chased') |

| Resultative and relative meaning | The meaning of a particular single action | The meaning of a repeated, customary action |

MOOD

Núosaka

5.41 Mood expresses modality, i.e. the speaker's attitude towards the contents of an utterance. Modality subsumes a number of meanings which find expression in a variety of morphological, syntactical and lexical means.

Three kinds of modal oppositions are indicated in Lithuanian by means of the morphological mood forms of the verb:

(1) on the basis of the speaker's attitude to the factual status of the action with respect to the source of information (evidence, direct or indirect experience);

(2) on the basis of the speaker's will that something should or shouldn't take place or happen (volition);

(3) on the basis of the speaker's attitude to the reality or possibility, probability of the action (possibility).

The oblique mood (*modus relativus*), having the distinctive feature of indirect experience, is opposed to all the other moods taken together. The notion of volition is characteristic of the imperative mood, whereas the meaning of possibility is typical of the subjunctive mood. Thus, the mood system in Lithuanian consists of three opposition levels.

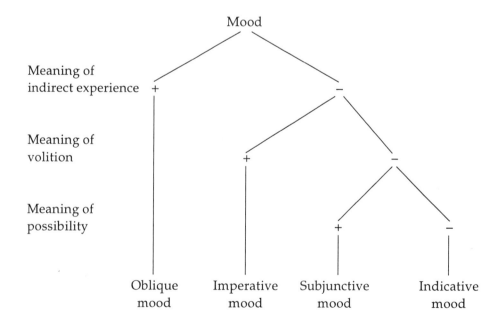

5.42 The category of mood is not a homogeneous category either in its meaning or its form. The first level of opposition, which is defined on the basis of the meaning of evidence or indirect experience, characterizes the speaker's attitude toward the content of the utterance in a way which is different from both the second and third levels of opposition. In addition, it is expressed by the nominative case of an active participle, cf.: *brólis dìrba* 'brother works' : *brólis dìrbąs* 'brother is said to work'. Therefore it would be quite valid to consider these forms to represent an independent evidential category. These forms are included in the mood system taking into account their paradigmatic character and the regular correlation with the tense forms of the indicative mood.

The imperative mood is opposed to the indicative and subjunctive moods on the semantic basis of volition. The latter two moods, being the unmarked members of this opposition, can also sometimes indicate volition or request (*Eĩnam namõ!* 'Let's go home!'; *Eĩtume dabař namõ!* 'I wish we could go home now!'). But these meanings cannot be considered to be the grammatical features of the indicative and subjunctive moods because in these cases they are entirely dependent upon the situation and the intonation of the utterance. The speaker's attitude of volition expressed by the imperative mood can refer both to an action which is really taking place (*Dìrbk ir toliaũ taĩp!* 'Go on working like this!') and a possible or desirable action.

The subjunctive mood is opposed to the indicative mood on the semantic basis of irreality: the subjunctive mood indicates an action which the speaker considers possible, whereas the indicative mood indicates, as a rule, an action which the speaker considers to be real. Being, however, the unmarked member of all the oppositions within the mood system, the indicative mood can sometimes be used in the meaning of the other moods, i.e. it can also indicate a desirable, possible, probable or indirectly experienced action.

The indicative mood and the oblique mood have four tenses: the present, the past, the past frequentative and the future. The imperative and subjunctive moods are not inflected for tenses, except that the distinction of temporal meaning within the subjunctive mood is based on the opposition of its simple and compound forms (see 5.47).

5.43 The morphological forms of the imperative and subjunctive moods are formed mostly with the help of inflectional suffixes: the indicator of the imperative mood is the suffix *-k(i)*, while those of the subjunctive mood are the suffixes *-čia-* (1st person singular), *-tum(ė)-* (2nd person singular, 1st and 2nd person plural) and *-tų* (3rd person). The imperative 3rd person forms with the prefix *te-* and the endings *-ie* and *-i* are obsolescent and disappearing. Apart from the tense, person and number markers the indicative mood does not have any other particular affixes. Thus, the indicative mood is the unmarked member of all the oppositions in the mood system not only in its meaning but also in its form.

Indicative mood
Tiesióginė núosaka

5.44 The indicative mood mostly expresses actions which the speaker considers to be real and attributes either to the present, past or future:

Žiẽmą mẽs visì draugè dìrbame/dìrbome/ 'In the winter we work/worked/
dìrbdavome/dìrbsime. used to work/will work all together.'

The main meanings of the tense forms of the indicative mood are described in 5.27–40. Sometimes the various tense forms of the indicative mood can acquire certain modal meanings, such as uncertainty, desirability, wish, determination, possibility, probability, volition, persuasion, etc. These modal meanings are determined by the linguistic context or the extra-lingual situation and they are usually emphasized by various particles, modal or parenthetical words.

5.45 In sentences with verbs of reporting, sensation, inert perception and cognition (e.g. *kalbė́ti* 'speak', *sakýti* 'say', *pāsakoti* 'tell', *pranèšti* 'inform', *rašýti* 'write', *jaũsti* 'feel', *girdė́ti* 'hear', *žinóti* 'know', *manýti* 'think', etc.), also with modal words (*gál* 'perhaps', *galbū́t* 'maybe', *turbū́t* 'most probably'), the indicative mood may indicate an indirectly experienced, reported or doubtful action, i.e. the forms of the indicative mood may be used in the meaning of the oblique mood.

Tė́vas sãkė, kad Kazỹs tik pāryčiu 'Father said that Kazys had
grį̃žo (cf. *grį̃žęs*). returned only in early morning.'
Turbū́t čià dár neseniaĩ žmónės 'Obviously it hasn't been long
gyvẽno (cf. *gyvẽnę*). since people lived here.'
Rytój jìs gál ir sugrį̃š (cf. *sugrį̃šiąs*). 'Tomorrow he will perhaps come back.'

The use of the indicative mood instead of the oblique mood is becoming frequent in publicistic, scientific and official styles.

5.46 In certain contexts the present and future tenses of the indicative mood (except their 1st person singular forms) may carry the meaning of persuasion, becoming in this way similar in meaning to the imperative mood.

2nd person singular:

Rytój einì ir àtneši mán dažų̃. 'Tomorrow you go and bring me some paint.'
Tù láuksi manę̃s miškè. 'You'll wait for me in the forest.'

2nd person plural:

Atsimiñkite: rytój pràdedate dìrbti pirmojè pamainojè.	'Remember: tomorrow you start work in the first shift.'
Po pietų užeĩsite pas manè.	'After lunch you come to see me.'

1st person plural (verbs of motion in particular, such as *eĩti* 'go', *lė̆kti* 'fly', *lìpti* 'climb'):

Eĩnam dabař į laukùs!	'Let's go now to the fields!'
Važiúojam!	'Let's go!'
Žinaĩ, brolėli, geriaũ nekalbė̆sim apie taĩ.	'You know, brother, let's not talk about it.'

The old athematic 1st person dual and plural forms of the present tense of the verb *eĩti* 'go' – *eivà* and *eimè*, respectively – nowadays are used exclusively in persuasive meaning:

Eimè visì kartù!	'Let's go all together!'
Eivà, sẽni, pir̃kion.	'Let's go, old man, (with me) into the house.'

The present and future tense forms with the prefix *te-* or the particle *tegu(l)* now replace the disappearing 3rd person forms of the imperative mood (see 5.49). The present tense forms indicate a desirable action in the present or in the future, while the future tense forms refer to a desirable action only in the future.

Tepasidžiaũgia sūneliù patì!	'Let her enjoy her sonny herself!'
Pagaliaũ tebū̃na (tebùs), kaĩp tù nóri.	'After all, let it be as you wish.'
Tegùl jì kartù su màno vaikaĩs gyveñs, kartù válgys, iš vienų̃ knỹgų mókysis.	'Let her live together with my children, let her eat together with them and learn from the same books.'

An action that the speaker desires for himself/herself is usually denoted by the 1st person form of the future tense:

Geriaũ težū̃siu aš víenas!	'I had better die alone!'

When the extra-lingual situation or the linguistic context indicate the possibility, probability or conditionality of the action, the meaning of the present and future tense forms of the indicative mood becomes similar to that of the subjunctive mood.

Į šìtą kam̃barį ne víenas, o trỹs stalaĩ lengvaĩ tel̃pa/til̃ptų.	'This room can easily accomodate three tables rather than one.'

Subjunctive mood
Tariamóji núosaka

5.47 The subjunctive mood indicates a possible action. It possesses both simple and compound forms (see 5.103, 110ff.).

The simple subjunctive forms indicate actions which under certain circumstances would be possible or desirable in the present or in the future.

Jéigu galė́čiau, dabař kitaĩp gyvénčiau.	'If I could, I would live differently now.'
Õ kad daugiaũ tų̃ žõdžių nebetařtum!	'(I wish) you wouldn't utter these words any more.'

The compound subjunctive forms consist of the simple forms of the auxiliary *bū́ti* 'be' and active or passive participles.

The compound continuative forms of the subjunctive mood with present active participles containing the prefix *be-* (see 5.110) are used very rarely. They differ from the simple forms in that they convey the duration of a possible action more distinctly.

Kõ jìs láukė šiõ laĩko nevẽdęs, bū́tų beturį̃s šeiminiñkę!	'Why did he wait so long and didn't marry, he would be having a housewife now!'

The compound perfect forms of the subjunctive mood with past active participles (see 5.109) denote a possible or imaginary action in the past or a state resulting from such an action.

Bū́čiau žinójęs, bū́čiau ir kójos iš namų̃ nekė́lęs.	'If I had known, I wouldn't have set my foot outside my home.'
Õ, kad jū̃s bū́tumėte mãtę, kaĩp jìs manè šokdìno!	'I wish you had seen how he danced with me!'

The compound perfect subjunctive forms relate to the simple forms of the subjunctive mood as past tense forms, cf.:

Jéi tavè bū́tų ištìkusi/ištìktų kokià neláimė, ką̃ dabař veĩktum?	'If a disaster had struck/struck you, what would you do now?'

The meaning of a past action is still more emphasized in the rare compound perfect forms containing the compound forms of the auxiliary *bū́ti* 'be':

1. Sg. *bū́čiau bùvęs* (m), *bùvusi* (f)
2. Sg. *bū́tum bùvęs, bùvusi*
3. Sg. *bū́tų bùvęs, bùvusi*

1. Pl. *bū́tume bùvę, bùvusios*
2. Pl. *bū́tumėte bùvę, bùvusios*
3. Pl. *bū́tų bùvę, bùvusios*

Jám bùvo neramù, tart̃um bū́tų bùvęs kuõ prasikal̃tęs.	'He felt uneasy as if he had done something wrong.'

Such compound subjunctive forms are nowadays more and more often replaced by forms containing the simple forms of the auxiliary *bū́ti* (cf. *tart̃um bū́tų kuõ prasikal̃tęs*).

The compound forms of the subjunctive mood with passive participles are opposed in their passive meaning to all the other forms of the subjunctive mood, cf.:

Active forms / Passive forms

mèsčiau 'I would throw' ——— *bū́čiau mẽtamas* 'I would be thrown'

bū́čiau bemetą̃s 'I would be throwing' ——— *'bū́čiau mẽstas* 'I would be thrown

bū́čiau mẽtęs 'I would have thrown' ——— *bū́čiau bùvęs mẽtamas* 'I would have been thrown'

bū́čiau bùvęs mẽstas 'I would have been thrown'

Jinaĩ taip pàt norė́tų, kad jõs išėjìmas iš šių̃ namų̃ bū́tų baĩgiamas maldà.	'She would also like it that her departure from this house should end in a prayer.'
Kad bū́tų taĩp ger̃biamas bùvęs, ar̃gi bū́tų galė́jęs taĩp visíems įkyrė́ti?	'If he had been so respected, could he have become such a bore to everybody?'
Mán liẽpta, kad visì darbaĩ per vãlandą bū́tų pabaigtì.	'I've been told that all work should be finished in an hour.'

5.48 Depending on the extra-lingual situation or the linguistic context the subjunctive mood can acquire the meaning of ability, condition, wish or persuasion.

(1) Ability:

Kàs įspė́tų tą̃ pãslaptį?	'Who could guess that secret?'
Tókią grãžią diẽną bū́tume visùs dárbus pabaĩgę.	'On such a nice day we could have finished all chores.'

(2) Condition:

Jéi tàs ãšaras suriñktum, pasi-darýtų sraunì ùpė.	'If you gathered all the tears, they would make a mighty river.'
Kad bū́čiau tą̃ diẽną atsikė́lęs vãlanda vėliaũ, bū́tume ir šiañ-dien gerúoju gyvẽnę.	'If I had got up an hour later that day, we would be getting on nicely today.'

In such cases the simple subjunctive forms usually indicate an action which under certain circumstances would be possible, whereas the compound forms denote an action which could have taken place but never did.

(3) Wish (very often together with the particles *kàd* 'that', *beñt* 'at least', the interjections *õ* 'oh', *àk* 'oh', etc.):

Õ kad turė́čiau nór̃s motinė̃lę!	'Oh I wish I had at least my mother!'
Beñt vãkaro bū́tum paláukęs.	'You should have waited at least until evening.'

In curses:

Velniaĩ griẽbtų!	'Damn!' (lit. 'The devils would snatch!')

In polite requests, suggestions, advice the indicative mood of such verbs as *norė́ti* 'want', *pageidáuti* 'wish', *prašýti* 'ask', *pasiū́lyti* 'suggest' and the like is frequently replaced by the subjunctive mood:

Prašýčiau miẽlus svečiùs tvarkõs neardýti.	'I would request our dear guests not to introduce disorder.'
Patar̃čiau jùms daugiaũ bū́ti grynamè orè.	'I would suggest you spend more time in fresh air.'

In explicative subordinate clauses and clauses of purpose the subjunctive mood of verbs denoting wish, volition or fear (*norė́ti* 'want', *prašýti* 'ask', *ver̃sti* 'force', *rãginti* 'urge', *liẽpti* 'order', *bijóti* 'fear', etc.) is used in the optative meaning:

Bijaũ, kad neapsirìkčiau.	'I'm afraid I may make a mistake.'
Paprašýk ją̃, kad dažniaũ ateĩtų.	'Ask her to come more often.'

(4) Stimulation (on the basis of optative meaning):

Eĩtum (cf. *eĩk*) *tù greičiaũ namõ.*	'I wish you would go home as soon as possible.'
Paieškótumėt (cf. *paieškókit*) *jū̃s mán lengvèsnio dárbo.*	'I wish you would find some easier work for me.'

In such cases the subjunctive mood becomes similar in meaning to the imperative mood, but it is more polite and less categorical.

A forceful order can be expressed by the subjunctive mood when it is used in utterances with the particle *kàd*:

Kad mán laikù sugrį̃žtum!   'Be sure to come back in time!'

Imperative mood
Liepiamóji núosaka

5.49   The meaning of volition and persuasion, typical of the imperative mood, fluctuates over a wide semantic range, from polite wish to categorical order. These various shades of persuasive meaning are generally indicated by the intonation of the utterance.

The grammatical paradigm of the imperative mood is defective (see 5.104–105) in that it lacks the 1st person singular form. By using the 2nd person singular the speaker appeals to the addressee to act (*Skubė́k namõ, vaĩke!* 'Hurry home, child!') while the 2nd person plural is directed toward several addressees (*Taĩp gyvénkit, kaip mẽs gyvẽnom.* 'Live as we have lived'). The 1st person plural denotes a suggestion about what the speaker and the addressee or several addressees should do together (*Kaip výrai be báimės mẽs stókim į̃ kõvą.* 'Like men let's join the struggle without fear').

The 3rd person forms with the prefix *te-* and the endings *-ie* and *-i* (*teein-iẽ* 'let him go', *terãša-i* 'let him write') are almost extinct in present-day Standard Lithuanian. They are sometimes to be found only in dialects and fiction. More frequent are the respective forms of the verb *bū́ti* 'be': *teesiẽ (tesiẽ), tebūniẽ* 'let him/her/it/them be'. These forms are used to express a wish, suggestion or instruction that the persons, who do not participate in the speech act, should or should not perform a certain action, or that an action should or should not take place.

Tesižìnai ir teeiniẽ visì, kuř̃   'Let them all do what they want and go
panorė́ję.   wherever they wish.'

Tebūniẽ taĩp, kaĩp pasakýsi.   'Let it be as you say.'

In present-day Standard Lithuanian these forms are usually replaced by the 3rd person forms of the present or future tense of the indicative mood used with the prefix *te-* or the particle *tegùl*: *teeĩna, tegù(l) eĩna; teeĩs, tegù(l) eĩs* 'let him/her/it/them go'; *terãšo, tegù(l) rãšo; terašỹs, tegù(l) rašỹs* 'let him/her/it/them write' (see 5.46).

In a number of Lithuanian grammars 3rd person forms of the imperative and sometimes even the 3rd person forms of the indicative used in the meanings typical of the imperative are considered to be a separate optative mood.

In set idiomatic phrases, expressing wish or desire, the 2nd person forms of the imperative mood can sometimes acquire the meaning of the 3rd person of the imperative mood.

Im̃k (cf. *teimiẽ*) *tavè velniaĩ!*   'Let the devils take you!'
Diẽvui bū́k (cf. *tebūniẽ*) *garbẽ.*   'Let it be to the greater honour of God.'

5.50 The imperative mood also possesses compound (periphrastic) forms, which include continuative, perfect and passive forms.

The compound continuative forms (2. Sg. *bū́k bedìrbąs, bedìrbanti* 'be working'; 2. Pl. *bū́kite bedìrbą, bedìrbančios* 'be working'; 1. Pl. *bū́kime bedìrbą, bedìrbančios* 'let's be working') are almost extinct now. The compound perfect forms (see 5.109) convey persuasion to achieve a certain resultant state.

Àš tuojaũ atvažiúosiu, tik tù   'I'm coming immediately, you
bū́k paválgęs ir apsirèngęs.   just have a meal and be dressed.'

The 2nd person forms of the imperative mood often acquire a variety of modal meanings such as necessity, possibility, etc.:

Tuõs vaikùs tik ganýk ir ganýk   'You have to shepherd and shepherd
per dienàs, nė̃r kadà nei dárbo   those children from morning till
nusitvérti.   night, there's no time to do any work.'
Ant tókio árklio tik sė́sk ir jók.   'On a horse like this you just mount and ride.'

When used with the set phrase *tù mán* (lit. 'you for me'), the 2nd person singular of the imperative mood expresses surprise or threat:

Ir turė̃k tù mán tíek drąsõs.   'That he/she should have so much courage.'
Tù mán netingė̃k!   'Just don't be lazy!'

Oblique mood
Netiesióginė núosaka

5.51 The oblique mood (*modus relativus*) is used to convey actions which the speaker got to know indirectly (through other persons or sources of information) and the truth of which he is not quite sure of.

The oblique mood forms consist of active participles in the nominative case without any auxiliary verb, used in the function which is usually typical of a finite form of the verb. These participles retain their gender forms, which agree with the nominative case of nouns and pronouns. They correlate with the finite forms of the verb on the basis of the category of tense and voice.

The oblique mood forms are simple and compound: the simple forms consist of active participles in various tenses; the compound forms consist of active and passive participles of the present and past tense and the active participial forms of the auxiliary *būti* 'be' (*ẽsąs, ẽsanti; bùvęs, bùvusi; bū́davęs, bū́davusi; bū́siąs, bū́sianti*). The paradigm of the oblique mood is symmetrical with that of the indicative mood, i.e. the simple and compound forms of the oblique mood are correlated with the respective forms of the indicative mood (see Table 9).

5.52 The main formal difference between the oblique mood and the compound forms of the indicative mood is the obligatory absence of the auxiliary verb. But since the auxiliary verb of the present tense of the indicative mood is sometimes omitted, three forms of the oblique mood may formally coincide with those of the indicative mood and therefore they may become ambiguous.

Oblique mood	Indicative mood
mẽtęs (Past)	*(yrà) mẽtęs* (Present perfect)
bùvęs mẽtamas (Past imperfect passive)	*(yrà) bùvęs mẽtamas* (Present imperfect passive)
bùvęs mẽstas (Past perfect passive)	*(yrà) bùvęs mẽstas* (Present perfect passive)

The meaning of such forms is usually disambiguated in the context.

To avoid ambiguity, the simple active voice forms of the oblique mood are sometimes replaced by compound forms (e.g. *mẽtęs* would be replaced by *ẽsąs mẽtęs*) while the compound passive forms of the oblique mood are replaced by forms including a compound participial form of the verb *būti* (e.g. *bùvęs mẽtamas* is replaced by *ẽsąs bùvęs mẽtamas; bùvęs mẽstas* by *ẽsąs bùvęs mẽstas*). In this way the difference in meaning between indirect experience and doubt is made more distinct.

Svẽčias ẽsąs kìlęs iš kaimiẽčių ir tõ nesìgina.	'The guest is said to be descended from the peasants and he doesn't deny it.'
Jìs jau kar̃tą ẽsąs bùvęs baũstas.	'He is said to have been punished once before.'

Certain active participles (the present tense participles without the prefix *be-*, frequentative past and future tense participles) are not used in compound tenses of the indicative mood at all.

5.53 Depending on the contextual and situational conditions, the oblique mood can indicate the following meanings:

(1) A fact learnt from report, hearsay or other sources of information; reported speech:

Table 9. **Correlation between the oblique mood and the indicative mood**

Tense	Simple forms		Compound	
			Continuative	
	Obl. m.	Ind. m.	Obl. m.	Ind. m.
Present	*mẽtąs*	*mẽta*	–	–
Past	*mẽtęs*	*mẽtė*	*bùvęs bemetąs*	*bùvo bemetąs*
Past frequentative	*mèsdavęs*	*mèsdavo*	*bū́davęs bemetąs*	*bū́davo bemetąs*
Future	*mèsiąs*	*mès*	*bū́siąs bemetąs*	*bùs bemetąs*

Girdėjau, jìs gyvẽnąs miestè.   'I heard he lives in town.'

Čià, sāko, miškaĩ bùvę.   'They say forests grew here once.'

Bū́davo, iñs pāsakoti, prie kokių̃ darbų̃ jìs bùvęs stùmdomas.   'Sometimes he would start telling us what kind of jobs he had been made to do.'

Sužinójau, kad per mū́sų sõdą bū́siąs tiẽsiamas kẽlias.   'I have learnt that a new road is going to be laid across our garden.'

(2) A doubtful action, the information about which is not quite reliable:

Užkastíeji pinigaĩ degą̃.   'The buried money is said to burn.'

Jiẽ màt bùk tai lenktỹnių ė̃ję.   'They are believed to have been racing.'

Jìs mė̃gdavo svajóti apie veĩkalus, kuriuõs jìs parašýsiąs ir kaĩp dėl tõ pakìlsiąs baroníenės akysè.   'He liked to daydream about the books he was going to write and the esteem they would gain him in the duchess' eyes.'

Benè nuo žmonõs jìs atsiskýręs ė̃sąs.   'Perhaps he is separated from his wife.'

(3) An action implied by its results:

Àk, žiūrė̆k, támsta jau besuprañtąs lietùviškai.   'Oh, look, you seem to understand Lithuanian already.'

Jaũ tie vaikaĩ pùpose bùvę: didžiáusios brỹdės pàliktos.   'Those children must have been in the beans again, wide tracks were left.'

(4) An unexpected or surprising action:

Po trijų̃ dienų̃ tėvaĩ žiū̃ri – vìsas žalčių̃ puĩkas bešliaužią̃s į jų̃ kiẽmą.   'In three days the parents saw a whole pack of grass-snakes crawling into their yard.'

	active forms		Compound passive forms			
	Perfect		Imperfect		Perfect	
Obl. m.	Ind. m.	Obl. m.	Ind. m.	Obl. m.	Ind. m.
ẽsąs mẽtęs	yrà mẽtęs	ẽsąs mẽtamas	yrà mẽtamas	ẽsąs mẽstas	yrà mẽstas
bùvęs mẽtęs	bùvo mẽtęs	bùvęs mẽtamas	bùvo mẽtamas	bùvęs mẽstas	bùvo mẽstas
bū́davęs mẽtęs	bū́davo mẽtęs	bū́davęs mẽtamas	bū́davo mẽtamas	bū́davęs mẽstas	bū́davo mẽstas
bū́sią̨s mẽtęs	bùs mẽtęs	bū́sią̨s mẽtamas	bū́sią̨s mẽstas	bū́sią̨s mẽstas	bùs mẽstas

Jìs atsigrę̃žęs žiū̃ri – stóvįs vélnias.   'He looked back and there a devil was standing.'

Žiūrẽk, kóks dìdelis lazdýnas išáugęs.   'Look, how big the hazel-nut bush has grown.'

The most frequent meaning of the oblique mood forms is that of an indirectly perceived action. They are often used in the context of verbs of saying, perception, bodily sensation and thinking. The indirect or doubtful nature of action is sometimes emphasized by modal particles, such as *tar̃tum* 'as if', *lýg* 'as if', *gál* 'perhaps', *galbū́t* 'maybe', *turbū́t* 'most probably', etc.

The oblique mood participles are mostly used with nouns and 3rd person pronouns. With 1st and 2nd person pronouns the oblique mood sometimes appears in reported speech.

Jìs pãsakojo, kad àš sergą̃s.   'He said I was ill.'

Tù tik sugaĩšią̨s tenaĩ nuvažiãvęs.   'You'll probably just lose time by going there.'

The oblique mood is often used in tales and legends, e.g.:

Víeno põno mìrusi patì ir palìkusi dvýlika sūnų̃ ir dár víeną dukterė̃lę. Po kíek laĩko tė́vas pamìlęs kìtą mergìną, rãganą. Tà sãkanti: „Duktė̃ tesiẽ, bet sàvo sū́nus sudẽgink..." Tė́vas mą̃stęs šiaĩp, mą̃stęs taĩp, nebežìną̨s, kàs čià bebùs darýti.   'The wife of a lord died and left twelve sons and a little daughter. After some time the father fell in love with another young woman, a witch. She said: "Your daughter may stay, but you must burn all your sons..." The father thought one way and another

Ir pasãkęs vienám sàvo tafnui. and didn't know what to do. Then he told one of his servants about it.'

5.54 In sentences where indirect experience or the uncertainty of the action is conveyed by verbs of saying, thinking or modal words, the oblique mood is often (in publicistic style, in particular) replaced by the indicative mood (*Sãko, jìs gyvẽna káime* 'They say he lives in the countryside,' see 5.45). This neutralization is stimulated by the fact that the southern Lithuanian dialects do not use the oblique mood and it has been accelerated by the influence of the Russian language during the period of the Soviet occupation. Cases of neutralization, however, do not make the indicative mood synonymous with the oblique mood. The latter as the marked member of the opposition is used only in certain modal meanings and cannot replace the indicative mood in other cases.

PERSON
Asmuõ

5.55 Distinctions of person indicate the relation of the action to the participants of the speech act from the point of view of the speaker. The 1st person forms refer to the speaker himself; the 2nd person forms refer to the addressee(s), while the 3rd person forms refer to something or someone who does not participate in the speech act. In this way distinctions of person constitute two-level oppositions on the basis of two semantic features: (**1**) participation in the speech act, and (**2**) relation between the participants of the speech act.

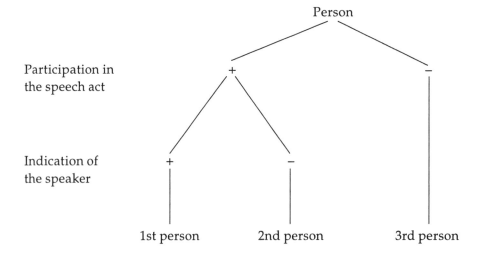

The 3rd person forms constitute the unmarked member of the first level opposition, which is in line with their specific endingless form and possible impersonal employment.

5.56 The category of person is very closely related to the categories of number, tense and mood. Its relation to the category of number is especially close, for both categories are expressed by the same endings, and the meaning of number exerts a marked influence on the use of personal forms. In fact, it determines the semantic differences between the forms of the 1st and 2nd person plural. Many tense forms of verbs, e.g. the present tense 3rd person forms *bėga* 'run(s)', *nėša* 'carry(ies)', the past tense 3rd person forms *bėgo* 'ran', *nėšė* 'carried' denote both tense and person.

The distinction of all three persons is typical only of the indicative and subjunctive moods. The imperative mood usually possesses only the 2nd person singular and the 1st and 2nd persons plural (except for the old and rare forms of the type *tenešiė* 'let him/her/it/them carry', *terāšai* 'let him/her/it/them write'. The oblique mood participles do not indicate any distinction of person, it is usually indicated by the accompanying nouns and pronouns (e.g. *àš, tù, jìs rāšąs* 'I, you, he am/are/is (said) to be writing').

5.57 The indicators of person distinction are the endings of the 1st and 2nd person forms. The 3rd person forms coincide with the stem of the verb and are opposed to the other forms of the verb as forms with a zero ending (see 5.86).

The same 3rd person forms are used both with the singular and plural forms of nouns and pronouns. They differ from the other personal verb forms in that they indicate actions or states performed or experienced both by animate and inanimate agents or patients, e.g.:

Šuõ/akmuõ gùli kryžkelėje.	'A dog/stone lies at the crossroads.'
Jūroje pakìlo bañgos.	'Waves appeared on the sea.'

5.58 All the personal forms of the verb can be used with the respective personal pronouns: 1st person pronouns *àš* 'I', *mẽs* 'we'; 2nd person pronouns *tù* 'thou', *támsta* 'you', *pàts* 'you', *jūs* 'you'; 3rd person pronouns *jìs* 'he', *jì* 'she', *jiē, jõs* 'they'; 3rd person verb forms can also be used with pronouns of other classes and nouns.

1st and 2nd person forms of the verb are usually (especially in colloquial speech) used alone, without any pronoun.

Viską geraĩ prisìmenu.	'I remember everything well.'
Ar manęs nepažį́sti?	'Don't you recognize me?'
Ieškójome tavęs ilgaĩ.	'We have looked for you a long time.'

Personal pronouns are almost never used with the imperative mood or in sentences of general meaning. On the other hand, they are applied in cases when emphasis on the participants of the speech act or their opposition to other persons is required, e.g.:

Dabař àš eĩsiu, o tù paláuksi   'Now I'll go, and you will wait
manę̃s čià.   for me here.'

While addressing someone:

Ar jū̃s, vaikaĩ, vienì pabū̃vat   'Do you, children, ever stay at
namiẽ?   home alone?'

The use of 1st and 2nd person forms of the verb without personal pronouns is one of the prominent features of Lithuanian which makes it different from many other languages where the 1st and 2nd person pronouns are much more frequent or even required when a finite form of the verb is used.

The 3rd person finite forms of the verb, however, require the presence of subject nouns or pronouns, except in cases where the context or situation makes them absolutely clear. The absence of a 3rd person pronoun can also be the indication of the impersonal or generalized personal meaning of the sentence:

Visuř šaũkė, klỹkė, spiẽgė, daũžė,   'There were screams, shrieks, yells, slams
trañkė dùrimis.   and the banging of doors all over the place.'

5.59 The generalized, expanded and figurative uses of verbal personal forms are based on their primary meaning.

Generalized reference is typical of 2nd person singular and 1st person plural forms in proverbs, saws and similar standard phrases.

Daũg norė́si, mažaĩ turė́si.   'If you want much, you'll get little.'
Eidamì eĩti, dirbdamì dìrbti   'We learn to walk by walking,
mókomės.   we learn to work by working.'

1st person singular and 2nd person plural verbal forms retain their association with the speaker or the addressee(s) even when they are used in generalized reference.

Kaĩp móku, taĩp šóku.   lit. 'I dance as I know how' (i.e. 'I work
                                        as I can').

Kuř tik pažvel̃gsit, visuř   'Wherever you look, you see
geltonúoja rugiaĩ.   yellow fields of rye.'

3rd person verbal forms are used to refer an action to an indefinite agent, i.e. to people in general, e.g.:

Kuř medžiùs keřta, teñ skíedros lēkia.	'Where trees are being cut, chips are flying around.'

However, the most usual way to convey that the agents of an action are people in general is to use the neuter form of a passive participle:

Iš turtìngo daugiaũ reikaláujama.	'More is required from a rich person.'

1st person plural forms, the so called *editorial we*, is sometimes used in writing instead of the 1st person singular, which is felt to be a little egotistic and, therefore, the author may wish to avoid it:

Rãšinį, šiaĩp ar taĩp, pàtariame skaitýti mū́sų rãštų istòrijos reĩkalui, teĩkiame jį̃ ir mokiniũ skaitỹkloms.	'However it may be, we advise one to read this piece in connection with the history of our literature; we also supply it to school libraries.'

When addressing a person directly, the 1st person plural form can also indicate an action performed by the addressee:

Tai vìs veřpiam, močiùte?	'So we are still spinning, granny?'

In emotionally vivid speech, the 2nd person singular may indicate an action, performed by the speaker, but typical of people in general.

Daraĩ, sténgiesi, o jái vìs negeraĩ ir negeraĩ.	'You just toil, try hard, but she is never pleased.'

2nd person plural is used instead of 2nd person singular when addressing the interlocutor politely:

O jū̃s mán tė́vas ė̃sat.	'And you are my father.'
Ar iš tólo eĩnate?	'Are you coming from far away?'

With the pronoun *támsta* 'you' the 2nd person singular form of the verb is commonly used:

Ar nežinaĩ támsta, kuř màno Petriùkas?	'Do you know, mister, where my Petriukas is?'

IMPERSONAL USE OF FINITE FORMS OF THE VERB

5.60   3rd person forms, which by definition do not associate the action with the participants of the speech act, can be used impersonally. This is very typical of so called impersonal verbs which indicate natural phenomena or processes which do not depend upon the will of the doer. Lithuanian possesses a very great number and variety of such impersonal verbs.

(1) Verbs denoting natural phenomena associated with changes in time and weather: *aũšti, aušróti, brė́kšti, švìsti, dienóti* 'dawn', *tamsúoti, témti, vakarė́ti* 'be getting dark', *dárganoti* 'be rainy', *dreñgti, drobliúoti* 'sleet', *dul̃kti, dulksnóti, rasénti, lašnóti, lynóti* 'drizzle', *lýti* 'rain', *snaigýti, snìguriuoti* 'snow (slightly)', *snìgti* 'snow', *spéigėti* 'freeze hard', *pustýti* 'drift, a blizzard', *griáudėti, griáusti* 'thunder', *giedrė́ti* 'be clearing up', *žaibúoti* 'flash (about lightning)', etc.

Vaikaĩ, kélkitės, jau aũšta/šviñta!	'Children, get up, day is breaking!'
Võs tik pràdeda dienóti, jaũ jìs ir rìtasi iš lóvos.	'As soon as day breaks, he rolls out of bed.'
Sniẽgti, lỹja, darganója, negiedrà dienẽlė.	'It's snowing, raining, sleeting, the day is nasty.'
Per vìsą diẽną dul̃kė.	'It was drizzling all day long.'
Kẽlias užpustýtas ir dár pùsto.	'There are snow drifts on the road, and the blizzard doesn't stop.'

The verb *brė́kšti* has two opposite meanings: 'to dawn' and 'to be getting dark'.

(2) Verbs denoting a person's physical and mental state: *gélti, maũsti* 'ache', *niežė́ti* 'itch', *perštė́ti* 'smart', *skaudė́ti* 'ache', *sopė́ti* 'ache', *knietė́ti* 'itch to do sth.', *ganė́ti* 'be enough', *pakàkti, užtèkti* 'be enough', *stìgti* 'lack', *trū́kti* 'lack', *pabaĩsti* 'be frightened', *atródyti* 'seem', *reikė́ti* 'need', *priderė́ti* 'be proper, be fit', *vertė́ti* 'be worth', *tèkti* 'fall (on/to sb.)', *derė́ti* 'be proper, fit', etc.

Mán taĩp gálvą skaũda/gẽlia!	'I have such a headache!'
Liežùvį jái niẽžti.	'Her tongue (ACC) itches.'
Gérklę peršti nuo dū́mų.	'The smoke makes my throat smart.'
Tárpais kniẽti pasakýti, kad jisaĩ melúoja.	'Sometimes I itch to say he is lying.'
Màno ámžiui vìsko užtèks.	'It'll be enough for me all my life.'
Mán svẽtimo turt̃o nereĩkia.	'I don't need what belongs to others.'

5.61 Among the impersonal verbs we can also find a large number of reflexive verbs denoting a spontaneous state:

(1) *blaustýtis* 'grow cloudy', *giẽdrytis* 'be clearing up', *niáuktis* 'grow cloudy':

Po lietaũs nusigiẽdrijo.	'After the rain it cleared up.'
Šiañdien lietaũs bùs – blaũstosi.	'It's going to rain today – it's getting cloudy.'

(2) *matýtis* 'be seen', *norė́tis* 'experience a wish', *regė́tis* 'seem', *ródytis* 'seem', *sèktis* 'go well; be lucky', *atsitìkti* 'happen':

Mán nórisi miẽgo.	'I'm sleepy' lit. 'I (DAT. SG) want (3. PRES. REFL) to sleep (GEN. SG).'
Kodė̃l jám taĩp sẽkasi?	'Why is he (DAT. SG) so lucky (3. PRES. REFL)?'

The corresponding verbs without the reflexive suffix are most often used as personal verbs:

Kàs dainúoja, tàs var̃go nejaũčia.	'He who sings, doesn't feel his troubles.'
Cf.: *Ligõs nesijaũčia.*	'The illness (GEN. SG) is not felt (3. PRES. REFL).'

5.62 The morphological paradigm of impersonal verbs includes the 3rd person forms of the indicative, subjunctive and oblique moods, the infinitive and gerunds. Some impersonal verbs also have the neuter form of passive participles, e.g.:

snìgti 'snow'	*sniñga, snìgo, snìgdavo, snìgs;* *bùvo/bū́davo/bùs besniñgą, snìgę; snìgtų;* *sniñgą, snìgę, snìgdavę, snìgsią; snìgta*
reikė́ti 'need'	*reĩkia, reikė́jo, reikė́davo, reikė̃s;* *bùvo/bū́davo/bùs bereĩkią; reĩkėtų; reĩkią,* *reikė́ję, reikė́davę, reikė́sią; reĩkėta*

But reflexive verbs which possess a complete morphological paradigm, i.e. all the forms indicated above, are rare. For example, the verbs *pabaĩso* 'became frightened', *pagaĩlo* 'became sorry', *pagar̃do* 'became tasty', are usually used only in the past tense, more rarely in the past frequentative. Instead of the other forms of these verbs the neuter forms of adjectives of a similar meaning in conjunction with the verb *darýtis* 'become' are mostly used:

Present:	*(dãrosi) baisù*	'it's becoming frightening'
	(dãrosi) gaĩla	'I'm becoming sorry'
Past:	*pabaĩso/pasidãrė baisù*	
	pagaĩlo/pasidãrė gaĩla	
Past frequentative:	*pabaĩsdavo/pasidarýdavo baisù* *pagaĩldavo/pasidarýdavo gaĩla*	
Future:	*pasidarỹs baisù*	
	pasidarỹs gaĩla	

In the present the verb *vertė́ti* 'be worth' is replaced by the neuter adjectival form *ver̃ta* with a link verb:

Present:	*(yrà) ver̃ta*	'it's worth'
Past:	*vertė́jo/bùvo ver̃ta*	'was worth'

Past
frequentative: *vertĕdavo/bŭdavo veřta* 'used to be worth'

Future: *vertẽs/bùs veřta* 'will be worth'

In certain contexts the 3rd person forms of other verbs can also be used impersonally when they denote natural processes: *kaĩtina* 'it's hot', *kvẽpia* 'it smells nice', *šą̃la* 'it's freezing', *atšỹla* 'it's getting warmer', *baltúoja* 'it appears (is) white', *palengvĕjo* 'it has become easier', etc.

Laukuosè jau geraĩ kaĩtino.	'It was already rather hot in the fields.'
Šiañdien staigà atšĩlo/atšãlo.	'Today it suddenly has become warmer/colder.'

In other cases such verbs, differently from the impersonal verbs proper, possess the 1st and 2nd person forms, cf.:

Kaĩtinu píeną.	'I'm warming up the milk.'
Rankàs atšálsi.	'Your hands will get cold.'

NUMBER

Skaĩčius

5.63 In the simple tenses number is reflected in the different endings of the 1st and 2nd person forms of finite verbs (which also reflect person), e.g. *einù* 'I go', *einì* 'you go' (singular); *eĩname* 'we go', *eĩnate* 'you go' (plural). The 3rd person forms contain no grammatical indicators of number, e.g.:

jìs/jì eĩna 'he, she goes' – *jiẽ/jõs eĩna* 'they go'.

In the compound tenses the distinction of number is indicated by the 1st and 2nd person forms of the auxiliary verb and the endings of the participial form of the main verb which is inflected only for number but not for person, e.g.:

(*àš*) *esù ẽjęs* 'I have walked (SG)' – (*mẽs*) *ẽsame ẽję* 'we have walked (PL)';

(*tù*) *buvaĩ nẽšamas* 'you were/had been carried (SG)' – *jũs bùvote nešamì* 'you were/had been carried (PL)'.

Number is also distinguished by the endings of the oblique mood participles, e.g.:

àš/jìs nešą̃s 'I am/He is said to be carrying (SG)' – *mẽs/jiẽ nešą̃* 'we/they are said to be carrying (PL)'.

In participles, just like in adjectives, number is indicated by the same inflections which convey case and gender distinctions.

Since the plural forms are the marked members of the opposition based on number, their meaning is always more definite than that of the singular forms, which can denote people in general, i.e. an indefinite agent. This is especially typical of the 2nd person forms:

Gyvenì ir mókaisi.	'You live and you learn.'
Kaĩp pasiklósi, taĩp išmiegósi.	lit. 'As you make your bed, so you will sleep on it' (i.e. one gets what one deserves).

Some other meanings of the singular and plural forms are indicated in 5.56–59 together with a description of the semantic distinctions which depend on person.

Finite forms of the verb agree with nouns and pronouns in number.

The now obsolete dual forms of the finite verb are still used in some dialects and literary writings, e.g.:

Eĩsiva namõ.	'We two will go home.'
Eivà namõ.	'Let's we two go home.'

VOICE
Rū́šis

5.64 The category of voice comprises two voices, active (*veikiamóji rū́šis*) and passive (*neveikiamóji rū́šis*). It finds expression in two sets of verbal forms indicating a different relation of the semantic subject to the syntactic subject.

The main formal means of marking the voice opposition is the participle which has active and passive forms, viz.:

nešą̃s 'carrying (ACT. PRES)'	– *nẽšamas* 'being carried (PASS. PRES)'
nẽšęs 'carried (ACT. PAST)'	– *nẽštas* 'carried (PASS. PAST)'

The present and past passive participles and the auxiliary *bū́ti* 'be' constitute periphrastic passive forms opposed to both simple and periphrastic active forms (cf. Table 10).

5.65 The active voice is represented by all the simple finite verb forms, infinitive, active participles (including gerunds) and the periphrastic forms with the active participles:

nešù '(I) carry'	*nešą̃s, -anti, nèšdamas,- à, nẽšant* 'carrying'
nešiaũ '(I) carried'	*nẽšęs, -usi, nẽšus* 'carried'

Table 10. **The correspondences between active and passive forms** *šaũkti* 'call', *eĩti* 'walk'

Types of active forms	Tense	Mood			
		Indicative		Subjunctive	
		Active	Passive	Active	Passive
Simple	Present	*šaũkia*	*yrà šaũkiamas, -à/ yrà šaũkiama*	*šaũktų*	*bū́tų šaũkiamas, -à/ bū́tų šaũkiama*
		eĩna	*yrà eĩnama*		
	Past	*šaũkė*	*bùvo šaũkiamas, -à/ bùvo šaũkiama*	*eĩtų*	*bū́tų eĩnama*
		ė̃jo	*bùvo eĩnama*		
	Past freq.	*šaũkdavo*	*bū́davo šaũkiamas, -à/ bū́davo šaũkiama*		
		eĩdavo	*bū́davo eĩnama*		
	Future	*šaũks*	*bùs šaũkiamas, -à/ bùs šaũkiama*		
		eĩs	*bùs eĩnama*		
Periphrastic	Present	*yrà šaũkęs, -usi*	*yrà šaũktas, -à/ yrà šaũkta*	*bū́tų šaũkęs, -usi*	*bū́tų šaũktas, -à/ šaũkta*
		yrà ė̃jęs, -usi	*yrà eĩta*		
	Past	*bùvo šaũkęs, -usi*	*bùvo šaũktas, -à/ bùvo šaũkta*	*bū́tų ė̃jęs, -usi*	*bū́tų eĩta*
		bùvo ė̃jęs, -usi	*bùvo eĩta*		
	Past freq.	*bū́davo šaukęs, -usi*	*bū́davo šaũktas, -à bū́davo šaũkta*		
		bū́davo ė̃jęs, -usi	*bū́davo eĩta*		
	Future	*bùs šaũkęs, -usi*	*bùs šaũktas, -à/ bùs šaũkta*		
		bùs ė̃jęs, -usi	*bùs eĩta*		

Mood			
Imperative		Oblique	
Active	Passive	Active	Passive
		šaūkiąs, -ianti	ẽsąs šaũkiamas, ẽsanti šaukiamà/ẽsą šaũkiama
		eĩnąs, -anti	ẽsą eĩnama
tešaukiẽ	tebūniẽ šaũkiamas,-à/ šaũkiama	šaũkęs, -usi	bùvęs šaũkiamas, bùvusi šauktà/bùvę šaũkiama
teeiniẽ	tebūniẽ eĩnama	ė̃jęs, -usi	bùvę eĩnama
		šaũkdavęs, -usi	bū́davęs šaũkiamas, bū́davusi šaukiamà/bū́davę šaũkiama
		eĩdavęs, -usi	bū́davę eĩnama
		šaũksiąs, -ianti	bū́siąs šaũkiamas, bū́sianti šaukiamà/bū́sią šaũkiama
		eĩsiąs, -ianti	bū́sią eĩnama
		ẽsąs šaũkęs, ẽsanti šaũkusi	ẽsąs šaũktas, ẽsanti šauktà/ẽsą šaũkta
		ẽsąs ė̃jęs, ẽsanti ė̃jusi	ẽsą eĩta
tebūniẽ šaũkęs, -usi	tebūniẽ šaũktas, -à/šaũkta	bùvęs šaũkęs, bùvusi šaũkusi	bùvęs šaũktas, bùvusi šauktà/bùvę šaũkta
tebūniẽ ė̃jęs, -usi	tebūniẽ eĩta	bùvęs ė̃jęs, bùvusi ė̃jusi	bùvę eĩta
		bū́davęs šaũkęs, bū́davusi šaũkusi	bū́davęs šaũktas, bū́davusi šauktà/bū́davę šaũkta
		bū́davęs ė̃jęs, bū́davusi ė̃jusi	bū́davę eĩta
		bū́siąs šaũkęs, bū́sianti šaũkusi	bū́siąs šaũktas, bū́sianti šauktà/bū́sią šaũkta
		bū́siąs ė̃jęs, bū́sianti ė̃jusi	bū́sią eĩta

nèšdavau 'I used to carry' *nèšdavęs, -usi, nèšdavus* 'carried (FREQ)'
nèšiu '(I) shall carry' *nèšiąs, -ianti, nèšiant* 'carrying (FUT)'
nèšti 'to carry' *esù / buvaũ / bū́davau / bū́siu nẽšęs, nẽšusi*
'(I) have / had / used to have carried / shall have carried' etc.

The passive voice is represented by passive participles and the periphrastic finite forms with the present and past passive participles, e.g.:

nẽšamas, -à 'being carried'
nẽštas, -à 'carried'
nèšimas 'carried (FUT)'
esù/buvaũ/bū́siu nẽšamas, -à/nẽštas, -à '(I) am / was / used to be / shall be carried'

The category of voice covers all the verbs, both transitive and intransitive, personal and impersonal, reflexive and non-reflexive, i.e. every single verb form is either active or passive. But not all active forms have passive counterparts; the restrictions on the passive voice are discussed below (5.75–78).

The correspondences between active and passive verb forms are influenced by the tense and aspect meanings of the verb. For instance, the present passive with the past participle (e.g. *láiškas yrà àtneštas kaimýno* 'a letter is brought by the neighbour') corresponds in the temporal and aspectual meaning both to the active periphrastic past (*kaimýnas yrà àtnešęs láišką* 'the neighbour has brought a letter') and to the simple past with the perfective meaning (*kaimýnas àtnešė láišką* 'the neighbour (has) brought a letter').

5.66 The marked member of the voice opposition is the passive. A passive verb form indicates that the semantic subject is not expressed by the syntactic subject or, in the case of an attributive passive participle, by the head noun. In the passive construction the semantic subject is expressed by the genitive or it is omitted, cf.:

Mótina mylė́jo dùkterį. 'Mother loved her daughter.'
Duktė̃ bùvo (mótinos) mylimà. 'The daughter was loved (by her mother).'

The choice of an active or a passive form of the verb determines the syntactic structure of the sentence.

If the subject of an active verb is the pronoun *àš* 'I' or *tù* 'you: SG', in the corresponding passive construction it acquires the possessive genitive form *màno* 'my', *tàvo* 'your' instead of *manę̃s, tavę̃s*:

Àš pàkviečiau draũgą. 'I invited a friend.'
Draũgas bùvo màno (*manę̃s) pàkviestas. 'The friend was invited by me.'

Tù pàmetei rãktą. 'You lost the key.'
Rãktas bùvo tàvo (*tavęs) pàmestas. 'The key was lost by you.'

The passive of transitive verbs and the passive of intransitive verbs differ in a number of grammatical properties.

THE PASSIVE OF TRANSITIVE VERBS

5.67 Active transitive constructions may have two passive equivalents: with and without agreement in gender between the syntactic subject and the passive participle of the predicate:

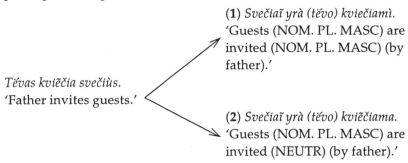

Tévas kviẽčia svečiùs.
'Father invites guests.'

(1) *Svečiaĩ yrà (tévo) kviečiamì.*
'Guests (NOM. PL. MASC) are invited (NOM. PL. MASC) (by father).'

(2) *Svečiaĩ yrà (tévo) kviẽčiama.*
'Guests (NOM. PL. MASC) are invited (NEUTR) (by father).'

Of the two types, the former is regularly used in Standard Lithuanian. Masculine and feminine forms of passive participles agree with the subject in number and case as well, cf.:

Mergáitės bùvo tévo kviẽstos. 'The girls (NOM. PL. FEM) were invited (NOM. PL. FEM) by father.'

Constructions of the latter type (with the neuter forms of participles without agreement) are peripheral in Standard Lithuanian.

Unprefixed reflexive verbs have passive forms with a neuter participle only, cf.:

peřkasi '(he) buys for himself' → *yrà peřkamasi* '(it is) bought for oneself'
mùšėsi '(they) fought' → *yrà mùštasi* '(it was) being fought (by them)'

The prefixed reflexives have passive forms of both types:

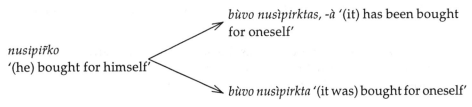

nusipiřko
'(he) bought for himself'

bùvo nusìpirktas, -à '(it) has been bought for oneself'

bùvo nusìpirkta '(it was) bought for oneself'

5.68 The accusative object of an active transitive verb is promoted to the nominative subject in the corresponding passive construction, while the active subject is demoted to the genitive object:

Visì manè skriaũdžia. →	'Everybody (lit. All) offends me.'
Àš esù visų̃ skriaũdžiamas.	'I am (being) offended (NOM. SG) by everybody (GEN. PL).'
Jìs yrà pir̃kęs šìtą žẽmę. →	'He has bought this land.'
Šità žẽmė yrà jõ pirktà.	'This land has been bought by him.'

5.69 The passive transformation with object promotion applies also to a number of verbs governing other than the accusative case forms. They are:

(1) Verbs taking the genitive object, e.g.: *norĕti* 'want', *geĩsti* 'desire, long', *(pa)geidáuti* 'wish, desire', *ieškóti* 'look (for)', *láukti* 'wait', *síekti* 'strive (for), seek', *véngti* 'avoid', *bijóti* 'be afraid (of)'; cf.:

Mótina íeško dukter̃s. →	'Mother is looking for her daughter (GEN).'
Duktė̃ yrà mótinos íeškoma.	'The daughter (NOM) is being looked for by her mother (GEN).'
Visì láukė svečių̃.→	'Everybody (NOM) was waiting for the guests (GEN).'
Svečiaĩ bùvo visų̃ laukiamì.	'The guests (NOM) were awaited by everybody (GEN).'

(2) Some verbs taking the dative object, e.g.: *atstováuti* 'represent', *įsakýti* 'order', *liẽpti* 'order, tell', cf.:

Mẽs atstovãvome darbiniñkams. →	'We represented the workers (DAT).'
Darbiniñkai bùvo mū́sų atstováujami.	'The workers (NOM) were represented by us.'
Tėvaĩ liẽpė jám dìrbti. →	'(His) parents ordered him (DAT) to work.'
Jìs bùvo tėvų̃ liẽptas dìrbti.	'He (NOM) was ordered to work by his parents (GEN).'

The obligatory locative required by the verb *gyvénti* 'inhabit, live (in)' may also be converted into the nominative subject:

Žvérys gyvẽna urvuosè. →	'Beasts live in burrows (LOC).'
Urvaĩ yrà žvėrių̃ gyvẽnami.	'The burrows (NOM) are inhabited by beasts (GEN).'

However, in the latter two cases the dative and the locative can be retained in the passive construction, in which the neuter form of the passive participle is used and the resultant sentence is subjectless:

Jám bùvo tėvų liẽpta dìrbti.	lit. 'To him (DAT) (it) was ordered (NEUTR) by (his) parents (GEN) to work.'
Urvuosè yrà žvėrių gyvẽnama.	lit. 'In the burrows (LOC) (it) is inhabited (NEUTR) by beasts (GEN).'

5.70 The verb *prašýti* 'ask' governing two objects (accusative and dative) may form two passive constructions, since either object can be converted into subject:

Berniùkas prãšė mókytoją knýgos. →	'The boy asked the teacher (ACC) for a book (GEN).'
(a) *Mókytojas bùvo (berniùko) prãšomas knýgos.*	'The teacher (NOM) was asked (by the boy) for a book (GEN).'
(b) *Knygà bùvo (berniùko) prãšoma.*	'The book (NOM) was requested (by the boy).'

The dative of addressee governed by the verb *dúoti* 'give' sometimes (very rarely) can also be converted into the subject of a passive construction, e.g.

Tėvas dãvė vaĩkui óbuolį.	'Father gave the child an apple (ACC).'
Vaĩkas bùvo dúotas óbuolį.	'The child (NOM) was given an apple (ACC).'

Cf. the regular passive:

Obuolỹs bùvo dúotas vaĩkui.	'The apple (NOM) was given to the child (DAT).'

5.71 The passive voice is a means of expressing an action irrespective of its agent. The agentive genitive is often omitted if the agent is unknown, unimportant to the speaker or implied by the situation and context, e.g.:

Tàs ligónis yrà gýdomas seniaĩ.	lit. 'This patient is being treated for a long time.'
Jám bùvo pasiū́lytas gerèsnis dárbas.	'He (DAT) was offered a better job (NOM).'

The agentive genitive is also omitted if the Agent is indefinite or generalized, e.g.:

Šiañdien vaĩsiai parduodamì visur̃.	'Today fruit is sold everywhere.'
Netrùkus visì darbaĩ bùs baigtì.	'Shortly all work will be finished.'
Jìs bùvo labaĩ ger̃biamas.	'He was highly esteemed.'

5.72 The passive of transitive verbs with the neuter participle (second type) is mainly used in the following cases:

(1) With the subject expressed by the pronouns unmarked for gender: *kàs* 'who, what', *kaĩ kàs* 'somebody, anybody, something', *kas nórs* 'anybody, anything', *kažkàs* 'somebody, something', *niēkas* 'nobody, nothing', *vìskas* 'everything', etc., and by adverbs or word groups with the genitive of quantity, e.g.: *daũg* 'many, much', *mažaĩ* 'few, little': *daũg vandeñs* 'much water', *kéletas vaikų̃* 'several children', *tū́kstančiai žmonių̃* 'thousands of people', etc.:

Kàs bùvo liẽpta, tùri bū́ti àtlikta.	'What was ordered must be carried out.'
Vìskas geraĩ dãroma.	'Everything is being done well.'
Niēkas nẽrà pardúota.	'Nothing is sold.'
Išléista šimtaĩ knỹgų.	'Hundreds of books are published.'

(2) In impersonal (subjectless) sentences with the genitive of indefinite quantity (a) or with an infinitive (b):

(a) *Priẽ pamiñklo bùvo padė́ta gė̃lių.*	'(Some) flowers (GEN) were laid (NEUTR) at the monument.'
(cf.: *Gė̃lės bùvo padė́tos priẽ pamiñklo.*)	('The flowers (NOM) were laid at monument.')
Vakarè láukiama / tìkimasi gerų̃ naujíenų.	'Good news (GEN. PL) was expected (NEUTR) in the evening.'
(b) *Paskuĩ bùvo àtnešta válgyti ir gérti.*	'Food and drinks were brought (NEUTR) later (lit. Then it was brought to eat and drink).'
Čià draũdžiama rūkýti.	'(It) is forbidden (NEUTR) to smoke.'
Jám bùvo liẽpta išeĩti.	'He (DAT) was ordered (NEUTR) to leave.'

5.73 The neuter passive participle is sometimes used also in personal sentences with the masculine or feminine subject, though agreement in gender is more common, cf.:

Pavãsarį rugiaĩ bùvo sė́jama / sė́jami.	'In spring, rye (MASC) was sown (NEUTR/MASC).'
Bùlvės jaũ bùvo nùkasta / nùkastos.	'The potatoes (FEM) were already dug up (NEUTR/FEM).'

The passive voice of some verbs governing the accusative object of quantity (*kainúoti* 'cost', *svérti/svérti* 'weigh', *trùkti* 'last', *sukàkti* 'turn (about age)') is formed with neuter passive participles only, e.g.:

Vištà	*svẽria*	*dù*	*kilogramùs.*
hen: NOM. SG	weigh: 3. PRES	two	kilograms (ACC. PL)

'The chicken weighs two kilograms.'

Vištos	*svēriama*		*dù*	*kilogrãmai/kilogramùs.*
hen: GEN. SG	weigh: PASS. PRES. PART. NEUTR		two	kilograms: NOM. PL/ACC. PL

'The weight of the chicken is two kilograms.'

5.74 Neuter passive participles with the preposed agentive genitive, especially when used without an auxiliary, can acquire the evidential meaning close to that of the indirect mood. It denotes an action inferred from its consequences or hearsay, or assumed, or an action causing surprise:

Girdėjau,	*jõ*	*miestè*	*nãmas*	*stãtoma.*
hear: 1. PAST	he: GEN	town: LOC	house: NOM	build: PRES. PASS. PART. NEUTR

'I hear, he is building a house in the town.'

Gál	*Jonùko*	*tiẽ*	*grỹbai*	*àtnešta.*
maybe	Jonukas: GEN	this: NOM. PL	mushroom: NOM. PL	bring: PAST. PASS. PART. NEUTR

'Maybe it is Jonukas (Johnny) who has brought those mushrooms.'

Senų̃	*miškaĩ*	*mylė́ta,*	*tūloñ*	*giesmeñ*	*dė́ta.*
old: GEN. PL	forest: NOM PL. MASC	love: PAST. PASS. PART. NEUTR	many: ILLAT. SG	song: ILLAT. SG	put: PAST. PASS. PART. NEUTR

'(In the days of old) people loved forests and made many songs about them.'

Such constructions with the neuter participle of transitive verbs are characteristic of eastern Lithuanian dialects. In the standard language they are rare and stylistically marked.

THE PASSIVE OF INTRANSITIVE VERBS

5.75 Intransitive verbs have periphrastic passive forms with the neuter participles only. The passive forms of intransitive verbs are correlated with the respective active forms as in the case of transitive verbs (see Table 10).

The periphrastic passive of intransitive verbs is used with or without the agentive genitive.

Constructions without the genitive are mostly used if the semantic subject is generalized, or indefinite or implied by the situation or context:

Čià nerūkoma.	'No smoking here (lit. Here is not smoked (PRES. PASS. PART. NEUTR).'
Rùdenį bùvo ilgaĩ miẽgama.	'People slept long in autumn (lit. In autumn was slept (PRES. PASS. PART. NEUTR) long).'
Ar nebùs pavėlúota?	'Won't it be too late (PAST. PASS. PART. NEUTR)?'

Some impersonal verbs (e.g. *lýti* 'rain', *snìgti* 'snow', *pustýti* 'drift (of snow)' also have passive forms with the neuter past participle, cf.:

Šiąnakt palìjo, yrà/bùvo palìję. →	'It rained (lit. it has/had rained) last night.'
Šiąnakt (bùvo) palýta.	'It had rained (lit. it was rained) last night.'
Rytój pasnìgs, bus pasnìgę. →	lit. 'It will snow/will have snowed tomorrow.'
Rýtoj bùs pàsnigta.	lit. 'Tomorrow will be snowed.'

5.76 Passive constructions with the agentive genitive correspond to active constructions as follows:

Tėvas suñkiai seȓga. →	'Father is seriously ill.'
Tėvo suñkiai seȓgama.	'Father (GEN) is seriously ill (PRES. PASS. PART. NEUTR).'
Vaikaĩ miegójo sodè. →	'The children slept in the garden.'
Vaikų̃ bùvo miẽgama sodè.	lit. 'By the children (GEN) was being slept (PRES. PASS. PART. NEUTR) in the garden.'
Jìs jaũ bùvo išė̃jęs. →	'He was already gone.'
Jõ jaũ bùvo ìšeita.	lit. 'By him (GEN) was already gone (PAST. PASS. PART. NEUTR).'

5.77 Passive constructions with the neuter participle and agentive genitive, especially without an auxiliary, are used in the evidential meaning (of an action not observed directly, but inferred from its consequences, assumed or hearsay). In such cases the agentive genitive is usually preposed to the verb, the word order of the respective active construction being retained, e.g.:

Čià	turbū̃t	iȓ	grỹbų	ẽsama.
here	maybe: PTCL	and	mushroom: GEN. PL	be: PRES. PASS. PART. NEUTR

'There must be mushrooms here.'

Teñ	šuñs	bė́gta.
there	dog: GEN. SG	run: PAST. PASS. PART. NEUTR

'A dog must have run here (there are foot-marks).'

Užeinù,	o	jõs	jaũ	miškañ	išeita.
drop-in: 3. PRES	but	she: GEN	already	wood: ILL. SG	go: PAST. PASS. PART. NEUTR

'I drop in, but she (it turns out, to my surprise) is gone to the woods.'

Čià	kìškio	gulė́ta,	čià	lãpės	kàsta –
here	rabbit: GEN	lie: PAST. PASS. PART. NEUTR	here	fox: GEN	dig: PAST. PASS. PART. NEUTR

àš	vìską	regiù.
I	everything: ACC	see: 3. PRES

'Here a rabbit has been lying, here a fox has been digging, – I see everything.'

The evidential passive with the neuter participle of intransitive verbs is more common than that of transitive verbs.

5.78 A sentence with a nominal (mostly adjectival) predicate can also be transformed into the passive voice having evidential meaning. In this case the copula *bū́ti* 'be' assumes the neuter form of a passive participle while the predicative assumes the genitive case form:

Jìs tebèrà gývas.   'He is still alive.' →

Jõ	tebė́sama	gývo.
he: GEN. SG	be: PRES. PASS. PART. NEUTR	alive: GEN. SG

'(They say) he is still alive.'

Pùšys bùvo stóros.   'The pinetrees were thick.' →

Pušų̃	bū́ta	storų̃.
pinetree: GEN. PL	be: PAST. PASS. PART. NEUTR	thick: GEN. PL

'The pinetrees turned out to be thick.'

Jõ tė́vas bùvo medžiótojas.   'His father was a hunter.' →

Jõ	tė́vo	bū́ta	medžiótojo.
he: GEN. SG	father: GEN. SG	be: PAST. PASS. PART. NEUTR	hunter: GEN. SG

'(I heard) his father was a hunter.'

If an active periphrastic verb form undergoes passivization (to express evidential meaning explicitly), both the auxiliary and the main verb assume the form of the passive neuter participle, e.g.:

Jìs bùvo išė́jęs.		'He was gone out.' →
Jõ	*bū́ta*	*išeita.*
he: GEN	be: PAST. PASS. PART. NEUTR	go-out: PAST. PASS. PART. NEUTR

'(They say/Evidently) he was gone out.'

Tadà mẽs jaũ bùvome atsigùlę.				'We had gone to bed then.' →
Tadà	*mū́sų*	*jaũ*	*bū́ta*	*atsìgulta.*
then	we: GEN	already	be: PAST. PASS. PART. NEUTR	lie-down: PAST. PASS. PART. NEUTR

'(Maybe/Evidently) we had already gone to bed then.'

The active form of the auxiliary can be retained, but in this case the evidential meaning is less clear, cf.: *Jõ bùvo ìšeita. Mū́sų bùvo atsìgulta.*

Finite forms of the verb

Veiksmãžodžių asmenúojamosios fòrmos

5.79 The finite forms of the verb include: the forms of three persons and two numbers (singular and plural), the forms of four tenses (present, past, past frequentative and future) in the indicative mood and in the oblique mood, and the forms of the subjunctive and imperative moods.

All the finite forms of the verb are formed from the three main verbal stems – that of the present, the past and the infinitive.

The present stem is the 3rd person form of the present tense, e.g. *sùpa* 'surrounds', *kẽlia* 'raises', *lỹdi* 'accompanies', *rãšo* 'writes'. This stem is used to build the present tense forms of the indicative and the 3rd person form of the imperative.

The past stem is the 3rd person form of the past tense, e.g. *sùpo* 'surrounded', *kė́lė* 'raised', *lydė́jo* 'accompanied', *rãšė* 'wrote'. This stem is used to create the past tense forms of the indicative.

In the present and past tenses the 3rd person forms coincide with the stem and do not contain any morphemes of person or number.

The infinitival stem is the part of the verb which remains after dropping the suffix *-ti*, e.g. *sùp-ti* 'to surround', *kél-ti* 'to raise', *lydė́-ti* 'to accompany', *rašý-ti* 'to write'. The infinitival stem is used to create the past frequentative and future tense forms of the indicative, the forms of the imperative with the suffix -k(i), and the subjunctive.

Verbal stems and thematic vowels

5.80 According to the morphemic structure of their stems all the verbs can be divided into three groups: primary, mixed and suffixal verbs.

All the three stems of the primary verbs are simple, although they may contain certain infixes or formants, e.g.:

bėga, bėgo, bėg-ti 'run'
spru-ñ-ka, sprùko, sprùk-ti 'take to one's heels'
pỹk-st-a, pỹko, pỹk-ti 'to be angry'

Among the stems of the mixed verbs we find both simple and suffixal stems, e.g.:

miẽga, mieg-ój-o, mieg-ó-ti 'sleep'
bráižo, bráižė, bráiž-y-ti 'scratch'

All the stems of the suffixal verbs contain a suffix, e.g.:

dìd-in-a, dìd-in-o, dìd-in-ti 'increase'

5.81 The present and past tense stems of many verbs differ in their thematic vowels only (they have the same root and the same affixes):

áug-a – áug-o 'grow'
atbėg-a – atbėg-o 'come running'
jùdin-a – jùdin-o 'move'

Almost all of the suffixal and a great number of primary verbs belong to this group. The stems of the other primary verbs differ quite often in their root vowels (apophonic change) or in certain consonant infixes, e.g. skìn-a, skýn-ė, skìn-ti 'pluck', šlam̃p-a, šlãp-o, šlàp-ti 'become wet' (see Table 11). There are several primary verbs which show irregular stem formation, e.g. dúod-a, dãv-ė, dúo-ti 'give'.

Mixed verbs have a suffix in the infinitive and the past tense stems or only in the infinitive stem (see Table 12).

5.82 The conjugation of verbs involves a number of systemic morphonological stem changes, which do not affect the morphological form of the stem in any way. The most important changes are the following ones:

(1) Before -*a* and -*u* the soft consonants *d*, *t* [dʲ tʲ] become soft affricates *dž*, *č* [ʤʲ ʧʲ] cf.:

áudė – áudžia 'weave' (3 PRES)
keĩtė – keičiù 'change' (1 PRES)

The consonants *d*, *t* become *s* between a vowel and the consonant *t* (that means also before the infinitival suffix *-ti*):

sėda, sėdo, sėsti (< *sėd-ti*) 'sit down'
mėta, mėtė, mèsti (< *mèt-ti*) 'throw'

The consonants *d*, *t* disappear between the sibilants *s*, *š*, *z*, *ž* and the infinitival suffix *-ti*:

brùzdo, brùzti (< *brùzd-ti*) 'bustle about'
beřgždė, beřgžti (< *beřgžd-ti*) 'become barren'
druм̃stė, druм̃sti (< *druм̃st-ti*) 'stir up'
pruñkštė, pruñkšti (< *pruñkšt-ti*) 'snort'

In the present stem the consonants *d*, *t* disappear also before *-st-*:

klýdo, klýsta (< *klýd-st-a*) 'err'
kaĩto, kaĩsta (< *kaĩt-st-a*) 'be getting hot'

(2) In the present tense stem after the sibilants *s*, *š*, *z*, *ž* the formant *-st-* loses *s*:

ilso, ilsta (< *ils-st-a*) 'become tired'
aũšo, aũšta (< *aũš-st-a*) 'dawn'
iřzo, iřzta (< *iřz-st-a*) 'get annoyed'
dū̃žo, dū̃žta (< *dū̃ž-st-a*) 'break'

(3) Before consonants the sound clusters *sk*, *šk*, *zg*, *žg* become *ks*, *kš*, *gz*, *gž*:

drỹska – drìsko – drìksti 'grow worn out, tear'
brėško – brėkšta – brėkšti 'dawn'
mėzga – mėzgė – mègzti 'knit'
džeřžgia – džeřžgė – džeřgžti 'jingle, clang'

(4) Changes of the consonant *j* which

(a) becomes *i* between the vowel *u* and a consonant:

gùja, gùjo, guĩti 'drive out; maltreat'

(b) disappears after *i* and before a consonant by making the latter vowel longer:

dalìja, dalìjo, dalýti 'divide'

(c) disappears after all the other vowels and before a consonant without a trace:

sėja, sėjo, sėti 'sow, plant'
jója, jójo, jóti 'ride'

(5) Between the vowel *u* and a consonant, the consonant *v* disappears, thereby lengthening the preceding vowel:

siùva, siùvo, siúti 'sew'

After all the other vowels the consonant *v* becomes *u*:

gãvo, gáuna, gáuti 'get'

(6) Before the consonants *l, m, n, r, s, š, z, ž, v* the present tense infix *n* and the same consonant in the infinitival stem disappears, thereby lengthening the preceding vowel:

bỹra (< biñra, cf. bìro) 'trickle'
spū̃ra (< spuñra, cf. spùro) 'fray'
bą́la (< bañla, cf. bãlo) 'become white'
keñtė, kę́sti (< keñs-ti < keñt-ti) 'suffer'
skùndė, skų́sti (< skùns-ti < skùnd-ti) 'report (against sb.)'

Concerning the changes of *s, š, z, ž* before the future tense suffix -*s(i)* see 5.102.

5.83 A large number of primary verbs possess different stems (see Table 11).

Table 11. **Stems of primary verbs**

Present	Past	Infinitive
The root contains *a, e, u*:	The root contains *o, ė, ū*:	The root contains *o, ė, ū*:
vãgia	võgė	võgti 'steal'
lẽkia	lė̃kė	lė̃kti 'fly'
tùpia	tū̃pė	tū̃pti 'alight'
The root contains *a, e, i, u*:	The root contains *o, ė, y, ū*:	The root contains *a, e, i, u*:
kãria	kórė	kárti 'hang'
kẽlia	kė̃lė	kélti 'raise'
gìria	gýrė	gìrti 'praise'
dùmia	dū́mė	dùmti 'dash'
The root contains *y, ū* (after dropping the -*n*-):	The root contains *i, u*:	The root contains *y, ū*:
gỹja	gìjo	gýti 'heal'
griū́va	griùvo	griū́ti 'fall'

Continuation of Table 11

Present	Past	Infinitive
The root contains *u, e:*	The root contains *u, i:*	The root contains *ū, y:*
siùva	siùvo	siū́ti 'sew'
vẽja	vìjo	výti 'chase'
The root contains *e:*	The root contains *i:*	The root contains *i:*
velka	vilko	vilkti 'drag'
kem̃ša	kim̃šo	kim̃šti 'stuff'
reñka	riñko	riñkti 'choose'
per̃ka	pir̃ko	pir̃kti 'buy'
gẽna	gìnė	giñti 'drive'
The root contains *au* and the infix *-n-* or *-j-* before the thematic vowel:	The root contains *ov* and no infix:	The root contains *au* and no infix:
džiáuna	džióvė	džiáuti 'hang to dry'
liáuja	lióvė	liáuti 'stop doing'
The root contains the infix *-n-* (*-m-* before *b, p*):	The root contains no infix:	The root contains no infix:
añka	ãko	àkti 'go blind'
señka	sẽko	sèkti 'sink'
stiñga	stìgo	stìgti 'be not enough'
spruñka	sprùko	sprùkti 'take to his/her heels'
šlam̃pa	šlãpo	šlàpti 'get wet'
glem̃ba	glẽbo	glèbti 'become flabby'
drim̃ba	drìbo	drìbti 'tumble'
čium̃pa	čiùpo	čiùpti 'grab'
bą́la (< bañla)	bãlo	bálti 'pale'
šỹla (< šiñla)	šìlo	šìlti 'become warm'
spū́ra (< spuñra)	spùro	spùrti 'fray'
The root contains the formant *-st-*	The root contains no formant:	The root contains no formant:
alpsta	alpo	alpti 'faint'
ilsta (< ils̃-st-a)	ilso	ilsti 'get tired'
aũšta (< aũš-st-a)	aũšo	aũšti 'dawn'
ir̃zta (< ir̃z-st-a)	ir̃zo	ir̃zti 'get irritated'
lū́žta (< lū́ž-st-a)	lū́žo	lū́žti 'break'

Irregular stems

Present	Past	Infinitive
aũna	ãvė	aũti 'put on or take off shoes'
yrà, ẽsame	bùvo	bū́ti 'be'
dė̃da	dė́jo	dė́ti 'put'
dúoda	dãvė	dúoti 'give'
eĩna	ė̃jo	eĩti 'go'
gáuna	gãvo	gáuti 'get'
ìma	ė̃mė	im̃ti 'take'
lieka	lìko	lìkti 'remain'
mìršta	mìrė	mir̃ti 'die'
púola	púolė	pùlti 'attack'
šlúoja	šlãvė	šlúoti 'sweep'
vérda	vìrė	vìrti 'boil'

Mixed verbs have different stems as well. Their present tense stem is usually simple, while the other two stems contain suffixes except for one group of verbs which contain a suffix only in the infinitival stem (see Table 12).

Table 12. **Stems of mixed verbs**

Present	Past	Infinitive
The simple stem ends in *a*:	The suffix *-ojo*:	The suffix *-oti*:
gíeda	giedójo	giedóti 'chant; crow'
miẽga	miegójo	miegóti 'sleep'
ráuda	raudójo	raudóti 'weep'
The simple stem ends in *o*:		
bìjo	bijójo	bijóti 'be afraid'
íeško	ieškójo	ieškóti 'look for'
pū̃pso	pūpsójo	pūpsóti 'lie puffed up'
teĩkšo	telkšójo	telkšóti 'lie (about water)'
The simple stem ends in *a*:	The suffix *-ėjo*:	The suffix *-ėti*:
bȳra	byrė́jo	byrė́ti 'trickle'
dùlka	dulkė́jo	dulkė́ti 'get dusty'
žìba	žibė́jo	žibė́ti 'sparkle'
The simple stem ends in *ia*:		
keñčia	kentė́jo	kentė́ti 'suffer'

Present	Past	Infinitive
kvėpia	kvepėjo	kvepėti 'smell good'
reĩkia	reikėjo	reikėti 'be necessary'
The simple stem ends in *i*:		
gùli	gulėjo	gulėti 'lie'
kriùksi	kriuksėjo	kriuksėti 'grunt'
bàrkši	barkšėjo	barkšėti 'rattle'
Simple stem ends in *-o*:	Simple stem ends in *-ė*:	Suffix *-yti*:
rãšo	rãšė	rašýti 'write'
gãno	gãnė	ganýti 'shepherd'
gìrdo	gìrdė	gìrdyti 'give water'
láisto	láistė	láistyti 'water'

Suffixal verbs usually retain their suffixes in all the principal forms, although in different phonetic environments some suffixes may undergo certain changes. For example, since the vowel cluster *au* becomes *av* before *o*, the present tense suffix -*(i)auja* and the infinitival suffix *-(i)auti* become *-(i)avo* in the past. The difference in the stems *dalìjo – dalýti* 'distribute' is explained by the disappearance of *j* before a consonant (cf. 5.82(4), I.3.6). There is only one group of verbs containing two different suffixes in their principal forms, e.g. *bangúoja, bangãvo, bangúoti* 'have waves'. Their stem in the past is like that of the verbs with the suffix *-(i)auti* (see Table 13).

Table 13 **Differences in the stems of suffixal verbs**

Present	Past	Infinitive
Suffix *-(i)uoja*:	Suffix *-(i)avo*:	Suffix *-(i)uoti*:
dainúoja	dainãvo	dainúoti 'sing'
važiúoja	važiãvo	važiúoti 'go (by a vehicle)'
lūkuriuoja	lūkuriavo	lūkuriuoti 'linger'
Suffix *-(i)auja*:		Suffix *-(i)auti*:
uogáuja	uogãvo	uogáuti 'pick berries'
keliáuja	keliãvo	keliáuti 'travel'
rėkauja	rėkavo	rėkauti 'shout (repeatedly)'
Suffix *-ija*:	Suffix *-ijo*:	Suffix *-yti*:
dalìja	dalìjo	dalýti 'distribute'
rūdìja	rūdìjo	rūdýti 'rust'
virŝija	virŝijo	virŝyti 'exceed'

5.84 There is a regular relationship between the form of the main stems and the thematic vowels in the present and the past.

In the present tense the stem of primary verbs ends in *a* (after a hard consonant or *j*) or in *ia* (after a soft consonant). The stems of the following verbs end in *a* if:

(1) they have an infix (or a formant) in the present tense stem or if the thematic vowel is preceded by *n, j, v*, e.g.:

kriñta, krìto, krìsti 'fall'
bȳra, bìro, bìrti 'trickle'
gęsta, gęso, gèsti 'get low (about fire, lights)'
šáuna, šóvė, šáuti 'shoot'
jója, jójo, jóti 'ride'
griũva, griùvo, griũti 'crumble; fall'

(2) they retain the root vowels *a, e, i, u* in all their stems, e.g.:

kāla, kālė, kálti 'hammer'
lìpa, lìpo, lìpti 'climb'
nẽša, nẽšė, nèšti 'carry'
lùpa, lùpo, lùpti 'peel'

(3) *i* and *y* alternate before *n*, e.g.:

pìna, pýnė, pìnti 'braid'

(4) *e* interchanges with *i*, e.g.:

kem̃ša, kim̃šo, kim̃šti 'stuff'
gẽna, gìnė, giñti 'drive'

The present tense stem of all other primary verbs ends in *ia* (with a few exceptions) (see Table 14).

The past stem of primary verbs ends in *o* or *ė*. The final vowel *o* of the past stem is to be found in verbs which:

(1) in the present tense stem have an infix (or a formant) or *j, v* before the thematic vowel, e.g.:

kriñta, krìto, krìsti 'fall'
gęsta, gęso, gèsti 'get low (about fire, lights)'
jója, jójo, jóti 'ride'

(2) have the short vowels *i, u*, in all their stems and no infixes or formants, e.g.:

lìpa, lìpo, lìpti 'climb'
sùka, sùko, sùkti 'rotate'

(3) have semidiphthongs with alternating *e* and *i*, e.g.:

telpa, tilpo, tilpti 'accommodate'

The past stem of all other primary verbs ends in *ė* (with a few exceptions) (see Table 14).

Table 14. **Correlation of the present and past stems of primary verbs and the thematic vowels**

Characteristics of the stem	Present thematic vowel	Past thematic vowel
	a	o
The actual or lost infix -*n*- (before *b, p*: -*m*-) in the present stem	añka 'goes blind'	āko
	geñda 'gets bad'	gẽdo
	kiñta 'changes'	kìto
	juñta 'feels'	jùto
	šlam̃pa 'gets wet'	šlãpo
	dum̃ba 'caves in'	dùbo
	bą̃la 'pales'	bãlo
	gvẽra 'gets rickety'	gvẽro
	bỹra 'trickles'	bìro
	spū̃ra 'frays'	spùro
	a	o
Infix -*st*- (following *s, š, z, ž*: -*t*-) in the present stem	álksta 'gets hungry'	álko
	mė́gsta 'likes'	mė́go
	aũšta 'dawns'	aũšo
	tū̃žta 'gets furious'	tū̃žo
	mą̃žta 'diminishes'	mą̃žo
	gỹžta 'gets sour'	gìžo
		Exception:
	gìmsta 'is born'	gìmė
	a	o
v, j preceding the thematic vowel in the present and past stems	griũva 'falls'	griùvo
	siũva 'sews'	siùvo
	gỹja 'heals'	gìjo
	jója 'rides'	jójo
	vė́ja 'pursues'	vìjo
	zùja 'zooms'	zùjo

Characteristics of the stem	Present thematic vowel	Past thematic vowel
	a	o
i, u in the stems	kìša 'stuffs'	kìšo
	lìpa 'climbs'	lìpo
	lùpa 'peels'	lùpo
	sùka 'rotates'	sùko
		Exceptions:
	gùla 'lies down'	gùlė
	mùša 'beats'	mùšė
	a	o
Apophonic change *e : i* (in semidiphthongs)	kem̃ša 'stuffs'	kim̃šo
	leñda 'gets into'	liñdo
	telpa 'is accommodated'	tilpo
	per̃ka 'buys'	pir̃ko
	a	ė
Apophonic change *e : i* (not in semidiphthongs)	gẽna 'drives'	gìnė
	mẽna 'remembers'	mìnė
	a	ė
Apophonic change *i : y* (preceding *n*)	gìna 'defends'	gýnė
	mìna 'treads'	mýnė
	skìna 'plucks'	skýnė
	a	ė
-(i)auna, -(i)auja : -(i)ovė	bliáuna 'brays'	blióvė
	ráuna 'uproots'	róvė
	liáuja 'desists'	lióvė
	a	ė
a, e in the stems	bãra 'scolds'	bãrė
	kãla 'hammers'	kãlė
	dẽga 'burns'	dẽgė
	nẽša 'carries'	nẽšė
	Exceptions:	
	ãria 'ploughs'	ãrė
	tãria 'pronounces'	tãrė
	žãgia 'steals'	žãgė

Continuation of Table 14

Characteristics of the stem	Present thematic vowel	Past thematic vowel
	ia	ė
ė, y, o, ū, ę in the stems	grėbia 'rakes' krỹkščia 'exults' dróžia 'planes' plū́kia 'rams' tę̃sia 'continues' Exceptions: ė́da 'eats' bė́ga 'runs' sė́da 'sits down' šóka 'dances' grū́da 'stuffs'	grė̃bė krỹkštė dróžė plū́kė tę̃sė Exceptions: ė́dė bė́go sė́do šóko grū́do
	ia	ė
Diphthongs in the stems	baĩgia 'finishes' braũkia 'brushes' kéikia 'curses' díegia 'implements' puõšia 'decorates' kuĩčia 'rummages' léidžia 'permits' Exception: áuga 'grows'	baĩgė braũkė kéikė díegė puõšė kuĩtė Exceptions: léido áugo
	ia	ė
Semidiphthongs in the stems (without apophonic change e : i)	skalbia 'washes' karšia 'cards' deñgia 'covers' tem̃pia 'drags' švil̃pia 'whistles' griñdžia 'grounds' drum̃sčia 'makes turbid' mur̃kia 'purrs' Exceptions: galánda 'sharpens' kánda 'bites' dìrba 'works' žìnda 'sucks'	skalbė karšė deñgė tem̃pė švil̃pė griñdė drum̃stė mur̃kė Exceptions: galándo kándo dìrbo žìndo

Continuation of Table 14

Characteristics of the stem	Present thematic vowel	Past thematic vowel
	ia	ė
Apophonic changes	kãria 'hangs'	kórė
a : o, e : ė, u : ū	vãgia 'steals'	võgė
	bẽria 'pours'	bė̃rė
	slẽpia 'hides'	slė̃pė
	kùlia 'threshes'	kū́lė
	tùpia 'alights'	tū̃pė
	ia	ė
Apophonic change	gìlia 'stings'	gýlė
i : y (preceding l, r)	vìlia 'gives hope'	výlė
	gìria 'praises'	gýrė
	tìria 'investigates'	týrė
	Exception:	
	pìla 'pours'	pýlė

5.85 A relationship between the thematic vowels in the present and in the past is also to be noticed.

The past stem in *o* corresponds, as a rule, to the present stem in *a*, whereas the past stem in *ė* corresponds to the present stem in *ia* (exceptions are few, see Table 14).

All the present stems of suffixal verbs end in *a* (after *n* or *j*) whereas all the past stems (both of suffixal and mixed verbs) end in *o*.

If the past stem of mixed verbs contains no suffix, their present and past tense stems end in *o* and *ė* respectively, e.g., *rãšo – rãšė* 'write'.

If the past stem of mixed verbs contains the suffix -*ojo* and if the infinitive contains the suffix -*oti*, the present tense stem also ends in *o*, e.g.:

íeško, ieškójo, ieškóti 'look for'
riógso, riogsójo, riogsóti 'stand, stick'

The following three verbs with the present tense stem ending in *a* constitute an exception to the above rule:

gíeda, giedójo, giedóti 'chant; crow'
miẽga, miegójo, miegóti 'sleep'
ráuda, raudójo, raudóti 'weep'

If the past stem of mixed verbs contains the suffix -*ėjo* and the infinitival stem contains the suffix -*ėti*, the present tense stem ends in *a* or *i*:

bỹra, byrė́jo, byrė́ti 'trickle'
gùli, gulė́jo, gulė́ti 'lie'

The following three verbs with the present stem ending in *ia* constitute an exception to the above rule:

keñčia, kentė́jo, kentė́ti 'suffer'
kvẽpia, kvepė́jo, kvepė́ti 'smell well'
reĩkia, reikė́jo, reikė́ti 'be necessary'

Endings indicating person and number

5.86 Person is indicated by adding the following endings to the verbal stem:

	Singular	Plural
1st person	-u	-me
2nd person	-i	-te
3rd person	-ø	-ø

The third person forms contain no special ending, coinciding with the pure stem (in other words, the absence of an ending is the indication of the third person form).

Before endings which begin with a consonant, the thematic vowels do not undergo any changes, e.g.:

sùpa-me 'we rock' *sùpa-te* 'you rock'
mýli-me 'we love' *mýli-te* 'you love'
rãšo-me 'we write' *rãšo-te* 'you write'
nẽšė-me 'we carried' *nẽšė-te* 'you carried'

Before vowel endings, the long thematic vowels *o, ė* become *a* and *e* respectively, whereas the short thematic vowels *a, i* disappear altogether, e.g.:

Pres. 2. Sg. *raša-ĩ* (cf. *rãšo*) 'you write'
Past. 2. Sg. *neše-ĩ* (cf. *nẽšė*) 'you carried'
Pres. 1. Sg. *sup-ù* (< *sùpa+u*) 'I rock'
Pres. 2. Sg. *sup-ì* (< *sùpa+i*) 'you rock'
Pres. 1. Sg. *mýli-u* (< *mýli+u*) 'I love'
Pres. 2. Sg. *mýl-i* (< *mýli+i*) 'you love'

(In *mýliu* the letter *i* indicates that the preceding consonant is palatalized.)

The 1st and 2nd person endings convey also the meaning of number, whereas the 3rd person form (which coincides with the pure stem) does not carry any meaning of number – it is used with nouns and pronouns both in the singular and in the plural.

The 1st and 2nd person plural forms may be shortened by dropping the final *e*, e.g.:

bė́gam 'we run' *bė́gat* 'you run'
bė́gom 'we ran' *bė́got* 'you ran'
bė́gdavom 'we used to run' *bė́gdavot* 'you used to run'
bė́gsim 'we'll run' *bė́gsit* 'you'll run'
bė́gtumėm 'we would run' *bė́gtumėt* 'you would run'
bė́kim 'let's run' *bė́kit* 'run!'

5.87 In present-day Lithuanian there are several verbs which in the present tense have retained the old athematic 3rd person forms, which consist of the stem without the thematic vowel and the ending *-ti*, e.g.:

ẽsti 'is, are' *sniẽgti* 'snows'
kósti 'coughs' *per̃šti* 'smarts'
niẽžti 'itches'

The verb *bū́ti* 'be' has several 3rd person forms in the present tense: *ẽs-ti, bū̃n-a, bū̃v-a, yrà*. The latter is the most frequently used form in present-day Lithuanian. The present 3rd person forms *kósėja* 'coughs', *sniñga* 'snows' are widely used as well.

The 3rd person forms of the imperative mood, which are rapidly disappearing, possess the ending *-ie* and *-i* (see 5.49, 105), e.g.:

tegul-iẽ 'let him/her/it/them lie'
terãša-i 'let him/her/it/them write'

5.88 The endings of the 1st and 2nd person plural forms of all the **reflexive verbs** containing the formant *-s(i)* at the end are slightly different from those of the respective non-reflexive verbs, whereas the endings of *a*-stem and *i*-stem reflexive verbs differ from those of the respective non-reflexive verbs not only in the 1st and 2nd person plural, but also in the 1st and 2nd person singular.

Singular	Plural
(*a*-stem and *i*-stem reflexive verbs)	(all the reflexive verbs)
1st person: *-uo-si*	*-mė-s*
2nd person: *-ie-si*	*-tė-s*

Cf. the non-reflexive and reflexive present forms of the verb *sùkti/sùktis* 'turn': 1st Sg. *suk-ù – suk-úo-si*, 2nd *suk-ì – suk-íe-si*, 1st Pl. *sùka-me – sùka-mės*, 2nd *sùka-te – sùka-tės*.

The difference in the endings of such reflexive verbs can be accounted for by the position of the ending before the reflexive formant -s(i), which has helped them to retain their length. Cf. a similar difference in the endings of simple and definite adjectives, e.g.:

Instr. Sg.: *ger-ù* : *gerúo-ju* 'good'
Nom. Pl.: *ger-ì* : *gerie-ji*

In the 3rd person form the reflexive formant -s(i) is preceded by a pure thematic vowel, e.g.:

sùka-si 'turns, turn'
mýli-si 'they love each other'
ródo-si 'it seems'

In prefixed verbs the formant -si- is placed between the prefix and the root. Such reflexive verbs are conjugated in the same way as non-reflexive verbs.

The reflexive formant at the end of the 1st and 2nd person plural forms in all tenses as well as the 3rd person form of the future and the 2nd person form singular of the imperative is used without the final vowel *i*, e.g.:

sùkamės 'we turn'	*sùkatės* 'you turn'
sùkomės 'we turned'	*sùkotės* 'you turned'
sùkdavomės 'we used to turn'	*sùkdavotės* 'you used to turn'
sùksimės 'we'll turn'	*sùksitės* 'you'll turn'
sùksis 'he/she/it/they will turn'	
sùkis 'turn!'	

The final *i* of the reflexive formant can sometimes also be dropped in the 1st and 2nd person singular and sometimes even in the 3rd person, e.g.:

sukúos 'I turn'	*sukíes* 'you turn'	*sùkas* 'turns'
sukaũs 'I turned'	*sukaĩs* 'you turned'	*sùkos* 'he/she/it/they turned'
sùkdavaus 'I used to turn'	*sùkdavais* 'you used to turn'	*sùkdavos* 'he/she/it/they used to turn'
sùksiuos 'I'll turn'	*sùksies* 'you'll turn'	
sùkčiaus 'I would turn'	*sùktumeis* 'you would turn'	*sùktųs* 'they would turn'

CONJUGATIONS

5.89 There are three conjugations which are distinguished according to the thematic vowels in the present tense.

The present stems of the 1st conjugation verbs end in *(i)a*:

kãla 'hammers' *kẽlia* 'raises'

The stems of the 2nd conjugation verbs end in *i*:

mýli 'loves' *tìksi* 'ticks'

The stems of the 3rd conjugation verbs end in *o*:

kãso 'scratches' *klũpo* 'kneels'

According to additional peculiarities of the present and past tense stems and their mutual relationships, verbs belonging to the 1st and 3rd conjugations are divided into several distinct groups.

Conjugation 1

5.90 Conjugation 1 comprises verbs the present tense stems of which end in *a* after a hard or soft consonant (in the latter case it is spelled as *ia*) and their past tense stems end in *o* or *ė*. Among the verbs which belong to Conjugation 1 we can find primary, mixed and suffixal verbs. They fall into four major groups.

GROUP 1

5.91 Group 1 comprises primary, mixed and suffixal verbs the present tense stems of which end in *a*, and the past stems of which end in *o*. Here belong:

(1) Primary verbs with:

(a) the infix *-n-* (*-m-* before *b, p*) in the present stems (the infix *-n-* has disappeared before *l, m, r, s, š, z, ž* causing the lengthening of the preceding vowel; see II.3.9), e.g.:

rañda 'finds'	*rãdo* 'found'
señka 'gets lower'	*sẽko* 'got lower (of water)'
stiñga 'lacks'	*stìgo* 'lacked'
truñka 'lasts'	*trùko* 'lasted'
dum̃ba 'caves in'	*dùbo* 'caved in'
šlam̃pa 'gets wet'	*šlãpo* 'got wet'
šą̃la 'freezes'	*šãlo* 'froze'
svỹla 'burns a little'	*svìlo* 'burnt a little'
gū̃ra 'crumbles'	*gùro* 'crumbled'
pliũška 'sags'	*pliùško* 'sagged'

(b) the formant *-st-* (or *-t-* following *s, š, z, ž*) in the present stem, e.g.:

álpsta 'faints'	álpo 'fainted'
leĩpsta 'swoons'	leĩpo 'swooned'
pỹksta 'is angry'	pỹko 'was angry'
sprógsta 'explodes'	sprógo 'exploded'
geĩsta 'becomes yellow'	geĩto 'was becoming yellow'
klýsta 'errs'	klýdo 'erred'
gaĩšta 'tarries'	gaĩšo 'tarried'
grį̃žta 'returns'	grį̃žo 'returned'

Exception – the verb *gìmsta – gìmė* 'is/was born' which belongs to Group 2.

(c) *v* or *j* preceding the thematic vowels in the present and the past, e.g.:

griũva 'crumbles'	griùvo 'crumbled'
pū́va 'rots'	pùvo 'rotted'
siùva 'sews'	siùvo 'sew'
lỹja 'rains'	lìjo 'rained'
vẽja 'chases'	vìjo 'chased'
plója 'claps'	plójo 'clapped'
líeja 'pours'	líejo 'poured'
ùja 'nags'	ùjo 'nagged'

Exceptions: verbs like *liáuja – lióvė* 'stop, cease', which belong to Group 2.

(d) the short vowel *i* or *u* in present and past stems, e.g.:

knìsa 'roots'	knìso 'rooted'
rìša 'ties'	rìšo 'tied'
rìta 'rolls'	rìto 'rolled'
brùka 'thrusts'	brùko 'thrust'
lùpa 'peels'	lùpo 'peeled'
sùpa 'surrounds'	sùpo 'surrounded'

Exceptions are the following verbs, which belong to Group 2:

gùla 'lies down'	gùlė 'lay down'
mùša 'beats'	mùšė 'beat'

(e) semidiphthongs with alternating *e* and *i* in present and past stems, e.g.:

ker̃pa 'cuts'	kir̃po 'cut'
krem̃ta 'bites'	krim̃to 'bit'
reñka 'gathers'	riñko 'gathered'
veĩka 'drags'	viĩko 'dragged'

(f) irregular stems, e.g.:

yrà 'is/are'	*bùvo* 'was/were'
dė́da 'puts'	*dė́jo* 'put'
eĩna 'goes'	*ė̃jo* 'went'
gáuna 'gets'	*gãvo* 'got'
liẽka 'remains'	*lìko* 'remained'

(2) Mixed verbs with:

(a) the suffix *-ėjo* in their past stem, e.g.:

drė̃ba 'trembles'	*drebė́jo* 'trembled'
jùda 'moves'	*judė́jo* 'moved'
krùta 'stirs'	*krutė́jo* 'stirred'
mìrga 'shimmers'	*mirgė́jo* 'shimmered'
móka 'knows how to'	*mokė́jo* 'knew how to'
sópa 'hurts'	*sopė́jo* 'hurt'
stė̃na 'groans'	*stenė́jo* 'groaned'

(b) the suffix *-ojo* in their past stem. Here belong only three verbs:

gíeda 'chants, crows'	*giedójo* 'chanted, crowed'
miẽga 'sleeps'	*miegójo* 'slept'
ráuda 'weeps'	*raudójo* 'wept'

(3) All the derived verbs with the following seven suffixes:

(a) *-(i)au-ti* (*draugáuti, keliáuti*, etc.)

draugáuja 'are friends'	*draugãvo* 'were friends'
keliáuja 'travels'	*keliãvo* 'travelled'
riešutáuja 'picks nuts'	*riešutãvo* 'picked nuts'
studentáuja 'is a student'	*studentãvo* 'was a student'

(b) *-(i)uo-ti* (*dainúoti, eiliúoti*, etc.)

dainúoja 'sings'	*dainãvo* 'sang'
eiliúoja 'creates rhymes'	*eiliãvo* 'created rhymes'
miltúoja 'covers with flour'	*miltãvo* 'covered with flour'
važiúoja 'drives'	*važiãvo* 'drove'

(c) *-(i)o-ti* (*galvóti, medžióti*, etc.)

galvója 'thinks'	*galvójo* 'thought'
medžiója 'hunts'	*medžiójo* 'hunted'
pláukioja 'swims'	*pláukiojo* 'swam'
putója 'foams'	*putójo* 'foamed'

žiemója 'winters' *žiemójo* 'wintered'
vedžiója 'leads' *vedžiójo* 'led'

(**d**) *-ė-ti* (*áuklėti, akmenėti*, etc.)

áuklėja 'educates' *áuklėjo* 'educated'
akmenėja 'petrifies' *akmenėjo* 'petrified'
gražėja 'becomes more beautiful', *gražėjo* 'became more beautiful'
pavasarėja 'comes (of spring)' *pavasarėjo* 'came (of spring)'
siūlėja 'hems' *siūlėjo* 'hemmed'
vaikėja 'becomes infantile' *vaikėjo* 'became infantile'

(**e**) *-y-ti* (*akýti, dalýti*, etc.)

akìja 'becomes porous' *akìjo* 'became porous'
dalìja 'distributes' *dalìjo* 'distributed'
núodija 'poisons' *núodijo* 'poisoned'
rūdìja 'rusts' *rūdìjo* 'rusted'
skiĕpija 'innoculates' *skiĕpijo* 'innoculated'
vilnìja 'ripples' *vilnìjo* 'rippled'

(**f**) *-in-ti* (*bárškinti, lēsinti*, etc.)

bárškina 'knocks' *bárškino* 'knocked'
lēsina 'feeds birds' *lēsino* 'fed birds'
prātina 'habituates' *prātino* 'habituated'
sodìna 'plants' *sodìno* 'planted'
šnēkina 'talks to' *šnēkino* 'talked to'
šlāpina 'wets' *šlāpino* 'wetted'

(**g**) *-en-ti* (*gyvénti, kedénti*, etc.)

gyvēna 'lives' *gyvēno* 'lived'
kedēna 'picks' *kedēno* 'picked'
kūrēna 'heats' *kūrēno* 'heated'
purēna 'loosens' *purēno* 'loosened'
ridēna 'rolls' *ridēno* 'rolled'

Additional derivative formants can make the suffixes longer, but the conjugation of the verb remains the same, e.g.:

mirguliúoja 'shimmers' *mirguliãvo* 'shimmered'
lūkuriuoja 'lingers' *lūkuriavo* 'lingered'
cf. *dainúoja* 'sings' *dainãvo* 'sang'

lìnkčioja 'nods' *lìnkčiojo* 'nodded'
vartaliója 'keeps turning' *vartaliójo* 'kept turning'
cf. *kartója* 'repeats' *kartójo* 'repeated'

šokinėja 'jumps up and down' *šokinėjo* 'jumped up and down'
cf. *áuklėja* 'educates' *áuklėjo* 'educated'

GROUP 2

5.92 Group 2 of Conjugation 1 includes primary verbs the present stem of which ends in *a* and the past stem of which ends in *ė*. Here belong primary verbs with:

(1) the vowels *a* or *e* in their stems, e.g.:

bãra 'scolds'	bãrė 'scolded'
kãsa 'digs'	kãsė 'dug'
lãka 'drinks'	lãkė 'drank (of a cat)'
mãla 'mills'	mãlė 'milled'
bēda 'stick'	bēdė 'stuck'
mēta 'throws'	mētė 'threw'
pēša 'pluck'	pēšė 'plucked'
sēga 'fastens'	sēgė 'fastened'
tēpa 'smears'	tēpė 'smeared'
vēža 'carry by a vehicle'	vēžė 'carried by a vehicle'

Exceptions (belonging to Group 3):

ãria 'ploughs'	ãrė 'ploughed'
tãria 'pronounces'	tãrė 'pronounced'
žãgia 'pollutes'	žãgė 'polluted'

(2) *i* preceding *n* in the present stem changing to *y* in the past stem, e.g.:

pìna 'weaves, twines'	pýnė 'wove, twined'
skìna 'plucks'	skýnė 'plucked'
trìna 'rubs'	trýnė 'rubbed'

(3) *e* in the present stem, changing to *i* in the past (this group includes only two verbs):

gēna 'drives'	gìnė 'drove'
mēna 'remembers'	mìnė 'remembered'

(4) -(i)auna or -(i)auja in the present stem changing into -(i)ovė in the past, e.g.:

bliáuna 'brays'	bliõvė 'brayed'
džiáuna 'hangs out to dry'	džiõvė 'hung (washing)'
griáuna 'destroys'	griõvė 'destroyed'
kráuna 'loads'	krõvė 'loaded'
pjáuna 'cuts'	pjõvė 'cut'
liáuja 'desists'	liõvė 'desisted'

(5) irregular present and past stems, e.g.:

aūna 'puts on shoes'	ãvė 'put on shoes

dúoda 'gives'   *dãvė* 'gave'
ìma 'takes'   *ẽmė* 'took'
mìršta 'dies'   *mìrė* 'died'
púola 'attacks'   *púolė* 'attacked'
šlúoja 'sweeps'   *šlãvė* 'swept'
vérda 'boils'   *vìrė* 'boiled'

GROUP 3

5.93 This group includes primary verbs the present stem of which ends in *ia* and the past stem ends in *ė*. It is a group of verbs characterized by the presence of the following stem vowels or diphthongs:

(1) the long vowels *ė, y, o, ū, ę*, e.g.:

glė̆bia 'embraces'   *glė̆bė* 'embraced'
plė̆šia 'tears'   *plė̆šė* 'tore'
trỹpia 'tramples'   *trỹpė* 'trampled'
žnýbia 'pinches'   *žnýbė* 'pinched'
vóžia 'puts a lid on'   *vóžė* 'put a lid on'
triũsia 'labours'   *triũsė* 'laboured'
ū̃žia 'drones'   *ū̃žė* 'droned'
grę̃žia 'drills'   *grę̃žė* 'drilled'

Exceptions (which fall under Group 1):

bė̆ga 'runs'   *bė̆go* 'ran'
sė̆da 'sits down'   *sė̆do* 'sat down'
šóka 'dances'   *šóko* 'danced'
grū̃da 'stuffs'   *grū̃do* 'stuffed'

(2) diphthongs:

baĩgia 'ends'   *baĩgė* 'ended'
žaĩdžia 'plays'   *žaĩdė* 'played'
spáudžia 'presses'   *spáudė* 'pressed'
šaũkia 'shouts'   *šaũkė* 'shouted'
keĩčia 'changes'   *keĩtė* 'changed'
steĩgia 'founds'   *steĩgė* 'founded'
díegia 'plants'   *díegė* 'planted'
liẽpia 'orders'   *liẽpė* 'ordered'
kuõpia 'cleans out'   *kuõpė* 'cleaned out'
sliuõgia 'crawls'   *sliuõgė* 'crawled'

Exceptions:

áuga 'grows'	*áugo* 'grew' (Group 1)
púola 'attacks'	*púolė* 'attacked' (Group 2)
léidžia 'permits'	*léido* 'permitted' (Group 4)

(3) semidiphthongs (without the apophonic change *e : i*):

deñgia 'covers'	*deñgė* 'covered'
reñgia 'prepares'	*reñgė* 'prepared'
kařšia 'cards'	*kařšė* 'carded'
čiřpia 'chirps'	*čiřpė* 'chirped'
iñkščia 'whines'	*iñkštė* 'whined'
dul˜kia 'drizzles'	*dul˜kė* 'drizzled'
skùndžia 'reports on'	*skùndė* 'reported on'

Exceptions (which fall under Group 1):

kánda 'bites'	*kándo* 'bit'
galánda 'sharpens'	*galándo* 'sharpened'
dìrba 'works'	*dìrbo* 'worked'
žìnda 'suck'	*žìndo* 'sucked'

(4) apophonic changes *a : o, e : ė, u : ū, i : y* (the latter takes place only before *l* and *r*), e.g.:

kāria 'hangs'	*kórė* 'hanged'
vãgia 'steals'	*võgė* 'stole'
gēlia 'stings'	*gḗlė* 'stung'
lēkia 'flies'	*lḗkė* 'flew'
kùria 'creates'	*kū̃rė* 'created'
pùčia 'blows'	*pūtė* 'blew'
gìlia 'stings'	*gýlė* 'stung'
spìria 'kicks'	*spýrė* 'kicked'

The verb *pìla* 'pours', *pýlė* 'poured' is an exception and it falls under Group 2.

GROUP 4

5.94 Group 4 of Conjugation 1 includes verbs the present stem of which ends in *ia* and the past stem ends in *o*. This is the smallest group; it has only three mixed verbs and one primary verb:

keñčia 'suffers'	*kentėjo* 'suffered'
kvẽpia 'smells good'	*kvepėjo* 'smelled good'

reĩkia 'it is necessary'   reikėjo 'it was necessary'
léidžia 'allows'   léido 'allowed'

Conjugation 2

5.95 Conjugation 2 comprises verbs the present stem of which ends in *i* and the past stem of which ends in *o*. All these verbs are of mixed derivation – in the present tense their stems are simple, but in the past they have the suffix *-ėjo*, e.g.:

gãli 'can'   galėjo 'could'
girdi 'hears'   girdėjo 'heard'
lỹdi 'accompanies'   lydėjo 'accompanied'
rãvi 'weeds'   ravėjo 'weeded'
sėdi 'sits'   sėdėjo 'sat'
žýdi 'blossoms'   žydėjo 'blossomed'
čėpsi 'smacks his/her lips'   čepsėjo 'smacked his/her lips'
pókši 'bangs'   pokšėjo 'banged'

Conjugation 3

5.96 Conjugation 3 includes verbs the present tense of which ends in *o* and the past stem of which ends in *ė* or *o*. All these verbs are of mixed derivation and fall into two groups.

GROUP 1

Group 1 includes verbs which have no suffix either in the present or in the past, but their infinitival form contains the suffix *-yti*. Their past stem ends in *ė*, e.g.:

bãdo 'butts'   bãdė 'butted'
daũžo 'breaks'   daũžė 'broke'
gãno 'shepherds'   gãnė 'shepherded'
kãso 'scratches'   kãsė 'scratched'
láužo 'breaks'   láužė 'broke'
mėto 'throws'   mėtė 'threw'
rãšo 'writes'   rãšė 'wrote'
var̃žo 'restricts'   var̃žė 'restricted'
ar̃do 'dismantles'   ar̃dė 'dismantled'
mìgdo 'puts to sleep'   mìgdė 'put to sleep'
spárdo 'kicks'   spárdė 'kicked'

baȓsto 'strews' baȓstė 'strewed'
kráusto 'moves' kráustė 'moved'

GROUP 2

The past stem of the verbs in this group contains the suffix -*ojo* (i.e., they end in *o*), e.g.:

bìjo 'is afraid' bijójo 'was afraid'
íeško 'looks for' ieškójo 'looked for'
kãbo 'hangs' kabójo 'hung'
klū́po 'kneels' klū́pojo 'knelt'
sáugo 'guards' sáugojo 'guarded'
týko 'stalks' týkojo 'stalked'
žìno 'knows' žinójo 'knew'
duñkso 'looms' dunksójo 'loomed'
spõkso 'gapes' spoksójo 'gaped'
teĩkšo 'lies' telkšójo 'lay (of a water body)'

CONJUGATION AND ACCENTUATION OF SIMPLE FINITE VERBS

Indicative mood

PRESENT

5.97 Present tense forms are created by adding personal endings to the present tense stem. The three paradigms correspond to the three verb conjugations.

Paradigm 1

((*i*)*a*-stem)

Non-reflexive verbs

mokė́ti 'know', sùpti 'rock'
nèšti 'carry', šukúoti 'comb'
tráukti 'pull', kentė́ti 'suffer'

Reflexive verbs

sùptis 'rock oneself', nèštis 'bring for oneself'
šukúotis 'comb oneself'
tráuktis 'retreat'

Singular

1. móku, supù, nešù   supúosi, nešúosi
2. móki, supì, nešì   supíesi, nešíesi
3. móka, sùpa, nẽša   sùpasi, nẽšasi

1. šukúoju, tráukiu, kenčiù   šukúojuosi, tráukiuosi
2. šukúoji, tráuki, kentì   šukúojiesi, tráukiesi
3. šukúoja, tráukia, keñčia   šukúojasi, tráukiasi

Plural

1. mókame, sùpame, nẽšame   sùpamės, nẽšamės
2. mókate, sùpate, nẽšate   sùpatės, nẽšatės
3. móka, sùpa, nẽša   sùpasi, nẽšasi

1. šukúojame, tráukiame, keñčiame   šukúojamės, tráukiamės
2. šukúojate, tráukiate, keñčiate   šukúojatės, tráukiatės
3. šukúoja, tráukia, keñčia   šukúojasi, tráukiasi

Paradigm 2
(*i*-stem)

Non-reflexive verbs   Reflexive verbs

sėdė́ti 'sit', tikė́ti 'believe',   tikė́tis 'hope'
trinksė́ti 'bang'

Singular

1. sė́džiu, tikiù, trìnksiu   tikiúosi
2. sė́di, tikì, trìnksi   tikíesi
3. sė́di, tìki, trìnksi   tìkisi

Plural

1. sė́dime, tìkime, trìnksime   tìkimės
2. sė́dite, tìkite, trìnksite   tìkitės
3. sė́di, tìki, trìnksi   tìkisi

In the 1st and 2nd person singular the thematic vowels *a* and *i* in the stem of the verbs conjugated according to Paradigms 1 and 2 disappear (in Paradigm 2, *-i* at the end of the 2nd person singular is an ending).

Paradigm 3
(*o*-stem)

Non-reflexive verbs   Reflexive verbs

mókyti 'teach', bijóti 'fear',   mókytis 'learn', bijótis 'fear'
žiopsóti 'gape'

Singular

1. mókau, bijaũ, žiopsaũ   mókausi, bijaũsi
2. mókai, bijaĩ, žiopsaĩ   mókaisi, bijaĩsi
3. móko, bìjo, žiõpso   mókosi, bìjosi

Plural

1. mókome, bìjome, žiõpsome   mókomės, bìjomės
2. mókote, bìjote, žiõpsote   mókotės, bìjotės
3. móko, bìjo, žiõpso   mókosi, bìjosi

In Paradigm 3, before the endings of the 1st and 2nd person singular, the thematic vowel *o* changes into *a*.

5.98 The accentuation of present tense forms follows two patterns. If the acute toneme falls on the penultimate syllable of the stem or if a syllable more distant from the end irrespective of the toneme is stressed, all the forms carry the same toneme on the same stressed syllable, e.g.:

3. Sg./Pl.: *šóka* 'dance(s)', *mýli* 'love(s)', *važiúoja* 'drive(s)', *kìlsčioja* 'keep(s) lifting', *prátina* 'habituate(s)', *snúduriuoja* 'doze(s)'

1. Sg.: *šóku, mýliu, važiúoju, kìlsčioju, prátinu, snúduriuoju*
2. Sg.: *šóki, mýli, važiúoji, kìlsčioji, prátini, snúduriuoji*

1. Pl.: *šókame, mýlime, važiúojame, kìlsčiojame, prátiname, snúduriuojame*
2. Pl.: *šókate, mýlite, važiúojate, kìlsčiojate, prátinate, snúduriuojate*

If the stressed penultimate syllable of the stem is short or carries the circumflex toneme, the same kind of accentuation is retained in the 1st and 2nd person plural, but in the 1st and 2nd person singular the stress shifts to the ending, e.g.:

3. Sg./Pl.: *nẽša* 'carries/carry', *gyvẽna* 'live(s)', *skùta* 'peel(s)', *gaivìna* 'resuscitate(s)', *žìno* 'know(s)'

1. Sg.: *nešù, skutù, žinaũ, gyvenù, gaivinù*
2. Sg.: *nešì, skutì, žinaĩ, gyvenì, gaivinì*

1. Pl.: *nẽšame, skùtame, žìnome, gyvẽname, gaivìname*
2. Pl.: *nẽšate, skùtate, žìnote, gyvẽnate, gaivìnate*

PAST

5.99 The past tense forms are created by adding person endings to the past stem. The conjugation of verbs in the past follows two paradigms – those of the *o*-stem are conjugated according to Paradigm 3 (i.e. they have the same endings that verbs conjugated according to Paradigm 3 of the present tense have); those of the *ė*-stem are conjugated according to Paradigm 4, which is typical only of the past tense.

Paradigm 3
(*o*-stem)

Non-reflexive verbs

sùpti 'swing', kentė́ti 'suffer',
šukúoti 'comb',
tikė́ti 'believe', sáugoti 'guard'

Reflexive verbs

sùptis 'swing oneself',
šukúotis 'comb one's hair',
tikė́tis 'hope', sáugotis 'be careful'

Singular

1. supaũ, kentė́jau, šukavaũ
2. supaĩ, kentė́jai, šukavaĩ
3. sùpo, kentė́jo, šukãvo

supaũsi, šukavaũsi
supaĩsi, šukavaĩsi
sùposi, šukãvosi

1. tikė́jau, sáugojau
2. tikė́jai, sáugojai
3. tikė́jo, sáugojo

tikė́jausi, sáugojausi
tikė́jaisi, sáugojaisi
tikė́josi, sáugojosi

Plural

1. sùpome, kentė́jome, šukãvome
2. sùpote, kentė́jote, šukãvote
3. sùpo, kentė́jo, šukãvo

sùpomės, šukãvomės
sùpotės, šukãvotės
sùposi, šukãvosi

1. tikė́jome, sáugojome
2. tikė́jote, sáugojote
3. tikė́jo, sáugojo

tikė́jomės, sáugojomės
tikė́jotės, sáugojotės
tikė́josi, sáugojosi

Paradigm 3 is typical of verbs which belong to (**a**) Group 1 and 4 of Conjugation 1, (**b**) Conjugation 2, and (**c**) Group 2 of Conjugation 3.

Paradigm 4
(*ė*-stem)

Non-reflexive verbs

mókyti 'teach', nèšti 'carry',
keĩsti 'change'

Reflexive verbs

mókytis 'learn', nèštis 'dash',
keĩstis 'change oneself'

Singular

1. mókiau, nešiaũ, keičiaũ
2. mókei, nešeĩ, keiteĩ
3. mókė, nẽšė, keĩtė

mókiausi, nešiaũsi, keičiaũsi
mókeisi, nešeĩsi, keiteĩsi
mókėsi, nẽšėsi, keĩtėsi

Plural

1. mókėme, nẽšėme, keĩtėme
2. mókėte, nẽšėte, keĩtėte
3. mókė, nẽšė, keĩtė

mókėmės, nẽšėmės, keĩtėmės
mókėtės, nẽšėtės, keĩtėtės
mókėsi, nẽšėsi, keĩtėsi

In verbs conjugated according to Paradigm 4 the thematic vowel ė is shortened and changes into e before the inflexional vowel of the 1st and 2nd person singular. The resulting cluster eu at the end of the 1st person singular is spelled as *iau* like other forms containing the diphthong *au* after soft consonants.

Paradigm 4 is typical of verbs which belong to Groups 2 and 3 of Conjugation 1 and Group 1 of Conjugation 3.

5.100 The accentuation of past tense forms follows the same rules that present tense forms do (see 5.98).

Examples of fixed accentuation of all the forms of a verb:

3. Sg./Pl.: *kė̃lė* 'lifted', *bė̃go* 'ran', *ravė́jo* 'weeded', *káltino* 'accused', *skiẽpijo* 'inoculated'

1. Sg.: *kė̃liau, bė̃gau, ravė́jau, káltinau, skiẽpijau*
2. Sg.: *kė̃lei, bė̃gai, ravė́jai, káltinai, skiẽpijai*
1. Pl.: *kė̃lėme, bė̃gome, ravė́jome, káltinome, skiẽpijome*
2. Pl.: *kė̃lėte, bė̃gote, ravė́jote, káltinote, skiẽpijote*

Examples of shifting accentuation:

3. Sg./Pl.: *keĩtė* 'changed', *sùpo* 'rocked', *kū́rėno* 'heated', *važiãvo* 'drove'

1. Sg.: *keičiaũ, supaũ, kūrenaũ, važiavaũ*
2. Sg.: *keiteĩ, supaĩ, kūrenaĩ, važiavaĩ*
1. Pl.: *keĩtėme, sùpome, kū́rėnome, važiãvome*
2. Pl.: *keĩtėte, sùpote, kū́rėnote, važiãvote*

PAST FREQUENTATIVE

5.101 The past frequentative forms are created by adding the suffix *-dav-* and personal endings to the infinitival stem and they are conjugated according to Paradigm 3 (*o*-stem).

Non-reflexive verbs   Reflexive verbs

                        Singular

1. *sùpdavau, sėdė́davau, mókydavau*   *sùpdavausi, mókydavausi*
2. *sùpdavai, sėdė́davai, mókydavai*   *sùpdavaisi, mókydavaisi*
3. *sùpdavo, sėdė́davo, mókydavo*   *sùpdavosi, mókydavosi*

Plural

1. sùpdavome, sėdėdavome, mókydavome   sùpdavomės, mókydavomės
2. sùpdavote, sėdėdavote, mókydavote   sùpdavotės, mókydavotės
3. sùpdavo, sėdėdavo, mókydavo   sùpdavosi, mókydavosi

Past frequentative tense forms always retain the place of the accent and the same toneme of the accented syllable that is encountered in the infinitive.

FUTURE

5.102 Future tense forms are created by adding the suffix *-s(i)* and personal endings to the infinitival stem. The future tense of all verbs has the same conjugation.

Non-reflexive verbs   Reflexive verbs

Singular

1. sùpsiu, sėdėsiu, mókysiu   sùpsiuosi, mókysiuosi
2. sùpsi, sėdėsi, mókysi   sùpsiesi, mókysiesi
3. sùps, sėdės, mókys   sùpsis, mókysis

Plural

1. sùpsime, sėdėsime, mókysime   sùpsimės, mókysimės
2. sùpsite, sėdėsite, mókysite   sùpsitės, mókysitės
3. sùps, sėdės, mókys   sùpsis, mókysis

Future tense forms are conjugated according to Paradigm 2 (*i*-stem), except that the 3rd person forms of non-reflexive verbs do not have the thematic vowel (e.g., *sùps* 'will rock'). The 3rd person singular/plural and the 2nd person singular forms of non-reflexive verbs are created by adding the shortened variant of the future tense suffix *-s-* (in the 2nd person singular (*sùps-i*) the final *i* is the ending).

The 3rd person form of reflexive verbs ends in *-s* (the shortened variant of the reflexive affix) preceded by the inserted vowel *i*, which appears after a consonant, cf.: *sùps – sùps-i-s; nèš – nèš-i-s*.

After the final consonants *s, š, z, ž* of the infinitival stem the consonant *s* of the future tense suffix disappears while the consonants *z, ž* change to *s, š*, e.g.:

mèsiu < mès-s-iu   nèšiu < nèš-s-iu
mèsi < mès-s-i   nèši < nèš-s-i
mès < mès-s   nèš < nèš-s

mègsiu < mègz-s-iu grĩšiu < grĩž-s-iu
mègsi < mègz-s-i grĩši < grĩž-s-i
mègs < mègz-s grĩš < grĩž-s

The 3rd person future of the primary verbs with the long vowels y and ū in the infinitive and the present tense and the short vowels i and u in the past have the short vowels i and u in the root, e.g.:

Infinitive	3rd person present	3rd person past	3rd person future
gýti 'heal'	gỹja	gìjo	gìs
griúti 'fall'	griũva	griùvo	griùs
púti 'rot'	pũva	pùvo	pùs
žúti 'perish'	žũva	žùvo	žùs

Cf. verbs which do not contain long y or ū in the present tense:

| siúti 'sew' | siùva | siùvo | siũs |
| výti 'chase' | vėja | vìjo | vỹs |

Future tense forms usually retain the same accentuation as that of the infinitive except that the acute toneme changes into the circumflex toneme in monosyllabic 3rd person forms and in the final syllable of polysyllabic 3rd person forms, e.g.:

Infinitive: klýsti 'err' sakýti 'say' aimanúoti 'moan'

1. Sg.: klýsiu, sakýsiu, aimanúosiu
2. Sg.: klýsi, sakýsi, aimanúosi

1. Pl.: klýsime, sakýsime, aimanúosime
2. Pl.: klýsite, sakýsite, aimanúosite

But:

3. Sg./Pl.: klỹs, sakỹs, aimanuõs

Subjunctive mood

5.103 The 1st and 2nd person singular and plural of the subjunctive mood are created by adding the suffixes -čia-, -tum(ė)- and personal endings to the infinitival stem. The 3rd person forms contain the suffix -tų.

Singular	Plural
1. -čia-u	-tu(mė)-me
2. -tum(e-i)	-tumė-te
3. -tų	-tų

In the 2nd person singular, before the ending *-i* the final vowel *ė* changes into *e* (similarly to the change which occurs in the past, cf., *neš-e-ĩ* (past) and *nèštum-e-i* (subjunctive)).

In present day Lithuanian, especially in colloquial speech, the shortened form of the 2nd person singular with *-tum* is mostly used.

The subjunctive mood of reflexive verbs is formed in the same way as the present and past tenses of the indicative mood.

Non-reflexive verbs   Reflexive verbs

Singular

sùpčiau, sėdė́čiau, mókyčiau   sùpčiausi, mókyčiausi
sùptum, sėdė́tum, mókytum   sùptumeisi, mókytumeisi
sùptų, sėdė́tų, mókytų   sùptųsi, mókytųsi

Plural

sùptum(ė)me, sėdė́tu(mė)me, mókytu(mė)me   sùptu(mė)mės, mókytu(mė)mės
sùptumėte, sėdė́tumėte, mókytumėte   sùptumėtės, mókytumėtės
sùptų, sėdė́tų, mókytų   sùptųsi, mókytųsi

The 1st person plural forms (e.g., *sùptumėme*, *sùptumėmės*) are rather often shortened by omitting the *-mė-* part of the suffix: *sùptume*, *sùptumės*. The 2nd person plural forms can also be shortened in the same way (*sùptumėte > sùptute*, *sùptumėtės > sùptutės*), but this occurs less frequently than in the first person plural.

Subjunctive forms retain the same place of the accent and the same toneme of the accented syllable which is encountered in the infinitive, cf.:

Infinitive: *áugti* 'grow', *pū́sti* 'blow', *dìdinti* 'increase'

Sg. 1. *áugčiau, pū́sčiau, dìdinčiau*
2. *áugtum, pū́stum, dìdintum*
3. *áugtų, pū́stų, dìdintų*

Pl. 1. *áugtu(mė)me, pū́stu(mė)me, dìdintu(mė)me*
2. *áugtumėte, pū́stumėte, dìdintumėte*
3. *áugtų, pū́stų, dìdintų*

Imperative mood

5.104 The paradigm of the imperative mood is not complete – it does not have 1st person singular forms because the imperative mood conveys the volition of the speaker directed toward another person (or other persons).

The 2nd person singular and the 1st and 2nd person plural forms are created by adding the suffix -k(i) to the infinitival stem. The shorter variant -k of the suffix occurs in the 2nd person singular of non-reflexive verbs, e.g.:

sùp-k 'rock'   sėdė̃-k 'sit'   móky-k 'teach'

In some dialects, however, and sometimes in fiction (poetry in particular) the 2nd person singular forms are made with the longer variant -ki of the suffix, e.g.:

eĩ-ki 'go'   bū́-ki 'be'   nèš-ki 'carry'

The longer variant -ki- of the suffix is retained in the 2nd person singular of reflexive verbs (nèš-kis 'take for yourself', praũs-ki-s 'wash yourself', móky-ki-s 'learn') and the 1st and 2nd person plural forms of both reflexive and non-reflexive verbs (sùp-ki-me, sùp-ki-mės, sùp-ki-te, sùp-ki-tės).

Before the suffix -k(i) the final consonants g and k of the infinitival stem disappear, e.g.:

áuk < áug-k 'grow'
sùk < sùk-k 'turn'

Non-reflexive verbs	Reflexive verbs
Singular	
2. sùpk, sėdė̃k, mókyk	sùpkis, mókykis
Plural	
1. sùpkime, sėdė̃kime, mókykime	sùpkimės, mókykimės
2. sùpkite, sėdė̃kite, mókykite	sùpkitės, mókykitės

Imperative forms with the suffix -k(i) retain the place and kind of accentuation which is encountered in the infinitive, e.g.:

Infinitive: sùpti 'rock' rašýti 'write'

Sg. 2. sùpk, rašýk
Pl. 1. sùpkime, rašýkime
    2. sùpkite, rašýkite

5.105 The 3rd person form of the imperative mood, which in some grammars is considered to be a separate mood in its own right and called the optative, is used in Standard Lithuanian very rarely and is recognized as being archaic. It is made by adding the prefix te- to the present tense stem and the endings -ie or -i. The ending -ie is added to the (i)a- and i-stem verbs, e.g.:

te-sup-iẽ, te-praus-iẽ, te-sėd-iẽ
te-si-sup-iẽ, te-si-praus-iẽ

The ending *-i* is added to the *o*-stem verbs, e.g.:

te-móka-i, te-sáuga-i, te-dãra-i
te-si-móka-i, te-si-sáuga-i

The only verb whose 3rd person form of the imperative is fairly often used in Standard Lithuanian is the verb *bū́ti* 'be': *tees-iẽ, tebūn-iẽ*.

If the present tense stem is simple (i.e. if it does not contain a suffix), the imperative forms with the ending *-ie* carry the stress on the ending, e.g.:

tesukiẽ 'let him turn'
telydiẽ 'let him accompany'
teprausiẽ 'let him wash'

If the present tense stem contains a suffix, the imperative forms with the ending *-ie* retain the stress on the stem, e.g.:

teváikščiojie 'let him walk'
tevažiúojie 'let him drive'
tegyvẽnie 'let him live'
teskùbinie 'let him hurry'

Forms with the ending *-i* usually retain the stress on the same syllable and have the same toneme which are encountered in the present tense, e.g.:

teskaĩtai 'let him read'
terãšai 'let him write'
temókai 'let him teach'

In Standard Lithuanian the meaning of the 3rd person of the imperative is usually conveyed by the 3rd person present (sometimes future) tense forms containing the prefix *te-*, or by these forms used in conjunction with the particles *te* or *tegù/tegùl*, e.g.:

tèsupa, tegù/tegùl sùpa, tè (jìs) sùpa 'let him rock'
tesìsupa, tegù/tegùl sùpasi 'let him rock himself'
tesė́di, tegù/tegùl sė́di 'let him sit'
temóko, tegù/tegùl móko 'let him teach'
tesimóko, tegù/tegùl mókosi 'let him learn'
tebùs, tegù/tegùl bùs 'let it be'

Oblique mood

5.106 The oblique mood forms coincide with the nominative case of active participles. The oblique mood, like the indicative mood, has four tenses: the present, past,

past frequentative and future. The forms of the oblique mood are inflected for gender and number. They are not inflected for person, therefore the same form is used for all the three persons.

Table 15. **Forms of the oblique mood**

			Non-reflexive verbs	Reflexive verbs
Present	Sg.	masc.	supą̃s sė́dįs mókąs	sùpąsis mókąsis
		fem.	sùpanti sė́dinti mókanti	sùpantis mókantis
	Pl.	masc.	supą̃ sė́dį móką	sùpąsi mókąsi
		fem.	sùpančios sė́dinčios mókančios	sùpančiosi mókančiosi
Past	Sg.	masc.	sùpęs sėdė́jęs mókęs	sùpęsis mókęsis
		fem.	sùpusi sėdė́jusi mókiusi	sùpusis mókiusis
	Pl.	masc.	sùpę sėdė́ję mókę	sùpęsi mókęsi
		fem.	sùpusios sėdė́jusios mókiusios	sùpusiosi mókiusiosi
Past freq.	Sg.	masc.	sùpdavęs sėdė́davęs mókydavęs	sùpdavęsis mókydavęsis
		fem.	sùpdavusi sėdė́davusi mókydavusi	sùpdavusis mókydavusis
	Pl.	masc.	sùpdavę sėdė́davę mókydavę	sùpdavęsi mókydavęsi
		fem.	sùpdavusios sėdė́davusios mókydavusios	sùpdavusiosi mókydavusiosi
Future	Sg.	masc.	sùpsiąs sėdė́siąs mókysiąs	sùpsiąsis mókysiąsis
		fem.	sùpsianti sėdė́sianti mókysianti	sùpsiantis mókysiantis
	Pl.	masc.	sùpsią sėdė́sią mókysią	sùpsiąsi mókysiąsi
		fem.	sùpsiančios sėdė́siančios mókysiančios	sùpsiančiosi mókysiančiosi

The oblique mood forms are accented like the active participles of the respective tense.

Conjugation of the verb *bū́ti* 'be'

5.107 The verb *bū́ti* possesses suppletive finite forms, containing different stems: *es-*, *bu-/bū-*; the 3rd person present possesses its own unique stem *yrà*.

Table 16 **Forms of the verb *bū́ti***

Mood	Tense	Singular	Plural
Indicative	Present	1. *esù* 2. *esì* 3. *yrà*	*ẽsame* *ẽsate* *yrà*
	Past	1. *buvaũ* 2. *buvaĩ* 3. *bùvo*	*bùvome* *bùvote* *bùvo*
	Past freq.	1. *bū́davau* 2. *bū́davai* 3. *bū́davo*	*bū́davome* *bū́davote* *bū́davo*
	Future	1. *bū́siu* 2. *bū́si* 3. *bùs*	*bū́sime* *bū́site* *bùs*
Subjunctive		1. *bū́čiau* 2. *bū́tum* 3. *bū́tų*	*bū́tu(mè)me* *bū́tumėte* *bū́tų*
Imperative		1. —— 2. *bū́k* 3. *tebū̃nie*	*bū́kime* *bū́kite* *tebū̃nie*
Oblique mood	Present	*ẽsąs, ẽsanti*	*ẽsą, ẽsančios*
	Past	*bùvęs, bùvusi*	*bùvę, bùvusios*
	Past freq.	*bū́davęs, bū́davusi*	*bū́davę, bū́davusios*
	Future	*bū́siąs, bū́sianti*	*bū́sią, bū́siančios*

In addition to the present tense forms given in the table, more recent forms created by adding the formants -*n*- or -*v*- to the infinitival stem exist in Standard Lithuanian:

Singular

1. bū́nù, bū́vù
2. bū́nì, bū́vì
3. bū́na, bū́va

Plural

bū́name, bū́vame
bū́nate, bū́vate
bū́na, bū́va

There is a slight semantic difference between the forms in the table *esù*, *esì*, etc. and the forms created from the infinitival stem *bū*- (*bū́nù*, *bū́vù*, *bū́nì*, *bū́vì*, etc). The latter forms usually convey a regular process, a regular presence of something or somebody. The same meaning can also be expressed by the athematic 3rd person form *ẽsti*. The 3rd person of the imperative has two coexistent forms *tebū́niẽ* and *teesiẽ* 'let it be'.

COMPOUND (PERIPHRASTIC) FINITE FORMS

5.108 Compound finite forms of the verb are created with the help of the finite forms of the auxiliary *bū́ti* 'be' and the present or past active or passive participle. Compound forms containing active participles belong to the active voice, and those containing passive participles belong to the passive voice.

Compound forms with a present active participle are termed compound continuative tenses and moods, and those with a present passive participle are termed compound imperfect tenses and moods. Compound forms containing a past participle (active or passive) are known as compound active or passive perfect tenses and moods.

The auxiliary *bū́ti* in such compound tenses is usually used in one of its simple forms. Compound forms in which the auxiliary itself is used in a compound finite form are less frequent, e.g.:

yrà bùvęs atė̃jęs 'has been here' (lit. 'has been come')
bū́tų bùvęs padarýtas 'would have been done'

In present the auxiliary can be omitted, e.g.:

Àš jaũ paválgęs. 'I have eaten already.'

Not every sequence consisting of the verb *bū́ti* and a participle is a compound tense. Some combinations of this kind are simply free collocations. That depends upon the meaning of the participle, whether it has a prevailing qualitative meaning and is similar to an adjective (e.g.:, *Vaĩkas bùvo sil̃pnas, išbãlęs.* 'The child was weak, pale'; *Tėvaĩ sàvo vaikaĩs bùvo paténkinti.* 'The parents were pleased with their children.'), or whether its semantics is more verbal than adjectival.

The distinctive feature of compound tense forms which sets them apart from free collocations is their correlation with simple tenses.

Active voice
COMPOUND PERFECT TENSES

5.109 Compound perfect tenses are formed with the help of the auxiliary *bū́ti*, which is used in one of its finite forms, and the past active participle of a notional verb. It is the person, tense and mood of the auxiliary which determines the person, tense and mood of the compound perfect form. Thus, compound perfect forms occur in the present, past, past frequentative and future of the indicative and oblique mood and also in the subjunctive and imperative.

Table 17 **Perfect tenses**

Mood	Tense	Singular	Plural
Indicative	Present	1. *esù (at)nė́šęs*	*ẽsame (at)nė́šę*
		esù (at)nė́šusi	*ẽsame (at)nė́šusios*
		2. *esì (at)nė́šęs*	*ẽsate (at)nė́šę*
		esì (at)nė́šusi	*ẽsate (at)nė́šusios*
		3. *yrà (at)nė́šęs*	*yrà (at)nė́šę*
		yrà (at)nė́šusi	*yrà (at)nė́šusios*
	Past	1. *buvaũ (at)nė́šęs*	*bùvome (at)nė́šę*
		buvaũ (at)nė́šusi	*bùvome (at)nė́šusios*
		2. *buvaĩ (at)nė́šęs*	*bùvote (at)nė́šę*
		buvaĩ (at)nė́šusi	*bùvote (at)nė́šusios*
		3. *bùvo (at)nė́šęs*	*bùvo (at)nė́šę*
		bùvo (at)nė́šusi	*bùvo (at)nė́šusios*
	Past freq.	1. *bū́davau (at)nė́šęs*	*bū́davome (at)nė́šę*
		bū́davau (at)nė́šusi	*bū́davome (at)nė́šusios*
		2. *bū́davai (at)nė́šęs*	*bū́davote (at)nė́šę*

Mood	Tense	Singular	Plural
Indicative		būdavai (at)nėšusi	būdavote (at)nėšusios
		3. būdavo (at)nėšęs	būdavo (at)nėšę
		būdavo (at)nėšusi	būdavo (at)nėšusios
	Future	1. būsiu (at)nėšęs	būsime (at)nėšę
		būsiu (at)nėšusi	būsime (at)nėšusios
		2. būsi (at)nėšęs	būsite (at)nėšę
		būsi (at)nėšusi	būsite (at)nėšusios
		3. bùs (at)nėšęs	bùs (at)nėšę
		bùs (at)nėšusi	bùs (at)nėšusios
Subjunctive		1. būčiau (at)nėšęs	būtum(mė)me (at)nėšę
		būčiau (at)nėšusi	būtu(mė)me (at)nėšusios
		2. būtum (at)nėšęs	būtumėte (at)nėšę
		būtum (at)nėšusi	būtumėte (at)nėšusios
		3. būtų (at)nėšęs	būtų (at)nėšę
		būtų (at)nėšusi	būtų (at)nėšusios
Imperative		1. ———	būkime (at)nėšę
			būkime (at)nėšusios
		2. būk (at)nėšęs	būkite (at)nėšę
		būk (at)nėšusi	būkite (at)nėšusios
		3. tebūniē (at)nėšęs	tebūniē (at)nėšę
		tebūniē (at)nėšusi	tebūniē (at)nėšusios
Oblique mood	Present	ėsąs (at)nėšęs	ėsą (at)nėšę
		ėsanti (at)nėšusi	ėsančios (at)nėšusios
	Past	bùvęs (at)nėšęs	bùvę (at)nėšę
		bùvusi (at)nėšusi	bùvusios (at)nėšusios
	Past freq.	būdavęs (at)nėšęs	būdavę (at)nėšę
		būdavusi (at)nėšusi	būdavusios (at)nėšusios
	Future	būsiąs (at)nėšęs	būsią (at)nėšę
		būsianti (at)nėšusi	būsiančios (at)nėšusios

COMPOUND CONTINUATIVE TENSES

5.110 Compound continuative tenses are formed with the help of the finite forms of the auxiliary *būti* 'be' and the present active participle with the prefix *be-*.

There are no present tense forms among the compound continuative tenses. The past continuative is most frequently used. The other compound continuative tenses are rare in present-day Lithuanian and occur mostly in the Low Lithuanian (Samogitian) dialect.

Table 18. **Continuative tenses**

Mood	Tense	Singular	Plural
Indicative	Past	1. *buvaũ be(at)nẽšąs* *buvaũ bè(àt)nešanti* 2. *buvaĩ be(at)nẽšąs* *buvaĩ bè(àt)nešanti* 3. *bùvo be(at)nẽšąs* *bùvo bè(àt)nešanti*	*bùvome be(at)nẽšą* *bùvome bè(àt)nešančios* *bùvote be(at)nẽšą* *bùvote bè(àt)nešančios* *bùvo be(at)nẽšą* *bùvo bè(àt)nešančios*
	Past freq.	1. *búdavau be(at)nẽšąs* *búdavau bè(àt)nešanti* 2. *búdavai be(at)nẽšąs* *búdavai bè(àt)nešanti* 3. *búdavo be(at)nẽšąs* *búdavo bè(àt)nešanti*	*búdavome be(at)nẽšą* *búdavome bè(àt)nešančios* *búdavote be(at)nẽšą* *búdavote bè(àt)nešančios* *búdavo be(at)nẽšą* *búdavo bè(àt)nešančios*
	Future	1. *búsiu be(at)nẽšąs* *búsiu bè(àt)nešanti* 2. *búsi be(at)nẽšąs* *búsi bè(àt)nešanti* 3. *bùs be(at)nẽšąs* *bùs bè(àt)nešanti*	*búsime be(at)nẽšą* *búsime bè(àt)nešančios* *búsite be(at)nẽšą* *búsite bè(àt)nešančios* *bùs be(at)nẽšą* *bùs bè(àt)nešančios*
Subjunctive		1. *búčiau be(at)nẽšąs* *búčiau bè(àt)nešanti* 2. *bútum be(at)nẽšąs* *bútum bè(àt)nešanti* 3. *bútų be(at)nẽšąs* *bútų bè(àt)nešanti*	*bútu(mè)me be(at)nẽšą* *bútum(mè)me bè(àt)nešančios* *bútumėte be(at)nẽšą* *bútumėte bè(àt)nešančios* *bútų be(at)nẽšą* *bútų bè(àt)nešančios*
Imperative		1. ——— 2. *búk be(at)nẽšąs* *búk bè(àt)nešanti* 3. *tebūniẽ be(at)nẽšąs* *tebūniẽ bè(àt)nešanti*	*búkime be(at)nẽšą* *búkime bè(àt)nešančios* *búkite be(at)nẽšą* *búkite bè(àt)nešančios* *tebūniẽ be(at)nẽšą* *tebūniẽ bè(àt)nešančios*

Mood	Tense	Singular	Plural
Oblique mood	Past	bùvęs be(at)nešąs bùvusi bè(àt)nešanti	bùvę be(at)nešą bùvusios bè(àt)nešančios
	Past freq.	bū́davęs be(at)nešąs bū́davusi bè(àt)nešanti	bū́davę be(at)nešą bū́davusios bè(àt)nešančios
	Future	bū́siqs be(at)nešąs bū́sianti bè(àt)nešanti	bū́sią be(at)nešą bū́siančios bè(àt)nešančios

Passive voice

5.111 There are two groups of compound passive tenses: the imperfect passive and the perfect passive tenses. The forms of the 1st group contain present passive participle, those of the second group contain past passive participle. Concerning their meaning see 5.39, 40.

Table 19. **Imperfect passive tenses**

Mood	Tense	Singular	Plural
Indicative	Present	1. esù (àt)nẽšamas, esù (at)nešamà 2. esì (àt)nẽšamas esì (at)nešamà 3. yrà (àt)nẽšamas yrà (at)nešamà	ẽsame (at)nešamì ẽsame (àt)nẽšamos ẽsate (at)nešamì ẽsate (àt)nẽšamos yrà (àt)nẽšamì yrà (àt)nẽšamos
	Past	1. buvaũ (àt)nẽšamas buvaũ (at)nešamà 2. buvaĩ (àt)nẽšamas buvaĩ (at)nešamà 3. bùvo (àt)nẽšamas bùvo (àt)nešamà	bùvome (at)nešamì bùvome (àt)nẽšamos bùvote (at)nešamì bùvote (àt)nẽšamos bùvo (at)nešamì bùvo (àt)nẽšamos
	Past freq.	1. bū́davau (àt)nẽšamas bū́davau (at)nešamà 2. bū́davai (àt)nẽšamas bū́davai (at)nešamà 3. bū́davo (àt)nẽšamas bū́davo (at)nešamà	bū́davome (at)nešamì bū́davome (àt)nẽšamos bū́davote (at)nešamì bū́davote (àt)nẽšamos bū́davo (at)nešamì bū́davo (àt)nẽšamos

Mood	Tense	Singular	Plural
Indicative	Future	1. bū́siu (àt)nẽšamas	bū́sime (at)nešamì
		bū́siu (at)nešamà	bū́sime (àt)nẽšamos
		2. bū́si (àt)nẽšamas	bū́site (at)nešamì
		bū́si (at)nešamà	bū́site (àt)nẽšamos
		3. bùs (àt)nẽšamas	bùs (at)nešamì
		bùs (at)nešamà	bùs (àt)nẽšamos
Subjunctive		1. bū́čiau (àt)nẽšamas	bū́tum(mė)me (at)nešamì
		bū́čiau (at)nešamà	bū́tu(mė)me (àt)nẽšamos
		2. bū́tum (àt)nẽšamas	bū́tumėte (at)nešamì
		bū́tum (at)nešamà	bū́tumėte (àt)nẽšamos
		3. bū́tų (àt)nẽšamas	bū́tų (at)nešamì
		bū́tų (at)nešamà	bū́tų (àt)nẽšamos
Imperative		1. ———	bū́kime (at)nešamì
			bū́kime (àt)nẽšamos
		2. bū́k (àt)nẽšamas	bū́kite (at)nešamì
		bū́k (at)nešamà	bū́kite (àt)nẽšamos
		3. tebūniẽ (àt)nẽšamas	tebūniẽ (at)nešamì
		tebūniẽ (at)nešamà	tebūniẽ (àt)nẽšamos
Oblique mood	Present	ẽsąs (àt)nẽšamas	ẽsą (at)nešamì
		ẽsanti (at)nešamà	ẽsančios (àt)nẽšamos
	Past	bùvęs (àt)nẽšamas	bùvę (at)nešamì
		bùvusi (at)nešamà	bùvusios (àt)nẽšamos
	Past freq.	bū́davęs (àt)nẽšamas	bū́davę (at)nešamì
		bū́davusi (at)nešamà	bū́davusios (àt)nẽšamos
	Future	bū́siąs (àt)nẽšamas	bū́sią (at)nešamì
		bū́sianti (at)nešamà	bū́siančios (àt)nẽšamos

Table 20. **Perfect passive tenses**

Mood	Tense	Singular	Plural
Indicative	Present	1. esù (àt)nẽštas,	ẽsame (at)neštì
		esù (at)neštà	ẽsame (àt)nẽštos
		2. esì (àt)nẽštas	ẽsate (at)neštì

Mood	Tense	Singular	Plural
Indicative		esì (at)neštà	ẽsate (àt)neštos
		3. yrà (àt)nẽštas	yrà (at)neštì
		yrà (at)neštà	yrà (at)nẽštos
	Past	1. buvaũ (àt)nẽštas	bùvome (at)neštì
		buvaũ (at)neštà	bùvome (at)nẽštos
		2. buvaĩ (àt)nẽštas	bùvote (at)neštì
		buvaĩ (at)neštà	bùvote (àt)nẽštos
		3. bùvo (àt)nẽštas	bùvo (at)neštì
		bùvo (at)neštà	bùvo (àt)nẽštos
	Past freq.	1. bū́davau (àt)nẽštas	bū́davome (at)neštì
		bū́davau (at)neštà	bū́davome (àt)nẽštos
		2. bū́davai (àt)nẽštas	bū́davote (at)neštì
		bū́davai (at)neštà	bū́davote (àt)nẽštos
		3. bū́davo (àt)nẽštas	bū́davo (at)neštì
		bū́davo (at)neštà	bū́davo (at)nẽštos
	Future	1. bū́siu (àt)nẽštas	bū́sime (at)neštì
		bū́siu (at)neštà	bū́sime (àt)nẽštos
		2. bū́si (àt)nẽštas	bū́site (at)neštì
		bū́si (at)neštà	bū́site (àt)nẽštos
		3. bùs (àt)nẽštas	bùs (at)neštì
		bùs (at)neštà	bùs (àt)nẽštos
Subjunctive		1. bū́čiau (àt)nẽštas	bū́tum(mė)me (at)neštì
		bū́čiau (at)neštà	bū́tu(mė)me (àt)nẽštos
		2. bū́tum (àt)nẽštas	bū́tumėte (at)neštì
		bū́tum (at)neštà	bū́tumėte (àt)nẽštos
		3. bū́tų (àt)nẽštas	bū́tų (at)neštì
		bū́tų (at)neštà	bū́tų (at)nẽštos
Imperative		1. ———	bū́kime (at)neštì
			bū́kime (àt)nẽštos
		2. bū́k (àt)nẽštas	bū́kite (at)neštì
		bū́k (at)neštà	bū́kite (àt)nẽštos
		3. tebūniẽ (àt)nẽštas	tebūniẽ (at)neštì
		tebūniẽ (at)neštà	tebūniẽ (àt)nẽštos
Oblique mood	Present	ẽsąs (àt)nẽštas	ẽsą (at)neštì
		ẽsanti (àt)neštà	ẽsančios (àt)nẽštos

Continuation of Table 20

Mood	Tense	Singular	Plural
Oblique mood	Past	bùvęs (àt)nēštas bùvusi (at)neštà	bùvę (at)neštì bùvusios (àt)nēštos
	Past freq.	bū́davęs (àt)nēštas bū́davusi (at)neštà	bū́davę (at)neštì bū́davusios (àt)nēštos
	Future	bū́siąs (àt)nēštas bū́sianti (at)neštà	bū́sią (at)neštì bū́siančios (àt)nēštos

Non-finite forms of the verb

PARTICIPLES

Dalỹviai

5.112 Participles possess both verbal and adjectival properties; sometimes they possess also adverbial properties.

Participles are associated with verbs through their verbal stem and the categories of tense and voice, which form the basis for the classification of participles. A large number of participles possess both reflexive and non-reflexive forms, e.g.:

suką̃s	*suką̃sis*	'rotating'
sùkęs	*sùkęsis*	'which rotated'
sùkdavęs	*sùkdavęsis*	'which used to rotate'
sùksiąs	*sùksiąsis*	'which will rotate'

In the sentence, active participles retain the valency typical of the finite forms of the respective verb, e.g.:

Vaĩkas nẽša óbuolius.   'The child is carrying apples.'
Nẽšantis óbuolius vaĩkas.   'A child carrying apples.'

The valency of passive participles changes according to the regularities of the passive transformation, e.g.:

Tė́vas nẽša vaĩką.   'The father is carrying a child.'
Tė́vo nẽšamas vaĩkas.   'A child carried by the father.'

All participial constructions can be considered to be transforms of clauses containing the corresponding finite forms of the verb.

Most participles share with adjectives the categories of gender, number and case. All the masculine and feminine forms of declinable participles possess case and number forms. They agree with nouns and pronouns like adjectives, e.g.:

tėkanti ùpė	'flowing river'
prinókę vaĩsiai	'ripe fruit'
nuláužtas mẽdis	'broken tree'

The neuter forms of participles (see 5.124) are indeclinable. They cannot be used as modifiers of nouns or pronouns.

Like adjectives, participles can also possess definite forms, e.g.:

stóvinčioji móteris	'the standing woman'
praėjusieji mẽtai	'last year'
šnekamóji kalbà	'colloquial speech'

Indeclinable participles, termed gerunds (Lith. *pãdalyviai*), are similar to adverbs both by being indeclinable and by their syntactical usage, cf.:

Grĩžome sutėmus/vėlaĩ.	'We returned at dusk (PAST. GER)/late (ADV).'

Adverbial functions are also typical of the nominative case forms of certain declinable participles (see 5.142).

There is a group of participial forms which are called half-participles (Lith. *pùsdalyviai*). These forms are created with the suffix *-dam-* and are inflected for gender and number, e.g.:

eĩdamas – eidamà – eidamì – eĩdamos 'while going'
nèšdamas – nešdamà – nešdamì – nèšdamos 'while carrying'

Some Lithuanian grammars do not classify these forms as participles, but consider them to be a separate group in their own right. However, these forms present, in fact, a specific nominative case of the present active participle designed to be used for adverbial functions (see 5.143).

Participles are clasified into two groups – active and passive participles.

Active participles have four tense forms:

	Masculine	Feminine
Present participle:	nešą̃s, nèšdamas	nẽšanti, nešdamà
Past participle:	nẽšęs	nẽšusi
Past frequentative participle:	nèšdavęs	nèšdavusi
Future participle:	nèšiąs	nèšianti

Active participles can be formed both from transitive and intransitive verbs, e.g.:

āriantis laũką žmogùs   'a man ploughing a field'
važiúojantis vežìmas   'a travelling cart'
rugiùs išguĺdžiusi krušà   'hail which has beaten down the rye'
pavar̃gusi moterìškė   'a tired woman'

According to their formal properties and verbal voice all gerunds can be grouped together with active participles:

Present gerund: *nẽšant* 'while carrying'
Past gerund: *nẽšus* 'having carried'
Past frequentative gerund: *nèšdavus* 'after (somebody) used to carry'
Future gerund: *nèšiant* 'while (somebody) carries in the future'

Passive participles have three tense forms:

Present participle: *nẽšamas*   *nešamà* 'being carried'
Past participle: *nẽštas*   *neštà* 'which was carried'
Future participle: *nèšimas*   *nešimà* 'which will be carried'

Not all the formally passive participles are used in the meaning of the passive voice. Those participles which have passive meaning are mostly formed from transitive verbs (e.g., *skaĩtomos knýgos* 'books being read', *àtneštas kir̃vis* 'an axe which has been brought') including verbs governing the objective genitive case (e.g., *laukiamà šveñtė* 'an anticipated holiday', *nèkviestas svẽčias* 'uninvited guest').

Formally passive participles lacking passive meaning are formed both from transitive and intransitive verbs, e.g.: *kepamóji krósnis* 'baking oven', *miegamàsis kambarỹs* 'bedroom', *gimtàsis krãštas* 'native country'.

5.113 There is a special non-finite verbal form having a meaning of necessity which in certain Lithuanian grammars is classed as a passive participle. It is derived from the infinitival stem by adding the suffix *-tin-* and the adjectival *a*-stem (masculine) or *o*-stem (feminine) endings:

nèšti: *nèštinas*   *neštinà* 'which should be carried'
minėti: *minėtinas*   *minėtina* 'which should be mentioned'

These forms are declined like *a*-stem (masculine) or *o*-stem (feminine) adjectives. If their infinitival derivational base contains a suffix, the necessity form retains the accent of the infinitive. If the infinitival derivational base is simple (i.e., if it does not contain a suffix), the necessity forms are accented like adjectives of Accentuation Class 3, e.g.:

	Masc.	Fem.
Nom.	*dìrbtinas*	*dirbtinà* 'artificial, that should be done'
Gen.	*dìrbtino*	*dirbtinõs*

Dat.   *dirbtinám*   *dìrbtinai*
Acc.   *dìrbtiną*   *dìrbtiną*
Instr. *dìrbtinu*   *dirbtinà*, etc.

Necessity forms denote qualities associated with an action which is supposed to be carried out, e.g.:

pjautinì rugiaĩ	'rye which should be harvested'
atmiñtinas pavãsaris	'a memorable spring'

From the semantic point of view, these forms stand in opposition to all the other participles. The most frequent forms, however, containing the suffix *-tin-*, do not bear any of the meaning of necessity and function merely as verbal adjectives, e.g.:

abejótinas pāsakojimas	'doubtful story'
bū́tinas reĩkalas	'urgent matter'
įtar̃tinas žmogùs	'suspected man'
mir̃tinas pavõjus	'deadly danger'
pageidáutinas svẽčias	'desirable guest'
stebė́tinas dalỹkas	'surprising thing'

Active participles
Veikiamíeji dalỹviai

PRESENT ACTIVE PARTICIPLES

5.114 Present active participles are formed by adding the suffix *-nt-* and the *ia*-stem (masculine) or *io*-stem (feminine) adjectival endings to the present tense verbal stem, e.g.:

dìrba – dìrba-nt-is, dìrba-nt-i 'working'
tỹli – tỹli-nt-is, tỹli-nt-i 'being silent'

In *o*-stem verbs, belonging to Conjugation 3, the final vowel *o* of the stem changes into *a* before the suffix *-nt-*:

rãšo – rãša-nt-is, rãša-nt-i 'writing'

In the nominative case the masculine forms of present active participles also have the short variant in which the suffix *-nt-* merging with the final vowel of the stem has produced the endings *-ąs, -įs* (nominative singular) and *-ą, -į* (nominative plural). The endings *-ąs, -ą* appear in participles formed from verbs belonging to Conjugations 1 and 3. The endings *-įs, -į* appear in participles formed from verbs belonging to Conjugation 2, e.g.:

dìrba 'works' – dìrbąs/dirbą̃s, dìrbą/dirbą̃
rãšo 'writes' – rãšąs, rãšą
tỹli 'is silent' – tỹlįs/tylį̃s, tỹlį/tylį̃

In the nominative plural the long forms of masculine present participles have the ending -ys, which is typical of i-stem nouns:

dìrbantys, tỹlintys, rãšantys
cf.: ántys 'ducks', plėnys 'flake ashes'

The usage of the long and short forms of masculine nominative case participles is slightly different – the long forms are used to indicate a quality, e.g.:

tėkantis vanduõ	'flowing water'
blìzgantis põpierius	'shining paper'
žýdintys mẽdžiai	'blossoming trees'

The short forms are used to indicate the main or attending action, process or state in the sentence, e.g.:

Girdėjau, jìs sergą̃s.	'I hear he is ill.'
Tėvas bùvo beeĩnąs pro durìs.	'Father was on the point of stepping out through the door.'
Niẽkas jõ darbštùmo nepasiródė mãtą.	'Nobody let it be known that they saw his diligence.'

In the nominative plural, the short forms of masculine participles (the original neuter forms) are sometimes used to replace feminine participles, e.g.:

Móterys sãkėsi eĩnančios/eĩną grybáuti.	'The women said they were going to pick mushrooms.'

The present participle of the verb bū́ti 'be' is formed from the present tense stem es- (cf.: es-ù, es-ì, ẽs-ti), although the other 3rd person form yrà is more frequently used in present-day Lithuanian:

ẽs-ti – ẽsąs/esą̃s, ẽsantis, ẽsanti
ẽsą/esą̃, ẽsantys, ẽsančios

5.115 With the exception of certain short forms ending in -ąs, -įs in the nominative singular and in -ą, -į in the nominative plural, all the case forms of present active participles retain the place of the accent and the toneme of the accented syllable which are observed in the 3rd person present of the respective verb.

The short forms of participles formed from the verbs belonging to Conjugations 1 and 2 which shift their stress to the prefix in the 3rd person of the present tense bear their accent on the ending, e.g.:

nēša 'carries' – *ìšneša* 'carries out' – *nešą̃s, nešą̃*
kaĺba 'speaks' – *nèkalba* 'doesn't speak' – *kalbą̃s, kalbą̃*
tìki 'trusts' – *pàtiki* 'entrusts' – *tikį̃s, tikį̃*
mìni 'remembers' – *nèmini* 'doesn't remember' – *minį̃s, minį̃*

In Standard Lithuanian, however, the tendency to move the stress to the ending can be observed in a large number of other short form participles formed from verbs of Conjugations 1 and 2. Thus, although the following verbs do not shift the stress to the prefix in the 3rd person of the present tense, their respective short form participles often bear the stress on the ending:

dìrba 'works' – *nedìrba* 'doesn't work' – *dìrbąs, dìrbą/dirbą̃s, dirbą̃*
eĩna 'goes' – *ateĩna* 'comes' – *eĩnąs, eĩną/einą̃s, einą̃*
bė́ga 'runs' – *atbė́ga* 'comes running' – *bė́gąs, bė́gą/bėgą̃s, bėgą̃*
tỹli 'is silent' – *patỹli* 'is silent for a while' – *tỹlįs, tỹlį/tylį̃s, tylį̃*
mýli 'loves' – *nemýli* 'doesn't love' – *mýlįs, mýlį/mylį̃s, mylį̃*

The tendency to move the stress to the ending is less pronounced in short form participles formed from verbs of Conjugation 3. However such short form participles are also sometimes stressed in either way – on the root, or on the ending, e.g.:

válgo 'eats' – *válgąs/valgą̃s, válgą/valgą̃*
rãšo 'writes' – *rãšąs/rašą̃s, rãšą/rašą̃*
mìgdo 'puts to sleep' – *mìgdąs/migdą̃s, mìgdą/migdą̃*

Short form participles formed from polysyllabic verbs usually keep their stress on the root, e.g.:

kartója 'repeats' – *kartójąs, kartóją*
gą̃sdina 'frightens' – *gą̃sdinąs, gą̃sdiną*
keřšija 'takes revenge' – *keřšijąs, keřšiją*

The accentuation of prefixed short form participles follows the same rules as described above, e.g.:

ìšmeta 'throws out' – *išmetą̃s, išmetą̃*
nemýli 'doesn't love' – *nemýlįs, nemýlį/nemylį̃s, nemylį̃*
atkeřšija 'takes revenge' – *atkeřšijąs, atkeřšiją*

DECLENSION OF PRESENT ACTIVE PARTICIPLES

Masculine gender (*ia*-stem)

Singular

Nom.	*dìrbąs*	*tikį̃s*	*válgąs*	*kartójąs*
	dìrbantis	*tìkintis*	*válgantis*	*kartójantis*

Gen.	dìrbančio	tìkinčio	válgančio	kartójančio
Dat.	dìrbančiam	tìkinčiam	válgančiam	kartójančiam
Acc.	dìrbantį	tìkintį	válgantį	kartójantį
Instr.	dìrbančiu	tìkinčiu	válgančiu	kartójančiu
Loc.	dìrbančiame	tìkinčiame	válgančiame	kartójančiame

Plural

Nom.	dìrbą/dìrbantys	tìkį/tìkintys	válgą/válgantys	kartója̜/kartójantys
Gen.	dìrbančių	tìkinčių	válgančių	kartójančių
Dat.	dìrbantiems	tìkintiems	válgantiems	kartójantiems
Acc.	dìrbančius	tìkinčius	válgančius	kartójančius
Instr.	dìrbančiais	tìkinčiais	válgančiais	kartójančiais
Loc.	dìrbančiuose	tìkinčiuose	válgančiuose	kartójančiuose

Feminine gender (*io*-stem)

Singular

Nom.	dìrbanti	tìkinti	válganti	kartójanti
Gen.	dìrbančios	tìkinčios	válgančios	kartójančios
Dat.	dìrbančiai	tìkinčiai	válgančiai	kartójančiai
Acc.	dìrbančią	tìkinčią	válgančią	kartójančią
Instr.	dìrbančia	tìkinčia	válgančia	kartójančia
Loc.	dìrbančioje	tìkinčioje	válgančioje	kartójančioje

Plural

Nom.	dìrbančios	tìkinčios	válgančios	kartójančios
Gen.	dìrbančių	tìkinčių	válgančių	kartójančių
Dat.	dìrbančioms	tìkinčioms	válgančioms	kartójančioms
Acc.	dìrbančias	tìkinčias	válgančias	kartójančias
Instr.	dìrbančiomis	tìkinčiomis	válgančiomis	kartójančiomis
Loc.	dìrbančiose	tìkinčiose	válgančiose	kartójančiose

Half-participle

Pùsdalyvis

5.116 In the nominative singular and plural present active participles have another form which is used in adverbial function. This form is known in Lithuanian grammars as the half-participle.

Half-participles are used to indicate an attendant action or process simultaneous with the action or process denoted by the predicate and carried out by the subject of the sentence. Half-participles are inflected for gender and number and they agree with the subject of the sentence in gender and number, e.g.:

Vaĩkas skaitýdamas užmìgo.   'The child fell asleep while reading.'
Móterys grį̃žo dainúodamos.   'The women came back singing.'

Half-participles are formed by adding the suffix -*dam*- and *a*-stem (masculine) or *o*-stem (feminine) endings of the nominative case to the infinitival stem, e.g.:

	Singular	Plural
dìrb-ti 'work'	Masc. *dìrb-dam-as*	*dirb-dam-ì*
	Fem. *dirb-dam-à*	*dìrb-dam-os*
mylė́-ti 'love'	Masc. *mylė́-dam-as*	*mylė́-dam-i*
	Fem. *mylė́-dam-a*	*mylė́-dam-os*
kartó-ti 'repeat'	Masc. *kartó-dam-as*	*kartó-dam-i*
	Fem. *kartó-dam-a*	*kartó-dam-os*

Haf-participles formed from infinitives containing suffixes retain the same accentuation as the infinitive, e.g.:

sáugoti 'guard'	*sáugodamas*	*sáugodami*
	sáugodama	*sáugodamos*
žadė́ti 'promise'	*žadė́damas*	*žadė́dami*
	žadė́dama	*žadė́damos*
skaitýti 'read'	*skaitýdamas*	*skaitýdami*
	skaitýdama	*skaitýdamos*

Half-participles formed from simple (underived) infinitives retain the stress of the infinitive in the masculine singular form and the feminine plural, e.g.:

grė̃bti 'rake'	*grė̃bdamas*	*grė̃bdamos*
nèšti 'carry'	*nèšdamas*	*nèšdamos*

The plural masculine forms and the singular feminine forms of the above half-participles are stressed on the ending:

grėbdamì   *grėbdamà*
nešdamì   *nešdamà*

Prefixed half-participles are stressed like the respective non-prefixed half-participles, except those which have the prefix *per-*, which always attracts the stress.

PAST ACTIVE PARTICIPLE

5.117 Past active participles are formed by adding the suffix *-(i)us-* (except in the nominative singular and plural of the masculine forms) and the *ia*-stem (masculine) or *io*-stem (feminine) adjectival endings to the past stem of the verb. The final vowels *o* and *ė* of the stem are dropped, e.g.:

		Nom. Sg.	Gen. Sg.	Dat. Sg.
dìrbo 'worked'	Masc.		*dìrb-us-io*	*dìrb-us-iam*
	Fem.	*dìrb-us-i*	*dìrb-us-ios*	*dìrb-us-iai*
gḗrė 'drank'	Masc.		*gḗr-us-io*	*gḗr-us-iam*
	Fem.	*gḗr-us-i*	*gḗr-us-ios*	*gḗr-us-iai*
dainãvo 'sang'	Masc.		*dainãv-us-io*	*dainãv-us-iam*
	Fem.	*dainãv-us-i*	*dainãv-us-ios*	*dainãv-us-iai*

The variant *-ius-* of the preterit participial suffix occurs after a soft consonant in participles formed from verbs which have the suffix *-yti* in the infinitive and the vowel *ė* at the end of their past stem, e.g.:

		Nom. Sg.	Gen. Sg.
rašýti 'write' – *rãšė*	Masc.		*rãš-ius-io*
	Fem.	*rãš-ius-i*	*rãš-ius-ios*
laikýti 'hold' – *laĩkė*	Masc.		*laĩk-ius-io*
	Fem.	*laĩk-ius-i*	*laĩk-ius-ios*

Before the suffix *-ius-* the consonants *t, d* change into *č* and *dž*, e.g.:

		Nom. Sg.	Gen. Sg.
skaitýti 'read' – *skaĩtė*	Masc.		*skaĩč-ius-io*
	Fem.	*skaĩč-ius-i*	*skaĩč-ius-ios*
sklaidýti 'disperse' – *sklaĩdė*	Masc.		*sklaĩdž-ius-io*
	Fem.	*sklaĩdž-ius-i*	*sklaĩdž-ius-ios*

The short forms of the nominative case of masculine past participles are formed by adding the endings *-ęs* (singular) and *-ę* (plural) to the past stem of the verbs after dropping the final vowel, e.g.:

dìrb-o –   *dìrb-ęs*   *dìrb-ę*
gḗr-ė –   *gḗr-ęs*   *gḗr-ę*
bḗg-o –   *bḗg-ęs*   *bḗg-ę*
dainãv-o – *dainãv-ęs*   *dainãv-ę*

The long forms of the nominative case of masculine past participles occur much more rarely than the short forms. They are formed by adding the suffix *-(i)us-* and the endings *-is* (singular) and *-ys* (plural), e.g.:

dìrb-o – dìrb-us-is	dìrb-us-ys
rãš-ė – rãš-ius-is	rãš-ius-ys

These long forms have a dialectal colour and are used only as preposed attributes to indicate a quality, e.g.:

pargrį̃žusis põnas	'the gentleman who has come back'
diñgusis brólis	'the brother who has disappeared'
praẽjusys mẽtai	'bygone years'

The short form of the nominative plural of masculine past participles is originally neuter and can fulfill the functions of the neuter forms, cf. *Bùvo jaũ sutẽmę/tamsù.* 'It was already dark' (see 5.124). It is also used instead of the nominative plural of feminine participles, e.g.:

nušãlusios/nušãlę rañkos	'frost-bitten hands'
supùvusios/supùvę bùlvės	'rotten potatoes'

All preterit participles of the active voice follow the stress pattern of the respective infinitives. Since verbal prefixes in these participles do not attract the stress (except for the prefix *per-*), all prefixed participles are stressed like non-prefixed participles.

DECLENSION OF PAST ACTIVE PARTICIPLES

Masculine gender (*ia*-stem)

Singular

Nom.	dìrbęs	tikėjęs	válgęs	atnẽšęs
Gen.	dìrbusio	tikėjusio	válgiusio	atnẽšusio
Dat.	dìrbusiam	tikėjusiam	válgiusiam	atnẽšusiam
Acc.	dìrbusį	tikėjusį	válgiusį	atnẽšusį
Instr.	dìrbusiu	tikėjusiu	válgiusiu	atnẽšusiu
Loc.	dìrbusiame	tikėjusiame	válgiusiame	atnẽšusiame

Plural

Nom.	dìrbę	tikėję	válgę	atnẽšę
Gen.	dìrbusių	tikėjusių	válgiusių	atnẽšusių
Dat.	dìrbusiems	tikėjusiems	válgiusiems	atnẽšusiems
Acc.	dìrbusius	tikėjusius	válgiusius	atnẽšusius
Instr.	dìrbusiais	tikėjusiais	válgiusiais	atnẽšusiais
Loc.	dìrbusiuose	tikėjusiuose	válgiusiuose	atnẽšusiuose

Feminine gender (*io*-stem)

Singular

Nom.	dìrbusi	tikėjusi	válgiusi	atnẽšusi
Gen.	dìrbusios	tikėjusios	válgiusios	atnẽšusios
Dat.	dìrbusiai	tikėjusiai	válgiusiai	atnẽšusiai
Acc.	dìrbusią	tikėjusią	válgiusią	atnẽšusią
Instr.	dìrbusia	tikėjusia	válgiusia	atnẽšusia
Loc.	dìrbusioje	tikėjusioje	válgiusioje	atnẽšusioje

Plural

Nom.	dìrbusios	tikėjusios	válgiusios	atnẽšusios
Gen.	dìrbusių	tikėjusių	válgiusių	atnẽšusių
Dat.	dìrbusioms	tikėjusioms	válgiusioms	atnẽšusioms
Acc.	dìrbusias	tikėjusias	válgiusias	atnẽšusias
Instr.	dìrbusiomis	tikėjusiomis	válgiusiomis	atnẽšusiomis
Loc.	dìrbusiose	tikėjusiose	válgiusiose	atnẽšusiose

PAST FREQUENTATIVE PARTICIPLES

5.118 Past frequentative active participles are formed by adding the compound suffix *-dav-us-* (which combines the past frequentative suffix *-dav-* and the past participial suffix *-us-*) and the appropriate endings to the infinitival stem of the verb, e.g.:

	Nom. Sg. Fem.	Nom. Pl. Fem.
dìrb-ti 'work'	dìrb-dav-us-i	dìrb-dav-us-ios
gér-ti 'drink'	gér-dav-us-i	gér-dav-us-ios
kartó-ti 'repeat'	kartó-dav-us-i	kartó-dav-us-ios

The formation of masculine past frequentative participles is similar to that of masculine past participles in that they are also formed by adding the endings *-ęs* (Nom. Sg.) and *-ę* (Nom. Pl.) to the suffix *-dav-*, e.g.:

Nom. Sg. Masc.	Nom. Pl. Masc.
dìrb-dav-ęs	dìrb-dav-ę
gér-dav-ęs	gér-dav-ę
kartó-dav-ęs	kartó-dav-ę

Past frequentative participles are usually used only in the nominative case (singular or plural) and they usually indicate an indirectly experienced action or process (see 5.152).

The short form of the nominative plural of masculine future participles may replace the respective case form of feminine future participles, e.g.:

Dabar̃ grãžios diẽnos bū́siančios/ bū́sią. 'Now (maybe) the days will be beautiful.'
Ãvys ištrū́ksiančios/ištrū́ksią. 'The sheep (I think/probably) will escape.'

Future active participles are declined in the same way as present active participles. In all the cases, future participles retain the same accentuation as the infinitive. Prefixes, except for the prefix *per-*, do not attract the stress.

Most frequently future participles are used in the nominative case.

DECLENSION OF FUTURE ACTIVE PARTICIPLES

Masculine gender (*ia*-stem)

Singular

Nom.	dìrbsiąs	eĩsiąs	rašýsiąs
Gen.	dìrbsiančio	eĩsiančio	rašýsiančio
Dat.	dìrbsiančiam	eĩsiančiam	rašýsiančiam
Acc.	dìrbsiantį	eĩsiantį	rašýsiantį
Instr.	dìrbsiančiu	eĩsiančiu	rašýsiančiu
Loc.	dìrbsiančiame	eĩsiančiame	rašýsiančiame

Plural

Nom.	dìrbsiantys	eĩsiantys	rašýsiantys
Gen.	dìrbsiančių	eĩsiančių	rašýsiančių
Dat.	dìrbsiantiems	eĩsiantiems	rašýsiantiems
Acc.	dìrbsiančius	eĩsiančius	rašýsiančius
Instr.	dìrbsiančiais	eĩsiančiais	rašýsiančiais
Loc.	dìrbsiančiuose	eĩsiančiuose	rašýsiančiuose

Feminine gender (*io*-stem)

Singular

Nom.	dìrbsianti	eĩsianti	rašýsianti
Gen.	dìrbsiančios	eĩsiančios	rašýsiančios
Dat.	dìrbsiančiai	eĩsiančiai	rašýsiančiai
Acc.	dìrbsiančią	eĩsiančią	rašýsiančią
Instr.	dìrbsiančia	eĩsiančia	rašýsiančia
Loc.	dìrbsiančioje	eĩsiančioje	rašýsiančioje

dìrb-ti *dìrb-si-a-nt*
láuk-ti *láuk-si-a-nt*
tikė̃-ti *tikė̃-si-a-nt*
rašý-ti *rašý-si-a-nt*

Before the future tense suffix *-si-* the final consonants *s, z, š, ž* of the infinitival stem undergo the same changes as in the future tense finite forms and future active participles (see 5.119), i.e.:

$s + s \Rightarrow s$ $\quad$ $š + s \Rightarrow š$
$z + s \Rightarrow s$ $\quad$ $ž + s \Rightarrow š$

vès-ti *vèsiant* $\quad$ *nèš-ti* *nèšiant*
mègz-ti *mègsiant* $\quad$ *vèž-ti* *vèšiant*

Gerunds retain the infinitive accentuation.

The formation of gerunds can be described in another way. One may derive them by dropping the ending *-į* from the accusative singular of the respective active participle:

dìrbant-į – dìrbant $\quad$ *dìrbdavus-į – dìrbdavus*
dìrbus-į – dìrbus $\quad$ *dìrbsiant-į – dìrbsiant*

Historically, however, gerunds evolved from the old dative masculine forms with a consonantal stem which have lost the ending *-i*.

Passive participles
Neveikiamíeji dalỹviai

PRESENT PASSIVE PARTICIPLE

5.121 Present passive participles are formed by adding the suffix *-m-* and *a*-stem (masculine) and *o*-stem (feminine) adjectival endings to the present tense stem of the verbs.

dìrb-a 'works' – *dìrba-m-as, dirba-m-à*
mýl-i 'loves' – *mýli-m-as, myli-m-à*
rãš-o 'writes' – *rãšo-m-as, rãšo-m-a*

The passive participle of the verb *bū́ti* 'be' is formed from the stem *es-* (cf., *es-ù, es-ì, ẽs-ti*), which is different from the usual 3rd person form *yrà*. The passive participial suffix *-m-* is joined to the stem *es-* with the vowel *a*:

ẽs-a-m-as, es-a-m-à

Participles created from verbs of the 3rd conjugation and verbs containing suffixes retain the same stress pattern which is encountered in the finite forms of the present tense. Their stress pattern is the same as that of the adjectives belonging to Accentuation Class 1.

		Singular		Plural	
skaĩto 'reads'	Nom.	*skaĩtomas*	*skaĩtoma*	*skaĩtomi*	*skaĩtomos*
	Gen.	*skaĩtomo*	*skaĩtomos*	*skaĩtomų*	*skaĩtomų*
	Dat.	*skaĩtomam*	*skaĩtomai*	*skaĩtomiems*	*skaĩtomoms*
gyvẽna 'lives'	Nom.	*gyvẽnamas*	*gyvẽnama*	*gyvẽnami*	*gyvẽnamos*
	Gen.	*gyvẽnamo*	*gyvẽnamos*	*gyvẽnamų*	*gyvẽnamų*
	Dat.	*gyvẽnamam*	*gyvẽnamai*	*gyvẽnamiems*	*gyvẽnamoms*

Participles formed from bisyllabic verbs of the 1st and 2nd conjugations usually follow the stress pattern typical of adjectives belonging to the 3rd accentuation class, e.g.:

		Singular		Plural	
nẽša 'carries'	Nom.	*nẽšamas*	*nešamà*	*nešamì*	*nẽšamos*
	Gen.	*nẽšamo*	*nešamõs*	*nešamų̃*	*nešamų̃*
	Dat.	*nešamám*	*nẽšamai*	*nešamíems*	*nešamóms*
láukia 'waits'	Nom.	*láukiamas*	*laukiamà*	*laukiamì*	*láukiamos*
	Gen.	*láukiamo*	*laukiamõs*	*laukiamų̃*	*laukiamų̃*
	Dat.	*laukiamám*	*láukiamai*	*laukiamíems*	*laukiamóms*

However, if the verbs belonging to the 1st and 2nd conjugations carry the acute toneme, the accentuation of present passive participles formed from them may follow the pattern typical of adjectives of the 1st accentuation class, i.e. their accentuation may be fixed, e.g. *mýlimas, mýlima; láukiamas, láukiama*.

Prefixed participles are accented like their respective non-prefixed counterparts if the prefix does not attract the stress in the finite present tense verb from which the participle is formed, e.g.:

| *nemýli* 'doesn't love' | *nemýlimas* | *nemylimà* | cf. *mýlimas, -à* |
| *sulañksto* 'folds' | *sulañkstomas* | *sulañkstoma* | cf. *lañkstomas, -a* |

If the prefix attracts the stress in the finite present tense forms, the prefixed present passive participle is stressed like adjectives belonging to the 3[4b] accentuation class, i.e. some of the case forms are stressed on the prefix, some on the ending (see the declension pattern below).

DECLENSION OF PRESENT PASSIVE PARTICIPLES

Masculine gender (*a*-stem)

Singular

Nom.	dìrbamas	gãlimas	rãšomas	įžiūrimas	nùgalimas
Gen.	dìrbamo	gãlimo	rãšomo	įžiūrimo	nùgalimo
Dat.	dirbamám	galimám	rãšomam	įžiūrimám	nugalimám
Acc.	dìrbamą	gãlimą	rãšomą	įžiūrimą	nùgalimą
Instr.	dìrbamu	gãlimu	rãšomu	įžiūrimu	nùgalimu
Loc.	dirbamamè	galimamè	rãšomame	įžiūrimamè	nugalimamè

Plural

Nom.	dirbamì	galimì	rãšomi	įžiūrimì	nugalimì
Gen.	dirbamų̃	galimų̃	rãšomų	įžiūrimų̃	nugalimų̃
Dat.	dirbamíems	galimíems	rãšomiems	įžiūrimíems	nugalimíems
Acc.	dìrbamus	gãlimus	rãšomus	įžiūrimus	nùgalimus
Instr.	dirbamaĩs	galimaĩs	rãšomais	įžiūrimaĩs	nugalimaĩs
Loc.	dirbamuosè	galimuosè	rãšomuose	įžiūrimuosè	nugalimuosè

Feminine gender (*o*-stem)

Singular

Nom.	dirbamà	galimà	rãšoma	įžiūrimà	nugalimà
Gen.	dirbamõs	galimõs	rãšomos	įžiūrimõs	nugalimõs
Dat.	dìrbamai	gãlimai	rãšomai	įžiūrimai	nùgalimai
Acc.	dìrbamą	gãlimą	rãšomą	įžiūrimą	nùgalimą
Instr.	dìrbama	gãlima	rãšoma	įžiūrima	nùgalima
Loc.	dirbamojè	galimojè	rãšomoje	įžiūrimojè	nugalimojè

Plural

Nom.	dìrbamos	gãlimos	rãšomos	įžiūrimos	nùgalimos
Gen.	dirbamų̃	galimų̃	rãšomų	įžiūrimų̃	nugalimų̃
Dat.	dirbamóms	galimóms	rãšomoms	įžiūrimóms	nugalimóms
Acc.	dìrbamas	gãlimas	rãšomas	įžiūrimas	nùgalimas
Instr.	dirbamomìs	galimomìs	rãšomomis	įžiūrimomìs	nugalimomìs
Loc.	dirbamosè	galimosè	rãšomose	įžiūrimosè	nugalimosè

PAST PASSIVE PARTICIPLE

5.122 Past passive participles are formed by adding the suffix -*t*- and the adjectival *a*-stem (masculine) or *o*-stem (feminine) endings to the infinitival stem, e.g.:

dìrb-ti 'work' –	dìrb-t-as, dirb-t-à
eĩ-ti 'go' –	eĩ-t-as, ei-t-à
mylė́-ti 'love' –	mylė́-t-as, mylė́-t-a
kartó-ti 'repeat' –	kartó-t-as, kartó-t-a

Participles formed from infinitival stems containing suffixes retain the stress pattern of the infinitive, i.e., they belong to Accentuation Class 1, e.g.:

girdė́ti 'hear' –	girdė́tas, girdė́ta
rašýti 'write' –	rašýtas, rašýta

Participles formed from verbs which contain no suffixes and bear the acute toneme on the stressed syllable follow the stress pattern of Accentuation Class 3, e.g.:

dìrbti 'work' –   dìrbtas, dirbtà (like báltas, baltà 'white')

Due to dialectal influences, however, these participles may sometimes have fixed stress on the same syllable in all forms, e.g.:

láukti 'wait' –	láuktas, lauktà/láukta
léisti 'permit' –	léistas, leistà/léista

Participles with a short accented root vowel or the circumflex toneme on the root syllable follow the stress pattern of Accentuation Class 4, e.g.:

mùšti 'beat' –	mùštas, muštà
eĩti 'go' –	eĩtas, eità (cf. gẽras, gerà 'good')

The stressed vowels *a* and *e* in the root of past participles of the passive voice are (according to the traditional norm) long and have the circumflex toneme, e.g.:

mèsti 'throw' –	mẽstas, mestà
nèšti 'carry' –	nẽštas, neštà
ràsti 'find' –	rãstas, rastà
kàsti 'dig' –	kãstas, kastà

In colloquial speech, however, these participles now tend to retain the short vowel of the infinitive, cf.:

mèstas, nèštas, ràstas, kàstas

Prefixed participles formed from infinitival stems containing suffixes retain the stress pattern of the infinitive in all their forms, e.g.:

aprašýti 'describe' – *aprašýtas, aprašýta*
įžiūrė́ti 'discern' – *įžiūrė́tas, įžiūrė́ta*
pakartóti 'repeat' – *pakartótas, pakartóta*

Prefixed participles formed from infinitival stems which contain no suffixes are accented in two ways. If the infinitive bears the acute toneme, the stress in the participle is not attracted to the prefix and thus the prefixed participles are stressed like their respective non-prefixed counterparts, e.g.:

išráuti 'uproot' – *išráutas, išrautà*
praléisti 'omit' – *praléistas, praleistà*

If the infinitive contains a short stressed vowel or its root bears the circumflex toneme, the stress in the participle is attracted to the prefix or moved to the ending (accentuation class 3^b), e.g.:

nukir̃pti 'cut off' – *nùkirptas, nukirptà*
atnèšti 'bring' – *àtneštas, atneštà*
atràsti 'find' – *àtrastas, atrastà*

DECLENSION OF PAST PASSIVE PARTICIPLES

Masculine gender (*a*-stem)

Singular

Nom.	*dìrbtas*	*mùštas*	*rašýtas*	*nùkirptas*	*àtneštas*
Gen.	*dìrbto*	*mùšto*	*rašýto*	*nùkirpto*	*àtnešto*
Dat.	*dirbtám*	*muštám*	*rašýtam*	*nukirptám*	*atneštám*
Acc.	*dìrbtą*	*mùštą*	*rašýtą*	*nùkirptą*	*àtneštą*
Instr.	*dìrbtu*	*mùštù*	*rašýtu*	*nùkirptu*	*àtneštu*
Loc.	*dirbtamè*	*muštamè*	*rašýtame*	*nukirptamè*	*atneštamè*

Plural

Nom.	*dirbtì*	*muštì*	*rašýti*	*nukirptì*	*atneštì*
Gen.	*dirbtų̃*	*muštų̃*	*rašýtų*	*nukirptų̃*	*atneštų̃*
Dat.	*dirbtíems*	*muštíems*	*rašýtiems*	*nukirptíems*	*atneštíems*
Acc.	*dìrbtus*	*mùštùs*	*rašýtus*	*nùkirptus*	*àtneštus*
Instr.	*dìrbtaĩs*	*muštaĩs*	*rašýtais*	*nukirptaĩs*	*atneštaĩs*
Loc.	*dìrbtuosè*	*muštuosè*	*rašýtuose*	*nukirptuosè*	*atneštuosè*

Feminine gender (o-stem)

Singular

Nom.	dirbtà	muštà	rašýta	nukirptà	atneštà
Gen.	dirbtõs	muštõs	rašýtos	nukirptõs	atneštõs
Dat.	dìrbtai	mùštai	rašýtai	nùkirptai	àtneštai
Acc.	dìrbtą	mùštą	rašýtą	nùkirptą	àtneštą
Instr.	dìrbta	muštà	rašýta	nùkirpta	àtnešta
Loc.	dirbtojè	muštojè	rašýtoje	nukirptojè	atneštojè

Plural

Nom.	dìrbtos	mùštos	rašýtos	nùkirptos	àtneštos
Gen.	dirbtų̃	muštų̃	rašýtų	nukirptų̃	atneštų̃
Dat.	dirbtóms	muštóms	rašýtoms	nukirptóms	atneštóms
Acc.	dìrbtas	mùštàs	rašýtas	nùkirptas	àtneštas
Instr.	dirbtomìs	muštomìs	rašýtomis	nukirptomìs	atneštomìs
Loc.	dirbtosè	muštosè	rašýtose	nukirptosè	atneštosè

FUTURE PASSIVE PARTICIPLES

5.123 Future passive participles are formed by adding the compound suffix -*si-m*-, which includes the future tense suffix -*si*- and the suffix -*m*- of present passive participles, and the adjectival *a*-stem (for the masculine gender) or *o*-stem (for the feminine gender) endings, e.g.:

dìrbti 'work' – dìrb-si-m-as, dirb-si-m-à
bū́ti 'be' – bū́-si-m-as, bū-si-m-à

Before the compound suffix -*si-m*- the final consonants *s*, *z*, *š*, *ž* of the infinitival stem undergo changes similar to those in the formation of the finite forms of the future tense, i.e.:

$s + s \Rightarrow s$ $š + s \Rightarrow š$
$z + s \Rightarrow s$ $ž + s \Rightarrow š$

vèsti 'lead' – vèsimas, vesimà
mègzti 'knit' – mègsimas, megsimà

nèšti 'carry' – nèšimas, nešimà
vèžti 'transport with a vehicle' – vèšimas, vešimà

Except for the participle bū́simas, būsimà, future passive participles are rarely used.

Future passive participles are declined like present passive participles.

Future passive participles are accented as follows:

(1) participles formed from infinitival stems containing a suffix retain the same accentuation which is encountered in the infinitive, e.g.:

rašýti 'write' – rašýsimas, rašýsima

(2) participles formed from simple infinitival stems which contain no suffix follow the stress pattern of adjectives of Accentuation Class 3, e.g.:

	Singular		Plural	
Nom.	búsimas	būsimà	būsimì	búsimos
Gen.	búsimo	būsimõs	būsimų̃	būsimų̃
Dat.	būsimám	búsimai	būsimíems	būsimóms
Acc.	búsimą	búsimą	búsimus	búsimas
Instr.	búsimu	búsima	būsimaĩs	būsimomìs
Loc.	būsimamè	būsimojè	būsimuosè	būsimosè

Neuter participles

5.124 Participles (with the exception of half-participles) possess neuter forms, which most often function as predicates in impersonal sentences, in sentences with the pronouns vìskas, vìsa, taĩ and several others as the subject, and in other sentence patterns typical of neuter adjectives (see 2.4).

The neuter forms of active participles coincide with the short masculine forms of the nominative plural. Most frequent are neuter forms in the past and past frequentative, e.g.:

Vìskas sušlãpę.	'Everything has got wet.'
Nãktį palýdavę.	'At night it used to rain.'
Kíek daũg prisnìgę.	'How much snow there is.'
Bùvo jaũ sutémę.	'It was already dark.'
Visuř priplékę.	'There's mold everywhere.'

The neuter forms of passive participles have the ending -a, which is never stressed, e.g.:

Taĩp nedãroma.	'This is not done.'
Nùtarta visíems eĩti draugè.	'It has been decided that all should go together.'
Sãkoma, kad šiuosè namuosè vaidénasi.	'They say this is a haunted house.'
Kàs čia parašýta?	'What is written here?'

Reflexive participles

5.125 The reflexive active participles without prefixes are formed by adding the reflexive formant to the ending of the nominative case. Only short nominative singular and plural masculine forms of active non-prefixed participles can be reflexive. In the singular they have the vowel *i* inserted before the shorter variant of the reflexive formant, e.g.:

	Masc.	Fem.
Present	dìrbqs-i-s	dìrbanti-s
Past	dìrbęs-i-s	dìrbusi-s
Past freq.	dìrbdavęs-is	dìrbdavusi-s
Future	dìrbsiqs-is	dìrbsianti-s

In the plural the reflexive formant in its full form *-si* is added. It undergoes contraction with the final *-s* in feminine forms (*dìrbančios-si* → *dìrbančiosi*), e.g.:

	Masc.	Fem.
Present	dìrbq-si	dìrbančiosi
Past	dìrbę-si	dìrbusiosi
Past freq.	dìrbdavę-si	dìrbdavusiosi
Future	dìrbsiq-si	dìrbsiančiosi

The same contraction is observed in the feminine plural forms of the reflexive half-participles (*dìrbdamos-si* → *dìrbdamosi*). The reflexive half-participles retain the nominative plural ending *-ie-* before the reflexive formant, e.g.:

	Masc.	Fem.
Sg.	dìrbdamas-i-s	dìrbdama-si
Pl.	dìrbdamie-si	dìrbdamosi

The singular feminine form of reflexive half-participles sometimes preserves the long vowel *-o-* before the reflexive formant and coincides with the plural feminine form, e.g.: *dìrbdamosi, nèšdamosi*.

The non-prefixed reflexive gerunds are formed by adding the shorter form of the reflexive formant with the inserted vowel *i* (i.e. *-is*) to the suffix, e.g.:

Present	dìrbant-i-s	Past freq.	dìrbdavus-i-s
Past	dìrbus-i-s	Future	dìrbsiant-i-s

The non-prefixed reflexive active participles (including gerunds) retain the stress and toneme of the corresponding simple (non-reflexive) participles.

5.126 In the sentence the nominative forms of non-prefixed reflexive participles usually function as predicates denoting indirect experience, e.g.:

Pirklỹs gulį̃s sàvo vežimè ir juñtąs, kad po lángu laũmės šnẽkančiosi.	'The merchant (the say) is lying in his cart and he hears the fairies talking under the window.'
Tai tóks mìškas tráukęsis per Lietuvõs žẽmę.	'So such were (according to hearsay) the woods that extended across the Lithuanian land.'
Girdė́jau, rytój jiẽ rengią̃si į̃ kelionę.	'I heard they are going on a journey tomorrow.'

The non-prefixed reflexive participles in Modern Lithuanian are not inflected for case. In the various case functions (except the nominative) they are replaced by the forms of the corresponding reflexive participles with the affix *be-*, e.g.:

Present participle

	Singular	Plural
Nom.	*juõkiąsis, juõkiantis*	*juõkiąsi, juõkiančiosi*
Gen.	*besijuõkiančio, besijuõkiančios*	*besijuõkiančių*
Dat.	*besijuõkiančiam, besijuõkiančiai*	*besijuõkiantiems, besijuõkiančioms*
Acc.	*besijuõkiantį, besijuõkiančią*	*besijuõkiančius, besijuõkiančias*, etc.

Past participle

	Singular	Plural
Nom.	*juõkęsis, juõkusis*	*juõkęsi, juõkusiosi*
Gen.	*besijuõkusio, besijuõkusios*	*besijuõkusių*
Dat.	*besijuõkusiam, besijuõkusiai*	*besijuõkusiems, besijuõkusioms*
Acc.	*besijuõkusį, besijuõkusią*	*besijuõkusius, besijuõkusias*, etc.

5.127 In prefixed active participles, half-participles and gerunds, the reflexive formant *-si-* is inserted between the prefix (including the affixes *be-*, *te-*, *tebe-*, *ne-*) and the root, e.g.:

Infinitive	*apsidairýti*	*nesitikė́ti*
	'look around'	'not to expect'
Present	*ap-si-daĩrantis*	*ne-sì-tikintis*
	ap-si-daĩranti	*ne-sì-tikinti*
Past	*ap-si-daĩręs*	*ne-si-tikė́jęs*
	ap-si-daĩriusi	*ne-si-tikė́jusi*
Past freq.	*ap-si-dairýdavęs*	*ne-si-tikė́davęs*
	ap-si-dairýdavusi	*ne-si-tikė́davusi*

Future	*ap-si-dairýsiąs*	*ne-si-tikė́siąs*
	ap-si-dairýsianti	*ne-si-tikė́sianti*
Half-participle	*ap-si-dairýdamas*	*ne-si-tikė́damas*
	ap-si-dairýdama	*ne-si-tikė́dama*
Present gerund	*ap-si-daĩrant*	*ne-sì-tikint*
Past gerund	*ap-si-daĩrius*	*ne-si-tikė́jus*
Past freq. gerund	*ap-si-dairýdavus*	*ne-si-tikė́davus*
Future gerund	*ap-si-dairýsiant*	*ne-si-tikė́siant*

Reflexive active participles are declined like their non-reflexive counterparts with one exception concerning the present participles and gerunds. If the stress falls on the prefix of a present active participle or gerund, it shifts to the reflexive formant *-si-* in their reflexive counterparts (just like in the reflexive finite forms), e.g.:

àtnešantis – atsìnešantis	*atsìnešant*	cf.: *atsìneša* 'brings'
àtnešanti – atsìnešanti		
nùperkantis – nusìperkantis	*nusìperkant*	cf.: *nusìperka* 'buys'
nùperkanti – nusìperkanti		

The masculine and feminine forms of reflexive passive participles are created only from prefixed verbs (including those with the negative prefix *ne-*). The reflexive formant *-si-* is inserted between the prefix and the root, e.g.:

Present Passive		Past Passive	
pa-si-dìrbamas	*pa-si-dirbamà*	*pa-si-dìrbtas*	*pa-si-dirbtà*
nu-si-rãšomas	*nu-si-rãšoma*	*nu-si-rãšytas*	*nu-si-rãšyta*
nu-sì-vežamas	*nu-si-vežamà*	*nu-sì-vežtas*	*nu-si-vežtà*

These forms are declined and accented like their non-reflexive counterparts, except that those with a stressed prefix move the stress to the formant *-si-*, e.g.:

àtnešamas	*atnešamà –*	*atsìnešamas*	*atsinešamà*
àtneštas	*atneštà –*	*atsìneštas*	*atsineštà*

5.128 The neuter forms of reflexive passive participles can be formed both from prefixed and non-prefixed verbs. In non-prefixed neuter passive participles the formant *-si-* is added to the ending *-a*. These forms are accented like their non-reflexive counterparts, e.g.:

juõkiama-si	*praũsiama-si*
juõkta-si	*praũsta-si*

In prefixed neuter participles the formant *-si-* is inserted, as in all the other forms, between the prefix and the root. The accentuation of prefixed neuter participles is the same as that of the accusative singular of the corresponding masculine and feminine forms, e.g.:

pa-si-dároma   *nu-si-rášoma*   *ne-sì-vežama*
pa-si-darýta   *nu-si-rašýta*   *ne-sì-vežta*

Definite participles

5.129 The definite forms of active participles are derived and declined like definite *ia*-stem (masculine) and *io*-stem (feminine) adjectives (see *geresnỹsis, geresnióji* 'the better one' in 2.34). In forming definite masculine forms of active participles, the definite formant is added to the long nominative case forms, which retain the long vowel before the definite formant:

	Simple form	Definite form
Present	*dìrbantis*	*dìrbantysis*
	tỹlintis	*tỹlintysis*
	rãšantis	*rãšantysis*
Past	*dìrbusis*	*dìrbusysis*
	tylėjusis	*tylėjusysis*
	rãšiusis	*rãšiusysis*
Future	*dìrbsiantis*	*dìrbsiantysis*
	tylėsiantis	*tylėsiantysis*
	rašýsiantis	*rašýsiantysis*

In the nominative plural, masculine forms retain the diphthong *ie* in their endings, e.g.:

Present	Past	Future
dìrbantieji	*dìrbusieji*	*dìrbsiantieji*
tỹlintieji	*tylėjusieji*	*tylėsiantieji*
rãšantieji	*rãšiusieji*	*rašýsiantieji*

The nominative singular feminine definite participles are formed like feminine definite adjectives:

Present	Past	Future
dìrbanč-io-ji	*dìrbus-io-ji*	*dìrbsianč-io-ji*
tỹlinč-io-ji	*tylėjus-io-ji*	*tylėsianč-io-ji*
rãšanč-io-ji	*rãšius-io-ji*	*rašýsianč-io-ji*

The old nominative singular forms of feminine definite participles, containing the participial ending -*i* (*dìrbanti-ji, gìmusi-ji*, etc.) have become almost entirely extinct and are only to be found in old writings and some dialects.

Since half-participles and gerunds are not used to denote qualities, they do not possess any definite forms. This fact can also explain why definite forms are not typical of frequentative past active participles.

The definite forms of active participles are accented like the respective simple forms, but if the short masculine form of the simple participle carries the stress on the ending, the nominative form of the respective definite participle also moves the stress to the ending, e.g.:

nešą̃s	*nešantỹsis*
tikį̃s	*tikintỹsis*
slenką̃s	*slenkantỹsis*

5.130· The definite forms of passive participles are derived and declined exactly in the same way as *a*-stem (masculine) and *o*-stem (feminine) definite adjectives, e.g.:

dirbamàsis	*dirbamóji*
dirbtàsis	*dirbtóji*
cf.: *geltonàsis*	*geltonóji*
geràsis	*geróji* (see 2.34).

Definite passive participles formed from *o*-stem verbs (Conjugation 3) or from verbs with a suffix retain the same stress pattern as the respective simple participles, e.g.:

vartójamas	*vartójamo*	–	*vartójamasis*	*vartójamoji*
vartótas	*vartóta*	–	*vartótasis*	*vartótoji*
ródomas	*ródoma*	–	*ródomasis*	*ródomoji*
ródytas	*ródyta*	–	*ródytasis*	*ródytoji*

Definite passive participles formed from simple verbs belonging to Conjugation 1 or 2 are accented like definite adjectives with a shifting stress, e.g., *nešamàsis, nešamóji, gulimàsis, gulimóji* are accented like *geltonàsis, geltonóji; neštàsis, neštóji, dirbtàsis, dirbtóji* are accented like *baltàsis, baltóji* (see 2.41).

The stress in the definite forms of present passive participles formed from verbs of Conjugation 3 or from verbs with a suffix also tends to become mobile, particularly when the participle acquires an adjectival or substantival meaning, e.g.:

rašomàsis	*rašomóji* 'writing' (e.g. table)
gyvenamàsis	*gyvenamóji* 'living' (e.g. room)

DECLENSION OF DEFINITE ACTIVE PARTICIPLES

Masculine gender (*ia*-stem)

Singular

Nom.	*dìrbantysis*	*dìrbusysis*	*dìrbsiantysis*
Gen.	*dìrbančiojo*	*dìrbusiojo*	*dìrbsiančiojo*
Dat.	*dìrbančiajam*	*dìrbusiajam*	*dìrbsiančiajam*
Acc.	*dìrbantįjį*	*dìrbusįjį*	*dìrbsiantįjį*
Instr.	*dìrbančiuoju*	*dìrbusiuoju*	*dìrbsiančiuoju*
Loc.	*dìrbančiajame*	*dìrbusiajame*	*dìrbsiančiajame*

Plural

Nom.	*dìrbantieji*	*dìrbusieji*	*dìrbsiantieji*
Gen.	*dìrbančiųjų*	*dìrbusiųjų*	*dìrbsiančiųjų*
Dat.	*dìrbantiesiems*	*dìrbusiesiems*	*dìrbsiantiesiems*
Acc.	*dìrbančiuosius*	*dìrbusiuosius*	*dìrbsiančiuosius*
Instr.	*dìrbančiaisiais*	*dìrbusiaisiais*	*dìrbsiančiaisiais*
Loc.	*dìrbančiuosiuose*	*dìrbusiuosiuose*	*dìrbsiančiuosiuose*

Feminine gender (*o*-stem)

Singular

Nom.	*dìrbančioji*	*dìrbusioji*	*dìrbsiančioji*
Gen.	*dìrbančiosios*	*dìrbusiosios*	*dìrbsiančiosios*
Dat.	*dìrbančiajai*	*dìrbusiajai*	*dìrbsiančiajai*
Acc.	*dìrbančiąją*	*dìrbusiąją*	*dìrbsiančiąją*
Instr.	*dìrbančiąja*	*dìrbusiąja*	*dìrbsiančiąja*
Loc.	*dìrbančiojoje*	*dìrbusiojoje*	*dìrbsiančiojoje*

Plural

Nom.	*dìrbančiosios*	*dìrbusiosios*	*dìrbsiančiosios*
Gen.	*dìrbančiųjų*	*dìrbusiųjų*	*dìrbsiančiųjų*
Dat.	*dìrbančiosioms*	*dìrbusiosioms*	*dìrbsiančiosioms*
Acc.	*dìrbančiąsias*	*dìrbusiąsias*	*dìrbsiančiąsias*
Instr.	*dìrbančiosiomis*	*dìrbusiosiomis*	*dìrbsiančiosiomis*
Loc.	*dìrbančiosiose*	*dìrbusiosiose*	*dìrbsiančiosiose*

Meaning and usage of participles

5.131 Lithuanian participles possess a great variety of grammatical meanings, which depend upon the syntactic relations of the participle within a sentence. From the syntactic point of view it is possible to distinguish three kinds of participial usage: attributive, semi-predicative and predicative.

ATTRIBUTIVE USAGE

5.132 Attributive participles combine with nouns and agree with them in gender, number and case. They denote properties which, depending upon the tense of the participle, are associated with the present, past or future.

Attributive usage is typical of all declinable participial forms, except half-participles (which are, in fact, adverbial present active participles) and frequentative past active participles. The meanings of attributive participles can best be described by oppositions based on three distinctive semantic features: passivity, anteriority and posteriority.

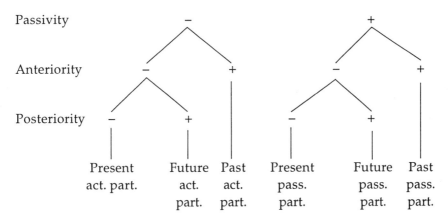

Relations among attributive participles

5.133 Present active participles being the unmarked members of the above oppositions indicate properties associated with (1) an action taking place simultaneously with the action denoted by the predicate, or (2) a regular, habitual action, e.g.:

(1) *Visì geraĩ mãtė artėjantį tráukinį.*	'Everybody could see well the approaching train.'
(2) *Tẽkantis vanduõ švarèsnis už stóvintį.*	'Flowing water is cleaner than still (water).'

Present active participles are most often formed from verbs of imperfective meaning. Even when they denote properties associated with regular, habitual actions present participles mostly retain the meaning of the active voice and the verbal government of cases, cf.:

ligàs gýdantis vanduõ	'water curing diseases'
dárbus išmãnantis ūkininkas	'a farmer knowledgeable about various jobs'

5.134 **Past active participles** possess the meaning of anteriority and indicate properties, associated with actions which took place prior to the action or state denoted by the predicate, e.g.:

Móters žvil̃gsnį patráukė tolumõj pasiródęs žmogùs.	'The woman's eye was attracted by the man who had appeared in the distance.'
Vaĩkas ilgaĩ trýnė sušãlusias rankàs.	'The child rubbed his frozen hands for a long time.'

Past active participles are most often made from prefixed resultative verbs with the perfective meaning. If the resultative meaning is predominant, its relation to the previous action may fade out and then the participle denotes a permanent property, e.g.:

pasiùtęs šuõ	'rabid dog'
išdýkęs vaĩkas	'naughty child'
suáugusi merginà	'grown up girl'

Perfective meaning is also typical of a great number of participles which are made from non-prefixed verbs, e.g.:

vẽdęs jaunikáitis	'married young man'
rū́gusis píenas	'sour milk'
mìrusi sesuõ	'dead sister'

Even in such cases active participles don't lose the meaning of the active voice and they never become true adjectives.

Past active participles formed from non-prefixed verbs sometimes can possess imperfective meaning and denote properties derived from an action which had been taking place for some time in the past, but such cases are not frequent, and they mostly occur in written language, e.g.:

Sárgas, stovėjęs už dùrų, įėjo į kam̃barį.	'The watchman, who had been standing behind the door, entered the room.'

5.135 **Future active participles** indicate properties associated with a foreseen (posterior) action. These participles are rarely used as attributes.

Laũmės pradėjo lem̃ti gìmsiančiam kū̃dikiui ateitiẽs gyvẽnimą.	'The fairies began to foretell the future life of the baby who was to be born.'
Ateĩsiančios žiemõs ilgùmo nežìnom.	'We do not know the length of the coming winter.'

5.136 **Present passive participles** denote properties associated with the action taking place at present or with a habitual regular action.

Participles with the passive meaning are formed from verbs (mostly transitive verbs) which govern a direct object. The object of a passive participle is usually expressed by the head word modified by that participle, e.g.:

mýlimas draũgas	'beloved friend'
pažį́stamas žmogùs	'an acquaintance' (lit. 'acquainted man')
žìnomas kẽlias	'(well-)known way'
láukiamas svẽčias	'welcome visitor'

Some of these participles, particularly those formed from prefixed verbs, denote a property associated with a habitual (generalized) action and, at the same time, the possibility of performing that action, e.g.:

suprantamà kalbà	'comprehensible speech'
sùkalbamas žmogùs	'compliant man'
pàkeliamas var̃gas	'endurable misery'
įskaĩtomas rãštas	'legible handwriting'

This is particularly true of negative participles, e.g.:

neapsãkoma galià	'indescribable might'
neišbrendamì uogienójai	'berry-plants which are impossible to wade through'
nenumaĩdomas príešas	'implacable enemy'
nepasíekiamas tìkslas	'unattainable goal'
nepàkeliamas akmuõ	'a stone which cannot be lifted'

Owing to their adjectival meaning such participles combine, like adjectives, with the dative rather than the agentive genitive, e.g.:

Ne kiekvienám prieĩnamas skanė̃stas.	'A delicacy which is not affordable by everyone.'
Kitíems nèregimas būdas.	'A method invisible to others.'
Dùrys visíems eĩnamos.	'A door everybody can walk through.'

(Cf.: *Dùrys visíems ãtviros.* lit. 'A door open to everybody.')

A similar semantic group of present passive participles consists of those which possess the meaning of destination. This meaning is typical of a great number of participles characterized by adjectival usage, e.g.:

dirbamà žẽmė	'tilled land'
ariamì laukaĩ	'arable fields'
gyvẽnamas nãmas	'dwelling house'

Similarly to classifying adjectives, these participles are often used in the definite form and can form terminological collocations, e.g.:

geriamàsis vanduõ	'drinking water'
melžiamóji kárvė	'milking cow'
pučiamàsis instrumeñtas	'wind instrument'
mušamàsis instrumeñtas	'percussion instrument'

The meaning of necessity is not very typical of these participles and it mostly occurs in dialects, e.g.:

Keliamõs kárvės blogà varškẽ.	'The milk of a puny (lit. 'to be lifted') cow is bad for curd.'

Present passive participles can also enter into a number of other relations with the modified noun.

(1) The modified noun denotes an instrument while the attributive participle specifies the action for the performance of which the instrument is used.

válgomasis šáukštas	'eating spoon'
jójamas arklỹs	'riding horse'
gėriamas puodėlis	'drinking cup'

In their definite form such participles are often used to designate tools and implements, e.g.:

kuliamóji mašinà	'threshing machine'
siuvamóji mašinà	'sowing machine'
pjaunamóji mašinà	'cutting machine'
šaunamàsis giñklas	'fire arm'
braĩžomoji/braižomóji lentà	'drawing board'
rãšomoji/rašomóji mašinėlė	'typewriter'

(2) An attributive participle (most often in its definite form) derived either from a transitive or intransitive verb is used to modify a noun which indicates (a) a place, or (b) time, e.g.:

(a) *miegamàsis kambarỹs*	'bedroom' (lit. 'sleeping room')
válgomasis/valgomàsis kambarỹs	'dining room'

gyvẽnamoji/gyvenamóji trobà	'dwelling house'
stovimóji vietà	'standing accomodation' (lit. 'place')
sėdimóji vietà	'sitting accomodation'
rū̃komasis/rūkomàsis vagònas	'smoking railcar'
(b) dirbamóji dienà	'working day'
péreinamasis laikótarpis	'transition period'
prìimamosios vãlandos	'reception hours'

When a participle formed from a transitive verb modifies a noun denoting an instrument, place or time, the object of the action can be designated by a noun in the genitive, e.g.:

alaũs	dãromas	kùbilas
beer: GEN. SG	make: PART. PRES. PASS	tub: NOM. SG

'tub for making beer', cf. also:

aviŲ kẽrpamos žìrklės	'shears for cutting sheep'
bùlvių sodìnamas laũkas	'field for planting potatoes'

(3) A participle (formed most often from an intransitive verb) denotes a property attributed to the semantic subject of the action or state, e.g.:

(a) participles formed from intransitive verbs:

skaudamà nùgara	'aching back'
tiñkamas dáiktas	'suitable thing'
limpamà ligà	'contagious disease'
atliekamì pinigaĩ	'extra (lit. 'remaining') money'

(b) participles built from transitive verbs:

gýdomas vanduõ	'healing water'
viliójamas pavéikslas	'enticing picture'

In their relations with the modified noun these participles are similar to present active participles (cf.: skaũdanti nùgara, gýdantis vanduõ, viliójantis pavéikslas). The difference lies in their more pronounced qualitative character and the meanings of suitability and possibility, which are responsible for the wide use of such passive participles in building terms, e.g.:

grįžtamóji šìltinė	'relapsing fever'
atsãkomasis/atsakomàsis redãktorius	'chief (lit. 'responsible') editor'
výkdomoji/vykdomóji valdžià	'executive power'
nejudamàsis turtas	'real (lit. 'non-movable') estate'

(4) The participle indicates a property which derives from an action related to the head noun by causal, manner or some other kind of relation, e.g.:

mirštamà ligà	'lethal (lit. 'dying') illness'
gulimà dúona	lit.'lying bread' (bread that can be earned simply by being in a lying position)
priverčiamíeji darbaĩ	'forced labour'
baigiamóji kalbà	'closing speech'

Some linguistic terms belong here, e.g.:

geidžiamóji núosaka	'optative mood'
liepiamóji núosaka	'imperative mood'
tariamóji núosaka	'subjunctive mood'
veikiamóji rū́šis	'active (lit. 'doing') voice'
esamàsis laĩkas	'present tense'
rãšomoji kalbà	'written language'
šnekamóji kalbà	'spoken language'

5.137 **Past passive participles** denote properties which derive from a past (anterior) action. They are formed mostly from transitive, particularly prefixed, verbs, and carry a resultative meaning, e.g.:

pradė́tas dárbas	'work which has been started'
ùžbaigtas dárbas	'finished work'
pamir̃štà dainà	'forgotten song'
ìšmuštas lángas	'broken window'

The resultative meaning is sometimes carried by participles which are formed from non-prefixed and non-perfective verbs, e.g.:

keptà dúona 'baked bread'	*sū́dyta mėsà* 'salted meat'
virtà žuvìs 'cooked fish'	*raugìnti agur̃kai* 'pickled cucumbers'
grį̃stas kẽlias 'paved road'	*mókytas žmogùs* 'learned man'
tašýtas akmuõ 'hewn stone'	

These participles often indicate constant properties of things or persons, particularly when these are based on their figurative or peripheral meaning:

àtmestas dárbas	'careless work'
cf.: *àtmestas prãšymas*	'rejected petition'
paténkintas žmogùs	'pleased man'
cf.: *paténkintas prãšymas*	'accepted petition'

Non-prefixed participial forms which possess a highly generalized qualitative meaning and which do not enter into any oppositions with participles in other tenses are considered to be verbal adjectives, e.g.:

drum̃stas 'turbid'   *glaũstas* 'concise'
riẽstas 'bent'   *sùktas* 'sly'

A great number of such forms derived from intransitive verbs are also considered to be verbal adjectives, e.g.:

báltas, baltà 'white' (: *bálti* 'to pale')
rim̃tas, rimtà 'serious' (: *rìmti* 'become quiet')
prãstas, prastà 'bad' (: *prãsti* 'become accustomed')
skýstas, skystà 'thin' (: *skýsti* 'become thinner' (about liquid))

But forms which constitute tense oppositions to other participial forms are considered to be participles, e.g.:

mirtà dienà	'dying day' (in the past)
cf.: *mirštamà dienà*	'dying day'
mirštamì nuodaĩ	'lethal poison'
būtà vietà	'past place'
cf.: *esamà vietà*	'present place'
eĩtas kẽlias	'road which has been travelled'
cf.: *eĩnamas kẽlias*	'road which is being travelled, which can be travelled'
gyvéntas nãmas	'house which was inhabited'
cf.: *gyvĕnamas nãmas*	'house which is inhabited, a dwelling house'

5.138 **Future passive participles** indicate properties associated with a posterior (foreseen) action, e.g.:

Àptarėme dìrbamus ir dìrbsimus dárbus.   'We discussed our present and future work.'

Jìs skaičiúoja turėsimus pìnigus.   'He is counting money which he is going to have.'

These participles are rarely used in present-day Lithuanian, except for the participle *būsimas, būsimà* 'future' which has no passive meaning, but constitutes a tense opposition to the present participle *ẽsamas, esamà* 'present'.

5.139 Some attributive participles which denote permanent properties possess **degrees of comparison**. Degrees of comparison are mostly typical of present passive participles., e.g.:

mýlimas, mylimà 'beloved' *rēgimas, regimà* 'apparent'
mylimèsnis, mylimèsnė   *regimèsnis, regimèsnė*
mylimiáusias, mylimiáusia *regimiáusias, regimiáusia*

tìkimas, tikimà 'credible'
tikimèsnis, tikimèsnė
tikimiáusias, tikimiáusia

Only singular past passive and past active participles possess degrees of comparison, e.g.:

mókytas, mókyta 'learned'   *pasiùtęs, pasiùtusi* 'mad'
mokytèsnis, mokytèsnė   *pasiutèsnis, pasiutèsnė*
mokyčiáusias, mokyčiáusia   *pasiučiáusias, pasiučiáusia*

5.140 Attributive participles of all tenses may be used in nominal positions, but fully substantivized participles occur only among present passive participles (except for the past active participle *suáugęs, suáugusi* 'grown-up'), e.g.:

miegamàsis   'bedroom'
kuliamóji   'threshing machine'
pažį́stamas, pažį́stamà/pažį́stama 'acquaintance'

In colloquial speech some feminine forms of past passive participles can be used in a peculiar substantivized meaning, e.g.:

Kaip sãkoma, praeitóji –   'As they say, what is past is
užmirštóji.   forgotten.'

SEMI-PREDICATIVE USAGE

5.141 In the sentence semi-predicative participles enter into two kinds of relations – with nouns and with finite verbal forms. They usually denote a secondary action which is associated with the main action of the sentence (designated by the predicate) through various semantic relations. Semi-pradicative usage is the most typical usage of Lithuanian participles.

According to their relations with the main action of the sentence, semi-predicative participles fall into two groups – adverbial participles and completive participles.

5.142 Adverbial participles are used in only one case form – the nominative, which agrees with the subject of the sentence (designated by a noun or a pronoun) in gender and number. Gerunds, being not inflected for case, show no concord with the nouns or pronouns. The semantic relations of adverbial participles with the finite verbal form in the sentence can be characterized as temporal, causal, conditional, or concessional. These semantic relations are often closely intertwined and are difficult to categorize.

Adverbial usage is most typical of half-participles, past active participles and gerunds. It is less typical of present and past passive participles.

Adverbial participles are opposed to one another on the basis of voice and tense, i.e. on the basis of the semantic distinctive features of passivity and anteriority.

Relations between adverbial participles

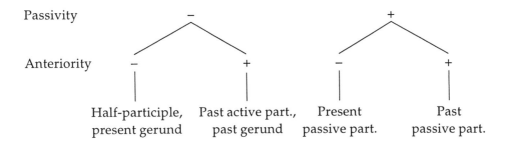

5.143 **Half-participles** are, in fact, present active participles designed for adverbial (appositive) use. They indicate a secondary action which is simultaneous with the main action of the sentence. Half-participles are most often formed from non-resultative imperfective verbs, e.g.:

Gaĩliai veřkia dukružėlė nuo močiùtės eidamà.	'The daughter cries bitterly leaving her mother.'
Tėvas visą kẽlią važiúodamas daīrėsi.	'Father kept looking around all the time while he drove.'

Those half-participles which are made from prefixed perfective verbs indicate the simultaneity of the main and secondary actions, but they do not indicate duration, e.g.:

Užmigdamà palikaũ, nubusdamà neradaũ ant galvõs vainikùžio.	'I had my wreath on my head when I fell asleep, I did not find it when I awoke.'

Being the unmarked member of the temporal opposition, the half-participle can sometimes indicate an action which is posterior to the main action, e.g.:

Lángas atsidãrė, įléisdamas gaivaũs óro.	'The window opened letting in some fresh air.'

Half-participles can also indicate:

(1) a secondary action which predetermines the main action, e.g.:

Võgdamas nepraturtė́si.	'You cannot get rich by stealing.'

(2) the content of the main action, e.g.:

Kazȳs mė́gdavo paišdykáuti gą̨sdindamas mergiotės.	'Kazys liked to amuse himself by frightening the girls.'

(3) the result of the main action, e.g.:

Màno žmonà mìrė palikdamà trìs vaikùs.	'My wife died leaving three children.'

(4) half-participles can emphasize the action which is denoted by another verb form of the same root, e.g.:

Dìrbk dìrbdamas, nežiūrė́k, kàs kur šnė̃ka.	'Do whatever you are doing, don't listen to whatever anyone is saying.'

5.144 Past active participles indicate a secondary action which is usually completed before the main action.

Vaĩkas pabùdęs apsidaĩrė.	'Waking up the child looked around.'
Kìškis išsigañdęs nukū́rė į̇̃ mìšką.	'The hare got scared and ran away into the forest.'

On the basis of their relative temporal meaning past active participles are opposed to half-participles. Their distinctive semantic feature is the meaning of anteriority, cf.:

Eidamà miškù, Verònika išgą̨sdino kažin kókį žvėrė̃lį.	'Walking in the forest, Veronika scared some animal.'
Išė̃jusi iš mìško, jì net stàbtelėjo.	'Having left the forest, she (suddenly) stopped.'

Non-prefixed past active participles can sometimes denote a process which continued for some time in the past, e.g.:

Trìs dienàs ė̃jęs priėjo trobė̃lę.	'Having walked for three days, at last he came to a small hut.'

Similarly to half-participles, past active participles can also be used to emphasize the main action indicated by a verb form with the same root as that of the participle, e.g.:

Lakstýk belãksčiusi.	'You may run as much as you like.'

Used with the negative prefix and in combination with cognate verbs, past active participles indicate an alternative, e.g.:

Galvók negalvójęs, vìs tas pàts.	'You may think as much as you like (lit. 'think not thinking'), nothing will change.'

Used in combination with verbs of a different root, negative past active participles can indicate an opposite action, e.g.:

Nutìlk neraudójęs.	'Stop, don't cry.'

5.145 Gerunds are similar to active participles in their tense and voice meanings. The difference between them lies in their relation to the agent of the main action.

If the performer of the secondary action is the same as the performer of the main action, the secondary action is indicated by a participle (or half-participle) in the nominative case, e.g.:

Vaikaĩ grį̃ždamì dainãvo.	'The children sang while coming back.'
Vaikaĩ sugrį̃žę dainãvo.	'After coming back, the children sang.'

If the secondary action and the main action are performed by different agents (or if the secondary action is spontaneous and impersonal), the secondary action is indicated by a gerund.

Vaikáms grį̃žtant, pragýdo lakštiñgala.	'When the children were coming back, a nightingale burst into song.'
Vaikáms sugrį̃žus, pragýdo lakštiñgala.	'After the children came back, a nightingale burst into song.'

Relations between adverbial active participles and gerunds

	Simultaneity	Anteriority
The agents are the same	half-participle	past active participle
The agents are different	present gerund	past gerund

Similarly to half-participles, adverbial gerunds of the present tense usually indicate a continuing action, whereas past gerunds indicate a secondary action completed before the main action.

5.146 The agent of the gerundial action (i.e., the gerund's semantic subject) is most often expressed by a noun or pronoun in the dative, forming a clause which is usually known as the **dative absolute** construction, e.g.:

Sáulei tēkant pàsiekėme krỹžkelę.	'We reached the crossroads when the sun was rising.'
Sáulei patekėjus pàsiekėme krỹžkelę.	'We reached the crossroads after the sun rose.'

Gerunds are also formed from impersonal verbs.

Lỹjant geraĩ dýgsta grỹbai.	'When it rains, mushrooms grow well.'
Palìjus geraĩ dýgsta grỹbai.	'Mushrooms grow well after it has rained.'
Prireĩkus jìs ir mūrininką pavadúoja.	'When it is necessary he can also work as a bricklayer.'

Some adverbial gerunds may lose their meaning of a secondary action and function as adverbs, e.g.:

bemãtant, bèregint mean not only 'while somebody is seeing', but also 'immediately';

veřkiant means (**1**) 'while (somebody) is crying', and (**2**) 'necessarily, by all means';

netrùkus means 'soon, immediately'.

The gerunds nepáisant 'notwithstanding', neskaĩtant, išskýrus 'except for' are functionally very similar to the preposition bè 'without'. Gerunds are also used as parenthetical words (see IV.4.19 (7), 4.20). In combination with neuter adjectives and adverbs or with the particle kàd (used to express a wish), past gerunds bear a semantic resemblance to the infinitive, e.g.:

Gal geriaũ bū́tų namõ grĩžus (cf. grĩžti)?	'Wouldn't it be better to go home?'
Kad taĩp įsigìjus žąsẽlę!	'I wish I could get a goose.'

5.147 Present passive participles are similar to half-participles in that they also indicate a secondary action simultaneous with the main action. The difference, however, lies in the meaning of the passive voice, e.g.:

Lãpė vejamà dar paspė́jus pérlįst pro vartùs. Šuvà gi výdamas įkliùvęs.	'The fox being chased managed to get through the gate. The dog chasing the fox got stuck.'
Ugnìs gesìnama pỹksta.	'When fire is being extinguished, it gets angry.'

Ir katė̃ glóstoma nùgarą riẽčia. 'A cat also bends its back when it is being stroked.'

Present passive participles are usually built from non-prefixed verbs.

5.148 **Past passive participles** indicate a secondary action which was completed before the main action began. They are usually formed from prefixed perfective verbs. Preterit passive participles correlate with preterit active participles in the meaning of tense, but are opposed to them in the meaning of voice.

Vil̃kas, geraĩ išpértas, nutráukęs úodegą pabė̃go. 'After a good hiding, the wolf ran away breaking off his tail.'

Akmuõ paléistas nùbimbė per stógą. lit.: 'The thrown stone zoomed over the roof.'

While indicating a secondary action, adverbial participles often carry an indication of time, manner, cause, condition or concession.

5.149 When used with the relative adverbs *kíek, kur̃, kadà,* the relative pronoun *kàs,* the particle *kaĩp,* and similar words, participles enter into syntactical constructions which are synonymous to subordinate clauses introduced by the same conjunctive words, e.g.:

Half-participles:

Sakýk ką̃ išmanýdamas. 'Say what you can think of.'
Cf.: *Sakýk, ką̃ išmanaĩ.*

Laukùs arinėja kadà atsi-miñdamas. 'He ploughs the fields when he remembers.'
Cf.: *Laukùs arinėja, kadà atsìmena.*

Bóbos išsigañdo, skùba kíek begalė̃damos. 'The women got scared and are hurrying away as fast as they can.'
Cf.: *Bóbos išsigañdo, skùba, kíek begãli.*

Kiáurą nãktį kaĩp galė̃dami dìrbo. 'All night through they worked as much as they could.'
Cf.: *Kiáurą nãktį dìrbo, kíek galė́jo.*

Past active participles:

Visì pajùto kõ netékę. 'Everybody felt whom/what they had lost.'
Cf.: *Visì pajùto, kõ netéko.*

Einù kuř panorė́jęs. Cf.: *Einù, kuř nóriu.*	'I go wherever I want.'
Kõ vaikštinė́ji užúot dìrbęs? Cf.: *Kõ vaikštinė́ji, o nedìrbi?*	'Why are you walking around instead of working?'

Present passive participles:

Vaikaĩ dū̃ko ir neklaũsė ką̃ liepiamì. Cf.: *Vaikaĩ dū̃ko ir neklaũsė, ką̃ jíems liẽpė.*	'The children romped and didn't listen to what they were told.'
Dabař vìsko turė́si kíek tiñkamas. Cf.: *Dabař vìsko turė́si, kíek norė́si.*	'Now you'll have everything as much as you want.'

Past passive participles:

Vìską padariaũ kaĩp paliẽptas. Cf.: *Vìską padariaũ, kaĩp mán liẽpė.*	'I did everything the way I was told to.'
Taĩp tas šuõ kuř pasių̃stas nešiójo pyragùs, dúoną, mė̃są. Cf.: *Taĩp tas šuõ, kuř tik jį̃ siuñtė, nešiójo pyragùs, dúoną, mė̃są.*	'So this dog took pies, bread, meat wherever it was sent to.'

Present and past gerunds:

Reĩkia kíek/kaĩp gãlint paskubė́ti. Cf.: *Reĩkia paskubė́ti, kíek/kaĩp gãlima.*	'We should hurry as much as we can.'
Nežinaũ, ką̃ čia mán padãrius. Cf.: *Nežinaũ, ką̃ čia mán darýti.*	'I don't know what I should do.'
Jám patiñka vaikštinė́ti užúot dìrbus. Cf.: *Jám patiñka vaikštinė́ti, bèt ne dìrbti.*	'He likes to walk around instead of working.'

5.150 Present active participles and future active participles can also sometimes form constructions with conjunctive words. The meaning of present active participles in such cases is identical to that of half-participles:

Dìrbk ką̃ gãlįs/ *Dìrbk ką̃ galė́damas/* *Dìrbk, ką̃ galì.*	'Do whatever job you can do.'
Su šienù darýkit kaĩp išmãnantys/ *Su šienù darýkit kaĩp išmanýdami/* *Su šienù darýkit, kaĩp išmãnot.*	'Do with hay whatever you think.'

Susirašiaũ ką̃ sakýsiąs/	'I put down what I was going to say.'
Susirašiaũ, ką̃ sakýsiu.	
Darbúokis ìt amžinaĩ gyvénsiąs/	'Work as if you were going to live for ever.'
Darbúokis, ìt amžinaĩ gyvénsi.	

Note should be made of the syntactical construction *nebū́ti* 'not be' (3rd person, any tense) + *kàs* + present active participle (masculine):

Nèrà kàs dúodąs.	'There's nobody (here) who might give.'
Nebùvo kàs dìrbąs.	'There was nobody who would work.'

This construction is synonymous to the following clauses:

(1) *nebū́ti* 'not be' (3rd person, any tense) + *kàs* + finite verb (3rd person, present):

Nebùvo kàs dìrba;

(2) *nebū́ti* 'not be' (3rd person, any tense) + *kám* + infinitive:

Nebùvo kám dìrbti.

In combination with the pronoun *kàs* the neuter form of present active participles can replace the infinitive:

Nèrà kàs dãrą/darýti.	'There's nothing to be done.'
Nèrà kàs pjáuną/pjáuti.	'There's nothing to be cut.'

5.151 Completive participles disclose the contents of the verbs of sensation, mental activity or saying and function (alone or in combination with their dependent words) as synonyms to completive subordinate clauses.

Completive usage is characteristic of participles in the nominative case (with the exception of half-participles and future passive participles) and gerunds.

In the sentence the nominative case of completive participles most frequently depends on a reflexive verb and indicates a secondary action performed by the same agent, e.g.:

Tė́vas sãkėsi geraĩ gyvẽnąs.	'Father said he lived well.'
Tė́vas sãkėsi geraĩ gyvẽnęs.	'Father said he had lived well.'
Tė́vas sãkėsi geraĩ gyvénsiąs.	'Father said he would live well.'

Completive participles usually depend on non-reflexive verbs and indicate a secondary action performed by a different subject, which is most often designated by the accusative, e.g.:

Sakiaũ tė́vą geraĩ gyvẽnant.	'I said father lived well.'
Sakiaũ tė́vą geraĩ gyvẽnus.	'I said father had lived well.'
Sakiaũ tė́vą geraĩ gyvénsiant.	'I said father would live well.'

The performer of the secondary action may also be designated by a genitive if the finite verb of the sentence has a negative prefix or requires an object in the genitive.

Ar nemateĩ tėvo pareĩnant?   'Did you see father coming?'

In combination with the infinitives *matýti, girdė́ti* the performer of the secondary action indicated by a gerund may also be expressed by a nominative.

Tolumojè matýti laĩvas plaũkiant.   'In the distance you can see a boat sailing.'

Relations among completive participles can be described on the basis of oppositions according to passivity, anteriority, posteriority and frequency of action.

Relations among completive participles

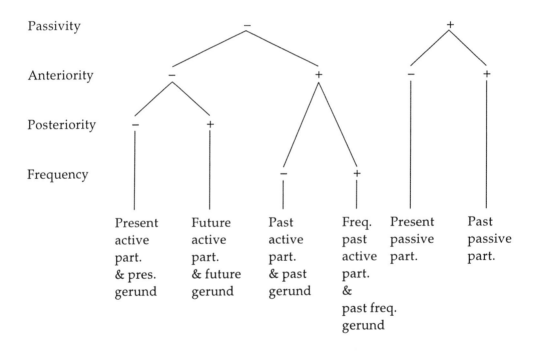

Examples of completive participial usage:

(1) Participles in the nominative case.

(a) Present active pariciples:

Viñcas tãrėsi gãlįs/galį̃s brólį pavadúoti.	'Vincas thought he could substitute for his brother.'
Senẽlė mán skùndėsi serganti.	'Granny complained to me she was ill.'

(b) Past active participles:

Àš nesijaučiù niẽko blõgo padãręs.	'I don't feel as if I have done anything wrong.'
Mótina apsìmetė niẽko nepastebėjusi.	'Mother pretended she hadn't noticed anything.'

In combination with verbs denoting termination of a process the past active participle is synonymous with the infinitive:

Lietùs nustójo lìjęs/lýti.	'It has stopped raining.'
Paliaũs ir vėjas mẽdžių šakàs láužęs/láužyti.	'The wind will stop breaking tree branches.'

(c) Frequentative past active participles:

Jìs sãkėsi visadà tuõ keliù važiúodavęs.	'He said he always used to go along that road.'
Jõs sãkosi daũg dìrbdavusios Amèrikoje.	'They say they worked a lot in America.'

(d) Future active participles:

Tikėjausi miestè išgir̃siąs naujíeną.	'I hoped I would hear some news in town.'
Gýrėsi gaidỹs vãnagą pagáusiąs.	'The cock bragged he would catch the hawk.'

(e) Present passive participles:

Tikiúosi ištéisinama.	'I hope I will be acquitted.'
Nesidžiaũk gìriamas, nevérk bãramas.	'Don't be overjoyed when being praised, don't cry when being scolded.'

These participles are also used with verbs denoting agreement, disagreement, wish, request, fear, etc.:

Nepasidúosim skriaudžiamì.	'We'll not allow ourselves to be wronged.'
Móteris prãšosi pavežamà.	'The woman is asking to be given a lift.'
Arklỹs bìjo mùšamas.	'The horse fears beating.'

(f) Past passive participles:

Jū̃s neprisipažìnsite nugalė́tas.	'You will not admit you are defeated.'
Keleĩvis susiprãto apgáutas.	'The traveller understood he had been taken in.'

(2) Gerunds

(a) Present gerunds:

Maniaũ jį̃ gyvẽnant miestè.	'I thought he lived in town.'
Visì sãko jį̃ ẽsant labaĩ mókytą.	'Everybody says he is very learned.'

(b) Past gerunds:

Eĩk ir pranèšk svẽčią atvažiãvus.	'Go and announce the arrival of the visitor.'
Radaũ visùs sumìgus.	'I found everybody asleep.'

(c) Past frequentative gerunds (very rare):

Sãko kar̃tais užeĩdavus tókią liū́tį.	'They say such torrential rains would sometimes come.'
Girdė́jau jį̃ priil̃sdavus tenái.	'I hear he used to get very tired.'

(d) Future gerunds:

Kaĩp jautì tė́vą pasiel̃gsiant?	'What's your feeling about father's future behaviour?'
Tikiù jį̃ netrùkus sugrį̃šiant.	'I believe he will soon come back.'

The absence of passive gerunds is compensated for by combining gerunds of the verb *bū́ti* 'be' with passive participles.

Girdė́jau jį̃ ẽsant mùšamą.	'I heard they beat him.'
Girdė́jau jį̃ bùvus mùšamą.	'I heard they used to beat him.'
Cf.: *Jis sãkėsi mùšamas.*	'He said they used to beat him.'

PREDICATIVE USAGE

5.152 Predicative participles function as predicates in the sentence and they differ from finite verbs in certain shades of modal meaning. Predicative usage is typical only of participles in the nominative case and neuter forms.

Relations among predicative active participles are identical with those among completive participles.

Predicative active participles are used as oblique mood forms, e.g.:

Girdė́jau, tù ẽsąs mókytas žmogùs.	'I heard you are a learned man.'
Tai tóks mìškas tráukęsis per Lietuvõs žẽmę.	'That was the kind of forest that extended (according to hearsay) across the Lithuanian land.'

Seniaũ žmónės namų̃ nerakìndavę. '(I heard) People didn't lock their doors in olden times.'

Jìs sãko, kad pinigaĩ vistíek nebū́sią pinigaĩ, o vir̃sią põpieriumi. 'He says money will stop being money and will become paper.'

(See also 5.52ff.).

5.153 Neuter forms of active participles are mostly used as predicates of impersonal sentences indicating indirectly experienced or doubtful events.

Present active participle:

Jái nuo dárbo rankàs suką̃. '(She said) Her arms ache from work.'

Past active participle:

Čia daũg grỹbų bùvę. '(I heard) There used to be a lot of mushrooms here.'

Frequentative past active participle:

Kaĩp gražù bū́davę! 'How beautiful it used to be!'

Future active participle:

Kìtąmet bū́sią ir žąsų̃. 'Next year there'll be (probably) geese as well.'

Neuter forms of passive participles, which combine with an agentive genitive, are also similar semantically to the oblique mood, but differ from the latter in that they usually convey an unexpected event or an event judged by its results and often causing surprise (see also 5.73, 77).

Present passive participle:

Kaĩp gamtõs mókama vìsa pìnti į́ víeną vìsumą! 'How well nature can weave everything into one unified whole!'

O gandaĩ skélbė, kad ēsama ir užmuštų̃. 'Rumour had it there were casualties as well.'

Past passive participle:

Matýt, jõ žinóta apiẽ sukaktuvès. 'He must have known about the anniversary.'

Keliù tik víenos vė́žės – màno važiúota. 'There's only one track on the road – that was me driving.'

Neuter forms of passive participles of the verb *bū́ti* 'be' combine with the genitive case to function as compound predicates which are similar in meaning to compound predicates with the nominative, e.g.:

Nežinójau, kad jõ ēsama turtìngo. (Cf.: *Nežinójau, kad jìs yrà/ẽsąs turtìngas.*)	'I didn't know he was rich.'
O tõs mergẽlės bū́ta víeno karãliaus dukteřs. (Cf.: *O tà mergẽlė bùvo/bùvusi víeno karãliaus duktė̃*)	'And the girl was (appeared to be) the daughter of a king.'

The semantic object of the neuter forms of transitive passive participles is denoted by the nominative case, e.g.:

Jų̃ jaũ ir namaĩ stãtoma, stogaĩ deñgiama.	'They are already building houses and putting on the roofs.'
Mū́sų tėvẽlių vìsos tõs gíesmės mokė́ta.	'Our parents used to know all those hymns.'

By combining with the finite forms of the verb *bū́ti* 'be' predicative participles form compound tenses (see 5.35–40).

THE INFINITIVE

Bendratìs

Formal properties

5.154 The infinitive is an uninflected verbal form which indicates an action without specifying tense, voice, person or number.

Formally, the infinitive is signalled by the presence of the suffix *-ti*, which is joined directly to the stem, e.g.:

eĩ-ti 'to go'	*matý-ti* 'to see'
mès-ti 'to throw'	*ieškó-ti* 'to look for'

In colloquial speech the infinitive is widely used in its short form (with the shortened suffix *-t*), e.g.:

eĩ-t	*matý-t*
mès-t	*ieškó-t*

The infinitival stem is one of the three principal verbal stems (see 5.79).

The infinitival stem of primary verbs may end in a consonant (*bė́g-ti* 'run', *ràs-ti* 'find'), a long vowel (*jó-ti* 'ride a horse', *dė́-ti* 'place', *vý-ti* 'chase'), a diphthong (ráu-ti 'uproot', eĩ-ti 'go', líe-ti 'pour') or a semi-diphthong (vìr-ti 'boil', reñ̃-ti 'support', pùl-ti 'attack').

The infinitival stem often differs from present and past stems in its stem vowel (due to morphonological vowel gradation), cf.:

dė́-ti	dẽda	dė́jo	'place'
vý-ti	vẽja	vìjo	'chase'
võg-ti	vãgia	võgė	'steal'

The infinitival stem of mixed and suffixal verbs may end in one of the following long vowels: y, o, ė (rašý-ti 'write', miegó-ti 'sleep', turė́-ti 'have', kartó-ti 'repeat', akė́-ti 'harrow'); one of the two diphthongs au, uo (rė́kau-ti 'shout', dainúo-ti 'sing'), or in one of the following semidiphthongs: en, el, er, in (gyvén-ti 'live', mė́gin-ti 'try', trìnktel-ti 'make a bang', žvìlgter-ti 'have a look'). The infinitival stems of mixed and suffixal verbs never end in a short vowel. The root vowel of the infinitival stem of these verbs is the same as in the present and past tense forms.

Reflexive infinitives are formed with the help of the affix -s(i), which is placed after the infinitival suffix if the verb does not have a prefix, or between the prefix and the root if the verb contains a prefix, e.g.:

praũsti 'wash' –	praũstis 'wash oneself'	
ródyti 'show' –	ródytis 'show oneself'	
kartóti 'repeat' –	kartótis 'repeat oneself'	
nupraũsti –	nu-si-praũsti	
paródyti –	pa-si-ródyti	
nekartóti –	ne-si-kartóti	

Meaning and usage

5.156 **Verbal properties**. The infinitive usually retains the valency typical of the finite forms. It can have dependent cases, adverbs or prepositional phrases. However, lacking tense, mood and voice forms, the infinitive most often combines with finite forms of the verb or other predicative words.

The infinitive is indispensable in combination with phasal verbs which denote the ingressive or completive phase of the action but not the action itself, such as pradė́ti 'begin', im̃ti 'start', baĩgti 'finish', liáutis 'stop', nustóti 'stop' and others, or in combination with modal verbs indicating ability, obligation, wish, etc. such as galė́ti 'can', turė́ti 'must', norė́ti 'wish', ketìnti 'intend', bandýti 'try', mė́ginti 'attempt', etc., e.g.:

pràdeda dìrbti	'begins to work'
gãli váikščioti	'can walk'
norė́jo išvỹkti	'wanted to leave'
ketìno grį̃žti	'intended to return'
bandýsiu užmìgti	'I'll try to fall asleep'

The infinitive can also combine with the respective verbal nouns, e.g.:

nóras grį̃žti	'desire to come back'
bañdymas pabė́gti	'attempt to escape'
gebė́jimas skaitýti	'ability to read'

In expressive speech the finite form of an ingressive verb can sometimes be omitted, e.g.:

Jì – bė́gti, jìs – výtis.	'She started running, he chased her.'

The infinitive also combines with impersonal verbs, such as *reikė́ti* 'be necessary', *tèkti* 'have to', with neuter adjectives and other words denoting states. The patient of the state is then designated by a dative, e.g.:

Mán reĩkia grį̃žti.	'I have to go back.'
Ligóniui sunkù váikščioti.	'It is difficult for the patient to walk.'
Ar táu ne gė́da melúoti?	'Aren't you ashamed to tell lies?'

The object of the transitive infinitive in such cases is denoted by an accusative or sometimes (in dialects and informal speech) by a nominative, e.g.:

Táu pačiám reikė̃s rugiùs/ rugiaĩ pjáuti.	'You'll have to cut the rye yourself' lit. 'For you (DAT) it will be necessary the rye (ACC/NOM) to cut.'

The infinitive can sometimes carry the meaning of obligation even when it stands alone, i.e., without a modal verb, e.g.:

Jùm tik juodà dúona krim̃sti.	'You should be given only brown bread' lit. 'For you (DAT) only brown bread (NOM) to nibble.'

In combination with the auxiliary verb *bū́ti* (which is usually omitted in the present tense) the infinitives *matýti* 'see', *girdė́ti* 'hear', *jùsti* 'feel', *jaũsti* 'feel' are used with a nominative denoting the content of perception, e.g.:

Jaũ namaĩ matýti.	'The house (NOM) is already visible (INF).'
Iš tolì bus matýti dū́mai.	'You'll be able (lit. 'it will be') to see the smoke from afar.'

In combination with finite verbs of stimulation the infinitive indicates an action which is performed by another agent different from that of the action expressed by the finite verb:

Ji prãšo manę̃s valdýti tavè.	'She asks me to manage you.'
Sárgas rė̃kė mán grį̃žti.	'The watchman shouted for me to come back.'
Uždráuskite dùkteriai su juõ matýtis.	'Forbid your daughter to meet him.'

In expressive speech the infinitive can indicate order, stimulation, or surprise even when it is used alone without a finite verb, e.g.:

Tuojaũ vìsíems išeĩti!	'Everybody (DAT) is to leave immediately!'

The infinitive can collocate with a finite verb of the same root. Such collocations are used for emphasis sake.

Ir pažìnti támsta jõ geraĩ nepažį̃sti.	'You don't even know him well.'

5.156 Nominal properties. Being historically derived from the dative of verbal nouns, the infinitive also possesses certain nominal properties. In combination with finite verbs the infinitive can indicate the purpose of an action or the intention to perform an action:

O pinigų̃ aš jái palikaũ ne tìk gyvénti.	'I left money for her not only for subsistance (INF).'
Atvažiavaũ dìrbti, o nè ilsė́tis.	'I've come here to work, not to rest.'

In such cases the infinitive is semantically similar to the dative case.

When a transitive infinitive combines with verbs of motion, its object is expressed by a genitive, e.g.:

Ir atjója bernužė̃lis bė́ro žìrgo pagìrdyti.	'Here comes a young laddie to water his bay steed (GEN).'

In eastern Lithuanian dialects and sometimes in fiction the special verb form with a suffix -tų termed supine (siekinỹs) replaces the infinitive in combination with verbs of motion, e.g.:

Vaikaĩ išė́jo grybáutų.	'The children went out to gather mushrooms.'

In combination with other verbs the object as well as the semantic subject of the infinitive is expressed by a dative, e.g.:

Niẽko neruõškite mán priimti.	'Don't prepare anything for my reception (lit. 'for me to receive').'
Àtnešė knỹgą vaikáms pasiskaitýti.	'They brough a book for the children to read.'

When the infinitive, alone or with a dative, denotes purpose, it often collocates with:

(a) a noun:

peĩlis dúonai riẽkti	'a knife for cutting (INF) bread (DAT)'
lentýna iñdams sudėti	'a shelf to put the dishes (DAT) on'
vietà apsistóti nãkčiai	'a place to put up for the night'

(b) an adjective:

gražùs pažiūrėti	'nice to look at'
siaũras nešióti	'tight to wear'

Some infinitives (e.g., válgyti 'eat', rūkýti 'smoke', praũstis 'wash oneself', gérti 'drink', dėvėti 'wear') can also be used to indicate an object, e.g.:

Pasiėmė válgyti ir gérti.	'They took (something) to eat and drink.'
Katrė įnešė praũstis.	'Katrė brought in (a bowl) to wash (ourselves).'

When used as the subject or the predicative of the sentence, the infinitive is similar in its meaning and function to verbal nouns in the nominative:

Ūkininkáuti – taĩ ne tvõrą tvérti.	'To be a farmer is not making a fence.'

The infinitive matýti is very widely used as a parenthetical word, e.g.:

Tù, matýt, manę̃s neláukei.	'You seem (lit. 'to see') not to have expected me.'

The infinitive (ne)palýginti is often used as a modal adverb, e.g.:

Jìs dar palýginti jáunas žmogùs.	'He is a comparatively (INF) young man.'
Tėvas nepalýginti didèsnis už sū́nų.	'The father is much (lit. 'not to compare') taller than the son.'

More on the usage of the infinitive see in the chapters on syntax.

6 ADVERB

Príeveiksmis

6.1 Adverbs are a class of uninflected words which express qualitative and quantitative, spatial and temporal characteristics of actions, states, properties, sometimes of things, and also, the circumstances under which actions and states occur. Accordingly, they are used to modify verbs, adjectives and adverbs, and clauses.

When used with verbs, adverbs function as adverbials:

gražiaĩ dainúoja	'(he) sings well'
daũg skaĩtė	'(he) read much'
parvažiãvome namõ	'(we) returned home'
vãkar lìjo	'it rained yesterday'

A number of adverbs typically serve as modifiers of adjectives and adverbs:

labaĩ gĕras/geraĩ	'very good/well'
pakañkamai áukštas/aukštaĩ	'sufficiently tall/high (ADV)'

Less commonly, adverbs modify nouns:

gyvēnimas vãkar	'the life yesterday'

A number of qualitative adverbs can be used as predicatives, e.g.:

Mán čià geraĩ.	lit. 'It's good for me here'

or as sentence modifiers, e.g.:

Tikriáusiai *grį̃šime kitaĩs mētais.*	'We'll probably return next year.'

The class of adverbs overlaps with particles and prepositions. For instance, words like *dár, vẽl, jaũ* function as adverbs if they have a separate syntactic function and they are used as particles if they emphasize the same part of a sentence, cf. respectively:

Dúok mán dár *dúonos.*	'Give me some more bread (ADV).'
Tėvas dár *negrį̃žo.*	'Father has not returned yet (PRTCL).'

Some adverbs are pressed into service as prepositions when they govern a noun, cf.:

Nuẽjom netolì.   lit. 'We didn't walk far (ADV).'
Sėdėjau netolì mótinos.   'I was sitting not far from (my) mother (PREP).'

It should be noted that assigning words to one class or another is sometimes arbitrary. Thus, the words *galbū́t* 'maybe' and *turbū́t* 'probably' (lit. 'must be') are traditionally classed as modal particles rather than adverbs.

Formal properties

6.2   From the point of view of form and derivative relations, adverbs may be divided into two main types, primary and secondary adverbs.

Primary (non-derived) adverbs are not motivated by words of other classes in Modern Lithuanian and they have no formal markers, e.g.:

dár 'more; yet'   *vẽl* 'again'
teñ 'there'   *čià* 'here'
dabař 'now'   *daũg* 'much'

This class of adverbs is not numerous.

Secondary (derived) adverbs are extremely numerous and they display a wide range of derivative patterns. Most adverbs are formed by one of three principal means, either suffixes, or prefixes, or both.

6.3   The most productive means of adverb derivation is the suffix *-(i)ai*. Adverbs derived from *a*-stem (MASC) and *o*-stem (FEM) adjectives have the allomorph *-ai*:

ret-aĩ 'sparsely; rarely'   (: *rẽt-as, -à* 'sparse; rare')
žem-aĩ 'lowly'   (: *žẽm-as, -à* 'low')

Adverbs derived from *ia*, *u*-stem. (MASC) and *io*, *ė*-stem (FEM) adjectives take the allomorph *-iai*, e.g.:

suñk-iai 'heavily; with difficulty'   (: *sunk-ùs, -ì* 'heavy; difficult')

apýger-iai 'rather well'   (: *apýger-is, -ė* 'rather good')

Before the suffix *-iai*, the consonants *t* and *d* alternate with the affricates *č* and *dž*, e.g.:

stač-iaĩ 'straight; upright'   (: *stat-ùs, -ì* 'straight; upright')
gardž-iaĩ 'tastefully'   (: *gard-ùs, -ì* 'tasty')

6.4   Adverbs with the suffix *-(i)ai* display two basic stress patterns.

(1) In adverbs formed from two-syllable *(i)a* stem adjectives, the last syllable is stressed:

aukštaĩ (: áukštas)   *doraĩ (: dõras)*
but: greĩtai (: greĩtas)

Short stem adverbs formed from two-syllable *u* stem adjectives are also finally stressed, e.g.:

aštriaĩ (: aštrùs)   *budriaĩ (: budrùs)*

Those with a long stem retain as a rule the stress of the Acc. Sg. form of the respective adjective:

baĩsiai(: baisùs, Acc. Sg. *baĩsų)*
meĩliai (: meilùs, Acc. Sg. *meĩlų)*
sóčiai (: sótus, Acc. Sg. *sótų)*

Exceptions:

gardžiaĩ (: gardùs, Acc, Sg. *gárdų)*   *rūgščiaĩ (: rūgštùs,* Acc. Sg. *rū́gštų)*
karčiaĩ (: kartùs, Acc. Sg. *kařtų)*   *saldžiaĩ (: saldùs,* Acc. Sg. *sáldų)*
riebiaĩ (: riebùs, Acc. Sg. *riēbų)*   *sūriaĩ* 'saltily' *(: sūrùs,* Acc. Sg. *sū́rų* 'salty')

(2) Adverbs formed from polysyllabic adjectives with permanent stress retain its position, e.g.:

laimìngai 'happily'   (: *laimìngas* 'happy')
mažókai 'somewhat little'   (: *mažókas* 'somewhat small')
lietùviškai 'in Lithuanian manner' (:*lietùviškas* 'Lithuanian')
apýtikriai 'approximately'   (: *apýtikris* 'approximate')

Adverbs are usually stressed on the final syllable if the base adjective has mobile stress, e.g.:

atidžiaĩ 'attentively'   (: *atidùs,* Acc. Sg. *atìdų* 'attentive')
mandagiaĩ 'politely'   (: *mandagùs,* Acc. Sg. *mandāgų* 'polite')
prabangiaĩ 'luxuriously'   (: *prabangùs,* Acc. Sg. *prabañgų* 'luxurious')
but: *malõniai* 'amiably'   (: *malonùs,* Acc. Sg. *malõnų* 'amiable, pleasant')
patõgiai comfortably'   (: *patogùs,* Acc. Sg. *patõgų* 'comfortable')
padõriai 'decently'   (: *padorùs,* Acc. Sg. *padõrų* 'decent')

6.5   The suffix *-(i)ai* is also used to derive adverbs from participles with an adjectival meaning.

Adverbs formed from present active and simple past participles retain the stress of the participle:

ãkinančiai 'blindingly'   (: *ãkinant-is, -i* 'blinding')

vỹkusiai 'successfully'	(: *vỹk-ęs, -usi* 'successful')
prìderančiai 'becomingly'	(: *prìderant-is, -i* 'becoming')
užsispýrusiai 'obstinately'	(: *užsispýr-ęs, -usi* 'obstinate')

Adverbs formed from present passive participles with fixed stress and some participles with a long stem, also retain their stress and tone, e.g.:

mãtomai 'visibly'	(: *mãtom-as, -a* 'visible')
suprañtamai 'intelligibly'	(: *suprañtam-as, -à* 'intelligible')

Those derived from participles with mobile stress are mostly stressed on the final syllable:

girdimaĩ 'audibly'	(: *gir̃dim-as, -à* 'audible')
patikimaĩ 'reliably'	(: *pàtikim-as, -à* 'reliable')

Adverbs related to past passive participles with fixed stress retain its position and tone, e.g.:

negirdĕtai 'unprecendently'	(: *negirdĕt-as, -a* 'unheard-of, unprecedented')
apgalvótai 'deliberately'	(: *apgalvót-as, -a* 'deliberate')

They are stressed on the final syllable if the base participle has mobile stress:

nelauktaĩ 'unexpectedly'	(: *neláukt-as, -à* 'unexpected')
įtemptaĩ 'strenuously'	(: *įtempt-as, -à* 'strained, strenuous')

The suffix *-(i)ai* does nor derive adverbs from past frequentative and future participles.

6.6   The suffix *-ai* is used to form adverbs from non-finite necessity verbal forms. If the latter form has fixed stress the derived adverb retains it, e.g.:

abejótin-ai 'doubtfully'	(: *abejótin-as, -a* 'doubtful')
pakartótin-ai 'repeatedly'	(: *pakartótin-as, -a* 'repeated, (that) which needs to be repeated')

In the case of mobile stress in the base form, the adverb is stressed on the final syllable:

būtin-aĩ 'necessarily'	(: *bū́tin-as, -à* 'necessary')
atmintin-aĩ 'memorably; by heart'	(: *atmiñtin-as, -à* 'memorable')

6.7   The suffix *-yn* serves to form adverbs from two-syllable (sometimes polysyllabic) qualitative adjectives. It adds the meaning of direction or increase in quality, cf.:

žem-ỹn 'down'	(: *žẽm-as, -à* 'low')

raudon-ỹn '(growing) redder' (: *raudón-as, -à* 'red')
tobul-ỹn '(growing) more perfect' (: *tóbul-as, -à* 'perfect')

This suffix is occasionally used to derive adverbs from nouns, participles and, even, adverbs, e.g.:

krašt-ỹn 'edge-wards' (: *krãšt-as* 'edge')
dugn-ỹn 'bottom-wards' (: *dùgn-as* 'bottom')
ištvirk-ỹn 'to depravity' (: *ištvìrk-ęs* 'depraved')
daug-ỹn 'increasingly' (: *daũg* 'much')
tol-ỹn 'farther, into the distance' (: *tolì* 'far')

The adverb *pirm-ỹn* 'forward' is a recent derivative from the ordinal numeral *pìrm-as, -à* 'first'. As is clear from the examples, in these adverbs the suffix carries the stress.

6.8 The adverbs *kur̃* 'where', *kadà* 'when', *tadà* 'then' and *kaĩp* 'how', *taĩp* 'so, this way' comprise a separate group. Historically, they are related to the pronouns *kàs* 'who, what', *tàs, tà* 'that', but in Modern Lithuanian they have lost derivative relations with these pronouns. By analogy, a great many other adverbs have been formed, e.g.:

kit-ur̃ 'elsewhere' (: *kìt-as, -à* 'other, another')
vien-ur̃ 'in one place' (: *víen-as, -à* 'one') (cf. *vienur̃ kitur̃* 'here and there')
vis-ur̃ 'everywhere' (: *vìs-as, -à* 'all')
svet-ur̃ 'in a strange place/land' (: *svet-ỹs* 'guest', cf. *svẽtim-as, -à* 'strange, foreign')
kita-dà 'sometime' (: *kìt-as, -à* 'other, another')
visa-dà 'always' (: *vìs-as, -à* 'all, whole')
an-aĩp 'that way' (: *an-às, -à* 'that (one)')
ši-aĩp 'this way' (: *šìs, -ì* 'this')
tav-aĩp 'in your way' (: *tãv-as, -à* 'thine, your')
antr-aĩp 'otherwise' (: *añtr-as, -à* 'second')
nauj-aĩp 'in a new way' (: *naũj-as, -à* 'new')

In these adverbs, the suffixes *-(i)ur̃*, *-dà* and *-(i)aĩp* can be distinguished. They are nearly always stressed, with the exception of *niẽkur* 'nowhere', *niẽkaip* '(in) no way', and *šìtaip* 'this way'.

The suffix *-dà* often alternates with its allomorph *-dõs*, e.g.: *visadà/visadõs* 'always', *kitadà/kitadõs* 'some other time, sometime', *niekadà/niekadõs* 'never'; it also has an abbreviated variant *-d*, cf.: *niẽkad* 'never', *visàd* 'always'.

6.9 A great many adverbs are adverbialised case forms of nouns, sometimes of pronouns and adjectives; here belong:

(1) nominative: *ganà* 'enough', *valià* '(it) is allowed, one may', *nevalià* '(it) is not allowed, one can't', *žinià* 'of course'; *nežinià* '(it) is not known';

(2) genitive: *kõ* 'why' (: *kàs* 'what'), *kūlio* 'upside down', *šúolio* 'by jumps';

(3) dative: *kám* 'why, what for' (: *kàs* 'what'), *ilgám* 'for long', *trumpám* 'for a short while';

(4) accusative: *trùputį* 'a little', *mãžumą* 'a little', *truputėlį* 'just a little', *mažumėlę* 'just a little';

(5) instrumental: *pùsbalsiu* 'in a low voice', *gretà* 'side by side', *šalià* 'near, close by', *tyčia* 'on purpose', *draugè* 'together', *sykiù* 'together', *slaptà* 'secretly', *žiñgine* 'at a slow pace', *piktúoju* 'maliciously', *kartais* 'sometimes', *mainaĩs* 'in exchange';

(6) locative: *šalyjè* 'side by side', *tarpùsavyje* 'between themselves (ourselves)'.

6.10 The following adverbs are descended from the old locative case of numerals which came to be used adverbially through functional shift: *dvíese* 'the two together', *trisè* 'the three together', *keturíese* 'the four together' ... *devyníese* 'the nine together', as in *Jiẽ dvíese taĩ padãrė* 'They did it the two of them together'. Likewise, the adverb *kelíese* 'how many together' is formed from the pronoun *kelì, kẽlios* 'how many'. The adverbs *namiẽ* 'at home', *artì* 'near(by)', *tolì* 'far(away)' retain the archaic locative case form of the respective noun and adjectives.

In Modern Lithuanian, a number of archaic postpositional locative forms, viz. the allative and the illative, with the fused postpositions *-n* and *-p*, are used as adverbs, e.g.: *laukañ* 'outside' (as in *Eĩk laukañ* 'Get out'), *šaliñ* 'away, off', *viduñ* 'inside', *viršuñ* 'up'; *galóp* 'to the end, finally', *vakaróp* 'towards evening', *velnióp* 'to hell'.

6.11 A great many adverbs are derived by means of the generalized suffix *-(i)ui* (which is traced back to the ending of the dative singular case), usually with the prefix *pa-*, from nouns and adjectives, and occasionally from words of other classes, e.g.:

véltui 'in vain'
ìlgainiui 'afterwards, eventually'
apliñkui 'around'
padieniuĩ 'by the day, every other day' (cf. *dienà* 'day')
paeiliuĩ 'in turn, by turns' (cf. *eilė̃* 'turn, queue')
pakeliuĩ 'on the way, the same way' (cf. *kẽlias* 'way')
paryčiuĩ 'early in the morning' (cf. *rýtas* 'morning')

pavėjuĩ 'with/before the wind' (cf. *vė́jas* 'wind')
pavieniuĩ 'one by one' (cf. *víenas* 'one')

The instrumental plural ending *-mis* and to a lesser degree *-ais*, have developed into adverbial suffixes through the adverbial use of the respective case forms, cf.:

-*mis*: *lygiomìs/lygiõm* 'in equal parts, equally' (cf. *lýgus* 'equal')
noromìs/norõm 'willingly' (cf. *norùs* 'willing')
slaptomìs/slaptõm 'secretly' (cf. *slãptas* 'secret', ADJ)
(pa)tylomìs/patylõm 'silently, on the quiet' (cf. *tylùs* 'silent')
negirdomìs/negirdõm 'without hearing'
pakaitomìs/pakaitõm 'by turns' (cf. *pakaità* 'change')
paskubomìs 'in a hurry' (cf. *skubà* 'hurry')

-*ais*: *príešais* 'in front, opposite' (cf. dial. *príešas* 'front, fore-part')
patyliùkais 'silently, on the sly' (cf. *tylùs* 'silent')
rėtkarčiais 'now and then' (cf. *rėtas kartas* 'rare case')
šalimaĩs 'close by, side by side' (cf. *šalimas* 'near, close')

Numerous adverbs are formed by analogy with other adverbialized case forms; cf. the following adverbs with affixes traced back to the genitive: *tolydžio* 'continuously, constantly' (cf. *tolydùs* 'continuous'), *nuolatõs* 'constantly' (cf. *nuõlat* 'constantly'), *atgaliõs* 'back(wards)' (cf. *atgal̃* 'back(wards)').

On the other hand, there are case forms of nouns of that retain their status despite their frequent adverbial use, e.g.: *ratù* 'in a circle' (Instr. of *rãtas* 'circle'), *būriù* 'in a crowd' (Instr. of *būrỹs* 'crowd, group'), *žaibù* 'like lightning' (Instr. of *žaĩbas* 'lightning'), etc.

6.12 A great many prepositional phrases used as adverbial modifiers have acquired adverbial meanings; here belong:

(1) genitive with the prepositions *dė̃l* 'because of', *iš* 'from, out of', *bè* 'without, except', *ikì(ìk)/lìgi(lìg)* 'until, up to', *nuõ* 'from', *põ* 'after', e.g. *dė̃l kõ* 'why' (lit. 'because of what'), *dėl tõ* 'therefore' (lit. 'for that'), *iš kar̃to* 'at once', *iš tikrųjų* 'indeed', *be gãlo* 'extremely' (lit. 'without end'), *lig laĩko* 'in advance' (lit. 'before time'), *po laĩko* 'too late' (lit. 'after the time'), *nuo mažeñs* 'since childhood';

(2) dative with the prepositions *põ* 'after' and *ikì(ìk)/lìgi(lìg)* 'until, up to' (mostly in colloquial speech); *iki/lig(i) vãliai* 'to one's heart's content', *po draũgei* 'together', *po senóvei* 'as of old, still', *po visám* 'after all (is over)';

(3) accusative with the prepositions *į̃* 'to, in', *per̃* 'over, in', *prõ* 'through, by'; e.g. *į̃ vãlią/valiàs* 'sufficiently', *per víeną* 'together', *pro tam̃są* 'while it's dark'.

Quite a number of similar prepositional phrases, having lost case endings and blended into a single word, have developed into prefixed adverbs, cf.:

iškart̃ 'at once' (: *iš kart̃o*)
issỹk 'at once' (: *iš sỹkio*)
išvìs 'altogether, on the whole' (: *iš vìso*)
ištiẽs 'really, indeed' (: *iš tiesų̃*)

išvíen 'together' (: *iš víeno*)
perdiẽn 'all the day (long)' (: *per díeną*)
pernãkt 'overnight' (: *per nãktį*)
priẽšpiẽt 'before lunch' (: *priẽš pietùs*)

A variety of adverbs have developed in the same way from nonprepositional word groups, e.g.:

kasvãkar 'every night' (: *kàs vãkaras* or *kàs vãkarą*)

šią̃nakt 'tonight' (: *šią̃ nãktį*)

šiamsỹk 'for this occasion' (: *šiám sỹkiui*)

aną̃kart 'that time' (: *aną̃ kar̃tą*)

anuõsyk 'that time' (: *anuõ sykiù*)
tuomèt 'then, at that time' (: *tuõ metù*)
šiuõkart 'this time' (: *šiuõ kartù*)

6.13 In Lithuanian, there is a productive class of adverbs derived from verbs by means of the suffix *-te* or *-tinai*:

nèš-ti 'carry' : *neš-tè, neš-tinaĩ*
žiūrė́-ti 'look' : *žiūrė́-te, žiūrė́-tinai*

These adverbs are traditionally classed as non-finite verb forms termed *būdinỹs*. They are used with verbs of the same root to intensify or emphasize their meaning. Due to their function they are contiguous to both adverbs and intensifying particles.

In deverbal intensifying adverbs the suffix is added to the infinitival stem. When formed from reflexive verbs, these adverbs lose the reflexive morpheme *-si/-s*, cf.: *džiaũgti-s* 'rejoice': *džiaug-tè*, as in *džiaugtè džiaũgiasi* '(he) rejoices greatly' (lit. 'rejoices rejoicing'). With prefixed verbs, a derivative from the respective non-prefixed verb is used, e.g. *bėg-tè* (: *bė́g-ti* 'run') *at-bė́go* '(he) came running'.

When formed from infinitival stems without a prefix these adverbs carry final stress:

bė́g-ti 'run' – *bėg-tè, bėg-tinaĩ* 'on a run'
eĩ-ti 'go, walk' – *eitè, ei-tinaĩ* 'walking'

Those derived from suffixed stems retain the stress and accent of the infinitive:

matý-ti 'see' – *matý-te, matý-tinai*
kartó-ti 'repeat' – *kartó-te, kartó-tinai*
válgy-ti 'eat' – *válgy-te, válgy-tinai*

6.14 Both forms of an intensifying adverb are interchangeable, though *-te* forms are more common. In emphatic speech they modify both prefixed and unprefixed verbs of the same root, cf.:

Žmónès grūs-tè grúdosi prie vartų.	'People jostled and tussled (lit. 'jostled jostling') at the gate.'
Jis grūs-tè pra-si-grúdo prie vartų.	'He forced his way by force to the gate.'

Sometimes these adverbs express the manner of action, e.g.:

Jéi válgyte nepriválgysi, laižýte neprilaižýsi.	'If you can't get your fill by eating (lit. eat enough eating') you won't get enough by licking.'

In this case they do not differ from ordinary adverbs.

When used with verbs with the negative prefix, intensifying adverbs are interchangeable with an infinitive used for emphasis:

Tėvas nè girdėte (= girdėti) negirdėjo.	'Father didn't hear it at all.'

Deverbal intensifying adverbs with the suffix *-tinai* are formally identical with other adverbs in *-tinai* (e.g. *Pirkaū nāmą iššimokėtinai* 'I have bought a house on credit'), but they are more restricted in use since they modify verbs of the same root exclusively, e.g.:

Grėtė nusigañdo ir bėgtinaī pabėgo nuo Vìliaus.	'Grete got frightened and rushed away from Vilius.'

6.15 The following and similar word groups, which are unanalysable semantically and unchangeable formally, may be regarded as complex adverbs: *kai kadà* 'sometimes', *kol kàs* 'so far, so long', *kada nórs* 'some day, ever', *bet kaĩp* 'somehow, anyhow', *bet kuř* 'anywhere', *kai kuř* 'here and there', *kuř ne kuř* 'here and there'.

Degrees of comparison

6.16 Like adjectives, a great many adverbs have degrees of comparison, the comparative and the superlative. They are characteristic of two types of adverbs denoting gradable concepts:

(1) adverbs with the suffix *-(i)ai* derived from adjectives and some participles with adjectival meanings, such as *aukštaĩ* 'high(ly)', *laimìngai* 'happily'; *suprañtamai* 'understandably';

(2) the adverbs *daũg* 'much, many', *anksti* 'early', *tolì* 'far', *artì* 'near(by)', *šalià* 'near(by), next to', *paskuĩ* 'afterwards' and the like.

6.17 The **comparative** degree is formed by adding the suffix *-iaũ* (identical with the comparative degree marker in neuter adjectives) to the stem of the positive form of an adverb. The suffix is always stressed, e.g.:

ger-aĩ 'well' — *ger-iaũ* 'better'
aukšt-aĩ 'high(ly)' — *aukšč-iaũ* 'higher'

The **superlative** degree is marked with the suffix *-iáusiai* or *-iáusia*. The former allomorph is used in *-(i)ai* adverbs:

ger-aĩ 'well' — *ger-iáusiai* 'best'
aukštaĩ 'high(ly)' — *aukšč-iáusiai* 'highest, most highly'

With other adverbs the latter allomorph is more common, though the former one is also possible, cf.:

daũg 'much, many' — *daugiáusia / daugiáusiai* 'mostly'
tolì 'far' — *toliáusia/toliáusiai* 'farthest'

The suffix *-iáusiai/-íausia* is a complex marker incorporating the formant *-iaus-* which marks the superlative degree of adjectives, cf.: *tol-ùs* 'far' – *tol-iáus-ias* 'farthest'. Therefore it is analysable into the superlative degree marker *-iaus-* and the adverbial suffix *-iai* or *-ia*: *tol-iáus-iai/-ia*. The suffix is always stressed.

The comparative and superlative forms of adverbs are identical with those of the respective neuter adjectives, cf.: *(buvo) gražù* – (it was) nice' – *graž-iaũ* 'nicer', *graž-iáusia* 'nicest'.

The same morphonological rules apply here as in the formation of adverbs by means of the suffix *-iai* (see 6.3), cf.:

aukšt-aĩ – aukšč-iaũ, aukšč-iáusiai
juod-aĩ – juodž-iaũ, juodž-iáusiai

In a number of cases, the degrees of comparison are related to an adverbially used case form of a noun, e.g.:

apač-iaũ 'lower', *apač-iáusiai* 'lowest' (: *apač-iojè* 'at the bottom')
šiaur-iaũ 'more to the north', (: *šiáur-ėje* 'in the north')
šiaur-iáusiai 'farthest to the north'
kair-iaũ 'more to the left', (: *kairėjè/į̃ kaĩrę* 'on the left')
kair-iáusiai 'farthest to the left'
gal-iaũ 'closer to the end', (: *gal-è* 'in the end')
gal-iáusiai 'at the very end'

6.18. There is a variant of the comparative degree of adverbs formed by means of the complex stressed suffix *-ėliaũ* comprised of the diminutive suffix *-ėl-* and the comparative degree marker *-iau*, e.g.:

ger-ėliaũ 'a little better'
aukšt-ėliaũ 'a little higher'
daug-ėliaũ 'a little more'

These forms are viewed as diminutive forms of the principal comparative form of adverbs.

6.19 The **comparative** degree usually denotes a stronger, greater, or more intense characteristic of an action or process as compared with another action or process or with an earlier stage of the same action or process, cf.:

Šiañdien jìs grĩžo namõ anksčiaũ negù vãkar.	'Today he returned home earlier than yesterday.'
Jìs grĩžo namõ anksčiaũ / ankstėliaũ už sẽserį.	'He returned home earlier / a little earlier than his sister.'
Paáiškink taĩ suprantamiaũ.	'(Please) explain it more clearly.'
Láužas labiaũ įsìdegė.	'The bonfire started burning more brightly.'

The comparative form of adverbs is often used with a noun with the preposition *ùž* 'than' or with the conjunctions *negù/neĩ* 'than' and *kaĩp* 'as' (see the above examples). The basis of comparison can also be expressed by the genitive case of a noun, e.g.:

Vandeñs bùvo aukščiaũ júostos.	'The water reached above (lit. higher) waist.'
Neĩk toliaũ sàvo kiẽmo.	'Don't go farther than your yard.'

These comparative adverbs are functionally similar to prepositions that take the genitive case.

To specify the content of the comparative form of an adverb, a prepositional phrase may also be used; cf.:

Mìškas tęsėsi toliaũ į vãkarus.	'The woods stretched farther to the west.'
Atsisėdau arčiaũ prie dùrų.	'I took a seat nearer to the door.'

6.20 When used with the adverb *užvìs* '(most) of all' and synonymous prepositional phrases *už visùs (vìsa)* 'of all' *už vìską (vìsa)* 'of everything', and the emphatic particles *kuõ, kõ*, the comparative form expresses the highest degree or quantity of the adverbial meaning and thus approaches the meaning of the superlative forms, cf.:

Skraĩdė užvìs greičiaũ (cf. greičiáusiai).	'(He) was flying faster than everybody else (cf. the fastest).'
Atsikėliau už visùs anksčiaũ (cf. anksčiáusiai).	'I got up earlier than everybody else (cf. the earliest).'
Grį̃žkite namõ kuõ/kõ greičiaũ (cf. greičiáusiai).	'Return home as soon as possible (cf. the soonest).'

On the other hand, the comparative form of some temporal adverbs, especially when used with prepositions, is practically synonymous with the positive form, cf.:

pirmiaũ	– pirmà 'first, earlier (than)'
paskiaũ	– paskuĩ 'afterwards, later'
iš anksčiaũ	– iš añksto 'from the time before/earlier'
nuo seniaũ	– nuo sẽno 'since earlier (time)'

6.21 The **superlative** forms denote the highest degree or quantity of a characteristic referred to by the adverb on the scale of comparison, cf.:

Tà knygà jį labiáusiai sudõmino.	'That book caused his interest most (of all).'
Jì dainúoja gražiáusiai.	'She sings the best.'
Jìs yrà blogiáusiai pasirengęs.	'He is prepared the worst.'

The superlative form of adverbs may express the elative meaning, i.e. a very high degree of a qualitative manner of action without implying comparison (cf. the respective use of the superlative form of adjectives, see 2.14). This meaning is often emphasized by the particles kuõ, kõ, e.g.:

Gyvénsim (kuõ/kõ) puikiáusiai.	'We shall live very well (lit. quite the best).'

The superlative form may be used with the adverbs užvìs, pervìs 'most of all' and prepositional phrases už visùs, -às 'of all' už vìską/vìsa 'of everything', which emphasize its meaning, e.g.:

Užvìs labiáusiai mylėjau senẽlę.	'I loved my grandmother best of all.'
Jìs mókėsi už visùs geriáusiai.	lit. 'He studied best of all.'

A favoured means of emphasis is the genitive plural visų̃ from the pronoun visì, vìsos 'all, everybody', cf.:

Sugrį̃žom visų̃ vėliáusiai.	'We returned the latest (latest of all).'
Mū́sų káime vaikų̃ visų̃ daugiáusia.	'There are more children in our village than in all the others (lit. most of all).'

The elative meaning is also emphasized by the genitive plural case of the respective adjective, e.g.: *senų seniáusiai* 'very, very long ago', *ramių ramiáusiai* 'quietly as possible'. To emphasize the superlative degree of the adverb *daũg* 'much, many', the form *daugių* is used which is derived by analogy with the genitive of adjectives, cf.:

Prisirinko daugių daugiáusia šim̃tas žmonių.	'There gathered a hundred people at the most.'

The comparative and the superlative forms of the adverb *labaĩ* 'very', which typically combines with adjectives as an intensifier (cf. *labaĩ šáltas* 'very cold', *labaĩ gražùs* 'very beautiful'), are never used with adjectives; instead, the respective form of the adjective itself is used: *šaltèsnis* 'colder', *šalčiáusias* '(the) coldest'; *gražèsnis* 'more beautiful', *gražiáusias* '(the) most beautiful' (**labiaũ, labiáusiai šáltas; *labiaũ, labiáusiai gražùs*). However, *labiaũ* and *labiáusiai* are used with those participles which do not have the degrees of comparison: *labiaũ, labiáusiai pavar̃gęs* 'more/(the) most tired'.

6.22 The comparative and the superlative forms of a number of adverbs, e.g. *verčiaũ* 'rather, better', *veikiaũ, veikiáusiai* 'most likely, probably', *greičiáusiai* 'probably, very likely', *tikriáusiai* 'probably, most likely, surely', express modal assessment, certainty, doubt, etc. rather than manner or quantity of an action, cf.:

Jìs tikriáusiai niẽko nesuprãto.	'He probably didn't understand anything.'
Àš verčiaũ paláuksiu jõ čià.	'I'd rather wait for him here.'
Jìs greičiáusiai pavėluõs.	'He will most likely be late.'

Semantic types of adverbs

6.23 With respect to meaning, adverbs are divided into adverbs of manner, place, time, cause, purpose and modality.

6.24 **Adverbs of manner** denote qualitative (i.e. quality, manner or intensity) and quantitative characteristics of an action, or a state, or a property.

Quality is expressed by most of the *-(i)ai* adverbs formed from adjectives and participles. They commonly modify verbs, e.g.:

ramiaĩ miegóti 'sleep quietly'	*blogaĩ dìrbti* 'work poorly'
žiauriaĩ nubaũsti 'punish severely'	*prìderančiai el̃gtis* 'behave properly'

Depending on their lexical meaning, some adverbs may also modify adjectives (cf. *juokìngai liũdnas* 'funnily sad', *tam̃siai žãlias* lit. 'darkly green') and in exceptional cases, adverbs, cf.: nudažýti *tam̃siai raudónai* 'paint dark (lit. 'darkly') red' (ADV) (: *tam̃siai raudónas* lit. 'darkly red').

The meaning of the manner of an action is rendered by numerous adverbs formed in a variety of ways, many of them traced back to adverbialized case forms; these adverbs usually modify verbs; here belong:

apgraibomìs 'groping(ly)' *kitaĩp* 'otherwise'
vogčiomìs 'surreptitiously' *iškar̃t* 'at once'
véltui 'in vain' *gerúoju* 'in a friendly way'

Quantity is expressed mostly by adverbs related to numerals, e.g.:

dvìgubai (atlýginti) '(pay) double'
dvíese (dìrbti) '(work) two-together'
añtrąsyk (pakartóti) '(repeat) a second time'
dvìgubai (ilgèsnis) 'twice (as long)'

Other adverbs have a generalized meaning of quantity: *daũg* 'much, many', *gaũsiai* 'abundantly', *trùputį* 'a little', *galutinaĩ* 'finally'. A number of adverbs of quantity can modify the comparative and superlative forms of adjectives and adverbs, e.g.:

dvìgubai didèsnis 'twice as large (lit. twice larger)'
dvìgubai daugiaũ 'twice as much/many (lit. twice more)'
trùputį stiprèsnis 'a little stronger'
trùputį stipriaũ 'a little more strongly'

The most common adverb of intensity is *labaĩ* 'very'. It modifies the positive degree of both adjectives and adverbs, cf. respectively: *labaĩ pìktas/piktaĩ* 'very angry/angrily'. It is also used as a verbal intensifier, e.g.: *labaĩ pỹkti/džiaũgtis* 'be angry/ rejoice very much', *labaĩ juõktis* 'laugh hard'; but there are lexical restrictions on its co-occurrence with verbs, cf.: **labaĩ miegóti/sėdėti* 'sleep/sit very'. Other intensifying adverbs are:

ypatìngai/ýpač 'especially' *smar̃kiai* 'hard, heavily'
nuostabiaĩ 'wonderfully, remarkably' *gerókai* 'pretty (hard)
puĩkiai 'perfectly' considerably', etc.
stipriaĩ 'strongly'

Here also belong deverbal adverbs in *-te/-tinai* which are in fact specified intensifiers (see 6.13), e.g.:

bėgtè bėgti lit. 'run running' *verktinaĩ ver̃kti* 'cry very hard'

To express an increasing degree of quality, quantity or intensity, adverbs with the suffix *-yn* are used, mostly in collocation with the verb *eĩti* 'go' which acquires the processual meaning 'become, grow'; these verbal groups are synonymous with process verbs derived from respective adjectives by means of the suffix *-ėti*, cf.:

eīti ilg-ỹn   – *ilg-ěti* 'become/grow longer'
eīti giedr-ỹn 'grow clearer (of weather)'   – *giedr-ěti* 'clear up'
eīti plat-ỹn 'become wider'   – *plat-ěti* 'widen'

6.25 **Adverbs of place** denote the place of action, direction, of the initial or final point of motion.

Place adverbs are extremely numerous and formally varied; here belong:

aukštaĩ 'high above'	*teñ* 'there'
žemaĩ 'below'	*artì* 'nearly'
namiẽ 'at home'	*tolì* 'far (away)'
visuř 'everywhere'	*šalimaĩs* 'side by side'
čià 'here'	*apliñkui* 'around', etc.

Direction of motion is mostly rendered by adverbs with the suffix *-yn* (1), or those descended from the illative case (2), and other adverbialized cases (3), or other forms (4), e.g.:

(1) *(kìlti) aukšt-ỹn* '(rise) upwards'
(léistis) žemỹn '(go) downwards'
(eīti) pirm-ỹn '(go) forwards'

(2) *(pasùkti) dešin-ẽn* '(turn) to the right'
(užlìpti) virš-uñ '(ascend) to the top'
(eīti) lauk-añ '(go) outside'

(3) *(plaũkti) pavějui/pasroviuĩ/pavandeniuĩ* '(swim) with the wind/downstream'
(skuběti) namõ '(hurry) home (ward)'

(4) *(grį̃žti) atgaĩ/atgaliõs* '(return) back'
(važiúoti) tiesióg '(go) straight forward'
(atběgti) príešpriešiais '(come running) from the opposite direction'

The **starting point** of motion is usually expressed by place adverbs with the prepositions *iš* 'from', *nuõ* 'from' (1), and the **final point** by place adverbs with the prepositions *ikì/lìgi* 'to, as far as' (2):

(1) *Iš kuř keliáujate?*	'Where are you coming from?'
iš aukštaĩ nukrìsti	'fall from high above'
praděti nuo čià	'begin from here'
(2) *ikì čià*	'as far as here'
lìgi kuř	lit. 'as far as where'

Most of the adverbs of place can denote both place and direction, either interpretation being determined by the verbal meaning: with verbs of motion these adverbs usually refer to direction, and with verbs of stationary action to place, cf. respectively:

eĩsim kitur̃ 'we'll go elsewhere' – *gyvenù kitur̃* 'I live elsewhere'
skubė́kim teñ 'let's hurry there' – *teñ užáugau* 'I grew up there'

6.26 **Adverbs of time** denote various temporal characteristics of verbal actions, such as period or duration, point of time, frequency or repetition.

Adverbs expressing generalized temporal concepts occur mostly with verbs, e.g.:

dabar̃ pailsė́sim	'we'll have a rest now'
paskuĩ dìrbsim	'we'll work afterwards'
seniaĩ nesimãtėme	'we haven't met for a long time'
niekadà nebegrį̃šiu	'I'll never return'
ankstì/vėlaĩ sutė́mo	'it grew dark early/late'

They can also express an indefinite period of time, e.g.:

ilgaĩ/laikinaĩ gyvẽno	'(he) stayed for a long time/temporarily'
greĩtai apsìrengė	'(he) dressed quickly'
ìlgainiui apsiprãtome	'we got used in due course'
tuojaũ ateĩsiu	'I'll come immediately'

An approximate time period is usually rendered by adverbialized dative case forms, e.g.:

ilgám atvažiãvo	'he's come for a long time'
trumpám išė́jo	'he's left for a short while'

The following adverbs refer to (1) days and (2) time of the day and (3) year relative to the moment of utterance:

(1) *šiañdien* 'today'	*ùžvakar* 'the day before yesterday'
rytój 'tomorrow'	*porýt* 'the day after tomorrow'
vãkar 'yesterday'	*kìtądien* 'some other day'
(2) *šìąnakt* 'tonight'	*popiẽt* 'after lunch'
nakčià 'at night'	*priešpiẽt* 'before lunch'
(3) *šiẽmet* 'this year'	*pérnai* 'last year'
rudenióp 'towards autumn',	*ùžpernai* 'the year before last'

Repetition and **frequency** of action are also rendered by specialized adverbs such as:

dažnaĩ 'often'	*vė̃l* 'again'
retaĩ 'seldom'	*kai kadà* 'sometimes'

rẽtkarčiais 'now and then'   *visadà* 'always'
kar̃tais 'sometimes'   *visuomèt* 'always' etc.

They modify mostly verbs and sometimes, adjectives and adverbs, e.g.:

jìs visadà juõkiasi 'he is always laughing' – *visadà liñksmas* 'always merry' – *(gyvénsim) visadà linksmaĩ* '(we'll live) always merrily'

vẽl pýksta 'he is in a bad temper again' – *vẽl pìktas* 'angry again' – *vẽl piktaĩ* 'angrily again'

The **starting** and the **final temporal** points of action are mostly signified by adverbs with the prepositions *nuõ* 'from, since', *ikì/lìgi* 'until', which may be merged into a single adverb: *iki šiõl/lig šiõl* 'until now', *ikipiẽt* 'until lunch', cf.: *iki dabar̃* 'until now', *nuo vãkar* 'since yesterday'.

6.27 **Adverbs of cause and purpose** make up a very small group; the most common adverbs are:

dėl kõ 'why'   *kám* 'why'
dėl tõ 'therefore'   *todẽl* 'therefore'
kodẽl 'why'   *užtàt* 'that's why'
kõ 'what for'

There is no distinct border-line between the two meanings in these adverbs, cf.: *Dėl kõ/kodẽl/kõ tù taĩp suñkiai dìrbi?* 'Why do you work so hard?' – *Dėl vaikų̃* 'For the children' (purpose); *Dėl netur̃to* 'Out of poverty' (cause). The adverbs *týčia (týčiomis)* 'on purpose, intentionally', *netýčia (netýčiomis)* 'inadvertently, unintentionally', *šiaĩp sáu* 'without particular purpose', *véltui* 'in vain, to no purpose' are semantically contiguous to adverbs of purpose; cf.: *jìs týčia melúoja* 'he is lying on purpose', *véltui sténgėsi* 'he tried in vain'.

6.28 **Modal adverbs** express the speaker's assessment of the content of a statement. They may express modality ranging from certainty to greater or lesser doubt and supposition, e.g.:

tikraĩ 'surely, certainly'   *tikriáusiai* 'probably'
greičiáusiai 'doubtless'   *veikiáu(siai)* 'very likely, probably'
būtinaĩ 'by all means'   *verčiaũ* 'rather, better'
neišvéngiamai 'inevitably'

A few adverbs express neutral assessment, e.g.:

apskritaĩ 'in general, generally'
paprastaĩ 'usually, commonly'
pirmiáusiai 'in the first place'

The adverb *verčiaũ* can express advice:

Tù verčiaũ patylė́k.   'You'd better keep silence.'

The modal adverbs usually precede a verb: *Jìs tikraĩ/greičiáusiai ateĩs* 'He will surely/doubtless come', though most of them can be used in the initial position as sentence modifiers, cf.: *Tikriáusiai/veikiáusiai jìs vėlúoja* 'Probably/very likely he is late'. All of them, with the exception of *neišvéngiamai, verčiaũ* and adverbs of neutral assessment, may be used in response to a question, e.g.:

Ar tù ateĩsi? 'Will you come?' – *Tikraĩ/tikriáusiai/veikiáusiai.* 'Of course/most probably/probably.'

A number of other word forms (the infinitive *matýt* 'probably', lit. 'see', the nominative case *láimė* 'luck' and its dative case forms *láimei* 'luckily' and *neláimei* 'unluckily', the present passive participles *žìnoma* 'of course' (lit. 'known') and *suprañtama* 'of course, understandably' and the prepositional phrase *be ābejo* 'without doubt' are used very much like modal adverbs and are interchangeable with them, cf.:

Jìs matýt/žìnoma/tikriáusiai vėlúoja. 'He is probably/of course/most likely late.'

7 PARTICLES

Dalelỹtės

7.1 Particles are a class of words which serve to give modal or emotional emphasis to other words, or word groups, or clauses. Particles are unchangeable words and they have no particular syntactic function in a sentence.

In Lithuanian, particles are extremely numerous and varied semantically. Particles can specify, or limit, or intensify the meaning of a word or phrase. Some of them also serve as connectives between clauses and sentences and thus are a means of achieving coherence in a text.

A number of particles have a broad range of semantic functions; e.g. the particle *tìk* 'only' is used to limit, or single out, or intensify the meaning of a word (see 7.6, 13).

Interrogative and negative particles modify and even change the meaning of an utterance (see 7.9, 10).

A number of particles are identical in form with other parts of speech, e.g. with conjunctions (*af̃* 'if, whether', *if̃* 'and', *kàd* 'that', *nórs* 'though'), adverbs (*kaĩp* 'how', *taĩp* 'thus, so', *čià* 'here'), pronouns (*kõ* 'what' (GEN), *kuõ* 'what' (INSTR).

The particles *bevéik* 'almost', *dár* 'yet', *jaũ* 'already', *vė̃l* 'again', *võs võs* 'hardly', etc. are semantically close to adverbs; *neĩ* 'neither, nor', *tìk* 'only', *vos tìk* 'as soon as', *nebeñt* 'if only', are very similar to conjunctions in certain contexts, without losing their meaning and their limiting or specifying function; the particles *õgi* 'surely', *và* 'there, here', *vái* 'oh' border on interjections.

7.2 Particles are usually preposed to the subordinating word or phrase:

Jìs bevéik pasveĩko.   'He (has) almost recovered.'

The particles *gì* and *pàt* which are used in post-position are exceptions:

Ateĩsiu tuojaũ pàt.   'I'll come right now'.
Gė̃ros gi tàvo ākys!   'Aren't your eyes good!'

When used with a prepositional noun phrase, *pàt* is placed between the preposition and noun: *nuo pàt rýto* 'since very morning'.

396 MORPHOLOGY

Monosyllabic particles are usually unstressed (they are proclitics or enclitics). Other particles, including compounds, tend to retain their stress, e.g.: *galbu̇́t* 'maybe', *nejaũgi* 'really(?)', *võs ne võs* 'hardly'.

7.3   With respect to their structure, particles may be simple, compound and complex.

Simple particles are short, mostly monosyllabic words which are not analysable into components in Modern Lithuanian, e.g.: *ar̃, bè, dár, gì, jaũ, nè, nẽ, nèt, pàt, vìs, vė̃l*.

Compound particles usually comprise two (rarely three) fused components and most of them contain either the negative particle *nè* 'not' or the intensifying *gì*:

nèbe 'not any longer'   *ar̃gi* 'really(?)'
nebeñt 'if only'   *nègi* 'really(?)'
benè (emphatic)   *nètgi* 'even'
konè 'almost'   *nejaũgi* 'really(?)' (= *nejaũ+gì*)
màžnè 'almost'   *nejaũ* (= *nè+jaũ*)

A few particles contain other components:

nèmàž 'not at all' (= *nẽ+màž*)
tiktaĩ 'only' (= *tìk+taĩ*)
begù (*bè+gù*) (interrogative)

The compound particle *kažìn* 'hardly' is a contraction of the phrase *kàs žìno* 'who knows', *galbū́t* 'perhaps' derives from *gã̃li bū́ti* '(it) may be'.

Complex particles comprised of two separate components can be semantically indivisible, cf. *võs tik* (as in *Sẽnis võs tik pàjuda* 'The old man is hardly capable of moving') and *võs* 'hardly' and *tìk* 'only'; here also belong *kõ tik, tìk tìk* 'just'. Most of the complex particles, however, are free combinations of simple particles retaining their own meaning, e.g. *ar nè* 'isn't it', *kad ir̃* 'even', *lýg tai* '(it) seems', *víen tik* 'just only'; cf. *Taĩ beñt výras!* 'He is quite a man!'

7.4   According to their relatedness to other words, particles fall into primary (non-derived) and secondary (derivative).

The monosyllabic simple particles *ar̃, beñt, gì, jaũ, nè, tè, tìk*, etc. are primary, since they are not relatable to any other words in Modern Lithuanian.

Secondary particles are related to words of other classes (parts of speech), e.g.:

pronouns:

anà 'there'   – *anàs, anà* 'that'
vìs 'still'   – *vìsas, visà* '(the) whole', 'entire', also the
                                   adverb *visái* 'entirely'
štaĩ   – *šìtas, šìta/šità* 'this'

adjectives and/or adverbs:

ýpač 'especialy'	– ypatìngas 'special'
lýg 'like, as'	– lýgus 'flat, smooth', also the the adverb
lýgiai 'smoothly, evenly'	
bemàž 'almost, nearly'	– be mãžo 'without a little'

verbs:

gál 'maybe'	– galì '(you) can (2. SG. PRES)'
galbū́t 'maybe'	– gãli bū́ti '(it) may be'
ràsi 'maybe'	– ràsi '(you will) find (2. SG. FUT)'
tar̃tum 'like'	– tar̃tum '(you would) say (2. SG. SUBJ)'

All the compound and complex particles are also secondary.

A number of particles have lost their status of words and become bound morphemes within words of other classes, viz. of complex pronouns (bet kàs 'anyone', kažìn kàs 'somebody, something', koks nórs 'any, some') and adverbs (kažìn kaĩp 'somehow', kaip nórs 'somehow', tiek pàt 'as much/many'). The prefixes ne- 'not', nebe- 'not any more', te- 'yet', tebe- 'yet' originate from respective particles (cf. láimė 'happiness' – neláimė 'misfortune', dìrba '(he) works' – nebedìrba '(he) does not work any more', gyvẽna '(he) lives' – tebegyvẽna '(he) goes on living'). The components -gi and -gu in taĩgi 'now then, then', negù 'than' also derive from particles.

Semantic types of particles

7.5 The meaning of a particle usually varies within certain limits since it is largely dependent on the meaning of words and phrases it occurs with as well as on broader context and/or intonation. Therefore their semantic classification presents considerable difficulties. Nevertheless, they can be tentatively categorized into the following semantic-functional types: (1) specifying and limiting, (2) demonstrative, (3) negative, (4) affirmative, (5) interrogative and dubitative, (6) comparative, (7) optative, (8) intensifying-emphatic, and (9) connecting.

Affirmative, interrogative, comparative and optative particles are modal words, i.e. they express the speaker's attitude to the content of the utterance; intensifying-emphatic particles can also express the speaker's subjective evaluation.

7.6 **Specifying and limiting particles.** The particles (1) bevéik 'almost', bemàž, maž-daũg, konè and màžnè 'nearly, almost', per̃ 'too', võs 'hardly', etc. are used to specify quantity or degree, and (2) dár 'yet', jaũ 'already', pàt 'right', vė̃l 'again', vìs 'still', võs 'hardly', etc. specify the mode of action or state; cf. respectively:

(1) *Kambarỹs* bevéik/bemàž *pìlnas žmoniū̃*.	'The room is almost full of people.'
Čià peř *tamsù*.	'It is too dark here.'
(2) *Jiē̃* dár *negrį̃žo*.	'They haven't returned yet.'
Sáulė jaũ *nusiléido*.	'The sun has already set.'

The particle *pàt* specifies spatial or temporal limits expressed by other words, cf.:

Prie pàt *trobė̃lės bùvo šulinỹs*.	'There was a well right by the hut.'

The particles *beñt* 'at least', *tìk* 'only', *tiktaĩ* 'only', *nèt* 'even', *ýpač* 'especially', *kad iř* 'even', *nebeñt* 'if only', *nórs* 'though', *víen* 'at least', *víen tik* 'even only', usually serve to single out a thing or to limit the meaning of a word.

The particles *tìk, tiktaĩ, víen, víen tik* have no additional connotations, whereas *nèt, nètgi, nèt ir, nė̃* imply wonder, surprise; cf. respectively:

Mẽs rãdome tìk/tiktaĩ *jõ ãkinius*.	'We found only his glasses.'
Jìs nètgi *nežinójo jõs ãdreso*.	'He didn't even know her address.'
Nèt *jìs atė̃jo*.	'Even he turned up.'

The limiting particles *beñt* 'at least', *nórs* 'though', *kad iř, nebeñt* imply concession, e.g.:

Pasiim̃k beñt/nórs *lãzdą šunìms atsigìnti*.	'Take at least a stick to defend yourself against the dogs.'
Tà mergìnà nebeñt *ūgiù panašì į Õną*.	'That girl is at least as tall as Ona (Ann).'

The particle *ýpač* has a very strong specifying and limiting force, e.g.:

Ýpač *àš nemė̃gstu bailiū̃*.	'Especially I don't like cowards.'

There is no distinct borderline between specifying and limiting particles.

7.7 **Demonstrative particles.** The particles *anà* 'there', *antaĩ* 'there', *aurè* 'there', *štaĩ* 'here', *šìt* 'here', *và* 'here, there', semantically close to demonstrative pronouns, are used to introduce a statement by pointing out the place of an action or a thing, etc.; cf.:

Antaĩ *bė̃ga lãpė*.	'There is a fox running.'
Štaĩ *sė̃džiu àš prie lángo*.	'Here I am sitting by the window.'
Štaĩ *tàvo knygà*.	'Here (is) your book.'

7.8 **Affirmative particles.** In Standard Lithuanian the only affirmative particle in use is *taĩp* 'yes'; in colloquial Lithuanian the particles *taĩgi* 'yes' and *ahà* 'yea' sometimes are used instead. The particle *taĩp* is often used alone as an affirmative reply to a question:

Ar važiúosi namõ? – Taĩp.	'Will you go home? – Yes.'

It is also used:

(1) when confirming negation:

Juk jũs teñ nebùvote? – Taĩp, *nebuvaũ*.	'But you weren't there, were you? – No, I wasn't (lit. Yes, I wasn't).'

(2) in echo questions to express surprise:

Ar žinaĩ, kad jìs grį̃žo? – Taĩp? *Nežinójau*.	'Do you know he is back? – Really? No, I didn't.'

It is emphatic in contexts like *Čià* taĩp *gražù*. 'It is so nice here', and with adverbs, cf. *taĩp gražiaĩ* 'so nicely'.

7.9 Negative particles. In Standard Lithuanian, four negative particles are in use: the principal particles *nè* 'no, not' and *nebè* 'not (any more/longer)', and also *nẽ* and *neĩ* 'not (a)', 'not even'.

The particle *nebè* differs from *nè* in that it is used to negate continuation of an action or state that has gone on for some time; cf.:

Màno sūnùs ne *tóks gẽras*.	'My son is not so good.'
Màno sūnùs (jaũ) nebe *tóks gẽras*.	'My son is not so good any longer.'

The particles *nè* and *nebè* also double as negative prefixes:

Jìs bùvo negẽras.	'He was not good.'
Jìs neberãšo.	'He does not write any more.'

In fact, they are spelt together with verbs, adjectives, etc., in accordance with Lithuanian orthography.

The particle *nè* can be used singly in response to a general question. In a reply to a negative question, this particle expresses confirmation and in a reply to a positive question, it expresses negation; cf. respectively:

Nemateĩ jõ? – Nè.	'You didn't see him? – No.'
Ar grį̃ši šiañdien? – Nè.	'Will you return today? – No.'

In response to the question *Juk jũs teñ nebùvote?* 'You weren't there, were you?' one can say *Nè, buvaũ* lit. 'No, (but) I was', which denies the implied negative presupposition and affirms the opposite (cf. the response *Taĩp, nebuvaũ* 'No, I wasn't' above).

The particle *nẽ* denotes emphatic negation (a sentence usually contains another negative marker), cf.:

Àš jõ nepastebė́jau.	'I didn't notice him.'
Àš jõ nẽ *nepastebė́jau*.	'I didn't even notice him.'

If two or more coordinated words (or clauses) are negated, the reduplicated negative conjunction *neĩ ... neĩ* 'neither ... nor', identical in meaning with the particle *neĩ*, is often used if the predicate has the negative prefix):

Nedžiùgino jõs neĩ *šviesì saulùtė,* neĩ *giẽdras dangùs.*	'Neither the bright sun nor the clear sky gave her joy.'

7.10 Interrogative and dubitative particles. The most common interrogative particle used to introduce general questions is *ar̃*:

Ar *teisýbę jìs sãko?*	'Does he tell the truth?'

Its functional equivalent is *bè*, which is rarely used; cf.:

Bet patì, be *vìską padareĩ?*	'But yourself, have you done everything?'

Questions with these particles and negation acquire the meaning of doubt or supposition. This combined meaning is also rendered, in most cases, by the particle *benè*:

Benè *vẽl bùs kàs atsitìkę?*	'Has anything again happened (I wonder)?'

The interrogative particles *nègi/nejaũ/nejaũgi* 'really(?)', *ar̃gi* 'indeed(?), really(?)' strongly imply the speaker's surprise, disbelief or doubt:

Nejaũgi/nejaũ/negi *tù skìrsies su manim̃?*	'Will you really divorce me (= I can't believe it)?'
Ar̃gi *tù vìską padareĩ?*	'Have you really done everything?'

When used in rhetorical questions, these particles express doubt.

Doubt or uncertainty are explicitly rendered by the particles *gál* 'probably', *galbū́t* 'maybe', *kažìn* 'I doubt/wonder', *ràsi* 'perhaps, maybe', *turbū́t* 'probably'; cf.:

Jìs gál/galbū́t *pavėluõs.*	'He will be probably late.'
Kažìn *ar jìs grį̃žo.*	'I doubt if he is back.'

The modal words *gál* 'probably', *galbū́t* 'maybe', *turbū́t* 'probably' are classed with particles here, due to their functional affinity to the latter, since modal words are not distinguished as a special word class in Lithuanian grammar.

7.11 Comparative particles. Here belong *lýg* and *lýg ir* 'like, as if, kind of', *lýg kad* and *nevà* 'ostensibly, as if', *tar̃si/tar̃tum/tarýtum* 'as if, as though' which are used to express ostensible comparison and uncertainty, doubt at the same time; cf.:

Lýg *debesìs,* lýg *miglà kokià nusiléido iš viršaũs.*	'It seemed as if a cloud, a kind of mist came from above.'

Dabař jám tarýtum *pasidārė lengviaū*.	'Now he, it seemed, felt better.'
Jìs tařsi *atjaunėjo*.	'He kind of grew younger.'

These particles may introduce comparative phrases and clauses, in which case they function as conjunctions; cf.:

Jìs gyvēna lýg/tařsi *atsiskýrėlis*.	'He lives like a hermit.'

7.12 **Optative particles** serve to convey the speaker's will, wishes, and the like. The particles *tegù(l)* and *tè* 'let' are often used with the present or (less commonly) future tense 3rd person form to render the imperative mood 3rd person meaning; cf.:

Jeigu nóri, tegùl *skraĩdo* (PRES).	'If he feels like it, let (him) fly.'
Te *kiekvíenas parašỹs* (FUT).	'Let everyone write.'

These particles may also occur with the future or present tense 1st person or with the subjunctive mood:

Geriaū tegù *àš miřsiu, negù jį išdúosiu*.	'Better let me (I'd rather) die (FUT) than betray him.'

In dialects and sometimes in written Standard Lithuanian, the particle *laĩ* is used to render the optative meaning; e.g.:

Laĩ *tàs bùs karālius*.	'Let that one be the king.'

To express request, order, wish, threat the particle *kàd* can be used with the subjunctive mood of verbs:

Kad *tù sudègtum* (SUBJ)!	'May you burn! (I wish you would burn!)'
Kad *turéčiau* (SUBJ) *šią knỹgą!*	'I wish I had this book!'

The particles *šè, tè, nà* which express inducement are used (mostly in colloquial Lithuanian since they sound familiar) when offering or giving something:

Šè *táu maĩšą pinigų*.	'Here, take this bag of money' (lit. Here a bag of money for you).'

The particles *šèkit* and *tèkit* which are contiguous to interjections are formed from the particles *šè, tè* with the imperative suffix and 2. PL ending:

Šèkit, *iñkite vìską*.	'Here, take everything.'

7.13 **Intensifying-emphatic particles** are used to emphasize a word or a clause. The most common intensifiers are the particles *gì, jùk* and *iř*:

Jìs gi *kvaĩlas*.	'He is just stupid.'
Žinaĩ gi *jō pāpročius*.	'You do know his ways (or: You know his ways, don't you).'

Jùk ir *àš tàvo duktē̃*.	'I am your daughter, too, aren't I.'
Jìs ir *yrà tàs žmogùs, apiē kurį kalbame*.	'He is just the man (the very man) we are talking about.'

The particle *gì*, usually postposed to the word it intensifies, sometimes occurs in the initial position:

Gi *žinaĩ, kõ jám reĩkia*.	'You do know what he wants.'

The particles *kàd, kàdgi* 'simply', *taĩ* 'that', *tìk* 'only', *nèt* 'even', *jaũ kad* 'simply' are also used as emphasizers:

O *tàs gaidỹs ant tvorõs* kad *gíeda*.	'That rooster on the fence is simply bursting with crowing (lit. just crows).'
Jìs nèt *pravir̃ko*.	'He even burst into tears'.
O jì tik *ver̃kia!*	'And she is crying and crying!'
Taĩ *bùs juõko!*	'That'll be a good laugh, won't it!'

The particles *kuõ, kõ* are used with the superlative (sometimes comparative) degree of adjectives and adverbs:

kuõ geriáusias / geriáusiai 'the best possible / in the best possible way'
kõ geriaũ 'as well as possible'

7.14 **Connecting particles.** The particles *ir̃gi* 'also, too' and *taip pàt* 'also, too' are used as connectors between clauses and sentences to achieve logical coherence:

Pẽtras pradėjo juõktis, kitì taip pàt *nusìjuokė*.	'Peter burst out laughing, the others laughed too.'
Àš ką̃ tìk sutikaũ Jõną. – Àš ir̃gi/taip pàt *jį sutikaũ*.	'I've just met John. – I have also met him.

The intensifying particle *ir̃*, which is identical in form with the conjunction *ir̃* 'and', is also used a connector:

Neválgyk pyrãgo. – Àš ir *nenóriu*.	'Don't eat the cake. – [But] I don't even want it.'

The particle *dár* has an additive force, usually when used with interrogative pronouns:

Kàs dár *nóri arbãtos?*	'Who else wants tea?'

7.15 A number of adverbs and other words and word groups can function as particles in certain contexts, the boundary between particles and other word classes being rather fuzzy.

This is characteristic of the following words:

(1) adverbs, e.g. *tiesióg* 'straight, right', *stačiaĩ* 'straight', *ganà* 'enough, rather', used as intensifiers; cf.:

Tiẽ kalnaĩ tiesióg *pãsakiški.*	'Those mountains are just fabulous.'
Jìs grĩžo ganà *greĩt.*	'He returned quite soon.'

(2) the dative case form *mán* 'to me', *táu* 'to you', *sáu* 'to oneself' of the respective personal and reflexive pronouns, used as intensifiers, cf.:

Tù mán *nejuokáuk!*	'Don't you dare to joke!'
Gyvénsi sáu *kaip ponià.*	'You'll live just like a lady.'

(3) the pronoun *víenas* 'one', used as an intensifier:

Vienì *vargaĩ su tavim̃.*	'What a lot of trouble you cause.'

(4) verbal forms like *nelýginant* 'without comparing', *sakýtum(ei)* 'you'd say':

Mẽs čià nelýginant/sakýtumei *visái svetimì.*	'We are here just like strangers.'

(5) in exclamatory sentences and rhetorical questions, word clusters like *kàs per* 'what(a)', *tai táu, šè tau, ką tìk* 'just', *tai štaĩ* 'so' are used very much like particles to emphasize surprise:

Viẽšpatie, kàs per *gražùmas!*	'Oh dear, what a wonderful sight!'
Tai štaĩ *kuř tù buvaĩ pasislẽpęs.*	'Ah, so that's where you were hiding.'

8 PREPOSITIONS
Príelinksniai

8.1 Prepositions constitute a class of invariable words which denote the dependence of nouns on other words in the sentence. They express a variety of relational meanings of which spatial relations (e.g. *knygà ant stãlo* 'a book on the table', *eĩti į mìšką* 'go to the woods') are the most prominent. A preposition followed by a noun or pronoun forms a compact unit with it, called a prepositional phrase. In word groups, a prepositional phrase is subordinated to the head word, which may be a verb, a noun, an adjective, etc. A complement may be a noun or a pronoun or sometimes an adverb, never a clause. Certain Lithuanian prepositions may also be used as postpositions, e.g. *liñk(ui)* 'towards', *dė̃lei* 'because of' and *viẽtoj* 'instead of'. Postpositions which function similarly to prepositions are placed after the case form of a noun or pronoun. The postposition *dėkà* 'due to' may not function as a preposition.

8.2 Lithuanian prepositions are either primary (non-derived) or secondary (derivative).

Primary prepositions are simple (mostly monosyllabic) words which are not formally related to other words in Modern Lithuanian. They are the oldest prepositions historically. Many primary prepositions are identical in form with verbal prefixes, cf.:

į̃ 'into, to'	– *į-*, as in *į-vèsti* 'lead in(to), introduce'
ìš 'out of'	– *iš-*, as in *iš-vèsti* 'lead out(of)'
sù 'with'	– *su-*, as in *su-eĩti* 'come together'
ùž 'on, over'	– *už-*, as in *už-dė́ti* 'put on'

Sometimes they differ due to vowel alternation, e.g.:

apiẽ 'about'	– *ap(i)-*, as in *ap-eĩti* 'go round'
nuõ 'from'	– *nu-*, as in *nu-eĩti* 'go away'
prõ 'by'	– *pra-*, as in *praeĩti* 'pass by'

The prepositions *añt* 'on', *anót* 'according to', *dė̃l* 'because of', *ikì* 'to, till', *lìg(i)* 'till', *pàs* 'at, by, to', are also primary.

Secondary prepositions are those which are related to other words, mostly adverbs, or formally coincide with them, e.g.:

abìpus 'on both sides of'	*išìlgaĩ* 'along'
anãpus and *kìtapus* 'on the other side of'	*įstrižaĩ* 'slantwise'
šiãpus 'this side of'	*skersaĩ* 'across'
apliñk(ui) '(a)round'	*liñk(ui)* 'towards, in the direction of'
pãskui/pãskum 'behind, after'	*priẽš* 'against'
gretà 'next to'	*tiẽs* 'by, at'
šalià 'by, next to'	*kiauraĩ* 'through'
artì/arčiaũ 'near, by'	*viẽtoj* 'instead of'
artỹn 'nearer to'	*vidurỹ/vidur̃* 'in the middle of'
netolì 'not far from'	*vidùj* 'inside'
pirmà/pirmiaũ 'before'	*virš̃/viršùj/viršum̃* 'above'

They may be referred to as adverbial prepositions. Most of them, except *liñk(ui)*, *tiẽs*, *virš̃*, *vidur̃* and *pasàk* 'according to', *pagal̃* 'along, according to', *tar̃p* 'between', *dėkà* 'thanks to' are also used as adverbs, cf.:

Gyvenù artì ùpės.	'I live near the river.'
Jìs gyvẽna artì.	'He lives nearby.'

These adverbs are in their turn mostly derived either from adjectives (e.g. *ìlg-as* 'long': *iš-ilg-aĩ* 'along', *įstriž-as* 'slanting': *įstriž-aĩ* 'slantwise, across'), or nouns (e.g. *viet-à* 'place' : *viẽt-oj* 'instead of' (lit. 'in place of'), *vidur-ỹs* 'middle' : *vidur-ỹ(jè)* 'in the middle of'), a numeral (*pìrm-as* 'first' : *pirm-à* 'before'), etc.

The locative case of a number of nouns meaning 'end', 'side', and the like may acquire a function similar to that of prepositions; cf.:

galè laũko	'at the end of the field'
šóne kẽlio	'on the side of the road'
kraštè mãrių	'by (lit. 'at the edge') lagoon'
príeky/priešakỹ vežìmo	'in front of the cart'
užpakalỹ kolònos	'behind the column'

Secondary prepositions are more complex with respect to morphemic structure than primary prepositions, since they mostly retain the form of the respective adverbs or case forms.

In Lithuanian, there is also a number of complex prepositions composed of two primary (*iš põ* 'from under' and *iš ùž* 'from behind') or a primary and a secondary (*į anãpus* 'to the other side of', *iš tar̃p* 'from among') prepositions. In Standard Lithuanian only two of them, viz. *iš põ* and *iš ùž*, are frequent.

8.3 Primary and secondary prepositions also differ semantically. Primary prepositions are usually polysemous; as a rule, their meanings tend to be more abstract than those of secondary prepositions, cf. *ant miẽsto* (= *viršùj miẽsto*) 'above the town' and *pỹkti ant draũgo* 'to be angry with a friend'. They may express a variety of semantic relations within a word group, e.g.:

ateĩti iš mìško	'to come from the woods' (spatial relation)
ateĩti iš rýto	to come in the morning' (temporal relation)
nãmas iš plýtų	'a house (built) of bricks' (relation between a thing and material)
šokinėti iš džiaũgsmo	'jump with joy' (causal relation)

These meanings are usually determined by the lexical meaning of the complement and, sometimes, of the head word a prepositional phrase depends on.

Secondary prepositions usually retain the lexical meaning of the corresponding adverb, therefore they are concrete and monosemous.

8.4 Primary prepositions which have identical correlates among verbal prefixes typically occur with respective prefixed verbs, when used in their spatial meaning, e.g.:

ap-eĩti apie nãmą	'go around the house'
į-eĩti į nãmą	'go into the house'
iš-eĩti iš nãmo	'go out of the house'
nu-mèsti nuo stãlo	'throw from the table'
pér-bėgti per kẽlią	'run across the road'
pri-eĩti prie ùpės	'to come up to the river'

8.5 A preposition may have a distinct lexical meaning, especially if it denotes direction, cf.:

į miẽstą	'to the town'
iš miẽsto	'from the town'
pro miẽstą	'past the town'
už miẽsto	'beyond the town'

In most cases, however, the meaning of a preposition is dependent on that of the complement and its case form (cf. 8.3) therefore it is hard to distinguish one from the other and the meaning of a preposition can be identified with that of the prepositional phrase it occurs in.

8.6 In Standard Lithuanian, the genitive, accusative and the instrumental cases occur with prepositions. Most of the prepositions combine with one of these cases only.

The preposition *ùž* takes two case-forms, the genitive and the accusative, and *põ* alone combines with all the three case-forms.

Prepositions with the genitive case

8.7 The majority of prepositions are used with the genitive case, here belong:

(a) the primary prepositions *anót, añt, bè, dė̃l(ei), ikì, lìg(i), ìš, nuõ, priẽ*;

(b) the derivative prepositions *artì (arčiaũ, artỹn), aukščiaũ, dėkà, gretà, įkandin, liñk(ui), netolì, pasàk, pirmà (pirmiaũ, pir̃m), pusiáu, šalià, tar̃p, toliaũ, vidùj, vidurỹ (vidur̃), viẽtoj, virš̃ (viršùj, viršum̃), žemiaũ; anàpus, abìpus, antràpus, šiàpus, abìšal, anàšal*;

(c) the complex prepositions *iš ùž, iš põ, iš tar̃p, iš anàpus, į anàpus, už anàpus*.

With *išilgaĩ, įstrižaĩ, skersaĩ, kiauraĩ*, etc. the genitive alternates with the accusative without a change in meaning (see 8.16, 3). The most characteristic meanings of the more common prepositions are listed below, the primary prepositions being treated first.

8.8 The preposition *añt* denotes the following:

(1) position on top, or on the surface, e.g.:

gulė́ti ant grindų̃	'lie on the floor'
bū́ti ant kálno	'be on the hill'

(2) the final point of movement:

padė́ti ant stãlo	'put (sth) on the table'
atsigulĩti ant súolo	'lie down on the bench'

(3) manner or means, depending on the lexical meanings of the complement noun and head verb, cf.:

gulė́ti ant nùgaros	'lie on (one's) back'
jóti ant žìrgo	'ride on horseback'
plaũkti ant lentõs	'swim on a board'
pakélti ant šãkių	'raise (sth) on a pitchfork'

(4) stimulus or target, with verbs expressing negative emotions or their manifestation, cf.:

pỹkti ant kõ	'be angry at sb'
rė́kauti/bártis ant kõ	'shout/swear at sb'

8.9 The preposition *anót* 'according to' and its synonym *pasàk* refer to the source of information; they are used in introductory parenthetic phrases:

Jìs, anót tévo, kvaĩlas.	'As his father says, he is stupid.'
Pasàk laĩkraščių, bus káršta.	'According to newspapers, it will be hot.'

Anót is colloquial and implies the speaker's agreement with the source, and *pasàk* is rather bookish and carries no implications.

8.10 The preposition *bè* 'without, except' (antonymous to *sù* 'with') has no spatial meanings. It is commonly used to denote absence or lack of something. The prepositional phrase *bè* + GEN indicates:

(1) absence or lack of a thing or a person when used with a verb, e.g.:

siúti be ãdatos	'sew without a needle'
grį̃žti be kepùrės	'return without a cap'
ateĩti be žmonõs	'come without (one's) wife'
dìrbti be póilsio	'work without a rest'
gyvénti be džiaũgsmo	'live without joy'

(2) absence of a property or a part, when subordinated to a noun:

nãmas be stógo	'the house without a roof'
žmogùs be są́žinės	'a man without conscience'

(3) being short of some quantity:

lìtas be ceñto	lit. 'a litas without a cent' (= 99 cents)
šim̃tas be víeno	'a hundred minus one' (= almost a hundred)

(4) the temporal limit before which an action takes (or does not take) place (usually with negated verbs):

Atsikėliau be šviesõs.	'I got up before daylight.'
Be pavãsario negrį̃šiu.	'I won't return before (lit. 'without') spring.'

(5) it has an additive sense in cases like *Be brólio, àš turiù dvì sẽseris* 'Besides a brother, I have two sisters'; it denotes exception when used after negated verbs:

Be brólio, àš daugiaũ niẽko neturiù 'Except for a brother, I have no relatives.'

8.11 The preposition *dė̃l(ei)* 'because of, due to, thanks to' expresses abstract relations such as the following:

(1) cause or reason (very often with verbs of emotion and speech):

Žvaĩgždės atródo mãžos dėl didelių̃ atstùmų.	'Stars look small because of the great distances.'

Supykaĩ dėl niẽkų.	'You got angry because of nothing.'
Jis skùndėsi dėl nesėkmių̃.	'He complained of failures.'

(2) purpose or goal, mostly with verbs of volitional actions especially those of motion:

kovóti dėl láisvės	'fight for freedom'
išgérti dėl drąsõs	'take a drink for courage'
ateĩti dėl mergẽlės	'come to see (lit. 'because of') the fair girl'

(3) concession:

Dėl tókio lietaũs galì eĩti be skė̃čio	'With this rain, you can go out without an umbrella.'
Dėl manę̃s galì ir pasikárti.	'As far as I am concerned, you can go hang yourself.'

(4) content, with verbs of speech and mental processes:

tartis dėl paliáubų	'negotiate a truce'
suabejóti dėl tų̃ žõdžių	'doubt the statement'
susirū́pinti dėl sveikãtos	'get worried about (one's) health'

8.12 The synonymous prepositions *ikì* and *lìg(i)* 'as far as, until' specify:

(1) the final limit of movement, or extent of a thing in space:

nueĩti ikì / lìgi mìško	'go as far as the woods'
pakìlti ikì debesų̃	'rise up to the clouds'
(mìškas) tę̃siasi ikì jū́ros	'(the forest) stretches as far as the sea'
ikì stotiẽs tolì	'it is far to the station'

(2) the temporal limit of an action:

dìrbti ikì naktiẽs	'work till/until night'
grį̃žti ikì šeštãdienio	'return before Saturday'

(3) the upper limit of quantity:

suskaičiúoti ikì dẽšimt	'count to ten'
susiriñko lig šim̃to žmonių̃	'as many as a hundred people gathered'

(4) the highest degree of a state or an action:

(geležìs) įkaĩto ikì baltùmo	'(the iron) got white hot' (lit. 'until whitness')
juõktis ikì ãšarų	'laugh to the point of tears'

8.13 The preposition *ìš* 'out of', 'from', 'for' has a very broad range of meanings; depending on the meaning of the complement, it may identify:

(1) the initial point of movement:

(a) from inside a place or a thing:

išeĩti iš kam̃bario	'go out of the room'
išim̃ti iš spìntos	'take (sth) out of a cupboard'

(b) from a place, which can be denoted metonymically by a human noun:

grį̃žti iš miẽsto / iš seser̃s	'return from the town/from one's sister'
parsinèšti páltą iš siuvė́jo	'fetch the coat from the tailor'

(c) from the place of activity, the complement denoting an action or process:

grį̃žti iš kãro	'return from a war'
pareĩti iš medžiõklės	'come back from hunting'

(2) the initial state, with verbs denoting a change of state:

pabùsti iš miẽgo	'awake from sleep'
atsipéikėti iš ìšgąsčio	'recover from fright'
išeĩti iš pusiáusvyros	'lose (lit. 'go out of') composure'

(3) material or ingredients of the whole:

Pastãtė nãmą iš plýtų.	'(He) built a house from bricks.'
Kalbà susìdeda iš žõdžių.	'A language is composed of words.'

(4) a thing which changes into something else:

Iš nãmo lìko pelenaĩ.	'Ashes was all that remained of the house.'
Iš erẽlio pavir̃to žmogùs.	'An eagle turned into a man.' (lit. 'A man became out of a eagle.')

(5) the source, especially of information:

sužinóti iš laĩkraščių	'learn from newspapers'
pažìnti iš eĩsenos	'recognize by (lit. 'from') the gait'
supràsti iš akių̃	'understand from the eyes'
pir̃kti iš kaimýno	'buy from a neighbour'

(6) origin with respect to place, social class or family:

Jìs (kìlęs) iš Kaũno / iš valstiẽčių / iš Radvilų̃.	'He is (comes) from Kaunas/from peasants/from the Radvila family.'

(7) a class or a whole from which a part or component is distinguished:

išsiskìrti iš visų̃	'stand out among all'
víenas iš mokinių̃	'one of the students'
jauniáusia iš seserų̃	'the youngest of the sisters'

(8) the object of verbs denoting manifestation of negative emotions:

týčiotis/juõktis iš žmonių	'jeer/laugh at people'

(9) the cause of negative emotions, states, etc.:

pabálti iš pykčio	grow pale with anger'
virpėti iš báimės	'shake with fear'
mir̃ti iš (nuo) bãdo	'die of hunger'

(10) the initial time limit of an action (with temporal nouns):

skaudėti iš (nuo) rýto	'ache since morning'
sir̃gti iš (nuo) pavãsario	'be ill since spring'

(11) the manner of action (in set phrases):

supràsti iš kar̃to	'understand at once'
padėti iš širdiẽs	'help sincerely' (lit. 'from heart')
iš petiẽs	'with all one's might'
iš esmẽs	'in essence'

8.14 The preposition nuõ 'from, off' specifies:

(1) negative direction, viz.

(a) from the initial point downward or upward:

nukrìsti nuo stãlo	'fall from the table'
nusiléisti nuo kálno	'descend from the hill'
pakélti nuo žẽmės	'pick up from the ground'

(b) away from the initial point:

ateĩti nuo mìško	'come from the direction of the woods'
atsitráukti nuo síenos	'pull away from the wall' (antonymous with liñk 'towards', see 8.16, 2)

(c) an entity from which a part is taken or another entity detached (with verbs of respective lexical meanings):

atrìšti žìrgą nuo tvorõs	'untie a horse from the fence'
nusivalýti sniẽgą nuo bãtų	'brush snow from (one's) shoes'

(2) relative static position:

Mẽdis (áuga) netolì nuo nãmo.	'The tree (grows) not far from the house.'

(3) limits of space or distance:

eĩti nuo miẽsto iki ẽžero	'go from the town to the lake'

(4) the initial time limit of an action (with temporal nouns):

lýti nuo rýto	'rain since morning'

(5) cause, either external or internal (with verbs of physical and psychological states):

susvyrúoti nuo smū̃gio	'stagger from (under) the blow'
užsnū́sti nuo (iš) núovargio	'fall asleep from fatigue'
	(iš is more common in the latter case)

(6) the person(s) as the initiator(s) in collocations like:

Pérduok linkė́jimų nuo manę̃s.	'Give my best regards to ...' (lit. 'from me')
Pasiuntinỹs atvỹko nuo karãliaus.	'The envoy has arrived from the king.'

(7) purpose, when modifying a noun:

váistai nuo grìpo	'medicine against the flu'
pastógė nuo lietaũs	'shelter from rain'

8.15 The preposition priẽ 'at, by, to' specifies mostly spatial relations:

(1) position next to a place or a thing:

stovė́ti prie var̃tų	'stand at the gate'
gyvénti prie ùpės	'live by the river'

(2) final point of movement (with or without coming into contact):

nueĩti prie ẽžero	'go to the lake'
prisiglaũsti prie síenos	'press to the wall'
sė́sti prie stãlo	'sit down at the table'

(3) the person(s) in whose presence the action takes place:

kalbė́ti prie vaikų̃	'speak in children's presence'

(4) relation of subordination to an institution:

komìsija prie universitèto	'a committee at (attached to, subordinated to) the university'

8.16 The secondary prepositions, including adverbial prepositions, explicate a variety of spatial relations. They identify:

(1) relative place or position (artì 'near to', gretà 'next to', šalià 'next to, on the side of', netolì 'not far from', pirmà 'in front of', vidurỹ 'in the middle of', vir̃š 'above', žemiaũ 'under, below', tar̃p 'between, among', abìpus 'on both sides of', abìšal 'on both sides of', anàpus/kìtapus 'on the other side of') cf.:

bė́gti pirmà vežìmo	'run in front of the cart'
skraidýti vir̃š miẽsto	'fly above the town'
sėdė́ti šalià / gretà tė́vo	'sit next to (one's) father'
áugti tarp mẽdžių	'grow among the trees'

(2) direction, the final point of movement (artì 'next to', also arčiaũ 'near to', artỹn 'nearer to', liñk(ui) 'towards', tar̃p 'between, among', vidurỹ 'in the middle of'), cf.:

prieĩti artì nãmo	'come up to the house'
diñgti tarp mẽdžių	'disappear among trees'
eĩti namų̃ liñk	'go towards home'

(3) route, i.e. direction of movement with reference to the path (išilgaĩ 'along', skersaĩ 'across', įstrižaĩ 'slantwise', kiauraĩ 'through' (with these prepositions, the genitive is interchangeable with the accusative), cf.:

nubė́gti skersaĩ kẽlio / kẽlią	'run across the road'

8.17 Few of the secondary (including adverbial) prepositions express other than spatial relations. The following prepositions are used to identify:

(1) temporal relations:

(a) *pirmà* expresses precedence in time:

atė́jo pirmà mū́sų / pùsryčių	'(he) came before us / breakfast'

(b) *tar̃p* indicates temporal limits:

atė́jo tarp pirmõs ir antrõs valandõs	'(he) came between one and two o'clock'

(c) *vidur̃(ỹ)*, and rarely *vidùj* express the middle of a period of time:

vidur̃ / vidurỹ / vidùj naktiẽs	'in the middle of the night'

(d) *artì* indicates approximate time:

bùvo artì vidùrnakčio	'it was close to midnight'

(2) *artì* is also used to specify the approximate time or quantity:

artì kilogrãmo / kilomètro	'near to (almost) a kilogram / a kilometre'

tar̃p is used to indicate the limits of quantity:

kainúoja tar̃p penkių̃ ir dešimtiẽs lìtų	'it costs between five and ten litas'

(3) *dėkà* 'due to, thanks to', which has no locative meaning, denotes (positive) cause:

jõ dárbo dėkà	'thanks to his work'
daũg pasíekti gabùmų dėkà	'achieve much due to talents'

(4) *viẽtoj* 'in place of' specifies the relations of substitution:

gérti píeną viẽtoj vandeñs	'drink milk instead of water'
viẽtoj tė́vo atė́jo sūnùs	'instead of the father, the son came'

(5) *šalià* 'along with, next to' is used figuratively to express oppositeness:

šalià pilnų̃ fòrmų vartójamos ir sutrum̃pintos	'along with full forms, abbreviated forms are also used'

8.18 The complex preposition *iš põ* 'from under' can specify spatial and temporal relations:

iš po stãlo	'from under the table'
iš po žiemõs	'after (lit. 'from under') winter'

The prepositions *iš ùž* 'from behind', *į̃ anàpus* 'to the other side', *iš anàpus* 'from the other side' and others specify spatial relations exclusively:

iš už mìško	'from behind the forest'
iš anàpus ùpės	'from the other side of the river'

Prepositions with the accusative case

8.19 The prepositions that require the accusative case of the complement are:

apiẽ/apliñk(ui) 'about, around'	*pãskui/pãskum* 'after, behind'
į̃ 'to, in, into'	*peř* 'through, over, in, by'
pagaĩ 'by, according to, along'	*priẽš* 'against, before'
paleĩ 'by, near, along'	*prõ* 'through, by'
pàs 'by, to, with'	

Most of these prepositions are polysemous.

8.20 The prepositions *apiẽ* 'about, around' and *apliñk* 'around' are synonymous as regards their spatial meanings, and the latter, being a secondary preposition, has no other meanings. They are used to specify:

(1) the place of an action or position round an object:

stovė́ti apiẽ/apliñk láužą	'stand round the fire'
triū̃sti apiẽ namùs	'work about the house'

(2) the route of movement (after verbs of motion):

(api)bė́gti apiẽ/apliñk nãmą	'run round the house'

(3) approximate time (with temporal nouns):

apiẽ vidùrdienį	'at about midday'
apiẽ peñktą vãlandą	'at about five o'clock'

(4) approximate quantity:

sverti (svérti) / nupir̃kti apiẽ dù kilogramùs	'weigh/buy about two kilograms'

(5) content (after verbs of speech and mental processes):

kalbė́ti apiẽ kelionès	'speak about travels'
pãsakoti apiẽ keliõnę	'tell about the trip'
(but pãsakoti naujíenas, įspū́džius	'tell the news, impressions')
galvóti apiẽ vaikùs	'think about (the) children'

8.21 The preposition į̃ 'in, to, into' denotes:

(1) direction of movement into, inside a place:

eĩti į̃ miẽstą	'go to the town'
padė́ti į̃ stálčių	'put into the drawer'
įeĩti į̃ kam̃barį	'come into the room'

The meaning 'inside' is neutralised after verbs of other semantic types:

pasùkti į̃ dẽšinę	'turn to the right'
atsirem̃ti į̃ mẽdį	'lean against a tree'
bélstis į̃ durìs	'knock at the door'

(2) when used metaphorically, destination of movement (with nouns denoting activities, events):

išvỹkti į̃ kãrą	'go to war'
nueĩti į̃ susirinkìmą, į̃ šokiùs, į̃ pãskaitą	'go to a meeting, to dance, to a lecture'

(3) the target of an action (with certain verbs):

žiūrė́ti į̃ sáulę	'look at the sun'
táikytis į̃ žmõgų	'aim at a man'

(4) the result of process (after verbs of change):

Žmõnės pavir̃to į̃ ãkmenis.	'People turned into stones.'
Sūnùs išáugo į̃ výrą.	'The son has grown into a man.'
Stiklìnė sudùžo į̃ šukès.	'The glass broke into pieces.'

(5) the approximate time of action:

Atė́jo į̃ vãkarą.	'He came when it was almost evening.'

(6) the standard of comparison:

Sūnùs panašùs į̃ tė́vą	'The son resembles the father.'

8.22 The prepositions *pagal̃* 'according to; by, along' and *palei̇̃* 'along, by, near' are synonymous in their spatial meanings; the former preposition has a broader range of meanings than the latter. They specify:

(1) the route of movement along and outside object:

eĩti pagal̃ ùpę	'walk along the river'

(2) location next to an object (usually long, or of large dimensions):

gulė́ti pagal̃/palei̇̃ tvõrą	'lie under (along) the fence'
gyvénti palei̇̃ ẽžerą	'live next to/by the lake'

(3) the standard or basis of action:

veĩkti pagal̃ plā́ną	'act according to plan'
reñgtis pagal̃ mã́dą	'dress in accordance with fashion'

(4) the criterion of comparison:

áukštas pagal̃ ámžių	'tall for (his) age'

(5) the source of information (in parenthetical phrases):

Pagal̃ laĩkraščius, teñ šáudoma.	'According to newspapers, shooting goes on there.'

8.23 The preposition *pàs* 'by, at; with' has spatial meanings only; it identifies:

(1) location referred to by a human (or animate) noun:

gyvénti pas tė́vùs	'live with one's parents (at their place)'
pas mùs gražù	'it's beautiful at our place' (lit. 'with us')

(2) the final point of movement also referred to by a human (or generally animate) noun:

sueĩti pas draũgą	'go together to a friend'
nuvèsti pas dãktarą	'take (sb) to a doctor'

(3) with inanimate nouns it is used as a synonym of *priẽ* in colloquial speech:

stovė́ti pas lángą/prie lángo	'stand at/by the window'
nueĩti pas ùpę/prie ùpės	'go to the river'

8.24 The preposition *pãskui/pãskum* 'after, behind' differs from all the others (except its antonym *pirmà* 'in front of') in that it denotes a spatial relation between two moving objects:

jìs bė́go pāskui/pāskum manè	'he was running behind me'
Cf. *pirmà manę̃s*	'in front of me'
šalià manę̃s	'at my side, next to me'

8.25 The preposition *peř* 'through, across; in, within' specifies a variety of spatial and other relations:

(1) passage through, within, across, over an object or space:

eĩti per mìšką	'go through the forest'
išeĩti per durìs	'go out through the door'
žeñgti per sleñkstį	'step across the threshold'
šókti per tvõrą	'jump over the fence'
važiúoti į Lòndoną per Parỹžių	'go to London via Paris'

the path of movement from one place to another, covering many:

eĩti per kráutuves	'go shopping' (lit. 'through shops')

(2) the target (usually a body part) at which a blow is aimed:

mùšti per gálvą	'beat on the head'

a part (a body part, as a rule) of the whole to which an action or state is related:

bãtai siaurì per pirštùs	'the shoes are narrow at the toes'
lū́žo rankà per ríešą	'the hand broke at the wrist'

(3) the distance relative to an object:

stovė́ti per žiñgsnį nuo dùrų	'stand a step away from the door'

(4) period of time during which an action takes place, or duration of an action:

ateĩti per pietùs	'come during dinner'
per (vìsą) diẽną	'all day long'
padarýti per dvì dienàs	'do (sth) in (within) two days'

(5) the cause of a (negative) event:

nukentė́ti per draugùs	'suffer because of (through the fault of) friends'
cf. *nukentė́ti nuo draugų̃*	'suffer from friends'

(6) the mediator or means:

kalbė́ti per vertė́ją	'speak through an interpretor'
pranèšti per spaũdą	'announce through the press'

(7) exceeding the quantity:

sumokė́ti per dù šimtùs	'pay more than (over) two hundred'
jái per trìsdešimt	'she is over thirty (years old)'

8.26 The preposition *priẽš/príešais* 'against, in front of, before' identifies:

(**1**) position relative to an object (facing it):

Gyvenù prieš parduotùvę.	'I live opposite a shop.'
Kėdė̃ stóvi prieš stãlą.	'A chair is before (in front of) the table.'

(**2**) the opposite direction of motion:

Plaukiaũ prieš sróvę.	'I swam against the current.'
Vaikaĩ bė́ga príešais mótiną.	'The children are running to meet (their) mother.'

(**3**) position in front of a moving object (*pirmà* is more frequent in this case, see 8.16, 1):

Prieš vežìmą bė́go šuõ.	'In front of the cart a dog ran.'

(**4**) precedence in time, viz.:

(**a**) the period of time before which an action takes place:

ateĩti prieš rýtą	'come before morning'
susitìkti prieš kãrą	'meet before the war'

(**b**) the period of time that separates the action from the moment of utterance:

Grįžaũ prieš mė́nesį.	'I returned a month ago.'

(**5**) opposition to the person:

(**a**) at whom hostile action is directed:

kovóti prieš engė́jus	'fight against oppressors'
šiáuštis prieš tė́vą	'stand against (one's) father'

(**b**) with respect to whom a psychological state or its manifestation takes place:

žẽmintis prieš viršininką	'abase oneself with one's superior'
raudonúoti prieš žmónes	'blush in the presence of people'

(**6**) the standard of comparison:

Sūnùs prieš tė́vą negražùs.	'The son is not handsome in comparison (lit. 'against') with father.'

8.27 The preposition *prõ* 'past, through' is used to denote spatial relations:

(**1**) the route of movement past an object or place:

važiúoti pro mìšką	'ride past a forest'
jìs praė́jo pro manè	'he passed by me'

(**2**) the route of movement through an object, obstruction:

išeĩti pro durìs	'go out through the door'
bráutis pro mìnią	'force one's way through a crowd'
šviẽsti pro rū̃ką	'shine through fog'
žiūrė́ti pro žiūronùs	'look through binoculars'

Prepositions with the instrumental case

8.28 The prepositions *sù* 'with', *sulìg* 'up to' and *tiẽs* 'by, at, against, opposite, over' are used with the instrumental case exclusively. The most frequent and polysemous of them is *sù* which has no spatial meanings.

8.29 The preposition *sù* 'with' renders a broad variety of comitative and sociative and other relations. It may identify:

(1) the object of verbs denoting reciprocal actions:

giñčytis / draugáuti su mókytoju	'argue/be friends with the teacher'
kovóti su príešu	'struggle with the enemy'

(2) the accompanying person(s) or thing(s), cf. respectively:

(a) *Tė́vas su vaikaĩs bùvo namiẽ.*	'The father and children (lit. 'father with children') were at home.'
pakviẽsti tė́vą su vaikaĩs	'invite the father and his children'
gyvénti su tėvaĩs	'live with one's parents'
(b) *žmogùs (atė́jo) su kirviù*	'the man (came) with an ax'
válgyti dúoną su svíestu	'eat bread with (= and) butter'

(3) an ingredient, or a feature, or the content of a whole:

nãmas su balkonù	'a house with a balcony'
žmogùs su charãkteriu	'a man with (= of) character'
maĩšas su mìltais (= mìltų: GEN)	'a bag with (= of) flour'

(4) the time of action (simultaneity with an event, usually a natural phenomenon):

kéltis su sáule	'rise with the sun (= at dawn)'
grį̃žti su šviesà	'return with light (= while it is light yet)'

(5) the standard of comparison after expressions of similarity and identity:

tapatùs su kuõ nórs	'identical with sb/sth'

(6) the state of the subject during an action:

kalbė́ti su užsidegimù	'speak with enthusiasm'
láukti su nekantrumù	'wait with impatience'
klausýtis/kalbė́ti su šỹpsena	'listen/speak with a smile'

(7) the instrument:

rašýti su pieštukù	'write with a pencil'

(synonymous with the instrumental case without a preposition: rašýti pieštukù)

8.30   The secondary preposition sulìg 'up to' (= 'equally') indicates:

(1) the spatial limits of an action on the vertical axis:

vanduõ pakìlo sulìg tìltu	'water rose up to the bridge'
nusileñkti sulìg žẽmè	'bow down to the ground'

(2) the standard of comparison in expressions of equivalence:

mẽdis sulìg namù	'a tree as tall as the house'
sulìg tė́vu storùmo	'as fat as (his) father'

(3) simultaneity with another event or time:

atsikélti sulìg sáulės tekė́jimu	'get up at (= at the same time as) sunrise'

8.31   The secondary preposition tiẽs specifies position relative to an object:

sustóti ties var̃tais	'stop at the gate'
áugti ties takeliù	'grow by the path'

It is also synonymous with vir̃š 'over, above':

lémpa kãbo ties stalù	'a lamp hangs over the table'

Prepositions with two and more case forms

8.32   The preposition ùž 'behind, over, outside; later; by, for, etc.', takes either an accusative or a genitive complement. When used with the **genitive** case, it indicates:

(1) position behind or outside the reference point:

bū́ti/áugti už nãmo	'be/grow behind the house'
gyvénti už miẽsto	'live out of town'
sė́sti(s) už stãlo	'sit down at the table'

(2) distance relative to a place:

gyvénti/nuvèžti už dviejų kilomètrų nuo namų	'live/take (sb) two kilometers away from home'

(3) the time period after which an action took or will take place:

atėjo/ateĩs už valandõs	'(he) came/will come in an hour'

(*põ* + GEN is more common in this sense, see 8.33, 1b)

(4) part of a whole of which hold is taken:

vèsti/paim̃ti už rañkos	'lead/take by the hand'
laikýtis už turėklo	'hold onto the rail'

When used with the **accusative** case, *ùž* identifies:

(5) the goal or beneficiary:

kovóti už tėvýnę/láisvę	'struggle/fight for the homeland/ freedom'
balsúoti už prezideñtą	'vote for the president'

(6) the motive of actions like paying, rewarding, punishing, etc.:

apdovanóti/mokėti/baũsti už ką nórs	'award/pay/punish for sth'

(7) the sum of money for which a thing is sold or bought:

pir̃kti/pardúoti už dēšimt dólerių	'buy/sell for ten dollars'

(8) the motive or stimulus of an emotion or its manifestation:

mylėti/gìrti/nekęsti/bárti už ką nórs	'love/praise/hate/scold for sth'

(9) (interchangeably with *viẽtoj* 'instead of') the person instead of whom an action is performed:

dìrbti už kolègą	'stand in for a colleague'
pasirašýti už sū́nų	'sign in one's son's name'

(10) the status (social, professional, etc.) or function of the subject (in colloquial speech):

dìrbti už sekretõrių	'work as a secretary'

(11) the standard of comparison, with the comparative (rarely superlative) degree of adjectives and adverbs:

sunkèsnis už ãkmenį	'heavier than stone'

8.33 The preposition *põ* 'about, around, after' is used with all the three cases. When used with the **genitive** case, it specifies:

(1) temporal sequence, viz.:

(a) the period of time which precedes an action:

Po naktiẽs pàteka sáulė.	'The sun rises after the night.'
Grįžaũ po pamokų̃.	'I returned after the classes.'

(b) the period of time separating an action from the preceding point of reference:

Grįžaũ po valandõs.	'I returned in an hour.'
cf. also *dẽšimt (minùčių) po šešių̃*	'ten (minutes) past six'

It is also used in sequences like *dienà po dienõs* 'day after day'

(2) (in colloquial speech) the object which is destroyed or disappears as a result of the action, as in the pattern:

Ištekėjai, ir po gražùmo.	'You marry, and your beauty is gone' (lit. 'and after beauty').

When used with the **accusative** case, *põ* identifies:

(3) the place within the limits of which an iterative action takes place:

váikščioti po kam̃barį/laukùs	'walk about the room (pace the room)/in the fields'
ieškóti po kišenès	'search in all the pockets'
keliáuti po krãštą	'travel all over the country'

(4) the route of movement from one place to another or a pervasive movement, with the complement in the plural number:

váikščioti po parduotuvès	'go shopping (visit many shops)'
váikščioti po susirinkimùs/draugùs	'attend meetings/visit friends'

(5) the places over which an action or state of a thing is distributed (pervasive static meaning):

Màno gìminės gyvẽna po vìsą pasáulį.	'My relatives live all over the world.'

(6) distributive quantity:

dúoti vaikáms po dù óbuolius	'give children two apples apiece'
váikščioti po dù	'walk in pairs (= in twos)'

When used with the **instrumental** case, *põ* indicates:

(7) relative position or place of an action under a thing or in proximity to the lower part of it (spatial proximity):

gulěti / palį̃sti po stalù   'lie/creep under the table'
sėdėti po lángu   'sit at the window'
áugti po kálnu   'grow at the bottom of the hill'

9 CONJUNCTIONS
Jungtùkai

9.1 Conjunctions are a class of invariable words which serve to connect notional words, word groups and/or clauses collectively termed conjuncts, cf.:

Jìs gražùs, bet mãžas.	'He is handsome but small.'
Àš žinaũ, kad jìs čià.	'I know that he is here.'

Conjunctions differ from prepositions in that they do not determine the grammatical form of nouns, cf.: *mótin-a ir vaik-aĩ* 'mother (NOM) and children (NOM)' and *mótin-a su vaik-aĩs* lit. 'mother (NOM) with (the) children (INSTR)'.

9.2 With regard to form, conjunctions are divided into **simple** (one-word) and **complex** (of more than one words) conjunctions.

Most of the **simple conjunctions** are monosyllabic words, e.g.:

õ 'and, but'	*nès* 'as'
iř 'and'	*kàd* 'that'
ař 'or'	*jóg* 'that'
bèt 'but'	*nórs* 'though'

A number of simple conjunctions consist of two or more syllables. Some of them are descended from two- (or more) word clusters, e.g. *bètgi* 'but' (*bèt + gì*), *užtàt/užtaĩ* 'therefore' (*ùž + tàt/ùž + taĩ*); but in Standard Lithuanian most of them are unanalysable into segments. Here belong:

arbà 'for'	*benè* 'perhaps'
jéigu 'if'	*õgi* 'but'
negù 'than'	*taĩgi* 'so'
nekaĩp 'than'	*kadángi* 'because'
nebeñt 'unless'	*tiktaĩ* 'only'

A few conjunctions have retained their derivative relations with other words and word forms, thus *taŕtum / tarýtum / taŕsi* 'as if' are descended from tense and mood forms of the verb *taŕti* 'say', *nelýginant* 'like' is originally a gerund of *(ne)-lýginti* '(not) compare'.

Simple conjunctions either function as conjunctions exclusively (e.g. *jóg* 'that', *nès* 'as', *kadángi* 'because', *beĩ* 'and', *tačiaũ* 'but, though'), or they double as particles (*ař* 'or', *neĩ* 'than', *tařsi / tařtum / tarýtum* 'as if', *tegùl* '(even) though', *tìk* 'but', *võs, võs tik* 'hardly [ever]'; *bèt* 'but', *iř* 'and', *kàd* 'that', *lýg* 'as if', *nórs* 'though'), adverbs (*kadà* 'when', *kõl* 'while', *kaĩp* 'how', *kuř* 'where'), or prepositions (*ikì* 'until', *lìgi* 'until, till'), or interjections (*õ* 'but').

Complex conjunctions are composed of two or more words at least one of which is a simple conjunction. They may be comprised of:

(1) two semantically contiguous conjunctions:

õ tačiaũ 'but however'	*lìgi kõl(ei)* 'until, till'
õ bètgi 'but however'	*lýg kaĩp* 'as if'
õ vìs dėltõ 'but still'	*lýg tařtum* 'as if'
ikì kõl(ei) 'until'	*nelýginant kaĩp* 'like, as if'

(2) a (subordinating) conjunction or adverb and the particle *tìk* 'only':

kaĩ tìk 'as soon as'	*lìg tìk* 'as soon as'
võs tìk 'as soon as'	*kõl tìk* 'while'
jéi tìk 'if only'	*kadà tìk* 'just when'

(3) a (comparative) conjunction and the particle *kàd*:

kaĩp kàd 'as, like'	*negù kàd* 'than'
lýg kàd 'as, if'	*nebeñt kàd* 'unless'

(4) a conjunction such as *kàd* 'that' or *nórs* 'though', etc., and the particle *iř*:

kàd iř 'though'	*nórs iř* 'though'
tegùl iř 'though'	*kaĩp iř* 'as if, like'

If a particle retains its intensifying force, the conjunction is regarded as a simple one, i.e. the particle does not become a part of the latter; e.g.:

Malonù aplankýti svētimas	'It is a pleasure to visit foreign
šalìs, bèt ir teñ galvóji apiē	countries, but even there one
namùs.	keeps thinking about home.'

9.3 According to the number of positions they occupy in a sentence, conjunctions are divided into one-place (single) and two-place (multiple-place) units.

One-place (single) conjunctions (simple and complex) are positioned either between conjuncts (e.g. *brólis ir sesuõ* 'brother and sister'; *Ateĩsiu, jéigu nelìs* 'I'll come if it does not rain') or they precede the first one (e.g. *Jéigu nelìs, ateĩsiu* 'If it doesn't rain I'll come').

Multi-place conjunctions consist of two, rarely more elements each introducing a conjunct, e.g.: *Kuõ giliaũ į mìšką, tuõ daugiaũ mẽdžių* 'The deeper into the forest, the more trees.' They are subdivided into paired and reduplicated conjunctions.

Paired conjunctions consist of two formally different elements each introducing a conjunct. Two types of paired conjunctions are distinguished:

(1) the first part corresponds to a concessive (subordinating) conjunction, and the second to an adversative (coordinating) conjunction; here belong:

kad iř ... bèt	'however ... but'
kad iř ... õ/tačiaũ	'though ... but'
nórs (iř) ... bèt/õ/tačiaũ	'though ... but'
tegù ... bèt	'even if ... but'; e.g.:

Nors/Kad ir labaĩ sténgėmės, bet niẽko negalėjom padarýti.	'However hard we tried (but) we couldn't do anything.'
Nors naktìs bùvo tamsì ir šaltà, tačiaũ vaikaĩ laimìngai pasíekė namùs.	'Though the night was dark and cold, (but) the children reached home safely.'

(2) the first part corresponds to a coordinating conjunction (or another type of conjunctive word), and the second to the particle *taĩ*, sometimes *taĩp*; here belong: *kaĩ ... taĩ/taĩp* 'if/when ... then', *kadà ... taĩ* 'when ... then', *kõl ... taĩ* 'while ... then', *ikì ... taĩ* 'until ... then', *kadángi ... taĩ/tàd* 'because ... then', *jéi(gu) ... taĩ* 'if ... then', *kàd (iř) ... taĩ* 'even if ... then', *tegùl (ir) ... taĩ* 'even if ... then'; e.g.:

Kai àš kur nórs iškeliáuju, tai vaikaĩ galvõm eĩna.	'As soon as I go away, the children start romping.'
Kadángi labaĩ káršta bùvo, tai dùrys bùvo ikì gãlo atìdaros.	'As it was very hot, the door was wide open.'
Jei beñt kíek pavėlúosi, tai tikraĩ niẽko namiẽ neràsi.	'If you are even a little late, you are sure to find no one at home.'

There is a special group of conjunctions *kuõ ... tuõ* 'the ... the', *juõ ... tuõ, juõ ... juõ* with the same meaning, comprised of components which are never used as simple conjunctions; cf.:

Kuõ/Juõ daugiaũ skaitýsi, tuõ daugiaũ sužinósi.	'The more you will read the more you will learn.'

Reduplicated conjunctions are comprised of identical elements which can be repeated any number of times. The component elements are either simple conjunctions or they are identical with adverbs, cf. respectively:

iř ... iř 'both ... and', *ař ... ař* 'whether ... or', *arbà ... arbà* 'either ... or', *neĩ ... neĩ* 'neither ... nor', *taĩ ... taĩ* 'now ... now'; and *čià ... čià* 'now ... now', *tíek ... tíek* 'both ... and'.

9.4 With regard to the type of relations they express, coordinating and subordinating conjunctions are distinguished.

Coordinating conjunctions (coordinators) serve to connect units, (either words or clauses) of equal syntactic status.

Subordinating conjunctions (subordinators) serve to express the relation of subordination between clauses (rarely words).

The conjunction *ar̃* is polyfunctional: it is used to denote both coordination and subordination, cf. respectively:

Jìs bùvo jõs gimináitis ar nèt brólis.	'He was her relative or even brother.'
Pažiūrėk, ar jìs čià.	'See if he is here.'

COORDINATING CONJUNCTIONS

9.5 The coordinators *beĩ* 'and' and *neĩ* 'nor' are used to connect words and word groups exclusively, whereas *taĩ* 'so', *taĩgi* 'so', *tàd* 'so, thus', *vìs dėltõ* 'still, however', *vis tíek* 'all the same, nevertheless' are used to connect clauses. The other conjunctions can join both words within a clause and clauses within a composite sentence. With regard to meaning, coordinators are subcategorized into the following types:

(1) **Copulative (cumulative)** conjunctions: *ir̃* 'and', *ir̃* ... *ir̃* 'both ... and', *beĩ* 'and', *čià* ... *čià* 'now ... now', *neĩ* 'nor', *neĩ* ... *neĩ* 'neither ... nor', *taĩ* ... *taĩ* 'now ... now', *tíek* ... *tíek* 'both ... and'; they have additive force, e.g.:

Sodè sir̃po obuoliaĩ ir vỹšnios.	'In the garden apples and cherries were ripening.'
Rùdenį daũg dárbo ir namiẽ, ir laukuosè.	'In autumn there is much work both at home and in the fields.'
Láužas taĩ/čià suliepsnódavo, taĩ/čià vėl gèsdavo.	'Now the bonfire flared up up now it died out.'
Mergáitė neturėjo tėvo neĩ mótinos.	lit. 'The girl had neither father nor mother.'
Jìs táu neĩ patãrs, neĩ padė̃s.	'He will neither give you advice nor help you.'

The conjunction *beĩ* coordinates words and word groups that are very close in meaning. This coordinated group may in its turn be linked to a word group by the conjunction *ir̃*:

Pavãsaris beĩ vãsara iř ruduõ	'Spring and summer, and autumn
beĩ žiemà skìria metùs į šviẽsųjį	and winter constitute the light
iř tam̃sųjį mẽtą.	and the dark periods of the year.'

(2) **Adversative** conjunctions: *bèt(gi)* 'but', *õ(gi)* 'but', *tačiaũ* 'but, while, whereas', *tìk(taĩ)* 'only, but', *vìs dėltõ* 'still, however', *vìs tìk* 'still', *(bet) užtàt* 'but, but then', *o bètgi* 'and nevertheless', *o tačiaũ* 'but, whereas', *o vìs dėltõ* 'and still', *bet vìs dėltõ* 'but still'; they express contrast between conjuncts; e.g.:

Mókslo šãknys kárčios, bèt jõ	'The roots of learning are bitter,
vaĩsiai sáldūs.	but its fruit is sweet.'
Sẽserys lìko namiẽ, õ brólis	'The sisters stayed at home, and the brother
išẽjo apsižvalgýti.	went out to have a look around.'
Šaũkė jì ilgaĩ, (õ) tačiaũ niẽkas	'She shouted for a long time but
neatsìliepė.	no one answered.'
Visì dìrbo lìgi vãkaro, tìk	lit. 'Everybody worked until evening
Pẽtras vaikštinėjo švìlpaudamas.	only Peter loitered about whistling.'
Ẽsame dabař neturtìngi, (bèt)	'We are poor now, but (we are)
užtàt laisvì.	free.'
Netikėjau jõ pagyromìs, (õ) vìs	'I didn't believe his praise, but
dėltõ klausýtis bùvo malonù.	all the same it was pleasant to listen.'

(3) **Disjunctive (alternative)** conjunctions: *ař* 'or', *ař ... ař* 'either ... or', *arbà* 'or', *arbà ... arbà* 'either ... or'; they offer a choice between conjuncts; e.g.:

Šiañdien ař rytój grį̃ši?	'Will you return today or tomorrow?'
Ař tù šaũksi, ar nešaũksi, niẽkas	'Whether you shout or not
čià neišgiřs.	(shout), – nobody will hear you here.'
Dabař reikėjo (arbà) nugalėti	'Now we had (either) to win or to die.'
arbà miřti.	

(4) **Consecutive (inferential)** conjunctions: *taĩ/taĩgi* 'so, thus, therefore', *tàd* 'so, therefore', they denote consequence or result; e.g.:

Mergáitė pasijùto blogaĩ, tàd	'The girl felt unwell, therefore
(taĩ/taĩgi) paprãšė brólį váistų	she asked her brother to give her
padúoti.	some medicine.'

A number of adverbs, e.g. *todėl* 'therefore', *per taĩ* 'for that', are also used to express consecutive relations. The explanatory relation can be expressed by words like *bū́tent* 'namely', *dėstis* 'depending on', *nelýgu* 'unlike', *taĩ yrà* 'that is', *kaĩp antaĩ* 'for example', which function very much like conjunctions.

To cover both conjunctions proper and words of other classes (some adverbs, pronouns and particles), that have a connective function, the term **conjunctives** is used.

SUBORDINATING CONJUNCTIONS

9.6 These conjunctions introduce a subordinate constituent (typically a clause) by connecting it with the principal constituent. A subordinate clause is dependent either on the main clause or on a word or word group in the latter.

9.7 Subordinating conjunctions are subcategorized into semantically loaded and asemantic conjunctions. The latter indicate syntactic subordination of a conjunct without explicating the semantic relationship which is dependent upon the structural properties of a sentence. Here belong the subordinators *kàd* 'that' and *jóg* 'that'. They subordinate completive and correlative clauses; on the other hand, the conjunction *kàd* is also used to express the semantic relations of cause, concession, condition, and purpose. The other conjunctions express both syntactic and semantic relations between conjuncts. Subordinators may be categorized into the following semantic types:

(1) **temporal** subordinators: *kaĩ* 'while, as', *kadà* 'when', *ikì/lìg(i)* 'until', *kõl* 'while, till', *võs* 'as soon as', *tìk* 'as soon as', *kadà tìk* 'just when', *kaĩ tìk* 'as soon as', *lìg(i) tìk* 'only until', *vós tìk* 'as soon as', *kõl tìk* 'only while/till', *ikì kõl(ei)* 'until', *kaĩ ... taĩ* 'when ... then', *kaĩ tìk ... taĩ iř* 'as soon as ... then', *kadà ... taĩ* 'when ... then', *kõl ... taĩ* 'while ... then', *ikì ... taĩ* 'until ... then'; e.g.:

Kaĩ sáulė tekėjo, mū́sų linaĩ žydėjo.	'When the sun rose our flax was blossoming.'
Pasilìk čià, kõl/ikì tavè pašaũksiu.	'Stay here until I call you.'
Võs (tìk) nuaidėjo pirmíeji šū̃viai, iš visų̃ pùsių subėgo daugýbė žmonių̃.	'As soon as the first shots sounded, many people came running from everywhere.'
Kaĩ tìk aš išvažiúoju, taĩ vìs kàs nórs atsitiñka.	'As soon as I leave, (then) something always happens.'

(2) subordinators of **cause**: *nès* 'as', *kadángi* 'because', *kadángi ... taĩ* 'as ... then', *kadángi ... tàd* 'as ... therefore'; e.g.:

Negalė́jau táu parašýti láiško, nès nežinójau ā́dreso.	'I couldn't write you a letter as I didn't know your address.'
Kadángi bùvo jaũ vėlùs vãkaras, (taĩ) reikė́jo kur nórs apsistóti pailsė́ti.	'As it was late night, we had to stop for a rest.'

(3) subordinators of **condition**: *jéi* 'if', *jéigu* 'if', *jéi(gu) ... taĩ (iȓ)* 'if ... then'; e.g.:

Jéigu ką̃ nùveikiau gẽra, pasakỹs kitì.	'If have done any good, others will say (about it).'
Jéi per daũg norė́si, taĩ niẽko neturė́si.	'If you want too much you will have nothing.'

(4) the subordinator of **purpose** *idañt* 'in order that'; it is rarely used in Standard Lithuanian; the asemantic conjunction *kàd* 'that' is more common in this function; e.g.:

Užė́jome į̃ šį̃ nãmą, idañt/kàd pamatýtume víeną įdomiáusių reginių̃.	We went into this house in order to see (lit. so that we could see) one of the most interesting sights.'

(5) subordinators of **concession**: *nórs (iȓ)* 'though', *kàd iȓ* 'even though', *tegùl (iȓ)* 'even if'; *nórs (iȓ) ... tačiaũ* 'though ... but', *nórs (iȓ) ... õ* 'though ... but', *nórs (iȓ) ... bèt (vìs dė́ltõ)/(vìs) dė́ltõ/vìs tìk* 'though ... but/all the same', *kàd iȓ ... tačiaũ/õ/ bèt (vìs dė́ltõ)/vìs dė́ltõ/taĩ* 'even if ... but/all the same', *tegùl (iȓ) ... bèt (vìs dė́ltõ)/ vìs (dė́ltõ)/taĩ* 'even if ... but/all the same'; e.g.:

Nórs (iȓ) labaĩ sténgėmės, (bèt) niẽko negalė́jome pamatýti.	'Though we tried hard, we couldn't see anything.'
Tegùl jìs iȓ blógas žmogùs, tačiaũ/vìs dė́ltõ víeną kaȓtą mán pagélbėjo.	'Even if he is a bad man (but)/ all the same he helped me once.'
Kàd iȓ áiškiai sakaĩ, nesuprantù.	'Though you speak clearly, I don't understand.

(6) subordinators of **comparison**; they are further divided into three subtypes:

(a) subordinators of similarity: *kaĩp* 'like', *lýg* 'as if', *taȓtum/tarýtum/taȓsi* 'as if, as though', *ìt* 'as if, like', *nelýginant* 'like'; *lýg taȓtum* 'as if/though', *lýg kaĩp* 'like', *lýg kàd* 'like, as if', *kaĩp kàd* 'like', *nelýginant kaĩp* 'like'; e.g.:

Čià gyvénsi kaĩp ponià.	'You will live here like a lady.'
Vìsas gyvẽnimas praė́jo lýg/taȓtum sunkùs sãpnas.	'All life has passed like a nightmare.'
Ramiaĩ sėdė́k, lyg kàd niẽko nebū́tum mãtęs.	'Stay quiet, as if you have not seen anything.'

(b) subordinators of proportion: *juõ ... juõ* and *juõ ... tuõ* 'the ... the', *kuõ ... tuõ* 'the ... the'; e.g.:

Juõ/Kuõ aukščiaũ kópsi, juõ/ tuõ daugiaũ pamatýsi.	'The higher you will climb the more you will see.'

(c) subordinators of difference: *negù* 'than', *nekaĩp* 'than', *neĩ* 'than' (rarely used), *kaĩp* 'than', *negù kàd* 'than'; e.g.:

Kálnas bùvo aukštèsnis, negù (kàd) iš pradžių̃ atródė.	'The mountain was higher than it had seemed at first.'
Jì visadà reñgėsi puošniaũ neĩ/nekaĩp kìtos.	'She was always better dressed than the others.'

10 INTERJECTIONS
Jaustùkai

10.1 Interjections are a class of invariable words which express emotions, reactions or commands without naming them. They do not enter into syntactic relations with any other words in a sentence.

Interjections have no referential meaning: they serve as verbal signals, often in conjunction with extralinguistic signs of communication such as gestures and facial expression, which also indicate the speaker's emotions, mood or will.

Interjections fall under two types, interjections proper (e.g. *àk* 'oh', *ói* 'ouch', *nà* 'well', *éi* 'hey') and vocative interjections used to call or drive away domestic animals (e.g. *kàt kàt* 'puss puss', *škàc* 'shoo').

Interjections proper are further subdivided into emotive and imperative interjections. Vocative interjections may also be regarded as a subclass of imperative interjections.

Emotive interjections express a broad range of the speaker's emotions, e.g. surprise, admiration, regret, pain, disgust, etc.; here belong *ã, àk, ẽ, éi, ài, ói, ojè, br̃r, èt* and a great many others.

Imperative interjections express the speaker's will, commands, encouragement or appeal to the listener, e.g. *éi* 'hey', *òpa!* 'hop', *šã (šà)* 'hush', *šš, tìč, tš(š), tss* 'sh-sh', *márš!* 'march!', etc. There are other exclamatory words which function very much like interjections, viz. formulaic words required by speech etiquette, such as *ãčiū* and *dẽkui* 'thanks', *sudiẽ* 'goodbye', *labãnakt* 'goodnight', etc., which retain their initial meaning. In grammars of Lithuanian, they are traditionally classed with imperative interjections, due to their functional affinity.

The lexical and grammatical meaning of interjections is not easy to define, since their content is purely emotive. Syntactically, interjections function either as emotive-expressive elements in a sentence (cf. *Ái, skaũda!* 'Ouch, it hurts!') or as sentence equivalents like *ãčiū* 'thank you' and *sudiẽ* 'good-bye'.

According to their structure, interjections can be divided into primary (non-derived) and secondary (derived) units.

10.2 **Primary interjections** have indeterminate morphological structure. They may consist either of a single vowel, viz. a monophthong (e.g. *ã, à, ẽ, è, ỹ, õ, ù, ũ*) or a diphthong (*ái, ói, éi, ùi*), or a cluster of two or more phonemes (*ojẽ, ovà*). The vowel in an interjection may be lengthened or reduplicated: *Aà!, Ėẽ! Oõ(õ)!*, e.g.:

Oõ, kíek žmoniŭ!   'Gee, what a crowd!'

An interjection may be a combination of a short and a long vowel, e.g. *aã, eẽ*. The consonants *h* and *j* are often inserted between two identical vowels (*ahà, ohò, ohohò; ajà, ajajà*) and sometimes between different vowels (*ojè, ajè, ajà*).

Diphthongs may be reduplicated: *ai ái, ai ai ái*. The consonant *j* may be inserted here, too (in other words, the second component of the diphthong changes into *j*): *ai + ai = ajái, ajajái*.

A number of primary conjunctions have variants with the initial consonant *v*: *vái, vói, vùi, vajái*.

Quite a number of primary interjections consist of a vowel and a consonant: *àk, àt, èg, èt, èch, èk, òt, òpa, nà, šà, tè*. Some of them are usually reduplicated in speech (*ta tà, te tè, tiũ tiũ*), often with an added initial vowel, e.g. *ãtata, ẽtete, ũtiti (ùtiti), òpapa, òčiačia, òlialia, ẽpapa, àpapa*, etc.

There are also a few interjections comprising a prolonged consonant: *ss(s)! šš(š)*, also *mm(m)*.

The interjection *mm(m-m)* has variants with *h*, viz. *hm* and *mhm*, cf.:

M-m, labaĩ skanù...   'Mm, (it) tastes good...'
M-h-m, nežinaũ...   'Mm, I don't know...'

A number of primary interjections are of onomatopoeic origin. For instance, the interjections *viaũ, éu* and the like imitate sounds caused by disgust or retching. The interjections *tfù, tfúi, pfù, pfúi, pfũ, fù, fè, fi* imitate spitting; *br̃r* and *ũtiti* are used when shivering with cold or fright. Cf.:

Pfúi, vėl apsirikaũ!   'Darn it, I'm wrong again!'
Br̃r... visái sustiraũ nuõ šalčio!   'Brr, I'm stiff with cold!'

10.3 **Secondary interjections** are descended from words of other classes through loss of their referential meaning and, as a rule, morphological properties.

Most secondary interjections are related to the vocative case of nouns and imperative verb forms (2. Sg.). Thus the interjections *diẽ, bról* are abbreviated desemanticized forms of the vocatives *Diẽve!* 'God!', *Bróli!, Brolaũ!* 'Brother!', e.g.:

Diẽ, Petrùli, neminėk tù jõ nakčià.   'Gosh, Peter, never mention him at night.'
Taĩp jaũ, bról, yrà, nieko nepadarýsi.   'That's how it is, dear, nothing doing.'

The full vocative forms of these nouns (*Diẽve* 'God', *bróli* 'brother'), also with a diminutive suffix and the ending of a different stem (*Dievùliau* (= *Dievùli*) and *Dievulė́liau* (= *Dievulė́li*) 'Dearest God', *brolaũ* (= *bróli*) 'brother', *motinė́liau* (= *motinė́le*) 'dearest mother') are also used as interjections, usually in conjunction with a primary interjection, cf.:

Ùi, Dievùliau, ar ikì pietų̃ miegósite!	'Oh, Dearest God, are you going to sleep until noon!'

A number of interjections are related to other case forms. Thus, *dejà* 'alas' is the petrified nominative case form of a noun; *velnióp* 'to hell', expressing disgust or anger, is the archaic allative form of the noun *vélnias* 'devil'.

The interjections *žiū̃, paĩ, palà, išgraũš, išgraũ, išgraũž* are descended from 2. SG imperative verb forms *žiūrė́k* 'look', *paláuk* 'wait', and *išgráužk* 'cut (it) out' respectively; cf.:

Žiū̃, jau atvažiúoja!	'Look, they are coming already!'
Palà, ką̃ tù norė́jai pasakýti?	'Wait, what did you want to say?'

The 2. SG imperative forms *eĩk* (: *eĩti* 'go'), *išliùpk* (: *išliùpti* 'pull out') are also used as interjections to express disbelief, resp. ingratitude:

Eĩk, eĩk, negãli tõ bū́ti!	'Don't say so (lit. go, go) that's impossible!'

The interjections *valiõ* 'hurray' (: *valióti* 'be able'), *ėdrõ* (: *ėdróti* 'eat' (of animals)) expressing joy, encouragement, are also deverbal derivatives.

The units *lãbas* 'hello', *sveĩkas* (-à, -ì) 'hello', *skalsù* 'bon appétit!', used as interjections are formally identical with the adjectives *lãbas* (*rýtas*) 'good (morning)', *sveĩkas* 'healthy', *skalsùs* 'long-lasting, abundant, nourishing', respectively.

The words *dė̃kui* 'thank you' and *ãčiū* 'thank you' are Slavic borrowings.

A number of interjections, e.g. *šè*, *tè*, are formally identical with particles, the difference being semantic and functional, cf.:

Šè, jaũ ir tàs miẽga.	'Well, even this one is asleep already (interjection).'
Šè táu knỹgą.	'Here is the book, take it (particle).'

A few interjections are related to other word classes, e.g. *taĩ* is identical with the pronoun *taĩ* 'that', *šim̃ts* with the numeral *šim̃tas* 'hundred'; cf.:

Taĩ! Ikì paskutìnio skatìko nulùpo.	'Oh dear, he's robbed me clean.'

10.4 A number of interjections are clusters of two or more words merged into one word that has acquired the emotional meaning and other properties characteristic of interjections. The most common type here is a blend of an interjection and a particle, e.g.: *ajaũ < a + jaũ, avà < a + và, evà < e + và, avè < a + vè*. The emphatic particle *gì* is the most frequent one here, cf.: *ė̃gi, õgi, eĩgi, ètgi, nàgi*.

Two interjections are often blended into one: *ojái, ajùi*; they may be extended by an additional formant: *ajèg, ajègi, ajė̃jau, ajèti*. The interjection *aimán* is composed of the primary interjection *ài* and pronoun *mán* 'me (DAT)'.

An interjection can have a number of variants, e.g., alongside *ojà* 'oh', its variants *ojè, ojègi, ojègis, ojeĩ, ojejáičiau, ojètus* are used.

There are also complex interjections composed of (**a**) two interjections, e.g. *o véi, oi véi, ei véi*; (**b**) interjection + particle, e.g. *èt jau, àk jau*; (**c**) interjection + pronoun, e.g. *eĩ tu* lit. 'oh you', *vajè tu, àk tu*; cf.:

Àk jau, nenóriu niẽko.	'Oh, dear, I don't anything.'
Vajè tu, neĩk teñ.	'Oh dear, don't go there.'

10.5 The following interjections (formulaic exclamations) are word groups blended into one:

dievažì, dievàž, dievažiñ	(< *Diẽvas žìno* 'God knows')
sudiẽ, sudiẽv, sudiẽu	(< *su Dievù* 'with God')
dievmýlėk, diemýlėk, die(v)mylỹ	(< *Diẽve, mylė́k* 'God, love (us)')
dievegìn	(< *Diẽve, gìnk* 'God forbid')
amžinãtilsį	(< *Ámžiną ãtilsį* 'Eternal rest (ACC)' = 'Rest in peace')
labarýt, labrýt	(< *Lãbas rýtas* 'Good morning')
labadiẽn	(< *Labà dienà* 'Good afternoon' (lit. 'Good day'))
labãnakt, labãnaktis	(< *Labà naktìs, Lãbą nãktį* 'Good night')

The respective full words groups are also used in speech.

There is an number of idiomatic phrases containing words like *Diẽvas* 'God', *Viẽšpats* '(God) Almighty', *vélnias* 'devil', *perkū́nas* 'thunder'; 'Thunderer (god of thunder)', that are used very much like interjections, cf.:

Diẽve nedúok	'God forbid'
Diẽve sérgėk	'God protect'
po velnių̃ / velniaĩs	'damn'
velniaĩ raũtų	'confound it'
nė̃ vélnio	'no, the hell' (emph.)
po perkū́nų	'damn'

The nouns *gãlas* 'end', *šuõ* 'dog', *bùdelis* 'hangman', *bėdà* 'misfortune', *var̃gas* 'misery, trouble', and the numeral *šim̃tas* 'hundred' are frequent in this kind of idioms; the latter often contain the particle *kàd* and pronouns *tù* 'thou', *jìs* 'he', *jì* 'she'; cf.:

kad tavè gãlas	'Oh damn!'
po galaĩs	'damn'
var̃ge tu màno	'Oh dear, dear'
po šim̃ts velnių̃ (pỹpkių, kalakùtų)	'confound it' (lit. 'a hundred devils (pipes, turkeys)')
nà dabar̃ táu	'oh my, oh well'
tùsčia jõ (jõs, jų̃)	'damn him (her, them)'.

Quite a number of interjectional set phrases, used to express surprise, disappointment, admiration, etc., contain the desemanticized adverb *kur̃* 'where', sometimes *kíek* 'so (how) many', *kaĩp* 'how', e.g.: *kur̃ tau, kur̃ čia, kur̃ nè*, cf.:

Maniaũ, jìs grĩš. Bèt kur̃ tau!	'I thought he would come back. But alas!'

Meaning and usage of interjections

10.6 As was mentioned above, interjections proper can be emotive and imperative. Due to the absence of referential meaning, the majority of interjections are used to express a variety of feelings each. The meaning is often determined by context and speech situation. Intonation plays a particularly important role. For instance, the interjection *ã* can express quite different emotions depending on the factors mentioned, e.g.:

remorse:
Ã, negeraĩ padariaũ.	'Oh dear, I've done the wrong thing.'

surprise:
Ã! Kàs gi čià tóks?	'Oh! Who's this one?'

relief:
Ã, dabar̃ tavè prisìmenu.	'Oh, now I remember who you are.'

Similarly, the interjections *õ, ẽ, àk!, ái*, and many other primary interjections can express admiration, joy, surprise, or sorrow, pity, regret, indignation, complaint, etc., e.g.:

surprise:
Õ! Jì jaũ parẽjo.   'Oh! She is back already.'

admiration:
Õ! Tai beñt výras!   'Oh! He is a real man!'

contentment:
Õ, kad miegójau, tai miegójau.   'Oh, I slept like a log.'

The meaning of a number of interjections is less dependent on the factors mentioned. In the first place, this is true of secondary interjections like *dejà* 'alas', *valiõ* 'hurrah', *palà* 'here', *velnióp* '(to) hell', *diẽ* '(oh) dear', etc. The following interjections are also specialized with respect to meaning and usage: *tfù* and *viáu* express contempt, *ātata* is used when one is hot or pleased; *ss, šš(š), ts(s)* and *tš(š)* are used to request silence, (e.g.: *Šš, pasiklausýk* 'Hush, listen'); the interjections *òp (òpa, òpapa)* and *ùpa (ùpapa)* are used when lifting a heavy thing or jumping over an obstacle, or urging someone to do it.

Interjections are characteristic of expressive, emotional speech. Their repetition serves to create an emphatic colouring for speech. They can be used instead of descriptive notional words to give an emotional evaluation, e.g.: *Jōnas – tai výras oho-ohò!* 'John, he is super' (lit. 'John, he is a man oho!'). They can also function as sentence equivalents, e.g.: *Br̃r...* (when scared or cold); *Valiõ!* 'Hurray!', 'Bravo!'; *Ái!* 'Ouch!' (sudden pain) or *Ói!* 'Oh!' (fright). Emotive interjections are a property of colloquial everyday speech: they make conversation lively, emotional, and add familiarity and intimacy.

A number of interjections also serve to intensify rhetorical questions, addressing somebody and exclamatory sentences and thus make speech elevated and solemn, e.g.:

O láisve, tu kar̃tais už grandinès sunkèsnė.   'Oh freedom, you can be heavier than chains.'

For all these reasons, interjections are also frequent in Lithuanian poetry and fiction.

VOCATIVE INTERJECTIONS

10.7 Vocative interjections are a special subclass of interjections used to call or drive away domestic animals and poultry. For instance, *nā, nō-o, šiū̃-ū* are used to drive oxen; *nà, nà* or *nù, nū(ū), nē(ē), kùž kùž* are used to urge horses and *tr(r̃), pr(r̃)* are used to stop a horse.

There is a variety of ways to address a cow: *šiũ* is a general "address", along with *mùže mùže* and *mužì mužì*; *õha* is used to make a cow stand still when milking; *kūre* is an order to stay in the herd. Oxen are summoned by saying *bulì bulì* (*bulià bulià*) and they are teased with *mỹ mỹ*. A dog is summoned with *čiù čiù, ciù ciù, nà nà*, or *čiùč, ss(s), sà*, e.g.:

Sà, šunēli, sà.   'Here, doggie, here.'

Pigs are summoned with *čiùk(a) čiùk(a), kriù kriù, ūdžiù (ūdžiù)* and driven away with *ucì, ajùis* and *aūkš*. One may call hens with *pùt(ì) pùt(ì)*, and chickens with *cìp(a) cìp(a)*; ducks are called with *pùl pùl, pulì pulì*, geese – *žiùr žiùr, žiùri žiùri*.

10.8 Some vocative interjections are similar to or identical with primary interjections in their phonemic structure (*nà, õ*, and the like). In the majority of cases, however, ways of addressing animals have distinctive phonemic and derivative properties, since they are related to the names of animals and/or to their onomatopoeic origin, viz. they imitate the sounds produced by animals.

Some of them are derived from the vocative case of animal names, e.g.:

bulì bulì (bulià bulià)   (cf. *bùlius* 'bull, ox')
kiául kiául   (cf. *kiaũlė* 'pig')
kàt kàt (kàc kàc)   (cf. *katẽ* 'cat')
triùš triùš   (cf. *triùšis* 'rabbit')

The following are onomatopoeic invocations:

ciù ciù, čiù čiù   (imitating a dog's whimpering)
kriù kriù, čiùk(à) čiùk(à), čiukì čiukì   (imitating pigs)
kùt kùt, cìp(à) cìp(à)   (hens and chickens)
gìr gìr   (geese)
r-r-r and *uř-uř*   (used to tease dogs imitating dogs' growling)

As is clear from the examples, interjections of this class are usually reduplicated units.

Invocations used to drive away or shoo animals are also mostly onomatopoeic: *šš, št, t(ì)š, pū, più, čis*.

A limited number of vocative interjections are compound derivatives composed of an interjection or a particle and an infinitive, e.g.:

uzgỹt < *ùz* + *gýti/gìnti* 'drive' (to drive away pigs)
šegul̃t < *šè* + *gul̃ti* 'lie down'
šelaũk < *šè* + *laũk* 'out', etc.

The vocative *kũre* (stopping a cow) is a contraction of *Kuř eini?* 'Where are you going?'

10.9 Most of the reduplicated vocatives with a final consonant can take the vowel formant *-i* or *-a*:

kàt kàt – katì katì	kìz kìz – kizì kizì
cìp cìp – cipà cipà	čiùk čiùk – čiukà čiukà.

In a number of invocations, the formant *a-* is also added initially:

a(š)tìš, apruč, atiũ, ažiuř.

The formant *š-* is also sometimes added initially. All these formants change the meaning of an invocation: *kàc, pùl, žiuř* are used to call cats, ducks and geese respectively and *škàc, špùl* and *ažiuř* are used to shoo them away.

There are ways of addressing animals with both formants *a* and *š*, e.g.: *aštìš, aškàc, ašpùl*; these have numerous dialectal variants, too, cf.:

aškàc, aškàč, aškacỹ, aškatỹ
aškìc, aškỹc, askỹč

11 ONOMATOPOEIC WORDS
Ištiktùkai

11.1 This is a class of invariable words which are mostly a deliberate imitation of sounds or acoustic and visual effects or impressions of human actions, animals, natural phenomena, artifacts, etc., e.g.:

trìnkt! 'bang!' *bàkst!* 'prick!'
diñ diñ 'ding dong' *apčỹ* (imitation of sneezing)
miáu 'meaow' *guř guř* (of running water)
káukšt! 'tap!, bang!' *blýkst* (of a flash of light)

Onomatopoeic words are distinguished from interjections and other parts of speech since they are characterized by specific semantic features and syntactic properties as well as by common formal properties. Semantically, most of them refer to actions by imitating the acoustic impression or association with the latter. Syntactically, they function as predicates (predicate substitutes) or verbal modifiers. Formally, they display a number of specific derivative patterns.

Due to their expressive force, onomatopoeic words are a property of informal everyday speech. They are particularly numerous and varied in dialects.

Onomatopoeic words are either verb-related or imitative.

11.2 Verb-related words share the stem (with or without a special formant) with respective verbs. In the stem, vowel and tone alternation are frequent enough. Verb-related words are an expressive means of referring to an action, therefore they have a distinct lexical meaning. This type comprises a limited number of units; here belong:

drìbt (: *drìbti* 'fall, drop, tumble')
glùst (: *glaũsti* 'clasp', *glùsti* 'snuggle, cuddle up')
klùp (: *klùpti* 'stumble')
krýp, krýpt, krỹpu, krypái (: *krỹpti* 'turn, swing, bend')
lìnkt (: *liñkti* 'bend, stoop', *leñkti* 'bend, bow')
lilìngt (: *lingúoti* 'rock, swing')
mìrkt (: *mérkti* 'shut (one's eyes), wink')
pakýšt (: *kìšti* 'thrust, shove')
pèšt, pěšt (: *pèšti* 'pull, pluck')

rìkt, rýkt (: *rė̃kti* 'scream, shout')
skě̃st (: *skė̃sti* 'spread')
slýst (: *slýsti* 'slip, slide')
smùkt (: *smùkti* 'slip down')
spỹg (: *spiẽgti* 'squeal, shriek')
spùst (: *spáusti* 'squeeze, press')
stùmt (: *stùmti* 'push')
šìpt, šýpt (: *šypsótis* 'smile')
šlam̃ (: *šlamė́ti* 'rustle')
švìlpt (: *švil̃pti* 'whistle')
tèpt, těpt (: *tèpti* 'smear, stain')
trìnkt (: *treñkti* 'bang, hit, knock')
trùkt (: *tráukti* 'pull')
virtìnkš (: *vir̃sti* 'overturn, tumble')
žìrgt, žérgt (: *žer̃gti* 'spread (one's legs) wide, stride')
žvìlgt (: *žvel̃gti* '(cast a) glance'), etc.

11.3 Most onomatopoeic words are **imitation words.** Their meaning is usually diffuse and hard to define. With respect to phonetic structure, they vary within a broad range, cf.: *diñ, kar̃, kriù, miáu, klèpu, mataŕai, raràp, gurgulìnkšt, šir̃kšt, šiù, rrr, zz.*

Natural sounds are imitated more or less within the limits of the phonetic system of Lithuanian; one and the same sound may be imitated in a variety of ways, thus *gur̃ gur̃, šliùkšt, gurgulìùkšt* imitate the sound of running water.

Impressions and sensations are rendered in an entirely arbitrary way, e.g. *mataŕai* denotes irregular, disorderly motion, *blýkst* refers to a flash of light.

Onomatopoeic words are very frequent in colloquial Lithuanian. Most of them have no equivalents in English (and in other languages), therefore most of them are cited without translation.

Formal properties

11.4 Most onomatopoeic words are monosyllabic (they may comprise only consonants), less common are words of two and three syllables, and a few comprise as many as four syllable.

According to the final element, onomatopoeic words are divided into two subsets: those with a specific final formant and those without a formant. The **formant** is a final phoneme or a cluster of phonemes added to the root and thereby distinguished from a related verb or another onomatopoeic word. Words with the same formant are usually similar in meaning.

11.5 The most common formant is *-t*, typical mostly of monosyllabic words. As a rule, it is preceded by the voiceless consonants *k, p, s, š* and clusters *kš, ks*, e.g.:

càkt, stùkt, čiùlpt, kàpt, krúpt, sliúopt
rìst, snùst, švýst
kìšt, pèšt, šlýst
káukšt, pùkšt, šmùkšt
bàkst, drýkst

Less commonly it is preceded by voiced *b, g, ž, m, r*:

bùrbt, stàbt, klìngt, spràgt, lýžt, ūžt, plùmt, biřt

Most of onomatopoeics in *-t* are imitation words. Some of them have counterparts without this formant, e.g.:

kriùk – kriùkt	bràkš – bràkšt
càp – càpt	tvóks – tvókst

A great many deverbal onomatopoeics also display this formant, e.g.:

lìnkt (: liñkti)
čiùlpt (: čiulpti)
drìkst, drýkst (: drìksti, drĕksti)
(see also the list in 11.2.)

In words of two and three syllables, the formant can follow a cluster of consonants, which forms with *-t* a kind of a suffix, e.g.: *mugùrkt, kuldìnkšt, šabaldókšt, gurguliùkšt*.

As was mentioned, onomatopoeic words with the same formant (and similar phonetic structure) may be similar in meaning. For instance, bi-syllabic and tri-syllabic words with *-(i)okšt* usually denote a sudden overturning, or fall: *kabókšt, šlamókšt, keberiókšt, tabarókšt*.

Onomatopoeic words with the formants *-t* and *-š* have an acute toneme if the vowel of the stressed syllable is either long or a diphthong. The vowels *a* and *e* alone, if they are lengthened under stress, have a circumflex.

11.6 The formants *-š* and *-s* also occur, usually after the consonant *k*, less frequently after *p, b, m, l* and *r*, e.g.: *bàkš, šmáukš, šnýpš, grýbš, krùms, káls, dùrs*. Words with these formants are not numerous. They are being ousted by their very common respective equivalents with the final *-t*: *bàkšt, šmáukšt, šnýpšt, krùmst, kàlst, dùrst*.

A number of the onomatopoeic words in question have shortened variants without the formants *-š, -s*, e.g.: *bàk, kàp*.

11.7 A considerable number of onomatopoeic words display the final vowel formants *-i, -y, -u* and *-ū* preceded by a consonant, e.g.:

birì, svyrì, vizgì
baldỹ, sukỹ, svirdikulỹ
lapatù, lìngu, šlèpu
burkū̃, sukū̃, supū̃

Some of them also occur without a final formant. The vowel formants alternate in some words, e.g.:

čiupì / čiupỹ / čiùpu *lapatì / lapatù*
šlamì / šlamỹ / šlamù *spuřdi / spurdỹ*

Words with the formants *-i, -u* and *-y, -ū* differ in meaning: those with the short formants convey weaker actions or impressions, and those with the long formants refer to a stronger, louder effect; cf.:

Tuõj ponià atsikėlė iš lóvos –	'The mistress at once got out of
šiurì šiurì ateĩna.	bed – and here she comes rustling.'
Šiurỹ šiurỹ vėjas pláukus šiurẽna.	'The wind ruffles greatly the hair.'
Brazdù brazdù kažkàs už	it. 'Something scratched scratch
síenos subrazdėjo.	scratch (softly) behind the wall.'
Kažin kàs už grỹčios brazdū̃	'Somebody there behind the hut
brazdū̃!	was scratching (hard)!'

11.8 The formant *-(i)ai* is also used to form onomatopoeic words, mostly of three syllables (e.g.: *klebetái, reketái, šlapatái*) and sometimes of two syllables (e.g.: *lingái, rūkái*). Practically all of them have variants without a formant: *capái – càp, klebetái – klebèt, makalái – màkal*.

The formant *-(i)ai* is always stressed and receives an acute toneme.

11.9 Onomatopoeic words ending in sounds and sound clusters other than those enumerated in the above sections do not make up any distinct groups, but the more frequent final elements are also similar to formants and can be distinguished from other respective onomatopoeic words or verbs. Here belong the segments *-um, -ur, -e, -(i)o, -ui*, e.g.:

klèktum (cf. *klèkt*), *cāpum* (cf. *càp*)
kỹbur (cf. *kybóti* 'hang'), *viñgur* (cf. *vingiúoti, vinguriúoti* 'meander')
càpe (cf. *càp*), *rùzge* (cf. *ruzgėti* 'stir')
bizeliõ (cf. *bizelióti* 'run about madly'), *kumpõ* (cf. *kumpóti* 'nod')
lapatuĩ (cf. *lapatái, lapatì; lapatúoti* 'run with long strides')

Onomatopoeic words in *-t, -s*, and *-š* usually refer to sudden actions and those in *-i, -y, -u, -ū, -(i)ai*, etc. refer to slow, longer actions and sounds.

444 MORPHOLOGY

11.10 Onomatopoeic words without formants are few in number, and their phonetic structure varies, e.g.: *gà, mẽ, cỹ, tfù, ũ, miáu, dziñ, dař, muř, spiř, šabál, càk, spàk, làp, čýv, bžž, prr, šš*. They are mostly sound imitations.

These words are mostly monosyllabic. Short syllable onomatopoeics of this subset usually express sudden, brief sound effects or actions and those with a long syllable, slow sound effects of longer duration, cf.:

Jìs dràk bóbai pāgaliu per gálvą.	'He hit the woman on the head with a stick.'
Avėlė rēkia bẽ, ožkà mẽ, vìsos nóri válgyti.	'The sheep bleats be-e, the goat me-e, all of them are hungry.'

Deverbal onomatopoeic words without a formant are identical in form with the verbal root, e.g.:

biř (: *bìr-ti, byrĕti* 'pour' (of sand etc.))
jùd (: *jud-ĕti* 'move')

A number of onomatopoeic words are formed with the prefix *pa-*, mostly from words in *-t*, e.g.:

pabràkšt (: *bràkšt* 'crack', cf. *brakšĕti* 'to crack')
pastrìkt (: *strìkt*, cf. *striksĕti* 'hop')
pašnìpšt (: *šnìpšt*, cf. *šnipšĕti* 'hiss, sputter')

The prefix also occurs in a few other onomatopoeic words, e.g.: *patáukš, patvýks, pašmàkštu, pablìnk, pastràk*. The prefix *pa-* adds the meaning of onset, preparation of the action or sound expressed by the base word.

11.11 A characteristic feature of onomatopoeic words is reduplication of a segment (initial, middle, or final element) twice or more times (repetition of an entire imitation word is not considered to be reduplication; see below).

The most frequent instance is reduplication of the initial consonant(s) and the following vowel or first element of a diphthong, e.g.:

balàkšt (: *bàkšt*)	*kleklèbt* (: *klèbt*)
brabràkš (: *bràkš*)	*tvitvìsk* (: *tvìsk*)
čičìnkt (: *čìnkt*)	*klekleĩkt* (: *kleĩkt*)
dudùn (: *dùn*)	*kvakváukt* (: *kváukt*)

It may involve vowel alternation, e.g.:

dridrýkt (: *drýkt*)   *kliklánkt* (: *klánkt*).

A number of onomatopoeic words are derived from other onomatopoeic words by infixing *l* or *r* after the stem vowel and repeating the latter; e.g.:

talàk (: *tàk*)   *dziliñ* (: *dziñ*)
caràp(t) (: *càp(t)*)   *čirìk* (: *čìk*)

Infixed words sometimes have a repeated middle segment, e.g.: *cililiñgt* (: *ciliñgt*), *talalañ* (: *talañ*). These infixed words usually co-occur with the base onomatopoeic word, e.g.: *càp(t) caràp(t)*, *čìk čirìk*, *dañ dalañ*.

Reduplicated and infixed words imitate a complex sound or impression.

11.12 Onomatopoeic words that are formally similar can combine into pairs. Paired words differ either in the vowel or the initial consonant (cf. *bìm bám*, *pýkšt pàkšt*, *brùzdu bràzdu*, *cāpu lāpu*, *čȳru vȳru*, *šuldù buldù*), or one of the components (as a rule, the second one) has the prefix *pa-*, or an infix, or another additional element, e.g.:

kàpst pakàpst   *kniáu kurniáu*
striŭokt pastriŭokt   *stràk strākum*
ciñ ciliñ   *tèkšt tebelèkšt*

The two words in a pair may differ considerably, e.g.:

cèpt làpt
džìngt brìngt
cilìm bám
šālum drȳlum

All these pairs refer to a complex sound or impression produced by one action; cf.:

Stikliùkas ciñ ciliñ ant   'The glass fell tinkling on the
akmeñs ir subyrė́jo.   stone and broke into pieces.'
Dziuñ dzàp – sùzvembė kulkà.   'Bleep blip – a bullet whined by.'
Dzìngu lìngu į júsų sveikãtą!   lit. 'Chin chin to your health!'

To imitate a repeated sound, an onomatopoeic word may be repeated two or more times, e.g.:

Jõ širdìs dùkt dùkt plākė.   'His heart went tuck tuck.'
Šiùr šiùr šiùr, – šnābžda   'Sh, sh, sh, – something is
kažkàs šiauduosè.   rustling in the hay.'

A number of onomatopoeic worde have variants with a short and a long vowel, e.g.:

kèpšt / kė́pšt   *šliùkšt / šliū́kšt*
šlèpt / šlė́pt   *krìpu / krȳpu*
sriùbt / sriū́bt   *rìkt / rȳkt*

The difference in vowel length is meaningful: the short root usually imitates a weaker and shorter sound, and the long root a stronger, longer (usually sudden) sound or action, cf.:

Šiùpt drùskos žiupsnẽlį.	lit. '(She) poured a little salt.'
Šiū́pt vìsą sáują.	lit. '(She) poured (emph.) a full handful'.
Senùtė stìp stìp nuskubė́jo.	'The old woman hurried away with tiny steps.'
Didžiáusias kãtinas stýp stýp paliñdo põ stalù.	'With long strides the huge tomcat stole under the table.'

Lengthening is also observed in onomatopoeic words *čir̃ – čýr* and *šliòpt – šliópt*. To emphasize longer duration, in some onomatopoeic words the middle or final vowel or consonant (*r, n, z, ž*) is lengthened, e.g.:

Trýk trýk trýyk *trimitúoja medžiótojo rãgas.*	lit. 'Tryk tryk tryyk went the hunter's horn.'
Dzinñ ... dzz ... dzinñ – *skambė́jo telefònas.*	lit. 'Dzinn ... dzz ... dzinn, rang out the telephone.'

In pairs with different vowels, onomatopoeic words with a front vowel are commonly used to imitate high-pitched sounds or weaker impressions whereas those with a back vowel imitate low sounds or stronger perceptions, cf.:

Diñ diñ diñ *varpẽlis suskambė́jo.*	lit. 'The little bell went din din din.'
Dañ dañ dañ – *skam̃ba var̃pas.*	'The bell booms dong dong dong.'
Liepsnà kýšt, *ugnẽlė* blì blì blì.	'The flame jumped, tiny flames started dancing.'
Į́metė kelià̃s skíedras, tìk – blà blà blà *ir staigà užsiliepsnójo.*	'He threw a few chips (into the fireplace) and suddenly (the logs) blazed up.'

11.13 Onomatopoeic words beginning with the consonant cluster *šm* usually imitate sounds caused by swift motion through the air (*šmýkšt, šmìrkš(t), šmùrkšt*), those with the initial *bl* refer to flashes of light (*blàkt, blýks(t), blizgù*). Words with the final *m* and *n* customarily imitate jingling and pealing (*bám, diñ*); those with the final *r* imitate vibrating sounds (*čir̃, dar̃, tir̃*).

Onomatopoeic words can include only those consonants which are associated with similar natural sounds, e.g.:

Mùsės bzz bzz *apliñk.*	'Flies buzzed around.'
Džž *pradė́jo ver̃žtis vanduõ.*	'Water spouted out babbling.'

Alongside the onomatopoeic words discussed above, occasional imitation words are ofter created to render specific sounds or impressions, e.g.: *ku ku ũk* (imitating stammering), *ž ž ž koh* (imitating shell fire), *vatakūūū!* (imitating water poured into an engine).

Meaning and usage

11.14 Most onomatopoeic words are used to express the acoustic effect or impression of dynamic actions, mostly of motion (e.g. of walking, running, flying, throwing, falling, jumping, beating, cutting, breaking, grasping, and the like); cf.:

Klausaũs – kažin kàs tik šlèp šlèp į̃ màno pùsę.	'I listen – someone is shuffling towards me.'
Strãzdas tik pùrpt – ir nuskrìdo.	'The blackbird just took wing – and flew away.'
Plùmpt nukrìto kaĩp pelų̃ maĩšas.	'He fell with a thud like a sack of chaff.'
Cāpum àš jį̃ už plaukų̃ ir iš-tráukiau.	'I grabbed him by the hair and pulled him out.'

Numerous onomatopoeic words imitate birds, animals, insects, e.g.:

Antys „prỹ! prỹ! prỹ!"	'The ducks (quacked) "quack! quack! quack!"'
Kiaũlė kriùkt kriùkt šaũkia sàvo paršeliùs.	'The sow calls her piglets grunting.'
Stũgt sustáugė vil̃kas.	'A wolf gave out a loud howl.'

Onomatopoeic words can also express the sound effects of physiological processes as well as actions of human beings and animals, e.g. talking (*plè plè plè* 'bla bla bla', cf. *plepėti* 'chatter, jabber'), laughter (*kà kà kà*), weeping (*vẽ*), sneezing (*apčỹ*), eating (*krìmst*, cf. *krim̃sti* 'eat, nibble'), drinking or lapping up (*màk, gùrkšt*), fear (*brrr̃, šiùrpt*, cf. *šiur̃pti* 'shudder with fright'), etc.

Onomatopoeic words also imitate the sound effects of natural phenomena, such as flowing water (*gur̃ gur̃, gurguliùkšt, šliùkšt*), rain (*pliũpt*), thunder (*dù dù dù, dar̃ dar̃*), and the like.

A number of onomatopoeic words imitate musical and other instruments, e.g. a trumpet (*turū̃ turū̃*), a fiddle (*knir̃ knir̃, čỹru vỹru*), a hammer (*tùk tùk*), a saw (*džỹru dzỹru*) and a great many others.

A number of onomatopoeic words emphasize the suddenness or unexpectedness of an action, or a poorly performed action, cf.:

Bráukšt ir nùmirė.	'Bang, and he is dead.'
Jìs tik pýkšt ir pastãtė nãmą.	lit. 'He just pop and built the house.'
Dìrbo, dìrbo ir padìrbo šnìpšt.	'He worked and worked, and produced a flop.'
Dìrbi kaip pakliũva – šiùrum bùrum.	'You work just anyhow – helter-skelter.'

11.15 Onomatopoeic words can be monosemous or polysemous. Almost all **monosemous** onomatopoeic words are related to verbs. Only some of them are sound imitations. Here belong *čiùpt, càpt, kàpt*, expressing grabbing a thing, *žvìlgt, dìlbt, dě̃bt* referring to a glance, *chà chà, kà kà, kè ké, kì kì* imitating laughter. Very few of them (e.g., *žýbt, brū́kš(t)*) are also used to emphasize a sudden action.

Words imitating specific sounds produced by animals, are also usually monosemous.

Polysemous units are mostly sound imitations. For instance, the word *tař tař* is used to imitate a variety of vibrating sounds, e.g. those of a spinning wheel, rattling windows, cart wheels, and also thunder; *màkt* is used to denote downing a glass of alcohol at one draught, plunging (sth.) into water, giving (sb) a punch, and a number of other sudden swift actions.

Onomatopoeic words function mostly as predicates instead of a verb or as verbal intensifiers.

In the former instance the meanings of tense, mood, person and number are implied by the context. They are particularly frequent as substitutes of Simple Past tense verbs, cf.:

Pérsigando, ir pliùpt *kiřvis iš rañkų.*	'He got a fright, and the ax fell out of his hands.'
Tìk šakà trióks̆t, *àš žẽmèn* blùmpt.	'The branch (went) crack, (and) I (went) bang down.'
Paválgyk ir driùn *į lovẽlę.*	'Finish your supper and jump into bed.'

When used as intensifiers, they modify a verb as a kind of illustration, e.g.:

Šà šà kriñta lãpai.	'The leaves fall with a rustle.'
Bùm bùm pradẽjo šáudyt.	'They started shooting bang bang.'

An onomatopoeic word can be conjoined with a verb by means of the conjunction *iř* 'and'; e.g.:

Šuõ knàbš *į kója ir* įkándo.	lit. 'The dog went snap and bit him in the leg.'

Less frequently, onomatopoeic words are used instead of a noun or an adverb; cf.:

Giřdime kažkókį ūžìmą, kažkókį lýg tai bù bù bù.	'We hear a kind of noise, a kind of bu bu bu.'
Còp còp šito dárbo nepadìrbsi.	'This job can't be done just anyhow in a jiffy.'

IV/Syntax

1 **Sentence and its structure** (1.1–41) 453
   Syntactic relations (1.3) 454
   Parts of a sentence (1.10–41) 461
   The predicate (1.13–20) 463
      Simple predicate (1.14) 464
      Compound verbal predicate (1.15-17) 466
      Compound nominal predicate (1.18–20) 468
   The subject (1.21–23) 475
      Simple subject (1.22) 475
      Complex subject (1.23) 477
      Subject – predicate concord (1.24–27) 478
   The object (1.28–31) 486
   The adverbial (1.32) 489
   The predicative complement (1.33–35) 491
   Modifiers (1.36–41) 493

2 **Word groups** (2.1–156) 497
   Subordinative word groups (2.2–143) 498
   A. Verbal groups (2.5–87) 500
      Verb – noun (2. 6–35) 500
      Verb – prepositional phrase (2.36–78) 521
      Verb – infinitive (2.79–85) 554
      Verb – participle, gerund (2.86) 558
      Verb – adverb (2.87) 559
      Nominalisations (2.88, 89) 560
   B. Nominal groups (2.90–133) 561
      Noun – noun (2.91–109) 561
      Noun – prepositional phrase (2.111, 112) 574
      Noun – adverb, gerund (2.113) 577
      Noun – adjective (2.114) 578

    C. Adjectival groups (2.115–131) 579
        Adjective – noun (2.115–119) 579
        Adjective – prepositional phrase (2.120–127) 582
        Adjective – pronoun (2.128) 584
        Adjective – adverb (2.129) 584
        Adjective – infinitive (2.130) 585
        Adjectival nominalisations (2.131) 586
    D. Numeral groups (2.132–135) 586
        Numeral – genitive case (2.132–134) 587
        Numeral – prepositional phrase (2.135) 588
    E. Pronominal groups (2.136–138) 588
        Pronoun – genitive case (2.136) 588
        Pronoun – adjective (2.137) 589
        Pronoun – adverb (2.138) 590
    F. Adverbial groups (2.139–145) 590
        Adverb – adverb (2.139) 590
        Adverb – noun (2.140–143) 590
        Adverb – prepositional phrase (2.144, 145) 592
    Coordinative word groups (2.146–158) 592
        Syndetic coordination (2.151–156) 595
        Asyndetic coordination (2.157) 598
        Mixed coordination (2.158) 598

3 The simple sentence (3.1–125) 599

Simple sentence patterns (3.4–125) 601
Verbal sentences (3.9–74) 604
    Personal sentence patterns (3.10–53) 604
    Impersonal sentence patterns (3.54–74) 627
Nominal sentences (3.75–97) 641
    Personal sentence patterns (3.76–85) 642
    Impersonal sentence patterns (**3.86–97**) 649
    Variation of constituents in sentence patterns (3.98–104) 654
    Omission and interchangeability of constituents (3.105–107) 658
    Relations between sentence patterns (3.108–125) 660
    Active and passive sentences (3.108–110) 660
    Personal and impersonal sentences (3.111–113) 663
    Affirmative and negative sentences (3.114–125) 663

4 Expanded sentences (4.1–24) ... 674
Participial clauses (4.2–7) ... 674
Comparative phrases (4.8–11) ... 678
Apposition (4.12, 13) ... 681
Direct address (4.14–17) ... 683
Interpolation (4.18–24) ... 685

5 Word order (5.1–31) ... 690
The order of the main sentence connstituents (5.4–17) ... 692
Word order in subordinative groups (5.18–31) ... 699
Verb groups (5.19–22) ... 699
Nominal groups (5.23–31) ... 701

6 The communicative types of sentences (6.1–22) ... 707
Declarative sentences (6.2) ... 707
Volitional sentences (6.3) ... 708
Imperative sentences (6.4–9) ... 708
Optative sentences (6.10–12) ... 710
Interrogative sentences (6.13–19) ... 711
Exclamatory sentences (6.20–22) ... 715

7 The composite sentence (7.1–129) ... 717
Complex sentence (7.5–71) ... 719
Integrated clauses (7.16–35) ... 725
    COMPLETIVE CLAUSES (7.16–23) ... 725
    ATTRIBUTIVE CLAUSES (7.24–32) ... 731
    CORRELATIVE CLAUSES (7.33–35) ... 735
Non-integrated clauses (7.36–71) ... 737
    CLAUSES OF TIME (7.36–43) ... 737
    CLAUSES OF CAUSE (7.44–50) ... 741
    CLAUSES OF CONDITION (7.51–57) ... 743
    CLAUSES OF CONCESSION (7.58–60) ... 746
    CLAUSES OF PURPOSE (7.61, 62) ... 747
    CLAUSES OF PLACE (7.63, 64) ... 748
    COMPARATIVE CLAUSES (7.65–70) ... 748
    ADDITIVE CLAUSES (7.71) ... 751
Compound sentence (7.72–106) ... 752
Copulative coordination (7.77–86) ... 754

Juxtapositive and adversative coordination (7.87–100) 759
Disjunctive coordination (7.101) 766
Consecutive coordination (7.102–105) 767
Continuative coordination (7.106) 768
Asyndetic sentence (7.107–123) 769
Open-structure sentences (7.108–111) 770
Closed-structure sentences (7.112–122) 773
Asyndetic sentences of complex xtructure (7.123) 777
Mixed complex sentence (7.124–129) 779

1 SENTENCE AND ITS STRUCTURE

1.1 This section is concerned with the sentence and its structure in Lithuanian. Word forms described in Morphology from the viewpoint of their interior structure, meaning and categorial contrasts, are the primary units of syntax. They are regarded here as components of word groups, sentences and clauses which are determined by and described in terms of their mutual relations.

The sentence is viewed here as the minimal communicative unit represented by a grammatically independent form. In speech, a sentence displays a complete intonation pattern and is separated from other sentences by pauses; in writing punctuation marks are used as sentence boundaries.

In Lithuanian, a sentence may consist either of a single word form (cf. *Rudenė́ja* 'Autumn is coming'), a word group (cf. *Tylì naktìs* lit. 'Quiet night'), or a number of interrelated word groups.

1.2 According to their communicative function, sentences are classified into a number of communicative types (declarative, interrogative, imperative, exclamatory) each characterized by specific structural properties and intonation. The grammatical form of sentences is represented by a finite number of structural sentence patterns which are realized in an infinite number of utterances produced in speech. Sentence patterns are described in terms of the syntactic functions of constituent word forms (predicate, subject, object, etc.) and in terms of their semantic functions (agent, patient, content, instrument, etc.).

The syntactic structure of a sentence is regarded as a complex of interrelations between its constituents. The semantic structure of a sentence is determined by the semantic relations between the predicate and its actants. The semantic structure of a sentence is not necessarily isomorphic to its syntactic structure: the same content can be expressed by different syntactic structures, cf. *Tė́vas* (NOM) *išvažiãvo* (PAST. ACT) and *Tė́vo* (GEN) *išvažiúota* (PASS. PART. NEUTR) both meaning 'Father has left.'

Syntactic relations

Sintaksìniai ryšiaĩ

1.3 The term syntactic relations is used here to refer to immediate linear relations between word forms, word groups and clauses in a sentence.

The grammatical means of marking syntactic relations in Lithuanian are **endings** and, less commonly, **inflexional suffixes**, often supplemented by structural words, viz. prepositions, conjunctions, and particles. **Word order** is of secondary importance as a means of expressing grammatical relationships in Lithuanian. For instance, it signals the syntactic function of the adjective in phrases like *grãžios gėlės* (attribute; cf. *Grãžios gėlės áuga sodè* 'Beautiful flowers grow in the garden') and *Gėlės grãžios* (predicative), meaning *Gėlės yrà grãžios* 'The flowers are beautiful.' Within a sentence, **intonation** binds word forms into groups and serves to reinforce their syntactic relations (immediately related word forms usually form an intonational unit); it also signals communicative sentence types.

Three principal types of syntactic relations are distinguished: interdependence, subordination and coordination.

Interdependence

1.4 The term *interdependence* is used to refer to the syntactic relation between sentence constituents which mutually presuppose each other. Thus the central constituent, viz. the predicate, presupposes the second constituent, viz. the subject and is in its turn formally dependent on the latter. The relation is bilateral, which can be shown as follows:

Mẽs ↔ *gailėjomės* *draũgo.*
we: NOM   pity: 1. PL. PAST. REFL   friend: GEN
'We were sorry for (our) friend.'

The predicate here determines the nominative case form of the pronoun *mẽs* 'we', while the person and number of the verb are in concord with the pronoun (cf. *àš gailėjausi* 'I was sorry', *tù gailėjaisi* 'you were sorry (2. SG)', *jiẽ gailėjosi* 'they were sorry (3. PL)'. If we use the verb *pagaĩlo* the dative case of the pronoun should be used, and the verb does not agree with it in person and number, cf.:

Mùms ← *pagaĩlo* *draũgo.*
we: DAT   pity: 3. PAST   friend: GEN
'We began feeling sorry for (our) friend.'

In this instance the relationship between *mùms* and *pagaĩlo* is that of subordination.

The finite forms of *bū́ti* 'be', used as a copula, also predetermine the nominative case of the subject and, in their turn, they are dependent on the latter for person and number, e.g.:

Pẽtras ↔ *bùvo* → *pìktas.*
Peter: NOM   be: 3. PAST   angry: NOM. SG
'Peter was angry.'

The predicative adjective agrees with the subject in case, number, and gender. Substitution of a passive participle (present or past), which also functions as a predicate, or an infinitive for the finite form of *bū́ti* 'be' entails a change of the nominative into the genitive or dative respectively:

Pẽtro   *bū́ta*   *pìkto.*
Peter: GEN   be: PAST. PASS. PART. NEUTR   angry: GEN
'Peter was angry.'

Pẽtrui   *(sunkù)*   *bū́ti*   *piktám.*
Peter: DAT   (difficult: ADJ. NEUTR)   be: INF   angry: DAT
'(It is difficult) for Peter to be angry.'

As was mentioned, the number and person of the finite link verb are determined by the subject in the nominative case:

Mẽs   *bùvome*   *piktì.*
we: NOM   be: 1. PL. PAST   angry: NOM. PL. MASC
'We were angry.'

Jũs   *bùvote*   *pìktos.*
you: NOM   be: 2. PL. PAST   angry: NOM. PL. FEM
'You were angry.'

The nominative case of the subject related to the predicate by interdependence is sometimes interchangeable with uninflected word forms, e.g. an infinitive or a gerund (*pādalyvis*), cf.:

Gyvénti   (cf. *gyvēnimas*)   *yrà*   *láimė.*
live: INF   life: NOM. MASC   be: 3. PRES   happiness: NOM
lit. 'To live (cf. life) is happiness.'

Bùvo   *girdė́ti*   *griáudžiant*   (cf. *griaustìnis*).
be: 3. PAST   hear: INF   thunder: GER   thunder: NOM
'One could hear thunder.'

In these instances interdependence has no formal expression by means of concord, but it is explicated by substitution, i.e. by alternation with the nominative case of a noun. But these are atypical, marginal cases of interdependence.

Subordination

1.5 Subordination (*prijungimas*) is a syntactic relation between sentence constituents of which one (the principal constituent) determines the other (dependent constituent). Subordination is a unilateral relation shown by an arrow:

Skýniau → gėlės
'I picked flowers.'

baĩgė → rašýti
lit. 'he finished to write', i.e. 'he finished writing'

labaĩ ← gražùs
'very beautiful'

ankstì ← sutėmo
early   get dark: 3. PAST
'it grew dark early'

Subordination can be strong (obligatory) and weak (optional). In the case of strong (obligatory) subordination the dependent word form is necessary to produce a grammatically well-formed sentence structure, e.g.:

Vaĩkas pradėjo válgyti.	'The child began to eat.'
Kareĩvis prànešė naujíeną.	'The soldier reported the news.'

(The sentences **Vaĩkas pradėjo* 'The child began' and **Kareĩvis prànešė* 'The soldier reported' are grammatically incomplete and they are admissible in certain contexts only, as elliptical sentences).

In the case of weak (optional) subordination the dependent constituent can be omitted without violating the sentence structure, though its meaning may be important for the content of the sentence, e.g.:

Mótina grįžo vakarè.	'Mother returned in the evening.'
Jìs véngia blogų̃ žmonių̃.	'He avoids bad people.'

(*Mótina grįžo* 'Mother returned' and *Jìs véngia žmonių̃* 'He avoids people' are grammatically complete, though they differ in meaning from the above sentences).

According to the means of formal expression, three types of subordination are distinguished: agreement, government, and adjunction.

1.6 **Agreement** (*dẽrinimas*) is a formal link between two words whereby the form of the principal word (head) requires that the dependent word should assume the same form. In the case of agreement the case, number and gender of the dependent word repeat the case, number and gender of the head word; cf.:

báltas	*akmuõ*
white: NOM. SG. MASC	stone: NOM. SG. MASC
'a white stone'	
baltà	*várna*
white: NOM. SG. FEM	crow: NOM. SG. FEM
'a white crow'	
devynì	*bróliai*
nine: NOM. PL. MASC	brother: NOM. PL. MASC
'nine brothers'	
devýnios	*mergáitės*
nine: NOM. PL. FEM	girl: NOM. PL. FEM
'nine girls'	

If the morphological form of the head word is changed, the dependent word obligatorily changes its form too, cf.:

devynių̃	*brólių*
nine: GEN. PL. MASC	brother: GEN. PL. MASC
'of nine brothers'	
devyniaĩs	*bróliais*
nine: INSTR. PL. MASC	brother: INSTR. PL. MASC
'with nine brothers'	

Agreement typically links adjectives, participles, adjectival pronouns and ordinal and some cardinal numerals to a head noun or pronoun.

1.7 **Government** (*valdymas*) is a formal link between the principal word (head) and a specific case form of the dependent word (determined by the grammatical valency of the head word) with or without a preposition. Accordingly, non-prepositional and prepositional government is distinguished; cf. respectively:

parašýti láišką	'write a letter: ACC. SG'
láukti rudeñs	'await autumn: GEN. SG'

pavar̃gti nuõ darbų̃	'get tired of work: Prep + GEN. PL'
láukti ikì rudeñs	'wait until autumn: Prep + GEN. SG'

The head word can be:

(1) a verb (finite and non-finite form) or a deverbal derivative, e.g.:

rašaũ láišką	'I am writing a letter: ACC. SG'
sáulei tẽkant	lit. '(with) the sun: DAT. SG rise: GER'
láiško rãšymas	'the writing of a letter: GEN. SG'

(2) a noun, e.g.:

áukso žíedas	'a ring of gold: GEN'
dovanà tėváms	'a gift for parents: DAT. PL'
kẽlias pàupiu	'the road along the river: INSTR'

(3) an adjective, e.g.:

pìlnas vandeñs	'full of water: GEN'
ištikimas draugáms	'loyal to friends: DAT. PL'

(4) a numeral, e.g.:

dvýlika brólių	'twelve brothers: GEN. PL'
dẽšimt výrų	'ten men: GEN. PL'

(5) an adverb, e.g.:

daũg rū̃pesčių	'many cares: GEN. PL'
ganà vargų̃	'enough hardships: GEN. PL'

(6) less commonly, a particle, an interjection or an onomatopoeic word, e.g.:

šè pinigų̃	lit. 'here (is some) money: GEN. PL'
ãčiū visíems	'thanks to all: DAT. PL'
pliáukšt botagù	'crack with a whip: INSTR'

A great many words (especially verbs) can govern two or more case forms, e.g.:

Tėvas	*dovanójo*	*sū́nui*	*laĩkrodį.*
father	presented	son: DAT. SG	watch: ACC. SG

'Father gave a watch to his son as a present.'

Kreĩpkis	*į̃*	*draugùs*	*patarìmo.*
appeal	to	friends: ACC. PL	advice: GEN. SG

'Ask your friends for advice.'

Government can be strong (obligatory) and weak (optional); cf.:

strong government:

Šiañdien baĩgsiu dárbą.	'Today I'll finish the work: ACC. SG'
Miestè trū́ksta vandeñs.	'There is a shortage of water: GEN. SG in the town.'
Jìs atstovãvo darbiniñkams.	'He represented the workers: DAT. PL'
Vaikaĩ domė́josi pãroda.	'The children were interested in the exposition: INSTR. SG.'
Mē̃s gyvẽnome miestè.	'We lived in a town: LOC. SG.'

weak government:

Atėjaũ kir̃vio.	'I've come for an ax: GEN. SG.'
Dìrbame sáu.	'We work for ourselves: DAT. SG'
Ė̃jome miškaĩs / į́ kálnus / pas tė́vus.	'We went across the woods: INSTR. PL / to the hills: Prep + ACC. PL / to (our) parents: Prep + ACC. PL.'
Sėdė́jom po medžiù / sù draugaĩs / paùnksnėje.	'We sat under a tree: Prep + INSTR. SG / with friends: Prep + INSTR. PL / in shadow: LOC. SG.'

1.8 **Adjunction** (*šliejìmas*) is a syntactic link which has no formal expression through inflection, words being linked solely through juxtaposition. Thus adjunction is opposed formally to both agreement and government.

By means of adjunction, verbs subordinate all unchangeable words and word forms, e.g.:

važiúojame namõ	'we are going home: ADV'
atsisė́dome pailsė́ti	'we sat down to rest: INF'

Adjectives subordinate adverbs and sometimes infinitives:

labaĩ gražùs	'very beautiful'
perpùs mažèsnis	'smaller by half'
malonùs pažiūrė́ti	'nice to look at: INF'

Infinitives can also be linked by adjunction to some nouns:

viltìs sugrį̃žti	'the hope to return'
próga apsilankýti	'an occasion to pay a visit'

Less commonly, adverbs are also adjoined to nouns:

žiñgsnis atgaĩ	'a step backwards'
gyvẽnimas svetur̃	'life abroad'

Adverbs subordinate only adverbs by adjunction:

labaĩ daũg	'very much'
kíek geriaũ	'somewhat better'

Adjunction is usually a weak (optional) syntactic relation. Strong adjunction occurs in the case of verbs that obligatorily require an infinitive, e.g.:

liáutis dìrbti	'stop working' (lit. 'to work')
bandýti grį̃žti	'try to return'
mokė́ti skaitýti	'be able to read'
mė́gti skaitýti	'like to read'

A number of verbs obligatorily take adverbs:

atródai geraĩ	'you look well (fine)'
jìs elgiasi výriškai	'he behaves in a manly way'

Coordination

1.9   Coordination (*sujungimas*) is a syntactic relation between two or more sentence constituents of equivalent syntactic status. They are included in a sentence either independently of each other or by means of an identical dependence some head constituent.

Coordination links clauses within a complex sentence, and also phrases and word forms in a simple sentence. As a rule, coordinated clauses are not dependent on any other sentence constituent, cf.: *Pūtė vėjas, iř mẽdžiai lingãvo* 'It was windy, and the trees were swaying.' Coordinated word forms have an identical dependence relation to another word, cf.: *Atėjo ìlgas iř lietìngas ruduõ* 'A long and rainy autum came' (two adjectives are in agreement with the noun).

Due to its specific nature, coordination is opposed to both interdependence and subordination. Each coordinated word form (or clause) can be used without the other; the link between them has no direction and is indicated by a line without an arrow head; e.g., the phrase *giẽdras iř tylùs vãkaras* 'a clear and quiet evening' can be represented graphically as follows:

vãkaras

giẽdras ir tylùs

Explicit markers of coordination are coordinating conjunctions (cf. *iř* 'and' in the above example); constituents can also be coordinated without any explicit markers (asyndetic coordination), in which case coordination is indicated by juxtaposition of constituents and their equivalent syntactic status (cf. *giẽdras, tylùs vãkaras* 'a clear quiet evening'). Thus word order and intonation play a major role in the latter instance.

Parts of a sentence

Sākinio dālys

1.10 The structure of a sentence can be described in terms of the predicate, subject, object, adverbial, predicative complement and modifiers, which are the syntactic functions of the constituent word forms. The syntactic function of a word form is identified by its syntactic relation(s) with another word form (or other word forms) in a sentence, and by its substitution potential.

The most important syntactic function is that of the predicate. The predicate is the principal part of the sentence and its structural centre to which the subject, object(s) and adverbial modifiers are linked.

The syntactic relation of interdependence holds between the predicate and subject and the relation of subordination holds between the predicate and an object (objects) and adverbials. A twofold syntactic relation links a predicative complement to the predicate and subject or object.

An attribute dependent on a noun is not directly linked to the predicate and therefore it is not regarded as a part of sentence structure. It is a modifier hierarchically subordinated to the subject or another sentence part linked to the predicate.

Each part of a sentence is characterized by its syntactic relations with other sentence parts and by specific formal properties. Special questions help to identify the syntactic function of a word form in ambiguous cases.

According to their internal structure, simple and complex parts of a sentence are distinguished. A simple part of a sentence consists of a single word form, and a complex one is a word group or a cluster of two or more word forms.

1.11 The units of the syntactic structure of a sentence or clause commonly serve to encode the elements of its semantic structure, i.e. the agent, patient, instrument, and other semantic functions. The syntactic structure of a sentence does not always correlate with its semantic structure. It is only in straightforward cases that the syntactic structure and semantic structure of a sentence are isomorphic, the subject encoding the agent, the object encoding the patient, etc. In Lithuanian, as in other accusative-type languages, a certain case form (typically accusative) encodes the patient (Pat) of a two-place predicate, while the agent (Ag) of a two-place predicate and the patient of a monovalent (one-place) predicate (both collectively referred to as semantic subject) are encoded by the same case form (typically nominative), cf.:

Mergáitės   *augìna*   *gėlès* (Pat).
girl: NOM. PL   grow: 3. PRES   flower: ACC. PL
'The girls grow flowers.'

Gė̃lės (Pat)   *áuga.*
flower: NOM. PL   grow: 3. PRES
'Flowers grow.'

The agent, however, is not always encoded by the syntactic subject. Thus, in the sentence

Kambaryjè   *prisiriñko*   *žmonių̃* (Ag).
room: LOC. SG   gather: 3. PAST   people: GEN. PL
'Some people gathered in the room.'

the agent is encoded by the genitive case form which is a syntactic object, as the verb, due to the prefix denoting indefinite quantity, has no subject valency. In a number of other cases, the semantic relationship between the predicate and its agent, patient, or content is often expressed by a syntactically impersonal (subjectless) sentence, cf.:

Čià   *kìškio* (Ag)   *bė́gta.*
here   rabbit: GEN. SG   run: PAST. PASS. PART. NEUTR
'A rabbit has been (running) here' (evidential passive).

Mán (Pat)   *trū́ksta*   *dúonos.*
I: DAT   lack: 3. PRES   bread: GEN
'I am short of bread.'

Moreover, since the verb is inflected for person and number, the 1st and 2nd person subject need not be represented in the syntactic structure by a separate constituent. Therefore many personal sentences in Lithuanian have no overt subject.

Nešù   *lãzdą.*
carry: 1. SG. PRES   stick: ACC
'I am carrying a stick.'

1.12 Participial (including gerundial) constructions and subordinate clauses can also function as sentence parts related to the predicate; cf.:

(1) *Bùvo   girdėti   lāšant / vanduō lāšant / kàd   lāša   (vanduō).*
    be: 3 PAST hear: INF drip: water: drip: that drip: water:
                          GER   NOM   GER   3. PRES   NOM
'One could hear dripping/water dripping/that it (water) is dripping.'

(2) *Jìs   gýrėsi   laimėjęs   (rungtynès) / jóg   laimėjo   (rungtynès).*
    he: boast: win: PAST.   competition: that   win: competition:
    NOM   3. PAST.   ACT. PART.   ACC   3. PAST   ACC
              REFL   NOM
'He boasted having won (the competition)/that he had won (the competition).'

(3) *Išgirdome   (ratùs)   bìldant /   kàd   (rãtai)   bìlda.*
    hear: wheel: rumble: that   wheel: rumble:
    1. PL. PAST   ACC. PL   GER   NOM. PL   3. PRES
'We heard (the wheels) rumbling/that wheels were rumbling.'

In (1) the gerund, the gerundial construction (*vanduō lāšant*) and the subordinate clause (*kàd vanduō lāša*) are identified as the syntactic subject since they can be replaced by a noun subject, cf.:

Bùvo   girdėti   lietùs.
be: 3. PAST   hear: INF   rain: NOM
'One could hear rain.'

In (2) and in (3) they are identified as objects, since they are interchangeable with a noun object, cf.:

Jìs   gýrėsi   laimėjimu (pérgale).
he: NOM   boast: 3. PAST. REFL   victory: INSTR
'He boasted of (his) victory.'

Išgirdome   bìldesį.
hear: 1. PL. PAST   rumble: ACC. SG
'We heard a rumble.'

A gerund (gerundial construction) or a clause is an obligatory sentence constituent here. (For further discussion see 2.86, 3.101, III.5.151.)

THE PREDICATE

1.13 The predicate (*tarinỹs*) is the grammatical centre which determines the syntactic relations in a sentence. The other main syntactic constituents of sentence structure are immediately related to the predicate. Thus, in the sentence

Príemiesčio	*gatvės*	*užpìldė*	*mìnios*	*žmonių*.
suburb: GEN	street: ACC. PL	fill: 3. PAST	crowd: NOM. PL	people: GEN. PL

'Crowds of people filled the streets of the suburb.'

the subject *mìnios* 'crowds' and the (direct) object *gatvės* 'streets' are immediately linked to the predicate *užpìldė* 'filled', and the attributes *príemiesčio* 'of the suburb' and *žmonių* 'of people' are linked to the object and subject respectively at the lower stage of sentence parsing. The subject is not immediately linked with the object: they are related via the predicate.

The predicate signifies a fact, which may be an action, or a state, or a qualitative or quantitative characteristic of the subject referent, or it attributes the subject referent to a class (as in *Šuõ yrà nãminis gyvulỹs* 'The dog is a domestic animal').

According to their internal structure, predicates are classified into simple and compound predicates. The latter are further subdivided into verbal and nominal predicates, depending on the grammatical class of the second component.

Simple predicate

1.14 In personal sentences, the simple predicate can be expressed by the following word forms:

(1) Any syntactic finite verb form, in whatever mood and tense, e.g.:

Miškè	*visì*	*dainúoja* /	*dainãvo* /	*dainúokite*.
wood: LOC	all: NOM. PL. MASC	sing: 3. PRES	sing: 3. PAST	sing: 2. PL. IMPER

'In the woods everybody is singing/sang/sing.'

(2) An active participle without an auxiliary verb, used to express unexpectedness of the event, or doubt, or hearsay information about it, e.g.:

Tėvas	*jaũ*	*beateĩnąs*.
father: NOM	already	PREF-come: PRES. ACT. PART. NOM

'Father is coming already.'

Kitadõs	*gyvẽnę*	*dù*	*brõliai*.
sometime	live: PAST. ACT. PART. PL. MASC	two	brother: NOM. PL. MASC

'(They say) once upon a time there lived two brothers.'

These participles differ from finite verb forms by their modal meaning of the indirect mood (*modus relativus*), but they agree with the subject in the same way as the second part of a compound nominal predicate, e.g.:

Jìs   eĩsiąs.
he: NOM. MASC   go: FUT. ACT. PART. NOM. SG. MASC
'He will (probably) go.'

Jiẽ   eĩsią.
they: NOM. MASC go: FUT. ACT. PART. NOM. PL. MASC
'They will (probably) go.'

(3) An onomatopoeic word interchangeable with the respective verb, e.g.:

Brólis   šmáukšt   (= šmáukštelėjo)   botagù.
brother: NOM. SG   crack   crack: 3. PAST   whip: INSTR
'Brother cracked (lit. 'crack') a whip.'

(4) An interjection or a particle, e.g.:

Márš   namõ!
march   home
'Go home!'

Šè   iř̃   táu   lašẽlį.
here   also   you: DAT   drop: ACC
'Here, have a drop, too.'

(5) In expressive emotive speech an infinitive can be used to express a (sudden) energetic action, e.g.:

Zuĩkis   bė́gt   vil̃kas   výtis.
hare: NOM. SG   run: INF   wolf: NOM. SG   chase: INF. REFL
'The hare dashed away, the wolf chased after.'

(6) In impersonal sentences, a past gerund or an infinitive can be used as a simple predicate, e.g.:

Ką̃   čià   dár   prasimānius /   prasimanýti?
what: ACC   here   else   think up: PAST. GER think up: INF
'What else could we think up?'

Visíems   išeĩt!
all: DAT. PL   go out: INF
'Get out, everybody!'

(7) The function of a simple predicate is also assigned to the neuter form of a passive participle, used in the meaning similar to that of the indirect mood (evidential passive), e.g.:

Čià   vilkų̃   ẽsama /   bū́ta.
here   wolf: GEN. PL   be: PRES. PASS.   be: PAST. PASS.
                             PART. NEUTR   PART. NEUTR
'(It seems/evidently) There are wolves here/Wolves have been here.'

Compound verbal predicate

1.15 The following types of verb phrases are qualified as compound verbal predicates.

(1) The finite form of a modal or phasal verb, which is obligatorily supplemented by the infinitive of a lexical verb, e.g.:

Jūs	*gãlite*	*eĩti.*
you: NOM	can: 2. PL. PRES	go: INF

'You can go.'

Jì	*ėmė̃*	*veřkti.*
she: NOM	take: 3. PAST	cry: INF

'She began to cry.'

Likaũ		*sėdėti.*
stay: 1. SG. PAST		sit: INF

'I kept sitting.'

Jám	*reikėjo /*	*rūpėjo*	*išeĩti.*
he: DAT	need: 3. PAST	worry: 3. PAST	leave: INF

'He had/was anxious to leave.'

The finite verb subordinates the infinitive formally, but semantically the infinitive is the main word.

(2) Phasal verbs denoting the end of an action (*nustóti* 'stop', *liáutis* 'stop, cease', *mèsti* 'give up, stop' and the like) with the active past participle of a notional verb, e.g.:

Našláitė	*lióvėsi*	*veřkusi.*
orphan: NOM. SG. FEM	stop: 3. PAST. REFL	cry: PAST. ACT. PART. NOM. SG. FEM

'The orphan stopped crying.'

Lietùs	*nustójo*	*lìjęs.*
rain: NOM. SG. MASC	stop: 3. PAST	rain: PAST. ACT. PART. NOM. SG. MASC

'It stopped raining.'

(3) The finite form of the copula *bū́ti* 'be' (zero form in the present tense) with the infinitive of a verb of perception (*matýti* 'see', *girdėti* 'hear', *jaũsti/jùsti* 'feel', *numanýti* 'anticipate'), e.g.:

Kàs	*naũja*	*girdė́ti?*	
what: NOM	new: NOM. NEUTR	hear: INF	

'What's the news?'

Tolumojè	*mìškas*	*bùvo* /	*bū́davo* /	*bùs*		*matýti.*
distance: LOC	forest: NOM	was	used to be	will be		see: INF

'In the distance, one can/could/used to/will see a forest.'

1.16 In emphatic speech the following formal expressions of a compound verbal predicate occur:

(1) Repeated form of the same verb, or of two verbs with the same root, or of two synonymous verbs; cf. respectively:

Ė̃jom	*ė̃jom*	*vìsą*	*diẽną.*
go: 1. PL. PAST	go: 1. PL. PAST	all	day

'We walked on all day long.'

Griáudė	*nugriáudė*	*áudra.*
thunder: 3. PAST	PREF-thunder: 3. PAST	storm: NOM

'The storm thundered and spent itself.'

Sūnùs	*tiẽsė*	*vãrė*	*pìrmas*	*vagàs.*
son: NOM	lay: 3. PAST	cut: 3. PAST	first: ACC. PL	furrow: ACC. PL

'The son ploughed and cut the first furrows.'

(2) A finite verb form with the infinitive of the same verb added for emphasis, e.g.:

Matýt	*mačiaũ,*	*bèt*	*nenutvė́riau.*
see: INF	see: 1. SG. PAST	but	not-seize: 1. SG. PAST

'I did see (him) but didn't catch him.'

(3) A finite verb form with a participle of the same verb, e.g.:

Kukúoja	*gegẽlė*	*kukúodama.*
cuckoo: 3. PRES	cuckoo: NOM. SG. FEM	cuckoo: HALF-PART. NOM. FEM

'The cuckoo is calling and calling.'

Rašýk	*berãšiusi!*
write: 2. SG. IMPER	PREF-write: PAST. ACT. PART. FEM

'Write and write!'

(4) A verb in combination with its adverbial derivative in *-te/-tinai* which has a purely emphatic function, e.g.:

Jì	*stingtè*	*sustìngo.*
she	freeze: ADV	PREF-freeze: 3. PAST

'She froze stiff.'

(5) A finite verb form with an onomatopoeic word, e.g.:

Várna *šàst* *nùtūpė.*
crow: NOM   ONOMAT   alight: 3. PAST
'A crow suddenly alighted.'

1.17 Periphrastic finite verb forms are an integral part of the tense-mood-voice paradigm and with respect to their grammatical categorial meanings of tense and voice they are regularly opposed to simple finite forms; therefore they can be regarded as simple verbal predicates. On the other hand, they are structurally similar to nominal predicates with the copula *bū́ti* 'be' and an adjective, e.g.:

Šìtame   *káime*   *jì*   *yrà*   *gyvẽnusi.*
this: LOC   village: LOC   she: NOM   be: 3. PRES   live: PAST. ACT. PART. NOM. FEM

'She has lived in this village.'

Cf.:

Šìtame   *káime*   *jì*   *gyvẽna.*
this: LOC   village: LOC   she: NOM   live: 3. PRES
'She lives in this village.'

Jì   *yrà*   *jauniáusia.*
she: NOM   be: 3. PRES   young: ADJ. SUPERLAT. NOM. FEM
'She is the youngest.'

Compound nominal predicate

1.18 A compound nominal predicate consists of two parts, a copula and a predicative. The copula is expressed by the finite form of the auxiliary verb *bū́ti* 'be' or of a semi-notional verb, and the predicative is either a noun (or its substitute), an adjective or an adjectivized participle. The predicative is linked to the copula by adjunction and to the subject by agreement, cf.:

Onùtė   *bùvo*   *píenininkė.*
Annie: NOM   be: 3. PAST   milkmaid
'Annie was a milkmaid.'

Vaikaĩ   *bùs*   *paténkinti.*
child: NOM. PL. MASC   be: 3. FUT   pleased: NOM. PL. MASC
'The children will be pleased.'

In this respect a predicative is very much like a predicative attribute, cf.:

Vaikaĩ grį̃žo paténkinti.
children: NOM. PL. MASC   return: 3. PAST   pleased: NOM. PL. MASC
'The children returned pleased.'

THE COPULA

1.19 *Bū́ti* 'be' is a link verb most frequently used in compound nominal predicates. It is devoid of any lexical meaning in this function and has a full paradigm of finite tense-mood forms. It denotes assigning the subject referent to a class of things or a property to the subject-referent within a temporal modal frame.

A compound nominal predicate can incorporate a modal verb (e.g. *galė́ti* 'be able to', *turė́ti* 'have to', *privalė́ti* 'be obliged to', *reikė́ti* 'need'), e.g.:

Tù turì bū́ti teisìngas.
thou: NOM   must: 2. SG. PRES   be: INF   just: NOM. SG. MASC
'You must be just.'

Tàs žiñgsnis gãli bū́ti paskutìnis.
that   step: NOM.   can: 3.   be: INF   last: NOM. SG. MASC
        SG. MASC   PRES
'That step can be the last (one).'

The present tense form of *bū́ti* 'be' can be omitted (zero form), its absence indicating the present tense of the indicative mood, e.g.:

Màno tė́vas sveĩkas.
my   father   healthy
'My father is well.'

(Cf.: *bùvo / bū́davo / bùs / yrà bùvęs / bū́tų sveĩkas* 'was / used to be / will be / has been / would be well'.)

With a noun or a 3rd person pronoun as subject, the zero copula is equivalent to the 3rd person present form of *bū́ti* 'be' (*yrà* 'is, are', *ẽsti* 'is, are'); with a 1st or 2nd person pronoun it is equivalent to the 1st or 2nd person singular or plural forms, cf.:

àš (esù) jáunas   'I am young'
tù (esì) jáunas   'thou (are) young'
jū̃s (ẽsate) jaunì   'you (are) young'

In sentences with the zero copula the syntactic link between subject and predicative can be reinforced by the pronoun *taĩ* 'that' or emphasized by intonation, marked by a dash in writing:

Kelionė –	taĩ	nè	juõkas.
travel	that	not	joke

'A trip is no joke.'

Dù	ir	dù –	keturì.
two	and	two	four

'Two and two is four.'

In most cases, an overt present tense form of *bū́ti* is interchangeable with the zero form, cf.: *Tù pàts esì kaĩtas = Tù pàts kaĩtas* 'You are guilty yourself.'

The zero form is commonly used in compound predicates denoting a permanent feature of the subject referent or assigning the latter to a class irrespective of time, e.g.:

Genỹs márgas, pasáulis dár margèsnis.	'The woodpecker is motley, the world is even more motley.'
Janùlis teisìngas žmogùs.	'Janulis is a just man.'

The copula *bū́ti* is obligatory if the 1st or 2nd person subject is omitted (which is often the case) and has to be inferred from the predicate, e.g.:

Esì	*jáunas*	*iř*	*stiprùs.*
be: 2. SG. PRES	young: NOM. SG. MASC	and	strong: NOM. SG. MASC

'You are young and strong.'

Ẽsame	*jáunos*	*iř*	*grãžios.*
be: 1. PL. PRES	young: NOM. PL. FEM	and	pretty: NOM. PL. FEM

'We are young and pretty.'

A number of semi-notional verbs are also used like copulas: they express either a change (e.g., *tàpti* 'become, grow', *darýtis* 'become'), or remaining in a state (e.g., *(pa)lìkti* 'remain'), or pretending (e.g., *dė́tis* 'pretend', *apsimèsti* 'pretend, feign'), the state being denoted by the predicative; cf.:

Jìs tãpo turtìngas.	'He grew rich.'
Jìs lìko víenišas.	'He remained alone.'

The verbs denoting pretending can take participles, e.g.:

Darbiniñkai	*dė́josi*	*pavařgę.*
worker: NOM. PL	pretend: 3. PAST. REFL	tired: PAST. ACT. PART. NOM. PL

'The workers pretended to be tired.'

THE PREDICATIVE

1.20 The predicative can be expressed by the following word forms and phrases.

(1) The nominative case of a noun, single or with dependent words, cf. respectively:

(a) *Geležìs yrà metãlas.* 'Iron is a metal.'
Bùvo žiemà. 'It was winter.'

(b) *Kaimýnas bùvo gēras žmogùs.* 'The neighbour was a good man.'

The predicative can also be expressed by a comparative phrase with the nominative case form:

Sūnùs bùvo kaĩp ą́žuolas. '(His) Son was like an oak-tree (= strong and handsome).'

(2) The nominative case of an adjective, (ordinal) numeral, pronoun, or participle, cf.:

(a) *Dangùs bùvo giẽdras.* 'The sky was clear.'

(b) *Berniùkas lìko víenas.* 'The boy remained alone.'
Jìs bùvo añtras. 'He was the second.'

(c) *Laikaĩ bùvo kitókie.* 'The times were different' (lit. 'other').

(d) *Mótina bùvo tikinti.* 'Mother was a believer' (lit. 'believing': PRES. ACT. PART).

(3) The genitive case of a noun (single or with dependent words):

Žíedas bùvo áukso. 'The ring was of gold.'
Tàs ū́kis yrà màno tė́vo. 'That farm is my father's.'

The predicative noun (or adjective) is in the genitive case (and the semantic subject, too) if the copula is used with the negative particle or if it has the neuter form of a passive participle:

Tė́vo   nebėrà   gývo.
father: GEN not-be: 3. PRES alive: GEN
'Father is dead.'

Jõ   ẽsama /   bū́ta   ragãniaus.
he: GEN   be: PRES. PASS.   be: PAST. PASS.   wizard: GEN. SG
          PART. NEUTR   PART. NEUTR
'(They say) he is/was a wizard.'

(4) The instrumental case of a noun is used as a predicative to express a temporary or changing state. To express a permanent state, the nominative is used; cf.:

Jìs	bùvo	mókytojas.
he	was	teacher: NOM

'He was a teacher' (permanent profession).

Jìs	bùvo	mókytoju.
he	was	teacher: INSTR

'He worked as a teacher' (temporary occupation).

As a rule, the nominative can be substituted for the instrumental, but not vice versa; cf. also:

Kēletą mētų dėdė bùvo   'For a number of years my uncle
seniūnù (INSTR)/seniūnas (NOM). was the village elder.'

The instrumental is more common than nominative with semi-notional copulative verbs denoting a change of state or a seeming state, than with *bū́ti* 'be', e.g.:

Patì	eglè	tāpo.
herself: NOM	fir-tree: INSTR	became

'She herself turned into a fir-tree.'

Jìs	apsìmetė	viršininku.
he	pretended	boss: INSTR

'He pretended to be the boss.'

In the case of a descriptive part-whole relationship with the subject, the predicative noun denoting a (body) part must take an attribute, e.g.:

Vaikaĩ	bùvo	įdùbusiais	skrúostais.
children	were	sunken: INSTR. PL	cheek: INSTR. PL

'The children had sunken cheeks.'

In Standard Lithuanian, adjectives and their equivalents in the predicative position are not used in the instrumental case, e.g.:

Mẽs	bū́sime	laisvì	(not *laisvaĩs).
we	will be	free: NOM. PL	(free: INSTR. PL)

'We will be free.'

(5) Prepositional phrases describe the subject referent when used predicatively, e.g.:

iš 'from, of' + GEN:

Nãmo síenos iš rą̃stų.   'The walls of the house are of timber.'

bè 'without' + GEN:

Mẽdžiai jaũ be lãpų.　　lit. 'The trees are already without leaves.'

ikì 'up to' + GEN:

Rankóvės bùs iki alkúnių.　lit. 'The sleeves will be down to the elbows.'

sù 'with' + INSTR:

Dẽdė bùvo su ū̃sais.　　'The uncle had a moustache.'

The preposition *iš* 'from' is also used with the genitive plural form of nouns (commonly denoting social status or origin), pronouns, pronominal adjectives and the superlative form of adjectives, cf.:

Jõ	senẽlis	bùvo	iš	bajõrų.
his	grandfather	was	from	gentry: GEN. PL

'His grandfather was descended from landed gentry.'

Màno	duktẽ	nè	iš	tokių̃ /	nè	iš	prastų̃jų
my	daughter	not	from	such:	not	from	common:
				GEN. PL			PRON. GEN. PL

cf.: ne	tokià /	neprastà.
not	such: NOM	not common: NOM

'My daughter is not one of those/not one of the common wenches' (cf.: '(she) is not like that/not a common wench').

Jìs	bùvo	nè	iš	kvailiáusių.
he	was	not	from	stupid: ADJ. SUPERL. GEN. PL

'He was not one of the stupidest' (i.e. 'not very stupid').

(6) The neuter form of an adjective (the ending -*a*, -*u*) is used as a predicative in a personal sentence if the subject is either (**a**) a neuter adjective or (**b**) the pronoun *taĩ* 'that', or *vìsa* 'all, everything', *víena* 'one', *kìta* 'another (thing)', or (**c**) the indefinite pronoun *kàs* 'who, what' (or *kažkàs* 'something, somebody'), *kai kàs* 'something, someone', *daũg kas* 'much, many', *bet kàs* 'anything, anyone', *kàs ne kàs* 'something, somebody', *niẽkas* 'nothing, nobody', *vìskas* 'everything'; cf.:

(a) *Sẽna bùvo nuobodù, õ*　　　'(What was) old was dull, and
naũja neáišku.　　　　　　　(what was) new was uncertain.'

(b) *Taĩ labaĩ įdomù.*　　　　　'That is very interesting.'
Víena yrà tìkra.　　　　　　'One (thing) is true.'

(c) *Kàs táu malonù?*   'What is pleasant for you?'
Kai kàs / daũg kàs / kažkàs bùvo negẽra.   'Some things / much (many things) / something was wrong' (lit. 'not good').
Čià niẽkas nemíela.   lit. 'Nothing is pleasant here' (= 'I hate it here').

The neuter form of an adjective is used with the nominative subject to express a generalized assessment, cf.:

Svẽčias visadà malonù.   'A guest is always a pleasure' (lit. 'pleasant').
Nè pinigaĩ, õ drąsà svarbù.   'Not money but courage is important.'

The neuter form of ordinal numerals, adjectival pronouns and passive participles is also used in this way, e.g.:

Kalbà yrà víena, õ darbaĩ kìta.   'Talking is one (thing) and deeds (quite) another.'

Neuter adjectives are widely used as predicatives in impersonal sentences to express a state, e.g.:

Bùvo	*káršta.*
was	hot: NEUTR

'It was hot.'

Jám	*bùvo*	*nesmagù.*
he: DAT	was	not pleasant: NEUTR

'He felt uneasy.'

Neuter adjectives can also take an infinitive, e.g.:

Čià	*gẽra*	*gyvénti.*
here	good: NEUTR	live: INF

'It's good to live here.'

Mán	*bùvo*	*neįdomù*	*klausýti.*
I: DAT	was	not interesting: NEUTR	listen: INF

'It was dull for me to listen.'

(7) A number of adverbs of manner can also be used predicatively, to express meanings similar to those of neuter adjectives, cf.:

Čià	*kažkàs*	*negeraĩ /*	*negẽra.*
here	something	not good: ADV	not good: NEUTR

'Something is wrong here.'

Táu	*bùs*	*riestaĩ /*	*riẽsta.*
you: DAT	will be	hard: ADV	hard: NEUTR

'You'll be in a spot.'

(8) An infinitive is also used in compound nominal predicates if the subject is a noun or an infinitive, e.g.:

Jõ	vìsas	dárbas	bùvo	dykinė́ti.
his	all: NOM	work: NOM	was	idle: INF

'His job was to do nothing.'

Gyvénti –	taĩ	kùrti.
live: INF	that	create: INF

'To live is to create.'

THE SUBJECT

1.21 The part of a sentence immediately linked to the predicate by the syntactic relation of interdependence is regarded as subject (*veiksnỹs*). A specialized grammatical form for encoding the subject is the nominative case of a noun, e.g.:

Kviečiaĩ pribréndo.
wheat: NOM. PL ripen: 3. PAST
'The wheat has ripened.'

Mergáitė	bùvo	linksmà.
girl: NOM. SG. FEM	be: 3. PAST	cheerful: NOM. SG. FEM

'The girl was cheerful.'

Any other word form (or word group) interchangeable with a noun in the nominative case is also viewed as subject, if it accepts a question beginning with *kàs* 'who, what.'

The subject denotes an entity whose processual, qualitative, quantitative or any other characteristic, or assignment to a class is expressed by the predicate.

According to internal structure, simple and complex subjects are distinguished.

Simple subject

1.22 A simple subject is expressed by the following word forms.

(1) The nominative case of a personal pronoun, e.g.:

| Àš dár niẽko nežinójau. | 'I didn't know anything yet.' |
| Jìs labaĩ jáunas. | 'He is very young.' |

The 1st and 2nd person pronouns in subject position are often omitted, since the verbal ending implies the subject unambiguously, e.g.:

Einù *iř* *dainúoju.*
go: 1. SG. PRES   and   sing: 1. SG. PRES
'I am walking and singing.'

Mokėjot *ateĩt,* *mokėkit* *išeĩt.*
know: 2. PL. PAST   come: INF   know: 2. PL. IMPER   leave: INF
'You knew how to come, you must know how (and when) to leave.'

(2) The nominative case of other than personal pronouns, also numerals, adjectives, etc. used in the position of a noun, e.g.:

Kiekvíenas jį̃ pažį́sta.	'Everyone knows him.'
Jaunì šóka, senì žiū̃ri.	'The young are dancing, the old are watching.'
Dù bė́ga, trẽčias vė́jasi.	'Two are running, the third is pursuing.'

(3) The neuter form of an adjective or pronoun, e.g.:

Iš sẽna gìmsta jáuna.	'The young is born out of old.'
Taĩ bùvo netikė́ta.	'It was unexpected.'
Vìsa prapúolė.	'All is lost.'

(4) The genitive case of a noun with the meaning of indefinite quantity, e.g.:

Pavāsariais *atplaũkdavo* *laivų̃* (cf. *laivaĩ*).
spring: INSTR. PL   come: 3. PAST. FREQ   ship: GEN. PL   ship: NOM. PL
'Each spring, some ships (cf. 'ships') used to arrive.'

The genitive case is used instead of the nominative with the negative form of *bū́ti* 'be' to express absence of the indefinite subject referent in the place indicated, e.g.:

Výrų *kiemè* *nebùvo.*
man: GEN. PL   yard: LOC. SG   not be: 3. PAST
'There were no men in the yard.'

Cf.: *Výrai* *bùvo* *kiemè.*
man: NOM. PL   were   yard: LOC. SG
'The men were in the yard.'

Výrai *kiemè* *nebùvo.*
man: NOM. PL   yard: LOC   not be: 3. PAST
'The men were not in the yard.'

If a compound nominal predicate is used with negation the subject retains the nominative case form:

Naujíena	nebùvo	maloní.
news: NOM. SG	not be: 3. PAST	pleasant: NOM. SG

'The news wasn't pleasant.'

(5) An infinitive occurs in subject position in sentences with a compound nominal predicate, or with another infinitive as predicate, e.g.:

Šienáuti yrà neleñgvas dárbas.	'To make hay is hard work.'
Supràsti – taĩ atléisti.	'To understand is to forgive.'

The infinitive is regarded as a part of a compound predicate when it co-occurs with a modal or another semi-notional verb or with a neuter adjective.

Complex subject

1.23 The following word clusters in subject position are qualified as complex subjects.

(1) A personal pronoun with an intensifying or specifying pronoun (pàts 'oneself', vìsas, -à 'all, (the) whole', víenas, -à 'one, alone', abù, abì 'both', kiekvíenas, -à 'each'), e.g.:

Àš pàts skubėjau išeĩti.	'I myself was in a hurry to leave.'
Jì vienà teisýbę pasãkė.	'She alone told the truth.'
Mẽs visì (mẽs kiekvíenas) taĩ žìnome.	'All of us (each of us) (lit. 'we all, we each') know it.'
Jiẽ abù vienódi.	'Both of them (lit. 'they both') are the same.'

(2) An indefinite pronoun with another pronoun, e.g.:

Niẽkas kìtas tõ negalė́jo padarýti.	'No one else could do it.'
Vìsa taĩ atródė juokìnga.	'All that seemed funny.'

(3) The pronoun kàs 'who, what' (and its compounds kažkàs 'somebody, something', kas nórs 'somebody, someone, something', etc.) used with an adjective, numeral or an adverb, e.g.:

Kàs ketviŕtas káime siŕgo.	Each fourth (person) in the village was ill.'
Kàs gývas bė́go gélbėtis.	'Everyone alive tried to escape.'
Daũg kàs čià bùvo.	'Many people (lit. 'many who') have been here.'
Teñ atsitìko kažkàs negẽra.	lit. 'Something bad happened here.'

A cluster of two pronouns can be replaced by one of them, mostly the second one, e.g.:

Patì (= Àš patì) pietùs išvìrsiu.	'I myself will cook dinner.'
Visì (= Mẽs visì) taĩ mãtėme.	'All of us have seen it.'

(4) A quantitative adverb (*daũg* 'much, many', *kíek* 'how much/many', *tíek* 'so much/many', *šíek tíek* 'a little, a few', *mãža* 'little') or the neuter adjectives *mãža* 'little', and *apstù* 'a lot' used with the genitive case of a noun, e.g.:

Daũg mẽtų praėjo.	'Many years (have) passed.'
Tíek žmonių čià gyvẽna.	lit. 'So many people live here.'

The status of a complex subject is also assigned to a combination of (**a**) two synonymous words in the nominative case or (**b**) the nominative and emphatic genitive of the same noun, e.g.:

(**a**) Bar̃s tavè močiùtė motinėlė.
scold: FUT you: ACC mother: DIMIN. NOM mother: DIMIN. NOM
'Your mummy will scold you.'

Tyvuliãvo ežeraĩ ežeriùkai.
stretch: 3. PAST lake: NOM. PL lake: DIMIN. NOM. PL
'Many great and small lakes stretched around.'

(**b**) Prabė́go mẽtų mẽtai.
pass: 3. PAST year: GEN. PL year: NOM. PL
lit. 'Years of years (i.e. many years) passed by.'

(For the gerundial clauses in subject position see 3.103.)

Subject-predicate concord

1.24 In most cases, the subject and predicate are dependent upon each other with respect to form: the number and person of the predicate are determined by the subject while the overt subject assumes the case form imposed by the predicate. In other words, they are in concord with each other. In a number of cases, concord is not complete or limited.

In the 1st and 2nd person, the subject (expressed by a personal pronoun) and predicate in a simple tense form agree in person and number, e.g.:

àš	sė́džiu	mẽs	sė́dime
I: NOM	sit: 1. SG. PRES	we: NOM	sit: 1. PL. PRES
'I am sitting'		'We are sitting'	

tù	*sėdi*	*jũs*	*sėdite*
thou: NOM	sit: 2.PRES	you: NOM	sit: 2. PL. PRES
'You are sitting'		'You are sitting'	

If the subject is a noun or a 3rd person pronoun, the predicate agrees with it in person (number being unmarked in this form):

jìs/	*jì/*	*jiẽ /*	*jõs /*	*vaikaĩ /*	*móterys*	*sėdi*
he	she	they: MASC	they: FEM	children	women	sit: 3. PRES

'he/she/they/children/women is/are sitting'

As a polite form of address to one person, the plural pronoun *jũs* 'you' and the nouns *põnas* 'Mister', *ponià* 'Madam', *panẽlė* 'Miss' are used with the 2nd person plural form of a verb, e.g.:

Ką̃	*jũs*	*kal̃bate,*	*mielàsis?*
what: ACC	you: PL	talk: 2. PL. PRES	dear: SG. MASC

'What are you talking about, dear?'

Ar̃	*ponià/*	*panẽlė*	*jaũ*	*papietãvote?*
PARTICLE	madam/	miss	already	dine: 2. PL. PAST

'Have you had your dinner, Madam/Miss?'

As a polite address, the pronoun *támsta* 'you', *pàts* 'yourself' and the adjective *sveĩkas, -à* 'healthy, sound' in the meaning of *támsta* are used with the 2nd person singular verb form:

Kaĩp	*támsta*	*gyvenì?*
how	you	live: 2. SG. PRES

'How are you getting on?'

Kur̃	*pàts*	*einì?*
where	yourself	go: 2. SG. PRES

'Where are you going?'

Kodė̃l	*sveĩkas*	*nesiródai?*
why	healthy	not show: 2. SG. PRES. REFL

'Why do you never come (here)?'

They are also used in the plural form:

Kaĩp	*támstos*	*gyvẽnate?*
how	you: PL	live: 2. PL. PRES

'How are you all getting on?'

The subject can be extended by the prepositional phrase *ìš* + GEN, in which case the person and number of the predicate correlate either with the subject or with the noun (pronoun) of the prepositional phrase, e.g.:

Kelì	*iš*	*júsų*	*sėdėjo /*	*sėdėjote*	*namiẽ?*
how many	from	you: Prep + GEN. PL	sit: 3. PAST	sit: 2. PL. PAST	at home

'How many of you stayed at home?'

The subject may be expressed by a personal pronoun with another pronoun (*pàts* 'oneself', *víenas* 'one, alone', *kiekvíenas* 'each', *abù* 'both'), and in this cluster the personal pronoun can be omitted, the second component representing the subject group. In this case the person of the omitted pronoun is marked in the predicate:

Pàts	*nuėjaũ/*	*nuėjaĩ/*	*nuėjo.*
self: MASC	go: 1. SG. PAST	go: 2. SG. PAST	go: 3. PAST

'I myself/you yourself/he himself went there.'

Vienà	*vìską*	*padariaũ/*	*padareĩ/*	*padãrė.*
one: FEM. NOM	all: ACC	do: 1. SG. PAST	do: 2. SG. PAST	do: 3. PAST

'I/thou/she alone did everything.'

Abù	*grį̃žome/*	*grį̃žote/*	*grį̃žo.*
both	return: 1. PL. PAST	return: 2. PL. PAST	return: 3. PAST

'Both of us/you/them returned.'

With the pronouns *kàs* 'who' (and its derivatives *daũg kàs* 'many', *kàs ne kàs* 'some (people)', *katràs* 'which (of the two)', *kurìs* 'which', *kẽletas* 'a few', *niẽkas* 'no one', *kelì* 'several', *kai kuriẽ* 'some (people)' in subject position the verb is in the 1st and 2nd plural or in the 3rd person form, cf.:

Kàs/	*katràs/*	*kurìs*	*dabař*	*eĩsite?*
who	which	which	now	go: 2. PL. FUT

'Who/which of you two/which one will go now?'

Daũg kàs/	*kai kàs*	*apiẽ*	*taĩ*	*girdėjome.*
many	some	about	that	hear: 1. PL. PAST

'Many of us/some of us (have) heard about it.'

Niẽkas	*nesuprañtame/*	*nesuprañta.*
no one	not understand: 1. PL. PRES	not understand: 3. PRES

'None of us/No one understand(s) it.'

Kai kuriẽ	*pasilìkome /*	*pasilìko.*
some	stay: 1. PL. PAST	stay: 3. PAST

'Some of us/Some (people) stayed.'

The plural form of a verbal predicate can also combine with the singular form of some collective nouns:

Daugùmas   *grĩžome.*
majority: NOM. SG   return: 1. PL. PAST
'Most of us returned.'

Tadà   *daũgelis*   *tylė́jote.*
then   many: NOM. SG   be silent: 2. PL. PAST
'At that time many of you kept silent.'

1.25   The link verb of a compound nominal predicate correlates with the subject according to the same rules as a simple verbal predicate.

The predicative of a compound predicate is also formally correlated with the subject, different sets of rules applying to predicative nouns and adjectives.

Nouns and nominal substitutes do not agree with the subject in gender (cf. (1)), unless there is a choice between two words differing in gender (cf. (2)) or the noun has different gender forms (cf. (3)):

(1) *Túopa*   *yrà*   *mẽdis.*
     poplar: FEM   is   tree: MASC
'A poplar is a tree.'

Nẽmunas   *yrà*   *ùpė.*
Nemunas: MASC   is   river: FEM
'The Nemunas is a river.'

(2) *Jõnas*   *bùvo*   *sūnùs,*   *o*   *Marýtė*   *jauniáusia*   *duktė̃.*
     John: was   son: and   Mary: youngest: daughter:
     MASC   MASC   FEM   FEM   FEM
'John was (their) son, and Mary (was) the youngest daughter.'

(3) *Jìs*   *bùvo*   *mókytojas.*
     he   was   teacher: MASC. SG
'He was a teacher.'

Jì   *bùvo*   *mókytoja.*
she   was   teacher: FEM. SG
'She was a teacher.'

The predicative noun usually agrees with the subject in number, e.g.:

Brólis   *bùs*   *ū́kininkas.*
brother: NOM. SG   be: FUT   farmer: NOM. SG
'(My) brother will be a farmer.'

Bróliai   *bùs*   *ū́kininkai.*
brother: NOM. PL   be: 3.FUT   farmer: NOM. PL
'(My) brothers will be farmers.'

This is not the case if one of the two nouns belongs to the class of *pluralia tantum*, cf.:

Jų	*maĩstas*	*bùvo*	*bùlvės.*
their	food: NOM. SG	be: 3. PAST	potato: NOM. PL

'Their food was potatoes.'

Akėčios –		*pasẽnęs*	*įrankis.*
harrow: NOM. PL. FEM		outdated	tool: NOM. SG. MASC

'The harrow is an outdated tool.'

An abstract noun used as a predicative does not always agree with the subject in number, cf.:

Vaikaĩ	*bùvo*	*mū́sų*	*viltìs.*
child: NOM. PL	be: 3. PAST	our	hope: NOM. SG

'The children were our hope.'

If the pronoun *jū̃s* 'you' is used as a polite address instead of *tù* 'thou' the predicative noun is in the singular:

Jū̃s	*ẽsate*	*dìdvyris.*
you	be: 2. PL. PRES	hero: NOM. SG

'You are a hero.'

If the subject is a noun or a pronoun in the singular, but referring to a number of persons or things (it may subordinate a prepositional phrase), the predicative has the plural form, e.g.:

Kẽletas	*(iš*	*jų)*	*bùvo*	*studeñtai.*
several: NOM. SG	from	them	be: 3. PAST	student: NOM. PL

'Some (of them) were students.'

Vìsa	*taĩ –*	*nesą́monės.*
all: NOM. SG	that	nonsense: NOM. PL

'All that is nonsense.'

Kàs	*bùs*	*nugalėtojai?*
who	be: FUT	winner: NOM. PL

'Who will be the winners?'

The predicative noun is also plural if the subject is a collective noun or the phrase NOM + *sù* 'with' + INSTR, e.g.:

Daugùmas	*bùvo*	*výrai.*
majority: SG	be: 3. PAST	man: NOM. PL

'The majority were men.'

Tėvas   su   mótina   bùvo   darbiniñkai.
father: NOM. SG   with   mother: INSTR   be: 3. PAST   worker: NOM. PL
'Father and mother were workers.'

The instrumental case of a predicative noun agrees with the subject in number in the same way as the nominative, e.g.:

Visì   bróliai   tãpo   júodvarniais.
all: NOM. PL   brother: NOM. PL   become: 3. PAST   raven: INSTR. PL
'All the brothers turned into ravens.'

Cf.: *Jìs   tãpo   júodvarniu.*
    he   became   raven: INSTR. SG
'He turned into a raven.'

No agreement in number or in gender takes place if a collective or an abstract noun occurs in either position, e.g.:

Karõliai   tãpo   jõs   mėgstamu   pãpuošalu.
bead: NOM. PL   became   her   favourite   adornment: INSTR. SG
'Beads became her favourite adornment.'

1.26 **Adjectives** and other adjectival words in predicative position agree with the subject in the nominative case in gender, number, and case, e.g.:

Vaikaī   *bùvo*   *laimìngi.*
child: NOM. PL. MASC   be: 3. PAST   happy: NOM. PL. MASC
'The children were happy.'

Mergáitės   *bùvo*   *laimìngos.*
girl: NOM. PL. FEM   were   happy: NOM. PL. FEM
'The girls were happy.'

Jì   bùvo   pasipūtusi.
she   be: 3. PAST   conceit: PART. NOM. SG. FEM
'She was conceited.'

Gender is marked in the predicative noun or adjective if the subject is a 1st or 2nd person pronoun with no gender contrast, e.g.:

Àš   buvaũ   laimìngas/   laimìnga.
I   was   happy: MASC   happy: FEM
'I was happy.'

Jūs   būsite   laimìngi /   laimìngos.
you   be: 2. PL. FUT   happy: PL. MASC   happy: PL. FEM
'You will be happy.'

If the subject pronoun *jūs* 'you' is used as a polite address to one person, the predicative is in the singular, though the copula is in the plural:

Jūs   *ēsate*   *gražì.*
you   be: 2. PL. PRES   pretty: SG. FEM
'You are pretty.'

On the other hand, if a subject in the singular refers to several persons or things, the predicative is in the plural:

Daũgelis   *bùvo*   *piktì.*
many: SG   were   angry: PL. MASC
'The majority were angry.'

To sum up, in most cases semantic agreement underlies the choice of the grammatical categories of subject and predicative.

If a neuter adjective, or a pronoun, or an indefinite pronoun with no gender contrast is used as subject, the predicative adjective also assumes the neuter form (see (3) in 1.22).

Neuter adjectives used in a generalized sense do not agree with a subject noun, e.g.:

Medùs   *gardù.*
honey: MASC   tasty: NEUTR
'Honey is delicious.'

1.27   The participle of a periphrastic verb form agrees with the subject according to the same rules as the adjectival predicative of a compound nominal predicate, the auxiliary verb *bū́ti* 'be' assuming the person and number of the subject; cf.:

Àš   *esù*   *kalbė́jęs /*   *kalbė́jusi.*
I   be: 1. SG. PRES   speak: PAST. ACT. MASC   speak: PAST. ACT.
                             PART. SG.   PART. SG. FEM
'I have spoken.'

Tù   *esì*   *kalbė́jęs /*   *kalbė́jusi.*
thou   be: 2. SG. PRES   speak: PAST. ACT. PART. SG. MASC   speak: SG.FEM
'You have spoken.'

Mẽs   *bùvome*   *grį̃žę /*   *grį̃žusios.*
we   be: 1. PL. PAST   return: PAST. ACT.   return: PL. FEM
                             PART. PL. MASC
'We had returned.'

Jū̃s   bùvote   kviečiamì/   kviečiamos.
you   be: 2. PL. PAST   invite: PRES. PASS. PART. PL. MASC   invite: PL. FEM
'You were invited.'

(But: *Jū̃s bùvote kviečiamas* (SG. MASC)/*kviečiamà* (SG. FEM) 'You were invited', when addressing one person.)

If the subject is an indefinite pronoun (*kàs* 'what', *niẽkas* 'nothing, nobody', *kelì* 'some, several', etc.; see 1.24) or a word or word group denoting quantity, which are neutral with respect to gender, the participle usually assumes the neuter form, e.g.:

Vìskas   bùvo   pàmiršta.
everything   be: 3. PAST   forget: PAST. PASS. PART. NEUTR
'Everything was forgotten.'

Daũg   grūdų̃   bùvo   vėžama   į̇̃   miẽstą.
much   grain: GEN. PL   was   carry: PRES.   to   town: ACC. SG
                                              PASS. PART. NEUTR
'Much grain was taken to the town.'

Vìskas   bùvo   sugė́dę.
everything   was   spoil: PAST. ACT. PART. NEUTR
'Everything was spoiled.'

The neuter form of passive participles can also be used with subject nouns of either gender and number, cf.:

Rugiaĩ   jaũ   sė́jama.
rye: MASC. PL   already   sow: PRES. PASS. PART. NEUTR
'Rye is being sown already.'

Nãmas   pastatýta.
house: MASC. SG   build: PAST. PASS. PART. NEUTR
'The house is built.'

Bùlvės   bùvo   nùkasta.
potato: FEM. PL   be: 3. PAST   dig up: PAST. PASS. PART. NEUTR
'Potatoes have been dug up.'

The neuter form of a participle in a periphrastic verb form is also used if there are two or more conjoined subjects (especially if they differ in gender):

Pirmiáusia   bùs   nẽšama   gė́lės   iř̃   pavéikslai.
first   be: 3. FUT   carry: PRES.   flower: and   picture:
                                            PASS. PART. NEUTR   PL. FEM   PL. MASC
'First, flowers and pictures will be carried (out).'

THE OBJECT

1.28 The object (*papildinỹs*) is immediately subordinated to the predicate and expressed by a noun in an oblique case form (with or without a preposition) or by its substitute (a word form or a word group) in the same position.

Direct and indirect objects are distinguished.

1.29 The status of a **direct object** (*tiesióginis papildinỹs*) is assigned to a noun, a pronoun or a cardinal numeral in the accusative, and sometimes in the genitive case without a preposition, which change into the nominative case in a passive sentence, e.g.:

Jì àpdengė stãlą.	'She laid the table (ACC. SG).'
Stãlas bùvo jõs àpdengtas.	'The table (NOM. SG) was laid by her.'
Láukėme svečių̃.	'We expected visitors (GEN. PL).'
Svečiaĩ bùvo laukiamì.	'Visitors (NOM. PL) were expected.'

The accusative case is a specialized form of the direct object. If a transitive verb is used with negation the genitive is obligatorily substituted for the accusative, e.g.:

Mataũ paũkštį.	'I see a bird (ACC. SG).'
Nemataũ paũkščio.	'I don't see a bird (GEN. SG).'
Turiù sẽserį.	'I have a sister (ACC. SG).'
Neturiù seser̃s.	'I don't have a sister (GEN. SG).'

If a direct object refers to an indefinite quantity, the genitive case is also used instead of the accusative, e.g.:

Àtnešiau obuolių̃.	'I brought some apples (GEN. PL).'
Cf. *Àtnešiau óbuolius.*	'I brought the apples (ACC. PL).'
Gavaũ laiškų̃.	'I received some letters (GEN. PL).'
Cf. *Gavaũ láiškus.*	'I received the letters (ACC. PL).'

The following verbs always require a direct object in the genitive case: *láukti* 'wait (for)', *ieškóti* 'look (for)', *geĩsti* 'desire', *trókšti* 'desire, wish', *norėti* 'want', *síekti* 'strive (for)', *stokóti* 'be short (of)', *bijóti* 'be afraid (of)', *véngti* 'avoid', and the like.

The accusative (or genitive) case of a direct object is interchangeable with an **infinitive** after some verbs, e.g.:

Jì dãvė paválgyti / valgio.	'She gave some food: INF/GEN.'
Vaikaĩ kar̃tais gáuna lùpti / rýkščių.	'Sometimes (the) children get a beating (INF)/the birch (GEN).'

An infinitive often used with verbs like *véngti* 'avoid', *mókytis* 'learn', *sáugotis* 'take care (of)', *bijóti* 'be afraid (of)', *at(si)miñti* 'remember', *užmiřšti* 'forget', etc. also occupies the position of a direct object; cf.:

mókosi rašýti / rãšto	'he learns to write (INF)/writing (GEN)'
užmiršaũ pasisvéikinti	'I forgot to say hello (INF)'
bijaũ gr̃žti	'I am afraid to come back (INF)'

A direct object can also be expressed by the neuter form of an adjective, a pronoun or a passive participle unmarked for case; e.g.:

Šìtas	*žmogùs*	*šìlta*	*iř*	*šálta*	*mãtęs.*
this	man	warm: NEUTR	and	cold: NEUTR	see: PAST. ACT. PART

'This man has experienced everything' (lit. 'has seen hot and cold').

Jìs	*pàts*	*vìsa*	*padãrė.*
he	himself	all: NEUTR	do: 3. PAST

'He did everything himself.'

Ligónė	*nebeválgo*	*neĩ*	*vìrta,*	*neĩ*	*kẽpta.*
patient: NOM. FEM	not any longer eat: 3. PRES	neither	boil: PAST. PASS. PART. NEUTR	nor	fry: PAST. PASS. PART. NEUTR

'The patient does not eat either boiled or fried food any longer.'

A direct object, like the subject, can be expressed by a variety of word clusters groups consisting, for instance, of (1) a personal and an intensifying pronoun; (2) a noun and another word, or (3) two nouns in the accusative; cf.:

(1) *Šiañdien àš jĩ pãtį mačiaũ.*	lit. 'Today I saw him himself.'
(2) *Sutikaũ daũg draugų̃.*	'I met many friends.'
(3) *Rankàs kójas pavargaũ.*	lit. 'I tired (my) hands and feet.'

1.30 The status of an **indirect object** (*netiesióginis papildinỹs*) is assigned to a noun in an oblique case (with or without a preposition) or its substitute, which retains its form with the passive form of the predicate, cf.:

Mergáitė	*gėlès*	*àtnešė*	*mótinai.*
girl: NOM. SG	flower: ACC. PL	bring: 3. PAST	mother: DAT. SG

'The girl brought flowers to her mother.'

Gẽlės	*bùvo*	*àtneštos*	*mótinai.*
flower: NOM. PL	be: 3. PAST	bring: PAST. PL PART. NOM.	mother: DAT. SG

'Flowers were brought to the mother.'

Jiẽ   džiaũgėsi   pérgale.
They   rejoice: 3. PAST. REFL   victory: INSTR
'They rejoiced at the victory.'

Bùvo   džiaũgiamasi   pérgale.
be: 3. PAST   rejoice: PRES. PASS. PART. NEUTR. REFL   victory: INSTR
'There was rejoicing at the victory.'

An indirect object is most commonly expressed by (1) the dative, (2) the instrumental, (3) a prepositional phrase; cf. respectively:

(1) *Sáulė visíems šviẽčia.*	'The sun shines for all (DAT. PL).'
Jái neláimė atsitìko.	lit. 'A misfortune happened to her (DAT. SG).'
(2) *Jiẽ didžiúojasi sàvo sūnumĩ.*	'They are proud of their son (INSTR. SG).'
Jìs vìskuo abejója.	'He doubts everything (INSTR. SG).'
Atvažiavaũ tráukiniu.	'I have come by train (INSTR. SG).'
(3) *Jìs juõkiasi ìš tavę̃s.*	'He laughs at you (Prep + GEN. SG).'
Papāsakok apiẽ sàvo kelionès.	'Tell (me) about your travels (Prep + ACC. PL).'

The genitive case without a preposition also occurs as indirect object, but in active constructions it is less common than the dative or the instrumental, e.g.:

Merginà drovėjosi svečių̃.   'The girl felt shy with visitors (GEN. PL).'

On the other hand, the genitive is very common in passive constructions where it denotes the agent (*genetivus auctoris*); cf.:

Stógas   bùvo   vėjo   nùneštas.
roof: NOM. SG. MASC was   wind: GEN. SG carry away: PAST. PASS.
                                             PART. NOM. SG. MASC
'The roof was blown away by the wind.'

Teñ   vaikų̃   žaĩdžiama.
there   child: GEN. PL   play: PRES. PASS. PART. NEUTR
'There are children playing there.'

The genitive is also required by adjectives and some adverbs of state used predicatively, cf.:

Jìs   bùvo   godùs   pinigų̃.
he   was   greedy: NOM. MASC   money: GEN. PL
'He was greedy for money.'

Kalbõs   bùvo   apstù.
talk: GEN. SG   was   abundantly
'There was much talk (about it).'

1.31 An indirect object is often governed by a predicate having a direct object, e.g.:

Àš gẽrą naujíeną jùms *pařnešiau.*	'I've brought you (DAT) good news (ACC. SG).'
Seniaũ rugiùs pjáutuvais pjáudavom.	'In the old days we reaped rye (ACC. PL.) with sickles (INSTR. PL).'
Pasidariaũ kìbirą iš *lentų̃* bè *kiřvio.*	'I have made a pail (ACC. SG) from planks (Prep + GEN. PL) without an ax (Prep + GEN. SG).'

In these cases, the difference between a direct and indirect object is made explicit in a passive transform:

Rašiaũ   láišką   pieštukù   draũgui.
write: 1. SG. PAST   letter: ACC. SG   pencil: INSTR. SG   friend: DAT. SG
'I was writing a letter to a friend with a pencil.'

Láiškas   bùvo   rãšomas   pieštukù   draũgui.
letter: NOM. SG   was   write: PRES. PASS.   pencil: friend: DAT. SG
                          PART. NOM. SG   INSTR. SG
'The letter was being written to a friend with a pencil.'

The word groups singled out in the following sentences are viewed as complex indirect objects:

Juõdu bùvo víenas kitám skirtì.	'The two of them were made (lit. 'destined') for each (NOM) other (DAT).'
Nórs manè áuksu sidabrù apipìltų, neĩsiu.	'Even if they shower me with gold silver (INSTR), I won't go.'

THE ADVERBIAL

1.32 The status of the adverbial (*aplinkýbė*) is assigned to the part of a sentence immediately subordinated to the predicate and expressed by an adverb, a prepositional phrase replacing an adverb or by a noun in an oblique case (the locative, accusative and instrumental being the most frequent forms), also interchangeable with an adverb.

Adverbials may serve as the answer to the questions expressed by adverbs *kadà* 'when', *kaĩp* 'how', *kíek* 'how much/many', *kodė̃l* 'why', *kuř* 'where'; *nuo kadà* 'since when', *iki kõl* 'until when', *už kíek* 'for how much', *iš kuř* 'from where', etc. Adverbials denote the following:

(1) place, (including location and direction), e.g.:

Namiė niẽko neradaũ.	'I didn't find anyone at home.'
Apliñkui bùvo tylù.	'It was quiet all around (ADV).'
Miškè nuaidėjo šũviai.	'Shots were heard in the forest (LOC).'
Grĩžome iš miestẽlio.	'We returned from the town (Prep + GEN).'

(2) time:

Anksčiaũ tù taĩp nekalbėjai.	'You never spoke so before (ADV).'
Vidùdienį dẽbesys išsisklaĩdė.	'At noon (ACC) the clouds disappeared.'
Põ dviejų dienų sugrĩšiu.	'In two days (Prep + GEN) I'll be back.'

(3) manner:

Arkliaĩ bė́go risčià.	'The horses ran at a trot (ADV).'
Kraũjas suñkėsi põ lãšą.	'The blood seeped drop by drop (Prep + ACC).'
Čià pusėtinai švarù.	'It is rather (ADV) clean here.'
Gyvẽnome atskiraĩ, põ víeną.	'We lived separately, one to a room (Prep + ACC).'

(4) cause:

Mìrė iš síelvarto.	'He died of grief (Prep + GEN).'
Peř tavè pavėlavaũ į́ tráukinį.	'Because of you (Prep + ACC) I missed the train.'

(5) purpose:

Visì išėjo grybáuti.	'They have all gone out to gather mushrooms (INF).'
Jìs pàkvietė mùs pietų́.	'He invited us to dinner (GEN).'

Among adverbials of manner, modifiers of quantity (*Jìs daũg šnẽka, mažaĩ dãro* 'He talks much and does little') and of comparison (*Bė́ga kaĩp kìškis* 'He runs like a rabbit') can be distinguished.

Generally, adverbials are classified according to their semantic relationship with the predicate, the types distinguished displaying no specific grammatical features.

Some case forms and prepositional phrases may serve to answer two kinds of questions, cf.:

Grĩžome iš vakarõnės.   'We returned from an evening-party.'
(*Iš kuř?* 'From where?' / *Iš kõ?* 'From what?').

Išėjaũ pàs mótiną.   lit. 'I went to my mother.'
(*Kuř?* 'Where?' / *Pas ką?* 'To whom?').

Skaičiaũ láišką põ stalù.   'I read the letter under the table.'
(*Kuř?* 'Where?' / *Po kuõ?* 'Under what?').

These intermediate instances are interpreted as adverbials. Only those instances are classed as indirect objects which cannot serve as the answer to a question with a generalized interrogative adverb (*kuř?* 'where', *kadà?* 'when', etc.). The only exception is an adverbial modifier of purpose for which there is no specific interrogative adverb and which can serve as the answer to the question *kuriuõ tikslù? / kõ?* 'for what purpose?'. Therefore it may also be regarded as an indirect object.

An adverbial, like an indirect object, retains its form in a passive construction.

The structure and meanings of objects and adverbials are treated in more detail in the sections on word groups and sentence patterns.

THE PREDICATIVE COMPLEMENT

1.33 A part of a sentence immediately subordinated both to the predicate and to the subject or object is termed a predicative complement.

A predicative complement (like a predicative) agrees with the subject or with the object and is adjoined to the predicate, e.g.:

Berniùkas	*bėgiójo*	*bãsas.*
boy: NOM. SG. MASC	ran about	barefoot: NOM. SG. MASC

'The boy was running about barefooted.'

The syntactic relations in this sentence can be shown by the following scheme:

A predicative complement, expressed by an adjective, other adjectival word or participle and related to the subject takes the nominative case form and is in agreement with the subject in number and gender, e.g.:

Jì   grį̃š   turtìnga.
she: NOM   return: FUT   rich: NOM. SG. FEM
'She will return rich.'

Vaikaĩ   išėjo   alkanì.
child: NOM.   left   hungry: NOM. PL. MASC
PL. MASC
lit. 'The children went away hungry.'

Jìs   stovėjo   susiraũkęs,   niũrùs.
he: NOM   stood   frown: PAST. ACT.   gloomy: NOM. SG.
                      PART. NOM. SG. MASC   MASC
'He stood frowning and gloomy.'

When related to an object, the predicative complement agrees with it in case and in number and gender as well, cf.:

Àš   jį̃   pažinaũ   dár   studeñtą.
I   he: ACC. SG. MASC   knew   yet   student: ACC. SG. MASC
'I knew him as a student yet.'

Radaũ   sū́nų   neválgiusį.
find: 1. SG. PAST son: ACC. SG. MASC   not eat: PAST. PART. ACC. SG. MASC
'I found (my) son hungry' (lit. 'not having eaten').

Vaĩkui   nusibódo   vienám.
child: DAT. SG. MASC   be bored: 3. PAST   alone: DAT. SG. MASC
'The child got bored (being) alone.'

Nelaikýk   šuñs   paláido.
not keep: IMPER   dog: GEN. SG. MASC   loose: GEN. SG. MASC
'Don't keep the dog unleashed.'

1.34 A predicative complement can be realized by a noun with the conjunction *kaĩp* 'as, like' which in this case does not express comparison:

Sūnùs grį̃žo namõ kaĩp šeimininkas.	'The son returned home as (in the capacity of) its owner (NOM).'
Jìs atvýko kaĩp pasiuntinỹs. (Cf. *atvýko pãsiuntiniu.*)	'He came as an envoy (NOM)' ('(He) came as an envoy (INSTR).')
Mẽs gerbėme Motiẽjų kaĩp gãbų méistrą.	'We respected Matthew ACC. SG as a gifted master ACC. SG.'

1.35 A predicative complement (like a predicative, cf. 1.20, 4–5) can also be expressed by the instrumental case of a noun with a modifier or by a prepositional phrase, in which case there is no agreement with the subject (1) or object (2); cf. respectively:

(1) *Pabùdo jaunãmartė neramià širdimĩ.* lit. 'The bride woke up with a heavy heart (INSTR).'

Jìs grį̃žo namõ su unifòrma. 'He returned home in uniform (INSTR).'

(2) *Àtvedė vaikìną surištomìs rañkomis.* 'They brought in a lad (ACC) with bound hands (INSTR. PL).'

Surãdo manè be sąmonės. 'They found me unconscious' (lit. 'without consciousness (Prep + GEN)').

Participles in the predicative complement position often have an adverbial meaning and form participial clauses (see 4.2).

MODIFIERS

1.36 The parts of a sentence immediately related to the predicate are often extended by modifiers which in their turn may also have modifiers. Thus a sentence may have a structure of several consecutively subordinated levels, or ranks. On the first level the parts of a sentence related to the predicate are the subject, objects, adverbials and the predicative complement. On the lower levels, they are subordinated modifiers. For instance, a structure of several levels characterizes the sentence *Màno senẽlės nãmą sùpo sõdas, pìlnas skaĩsčiai raudonų̃ rõžių* 'A garden full of bright(ly) red roses surrounded my grandmother's house'; cf.:

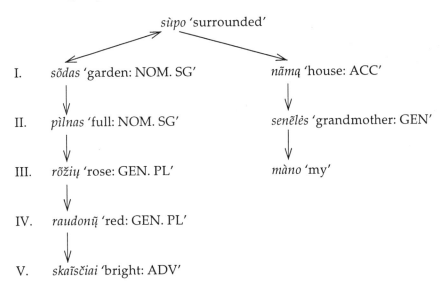

The object group contains here modifiers on two lower levels, and the subject group on four lower levels. The modifiers of lower levels are linked to the sentence parts and to one another either by agreement (pìlnas sõdas 'full garden', raudonų rõžių '(of) red roses'), or government (pìlnas rõžių 'full of roses', màno senẽlės 'my grandmother's'), or adjunction (skaĩsčiai raudonų '(of) bright(ly) red'). According to the type of syntactic relation with the head word these internal modifiers can be classified into attributive modifiers, or attributes (pìlnas sõdas, raudonų rõžių, màno senẽlės), objective modifiers (pìlnas rõžių) and adverbial modifiers (skaĩsčiai raudonų).

1.37 With respect to its syntactic relations, an **attribute** (viewed as a part of the sentence in traditional grammar) is but a modifier of a sentence part or of another higher level modifier, since it is distinguished on a lower level of sentence analysis.

An attribute agrees with the head word in gender, number and case if it is an adjective, an ordinal numeral, an adjectival pronoun, or a participle:

mė́lynas dangùs	'blue sky (NOM. SG. MASC)'
karštà vãsara	'hot summer (NOM. SG. FEM)'
pìrmos diẽnos	'first days (NOM. PL. FEM)'
kitì žmónės	'other people (NOM. PL. MASC)'
įdùbę skrúostai	'sunken (PAST. ACT. PART. NOM. PL. MASC) cheeks (NOM. PL. MASC)'

An attribute with dependent word forms constitutes an attribute group, cf.:

pìlnas raudonų rõžių sõdas   lit. 'full of red roses garden'

1.38 An attribute expressed by a noun which agrees with the head noun in case and often in gender and number, is termed **apposition**. Both the head noun and apposition are termed appositives. An apposition can either precede (cf. broliùkas Lìnas 'little brother Linas', generõlas Rãštikis 'General Rãštikis') or follow (cf. žõdis láisvė 'the word freedom') the head noun. It differs from other attributes in that it can be used instead of the entire word group, cf.:

Sutikaũ kaimýną Pẽtrą.	'I met (my) neighbour (ACC. SG. MASC) Peter (ACC. SG. MASC).'
Cf.	
Sutikaũ kaimýną.	'I met (my) neighbour.'
Sutikaũ Pẽtrą.	'I met Peter.'

The postmodifiers in the following word groups are very similar to appositional constructions:

visì kitì lit. 'all others (MASC. PL)'
kažkàs júodas 'something black (MASC. SG)'
vìsa gẽra 'everything good (NEUTR)'

1.39 An attribute does not agree with the head word if it is a noun (or its substitute) in the genitive case (*mū́sų núomonė* 'our (GEN. PL) opinion', *vaikų̃ žaislaĩ* 'children's (GEN. PL) toys'), in the instrumental case with dependent words (*mergáitė mė́lynomìs akimìs* 'a girl with blue eyes (INSTR. PL)' or a prepositional phrase (*žmogùs bè kójos* 'a man without a leg (Prep + GEN. SG)', *nãmas priẽ kẽlio* 'a house by the road (Prep + GEN. SG)'.

1.40 With respect to form, attributes are similar to predicatives and predicative complements. This similarity is not accidental: a phrase with an attribute may be regarded as a syntactic transform of a clause with a compound nominal predicate embedded in another clause, cf.:

Teñ sėdė́jo žmogùs. 'A man was sitting there.'
Žmogùs bùvo bè kójos. lit. 'The man was without a leg.'
⇒ *Teñ sėdė́jo žmogùs bè kójos.* 'A man without a leg was sitting there.'

1.41 Active participles (including gerunds) retain the valency of the base verb. A participial or a gerundial clause (i.e. participle or a gerund with dependent word forms) subordinated to the predicate is syntactically similar to a subordinate clause with a finite verb form. Therefore the constituents of participial and gerundial clauses (like the constituents of finite subordinate clauses) are also regarded as objects and adverbials. Thus the syntactic relations in the extended sentence *Vėlaĩ vakarè pabaĩgęs dárbą, Jõnas išė́jo namõ* 'Having finished work late at night, John went home' can be represented as follows:

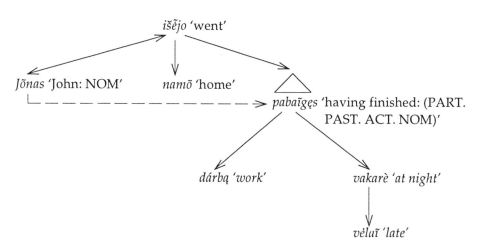

The syntactic relations within a gerundial phrase are analysable in the same way; cf. the sentence *Jõnui pabaĩgus dárbą, visì vaikaĩ išẽjo namõ* 'John having finished work, all the children went home':

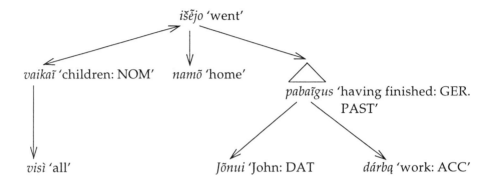

2 WORD GROUPS
Žõdžių junginiaĩ

2.1 In a sentence, at least two notional words related by an immediate syntactic relation constitute a word group. According to the type of syntactic relation, they are classified into interdependent, subordinative and coordinative word groups.

Interdependent word groups are distinguished on the highest level of sentence analysis and they are discussed in the sections concerned with the subject and predicate (see 1.13–27).

Subordinative and coordinative word groups are distinguished on all the levels of sentence analysis. For instance, the following word groups are distinguished in the sentence *Mergáitės riñko ant kálno pìlkas, saldžiaĩ kvėpiančias žolès* 'Girls gathered grey, sweet(ly) smelling herbs on the hill':

(1) the interdependent group *mergáitės riñko* 'girls gathered';

(2) the subordinative groups *riñko žolès* 'gathered herbs', *riñko ant kálno* 'gathered on the hill', *pìlkas žolès* 'grey herbs', *kvėpiančias žolès* 'smelling herbs', *saldžiaĩ kvėpiančias* 'sweet(ly) smelling';

(3) the coordinative group *pìlkas, kvėpiančias* 'grey, smelling'.

The following scheme shows the syntactic relations within the sentence:

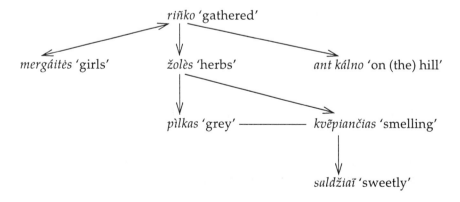

A word form may enter into more than one group on different levels of analysis. Thus in the above sentence, the accusative *žolès* 'herbs' is a dependent constituent of the group *riñko žolès* and a head word in *pìlkas žolès* and *kvėpiančias žolès*. The dependent word of the latter group is in its turn the head word of *saldžiaĩ kvėpiančias*.

Word groups, especially those with the interdependence relation, can be structurally identical to a simple sentence, e.g. *vaikaĩ žaĩdžia* 'children are playing', *laukè pasnìgo* 'it has snowed outside'.

Subordinative word groups

2.2 A **simple** subordinative word group is comprised of two word forms of which one is the head and the other is subordinated to it. A subordinative word group is incorporated in the sentence structure via its head word. A word form used with a preposition is termed a prepositional phrase, and it forms a single dependent constituent, as in *riñko ant kálno* 'gathered on the hill' (see the above example).

The structure of a subordinative word group is determined by the grammatical class and combinability of the head word. Accordingly, the verbal, nominal, adjectival, pronominal and adverbial groups are distinguished. They express a broad range of semantic relations: relations between an action and its agent (e.g. *paũkščio skridìmas* 'a bird's flight'), or its patient (*ieties metìmas* 'throwing a spear', *mèsti ietį* 'to throw a spear'), or content (*sakýti tiẽsą* 'to tell the truth'), or beneficiary (*dúoti vaĩkui* 'give to the child'), relations between an entity and its property (*raudóna rõžė* 'red rose'), and also various relations of time, place, manner, etc. (*miegóti nãktį/namiẽ/ramiaĩ* 'sleep at night/at home/quietly').

A word group may be a complex naming unit or an idiom, e.g.:

dėmė́toji šiĩtinė	'typhus'
laũmės júosta	'rainbow'
kiáuras maĩšas	'glutton' (lit. 'a bag full of holes')
gáudyti várnas	'gape' (lit. 'catch crows')

Structurally, however, these phrases are not different from regular neutral word groups.

2.3 A **complex** subordinative word group consists of a head word and two or more components subordinated to the latter on the same level of analysis, e.g.:

dúok mán rañkšluostį	'give me a towel'
labaĩ godùs pinigų̃	'very greedy for money'

A complex word group can be regarded as a combination of simple ones:

dúok mán 'give me' + *dúok rañkšluostį* 'give a towel'
godùs pinigų̃ 'greedy for money' + *labaĩ godùs* 'very greedy'

Therefore, the subsequent analysis is concerned mostly with simple word groups, except in cases when complex groups are indivisible for semantic or syntactic reasons.

The dependent constituent of a word group may be obligatorily modified by another dependent word form, i.e. the head word is necessarily related to the whole dependent group, e.g.:

trečià dienà lỹja	'it has been raining for three days'
(but **dienà lỹja*)	
vaĩkas įdùbusiais skrúostais	'a child with sunken cheeks'
(but **vaĩkas skrúostais*)	

2.4 Derivative words either retain or change the combinability of the base word. Thus, if a verbal group is transformed into a nominal one, optional modifiers of place, time, etc. usually retain their form; e.g.:

pailsė́jau vãsarą priẽ jū́ros	'I rested at the seaside in summer'
⇒ *màno póilsis vãsarą priẽ jū́ros*	'my rest at the seaside in summer'

A word group in such cases retains its verbal character.

On the other hand, the accusative case form governed by the verb is changed into the genitive in a derivative group:

rašýti láišką	'to write a letter (ACC)'
⇒ *láiško rãšymas*	lit. 'the writing of a letter (GEN)'

A verbal group with a qualitative adverb is often transformed into a nominal group with an adjective:

suñkiai dìrbti	'to work hard (ADV)'
⇒ *sunkùs dárbas*	'hard (ADJ) work'

The structure of a word group also changes if an adjective is transformed into a noun:

gražì móteris	'a beautiful woman'
⇒ *móters grõžis*	'the beauty of a woman (GEN)'

A. VERBAL GROUPS

2.5 Verbal groups are formed by all finite and non-finite verbs and by some deverbal nouns. The subordinate constituent can be an oblique case of a noun (or its substitute), a prepositional phrase, an infinitive, an adjective or an adverb. Accordingly, a number of subtypes are distinguished.

Verb – Noun

THE ACCUSATIVE CASE

2.6 The **objective accusative** obligatorily governed by a transitive verb denotes the following:

(1) an affected object of the verbal action (**a**) or an entity whose position is changed (**b**), e.g.:

(**a**) *skáldyti málkas*	'chop wood'
dažýti pláukus	'dye hair'
(**b**) *nèšti vándenį*	'carry water'
varýti bañdą	'drive a herd'

(2) an effected object, or the result of an action:

statýti namùs	'build houses'
mègzti pirštinę	'knit a glove'

(3) the content of an experience, or state, or speech:

girdėti mùziką	'hear music'
užmiršti var̃dą	'forget a name'
pranešti naujíeną	'report news'
mylėti vaikùs	'love children'

With a number of verbs denoting physical sensation the accusative is interchangeable with the nominative:

skaũda gálvą/galvà	lit. '(the) head (ACC/NOM) aches'
ausìs/aũsys gẽlia	lit. '(the) ears (ACC/NOM) ache'
délnus/delnaĩ niẽžti	'(the) palms (ACC/NOM) are itching'

2.7 The objective accusative is governed by numerous prefixed verbs derived from non-prefixed verbs governing other case forms or prepositional phrases; cf.:

siúti (drabužiùs) šeĩmai	'sew (clothes) for the family (DAT)'
– apsiúti šeĩmą	lit. 'provide the family (ACC) with clothes'
ganýti (avìs) píevoje	'graze (sheep) in a meadow (LOC)'
– nuganýti píevą	'damage a meadow (ACC) by grazing'
brìsti su bãtais	'wade with shoes (Prep + INSTR) on'
– išbrìsti batùs	'damage shoes (ACC) by wading'
lõšti iš pinigų̃	'play for money (Prep + GEN)'
– pralõšti pìnigus	'lose money (ACC) (at cards, etc.)'

Tautological combinations of a verb and a cognate object are distinguished as a special type:

dainúoti daĩną	'sing a song'
dìrbti dárbą	lit. 'to work work'
kariáuti kãrą	'wage a war'
keliáuti kẽlią	lit. 'walk/travel a path'

2.8 The **adverbial accusative** conveys temporal, spatial and quantitative meanings.

The optional accusative of temporal nouns (e.g. dienà 'day', naktìs 'night', pirmãdienis 'Monday', žiemà 'winter', etc., and nouns like valandà 'hour', mė́nuo 'month' used with specifiers) denotes the **time** of an action:

pabùsti nãktį	'wake up at night'
grį̃žti rùdenį	'return in autumn'
ateĩti antrãdienį	'come on Tuesday'
miegóti diẽną	'sleep in the daytime'
atostogáuti vãsarą	'have (one's) leave in summer'
pietáuti peñktą vãlandą	'have dinner at five o'clock'
žydė́ti gegužė̃s mė́nesį	'blossom in May'

The optional accusative of nouns denoting stretches of time denotes **duration** of an action:

lìjo vãlandą	'it rained for an hour'
sirgaũ mė́nesį	'(I) was ill for a month'
mókėmės metùs	'(we) studied for a year'

The accusative of duration may have a quantitative attribute (a numeral, pronoun or adjective):

snìgo dvì/kelìas paràs	'it snowed for two/several days'
miegójau vìsą/ìštisą diẽną	'(I) slept all/entire day'

The accusative of a numeral or pronoun is also used with the genitive of a temporal noun:

láukti dẽšimtį/kelió̃lika valandų̃	'wait for ten/several hours'

The accusative of **subsequent period**, in most cases synonymous with the more common dative, is used with a limited number of verbs such as *pakviẽsti* 'invite', *pasiųsti* 'send (sb)', *išléisti* 'let out', *sustóti* 'stop over', *apsistóti* 'stay, stop (at)', *apsigyvénti* 'put up, stay (for a while)', e.g.:

išvažiúoti mė́nesį/mė́nesiui	'to go away for a month'
sustóti vãlandą/vãlandai	'to stop for an hour'

2.9 The accusative of temporal nouns used with the pronouns *kàs* 'what' (without agreement in case), *kiekvíenas, -à* 'each, every', adjectives *dãžnas, -à* 'frequent', *rẽtas, -à* 'far between, rare' denotes **frequency** of action, i.e. intervals of time at which an action is regularly repeated, e.g.:

ateĩna kàs/kiekvíeną rýtą	'(he) comes every morning'
aplañko dãžną sekmãdienį	'(he) pays visits frequently on Sundays' (lit. 'on a frequent Sunday')
rẽtą díeną nelỹja	'it seldom (lit.'on a rare day') does not rain'

A phrase *kàs* + ACC can be extended by a numeral or a quantitative pronoun:

susitiñkame kàs añtrą díeną	'we meet every other (lit.'second') day'

In these cases, the nominative can be used instead of the accusative: *ateĩna kàs/kiekvíenas rýtas, dažnà dienà* 'he comes every morning, frequently (lit. '(on) a frequent day')'.

2.10 The accusative of nouns denoting linear measures, when used with motion verbs, expresses **distance**:

nueĩti kilomètrą	'walk a kilometre'
pasitráukti žiñgsnį	'draw aside a step'

It can be extended by a numeral or a quantitative pronoun:

nušókti trìs/kelìs metrùs	'jump three/several metres'.

In such verbal groups as *nujóti šim̃tą/kėletą mýlių* 'ride a hundred/several miles' the numeral or nominal pronoun assumes the accusative form, the noun of distance being used in the genitive (see 2.130, 2.134).

The accusative of nouns denoting other measures (often modified by a numeral or its pronominal substitute) occurs with the verbs *svẽrti/svérti (tòną)* 'weigh (a ton)', *sumokė́ti (dù litùs)* 'pay (two litas)', *kainúoti* 'cost', *sukàkti* (as in *jìs sukãko peñkerius metùs vãkar* (cf. *jám sukãko penkerì mẽtai*) ' he turned five years old yesterday'.

THE GENITIVE CASE

2.11 The **objective genitive** is obligatorily governed by verbs denoting the following:

(1) desire and other similar feelings: *norėti* 'want', *geĩsti/trókšti* 'desire', *ilgė́tis* 'long (for)', *tikė́tis* 'hope (for)', *láukti* 'expect', *pavydė́ti (draugáms sė̃kmės)* 'envy (friends, their success)', *klausýti (tėvų̃)* 'obey (parents)';

(2) fear, shame, and the like: *bijóti* 'be afraid (of)', *báimintis* 'be afraid (of)', *išsigą̃sti* 'be frightened', *baidýtis* 'take fright (of)'; *drovė́tis* 'be shy', *gė́dytis* 'be ashamed (of)', *gailė́tis* 'be sorry ', *gedė́ti* 'mourn'; *véngti* 'avoid', *šãlintis* 'avoid', *sáugotis* ' beware (of)', *atsikratýti* 'get rid (of)', *atsižadė́ti (įsitikinimų̃)* 'renounce (one's views)';

(3) want, loss or having enough (of sth.): *stìgti* 'be short of', *stokóti* 'lack', *trū́kti* 'be lacking', *nustóti* 'lose, be deprived (of)', *užtèkti* 'have enough (of)', *pakàkti* 'have/be enough', *ganė́ti* 'have/be enough', *reikė́ti* 'need (sth)';

(4) asking or requesting: *kláusti* 'ask', *meĩsti/maldáuti* 'beg', and *prašýti* 'ask (for sth)' which sometimes governs two genitives: *prašýti tė́vo pinigų̃* 'ask father (GEN) for money'. The genitive of the noun denoting a human being is interchangeable with the accusative (which is more common): *prašýti tė́vą pinigų̃* 'ask father (ACC) for money (GEN)';

(5) the genitive of object is also obligatorily governed by verbs with the prefixes *pri-, per-, at-, už-* derived from transitive verbs; it denotes a large or indefinite quantity:

pri(si)riñkti úogų	'to gather (enough) berries'
pri(si)skìnti gėlių̃	'pick (enough) flowers'
pérsivalgyti obuolių̃	'overeat of apples'
atsiválgyti medaũs	'have one's fill of honey'
už(si)ką́sti dúonos	'eat (a little) bread'

The objective genitive is also obligatorily governed by transitive verbs with the negation *ne-* 'not':

neparãšė láiško	'he didn't write a letter'
nežìno tiesõs	'he doesn't know the truth'

(see 3.115).

2.12 Some transitive verbs may take the **genitive of indefinite quantity**. The genitive is used to denote a part or indefinite quantity of the object expressed **(a)** by the plural form of a count noun, or **(b)** by the singular of a mass noun:

(a) *dúoti pinigų*	'give some money'
atnèšti obuolių	'bring some apples'
turėti ýdų	'have (some) faults'
(b) *pir̃kti cùkraus*	'buy some sugar'
turėti kantrýbės	'have patience'

The accusative is used to refer to the whole object or entire quantity, cf.:

išgérti vandeñs	'drink some water (GEN)'
išgérti vándenį	'drink (all) the water (ACC)'

2.13 The genitive denoting the **semantic subject** is required by passive participles (both present and past) used as attributes or predicates:

tėvo mýlimas (sūnùs)	'(son) loved by (his) father'
žolė bùvo išdžiovìnta sáulės	'the grass was dried by the sun'
(čià) žmonių gyvẽnama	'there are people living (here)' (lit. 'it is lived by people (here)'
čià kìškio gulėta	'a rabbit evidently has been lying (here)' (lit. '(here) has been lain by a rabbit')

(see II.5.65–78).

2.14 Some intransitive verbs take the genitive of indefinite quantity instead of the nominative; here belong:

(1) perfective verbs with the prefix *pri-*, denoting an action in which a quantity of things is involved; cf.:

krìto lãpai	'leaves (NOM) were falling'
– *prikrìto lãpų*	'some leaves (GEN) have fallen'
riñkosi žmónės	'people were gathering'
– *prisiriñko žmonių*	'some, many people have gathered'
dýgo grỹbai	'mushrooms were sprouting'
– *pridýgo grỹbų*	'(a lot of) mushrooms have sprouted'

(2) verbs denoting a change of quantity:

(pa)daugėjo žmonių	'the number of people increased'
(su)mažėjo/apmažėjo mùsių/drėgmės	'(the number of) flies/dampness decreased'

(3) the verbs *ràstis* 'become, appear', *pasitáikyti* 'be found', *bū́ti* 'be', *lìkti* 'remain', etc.; cf.:

rañdasi úogų	'some berries (are ripening)'
pasitáiko klaidų̃	'there are (some) mistakes (to be found)'

yrà/bùvo/bū́davo/ bùs žmonių̃	'there are/were/used to be/will be some people'
lìko rugių̃ (laukè)	'some rye remained (in the field)'
užeĩna žmonių̃	'(some) people drop in'

2.15 The **adverbial genitive** when used with verbs may denote purpose or (indefinite) quantity. The genitive of purpose occurs with verbs of motion or interruption of motion: eĩti 'go, walk', važiúoti 'ride, go', vỹkti 'go, travel', bė́gti 'run', skrìsti 'fly', grį̃žti 'return', riñktis 'gather', sustóti 'stop', apsistóti 'stop (at)'; cause to move: sių̃sti 'send', varýti 'drive', léisti 'let', kviẽsti 'invite', prašýti 'ask'; change of position: atsisė́sti 'sit down', pasodìnti 'seat (sb)', gul̃ti 'lie down', klaũptis 'kneel', atsistóti 'stand up', pasileñkti 'lean'.

The meaning of **purpose** may be acquired by the genitive of nouns denoting:

(1) concrete things:

išeĩti vandeñs	lit. 'go out for water'
išsių̃sti gýdytojo	'send for a doctor'
pakviẽsti arbãtos	'invite to tea'
síekti lazdõs	'try to reach a stick'

In this case the genitive often co-occurs with an infinitive:

išeĩti rugių̃ pjáuti	lit. 'go out to cut rye' (see 2.84)

(2) processes, temporal concepts, meals, holidays, social events and the like:

pakviẽsti vakariẽnės	'invite to supper'
atsigul̃ti pógulio	'lie down for a nap'
grį̃žti Kalė̃dų	'return for Christmas'
susiriñkti išleistùvių	'gather for a farewell party'
išvỹkti gastròlių	'go on tour'

The genitive of a noun denoting process, action or event may be synonymous with the respective infinitive:

sė́sti vakariẽnės/ vakarieniáuti	'sit down to supper (GEN)/ have supper (INF)'
atsigul̃ti póilsio/pailsė́ti	'lie down for a rest/to rest'

The genitive of **quantity** corresponds to the accusative of quantity (see 2.8), but it is used with negative verbs often emphasized by the negative particle nẽ 'not'; cf.:

neláukė (nẽ) valandõs/ (nẽ) dviejų̃ valandų̃	'he didn't (even) wait an hour/ two hours'
(cf. láukė vãlandą	'he waited (for) an hour')

nenuėjo (nė̃) kilomètro/   'he didn't (even) cover a kilometer/
(nė̃) kelių̃ kilomètrų   several kilometers'

nèsveria (nė̃) šim̃to grãmų   'it doesn't (even) weigh a hundred grams'

THE DATIVE CASE

2.16 The **objective dative** denotes the beneficiary or addressee, sometimes a patient, – usually a person to whose advantage (or disadvantage) the action is performed. A number of instances can be distinguished:

(**1**) verbs taking the dative alone:

atstováuti taũtai	'represent a nation'
aukótis žmonė́ms	'sacrifice oneself to the people'
tarnáuti atėjū́nams	'serve invaders'
vadováuti į́staigai	'be a chief of an office'
vergáuti põnams	'be a slave to lords'
pataikáuti val̃džiai	'be obsequious to the authorities'
nuolaidžiáuti mokiniáms	'make concessions to pupils'
nusileñkti karãliui	'obey, bow to a king'
pasidúoti príešui	'surrender to the enemy'
pritar̃ti draũgui	'give support (approval) to a friend'
ker̃šyti giminė́ms	'take revenge on (one's) relatives'
keñkti kaimýnams	'do harm to the neighbours'
prieštaráuti mókytojui	'contradict the teacher'
príešintis polìcijai	'resist the police'
dėkóti kám (už ką̃)	'thank sb (for sth)'

(**2**) verbs subordinating the dative and an infinitive:

liẽpti (įsakýti, patar̃ti, pasiū́lyti, léisti) jám pasilìkti	'tell (order, advise, offer, allow) him to stay'
uždraũsti (sutrukdýti) žmonė́ms išvỹkti	'forbid (prevent) people to leave (from leaving)'
padė́ti (pagélbėti) ligóniui atsisė́sti	'help (aid) the patient to sit up'

(see also 2.83)

(**3**) transitive verbs governing the accusative (or partitive genitive) and the dative of beneficiary or addressee:

pardúoti kaimýnui árklį/grūdų̃	'sell a horse/some grain to a neighbour'
dovanóti mótinai skarẽlę	'give mother a scarf (as a present)'

įteĩkti mókytojai gėlių	'give (hand) flowers to the teacher'
dúoti ligóniui vandeñs	'give some water to the patient'
pranèšti viršininkui naujíeną	'report the news to the chief'
pasèkti vaĩkui pãsaką	'tell the child a fairytale'
pir̃kti sūnui kepùrę	'by one's son a cap'

2.17 The dative case governed mostly by impersonal (or impersonally used) verbs denotes the following:

(1) the experiencer of a psychological or psycho-physical state (usually with prefixed verbs), as in the syntactic pattern:

Pagaĩlo   berniùkui   senẽlio.
pity: 3. PAST   boy: DAT. SG   grandfather: GEN. SG
'The boy felt sorry for his grandfather';

cf. also:

pabaĩso/paklaĩko mergáitei (miškè)	'the girl (DAT) got scared (in the woods)'
palengvėjo/pagerėjo ligóniui	'the patient (DAT) felt better '
atsibódo/įkyrėjo/įgrìso vaikáms (káime)	'the children (DAT) got bored (in the village)'
patìko svečiáms váišės	'the guests (DAT) liked (enjoyed) the feast'
tiñka mótinai skarẽlė	'the scarf becomes mother (DAT)'

(2) the person (or thing) who lacks, or needs, or has enough of what is referred to by the obligatory genitive case, as in:

Stiñga   žmonėms   pinigų̃.
lack: 3. PRES   people: DAT. PL   money: GEN. PL
'People are short of money';

cf. also:

kiekvienám reĩkia užúojautos	'everyone needs compassion'
užteñka/pakañka visíems dúonos	'there is enough bread for everybody'

(cf. 2.11, 3)

(3) a person (or, broader, an animate being) experiencing a psychological or psycho-physical state denoted by a reflexive verb, personal or impersonal:

bróliui nórisi miẽgo	'(my) brother (DAT) is sleepy' (lit. 'wants sleep')

kātei sapnúojasi pēlės	'the cat (DAT) is dreaming of mice'
jám ródėsi/vaidėnosi šmėklos	'he (DAT) saw ghosts'
prisìminė vaĩkui (vāsara)	'the child (DAT) remembered the summer'
mán giřdisi (mùzika)	'I (DAT) hear (music (NOM))'
jám visadà sẽkasi	'he (DAT) is always lucky'

A number of verbs govern the dative along with an infinitive:

rūpėjo vaĩkui mókytis/mókslas	'The child (DAT) was eager to study (INF/NOM)'
atsibódo mán láukti	'I (DAT) got tired of waiting (INF)'
kiekvienám pasitáiko suklýsti	'everyone (DAT) happens to make mistakes'
mán tẽko išvažiúoti	'(it so happened that) I (DAT) had to go away'
vertėjo jám patylėti	'he (DAT) should have kept silent' (see 2.82)

2.18 The dative case governed by verbs with another obligatory constituent has a **possessive** meaning in combinations like the following:

Jìs	pabučiãvo	mótinai	rañką.
he: NOM	kissed	mother: DAT	hand: ACC

'He kissed (his) mother's hand.'

Skaũda	senẽliui	kóją	/kója
ache: 3. PRES	grandfather: DAT	foot: ACC	/foot: NOM

'Grandfather's foot aches.'

The obligatory constituent naming an alienable or inalienable possession can be expressed by the following word forms:

(1) the nominative case, with intransitive verbs:

jám mìrė žmonà	'(his) wife (NOM) died on him (DAT)'
diñgo kaimýnui arklỹs	'the neighbour's (DAT) horse (NOM) is missing' (lit.'disappeared')
karãliui gìmė sūnùs	'a son (NOM) was born to the king (DAT)'
įdùbo nãmui stógas	'the roof (NOM) of the house (DAT) has caved in'

(2) the accusative, with transitive verbs:

mazgóti vaĩkui kójas	'wash the child's (DAT) feet (ACC)'
pavõgti árklį kaimýnui	'steal a horse (ACC) from the neighbour (DAT)'
nuláužti stãlui kóją	'break a leg (ACC) off the table (DAT)'

also with impersonal transitive verbs, cf.:

peřšti vaĩkui akìs	'the child's (DAT) eyes (ACC) smart'

(3) the locative case, with impersonally used verbs:

mán cýpia ausysè	'there is a ringing in my (DAT) ears (LOC)' (lit. 'in (the) ears is ringing to me')
mán mìrga akysè	'my (DAT) eyes (LOC) are dazzled'
mán apkar̃to burnojè	'I (DAT) have a bitter taste in my mouth (LOC)'

(4) a prepositional phrase, mostly with intransitive verbs:

treñkė mán per gálvą	'(they) hit me (DAT) on the head (Prep + ACC)'
(plaukaĩ) kriñta mergáitei ant akių̃	'(hair) covers the girl's (DAT) eyes (Prep + GEN)'
(skarėlė) nusmùko senẽlei nuo galvõs	'(the kerchief) slipped off granny's head (Prep + GEN)'
nutvė́rė kātei už uodegõs	'(he) caught the cat by the tail (Prep + GEN)'

The dative is often interchangeable with the possessive genitive in attributive position. The possessive genitive is a more immediate expression of possessivity, cf.:

diñgo dėdei/ dė́dės arklỹs	'(my) uncle's (DAT/GEN) horse is missing'
į̇dùbo nãmui/nãmo stógas	'the roof of the house (DAT/GEN) caved in'

2.19 The **adverbial dative** optionally dependent on a verb expresses time or purpose (or destination).

The temporal dative denotes the **time** for which the action or its result is intended rather than the time of action; e.g.:

taupýk dúoną rytójui	'save bread for tomorrow (DAT)'
prisiriñko žmonių̃ nãkčiai	'(many) people gathered for the night (DAT)'
apsišvãrino šveñtėms	'(they) tidied up for the holiday (DAT)'
sugrį̃žo (į̇ káimą) vãsarai	'(they) returned (to the village) for the summer (DAT)'
užsidìrbo senãtvei	'(he) has earned enough for old age (DAT)'

A number of generalized temporal nouns require a specifying attribute:

pasilìkti pinigų̃ júodai diẽnai	'put aside some money for a rainy (lit.'black') day'
atidė́ti paskutìnei minùtei	'put (sth) off for the last minute'
pir̃kti bìlietą dvýliktai vãlandai	'buy a ticket for twelve o'clock'

A noun in the dative case may refer to a subsequent period or duration of the resultant state, e.g.:

atvažiúoti saváitei	'come for a week'
apsistóti diēnai	'stop for a day'
parsisamdýti mētams	'hire oneself out for a year'
paveȓgti šiȓtmečiams	'enslave for centuries'

The dative of duration is also used with quantitative attributes:

išvýkti ketveríems/keleríems mētams	'leave for four/several years'
ateīti visám vākarui	'come for the whole evening'

The dative of a quantitative word is often connected with the subordinated genitive of a temporal noun:

sustóti dēšimčiai/ kēletui dienų	'stop (at a place) for ten (DAT)/several (DAT) days (GEN)'
įsikùrti daũgeliui/ pùsei mētų	'take up residence for many (DAT) years (GEN)/half (DAT) a year (GEN)'

(see 2.130, 2.134)

2.20 The optional dative with transitive verbs taking an obligatory object denotes **purpose** or **destination**:

turḗti pinigų nãmui	'have (enough) money for a house'
piȓkti (įsigýti, gáuti) lentų grindìms	'buy (acquire, get) planks for the floor'
išsinúomoti kaȓbarį mezgýklai	'take a room on lease for a knitting shop'
atnèšti vandeñs daržáms	'bring water for the kitchen-garden'
suveȓpti linùs dróbei	'spin flax for linen'

The dative of purpose may co-occur with the dative of addressee, e.g.:

dãvė mán siū́lų megztìniui	'(she) gave (me) some yarn for a sweater'
paȓdavė kaimýnui rugių sėklai	'(he) sold some rye (to his neighbour) for seed'

2.21 The dative of purpose also occurs in the following cases:

(1) it is governed by some verbs with the obligatory genitive; e.g.:

mán trū́ksta pinigų váistams	'I am short of money for medicines'
pagailė́jo knýgoms pinigų	'(he) grudged money for books'

(see 2.11, 3)

(2) it is often used with an infinitive:

àtnešė vandeñs gėlėms paláistyti	lit.'(he) brought some water for flowers'

(see 2.84)

(3) it is governed by some intransitive verbs (it may be interchangeable with an infinitive):

ruõštis nãkčiai/miegóti	'prepare for the night/to sleep'
apsireñgti keliõnei	'get dressed for the trip'
gìmti kõvai	'be born for struggle'

THE INSTRUMENTAL CASE

2.22   The **objective instrumental** is used to denote an instrument of an action, or the content of a state or the means of an action.

The instrumental of **content** (obligatory in most cases) is used with verbs of a number of lexical semantic groups:

(1) *didžiúotis* 'be proud (of)', *domėtis* 'be interested (in)', *džiaũgtis* 'rejoice (at), be happy (with)', *grožėtis* 'be delighted (with)', *gėrėtis* 'be delighted (with)', *žavėtis* 'admire, be delighted (with)', *mėgautis* 'revel (in)', *stebėtis* 'wonder (at)', *gardžiúotis* 'relish';

(2) *gìrtis* 'boast (of)', *skų́stis* 'complain (of)', *pa(si)tikėti* 'trust', *abejóti* 'doubt', *gúostis/ramìntis* 'console oneself (with)', *rū́pintis* 'take care (of)';

(3) *įkyrė́ti (skuñdais)* 'plague (with complaints)', *įgrìsti* 'pester, bore (with)';

(4) *skìrtis (ū́giù)* 'differ (in height)', *pasižymė́ti (grožiù)* 'be notable (for beauty)';

(5) *prekiáuti* 'trade (in)', *ver̃stis* 'earn one's living (by)', *naudótis* 'make use (of), benefit (by)';

(6) *susir̃gti (gripù)* 'fall ill (with flu)', *užsikrė̃sti (šíltine)* 'catch (typhus)';

(7) *kvepė́ti* 'smell (of)', *smirdė́ti* 'stink (of)' and their synonyms; e.g.

kvepė́ti ramùnėmis	'to smell of camomiles'
dvel̃kti pavãsariu	'to smell of spring'
smirdė́ti dumblù	'to stink of silt'
dvõkti žuvim̃	'to stink of fish'

2.23   The instrumental of **means** is used optionally after numerous transitive verbs of action like:

rašýti rãšalu	'write with ink'
užtèpti dervà	'smear with tar'
láistyti vándeniu	'sprinkle with water'
prikálti vinimì	'fasten with a nail'

The instrumental of means, interchangeable with the accusative, is required by verbs of the following lexical groups:

(1) verbs denoting wearing and putting on clothes, footwear, decorations, etc., the verbs being specialized with respect to the kind of clothes:

avė́ti/aũtis bãtais/batùs	'wear/put on shoes (INSTR/ACC)'
juosė́ti/júostis diržù/dir̃žą	'wear/put on a belt'
mūvė́ti/máutis kélnėmis/kélnes	'wear/put on pants'
ryšė́ti/rìštis skarelè/skarẽlę	'wear/tie on a kerchief'
segė́ti/sègtis sijonù/sijõną	'wear/put on a skirt'
gobė́ti/gaũbtis skarà/skārą	'wear/wrap (around one's shoulders) a shawl'
vilkė́ti/vil̃ktis drabùžiais/drabužiùs (pálṭu, suknelè/pálṭą, suknẽlę)	'wear/put on clothes (a coat, a dress)'

The names of all kinds of clothes, footwear, etc. combine with the verbs *dėvė́-ti/nešióti* 'wear, have (sth) on':

dėvė́ti/nešióti bãtais/batùs, suknelè/suknẽlę	'wear shoes, a dress'

The un-prefixed reflexive verbs of this list are used in two antonymous meanings, e.g. *vil̃ktis* means both 'put on' and 'take off'. Verbs of taking off clothes are used with the accusative case of the object, e.g.:

vil̃ktis/nusivil̃kti pálṭą	'take off a coat'

The choice of the accusative or the instrumental is sometimes determined by the context. The instrumental is used if a verb has another accusative object, e.g.:

ap(si)rìšti gálvą skarelè (*skarẽlę)	'tie a kerchief (INSTR/*ACC) around one's head (ACC)'
susijúosti kélnes diržù (*dir̃žą)	'girdle (one's) trousers (ACC) with a belt (INSTR/*ACC)'

If a prepositional phrase is used in place of the accusative, the accusative is used instead of the instrumental:

užsirìšti ant galvõs skarẽlę (*skarelè)	'tie (up) a kerchief (ACC/*INSTR) on one's head'
susijúosti júostą (*júosta) ant marškinių̃	'girdle/put on a belt (ACC/*INSTR) on one's shirt'

The accusative is also used with the non-reflexive transitive verbs from which the above reflexive verbs are derived, e.g., *viľkti* 'dress/take off', *aūti* 'put on/take off (sb)':

aūti batukùs vaīkui ant kójų	'put on shoes (ACC) on the child's (DAT) feet (Prep + GEN)'
(į)sègti sãgę į suknēlę	'fasten a brooch (ACC) to the dress (Prep + ACC)'

(2) verbs denoting movement of body parts:

lingúoti (kinkúoti) gálva/gálvą	'shake one's head (INSTR/ACC)'
(but only: *gálvą kratýti, kraipýti, pùrtyti*	'shake, toss one's head (ACC)')
karpýti ausimìs/ausìs	'move one's ears (INSTR/ ACC)'
gríežti, kalénti dantimìs/dantìs	'gnash, (lit.) chatter one's teeth (INSTR/ACC)'
skėsčioti (skeryčióti) rañkomis/rañkas	'throw up one's arms (INSTR/ACC)'
(but: *sùpti kójas*	'swing one's legs (ACC)')
tráukyti (trūkčioti) pečiaīs/pečiùs	'shrug one's shoulders (INSTR/ACC)'
(but: *gūžčioti pečiaīs* (INSTR))	
vìzginti úodega/úodegą	'wag one's tail (INSTR/ACC)'

(3) verbs denoting sounds produced by means of the referent of the instrumental/accusative case:

bárškinti iñdais/indùs	'rattle (the) crockery (INSTR/ACC)'
žvánginti rāktais/raktùs	'jingle (the) keys'
skambinti taūrėmis/taurès	'tinkle (the) wineglasses'
treñkti dùrimis/durìs	'bang the door'
sumùšti kulnimìs/kulnìs	'click one's heels'
birbinti vamzdeliù/vamzdēlį	'paly a reed-pipe (INSTR/ACC)'
čirpinti smuikù/smuīką	'play (lit. 'make chirp') a fiddle'

Most of these verbs have the causative suffix *-in(-ti)*. With non-causative verbs, the instrumental alone is used:

(mergáitė) šilkaīs šlamėjo	lit.'(the girl) rustled with silk'
(žìrgas) kāmanomis žvangėjo	'(the steed) rattled (his) bridle'

2.24 The instrumental case of **instrument** is optionally used with verbs of action governing the following word forms:

(1) the accusative:

rašýti láišką pieštukù	'write a letter with pencil'

nusišlúostyti véidą rañkšluosčiu	'dry one's face with a towel'
kapóti málkas kirviù	'chop wood with an axe

(2) the genitive (rarely):

įsikìbti rañkomis turĕklų	'grasp the rail with (one's) hands'

(3) the dative (rarely):

pagrasýti vaĩkui pirštù	'shake (one's) finger at the child'

(4) a prepositional phrase:

atsigìnti nuo príešo kalavijù	'defend oneself against the enemy with a sword'

The instrumental case denoting means of transportation combines with verbs of motion:

važiúoti dvìračiu/tráukiniu	'go by bicycle/train'
skrìsti lėktuvù	'fly by plane'
plaũkti laivù	'sail by boat'
(at)vèžti prekès tráukiniu	'convey goods by train'

The instrumental case of instrument and means is sometimes (but rarely) used also with the preposition *sù* 'with', e.g.:

važiúoti su dvìračiu	'go by a bicycle'
láistyti su vándeniu	'sprinkle with water'

2.25   The **adverbial instrumental** is used to express place (route of motion), time, quantity and manner of an action.

The **spatial** instrumental denotes the route of motion along or inside a thing or place:

važiúoti keliù	'go along a road'
eĩti miškù	'walk through the forest'
plaũkti jūrà	'sail in the sea'
lìpti láiptais	'walk up the stairs'

The instrumental of nouns denoting an area is interchangeable with a prepositional phrase *peř* 'across' + ACC, e.g.:

eĩti laukù/per laũką	'walk across the field'
(ãšara) riĕda skrúostu/per skrúostą	'(a tear) rolls down a cheek'

The instrumental of nouns with the prefix *pa-* denoting the edge or side of a place is synonymous with the locative when used with verbs of motion and other verbs, e.g.:

váikščioti pãupiu/paupỹ	'walk along the river (side) (INSTR/LOC)'
áugti pãtvoriu/patvorỹ	'grow along a fence (INSTR/LOC)'

2.26 The instrumental of **time** expresses a variety of temporal meanings.

(1) The instrumental of nouns denoting time of a day or a season expresses the moment or period of time when the action takes place:

grĩžti vidùrnakčiu	'return at midnight'
susir̃gti vidù(r)vasariu	'fall ill in midsummer'
lýti pãryčiu	'rain at dawn'
darbýmečiu ir akmuõ krùta	'during a busy season even a stone moves'

In this cases the instrumental is interchangeable with the locative and the accusative:

grĩžti pãvakariu/pavakarỹ/pãvakarį   'return towards evening (INSTR/LOC/ACC)'

The instrumental of generalized temporal nouns (e.g. *momeñtas* 'moment', *mẽtas/laĩkas* 'time', *dienà* 'day') must be used with a specifying attribute:

tuõ momentù galvójo kitaĩp	'at that moment (he) thought otherwise'
diñgo áudros metù	'(he) disappeared during a storm'
nerimãvo pirmomìs dienomìs	'(he) was worried during the first days'

(2) The instrumental of temporal nouns in the plural number indicates **frequency** of action, i.e. intervals at which an action is regularly repeated:

išeĩti rytaĩs	'go away every morning'
dìrbti sekmãdieniais	'work on Sundays'

The instrumental plural form of some temporal nouns must be used with an attribute:

susitìkti kiekvienaĩs mētais	'meet every year'
išvažiúoti vãsaros mėnesiais	'go away in summer months'
skaitýti póilsio valandomìs	lit.'read in hours of rest'

(3) The instrumental plural form of nouns naming units of time denotes **duration** of an action:

valandomìs klausýtis (mùzikos)	'listen (to music) for hours'
kariáuti ámžiais	'be at war for centuries'
neišeĩti (iš namų̃) savàitėmis	'stay (at home) for weeks'

The meaning of duration can be emphasized by an attribute:

ištisomìs dienomìs miegóti	'sleep days and days'

Sometimes, duration is expressed by the instrumental singular form with an obligatory attribute:

išmókti trumpù laikù	'learn in a short time'
padarýti vienà dienà	'do (sth) in one day'

This meaning can also be rendered by an instrumental plural form with the subordinated genitive of time:

(Žẽmė) formãvosi tū́kstančiais mẽtų.	'(The earth) was formed in the course of thousands of years.'

2.27 **Manner** of action is expressed by the instrumental case of the following nouns:

(1) abstract nouns, with an obligatory attribute (adjective or adjectival pronoun):

važiúoti dìdeliu greičiù	'drive at great speed'
išsitiẽsti visù ūgiù	'sprawl at full length'
rė̃kti nesavù balsù	'scream with all one's might'
	(lit. 'in a voice not one's own')

(2) abstract nouns with an attribute in the genitive case implying comparison:

pùlti liū́to smarkumù	'attack with the might of a lion'
(cf. *pùlti smar̃kiai kaĩp liū́tas*	'attack (as) forcefully as a lion')
bė́gti vė́jo greitumù	'run at the speed of wind'

(3) a noun of the same stem as the verb, with an obligatory adjectival attribute:

miegóti kíetu miegù	lit.'sleep (with) a sound sleep'
nusijuõkti nemaloniù juokù	'laugh (with) an unpleasant laugh'

(4) nouns denoting a part (of the body or a thing), with a locational modifier:

stovė́ti nùgara į síeną	'stand (with one's) back to the wall'
atsisùkti véidu į sáulę	'turn (one's) face (INSTR) to the sun'
pakabìnti (bùtelį) kaklù žemỹn	' hang (a bottle) neck down'

The instrumental case can be used as a modifier of manner without an attribute, in which case it either implies comparison (**a**), or it is descriptive (**b**):

(**a**) *lóti šunimì* (cf. *lóti kaĩp šuõ*)	'bark like a dog'
áuksu žibė́ti	'shine like gold'
atlė̃kti vė́ju	'come running like the wind'
(**b**) *(ãšaros) bė́ga upeliù/upẽliais*	'(teas) are streaming in rivulets (SG/PL)'
(dū́mai) kìlo kamuoliaĩs	'(smoke) was rising in puff-balls'
bìtės pakìlo spiẽčiumi	'bees rose in a swarm'

2.28 Sometimes, the instrumental denotes the **cause** of a state. Two cases can be distinguished:

(1) the instrumental refers to a psycho-physical state of a person:

véidas nuraũdo ãpmaudu	'(her/his) face grow red with vexation'
jìs nušvìto džiaugsmù	'he brightened with joy'
véidas pérsikreipė pykčiù	'(his) face distorted with anger'
vaĩkas leĩpo juokù	'the child was dying with laughter'

The genitive with the preposition ìš 'from' is more common in this case (see 2.68, 1, 3)

(2) the instrumental implies cause by way of characterization of a thing:

šlaĩtas mėlynúoja žibùtėmis	'the slope is blue with violets'
dangùs mìrga žvaigždėmìs	'the sky sparkles with stars'
mìškas skaṁba (paũkščių) giesmėmìs	'the woods ring with (birds') songs'

Note: This instrumental is interchangeable with the prepositional phrase nuõ 'from' + GEN (see 2.69, 1)

THE LOCATIVE CASE

2.29 The locative case is used with verbs to express the adverbial meanings of place, time and (rarely) manner.

The **spatial** locative denotes location of an action or state inside or within the place named by the noun:

kabėti spìntoje	'hang in the wardrobe'
gyvénti miestè	'live in a town'
žaĩsti sodè	'play in the garden'
skraidýti dangujè	'fly in the sky'
skę̃sti ùpėje	'drown in the river'

Owing to the meaning of a noun, its locative case form may refer to the sphere of activity:

dalyváuti varžýbose/konfereñcijoje	'take part in a match/conference'
pirmáuti móksle/spòrte	'be the first in science/sports'

2.30 The **temporal** locative denotes the time of an action by locating it within a period named by the noun. Thus the meaning of the case form is necessarily determined by the lexical meaning of the noun which either denotes or implies a period of time:

kéltis apýaušry	'get up at (during) dawn'
žydėti balañdyje	'blossom in (during) April'

máudytis vidù(r)vasaryjè	'bathe in midsummer'
(but **vãsaroje*	'in summer')
mylė́ti jaunỹstėje	'love in (one's) youth'
žū́ti karè	'die in a war'
susipažìnti vestùvėse/per vestuvès	'get acquainted at a wedding'
tinginiáuti darbýmetyje	'idle in (during) a busy season'
triukšmáuti pamokosè/per pãmokas	'be noisy during lessons'

The locative case form of generalized temporal nouns must be used with a specifying attribute:

gyvénti trečiamè ámžiuje	'live in the third century'
žydė́ti balañdžio mė́nesyje/mė́nesį	'blossom in the month of April (LOC/ACC)'

2.31 **Manner** of action is expressed (rarely) by the locative case of nouns denoting:

(1) human states:

gyvénti taikojè, méilėje,	'live in peace, (lit.) in love, in unity,
vienýbėje, láisvėje, pértekliuje,	in freedom, in abundance, in wealth,
tuŕ̃tuose, skurdè, vargè,	in poverty, in hardship'
miŕti skausmuosè	'die in pain'
ilgė́tis vienumojè	'miss (sb) in solitude'

(2) collective concepts:

áugti šeimojè	'grow up in a family'
gyvénti krūvõj/kùpetoj	'live together (lit. 'in a heap')'
ganýtis bandojè	'graze in a herd'

(3) some means of transport (with verbs of motion) and containers:

važiúoti vežimè (ir dainúoti)	'go in a cart (and sing)'
atvèžti alaũs statìnėje	'bring some beer in a barrel'
atnèšti úogų sáujoje	'bring some berries in one's hand'

2.32 In the East High Lithuanian dialect and in fiction a variety of locative case – the **illative** (usually in the singular) is used with verbs of motion. It has the meaning of motion into or direction towards a place and is thus synonymous with the prepositional phrase *į̃* 'to' + ACC, cf.:

eĩti miestañ/į̃ miẽstą	'go to the town'
įmèsti ùpėn/į̃ ùpę	'throw into the river'
(nu)važiúoti tuŕ̃gun/į̃ tuŕ̃gų	'go to the market'
paim̃ti rañkon/į̃ rañką	'take into (one's) hand'
įkrìsti akiñ/į̃ ãkį	'get into the eye, catch attention'

In Standard Lithuanian, the illative is stylistically marked and it is going out of use.

THE NOMINATIVE CASE

2.33 The nominative case of nouns, besides its main function of the subject and predicative (see 1.20–27), in some instances is used with verbs to express an **adverbial** meaning.

Frequency of action is expressed by temporal nouns with (**1**) the pronouns *kàs* 'what; each', less commonly *kiekvíenas* 'each', and (**2**) the adjectives *dãžnas* 'frequent' and *rẽtas* 'rare' as obligatory attributes; compare respectively:

(**1**) *eĩdavo kàs rýtas*	'(they) used to go every morning'
atvažiúoja kàs mė́nuo	'(he) comes every month'
(varžýbos) vỹksta kiekvieni̇̀ mė́tai	'(contests) take place every year'
(**2**) *dažnà dienà lỹja*	lit. 'it rains a frequent day'
dãžnas sekmãdienis atvažiúoja	'(he) comes a frequent Sunday'
retà dienà neskaũda kójų	lit. 'a rare day (my) feet don't ache'

Words groups with *kàs* can be extended by a numeral or a quantitative pronoun:

ateĩna kàs antrà dienà	lit. '(he) comes every second day'
susitiñka kàs treji̇̀ (kelinti̇̀) mė́tai	'(they) meet once in three (several) years' (lit. 'every three years')

The accusative case is also used in this meaning (see 2.9)

2.34 **Quantity** of action may be expressed by the nominative case after non-finite verb forms (though the accusative is more common in Standard Lithuanian, cf. 2.8):

(**1**) with neuter passive participles (usually, with the agentive genitive):

jõ nùeita kilomètras	lit. 'a kilometre has been gone by him (GEN)', i.e. 'he has gone a kilometre'
màno išláukta valandà	lit. 'an hour has been waited by me'
jõ sumokė́ta lìtas (cf. lìtą)(už pãslaugas)	'one litas (NOM) has been paid by him (GEN) (for services)' (see 2.13)

(**2**) with a past gerund, used either as predicate or in a dependent position (mostly subordinated to neuter adjectives):

kad taĩp nors kilomètras (cf. kilomètrą) nuvažiãvus mašinà	'I wish I could ride in a car at least a kilometre (NOM/ACC)'

kad nórs saváitė (cf. *saváitę*) *paatostogãvus*	'I wish I could have a holiday at least for a week (NOM)'
bū́tų gẽra/geraĩ valandė̃lė (cf. *valandė̃lę*) *nusnū́dus*	'it would be nice to have a nap at least for a minute (NOM)'
bū́tų láimė nors gurkšnẽlis (cf. *gurkšnẽlį*) *vandeñs išgḗrus*	'it would be happiness if I had (drunk) at least a mouthful (NOM) of water'

(3) with an infinitive, used either as predicate or in a dependent position (usually, after a neuter adjective or an impersonal verb):

ne vaĩkui kilomètras (cf. *kilomètrą*) *nueĩti*	'it's not for a baby to walk a kilometre'
ne jám valandà (cf. *vãlandą*) *išláukti*	'it's not for him to wait an hour'
neleñgva ceñtneris (cf. *ceñtnerį*) *pakélti*	'it's not easy to lift a centner'
reĩkia nors lìtras (cf. *lìtrą*) *priuogáuti*	'it is necessary (impersonal verb) to gather at least a litre (NOM) of berries'

This usage of the nominative is restricted to impersonal sentences.

2.35 The nominative of temporal nouns (often with an attribute) can be used also with finite imperfective verbs (mostly in present tense forms) to denote the quantity of time (duration), e.g.:

mė́nuo seȓga tė́vas	'father has been ill (for) a month'
(but: *mė́nesį siȓgo*)	('(father) was ill for a month (ACC)')
saváitė kãsa bùlves	'(they) have been digging potatoes (for) a week'
parà nesìkelia iš lóvos	'he hasn't been out of bed all day and night'
tretì mẽtai (cf. *trečiùs metùs*) *mókosi*	lit.'he has been studying three years'
vìsas/ìštisas rýtas (cf. *vìsą/ìštisą rýtą*) *lỹja*	'it's been raining all/the whole morning'

The nominative of nouns denoting a measure of distance occurs with a dependent prepositional phrase:

lėktùvas nùtūpė kilomètras nuo mìško/nuo čià	'the plane (has) landed a kilometre from the forest/from here'
sustójo žiñgsnis nuo manę̃s	'(he) stopped a step from me'

Verb – prepositional phrase

OBJECTIVE PREPOSITIONAL PHRASES

Objective prepositional phrases are considered below according to the case form of the dependent noun and the preposition.

Prepositional phrases with the accusative

2.36 The phrase į̃ + ACC expresses a number of objective meanings determined mostly by the semantic character of the verb.

(1) With verbs of striking and touching this prepositional phrase names the affected object:

(a) bélstis į́ lángą	'knock on the window'
treñkti į́ síeną	'bang on the wall'
kliū́ti/patáikyti (ãkmeniu) į́ gálvą	'hit (sb) on the head (with a stone)'

With some verbs, this phrase is synonymous with the prepositionless accusative (daužýti į́ véidą/véidą lit. 'hit (sb) in the face/the face') or with the phrase peř + ACC:

treñkti per pečiùs	'strike (sb) on the shoulders'
gáuti per pirštùs	lit. 'get smacked on (one's) fingers'
(b) sudùžti į́ uolàs	'crash into rocks' (e.g., of a plane)
susižeĩsti į́ stìklą	'injure/hurt oneself on glass'
nusivalýti (batùs) į́ žõlę	'clean (one's) shoes on grass'
(c) įsikìbti į́ turė̃klus (also turė̃klų/už turė̃klų)	'grasp (at) the rail'
kìbti į́ pláukus	'seize (sb) by the hair'

With verbs of answering, responding and the like this phrase refers to the stimulus:

atsakýti į́ kláusimą	'answer a question'
atsiliẽpti į́ šaũksmą	'answer, respond to a call'

(2) This prepositional phrase denotes the result of change in the following cases:

(a) with verbs denoting breaking and dividing up it refers to resultant fragments:

sudùžti į́ šukès	'break into pieces (slivers)'

sudaužýti (ką̃) į̃ šukès	'smash (sth) into pieces'
suláužyti (lãzdą) į̃ šìpulius	'break (a stick) into splinters'
suskìrstyti (žẽmę) į̃ sklypùs/sklỹpais	'divide (land) into plots (į̃+ ACC/INSTR)'

(b) with verbs of uniting, putting and getting together it denotes the resultant whole:

sukráuti (málkas) į̃ krũvą	'pile (fire-wood) into a stack'
sugniáužti (sniẽgą) į̃ kãmuolį	lit. 'squeeze (snow) into a ball'

(c) with verbs (both transitive and transitive) denoting a change of state, it denotes the resultant state:

pavir̃sti į̃ ãkmenis/akmenimìs	'turn into stones'
išáugti į̃ výrus/výru	'grow up into a man'
išriñkti į̃ seniūnùs/seniūnù	'select as village elder'

In some of these cases the prepositional phrase is synonymous with the instrumental.

2.37 The phrase *ùž* + ACC also has a number of meanings dependent on the head verb.

(1) With verbs of rewarding, thanking, etc., the prepositional phrase refers to recompense or motivation:

sumokėti už dárbą	'pay for the work'
apdovanóti už drą̃są	'award for bravery'
dėkóti už páramą	'thank for help'
gìrti už póelgį	'praise for a deed'

It has the same meaning after the verbs *kovóti/kariáuti* (*už láisvę/dėl láisvės*) 'struggle/fight (for freedom)', *aukótis* (*už tėvýnę/dėl tėvýnės*) 'sacrifice oneself (for homeland)'.

(2) With verbs of buying, selling, and the like, the phrase denotes the form of payment (usually money):

pir̃kti (nãmą) už áuksą/pìnigus	'buy (a house) for gold/money'
dìrbti už val̃gį (o ne už pìnigus)	'work for food (not for money)'

(3) With a number of verbs, it denotes the person for whom the agent acts as proxy:

dìrbti už tė́vą	'work instead of (the) father'
išeĩti (į̃ rekrutùs) už brólį	'join (the army) instead of one's brother'

2.38 The phrase *apiẽ* + ACC is used with verbs of speech, mental processes and the like to denote content:

kalbė́ti apie namùs	'speak about home'
užsimiñti apie pìnigus	'mention money'
svajóti apie ãteitį	'dream about the future'
sužinóti apie neláimę	'learn about the misfortune'

2.39 The phrase *priẽš* + ACC is used with verbs of resistance to name the counteragent or opposition:

spìrtis/šiáuštis priẽš tėvùs	'resist/stand against the parents'
maištáuti priẽš val̃džią	'rebel against the authorities'
kìlti priẽš pavergė́jus	'revolt against the conquerors'

It is also used with *kovóti* 'struggle', *kariáuti* 'fight' instead of *sù* 'with' + INSTR; cf. also:

didžiúotis priẽš kaimýnus	'be proud with one's neighbours'
raudonúoti priẽš žmónes	'blush when facing people'

Prepositional phrases with the genitive

2.40 The phrase *ìš* + GEN has a number of objective meanings determined by the verbs it occurs with.

(1) It denotes the material from which the referent of the direct object is created, after verbs of 'making':

nupìnti (vainìką) iš gėlių̃	'weave (a garland) out of flowers'
pastatýti (nãmą) iš plýtų	'build (a house) out of bricks'
gamìnti (vỹną) iš piẽnių	'make (wine) from dandelions', etc.

It also denotes the component parts or source in word groups with intransitive verbs:

dainà susìdeda iš žõdžių	'a song consists of words'
dẽbesys susidãro iš garų̃	'clouds are formed from vapour'
gaĩsras kìlo iš kibirkštiẽs	'the fire grew from a spark'
obelìs išdýgo iš grū́do	'the apple-tree grew from a seed'

(2) This phrase denotes the source (of information, etc.) after verbs of the following types:

(a) *sužinóti/išgir̃sti iš žmonių̃*	'learn/hear from people'
išmókti iš mótinos (mègzti)	'learn from one's mother (how to knit)'
(b) *pažìnti/atpažìnti iš bal̃so, iš drabùžių*	'recognize/identify by the voice, by the clothes'

suprãsti iš akių	'understand from sb's eyes'
suvókti/spėti iš véido	'perceive/guess from sb's face'
(c) *pirkti iš kaimýno*	'by from a neighbour'
paimti iš draũgo	'take from a friend'
gáuti iš bánko	'get from a bank'
pavõgti/pasiskõlinti iš vaĩko/parduotùvės	'steal/borrow from a child/a shop'
išlõšti/atim̃ti (iš draũgo)	'take by force (from a friend)'
(d) *norėti (tikėtis, láukti) paramõs iš žmonių*	'want (hope for, expect) help from people'
reikaláuti/išprašýti iš tėvų (pinigų)	'demand/get (some money) from one's parents'

(3) After verbs like *tyčiotis (iš draugų)* 'mock (at friends)', *juõktis (iš vìsko)* 'laugh (at everything)', *šypsótis (iš kalbõs)* 'smile (at sb's words)', the prepositional phrase denotes the target of emotional reaction, e.g.:

pỹkti ant draugų	'be angry with (one's) friends'

(4) The phrase *iš* + GEN denotes the whole from which a part is distinguished or selected, when used after the verbs denoting choice or separation:

skìrtis iš kitų	'be different from others'
išskìrti iš visų	'single out, choose from all'
išsiskìrti iš miniõs	'stand out in a crowd'
riñkti(s) iš krūvõs	'choose from a pile'

2.41 The phrase *nuõ* + GEN denotes the following:

(1) the whole from which a part or a related entity is separated or separates (mostly after verbs with the prefixes *nu-* (related to the preposition *nuõ*)) and *at-*:

nuplėšti nuo mẽdžio (lapùs)	'tear off (leaves) from a tree'
nušlúostyti (dùlkes) nuo stãlo	'wipe (dust) from the table'
atšókti/atstóti nuo síenos	'come off the wall (of plaster)'
atsiskìrti nuo tėvų	'leave (lit. 'break away from') one's parents'
atsilìkti/atitrūkti nuo būrio	'fall behind/stray the platoon'
atsiribóti nuo žmonių	'dissociate oneself from people'

(2) the state one is relieved of:

atsigáuti nuo ligõs	'recover from an illness'
atsipéikėti nuo išgąsčio	'come to oneself after a fright'
atsipalaidúoti nuo rūpesčių	'get rid of worries'
atsikratýti nuo snáudulio	'shake off somnolence'
atpràsti nuo gėrìmo	'break oneself of drinking'

(3) the counteragent or a factor against which the agent takes precautions or defends himself or someone:

gìnti(s) nuo príešų	'defend (oneself) from the enemies'
gýdyti(s) nuo džiovõs	'treat (undergo treatment) for tuberculosis'
ap(si)draũsti nuo gaĩsro	'insure (oneself) against fire'
slė̃pti(s) nuo uodų̃/nuo sáulės	'protect oneself (lit. 'hide') from gnats/from the sun'

cf. also:

priklausýti nuo klìmato	'depend on the climate'

2.42 The phrase *priẽ* + GEN denotes the following:

(1) the entity to which the agent or patient is attached or added (usually, after verbs with the prefix *pri-* derived from the preposition *priẽ*):

pridė́ti prie visumõs	'add (sth) to the whole'
prikálti prie síenos	'nail (sth) to the wall'
prirìšti prie tvorõs	'tie to the fence'
mólis lim̃pa prie bãtų	'clay sticks to shoes'
prisidė́ti prie sukìlėlių/prie sukilìmo	'join the rebels/the rebellion'
prisiplàkti prie nepažį́stamų	'stick to strangers'

(2) the entity (inanimate or human) one gets used or adjusted to:

priprásti prie aplinkõs/prie šal̃čio	'get used to the environment/to the cold'
pri(si)táikyti/pri(si)dẽrinti (drabužiùs) prie figū̃ros	'fit (clothes) to (one's) figure'
prisitáikyti prie aplinkýbių	'adjust oneself to circumstances'
prisirìšti/prisigẽrinti/ prisiméilinti prie tėvų̃	'be attached/make up to one's parents'

cf. also:

(pri)tìkti prie akių̃	'match (one's) eyes' (of colour)
priklausýti prie gerų̃ žmonių̃	'be numbered among (lit. 'belong to') decent people'

2.43 The phrase *añt* + GEN denotes the target:

(**1**) of negative emotions after the verb *pỹkti* 'be angry (with)' and its synonyms *niřšti, šiřsti, tūžti, siùsti*, e.g.:

pỹkti ant kaimýnų	'be angry with one's neighbours'
niřšti ant vìso pasáulio	'be enraged against the whole world'

(**2**) of actions motivated by negative emotions:

bártis ant vaikų̃	'scold children'
(cf. *bárti vaikùs*)	('scold children (ACC)')
rė̃kti/šaũkti ant mokinių̃	'shout at pupils'
murmė́ti ant vadõvo/prieš vadõvą	'grumble at the chief/against the chief'

2.44 The phrase *bè* + GEN is used:

(**1**) obligatorily, with some intransitive verbs:

lìkti be namų̃	'be left without a home'
(cf. *netèkti namų̃*)	('lose one's home')
išsiveřsti be pinigų̃	'manage without money'
apsieĩti be pagálbos/draugų̃	'manage without help/friends'

(**2**) optionally, with transitive verbs of action to denote an instrument or means not used by the agent:

siū́ti be ā́datos	'sew without a needle'
(cf. *siū́ti su ā́data*)	('sew with a needle')
statýti be kiřvio	'build without an ax'

It is often used with negative verbs:

be tiñklo nesugáusi žuvų̃	'you won't catch fish without a net'
be pinigų̃ nenupiřksi	'you can't buy without money'

2.45 The phrase *ùž* + GEN denotes a support when used with the following verbs:

laikýtis už šakõs	'hold on to a branch'
įsikìbti/įsitvérti už šakõs/šakõs	'catch hold of a branch/a branch (GEN)'
griḗbtis už šiáudo	'catch at a straw'
užkliū́ti už sleñksčio/sleñksčio	'stumble (catch one's foot) over a threshold'

It also denotes a (body) part of the object, as in:

tampýti kãtę už uodegõs	'pull a cat by the tail'
paim̃ti vaĩką už rañkos	'take a child by the hand'
laikýti dvìratį už vaĩro	'hold the bicycle by the handlebar'

Prepositional phrases with the instrumental

2.46 The phrase *sù* + INSTR has two objective meanings determined by the head verb:

(1) With reciprocal (and more generally, symmetrical) predicates this prepositional phrase names:

(a) the second human actant (an obligatory comitative object):

bártis/giñčytis/pỹktis su draugaĩs	'quarrel/argue/be on bad terms with friends'
mùštis (pèštis) su bróliu	'fight with one's brother'
derĕtis su pirkĕjais	'bargain with buyers'
táikytis su draugù	'make peace with a friend'
bučiúotis/svéikintis/ tuōktis/skìrtis su žmonà	'kiss/greet/marry/divorce (one's) wife'
kovóti/kariáuti su užpuolìkais/prieš užpuolikùs	'struggle/fight with/against the agressors'
ruñgtis su varžovù	'compete with a rival'

(b) the second inanimate actant:

dangùs susisiékia/susiliẽčia su jū́ra	'the sky blends (lit. 'touches') with the sea'
mìškas ribójasi su ẽžeru	'the forest borders on the lake'
dienà susilýgino su naktim̃	lit. 'the day has become equal with the night'
cf.: *maišýti mólį su smėliù*	'mix clay with sand'

Many symmetrical predicates have the prefix *su-*: *susipažìnti* 'get acquainted', *susitìkti* 'meet', *susidùrti* 'encounter, collide', *susirašinĕti* 'correspond (with)', *sugyvénti* 'be on good terms', *susibárti* 'quarrel', *susitáikyti* 'make up (with)', etc. This prepositional phrase is also obligatory with some non-symmetrical predicates, e.g.:

susidoróti su dárbu/su príešu	'cope with the work/have done with the enemy'

This phrase is also used to denote an optional comitative object with non-symmetrical predicates, e.g.:

ateĩti su vaikaĩs	'come with (one's) children'
válgyti dúoną su svíestu	'eat bread and (lit. 'with') butter'

(2) The prepositional phrase *sù* + INSTR is interchangeable with the more common instrumental case (without a preposition) denoting instrument or means:

rašýti (su) pieštukù	'write with a pencil'
atvažiúoti (su) tráukiniu	'come by train' (see above 2.24)

ADVERBIAL PREPOSITIONAL PHRASES

Prepositional phrases of place

2.47 Meanings of place are expressed by prepositional phrases with concrete nouns (and their pronominal substitutes).

The following principal meanings are distinguished:

(1) location (static), e.g.:

stovéti ant stógo	'stand on the roof'

(2) direction, usually with verbs of motion. This includes (a) the initial point of motion (*išeĩti iš namų̃* 'leave home'), (b) the final point, or destination of motion (*grį̃žti į̃ namùs* 'return home'), and (c) route (*eĩti per kiẽmą* 'go across the yard').

LOCATION

2.48 Prepositional phrases of relative position are particularly associated with 'static' verbs denoting state, position and concrete action (but not with verbs of directed motion).

Prepositional phrases of position express a broad range of specific meanings, viz.:

(1) position relative to an object near or far from it (usually by the side); the following prepositions are used here:

priẽ + GEN (the least distance from an object):

áugti prie nãmo	'grow by the house'
susitìkti prie vartẽlių	'meet at the gate'

artì/netolì + GEN:

stovéti artì ugniẽs	'stand near the fire'
gyvénti netoli ùpės	'live not far from the river'

tolì nuo + GEN (the greatest distance from an object):

apsistóti tolì nuo miẽsto	'stay far from the town'

(2) position relative to a linear object (parallel to it):

pagaĩ/paleĩ +ACC:

(súolas) stóvi pagaĩ síeną	'(a bench) stands along the wall'
(žolẽ) áuga paleĩ griovį	'(grass) grows along a ditch'

(3) relative position by the side:

šalià/gretà + GEN:

sėdė́ti šalià krósnies	'sit by the stove' (lit. 'at the side of')
áugti šalià kẽlio	'grow by the road' ('on the roadside')

(4) position on both or all sides of an object:

abìpus + GEN:

abìpus kẽlio geltonúoja rugiaĩ	'rye is turning yellow/is yellow (lit. 'is yellowing') on both sides of the road'

apiẽ/apliñk + ACC:

sėdė́ti apie stãlą	'sit round a table'
áugti apliñk nãmą	'grow round a house'

(5) position on top or on the surface:

añt + GEN:

stūksóti ant kálno	'loom on (top of) a mountain'
sėdė́ti ant kélmo	'sit on a tree stump'
ryšė́ti skarẽlę ant galvõs	'have a kerchief on (one's) head'
áugti ant mẽdžio	'grow on a tree' (e.g. of moss)

The preposition *añt* with names of surfaces is synonymous with the locative case:

gyvénti ant krañto/krantè	'live on the shore'
pasiródyti ant viẽškelio/viẽškelyje	'appear on the highway'
laikýti ant délno/delnè	lit. 'hold on/in one's palm'
sėdė́ti ant žẽmės/žẽmėje	'sit on the ground'

(6) position above an object (without touching it):

virš̃/viršùj/viršum̃ + GEN:

kabė́ti virš galvõs	'hang above one's head'
skraidýti viršum̃ laukų̃	'fly above the fields'

aukščiaũ + GEN:

(rándas) bùvo aukščiaũ alkū́nės	'(the scar) was above the elbow'

(7) position under an object:

põ + INSTR:

tupė́ti po stalù	'squat under a table'
lìkti po sniegù	'remain under snow'
stovė́ti po medžiù	'stand under a tree'

(8) position in front, on this side of a thing:

priẽš + ACC (usually with names of objects with a front):

sustóti prieš rū́mus	'stop in front of a palace'
klūpóti prieš altõrių	'kneel in front of the altar'
staipýtis prieš véidrodį	'mince in front of a mirror'
šìldytis prieš ùgnį	'warm oneself in front of a fire'
stovė́ti prieš vė́ją	'stand facing the wind'

šiãpus + GEN (the place is determined relative to the observer):

gyvénti šiãpus gìrios	'live (on) this side of the forest'
pasivýti draũgą šiãpus tìlto	'catch up with a friend on this side of the bridge'

(9) position on the other side of an object (relative to its front side or to the observer's position):

ùž + GEN:

stovė́ti už prekýstalio	'stand behind the counter'
slė̃ptis už nãmo	'hide behind a house'

anãpus/kitapus/antrãpus/anãšal + GEN (the relative position is determined by the observer):

gyvénti anãpus ùpės	'live on the other side of the river'
sėdė́ti kitapus stãlo	'sit on the other side of the table'

(10) position between two or more objects:

tar̃p + GEN:

gyvénti tarp ùpės ir mìško	'live between a river and a forest'
tyvuliúoti tarp kalnų̃	'stretch (of a lake) between mountains'
slė̃ptis tarp lãpų	'hide among leaves'
stovė́ti tarp dùrų	'stand in the doorway' (with *pluralia tantum*)

(11) position on the surface or inside an object relative to its dimensions:

išilgaĩ/įstrižaĩ/įkypaĩ + GEN/ACC:

vežìmas stóvi skersaĩ kẽlio/kẽlią	'the wagon stands across the road (GEN/ACC)'
(kãsos) tį̃so išilgaĩ nùgaros/nùgarą	'(plaits) hang down the back'
gulė́ti įstrižaĩ lóvos	'lie across a bed'

Place of action is also expressed by the phrase *pàs* + ACC of a human noun:

gyvénti pas tėvùs	'live with one's parents'
bū́ti pas dirèktorių	lit. 'be at the manager's'

The preposition *pàs* is also occasionally used with concrete nouns instead of *priẽ*, e.g.:

stovė́ti pas lángą/prie lángo	'stand by the window'

Note: Static position is also expressed by the locative (see 2.29) and instrumental cases (see 2.25).

DIRECTION

The initial point of motion

2.49 Prepositional phrases may refer to the following concrete locations of the initial point of motion:

(1) inside an object (the head verb is often prefixed with *iš-*):

ìš + GEN:

(iš)važiúoti iš miẽsto	'go out of town'
paim̃ti/išim̃ti (knỹgą) iš spìntos	'take (a book) out of the bookcase'
(iš)krìsti iš rañkų	'fall out of the hands'
vė́jas pùčia iš pietų̃	'the wind is blowing from the south'

(2) next to an object:

nuõ + GEN (the verb is often prefixed with *at-*):

(at)jóti nuo mìško	'ride from (the direction of) the forest'
atsitráukti nuo ugniẽs	'draw from fire'

(3) the surface (or top) of an object:

nuõ + GEN (the verb can be prefixed with *nu-* or *pa-*):

nukrìsti nuo stãlo	'fall from the table'
pakìlti nuo žẽmės	'rise from the ground'

cf. the respective static location:

gulėti ant stãlo	'lie on the table'

(4) below a thing:

iš põ + GEN:

išlįsti iš po kélmo	'crawl out from under a tree stump'

cf. the respective static location:

lindėti po kélmu	'be under a tree stump'

(5) behind (another side) an object:

iš ùž + GEN:

išlįsti iš už debesų̃	'appear from behind the clouds'

cf. the respective static position:

bū́ti už debesų̃	'be behind the clouds'

iš anàpus/iš antràpus/iš kìtapus + GEN:

pérsikelti iš anàpus ùpės	'move (come) from the other side of the river'

cf. the respective static position:

bū́ti anàpus ùpės	'be on the other side of the river'

(6) between two or more objects:

iš tar̃p + GEN:

išbė́gti iš tarp mẽdžių	'run out from between/among trees'

cf. the respective static position:

bū́ti tarp mẽdžių	'be among trees'

2.50 The initial point of motion is also expressed by the same prepositions combined with the following adverbs:

(1) *iš, nuo* + *čià* 'here'/*teñ* 'there'/*kur̃* 'where'/*visur̃* 'everywhere'/*kitur̃* 'elsewhere'/*kažkur̃* 'somewhere'/*niẽkur* 'nowhere' (these adverbs can refer to both static position and direction), e.g.:

ateĩti iš teñ	'come from there'
susiriñkti iš visur̃	'gather from everywhere'
atsinèšti iš kitur̃	'bring from elsewhere'
atbė́gti iš kažkur̃	'come running from somewhere'
nuo čià tolì matýti	'one can see far from here'
nuo teñ nukrìto	'it fell from there'

(2) *iš* + *artì* 'nearby' / *tolì* 'far away' / *aukštaĩ* 'high above'; e.g.:

matýti iš artì	'see from a short distance'
grį́žti iš tolì	'return from far away'
nukrìsti iš aukštaĩ/iš aũkšto	'fall from high above'

(3) *iš* + *anàpus/kìtapus/antràpus, šiàpus, abìpus*; e.g.:

atvỹkti iš anàpus	'arrive from the other side'
ateĩti iš šiàpus	'come from this side'
žiūrė́ti iš antràpus	'look from the other side'
bė́gti iš abìpus	'run from both sides'

The final point of motion

2.51 Prepositional phrases of the final point of motion may refer to the following concrete destinations:

(1) inside a place or object:

į̃ + ACC (a perfective verb often has the prefix *į-*):

(į)važiúoti į mìšką	'come into the forest'
įsidė́ti į kišẽnę	'put into the pocket'
pasùkti į dẽšinę	'turn to the right'
pašókti į viršų̃	'jump upward'

cf. the respective static position expressed by the locative:

bū́ti miškè	'be in the forest'

(2) near to an object (in contact or not):

priẽ + GEN (the head verb often has the related prefix *pri-*):

prieĩti prie var̃tų	'come up to the gate'
prilìpti prie síenos	'stick to the wall'
pastatýti prie dùrų	'put at the door'
pasileñkti prie ligónio	'bend over the patient'

cf. the respective static position:

stovė́ti prie var̃tų	'stand at the gate'

artỹn + GEN:

sliñkti artỹn ẽžero	'move nearer to the lake'
cf. sliñkti prie ẽžero	'move towards the lake'

artì/arčiaũ + GEN:

prieĩti artì/arčiaũ nãmo	'come up near/nearer to the house'

(3) on the surface of an object:

añt + GEN (the verb may be prefixed with *už-*):

(už)lìpti ant stógo	'climb on to the roof'
padėti ant stãlo	'put on the table'
nukrìsti ant žēmės	'fall to the ground'

(4) above an object (without touching it):

viřš/viršum̃ + GEN:

užskrìsti virš miẽsto	'fly up above the town'
pakìlti viršum̃ stógo	'rise above the roof'

aukščiaũ + GEN:

pakìlti aukščiaũ debesų̃	'rise above (higher than) clouds'

(5) below an object:

põ + INSTR (often after verbs with the related prefix *pa-*):

palį̃sti po stalù	'crawl under the table'
padėti po pagálve	'put under a pillow'
atsisėsti po medžiù	'sit down under a tree'

cf. the respective static location:

lindėti po stalù	'stay under a table'

(6) behind, on the other side of an object:

ùž + GEN (often, with verbs with the prefix *už-*):

užlį̃sti už spìntos	'creep behind a cupboard'
nunèšti už vartų̃	'take outside the gate'
užkìšti (peĩlį) už diřžo	'stick (a knife) behind the belt'

cf. the respective static location:

lindėti už spìntos	'stay behind a cupboard'

(į) anàpus/kìtapus + GEN:

pérsikelti (į) anàpus ùpės	'cross to the other bank of the river'

(7) between two or more things:

tař̃p + GEN:

įstrìgti tarp mẽdžių	'get stuck between trees'
įbrìsti tarp méldų	'wade in among rushes'

2.52 Prepositional phrases can also express:

(1) the limit of movement:

ikì/lìgi + GEN:

nueĩti iki/ligi miẽsto	'walk as far as the town'
pakìlti ligi debesų̃	'rise up to the clouds'
įbrìsti (į vándenį) iki kẽlių	'wade (into the water) up to one's knees'

sulìg + INSTR:

(béržas) užáugo sulìg namù	'(the birch-tree) grew equal to the house (i.e. as tall as the house)'
(vanduõ) pakìlo sulìg lieptù	'(water) rose up to (as high as) the footbridge'

(2) direction (without indicating the limit):

GEN + *liñk(ui)* or *liñk(ui)* + GEN:

nueĩti miẽsto link/link miẽsto	'walk towards the town'
cf. *nueĩti į miẽsto pùsę*	'walk in the direction of the town'

The prepositional phrase *pàs* + ACC, with a human noun, denotes destination metonymically:

nuvažiúoti pas gìmines	'go to (one's) relatives' (i.e. the place where they live)
išeĩti pas kirpė́ją	'go to the hairdresser('s)'
nubė́gti pas brólį	'run to one's brother's (place)'

2.53 A number of other prepositional phrases of place denote the final point of movement when used with verbs of change of posture or position (*atsisė́sti* 'sit down', *pasodìnti* 'seat (sb)', *padė́ti* 'put down', etc.); when associated with verbs of state or motion, they denote location or passage (see 2.48, 2.55). Here belong:

apiẽ/apliñk + ACC:

susė́sti/susodìnti apie stãlą	'sit down/seat (people) round the table'
apvynióti šãliką apliñk kãklą	'wrap a scarf around (one's) neck'

pagaĩ/paleĩ + ACC:

atsiguĩti paleĩ síeną	'lie down along the wall'
patiẽsti (dróbę) pagaĩ ùpēlį	'stretch (a roll of linen) along the stream'

priẽš + ACC:

atsisė́sti prieš židinį	'sit down in front of the fire-place'
atsiklaũpti prieš tėvùs	'kneel in front of (before) the parents'

gretà/šalià + GEN:

atsisė́sti gretà/šalià mókytojo	'sit down next to the teacher'
pasidė́ti šalià lóvos	'put next to the bed'

skersaĩ, išilgaĩ, įstrižaĩ/įkypaĩ + GEN/ACC:

numèsti leñtą skersaĩ kẽlio/kẽlią	'throw a plank across the road'
atsigul̃ti įstrižaĩ lóvos/lóvą	'lie down across (= slantwise) the bed'
pastatýti súolą išilgaĩ síenos	'put a bench along the wall'

2.54 The final point or destination of movement is expressed by a number of prepositional phrases with adverbs:

(1) *į̃ + čià/teñ/kur̃*:

eĩk į̃ čià	'come here'
sùk į̃ teñ	'turn that way (there)'

(2) *į̃ + anàpus/kìtapus/antràpus/šiàpus/abìpus*:

išeĩti į̃ anàpus	lit. 'go to the other side' (i.e. die)
grį̃žti į̃ šiàpus	'return to this side'
ištiẽsti rankàs į̃ abìpus	'stretch out (one's) arms' lit. 'to both sides'

(3) *ikì/lìgi + čià/teñ/kur̃/kõl/tõl*:

atbė́gti iki čià	'run up to here'
nueĩti iki teñ	'go as far as there'
ateĩti iki tõl	'come up to here'
iki kur̃/kõl eĩsi?	'how far will you go'

Route

2.55 Two variants of this meaning can be distinguished: most prepositional phrases express the route of unidirectional motion, and *põ* + ACC expresses the route of multi-directional motion.

Prepositional phrases denoting the route of unidirectional motion are given below:

(1) route across an object from one end to the other:

per̃ + ACC:

eĩti per miẽstą	'go across the town'
važiúoti per tìltą	'drive across the bridge'
riedė́ti per véidą	'roll down (one's) face' (of tears)

These prepositional phrases are synonymous with the instrumental of place (see 2.25). After verbs with the prefix *per-* the preposition can be omitted, e.g.:

pérbėgti/péreiti per kiẽmą/kiẽmą	'run/go across the yard/cross the yard'
pérskristi per ẽžerą/ẽžerą	'fly across the lake/cross the lake flying'
péršokti per griõvį/griõvį	'jump across (over) a ditch'

skersaĩ, išilgaĩ, įstrižaĩ/įkypaĩ + GEN/ACC (reference to movement through or along the surface):

plaũkti skersaĩ ùpės/ùpę	'swim across the river'
péreiti išilgaĩ lentõs/leñtą	'walk the length of the plank'
nuriedėti įstrižaĩ aikštẽs/áikštę	'roll across (diagonally) the square'

(2) route of motion through an object (with names of things with holes or gaps):

prõ + ACC, with nouns as the following:

išeĩti pro durìs	'walk through the door'
žiūrėti pro grõtas	'look through the lattice'
išlį̃sti pro tiñklą	'get through a net (of fish)'
rūkti pro kãminą (also *iš kãmino*)	'go out though a chimney (of smoke)'

The phrase *peř* + ACC is occasionally used in the same sense:

įeĩti per durìs	'enter through the door'
žiūrėti per lángą	'look through a window '

peř + ACC (with names of solid objects and materials):

išlį̃sti per síeną	'pass through a wall (of a bullet)'
pérsigerti per drabužiùs	'soak through clothes (of water)'

The phrase *prõ* + ACC is occasionally used instead, cf.:

suñktis pro batùs	'soak through shoes (of water)'
prasimùšti pro stógą	'break out through the roof (of fire)'

kiauraĩ/skrãdžiai + ACC/GEN:

(*vinìs*) *išliñdo kiauraĩ leñtą*	'(a nail) came out the plank'
(*rõgės*) *kliñpsta skrãdžiai sniẽgą*	'(the sled) sinks through snow'
(*nãmas*) *nugrim̃zdo kiauraĩ/skrãdžiai žẽmę/žẽmės*	'(the house) sank through the earth'

(3) route of motion past an object, by its side:

prõ + ACC:

važiúoti pro ẽžerą	'go past a lake'
nueĩti pro sõdą (*į mìšką*)	'go past the garden (to the woods)'

After verbs with the related prefix *pra-*, the preposition can be omitted:

pravažiúoti pro miẽstą/miẽstą	'drive past a town/pass a town'
praeĩti pro óbelį/óbelį	'walk past an apple-tree/pass an apple-tree'

pagal̃/paleĩ + ACC (with names of things having length):

eĩti paleĩ ùpę	'walk along a river'
šliaũžti paleĩ/pagal̃ tvõrą	'crawl along a fence'

(4) route of motion around an object, on all sides:

apliñk/apiẽ + ACC (mostly with verbs with the prefix *ap(i)-*):

(api)bė́gti apie/apliñk nãmą	'run around a house'
žẽmė sùkasi apie sàvo ãšį	'the earth rotates round its axis'

(5) route of motion over, above an object (with verbs denoting motion in the air):

per̃ + ACC:

skrìsti per ẽžerą	'fly above a lake'
pér̃šokti per griõvį	'jump over a ditch'
pérmesti ãkmenį per tvõrą	'throw a stone over a fence'

vir̃š/viršum̃/viršùj + GEN:

skrìsti virš mìško	'fly above a forest'
pralė́kti virš galvõs	'fly over (sb's) head'

aukščiaũ + GEN:

skrìsti aukščiaũ/virš debesų̃	'fly above the clouds'

(6) route of motion between two or more objects:

tar̃p + GEN:

šliaũžti tarp bė́gių	'crawl between the rails'
bráutis tarp žmonių̃	lit. 'force one's way among the people'

(7) route is also occasionally expressed by the following prepositional phrases:

príešais + ACC:

praeĩti príešais tribū́ną	'pass in front of the stands'

ùž + GEN:

prabė́gti už nùgaros	'run behind (sb's) back'

põ + INSTR:

praplaũkti po tìltu	'swim by under a bridge'

artì/netolì + GEN:

praskrìsti netoli/arti žẽmės	'fly not far from/close to the ground'

tiẽs + INSTR:

skrìsti ties gálva	'fly past (sb's) head'

gretà/šalià + GEN:

eĩti šalià vežìmo	'walk next to the cart'

Route is also expressed by the instrumental case (see 2.25).

Multidirectional, iterative motion within the limits of an area is denoted by the prepositional phrase *põ* + ACC; it combines with verbs denoting:

(1) reiterated movement (also searching):

váikščioti po kiẽmą	'walk about a yard'
pláukioti po ẽžerą	'sail on a lake'
ieškóti po mìšką	'look for (sth) all over the forest'
graibýtis po kišenès	'grope in the pockets'

(2) dispersing, spreading:

pasklìsti po mìšką	'disperse (all) over the forest'
išmėtyti po laukùs	'scatter (sth) over the fields'
aidėti po mìšką	'echo over the forest'

The phrase *põ* + ACC can be interchangeable with the locative, cf.:

váikščioti po kiẽmą/kiemè	'walk over the yard/in the yard'
ieškóti po kišenès/kišẽnėse	'search through the pockets/in the pockets'
pasklìsti po píevą/píevoje	'spread over the meadow/in the meadow'

The spatial position of moving objects relative to each other is denoted by the prepositional phrases *pirmà* + GEN and *pãskui/pãskum* + ACC, when used with verbs of motion, e.g.:

šuõ bėga pirmà vežìmo/ *pãskui vežìmą*	'the dog is running in front of/behind the cart' (both the dog and the cart are moving)

The direction of motion is also indicated: both are moving along the same path and in the same direction. The prepositional phrases *príeky/priešakỹ* 'in front of' + GEN and *priẽš/príešais* 'in front' + ACC render the same meaning.

The phrase *priẽš* + ACC can also denote motion from the opposite direction, e.g.:

vaikaĩ išbėgo príešais mótiną	'the children ran out to meet (lit. 'opposite') their mother'

540 SYNTAX

2.57 Phrases with two prepositions, viz. *nuõ ... priẽ, nuõ ... añt, nuõ ... į̃, nuõ ... pà*... *ikì/lìgi*, and *ìš ... į̃* occur with imperfective (often iterative) multidirec verbs to describe a change of direction or to delimit the path of motion. prepositional phrases my contain:

(1) the relevant case-forms of the same noun, e.g.:

bėginėti nuo mẽdžio prie mẽdžio	'be running from tree to tree'
šokinėti nuo kùpsto ant kùpsto	'be jumping from mound to mound'
váikščioti iš kam̃bario į kam̃barį	'walk from room to room'

(2) indefinite pronouns as in:

váikščioti nuo víeno lángo prie kìto	'walk from one window to another'
nešióti iš vienõs víetos į kìtą	'carry from one place to another'

(3) two different nouns: *bėgióti nuo lángo prie dùrų* ' be running from the wi to the door'.

To emphasize iteration, a prepositional phrase can be repeated in reversed

váikščioti nuo lángo iki	lit. 'walk from the window to the d
dùrų, nuo dùrų iki lángo	from the door (back) to the window

Prepositional phrases of time

2.58 Temporal meanings are expressed by prepositional phrases with nouns der concepts of time, sometimes processes and seldom concrete things.

The following principal temporal meanings are distinguished:

(1) the time of an action,
(2) duration,
(3) the commencement and terminal points of an action,
(4) the limits of duration,
(5) anteriority and posteriority,
(6) simultaneity,
(7) frequency.

TIME OF ACTION

2.59 Two instances can be distinguished here.

(1) A stretch of time within which an action takes place is indicated b prepositional phrase *peř* + ACC. It is not necessarily implied that the event l for the entire period. The following nouns are used in this phrase:

(a) names of holidays, rituals, meals, some natural phenomena, etc.:

susitìkti per Kalėdàs/ per rugiapjū́tę/per atóstogas/per vakariẽnę	'meet at Christmas/at harvest time/ during holidays/at supper'
šókti per vestuvès	'dance at a wedding'
šienáuti per kaĩtrą	'make hay during a period of heat'

(b) names of parts of the day, seasons, and the like:

lýti per diẽną/per nãktį	'rain in the daytime/at night'
žydėti per vãsarą	'blossom in summer'
susir̃gti per darbýmetį	'fall ill during a busy season'

These phrases are close in meaning to phrases of duration (see 2.60).

(c) names of units of time (with an obligatory modifier):

pasikeĩsti per praėjusį dešim̃tmetį	'change in the past decade'

(2) The approximate time of an action is expressed by the following prepositional phrases with temporal nouns:

apiẽ + ACC:

grį̃žti apie rýtą/apie peñktą vãlandą	'return approximately in the morning/at about five o'clock'
išvažiúoti apie pietùs/apie pavãsarį	'go away at about lunchtime/ about spring time'

į̃ + ACC:

atvėsti į rýtą	'grow colder by (towards) morning'
pristìgti (dúonos) į pavãsarį	'be short (of bread) by spring'
sugrį̃žti į mė́nesio/mė́tų pãbaigą	'return by (towards) the end of the month/year'

artì/netolì + GEN (rare):

baĩgtis artì vidùrnakčio	'be over at about (lit. 'near to') midnight'

DURATION

2.60 Duration of an action (from the beginning to the end of a period) is expressed by *per̃* + ACC. In this phrase, temporal nouns are used usually with a quantitative modifier, viz. a numeral, the pronouns *kelì* 'several', *vìsas* 'all', the adjectives *ištisas* 'entire', *kiáuras* 'all, entire', and the like, e.g.:

šókti per vìsą/ìštisą/kiáurą nãktį	'dance all/the entire night'
dìrbti per vìsą vãsarą	'work all summer'

This prepositional phrase can also indicate the period of time in which a certain result is achieved, e.g.:

páltą pàsiuva per trìs mė́nesius	'(they) make a coat in three months' ('it takes three months to make a coat')

The prepositional phrase *apiẽ* + ACC with nouns denoting units of time (often with quantitative attributes) expresses approximate duration:

lýti apie vãlandą	'rain for about an hour'
láukti apie penkìs/kelìs mė́nesius	'wait for about five/several months'

Note: Duration of an action is also expressed by all the case forms without prepositions.

COMMENCEMENT AND TERMINAL POINTS

2.61 The initial temporal point of an action is expressed by *nuõ* + GEN and *ìš* + GEN. The former indicates the time when an action (which is still going on) began and it occurs mostly with imperfective verbs; cf.: *miegóti nuo vãkaro* 'sleep since evening'. The latter phrase is used mostly with perfective verbs to indicate the time when an action takes place and the implied resultant state (which still holds) begins, e.g.: *susiruõšti iš vãkaro* 'get ready in the evening (and be ready since)'.

The preposition *nuõ* has broader combinability with nouns than *ìš*; cf.:

ìš + GEN:

ateĩti iš vãkaro	'arrive in (lit. 'from') the evening (and be here since)'
sužaliúoti iš pavãsario	'turn green in (since) spring'

nuõ + GEN:

nekę̃sti iš/nuo pirmõs dienõs	'hate from/since the first day'
išlìkti iš/nuo senų̃ laikų̃	'exist from/since the olden times'
váikščioti nuo rýto	'walk since morning'
mókytis nuo vaikỹstės	'study since childhood'
láukti nuo antrõs valandõs	'wait since two o'clock'

The terminal point of an action or the period before which an action comes to an end is expressed by *ikì/lìgi* + GEN with temporal nouns:

láukti iki vãkaro/rudeñs/pirmãdienio	'wait until evening/autumn/Monday'

mókytis ligi egzaminų	'study until the examinations'
sugrį̃žti iki gegužė̃s mė́nesio	'return until the month of May'

The prepositional phrase *ikì/lìgi* + GEN with nouns denoting units of time specifies the limits of duration:

(jumis tèks) láukti iki valandõs/mẽtų	'(you have to) wait for about (as long as) an hour/a year'
(be vandeñs gãlima) išgyvénti ligi septynių̃ parų̃	'(without water one can) live up to (for about) seven days'

THE LIMITS OF DURATION

2.62 A limited period of time is expressed by *tar̃p* + GEN *ir̃* GEN, e.g.:

(žvė́rys) šẽriasi tarp rugpjū́čio ir spãlio mė́nesio	'(wild beasts) moult between September and October'
(žadė́jo) ateĩti tarp vienúolikos ir dvýliktos valandõs	'(they promised to) come between eleven and twelve o'clock'

The coordinated genitives can be sometimes replaced by the plural form of a noun:

susitìksim tarp šveñčių	'we'll meet between the holidays'

The limits of duration can also be expressed by a complex prepositional phrase *nuõ* + GEN – *ikì/lìgi* + GEN. The following nouns are used here:

(1) antonyms, e.g.:

dìrbti nuo rýto iki vãkaro	'work from morning till night'
keliáuti nuo pavãsario iki rudeñs	'travel from spring to autumn'

(2) nouns with the modifiers *víenas ... kìtas*:

láukti nuo víeno sekmãdienio iki kìto	lit. 'wait from one Sunday till the next'

ANTERIORITY AND POSTERIORITY

2.63 The prepositional phrases *priẽš* + ACC and *pirmà* + GEN relate an action to the following time or event. The phrase *põ* + GEN relates an action to the preceding time or event. Nouns used in these phrases denote:

(1) temporal concepts and also events, e.g.:

(a) kéltis prieš aũšrą/pirmà aušrõs	'get up before dawn'
ateĩti prieš vãkarą/pirmà vãkaro	'come before evening'
susitìkti prieš atóstogas	'meet before the vacation'

(b) *grį̃žti po pietų̃*   'return after dinner'
sužaliúoti po lietaũs   'break into young leaf after rain'
ràsti po naktiẽs   'find (sth) after a night'
išdýgti po žiemõs/iš po žiemõs   'sprout after the winter'

(*iš põ* is used with the nouns *naktìs* 'night' and *žiemà* 'winter' exclusively);

(2) animate beings, plants and things which refer to time by implying comparison:

(a) *gyvẽno (čià) priẽš*   '(they) lived (here) before the Lithuanians'
lietuviùs/pirmà lietùvių   (= 'before the Lithuanians had lived here')
(pémpė) atskrìdo priẽš gañdrą   '(the lapwing) returned before the stork'
atėjo priẽš manè/pirmà manę̃s   '(he) came before me'

(b) *(Výtautas) valdė Líetuvą po*   '(Vytautas) ruled Lithuania after
Kęstùčio   Kęstutis'
pjáuti kviečiùs po rugių̃   'cut rye after wheat'
sugrį̃žti po brólio   'return after (one's) brother'

(3) generalized temporal concepts (with an obligatory modifier):

(a) *išeĩti priẽš dvýliktą vãlandą*   'leave before twelve o'clock' (lit. 'twelfth hour')
palýti priẽš pjūtiẽs mẽtą   'rain before harvest time'
susitáikyti priẽš ámžiaus gãlą   'get reconciled before the end of life'

(b) *ateĩti po penktõs valandõs*   'come after five o'clock'
atšìlti po ledýnų laikótarpio   'grow warmer after the glacial period'

2.64 The prepositional phrase *bè* + GEN, with various temporal nouns, denotes a period of time before which an action cannot take place; it is used with the future tense and imperative form of verbs with negation, e.g.:

neišvažiúos be vãkaro   'he won't leave until (lit. 'without') evening'
(i.e. *išvažiuõs tik vakarè*)   ('he'll leave only in the evening')
negrį̃žk be rudeñs   'don't return until autumn'
nesusitìksi be šveñčių   'we won't meet until the holidays'

It is seldom used after verbs without negation, in which case it refers the verbal action to the time preceding the moment named:

atsikélti be sáulės (dienõs, šviesõs)   'get up before sunrise (daylight, light)'

2.65 A stretch of time separating the verbal action from a later reference point (usually the present moment) is specified by the prepositional phrase *priẽš* + ACC with a noun denoting a unit of time, e.g.:

susiriñko prieš vãlandą	'they gathered an hour ago'
atvýko prieš dù měnesius	'he arrived two months ago'
gyvẽno prieš šim̃tą mẽtų	'he lived a hundred (ACC) years (GEN) ago'

The synonymous prepositional phrases *põ* + GEN and *ùž* + GEN (less common), and also *bè* + GEN (with negative verbs) when used with nouns naming units of time, specify the stretch of time separating the verbal action from a prior reference point (implied by or given in the context), cf. respectively:

sugrį̃žo po/už valandõs	'he returned an hour later'
susitìko po trijų̃ (kelių̃) dienų̃	'they met three (a few) days later'
atẽjo po dešimtiẽs minùčių	'he came ten (Prep + GEN) minutes (GEN) later'
negérk váistų be valandõs	'take this medicine in an hour's time only' (lit. 'don't take this medicine without an hour')
ligónis nepasveĩks be dviejų̃ saváičių	'the patient will get well in two weeks only'

SIMULTANEITY

2.66 Simultaneity of an action with another event or moment is expressed by *sù* + INSTR with the names of parts of the day and seasons, and natural phenomena related to seasons of a year:

atsikélti su šviesà (*aušrà, dienà, sáule*)	lit. 'get up with the (day)light (dawn, day(light), sun(rise))'
báimė ateĩna su vãkaru	'fear comes with the night'
lìgos prasìdeda su rùdeniu	'illnesses begin with the autumn'
cf. also: *kéltis (kartù) su paũkščiais*	'get up (together) with the birds'
gul̃ti su vìštomis	'go to bed with the hens' (i.e. 'very early')

FREQUENCY

2.67 A period of time in which an action is regularly reiterated is denoted by prepositional phrases *peř* + ACC with the plural number of temporal nouns:

(vėjas) stúgauja per naktìs	'(the wind) howls at nights'
(šeimà) susitìkdavo per šventès	'(the family) used to meet during holidays'
(mokiniaĩ) išdykáuja per pértraukas	'(schoolchildren) romp during intervals'

When used with *pluralia tantum*, this phrase denotes frequency with the past frequentative tense form only, cf.:

atvažiúodavo per atóstogas	'he used to come (home) on holidays' (frequency)
– *atvažiãvo per atóstogas*	'he came (home) during holidays' (time of action)

Frequency of action is also expressed by the nominative (see 2.33), accusative (see 2.9) and instrumental (see 2.26, 2) used without a preposition.

Prepositional phrases of cause

In prepositional phrases of cause the prepositions *ìš* 'because of, out of, for', *nuõ* 'from, of', *dė̃l* 'because of', *ùž* 'for', less commonly *dėkà* 'thanks to', *peř* 'through, because of' are used.

ìš + GEN

2.68 The phrase *ìš* + GEN expresses the cause of volitional actions and emotional sates of human (and other animate) beings. The cause may be:

(1) an emotion or mood (either positive or negative):

šokinė́ti iš džiaũgsmo/ láimės/linksmùmo	'be jumping with joy/happiness/merriment'
paraũsti iš pỹkčio/gė́dos	'redden with anger/shame'
veřkti iš núoskaudos/ ãpmaudo/neviltiẽs	'cry out of mortification/vexation/despair'
drebė́ti iš báimės/ susijáudinimo/ìšgąsčio	'tremble with fear/agitation/fright'

(2) a psychological feature:

atsisakýti iš kuklùmo/mandagùmo	'refuse (sth) out of modesty/politeness'
padė́ti iš pareigingùmo/ gerùmo/draugiškùmo	'help (sb) out of a sense of duty/kindness/friendliness'
nusigyvénti iš tinginỹstės	'become impoverished because of laziness'

(3) a feeling or a physical state:

raitýtis iš skaũsmo	'writhe with pain'
užmìgti iš núovargio	'fall asleep from fatigue'
apal̃pti iš álkio/bãdo/trõškulio	'faint from hunger/starvation/thirst'
drebė́ti iš šal̃čio	'tremble with cold'

nuõ + GEN

2.69 The phrase *nuõ* + GEN specifies the cause of (a change of) a state, and, occasionally an action; the cause may be:

(1) a concrete thing, sometimes an animate being:

susir̃gti nuo obuolių	'fall ill from apples'
žúti nuo príešų	'perish at the hands of the enemies'
mėlynúoti nuo žibùčių	'be blue with violets'
pérmirkti nuo lietaũs	lit.'get wet through (of shoes, clothes) from rain'

(2) a natural phenomenon:

nudègti nuo sáulės	'get sunburnt from/in the sun'
sùktis nuo vėjo	'go round (of a windmill) because of the wind'
supelýti nuo drėgmė̃s	'grow mouldy because of humidity'
kentė́ti nuo kar̃ščio	'suffer from the heat'
cf. also: *mir̃ti nuo žaizdų̃*	'die from wounds'

dė̃l + GEN

2.70 The phrase *dė̃l* + GEN differs from the above two prepositional phrases in that it commonly refers to the reason of explanation, mental cause or logical motivation, seldom to the cause of an action and it usually modifies the entire clause, e.g.:

dėl blogų̃ kelių̃ atvažiúodavo nedaũg žmonių	'few people used to come because of (due to) poor roads'
dėl saldùmo geresnė̃ bùvo laĩkoma klevų̃ sulà	'because of its sweetness, maple sap was considered to be better'

The preposition *dė̃l* typically combines with nouns denoting:

(1) abstract concepts: *aplinkýbės* 'circumstances', *są́lygos* 'conditions', *brúožai* 'features', *ypatýbė* 'peculiarity', *padėtìs* 'position, state', *põbūdis* 'character', *stokà* 'shortage', *fõrma* 'form', *turinỹs* 'content', *idėja* 'idea', *laĩkas* 'time' and the like; cf.:

Dėl sàvo geogrãfinės padėtiẽs Lietuvà negalėjo lìkti uždarà.	'Because of its geographical position, Lithuania could not remain isolated.'
Žvaĩgždės dėl dìdelio atstùmo atródo mãžos.	'Stars look small due to the great distance.'

(2) permanent properties and features of humans: *gabùmai* 'abilities', *grõžis* 'beauty', *atkaklùmas* 'pertinacity', *įsitìkinimai* 'convictions', *svõris* 'weight', *ū́gis* 'height', *išvaizdà* 'appearance', *dỹdis* 'size', *ámžius* 'age', *sveikatà* 'health', etc., e.g.:

Dėl sãvo mokytùmo jìs greĩtai pagarsė́jo.	'Because of his learning, he soon became famous.'
Jìs negalė́jo dìrbti dėl sveikãtos.	'He could not work because of his health.'

(3) also concrete things:

Čià negãlima gyvénti dėl uodų̃.	'People can't live here because of gnats.'
Jì mán patìko dėl sãvo žydrų̃ akių̃.	'I liked her for her blue eyes.'

The preposition *dė̃l* is used with the noun *priežastìs* 'cause' with an obligatory modifier:

dėl šiõs/menkõs priežastiẽs	'for this/slight reason'
dėl kė́leto priežasčių̃	'for a number of reasons'

(this noun is never used with other prepositions).

2.71   *Dė̃l* + GEN typically combines with verbs denoting the following:

(1) emotional and physical states (usually negative): *nusimiñti* 'become dispirited', *jáudintis* 'be worried', *nerimáuti* 'be uneasy/worried', *gráužtis/kriñstis (dėl ateitiẽs)* 'be worried (about the future)', *liūdė́ti* 'be sad', *gedė́ti* 'mourn', *síelotis/sielvartáuti (dėl artimų́jų)* 'grieve (for one's near relatives)', *drebė́ti* 'tremble', *nusigą̃sti* 'get frightened', *nustèbti* 'be surprised', *susigė́sti/raudonúoti* 'get ashamed/blush', *džiaũgtis (dėl sėkmė̃s/sėkmè)* 'rejoice at one's success (Prep + GEN)/ (INSTR)', *pỹkti* 'be angry', etc.;

(2) negative actions: *bárti(s)* 'scold', *giñčytis (dėl mã̃žmožių)* 'argue (about trifles)', *mùštis (dėl pinigų̃)* 'fight (about money)', etc.;

(3) spontaneous events: *atsitìkti/įvỹkti* 'happen', *atsirãsti/kìlti* 'arise, appear', *pasikeĩsti* 'change', *padaugė́ti* 'increase', *sumažė́ti* 'decrease, diminish', etc.; cf.:

neláimė įvỹko dėl neatsargùmo	'the accident happened because of carelessness'
gaĩsras kìlo dėl sausrõs	'the fire started because of the drought'
uodų̃ padaugė́ja dėl drėgmė̃s	'gnats multiply (lit. 'increase in number') due to humidity'

Dė̃l + GEN is commonly used after verbs with negation, e.g.:

neatė́jo dėl ligõs	'he didn't come because of (his) illness'
negalė́jo atvažiúoti dėl lietaũs	'he couldn't come because of the rain'
neužáugo javaĩ dėl kaitrõs	'rye didn't grow because of the heat'

2.72   *Dė̃l* + GEN sometimes denotes concession, i.e. a cause in spite of which an action takes or can take place; it usually combines with (1) modal predicates (*galė́ti* 'be able to', *gālima* 'it is possible', less frequently *privalė́ti* 'be obliged', *reikė́ti* '(be) necessary', *turė́ti* 'have to' with an infinitive or (2) the future tense, imperative subjunctive form of a verb; cf. respectively:

(**1**) *Dėl tókio šalčio reikėjo ateĩti.*	'In spite of this cold (weather), you should have come.'
Dėl tókio lietaũs gālime važiúoti.	'In spite of such rain, we can drive.'
(**2**) *Dėl tókios ligõs gyvénsi šim̃tą mẽtų.*	'With such an illness, you'll live a hundred years.'
Dėl manę̃s eĩkit nors į̃ prãgarą.	'For me (= as far as I am concerned) you can go to hell.'

peř + ACC

2.73 The prepositional phrase *peř* + ACC is typically used in negative contexts. It naturally combines with negative verbs and usually contains a negative noun, or a noun that acquires negative connotations. Thus it combines with the following types of verbs:

(**1**) verbs with negation:

nepabaigė dárbo per tingė́jimą	'he didn't finish work because of (out of) his laziness'
nèdavė pinigų̃ per šykštùmą	'he didn't give money out of stinginess'
negalė́jo išeĩti per vaikùs	'he couldn't go out because of the children'
nepailsė́jo per dárbus	'he had (had) no rest because of work'

(**2**) verbs with negative meanings:

apàkti per apsileidìmą	'become blind through carelessness'
kentė́ti per gìmines	'suffer because of relatives'
išeikvóti (pìnigus) per móteris	'embezzle (money) because of women'
pavėlúoti per svečiùs	'be late because of the visitors'

(**3**) verbs acquiring negative connotations in context:

pasielgti kvailaĩ per nesusipratìmą	'do a silly thing through misunderstanding'
ne taĩp atsakýti per susijáudinimą	'give the wrong answer because of excitement'
paim̃ti ne peĩlį, o šakùtę per skubėjimą	'take a fork instead of a knife in a hurry'

Peř + ACC is usually interchangeable with the neutral *dė̃l* + GEN:

nusigyvénti per tingė́jimą/dėl tingė́jimo	'become impoverished through (one's) laziness'

GEN + *dėkà*

2.74 The phrase GEN + *dėkà* 'thanks to' renders a specialized causal meaning which is antonymous to that of *peř* + ACC: it expresses a positive cause of an action. It is used with nouns denoting persons or their positive qualities; cf.:

pasveĩkti gýdytojų dėkà	'recover thanks to doctors'
parašýti puĩkų romāną tālento dėkà	'write a perfect novel thanks to talent'

ùž + ACC

2.75 The prepositional phrase *ùž* + ACC expresses motive or reason with verbs denoting:

(1) punishment for misdeeds, or awarding:

baũsti už nusikaltimùs	'punish for crimes'
keřšyti už skriaudàs	'revenge for offences'
teĩsti už vagỹstę	'try (take to a court of law) for stealing'
apdovanóti už drąsą	'award for bravery'

(2) verbal and emotional behavior and assessment, e.g.: *bárti* 'scold', *kéikti* 'curse', *káltinti* 'accuse', *smeřkti* 'blame', *kritikúoti (už klaidùos)* 'criticize (for mistakes)', *priekaištáuti* 'reproach', *peĩkti* 'blame', *niẽkinti* 'scorn', *žẽminti* 'humiliate', *meñkinti* 'belittle', *mylė́ti* 'love', *mė́gti* 'like', *geřbti* 'respect', *vértinti* 'appreciate', *atsiprašýti* 'apologize', *gìrti* 'praise', etc.; these verbs are also used with *dė̃l* + GEN.

Note: Cause is also expressed by the instrumental case (see 2.28).

Prepositional phrases of purpose

2.76 The following prepositional phrases are used with verbs to express purpose.

(1) The phrase *dė̃l/dė̃lei* + GEN refers to the purpose of an active action (most frequently, movement):

atjóti dė̃l mergė̃lės	lit. 'come riding for the fair girl'
lenktyniáuti dė̃l pirmōs viẽtos	'compete for the first place'
kovóti dė̃l láisvės/už láisvę	'fight for freedom'
išgérti dė̃l drąsõs	'have a drink for courage'
pasislė́pti atsargùmo dė̃lei	'hide oneself for the sake of caution'

(2) The phrase *į̃* + ACC, used with verbs of motion (or inducement, e.g. *kviẽsti* 'invite'), refers to an event in which the agent (patient) intends (is urged) to participate; e.g.:

jóti į medžiõklę/medžióti	'ride to the hunt/to hunt'
pakviẽsti (bičiuliùs) į puõtą	'invite (friends) to a feast'

(3) The phrase *priẽ* + GEN, combined with verbs of motion or change of position (e.g. *sė́sti* 'sit down'), refers to a thing which implies motivation of an action:

nueĩti prie rugių̃	lit. 'go to the rye' (i.e. to cut rye)
sė́sti prie ratẽlio	'sit down to the spinning-wheel' (i.e. to do spinning)
pastatýti darbiniñką prie stãklių	'send (lit. 'stand') a worker to the machine-tool'
cf.: *stóti prie dárbo/dìrbti*	'take up work' (lit. 'stand to work (Prep + GEN)/to work (INF)')

Note: Purpose is also expressed by the genitive (see 2.15) and the dative case (see 2.19–21).

Prepositional phrases of quantity

2.77 Prepositional phrases with quantitative nouns (and numerals) subordinate to a verb express quantitative characteristics of an action (extent or amount), e.g.:

nueĩti apie kilomètrą	'walk about a kilometre'
pir̃kti už penkìs litùs	'buy for five litas'

Nouns of quantity are often modified by a numeral (*apie dù kilometrùs* 'about two kilometres') or they are subordinated to a numeral (*apie šim̃tą mỹlių* 'about a hundred miles'). Quantity is expressed by the following prepositional phrases.

(1) The phrase *apiẽ* + ACC refers to an approximate quantity:

nuvažiúoti apie mỹlią (*apie trìs mylià̀s/šim̃tą mỹlių*)	'cover (drive) about a mile (about three miles/hundred miles)'
sver̃ti/svérti apie tòną (apie penkià̀s tonàs/apie dẽšimt tònų)	'weigh about a ton (about five tons/ten tons)'

(2) *artì/netolì* + GEN denotes a somewhat smaller quantity than that named by the noun:

nueĩti artì kilomètro	'walk nearly a kilometre'
pardúoti artì ceñtnerio (grūdų̃)	'sell almost a centner (of grain)'
sumokė́ti netolì šim̃to lìtų	'pay nearly a hundred litas'

(3) *ikì/lìgi* + GEN indicates the upper limit of quantity:

nueĩti iki kilomètro (*iki šešių̃/dešimtiẽs kilomètrų*)	'walk as much as a kilometre (six/ten kilometres)'
suskaičiúoti iki šim̃to	'count up to a hundred'

(4) *peř* + ACC denotes a greater quantity than that named by the noun or numeral:

sverti/svérti per kilogrãmą	'weigh over (more than) a kilogram'
kainúoti per tū́kstantį dólerių	'cost over a thousand dollars'

(5) *ùž* + GEN denotes distance from the reference point:

sustóti už kilomètro (už dviejų̃/šim̃to kilomètrų) nuo miẽsto	'stop at the distance of a kilometre (two/a hundred kilometres) from the town'
nukrìsti už penkių̃ mètrų (nuo manę̃s)	'fall five metres away (from me)'

(6) *ùž* + ACC denotes price, the account of payment, etc. (see 2.37, 2):

pir̃kti už šim̃tą lìtų	'buy for a hundred litas'

For prepositional phrases of quantifying time see 2.60.

Prepositional phrases of manner

2.78 Prepositional phrases of manner describe the following:

(1) the state of the agent while performing an action (or characterization of the action), viz.:

(a) presence of a characteristic or possession, for which purpose *sù* + INSTR is used:

pùlti su įniršiu	'attack with fury'
pažvel̃gti su méile	'glance (at sb) with love'
láukti su nekantrumù	'wait with impatience'
išeĩti su páltu	'go out in a coat (wearing a coat)'
sėdė́ti su kepurè	'sit with one's cap on'

(b) absence of a characteristic or possession, which is rendered by *bè* + GEN:

pùlti be báimės	'attack without fear'
išvarýti be gaĩlesčio	'drive (sb) out without pity'
gulė́ti be są́monės	'lie unconscious' (lit. 'without consciousness')
ateĩti be kepùrės	'come without a cap'

(2) the maximum intensity of an action or process, which is rendered by *ikì/lìgi* + GEN:

prisiválgyti iki sóties	lit. 'eat to satiety'
įkaĩsti iki raudonùmo	'be heated red' (lit. 'to redness') (of iron)
įkyrė́ti iki gývo káulo	'bore (sb) to death' (lit. 'to the live bone')

(3) the motive or plan, or grounds for performing an action, for which purpose *pagal̃* + ACC is used:

statýti (rū́mus) pagal̃ projèktą	'build (a palace) according to a project'
nubaũsti pagal̃ įstãtymą	'punish in accordance with the law'
reñgtis pagal̃ mãdą	lit. 'dress according to fashion'
veĩkti pagal̃ plãną	'act according to a plan'

(4) the intermediary or medium, expressed by *per̃* + ACC:

kalbė́tis per vertė́ją	'talk through an interpreter'
pranèšti per rãdiją/laĩkraštį	'announce on (lit. 'through') the radio/ through a newspaper'
pasiųsti (linkė́jimus) per draũgą	'send (best wishes) with (lit. 'through') a friend'

(5) means:

įsiver̃žti per jė́gą	'break in by force'
išsivèsti per príevartą	'lead (sb) away under compulsion'

(6) an obstacle (which may be the agent's state), expressed by *prõ/per̃* + ACC:

šypsótis pro ãšaras/skaũsmą	lit. 'smile through tears/pain'
išgir̃sti pro triùkšmą	'hear through noise'
susikalbė́ti per síeną	'communicate through a wall'

(7) the mode of action relative to the position of a body part, expressed by *añt* + GEN:

stovė́ti ant vienõs kójos	'stand on one foot'
gulė́ti ant nùgaros	'lie on one's back'
pasirem̃ti ant rañkų	'lean on one's hands'
nèšti (vaĩką) ant pečių̃	'carry (a child) on one's shoulders'

With verbs of 'attaching' this prepositional phrase may refer to a means:

paléisti áitvarą ant siū́lo	'fly a kite on/with a thread'

(8) distribution of the plural agent or patient in equal numbers during an action, expressed by *põ* + ACC:

išsiváikščioti po víeną	'disperse one by one'
ateĩti po kelìs	'come in groups of several'
prinešióti (šiẽno) po glė̃bį	'bring (hay) in armfuls'

The manner of an action can also be expressed by *ìš* + GEN, e.g.:

surìkti iš visų̃ jėgų̃	'cry out with all one's might'
palinkė́ti (gẽro) iš širdiẽs	lit. 'wish (good luck) with/from one's heart'

There is a number of adverbialized phrases with this preposition, e.g.:

žiūrė́ti iš padilbų̃/paniūrų̃	'look scowlingly'
kalbė́ti iš lė́to	'speak slowly'
ateĩti iš (pa)leñgvo	'walk slowly'
pérrašyti iš naũjo	'rewrite anew'
užpùlti iš pasalų̃	'attack on the sly'

Verb – Infinitive

2.79 In verb groups with a dependent infinitive the semantic subject of the latter may coincide with the subject of the head verb (*jìs mókа skaitýti* 'he can read') or it may not coincide with it (*jìs liẽpė mán ateĩti* 'he told me to come'). The former infinitive is traditionally termed 'subjective', and the latter 'objective'. Syntactically, the infinitive is either a part of a compound verbal predicate (*galì eĩti* 'you can go'), or it takes the position characteristic of an object (*jìs mė́gsta skaitýti* 'he likes to read'), or it is an adverbial modifier of purpose (*atė́jo padė́ti* 'he came to help'); it may also take the subject position (*mán nusibódo láukti/laukìmas* lit. 'to wait/waiting (NOM) bored me', i.e. 'I was bored with waiting').

2.80 In verb groups with a 'subjective' infinitive, the head may be a semantically deficient verb, in which case it modifies the meaning of the infinitive and serves as a semi-auxiliary in a compound verbal predicate. Here belong:

(1) phasal verbs:

pradė́ti/im̃ti (mókytis)	'begin (to study)'
(pa)baĩgti (rašýti)	'finish (writing)'
mèsti (rūkýti)	'stop, give up (smoking)'
liáutis/nustóti (lýti)	'stop, cease (raining)'
lìkti (stovė́ti)	'continue, go on (standing)'
įpusė́ti (knýgą skaitýti)	lit. 'do half (to read a book)'

These verbs typically combine with imperfective infinitives excepting *baĩgti* which also takes a perfective infinitive:

baĩgia išdžiū́ti	lit. 'it finishes to dry' i.e. 'it has almost dried'

The following verbs are also used with an infinitive to express a sudden and/or unexpected intense beginning of an action: *šókti* 'jump', *pùlti* 'rush, attack', *mèstis* 'throw oneself, rush', *griẽbtis* 'seize, set to', *tvértis* 'seize, snatch', *subrùzti* '(begin to) bustle', 'start (quickly)', *sujùsti* '(begin to) move', 'start, set about', *prapliùpti* 'gush out , burst into', *prakiùrti* 'burst', *pašė̃lti* 'get furious', *įnìkti* 'apply oneself (to)'. The ending of an action is expressed by the verbs *nutìlti* 'fall silent', *nuščiúti* 'die away', etc. They acquire a phasal meaning in combination with an infinitive only, cf.:

šóko padė́ti	'(he) rushed to help'
praplýšo dainúoti	'(he) burst into singing'
nutìlo šū́kauti	'(he) (suddenly) stopped shouting'

(2) Verbs with a modal meaning: *galė́ti* 'be able', *sugebė́ti* 'be able, capable', *pajė́gti/isténgti/valióti* 'be able', *mokė́ti* 'be able, know (how to)', *iprásti/igùsti* 'get used, get into the habit (of)', *turė́ti* 'have (to)', *privalė́ti* 'be obliged (to)', *reikė́ti* 'have (to)', e.g.:

reĩkia tikė́ti	'one ought be believe'
gãli padė́ti	'he can help'
tùri išeĩti	'he must go'

2.81 The following types of verbs retain their lexical meaning and subordinate a 'subjective' infinitive as a syntactic object, often interchangeable with a case form of a noun or a prepositional phrase.

(1) Verbs of volition and the like: *norė́ti* 'want', *veř̃žtis* 'long', *geĩsti* 'wish, long', *trókšti* 'crave', *tikė́tis/vìltis* 'hope', *mė́gti* 'like', etc.; *mė́ginti* 'try', *bandýti* 'try', *sténgtis* 'strive, seek', *išdrį̃sti* 'dare', etc., e.g.:

nórime džiaũgtis/džiaũgsmo	'we want to enjoy/enjoyment (GEN)'
mė́gstu gérti/gė́rimus	'I like to drink/drinks (ACC)'

(2) Verbs of intention, agreement or refusal, or memory: *galvóti* 'think, plan', *manýti* 'think, intend', *svajóti* 'dream', *užmir̃šti* 'forget', *atsimiñti* 'remember', *nuspré̇sti/nutar̃ti* 'decide', *ketìnti* 'intend', *ruõštis/reñgtis* 'prepare, get ready', *susiprásti (išeĩti)* 'have the sense (to leave)', *apsiim̃ti* 'undertake (to do sth)', *sutìkti* 'agree', *isipareigóti* 'pledge oneself (to do sth)', *prisíekti* 'promise', *rýžtis* 'decide, resolve', *žadė́ti* 'promise', *susitar̃ti* 'arrange (to do sth)', *siū́lytis* 'offer', *atsisakýti* 'refuse', e.g.:

nuspréndė išeĩti	'(he) decided to leave'
užmir̃šo pranèšti	'(he) forgot to report'
žadė́jo padė́ti	'(he) promised to help'

(3) Verbs with negative connotations: *bijóti* 'be afraid', *véngti* 'avoid', *sáugotis* 'fear, avoid', *gė́dytis* 'be ashamed', *drovė́tis* 'be shy', *tingė́ti* 'be lazy'; e.g.:

bìjo péršalti	'(he) is afraid of catching a cold'
véngia kalbė́ti	'(he) avoids talking'

(4) Verbs denoting excess or insufficiency: *padáuginti/pamãžinti* 'add too much/little', *patánkinti* 'make too thick/frequent', *parė́tinti* 'make too thin', *nuìlginti*

'make too long', *patrumpinti* 'make too short', and the like. The infinitive can be omitted here, e.g.:

padáuginau/pamãžinau (*į̃dėti*) *drùskos*	'I added too much/little salt' lit. 'I exceeded/lessened (to add) salt'

2.82 A number of verbs take an infinitive and the dative case of a noun naming the semantic subject of both the head and the infinitive; the latter occupies the position of the nominative case:

Atsibódo	*mán*	*láukti*	/	*laukìmas*
bored	I: DAT	wait: INF		waiting: NOM

'I got bored with waiting'

Here belong verbs of psychological states, assessment, and the like: *įkyrė́ti/įgrìsti/įsipykti/praìlgti* 'bore', *rūpė́ti/magė́ti* 'worry, be anxious', *knietė́ti* 'have an urge', *patìkti* 'like', *tìkti/derė́ti* 'be suitable', *sèktis* 'go well', *vertė́ti/apsimokė́ti* 'be (well) worth', *atsitìkti/pasitáikyti* 'happen', *tèkti* 'fall to the lot of', *pavỹkti* 'succeed (in), manage', e.g.:

mán rūpė́jo dìrbti/dárbas	'I (DAT) was anxious to work'
mán patiñka dainúoti/daĩnos	'I like to sing/songs'
jám sẽkasi rašýti/rãšymas	'to write/writing goes well with him'
jíems tẽko láukti	'(it so happened that) they (DAT) had to wait'
mùms pavỹko grį̃žti	'we (DAT) managed to return'

The following verbs are impersonal, they also take the dative case of a noun and an infinitive interchangeable with the genitive case of a noun:

reĩkia žmõgui pailsė́ti/póilsio	'a person (DAT) needs to rest/a rest (GEN)'
užtèks táu veřkti	lit. 'it is enough for you to cry' (' you have cried enough, stop it')
kiekvienám nórisi džiaũgtis/džiaũgsmo	'everyone (DAT) wants to be joyful/joy (GEN)'

2.83 An 'objective' infinitive occurs with verbs of causation governing either (1) the accusative (*pàkvietė manè ateĩti* 'he invited me (ACC) to come') or (2) the dative case (*léido mán išeĩti* '(he) allowed me (DAT) to go out ') of a noun which names a person to whom the infinitival action is ascribed:

(1) *prašýti* 'ask', *kviẽsti/vadìnti* 'invite', *vilióti/gùndyti* 'allure, tempt', *rãginti* 'encourage, urge', *skãtinti* 'induce', *kùrstyti* 'incite, instigate', *drą̃sinti* 'encourage', *įpareigóti* 'obligate', *priveřsti/prispìrti* 'force, compel', *įkalbė́ti/prikálbinti* 'persuade', *išmókyti* 'teach', (*pri*)*prãtinti* 'train', e.g.:

priprãtino vaĩką ankstì gul̃ti	'(she) trained the child to go to bed early'

(2) *liẽpti* 'tell', *į̇sakýti* 'order', *léisti* 'let, allow', *padė́ti* 'help', *patar̃ti* 'advise', *(pa)siū́-lyti* 'suggest', *(už)draũsti/užgìnti* 'forbid', e.g.:

liẽpė mán atsisė́sti	'(he) told me to sit down'
pasiū́liau jám nueĩti teñ	'I suggested that he should go there'
padė́jau jám atsikélti	'I helped him stand up'

2.84 The infinitive can be used optionally with verbs denoting motion to express **purpose**. This can also be expressed by the genitive case of a noun, e.g.:

atė̃jome pasikalbė́ti/pókalbio	'we have come to talk (INF)/for a talk (GEN)'
atsisė́do pailsė́ti/póilsio	'(he) sat down to rest (INF)/for a rest (GEN)'
išsiuntė̃ vaikùs uogáuti/úogų	'(he) sent the children to gather berries (INF)/for berries (GEN)'

If the dependent infinitive is transitive its direct object is expressed in the genitive instead of the accusative:

išvažiãvo kẽlio taisýti	'(they) went to repair the road (GEN)'
(cf. *taisýti kẽlią*)	('repair the road (ACC)')
atė̃jo draũgo aplankýti	'(he) came to visit his friend (GEN)'
lìko namų̃ sáugoti	'(he) stayed to look after the house (GEN)'
siuñtė mergáitę vandeñs parnèšti	'(she) sent the girl to fetch water (GEN)'

In sentences of this type a transitive infinitive may be omitted if the genitive of a concrete noun is sufficient to express purpose:

išė́jo píeno parnèšti	'(he) went to bring milk'
(cf. *išė́jo píeno*)	(lit. '(he) went for milk')
išsiuñtė sū́nų dãktaro pakviẽsti	'(he) sent his son to get the doctor'
(cf. *išsiuñtė sū́nų dãktaro*)	(lit. '(he) sent his son for the doctor')

The infinitive of purpose, with the exception of sentences with motion verbs, is mostly combined with the dative case denoting the direct object of the infinitive:

pastãtė daržìnę šiẽnui sukráuti	'they built a hay-loft to keep hay' (lit. 'they built a hay-loft for hay (DAT) to keep')
iššóvė žmonė́ms pagą̃sdinti	'(he) fired to scare people (DAT)'

The infinitive may be either obligatory (cf. **iššóvė žmonė́ms* 'he fired for people') or optional, as in:

par̃vežėm lentų̃ nãmui (apmùšti)	lit. 'we brought some boards for the house (to cover)'

The dative case is also used if the semantic subject of the infinitive is the beneficiary of the head verb:

pastūmė kėdę svečiui atsisėsti	'he moved the chair for the visitor (DAT) to sit down'
daviaũ svíedinį vaikáms žaĩsti	lit. 'I gave a ball to the children (DAT) to play'
iškasė griõvį vándeniui nutekėti	lit. 'they dug a ditch for water (DAT) to flow away'

2.85 The infinitives *válgyti* 'eat', *užkąsti* 'have a snack', *lèsti* 'peck' (of hens), *ėsti* 'eat' (of animals), *gérti* 'drink', *lãkti* 'lap', *rūkýti* 'smoke', *skaitýti* 'read', *siūti* 'sew', *mègzti* 'knit', *dėvėti* 'wear', *apsivilkti* 'put on', when subordinated to the verbs *nèšti(s)* 'take/carry (for/with oneself)', *at(si)nèšti* 'bring (for oneself)', *vèžtis* 'take/drive for oneself', *pa(si)imti* 'take (for oneself)', *dúoti* 'give', *nu(si)pir̃kti* 'buy (for oneself)', *paruõšti* 'prepare', are equivalent to the accusative (or genitive) case of a noun as a direct object, cf.:

dãvė mán válgyti/maĩsto	lit. 'she give me to eat/some food (GEN)'
pasiėmiau válgyti/dúonos	lit. 'I took to eat/some bread (GEN)'
įsidėjau mègzti/mėzginį	lit.' I have put (in my bag) to knit/the knitting (ACC)'

Verb – Participle, Gerund

2.86 The grammatical properties and meaning of a number of verbs permit complemention by a participle, e.g.:

sākėsi	*ateĩsiąs*
say: 3. PAST. REFL	come: FUT. ACT. PART. NOM. MASC
'he said he would come'	
mėgsta	*pàgiriamas*
like: 3. PRES	praise: PRES. PASS. PART. NOM. MASC
'he likes being praised'	

In a number of cases, the nominative of a participle is interchangeable with an infinitive (a) or with the accusative or genitive of a deverbal noun (b), cf.:

(a) *tikisi laimėsiąs/laimėti*	'he hopes to win (FUT. ACT. PART/INF)'
prāšėsi įléidžiamas/įléisti	'he asked to bé let in (PRES. PASS. PART/ INF)'
(b) *mėgsta pàgiriamas/ pagyrimùs*	'he likes being praised (PRES. PASS. PART)/praises (ACC)'
bìjo bāramas/barìmo	'he fears being scolded (PRES. PASS. PART)/ scolding (GEN)'

Verbs of perception can also subordinate a gerund, or a gerundial phrase with the accusative or genitive case of a noun, e.g.:

girdėjau griáudžiant	'I heard thundering (PRES. GER)'
mačiaũ skreñdant paũkštį	'I saw a bird flying (PRES. GER)'
láukė mótinos pareĩnant	lit. 'he was waiting for mother coming (PRES. GER)'

For a detailed treatment of verbs joined with a participle and gerund see 3.101, II.5.151.

Verb – Adverb

2.87 Adverbs define the action of the head verb with respect to place, time, quality, quantity, and manner.

(1) Adverbs of **place**:

gyvénti tolì/artì/nuošaliaĩ/šalià	'live far/nearby/apart/near'
lìkti namiẽ	'stay at home'
sliñkti artỹn	'move near(er)'
žiūrėti aukštỹn	'look upwards'
eĩti namõ	'go home'

A number of adverbs refer either to location or direction:

gyvẽna/atvỹko čià, teñ	'(he) lives/arrived here, there'
niẽkur nebùvo/nenuẽjo	lit. 'he has been/gone nowhere'
gyvẽno/išėjo kituř	'he lived/went elsewhere'

(2) Adverbs of **time**:

dabař nelỹja	'it is not raining now'
vãkar lìjo	'it rained yesterday'
ankstì atsikėlė, vėlaĩ atsìgulė	'(he) got up early, went to bed late'
ateĩna kasdiẽn (kàs diẽną)	'(he) comes every day'
negyvẽno (čià) niekadà	'(he) never lived (here)'
vaikaĩ gìmė pamečiuĩ	'the children were born every year'

(3) Adverbs of **cause**:

kodė̃l/dė̃l kõ nepasãkė?	'why didn't he say?'
kažkodė̃l neatėjo	'he didn't come for some reason'
todė̃l/dė̃l tõ/ùž taĩ nukentėjo	'therefore/for that reason he suffered'
týčia taĩp pasãkė	'he said so on purpose'

(4) Quantitative adverbs:

daũg skaĩto	'he reads much'
mažaĩ válgo	'he eats little'
ilgaĩ gyvẽno	'he lived long'
padaugė́jo dvìgubai/dùkart	'it increased twice' i.e. 'it doubled'
ketùrgubai atlýgino	'(they) remunerated (him) four times (as much)'
labaĩ láukė	lit. 'he waited very (much)'
mirtinaĩ įkyrė́jo	'it bored (sb) to death'

(5) Adverbs of manner:

skaũdžiai sudejãvo	lit. '(he) groaned painfully'
klausiamaĩ pàžvelgė	'(he) glanced inquiringly'
kaĩba pašnibždõm	'they talk in a whisper'
dìrba pakaitõm	'they work by turns'

Adverbs in *-te/-tinai* are used exclusively as intensifiers (see II.6.13):

bė́gtè bė́ga	lit. '(he) runs running' i.e. '(he) runs fast'
gertinaĩ gẽria	lit. '(he) drinks drinking' i.e. '(he) drinks like a fish'

Nominalisations

2.88 Many deverbal nouns of action or result (action nominals, *nomina actionis*) retain the syntactic relationships characteristic of the base verbs. Therefore they form word groups with the same dependent constituents, e.g.:

tamsõs báimė	'fear of darkness (GEN)'
(cf. *bijóti tamsõs*)	('be afraid of darkness (GEN)')
tikė́jimas ateitimì	'belief in the future (INSTR)'
(cf. *tikė́ti ateitimì*)	('believe in the future (INSTR)')
gyvẽnimas miestè	'life in a town (LOC)'
(cf. *gyvénti miestè*)	('live in a town (LOC)')
svajõnės apie ãteitį	'dreams about the future (Prep + ACC)'
(cf. *svajóti apie ãteitį*)	('dream about the future (Prep + ACC)')
skrỹdis per Atlántą	'flight across the Atlantic (Prep + ACC)'
(cf. *skrìsti per Atlántą*)	('fly across the Atlantic (Prep + ACC)')
sustojìmas pakeliuĩ	'a stop(ping) on the way (ADV)'
(cf. *sustóti pakeliuĩ*)	('to stop on the way (ADV)')

Deverbal nouns also retain the same relationships with an infinitive of the base verb, e.g.:

pómėgis skaitýti	'liking for reading (INF)'
(cf. *mė́gti skaitýti*)	('like to read')
viltìs pasveĩkti	'the hope to get well'
(cf. *vìltis pasveĩkti*)	('to hope to get well')
leidìmas išeĩti	'permission to leave'
(cf. *léisti išeĩti*)	('allow to leave')

2.89 Deverbal nouns do not combine with the following:

(1) qualitative adverbs with the suffix *-(i)ai*, which are changed into the respective adjective, participle, or pronoun, e.g.:

gražiaĩ mègzti	'knit beautifully'
(cf. *gražùs mezgìmas*)	('beautiful knitting')
įtikinamai atsakýti	'answer convincingly'
(cf. *įtìkinamas atsākymas*)	('convincing answer')
kitaĩp supràsti	'understand otherwise'
(cf. *kitóks supratìmas*)	('different (PRON) understanding')

(2) the accusative of measure, which is transformed into the genitive case or some other form, cf.:

dìrbti metùs	'work for a year'
– *mẽtų/mẽtinis dárbas*	'the work of a year (GEN/ADJ)'
nueĩti kilomètrą	'walk a kilometre'
– *kilomètro ėjìmas*	'walking a kilometre (GEN)'
sverti/svérti kilogrãmą	'weight a kilogram (ACC)'
– *kilogrãmo svõris*	lit. 'weight of (equal to) a kilogram (GEN)'

(3) the accusative case of direct object and the nominative case of subject, which are transformed into the genitive case (see 2.102, 103).

B. NOMINAL GROUPS

2.90 A noun can be joined with an adjective (or another adjectival word, viz. a participle, an ordinal numeral, a pronoun), a case form of a noun, a prepositional phrase, an infinitive and, less commonly, a gerund and an adverb.

Subordinated word forms usually express a qualitative characteristic of the noun referent, sometimes a quantitative and, rarely, an adverbial (circumstantial) characteristic.

NOUN – NOUN

Nominal groups with the governed case of a noun are further described according to the latter case form and its meanings.

The genitive case

THE POSSESSIVE GENITIVE

2.91 The possessive relations between the head noun and a genitive premodifier subsume the following instances:

(1) The relation of inalienable possession between part and whole, the genitive case referring to the whole and the head noun to the part:

vaĩko rankà	'child's hand'
gulbės spar̃nas	'swan's wing'
béržo šakà	'branch of a birch-tree'
tráukinio vagònai	'carriages of a train'

(2) The relation of alienable possession between possessor denoted by the genitive and property denoted by the head noun:

tėvų̃ sodýba	'parents' farmstead'
valstýbės mìškas	lit. 'forest of the state'
universitèto bibliotekà	'university library'

(3) Blood and family relationships. The following cases are distinguished here:

(a) both the head noun and the genitive premodifier denote relatives:

mótinos tėvas (senẽlis)	'mother's father (grandfather)'
senẽlio tėvas (prósenelis)	'grandfather's father (great-grandfather)'
výro brólis (díeveris)	'husband's brother (brother-in-law)'
výro sesuõ (móša)	'husband's sister (sister-in-law)'
výro tėvas (šẽšuras)	'husband's father (father-in-law)'
seser̃s duktė̃ (dukterė́čia)	'sister's daughter (niece)'
seser̃s sūnùs (sūnė́nas)	'sister's son (nephew)'

The head noun often denotes a relative, and the genitive premodifier a person identified otherwise:

mókytojo brólis	'teacher's brother'
karãliaus sūnùs	'king's son'
Pẽtro tėvas	'Peter's father'

(b) the head noun denotes an animal with respect to age or gender and the genitive premodifier names the species:

vil̃ko jaunìklis (vilkiùkas)	'wolf's cub'
várnos vaĩkas (varniùkas)	lit. 'crow's child (young crow)'
ánties pãtinas (añtinas)	lit. 'duck's male (drake)'

(4) A human (animate) possessor can be referred to by the possessive genitive form of personal pronouns (*màno* 'my', *tàvo* 'your (SG)', *sàvo* 'one's own', *mū́sų* 'our', *jū́sų* 'your', *jų̃* 'their', *jõ* 'his', *jõs* 'her') or the same case form of indefinite pronouns:

màno knygà	'my book'
tàvo tėvaĩ	'your parents'
jų̃ draugỹstė	'their friendship'
kienõ kaltė̃	'whose fault'
kažkienõ žõdis	'someone's word'

THE DESCRIPTIVE GENITIVE

2.92 The genitive premodifier expresses a qualitative characteristic of the head noun referent:

prõto žmogùs	'a man of intellect'
láimės diẽnos	'days of happiness'
užúojautos žõdžiai	lit. 'words of condolences'
tylõs minùtė	'a minute of silence'

The genitive of the subordinated noun is often used with an obligatory limiting modifier:

gẽro bū́do móteris (but **bū́do móteris*)	lit. 'woman of good nature'
dìdelio tãlento rašýtojas	'writer of great talent'
nematýto gražùmo mergáitė	'girl of exceptional beauty'
pláčių pečių̃ jaunuõlis	lit. 'a youth of broad shoulders'

THE GENITIVE OF COMPARISON

2.93 The genitive describes the referent of the head noun by implying comparison with respect to (1) the basic characteristic or (2) inalienable possession of the referent of the dependent noun:

(1) *sidãbro šalnà*	lit. 'frost of silver' (i.e. 'frost like silver')
deĩmanto žvaĩgždės	'stars of diamond'
áukso žõdžiai	'words of gold'
(2) *erẽlio nósis*	'the nose of an eagle' (i.e. 'a nose like that of an eagle')
árklio sveikatà	'the health of a horse'

šuñs apetìtas	'the appetite (like that) of a dog'
várnos balsas	'the voice (like that) of a crow'

The genitive modifier (especially of abstract nouns) is in its turn often premodified by another genitive case form, e.g.:

pelenų̃ spalvõs plaukaĩ	lit. 'hair of the colour of ashes'
(cf. *pelenų̃ spalvà*)	('the colour of ashes')
mótinos bū̃do duktė̃	lit. 'the daughter of the temper of her mother'
kriáušės pavìdalo ąsõtis	'a pearshaped jug' (lit. 'jug of the shape of a pear')

In poetic speech, nominal groups with the opposite relation of comparison are used: the genitive modifier names the object described, and the head noun refers to the basis of comparison, e.g.:

mėnùlio pjáutuvas	'the sickle of a moon' (i.e. 'the moon like a sicle')
upẽlio kãspinas	'the ribbon of the river'
ežerų̃ ãkys	'the eyes of the lakes' (i.e. 'lakes like eyes')

THE GENITIVE OF MATERIAL

2.94 In this case, the genitive premodifier names the material the referent of the head noun is made of:

áukso žíedas	'gold (GEN) ring'
vãško žvãkė	'wax candle'
kìškio kepùrė	'cap of rabbit (fur)'
ą́žuolo stãlas	'oak table'

The genitive plural has a similar meaning in the following instances:

ẽglių mìškas	'fir forest'
vỹšnių sõdas	'cherry orchard'
rugių̃ laũkas	'rye field'

THE GENITIVE OF PURPOSE

2.95 The genitive premodifier refers to the purpose the referent of the head noun is intended for:

dúonos peĩlis	'bread knife' (i.e. 'a knife for cutting bread')

akių lašaĩ	'eye drops'
dúonos mìltai	'bread flour' (i.e. 'flour for making bread')
grindų leñtos	lit. 'floor planks'
kavõs puodėlis	'coffee cup'
(cf. puodėlis kavõs)	('a cup of coffee')
dárbo kambarỹs	'work room'
rugių mẽtai	lit. 'rye year' (i.e. 'a good year for growing rye')
kviečių žẽmė	lit. 'wheat soil' (i.e. 'soil suitable for growing wheat')
grỹbų laĩkas	'mushroom season'

THE GENITIVE OF NAME

2.96 The genitive premodifier is the proper name of, or a narrower term for, the referent of the head noun.

(1) The genitive can be the proper name of:

(a) geographical objects, places, countries, administrative units, seas, etc.:

Vìlniaus miẽstas (= Vìlnius)	'the City of Vilnius'
Rambýno kálnas	'Mount Rambynas'
Ròmos impèrija	'the Roman Empire'
Trãkų pilìs	'the castle of Trakai'

(b) institutions, factories, newspapers, magazines, pieces of art, e.g.:

"Lelìjos" fãbrikas (also "Lelijà", fãbrikas "Lelijà")	'the factory "Lelija"'
"Mókslo" leidyklà	'"Mokslas" publishing house'
"Mẽtų" poemà	'poem "Metai" ("Year")'

(c) holidays (with the nouns dienà 'day', šveñtė 'holiday'):

Mótinos dienà	'Mother's day'
Visų šventųjų dienà	'All Saints' day'
Velýkų šveñtė	'Easter holiday'

(2) The genitive premodifier denotes a narrower concept, and the head noun a broader concept, e.g.:

(a) plėšrū́nų būrỹs	'order of predators'
bangìnių póbūris	'whale suborder'

lèmingų gentìs	'lemming genus'
kirstùkų rū̃šis	'the shrew species'
(b) *erškė̃čių krū́mas*	'blackthorn bush'
lelìjų kẽras	lit. 'lily bush'
serbeñtų krū́mas	'currant bush'
(c) *saũsio mė́nuo*	'the month of January'
rýto mẽtas	'the time of morning' (i.e. 'morning time')
rudeñs laĩkas	'autumn time'
jaunỹstės laikaĩ	lit. 'times of youth'
(d) *fìzikos mókslas*	'the science of physics'
novèlės žánras	'the genre of the short story'
romantìzmo srovė̃	'the trend of romanticism'

THE GENITIVE OF PLACE

2.97 The genitive case describes the referent of the head noun relative to the place it names:

mìško paũkštis	'forest bird'
miẽsto žmogùs	'town dweller' (lit. 'man of town')
vandeñs lelijà	'water lily'
kalnų̃ upẽlis	'mountain stream'
gãtvės žibiñtas	'street lamp'
Rytų̃ Lietuvà	'East Lithuania'
Pietų̃ ašìgalis	'South Pole'

THE TEMPORAL GENITIVE

2.98 The temporal genitive (1) describes the referent of the head noun relative to time or (2) specifies the time denoted by the head noun:

(1) *rudeñs gėlė̃*	'autumn flower'
naktiẽs paũkštis	'night bird'
rýto rasà	'morning dew'
vãsaros darbaĩ	'summer work'
senóvės daĩnos	'songs of old times'
(2) *pavãsario rýtas*	'spring morning'
biržẽlio vãkaras	'June evening'
šeštãdienio pópietė	'Saturday afternoon'

THE QUANTITATIVE GENITIVE

2.99 In this case, the genitive case form, due to its lexical meaning, expresses a quantitative characteristic of the referent of the head noun:

kilogrãmo lydekà	lit. 'a pike of a kilogram' (i.e. 'a pike weighing a kilogram')
kilomètro kẽlias	'the way a kilometre long'
minùtės pértrauka	'a (one) minute interval'
mėnesio viščiùkas	'a month-old chicken'

A complex quantitative modifier may consist of two subsequently subordinated genitives or it may be a nominal group with a numeral; cf. respectively:

(1) *mètro ĩlgio lentà*	lit. 'a plank of (one) metre's length'
(cf. *mètro ĩlgis*)	('metre's length')
mẽtų senùmo vỹnas	lit. 'wine of (one) year's age' (i.e. 'wine a year old')
(2) *ketverių̃ mẽtų (ámžiaus) vaĩkas*	'a child of four years (of age)'
dviejų̃ kilogrãmų (svõrio) žuvìs	'a fish of two kilograms (of weight)'

THE INTENSIFYING GENITIVE

2.100 The genitive plural case form premodifying the same noun has an intensifying function: it emphasizes either (1) the highest degree with respect to the quality of the referent of a singular noun or (2) the quantity of the referent of a plural noun; cf. respectively:

(1) *draugų̃ draũgas*	'the best of friends' (lit. 'the friend of friends')
giesmių̃ giesmẽ	'the song of songs'
žvaigždžių̃ žvaigždẽ	'the brightest of stars'
var̃gšų var̃gšas	'the poorest of all'
kvailių̃ kvailỹs	'the stupidest of fools'
(2) *minių̃ mìnios*	lit. 'crowds of crowds' (i.e. 'huge crowds')
dienų̃ diẽnos	'many, many days'
ámžių ámžiai	'centuries and centuries'
žiedų̃ žiedaĩ	'lots of blossoms'
kartų̃ kar̃tos	'many generations'

THE GENITIVE OF QUANTIFIED CONTENT

2.101 In this case, the genitive denoting matter or a thing usually modifies nouns denoting:

(1) an indefinite quantity:

daugumà/daugýbė žmonių	'majority/a lot of people'
gausýbė/áibė daiktų̃	'plenty/a lot of things'
dalìs/pùsė mìško	'a part/half of the forest'
ketviřtis/trẽčdalis tuřto	'a quarter/a third (part) of the property'
trupùtis pinigų̃	'a little money'

(2) a unit of quantity:

kilogrãmas svíesto	'a kilo of butter'
lìtras píeno	'a litre of milk'
mètras dróbės	'a metre of linen'
kilomètras kẽlio	'a kilometre of the road'
sáuja mìltų	'a handful of flour'
gùrkšnis vandeñs	'a mouthful of water'
šiẽno glėbỹs	'an armful of hay'
gãbalas dróbės	'a piece of linen

(3) a container or a place:

stiklìnė vandeñs	'a glass of water'
lėkštẽ sriubõs	'a bowl of soup'
maĩšas mìltų	'a sack of flour'
vežìmas šiẽno	'a cart (load) of hay'
kloįìmas šiẽno	'a barn (full) of hay'
skrynià dróbių	'a coffer of linen'

The genitive premodifying nouns of this type is often ambiguous: it may refer either to the quantified content (like the postpositive genitive) or to the purpose of the container:

kavõs puodẽlis	1. 'a cup (full) of coffee'; 2. 'a cup for drinking coffee'

The meaning is disambiguated by the context.

(4) a group of things of one kind:

būrỹs kareĩvių	'a platoon of soldiers'
minià žmonių̃	'a crowd of people'
gaujà vilkų̃	'a pack of wolves'
spiẽčius bìčių	'a swarm of bees'

krūvà akmenų 'a heap of stones'
púokštė gėlių 'a bunch of flowers'

THE OBJECTIVE AND SUBJECTIVE GENITIVE

2.102 The **objective** genitive modifies (de)verbal nouns from:

(1) transitive verbs taking the accusative case of a direct object (transformed into the objective genitive):

obuolių rãškymas	'the picking of apples'
(cf. *raškýti óbuolius*)	('pick apples')
akių gýdytojas	'an eye specialist'
(cf. *gýdyti akìs*)	('treat eyes')
nãmo statýba	'the building of a house'
lãpių medžiõklė	'fox hunting'
namų sárgas	'a house watchman'

(2) verbs taking other case forms:

tėvo padėjėjas	lit. 'father's helper'
(cf. *padėti tėvui*)	('help father: DAT')
tautõs atstõvas	'representative of the nation'
(cf. *atstováuti taūtai*)	('represent a nation: DAT')
rañkų dárbas	lit. 'work of hands' (i.e. 'handiwork')
(cf. *dìrbti rañkomis*)	('work with (one's) hands: INSTR')
Birùtės dainà	lit. 'Birutė's song '
(cf. *dainúoti apie Birùtę*)	('sing about Birutė')

2.103 The **subjective** genitive modifies nouns formed from:

(1) Verbs, e.g.:

paūkščio skrỹdis	'a bird's flight'
(cf. *paūkštis skreñda*)	('a bird flies')
upēlio čiurlēnimas	'the babble of a stream'
tėvų sutikìmas	'(the) parents' consent'
draūgo atvykìmas	'a friend's arrival'

The genitive is thus a transform of the subject of the respective finite verb.

(2) Adjectives, e.g.:

sniẽgo baltùmas	'the whiteness of snow'
gamtõs grõžis	'the beauty of nature'

In this case the genitive corresponds to the subject of a nominal predicate, cf.:

sniẽgas (yrà) báltas   'snow is white '

The dative case (with the infinitive)

2.104 The dative case denotes the purpose for which the head noun is intended:

lašaĩ akìms	lit. 'drops for eyes'
põpierius laiškáms	'paper for letters'
kraĩtis dùkteriai	'trousseau for (the) daughter'
lẽsalas paũkščiams	'seed for birds'

In this meaning, the genitive of purpose (cf. *akių̃ lašaĩ* 'eye drops') is more common (see 2.95). The dative is more frequently used with an infinitive:

iñdas arbãtai vìrti	'a kettle for making tea' (lit. 'for tea to make')
sklỹpas nãmui statýti	'a plot for building a house' (see 2.84)

With some nouns, the infinitive alone is used to signify purpose:

vietà sėdė́ti	'a place for sitting' (lit. 'to sit')
vanduõ atsigérti	'water for quenching the thirst' (lit. 'to drink')
siū́lai mègzti	'yarn for knitting'
laĩkas žydė́ti	'the time for blossoming'
próga susitìkti	'an occasion for meeting'

The instrumental case

2.105 The instrumental case of a noun with an obligatory modifier is used to denote an exterior feature of the head noun referent; the modifier can be expressed by:

(1) an adjective, a participle, or a numeral which agrees with its head in case:

mergáitė geltonomìs kasomìs	'a girl with blond plaits'
paũkštis lenktù snapù	'a bird with a crooked beak'
šãkės trimìs pirštais	'a pitchfork with three prongs'

(2) the genitive case of a noun:

žíedas deĩmanto akimì	'a ring with a diamond' (lit. 'with a diamond eye')
vaĩkas sẽnio véidu	'a child with an old man's face'
vyrìškis kãrio unifòrma	'a man in a soldier's uniform'

(3) with two (or more) sequentially subordinated genitives:

paũkštis ryškių̃ spalvų̃ plùnksnomis	lit. 'a bird with feathers of brilliant collours'

karaláitė mė́nesio spalvõs rū̃bais	lit. 'a princess with clothes of the colour of the moon'
mēdis dviejų̃ mètrų ìl̃gio šaknimìs	lit. 'a tree with roots of the length of two metres'

(4) the adjective *panašùs* 'similar' governing a prepositional phrase *į̃* + ACC:

áugalas panašiaĩs į́ kárdą lãpais	'a plant with leaves like swords'

The locative case

2.106 The locative case of concrete nouns subordinated to concrete (rarely abstract) nouns denotes the place of the referent of the head noun:

ẽžeras miškè	'a lake in the woods'
ãšaros akysè	'tears in (sb's) eyes'
áudra jū́roje	'a storm in the sea'

The accusative case

2.107 The accusative case of temporal nouns describes the referent of the head noun relative to time:

miẽstas nãktį	'the town at night'
ẽžeras žiẽmą	'the lake in winter'
mokyklà rugsė́jo mė́nesį	'a school in the month of September'

Appositive groups

2.108 Here belong nominal groups consisting of two nouns termed appositives which are typically identical in form and in reference (or else the reference of one is included in the reference of the other):

kaimýnas Pė́tras	'the neighbour Peter'
ùpė Nẽmunas	'the river Nemunas'

Apposition can be full or partial. In the case of partial apposition one of the appositives is clearly the head, and the other is the modifier termed apposition (*mókytojas Petráitis* 'the teacher Petraitis', *žõdis láisvė* 'the word freedom'). In full apposition, both nouns are semantically of (more or less) equal importance and it is not obvious which of the appositives is the head noun.

In an appositive group, both nouns are not always coordinated in case, number, and in gender.

(1) The appositives may not be coordinated in case in the following instances:

(a) in addresses, the polite 'title' *põnas* 'Mister' commonly retains its nominative case form if the head is in the vocative case, though the vocative is also used:

põnas/põne Juozáiti!	'Mister (NOM/VOC) Juozaitis (VOC)!'
põnas/põne Prezideñte!	'Mister (NOM/VOC) President (VOC)!'

(b) titles of publications, names of organizations, institutions, etc., comprised of two or more words, in Standard Lithuanian retain the nominative case form if the head noun is used in a different case:

Prenumerúoju žurnãlą "Kultũros baraĩ".	'I subscribe to the magazine (ACC) "Kultūros barai" (NOM).'

In informal speech, however, the genitive case of a modifier is preferable:

Prenumerúoju "Kultũros barų̃" (GEN) *žurnãlą* (ACC) (cf. 2.96);

(c) invariable nouns cannot agree in case with the head noun:

(grį̃žome) iš Tártu miẽsto	lit. '(we returned) from Tartu town (GEN)'
álfa dalẽlės	'alpha particles'

(2) The appositives may not agree in number:

(a) if one of the appositives is invariable for number (it is either singular or plural only):

(miestẽlio) vaȓdas Taurãgnai	'(the town's) name (SG) Tauragnai (PL)'
ligà raupaĩ	'the disease (SG) smallpox (PL)'

(b) if two or more appositives are subordinated to the same plural head noun:

žõdžiai láisvė ir lygýbė	'the words freedom and equality'

(3) The appositives do not agree in gender if both are invariable with regard to it:

vabzdỹs bìtė	lit. 'the insect (MASC) bee (FEM)'
sóstinė Vìlnius	lit. 'the capital (FEM) Vilnius (MASC)'

If an appositive is neutral with respect to gender it combines with nouns of both genders:

padáuža sūnùs/duktě̃	'scapegrace son (MASC)/daughter (FEM)'
akìplėša mokinỹs/mokinẽ̃	'cheeky (NOUN: COMMON) pupil (MASC/FEM)'

In the case of nouns with gender contrast (*substantiva mobilia*), coordination in gender is obligatory; cf.:

poètas Mairónis	'the poet Maironis (MASC)'
– *poètė Salomėja Nėrìs*	'the poetess Salomėja Nėris (FEM)'
diẽvas Perkū́nas	'the god Perkūnas (MASC)'
– *deĩvė Mìlda*	'the goddess Milda (FEM)'

2.109 In the case of **partial apposition** subordinated appositives occur most frequently with proper personal names:

mókytojas Jonáitis	'the teacher Jonaitis'
karãlius Mìndaugas	'king Mindaugas'
Sigùtė našlaitė̃lė	'Sigutė (the little) orphan'

also with human nouns in general:

kaimiẽtės móterys	lit. 'villagers (FEM) women'
bróliai dvyniaĩ	'twin brothers' (lit. 'brothers twins')
pãmotė rãgana	'stepmother (the) witch'
sūnùs palaidū́nas	'the son debauchee'

sometimes also with animate and concrete nouns:

šárka vagìlė	'magpie (the) pilferer'
sáulė močiùtė	lit. 'the sun mother'

In official style, in order to achieve precision, appositive collocations like *ùpė Nėmunas* 'the river Nemunas', *ẽžeras Sartaĩ* 'lake Sartai', are used, with proper nouns in apposition, though otherwise the genitive case is more common: *Nėmuno ùpė* 'the river (NOM) of Nemunas (GEN)'.

2.110 Full apposition is realised by clusters of two juxtaposed nouns collectively referring to a single (often semantically complex) notion. Here belong:

(1) pairs of hyponyms, usually jointly synonymous to the respective hyperonym:

tėvas mótina (tėvaĩ)	'father and mother (parents)'
bróliai sẽserys (brolijà)	'brothers and sisters'
výrai móterys	'men and women'
rañkos kójos	'arms and legs'
žiemà vãsara	'winter and summer' (i.e. 'the year round')
dienà naktìs	'day and night' (i.e. 'all the time, round the clock')

(2) pairs of synonyms, e.g.:

laũmė rãgana	lit. 'witch sorceress'
vargaĩ bė̃dos	lit. 'worries troubles'

kẽlias viẽškelis	lit. 'road highroad'
kaĨbos šnẽkos	lit. 'talk chat'

They are used for emphasis, as well as those of the following groups:

(3) two nouns of the same stem, the second noun usually with a diminutive suffix:

keliaĩ kelẽliai	lit. 'roads little-roads'
kalnaĩ kalnẽliai	'hills'
žõdžiai žodẽliai	'words'

All these clusters are stylistically marked. They are common in folklore, dialectal speech and in fiction; e.g.:

Skrìsčiau pas mergẽlę rýtas vakarẽlis.	'I'd go rushing to my girl morning and evening.'
Tarp kalnų̃ tyvuliãvo ežeraĩ ežeriùkai.	'Among the hills there stretched countless lakes.'

NOUN – PREPOSITIONAL PHRASE

2.111 Prepositional phrases used to modify a noun express a variety of meanings.

(1) *iš/nuõ* + GEN denotes the origin, source, material or composition of the head noun referent, e.g.:

(a) *žmogùs iš miẽsto*	'a man from the city'
giminẽ iš tẽvo pùsės	lit. 'relatives from (the) father's side (of the family)'
komìsija iš trijų̃ žmonių̃	'a committee of three persons'
(b) *sūnùs nuo pìrmo výro*	'the son by the first marriage (lit. 'husband')'
láiškas nuo tėvų̃	'a letter from (one's) parents'

(2) the following prepositional phrases denote:

(a) the purpose for which the referent of the head noun is intended:

nuõ + GEN:

váistai nuo galvõs skaũsmo	'remedy for a headache'
žõlės nuo kósulio	'herbs for a cough'

į̃ + ACC:

bìlietas į teãtrą	'a ticket to the theatre'
stráipsnis į laĩkraštį	'an article for a newspaper'

priẽ + GEN (rare):

sausaĩniai prie alaũs	'biscuits for beer (to go with beer)'

(b) the purpose for which the head noun referent has been used, is expressed by *nuõ* + GEN (often interchangeably with the preposed genitive without a preposition), cf.:

buteliùkas nuo váistų/ *váistų buteliùkas*	'a medicine phial'
statìnė nuo silkių/ *silkių statìnė*	'a herring barrel'

(3) The phrase *sù* + INSTR has a comitative meaning and thus refers to an attendant entity or possession. The noun in the instrumental case names the following:

(a) an object or a person of the same class as the head noun:

mótina su vaikaĩs	lit. 'mother with the children'
stãlas su kėdėmìs	'a table and (lit. 'with') chairs'
sáulė su mėnuliù	'the sun and the moon'
žẽmė su dangumì	'the earth and the sky'

These groups are close in meaning to coordinated groups with the conjunction *iř* 'and':

mótina su vaikaĩs = mótina ir vaikaĩ	'mother and the children';

(b) the entity habitually associated with the head noun referent:

sẽnis su lazdà	'an old man with a cane'
pyrãgas su várške	'a cake with cottage cheese'
(cf. *varškẽs pyrãgas*)	('a cottage cheese (GEN) cake')
dúona su svíestu	'bread and (lit. 'with') butter'

(c) a part or a feature of the head noun referent:

mergáitė su kasomìs	'a girl with plaits'
puodėlis su gėlýtėmis	'a cup with flowers (on it)'
vaĩkas su kepurè	'a child in (lit. 'with') a cap'
žmogùs su charãkteriu	'a man of (lit. 'with') character'

Sometimes, the preposition can be omitted, e.g.:

kiřvis (su) ìlgu kótu	'an axe with a long handle' (see 2.104)

(d) the content of a place or thing denoted by the head noun:

vežìmas su šienù	'a cart (loaded) with hay'
pintìnė su úogomis	'a basket with berries'

These prepositional phrases are often close in meaning to the postpositive genitive:

puodėlis su píenu	'a cup of (lit. 'with') milk'
– *puodėlis píeno*	'a cup of milk' (see 2.101, 3).

(4) The phrase *bè* + GEN denotes lack or absence of the noun referent; the noun in the genitive case refers to the following:

(a) an object or person(s) usually associated with the head noun referent, e.g.:

vaikaĩ be tėvų̃	'children without parents'
mókytojas be mokinių̃	'teacher without pupils'
laĩvas be kapitõno	'a ship without a captain'

(b) a part or a feature of the head noun referent, e.g.:

paũkštis be spar̃no	'a bird without a wing'
nãmas be stõgo	'a house without a roof'
žmogùs be vãlios	'a man without character'
žolė̃ be kvãpo	'grass without a smell'
naktìs be žvaigždžių̃	'a night without stars'

(c) the quantity the head noun referent is short of:

mẽtai be mė́nesio	'almost a year' (lit. 'a year without a month')
mė́nuo be dviejų̃ dienų̃	'a month minus (lit. 'without') two days'
mètras be dešimtiẽs centimètrų	'ninety centimetres' (lit. 'a metre without ten centimetres')

(5) The following prepositional phrases indicate the size or limit of the head noun referent:

ikì/lìgi + GEN:

kãsos iki liemeñs	lit. 'plaits (reaching down) to the waist'
spìnta iki lubų̃	'a wardrobe up to the ceiling'
pùsnys iki langų̃	'snowbank up to the windows'

virš(um̃)/aukščiaũ, žemiaũ + GEN:

suknẽlė virš(um̃)/aukščiaũ kẽlių	'a gown/above the knees'
kalnaĩ virš(um̃) debesų̃	'mountains higher than clouds'
rankóvės žemiaũ alkū́nių	'sleeves longer (lit. 'lower') than elbows'
páltas žemiaũ kẽlių	'a coat (reaching) below the knees'
cf. also: *páltas pusiáu blauzdų̃*	lit. 'a coat (reaching) to midcalf'

sulìg + INSTR:

sijõnas sulìg kēliais	'a skirt up to the knees'
mēdis sulìg namù	'a tree as tall as the house'

(6) The phrase *pagaĨ* + ACC denotes the standard to which the head noun referent corresponds:

drabùžiai pagaĨ mãdą	lit. 'clothes according to fashion'
vãsara pagaĨ žiēmą	lit. 'summer according to (i.e. like) winter'

(7) The phrase *apiē* + ACC is used to refer to the content of the head noun referent:

stráipsnis apie žolès	'an article about herbs'
žõdžiai apie draugùs	'words about friends'

(8) The phrase *priē* + GEN, when modifying nouns referring to institutions, indicates subordination of one social body or institution to another:

komìsija prie Seĩmo	'a committee at the Parliament'

This phrase belongs to official style.

2.112 When modifying a noun, prepositional phrases sometimes may have adverbial meaning and denote:

(1) **place**, e.g.:

pilìs ant kálno	'a castle on the hill'
béržas prie kēlio	'a birch-tree by the road'
kēlias į kálną	'path up the hill'
tìltas per ùpę	'a bridge across the river'
akmuõ po slenksčiù	'a stone under the doorstep'

(2) **time**, e.g.:

Vìlnius priẽš áudrą	'Vilnius before a storm'
miẽstas po gaĩsro	'a town after a fire'

NOUN – ADVERB, GERUND

2.113 Nouns rarely subordinate (1) adverbs and (2) gerunds, which usually have adverbial meanings, cf. respectively:

(1) *kēlias atgaĨ*	'the way back'
žiñgsnis pirmỹn	'a step forward' (locative meaning)
(2) *miẽstas aũštant*	'the town at dawn' (lit. 'dawning') (temporal meaning)

NOUN – ADJECTIVE

2.114 Adjectival words are joined to nouns by way of agreement in gender, number, and case. Their combinability is subject to lexical restrictions only. The following classes of adjectival words modify a noun.

(1) Adjectives, simple and definite, e.g.:

gražùs rýtas	'a fine morning'
medìnis nãmas	'a wooden house'
baltà/baltóji lelijà	'a white/the white lily'
ilgèsnė dienà	'a longer day'

(2) Active and passive participles, both present, past and future, e.g.:

spindinčios ākys	'shining eyes'
išbālęs véidas	'a pale face' (lit. 'a whitened face')
ateĩsianti vāsara	'the summer that will come (FUT. ACT. PART)'
neìssiųstas láiškas	'unmailed letter'
būsimos kaŕtos	'future (FUT. PASS. PART) generations'

(3) Adjectival pronouns of all semantic types; e.g.:

šìs miēstas	'this town'
tóks grõžis	'such beauty'
kai kuriē augalaĩ	'some plants'
vìsas pasáulis	'all the world'
patì viršùkalnė	'the very mountain-top'

(4) Ordinal numerals, which agree with the head noun like adjectives, e.g.:

antrà dienà	'the second day'
aštuonioliktíeji mētai	'the eighteenth year'

Cardinal numerals from one to nine are used with the plural number of the head noun (excepting víenas, -à 'one'), with agreement in gender (except trỹs 'three') and case; e.g.:

dù bróliai, dvì sēserys	'two brothers, two sisters'

(but trỹs bróliai, sēserys 'three brothers, sisters')

peñkios sаváitės	'five weeks (FEM)'
penkì mėnesiai	'five months (MASC)'
trējos dùrys	'three doors (FEM)'

C. ADJECTIVAL GROUPS

ADJECTIVE – NOUN

Adjectives can govern all noun cases except the nominative.

The genitive case

2.115 (1) The genitive case specifies the meaning of the adjective denoting its content, e.g.:

pìlnas/kùpinas/sklìdinas vandeñs	'full of water'
turtìngas pinigų̃	'rich in money'
veřtas pagarbõs	'worthy of respect'
reikalìngas paramõs	'needful of support'
godùs turtų̃	'greedy for riches'
skolìngas pinigų̃	'owing money'

The meaning of content is also expressed by the genitive after the neuter adjectives used predicatively:

mãža pinigų̃	'(there is) little money'
ìlga dienõs	lit. '(it is) long of the day' (i.e. 'the day is (too) long')
trum̃pa naktiẽs	lit. '(it is) short of night' ('the night is (too) short')
siaũra viẽtos	lit. '(it is too) narrow of space'
baisù kãro	'(one is) afraid of war'
ilgù tėvỹnės	'(one is) homesick for the native country'

The masculine and feminine gender of these adjectives do not usually govern the genitive case.

(2) The superlative degree of adjectives governs the genitive case of the adjectival pronoun vìsas 'all' (alone or with a noun it modifies) which serves as an intensifier, e.g.:

visų̃ gražiáusia	'the most beautiful (FEM) of all'
visų̃ aukščiáusias (kálnas)	'the highest (mountain) of all'

The preposition ìš can be used with the genitive:

iš visų̃ gražiáusia	'the most beautiful of all' (see 2.119, 1)

(3) An adjective can take the genitive of the noun derived from it, to emphasize the truth of the statement, usually in adversative statements:

Gerùmo jis gĕras, bet negudrùs.	'He is really good (lit. 'of goodness he is good'), but not clever.'
Jis gražùmo tai gražùs, bet nedōras.	'He is really handsome, but dishonest.'

The dative case

2.116 When governed by an adjective, the dative case of object refers to the thing for which the quality named by the adjective is intended or suitable or manifests itself, e.g.:

gabùs mùzikai	'gifted for music'
kenksmìngas žiedáms	'harmful to flowers'
pavojìngas sveikātai	'dangerous to the health'
atsparùs ùgniai	'fire resistant'
príešingas prìgimčiai	'contrary to nature'
reikalìngas/naudìngas augaláms	'necessary/useful to plants'

The dative of human nouns (and personal pronouns) used with a predicative neuter adjective of state names the experiencer of the latter state:

gēra jauníems	lit. '(it is) good to the young' ('the young feel good')
liñksma berniùkui	lit. '(it is) merry to the boy') (i.e. 'the boy is (feeling) merry')
sunkù visíems	'(it is) hard for everyone'
ilgù mán	lit. '(it is) homesick to me' ('I feel homesick')

The instrumental case

2.117 (1) The instrumental case denotes the cause, or source, or basis of comparison, or content of the quality named by the adjective, e.g.:

gývas maldomìs	'alive due to prayers'
garsùs/žìnomas darbaīs	'famous/known for deeds'
įdomùs (sàvo) praeitimì	'interesting for (its) past'

(2) When governed by an adjective with the suffix -*in(as)* formed from a transitive verb implying motion, the instrumental case names a comitative object, the

adjectival group functioning as a modifier of manner of an intransitive verb of motion, e.g.:

išėjo kìbiru nẽšinas	'(he) went out with a bucket'
(cf.: *išėjo nèšdamas kìbirą*)	
išvỹko vėžinas sūnumì	'he left taking his son with him'

(3) The instrumental case used with the comparative degree of adjectives denotes:

(a) the feature (of an entity) subjected to comparison, e.g.:

sesuõ véidu skaistèsnė už bañgą	lit. 'sister (NOM) by face (INSTR) fresher than a wave' (i.e. 'sister's face is fresher than a wave')

(b) the difference in quantity:

metrù/dviẽm mètrais platèsnis	'a metre/two metres broader'
mẽtais/trim̃ mẽtais jaunèsnis	'a year/three years younger'

(c) The instrumental case of temporal nouns (usually with an obligatory modifier) indicates the time when the property denoted by the head adjective is manifested, e.g.:

garsùs taĩs laikaĩs	'famous in those days'
žìnomas vidùramžiais	'(well-)known during the Middle Ages'

The accusative case

2.118 (1) The accusative case of object can be used with very few adjectives, e.g.:

(jìs) skolìngas šim̃tą lìtų	'(he) owes a hundred litas'
kal̃tas kaimýnui batùs	'(he) owes (lit. 'guilty') shoes to his neighbour'

(2) The comparative degree of adjectives governs (a) the accusative of the nouns *kar̃tas/sỹkis* 'time' (as in *dù kartùs* 'two times') with a numeral or with the adjectival pronoun *kelì* 'several' as attribute, or (b) the accusative of cardinal numerals (*dẽšimt* 'ten', *šim̃tas* 'hundred') and nominal pronouns *kẽletas, keliólika* 'several' with the governed genitive of *kar̃tas/sỹkis*; cf. respectively:

(a) *dù (trìs ... devýnis) kartùs didèsnis*	'two (three ... nine) (ACC) times (ACC) as big' (lit. 'bigger')
kelìs sykiùs greitèsnis	'several times as fast'
(b) *šim̃tą kar̃tų brangèsnis*	'hundred (ACC) times (GEN) more expensive'
kẽletą/keliólika sỹkių didèsnis	'several (ACC) times (GEN) bigger'

(3) The accusative case of temporal nouns (rare with adjectives) indicates the time when the quality named by the head adjective manifests itself, e.g.:

žãlias vãsarą	'green in summer'
paklusnùs vìsą laĩką	'obedient all the time'

The locative case

2.119 The locative case of nouns denoting or implying place indicates the space where the quality named by the head adjective is manifested:

garsùs apýlinkėje	'famous in the area'
žìnomas káime	'(well-)known in the village'
didžiáusias pasáulyje	'the biggest in the world'
turtingiáusias miestè	'the richest in town'

The accusative case of temporal nouns and nouns denoting processes indicates the time the quality named by the head adjective manifests itself, e.g.:

garsùs senóvėje	'famous in the old times'
narsùs mū̃šyje	'courageous in battle'
sumanùs darbè	'clever in work'

ADJECTIVE – PREPOSITIONAL PHRASE

Adjectives, when used predicatively, govern a number of prepositional phrases.

2.120 The phrase ìš + GEN is used:

(1) with the superlative (less commonly, comparative) degree of adjectives to denote the whole or class from which an entity is singled out, e.g.:

Vienà žvaigždė̃ iš visų̃ šviesiáusia.	'One star is brightest of all.'
Šità mergáitė iš visų̃ gražiáusia.	'This girl is the prettiest of all.'

In this phrase, the genitive singular form of collective nouns is also used:

Iš (vìso) bū̃rio jìs bùvo tinkamiáusias.	'Out of the (whole) group he was the most suitable.'

(2) with the positive degree of some adjectives to denote the part or property of entity described by the head adjective, e.g.:

mergáitė gražì iš véido	lit. 'girl (is) pretty of the face'
(cf. mergáitė gražaũs véido)	(lit. 'the girl (is) of a pretty face (GEN)')
žmogùs protìngas iš kalbõs	lit. 'the man (is) clever of speech'

2.121 The prepositional phrase *ùž* + ACC is used:

(1) with the positive degree of some adjectives to denote cause or motive, e.g.:

dėkìngas už pagálbą	'grateful for the help'
skolìngas už dárbą	'indebted for the work'

(2) with the comparative degree of adjectives to denote the basis of comparison:

sunkèsnis už ãkmenį	'heavier than stone'
baltèsnis už sniẽgą	'whiter than snow'

This prepositional phrase containing the accusative plural case of the pronoun *vìsas, -à* (alone or with a head noun) is synonymous with *ìš* + GEN (cf. 2.120, 1):

Šità mergáitė už visàs gražèsnė.	'This girl is prettier than all.

2.122 The prepositional phrase *priẽš* + ACC occasionally denotes an object with which the subject is compared, e.g.:

Sūnùs prieš tėvą negražùs.	'The son is not handsome in comparison with (lit. 'against') the father.'

2.123 The prepositional phrase *pagal̃* + ACC denotes the basis of comparison, e.g.:

Šį̃met der̃lius pagal̃ kitùs metùs prãstas.	'The harvest this year is poor in comparison with the last year.'
Pagal̃ ámžių jìs ganà gudrùs.	'He is quite clever for his age.'

2.124 The prepositional phrase *sù* + INSTR is used:

(1) after adjectives denoting human properties to refer to persons (sometimes things), e.g.:

kuklùs su vyrèsniais	'modest with elder (people)'
mandagùs su visaĩs	'polite to everybody'

(2) after the adjectives *lýgus* 'equal', *gìminiškas* 'kindred, related', *tapatùs* 'identical', *panašùs* 'alike, similar' e.g.:

lýgus su visaĩs	'equal to everybody'
brólis su sēseria panāšūs	'brother and (lit. 'with') sister are alike'
(but: brólis panašùs į sẽserį)	('the brother looks like sister (ACC)')

2.125 The prepositional phrase *bè* + GEN combines with neuter adjectives (used predicatively) to denote a thing whose absence or lack causes the state expressed by the head adjective:

ilgù be tėvỹnės	'one is homesick (lit. 'it is homesick') without one's homeland'

baugù be šuñs	'it is scary without a dog'
sunkù be namų̃	'it is hard (for one) without (one's) home'

2.126 The following prepositional phrases are rare in adjectival word groups:

añt + GEN:

pìktas ant žmonių̃	'angry with people'
(cf. *pỹkti ant žmonių̃*)	('be angry with people')

nuõ + GEN:

laĩsvas nuo dárbo	'free from work'

2.127 Prepositional phrases are occasionally used with adjectives to express the same adverbial meanings as with verbs, e.g.:

reikalìngas prie namų̃	'necessary at home'
(cf. *jõ reĩkia prie namų̃*)	('he is needed at home')
ištikimas iki mirtiẽs	'faithful unto death'
(cf. *tarnáuti iki mirtiẽs*)	('serve until death')
ráišas nuo kãro	'lame since the war'
sil̃pnas po ligõs	'weak after an illness'
júodas iš pỹkčio	'black with anger'
kal̃tas dėl neláimės	'guilty of the accident'
be gãlo laimìngas	'extremely happy' (lit. 'without end happy')

ADJECTIVE – PRONOUN

2.128 Qualitative adjectives can be modified by the adjectival pronouns *tóks, -ià (pat)* 'such', *kóks, -ià* 'what', *šìtoks, -ia* 'such', etc. which assume the same gender, number and case. These pronouns are used for emphasis; cf.:

tóks nelaimìngas	'so unhappy'
kóks gražùs	'how beautiful'
šìtoks tólimas (kẽlias)	'such (a) long (way)'

They are also used in comparative sentences, e.g.:

Jìs tóks báltas kaĩp obelìs.	'He is as white as an apple-tree.'
Vaikaĩ tokie pàt grãžūs kaĩp ir tėvaĩ.	'The children are as handsome as their parents.'

ADJECTIVE – ADVERB

2.129 Adjectives can be modified by adverbs. The following instances can be distinguished.

(1) Most commonly, the modifying adverb is an intensifier, the very frequent one being *labaĩ* 'very', e.g.:

labaĩ gẽras	'very good'
per daũg brangùs	'too expensive'
vìsiškai naũjas	'quite new'
ypatìngai svarbùs	'especially important'
nepaprastaĩ gražùs	'exceptionally beautiful'

(2) The modifying adverb can specify the quality of the head adjective, e.g.:

šviẽsiai/tam̃siai pìlkas	'light/dark grey'
žalsvaĩ mel̃svas	'greenish blue'
saldžiaĩ rūgštùs	'sweetly sour'
savaĩp įdomùs	'interesting in its own way'

(3) Numerous adverbs denote quantity or difference in quantity (with the comparative degree of adjectives), e.g.:

(a) *trupùtį keĩstas*	'a little queer'
šiek tíek kreĩvas	'somewhat curved'
(b) *daũg/gerókai šviesèsnis*	'much/considerably lighter (in colour)'
kur kàs sunkèsnis	'a lot heavier'
dvìgubai brangèsnis	'twice as (lit. 'more') expensive'
perpùs mažèsnis	'smaller by half'

(4) Adjectives (especially neuter) are sometimes modified by adverbs of place and time, e.g.:

visuř bálta	'(it is) white everywhere'
apliñkui tamsù	'(it is) dark around'
visadà kárštas	'always hot'
šiañdien pigùs	'cheap today'

ADJECTIVE – INFINITIVE

2.130 Some adjectives can be modified by a postposed infinitive which may denote the following.

(1) The property named by the head adjective, which can also take the genitive case instead of the infinitive, e.g.:

veřtas pagìrti/pagyrìmo	'worthy of praise (INF/GEN)'
godùs gérti/pinigų̃	lit. 'greedy to drink/for money (GEN)'
reikalìngas parem̃ti/paramõs	'in need of support (INF/GEN)'

Neuter adjectives used predicatively also take an infinitive (though not the genitive case), e.g.:

sunkù gyvénti	'(it is) hard to live'
nuobodù láukti	'(it is) boring to wait'
liñksma šókti	lit. '(it is) merry to dance'

(2) The purpose or suitability of the property the head adjective denotes, e.g.:

báltas pažiūrėti	lit. 'white to look at'
(arklỹs) gēras árti	lit. '(the horse) good to plough'
(mėsà)kietà pjáustyti	'(meat) tough to cut'
(sniēgas) mìnkštas pačiupinėti	'(snow) soft to touch'

An infinitive denoting purpose can co-occur with the dative case (cf. 2.84), e.g.:

(dienà) gerà šiēnui džiovìnti	lit. '(a day) good for the hay (DAT) to dry'
(suolėlis) patogùs kójoms pasidėti	lit. '(a stool) convenient for the feet (DAT) to put on'

ADJECTIVAL NOMINALISATIONS

2.131 Nouns derived from the following adjectives retain their combinability properties; e.g.:

tuȓto godulỹs	'greed for money (GEN)'
(cf. godùs tuȓto)	('greedy for money')
gabùmai mùzikai	'talent for music'
(cf. gabùs mùzikai)	(lit. 'talented for music')
piktùmas ant kaimýnų	'anger with neigbours (Prep + GEN)'
(cf. pìktas ant kaimýnų)	('angry with neighbours')
dėkingùmas už pāramą	'gratitude for support'
(cf. dėkìngas už pāramą)	('grateful for support')
lipšnùmas su žmonėmìs	lit. 'sweetness with people'
(cf. lipšnùs su žmonėmìs)	('sweet with people')
malonùmas keliáuti	'the pleasure of travelling'
(cf. malonù keliáuti)	('(it is) pleasant to travel')

D. NUMERAL GROUPS

The cardinal numerals, and (less commonly) ordinal numerals are joined with the genitive or a prepositional phrase.

NUMERAL – GENITIVE CASE

2.132 The genitive case (plural) of a noun (or its substitute) is governed by the following numerals:

(1) basic cardinal numerals *dẽšimt(ìs)* 'ten', *vienúolika* 'eleven' ... *dvìdešimt* 'twenty', *trìsdešimt* 'thirty' ... *devýniasdešimt* 'ninety', *šim̃tas* 'hundred', *tū́kstantis* 'thousand', *milijõnas* 'million', *milijárdas* 'billion'; e.g.:

dẽšimt dienų̃/tū́kstančių	'ten days/thousand (GEN. PL)'
šim̃tas lìtų/milijõnų	'(one) hundred litas/million (GEN. PL)'

(2) the collective numerals (marked by the suffix *-et(as)*) *dvẽjetas* 'two', *trẽjetas* 'three' ... *devýnetas* 'nine', e.g.:

kẽtvertas vaikų̃/šim̃tų̃	'four children/hundred (GEN. PL)'
(cf. *keturì vaikaĩ*)	('four children (NOM. PL)')
septýnetas žirgų̃/tū́kstančių	'seven horses/thousand'
(cf. *septynì žirgaĩ/tū́kstančiai*)	('seven horses/thousand (NOM. PL)')

2.133 When used in the plural number, the numerals *dẽšimtys* 'tens', *šim̃taĩ* 'hundreds', *tū́kstančiai* 'thousands', *milijõnai* 'millions', *milijárdai* 'billions' denote an indefinitely great quantity of the entities in the dependent genitive plural:

šim̃taĩ keleĩvių/tū́kstančių	'hundreds of passengers/thousands'
dẽšimtys kilomètrų/milijõnų	'tens of kilometres/millions'

The meaning of an indefinitely great quantity is also rendered by the word groups *šim̃tų̃ šim̃taĩ* 'hundreds upon hundreds' (lit. 'hundreds of hundreds'), *tū́kstančių tū́kstančiai* 'thousands upon thousands' (lit. 'thousands of thousands') and the like. In these phrases the genitive is preposed to the head numeral and serves as an intensifier (cf. noun groups like *minių̃ mìnios* lit. 'crowds of crowds', see 2.100).

2.134 Composite fractional numerals formed from the root *pus-* (= *pùsė* 'half') and an ordinal numeral are used in the genitive case and take another genitive, e.g.:

pusañtro kilogrãmo/šim̃to	'one and a half kilograms/hundred' (lit. 'half of the second kilogram/hundred')
pustrečiõs dienõs	'two and a half days'
pusketvirtų̃ mẽtų	'three and a half years'

In these phrases, the fractional numeral governs the genitive and agrees with the dependent noun or numeral in gender and number.

Numeral – prepositional phrase

2.135 Cardinal numerals may subordinate the following prepositional phrases:

(1) *iš* + GEN:

dù iš dešimtiẽs	'two out of ten'
víenas iš tū́kstančio	'one out of a thousand'
víenas iš draugų̃	'one of (the) friends'

(2) *bè* + GEN:

šim̃tas be trejų̃ mẽtų	lit. 'one hundred (years) without three years', i.e. '97 years'
penkiólika valandų̃ be penkių̃ minùčių	'five minutes to fifteen hours' (lit. 'fifteen hours without five minutes'), i.e. '14:55'.

Ordinal numerals occur in phrases like:

pirmàsis iš eilė̃s	'the first in (lit. 'from') the sequence'
añtras nuo gãlo	'the second from the end'
trẽčias pagal̃ ū̃gį	'the third in height'

E. PRONOMINAL GROUPS

Word groups with a head pronoun are less varied than those with a head noun or adjective. Some pronouns can be used with the genitive case of noun, with an adjective or adverb.

Pronoun – Genitive case

2.136 The indefinite pronoun (with no gender contrast) *kàs* 'who, what' and complex pronouns incorporating *kàs* (*kas nórs* 'somebody, something', *kaĩ kàs* 'some (people)', *daũg kas* 'many (people), *kàs ne kàs* 'somebody, some people', *kažkàs/kažin kàs* 'somebody, something', *niẽkas* 'nobody, nothing', and *šìs tàs* 'something', and also indefinite adjectival pronouns (inflected for gender) *kurìs, -ì, katràs, -à* 'which' (MASC/FEM) and the derivative adjectival complex pronouns *kaĩ kurìs* 'some', *kažkurìs* 'some', *kurìs ne kurìs* 'some', *kìtas* 'other, another', *víenas kìtas* 'some, some people', *kiekvíenas* 'each, every', *nė víenas* 'no one' govern the genitive plural (with or without the preposition *iš* 'from') which refers to a group or class out of which a part is distinguished, e.g.:

kàs (iš) kaimýnų	'which of the neighbours'
kažkurìs (iš) draugų̃	'one (someone) of the friends'

vienà (iš) móterų	'one of the women'
niēkas (iš) keleĩvių	'no one among (lit. 'from') the passengers'
kiekvíenas (iš) mū́sų	'each of us'

Collective nouns are used in the singular, the preposition *ìš* 'from' being obligatory, cf.:

kàs iš vyriausýbės	'someone (lit. 'who') of the government'
nė víenas iš komìsijos	'no one from the committee'

The indefinite quantitative pronouns *kḗletas* 'several' (from 2 to 10), *keliólika* 'several' (from 11 to 19) and *kḗliasdešimt* (20, 30 ... 90) take the genitive plural of a noun without a preposition, e.g.:

kḗletas žmonių̃	'several people'
keliólika dienų̃	'several days'
kḗliasdešimt kilomètrų	'some dozens of kilometres'

Pronoun – Adjective

2.137 The indefinite pronouns *kàs* 'something', *kažkàs* 'something', *kas nórs* 'anything', *šìs tàs* 'something', *niēkas* 'nothing' which have no gender distinctions can be modified by the genitive plural masculine or the neuter form of adjectives interchangeably, e.g.:

kàs pìkto/pìkta	'something bad'
kas nórs svarbaũs/svarbù	'something important'
(turĕti) šį̃ tą̃ válgomo/válgoma	'(to have) something edible'
(pajùsti) kažką̃ blõgo/blõga	'(to feel) something bad'
(nepasakýti) niēko nereikalìngo/nereikalìnga	lit. '(not to say) nothing unnecessary'

The interrogative pronoun *kàs* 'what' is also used with the same adjective forms:

kàs gēro/gēra?	lit. 'what (is) good?' ('what's the good news?')
kàs naũjo/naũja?	'what's new?'

The same pronouns also occur (though very seldom) with the masculine singular of adjectives instead of the neuter form, cf.:

kažkàs júodas/júoda	'something black (NOM. MASC/NEUTR)'
(susidomĕti) kažkuõ ypatìngu	'(get interested) in something peculiar (INSTR. MASC)'

Pronoun – Adverb

2.138 The adjectival pronouns *kìtas, -à* 'other, another', *kitóks, -ià* 'another, different', *toks pàt* 'the same (as)', *vìsas* 'all' can be modified by the intensifying and specifying adverbs *visái/vìsiškai* 'quite, entirely' (*vìsas* 'all'), *bevéik* 'almost', cf.:

visái/vìsiškai kìtas, kitóks, toks pàt	'quite another, different, the same'
bevéik vìsas	'almost all'
bevéik toks pàts	'almost the same'

F. ADVERBIAL GROUPS
Adverb – Adverb

2.139 Adverbs are joined to other adverbs very much like to the respective adjectives (see 2.128–129), cf.:

labaĩ gražiaĩ (cf. *gražùs*)	'very beautifully (beautiful)
per daũg pigiaĩ (pigùs)	'too (much) cheaply (cheep)'
trupùtį keistaĩ (keĩstas)	'a little queerly (queer)'
savaĩp įdõmiai (įdomùs)	'interestingly (interesting) in its ow way'
tam̃siai rudaĩ (cf. *rùdas*)	'dark brown'
taĩp geraĩ (cf. *tóks gẽras*)	'so well' (cf. 'so good')
kaĩp áiškiai (áiškus)	'how clearly (clear)'
šìtaip ramiaĩ (ramùs)	'so quietly (quiet)'

Respective adverbial groups are formed with the comparative degree of adverbs (coinciding with that of the neuter adjectives):

kur̃ kàs sunkiaũ (sunkèsnis)	'much more heavily (heavier)'
dvìgubai brangiaũ (brangèsnis)	'twice as expensively (expensive)'

Adverb groups with the head *daũg* alone have no corresponding adjective groups, e.g.:

labaĩ/be gãlo/neišpasakýtai daũg	'very/extremely/unusually much'

Adverb – Noun

2.140 Adverbs of quantity combine with the genitive case of nouns denoting quantified entities, in which respect these adverbs are similar to numerals and nouns or neuter adjectives denoting quantity, e.g.:

daũg/daugiaũ/daugiáusia žmonių	'many/more/the greatest number of people'
mažaĩ (cf. *máža*: ADJ. NEUTR) *sniẽgo*	'little snow'
šíek tíek džiaũgsmo	'a little joy'
tíek vandeñs	'so much water'
sóčiai (cf. *sótu*: ADJ. NEUTR) *dúonos*	'(more than) enough bread'

2.141 The comparative degree of adverbs combines with (1) the accusative of a numeral word group indicating the extent of difference and (2) the instrumental case, these phrases being parallel to word groups with the respective adjectives, e.g.:

(1) *dù kartùs greičiaũ* (cf. *greitèsnis*)	'two times (ACC) faster (ADV (cf. ADJ)')
šim̃tą kar̃tų mažiaũ (cf. *mažèsnis*)	'a hundred (ACC) times (GEN) less (cf. smaller)'
(2) *metrù siauriaũ* (cf. *siaurèsnis*)	'a metre (INSTR) narrower (ADV/ADJ)'
dviẽm lìtais brangiaũ	'two litas (INSTR) more expensive'
dẽšimčia dienų ankščiaũ	'ten (INSTR) days (GEN) earlier'

Word groups with *daugiaũ* 'more' as the head are formed in the same way:

dù kartùs/šim̃tą kar̃tų daugiaũ	'twice/a hundred (ACC) times more'
penkiaĩs kilogrãmais/ dẽšimčia kilogrãmų daugiaũ	'five kilograms (INSTR)/ten (INSTR) kilograms (GEN) more'

2.142 Time adverbs can take (1) the accusative, (2) the instrumental and (3) locative case of a noun, cf. respectively:

(1) *vėlaĩ rùdenį*	'late in autumn'
pérnai pavãsarį/vãsarą/žiẽmą	'last year in spring/summer/winter'
(2) *vãkar apýaušriais*	'yesterday at dawn'
šiañdien pãvakariu/pavakarỹ	'today before evening (INSTR/LOC)'
(3) *rytój vakarè*	'tomorrow (in the) evening'
šiañdien rytè	'today in the morning'

2.143 Place adverbs commonly govern the locative case of a noun which modifies the meaning of the head adverb, e.g.:

aukštaĩ kalnuõs	'high in the mountains'
giliaĩ žẽmėje	'deep in the ground'
tolì šiáurėje	'far in the north'

Adverb – Prepositional phrase

2.144 Some of the place adverbs are commonly modified by the following prepositional phrases (usually with a locative meaning):

priẽ + GEN:

artì/arčiaũ/artýn prie mìško	'near/nearer to the woods'

nuõ + GEN:

tolì/toliaũ nuo namų̃	'far/farther from home'
nuošaliaĩ/nuošaliaũ nuo žmonių̃	'apart from people'
žemỹn nuo kálno	'down (from) the hill'

į̃ + ACC:

giliaĩ/giliaũ/gilỹn į̃ mìšką	'deep/deeper/deep into the woods'
aukštỹn į̃ kálną	'up the hill'
pakeliuĩ į̃ namùs	'on the way home'

peř + ACC:

skersaĩ per kẽlią	'across the road'
išilgaĩ/įstrižaĩ per kiẽmą	'along/across the yard'

2.145 The comparative and the superlative degrees of an adverb, like the respective basic adjectives, can be modified by the following prepositional phrases referring to the basis of comparison:

ùž + ACC:

geriaũ už brólį	'better than (one's) brother'
(cf. *gerèsnis už brólį* 'better (ADJ) than (one's) brother')	

ìš + GEN:

(bė́gti) greičiáusiai iš visų̃	'(run) the fastest of all' (see 2.120, 1)

Coordinative word groups

2.146 A coordinative word group is comprised of grammatically equivalent word forms which are related to the same word (or word group) in a sentence by an identical syntactic relation. They can be linked by means of a coordinating conjunction, as in (1) or by juxtaposition only, as in (2):

(1) *Lankaũ draugùs ir pažį́stamus.*	'I visit friends and acquaintances.'
(2) *Lankaũ draugùs, pažį́stamus.*	'I visit friends, acquaintances.'

Coordinative word groups may consist of three or more word forms or phrases, e.g.:

Jám vẽl grį̃žo nóras gyvénti, dìrbti, išeĩti iš namų̃, susitìkti su žmonėmìs.	'He again felt a desire to live, to work, to go out, to meet people.'

2.147 The grammatical equivalence of coordinated words usually finds expression in their identical class membership and morphological form; cf.:

Jìs dãvė mán alaũs, sū́rio, svíesto.	'He gave me (some) beer, cheese, butter.'
Dabar̃ trū́ksta dorų̃ ir išmintìngų žmonių̃.	'There is a shortage of honest and wise people now.'
Žmónės jõ nemė́go, bet bijójo.	lit. 'People didn't like, but feared him.'
Negrį̃šime nei šiañdien, nei rytój.	'We won't return either today or tomorrow.'

Coordinated word forms may belong to different word classes on condition that they have the same syntactic function, e.g.:

Tù dar jáunas ir galì paláukti.	'You are young (ADJ) yet and can wait (V).'
Gùstas kalbė́jo lėtaĩ, neskubė́damas.	'Gustas spoke slowly (ADV), without hurry (HALF-PART).'

In case of coordination of prepositional phrases with the same preposition, the latter can be omitted in the second and subsequent phrases, e.g.:

Iš miẽstų ir (iš) káimų skubė́jo žmónės.	'People hurried from towns and (from) villages.'
Jìs grį̃š po mė́nesio ar (po) savaĩtės.	'He'll be back in a month or (in) a week.'

The same word form (or co-referential word forms) is (are) repeated in a coordinative collocation if it occurs with different prepositions, especially if different cases are involved, cf.:

Mergáitė šokinė́jo ant akmeñs ir nuo jõ.	'The girl was jumping onto the stone and (down) from it.'
Põpieriai bùvo išmė́tyti ant stãlo ir po stalù.	'The papers were strewn on the table and under the table.'

The identical particle is usually omitted by the second and subsequent coordinated form to avoid unwanted emphasis, e.g.:

Ne keliaĩ, (ne) ùpės, (ne) jū́ros skìria žmónes.	'Not roads, (not) rivers, (not) seas separate people.'

2.148 If conjoined nouns share an identical modifier it may be used once with the first noun, especially if both nouns have the same form, e.g.:

Nemė́gstu jõ véido, (jõ) bal̃so, (jõ) el̃gesio.	'I don't like his face, (his) voice, (his) manners.'
Kiemè bùvo daũg mažų̃ mergáičių ir berniùkų.	'There were many little girls and boys in the yard.'

However, if conjoined nouns require different forms of the same modifier, it can not be omitted:

Šìto výro ir šitõs móters àš nepažį́stu.	'I don't know this (MASC) man or this (FEM) woman.'

On the other hand, a group consisting of a noun and two or more modifying adjectives can be viewed as a phrase with the first head noun omitted, cf.:

raudóni ir baltì obuoliaĩ	'red and white apples'
mū́sų (vaikaĩ) ir jū́sų vaikaĩ	'our (children) and your children'

Coordinative groups consisting of finite verb forms are naturally similar to compound sentences, cf.:

Žmónės jų̃ nemė́go už šykštùmą, bet gárbino už pìnigus.	lit. 'People disliked them for their stinginess, but respected (them) for (their) money.'

2.149 Coordinative groups can be structurally closed or open.

Structurally closed groups consist of two components conjoined by a single or a two-member conjunction, e.g.:

šáltas ir vėjúotas rýtas	'cold and windy morning'
(Ùpė bùvo) nors ir neplatì, bet sraunì.	'(The river was) though not wide but rapid.'

A closed group can be asyndetic, an adversative relation being implied, e.g.:

Džiaũkis dúonos tùrinti, ne svíesto!	'Rejoice at having bread, not butter!' (i.e. 'even if you don't have butter').

Structurally open groups may comprise any number of components conjoined by repeated conjunctions (1), or asyndetically by intonation and juxtaposition, as in (2), cf.:

(1) Tokių̃ šarvų̃ neprãmuša nei ãkmenys, nei kalavìjai, nei kìrviai, nei íetys.	'Such armor cannot be pierced either by stones, or swords, or axes, or spears.'

(2) *Jì kalbė́jo nedrą̃siai,*   'She spoke timidly, quietly, sweetly.'
taikìngai, švelñiai.

2.150 Coordinate word forms can be subordinated to a generalizing superordinate word whose meaning they specify and explain. The superordinate word can be preposed or postposed to the coordinate words, or it can be distanced from them (see the examples below).

The following words are commonly used as generalizers:

(1) the pronouns *visì* 'all', *vìskas* 'everything', *vìsa, vìsa kìta* 'all the rest', *niẽkas* 'nothing, nobody', *tóks (pàt)* 'such', etc., e.g.:

Jái vìskas bùvo įdomù: 'Everything interested her: the
ir sodýba, ir tvenkinỹs,   farm-stead, and the pond, and the
ir mìškas.   woods.'

Iš rýto jì atsikė́lė vėl   'In the morning she was her usual self
tokia pàt: gyvà, sveikà, linksmà.   again: alive, healthy, merry.'

(2) the adverbs *visur̃* 'everywhere', *visadà* 'always', *niẽkur* 'nowhere', e.g.:

Nei kiemè, nei sodè, nei   'There is no peace anywhere – neither
laukè – niēkur nèrà ramýbės.   in the yard, nor in the garden, nor in the
     field.'

(3) nouns related to the coordinated words as their hyperonym, e.g.:

Visur̃ bėgiójo žmónės –   'People – men, women and children –
výrai, móterys ir vaikaĩ   were running about everywhere.'

Syndetic Coordination

2.151 In this case coordinated forms are linked either by a coordinating conjunction or, sometimes, by a subordinating conjunction, viz. *juõ ... tuõ* 'the ... the', *juõ ... juõ* 'the ... the', *nórs ... bèt* 'though ... but', *nórs ... tačiaũ* 'though ... but', and the like.

According to the type of conjunction and the relation between the coordinated units, these groups are further divided into copulative, juxtapositive and adversative, disjunctive and consecutive.

COPULATIVE GROUPS

2.152 This is the most frequent type, the commonly used conjunction being *ir̃* 'and':

Tàvo vaĩką padarýsiu turtìngą ir garbìngą.	'I'll make your son rich and honorable.'

The conjunction *beĩ* 'and' (synonymous with *ir̃*) connects units that are very similar in meaning: it emphasizes their semantic proximity; e.g.:

šìs bei tàs	'this and that'
nesutarìmai bei konfliktai tarp šalių̃	'discord and conflicts between countries'
išvìrsiu bei iškèpsiu	'I'll cook and bake'

Word forms joined by the conjunction *beĩ* can be connected with other coordinated units by *ir̃* to indicate the hierarchy, e.g.:

Tamè miškè gyvẽna lãpės bei vilkaĩ ir kitì laukìniai žvė́rys.	'In that forest, there are foxes and wolves, and other wild beasts.'

In two-component groups, reduplicated conjunctions are also used, viz. *ir̃ ... ir̃* 'and ... and', *neĩ ... neĩ* 'neither ... nor', and sometimes *čià ... čià* 'now ... now', *taĩ ... taĩ* 'now ... now', *tíek ... tíek (ir)* 'both ... and'; e.g.:

Pasidãrė ir šilčiaũ, ir šviesiaũ.	'It grew both warmer and lighter.'
Dabar̃ nebeláukiu nei žiniõs, nei láiško.	'Now I don't expect either news or a letter any longer.'
Jìs jaũtė tai báimę, tai džiaũgsmą.	lit. 'He felt now fear, now joy.'

Three or more coordinated units are linked with reduplicated conjunctions:

Nereĩkia mán tàvo drabùžių, nei deĩmantų, nei tur̃tų.	'I don't want your clothes, or diamonds, or riches.'

JUXTAPOSITIVE AND ADVERSATIVE GROUPS

2.153 These groups consist of two units only, coordinated by adversative conjunctions, the most commonly used ones being *bèt* and *tačiaũ*, e.g.:

Jáunas, bet/tačiaũ/ užtàt protìngas výras.	'A young, but wise man.'
Niẽkas kìtas, tiktaĩ gyvẽnimas pamókys jį̃.	lit. 'Nothing other but only life will teach him.'

Adversative groups are sometimes formed with the subordinating conjunctions *nórs (ir)* 'although' and *nórs (ir) ... bèt* 'though ... but':

įdomùs, nors nelengvas uždavinỹs	'an interesting, though hard task'
šveñtėme nors ir trumpaĩ, bet linksmaĩ	lit. 'we celebrated though briefly, but merrily'

DISJUNCTIVE GROUPS

2.154 Disjunctive groups may consist of two or more components. In two-component groups the single conjunctions *ar̃* 'or' and *arbà* 'or' and reduplicated *ar̃ ... ar̃*, *arbà ... arbà* are commonly used and, sometimes, *jéi(gu) nè ... taĩ* 'if not ... then'; e.g.:

Dabar̃ privãlome laimė́ti arba žū́ti.	'Now we must win or perish.'
Jéi ne tėvùs, tai sẽserį tikiúosi pamatýsiąs.	lit. 'I hope to see if not my parents then my sister.'

Three or more components are linked by the reduplicated conjunctions *ar̃ ... ar̃ ...* and *arbà ... arbà ...* :

Kõ jinaĩ bijójo, patì geraĩ nežinójo: ar sàvo žmonių̃, ar príešų, ar kažiñ kõ kìto.	'She herself didn't know who she was afraid of: whether her own people, or enemies, or somebody else.'

CONSECUTIVE GROUPS

2.155 Consecutive groups may consist of two components only, linked by the consecutive conjunctions *taĩ (ir̃)* 'so', *taĩgi* 'so' and *tàd* 'so, therefore':

Mẽs visì bùvome pavar̃gę, tad nelinksmì.	'We were all tired, therefore not merry.'
Daũg dìrba, tai vìsko ir tùri.	'He works hard, therefore (he) has everything.'

GROUPS WITH VARYING CONJUNCTIONS

2.156 Copulative conjunctions may be combined with conjunctions denoting adversative, disjunctive or consecutive relations; e.g.:

Sàvo tìkslo jìs siẽkė tvirtaĩ ir drą̃siai, bet atsargiaĩ.	lit. 'He pursued his object firmly and boldly, but cautiously.'
Dabar̃ grỹbai daugiáusia dýgsta paleĩ ẽžerus ir pamiškėsè arba palaũkėse.	'Now mushrooms grow mostly by the lakes and woods or by the fields.'
Jìs bùvo sẽnas ir paliẽgęs, tad labaĩ irzlùs.	'He was old and ailing, therefore petulant.'

Asyndetic coordination

2.157 Asyndetic word groups can be comprised of two or more juxtaposed units:

Dìdelis, raudónas mėnùlis patekėjo.	'A huge, red moon rose.'
Svečiaĩ šóko, dainãvo, gė́rė ãlų.	'The guests danced, sang, drank beer.'

Mixed coordination

2.158 In this case at least three units are coordinated by at least two different means on the same level of syntactic structure:

Jìs válgo sū́rį, svíestą, mė̃są, tik ne lãšinius.	'He eats cheese, butter, meat, but not bacon.'

The coordinated units can be arranged in pairs, either syndetic or asyndetic, linked by the alternative means: thus in (1) two syndetic pairs are linked asyndetically and in (2) two asyndetic pairs are linked by an adversative conjunction:

(1) Mẽdžiai mė̃tė ìlgus šešė̃lius į̃ laukùs ir píevas, ant kẽlio ir takų̃.	'The trees threw long shadows on the fields and meadows, on the road and paths.'
(2) Žmogùs parklùpo, parpúolė, bet greĩt pašóko, apsidaĩrė.	'The man stumbled, fell, but at once jumped to his feet, looked around.'

3 THE SIMPLE SENTENCE
Vientisìnis sakinỹs

3.1 A simple sentence consists of one clause only, i.e. it has a single syntactic centre. The syntactic centre is the predicate to which all the other sentence components are related, either directly or through an intermediate word form or word group.

In Lithuanian, a simple sentence may contain the syntactic subject, or it may be subjectless. Accordingly, simple sentences are classified into personal and impersonal.

3.2 In a **personal sentence**, the predicate requires a subject:

Viršuñ	*mìško*	*patekė́jo*	*mė́nuo.*
above	forest: GEN	rise: 3. PAST	moon: NOM. SG

'The moon rose above the forest.'

Vìsos	*gė̃lės*	*bùvo*	*nuvýtusios.*
all	flower: NOM. PL. FEM	be: 3. PAST	wilted: NOM. PL. FEM

'All the flowers were wilted.'

The subject of a personal sentence does not always need to be expressed by a separate word. A sentence remains personal if the 1st or 2nd person subject is marked in the predicate only, an overt pronoun in subject position being redundant:

Atsikė́liau	*ankstì.*
get up: 1. SG. PAST	early

'I got up early.'

Vìsą	*diẽną*	*dìrbome*	*laukuosè.*
all	day	work: 1. PL. PAST	field: LOC. PL

'We worked in the fields all day.'

Rytój	*važiúosite*	*į̃*	*mìšką.*
tomorrow	drive: 2. PL. FUT	to	forest: ACC

'Tomorrow you'll go to the forest.'

Sentences with the 2nd person singular predicate and no overt subject may express a generalized statement:

Gyvenì	ir	mókaisi.
live: 2. SG. PRES	and	learn: 2. SG. PRES. REFL

'You live and learn.'

Prieš	vėją	nepapūsi.
against	wind: ACC	not-blow: 2. SG. FUT

'One can't blow against the wind.'

The subject is sometimes mentioned in these generic sentences:

Taĩp ir	gyvenì	žmogùs	niẽko	nematýdamas.
so and	live: 2. SG. PRES	man: NOM	nothing	not-see: HALF-PART. SG

'Thus one (a person) spends one's life without seeing anything.'

The subject is also omitted in sentences with a 3rd person predicate to imply an unspecified, indefinite or generalized human agent *(žmónės* 'people', *visì* 'all (people), everyone', etc.):

Jám	pàvogė	árklį.
he: DAT	steal: 3. PAST	horse: ACC. SG

'Someone stole a horse from him.'

These sentences with a zero subject are termed indefinite-personal.

3.3 An **impersonal sentence** consists either of the predicate alone (*Rudenėja* 'Autumn is coming') or the predicate with subordinated components, e.g.:

Mán	skaudėjo	gálvą.
I: DAT	ache: 3. PAST	head: ACC. SG

'I had a headache.'

Impersonal sentences are mostly formed by:

(1) the finite form of an impersonal or an impersonally used verb, e.g.:

Jám	visadà	sẽkasi.
he: DAT	always	go well: 3. PRES. REFL

'He is always lucky.'

Vãkar	snìgo.
yesterday	snow: 3. PAST

'It snowed yesterday.'

(2) the neuter form of an adjective or a passive participle used predicatively:

Tamsù	miškè.
dark: NEUTR	forest: LOC

'It is dark in the forest.'
(cf. *Miškè bùvo tamsù* 'It was dark in the forest.')

Teñ	*žmonių*		*gyvénta.*
there	people: GEN. PL		live: PAST. PASS. PART. NEUTR

'People lived there' (lit. 'There it was lived by people.')

(3) the infinitive of a personal verb:

Kaĩp	*mùms*	*dabař*	*gyvénti?*
how	we: DAT	now	live: INF

'How can/shall we live now?'

(4) the past tense form of a gerund:

Kaĩp	*čià*	*padārius?*
how	here	do: PAST. GER

'How should I/one do it? (What should I/one do?)'

The predicate of an impersonal sentence can also be a noun (usually the name of a state or natural phenomenon) with or without a link verb:

Vãkaras.   'Evening' (= 'It is evening').
Bùvo naktìs.   'It was night.'

Simple sentence patterns

3.4 The predicate and the constituents required for its complementation comprise the nucleus of a sentence. The obligatory elements are usually the subject, an object or two objects, and sometimes an adverbial, as in

Svečiaĩ	*suėjo*	*į*	*trõbą.*
guests	gathered	to	house: ACC

'The guests gathered in(side) the house.'
Cf. **Svečiaĩ suėjo.* 'The guests came into', which is ungrammatical.

The nucleus of a sentence can be expanded by various optional elements, which may change the informational content without changing the sentence pattern, cf. (the optional constituents are bracketed):

(Vakarè)	*(pavařgę)*	*keleĩviai*	*išvýdo*	*(nuo kálno)*	*(dìdelį)*	*miẽstą.*
evening: LOC	tired	traveller: NOM. PL	saw	from hill	big	town: ACC

'(In the evening) the (tired) travellers saw a (great) city (from the hill).'

Context may render it possible to omit sentence nucleus elements which are otherwise considered obligatory (see 3.105).

3.5 The sentence pattern realized in a concrete sentence is essentially determined by the syntactic properties of the predicate. The predicate may require from one to three positions for sentence constituents. Accordingly, two-member (*Patekė́jo sáulė* 'The sun rose'), three-member (*Arklỹs tráukė vežìmą* 'The horse was pulling a cart') and four-member (*Sūnùs paprãšė tė́vą pinigų̃* 'The son asked his father for money') sentence patterns can be distinguished.

3.6 The following major sentence types described in terms of sentence parts can be distinguished in Lithuanian:

(1) Subject – predicate:

Vaikaĩ miẽga.	'The children are sleeping.'

(2) Subject – predicate – object:

Jiẽ mùms yrà gìminės.	lit. 'They are relatives to us.'

(3) Subject – predicate – object – object:

Draũgas grąžìno mán knỹgą.	'A friend returned a book to me.'

(4) Subject – predicate – (object) – adverbial:

Jõnas el̃giasi negražiaĩ.	'John behaves badly.'
Berniùkas padė́jo svíedinį ant grindų̃.	'The boy put the ball on the floor.'

(5) Subject – predicate – (object) – predicative complement:

Mókytojas atródė pìktas.	'The teacher looked angry.'
Teĩsmas pripažìno jį̃ kal̃tą.	'The court declared him guilty.'

(6) Predicate:

Pasnìgo.	'It has snowed.'
Bùvo naktìs.	'It was night.'

(7) Predicate – object:

Draũgui sė́kasi.	'My friend (DAT) is in luck.'
Mán šálta.	'I (DAT) am cold (ADJ. NEUTR).'

(8) Predicate – object – object:

Mùms užteñka pinigų̃.	'We (DAT) have enough money (GEN).'

(9) Predicate – (object) – adverbial:

Laukè dùnda.	'It is thundering outside (LOC).'
Miestè trū́ksta vandeñs.	'There is a shortage of water (GEN) in the town (LOC).'

3.7 Each of the above sentence types covers a variety of sentence patterns which differ in respect of the formal expression of the constituents.

In the sections below, the most common sentence patterns are described in terms of word forms abbreviated as follows:

Vf – finite verb form, active voice,
Vf_p – finite verb form, passive voice,
Vf_{cop} – finite form of a copula verb,
N – noun,
Adj – adjective,
Num – numeral,
Pron – pronoun,
Adv – adverb,
Inf – infinitive,
PrepP – prepositional phrase,
AdvLoc – adverbial of place,
AdvDir – adverbial of direction or route,
AdvQuant – adverbial of quantity,
AdvMan – adverbial of manner;

abbreviations for the case forms:

n – nominative,
g – genitive,
d – dative,
a – accusative,
i – instrumental,
l – locative,
x – any oblique case;
neutr – neuter adjective or passive participle.

In the formulae of sentence patterns below, the abbreviation N_n is placed initially before Vf, to indicate the most common position of the subject and to emphasize its importance since the subject determines concord with the predicate.

3.8 The sentence patterns below are also considered in terms of the semantic functions of their constituents.

The predicate can express an action, or a state, or a process (change of state). The verbal meaning largely determines the semantic functions (roles) of the subject and object(s). The latter may encode a number of roles for which the following tentative terms are used below:

Agent,
Cause (including Force),
Experiencer,
Comitative (second Agent or Patient, etc.),

Beneficiary (including Addressee and Possessor),
Patient (affected semantic object),
Result (effected semantic object),
Counteragent,
Goal,
Content,
Comparative,
Instrument,
Means,
Source.

Each syntactic pattern may be associated with one or more sets of semantic roles.

According to the type of predicate, sentences can be classified into verbal and nominal. These two types are considered separately in the subsequent sections.

VERBAL SENTENCES
Veiksmažodìniai sakiniaĩ

3.9 The predicate of a verbal sentence is either a simple or periphrastic finite verb form (Vf), or it is a compound verbal predicate with a modal or phrasal semi-auxiliary.

Personal sentence patterns

3.10 A personal sentence pattern consists of at least two constituents, the predicate (Vf) and the subject nominative or its substitute (N_n).

The finite verb form of the predicate in a personal sentence may be omitted, in which case it is recoverable from the context or speech situation, e.g.:

Tù	žẽmei	prãkaitą,	jì	táu	vìską.
you	land: DAT	sweat: ACC	she	you: DAT	everything: ACC

'You give sweat to your land and it gives you everything.'

I. SUBJECT – PREDICATE

3.11 This sentence type is realized by a single formal pattern:

N_n – Vf
Vaĩkas miẽga.   'The child is asleep.'

It typically encodes the following semantic structures:

(1) Agent/Force – Action:

Laukuosè dainãvo mergìnos.	'Girls were singing in the fields.'
Kaminè kaūkia vėjas.	'The wind is howling in the chimney.'

(2) Patient – State/Process:

Lėkštẽ sudùžo.	'The plate broke.'
Ligónis jaũ gỹja.	'The patient is already recovering.'
Gyvẽno trỹs bróliai.	'(There) lived three brothers.'

II. SUBJECT – PREDICATE – OBJECT

This type is realized by a number of sentence patterns.

3.12 $N_n - Vf - N_a$
Vaĩkas skaĩto knỹgą.   'The child is reading a book.'

(1) Agent/Cause – Action – Patient/Result:

Vaĩkas sudaũžė lẽkštę.	'The child broke a plate.'
Šviesà érzina akìs.	'Light irritates the eyes.'
Daĩlininkas nutãpė pavéikslą.	'The artist has painted a picture.'

(2) Agent – Action – Content:

Výrai žaĩdžia krepšìnį.	'The men are playing basketball.'
Senẽlė sẽka pãsaką.	'Granny is telling a fairy-tale.'

(3) Instrumental – Action – Patient:

Peĩlis peĩlį pagalánda.	'A knife sharpens a knife.'
Rãktas rakìna visàs spynàs.	'The key opens all locks.'

(4) Experiencer – State/Process – Content:

Mataũ mìšką.	'I see a forest.'
Jìs apgalvójo plãną.	'He thought over a plan.'
Jì prisìminė jaunỹstę.	'She recollected (her) youth.'

(5) Beneficiary – State/Process – Patient:

Dẽdė tùri ū́kį.	'(My) uncle has a farm.'
Darbiniñkai gãvo algàs.	'The workers received wages.'
Brólis prarãdo dárbą.	'Brother lost (his) job.'

(6) Patient – State – Comparative.

This semantic structure is ascribed to sentences with relational verbs of state, e.g.:

Kòpija atitiñka originãlą.   'The copy corresponds to the original.'

(7) Sentences with desemanticized verbs of change, a noun in the nominative or accusative denoting the state of the Patient or Experiencer, or Beneficiary:

Tė́vą   sùėmė   miẽgas.
father: ACC   took   sleep: NOM
'Father fell asleep.'

Mergáitę   pagãvo   báimė.
girl: ACC   caught   fright: NOM
'The girl got scared.'

Sūnùs   lìgą   įgãvo (= susir̃go).
son: NOM   disease: ACC   got (= fell ill)
'The son caught a disease (fell ill).'

Príešas   patýrė   pralaimė́jimą (= pralaimė́jo).
enemy: NOM   experienced   defeat: ACC (= lost)
'The enemy suffered defeat.'

The accusative case of a noun can be a cognate object:

Jì   sapnãvo   blõgą   sãpną.
she   dreamed   bad   dream: ACC
'She had a bad dream.'

3.13 $N_n - Vf - N_g$

Sesuõ íeško brólių.   'The sister is looking for her brothers.'

(1) Agent – Action – Patient/Result:

Arklỹs   atsigė́rė   vandeñs.
horse: NOM   drank: PREF. REFL   water: GEN
'The horse drank some water.'

Jì   prìkepė   pyrãgų.
she: NOM   baked: PREF   cake: GEN. PL
'She (has) baked a lot of pies.'

(2) Agent – Action – Content:

Jìs mókosi matemãtikos.   'He learns mathematics.'
Tė́vas atsisãkė dárbo.   'Father gave up his job.'

(3) Agent – Action – Goal:

Mergáitė íeško lėlės.	'The girl is looking for her doll.'
Móteris šaūkėsi pagálbos.	'The woman called for help.'

(4) Experiencer – State/Process – Content:

Šuõ nóri mėsõs.	'The dog wants (some) meat.'
Láukiame pavāsario.	'We wait for spring.'
Kìškis lãpo išsigañdo.	'The rabbit got scared of a leaf.'
Mẽs pasiìlgome namų̃.	'We are homesick' (lit. 'We are missing our home').
Jìs nekeñčia brólio.	'He hates his brother.'

(5) Beneficiary – State/Process – Content:

Mẽs pritrū́kome pinigų̃.	'We fell short of money.'

(6) Patient (N_n) – State/Process – Content:

Jì netēko są́monės.	'She fainted' (lit.'She lost consciousness').
Laĩvas pribė̃go vandeñs.	'The boat filled with water.'

(7) This sentence pattern is also realized by sentences with transitive verbs used with negation *ne-*. These negative sentences are transforms of the respective affirmative sentences, (cf. 3.115–118), e.g.:

Katẽ	*sugãvo*	*pẽlę.*
cat	caught	mouse: ACC

'The cat caught a mouse.'

⇒ *Katẽ*	*nesugãvo*	*pelẽs.*
cat	not-caught	mouse: GEN

'The cat didn't catch a mouse.'

3.14 $N_n - Vf - N_d$

Jìs padė́jo draũgui.   'He helped (his) friend.'

This pattern encodes the following principal sets of semantic functions:

(1) Agent – Action – Beneficiary/Counteragent:

Sūnùs pàdeda tėváms.	'The son helps his parents.'
Gyvéntojai príešinosi okupántams.	'The inhabitants resisted the invaders.'

(2) Agent – Action – Patient:

Vaĩkui įspýrė arklỹs.	'A horse kicked the child (DAT).'
Mán įgė́lė bìtė.	'A bee stung me (DAT).'

(3) Agent – Action – Goal:

Žmónės ruõšiasi sė́jai. 'The people are preparing for sowing.'

(4) Experiencer – State/Process – Goal:

Laurýnas atsìdavė mẽnui. 'Laurynas gave himself up to art.'

(5) Experiencer – State/Process – Content:

Žmónės pasìdavė pãnikai. 'People gave in to panic.'

(6) Patient – State/Process – Beneficiary:

Nãmas priklaũso bróliui. 'The house belongs to (my) brother.'
Palikìmas atitẽko vyriáusiam sū́nui. 'The property was inherited (ACT) by the eldest son.'

(7) Patient – State – Goal:

Dobilaĩ tiñka pãšarui. 'Clover is suitable for fodder.'

(8) Content (N_n) – State – Experiencer (N_d):

Mán patiñka kãtės. 'I like cats.'
Mótinai rū́pi vaikaĩ. 'Mother is worried about the children.'

(9) Content (N_n) – State – Beneficiary:

Mùms grēsia bãdas. 'We (DAT) are threatened with starvation (NOM).'

(10) Patient – State – Comparative:

Sūnùs prilýgsta tėvui. 'The son is like (equals) his father.'
Fãktai prieštaráuja teĩginiui. 'The facts contradict the statement.'

3.15 $N_n – Vf – N_i$

Jìs dōmisi mùzika. 'He is interested in music.'

(1) Agent – Action – Patient:

Berniùkai apsìkeitė kepùrėmis. 'The boys swapped (their) caps.'
Mergáitės pasidalìjo óbuoliu. 'The girls shared an apple.'

(2) Agent – Action – Instrument/Means:

Vidùdienį Mýkolas skam̃bina varpaĩs. 'At midday, Mykolas rings the bells.'
Jìs susìjuosė diržù. 'He girded himself with a belt.'

(3) Agent – Action – Content:

Káimo gyvéntojai veřtėsi žvejýba. 'Villagers earned their living by fishing.'
Jì pasivadìno mótinos pãvarde. 'She assumed (lit. 'called herself') her mother's name.'

(4) Agent – Action – Result:

Vélnias pasìvertė šunimì. 'The devil turned himself into a dog.'

(5) Experiencer – State/Process – Content:

Svečiaĩ gėrėjosi pavéikslais. 'The visitors admired the pictures.'
Abejóju tàvo pažadaĩs. 'I doubt your promises.'

(6) Patient – State/Process – Content:

Mergáitė vilkė́jo bálta suknelè. 'The girl was wearing a white gown.'

(for the respective constructions with the accusative see (1) in 2.23)

Bãtai aplìpo móliu. 'The shoes got covered with mud.'
Vaĩkas užsìkrėtė tymaĩs. 'The child caught measles.'

(7) Patient – Process – Result:

Láužas viřto pelenaĩs. 'The campfire turned into ashes.'

N_n – Vf – PrepP

Tė́vas susitìko su sūnumì. lit. 'Father met with his son.'

Prepositional phrases functioning as object are discussed in detail above (see 2.36ff.); in this section, the most typical semantic structures encoded by this pattern will be enumerated.

3.16 Sentence patterns with an object expressed by a prepositional phrase with the genitive encode the following semantic functions:

(1) Agent – Action – Patient:

Tė́vas bãrasi ant vaikų̃. 'Father scolds the children.'
Jis gẽrinosi prie manę̃s. 'He was courting (making up to) me.'
Žmogùs nusitvė́rė už šakõs. 'The man clutched at the branch.'

(2) Agent – Action – Counteragent/Contentive:

Žemaĩčiai gýnėsi nuo kryžiuõčių. 'The lowlanders defended themselves from crusaders.'

Duktė̃ ištekė́jo už girtuõklio. 'The daughter married a drunkard.'

(3) Experiencer – State/Process – Content:

Tik kvailỹs džiaũgiasi iš neláimės. 'Only a fool rejoices at misfortune.'
Užpykaũ ant vaikų̃. 'I got angry with/at the children.'
Šuõ priprãto prie naũjo šeiminiñko. 'The dog got used to the new master.'
Tinginỹs nuo dárbo atprañta. 'A lazy man falls out of the habit of working.'

(4) Patient – State/Process – Content:

Metãlai susìdeda iš kristãlų.	'Metals consist of crystals.'

(5) Patient – State – Comparative:

Jì skýrėsi iš visų̃ vaikų̃.	'She was different (lit. 'differed') from all the children' (standard of comparison).
Dienà nuo naktiẽs nesiskýrė.	'The day did not differ from the night.'

(6) Less obvious is the semantic function encoded by the prepositional phrase in sentences with relational stative verbs, such as the following:

Vaikaĩ priklaũso nuo tėvų̃.	'Children depend on their parents.'

3.17 Sentence patterns with an object expressed by a prepositional phrase with the accusative encode the following principal semantic structures:

(1) Agent – Action – Content:

Žmónės dar tebekalbėjo apie kãrą.	'People were still talking about the war.'
Vyriausýbė atsìžvelgė į piliečiùs.	'The government took the citizens into account.'

(2) Agent – Action – Patient:

Jìs pabéldė į durìs.	'He knocked on the door.'
Žaĩbas treñkė į mẽdį.	'A bolt of lightning struck the tree.'

(3) Agent – Action – Goal:

Mẽs balsúosime už sàvo kandidãtą.	'We shall vote for our candidate.'
Jiẽ kovója už láisvę.	'They fight for freedom.'

(4) Agent – Action – Addressee:

Mokinỹs kreĩpėsi į mókytoją.	'A schoolboy addressed the teacher.'

(5) Experiencer – State – Content:

Visì galvója apie ãteitį.	'Everybody thinks about the future.'
Jìs atsãko už sàvo dárbą.	'He is responsible for his work.'

(6) Agent – Action – Counteragent:

Žmónės sukìlo priẽš okupántus.	'The people revolted against the invaders.'

(7) Patient – Process – Result:

Vanduõ pavir̃to į lẽdą.	'Water turned into ice.'

3.18 The frequently used prepositional phrase *sù* + INSTR encodes a variety of semantic roles in the following semantic patterns:

(1) Agent – Action – Comitative:

Jìs kalbė́josi su kaimýnais.	'He talked with the neighbours.'
Mẽs atsisvéikinome su draugaĩs.	'We said goodbye to our friends.'

(2) Agent – Action – Patient:

Polìcija susidorójo su gyvéntojais.	'The police dealt (harshly) with the people.'
Žmónės darbãvosi su šienù.	lit. 'People worked with hay (were making hay).'

(3) Experiencer – State – Comitative:

Tė́vas geraĩ sutiñka su kaimýnais.	'Father is on good terms with his neighbours.'
Jìs susipýko su draugù.	'He quarrelled with his friend.'

(4) Experiencer – State/Process – Content:

Vil̃kas apsiprãto su neláisve.	'The wolf got used to captivity.'

(5) Patient – State/Process – Comitative:

Šiáurėje Lietuvà susieĩna su Lãtvija.	'In the north Lithuania borders (on) Latvia.'

(6) Patient – Process – Comparative:

Ąžuoliùkas susilýgino su úosiu.	'The oak-tree has caught up with (has grown as tall as) the ash-tree.'

Sentences with an infinitive

3.19 Sentences with an infinitive in object position have patterns analogous to those with an inflected substantive or a prepositional phrase.

Three-member patterns with an infinitive as object (N_n – Vf – Inf) are formed by verbs denoting a prospective (future) action: *nutar̃ti* 'decide', *nusprę́sti* 'decide', *su(si)tar̃ti* 'agree, come to an agreement', *tikė́tis* 'hope', *vìltis* 'hope', *numatýti* 'foresee, plan', *manýti* 'think, intend', *svajóti* 'dream', etc., cf.:

Kaimýnai susìtarė kol kàs patylė́ti.	'The neighbours agreed to keep silent for the time being.'
Dar vìs tikė́jausi sugrį̃žti.	'I still hoped to return.'
Ką̃ manaĩ darýti?	'What do you intend to do?'
Svajóju tavè pamatýti.	lit. 'I dream (hope) to see you.'

After some of these verbs, the infinitive is interchangeable with a future active participle or a subordinate clause; cf.:

Jiẽ	susìtarė	patylė́ti /	patylė́sią /	kad	patylė́s.
they	agreed	keep silent: / INF	keep silent: / FUT. ACT. PART. NOM. PL	that	keep silent: 3. FUT

'They decided to keep silent/that they would keep silent.'

Àš	tikė́jausi	grį̃žti /	grį̃šiąs /	kad	grį̃šiu.
I	hoped	return: INF /	return: FUT. PART. NOM. SG. MASC	that	return: 1. SG.FUT

'I hoped to return/that I would return.'

The verbs *sutìkti* 'agree, consent', *ruõštis* 'prepare', *rū́pintis* 'take care', *rýžtis* 'resolve', *bijóti* 'fear', *tingė́ti* 'be lazy', and the like take an infinitive only (but not a participle or a clause), cf.:

Duktė̃ sutìko mókytis.	'The daughter agreed to study.'
Marcė̃ tìngi dìrbti.	'Marcė doesn't feel like working.'

Only an infinitive is used after verbs like *padáuginti* 'do (sth) too much', *numãžinti* 'do (sth) too little', *paañkstinti* 'do (sth) too early', *pavė̃linti* 'do (sth) too late', etc.:

Paañkstinau	ateĩti.
do too early: 1. SG. PAST	come: INF

'I came too early.'

Jìs	nenudáugina	dúoti.
he	not-do too much: 3. PRES	give: INF

'He does not give too much.'

The infinitive usually encodes the content of the verbal action or state.

III. SUBJECT – PREDICATE – OBJECT – OBJECT

3.20 The sentence patterns below are grouped by the form of the first object and further subdivided according to the form of the second object. For each formal pattern, the most common semantic functions of the constituents are pointed out. Among all the four-member patterns, the most common are patterns with the accusative direct object and the dative, or instrumental, or the prepositional phrase *iš* + GEN as a second object.

Sentence patterns with the accusative as first object

The second object can be expressed by the genitive, dative, instrumental and by a prepositional phrase.

Here belong the following variants.

3.21 $N_n - Vf - N_a - N_g$

Sēnis paklausė jį kẽlio.　　　'The old man asked him the way.'

The semantic patterns are:

(1) Agent – Action – Addressee – Goal:

Vaĩkas prãšė tė́vą pinigų̃.　　　'The child asked his father for money.'

(2) Agent – Action – Patient – Content:

Jì móko vaikùs lietùvių kalbõs.　　'She teaches children Lithuanian.'
Výrai statìnę pripỹlė vandeñs.　　'The men filled the barrel with (lit. 'of') water.'

3.22 $N_n - Vf - N_a - N_d$

Senẽlė	dãvė	mergýtei	óbuolį.
granny	gave	little girl: DAT. SG	apple: ACC. SG

'Granny gave the little girl an apple.'

The most common semantic structures encoded by this pattern are:

(1) Agent – Action – Patient – Beneficiary:

Tė́vas pàvedė sàvo tur̃tą sū́nui.　　'Father entrusted his property to his son.'
Jiẽ įdãvė vãgį polìcijai.　　'They delivered the thief to the police.'
Áuklė užrìšo vaĩkui šãliką.　　lit. 'The nurse tied a scarf to the child.'

The class of verbs taking the obligatory dative of Beneficiary is quite numerous in Lithuanian. With some verbs, the dative may denote purpose as well, cf.:

Komìsija paskýrė pìnigus švietìmui.　　'The committee allocated money for education.'

(2) Agent – Action – Content – Beneficiary:

Àš táu vìską paáiškinsiu.　　'I'll explain everything to you.'
Pasakýk mán tiẽsą.　　'Tell me the truth.'
Mótina atléidžia vaikáms visàs skriaudàs.　　'Mother forgives her children all the offences.'

Numerous verbs denoting communication are used in this pattern.

3.23 $N_n - Vf - N_a - N_i$

Áuklė	*àpavė*	*vaĩką*	*batùkais.*
nurse: NOM	put on	child: ACC. SG	shoes: INSTR. PL. MASC

lit. 'The nurse shod the child with boots.'

(1) Agent – Action – Patient – Instrument/Means/Content:

Šeimiñinkė tvoràs nudžióvė skalbiniaĩs.	'The housewife hung the wash on the fences (for drying).'
Kaimýnas užsiùndė kiaulès šunimìs.	'The neighbour set the dogs (INSTR) on the pigs (ACC).'
Draugaĩ apkáltino jį̃ išdavystè.	'Friends accused him (ACC) of betrayal (INSTR).'

(2) Agent/Cause – Action – Patient – Result:

Rãgana pàvertė brólius akmenimìs.	'The witch turned the brothers into stones (INSTR).'
Tàvo namùs jìs pelenaĩs paléido!	'He turned your house into ashes!'
Šaĩtis pàvertė vándenį ledù.	'Frost turned water into ice.'

3.24 $N_n - Vf - N_a - PrepP$

Berniùkas	*àtėmė*	*žaĩslą*	*iš*	*draũgo.*
boy: NOM. SG	took	toy: ACC. SG	from	friend: GEN. SG

'The boy took a toy from his friend (by force).'

Note: In sentences with verbs meaning 'buy', 'sell', 'lend', 'rent', 'pay', etc. three semantic valencies are often realized:

Tėvas par̃davė kaimýnui kárvę.	'Father sold a cow to the neighbour.'
Kaimýnas pir̃ko kárvę iš tėvo.	'The neighbour bought a cow from father.'
Šeimiñinkas atsiskaĩtė su manimi̇̃ už dárbą.	'The owner paid me (lit. 'settled an account with me') for the work.'

But the second object is often omitted, the sentence retaining its grammaticality:

Tėvas par̃davė kárvę.	'Father sold a cow.'
Jìs atsiskaĩtė su manimi̇̃.	'He settled accounts with me.'

THE PREPOSITIONAL GENITIVE AS SECOND OBJECT

3.25 The most common semantic structures are:

(1) Agent – Action – Patient – Source/Counteragent:

Pasiskólinau iš draũgo knỹgą.	'I borrowed a book from my friend.'
Mìkas apgýnė vaĩką nuo šuñs.	'Mikas (Michael) defended the child from a dog.'
Kažkàs pàvogė iš manęs žíedą.	'Somebody stole a ring from me.'

(2) Beneficiary – Process – Patient – Source:

Jìs gãvo iš draũgo láišką.	'He received a letter from his friend.'

(3) Experiencer – State/Process – Content/Patient – Source:

Vìsa taĩ sužinójau iš draũgo/laĩkraščių.	'I learned all that from a friend/ newspapers.'
Būdą jìs paveldėjo iš tėvo.	'He inherited his temper from his father.'

(4) Agent – Action – Patient – Content:

Visì atkalbinėjo manè nuo tõ sumãnymo.	'Everybody was trying to dissuade me from that intention.'

THE PREPOSITIONAL ACCUSATIVE AS SECOND OBJECT

3.26   The most common semantic structures are:

(1) Agent – Action – Addressee – Content:

Vaikaĩ klausinėjo mókytoją (also mókytojo) apie paukščiùs.	'The children were asking the teacher (cf. GEN) about birds.'

(2) Agent – Action – Patient – Beneficiary:

Jìs užsiùndė šùnį ant avių̃.	'He set the dog on the sheep.'

(3) Agent – Action – Patient – Goal:

Tėvaĩ sū́nų į kùnigus išléido.	'The parents had their son become a priest.'
Jìs iškeitė́ páltą į lãšinius.	'He exchanged a coat for bacon.'

(4) Agent/Cause – Action – Patient – Result:

Rãgana pavertė́ brólius į ãkmenis.	'The witch turned the brothers into stones.'
Šaltis pavertė́ vándenį į lẽdą.	'Frost turned water into ice' (cf. (2) in 3.23).

(5) Agent – Action – Patient – Counteragent:

Mótina užstójo/užtãrė manè priẽš tė́vą.	'Mother interceded for me with father.'
Mẽs sukélsime žmónes priẽš biurokratùs.	'We shall incite the people against bureaucrats.'

THE PREPOSITIONAL INSTRUMENTAL AS SECOND OBJECT

3.27 The common semantic structures are:

(1) Agent – Action – Patient – Comitative (second Patent):

Darbiniñkas sumaĩšė cemeñtą su žvyrù.	'The worker mixed cement with gravel.'

(2) Agent - Action - Patient - Comparative:

Jõs akìs poètas lýgina su žvaigždėmìs.	'The poet compares her eyes to stars.'

(3) Agent – Action – Patient – Comitative (second Agent):

Mergáitė pasidalìjo óbuolį su draugè.	'The girl shared an apple with her friend.'

(4) Agent – Action – Content – Comitative:

Jõnas àptarė planùs su šeimà.	'John discussed the plans with his family.'

Sentence patterns with the genitive as first object

Here belong the following patterns.

3.28 $N_n - Vf - N_g - N_g$

Senẽlė paprāšė manę̃s vandeñs.
granny asked I: GEN water: GEN
'Granny asked me for water.'

This pattern is a variant of the pattern with the accusative direct object: in fact, the accusative and the genitive of a direct object are used interchangeably with the same verbs (cf. 3.21 above). The semantic functions of the nominal elements are the same:

Agent – Action – Addressee – Goal:

Praeĩvis pasikláusė mergáitės/mergáitę kẽlio.	'A passerby asked the girl (GEN/ACC) the way.'
Visì prāšė Diẽvo/Diẽvą lietaũs.	'Everybody begged God (GEN/ACC) for rain.'

3.29 $N_n - Vf - N_g - N_d$

Àš linkiù táu sėkmė̃s.
I: NOM wish you: DAT success: GEN. SG
'I wish you luck.'

It encodes two sets of semantic roles:

(1) Agent – Action – Patient – Beneficiary:

Jaunìkis prìdavė jái brangių̃ dovanų̃.	'The bridegroom gave her (a lot of) expensive presents.'

(The genitive of indefinite quantity is required by this and other verbs with the prefix *pri-*; the accusative is ungrammatical here.)

(2) Experiencer – State – Content – Beneficiary (Possessor):

Katrė̃ pavýdi draũgei pasisekìmo. 'Katrė (Katherine) envies her friend her success.'

3.30 $N_n - Vf - N_g - PrepP$

Jìs	*reikaláuja*	*iš*	*manę̃s*	*pinigų̃.*
he: NOM	demands	from	I: GEN	money: GEN. PL

'He demands money from me.'

(1) Agent – Action – Goal/Patient – Source:

Atėjū̃nai prisiplė̃šė iš gyvéntojų tur̃to.	'The invaders looted (a lot of) property from the inhabitants.'

(See also the above example.)

(2) Agent – Action – Addressee – Content:

Jì visų̃ (cf. *visùs*) *klausinėjo apie sàvo výrą.*	'She asked everybody (cf. ACC) about her husband.'

The prepositional phrase *apiẽ* + ACC is used with the same verbs of speech as the genitive of content (cf. *klausinėti kẽlio* 'ask/inquire about the way').

Sentence patterns with the dative as first object

Here belong two patterns.

3.31 $N_n - Vf - N_d - N_i$ with verbs *skų́stis* 'complain', *gìrtis* 'boast', etc. encoding the semantic structure:

Agent – Action – Addressee – Content:

Tė́vas	*visíems*	*gìriasi*	*sūnumì.*
father	all: DAT. PL	boasts	son: INSTR. SG

'Father boasts to everybody of his son.'

3.32 $N_n - Vf - N_d - PrepP$

The prepositional phrase can be either *apiẽ* + ACC (with verbs denoting communication like *(pa)sakýti* 'say', *pāsakoti* 'tell', *pranèšti* 'report', etc.), or *ùž* + ACC; the semantic structure is:

Agent – Action – Addressee – Content:

Niẽkas	*mùms*	*neprànešė*	*apie*	*susirinkìmą.*
nobody: NOM	we: DAT	not-informed	about	meeting: ACC. SG

'Nobody informed us about the meeting.'

Redāktorius	*jám*	*padėkójo*	*už*	*láišką.*
editor: NOM	he: DAT	thanked	for	letter: ACC. SG

'The editor thanked him for the letter.'

Sentence pattern with the instrumental as first object

3.33 $N_n - Vf - N_i - PrepP$

Agent – Action – Comitative – Patient

The most productive pattern here is with *sù* + INSTR in which reflexive verbs of reciprocal action are used:

Àš pasìkeičiau/pasidalijaũ   'I exchanged/shared clothes (INSTR)
su draugè drabùžiais.   with my friend.'

After some verbs, e.g. *pasidalýti*, the instrumental is interchangeable with the accusative (cf. (3) in 3.27). These verbs, like all other symmetrical predicates, are also used in sentences with a plural subject and the accusative or instrumental case encoding the Patient:

Mẽs pasidalìjome/   'We shared/exchanged the clothes'
pasìkeitėme drabùžiais.   (cf. (1) in 3.12, 15).

SENTENCE PATTERNS WITH AN INFINITIVE

A number of verbs governing the accusative or dative case require an infinitive as the fourth member of a sentence pattern.

3.34 In sentences with the accusative case the following semantic functions can be assigned to the components:

(1) Agent – Action – Patient – Goal

(with the verbs *prašýti* 'ask', *rãginti* 'encourage', *įkalbinėti* '(try to) persuade', *kviẽsti* 'invite', *vilióti* 'tempt', *siųsti* 'send', etc.):

Šeiminiñkė rãgino svečiùs válgyti.   'The hostess urged the guests to eat.'
Jìs kviẽtė manè užeĩti.   'He invited me to come in.'

The infinitive is often interchangeable with an explicative subordinate clause (see 7.19ff.).

(2) Agent – Action – Patient – Content

(with the verbs *mókyti* 'teach', *veřsti* 'make, force', *paskìrti* 'appoint', etc.):

Mótina móko vaĩką kalbė́ti.   'The mother teaches the child to speak.'
Draugaĩ prìvertė jį̃ nutìlti.   'Friends made him stop talking.'

In both cases, the performer of the infinitival action is in the accusative.

3.35   Sentences with the dative case are formed by verbs denoting (a) permission or prohibition and the like (*liẽpti* 'order', *siū́lyti* 'suggest', *linkė́ti* 'wish', *léisti* 'allow', *draũsti* 'forbid', *trukdýti* 'prevent', etc.), (b) assistance in performing an action (*padė́ti* 'help', *pagélbėti* 'assist'), (c) promise to perform an action (*(pa)(si)žadė́ti* 'promise', *prisíekti* 'give an oath', etc.).

With group (a) verbs, the infinitive is interchangeable with an explicative subordinate clause, cf.:

Jìs mán liẽpė ateĩti rytój/   'He ordered me to come
kad ateĩčiau rytój.   tomorrow / that I come tomorrow.'

With (c) verbs it is interchangeable with a clause or a future active participle:

Jìs	pažadė́jo	mán	nevė́luoti /	nevė́luosiąs /	kad	nevė́luōs.
he	promised	me	not-be late: INF	not-be late: FUT. ACT. PART/	that	not-be late: 3. FUT

'He promised not to be late / that he wouldn't be late.'

In sentences with type (a) and (b) verbs, the dative encodes the performer of the infinitival action, whereas with type (c) verbs the latter is expressed by the nominative case of the subject.

In sentences with the dative and an infinitive, the following semantic functions can be assigned to the components:

Agent – Action – Addressee – Content:

Mán mamà liẽpė sugrį̃žti.   'Mother ordered me to return.'
Tù mán prisíekei tylė́ti.   'You gave me an oath to keep silent.'
Draũgas padė́jo mán pabė́gti.   'A friend helped me to escape.'
Mókytojas léido vaikáms pailsė́ti.   'The teacher allowed the children to have a rest.'

IV. SUBJECT – PREDICATE – (OBJECT) – ADVERBIAL

3.36 A number of verbs require an obligatory adverbial.

Some of these verbs determine the meaning of the adverbial (e.g. spatial or quantitative, rarely some other meaning) without determining its grammatical form, cf.:

Knygà	bùvo	spìntoje /	ant	spìntos /	po	spìnta /	čià.
book	was	bookcase: LOC/	on	bookcase: GEN/	under	bookcase: INSTR/	here

'The book was in/on/under the bookcase/here.'

There are also verbs that determine the grammatical form of an adverbial. Thus, many verbs with prefixes denoting direction require a prepositional phrase with a preposition reduplicating the prefix and its meaning:

Vaĩkas	įkrìto	į	vándenį.
child	into-fell	into	water

'The child fell into water.'

Jìs	iššóko	iš	duobẽs.
he	out-jumped	out of	pit: GEN. SG

'He jumped out of the pit.'

Arklỹs	péršoko	per	griõvį.
horse	over-jumped	over	ditch: ACC. SG

'The horse jumped over a ditch.'

An obligatory adverbial is most commonly a noun in the locative or instrumental case or a prepositional phrase, though it may often vary. Therefore, in sentence patterns below the type of an adverbial and its general meaning are indicated instead of the case form or preposition.

Intransitive verbs with an obligatory adverbial form three-member (subject – predicate – adverbial) patterns and transitives – four-member (subject – predicate – object – adverbial) patterns.

Sentence patterns with spatial adverbials

These sentence patterns contain either an adverbial of place (AdvLoc) or an adverbial of direction or route of motion (AdvDir).

SENTENCE PATTERNS WITH AdvLoc

An adverbial of place usually varies in form: it may be the locative or instrumental case of a noun or a prepositional phrase.

3.37 N_n - Vf - AdvLoc

Senẽlė gyvẽna káime. 'Granny lives in the country.'

(1) Patient – State – Place:

Dešinėjè bùvo píeva. 'On the right was a meadow.'
Vaĩkas tūnójo kampè. 'The child stayed in the corner.'
Pavéikslas kãbo ant síenos. 'A picture hangs on the wall.'

(2) Agent – Action – Place:

Jìs lañkėsi pas kaimýnus. 'He visited his neighbours.'
Šeiminiñkė sùkosi virtùvėje. 'The housewife was busy (working) in the kitchen.'

3.38 N_n – Vf – N_a – AdvLoc

Jìs palìko sū́nų namiẽ. 'He left his son at home.'

The semantic functions are:

Agent – Action – Patient – Place:

Senẽlė laikýdavo kiaušiniùs lentýnoje. 'Granny used to keep eggs on the shelf.'
Šuõ gáiniojo vištàs kiemè. 'The dog chased chickens in the yard.'
Súolus sustãtėme pasíeniais/prie stãlo. 'We put the benches along the walls/ at the table.'

SENTENCE PATTERNS WITH AdvDir

3.39 The expression of an adverbial in this case is determined by its meaning, which may be that of direction, i.e. the initial or final point of motion, route, or a variant of these (see 2.49ff.). Direction is often expressed by a prepositional phrase, though sometimes the instrumental can be used instead, e.g.:

Jìs	ė̃jo	per	liẽptą /	lieptù.
he	walked	across	foot-bridge: ACC/	foot-bridge: INSTR

'He walked across the foot-bridge.'

3.40 N_n – Vf – AdvDir

Raĩtelis	*nusėdo*	*nuo*	*árklio.*
rider	off-sat	off	horse: GEN. SG

'The rider dismounted from the horse.'

(1) Agent – Action (Motion) – Initial/Final Point/Route:

Iš krūmų išliñdo šuõ.	'A dog crawled out of the bushes.'
Kãtinas užšóko ant tvorõs.	'The cat jumped on the fence.'
Kárvės breñda per ùpę.	'The cows are wading across the stream.'

(2) Patient – Process – Initial/Final Point/Route:

Vijõklis vyniójosi apie stuĩpą.	'Ivy wound round a post.'
Pupà išáugo iki dangaũs.	'The bean has grown up to the sky.'

3.41 N_n – Vf – N_a – AdvDir

Gýdytojas nùsiuntė vaĩką į váistinę. 'The doctor sent the child to the drugstore.'

Agent/Force – Action – Patient – Initial/Final point/Route:

Vėjas plėšė lapùs nuo medžių.	'The wind tore leaves from the trees.'
Jis pridėjo aũsį prie dùrų.	'He pressed his ear to the door.'
Piemuõ vãrė bañdą keliù.	'The shepherd drove the herd along the road.'

3.42 Many intransitive and transitive verbs can take two (and even three) adverbials denoting the initial and final points of motion; cf. respectively:

(1) *Ji péreina iš kambario į kambarį.*	'She passes from room to room.'
Vaĩkas nušóko nuo kėdės žẽmėn.	'The boy jumped down from the chair onto the ground.'
(2) *Výrai nurìtino rąstùs nuo kálno į ùpę.*	'The men rolled (down) the logs from the hill into the river.'
Šituõ takù jiẽ vèsdavo kárves iš namų į ganỹklą.	'They used to drive the cows along this path from home to the pasture.'

However, only one of the adverbials with these verbs can be regarded as obligatory. Thus these sentences realize the three- or four-member patterns discussed in 3.40–41.

For a more detailed treatment of spatial adverbials in verb groups see 2.47ff.

SENTENCE PATTERNS WITH AdvQuant

3.43 A quantitative adverbial is obligatory in sentences with the verbs (mostly prefixed) whose lexical meaning implies a quantitative characteristic of the action or subject (object).

The grammatical form of quantitative adverbials is not rigidly determined.

Sentences with an obligatory quantitative adverbial can contain other obligatory components. A number of patterns are distinguished here.

N_n – Vf – AdvQuant

Dárbas trùko ilgaĩ.   'The work lasted long (ADV).'

The encoded semantic structure is:

Patient – State/Process – Quantity.

3.44 A temporal quantitative adverbial is usually dependent on verbs with the prefixes *iš-* and *pra-*:

Jìs prasir̃go/išgulėjo vìsą žiẽmą.   'He was ill/spent in bed all winter'
                                     (cf. **Jìs prasir̃go/išgulėjo*).

3.45 A spatial quantitative adverbial is obligatory with the verbs *síekti* 'reach, stretch (as far as), equal', *tę̃stis* 'stretch', *nusitę̃sti* 'last, extend' and the like:

Kū́no ìlgis síekia trìs metrùs.   'The length of the body equals three metres.'

Lygumà tę̃siasi/nusitę̃sia tolì.   'The plain extends far.'

3.46 Quantitative adverbials denoting other dimensions are obligatory with the verbs *sver̃ti* 'weigh', *kainúoti* 'cost', *atsieĩti* 'cost, come to', *įkáinoti* 'appraise, fix the price (of)', etc.:

*Kū̃dikis svė̃rė kẽturis   'The baby weighed four kilograms/
kilogramùs/daũg/mažaĩ.*   much/ little.'

Knygà kainãvo pigiaĩ.   'The book cost little (lit. 'cheaply').'

In the following sentence the Agent is added:

*Jõ tur̃tą añtstolis įkáinojo   'The sheriff appraised his property
dviẽm tū́kstančiais lìtų.*   at two thousand litas.'

To express the limits of a quantitative characteristic, two prepositional phrases are used, usually with the prepositions *nuõ* 'from' and *ikì* 'to':

*Operãcija trùko nuo rýto   'The operation lasted from morning till
iki vãkaro.*   evening.'

3.47 N_n – Vf – AdvLoc – AdvQuant

Pas sū́nų jì išbùvo neilgaĩ.   'She stayed at her son's place a short while.'

The encoded semantic structure is:

Patient – State – Place – Quantity of time.

A number of intransitive verbs, usually with the prefixes *iš-*, *pra-* and sometimes others, form four-member patterns of this type, with an obligatory quantitative adverbial.

Iki dvýlikos mẽtų ámžiaus   'She stayed in bed until (she was) twelve
jì išgulė́jo lóvoje.   years of age.'

3.48 N_n – Vf – N_a – AdvLoc – AdvQuant

Agent – Action – Patient – Place – Quantity of time:

Jì išlaĩkė sū́nų namiẽ iki   'She kept her son at home until (he was)
dvìdešimties mẽtų.   twenty years of age.'

Sentence pattern with AdvMan

3.49 The verbs *elg̃tis* 'behave', *atródyti* 'appear, look', *jaũstis* 'feel, be', *gyvúoti* 'get on', *laikýtis* 'hold oneself, behave', and a few others take an obligatory adverbial of manner expressed by a qualitative adverb or its substitute (a comparative phrase, sometimes a prepositional phrase).

N_n – Vf – AdvMan

Jis keistaĩ/kaip vaĩkas elg̃iasi.   'He behaves strangely/like a child.'
Tė́vas prastaĩ atródo/jaũčiasi.   'Father looks/feels unwell' (cf. also 3.50).

V. SUBJECT – PREDICATE – (OBJECT) – PREDICATIVE COMPLEMENT

3.50 N_n – Vf – $Adj_n/N_n/N_i$

Mókytojas	*atródė*	*pìktas.*
teacher: NOM. SG. MASC	seemed	angry: NOM. SG. MASC

'The teacher looked angry.'

With the verbs *atródyti* 'seem, look', *ródytis* 'look', *pasiródyti* 'turn out (to be)' used in this pattern the subject encodes the Patient; with the verbs *jaũstis* 'feel (oneself)', *pasijùsti* 'begin to feel (oneself)', and the like, it encodes an Experiencer.

These verbs require specification by a qualitative adjective or a class noun in the nominative (less commonly instrumental) case (cf. sentences with a semantically similar adverbial in 3.49).

An adjective can be replaced by a qualitative participle:

Jis	jaūtėsi	nùskriaustas /	atródė	pavar̃gęs.
he	felt	hurt: PAST. PASS. PART. MASC/	seemed	tired: PAST. ACT. PART. MASC

'He felt hurt/seemed tired.'

An adjective may also be replaced by a comparative phrase, the genitive case of a noun (often with an attribute) or a prepositional phrase; cf. respectively:

Jìs jaūtėsi kaip nesãvas.	'He didn't feel like his own self.'
Mergýtė atródė gerõs širdiẽs.	'The girl seemed to be kind-hearted lit. 'of kind heart').'
Jì pasiródė visái be núovokos.	'She turned out to be quite witless (lit. 'quite without quick wits').'

If the subject is the neuter pronoun or an indefinite pronoun with no gender contrast, the predicative adjective is used in the neuter form:

Vìsa /	vìskas	teñ	atródė	naũja,	gražù.
all: NEUTR	everything	there	looked	new: NEUTR	beautiful: NEUTR

'Everything there looked new and beautiful.'

In sentences with the verbs ródytis/atródyti/pasiródyti 'seem, look' the dative object of Experiencer can be used:

Jìs	mán	baisùs	keistuõlis /	baisiù	keistuoliù	pasiródė.
he	I: DAT	terrible	crank: NOM /	terrible: INSTR	crank: INSTR	seemed

'He seemed to me a terribly queer man.'

3.51 $N_n - Vf - N_a - Adj_a/Adj_i - N_i$

Kãras	padãrė	visùs	nelaimìngus.
war: NOM. SG	made	all: ACC. PL	unhappy: ACC. PL

'The war made everybody unhappy.'

N_n commonly encodes Agent with the verbs (pa)darýti 'make' (in the above example it encodes Cause), vadìnti 'name, call', pravardžiúoti 'call', pripažìnti 'recognize, acknowledge', and Experiencer with the verb laikýti 'consider'; cf. respectively:

(a) *Visì pravardžiãvo jį̃ bedieviù.* 'Everyone called him an atheist (INSTR).'

(b) *Mẽs laĩkėme jį̃* 'We considered him a wise man (N$_i$)/
išmiñčiumi /išmintìngu. wise (Adj$_i$).'

SENTENCE PATTERNS WITH THE POSSESSIVE DATIVE CASE

3.52 The possessive dative case of a (usually human) noun often occurs in sentences with the subject or an object denoting a body part (or rather, inalienable and, sometimes, alienable possession); cf.:

Mótinai	*drẽba*	*rañkos.*
mother: DAT	tremble	hand: NOM. PL

'Mother's hands tremble.'

The dative denotes the possessor or the whole and it is related both to the name of a (body) part and to the predicate:

Pabučiãvo	*rañką*	*mótinai.*
kissed	hand: ACC. SG	mother: DAT

'He kissed mother's hand.'

Lū́žo	*rankà*	*vaĩkui.*
broke	arm: NOM. SG	child: DAT

'The boy's arm broke' (or 'The boy broke his arm').

Sė́di	*ant*	*kẽlių*	*tė́vui.*
sits	on	knee: GEN. PL	father: DAT

'He sits in his father's lap.'

To denote a part – whole relation, inanimate nouns can also be used in the possessive dative case, e.g.:

Švar̃kui	*atìro*	*rankóvė.*
jacket: DAT. SG	ripped off	sleeve: NOM. SG

'A sleeve of the jacket got ripped off.'

The dative is also used to denote Beneficiary who is also the possessor of alienable property:

Tù	*mán*	*(iš*	*manę̃s)*	*žẽmę*	*norė́jai*	*atim̃ti.*
thou	I: DAT	from	I: GEN	land: ACC	wanted	take: INF

'You wanted to take my land from me.'

3.53 The noun denoting a body part may assume a number of case forms with or without a preposition: it may be in the nominative or accusative case as in the above examples, or the locative, as in:

Mán	jõ	žõdžiai	be	paliovõs	skambėjo	galvojè.
I: DAT	his	word: NOM. PL	without	pause	sounded	head: LOC. SG

'His words constantly sounded in my head.'

Here are examples with prepositional phrases:

Šãkos	brė̃žė	jám		per	véidą.
branches	scratched	he: DAT		across	face: ACC

'Branches scratched him on the face.'

Žuvìs	išslýdo	vaĩkui		ìš	rañkų.
fish	slipped-out	child: DAT		from	hand: GEN. PL

'The fish slipped out of the boy's hands.'

In sentences with momentary verbs like *smõgti* 'strike, hit' and its synonyms (*dróžti, skélti, treñkti, (su)dúoti*, etc.), *dùrti* 'stab', *įką́sti* 'bite' and its synonyms (*įgélti, įkir̃sti*) the name of a body part may be omitted, in which case the dative of possessor/whole can be interpreted as Patient, cf.:

Šuõ	įkándo	mán	į̃	kóją.
dog: NOM	bite: 3. PAST	I: DAT	into	leg: ACC. SG

'A dog bit me on the leg.'

Mán	įkándo	šuõ.
I: DAT	bite: 3. PAST	dog: NOM

'A dog bit me.'

Impersonal sentence patterns

3.54 Impersonal sentences are formed with impersonal verbs, i.e. verbs which have no subject valency. Though subjectless, impersonal verbs may have a number of other valencies, therefore sentence patterns are varied enough: they may consist of a predicate alone or a predicate and obligatory dependent components.

VI. PREDICATE

3.55 **Vf**

Aũšta.   'Day is breaking.'

This pattern is realized mostly by sentences with impersonal verbs denoting meteorological phenomena or processes associated with the times of the day or with seasons:

Sniñga.	'It is snowing.'
Laukè šą̃la.	'It is growing cold outside.'
Jaũ šviñta.	'Day is already breaking.'
Rudenė́ja.	'Autumn is coming.'
Žaibúoja.	'Lightning is flashing.'

Impersonal verbs of this class are extremely numerous and varied.

Most of these verbs can take a tautological subject, the noun being lexically identical with the verb:

Lỹja lietùs.	lit. 'Rain is raining.'
Aũšta aušrà.	lit. 'Dawn is dawning.'

The exceptions are very few, e.g. the verbs *rudenė́ja* 'autumn is coming', *vakarė́ja* 'evening is coming', and a few others.

Structurally, sentences with a tautological subject assume the pattern $N_n - Vf$, but they remain impersonal since they denote events unrelated to any agent, the subject noun naming the same event. A two-member structure is used for emphasis, or in case it is necessary to include a modifier:

Lìjo šìltas lietùs.	'A warm rain was raining.'

The verbs under consideration can also be used in personal two-member (usually metaphorical) sentences:

Išaũšo gražì dienà.	lit. 'A beautiful day (has) dawned.'

Some impersonal verbs are sometimes used with an optional instrumental:

Ledaĩs lỹja.	lit. 'It rains with icicles.'
Bóbų ką́sniais sniñga	'It snows with huge snowflakes.'

VII. PREDICATE – OBJECT

3.56 $Vf - N_g$

Prisiriñko   *reikalų̃.*
accumulated   affair: GEN. PL
'A lot of affairs have accumulated.'

The encoded semantic structure is:

State/Process – Patient/Content.

This pattern is realized by sentences with perfective verbs with the prefix *pri-* which require the genitive of indefinite quantity. These sentences are interpreted as impersonal, because the genitive is not interchangeable with the nominative; e.g.:

Šiemet prìvìso uodų̃ (*uodaĩ).   'This year lots of gnats (GEN) have hatched.'
Cf. Veĩsiasi uodaĩ.   'Gnats (NOM) are hatching.'

This pattern is also associated with the negative form of the verb *bū́ti* 'be' (and *lìkti* 'remain'):

Nėrà   jokiõs   išeitiẽs.
not-be: 3. PRES no   way-out: GEN. SG
'There is no way out.'

Cf. Yrà   išeitìs.
    is   way-out: NOM. SG
'There is a way out.'

Seniaĩ   nebėrà   tė́vo.
old: ADV   not-be: 3. PRES   father: GEN
'Father died a long time ago.'

3.57 Vf – N_d

Draũgui   sẽkasi.
friend: DAT. SG   go well: 3. PRES. REFL
'My friend is in luck.'

The encoded semantic structure is:

State/Process – Experiencer/Beneficiary/Patient (human).

This pattern is realized by sentences with impersonal and some impersonally used verbs denoting physical or psychological states, the dative encoding either an Experiencer, or a Beneficiary, or a Patient. Here belong a number of non-reflexive verbs (e.g. *pagerė́ti* 'become better', *palengvė́ti* 'become easier', *pabaĩsti* 'feel horror', etc.) which are used in sentences like

Kartais   jám   palengvė́ja.
sometimes   he: DAT   become better: 3. PRES
'Sometimes he feels better.'

Most of these verbs are also used in personal sentences, the dative being interchangeable with the nominative of the subject:

Ligóniui	pagerėjo	=	Ligónis	pagerėjo.
patient: DAT	became better		patient: NOM	became better

'The patient improved.'

A number of verbs are *reflexiva tantum*, e.g. *sėktis* 'go well', *klótis* 'get on', e.g.:

Kaĩp	táu	klójasi?
how	you: DAT	goes on

'How are you getting on? (How are things with you?)'

A few verbs are reflexives derived from personal intransitives to express a modal-potential meaning; they are commonly used with negation or with an adverb of manner:

Mán	nesidìrba /		nesimiegójo.
I: DAT	not-REFL-work: 3. PRES		not-REFL-sleep: 3. PAST

'I can't work (don't feel like working)/couldn't sleep.'

Žmonėms	kitur̃	geriaũ	gyvẽnasi.
people: DAT. PL	elsewhere	better	live: 3. PRES. REFL

'People live better in other places.'

Adverbs of manner are also common with the verbs *eĩtis/išeĩti* 'go, happen', *klótis* 'get on', and they are less common with their synonyms *sėktis/pasisėkti* 'go well'; e.g.:

Ne	kiekvienám	lýgiai	geraĩ	eĩnasi.
not	everybody: DAT	equally	well	goes: REFL

'Not everyone is equally lucky.'

The verbs *sėktis*, *eĩtis*, *išeĩti* can also take the prepositional phrase *sù* + INSTR:

Su	kelionè	jíems	neišėjo /	nepavýko.
with	journey: INSTR	they: DAT	not-went	not-succeeded

'They failed to make the trip.'

3.58 Vf – N_a

Manè	pýkina.
I: ACC	make sick: 3. PRES

'I feel sick.'

The encoded semantic structure is:

Process/State – Patient.

In this pattern, two types of verbs occur: (1) impersonal or impersonally used (mostly prefixed) verbs denoting spontaneous natural processes (e.g., *sulýti* 'get wet (in the rain)', *užsnìgti* 'snow over', *nutreñkti* 'strike dead (of a bolt of lightning)' and the like) and (2) impersonally used personal verbs denoting the physical state of a human patient; cf. respectively:

(1) *Visái*   *užpùstė*   *kẽlią.*
quite   cover up: 3. PAST   road: ACC. SG
lit. 'It snowed up the road.'

Vãsarą   *mū́sų*   *kárvę*   *nùtrenkė.*
summer: ACC   our   cow: ACC. SG   strike dead: 3. PAST
'In summer, our cow was struck dead.'

(2) *Vežimė̃*   *ligónę*   *labaĩ*   *krãtė.*
cart: LOC   patient: ACC. SG   very   jolt: 3. PAST
'The patient was being badly jolted in the cart.'

Gál   *prieš*   *óro*   *pérmainą*   *manè*   *taĩp láužo.*
maybe   before   weather: GEN   change: ACC   I: ACC   so   break: 3. PRES
'Maybe because of the change of weather I am aching all over.'

The latter sentences are similar in meaning to three-member impersonal sentences with the possessive dative, e.g.:

Mán   *skaũda*   *gálvą.*
I: DAT   aches   head: ACC
'I have a headache.'

VIII. PREDICATE – OBJECT – OBJECT

3.59 $Vf - N_g - N_d$

Mùms   *trū́ksta*   *dúonos.*
we: DAT   lack: 3. PRES   bread: GEN. SG
'We are short of bread.'

This pattern encodes two semantic structures.

(1) State/Process – Beneficiary – Content:

Mán   *nereĩkia*   *svetimų̃*   *turtų̃.*
I: DAT   not-need: 3. PRES   strange: GEN. PL   riches: GEN. PL
'I don't need other people's riches.'

Sáulės   *mùms*   *užteñka.*
sun: GEN. SG   we: DAT   is enough
'We have enough sun (light).'

Žmōgui   niēkad   viltiẽs   nestiñga.
man: DAT   never   hope: GEN   not-lacks
'A man is never short of hope.'

The dative sometimes can be replaced by the locative of the inanimate noun, e.g.:

Šulinyjè   trū́ksta   vandeñs.
well: LOC   lacks   water: GEN
'There is too little water in the well' (see 3.67).

The verbs *užtèkti* 'be/have enough', *stìgti* 'be short (of)', *pristìgti* 'fall short (of)', *trū́kti* 'lack' are also used, though less commonly, with the nominative subject instead of the dative object (cf. 3.13, 5):

Víeną   kar̃tą   pristìgo   jìs   dúonos.
one   time   fell short   he: NOM   bread: GEN
'One day he was short of bread.'

(2) State/Process – Experiencer – Content:

Mán   labaĩ   norė́josi   óbuolio.
I: DAT   very   want: 3. PAST. REFL   apple: GEN. SG
'I wanted an apple very much.'

Medžiótojui   pagaĩlo   stirniùkės.
hunter: DAT. SG   fell sorry: 3. PAST   roe: GEN. SG
'The hunter felt sorry for the little roe.'

This pattern is also realized by sentences with the negative form of the reflexive verbs of sense perception *ne-si-mãto* '(is) not to be seen', *ne-si-jaũčia* '(is) not to be felt', *ne-si-gir̃di* '(is) not to be heard'; these sentences are in fact negative transforms of their respective affirmative sentences; thus

Mán   nesigirdė́jo   balsų̃
I: DAT   not-REFL-hear: 3. PAST   voice: GEN. PL
'I couldn't hear any voices'

is a transform of

Mán   girdė́josi   balsaĩ.
I: DAT   hear: 3. PAST. REFL   voice: NOM. PL
'I could hear voices.'

Cf. the non-reflexive sentence:

Àš   girdė́jau   balsùs.
I: NOM   hear: 1. SG. PAST   voice: ACC. PL
'I heard voices.'

These reflexives, however, are more common without the dative case, thus implying a generalized Experiencer:

Laukuosè   *nebesimãtė*   *žmonių.*
field: LOC. PL   not-any longer-REFL-see: 3. PAST   people: GEN
'One could no longer see people in the fields.' Or: 'There were no longer any people to be seen in the fields.'

It should be noted that in Standard Lithuanian sentences with the infinitive of the respective non-reflexive verbs are more common:

Nebematýti   *žmonių.*
not-any longer see: INF   people: GEN
'One can see no people any longer' (see 3.95).

3.60 $Vf - N_a - N_g$

Sõdą   *prìnešė*   *sniẽgo.*
garden: ACC. SG   drift: 3. PAST   snow: GEN. SG
'The garden was snowed up.'

The encoded semantic structure is:

Process – Patient – Content.

This pattern is limited to a small lexical group of verbs with the prefix *pri-* referring to meteorological phenomena, the accusative case denoting place, and the genitive snow or rain:

Prilìjo   *pìlną*   *griõvį*   *vandeñs.*
PREF-rained   full: ACC   ditch: ACC   water: GEN
'Rain filled the ditch with water' or 'It rained the ditch full of water.'

3.61 $Vf - N_a - N_i$

Vaĩką   *mẽto*   *spuogaĩs.*
child: ACC. SG   throw   pimple: INSTR. PL
'The child is covered with pimples.'

(Spontaneous) Process – Patient (human or body part) – Content.

This pattern is characteristic of impersonally used verbs like *(iš)beřti/išbérti* 'break out (of a rash)', *(iš)kélti* lit. 'raise', *mėtyti* 'cover' (lit. 'throw'), *(iš)mùšti* 'break out, erupt', *(iš)pìlti* 'erupt' (lit. 'pour out'), *veřsti* 'erupt, break out' denoting an eruption of sores, pimples and the like, which makes them synonyms; cf. also:

Jį išbėrė/išbėrė spuogaĩs.   'He had an eruption of pimples.'
Manè kařtais ìšmuša dėmėmìs.   'Sometimes I have an eruption of spots.'

The instrumental can be omitted with the verb *(iš)beřti/(iš)bérti* since the meaning of the noun is incorporated in the verb:

Manè bùvo smařkiai išbė́rę.   'I had a bad rash.'

With all these verbs the accusative can be used to denote a body part, in which case the possessive dative is used to refer to the person (see 3.72):

Mán	*nukė́lė*	*spuogaĩs*	*liežùvį.*
I: DAT	raised	sore: INSTR. PL	tongue: ACC. SG

'My tongue was covered with sores.'

With a number of these verbs, the instrumental alternates with the nominative, in which case the sentence is syntactically personal:

Vaĩką	*pìla*	*spuogaĩ.*
child: ACC	pour: 3. PRES	pimple: NOM. PL

'Pimples erupt on the child's body.'

This pattern is also realized by sentences with meteorological verbs, e.g.:

Dañgų	*užtráukė*	*debesimìs.*
sky: ACC	covered	cloud: INSTR. PL

'The sky got covered with clouds'

which has an alternative personal variant:

Dañgų	*užtráukė*	*dė̃besys.*
sky: ACC	covered	cloud: NOM. PL

'Clouds covered the sky.'

3.62   Vf – N_d – nuo N_g

Jám	*kliùs*	*nuo*	*tė́vo.*
he: DAT	get: 3. FUT	from	father: GEN

'He will get it hot from his father.'

The dative here denotes Patient and the prepositional phrase may be interpreted as Source of the state.

In this pattern, two verbs only, viz. *kliū́ti* and *tèkti* 'get (it)', are used.

IX. PREDICATE – (OBJECT) – ADVERBIAL

3.63   The nucleus of a number of impersonal sentences contains an obligatory adverbial of place (AdvLoc) or direction (AdvDir). Its grammatical form is not as a rule rigidly determined by the predicate. The following patterns can be distinguished here.

3.64 Vf – AdvLoc/AdvDir

Apliñkui   dùnda.
around   roar: 3. PRES
'There is a roar around here.'

The encoded semantic structure is:

State/Process – Place/Direction.

Sentences of this type are formed by impersonal and impersonally used intransitive verbs denoting acoustic or visual effects or events not attributed to any agent or cause and specified with respect to place.

Vakaruosè   parausvėjo.
west: LOC. PL   grow reddish: 3. PAST
'It grew reddish in the west.'

Gìriose   švõkštė,   šlamėjo.
wood: LOC. PL   swish: 3. PAST   rustle: 3. PAST
'There was swishing and rustling in the woods.'

Po   kójomis   žliùgsi.
under   foot: INSTR. PL squelch: 3. PRES
'(Water) squelches underfoot.'

Nuo   stógo   var̃va.
from   roof: GEN   drip: 3. PRES
'It is dripping from the roof.'

The locative case is often interchangeable with the nominative, the subject designating place; cf.:

Gìrios šlamėjo.   'The woods (NOM) rustled.'
Dangùs parausvėjo.   'The sky grew red.'

3.65 Vf – N_i – AdvLoc/AdvDir

Čià   kvẽpia   gėlėmìs.
here   smell: 3. PRES flower: INSTR. PL
'It smells of flowers here.'

State/Process – Content – Place/Direction.

This pattern is characteristic of impersonally used intransitive verbs denoting the emitting of an odour or flowing usually with an adverbial either of place or direction, cf. respectively:

(a) *Laukuosè*   *kvepėjo*   *medumì.*
field: LOC. PL   smell: 3. PAST   honey: INSTR. SG
'In the fields it smelled of honey.'

(b) *Nuo   ėžero*   *patráukė*   *vėsumù.*
from   lake: GEN   draw: 3. PAST   freshness: INSTR
'There was a draught of fresh air from the lake.'

3.66 Vf – N_a – AdvDir

Manè   tráukia   namõ.
I: ACC   draw: 3. PRES   home
'I long to go home.'

State – Patient (human) – Direction.

This pattern is characteristic of impersonally used transitive verbs which acquire the meaning of an uncontrolled urge to go to the place designated by an adverbial; here belong *kélti* 'raise', *tráukti* 'draw, pull', *stùmti* 'push', etc.; also *vilióti/mãsinti* 'attract, lure'. Direction is expressed by a prepositional phrase or an adverb:

Manè   lyg   stūmė   į   ėžerą /   pirmỹn.
I: ACC   as if   push: 3. PAST   into   lake: ACC forwards
'Some force kind of pushed me into the lake/forwards.'

Sentences of this type are semantically similar to those of the pattern Vf – N_a denoting a person's physical state (see 3.58.).

3.67 Vf – N_g – AdvLoc/AdvDir

Šulinyjè   stiñga /   pakañka   vandeñs.
well: LOC. SG   lack: 3. PRES   be enough: 3. PRES   water: GEN
'There is too little/enough water in the well'

This pattern encodes two semantic structures.

(1) State/Process – Content – Place:

Kambaryjè   trū́ksta   óro.
room: LOC   lack: 3. PRES   air: GEN
lit. 'There is too little air in the room (i.e. it is stuffy)'
(cf. also the above example).

The pattern is formed by verbs denoting shortage, lack of sth. and their antonyms (cf. *pakàkti* 'be in sufficient quantity').

(2) State/Process – Patient/Content – Direction:

statinę	pribėgo	vandens.
Į	barrel: ACC. SG	PREF-run: 3. PAST	water: GEN. SG

into

'(Much) water filled the barrel.'

Pribyrėjo	tinko	nuo	lubų.
PREF-fall: 3. PAST	plaster: GEN. SG	from	ceiling: GEN. PL

'A lot of plaster flaked off down from the ceiling.'

This pattern is semantically similar to the two-member pattern, e.g.:

Prisirinko reikalų.   'A lot of affairs have accumulated'(see 3.56).

Most of these verbs are also used personally, with the nominative of spatial noun instead of an adverbial of place:

Į	kambarį /	Kambarys	prisirinko	žmonių.
into	room: ACC. SG	room: NOM. SG	PREF-REFL-gather: 3. PAST	people: GEN

'A lot of people gathered in the room/The room filled with (a lot of) people.'

With verbs of shortage and sufficient quantity an adverbial can alternate with the dative case of an object, unless it is a locative noun (see 3.59), cf.:

Knygoje	trūksta	dviejų	lapų.
book: LOC. SG	lack: 3. PRES	two: GEN	page: GEN. PL

'Two pages are missing in the book.'

Knygai	trūksta	dviejų	lapų.
book: DAT. SG	lack: 3. PRES	two: GEN	pages: GEN

'The book lacks two pages'

but:

*Šuliniui	trūksta	vandens.
well: DAT	lacks	water: GEN

'The well is short of water.'

SENTENCE PATTERNS WITH AN INFINITIVE

3.68 A number of verbs (*tèkti* 'have to', *patìkti* 'like', *rūpėti* 'care, be worried (about)', *tráukti* 'attract' and the like) can be semantically supplemented by an infinitive or a noun in object position, cf.:

Sūnui	patiko	dirbti /	dárbas.
son: DAT. SG	like: 3. PAST	work: INF	work: NOM. SG

'The son liked to work/the work.'

Mán	*nórisi*		*válgyti /*	*valˇgio /*	*dúonos.*
I: DAT	want: 3. PRES. REFL		eat: INF	food: GEN	bread: GEN

'I'd like to eat/some food/some bread.'

Manè	*tráukia*	*keliáuti /*	*kelionės.*
I: ACC	attract: 3. PRES	travel: INF	travelling: NOM. PL

'I'd like to travel/Travelling attracts me.'

According to the case form of the second subordinate nominal, two patterns are distinguished.

3.69 Vf – N$_d$ – Inf

Svečiáms	*reikės*	*paláukti.*
guest: DAT. PL	be necessary: FUT	wait: INF

'The visitors will have to wait a while.'

The encoded semantic structure is:

State – Experiencer/Beneficiary – Content.

The verbs *užtèkti/pakàkti* 'have/be enough', *sèktis* 'succeed, be a success', *derėti* 'be suited/suitable', *tèkti/pasitáikyti* 'happen', *patìkti* 'like', *at(si)bósti* 'get bored', *įkyrėti* 'bore', *rūpėti* 'be worried (about), care', *knietėti* 'be anxious (to do sth)', *pabaĩsti* 'feel terror', etc. are also used in this pattern; e.g.:

Jám pasìsekė išlõšti.	'He (DAT) was lucky enough to win.'
Ganės táu niekùs taũkšti.	lit. 'It is enough for you (DAT) to jabber.'
Táu neprìdera taĩp darýti.	'It isn't proper for you (DAT) to do so.'
Mán pakyrėjo láukti.	'I (DAT) got bored with waiting.'

The dative case of a human noun is often omitted if it is implied by the context or if it is generalized:

Rytój	*tèks*	*labaĩ*	*gailėtis.*
tomorrow	have-to: 3. FUT	very	be-sorry: INF

'Tomorrow one will be very sorry.'

Vakarè jau nórisi pailsėti.	'In the evening one feels like having a rest.'

The object of a transitive infinitive can take the form of the nominative instead of the accusative:

Jám	*nepatìko*	*laukėlis*	*(laukėlį)*	*árti.*
he: DAT	not-like: 3. PAST	field: NOM. SG	field: ACC. SG	plough: INF

'He didn't like to plough the field (NOM/ACC).'

3.70 Vf – N_a – Inf

Manè	tráukia	keliáuti.
I: ACC	attract: 3. PRES	travel: INF

'I'd like to travel.'

The encoded semantic structure is:

State – Experiencer/Patient – Content.

In fact, the semantic structure is similar to that in the previous case, the difference being in the case form of Experiencer or Patient: in this case impersonally used transitive verbs (such as *vilióti/māsinti* 'lure', and also *veřsti* 'force, compel', *gùndyti* 'tempt', etc.) require the accusative (cf. 3.66):

Ją veřčia vémti.	lit. 'It makes her (ACC) sick (INF).'
Manè seniaĩ viliója pamatýti jū́rą.	'I have been longing to see the sea for a long time.'

The accusative of Patient/Experiencer may be omitted if it is generalized or implied by the context, cf.:

Tỹlų vãkarą taĩp ir tráukia pasiváikščioti.	'On a quiet evening one feels like taking a walk.'

3.71 The infinitive of *bū́ti* 'be' and *tàpti* 'become' used as a copula after an impersonal verb takes either (a) the instrumental case of a noun, or (b) the dative or accusative of an adjective which agrees with the case of a human object:

(a)
Táu	tèks	pabū́ti /	tàpti	vertėju.
you: DAT	have-to: 3. FUT	PREF-be: INF	become: INF	translator: INSTR

'You'll have to act as an interpreter.'

Berniùką	tráukė	bū́ti /	tàpti	lakūnù.
boy: ACC. SG	draw: 3. PAST	be: INF	become: INF	pilot: INSTR

'The boy had an urge to be/become a pilot.'

(b)
Táu	reĩkia		bū́ti	atsargiám.
you: DAT	be necessary: 3. PRES		be: INF	careful: DAT

'You ought to be careful.'

Manè	gùndė		bū́ti	abejìngą	vìskam.
I: ACC	tempt: 3. PAST		be: INF	indifferent: ACC	all: DAT

'I was tempted to be indifferent to everything.'

PATTERNS WITH THE POSSESSIVE DATIVE

3.72 The possessive dative is included in impersonal sentence patterns in the same way as in personal sentences when the possessive part – whole relationship is to be expressed. The animate possessor (whole) is named by the dative and the (body) part, by various case forms and prepositional phrases:

Mònikai   kójas   įskaũdo.
Monica: DAT   foot: ACC. PL   begin-to-ache: 3. PAST
'Monica's feet began to ache.'

Jám   speñgia   ausysè.
he: DAT   ring: 3. PRES   ear: LOC. PL
'There is a ringing in his ears.'

Mán   smìlksi   per   šìrdį.
I: DAT   prick: 3. PRES   across   heart: ACC. SG
'I feel a stitch in the heart.'

The possessive dative is common with verbs denoting pain and similar sensations: *skaudė́ti* 'ache', *maũsti* 'ache', *gélti* 'ache', *dùrti* 'prick', etc.

INFINITIVAL SENTENCES

3.73 A special type of impersonal sentence is formed with the infinitive as a predicate. The semantic subject of the infinitive can be expressed by the dative case of an object (very much as in other types of impersonal sentences), but it often is not expressed if a generalized or indefinite agent is implied.

The pattern for infinitival sentences is:

Inf (– N_d)

Išeĩti   (visíems)!
leave: INF   all: DAT. PL
'Get out (everybody)!'

Personal verbs with a human agent are commonly used in this type of sentence. An infinitive retains its objects and adverbials, the subject being changed into the dative object.

Infinitival sentences are common in emphatic speech and express a variety of modal and emotive meanings by context and/or intonation.

Infinitival sentences are used to express:

(1) Order, request, prohibition (usually without the dative case of an agent):

Vaikaĩ,	dainúoti!
children	sing: INF

'Children, sing!'

(2) Wishing luck (to oneself or another person):

Laimìngai	sugrį̃žti!
happily	return: INF

'Happy return!'

Taĩ	kad	mán	taĩp	pasivažinė́ti!
PRT	PRT	I: DAT	so	travel: INF

'I wish I could travel so too!'

(3) Censure, disapproval:

Tokiám	rimtám	výrui	taĩp	pasiel̃gti!
such	serious	man: DAT	so	behave: INF

'That such a serious man should have behaved so (i.e. disgracefully)!'

Infinitival sentences can also be interrogative:

Ar	mán	čia	lìkti,	ar	išeĩti?
PRT	I: DAT	here	stay: INF	or	leave: INF

'Shall I stay or leave?'

These cases can be viewed as sentences with an omitted modal verb (cf. 3.98).

3.74 The infinitive often alternates with a past gerund in impersonal sentences expressing a question, intention, or a wish, especially in sentences beginning with the particle kàd or an interrogative or relative pronoun:

Kad	taĩp	tą̃	paũkštį	pagáuti /	pagãvus!
PRT	so	that	bird: ACC. SG	catch: INF	catch: PAST. GER

'I wish I (we) could catch that bird!'

Ką̃	čia	mùms	darýti /	padãrius?
what: ACC	here	we: DAT	do: INF	do: PAST. GER

"What could/should we do here (I wonder)?'

NOMINAL SENTENCES

Vardažodìniai sakiniaĩ

3.75 This term is used here to refer to sentences with a compound nominal predicate, i.e. a predicate consisting of a noun or an adjective (or any other nominal part of speech) and a copula (link verb). Instead of a noun, an adverb or an infinitive can be used. The most common link verb is *bū́ti* 'be' devoid of any lexical meaning and having the grammatical meanings of tense, mood, etc. The verbs *darýtis / pasidarýti* 'become', *tàpti* 'become' etc. denoting change and *lìkti* 'remain' are also used as copulas.

Most nominal sentences contain an obligatory subject, and they may contain other grammatically obligatory constituents, e.g.:

Sūnùs lýgus su tėvu.   lit. 'The son is equal with the father.'

They are entered in the sentence patterns below.

However, the obligatory valencies of infinitives and verbal nouns (*keřštas* 'revenge', *užduotìs* 'task', (cf. *uždúoti* 'give a task'), *atlýginimas* 'pay' (cf. *atlýginti* 'to pay') are not included in sentence patterns. They are described in the sections on word groups and verbal sentence patterns.

Since a compound nominal predicate is a syntactic unit, the copula and the nominal part (predicative) are not separated by a dash in the sentence patterns below.

Nominal sentences, like verbal sentences, are classified into personal and impersonal sentences.

Personal sentence patterns
Ia. SUBJECT – PREDICATE

3.76 $N_n - Vf_{cop}N_n$

Pėtras   *yrà*   *darbiniñkas.*
Peter: NOM   is   worker: NOM. SG. MASC
'Peter is a worker.'

This pattern is encountered in sentences which:

(1) Assign the subject referent to a class, e.g.:

Béržas yrà mẽdis.   'The birch is a tree.'
Àš vérgas nebuvaũ ir nebū́siu.   'I haven't been and won't be a slave.'

The predicative noun can have a modifier, especially if it is a noun of generalized meaning (*dáiktas* 'thing', *žmogùs* 'person', *výras* 'man', etc.).

Jū́sų sūnùs bùvo gẽras mokinỹs.   'Your son was an excellent student.'
Tõs bùlvės bùvo pigùs dáiktas.   'Those potatoes were a cheap thing.'

(2) Identify the subject referent:

Màno pavardẽ Stonỹs. 'My surname is Stonys.'

Taĩ bùvo vieniñtelis màno gyvẽnime šū́vis. 'That was the only shot in my life.'

The predicate noun often acquires this function only if modified, as in the latter example; cf. also:

Kir̃vis yrà màno mėgstamiáusias įrankis. 'An ax is my favourite instrument.'

(3) Show the relationship between the referents of a plural subject, whose meaning is determined by the predicate noun:

Mùdu su Jonù senì pažį́stami. 'Jonas and I (lit. 'We two with Jonas') are old acquaintances.'

Taĩp mẽs pasidãrėme gìminės. 'In this way we became relatives.'

3.77 $N_n - Vf_{cop}N_i$

Jìs	*bùvo*	*mókytoju.*
he: NOM	was	teacher: INSTR. SG

'He was a teacher.'

The instrumental case instead of the nominative expresses a temporary characteristic, cf.:

Jų̃ vestùvėse jìs bùvo pãbroliu. 'At their wedding he was best man.'

Ir grýnas vandenė̃lis mùms medumì bùvo. 'At that time pure water was honey to us.'

The instrumental is sometimes replaced by a prepositional phrase *per* + ACC:

Nà, tai lìksiu àš per píemenį. 'Well, I'll remain a shepherd.'

3.78 $N_n - Vf_{cop}Adj_n$

Peĩlis	*bùvo*	*aštrùs.*
knife: NOM. SG	was	sharp: NOM. SG

'The knife was sharp.'

The predicate denotes a qualitative (or quantitative) characteristic of the subject referent. The predicate can also be expressed by any other adjectival word (a participle, adjectival pronoun or an ordinal numeral) (see 1.20, 2).

An adjective is also interchangeable with the following:

(1) the genitive case of a noun or nominal pronoun:

Vìsos síenos bùvo (júodo) mẽdžio.	'All the walls were of (black) wood (GEN).'
Šìtas kambarỹs bùs tàvo.	'This room will be yours.'

(2) the instrumental case of a noun with an obligatory modifier:

Mergáitė bùvo juodaĩs plaukaĩs.	'The girl was black-haired (lit. 'with black hair').'

(3) a prepositional phrase:

Dárbas bùvo ne pagaĩ jėgàs.	'The job was beyond (his) abilities (lit. 'not according to strength').'

(4) the genitive or instrumental case of some nouns with a dependent prepositional phrase:

Àš   esù   vardù   į   dė̃dę.
I   am   name: INSTR   in   uncle: ACC. SG
'I have been named after my uncle.'

Pil̃vas   bùvo   didùmo   sulìg   mažù   kálnu.
belly: NOM. SG   was   bigness: GEN   equal to   small: INSTR   hill: INSTR
'The belly was as big as a small hill.'

(5) a comparative phrase:

Tàvo liežùvis lyg ãdata.	'Your tongue is like a needle.'

In all these sentences the predicate denotes a qualitative characteristic of the subject referent.

Due to the lexical meaning of the predicate adjective, the following sentences express comparison:

Mẽs   víenas   į   kìtą   panãšūs.
we   one: NOM   to   another: ACC   similar: NOM. PL. MASC
'We two are alike.'

Jõnas su Petrù labaĩ skirtìngi.	'John and Peter (lit. 'with Peter: INSTR') are quite different.'

A quantitative characteristic of the subject referent is expressed by cardinal numerals (and the quantitative pronouns *kelì, kelerì, kẽletas, keliólika* meaning 'several'):

Žuviẽs   patiekalaĩ   tebùs   tik   dù.
fish   dish: NOM. PL   will be   only   two: NOM
'There will be only two fish dishes.'

Mẽs bùvome teñ kelì.	lit. 'We were several there.'

3.79 Pron$_{neutr}$/N$_n$ – Vf$_{cop}$Adj$_{neutr}$

Taĩ	bùvo	puikù.
that: NEUTR	was	wonderful: NEUTR

'That was wonderful.'

If the predicate is a neuter adjective or a pronoun or adverb, the subject is either the pronoun *taĩ* 'it, that' or an indefinite pronoun (*kažkàs* 'something', *kas nórs* 'something', *kai kàs* 'something', *vìskas* 'everything'):

Vìskas atródė apsiblaũsę,   'Everything looked dull, commonplace,
kasdiēniška, niūrù.   gloomy.'

Nè,	čià	jaũ	kas nórs	negeraĩ.
no	here	already	something	not-good: ADV

'Well, something is wrong here.'

The subject can also be an infinitive:

Pavar̃gti	ùž	tėvỹnę–	gražù.
suffer: INF	for	homeland: ACC	beautiful: NEUTR

'To suffer for one's homeland is an honour.'

The nominative case of a noun in subject position is not common with a neuter adjective used predicatively; it occurs, however, in sentences like

Ne mētai, o drąsà svarbù.   'Not age, but courage is important.'

In the latter case, an adverb equivalent to a neuter adjective can be used:

Dárbas bùvo véltui.   'The work was in vain.'

Sentences of this type with a neuter adjective (or its equivalent) as a predicate express assessment, or a qualitative or quantitative characteristic of the subject.

3.80 N$_n$ – Vf$_{cop}$Inf

Tàvo	dárbas	yrà	mókytis.
your	work: NOM	is	study: INF. REFL

'Your job is to study.'

In sentences with an infinitive predicate, the subject is usually an abstract noun with a dependent modifier; cf. also:

Tàvo reĩkalas susiràsti   'Your business is to find a new master and
naũją šeimininką ir išeĩti.   leave.'

If the infinitive is a link verb, it takes (1) the dative case of an adjective or (2) the instrumental case of a noun:

(1) *Svarbiáusias dalỹkas*   'The most important thing was to stay
bùvo išlìkti gyvíems.   alive (DAT).'

(2) *Jõ troškìmas – bū́ti mókytoju.*   'His wish is to be a teacher (INSTR).'

3.81 Inf – Vf$_{cop}$N$_n$

Tylė́ti	*bū́tų*	*nusikaltìmas.*
be silent: INF	be: 3. SUBJ	crime: NOM. SG

'It would be a crime to keep silent.'

The predicate is usually an abstract noun, often with a modifier; cf.:

Dúona augìnti yrà alsùs dárbas.   lit. 'To grow (grain for) bread is a tiring job.'

A link verb in subject position combines with the dative case of an adjective or the instrumental of a noun (cf. 3.80):

Bū́ti gerù mókytoju – dìdelis dalỹkas.   'To be a good teacher is a great thing.'

Bū́ti mandagiám – taĩ svarbiáusias reikalãvimas.   'To be polite is the most important requirement.'

3.82 Inf – Vf$_{cop}$Inf

Dìrbti –	*taĩ*	*gyvénti.*
work: INF	it	live: INF

'To work is to live.'

The copula is usually omitted, because such sentences mostly state general truths. Semantically, the subject infinitive is equated with the predicate infinitive; cf. also:

Knygàs rašýti – taĩ ne ãlų gérti.   'To write books is not (the same as) to drink beer.'

Sentences of this type can contain a human noun in the dative case dependent on the subject infinitive:

Mán nedìrbti – taĩ negyvénti.   'For me, not to work is not to live' (cf. 3.84).

IIa. SUBJECT – PREDICATE – OBJECT

3.83   Nominal sentences realizing this pattern can be subdivided into two types.

In sentences of the first type, the predicate requires complementation by an object. The following word forms occur as predicates in these sentences:

(1) Nouns (like *tėvas* 'father', *brólis* 'brother', *giminė̃* 'relative', *draũgas* 'friend', *príešas* 'enemy', etc.) implying symmetrical relations, complemented by the dative or the prepositional phrase *sù* + INSTR:

Baĩtrus	*mán*	*dė̃dė.*
Baltrus: NOM	I: DAT	uncle: NOM. SG

'Baltrus is my uncle.'

Mẽs	*ẽsame*	*gìminės*	*su*	*Stoniaĩs.*
we: NOM	are	relative: NOM. PL	with	Stonys: INSTR.PL

'We are relatives with the Stonys family.'

The predicate is sometimes expressed by *ùž* + ACC:

Žìrgas bùs mán už draugẽlį   'The horse will be (like) a friend to me.'
(cf. *draugeliù*).

The dative case or prepositional phrase of an object is semantically equivalent to the possessive genitive, cf.:

Baĩtrus màno dė̃dė.	'Baltrus is my uncle.'
Mẽs ẽsame Stonių̃ gìminės.	'We are the Stonys' relatives.'
Žìrgas bùs màno draũgas.	'The horse will be my friend.'

(2) Adjectives, namely:

(a) the adjectives *pìlnas* 'full', *kùpinas* 'full', *reikalìngas* 'necessary, requiring', *veȓtas* 'worthy, worth', *turtìngas* 'rich', etc. which govern the genitive case:

Obelìs pilnà žiedų̃.	'The apple-tree is full of blossoms.'
Šìtas nãmas veȓtas dìdelių pinigų̃.	'This house is worth a lot of money.'

(b) the adjectives *aȓtimas* 'near, close (to)', *būdìngas* 'peculiar (to), characteristic (of)', *naudìngas* 'useful', *palankùs* 'favourable (to)', *pavojìngas* 'dangerous', *reikalìngas* 'necessary', etc. which require the dative case:

Vertìmas aȓtimas originãlui.	'The translation is close to the original.'
Jìs bùs mùms naudìngas.	'He will be useful to us.'

(c) the adjective *paténkintas* 'pleased' which governs the instrumental:

Jìs bùvo vìskuo paténkintas.   'He was pleased with everything.'

(d) a number of adjectives require a prepositional phrase:

Jìs su manimì bevéik lýgus.	'He is almost equal (in height) with me.'
Jìs panašùs į̃ tė́vą.	'He looks like (lit. 'is similar to') his father.'

The prepositional phrase *ùž* + ACC is obligatory with the comparative form of adjectives:

Vìlnius yrà didèsnis už Kaũną.   'Vilnius is bigger than Kaunas.'

This sentence is synonymous to:

Vìlnius yrà didèsnis kaip/negù Kaũnas. lit. 'Vilnius is bigger than Kaunas.'

If a predicative adjective is in the superlative form it requires *iš* + GEN:

Marýtė laimingiáusia iš visų mergáičių. 'Marytė is the happiest of all the girls.'

The genitive or the dative case form of a noun is sometimes interchangeable with an infinitive, cf.:

Žmogùtis tóks nevertas pažiūrėti/dėmesio.	lit. 'The little man is quite unworthy to look at/of attention (GEN).'
Sąlygos palañkios mókytis/mókslui.	lit.' The conditions are favourable to study (INF)/ for studies (DAT).'

Adjectives are used in the neuter form if the subject does not require agreement in gender, in which case they retain their object valency:

Taĩ verta pagyrìmo.	'That is worthy of praise (GEN).'
Tàs paskyrìmas bùvo lýgu ištrėmìmui.	'That appointment was equal to an exile (DAT).'
Taĩ bùvo panašù į skandãlą.	'That looked like a scandal.'
Geraĩ pailsėti dabar̃ svarbiaũ už vìską.	'To have a good rest is now more important than anything.'

3.84 Sentences of the second type contain the dative case of a human noun referring to the experiencer of a state. The predicate is a neuter adjective, sometimes an adverb or a noun with a similar meaning (*gėda* 'shame', *garbė̃* 'honour', *var̃gas* 'misery', and the like):

Vìsa taĩ mán naũja.	'All that is new to me.'
Jái niẽkas nemíela.	'Nothing gives her pleasure' (lit. 'is pleasant to her').
O taĩ jám bùvo dìdelė garbė̃.	'That was a great honour to him.'

The dative of a human noun is also possible in sentences of the pattern N_n – $Vf_{cop}Inf$ – N_d, where the predicate is the infinitive of a verb of perception (*matýti* 'see', *regėti* 'see', *girdėti* 'hear', *jaũsti* 'feel', etc.), e.g.:

Iš	teñ	jám	vìskas	aiškiaũ	matýti.
from	there	he: DAT	everything: NOM	clearer	see: INF

'He can see everything better from there.'

Cf. the corresponding sentence with a finite verb (without the modal meaning):

Jìs vìską aiškiaũ mãto.	'He sees everything better.'

These sentences often occur without the dative case of a human noun, e.g.:

Pro durìs bùvo girdė́ti balsaĩ.	'One could hear voices behind the door.'
Visuř numanýti šveñtė.	'One could feel a festive mood (lit. 'a holiday') everywhere.'

3.85 The adjective *skolìngas* 'indebted', when used predicatively, governs a direct and a dative object:

Jìs mán skolìngas dù litùs.	'He owes me two litas.'

Impersonal sentence patterns

3.86 Impersonal nominal sentences denote either a state that is not attributed to anything, or the state of a patient or an experiencer referred to by the dative case, or a qualitative characteristic of a thing referred to by the genitive case.

VIa. PREDICATE

3.87 $Vf_{cop}N_n$

Bùvo   žiemà.
was   winter: NOM
'It was winter.'

Nouns denoting temporal concepts such as seasons, weekdays, parts of the day, etc., and also natural phenomena and states are typically used in this pattern:

Bùvo vėlùs žiemõs vãkaras.	'It was a late winter evening.'
Rytój bùs sekmãdienis.	'Tomorrow will be Sunday.'
Vãkar bùvo audrà.	'There was a storm yesterday.'
Klãsėje bùvo mirtinà tylà.	'There was a dead silence in the classroom.'

The present tense form of the copula *bū́ti* 'be' is usually omitted (zero copula):

Kárštas vãsaros vidùrdienis.	'(It is) a hot summer afternoon.'
Šiañdien pirmãdienis.	'Today (is) Monday.'
Vãkaras. Visuř tylà.	'(It is) evening. Silence everywhere.'

Sentences of this pattern without a copula can be used to inform about a thing or a phenomenon.

Gražùs paupỹs. Kálvos. Lakštiñgalos.   lit. 'Beautiful riverside. Hills. Nightingales.'
Štaĩ táu trỹs rõžės.   'Here (are) three roses for you.'

Such sentences without a copula are often termed nominative sentences.

3.88   Vf$_{cop}$Adj$_{neutr}$/Adv

Bùvo   *káršta.*
was   hot: NEUTR
'It was hot.'

These sentences usually denote states, viz. (a) natural phenomena or states often related to a place or time, (b) psychological states or experiences, (c) descriptive assessments; cf. respectively:

(1) *Gūdù búdavo miškè.*   'It used to be gloomy in the forest.'
Saulė́ta, šviesù.   lit. '(It is) sunny, light (ADJ).'
Tylù vakaraĩs.   '(It is) quiet in the evenings.'

(2) *Dabař jõ síeloj taĩp ramù, džiugù.*   lit. 'Now (it is) so quiet, joyful in his soul.'
Taĩp malonù pavė́sy.   '(It is) so pleasant in the shade.'

(3) *O dabař vis prasčiaũ ir prasčiaũ.*   'And now (it is getting) worse and worse.'

Adverbs seldom occur predicatively, except those with the suffix *-yn* which are used with the desemanticized semi-link verb *eĩti* 'go, become':

Nuo pusiáukelės ė̃mė eĩti šviesỹn.   'From midway it began growing lighter.'

VIIa. PREDICATE – OBJECT

The obligatory structural component of a nominal sentence is the dative or genitive case of an animate noun encoding a patient or experiencer. Four patterns are distinguished here.

3.89   Vf$_{cop}$Adj$_{neutr}$/Adv – N$_d$

Jám   *bùvo*   *pìkta.*
he: DAT   be: 3. PAST   angry: NEUTR
'He felt anger.'

The predicate here denotes a psychological or physical state experienced by the object referent, sometimes its assessment by the speaker; cf.:

Mergáitei kasdiẽn blogiaũ.   'The girl's state is deteriorating each day' (lit. 'It is worse to the girl each day').

Bùs arkliáms sunkù.   'It will be hard on the horses.'

Ar táu pas mùs bùvo negeraĩ?   'Didn't you feel well at our place?'

The dative object can be omitted if its referent is implied by the context or generalized:

Burnojè šleikštù. 'There is a bad taste in the mouth.'

Instead of a neuter adjective, the neuter form of a pronoun can be used as a predicate:

Mán víena, táu kìta. 'One (thing) (is) for me, (something) another for you.'

3.90 $Vf_{cop}N_n - N_d$

Vaĩkui tiktaĩ mētai. 'The child is only one year old' (lit. '(It is) only a year to the child').

Kokià táu garbẽ visamè káime. lit. 'What glory for you in the whole village.'

The predicate noun in these sentences denotes a state.

3.91 $Vf_{cop}N_g - N_d$

Vaĩkui nèrà nè mētų. 'The child is not even a year old.'

Sentences of this pattern are negative transforms of affirmative sentences with the nominative case of a predicate noun (see 3.90); cf.:

Mán tenaĩ nebùvo gyvēnimo. lit. 'There wasn't any life for me there' (i.e. 'Life was hard for me there').

– Mán teñ tai bùvo gyvēnimas. lit. 'It was life for me there' (i.e. 'Life was easy for me there').

3.92 $N_g - Vf_{cop}AdvQuant$

Grỹbų	*bùvo*	*daũg.*
mushroom: GEN. PL	was	many

'Mushrooms were plentiful.'

In these sentences, the genitive of indefinite quantity is characterized by a predicate with a quantitative meaning. The predicate can be:

(1) an adverb of quantity, as in the above sentence and in:

Sniẽgo bùvo daũg/menkaĩ. 'There was much/little snow' (lit. 'Snow (GEN) was much/little').

(2) a quantitative pronoun:

Výrų bùvo tik kēletas. 'There were only a few men.'

If quantity is expressed by a cardinal numeral the genitive case can marginally alternate with the nominative:

Brólių bùvo penkì.	'There were five brothers.'
– *Bróliai bùvo penkì.*	lit. 'The brothers were five.'

(3) a noun denoting quantity:

Žmonių bùvo daugýbė.	'There was a multitude of people (there).'

(4) a neuter adjective implying a quantitative characteristic:

Sniẽgo gilù.	'The snow is deep' (lit. '(It is) deep of snow').
Dabař dienõs ìlga, naktiẽs trum̃pa.	'Now days are long, nights are short' (lit. 'Long of the day, short of the night').

(5) prepositional phrase:

Vandeñs čià iki kẽlių.	'There is water (GEN) up to the knees here.'
Vargų̃ bùvo be gãlo.	'There were troubles (GEN) without end.'

3.93 $N_g - Vf_{cop} Adj_g/Num_g$

Tė́vo	*nebẽrà*	*gývo.*
father: GEN	not-be: 3. PRES	alive: GEN

'Father is dead.'

This pattern is encountered in negative transforms of affirmative personal sentences with the nominative case of a predicate adjective or ordinal numeral, cf.:

Nė víeno óbuolio nebùvo sveĩko.	'Not a single apple was sound.'
– *Visì obuoliaĩ bùvo sveikì.*	'All the apples were sound' (cf. 3.78).
Niẽko nėrà ámžino.	'Nothing is eternal.'
Kriáušės teñ nė vienõs nėrà.	'There is not a single pear-tree there.'

In this pattern the predicate expressed by any adjective substitute (e.g. a participle) is also in the genitive case; e.g.:

Tókio žõdžio nėrà išlìkusio.	lit. 'Such a word (GEN) is not retained (GEN).'

The predicate can also be an emphatic phrase consisting of the negation *nẽ* 'not even' and the genitive case of a noun:

Arklių̃ nebùvo nẽ pė́dsako.	'There was not the slightest sign (lit. 'footprint') of the horses.'
Sáulės nẽ spindulė̃lio.	'There isn't a ray of sun(light).'

VIIIa. PREDICATE – OBJECT – OBJECT

There are two patterns of this type.

3.94 Vf_cop Adv – N_g – N_d

Mán	gaĩla	tavęs.
I: DAT	pity	you: GEN

'I am sorry for you.'

The adverbs *ganà* 'enough', *gaĩla* 'pity' and the nouns *stokà* 'lack, shortage', *gėda* 'shame' are used predicatively in this pattern. They express a state experienced by the human referent in the dative case:

| Šeĩmai bùvo ganà sàvo rūpesčių. | 'The family had enough of its own worries.' |
| Jám vìs stokà dúonos. | 'He is always short of bread.' |

Just as in the other patterns the dative case of a human noun can be omitted:

| Gaĩla ir tėvo, ir vaikų. | 'One is sorry for both the father and the children.' |

3.95 Vf_cop Inf – N_g – N_d

Mán	nematýti	sáulės.
I: DAT	not-see: INF	sun: GEN

'I can't see the sun.'

Sentences of this pattern are negative transforms of personal sentences like

| Mán matýti sáulė. | 'I (can) see the sun' (3.84). |

SENTENCES WITH AN INFINITIVE

3.96 In impersonal sentences a neuter adjective or an adverb denoting state when used predicatively (see 3.89) often takes an infinitive. These sentences express the state of an experiencer or a patient designated by the dative case:

Mán nepatogù sėdėti.	'It is awkward for me to sit.'
Sunkù Pėtrui gyvénti.	lit. 'It is hard for Peter to live.'
Jíems bùvo nepàkeliama dìrbti kartù.	'It was intolerable for them to work together.'
Bepìgu táu taĩp kalbėti.	'It is all very well for you to say that.'
(Cf. also *Táu laĩkas išeĩti.*	'It is time for you to go.')

The dative is often omitted here:

| Paskuĩ bùs vėlù grį̃žti. | 'After that it will be late to return.' |
| Blóga/Blogaĩ turėti daũg pinigų. | 'It is bad to have much money.' |

The infinitive is often interchangeable with a past gerund:

Gėra bū́tų su juõ susitìkus.   'It would be nice to meet (lit. 'meeting') him.'

3.97 The infinitive of a link verb is combined with (1) the dative case of an adjective or (2) the instrumental case of a noun, which agree with the dative case of the semantic subject in gender and number:

(1) Gėrà žmõgui bū́ti sveikám.   'It's good for a person (DAT. SG. MASC) to be healthy (DAT. SG. MASC).'

(2) Kiekvienám malonù pasidarýti dìdvyriu.   lit. 'It's pleasant for everyone (DAT. SG. MASC) to become a hero (INSTR. SG. MASC).'

Variation of constituents in sentence patterns

3.98 The constituents of most sentence patterns (designated by the abbreviations used above) may have alternative means of expression.

The finite form of a verb (Vf) can alternate with a verbal group comprised of a phasal (*pradė́ti* 'begin', *im̃ti* 'begin, start', *baĩgti* 'finish', *liáutis* 'stop', etc.) or a modal verb (*galė́ti* 'be able (to)', *pajė̃gti* 'be able', *turė́ti* 'have (to)', *privalė́ti* 'be obliged (to), have (to)') and an infinitive. A modal or phasal verb is semantically subordinated to the infinitive and modifies its meaning. The phasal meanings can also be expressed by prefixes, in which case a compound verbal phasal predicate can be interchangeable with a prefixed verb: *pradė́jo giedóti = pragýdo* '(he) began to chant'; *baĩgė válgyti = paválgė* '(he) finished eating'. The modal meaning 'be able (to)' can also be expressed by a prefix: *gãli eĩti = paeĩna* '(he) can walk'.

Verbal groups with a phasal or modal verb like *pradė́jo rė̃kti/váikščioti* '(he) began to shout/walk', *baĩgė dìrbti/rašýti* '(he) finished working/writing', *pradė́jo/baĩgė lýti/snìgti* 'it began/stopped raining/snowing'; *galiù váikščioti/dìrbti* 'I can walk/work' are viewed here as variants of the simple predicates *rė̃kė* 'shouted', *váikščiojo* 'walked', *dìrbo* 'worked', *rãšė* 'wrote', *lìjo* '(it) rained', *snìgo* '(it) snowed', etc., respectively. For this reason, no special patterns are given for them.

A number of phasal verbs are used either with an infinitive or a past active participle:

lióvėsi rašýti/rãšęs, -iusi, -ę   '(he, she, they) stopped writing'
nustójo lýti/lìję   '(it) stopped raining'

A phasal verb denoting beginning can be omitted in emphatic speech, an infinitive alone representing the predicate:

Žandãrai kósėt, čiáudėt,	'The gendarmes (started) to cough,
ir iškurnėjo kéikdamiesi.	sneeze, and hurried out cursing.'

3.99 Inflected nouns, prepositional phrases and adverbs can alternate with syntactically equivalent word groups. Thus, for instance, instead of the nominative or another case of a noun, word groups like *daũg žmonių̃* 'many people', *dẽšimt knỹgų* 'ten books', *tė́vas su sūnumì* lit. 'father with son (INSTR)', *mẽs su draugù* lit. 'we with the friend' (= 'my friend and I'), *minių̃ mìnios* 'crowds upon (lit. 'of') crowds', *áuksas sidãbras* lit. 'silver gold', *àš pàts* ' I myself', etc. can be used.

3.100 The accusative case of a direct object alternates with the genitive of indefinite quantity (see 2.12); e.g.:

Mergà àtnešė dúoną.	'The maid brought the bread (ACC).'
– *Mergà àtnešė dúonos.*	'The maid brought some bread (GEN).'

(On the use of the genitive of indefinite quantity determined by the verbal meaning see 2.11, 3.56, 60.)

The genitive of indefinite quantity can also be used instead of the nominative in subject position; cf.:

Atvažiãvo svečiaĩ/svečių̃.	'The guests (NOM)/Some guests (GEN) arrived.'

The genitive of the subject is in concord with the genitive of the predicate, cf.:

Viẽtos bùs láisvos.	'The seats will be vacant (NOM).'
– *Viẽtų bùs laisvų̃.*	'Some places will be vacant' (= 'There will be some vacant seats').

3.101 With verbs of sense and mental perception and the like the object position can be filled by (1) a gerund, (2) a gerundial phrase or (3) a subordinate clause:

(**1**) *Išgirdaũ griaũsmą/griáudžiant.*	'I heard a clap of thunder (ACC)/ thundering (PRES. GER).'
Visì láukė atšilìmo/atšỹlant.	'Everybody was waiting for a thaw (GEN)/ thawing (PRES. GER).'
(**2**) *Jaučiù vė́ją pùčiant.*	'I feel a wind (ACC) blowing (PRES. GER).'
(**3**) *Jiẽ supràto, kad vãsara baĩgėsi.*	'They realized that the summer was over.'

This alternation is often possible in the same sentence; cf.:

Mačiaũ, kaip jìs grį̃žo/jį̃ grį̃žtant/jõ sugrį̃žimą.	lit. 'I saw how he returned/him returning (GER)/his return (ACC).'

3.102 A gerund or a gerundial clause occurs in object position after verbs denoting:

(1) speech and related actions:

Tar̃nas prànešė žmõgų atė̃jus su reĩkalu.	'The servant announced a man (ACC) who had come (PAST. GER) on business.'

(2) perception:

Kur̃ girdė́jai gaidžiùs lójant, šunìs gíedant?	'Where have you heard roosters (ACC) barking (PRES. GER), dogs (ACC) crowing (PRES. GER)?'
Mačiaũ brólį ateĩnant.	'I saw my brother (ACC) coming (PRES. GER).'

(3) mental processes:

Jìs pramãnė manè ilgaĩ miẽgant.	'He thought I (ACC) slept (PRES. GER) (too) long.'

(4) hope, belief:

Reĩkia tikė́ti jį̃ greĩtai grį̃šiant.	'One should believe he (ACC) would return (FUT. GER) soon.'

(5) finding and leaving:

Senẽlė rãdo/palìko manè tùpint/tùpintį kampè.	'Grandmother found/left me (ACC) squatting (PRES. GER/PART) in the corner.'

The accusative (sometimes the genitive) here names the performer of the embedded gerundial action.

If the performer of the embedded action is coreferential with the subject of the sentence, a participle in the nominative case is used instead of a gerund; it occurs mostly with the corresponding reflexive verbs of the same lexical groups as above:

(1)
Jìs gýrėsi daũg mãtęs.	'He boasted of having seen (PAST. PART) much.'
Žmogùs pasiskùndė netẽkęs dárbo.	'The man complained of having lost (PAST. PART) his job.'

(2)
Jì ne(si)jaũčia klaĩdą padãriusi.	'She doesn't feel she has made (PAST. PART) a mistake.'
Tėvaĩ mãtė sūnaũs nepérkalbėsią.	'The parents saw they wouldn't talk (FUT. PART) their son out of it.'

(3)
Kitì tãriasi vìską žìną.	'Some people think they know (PRES. PART) everything.'

Viñcas įsitìkino geraĩ pir̃kęs.	'Vincas was convinced he had made a good purchase (lit. 'having bought well') (PAST. PART).'
(4) *Výlėsi turė́siąs gẽrą žmóną.*	'He hoped he would have (FUT. PART) a good wife.'
Dabar̃ tikiúosi ištéisinamas.	'Now I hope to be acquitted (PRES. PASS. PART).'
(5) *Pasilikaũ begulį̃s lóvoje.*	'I remained lying (PRES. PART) in bed.'

In the following case, the present passive participle alone is possible:

Katẽ láukia paglóstoma.	'The cat is waiting to be stroked (PRES. PASS. PART).'

The nominative case of a participle is also used in object position after verbs such as *apsimèsti* 'pretend, feign', *susilaikýti* 'refrain (from)' and the like:

Mažàsis brólis dė́josi niẽko nežìnąs.	'The little brother pretended he knew (PRES. PART) nothing.'
Jìs apsìmeta sergą̃s.	'He pretends to be ill (PRES. PART).'
Kareĩvis võs susilaĩkė neiššóvęs.	'The soldier hardly refrained from shooting (PAST. PART).'

Present passive participles can also occur after verbs meaning 'ask', 'want', 'agree' (and with their antonyms); e.g.:

Kõ norė́si màno dúodamas?
what: GEN want: 2. SG. FUT I: GEN give: PRES. PASS. PART. NOM. SG
'What will you want me to give you?'

Arklỹs bìjo mùšamas.	'The horse is afraid of being beaten (PRES. PASS. PART).'
Jìs léidosi įkalbamas.	'He let himself be talked into it (PRES. PASS. PART).'

In most of these cases the participle (or participial clause) is interchangeable with a completive subordinate clause (see II.5.151) ; cf.:

Jìs jaũtėsi negalį̃s dìrbti.	'He felt unable to work.'
– *Jìs jaũtė, kad negãli dìrbti.*	'He felt that he couldn't work.'
Džiaugiúosi sugrį̃žęs.	'I rejoice at having returned.'
– *Džiaugiúosi, kad sugrįžaũ.*	'I rejoice that I have returned.'
Sakeĩ ateĩsiąs	'You said you would come.'
(= *Sakeĩ, kad ateĩsi*).	

3.103 A gerund takes the subject position (or functions as part of a complex subject) if the predicate is expressed by the infinitive of the verbs of perception *girdė́ti* 'hear', *matýti* 'see', *numanýti* 'guess', *jaũsti* 'feel' or by their reflexive derivatives:

Jaũ matýti žą̃sys par̃skrendant	'One can already see the geese (NOM) return (PRES. GER/that the geese are returning).'
(cf.: *kad žą̃sys par̃skrenda*).	
Girdė́ti/Pasigir̃do griáudžiant.	'One can hear/One could hear thundering
(Cf.: *Girdė́ti griaũsmas/*	(GER)/thunder (NOM)/that it is thundering.'
kad griáudžia.)	

3.104 The objective infinitive in some patterns is interchangeable with a completive subordinate clause:

Prašiaũ tė́vą sugrį̃žti.	'I asked father to return.'
– *Prašiaũ tė́vą, kad sugrį̃žtų.*	'I asked father that he return.'

Omission and interchangeability of constituents

3.105 A usually obligatory constituent of a sentence pattern can be omitted as a result of the context or speech situation. This yields a grammatically incomplete sentence variant the meaning of which, however, is clear.

The meaning of a sentence may change if an object or an adverbial is not expressed. For instance, a sentence may denote a temporary or permanent characteristic of the subject, instead of a concrete action, if the object is omitted:

Arkliaĩ pasibaĩdė akmeñs.	'The horses took fright at a stone.'
– *Arkliaĩ baĩdosi.*	'The horses take fright (easily).'
Jìs labaĩ didžiúojasi sàvo arkliaĩs.	'He is very proud of his horses.'
– *Jìs labaĩ didžiúojasi*	'He is very proud (= is arrogant).'
(= *yrà labaĩ išdidùs*).	
Jì mą̃stė apie ãteitį.	'She thought of the future.'
– *Jì sėdėjo ir mą̃stė.*	'She sat deep in thought (lit. 'sat and thought').'

This case is traditionally referred to as the absolutive use of transitive verbs.

In other cases, an object is often omitted if it is unambiguously implied by the meaning of the verb (1), sometimes of the verb and other components (2):

(1) *Jìs*	*apsiãvė*	*(bãtais).*
he	put-on-shoes	(shoe: INSTR. PL)
'He put on shoes.'		

(2) *Móterys àpgaubė* 'The women veiled the bride (with a
jáunąją (núometu). married woman's head-dress).'

A direct object may be sometimes omitted to imply an unspecified or generalized referent, e.g.:

Visì dabař tik pardúoda, 'Everyone is only selling now, no one is
niēkas nèperka. buying.'

An indirect object is more often omitted in such cases, e.g.:

Raudóna spalvà primena rožès. 'The red colour reminds (one) of roses' (implied DAT – generalized referent).

Jìs žadėjo ateĩti. 'He promised to come' (implied DAT – unspecified referent).

Už gērą dárbą vyriausýbė 'The government awarded him for good
jį̃ apdovanójo. work' (implied INSTR – unspecified referent).

Kiaušìnis vìštą móko (kõ?). 'An egg teaches the hen' (implied GEN – generalized referent).

A prepositional phrase can also be omitted:

Màno duktẽ ìšteka (už kõ?). 'My daughter is getting married (to whom?)' (unspecified referent).

Jìs gãvo láišką (iš kõ?). 'He received a letter (from whom?)' (unspecified referent).

Pìktas šuõ namùs gìna (nuo kõ?). 'A fierce dog protects home (from whom?)' (generalized referent).

Omission of two objects is also possible:

Jì amžinaĩ skùndžiasi (kám? kuõ?). 'She always complains (to whom? about what?).'

In these cases the objects are omitted because the information is irrelevant.

3.106 In impersonal sentences the dative or the accusative object is often omitted to express a generalized or an unspecified semantic subject or object, cf.:

Mán	*geraĩ*	*miẽgasi.*
I: DAT	well	sleep: 3. PRES. REFL
'I (can) sleep well.'		

Lỹjant	*geraĩ*	*miẽgasi.*
rain: PRES. GER	well	sleep: 3. PRES. REFL

'One sleeps well when it rains.'

Manè dùsina.
I: ACC suffocate: 3. PRES
'I am suffocating.'

Tókiu	*óru*	*labaĩ*	*dùsina.*
such	weather: INSTR. SG	very	suffocate: 3. PRES

'In such weather it is hard to breathe.'

3.107 Sometimes, an object can be replaced by an adverbial modifier of place or manner; cf. respectively:

(1) *Anglių kasỹklai/kasỹkloje jìs atìdavė sàvo sveikãtą.*
'He lost (lit. 'gave') his health to the coal mine (DAT)/in the coal mine (LOC).'

Jonùkas reikalìngas namìškiams/priẽ namų̃.
'Johnny is needed (lit. 'necessary') by his family (DAT)/at home (PREP. GEN).'

(2) *Àš nugirdaũ visái kìtką/kitaĩp.*
lit. 'I heard something different (ACC)/quite otherwise (ADV).'

Turbū̃t Diẽvas tõ/taĩp norė́jo.
lit. ' God must have wanted that (GEN)/so (ADV).'

An adverbial of place can be omitted if its absence is compensated for by an adverbial of purpose:

Siunčiaũ jį̃ dúonos (į̃ parduotùvę).   'I sent him for bread (to the shop).'

Sometimes an adverbial can be substituted for an (inanimate) subject, which results in an impersonal sentence, e.g.:

Vaĩkui	*daržẽlyje /*	*daržẽlis*	*nepatìko.*
child: DAT. SG	kindergarten: LOC	kindergarten: NOM	not-liked

'The boy didn't like it in the kindergarten/didn't like the kindergarten.'

Štaĩ	*kaĩp /*	*kàs*	*kar̃tais*	*atsitiñka*	*žmõgui.*
thus	how	what: NOM	sometimes	happens	man: DAT. SG

'That's how it/what sometimes happens to a person.'

Relations between sentence patterns
ACTIVE AND PASSIVE SENTENCES

3.108 If the active voice of the predicate is changed into the passive, the sentence structure undergoes a number of changes: the nominative of the subject is replaced by the genitive or it is omitted. The object of a transitive verb becomes the subject in the nominative case. The sentence structure changes as follows:

$N_n^1 - Vf - N_a^2 \Rightarrow N_n^2 - Vf_p - N_g^1$

In a passive construction, the passive participle assumes either the masculine or feminine (1) or (rarely) the neuter form (2):

Tėvas skaĩto laĩkraštį.   'Father is reading a newspaper.' ⇒

(1) *Laĩkraštis   yrà   skaĩtomas   tėvo.*
newspaper: is   read: PRES. PASS.   father: GEN. SG
NOM. SG. MASC   PART. MASC

(2) *Laĩkraštis   yrà   skaĩtoma   tėvo.*
newspaper: is   read: PRES. PASS.   father: GEN
MASC   PART. NEUTR
'The newspaper is (being) read by father.'

In the sentences with the neuter form of the passive participle (without an agentive genitive) the object may retain its accusative case form:

Rãšoma   laĩškas /   laĩšką.
write: PRES. PASS.   letter: NOM. SG   letter: ACC. SG
PART. NEUTR
'A letter is (being) written.'

Per̃kama   grūdaĩ /   grū́dus.
buy: PRES. PASS.   grain: NOM. PL   grain: ACC. PL
PART. NEUTR
'Grain is (being) bought.'

Sentences with the neuter form of a passive participle may express special meanings (see II. 5.74, 77).

Sentences with the passive form of the transitive verbs *atstováuti* 'represent', *vadováuti* 'lead, guide' taking an object in the dative case and of verbs taking an object in the genitive case (*láukti* 'wait (for)', *ieškóti* 'look (for)', etc.) can be transformed in two ways:

(a) The object acquires the nominative case form and the passive participle agrees with it in gender, e.g.:

Jìs atstováuja kìtai pártijai.   'He represents another party.' ⇒
Kità pártija yrà (jõ) atstováujama.   'Another party is represented (by him).'
Šeimininkė̃ láukia svečių̃.   'The hostess is waiting for the guests.' ⇒
Svečiaĩ yrà laukiamì (šeimininkė̃s).   'The guests are expected (by the hostess).'

The sentence structure changes as follows:

$N_n^1 - Vf - N_{g/d}^2 \Rightarrow N_n^2 - Vf_p - N_g^1$

(**b**) The object retains its case form and the passive participle is neuter; thus the transform is an impersonal sentence:

Pártijai yrà (jõ) atstováujama.	'The party (DAT) is represented (PRES. PASS. PART. NEUTR) (by him)' (or: 'There is a representation of the party').
Svečių yrà láukiama.	'Guests (GEN. PL) are expected (PRES. PASS. PART. NEUTR).'

In this case the sentence undergoes the following change:

$N_n^1 - Vf - N_{g/d}^2 \Rightarrow N_g^1 - Vf_p - N_{g/d}^2$

The two passive transforms of an active sentence differ pragmatically in the distribution of emphasis: in (a) the object of the active sentence is made more prominent and raised to subject, whereas in (b) the verbal meaning is more prominent, the agentive genitive being usually omitted.

Personal sentences with intransitive verbs are also transformed into impersonal passive sentences, the participle assuming the neuter form:

Tėvas miẽga. 'Father is asleep.' $\Rightarrow$

Tėvo   miẽgama.
father: GEN   sleep: PRES. PASS. PART. NEUTR
'Father is asleep.'

The structure here changes as follows: $N_n - Vf \Rightarrow Vf_p - N_g$.

3.109 A compound nominal predicate can also take the passive form, both the subject and the predicate acquiring the genitive case form, cf.:

Jìs bùvo kareĩvis.   'He was a soldier.' $\Rightarrow$

Jõ	*bū́ta*	*kareĩvio.*
he: GEN	be: PAST. PASS. PART. NEUTR	soldier: GEN. SG

'(They say) he was a soldier.'

The agentive genitive is obligatory in these sentences, which distinguishes them from other passive constructions.

3.110 Passive transformation usually involves a change in the communicative sentence structure and deletion of the agent, therefore an active sentence and its passive transform are not always interchangeable. On the other hand, many passive sentences with a deleted agent cannot be replaced by the active counterpart.

Passive constructions with a deleted agent are widely used to express an action with an indefinite, or generalized, or unknown, or irrelevant agent, instead of so-called indefinite-personal sentences with a zero subject, whose usage is rather restricted in Lithuanian; e.g.:

Čià pardúodamos knỹgos.	'Books are sold here.'

Cf. also impersonal sentences with the neuter passive form:

Laiškų̃ negáuta.	'No letters are received.'
Taĩp nedãroma.	'This (lit. 'so') is not done' ('One can't do so').
Sālėje šókama.	'There is dancing in the hall.'

PERSONAL AND IMPERSONAL SENTENCES

3.111 In many cases, a personal sentence alternates with an impersonal sentence without a change in the predicate. Less commonly, this change is marked in the verb. The nominative case of the subject of a personal sentence usually alternates with an oblique case or a prepositional phrase.

3.112 The predicate retains its grammatical form (except person) in the following cases.

(1) $N_n - N_d$. A number of relational verbs (of the lexical type *užtèkti* 'have/be enough', *trū́kti* 'lack, be short (of)', etc.) and some others occur in two sentence patterns, either with the nominative or the dative case of the semantic subject (Possessor, Patient or Experiencer), cf.:

Mẽs pritrū́kome pinigų̃.	'We (NOM) ran short of money.'
– *Mùms pritrū́ko pinigų̃.*	'We (DAT) ran short of money.'
Ligónis/ligóniui pagerė́jo.	'The patient (NOM/DAT) improved.'
Jìs/jám gailė́jo šuñs.	'He (NOM/DAT) felt pity for the dog.'

(2) $N_n - N_a$. Verbs of physical sensations (like *skaudė́ti* 'ache', *gélti* 'ache', *niežė́ti* 'itch', *peršė́ti* 'smart', etc.) are used interchangeably with the nominative or the accusative case of noun denoting a body part and the dative case of a human noun, thus forming a personal or an impersonal sentence:

Mán skaũda galvà/gálvą.	'I have a headache' (lit. 'To me (the) head (NOM/ACC) aches').
Jám gerklė̃/gérklę peřši.	'His (DAT) throat (NOM/ACC) smarts' (i.e., 'He has a sore throat').
Mán gẽlia šónas/šóną.	'I (DAT) have a stitch in the side (NOM/ACC)' (i.e., 'My side aches').

Impersonal sentences with the accusative case are more common in speech.

(3) $N_n - N_i$. The nominative case alternates with the instrumental in sentences with numerous verbs of the lexical types illustrated here:

(a) *Vaĩką išbėrė spuogaĩ/spuogaĩs.*   'Pimples (NOM/INSTR) covered (lit. 'broke out') the child.'

(b) *Kambaryjè kvėpia gėlės/gėlėmìs.*   lit. 'Flowers (NOM/INSTR) smell sweet in the room.' (Or: 'In the room flowers smell sweet/it smells of flowers.')

(c) *Nuo ẽžero pàdvelkė vėsùmas/vėsumù.*   'Cool air (NOM/INSTR) drifted up from the lake.'

(d) *Dañgų užtráukė dėbesys/debesimìs.*   'Clouds (NOM/INSTR) covered the sky.'

Impersonal sentences emphasize the spontaneous nature of a state or process.

(4) $N_n - N_l$/PrepP. In sentences with a number of verbs of sensation the nominative of a body part alternates with the locative case, the Experiencer being denoted by the dative case:

Mán ūžia galvà/galvojè.   'There is a buzzing in my (DAT) head (NOM/LOC).'

A number of verbs take the nominative case of a noun with the meaning of location alternating with the locative case and/or a prepositional phrase denoting direction:

(a) *Daržaĩ/daržuosè/ po daržùs dar žaliúoja.*   'The gardens (NOM/LOC/prepACC) are green yet.'

This and similar verbs can also take a patient noun in subject position:

Daržuosè dar žaliúoja žolė̃.   'The grass is green yet in the garden.'

(b) *Manè tráukia ẽžeras/ prie ẽžero.*   'The lake (NOM) attracts me (ACC)'/'I (ACC) feel like going to the lake (Prep GEN).'

In both cases impersonal sentences emphasize the spontaneous character of a state.

Verbs with the prefix *pri-* of the following type governing the genitive case of indefinite quantity display a similar alternation in the form of a noun with the meaning of location:

Kiẽmas /   į   kiẽmą   privažiãvo   žmonių̃.
courtyard: NOM   to   courtyard: ACC   came   people: GEN
'A lot of people came into (filled) the courtyard.'

Trobà /	*trobojè /*	*į*	*trobą*	*prisirinko dū́mų.*
cottage: NOM	cottage: LOC	into	cottage: ACC	gathered smoke: GEN. PL

'The cottage filled with smoke.'

(5) N_n – Inf. In sentences with verbs taking the dative or accusative of a human noun, the nominative of a verbal noun in the semantic function of content alternates with an infinitive:

Jám	*sẽkasi*	*dárbas /*	*dìrbti.*
he: DAT	goes well	work: NOM	work: INF

'He works successfully.'

Vaĩkui nusibódo žaidìmas/žaĩsti.	lit. 'Playing/to play bored the child.'
Manè viliója kelionės/keliáuti.	lit. 'Travels/to travel lure(s) me.'

The infinitive denotes an action of the dative referent, whereas the referent of an action expressed by a verbal noun is not necessarily identical with that of the predicate, cf.:

Mán patiñka dainúoti.	'I like to sing.'
– Mán patiñka dainãvimas.	'I like singing' (my own or another person's).

(6) The subject of a personal sentence expressed by the nominative case may be omitted (N_n – Ø) if it is tautological or can be recovered unambiguously from the verbal meaning:

Nuo stógo var̃va lašaĩ.	'Drops drip from the roof.'
– Nuo stógo var̃va.	'It is dripping from the roof.'

Impersonal sentences with causative verbs and the accusative of a human noun, such as

Manè kẽlia į órą	lit. '(It) is lifting me into the air'

may be considered to be variants of personal sentences with a lexically expressed indefinite non-human subject:

Manè kažkàs kẽlia į órą.	'Something is lifting me into the air.'

3.113 Alternation of a personal sentence with an impersonal is encoded in the verb.

(1) An impersonal verb may be a reflexive derivative from a personal verb, the subject of the underlying verb being denoted by the dative object:

Àš nemiegù.	'I don't sleep.'

Mán	*nesimiẽga.*
I: DAT	not-REFL-sleep: 3. PRES

'I can't sleep.'

Jìs geraĩ dìrba.	'He works well.'
Jám geraĩ he: DAT well 'It is easy for him to work.'	*dìrbasi.* work: 3. PRES. REFL

An impersonal reflexive verb usually occurs either with negation or with an adverbial of modality, but:

Àš nóriu miẽgo.	'I am sleepy' lit. 'I want sleep (GEN).'
– Mán nórisi I: DAT want: 3. PRES. REFL 'I feel sleepy.'	*miẽgo.* sleep: GEN. SG

Impersonal reflexives differ semantically from the respective non-reflexive verbs in that they acquire a potential modal meaning of the human referent's involuntary predisposition to the action of the underlying verb (cf. 3.57).

(2) A number of intransitive verbs (*bū́ti* 'be', *lìkti* 'remain, be left', *matýtis* 'be seen', *girdė́tis* 'be heard', etc.) used with negation (*ne-* 'not' or *nebe-* 'not any longer') require the genitive rather than the nominative subject when the existence of something is denied, cf.:

Išeitìs yrà.	'There is a way out.'
– Išeitiẽs nėrà.	'There is no way out.'
Kambaryjè jaũčiasi drėgmė̃.	lit. 'Dampness is felt in the room.'
– Nesijaũčia drėgmė̃s.	'No dampness is felt.'

Compare also respective sentences with an infinitive:

Mán matýti šviesà. I: DAT see: INF light: NOM 'I can see light.'	*Mán nematýti šviesõs.* I: DAT not-see: INF light: GEN 'I can't see any light.'

(3) A personal sentence alternates with an impersonal sentence in which the infinitive is substituted for the imperative form of the predicate, the subject taking the dative form:

Visì tylė́kit!	'Everybody, keep silence!'
– Visíems tylė́ti! everybody: DAT. PL be silent: INF 'Everybody, silence!'	

Jū̃s dainúokit!	'(You) sing! (IMPER. PL).'
– Jùms dainúoti! you: DAT sing: INF 'Your turn to sing!'	

Infinitival sentences are similar in meaning to the respective imperative personal sentences (see 3.73).

(4) Impersonal sentences with the passive verb form are described above (see 3.108–110).

AFFIRMATIVE AND NEGATIVE SENTENCES

3.114 The principal means of expressing negation is the negative marker *ne* which has the status of prefix or a particle. Sentences in which the negative marker is attached to the predicate are termed negative. They can be regarded as negative counterparts of the respective affirmative sentences; cf.:

Tėvas grį̃š rytój.	'Father will return tomorrow.'
– *Tėvas negrį̃š rytój.*	'Father will not return tomorrow.'
Mán reĩkia ankstì kéltis.	'I have to get up early.'
– *Mán nereĩkia ankstì kéltis.*	'I don't have to get up early.'

If the negative marker is added to a constituent other than the predicate the sentence remains affirmative:

Jìs prāšė manè dár nevažiúoti.	'He asked me not to leave yet.'
Gyvẽname nè dėl turto.	lit. 'We live not for riches.'

Affirmation has no specific markers, excepting the particle *taĩp* 'yes' which can be used alone as a sentence substitute, or it can introduce an affirmative sentence, in response to a question (1) or in order to emphasize assertion (2). The particle *nè* is its negative counterpart. Cf.:

(1) *Ar pasakeĩ jám teisýbę? – Taĩp/Nè.*	'Did you tell him the truth? – Yes/No.'
Tėvas jaũ grį̃žo?	'Has father returned ? – Yes, he has/No, he hasn't.'
– *Taĩp, grį̃žo/Nè, negrį̃žo.*	
(2) *Taĩp, dabař àš suprantù/*	'Yes, now I understand it/No, now I don't understand it.'
Nè, dabař àš nesuprantù.	

3.115 With regard to their formal relation to respective affirmative sentences, two types of negative sentences are distinguished: those in which negation entails formal changes in the syntactic structure and those which retain the syntactic pattern of the respective affirmative sentence.

The direct object of a negated transitive verb is in the genitive case (cf. 3.13):

Studeñtai lañkė pãskaitas.	'The students attended lectures (ACC).'
– *Studeñtai nelañkė paskaitų̃.*	'The students did not attend lectures (GEN).'

Mótiną radaũ namiẽ.   'I found my mother (ACC) at home.'
– *Mótinos neradaũ namiẽ.*   'I did not find my mother (GEN) at home.'

3.116 Negative sentences with the predicates *bū́ti* 'be', *lìkti* 'remain' either retain the nominative case of the subject or change it into the genitive depending on the scope of negation. If the subject is not within the scope of negation it retains its case form and syntactic status:

Vaikaĩ bùvo/lìko namiẽ.   'The children were/stayed at home.'
– *Vaikaĩ nebùvo/*   'The children were not/did not stay at
nelìko namiẽ.   home (i.e. they were elsewhere).'

If the subject comes within the scope of negation it is transformed into an object in the genitive case; thus the negation is extended over the entire statement:

Vaikų̃ nebùvo/nelìko namiẽ.   'There were no children at home/No children stayed at home.'

This rule also applies to sentences without an adverbial of place:

Yrà kìtas kẽlias.   'There is another way.'
– *Nèrà kìto kẽlio.*   'There is no other (GEN) way (GEN).'
Lìko išeitìs.   'There was yet (lit. 'remained') a way out.'
– *Nelìko išeitiẽs.*   'There remained no way out (GEN).'

In negative sentences with the copula *bū́ti* 'be' the nominative case of the predicate as well as of the subject is also changed into the genitive:

Jìs yrà gýwas.   'He is alive.'
– *Jõ nèrà gývo.*   '(The state of things is such that) he (GEN) is not alive (GEN).'

The equivalent of the English sentence *He is dead* is *Jìs negývas* 'He (is) not alive.' In other words, the predicate retains case agreement with the antecedent.

3.117 The negative infinitive of the verbs of perception, viz. *ne(be)matýti* 'not to see (any longer)', *ne(be)girdė́ti* 'not to hear (any longer)', *nejaũsti* 'not to feel' and the negative form of their reflexive derivatives require the genitive case of a noun instead of the nominative, which makes the sentences impersonal (cf. 3.113, 2), cf.:

Čià	*matýti /*	*mãtosi*	*kẽlias.*
here	see: INF	see: 3. PRES. REFL	road: NOM

'One can see the road here.'

– *Čià*	*nematýti /*	*nesimãto*	*kẽlio.*
here	not-see: INF	not-REFL-see: 3. PRES	road: GEN

'One can't see the road here.'

3.118 In sentences with an obligatory infinitive dependent on the predicate the negative marker can be prefixed either to the infinitive or to the predicate. In the former instance the accusative case form governed by the finite verb is retained since it does not fall within the scope of negation:

Tėvaĩ mùs *mókė netingėti.*	'The parents taught us (ACC) not to idle.'
Jìs manè *privertė negrį̃žti.*	'He forced me (ACC) not to return.'

If the negation is prefixed to the predicate the genitive is used instead of the accusative:

Tėvaĩ mū́sų nemókė tingėti.	'The parents did not teach us (GEN) to idle.'
Jìs manę̃s *neprivertė grį̃žti.*	'He did not succeed in forcing me (GEN) to return.'

The direct object of the infinitive dependent on a negated modal or phasal finite verb is in the genitive:

Jìs mė́gsta rašýti láiškus.	'He likes to write letters (ACC).'
– *Jìs nemė́gsta rašýti* laiškų̃.	'He doesn't like to write letters (GEN).'
Šiañdien tùrime sodìnti medžiùs.	'We must plant trees (ACC) today.'
– *Netùrime sodìnti* mẽdžių.	'We don't have to plant (any) trees (GEN).'
Pradėjau skaitýti tàvo knỹgą.	'I have begun to read your book (ACC).'
– *Dár nepradėjau skaitýti tàvo* knỹgos.	'I haven't begun to read your book (GEN) yet.'

The object of a negated modal or phasal verb is usually also in the genitive case when it is governed by the last in a string of infinitives:

Negaliù prisirúošti parašýti láiško.	'I can't get myself (ready) to write a letter (GEN).'
Jiẽ nenóri léisti pradė́ti statýti mokỹklos.	lit. 'They don't want to allow to begin to build a school (GEN).'

The accusative case, however, may be retained in a negative sentence, especially if there are other words placed between the finite verb and the infinitive, e.g.:

Tìk nepamir̃šk mán kìtą diẽną parašýti láišką / láiško.	lit. 'Only don't forget on the next day to write me a letter (ACC/GEN).'
Nedrįsaũ táu tadà atviraĩ pasakýti tiẽsą / tiesõs.	'I didn't dare then to tell you the truth (ACC/GEN) frankly.'

3.119 In sentences with a compound adjectival predicate the negation can be prefixed either to the predicate or to the copula. In the former instance a sentence remains affirmative (it assigns the negated feature to the subject) and in the latter instance it becomes negative (the assignment of the feature to the subject is negated):

Duktė̃ bùvo/pasidãrė gražì.	'The daughter was/became pretty.' ⇒
(a) *Duktė̃ bùvo/pasidãrė negražì.*	lit. 'The daughter was/became not pretty.'
(b) *Duktė̃ nebùvo/nepasidãrė gražì.*	'The daughter wasn't/didn't become pretty.'

Similarly, the negative marker can be prefixed to either component of a periphrastic (active or passive) verb form:

Mẽdžių lãpai jaũ bùvo nuvýtę.	'The tree leaves were already withered.' ⇒
(a) *Mẽdžių lãpai bùvo dár nenuvýtę.*	'The tree leaves were not-withered yet.'
(b) *Mẽdžių lãpai dár nebùvo nuvýtę.*	'The tree leaves were not yet withered.'
Stãlas bùvo pàdengtas.	'The table was laid (for a meal).' ⇒
(a) *Stãlas bùvo nepàdengtas.*	'The table was not-laid.'
(b) *Stãlas nebùvo pàdengtas.*	'The table was-not laid.'

3.120 In sentences with a compound predicate (both verbal and nominal) and with periphrastic verb forms the negative prefix can be repeated with both components:

Àš negalėjau neateĩti.	lit. 'I couldn't not come' (= 'I couldn't help coming').
Duktė̃ nebùvo negražì.	lit. 'The daughter was not not-pretty (= 'She was pretty').
Stãlas nebùvo nepàdengtas.	lit. 'The table was not not-laid' (= 'It was laid').

These sentences are negative in form and affirmative in meaning, the two negations cancelling each other out. Double negation here is a variety of litotes and serves the stylistic purpose of deliberate understatement.

3.121 To intensify negation, the particle *nė̃* or (less commonly) *neĩ* is used. It can be placed either before the negative predicate (1) or before any other sentence constituent (2):

(1) *Mókytoja nė/nei nepàžvelgė į sąsiuvinį.*	'The teacher did not even glance at the copybook.'
Tókio džiaũgsmo jìs nė/nei nebùvo sapnãvęs/nebùvo nė/nei sapnãvęs.	'He had not even dreamed of such joy.'

(2) *Jìs nepàjėgė daugiaũ nė/nei žõdžio ištar̃ti.*	'He could not utter a single word'(lit. 'He could not utter not a word more').
Nė/Nei víenas iš jų̃ nenùjautė sàvo likìmo.	'Not even a single one of them had (lit. 'did not have') a premonition of his fate.'

3.122 To express negation with coordinated predicates (1) or other parts of the sentence (2), or clauses (3), the reduplicated conjunction *neĩ ... neĩ* 'neither ... nor' is used. It has emphatic force and it is a negative counterpart of the emphatic conjunction *ir̃ ... ir̃*, cf.:

(1) *Žmónės ir mãtė, ir girdėjo artėjančią aũdrą.*	'People both saw and heard the approaching storm.'
– *Žmónės nei nemãtė, nei negirdėjo artėjančios audrõs.*	'People neither saw (lit. 'not-saw') nor heard (lit. 'not-heard') the approaching storm.'
(2) *Galiù pasakýti tiẽsą ir táu, ir kitíems.*	'I can tell the truth both to you and to other people.'
– *Negaliù pasakýti tiesõs nei táu, nei kitíems.*	'I can't tell the truth either (lit. 'neither') to you or (lit. 'nor') to anyone else.'
(3) *Ir àš Jõną mačiaũ, ir tù galėjai jį̃ sutìkti.*	'(And) I have seen Jonas (John), and you could have met him.'
– *Nei àš Jõno nemačiaũ, nei tù negalėjai jõ sutìkti.*	'Neither have I seen (lit. 'not-saw') Jonas (John) nor could (lit. 'could not') you have met him.'

When the conjunction *neĩ ... neĩ* coordinates predicates or clauses the negative prefix can sometimes be omitted in the predicates, the negative conjunction compensating for it, cf.:

Žmónės nei mãtė, nei girdėjo artėjančios audrõs.	'People neither saw nor heard the approaching storm.'
Nei àš Jõną mačiaũ, nei tù galėjai jį̃ sutìkti.	'Neither have I seen Jonas (John) nor could you have met him.'
Nei àš táu ką̃ dúosiu, nei tù manę̃s prašýk.	lit. 'Neither will I give you anything nor (you) ask (IMPER) me.'

In sentences with the conjunction *neĩ ... neĩ* or with the particle *nè* the present tense form of *bū́ti* 'be' with negation can also be omitted (in expressive speech):

Apliñk (nerà) nei mẽdžio, nei krūmẽlio.	lit. 'Around (there is not) neither a tree nor a bush.'
Miestẽlyje (nerà) nè žiburẽlio.	'In the town (there is) not a light.'

3.123 In negative sentences alternating with the affirmative ones the following pronouns are often replaced by their negative counterparts:

vìskas 'everything', *kažkàs* 'somebody', 'something' – *niẽkas* 'nothing, nobody';

visì, -os 'everybody', *kiekvíenas, -à* 'everyone' – *niẽkas* 'nobody', *nė víenas, -à* 'not (a single) one';

visóks, -ia 'any (kind of)' – *jóks, -ià* 'no (kind of)'; cf.:

Tadà mán vìskas paaiškėjo.	'Everything then became clear to me.'
– Tadà mán niẽkas/niẽko nepaaiškėjo.	lit. 'That time nothing (NOM/GEN) became clear to me.'
Tėvas su kažkuõ šnekėjosi.	'Father was talking with somebody.'
– Tėvas su niẽkuo nesišnekėjo.	'Father was not talking with anyone (lit. 'with nobody').'
Jį̃ teñ visì pažį́sta.	'Everyone knows him there.'
– Jõ teñ niẽkas nepažį́sta.	'Nobody knows him there.'
Kiekvíenas výras taĩp tùri el̃gtis.	'Every man should behave so.'
– Nė víenas/Jóks výras taĩp netùri el̃gtis.	'Not one/no man should behave so.'
Dėdė vaikáms àtnešė visókių dovanų̃.	'The uncle brought the children all kinds of presents.'
– Dėdė vaikáms neàtnešė jokių̃ dovanų̃.	'The uncle did not bring the children any (lit. 'no') presents.'

This rule also applies to the following adverbs:

visaĩp 'in all ways', *kažkaĩp* 'somehow' – *niẽkaip* 'in no way, nowise'
visur̃ 'everywhere, *kažkur̃* 'somewhere' – *niẽkur* 'nowhere'
visadà/visadõs 'always' – *niekadà/niekadõs* 'never'
visuomèt 'always' – *niekuomèt* 'never'
šíek tíek 'somewhat, a little' – *nė kíek* 'not at all, not any'; cf.:

Sténgiausi visaĩp jám padėti.	'I tried to help him in all (possible) ways.'
– Nesisténgiau jám niẽkaip padėti.	'I did not try to help him in any (lit. 'no') way.'
Visur̃ bùvo daũg žmonių̃.	'There were many people everywhere.'
– Niẽkur nebùvo žmonių̃.	'There were no people anywhere (lit. 'nowhere').'
Mótina kažkur̃ išvažiãvo.	'Mother has gone somewhere.'
– Mótina niẽkur neišvažiãvo.	'Mother has not gone anywhere (lit. 'nowhere').'

Tàs sẽnis visadà / visuomèt *po pietų̃ pamiẽga.*   'That old man always has a nap after dinner.'

– *Tàs sẽnis* niekadà / niekuomèt *po pietų̃ nemiẽga.*   'That old man never has a nap after dinner.'

Váistai mán šiek tíek *padėjo.*   'The medicine has helped me a little.'

– *Váistai mán* nė kíek *nepadėjo.*   'The medicine hasn't helped me at all.'

The negative pronouns and adverbs in question are used in negative sentences only. They do not cancel the negative meaning of the sentence (unlike the second negation in 3.120); instead, they intensify negation and stress its total character.

3.124 A sentence may contain several negative pronouns and/or adverbs, e.g.:

Táu niẽkas niekadà *nedãrė* jokių̃ *príekaištų.*   'No one has ever reproached you for anything' (lit. 'No one never did not make you no reproaches').

Niẽko, niẽkur *ir* niẽkad *jíems neléidžiama.*   'They are never allowed anything anywhere' (lit. 'Nothing is not allowed them nowhere and never').

To limit the scope of negation, the pronouns and adverbs of the respective affirmative sentence can be retained, e.g.:

Jìs visur̃ *yrà bùvęs,* vìską *mãtęs.*   'He has been everywhere, seen everything.'

– *Jìs* visur̃ *nèrà bùvęs,* vìsko *nèrà mãtęs.*   'He hasn't been everywhere, hasn't seen everything' (i.e. 'He has been to some places only, has seen some things, but not everything').

Kiekvíenas *tõ neprivãlo darýti.*   lit. 'Everybody is not obliged to do it' (= 'Not everybody is obliged to do it').

Sentences of the following type are ambiguous:

Sẽnis visadà *po pietų̃ nemiẽga.*   'The old man does not always sleep after dinner' or 'The old man never sleeps after dinner.'

3.125 If the particle *dár* is used in a positive sentence, the particle *jaũ* is used in the negative counterpart. If the particle *jaũ* is used in a positive sentence, the particle *dár* is used in the negative counterpart:

Àš dár *tavę̃s paláuksiu.*   'I'll wait for you (for a while) yet.'

– Àš jaũ *tavę̃s nebeláuksiu.*   'I won't wait for you any longer.'

Traukinỹs jaũ *atvažiúoja.*   'The train is already pulling in.'

– *Traukinỹs* dár *neatvažiúoja.*   'The train is not arriving yet.'

4 EXPANDED SENTENCES

Išplėstìniai sakiniaĩ

4.1 The sentence patterns composed of obligatory constituents can be expanded by various optional elements expressed by word forms and by word groups whose structure and meaning are outlined in 2.2–2.145.

Simple sentences can also be expanded or amplified by participial clauses, comparative phrases, non-restrictive appositions, direct address and parenthetical constructions.

PARTICIPIAL CLAUSES

4.2 This term is used here to refer to non-finite clauses in which the head is a participle (including half-participles in *-dam-* and gerunds).

Participial clauses are functionally close to finite subordinate clauses. A participial clause is embedded in a sentence to express a secondary action modifying the action of the finite main verb with respect to time, manner, etc.

Cf. the following example:

Žmogùs stovėjo prie lángo.	'A man stood at the window.'
Jìs kalbėjosi su láiškanešiu.	'He was talking to the postman.'

In these sentences two actions are given equal syntactic status. The relation between them can be changed in two ways:

(1) *Stovėdamas prie lángo, žmogùs kalbėjosi su láiškanešiu.*	'Standing at the window the man talked to the postman.'
(2) *Žmogùs stovėjo prie lángo, kalbėdamas su láiškanešiu.*	'The man stood at the window, talking to the postman.'

Both are simple sentences expanded by a participial phrase: in **(1)** the action of standing is made secondary by transforming the first sentence into an embedded participial clause, while in **(2)** the other action is made secondary in the same way.

4.3 Participial clauses formed with half-participles (participles in *-dam-*), past active participles, and present and past passive participles are used to denote a secondary action if their subject is co-referential with the subject of the finite main verb and therefore need not and can not be expressed in the participial phrase. The participle agrees with the sentence subject in case, number and gender, cf.:

Senẽlis, žiūrẽdamas į darbininkùs, šypsójosi.	'Looking (HALF-PART) at the workers, grandfather smiled.'
Bérnas, vidurų pir̃kios atsistójęs, apsidaĩrė apliñkui.	'The lad, having stopped (PAST. ACT. PART) in the middle of the room, looked around.'
Visų pérsekiojamas, kareĩvis nùtarė gìntis.	'Pursued (PRES. PASS. PART) by everybody, the soldier decided to defend himself.'
Paleistà iš nárvo, kanarẽlė išskrìdo pro lángą.	'Set free (PAST. PASS. PART) from the bird-cage, the canary flew out of the window.'

The semi-participle of the link verb *būti* 'be' with an adjective, participle or its substitute is also used in participial clauses to denote a simultaneous state:

Jurgẽlis mìrė penkiólikos mẽtų bū́damas.	lit. 'Jurgelis (Georgie) died being (HALF-PART) fifteen years of age.'
Būdamà pavar̃gusi, negalẽjau apsigìnti.	lit. 'Being (HALF-PART) tired I could not defend myself.'

4.4 Participial clauses with a present or past gerund denote a secondary action whose semantic subject is not identical with that of the finite predicate. The semantic subject can be in the dative case, thereby forming (with the gerund) the dative absolute construction (*dativus absolutus*):

Mùms	*besìšnekant*	*atsidãrė*	*dùrys.*
we: DAT	talk: PRES. GER	open: 3. PAST	door

'While we were talking the door opened.'

Bróliui	*grį̃žus*	*àš*	*atsìguliau.*
brother: DAT. SG	return: PAST. GER	I	lie (down): 1. SG. PAST

'When (my) brother returned I went to bed.'

The semantic subject is not expressed overtly in a gerundial clause if it is (1) implied by the context, (2) generalized or indefinite, or (3) if the gerund is impersonal:

(1) *Draugaĩ išvažiãvo ankstì.*	'The friends left home early.
Važiuójant per mìšką sulū́žo rãtas.	While (they were) driving (PRES. GER) through the woods, the wheel broke.'
(2) *Bùlves kãsant dažnaĩ prasìdeda šalnos.*	'(When) digging up (PRES. GER) potatoes, it often starts freezing.'
(3) *Taĩp spar̃čiai sutẽmus mẽs nebegalė́jome nė tãko įžiūrė́ti.*	'(It) having grown dark (PAST. GER) so fast, we couldn't even see the path.'

The dative is redundant in the gerundial clause if it is named by an object or otherwise in the main clause:

Grį̃žus namõ mùs pasitìko tik šuõ.	'On return (PAST. GER) home, the dog alone came out meet us.'
Nãktį bežygiúojant suñkvežimis jám pérvažiavo kóją.	'When he was walking (PRES. GEN) at night, a lorry (ran him over and) crushed his (lit. to him, DAT) leg.'
Jõ véidas paniùro išgir̃dus atsãkymą.	'His face fell on hearing (PAST. GER) the answer.'

4.5   The choice of a participle (and half-participle) or a gerund is determined by the identity/non-identity of the semantic subject of the secondary action with that of the main action. If they are identical a participle or a half-participle (for a simultaneous action) is used. If they are not identical, a gerund has to be used.

A gerund is also used if the semantic subjects of both actions are only partly identical:

Iš pradžių̃ abù kaimýnai ė̃jo tylomìs. Ar̃tinantis prie dvãro, víenas prašnė̃ko.	'At the beginning two neighbours walked in silence. On approaching (PRES. GER) the manor, one of them began to talk.'

The participle or half-participle of a participial clause is replaced by a gerund in the respective impersonal sentence:

Taĩp suñkiai dìrbdamas/dìrbęs galì ir pailsė́ti.	'Working (HALF-PART)/having worked (PAST. ACT. PART) so hard, you can afford a rest.'
Taĩp suñkiai dìrbant/dìrbus gãlima ir pailsė́ti.	'Working (PRES. GER)/having worked (PAST. GER) so hard, one can (lit. it is allowed/possible to) have a rest.'

4.6   As a means of subordination, participial clauses differ from finite subordinate clauses in that they are more tightly integrated into the sentence structure and their semantic relations with the main predicate in most cases are not formally expressed.

Most commonly, participial clauses, especially those with gerunds, indicate the relative time of the main action. To specify the temporal relation, the subordinators *ikì* 'until, before', *priẽš* 'before', *võs* 'hardly, as soon as', *tìk* 'just' are used to introduce a participial clause, e.g.:

Prieš eĩdamas namõ, Jùrgis visadà užsùkdavo pas ją̃.	'Before going home, Jurgis (George) used to look in on her.'
Mótina išskubėjo į̃ miestẽlį vos rýtui prašvìtus.	'Mother went to the town as soon as it dawned (lit. morning: DAT dawn: PAST. GER).'

Participial clauses may acquire a number of additional meanings superimposed upon the temporal meaning. In relation to the main clause, they may denote:

(1) cause:

Per dienų dienàs niẽko nedirbdamà, jì tùri net per daũg laĩko.	lit. 'Doing (HALF-PART) nothing all day long, she has too much spare time.'
Nuolàt visų́ pérsekiojamas jìs priprãto gìntis.	'Constantly persecuted (PRES. PASS. PART) by all he got used to defending himself.'
Mótinai čià ẽsant, mán nebaisù.	lit. 'Mother being (PRES. GER) here, I am not afraid of anything.'

(2) condition:

Pabùvęs pas manè metùs, išmóktum ir laukùs árti.	'Having spent (PAST. ACT. PART) a year with me, you would even learn to plough the fields.'
Tavimì dė́tas aš bū́čiau kitaĩp pasielgę̃s.	'If I were you (you: INSTR. SG put: PAST. PASS. PART. NOM. SG) I'd have behaved differently.'
Dúodant vienám, reĩkia dúoti ir kitám.	'If you give (PRES. GER) to one, you should (lit. 'it is necessary' to) give to another.'

(3) concession (sometimes emphasized by *ir*, *kad ir*, *nors (ir)*):

Pàts varganaĩ gyvéndamas, jìs sténgėsi kitíems padė́ti.	'Being poor (lit. living poorly: HALF-PART) himself, he did his best to help others.'
Čià gìmęs ir užáugęs, gimtõsios kalbõs doraĩ neišmóko.	'Having been born and grown up here, he hasn't learnt his native language properly.'
Nors/kad ir sáugomas draugų̃, jìs neprarãdo viltiẽs pabė́gti.	'Though guarded (PRES. PASS. PART) by his friends, he did not lose hope of escaping.'

(4) manner:

Besirū̃pindamas kitų̃ láime ràsi ir sãvąją.	'(While) being concerned (HALF-PART) with other people's happiness, you'll find your own.'
Vaikaĩ sėdėjo kam̃bario kam̃pè prisiglaũdę víenas prie kìto.	'The children were sitting in a corner of the room cuddling up (PAST. ACT. PART) to each other.'

(5) purpose (with the *-dam-* participle or present gerund of verbs like *ieškóti* 'look for', *síekti* 'seek, strive', *norė́ti* 'want', mostly after verbs of motion):

Vìsą dië̃ną bėgiójau ieškódamas mergáitės tėvų̃.	lit. 'I ran about all day looking (HALF-PART) for the girl's parents.'
Jìs užė̃jo į̃ knygýną, tikė́damasis / norė́damas nusipir̃kti žodýną.	lit. 'He dropped into a bookshop hoping/wanting to buy a dictionary.'

These adverbial meanings of participial clauses are largely determined by the lexical meaning of sentence constituents and by context. In the majority of cases they are not distinctly differentiated and a participial clause may carry several shades of meaning. For instance, the participle clause in

Vaĩkas sušlãpo kójas braidýdamas po balàs.	'The boy got his feet wet wading (HALF-PART) in the puddles.'

conveys the time of the main action as well as cause and manner.

4.7 A participial clause may be separated by pauses (commas in written language) and/or uttered with a rising tone in order to give it more prominence. This is common if a participle clause is placed initially:

Gyvéndamas tolì nuo sàvo giminių̃, Jõnas retaĩ tegalė́jo júos aplankýti.	lit. 'Living (HALF-PART) far from his relatives, John could only seldom visit them.'

A single participle without dependent words can also be detached from the sentence:

Paválgę, medžiótojai tuojaũ nuė̃jo atgál į̃ mìšką.	'Having eaten (PAST. ACT. PART) the hunters at once went back into the woods.'

COMPARATIVE PHRASES

4.8 A comparative phrase consists of a word form (single or with dependent word forms) naming the standard of comparison and linked to the predicate or any other part of the sentence by a comparative conjunction (*kaĩp* 'like, as', *tar̃tum* 'as if', etc.). Comparative phrases subordinated to the predicate and performing an adverbial function are very close to comparative subordinate clauses (see 7.65–70), except that they contain no predicate; cf.:

Vargaĩ praeĩs kaip naktìs.	lit. 'Troubles will pass like a night' (comparative phrase).
Vargaĩ praeĩs, kaip praeĩna naktìs.	'Troubles will pass like a night passes' (comparative clause).

Comparative phrases linked to other parts of the sentence and their modifiers cannot be replaced by a subordinate clause:

Nusipirkaũ júodą kaip anglìs kepùrę.	'I bought a cap black as night.'

Comparative phrases can be subdivided into equational (qualitative and quantitative) and differentiating.

4.9 **Qualitative comparative phrases** denote similarity of qualitative characteristics and relate to verbs (1), nouns (2) and adjectives (3) or their substitutes. They are introduced by the neutral (with respect to modality) conjunction *kaĩp* 'like', or by *it̀, lýg, tar̃tum / tar̃si* implying a shade of modal meaning.

(1) *Tėvas dìrba kaip visì.*	'Father works like everybody else.'
Merginà žýdi lyg / tar̃tum rõžė.	'The girl is blooming like a rose.'
(2) *Sáugojo ją̃ trỹs bróliai kaip ąžuolaĩ.*	'She was guarded by three brothers like oak-trees.'
(3) *Jis grįžo namõ pìktas it/lyg/ tar̃tum žvėrìs.*	'He returned home angry as a beast.'

If a comparative phrase modifies an adjective the standard of comparison is usually in the nominative case, whatever the case of the adjective (and its head noun):

Mẽs ėjome lýgiu kaip stãlas keliù.	'We walked along the road (INSTR) (which was) flat (INSTR) as a table (NOM).'
Sáulė pasìslėpė už tamsaũs kaip naktìs šìlo.	'The sun hid behind the pine forest (GEN) (which was as) dark (GEN) as the night (NOM).'

If a comparative phrase modifies a noun the standard of comparison assumes the case form of the head noun:

Nóriu miẽgo kaip medaũs.	'I want sleep (GEN) like honey (GEN)'.
Cf. *Nóriu miẽgo saldaũs kaip medùs.*	lit. 'I want sleep (GEN) as sweet (GEN) as honey (NOM).'

The standard of comparison can also be denoted by an adjective, an adjectival word or by an adverb or its substitute:

Bókštas žìba kaip stiklìnis.	'The tower glitters like (made of) glass (ADJ).'
Jìs léidžia màno pìnigus kaip savùs.	'He spends my money (ACC) like his own (PRON. ACC).'
Dabař gãlim pasikalbė́ti kaip seniaũ.	'Now we can have a chat as of old (ADV).'

A comparative phrase often is parallel in structure to the main clause (except for the absence of a predicate):

Katrė̃ rū́muose kankìnasi lyg narvè paukštė̃lė.	'Katrė (Catherine) is suffering in the palace like a bird in a cage.'

Adverbial comparative phrases can be preceded by the correlative words *taĩp* 'so', *taip pàt* 'as':

Jaũ nebùs taip geraĩ kaip anksčiaũ.	'It won't be as good (ADV) as earlier.'
Išvažiãvome taip pàt ankstì kaip visadà.	'We left as early as always.'

The correlative words cooccurring with modifying comparative phrases are *tóks, -ià* 'such', *tóks pàt, tokià pàt* 'the same', sometimes *taĩp* 'so' and *taip pàt* 'as':

Ar tù regė́jai tókį dvãrą kaip màno?	'Have you seen such a manor as mine?
Jì tokià pàt / taip pàt gražì kaip jaunỹstėje.	'She is as beautiful as in her youth.'

4.10 Quantitative comparative phrases denote similarity with respect to quantitative characteristics. They are introduced by *kíek* 'how much/many', *kaĩp* 'how' and they are usually preceded by the correlatives *tíek* 'so (as) much' or *tiek pàt* 'as much'.

Šulinyjè vandeñs bùvo tíek, kiek statìnėje	'In the well there was as much water as (lit. how much) in the barrel.'

Comparative phrases preceded by *tíek (pàt)* are most frequently introduced by *kaĩp*:

Àš ne tíek pasikeĩtęs kaip jū̃s.	'I haven't changed as much as you.'
Niẽkam jìs tíek neįkyrė́davo kaip mán.	'He didn't worry anyone as much as me.'
Nusipirkaũ tiek pàt knỹgų kaip ir brólis.	'I've bought as many books as (my) brother.'

The correlative *tíek* often co-occurs with the adverb *daũg* 'much/many':

Susiriñko tiek daũg žmonių̃ kaip dar niekadà.	lit. 'So many people gathered as never before.'

4.11 Differentiating comparative phrases serve to express the difference between compared entities or actions. They are commonly introduced by the conjunction *negù* 'than', and sometimes by *nekaĩp, neĩ, kaĩp* with the same meaning. Differentiating phrases are used as postmodifiers and co-occur with the following head words only:

(1) the comparative form of adverbs:

Tą diẽną jìs išẽjo į dárbą anksčiaũ kaip / negu visadà.	'On that day he left for work earlier than usual (lit. 'always').'
Geriaũ mir̃ti nekaĩp svetimíems tarnáuti.	'It's better to die than to serve the invaders (lit. 'foreigners').'

(2) the comparative form of adjectives:

Jõ gyvuliaĩ visadà menkesnì negu jõ kaimýnų.	'His cattle are always scraggier than his neighbours.'
Čià lìkęs àš tikraĩ bū́siu laimingèsnis nei tù.	'Staying here, I will surely be happier than you.'

(3) the adverb *kitaĩp* 'differently' and the adjective *kitóks, -ià* 'different, another':

Žmónės čia kitaĩp gyvẽna negu mū́sų káime.	lit. 'The people here live otherwise (differently) than in our village.'
Jìs yrà kitóks / kitókio bū̃do negu visì vaikaĩ.	lit. 'He is different / of a different nature than all (the other) children.'

Comparative phrases dependent on comparative adverbs and adjectives are interchangeable with the prepositional phrase *ùž* + ACC:

Sūnùs žìno daugiaũ negu tėvas / daugiaũ už tė́vą.	'The son knows more than the father' (see 2.120, 143).

APPOSITION

4.12 Non-restrictive apposition modifies the head word by conveying additional information or explaining it. It follows the modified word and is detached from the sentence by a separate intonation (marked by commas or otherwise in writing). These features distinguish the non-restrictive apposition from restrictive apposition which serves to identify the head word (see 1.38).

Non-restrictive apposition can modify:

(1) nouns, in subject or object position:

Bùvo trỹs bróliai, dideli ir galìngi karãliai.	'There were three brothers, great and powerful kings.'
Jis àtnešė mùms dovanų̃: žaislų̃, knỹgų, saldaĩnių.	'He brought us gifts: toys, books, sweets.'

(2) adverbs and other word forms used as adverbial modifiers:

Teñ, prie lópšio, klū́po móteris.	'There, by the cradle, a woman is kneeling.'
Rýtą, dár neišaũšus, išė̃jome grybáuti.	'In the morning, before dawn yet (lit. 'having not dawned yet'), we went mushrooming.'
Už namų̃, paleĩ vìsą tvõrą, áugo aviẽtės.	'At the back of the house, along the fence, there grew raspberries.'

(3) adjectives and adjectival words:

Tàs kambarė̃lis bùvo labaĩ malonùs: saulė́tas, švarùs, baltomìs síenomis.	'That little room was very pleasant: sunny, clean, with white walls.'

(4) personal pronouns, in various syntactic positions:

Jái, (kaip) našláitei, bùvo labaĩ sunkù.	'For her, (as) an orphan, it was very hard.'
Dovanókite mán, sẽniui.	'Please forgive me, an old man.'

An appositional construction is occasionally used with a verbal predicate:

Mótina kambaryjè balsù raudójo, stãčiai šaũkė.	'In the room, mother was weeping loudly, screaming even.'

4.13 Non-restrictive appositional constructions can modify the meaning of the head in a number of ways which are indicated by special conjunctives.

(1) An appositional construction identifies the head referent, the relation between the appositives being that of equivalence; the indicators are *bū́tent* 'namely', *arbà* 'or, otherwise', *tai yrà* (abbreviated *t.y.*) 'that is':

Tik víenas klausýtojas, bū́tent Viñcas, pasilìko sãlėje.	'Only one listener, namely Vincas (Vincent), stayed in the hall.'
Atžalýnas, arbà/t.y. jáunas mìškas, ganýti neléidžiamas.	'The undergrowth, or/i.e. a young forest, is a forbidden place for grazing.'

(2) An appositional construction names the components or illustrates the head, in which case the relation between the appositives is that of inclusion which may be indicated by the conjunctive words *kaip antaĩ* 'as for instance', *pãvyzdžiui* 'for example' (abbreviated *pvz.*), the adverbs *ýpač* 'especially', *daugiáusia* 'mostly', and the like.

Namìniai paũkščiai, kaip antaĩ/   'Poultry, as for instance/for example
pãvyzdžiui, vìštos, ántys   hens, ducks and geese, are very
ar žą̃sys, labaĩ naudìngi žmõgui.   useful to man.'

Laukìnės bìtės apdùlkina áugalus,   'Wild bees pollinate plants,
ýpač/labiáusiai raudonúosius   especially/most of all red clover.'
dóbilus.

(3) An appositional construction has an additive force, which is indicated by *kaĩp ir* 'as well as', *taip pàt ir* 'and also':

Laukaĩ, kaĩp ir miškaĩ, ištuštėjo.   'The fields, as well as the woods, were deserted.'

Šiẽmet, kaĩp ir/taip pàt ir pérnai,   'This year, as well as/and also last
bùvo labaĩ kárštà vãsara.   year, we had a very hot summer.'

(4) An appositional construction is explanatory if it specifies the relevant aspect of the head and can be introduced by *kaĩp*:

Jõnas, (kaip) visų̃ vaikų̃ vyriáusias,   'Jonas (John) (as) the oldest of all
turėjo užkùrti láužą.   the children, was to light the bonfire.'

Jùms, kaip mótinai, reikėtų labiaũ   'You, as mother, should be more
rū́pintis sūnaũs ateitimì.   concerned with your son's future.'

DIRECT ADDRESS

4.14 Direct address (*kreipinỹs*) expands a sentence by referring to the person(s) who is (are) addressed. Its basic function is to establish contact with the listener(s). Direct address is a detached constituent set off from the sentence by pauses and intonation (commas or exclamation marks in writing). It is usually expressed by the vocative case of (1) proper or (2) common (mostly human) nouns:

(1) *Pètrai, paródyk tám žmõgui kẽlią.*   'Peter, show that man the way.'
Liètuva, pabùsk iš ìlgo miẽgo!   'Lithuania, awake from your long sleep!'

(2) *Tuojaũ skubėkit namõ, vaikaĩ!*   'Hurry home at once, children!'
Výrai, nesibárkite!   'Gentlemen (lit. Men) don't quarrel!'
Visì manè, motùle, mylėjo.   'Everybody loved me, mother.'

The nouns *põnas* 'Mister, Sir', *ponià* 'Madam', *panẽlė* 'Miss' are used for formal and polite address:

Atléiskite, põnia/panẽle, àš   'Sorry, Madam/Miss, I didn't mean
nenorėjau sutrukdýti.   to disturb you.'

The vocative of non-human nouns usually occurs in rhetorical speech:

Vai lẽkite, daĩnos!	'Oh fly, (my) songs!'

The noun in direct address can take all kinds of modifiers:

Ką̃ pasakýsite, garbìngi ir nar̃sūs výrai?	'What will you say, honourable and valiant men?'

The position of direct address in the sentence is not fixed. It is frequently placed in initial position.

4.15 Direct address can also be expressed by the following noun substitutes:

(1) adjectives and passive participles (usually the definite form):

Nusiramìnk, mielàsis / màno míelas.	'Be quiet, dear / my dear.'
Taĩ apie ką̃ mẽs čià kalbė́sime, gerbiamíeji?	'And what shall we talk about gentlemen (lit. 'honourable')?'

(2) the personal pronouns *tù* 'you: SG', *támsta*, *jū̃s* 'you':

Greičiaũ, tu!	'You, be quick!'
Sakýk, támsta, kuriuõ keliù reĩkia eĩti?	'Please tell me, sir, which way do I take?'
Ei, jū̃s, atnèškite mán vỹno!	'Hey, you, bring (2. PL)me some wine!'

4.16 For emphasis an interjection by itself or with a pronoun may be added to a sequence denoting direct address:

Ak, Paũliau, dabar̃ nebe tiẽ laikaĩ.	'Oh, Paul, the times have changed.'
Oi tu, mergẽle jaunóji, kur̃ taip vaikštinė́ji?	'Oh you, young maiden, where are you walking?'

But an interjection preceding direct address can also be separated from it by a pause (a comma in writing):

Èt, vyrẽli, geriaũ tylė́tum!	'Well, old chap, you'd better keep silent!'
Éi, vaĩke, prieĩk arčiaũ!	'Hey, child, come up nearer!'

4.17 Alongside the basic phatic function of establishing contact with the listener(s), direct address also serves to express the speaker's attitude towards the addressee and, even, to evaluate the latter. This emotive and evaluative function is especially prominent if direct address is expressed by a modified diminutive noun, e.g.:

Oi, bernẽli màno míelas, jau negreĩt pasimatýsim!	'Oh, my dearest sweetheart, we won't meet soon!'

A sentence may contain two occurrences of direct address: the first one, usually in sentence-initial position, has the phatic function and the other, placed finally, has an emotive-evaluative function:

Kaimýne, kõ taip skubì namõ, brangùsis?	'Neighbour, why are you hurrying home so, dearest?'

INTERPOLATION

4.18 Interpolation (*įterpinỹs*) is a syntactic means of amplifying a sentence by a broad (practically unlimited) range of meanings, which is reflected in its formal and semantic variety. An interpolated remark may be semantically related to the whole sentence or to a constituent, while formally it is not linked to the latter. It is singled out by a specific intonation:

Jìs, žìnoma, niēko teñ nerãdo.	'He, of course, didn't find anything there.'

The position of interpolation is not fixed, but it mostly appears in the initial or medial position.

4.19 Interpolated word forms either retain their morphological status or acquire specialized meanings losing, to a greater or lesser degree, their semantic relation with the respective original word.

The following word forms are commonly used in interpolation:

(1) the nominative case form of the evaluative nouns *bėdà* 'misfortune', *láimė* 'luck', *neláimė* 'misfortune', *teisýbė* 'truth', *tiesà* 'truth', *var̃gas* 'misery, grief' and the like (also the dative of *láimė* and *neláimė*):

Láimė / láimei, mótina bùvo netolíese.	'Luckily (NOM/DAT), mother was nearby.'
Teisýbė, jìs niēko nežinójo.	'True (lit. Truth), he didn't know anything.'

(2) The instrumental form *žodžiù* 'in a word':

Mẽs miegójome, žodžiù, niēko nemãtėme.	'We were asleep, in a word, we didn't see anything.'

(3) The vocative case forms *Diẽve* 'God', *Viẽšpatie* 'Good Lord', *var̃ge* 'woe, grief' and the like which function as interjections:

Viẽšpatie, kàs gi čià dẽdasi?	'Good Lord, what's going on here?'
Var̃ge, kàs gi táu atsitìko?	'Woe, what has become of you?'

(4) Interjections:

Dejà, dabaȓ jau gãli bū́ti per vėlù.	'Alas, it may be too late now.'
Dievažì, ir kõ jìs iš manę̃s nóri?	'O dear, what does he want of me?'

(5) The neuter adjectives *áišku* 'clear', *svarbiáusia* 'most important', the neuter passive participles *žìnoma* 'of course', *suprañtama* 'of course', and also the neuter form of the numerals *víena* 'first(ly)', *añtra* 'secondly', *pìrma* 'first', *pirmiáusia* 'first of all' and the like:

Tų̃ knỹgų, žìnoma, niẽkas neskaĩtė.	'No one read those books, of course.'
Víena, jis bùvo pavařgęs, añtra, pàts negalėjo apsisprę́sti.	'Firstly, he was tired, secondly, he couldn't make up his mind.'

(6) The synonymous adverbs *atvirkščiaĩ* and *príešingai* 'on the contrary':

Tàs jõ tylė́jimas, atvirkščiaĩ/ príešingai, kė́lė dár didèsnį nèrimą.	'That silence of his, on the contrary, caused even greater uneasiness.'

(7) The adverbialized gerunds *atsiprãšant* '(by way of) apologizing', *nepérdedant* 'without exaggerating':

Vèskis iš čià tą̃, atsiprãšant, kvailį̃.	'Get this, beg your pardon, fool out of here.'
Màno duktė̃, nepérdedant, gerà virė́ja.	'My daughter is, without exaggeration, a good cook.'

(8) The infinitives *matýt(i)* 'evidently (lit. 'see')', *girdė́t(i)* 'they say (lit. 'hear')' and the finite verb forms *ródos(i)* 'it seems', *rẽgis(i)* 'it seems', *vadìnasi* 'so, then, well then, consequently':

Vaĩkas, matýt, bùvo nekaĩtas.	'The child was, obviously, innocent.'
Ródos, čià niẽkas negyvẽna.	'It seems, no one lives here.'
Vadìnasi, turė́sime išsikélti kituȓ.	'Well then, we'll have to move elsewhere.'

(9) The particle *bejè* 'by the way':

Bejè, ar negalė́si mán padė́ti?	'By the way, could you help me?'

4.20 The following prepositional phrases are commonly used as interpolation:

(1) *anót/pasàk/pagaĩ* 'according to + GEN', with human nouns:

Pasàk Jõno, jiẽ tik pasiteirãvo apie kaimýnus.	'According to Jonas (John), they only inquired about the neighbours.'

(2) *bè* 'without, besides, except + GEN', especially set phrases like *be tõ* 'besides', *be ãbejo/be abejõnės* 'without doubt':

Be smuĩkininko, teñ dar bùvo kẽletas svečių̃.	'Besides the violinist, there were a few more guests.'

Be ābejo, tu vėl pavėlúosi į tráukinį.	'Doubtless, you will miss your train again.'

(3) the preposition *põ* 'after' with the Genitive or Instrumental case in set phrases used as swear-words, e.g.:

Nejaũgi, po velniũ, čia nė víeno padoraũs žmogaũs neliko?	'What the deuce, is there not a single decent man (left) here?'

(4) the phrases *tarp kìtko / tarp kìta kõ* 'by the way (lit. 'among others')'

Àš, tarp kìta kõ, turiù táu gerũ naujíenų.	'By the way, I have good news for you.'

All the above mentioned word forms and phrases can also be optionally expanded to form interpolated word groups, e.g.:

mū́sų (jũ, visũ, miẽsto gyvéntojų) láimei	'luckily for us (them, everybody, the towns people (lit. to my/ their, etc. luck)'
saváime áišku	'of course'
visũ pirmiáusia	'first of all'
príešingai negù visì	'contrary to everybody'
nė kíek nepérdedant	'without exaggerating at all'
añtra veȓtus	'on the other hand'
anót namũ gyvéntojų	'according to the inhabitants of the house'
pagaĩ tùrimus šaltiniùs	'according to the sources we have'
be jokiõs abejõnės	'without any doubt', etc.

There are also a great many interpolations composed of two (very seldom more than two) word forms, their head word never being used singly as an interpolation; here belong:

teisýbę pasākius	'to tell (lit. 'having told') the truth'
kitaĩp / víenu žodžiù sākant	'to put it (lit. 'putting it') otherwise / in one word'
atviraĩ kaĩbant	'frankly speaking'
išskýrus kitùs	'excepting the others'
áiškus / suprañtamas dalýkas	'of course'
turimaĩs duomenimìs	'according to the available information'
āčiū Diẽvui	'thank God', etc.

A great many set phrases containing a pronoun or an adverb are habitually used in interpolation, e.g.:

Ko gẽro, vẽl suláuksime nekviestų̃ svečių̃.	'I am afraid (lit. 'what good: GEN'), we shall have uninvited visitors gain.'
Jõnas, šiaĩp ar taĩp, gẽras mokinỹs.	'Jõnas (John) in any case, is a good pupil.'

4.21 A clause may be interpolated as well. The predicate of an interpolated clause is usually a verb denoting comprehension which can be used alone as an interpolation, e.g.:

Mán ródos, jis mùs pamir̃šo.	'I think, he has forgotten us.'
Tėvas, áiškiai matýti, dar niẽko nežìno.	'Father, to all appearance, doesn't know anything yet.'

Interpolated clauses are often introduced by the conjunctions *kaĩp* 'as' and *kíek* 'as':

Jõs výras, kaip visíems žìnoma, bùvo girtuõklis.	'Her husband, as everyone knows, was a drunkard.'
Kaĩp jaũ bùvo minėta, jìs tuõ metù gyvẽno káime.	'As it was mentioned, he lived in the country at that time.'
Kíek prisìmenu, jìs čià nebùvo apsilañkęs.	'For all I remember, he hasn't ever been here.'

4.22 The most prominent functions of interpolation are the following:

(1) expressing the speaker's attitude towards the content of the sentence, including all kinds of evaluation (modal, emotional, etc):

Tikiúosi, tu nepasèksi tėvo pėdomis.	'I hope, you won't follow in your father's steps.'
Vìlniuje, kaip girdėti, jìs nebegyvẽna.	'He doesn't live in Vilnius any longer, (as) one hears.'

(2) commenting or summarizing what is being said in the sentence:

Atviraĩ sãkant/pasãkius, àš tõ geraĩ nežìnau.	'Speaking honestly, I don't know much about that.'
Žodžių̃, reĩkia nedelsti nė valandėlės.	'In a word, we shouldn't waste a moment.'

(3) appealing to the listener:

Šìto, žìnote, àš jau nebegalėsiu pakęsti.	'This, you know, I won't put up with.'

(4) indicating the source of information:

Antràsis sūnùs bùvo, anót tėvo, nevýkėlis.	'The second son was, according to (his) father, a failure.'

(5) specifying the content of the sentence (by way of contrast, exception, comparison, enumeration etc.) or relating the sentence to the context:

Visì bùvo susiriñkę, išskýrus tuõs trìs.	'Everybody was there, excepting those three.'
Palýginti su kitaĩs, jìs atródė protìngas.	'In comparison with the others, he looked intelligent.'
Añtra veřtus, teñ galė́si mókytis.	'On the other hand, you'll be able to study there.'
Nepaklauseĩ màno patarìmo, vadìnasi, pàts bū́si kaĩtas.	'You didn't heed my advice, consequently, you yourself will be to blame.'

4.23 The following modal (and similar) words, and phrases function very much like interpolated expressions but they are included in the sentence intonationally (in writing they are not set off by commas):

pirmiáusia 'first of all'	*iš tiesų̃* 'really, indeed'
visų̃ pirmà 'first of all'	*iš tikrų̃jų* 'really, indeed'
tikriáusiai 'most probably, surely'	*galbū́t* 'maybe'
veikiáusiai 'most probably/likely'	*turbū́t* 'must be'
apskritaĩ 'in general, on the whole'	*ràsi/ràsit* 'maybe, perhaps'
paprastaĩ 'usually'	*berõds* 'it seems'
anaiptõl 'by no means'	*atseĩt* 'that is'
iš vìso 'all in all'	*antaĩ* 'there'
iš prìncipo 'on principle'	*taĩgi* 'now then, consequently'

4.24 An interpolation can also be inserted at will: the speaker is free to put into a sentence any remark as additional information or evaluation, or comment, etc., e.g.:

Mótina, jìs jaũtė, bùvo susirū́pinus, nórs ir šypsójosi.	'Mother, he felt, was worried, though she was smiling.'
Mū́sų kaimýnas (o jìs, nórs kar̃tais mė́gsta išgérti, bèt taĩp žmogùs ne melãgis) papãsakojo mùms keĩstą atsitikìmą.	'Our neighbour (and he, though a drinking man, is not a liar), told us a strange story.'

5 WORD ORDER
Žõdžių tvarkà

5.1 Word order in Lithuanian is a means of signifying the functional (theme – rheme) sentence perspective and, to a much lesser degree, the syntactic relations between sentence constituents. Word order can be variable and structurally fixed.

Variable word order is not rigidly determined by the syntactic sentence structure and it may vary depending on the functional sentence perspective and on expressive and stylistic factors. Variable word order is characteristic of Lithuanian. This is due to a highly developed system of inflections which signal the syntactic functions of words in a sentence and their semantic roles. The sequential arrangement of words does not usually change their syntactic or semantic functions.

Variable word order may be **neutral** and **inverted**. Neutral word order does not depend on the context or special intention. Inversion of regular neutral word order is a means of changing the communicative content of a sentence and expressing emphasis. Thus, the neutral position of an adverbial of manner or an adjectival modifier is before a verb (*geraĩ žinaũ* lit. '(I) well know', *áiškiai pasãkė* lit. '(he) clearly said') and a head noun (*brangióji tėvýnė* 'dear homeland') respectively; in the case of inversion they are post-posed to the head word and thus receive emphasis: *žinaũ geraĩ* '(I) know well', *pasãkė áiškiai* '(he) said clearly', and *tėvýnė brangióji* 'homeland dear'.

A number of restrictions are imposed on word order variation by the tendency to juxtapose immediately related word forms (or word groups). Immediately related word groups and word forms can be distanced if the communicative intention or distribution of emphasis require it. This may result in a "closed-in" construction; for instance, the copula of a compound predicate may be separated from the predicative adjective and noun by positioning the subject or an adverbial between them:

Bùvo	*tadà*	*jìs*	*dár*	*visái*	*jáunas*	*vaikìnas.*
was	then	he	yet	quite	young	youth

'He was quite a young boy then.'

5.2 **Structurally fixed** word order cannot be changed for communicative or stylistic reasons. Instances of structurally fixed order are:

(1) place of prepositions before a noun, e.g.:

(nãmas) be langų̃	'(a house) without windows'
(eĩti) į mìšką	'(go) to the woods'

(2) pre-position of negation, e.g.:

ne visì žmónės	'not all people'
ne jìs atẽjo	lit. 'not he came' ('it wasn't he who came')

(3) the initial position of an interrogative particle, e.g.:

Ar jìs čià?	'Is he here?'

(4) post-position of attributive clauses to the head noun, e.g.:

Išaũšo dienà, kuriõs visì láukė.	'The day dawned everyone had been waiting for.'

There is no distinct border-line between instances of variable and structurally fixed word order, which results in a number of intermediate cases. Thus, a modifier expressed by the genitive case of a noun is usually placed before the head noun in Standard Lithuanian (especially in scientific and official style):

tẽvo kambarỹs	'father's room'
mìško žvėrys	'forest beasts'

However, in colloquial (especially dialectal) speech and in fiction (especially in poetry), their sequence may be reversed (see 5.21).

5.3 In the case of variable word order, sequence of words in a sentence is determined by the communicative intention. From this viewpoint, a sentence is assigned a communicative structure consisting of two parts, **the theme** and **the rheme**. The theme carries given information already supplied by the context and the rheme carries the new information which is the most important part from the viewpoint of the purpose of communication. The theme usually precedes the rheme and in the case of neutral word order and neutral intonation pattern it corresponds to the subject (or subject group), while the predicate or the predicate group is the rheme. However, the theme – rheme structure does not necessarily coincide with the syntactic structure: the content of the theme and rheme can be changed by changing the sequence of words. Thus, if the sentence *Pẽtras àtvežė málkų* 'Petras (Peter) brought some firewood' contains a reply to the question 'What did Peter do?', the theme coincides with the subject and the rheme is the verb with the object. The subject can be made the rheme by moving it to clause final position, the object becoming the theme in clause initial position:

Málką àtvežė Pètras   'The firewood was brought by Peter.'

An alternative means of changing the theme – rheme structure is intonation: any part of a sentence can be rhematized by heavy stress and falling intonation.

Rhematization of the subject:

Kàs àtvežė málką? 'Who brought the firewood?' – *PĒTRAS àtvežė málką* 'PETER brought the firewood.'

Rhematization of the predicate:

Ką̃ padãrė Pètras? 'What did Peter do?' – *Pètras ÀTVEŽĖ málką* 'Peter BROUGHT the firewood.'

In written language, word order inversion (along with passivization) is the principal means of changing the theme – rheme content.

Word order sequences where the theme precedes the rheme, the theme corresponding to the subject and the rheme to the predicate or predicate group, being the most common cases, are regarded as the basic patterns.

It is not always easy to distinguish between theme and rheme or to determine the boundary between them. For instance, the opening sentence of a text usually contains no given information: it is rhematic and serves to introduce the theme for the subsequent sentences:

Gyvẽno dù brõliai. Jiẽ bùvo labaĩ neturtìngi.   'There lived two brothers. They were very poor.'

Word order in introductory sentences is usually opposite to the regular word order in sentences with a distinct theme – rheme structure.

Word order in interrogative, exclamatory and also in complex sentences has specific characteristics briefly discussed in the relevant chapters. The sections below are concerned with the basic tendencies of word order in declarative simple sentences.

THE ORDER OF THE MAIN SENTENCE CONSTITUENTS

5.4   The kernel of most simple sentences comprises either the predicate (V), subject (S) and direct object (O), or the predicate and subject (V,S), or the predicate alone

(V). Therefore it is important to establish the sequential arrangement of these components and its relatedness to the functional (theme – rheme) sentence perspective.

5.5 In the **two-constituent sentences** with the kernel structure consisting of the predicate and subject their basic neutral sequence is **SV**. They are usually divisible into theme and rheme. The subject is then the theme and the predicate (alone or with dependent words) is the rheme; cf.:

Laukaĩ ištuštėjo.	'The fields grew empty.'

This word order is also characteristic of sentences with a compound predicate (verbal or nominal):

Žmónės pradėjo skìrstytis.	'The people began to disperse.'
Ruduõ bùvo ìlgas.	'The autumn was long.'

In sentences with a zero copula and the genitive of a noun or an adjective in predicate position this sequence cannot be changed since the reversed word order is indicative of a noun with a preceding modifier:

Švar̃kas	*juodõs*	*spalvõs.*
jacket	black: GEN	colour: GEN

lit. 'The jacket is of black colour.'

Cf.: *juodõs spalvõs švar̃kas* lit. 'a jacket of black colour'

Dienà šiltà. 'The day is warm.'
Cf.: *šiltà dienà* 'a warm day' (see 5.22)

The rhematic predicate (V) preceding the subject (S) is usually marked by intonation:

ATSISTÓJO	*jìs*	*kiẽmo*	*vidurỹ*	*(iř pravir̃ko).*
stopped	he: NOM	yard: GEN	middle: LOC	(and cried)

'He stopped in the middle of the yard (and burst into tears).'

NUOBÕDŽIOS	*bū́davo*	*mùms*	*žiẽmos.*
tedious: NOM. PL. FEM	used-to-be	we: DAT	winter: NOM. PL. FEM

'Winters used to be tedious for us.'

If the rheme is the subject (S), the VS sequence is regular in sentences with the neutral intonation pattern, e.g.:

(*Kàs teñ stuksẽna? –*) *Teñ dìrba Pėtras.*	'(Who is knocking there? –) (lit.) There works petras (Peter).'
Mìrė tą̃ diẽną ir víenas kareĩvis.	'On that day one soldier died too.'

The VS sequence is also common in authorial remarks following direct speech:

"Šálta," – pasãkė Pẽtras.   '"It is cold," said Peter.'

5.6   In two-constituent rhematic sentences, where no theme is distinguished, the regular word order is **VS**:

Gyvẽno kar̃tą var̃gšas žmogė́lis.   'There once lived a poor man.'
Sodè áuga dìdelė líepa.   lit. 'In the garden (there) grows a big lime-tree.'

Less common are rhematic sentences with a compound nominal predicate and the VS sequence, as in

Senì bùvo laikaĩ.   lit. 'Old were the times' (= 'It was a long time ago').

In SV sentences the rhematic character (communicative indivisibility) is made clear by intonation or context, if, for instance, they are juxtaposed with rhematic VS sentences:

Prasidė́jo žiemà. Ùpės užšãlo.   lit. 'Began winter. The rivers froze.'

Since most sentences are divided into theme and rheme, the SV sequence is basic and the most common one in Lithuanian.

Sentences consisting of a predicate and object (VO), without an explicit subject, have the same word order as three-member sentences (SVO) (see 5.7–13).

5.7   In a compound predicate, the copula or the (semi-)auxiliary verb is usually placed before the notional component:

Diẽną bùvo vėjúota.   'The day was windy.'
Pẽtras atródė pavar̃gęs.   'Peter looked tired.'
Jìs gãli pavėlúoti.   'He may be late.'

The same rule applies to copulas with a neuter adjective:

Miestẽlyje bùvo ramù.   'It was quiet in the town.'
Bùs vėlù grį̃žti.   'It will be late to return.'

But their sequence is inverted if the predicate is fronted and (usually) emphasized by intonation:

RAMÙ bùvo miestẽlyje.   'It was QUIET in the town.'
VĖLÙ bùs grį̃žti.   'It will be LATE to return.'

5.8   The rhematic part of a **three-constituent sentence** may be either (1) the predicate and object (VO) or the object alone, or (2) the subject and predicate (S, V) or (3) the subject alone.

Theme – **S**, Rheme – **VO** or **O**

5.9 Under these circumstances the neutral word order is SVO which is also the basic word order in Standard Lithuanian, e.g.:

Vaikaĩ suválgė visùs óbuolius.	'The children have eaten all the apples.'

Corresponding sentences with an implied subject retain the VO word order:

Sužinójau naujíeną.	'I have heard the news.'

The SVO sequence is prevalent in the official styles of Standard Lithuanian. If the object is placed before the verb (**SOV**) it sometimes receives more emphasis:

Vaikaĩ visùs óbuolius suválgė.	'The children have eaten all the apples.'
Naujíeną sužinójau.	'I've heard the news.'

However, the (**S**)**OV** sequence is not always stylistically marked: in many cases SVO and SOV alternate without any marked difference. Moreover, SOV is neutral and more common in a number of cases, especially if the object is a pronoun:

Vìsas miẽstas manè gerbė.	'The whole town respected me.'
Šiañdien àš niẽko nesakýsiu.	'Today I won't say anything.'

The SOV sequence is also common in set phrases and general statements, e.g.:

Pirmì gaidžiaĩ vélnią baĩdo.	'Early roosters scare away the devil.'
Áitvaras pìnigus nẽša.	'The house-spirit brings money.'
Dárbas dárbą vẽja.	lit. 'Work chases work' (i.e. 'There is too much work').

In fact, SOV is more common in dialectal speech and in folklore than in Standard Lithuanian.

The position of an object is also dependent on the lexical meaning of the verbal predicate. For instance, the object mostly takes the final position after verbs of speech, perception and mental activities, e.g.:

Sesuõ pasākė naujíeną.	'My sister told me the news.'
Pamačiaũ kìškį.	'I saw a rabbit.'
Mẽs nežinójome kẽlio.	'We didn't know the way.'

5.10 In sentences with a thematic subject and rhematic predicate and/or object, any other sequence of the components is inverted. For instance, alongside sentences with the basic SVO sequence (e.g. *Tà žinià labaĩ sujáudino mótiną* 'That news excited mother very much') and SOV (*Tà žinià mótiną labaĩ sujáudino*) four inverted sequences are possible.

The pattern VSO is used to emphasize the predicate while VOS often emphasizes the predicate and subject:

(1) VSO: *Labaĩ sujáudino tà žinià mótiną.*

(2) VOS: *Labaĩ sujáudino mótiną tà žinià.*

The OSV pattern places emphasis on the object:

(3) *Mótiną tà žinià labaĩ sujáudino.*

OVS emphasizes both the object and the subject:

(4) *Mótiną labaĩ sujáudino tà žinià.* 'Mother was very excited by the news.'

The stressed component is usually in an atypical position: V is preposed to S, O precedes S, and S follows V.

Theme – O, Rheme – VS or S

5.11 In this type of communicative structure the neutral word order is **OSV**, sometimes **OSV**. It is characteristic of active sentences denoting the state of a human object or natural phenomena:

OVS: *Manè àpėmė báimė.*	'I (O) was gripped (3. PAST. ACT) by fear (S).'
Káimą gaũbė naktìs.	'The village (O) was engulfed (3. PAST. ACT) by night (S).'
OSV: *Manè báimė àpėmė.*	'I (O) was gripped by fear (S).'

Theme – SV, Rheme – O

5.12 In this case the common sequence is **SOV** alongside **SVO**. Thus, regular answers to the question *Ką̃ tėvas nušóvė?* 'What did father shoot?' may be:

SOV: *Tė́vas lãpę nušóvė.*	'Father shot a fox.'
SVO: *Tė́vas nušóvė lãpę.*	'Father shot a fox.'

In sentences without an overt subject the respective word order is **OV** and **VO**.

The OSV sequence is inverted, the rhematic object being emphasized by its initial position:

LÃPĘ tėvas nušóvė.   'It was a fox that father shot.'

The OVS, VSO, VOS sequences are not typical of sentences with a rhematic object.

Theme – VO, Rheme – S

5.13 In this case the common word order is **OVS** and **OSV**. Thus, the answer to the question *Kàs nušóvė lãpę?* 'Who shot the fox?' may be:

OVS: *Lāpę nušóvė* tėvas. 'It was father who shot the fox.'
OSV: *Lāpę* tėvas *nušóvė.* (Same translation).

These sentences may be regarded as variants of those discussed in 5.10 above, with the rhematic S. This accounts for the identical common word order. The rhematic subject is indicated by its unusual position after the object. If the word order is SVO (*JÌS nušóvė lãpę* 'He shot a fox') or SOV (*JÌS lãpę nušóvė*) the subject can be rhematized by heavy stress.

Rhematic sentences

5.14 In rhematic sentences the regular word order is either **VSO** or **OVS**, with the predicate preceding the subject (cf. respective two-constituent sentences in 5.5).

VSO: *(Kartą) Nēšė vélnias ãkmenį.* '(Once) a devil carried a stone.'
Turėjo karãlius grãžią dùkterį. '(There was) A king (who) had a beautiful daughter.'
OVS: *Píevas deñgė miglà.* 'Meadows (O) were enveloped in mist (S).'

Sentences with the most common SVO and SOV order may have no theme distinguished either, but in this case their communicative indivisibility is not marked by word order: it can be made clear by the context and it is often indicated by an indefinite adverbial in the initial position:

Kartą žmogùs bùlves kãsė/kãsė bùlves. 'Once a man was digging potatoes.'

In this kind of sentence, if the subject is not expressed, the object is usually placed in final position after the predicate:

Laukuosè jau kãsė bùlves. 'In the fields (the people) were already digging potatoes.'

THE POSITION OF OTHER SENTENCE CONSTITUENTS

Oblique objects

5.15 An oblique object usually precedes a direct object. This position is most typical of a dative (especially human) object, cf.:

Jis atléido vaikáms *visùs išdykãvimus.* 'He forgave (his) children (DAT) all (their) pranks.'
Àš táu pãčią sáulę atidúosiu. 'I will give you (DAT) the sun itself.'

Jìs paródė rankà *kaimýnų nãmą*. 'He pointed with his hand (INSTR) to the neighbours' house (ACC).'

However, the position of an oblique object may vary depending on its informative load. It can be shifted to the final position, as in (1), or to the initial position, as in (2):

(**1**) *Senẽlė vaišino Antanùką medumì.* 'Granny treated Anthony (ACC) to some honey (INSTR).'

(**2**) *Pẽtrui liẽpė indùs supláuti.* 'Peter (DAT) was ordered (lit. '(they) ordered') to wash up the dishes.'

Adverbials

5.16 There is no fixed position for all adverbials in a sentence: it is determined by the type of adverbial and/or its communicative function. If it is given no particular prominence, it is commonly placed between the predicate and a direct object:

Vaikaĩ rińko miškè úogas. 'Children picked berries in the woods.'

It may be given prominence by placing it either in the initial or in the final position, cf. respectively:

Miškè vaikaĩ rińko úogas. 'In the woods children picked berries.'
Vaikaĩ rińko úogas miškè. 'The children picked berries in the woods.'

An adverbial (of place or time) modifying the entire sentence is usually thematic and therefore fronted:

Válgomajame stalaĩ lū́žo nuo val̃gių. 'In the dining room, the tables were laden with food.'

Predicative complement

5.17 A complement related to the subject and predicate is commonly placed after both:

Mėnùlis pakìlo raudónas ir grėsmìngas. 'The moon rose red and menacing.'

A complement related to the object and predicate is commonly put after the object:

Šiañdien pagaliaũ pamãtėme jį̃ liñksmą. 'Today, at last, we saw him merry.'

A complement can be placed before the subject and predicate or the object to give it communicative prominence; cf. respectively:

Skaistì ir linksmà, *prašvìto pavakarìnė sáulė.*	'Bright and joyful, the evening sun came out.'
Ir àtnešė gývą tą̃ žvėrẽlį.	'And (they) brought that little animal (ACC) alive (ACC).'

WORD ORDER IN SUBORDINATIVE GROUPS

5.18 There is a general tendency to place a dependent constituent before the head. This tendency is particularly marked in noun groups, although it is less prominent in verb groups where word order may vary considerably. The position of a word is also dependent on its categorial status, e.g. some adverbs and particles may have a specific position.

Verb groups

5.19 The neutral and common position of an **adverb** in a verb group is usually before the head (**AdvV**). Pre-posing is particularly characteristic of the following classes of adverbs:

(1) adverbs of manner (and also inflected nouns and prepositional phrases denoting manner of action), e.g.:

geraĩ dìrbi	'(you) work well'
pėsčiõm váikšto	'(he/she/they) walk on foot'
balsù veřkė	'(he/she/they) wept loudly (lit. 'in a voice: INSTR')'
be tìkslo kláidžiojo	lit. '(he/she/they) wandered without aim'

(2) adverbs of place, time and cause (unrelated to inflected nouns) such as *čià* 'here', *teñ* 'there', *kituř* 'elsewhere', *niẽkur* 'nowhere', *visuř* 'everywhere', *dabař* 'now', *niekadà* 'never', *paskuĩ* 'later', *tadà* 'then', *tuojaũ* 'at once', *todẽl* 'therefore', *kažkodẽl* 'for some reason', etc.; e.g.:

Visì teñ sugrį̃šime.	'We shall all return there.'
Dabař visuř palìjo.	'Now it has rained everywhere.'
Traukinỹs tuõj pajudė̃s.	'The train will start immediately' (= 'the train is leaving').
Vaĩkas kažkodẽl susiřgo.	'The child has fallen ill for some reason.'

These adverbs are placed after the predicate if they are the rhematic focus:

Mẽs gyvẽname geraĩ.	'We live well.'
Kalbė́k ramiaĩ.	'(Please) speak calmly.'
Láuksime čià.	'We'll be waiting here.'
Važiúosime kitur̃.	'We'll go elsewhere.'
Padarýk taĩ dabar̃.	'Do it now.'

The position of other types of adverbs, adverbial case forms and prepositional phrases is less fixed; if the predicate is stressed they usually precede it:

Tė́vas iš rýto dìrba, vakaraĩs ìlsisi.	'In the morning father works, in the evening (he) rests.'
Traukinỹs pakeliuĩ sustójo.	'The train stopped on the way.'

There is a tendency to place adverbs after the verb if it denotes motion or a change of state, e.g.:

žeñgė atgaĩ	'(he) stepped back'
išvažiãvo namõ	'(he) went home'

A predicative adverb also usually follows the copula:

jám pasidãrė negeraĩ	'he (suddenly) felt unwell'

Adverbials of purpose are as a rule placed in final position:

pàkvietė pietų̃	'(he) invited for dinner'
susė́dom pusryčiáuti	'we sat down to have breakfast'
išė́jo obuolių̃ raškýti	'(he) went to pick apples'

In the case of multiple adverbial modification, an adverb of manner is commonly placed immediately before the verb, the other adverbs preceding it, e.g.:

Jìs visadà ramiaĩ miẽga.	'He always sleeps quietly.'
Vãkar týčia ilgaĩ láukėme.	'Yesterday we waited a long time on purpose.'

5.20 An adverb modifying another adverb always precedes it (**Adv₁ Adv**), e.g.:

visái geraĩ dìrba	'(he) works quite well'
labaĩ greĩtai skreñda	'(it) is flying very fast'
mataũ daũg geriaũ	'(I) see much better'

5.21 **Comparative phrases** introduced by the conjunctions *kaĩp* 'like', *lýg* 'as, like' and *tar̃tum/tar̃si* 'as if/though' are usually placed after the predicate (**VComp**):

Gíeda kaip gaidỹs.	'(He) Croaks like a rooster.'
Miegójo lyg ùžmuštas.	'(He) Slept like a log' (lit. 'like dead').

A comparative phrase may be placed in initial position for emphasis:

Kaip vienà dienà prabėgo mẽtai.   'The year passed like a single day.'

5.22 The neutral position of a **particle is** before the head word (**PrtV**), e.g.:

dár nemiẽga	'(they) are not asleep yet'
jaũ atẽjo	'(he has) already come'
bevéik suprataũ	'I almost understood'
nèt nežinaũ	'(I) don't even know'
võs jùda	'(he) hardly moves'
vẽl ateĩna	'(she) is coming again'

The interrogative particles *ar̃* and *benè* (cf. 5.2, 6.14) are also always placed initially. The particle *gì* usually follows the verb, e.g.:

Žinaĩ gi jõ pãpročius.   'You do know his habits, don't you.'
Tù gi žinaĩ jõ pãpročius.   (Same translation)

Nominal groups

5.23 The neutral position of an **adjective** is before the head noun (**AdjN**):

tamsùs debesìs   'dark cloud'
smarkùs vẽjas   'strong wind'

The adjective is post-posed in case of inversion for emphasis:

Pirkaũ trobẽlę mažýtę ir sẽną.   lit. 'I bought a hut small and old.'

Post-posing is characteristic of adjectives used as trite epithets (*rūtà žalióji* 'green rue'), and it is common in poetry, e.g.:

Teñ už ùpių plačių̃ spiñdi mū́sų pulkaĩ.   'There, beyond wide rivers, our regiments are shining.'

An adjective distanced from the head noun receives special emphasis:

Iš mažõs kibirkštiẽs dìdis kýla gaĩsras.   'From a small spark a great fire starts.'

An adjective usually follows the head for emphasis if it has dependent words, or an intensifier (*tóks, -ià* 'such', *nèt* 'even', *nórs* 'though', etc.), or if it is coordinated with another adjective, cf.:

Jìs rãdo óbelę, pìlną labaĩ gražių̃ obuolių̃.   'He found an apple-tree full of fine apples.'
Atẽjo ruduõ, liū̃dnas, nelaimìngas.   'Autumn came, sad, unhappy.'
Mán bùvo gaĩla mergáitės, tokiõs jaunõs, tokiõs gražiõs.   'I was sorry for the girl, so young, so beautiful.'

Adjectives used with the relative pronoun *kurìs* 'which', are also used as post-modifiers (very much like attributive clauses; see 7.24–27), e.g.:

Grybùs kuriuõs geresniùs (cf. *grybùs, kuriẽ (yrà) geresnì) dė́k į̃ krẽpšį̃.*	'Put (IMPER) the better mushrooms (lit. 'the mushrooms (ACC) which better (ACC)') into the basket' (sequence **NRel**).

The neutral position of participles, adjectival pronouns, and ordinal (and some cardinal) numerals when used attributively is also before the head noun (**PartN, PronN, NumN**):

žaĩdžiantis vaĩkas	'a playing child'
ãriamas laũkas	'a ploughed field'
kìtas krãštas	'another country'
tokià dienà	'such a day'
víenas mẽdis	'one tree'
pìrmas mė́nuo	'the first month'
penkì výrai	'five men'

5.24 **The genitive of a noun** used attributively is placed before the head (**GenN**):

tė́vo švar̃kas	'father's jacket'
áukso žíedas	'gold ring'
keliõnės tìkslas	'the purpose of the journey'
nãmo statýba	'building of a house'
Vìlniaus miẽstas	'the town of Vilnius'

Inverted sequence is rare and stylistically marked. It is used as a means of emphasis, especially in lofty poetic style (cf. *Kaĩp puikū̃s slė́niai srauniõs Dubýsos* 'How magnificent are the vales of the swift Dubysa'). It is common if the genitive case of a noun has a subordinate attributive clause (*Sunkùs gyvẽnimas žmogaũs, kuriuõ niẽkas nètiki* lit. 'Hard is the life of a man whom nobody believes'). Post-position of the genitive of a pronoun is a means of emphasizing the head noun:

Dar̃žas jų̃ mãžas ir apléistas.	'Their garden (lit. 'garden of them') is small and neglected.'

However, the genitive attribute usually follows head nouns of measure and quantity:

bùtelis alaũs	'a bottle of beer'
dalìs linų̃	'a part of the flax'
bū́rỹs žmonių̃	'a group of people'
lìtras píeno	'a litre of milk'

These head nouns are akin to adverbs of measure which are also placed before the genitive, e.g.:

daũg píeno	'much milk'
mažaĩ pinigų̃	'little money'
pakañkamai laĩko	'enough time'

The sequence of components in noun groups with a dependent genitive can be a means of distinguishing between two meanings: a pre-posed head noun refers to quantity (*stiklìnė píeno* 'a glass (full) of milk', *vežìmas málkų* 'a cart (load) of firewood') and if the head noun is postposed the meaning may be that of purpose, property, as well as of quantity, e.g.: *píeno stiklìnė* (1) 'a glass for milk', (2) 'a glass (full) of milk'; *šiẽno vežìmas* (1) 'a hay cart', (2) 'a cart (load) of hay'.

5.25 If a noun has two or more preceding modifiers, a pronoun and a numeral (in concord with the head) commonly precede an adjective:

tàs (tóks) gražùs pavãsaris	'that (such a) beautiful spring'
kiekvíenas dõras žmogùs	'every honest man'
dù mažì vaikaĩ	'two little children'
pirmóji šiltà dienà	'the first warm day'

The genitive is also placed immediately before the head:

kìtas pasáulio krãštas	'the other end of the world'
kiekvíenas màno žõdis	lit. 'each my (GEN) word'

A limiting modifier is commonly placed between a descriptive modifier and the head noun. The former is often expressed by the genitive, and the latter by an adjective:

báltas obels̃ žíedas	'a white apple (GEN) blossom'
sunkùs vãrio var̃pas	'a heavy copper (GEN) bell'

A limiting modifier can also be an adjective and it may be preceded by the possessive genitive:

mótinos vestùvinė suknẽlė	'mother's wedding (Adj) gown'
árklio príekinės kójos	'a horse's fore (Adj) legs'

5.26 A modifier expressed by the **instrumental** case of a noun (with a dependent modifier) is placed after the head (**NInstr**):

Pamačiaũ mergáitę ilgaĩs plaukaĩs.	'I saw a girl with long hair.'
Ar esì kuomèt mãtęs žáltį devyniomìs galvomìs?	'Have you ever seen a grass-snake with nine heads?'

The reversed sequence is also neutral but it is very rare; cf.:

Taĩ bùvo aukštà, žemaĩ palinkusiomis šakomìs ẽglė.	'It was a tall fir-tree with bowed branches.'

5.27 Modifiers expressed by any other case form of a noun or by a prepositional phrase also follow the head noun, as a rule:

įvykis dvarè	'the incident in the manor'
žmogùs be pastógės	'a person without a home'
puolìmas iš piliẽs	'attack from the castle'

5.28 In **adjectival groups**, a modifying adverb usually precedes the head (**AdvAdj**):

nepaprastaĩ tvankùs óras	'unusually sultry weather'
malõniai šíltas vanduõ	'pleasantly warm water'
per daũg išdidùs (svẽčias)	'too proud (guest)'
ganà gražì mergìna	'a rather pretty girl'

A qualitative prepositional group is also placed before the head adjective:

be gãlo gẽras	'very (lit. 'without end') good'
iš esmės klaidìngas	'basically (lit. 'from essence') erroneous'

Similarly, the instrumental case of a noun precedes a verbal adjective in *-inas, -a*:

ėjo kibiraĩs nešinà	'(she) walked carrying buckets (INSTR)'
grĩžo árkliu vėdinas	'(he) returned leading a horse (INSTR)'

The position of other case forms and prepositional phrases with respect to the head adjective varies, both pre-modification and post-modification being neutral:

vandeñs pìlnas ąsõtis/pìlnas vandeñs ąsõtis	'a jug full of water (GEN)'
tėvui reikalìngas peĩlis/reikalìngas tėvui peĩlis	lit. 'a knife necessary for father (DAT)'
į mótiną panašùs vaĩkas/panašùs į mótiną vaĩkas	'a child resembling (his) mother (Prep + ACC)'

5.29 In **comparative phrases**, the prepositional phrase *už* + ACC denoting the standard (St) of comparison can either precede or follow the head adjective in the comparative form (**StComp** and **CompSt** respectively). Its pre-position is frequent in dialectal speech, folklore, and, to a certain degree, in fiction; cf.:

už árklį didèsnis	'bigger than a horse'
už mẽdų saldèsnis	'sweeter than honey'

Its post-position is characteristic of official style, e.g.:

sunkèsnis už gẽležį	'heavier than iron'
greitèsnis už gar̃są	'faster than sound'

The prepositional phrase per̃ + ACC used in dialectal speech alternately with ùž + ACC also precedes the head:

per visùs vertèsnis	'worthier than all'
per ją̃ gražèsnis	'handsomer than she'

The genitive plural visų̃ 'of all' of the pronoun vìsas, -à (with or without the genitive of a noun) and the adverbs pervìs/užvìs '(most) of all' also precede the superlative (sometimes the comparative) form of an adjective:

visų̃ geriáusias	'the best of all'
visų̃ kalnų̃ aukščiáusias	'the highest of all the mountains'
pervìs didžiáusias	'the biggest of all'
pervìs baltèsnis/balčiáusias	'whiter than all/the whitest of all'

The standard of comparison expressed by a noun with the conjunctions negù/néi/(ne)kaĩp 'than' usually follows the head adjective:

kietèsnis negù (néi) geležìs	'harder than iron'
baltèsnis kaĩp (nekaĩp) sniẽgas	'whiter than snow'

The instrumental case expressing the compared characteristics precedes the head, as a rule:

ūgiù mažèsnis už brólį	lit. 'in height smaller than (his) brother'
dviẽm mẽtais vyrèsnis už brólį	'two years older than (his) brother'

It is placed after the head for emphasis:

pranašèsnis už kitùs išmintimì	'superior to others in wisdom'
už draugùs aukštèsnis visà gálva	'a head taller than his friends'

5.30 In comparative phrases with the comparative degree of an adverb the sequence is either variable as with adjectives (cf. už vė́ją greičiaũ/greičiaũ už vė́ją 'faster than wind'), or fixed, as in užvìs geriaũ 'better than anything', pervìs toliaũ 'farther than anything', anksčiaũ negù (nekaĩp, kaĩp) vãkar 'earlier than yesterday'. The position of the criterion is also variable: dviẽm minùtėm už tavè greičiaũ/už tavè greičiaũ dviẽm minùtėm 'two minutes faster than you'.

5.31 To sum up, the dependent constituent commonly precedes the head in the neutral word order patterns AdvV (with adverbs of manner, place, time and cause), PartV, AdjN, PronN, NumN, GenN, Adv$_1$Adv and AdvAdj with the adverbs of manner.

The dependent constituent usually follows the head in the patterns NInstr, Adj/AdvN with a quantitative meaning and in comparative phrases with conjunctions (CompSt).

Variability in position of constituents is more characteristic of prepositional phrases with regard to the head verb and noun (VPrepN/PrepNV, NPrepN/PrepNN), and of the standard of comparison in comparative phrases with prepositions (StComp/CompSt).

The tendency to place a dependent constituent before the head word typologically parallels the basic (S)OV order which is quite frequent in dialects and in folklore besides the (S)VO order, predominant in Standard Lithuanian.

The functional (theme – rheme) structure determines the order of the main sentence constituents to a greater degree than that of the constituents within subordinative word groups.

6 THE COMMUNICATIVE TYPES OF SENTENCES

6.1 According to their communicative function, sentences are classified into declarative, or statements, volitional and interrogative, or questions. These communicative types of sentences differ in syntactic properties and, in oral speech, intonation.

A sentence of any of these types may become exclamatory (exclamation) if it receives an emotional load which thereby changes the intonation pattern. Thus exclamatory sentences are opposed to the three basic communicative sentence types.

DECLARATIVE SENTENCES

6.2 A declarative sentence states a fact (in the affirmative or negative form). By means of a declarative sentence the speaker conveys information to the listener(s). Statements are generally uttered with a falling intonation at the end, though a rise (rises) may occur before the final fall to give prominence to the key word(s).

The predicative centre of a declarative sentence may be any mood form of a verbal or a compound nominal predicate. The imperative mood is not characteristic of declarative sentences unless it acquires a function close to that of the indicative mood and expresses necessity, obligation, or surprise, etc. In these cases, typical of colloquial speech, an imperative mood form is often used with the pronouns *tù* 'you', *mán* 'to-me (DAT)', or with the emphatic clusters *tù mán* lit. 'you to me', *tù jám* 'you to him', *tù žmogùs* 'you man', or with the particles *iř*, *tìk*, *taĩ*:

Tàvo namuosè nuo rýto iki vãkaro tik dìrbk ir dìrbk.	'At your house one has to work and work (lit. 'only work (IMPER) and work (IMPER)') from morning till night.'
Tù mán ir pridarýk tíek nētvarkos.	lit. 'Just make (IMPER) such a mess to me (DAT).' 'It's surprising what a mess one has made.'

Ir turẽk mán žmogùs tókias akìs.	'Just imagine a man having such eyes' (lit. 'Just have (IMPER) to me (DAT) a man (NOM) such eyes').
Dabař į rogès tik sẽsk ir važiúok.	'Just get (IMPER) into the sledge and go (IMPER).'

VOLITIONAL SENTENCES

6.3 Volitional sentences express the speaker's will ranging from a categorical command to a polite request or humble entreaty. The principal means of expressing this variety of meanings is intonation. Thus the sentence *Atidarýk lángą* 'Open the window' can be made to sound as an order, or a request, or a suggestion depending on the intonation contour. Alongside intonation, grammatical and lexical means and context also distinguish between the above meanings. For instance, various meanings can be explicated by the use of such appropriate verbs as *liẽpti* 'order', *reikaláuti* 'demand, insist', *norẽti* 'want', *prašýti* 'ask', *pageidáuti* 'desire, wish', *linkẽti* 'wish (sb sth)', and the like combined with an infinitive.

Volitional sentences are further divided into imperative and hortative sentences. The speaker uses imperative sentences to induce the addressee(s) to do something, while optative sentences are not as a rule specifically addressed to anyone and express the speaker's wish that something should be done or happen.

IMPERATIVE SENTENCES

6.4 Imperative sentences express the speaker's command (in the broad sense) to perform an action.

Imperative sentences are usually uttered at a high pitch.

The imperative mood is a specialized grammatical means of expressing commands. The singular and plural 2nd person forms express a more categorical command than the 1st person plural form which includes both the addressee(s) and the speaker; cf.:

Ateĩk pas manè rytój!	'Come to see me tomorrow!'
Neklausýkit jũs tokių šnekų!	'Don't you listen to such talk!'
Sẽskimės čià, ant akmeñs.	'Let's sit down here, on the boulder.'

The meaning of an imperative mood form can be modified or specified by various lexical means (especially in colloquial speech), such as the imperative form of the verb *žiūrẽti* 'look', forms of direct address, particles, etc. To intensify or tone down a request, expressions like *bū́k gēras, -à* 'be kind', *susimìldamas, -a* 'for goodness' sake', etc. are also used, e.g.:

Žiūrėk/Bū́k gēras/Susimìldamas neužmiřšk grąžìnti knỹgos.	'Look/Be good (and)/For goodness' sake, don't forget to return the book.'
Tù mán sàvo sūnaũs neužtarinėk!	'Don't you intercede for your son!'
Šè, im̃k sáu tą̃ árklį.	'Here, take that horse.'

The particle *tìk*, the adverb *dár* 'yet', and the dative *mán* 'to me' (functionally similar to a particle) can be used to add threat to an imperative form, while the particle *gál* is used to tone down an order:

Tìk pamėgìnk išbė́gti laukañ! – grasìna močiùtė.	'Just you try to run outside! – threatened granny.'
O tù mán tylė́k!	'And you just keep silent!'
Dabař̃ gál eĩk namõ.	'Now you (may) go home.'

6.5 The predicate of an imperative sentence can be also expressed by a present or future indicative:

Prisė́dam po tuõ medžiù!	'Let's sit down (lit. 'We sit down') under that tree!'
Tai gál nesipỹksim.	lit. 'May be we shall not quarrel.'
Tù láuksi manę̃s miškè.	'You'll wait for me in the woods.'
O rytój užeĩsite pas manè, – pridū́rė dirèktorius.	'And tomorrow you'll call on me, – added the director.'

6.6 The subjunctive mood (usually 2nd person) may express a milder command, but it can be strengthened by the particle *kàd (mán)* or softened by *gál/gal bū́t*:

Kad àš tokių̃ kalbų̃ daugiaũ negirdė́čiau!	'No more talk like this!' (lit. 'That I wouldn't hear any more talk like this!')
Kad mán daugiaũ čia kójos nekéltumėt!	'Don't you ever dare come here again!' (lit. 'That you should never come here again!')
Gal užsùktum pas mùs..?	'Maybe you might drop in at our place..?'

6.7 In expressive speech categorical commands can be conveyed by an infinitive or an intensifying deverbal adverb in *-te*, e.g.:

Tuojaũ išvarýti pùbliką iš čià!	'Turn out (INF) the people from here immediately!'
Bė́gtè márš!	'Quick march!' (lit. 'Running march!')
Tylė́t!	'You be quiet (INF)!'

These commands are uttered with a particularly forceful intonation.

6.8 A sharp command can be also expressed by an interjection with an imperative meaning:

Jùkš iš màno kiẽmo!	'(Get) out of my yard!'
Cìt, vaĩkai!	'Hush, children!'
Šè táu pìnigus!	'Here, take this money!'

6.9 Imperative sentences can have no overt predicate. A command may be implied by words which denote an object or circumstances of the requested action:

Rankàs aukštỹn!	'Hands up!'
Sesẽle, vandeñs!	'Nurse, water!'
Nè iš viẽtos!..	'Not a step (further)!'

OPTATIVE SENTENCES

6.10 Optative sentences express the speaker's wish or desire, or at least consent that something should be done or happen. They have a specific intonation contour with a low final fall.

Special means of rendering the optative meaning are the 3rd person imperative mood forms and also 3rd person indicative present and future tense forms with the prefix *te-* or with the particles *tè, tegù/teguĩ* 'let', e.g.:

Tebūniẽ vìskas pagaĩ tavè.	'Let everything be as you wish.'
Tegù Jokūbas greičiaũ ateĩna.	'Let Jacob come sooner.'
Teguĩ visàd laisvà bùs mū́sų žẽmė.	'Let our land be always free.'

2nd person imperative forms are also used occasionally:

Pasilìkit sveikì...	'Stay (2. PL) healthy...'
Im̃k tavè velniaĩ!	lit. 'Devils take (2. PL) you!'

Future and present tense forms of the indicative mood with the affix *te-* or particle *tegù/teguĩ*, and with the particle *tìk* 'only, just' are sometimes used to express a threat:

Teišdrį́sta tik jìs paliẽsti màno dùkterį...	'Let him just dare (3. PRES) touch my daughter...'
Tegù tik àš sužinósiu tõ vagiẽs var̃dą.	lit. 'Let me only find out (1. SG. FUT) the name of that thief.'

6.11 The subjunctive mood is widely used in optative sentences. Its meaning can be emphasized by the initially placed particle *kàd* 'that', alone or in conjunction with the interjections *ái, àk, õ, ói* or with the particle *tìk*, e.g.:

Õ, kad àš užmìgčiau nór̃s valandė̃lę!	'Oh, if (only) I could fall asleep for even a little while!'
Kad tìk mamýtė greičiaũ namõ grį̃žtų...	'If only mummy returned (3. SUBJ) home sooner...'

This type of optative sentence is often used to wish somebody ill, e.g.:

Kad juõs perkū́nas nutreñktų!	'Let thunder strike them!'
Õ, kad tù sudègtum!	'Oh, may you burn!'

Sometimes in these sentences subjunctive mood is implied:

Kad beñt lašẽlis vandeñs.	'If only (there were) at least a drop of water.'
Kad juõs kur gãlas!	'To hell with them!' (lit. 'That them (ACC) where end (NOM)!'

6.12 To wish something for oneself or another person, optative sentences with an infinitive or a past gerund (with or without a particle or an interjection) are also employed:

Numir̃ti, užmìgti amžinaĩ, niẽkad nejaũsti skaũsmo!	'To die, to sleep forever, never to feel pain!'
Kad tìk ištrū́kus iš čià!	'If only one could escape (PAST. GER) from here!'

The finite forms of verbs like *norė́ti* 'want', *pageidáuti* 'desire, wish', *linkė́ti* 'wish' with an infinitive or a noun are also used for the same purpose; e. g.:

Linkiù pasveĩkti.	'I wish you to get well.'
Linkiù laimìngų Naujū́jų Mẽtų/ gerõs sveikãtos.	'I wish (you) a Happy New Year / good health.'

The finite verb form is often omitted in these formulaic sentences:

Į̃ sveikãtą!	'To your health!'
Linksmų̃ Kalė̃dų!	'Merry Christmas!'
Laimìngai!	'Good luck!'

INTERROGATIVE SENTENCES

6.13 Interrogative sentences are a way of asking the addressee(s) for new or more complete information, usually though not necessarily requiring a reply from the latter.

Sometimes interrogative sentences may supply information rather than ask for it.

In Lithuanian most of interrogative sentences are similar in structure to declarative sentences. They may be even syntactically identical with the latter, but they are characterized by distinctive intonation patterns. Interrogative sentences are usually uttered with a final rise or with a rise on the key word(s) depending on the type of question. Word order can be changed also: the key word(s) can be placed either in initial or final position; cf.:

Čià   gyvénsiu   ilgaĩ. –   Ilgaĩ   čià   gyvénsi?
here   live: FUT. 1. SG   long   long   here   live: FUT. 2. SG
'I'll stay here a long time.' 'Will you stay here a long time?'

Àtnešiau   táu   gėlių̃.   –
bring: PAST. 1. SG   you: DAT   flowers: GEN
'I have brought you some flowers.'

Gėlès   àtnešei   mán?
flowers: ACC   bring: PAST. 2. SG   me: DAT
'Have you brought the flowers for me?'

Interrogative or dubitative particles, or interrogative pronouns and adverbs usually placed in the sentence-initial position are specialized markers of interrogative sentences, e.g.:

Ar tù ateĩsi vakarè? (or *Tù ateĩsi vakarè?*)   'Will you come in the evening?'
Kadà tėvas parašỹs láišką?   'When will father write a letter?'

Depending on the communicative purpose, interrogative sentences are classified into interrogative sentences proper, which require a reply, and rhetorical questions.

Interrogative sentences proper are further subcategorized into general (verifying) and special (particularizing) questions depending on the nature of the information the speaker seeks to obtain.

6.14 **General questions** are aimed at verifying the facts. They may be answered with *taĩp* 'yes' or *nè* 'no'.

General questions either (1) contain no interrogative marker and are distinguished from statements by intonation alone, and, sometimes, word order, or (2) they contain an interrogative or a dubitative particle, e.g.: *ar̃, ar̃gi, benè, gál, kažìn, nègi, nejaũ, nejaũgi,* etc.:

(1) *Tù jį̃ geraĩ pažį́sti?*   'Do you know him well?'
Guĺti dar neinì?   'Aren't you going to bed yet?'
Tàvo žmonà namiẽ?   'Is your wife at home?'

(2) *Ar galėčiau táu kuo nórs padėti?*   'Could I possibly help you?'
Gal ir tù per daũg reikaláuji?   'Maybe you too want too much?'
Benè táu įdomù?   'Is it of interest to you?'

Most general questions can be either positive or negative (irrespective of the expected reply). A question containing negation may sound more polite, cf.:

Táu reĩkia pinigų̃? 'Do you need (any) money?'   —   *Táu nereĩkia pinigų̃?* 'Maybe you need some money?'

Sometimes, negative questions with *ar̃* acquire the additional meaning of prohibition, restraint or threat, e.g.:

Ar tù pagaliaũ nenutìlsi?   'Won't you stop talking at last?'

The particle *ar̃* is a specialized formal marker of general questions, though it is not syntactically obligatory and does not change the question in any way; cf.:

Jìs ateĩs? / Ar jìs ateĩs?   'Will he come?'

The particle *ar̃* is especially characteristic of the written language which has few means of rendering the interrogative intonation.

6.15 The other particles may impart various modal meanings to the questions.

Sentences containing the particles *ar̃gi, benè, nègi, nejaũ, nejaũgi*, the cluster *ar tìk* convey uncertainty about what is being asked. These questions presuppose a contrary reply:

Ar̃gi šuõ jõ nepažiñs? 'Won't the dog recognize him?'   (expected response: *Taĩp, pažìns*. 'Yes, it will')
Nègi tù nóri teñ eĩti? 'Do you really want to go there?'   (expected response: *Nè, nenóriu*. 'No, I don't.')
Ar tik nemelúoji, sẽni?   'Are you really not lying, old chap?' (presupposition: the addressee is lying).

The particles *gál, kažìn* convey doubt with respect to what is being asked:

Gal manè prisìmeni?   'Maybe you remember me?'
Kažìn ar vaĩkas nóri gérti?   'I wonder if the child is thirsty?'

6.16 **Special questions** seek to obtain particularizing additional information. They usually require a concrete answer. These sentences are formed (1) with various case forms of the interrogative pronouns *kàs* 'who, what', *kurìs* 'which', *kóks* 'what (kind of)', *kelì* 'how many', *keliñtas* 'which (of the ordinal number)' and (2) with the interrogative adverbs *kur̃* 'where', *kadà* 'when', *kaĩp* 'how', *kodė̃l* 'why', *kíek* 'how many'. These markers are placed initially; cf. respectively:

(1) *Kàs teñ béldžiasi?*	'Who (NOM) is knocking there?'
Kuõ tai padareĩ?	'What (INSTR) did you do it with?'
Ką̃ mán dabar̃ darýti?	'What (ACC) shall I do now?'
Kienõ šìtas šáutuvas?	'Whose (GEN) rifle is this?'
Kokių̃ dažų̃ táu reĩkia?	'What (GEN. PL) paint (GEN. PL) do you need?'
Kelintà dabar̃ valandà?	'What's the time now?' (lit. 'Which (NOM) hour (NOM) is now?')
(2) *Kur̃ rengíesi eĩti?*	'Where are you going to go?'
Kadà grį̃ši namõ?	'When will you return home?'
Kodė̃l taip gar̃siai šaũkiate?	'Why are you shouting so loudly?'
Kíek svečių̃ tikíesi suláukti?	'How many visitors do you expect?'

6.17 Interrogative sentences can be related to the preceding sentences by the conjunctions *bèt, ir̃, õ, tìk* placed initially:

Bet kodė̃l taĩp rū́piniesi?	'But why are you so concerned?'
O ar pàts kar̃tais nebandeĩ jõ paklausinė́ti?	'But/And you by any chance didn't try to ask him a few questions?'
Tik kur̃ jìs gaũs tíek knỹgų?	'But (lit. 'Only') where will he get so many books?'

In speech, an interrogative word alone can substitute for an interrogative sentence:

(Nóriu jį̃ aplankýti.) – Kodė̃l?	'(I want to visit him.) – Why?'
(Jìs išvažiãvo.) – Kur̃?	'(He's gone away.) – Where?'

The addressee is urged to respond by means of the interjection *nà* in the initial position or by the tags *taĩp, ar nè, (ar) ką̃*, which makes them disjunctive questions:

Nà, ar àš ne karalíenė?	'Well, aren't I a queen?'
Táu reĩkia pinigų̃, taĩp?/ar nè?	'You need money, yes?/don't you?'
Juk táu jìs visái nepatiñka, ar nè?	'But you don't like him at all, do you?'
Čià susirinkìmas, ar ką̃?	'Is this a meeting, or what?'

6.18 The following questions offer a choice between possible alternative replies:

Ar pas mùs apsistósi, ar viẽšbutyje?	'Will you put up at our place, or at a hotel?'
O katràs bùvot kaĩtas: ar mamà, ar tù?	'And which (of you) was to blame: mother or you?'

6.19 **Rhetorical questions** do not require a response. In fact, they are forceful and expressive assertions. Rhetorical questions share the syntactic properties and intonation patterns with regular interrogative sentences, but functionally they are close to declarative sentences. They often have a generalized meaning.

A positive rhetorical question is in fact a negative assertion while a negative question is a positive assertion:

Kàs nenorė́tų sàvo jaunystę sugrą́žinti?	'Who wouldn't like to recover one's youth?' (= Everyone would like to.)
Kodė̃l mùms nepradė́jus (PAST. GER) vìsko iš naũjo?	'Why don't we start everything anew?'
Kàs gi galė́jo taĩ numatýti?	'Who could have foreseen it?' (= No one could have foreseen it.)

EXCLAMATORY SENTENCES

6.20 Exclamatory sentences differ from the other communicative sentence types in that their content is heavily underscored by emphatic intonation which may turn any declarative (1) or volitional (2) or interrogative (3) sentence into an exclamatory one.

(1) Àš táu niẽko nedúosiu! (rìktelėjo vaĩkas.)	'I won't give you anything! (shouted the boy.)'
(2) Diñk iš màno namų̃!	'Get out of my house!'
(3) Ką̃ čia padareĩ?!	'What have you done here?!'

Exclamatory sentences are uttered at a high pitch, the key word(s) bearing emphatic stress and a high fall.

Exclamatory sentences are often incomplete or they consist of a single word, e.g.:

Atvažiãvo!	'(They have) Arrived!'
Neteisýbė!	'(That's) Not right!'
Anaiptõl!	'Not at all!'

6.21 The emotional load of exclamatory sentences is often further reinforced by (1) interjections, (2) interrogative pronouns and pronominal adverbs, and (3) vocatives:

(1) Àk, nèrà tė́vo!	'Alas, Father is not with us!'
Ói, gélbėkit!	'Oh, help!'
Valiõ-o!	'Hurray!'
(2) Ir kàs per naktìs!	'Oh what a night!'
Kokià ramýbė!	'What peace!'
Kaĩp àš nepažìnsiu sàvo vaĩko?!	'Won't I recognize my child!'

(3) *Vaĩkai, greičiaũ!*   'Children, faster!'
Liáukitės, niekataũškiai!   'Stop it, chatterboxes!'
Ar neĩsi šaliñ, kvailỹ?!   'Won't you get out of the way, (you) fool?!'

6.22 Exclamatory intonation can be superimposed upon rhetorical questions (mostly those with negation):

Kàs nenorė́tų sàvo jaunỹstę sugrą̃žinti!   'Who wouldn't like to recover his youth!'

Exclamatory sentences formally identical with declarative sentences can imply the opposite assumption:

Padė̃s jìs táu!   lit. 'He'll help you!' (meaning 'He won't help you.')

Neim̃s jìs táu pinigų̃!   lit. 'Won't he take you (DAT. SG) the money!' (= 'He will certainly take the money!').

7 THE COMPOSITE SENTENCE
Sudėtìnis sakinỹs

7.1   A composite sentence is a syntactic unit comprised of two or more clauses each with a predicate of its own and structurally similar to a simple sentence.

The clauses within a composite sentence are linked syntactically and semantically, and also prosodically by intonation. For instance, the sentence *Óras bùvo gražùs ir mẽs išėjome pasiváikščioti* 'The weather was fine and we went out for a walk' is composed of two clauses each containing a separate predicate as well as a separate subject. But these clauses are not grammatically independent: they are linked by the conjunction *iř* 'and' indicating coordination, they also form a single intonation pattern and thus they constitute a larger syntactic unit.

Composite sentences are termed **syndetic** (conjunctive) if the constituent clauses are linked both by intonation and a conjunctive word and **asyndetic** (conjunctionless) if the only means of linking the clauses is intonation.

The link between clauses within a composite sentence can be reinforced by correlative words, sequence of clauses, the grammatical form and lexical meaning of the predicates, ellipsis of constituents and by other means. If the clauses are joined asyndetically or by an asemantic conjunction, these secondary means may acquire a distinctive function. Thus, for instance, the following example is a conditional sentence:

Kad   suieškótumei   màno   dùkteris,   àš   táu
that   find: SUBJ. 2. SG   my   daughter: ACC. PL   I: NOM   thou: DAT
dúočiau   pùsę   sàvo   tuřto.
give: SUBJ. 1. SG   half: ACC   my   wealth: GEN. SG
'If you found my daughters, I'd give you half of my riches.'

If the subjunctive form *dúočiau* '(I) would give' is changed into the indicative future tense form, the subordinate clause acquires the meaning of purpose:

Kad   suieškótumei   màno   dùkteris,   àš   dúosiu   tàu   pùsę sàvo tuřto.
that find: SUBJ.   my   daughters   I   give: thee   half my   wealth
      2. SG   FUT. 1. SG
'I'll give you half of my riches so that you could find my daughters.'

7.2 In Lithuanian, composite syndetic sentences are classified into **compound** (coordinative) and **complex** (subordinative). Coordination and subordination of clauses are marked by different sets of connectors.

In asyndetic sentences, the contrast between coordination and subordination is not marked by means of connectors.

Coordination of clauses differs from word coordination in that clauses are more independent and they are not related to any superordinate unit.

7.3 Clauses within a composite sentence usually realize the same syntactic patterns as simple sentences. However, they are more frequently incomplete, because a co-referential constituent expressed in one clause is often omitted in another. Thus the clauses often share a subject (1), an object (2), or an adverbial (3):

(1) Jõnas *pamiřšo, kad žadėjo padėti.*   'Jonas (John) forgot that (he had) promised to help.'

In the case of a 3rd person subject its absence in the subsequent clause indicates co-reference with the subject of the first clause; the following sentence is ambiguous:

Jõnas *pamiřšo, kad* jìs *žadėjo padėti.*   'Jonas (John) forgot that he (John himself or another person) had promised to help.'

(2) Výras pìnigus *uždìrba, o* žmonà *išléidžia.*   'The husband earns money and the wife spends (it).'

(3) Vãkar *bùvo šálta ir vaikaĩ bùvo namiẽ.*   'Yesterday it was cold and the children were at home.'

Repetition of a co-referential object or adverbial is redundant and a shared constituent serves to reinforce the bond between the clauses. In the case of initial position of an adverbial its scope is often extended to subsequent clauses.

Sentences with two or more coordinated predicates and one subject, such as

Jìs *bùvo didìko põno sūnùs, bet áugo* vargè.   'He was the son of noble parents, but grew up in poverty.'

should also be classed as composite sentences, but in accordance with the Lithuanian grammatical tradition, they are discussed in the section on coordinative collocations (see 2.144–156).

7.4 The clauses of a composite sentence can be separated from each other by a pause (marked by a full stop in writing), without any change in grammatical structure:

Àš niẽkur neĩsiu. Ir táu nepàtariu.	'I won't go anywhere. And (I) don't advise you (to do so).'
Àš vìską padarýsiu. Nórs ir labaĩ sunkù.	'I'll do everything. Though it is very hard.'

This kind of separation of clauses is determined by pragmatic and/or stylistic factors. They are not regarded as special structural types of sentences.

Complex sentence
Prijungiamàsis sakinỹs

7.5 A complex sentence is comprised of two (or more) clauses of which one is the main (or superordinate) clause and the other is a subordinate (or dependent) clause linked to the main clause by a subordinating conjunction (1), a relative pronoun (2) or an adverb (3) collectively referred to as subordinators:

(**1**) *Prašiaũ tėvužẽlio*, kad *manè aplankýtų*.	'I begged my dear father to visit me (lit. 'that (he) visit me').'
Sužinójau, kad *jìs dár negrį̃žęs*.	'I learnt that he hadn't returned yet.'
(**2**) *Tàs ne výras*, kurìs *taĩp elgiasi*.	'He is not a man who behaves so.'
(**3**) Kuř *žemà tvorà*, teñ *visì gyvuliaĩ šóka*.	'Where the fence is low, (there) all the cattle jump over.'

A subordinator (or the first component of a complex conjunction) is included in the structure of the subordinate clause. It indicates the dependent status of the latter. As a rule, the predicate of a subordinate clause has a relative rather than an absolute temporal meaning.

The main clause is in its turn correlated with the subordinate. It may also be incomplete, the clauses supplementing each other to form a complete sentence. Typically, a subordinate clause modifies the main clause, but sometimes it is the more important constituent semantically, and the main clause modifies it by lending modality or subjective evaluation, or introducing it; cf.:

Mãnoma, kad jìs slãpstosi.	'(It is) believed that he is in hiding.'
Ir ródos šiandiẽną, kad bùvo taĩ sãpnas.	'And it seems today that it was but a dream.'

7.6 A subordinate clause can be related to the main clause in two ways. According to the character of relatedness, integrated and non-integrated subordinate clauses are distinguished.

An **integrated** subordinate clause is related to a constituent of the main clause (termed the antecedent), and its dependence is determined by the grammatical and semantic properties of the antecedent. A subordinate clause may be often integrated in the main clause as its part. The relation between a subordinate clause and its antecedent is similar to that between the components of a subordinative word group, e.g.:

Mẽdis, kurìs gìrgžda, nelū̃žta.   'A tree that creaks never breaks.'

The subordinate clause in this sentence modifies the head word *mẽdis* 'tree' very much like an adjective (or its equivalent, in this case a participle) and has the same syntactic function as an attribute, cf.:

Gìrgždantis mẽdis nelū̃žta.   'A creaking tree never breaks.'

In the following sentence the subordinate clause is equivalent to an object, cf.:

Víenas žmogùs norẽjo išgir̃sti, ką̃ šnẽka jõ arkliaĩ.   'One man wanted to hear what his horses talk about.'

Víenas žmogùs norẽjo išgir̃sti sàvo arklių̃ šnẽką.   'One man wanted to hear his horses talk (ACC).'

Thus, an integrated clause is often interchangeable with a participle, an infinitive or a verbal noun. It functions as a subject, object, adverbial or an attribute. The antecedent of a subordinate clause may be a verb, a noun, an adjective, etc.

A **non-integrated** subordinate clause, as a rule, is related to the main clause as a whole or to the predicate group. Its structure is not determined by the properties of any constituent of the main clause, e.g.:

Žibuõklių kvãpas orè plaũko, nórs píevoj jų̃ ir nematýt.   'The fragrance of violets drifts in the air, though one cannot see them in the meadow.'

In this sentence the connection between the clauses is determined by the meaning of the conjunction *nórs* 'though' and by the content of the constituents. The connection between the clauses is less rigid than in the case of integrated subordinate clauses and in some respects it is more like coordination in a compound sentence.

For each type of subordination there are special markers of which the principal ones are conjunctive and correlative words.

7.7   A subordinating conjunction is contained in the subordinate clause but it does not enter into any constituent phrase and has no syntactic function of its own. Subordinating conjunctions are divided into asemantic and semantic conjunctions.

The **asemantic** (polyfunctional) **conjunctions** *kàd* 'that' and *jóg* 'that' indicate subordination without expressing the semantic relation between clauses. The latter is explicated by the structure of the clauses and the grammatical and semantic properties of the antecedent and other components, e.g.:

| Jìs pajùto, kad pasidãrė šálta. | lit. 'He felt that it became cold.' |

In this sentence the conjunction *kàd* subordinates a completive clause in object position to the transitive predicate verb *pajùto* 'felt'. The same conjunction is used in the following sentence, with an intransitive predicate and the subjunctive mood in the subordinate clause indicating the relation of purpose:

| Jìs sténgiasi, kad gyvẽnimas gerė́tų. | lit. 'He strives that life should improve.' |

Semantic conjunctions indicate subordination and at the same time they express the semantic relation between clauses. They can express temporal (*kaĩ* 'as, when', *ikì/lìgi* 'until', *kõl* 'while', etc.), causal (*kadángi* 'because', *nès* 'as'), and conditional (*jéi/jéigu* 'if', *nebeñt* 'unless') relations, and also the relations of concession (*nórs* 'though', *kad iř̃* 'even though', *tegùl* 'though'), purpose (*idañt* 'in order that'), and comparison (*kaĩp* 'like', *lýg* 'like, as if', *negù* 'than', etc.) (see III.9.6).

If a semantic conjunction is replaced by another (on condition the sentence permits it), the meaning changes too; cf.:

Paũkščiai pràdeda čiulbė́ti, 'Birds begin to sing
{
 kai óras atšýla.
 when the weather grows warm' (time).
 nes óras atšýla.
 because the weather grows warm' (cause).
 jei óras atšýla.
 if the weather grows warm' (condition).
}

Conjunctions are often used with the intensifying postpositive particles *kàd*, *iř̃*, *dár*, *tìk*, *nèt*, *nórs*, etc. Some of these combinations have become complex conjunctions, e.g. *kad iř̃* '(al)though', *kai tìk* 'as soon as', *võs tik* 'as soon as', etc. (see III.9.2).

If a conjunction comprises two components, the first one is placed in the subordinate clause, and the second in the main clause, e.g.:

| Nors *ir vėlù*, bet *netrùkus* ateĩsiu. | lit. 'Even though it is late but I'll come soon.' |
| Jei ateĩsim anksčiaũ, tai užim̃sim geriáusias vietàs. | lit. 'If we come earlier then we'll take the best seats.' |

Since all the two-place subordinating conjunctions, excepting *juõ... juõ*, *kuõ... tuõ*, *juõ... tuõ*, are comprised of simple conjunctions and retain the meaning of their first component, sentences with single and two-place conjunctions are treated together below.

7.8 The **relative pronouns** *kàs* 'what, who', *kóks, -ià* 'what', *kurìs, -ì* 'which', *katràs, -à* 'which (of the two)', *kelì, kēlios* and *kelerì, kēlerios* 'how many (of several)' and *keliñtas, -à* 'which (in number)' are included in the structure of the subordinate clause and have a syntactic function. They can function as:

(1) the subject of a subordinate clause:

Jìs žìno, kàs teñ atsitìko.	'He knows what (NOM) happened there.'

(2) an object:

Jìs žìno, kõ mán reĩkia.	'He knows what (GEN) I need.'

(3) a predicative:

Niẽkas nežìno, kóks bùs ruduõ.	'No one knows what the autumn will be like.'

(4) an attribute:

Jiẽ svařstė, kurį̃ projèktą pasiriñks komìsija.	'They discussed which project the committee would choose.'
Senẽlė kláusia, kēlios mergáitės eĩs į̃ vakarė̃lį.	'Granny asks how many girls are going to the party.'

7.9 The **relative adverbs** *kadà* 'when', *kuomèt* 'when', *kaĩp* 'how', *kíek* 'how much', *kuř̃* 'where', *kodė̃l* 'why', used to subordinate clauses in the form of an indirect question, function as adverbials within subordinate clauses:

Nekañtriai láukiau, kadà užáugsiu.	lit. 'I waited impatiently when I would *dìdelis* grow up.'
Nežinaũ, kuř̃ jìs išvažiãvo.	'I don't know where he has gone.'

Sometimes the syntactic function of relative adverbs is weakened and they approach the status of semantic conjunctions, cf.:

Jaũ bùvo sutémę, kadà (cf. *kaĩ*) *vaikaĩ grį̃žo namõ.*	'It was already dark when (cf. 'as') the children returned home.'

7.10 Subordinators (or the first components of the complex conjunctions) commonly occur in the initial position of a subordinate clause, but they may be moved to a middle position if the subject or another constituent is fronted for communicative prominence, cf.:

Tetùšis kadà mìrė, buvaũ dar mãžas.	'When father died I was small yet.'
Šìtą kepùrę jei kàs užsìdeda, tai niẽkas jõ nemãto.	'When anyone puts on this cap, then nobody can see him.'

7.11 **Correlative words** are pronouns and adverbs with generalized meanings used in the main clause and correlated with the conjunctives in the dependent clause.

They serve to stress and reinforce the link between the clauses. In a way, they represent the subordinate clause in the structure of the main clause. Therefore they have a syntactic function in the main clause, which distinguishes them from the second component of complex conjunctions:

Eĩsiu teñ, kur paliẽpsi.	lit. 'I'll go there where you tell me.'

The most commonly used correlatives are the demonstrative pronouns tàs, -à, taĩ 'that', tóks, -ià 'such' and the adverbs taĩp 'so', tíek 'so much', tadà 'then', tuomèt 'then', tõl 'until, till', teñ 'there', todė̃l/dė̀l tõ 'therefore'. The choice of a correlative word is determined by the semantic relation (spatial, temporal, causal, etc.) between the clauses. Thus, taĩp 'so' correlates with kàd 'that'; tíek 'so much/many' with kíek 'how much/many' and kàd 'that'; tadà 'then' may correlate with kadà 'when', kaĩ 'as, when'; tàs 'that' with kàs 'who, what' and kurìs 'which'; teñ 'there' with kur̃ 'where', etc.

Optional correlatives are used for reinforcing the link between clauses. In sentences with correlative clauses and with pronominal attributive clauses, a correlative word is obligatory as an essential feature of the structure of a complex sentence and, as a rule, it cannot be omitted; e.g.:

Mergáitė bùvo tokià pavar̃gusi, kad mùms jõs pagaĩlo.	'The girl was so (lit. 'such') tired that we felt sorry for her.'

Correlative words are not used in sentences with the conjunction jéi/jéigu 'if'.

7.12 The **order of clauses** in a complex sentence is either variable or fixed.

Variable order is characteristic of sentences with simple (one-component) semantic conjunctions (excepting nès 'as', negù, neĩ 'than'), asemantic conjunctions used without correlative words and in most sentences with subordinating relative pronouns and adverbs.

In sentences with variable order a subordinate clause may either precede or follow the main clause, or it may be interposed in the latter; cf. respectively:

Kai pradėjo lýti, minià išsiskìrstė.	'When it started raining the crowd dispersed.'
Minià išsiskìrstė, kai pradėjo lýti.	'The crowd dispersed when it started raining.'
Minià, kai pradėjo lýti, išsiskìrstė.	lit. 'The crowd, when it started raining, dispersed.'

Fixed order of clauses holds in the following types of sentences:

(1) In sentences with two-place conjunctions a subordinate clause is preposed to the main clause:

Jei *ateĩsi iš rýto*, tai *manè dar ràsi namiẽ*. 'If you come in the morning, (so) you'll find me in.'

(2) A subordinate clause is postposed to the main clause in sentences with the semantic conjunctions *nès*, *negù*, *neĩ*, asemantic conjunctions used with correlative words and with complex conjunctions such as *kaĩp kad, kad nèt*, etc.:

Mẽs turėjom eĩti namõ, nes *bùvo vėlù*. 'We had to go home, for it was late.'

Mẽs taĩp *džiaũgėmės*, kad *visái pamiřšome pavõjų*. lit. 'We so rejoiced that we quite forgot about the danger.'

Mìškas bùvo didèsnis, negu *vaikáms iš pradžiũ atródė*. 'The forest was bigger than it had first seemed to the children.'

In sentences with the relative pronouns *kurìs, -ì* 'which', *kóks, -ià* 'what (kind of)', a subordinate clause commonly follows the antecedent, e.g.:

Pamatýsi žmõgų, kókio *niekuomèt nesì dár užtìkęs*. 'You'll see a man whose like you have never met before.'

7.13 Some types of subordinate clauses function as a part of the main clause, taking the position of the subject, an object, an attribute, etc. However, numerous subordinate clauses do not have any equivalents among parts of the sentence or their modifiers. Moreover, if clauses are classified by the syntactic function, a great many structurally identical clauses are ascribed to different functional types; on the other hand, structurally different clauses are attributed to the same functional type. Therefore, in this grammar subordinate clauses are classified according to their structural properties, their functional relationship with the main clause being specified for each type separately.

7.14 **Complex sentences with more than one dependent clauses** display two basic types of organisation:

(1) Co-subordination; two or more clauses are subordinated to the same superordinate clause:

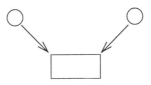

Kai *sutėmo, mẽs pagalvójom*, kad *jaũ laĩkas eĩti namõ*. 'When it grew dark we thought it was time to go home.'

(2) Chain subordination: a subordinate clause is superordinate to another which in its turn may be superordinate to another dependent clause:

              I   II   III

Mán pāsakojo, kad *teñ gyvéna daũg žmonių*, kuríems *reĩkia pagálbos*.   'They told me that many people lived there who needed help.'

Two types of subordination can be combined in various ways to form sentences of great complexity.

7.15 Subordinate clauses are classified here as follows:

A. Integrated clauses:

(1) completive clauses (subjects and objects);
(2) attributive clauses:
      (a) related to a noun antecedent,
      (b) related to a pronoun antecedent;
(3) correlative clauses.

B. Non-integrated clauses denoting:

(1) time,
(2) cause,
(3) condition,
(4) concession,
(5) purpose,
(6) place,
(7) comparison.

A special type of non-integrated clauses are additive clauses.

INTEGRATED CLAUSES

Completive Clauses

7.16 Completive clauses (*áiškinamieji sakiniaĩ*) are connected with the main clause by asemantic conjunctions and relative pronouns and adverbs. They are subordinated to a verb, a verbal noun or a neuter adjective or an adverb. They function as subjects or objects, or explicate the correlative word in the subject or object position. The antecedent of a completive clause commonly refers to speech, a mental process, perception, emotions or appraisal.

A completive clause can be related to the antecedent noun in the same way as to a verb; cf.:

Jìs bijójo, kad jiẽ nesugrį̃žtų.	'He was afraid lest they should return.'
Jám nèrà báimės, kad jiẽ sugrį̃š.	'He has no fear (lit. 'to him is no fear') that they will return.'

CLAUSES INTRODUCED BY CONJUNCTIONS

7.17 When used in completive clauses, the conjunctions *kàd* 'that' and *jóg* 'that' are often interchangeable. If a sentence contains two hierarchically subordinated completive clauses, both conjunctions are used in order to avoid monotonous repetition:

Jìs vìsą laĩką kalbėjo, kad gaĩla, jog abù sū́nūs išvỹkę.	'He said all the time that it was a pity that both his sons were away.'

Generally, the conjunction *kàd* is more common than *jóg* (the latter is nearly out of use in dialects). Only the former conjunction is used after the verbs *bijóti* 'fear', *láukti* 'wait', *mókyti* 'teach', *norė́ti* 'want', *prašýti* 'ask', *reikaláuti* 'demand', *reikė́ti* 'be necessary', *sáugotis* 'beware', etc., to introduce clauses with the subjunctive mood in the predicate:

Prašiaũ, kad (*jog) manè išléistų.	lit. 'I asked that (they) should let me out.'
Nóriu, kad (*jog) jìs ateĩtų.	'I want him to come (lit. 'that he should come').'

Completive clauses are introduced by the conjunctions *lýg* 'as if' and *tartum/taŕsi* 'as if' if an unreal, imaginary, or possible action is referred to:

Jám pasivaidė́no, lyg vil̃kas bū́tų.	'He fancied he saw something like a wolf.'
Iš tólo girdė́josi, tartum jìs ką̃ dainúotų.	'One could hear from afar what sounded like his singing something.'

Sometimes, the conjunction *kaĩ* 'when' is used in completive clauses. This adds a temporal meaning:

Àš mė́gstu, kai pas manè svečiaĩ.	'I like (it) when I have visitors.'

CLAUSES INTRODUCED BY RELATIVE PRONOUNS AND ADVERBS (EMBEDDED QUESTIONS)

7.18 Completive clauses can have the form of interrogative clauses, in which case subordination is marked by the following means:

(1) various case forms of the relative pronouns *kàs* 'what, who', *kóks, -ià* 'what (kind of)', *kurìs, -ì* 'which', *katràs, -à* 'which (of the two)', *keliñtas, -à* 'which (in number)', *kelì, kélios* 'how many'; e.g.:

Nežinaũ, kàs *ten bùvo.*	'I don't know who was there.'
Dabar̃ mataĩ, kokių *neláimių gãlima susiláukti.*	'Now you see what misfortunes may happen.'
Jìs žìno, kurį̃/katrą̃ *vaĩką reĩkia pabárti.*	'He knows which/which of the two children should be scolded.'
Pasakýk, varnéle, kelì *tàvo vaikaĩ.*	'Tell me, dear crow, how many children you have.'

(2) The relative adverbs *kadà* 'when', *kuomèt* 'when', *kur̃* 'where', *kaĩp* 'how', *kíek* 'how many', *kodė̃l* 'why', etc., and also the case forms *kõ* 'why' (GEN of *kàs* 'what'), *kám* 'what for' (DAT of *kàs* 'what'), *kamè* 'where, in what' (LOC of *kàs*):

Láukėm, kadà/kuomèt *pradė̃s lýti.*	lit. 'We were waiting for it to start raining.'
Ar tù žinaĩ, kaĩp/kamè *tàvo tėvaĩ gyvẽna?*	'Do you know how/where your parents live?'
Visíems papãsakok, kíek/kodė̃l *jìs mùms padė́jo.*	'Tell everybody how much/why he has helped us.'

(3) The above mentioned pronouns and some adverbs with the prepositions *į̃* 'to', *iš* 'out of', *nuõ* 'from', *ùž* 'for', etc.:

Jìs taĩp ir nesužinójo, už ką *bùvo baũstas.*	'He never learnt what he had been punished for.'
Pasakýk atviraĩ, iš kur̃ *atkeliavaĩ.*	'Tell us frankly where you have arrived from.'

(4) The particles *ar̃, benè, gál*:

Sakýk, ar *gãlime juõ pasikliáuti.*	'Tell me whether we can rely on him.'
Tikė́jausi, bene *pàts susipràs atsiprašýti.*	'I hoped maybe he would remember to apologize.'
Bė́k pasižiūrė́ti, gal *jìs jau šóka.*	'Go and see, maybe he is already dancing.'

7.19 Infinitival phrases after the verb *búti* 'be' can be used with the same subordinators as completive clauses:

Jíems	*nebùvo*	*kàs*	*veĩkti.*
they: DAT	not-be: PAST	what	do: INF

'They had nothing to do.'

Kai	*jìs*	*kaĩba,*	*tai*	*yrà*	*kõ*	*pasiklausýti.*
when	he	speaks	then	is	what	listen: INF

'When he speaks it is worthwhile listening to him.'

Váistų	*nėrà*	*kuř*	*gáuti.*
medicine	not-be: PRES	where	get: INF

'One can't get any medicine anywhere.'

Bùs	*kuř*	*laikýti*	*karvùtę.*
will be	where	keep: INF	cow

'We'll have somewhere to keep the cow.'

Infinitival phrases with subordinating relative pronouns and adverbs are also used after the verbs *turėti* 'have', *gáuti* 'get', *ràsti* 'find', etc.:

Ar turì kuõ rašýti?   lit. 'Do you have something to write with?'
Mùms atsirãdo kuř žiopsóti.   'We found something (lit. 'where') to gape at.'

Participles and 3rd person verb forms can also be used in subordinate clauses with the same subordinator (they have a dialectal colouring):

Nėrà	*kàs*	*ãria.*
not-is	who	ploughs

'There is no one to do the ploughing.'

Nėrà	*kám*	*tuřgun*	*važiúoja.*
not-is	who: DAT	to market	go: 3. PRES

'There's no one who could go to the market.'

Nėrà	*kàs*	*dãrą*	*su*	*tókiu*	*karãliumi.*
not-is	what: ACC	do: ACT. PRES. PART. NEUTR	with	such	king: INSTR. SG

'There is nothing one can do with such a king.'

In some sentences, the nominative form of the relative pronoun *kàs* 'who, what' may function either as subject or object; thus the following sentence is ambiguous:

Nėrà	*kàs*	*kùlia.*
not-is	who/what	thrash: 3. PRES

'There is no one to do the thrashing/There is nothing (no grain) to thrash.'

SYNTACTIC FUNCTIONS OF COMPLETIVE CLAUSES

The subject function

7.20 Completive subordinate clauses can take the subject position in a superordinate clause with a predicate expressed by the following:

(1) the 3rd person form of verbs denoting being, happening (real or ostensible), seeming, attitudes, etc. (e.g. *atródyti* 'seem', *atsitìkti* 'happen', *bū́ti* 'be', *dìngtelėti* 'cross one's mind', *matýtis* 'be seen', *paaiškė́ti* 'become clear', *ródytis* 'show itself', *rūpė́ti* 'be concerned', *patìkti* 'like'):

Mán atródė, jog jaũ vėlù.	'It seemed to me that it was already late.'
Bū́davo, kad ìštisą mė́nesį lỹja be pértraukos.	'It sometimes happened (lit. 'it used to be') that it would rain for a month without stopping.'
Jám patiñka, kad vìskas bū́tų padarýta laikù.	'He likes (it) when (lit. 'that') everything is (lit. 'should be') done in time.'

(2) The infinitive of the verbs *girdė́ti* 'hear', *matýti* 'see', *jaũsti, jùsti* 'feel':

Matýt, kad jám galvà sùkas.	'One can guess (lit. 'To see') that his head is swimming.'
Dabař bùvo girdė́ti, kaĩp skam̃ba varpaĩ.	'Now one could hear the bells ringing' (lit. 'Now was to hear how the bells ring').

(3) The neuter adjectives and passive participles of verbs denoting emotions, sensations, comprehension and speech:

Nèt keĩsta, kad ją̃ taĩp visì gìria.	'It is even strange that all (the people) praise her so.'
Žìnoma, kaĩp bùs.	'(It is) known how it will be.'
Bùvo pasakýta, kad jiẽ tùri padė́ti kaimýnams.	lit. '(It) was said that they must help the neighbours.'

(4) Adverbs of state:

Geraĩ, kad vìską mán pasakeĩ.	'(It is) good that you have told me everything.'
Nežinià, ką̃ jìs bū́tų padā́ręs.	'There is no knowing what he might have done.'

(5) The nominative case form of nouns denoting emotions and states (e.g. *džiaũgsmas* 'joy', *garbė̃* 'honour', *gė́da* 'shame', *láimė* 'luck', *kaltė̃* 'fault, guilt', *teisýbė* 'truth', etc.):

Ar̃gi màno kaltė̃, *kad jìs niẽko netùri.*   'Is it my fault that he has nothing.'

Táu džiaũgsmas, *kad vaikaĩ sveikì.*   'It's a joy for you that your children are healthy.'

The object function

7.21 Completive clauses can take the object position in the superordinate clause interchangeably with oblique case forms (the genitive (1), accusative (2) or instrumental (3)) or with a prepositional phrase (4):

(1) *Jìs kláusė, ką̃ jìs turė́tų darýti* (cf. *kláusė patarìmo*).   'He asked what he should do' (cf. 'asked for advice').

(2) *Pasakýk, kaĩp mán pabė́gti* (cf. *pasakýk teisýbę*).   'Tell me how I could escape' (cf. 'tell the truth').

(3) *Tė́vas patikė́jo, kad sẽnis sãko teisýbę* (cf. *patikė́jo seniù*).   'Father believed that the old man was telling the truth' (cf. 'believed the old man').

(4) *Nepỹk ant manę̃s, kad àš nóriu šìtai žinóti* (cf. *nepỹk už màno kláusimą*).   'Don't be angry with me that I want to know it' (cf. 'don't be angry at my question').

THE ORDER OF CLAUSES

7.22 A completive subordinate clause commonly follows the main clause. Inverted arrangement serves to emphasize the subordinate clause or to make it the theme of a sentence:

Kuomèt išsìrengiau važiúoti, negaliù tikraĩ pasakýti.   'When I got ready to go, I can't really say.'

Kuř laĩkomi degtùkai, žinójo tik tė́vas.   'Where the matches were kept, father alone knew.'

CORRELATIVE WORDS

7.23 Correlative words are not often used in sentences with completive clauses. They are in fact dummy substitutes representing the subordinate clause in the main clause, which distinguishes them from the respective antecedents of attributive clauses (cf. 7.29–32). The most common words used as dummy substitutes are *taĩ* 'that, it' and the case forms of *tàs* 'that':

Ar tai blõga, kad jìs žmonė́ms gẽra dãro.   lit. 'Is it bad that he does good to people.'

A correlative dummy word is obligatory in sentences with a few verbs only; cf.:

Jõs gerùmas réiškėsi tuõ, kad jì 'Her goodness expressed itself in that she
visíems padė́davo.   used to help everyone.'

Completive subordinate clauses can be represented by generalized pronouns (*víena* 'one', *vìskas* 'everything', *niẽko* 'nothing'), sometimes by abstract nouns, very much like the dummy *taĩ, tàs*:

Jìs vìską žìno, kàs teñ dãrosi. 'He knows everything that goes on there.'

Pasakýk mán vìsą teisýbę,   'Tell me all the truth how it happened.'
kaĩp tai atsitìko.

Attributive clauses

7.24 Attributive clauses (*pažymimíeji sakiniaĩ*) are typically introduced by the relative pronouns *kurìs, -ì* 'which, that', *kóks, -ià* 'what (kind of)', *katràs, -à* 'which (of the two)', *kàs* 'what'. Their head words are nouns or pronouns.

CLAUSES WITH NOUN ANTECEDENTS

7.25 If the antecedent of an attributive clause is a noun, or its substitute, it is introduced by the relative pronouns *kurìs, -ì* 'which, what', *kóks, -ià* 'what (kind of)', and, sometimes, by the adverbs *kadà* 'when', *kaĩ* 'as', *kodė́l* 'why', *kur̃* 'where', etc. (see 7.28). The antecedent nouns vary in lexical meaning and syntactic function; cf.:

Šuõ, kurìs lója, nekánda.   'A dog that barks does not bite.'

Vaikaĩ sužiùro į̃ tãką, kuriuõ bùvo 'The children stared at the path by which
atė̃ję.   they had come.'

The main clause may contain the pronoun *tàs, tà* 'that' or *tóks, -ià* 'such' as an optional correlative word which serves to single out the antecedent noun and to reinforce the link between the clauses; e.g.:

Paim̃k tą̃ knỹgą, kurì ant stãlo. lit. 'Take that book which is on the table.'

7.26 An attributive clause usually follows immediately after the antecedent, unless a post-posed attribute is placed between them:

Mergáitė *juodaĩs plaukaĩs*,   'The girl with black hair whom you saw
kurią mateĩ vãkar, yrà màno   yesterday is my niece.'
dukterė̃čia.

An attributive clause may also by distanced from the antecedent if the latter is a preposed genitive attribute itself, cf.:

Pìnigas nemė́gsta tõ žmogaũs rañkų, kurìs nemóka jõ vértinti.	'Money doesn't like the hands of the man who doesn't value it.'

7.27 Attributive clauses are divided into restrictive and non-restrictive, or continuative.

(1) **Restrictive clauses** serve to specify the meaning of the antecedent. They are essential for identifying its referent and cannot be omitted without impairing the meaning of the sentence:

Nemė́gstu žmonių̃, kuriẽ nemóka laikýti liežùvio už dantų̃.	'I don't like people who can't hold their tongues'.
Cf. Nemė́gstu žmonių̃.	'I don't like people.'

They are introduced by the relative pronoun *kurìs, -ì* 'which'. The pronouns *tàs, tà* 'that', *tas pàts, ta patì* 'that same' can be used as correlative words:

Taĩ tas pàts žmogùs, kurìs padė́jo jíems pabė́gti.	'It is the (very) same man who had helped them to escape.'

Restrictive clauses specifying the quality of the antecedent are introduced by the pronouns *kurìs, -ì* or *kóks, -ià*, with the correlative pronoun *tóks, -ià* 'such' used optionally:

Pamatýsi (tókį/*tą̃) sõdą, kókio niekuomèt nesì dar mãtęs.	'You'll see a garden (whose like) you have never seen yet.'
Jìs trósko (tokiõs/*tõs) audrõs, kurì išblaškýtų nerimą̃.	'He longed for (such) a storm that would dispel his worries.'

(2) **Continuative clauses** serve to provide additional information about the antecedent. They are introduced by the pronoun *kurìs, -ì* 'which' and never occur with a correlative word; e.g.:

Gyvẽno kar̃tą sẽnas žmogùs, kuriám mìrė žmonà.	'There lived an old man whose (lit. 'to whom') wife had died.'
Po dárbo manè aplañkė sẽnas bičiùlis, kurį̃ pàkviečiau vakarieniáuti.	'An old friend came to see me after work and (lit. 'whom') I invited him to supper.'

7.28 Attributive clauses can also be introduced by invariable words.

(1) If the antecedent is a locative noun in subject or object position, the relative adverb *kur̃* can be used:

Mẽs aplañkème nãmą, kuř̃/kuriamè kadáise gyvẽno rašýtojas.	'We visited the house where the writer had once lived.'

(2) If the antecedent is a temporal noun (*laĩkas* 'time', *dienà* 'day', etc.) the markers of subordination are the relative adverbs *kadà* 'when' and *kaĩ* 'as':

Prisìminiau dienàs, kadà/ kaĩ visái dar jáunas buvaũ.	'I remembered the days when I was quite young yet.'

(3) If the antecedent is a "causal" noun like *priežastìs* 'cause, reason' or *dingstìs* 'pretext', the adverb *kodḗl* 'why' can be used:

Bùvo ir kità priežastìs, kodḗl/dėl kuriõs jìs nenorėjo eĩti su mumìs.	'There was another reason why he didn't want to go with us.'

Note: Subordinate clauses introduced by the subordinators *kadà, kaĩ, kuř̃* and dependent on nouns which function as adverbials are classed as adverbial clauses of time and place respectively and therefore are considered in the corresponding sections (see 7.38, 64).

CLAUSES WITH PRONOUN ANTECEDENTS

7.29 The relative pronouns *kàs* 'who, what', *kurìs, -ì* 'which', *katràs, -à* 'which (of the two)', *kóks, -ià* 'what (kind of)', introducing the subordinate clause can be related to the demonstrative pronouns *tàs, tà* 'that', *tóks, -ià* 'such', included or implied in the principal clause. They agree with the antecedent in number and gender and refer to the same entity; cf.:

Kàs per daũg nóri, tàs mažaĩ gáuna.	'Whoever wants too much, (that one) gains little.'

The antecedent pronoun is sometimes omitted, but it is easily recoverable from the sentence structure:

Kàs daũg kaĨba, (tàs) mažaĩ dìrba.	lit. 'Whoever talks much, (that one) works little.'

Both the main and the subordinate clause usually have identical structure and both are semantically incomplete, due to the indefinite meaning of both pronouns.

In these sentences, the subordinate clause usually precedes the superordinate clause and each pronoun is placed initially in its respective clause. If the arrangement of the clauses is inverted, then the antecedent is placed either initially, or finally, cf. respectively:

Tàs laimẽs, kàs bùs pìrmas.	'That (one) will win who will be the first.'
Bū́siu gẽras ir tóks, kóks esù.	'I'll be good/suitable enough the way I am' (lit. 'I'll be good such as I am').

7.30 Subordinate clauses introduced by the relative pronouns *kàs* 'who, what', *kurìs, -ì* 'which, that' describe the entity (thing or person) referred to by the demonstrative pronoun *tàs, tà, taĩ* (explicit or implicit) in the main clause.

The most common pairs of pronouns in sentences of the type under consideration are *kàs... tàs, taĩ*. The case form of the relative pronoun and of its antecedent is determined by the syntactic function of each, therefore it may be the same or it may differ, cf.:

Kàs *lengvaĩ žãda*, tàs *suñkiai dúoda*/tám *sunkù dúoti*.	'Whoever (NOM) is quick to promise that one (NOM) is slow to give/for that one (DAT) it is hard to give.'
Ką̃ *lengvaĩ žadėsi*, tą̃ *suñkiai dúosi*/tàs *bùs sunkù dúoti*.	lit. 'What (ACC) you easily promise, that (ACC) you will give with difficulty/that (NOM) will be hard to give.'
Kám *lengvaĩ žadėsi*, tám *suñkiai dúosi*.	'Whom (DAT) you promise easily, to that one (DAT) you will give with difficulty,' etc.

The relative pronoun *kurìs, -ì* 'which' is less commonly used; sentence structure and relations between clauses correspond to sentences with *kàs*, e.g.:

Àš *ne* iš tų̃, kuriuõs *galì apgáuti*.	'I am not one of those whom (lit. 'which') one can cheat.'

An attributive clause can also be dependent on the pronouns *kažkàs* 'somebody, something', *kiekvíenas* 'everybody', *niẽkas* 'nobody', *vìsas, -à* 'all, the whole', *vìskas* 'everything':

Jìs *tùri savyjè* kažką̃, kàs *tráukia*.	lit. 'He has something in himself that attracts.'
Kviẽsk į̃ vìdų kiekvíeną, kàs *pasibel̃s*.	lit. 'Invite inside everyone who will knock at the door.'
Jìs pasiėmė vìską, kàs *bùvo ant stãlo*.	'He took everything that was on the table.'

7.31 Clauses introduced by the relative pronoun *kóks, -ià* 'what (kind of)' refer to the property indicated by the antecedent pronoun *tóks, -ià* in the main clause:

Kóks *tėvas*, tóks *ir sūnùs*.	'Like father, like son.' (lit. 'What (kind of man) is the father, such is the son.')
Kókio *norėsi*, tókį̃ *gáusi*.	'What (kind of man/husband) you will want, such (kind) you will get.'

Similar relations hold in sentences with the pronouns *tóks, -ià ... kurìs, -ì*:

Bùvo ir tokių, kuriẽ skýrėsi nuo kitų.	'There were also such (people) who (lit. 'which') stood out among the others.'

7.32 The demonstrative pronoun in the main clause can function as

(1) the subject:

Kàs *daũg žãda*, tàs *mažaĩ dãro.*	'Whoever promises much, (that one) does little.'

(2) an object:

Negìrk tõ, kõ *nemateĩ.*	'Don't praise that which (lit. 'what: GEN') you haven't seen.'
Vèsi (tą̃), kurią̃ *liẽpsiu.*	'You'll marry (that (one)), whom (lit. 'which') I tell you.'

(3) a predicative:

Ar esì tàs, kurĩõ *láukiame?*	'Are you the one (whom) we are waiting for?'

The demonstrative pronoun in the superordinate clause is related to the relative pronoun of the subordinate clause only; it does not represent the subordinate clause. This distinguishes attributive clauses from completive clauses introduced by the same relative pronouns *kàs* 'who, what', *kurìs, -ì* 'which', *kóks, -ià* 'what (kind of)' (cf. 7.18).

Correlative clauses

7.33 Subordinate clauses of this type are introduced by the conjunctions *kàd* 'that' and *jóg* 'that', while the demonstrative pronouns *tàs, tà* 'that', *tóks, -ià* 'such' and the adverbs *taĩp* 'so', *tíek* 'so (much)' serve as correlative words within the main clause. These clauses are termed correlative due to the obligatory use of a correlative word which stands in a specific relationship to the subordinate clause.

A correlative word functions as antecedent or it modifies a noun, an adjective or an adverb; e. g.:

Griaustìnis bùvęs tóks (baisùs), kad *nãmo síenos drebė́jusios.*	'The thunder was such (so terrible) that the walls of the house shook.'

Sentences with a correlative clause commonly express cause and effect relations.

Subordinate clauses (taken without a conjunctive word) are usually structurally identical with simple sentences. The main clause containing a correlative word is semantically incomplete. It always precedes the subordinate clause.

In sentences of this type the synonymous conjunctions *kàd* 'that' and *jóg* 'that' are not always interchangeable. The conjunction *kàd* alone is used to introduce clauses with the subjunctive mood of the predicate expressing purpose, aim, e.g.:

Kàs tùri tókią pìktą šìrdį, kad (*jog) *galė́tų taĩp padarýti?*	'Who has such an evil heart that he could do so?'

7.34 Both conjunctions (*kàd* and *jóg*) are often used with the emphatic particle *nèt* 'even', less frequently with *nórs* 'though, even' (the latter usually with the imperative):

Àš tíek apie jį̃ girdė́jau, kad / jog net *sapnavaũ kar̃tą.*	'I've heard so much about him that I even dreamed about him once.'
Jìs kalbė́jo taĩp *piktaĩ,* kad nors *apsisùk ir išeĩk.*	lit. 'He spoke in such an angry way that one felt like turning and leaving (lit.: 'that even turn (2. IMPER) and leave (2.IMPER)').'

These conjunctions are sometimes omitted, especially in dialectal speech and in fiction, and the particles *nèt* and *nórs* introduce a subordinate clause:

Čià taĩp skaniaĩ kvẽpia, net *séilės var̃va.*	lit. 'It smells so nice here, even one's mouth waters.'
Vandeñs pribė́go tíek, nors *kìbiru sémk.*	'There was so much water, one might scoop it up (lit. 'even scoop it up (2. IMPER)') with a bucket.'

If a subordinate clause follows the main clause, the conjunctions in question and the correlative word *taĩp* 'so' function as a complex conjunction, e.g.:

Vaikaĩ jų̃ mìrė víenas po kìto, taĩp kad *pagaliaũ neturė́jo nė víeno.*	'Their children died one after another, so that finally they had none.'

7.35 The antecedent of a subordinate clause can perform any syntactic function in the superordinate clause:

(1) The predicative:

Reĩkalas tóks, kad neberà pasitikė́jimo.	lit. 'The matter is such that there is no trust any longer.'
Skìrtumas tàs, kad esì už jã dẽšimt mẽtų vyrèsnis.	'The difference is (that) that you are ten years older than she is.'
Dienà bùvo tokià gražì, kad/jog nenorė́jom grį̃žti namõ.	'The day was so nice that we didn't want to return home.'

In this case the adverbs *taĩp* 'so' and *tíek* 'so much' are sometimes used instead of the correlative *tóks, -ià*, to stress the degree of the quality denoted by an adjective:

Senẽlė bùvo taĩp *senà, kad nebegalė́jo ir paeĩti.*	'Granny was so old that she could not even walk.'
Jìs dãrosi tíek *drąsùs, kad viską pàts ìma.*	'He is growing so (much) bold that he takes everything himself.'

The relative adverb *taĩp* is the principal correlative word used with the neuter form of adjectives and participles in predicative position:

Teñ bùvo taĩp *gẽra/liñksma, kad niẽkas nenorė́jo išeĩti.*	'It was so nice/merry there that no one wanted to leave.'

(2) The subject:

Prasidė́jo tokià áudra, kad net stógus kilnójo.	'Such a storm began that it even tore at the roofs.'

(3) An object:

Jìs pajùto tókį skaũsmą, kad nenoromìs sudejãvo.	'He felt such a pain that he moaned against his will.'

(4) An adverbial of manner:

Tíek/taĩp dìrbi, kad galė́jai ir praturtė́ti.	'You work so much/so that you could get rich.'
Dainúoja taĩp gražiaĩ, kad ver̃kt nórisi.	'They are singing so beautifully that one feels like crying.'

NON-INTEGRATED CLAUSES
Clauses of time

7.36 Clauses of time are commonly introduced by semantic temporal conjunctions *kaĩ* 'as', *kadà* 'when', *kõl* 'while, till', *ikì* 'until', *lìgi* 'until', *võs* 'as soon as', *tìk* 'only, but', etc. and corresponding complex conjunctions. Correlative words (*tadà* 'then', *tuomèt* 'then', *po tõ* 'after that', *tõl* 'until, till', etc.), also temporal in meaning, can be used optionally. The order of clauses is usually variable.

In sentences with the conjunctions *kaĩ* and *kadà* the temporal relationship between the clauses is unspecified and it is dependent on the meaning of the predicates and the properties of the correlative word and other structural features. The other conjunctions indicate specific temporal relations: the limit of the verbal action, priority of action, etc. In accordance with these distinctions, three subtypes of temporal clauses are distinguished.

Clauses with *kaĩ, kadà*

7.37 These conjunctions are the least specified semantically. The most neutral and common conjunction is *kaĩ* 'as, when'. Its synonym *kadà* 'when' is less frequently used and it cannot always substitute for *kaĩ* (see 7.39). The two-place conjunctions *kaĩ... taĩ* 'as... then', *kadà... taĩ* reinforce the formal link between the clauses.

In sentences with clauses of time, both predicates are as a rule used in the same tense form, their aspectual value determining the temporal relation of simultaneity or succession of actions expressed by the predicates.

The actions are simultaneous if one or both of the related predicates are imperfective; cf. respectively:

Tadà tavè atlankýsiu, *kadà mẽdžiai* žaliuõs.	'I'll come (PERF) to see you when the trees are green (IMPF).'
Kai saulẽlė tekėjo, *mū́sų linaĩ* žydėjo.	lit. 'As the sun was rising (IMPF), our flax was blossoming (IMPF).'

In the case of succession of actions, both verbs are perfective:

Kai/kada/kai tik sáulė nusėdo *už gìrių*, àtlėkė *pelė́da*.	'As/when/as soon as the sun set (PERF) beyond the woods, an owl came flying (PERF).'

If both verbs are perfective and denote momentary actions, their duration may be of no importance to the speaker and the sentence may convey simultaneity, e.g.:

Àš net nusigandaũ, *kai jìs mùs* prakálbino.	'I even got startled as he addressed us.'

7.38 The correlative words co-occurring with the conjunctions in question are *tadà* 'then' and, less commonly, *tuomèt* 'then, at that time'; they emphasize the temporal relationship between the clauses:

Kalbėsiu tiẽsą ir tuomèt/ *tadà, kai pavojìnga*.	'I will speak the truth even at the time/ then when it is dangerous.'

The phrases *tuõ metù* 'at that time', *tuõ tárpu* 'in the meanwhile' are functionally similar to these correlative words and stress simultaneity of actions:

Tuõ metù, kai jìs kalbėjosi su kaimýnu, mergáitė žaĩdė netolíese.	'At the time when he was talking to the neighbour, the girl was playing nearby.'

On the other hand, the temporal meaning of succession may be emphasized by the correlative *po tõ* 'after (that)':

Àš grįžaũ jau po tõ, *kai jìs užmìgo.*	'I returned already after [that as] he had fallen asleep.'

Temporal clauses can be dependent on nouns and other words with a temporal meaning in the function of an adverbial of time:

Dabar̃/Nãktį, *kai jau šõkiai pasibaĩgia, jaunìmas išsiskìrsto namõ.*	'Now/At night as the dances are over, the young people are leaving for home.'

The subordinate clause has a restrictive force in this case.

7.39 A temporal clause commonly denotes the relative time of the action expressed by the main predicate. However, the temporal relation may be reversed, in which case it is the main clause that denotes the time of the subordinate action:

Dienà jau sliñko vakaróp, kai *jiẽdu grį̃žo namõ.*	'The day was drawing to a close as/when they returned home.'

The main clause, if it is a nominal sentence comprising a temporal noun (single or with dependent words), may denote a stretch of time that has passed since the action of the subordinate clause, or the duration of the latter, owing to the perfective or imperfective aspect of the subordinate predicate; cf. respectively:

Jaũ valandà, kai/kaip *sáulė nusiléido.*	'It is an hour since (lit. 'as') the sun has set.'
Jaũ valandà, kai/kaip *jìs miẽga.*	'It is an hour that he has been asleep.'

The particles *dár* 'yet', *jaũ* 'already', *võs* 'hardly', *tìk* 'just, only', when used in the main clause, specify the temporal relation:

Võs (tik) *spėjau užmìgti,* kai *suskam̃bo telefònas.*	'I had hardly (just) fallen asleep when the telephone rang.'

(Cf. semantically similar sentences without *kaĩ* in which *võs* serves as a conjunction, in 7.43.)

A subordinate clause beginning with *kaĩ* may denote an action which had begun or taken place before the action of a negative main clause denoting the time of an action:

Nepraėjo *ir valandà,* kai *pradėjo lýti.*	lit. 'An hour wasn't over yet when it started to rain.'

In sentences with a reversed temporal relation, the main clause always precedes the subordinate clause. The conjunctive *kadà* is not used in these sentences.

7.40 Subordinate clauses of time with the conjunction *kaĩ* can also have a secondary causal meaning determined by context; e.g.:

| Kai *dabar̃ keliaĩ prastì, tai ir svečiaĩ neatvažiúoja.* | 'As the roads are poor now, there are few visitors.' |

Clauses with *kõl, ikì/lìgi*

7.41 In this case, the action of the main clause is limited to the time or period indicated by the subordinate action. As well as in sentences with *kaĩ* and *kadà*, the relation of simultaneity or succession is dependent on the predicates of both clauses. A subordinate clause with an imperfective verb, usually introduced by *kõl*, indicates a simultaneous action whose duration sets limits to the duration of the main action:

| *Jìs dìrbo, kol sáulė šviẽtė.* | 'He worked while (lit. 'till') the sun shone.' |

A subordinate clause with a perfective verb usually introduced by *kõl(ei)* (less commonly by *ikì, lìgi*) denotes the successive event limiting the duration of the main action:

| *Jìs dìrbo, kol/iki patekė́jo mėnùlis.* | 'He worked until the moon rose.' |

The predicate of a subordinate clause is used with negation in order to refer to an event that is not taking place yet, e.g.:

| *Tráukimės namõ, kol* neužlìjo /nelỹja. | 'Let's go home before it starts raining (PAST)/rains (PRES) (lit. 'till it did not start raining/does not rain').' |

If the subordinate predicate denotes an event taking place and limiting duration of the main action, negation is not used, cf.:

| *Mùšė, kol ùžmušė (kol *neùžmušė).* | '(They) beat him until (they) killed (him).' |

7.42 The most common **correlative word** in the main clause is the adverb *tõl* 'so long':

| *Kol gyvenì, tõl ir mókaisi.* | 'You learn as long as you live' (lit. 'While you live so long you learn'). |

A subordinate clause (like clauses introduced by *kaĩ* 'as') can have an antecedent that functions as an adverbial of time:

| *Po lietaũs, kol bùvo šlãpia, sėdė́jome namiẽ.* | 'After the rain, while it was wet, we stayed at home.' |

Clauses with *võs, tìk*

7.43 These conjunctions (homonymous with the particles *võs* 'hardly' and *tìk* 'only, just') denote an immediate succession of actions, the main action beginning or taking place immediately after the subordinate action is over. The latter action is always expressed by a perfective verb.

The conjunction *võs* and the complex conjunction *võs tik* are the most common subordinators used in this case, *tìk* and the complex conjunction *lìg tik(tai)* occurring in everyday speech and in fiction. Cf. respectively:

Vos (tik) nusiléido sáulė, jìs parbėgo namõ.	'As soon as the sun set, he came running home.'
Tìk (lìg tik) manè pamãto, tuõj veřkia.	'As soon as (he) sees me, he at once starts crying (lit. 'cries').'

Clauses of cause

7.44 Subordinate clauses of cause are introduced by the semantic conjunctions *kadángi* 'as, since, because', *nès* 'for, as, because' and by the asemantic *kàd* 'that, as' which is commonly paired with the correlative words *dėl tõ (todėl̃)* 'therefore, so', *už taĩ/užtàt* 'therefore'. These clauses denote the cause of the main action or the foundation of the assertion expressed by the main clause.

Three types of clauses of cause are distinguished according to the conjunction and structural properties.

Clauses with *nès*

7.45 This type is the most common in Standard Lithuanian. A subordinate clause is always postposed to the main clause. The relationship between the clauses is usually that of cause and effect.

Jìs netrùkus užmìgo, nes bùvo labaĩ pavařgęs.	'He fell asleep at once, for he was very tired.'

Such sentences are close in meaning to compound sentences with the coordinators *todėl̃/dėl tõ* 'therefore' denoting consequence:

Óbuolius pasìimu, nes namiẽ neturiù.	'I'm taking the apples, because I have none at home.'
Namiẽ obuolių̃ neturiù, todėl̃ juõs pasìimu.	'I have no apples at home, therefore I am taking these.'

7.46 The conjunction *nès* is also used to connect clauses related as assertion and its foundation (premise), the latter being expressed by the subordinate clause:

Rytój bùs vėjúota dienà, nes *dangùs raudónas.*	'It will be a windy day tomorrow, as the sky is red.'

Such sentences correspond to compound sentences with the conjunction *taĩgi*:

Dangùs raudónas, taĩgi *rytój bùs vėjúota.*	'The sky is red, so it will be a windy day tomorrow.'

Clauses with *kadángi*

7.47 This conjunction is less common in everyday speech than *nès*; it is characteristic of formal styles. The order of clauses varies, but the subordinate clause tends to precede the main clause.

The conjunction *kadángi* mostly expresses cause and effect relations:

Kadángi *pelĕdos gáudo pelès, jōs žmõgui naudìngos.*	'As owls hunt mice, they are useful to man.'

This conjunction is often paired with *taĩ* 'then', both comprising a two-place conjunction:

Kadángi *knỹgos brángios,* tai *pirkĕjų mažaĩ.*	lit. 'Since books are expensive, (then) there are few buyers.'

A sentence containing this conjunction can also denote relation between the assertion and its premise, in which case the subordinate clause follows the main clause:

Jiē, matýt, bùvo miestiẽčiai, kadángi *nešiójo júodus ākinius.*	'They were not villagers, obviously, because they were wearing dark glasses.'

Clauses with *kàd*

7.48 The conjunction *kàd* is commonly used with the correlative *dèl tõ* 'that is why, therefore'. The subordinate clause immediately follows the correlative, therefore its usual position is after the main clause or in the middle of it. This conjunction expresses cause and effect relations:

Mán jì patìko tik dèl tõ, kad *turĕjo grãžų baĩsą.*	'I liked her only because she had a beautiful voice.'

The correlative and the conjunction sometimes (especially in everyday speech) merge into a complex conjunction; e.g.:

Neatėjaũ, dėl tõ kad sirgaũ. 'I didn't come because I was ill.'

A less common correlative is the adverb *todė̃l* 'therefore':

Atėjaũ tik todė̃l, kad mán pasidãrė gaĩla tàvo sūnaũs. 'I have come only because I felt sorry for your son.'

The conjunction *kàd* in clauses of this type is rarely used without a correlative, this usage occurring in everyday speech:

Kad *tė́vas prãšė, turiù eĩt.* 'Because father asked, I have to go.'

More common are sentences with the two-place conjunctions *kàd... taĩ* 'because... then' and *kàd... tàd* 'because... therefore'; e.g.:

Kad *vaikaĩ maži,* tai/tad *reikė̃s sėdė́ti namiẽ.* lit. 'Because the children are small, therefore I'll have to stay at home.'

7.49 The conjunction *kàd* is commonly used without a correlative word if the main clause expresses a question or doubt, and the subordinate clause the reason for the inquiry or doubt:

Kàs čia bùs, kad *žmoniũ taip mãža?* lit. 'What's going to happen, as/since there are so few people?'

Gal jìs seȓga, kad *neatvažiãvo.* 'Maybe he is ill, since he hasn't come.'

In this case the conjunction *kàd* cannot be replaced by *nès* or *kadángi*.

7.50 Clauses of cause are sometimes introduced by the adverbialized case forms *kám* 'why, for what (DAT)' and *kõ* 'why, for what (GEN)' of the pronoun *kàs* 'what':

Tė́vas supy̆ko, kám *jì gìnasi.* lit. 'Father got angry, because she was defending herself.'

Mamà bãrėsi, kõ *taip vėlaĩ parėjaũ.* 'Mother scolded me because I had returned so late.'

Clauses of condition

7.51 To introduce clauses of condition, the semantic conjunctions *jéigu/jéi* 'if', less commonly *nebeñt* 'if only', the asemantic conjunction *kàd* 'that', and the two-place conjunctions (*jéi... taĩ* 'if... then', *kàd... taĩ* 'if... that') are used. The basic meaning of a conditional clause often implies a secondary meaning (of cause, time, contrast, etc.).

The order of clauses is variable, though a subordinate clause tends to assume initial position. An important feature (especially in sentences with the conjunction *kàd*) is the relationship between the mood/tense forms of the predicates.

Clauses with *jéigu, jéi*

7.52 Sentences with the **subjunctive mood** in both clauses (less commonly, the subordinate clause only) express an unreal condition. Simple inflexional mood forms refer to the present and future (1) and periphrastic forms refer to the past (2):

(1) Jei pamiřštume *sàvo kaĺbą ir prāeitį*, diñgtų ir Lietuvà.	'If we forgot our language and past, Lithuania would perish.'
(2) Jei bū́tum *rimtaĩ* kalbė́jęs, *gal* bū́čiau tekė́jusi.	'If you had spoken seriously, perhaps I would have married you.'

The main predicate can be used in the imperative form or in the indicative future tense form:

Jeigu *kàs táu ką blōga* norė́tų *padarýti*, šaũkis *manę̃s*.	'If anyone would want to mistreat you, call me.'
Jeigu *dár sýkį tù mán šìtaip* padarýtum, *tai* bū́si nužudýtas.	'If you would do it to me once more you will be killed.'

7.53 A subordinate clause with an **indicative** or **imperative** verb form may denote a real condition. The choice of tense forms is determined by the temporal relationship between predicates:

Jei turė́si / turì *pinigų̃*, gáusi *vìską*.	'If you have (FUT/PRES) money you will get everything.'
Jeigu *gegužė̃s mė́nesį* nebū́na *lietaũs*, *gḗro deřliaus* neláuk.	'If it does not rain (PRES) in May, don't expect a good harvest.'

The conjunction is often coupled with the particles *tìk* and *iř*:

Jei tik *geraĩ sutařsime*, *niẽkas mū́sų neišskiřs*.	'If only we get on well no one will separate us.'
Jeigu ir *niẽkas manim̃ nepatikė̃s, negaliù tylė́ti*.	'Even if nobody believes me I can't keep silent.'

7.54 The two-place conjunction *jéi(gu)... taĩ* is used in the same way as *jéi(gu)*:

Jeigu *rytój ateĩtum/ateĩsi*, tai *gál daugiaũ sužinótum/sužinósi*.	'If you came/come tomorrow then probably you would/will learn more.'

Sometimes the main clause (usually incomplete) has a restrictive meaning; e.g.:

Jei gr*į́*ždavo k*à*s iš kari*úo*menės, tai *jaũ sẽnas, palíegęs.*	lit. 'If anyone ever returned from the army, then (he was) already old and ailing.'

7.55 The conjunction *jéi(gu)... taĩ* is also used to express **contrastive relations**:

Jei *t*ù *ir nusiv*ý*lei*, tai *àš tik apsìdžiaugiau.*	'Even if you got disappointed, then I was only glad.'
Jeigu *táu su manim̃ blõga,* tai *víenai bùs dár blogiaũ.*	'If you don't like being with me, (then) you'll be worse off alone.'

Sentences such as these can be replaced by compound sentences with the conjunctions *õ* 'but', *tačiaũ* 'however', but they differ from the latter sentences in that both clauses are more closely related.

Clauses with *kàd*

7.56 Conditional sentences with this conjunction are more common in colloquial speech, folklore and fiction. The conditional meaning is unambiguous if both the main and the subordinate predicate are used in the subjunctive form:

Kad bū́čiau norė́jęs, *(tai)* bū́čiau *tavè* pralenk̃ęs.	'Had I wished I would have outstripped you.'
*K*ą̃ *àš* darýčiau, *kad tavę̃s* neturė́čiau.	'Whatever should I do if I did not have you.'

If the predicates are used in other than the subjunctive mood forms (viz. imperative or indicative future tense) the conditional meaning can be implied by the lexical meaning of the clause components and by the context:

Kad nedìrbsi, *tai niẽko ir* neturė́si.	'If you don't work then you'll have nothing.'

Clauses with *nebeñt*

7.57 The conjunction *nebeñt* 'unless' is used to express negative condition. It has the exclusive meaning 'only... if... not' or 'except on condition that'. The subordinate predicate has mostly a subjunctive mood form:

Sėdė́k namiẽ, nebeñt *pakviẽsčiau.*	lit. 'Stay at home, unless I should invite you.'
Daũg pel̃no iš tõ nebùs, nebeñt *im̃tumei sukčiáuti.*	'There will be little profit out of it, unless you should start cheating.'

Clauses of concession

7.58 Concessive clauses are introduced by the conjunctions *nórs* 'though, although', *kàd iř* 'even if', *tegù(l)* 'though, even if'. They imply contrast, the subordinate clause denoting the factor unfavourable or opposite to the content of the main clause.

Most concessive sentences are similar in meaning to compound sentences with the conjunctions *bèt* 'but', *õ* 'but', *tačiaũ* 'but, however', *vìs dẽltõ* 'nevertheless' (see 7.90, 95, 98, 100) which are also used as part of complex concessive conjunctions, e.g.: *nórs/kàd iř... bèt* 'although... but', *nórs/kàd iř... tačiaũ* 'although... but', *nórs/kàd iř... õ/vìs dẽltõ/õ vìs dẽltõ* 'even though... but/nevertheless'.

There are no restrictions on the use and combinations of various mood and tense forms in both clauses. The order of the clauses is not fixed, excepting sentences with two-place conjunctions.

The most common conjunction of concession in Standard Lithuanian is *nórs (iř)*.

The contrast expressed in sentences with this conjunction is stressed if the subordinate clause precedes the main clause:

Nors *veřkia širdìs, linksmaĩ juõktis galiù.*	'Although my heart is weeping, I can laugh merrily.'
Nors *tvirtóvės síenos griùvo, tačiaũ/bet kariaĩ nùtarė gyvì nepasidúoti.*	'Although the walls of the fortress were torn down, the defenders decided not to surrender alive.'

7.59 Sentences with the conjunction *kàd iř* (and respective two-place conjunctions) do not differ from those with *nórs (iř)* either structurally or semantically, but they are more common in informal speech and in fiction, e.g.:

Kad ir *labaĩ norėtum, neĩsiu į gìrią.*	'However much you ask me, I won't go to the woods.'
Kad àš ir *išgýsiu, bet/tačiaũ tàvo nebū́siu.*	'Even if I recover, (but) I won't be yours.'

7.60 Subordinate clauses introduced by the conjunction *tegù(l) (iř)* may denote (1) supposition or (2) a real fact, both contrasted to the content of the main clause:

(1) Tegù(l) *jìs nors ir atsiklaũpęs prašỹs/prašýtų, nieko jám nedúosiu.*	'Even if he begs (FUT/SUBJ) me on his knees, I won't give him anything.'
(2) Tegù(l) *(iř) niẽkas to nemãtė, (bet) àš vis víen negalė́siu jám melúoti.*	'Even if no one has seen it, (but) I won't be able to tell him a lie.'

Clauses of purpose

7.61 Clauses of purpose are introduced by the conjunction *kàd* and, very seldom, by the specialized semantic conjunction of purpose *idañt* 'in order that'. Since *kàd* is an asemantic conjunction, the meaning of purpose is determined by the relationship between the predicates: the predicate of the subordinate clause has to be a simple form of the subjunctive mood. The predicate of the principal clause denotes an active, purposeful action. The order of clauses varies, though the subordinate clause tends to be postposed to the main clause; cf.:

Padė́k rankàs ant stãlo, kad visì matýtų.	'Put your hands on the table so that everyone can see.'
Kad lengviaũ bū́tų atsigìnti nuo príešų, lietùviai stãtėsi pilìs.	'In order that it might be easier to defend themselves from the enemy, Lithuanians used to build fortresses.'
Išė́jome ankstì, kad nepavėlúotume į́ tráukinį.	'We left home early in order not to miss the train.'

The conjunction *kàd* can be used with the correlatives *tám* (which is the adverbialised dative case form of the pronoun *tàs* 'that') and the prepositional phrase *dėl tõ* 'for that', in which case the main clause precedes the subordinate clause:

Àš ne tám suñkiai dìrbau, kad tù galė́tum dykinė́ti.	'I didn't work hard so that you could idle.'
Dėl tõ atėjaũ, kad táu padė́čiau.	'I have come in order that I might help you.'

A correlative word is obligatory if the predicate of the main clause is used with negation:

Ne dėl tõ (tám) dainúoju, kad žmónės girdė́tų.	'I don't sing in order that people should hear me' (lit. 'I sing not in order that...').

Note: Subordinate clauses dependent on the verbs *bijóti* 'fear', *gailė́tis* 'be sorry', *norė́ti* 'want, wish', *láukti* 'wait', *prašýti* 'ask', etc., which substitute for the object of these verbs, are classed as completive clauses (see 7.17; 21).

7.62 Clauses of purpose with the conjunction *idañt* are somewhat archaic and formal. Structurally, they are identical with *kàd*-clauses:

Atvỹkome į̃ šį̃ krãštą, idañt geriaũ pažìntume jo gam̃tą ir žmónes.	'We have come to this land in order that we might get better acquainted with its nature and people.'

Clauses of place

7.63 Adverbial clauses of place are commonly introduced by the relative adverb *kuř* 'where' which is functionally close to a conjunction. They denote place or direction of the main action. There are no special restrictions on tense forms of the predicates in both clauses. The order of clauses is variable.

Jìs nuẽjo, kuř *kójos nẽša.*	'He went where his feet took him.'

For emphasis, the subordinator *kuř tik* 'wherever' is used:

Kuř tik *jì eĩdavo, kãtinas sẽkė iš paskõs.*	'Wherever she went, the cat followed in her steps.'

As a rule, clauses of place co-occur with a correlative word, viz. the adverb *teñ* 'there'; in this case a subordinate clause is usually preposed to the main clause, or it follows the correlative word:

Kuř *paũkštis lẽkia,* teñ *plùnksna kreñta.*	lit. 'Where a bird flies, there a feather falls.'
Niẽko neberadaũ teñ, kuř *kadáise stovėjo tėvų̃ namaĩ.*	lit. 'I found nothing there where my parents' house had been.'

Both the subordinator *kuř* and the correlative *teñ* can be used with the prepositions of direction *iš* 'out of', *nuõ* 'from', *peř* 'through, across', etc.:

Namõ grį̃šite, per kuř *norẽsite.*	'You'll return home by any road (lit. 'by where') you want.'
Nuo teñ, kuř *jì tadà gyvẽno, atskambėjo dainõs áidas.*	lit. 'From (there) where she lived then the echo of a song came.'

7.64 Clauses of place sometimes have an antecedent which functions as an adverbial of place in the main clause:

Jìs nùplaukė ganà tolì, kuř *bùvo negilì vietà.*	'He swam rather far, where there was a shallow place.'
Sẽnis sténgdavosi bū́ti tarp žmonių̃, kuř *daugiaũ triùkšmo, kalbų̃.*	'The old man strove to be among people, where there was more noise and talk.'

In everyday speech and in folklore, the locative case form *kamè* 'in what' is sometimes used as a subordinator instead of *kuř*:

Kamè *lósi, tenái ir làksi.*	'Where you bark (there) you will lap.'

Comparative clauses

Comparative clauses are subdivided into equational and differentiating clauses.

EQUATIONAL CLAUSES

Three types of equational clauses are distinguished.

Qualitative comparative clauses

7.65 They are introduced by the subordinators *kaĩp* 'as, like', *lýg* 'as if', *ìt* 'as if, like', *tar̃tum/tar̃si* 'as if' and denote a comparison of quality or manner. If no correlative word is used the main clause precedes the subordinate clause (which is often incomplete).

7.66 Sentences with the subordinator *kaĩp* denote comparison without implying any modal meaning:

Vìskas bùvo padarýta, kaĩp *sùtarta.*	'Everything was done according to agreement (lit. 'as agreed').'

In sentences with verbal predicates the correlative *taĩp* 'so' can be used:

Jìs vìską taĩp *padarỹs,* kaĩp *nóriu.*	'He will do everything the way (lit. 'so as') I want it.'

In sentences with a compound nominal predicate in the main clause the pronoun *tóks, -ià* 'such' is used:

Jìs bùvo tóks, kaĩp *mán pāsakojo.*	lit. 'He was such as they told me.'

7.67 Sentences with the subordinators *lýg, ìt, tar̃tum/tarýtum* and *tar̃si* which usually require a subjunctive mood form in the subordinate clause, denote comparison with a possible or unreal or imaginary event:

Vaikìnas dìrbo toliaũ, lyg/tarsi/it bū́tų niẽko nepastebė́jęs.	'The boy went on working as if he hadn't noticed anything.'

The subordinators here are interchangeable though they differ slightly in modality. However, they cannot be replaced by *kaĩp*.

In these sentences the correlative word *taĩp* 'so' is also used:

Jìs el̃gėsi taĩp, lýg *tikraĩ niẽko negirdė́tų ir nematýtų.*	'He behaved so as if he really didn't hear and see anything.'

If the standard of comparison is a quality, the correlative *tóks*, sometimes *tíek*, can be used:

Eglùtė jaũtė tókį *sópulį,* tar̃tum *bū́tų kas šìrdį jái ráižęs.*	'Eglutė felt such pain as if her heart were being stabbed.'

A clause of comparison can also have an adverbial antecedent in the main clause, e.g.:

Visì dabař sėdėjom týliai, lýg klaũsėme kõ.	'We were all sitting quietly, as if we were listening to something.'

Quantitative comparative clauses

7.68 These clauses are formed with the subordinator *kíek* 'how much' and the correlative *tíek* 'so much'. They denote a comparison of quantity or extent. The order of clauses is not fixed and there are no special restrictions on tenses and their combinations.

Kíek *atsiriẽksi*, tíek *ir suválgysi*.	'You'll eat as much as you will cut off for yourself' (lit. 'How much you will cut off so much you will eat').
Senẽlis jái dãvė tíek *obuolių̃*, kíek jì galėjo panèšti.	'Grandfather gave her as many apples as (lit. 'so many... how many') she could carry.'

A comparative clause can be related to the pronoun *vìsas* 'all' or to the adverb *visuř* 'everywhere' implying quantity:

Kíek *mū́sų bùvome*, visì *apsiřgome*.	lit. 'As many of us were there, all fell ill.'
Kíek *tik ãkys užmãto*, visuř *juodúoja dẽbesys*.	'As far as (lit. 'how much') the eye can see everywhere the clouds appear black.'

The correlative word is sometimes omitted:

Kíek *žíedą regėsi, manè atsimiñsi*.	'As long as (lit. 'how much') you see the ring, you will remember me.'

Comparative clauses of proportion

7.69 Sentences with a clause of proportion are formed with the two-place conjunctions *kuõ... tuõ, juõ... tuõ* and *juõ... juõ* all of them meaning 'the... the'. They denote comparison of the degree of intensity. Both clauses are usually structurally parallel and may contain the comparative form of an adjective or an adverb (1), though not necessarily (2). A subordinate clause usually precedes the main clause (therefore, in sentences with *juõ... juõ* the initially placed clause is regarded as the subordinate one):

(1) Kuõ (juõ) į̃ mìšką toliaũ, tuõ mẽdžių daugiaũ.	lit. 'The farther into the woods the more trees.'

Kuõ *daugiaũ* jìs dìrbo, tuõ *mažiaũ* gãvo.	'The more he worked the less he got.'
Juõ *senèsnis* jìs dãrosi, juõ *raukšlių* daugėja.	'The older he grows the more wrinkles appear.'
Juõ *gyvẽnimas* Sevèrją báilino, juõ jì stvė́rės tõ pakum̃pusio sẽnio.	'The (more) life scared Severja, the (more) she stuck to that bent old man.'

DIFFERENTIATING CLAUSES

7.70 These clauses are most commonly introduced by the conjunction *negù* 'than', and they are used to express a difference between compared entities. They are usually preceded by an antecedent which is either an adjective or an adverb in the comparative form, or a pronoun like *kìtas, -à* 'other, different', *kitóks, -ia* 'different, not such', or an adverb like *kitaĩp, kitóniškai* 'in a different way'.

Dabartìnių laikų̃ vaikaĩ gudresnì, negu *kadáise bùvo suáugę výrai*.	'Children these days are cleverer than adult men used to be before.'
Susitikìmas bùvo visái kitóks, negu *mẽs tikė́jomės*.	'The meeting was quite different from what (lit. 'than') we had expected.'

Differentiating clauses are also introduced by the conjunctions *nekaĩp, neĩ, kaĩp*. They do not differ from those with *negù* either structurally or in meaning, but they occur mostly in colloquial speech, cf.:

Negaliù suteĩkti jái daugiaũ *láisvės*, kaip/nekaip/nei *jì dabar̃ tùri*.	'I can't give her more freedom than she has now.'

Occasionally in colloquial speech differentiating clauses are introduced by the pronoun form *ką̃* 'what (ACC)' turned conjunction, in which case they may be placed initially as well:

Ką̃ *mán prašýt, tai* geriaũ *visái netúrėsiu*.	'I'd rather not have it at all than beg for it.'

Additive clauses

7.71 This term is used here to refer to subordinate clauses which have as their antecedent the whole main clause. They are commonly introduced by the case forms of the relative pronoun *kàs* and by the relative adverb *kaĩp*. These subordinators have a syntactic function in the subordinate clause, which distinguishes additive clauses from other types of non-integrated clauses.

The main clause is structured like a simple sentence and contains no correlative words. The subordinate clause, usually placed after the main clause, contains additional information and expresses a kind of evaluative statement concerning the content of the main clause:

Jiẽ neatẽjo, kàs *manè labaĩ nuliũdino*.	'They did not come, which worried me very much.'
Mergáitė miegódavo iki pusiáudienio, už ką *nuolàt gáudavo bárti nuo mótinos*.	'The girl used to sleep till noon, for which her mother always scolded her.'
Jám skaudėjo kójas, kaĩp paprastaĩ ēsti po ilgōs keliōnės.	'His feet were aching, as it usually happens after a long walk.'

With respect to the relationship between the clauses, these sentences are close to compound sentences with the conjunctions *iř* 'and', *õ* 'and', *nès* 'as' followed by a demonstrative pronoun (*tàs, tà, taĩ* 'that', *tóks* 'such') or the adverb *taĩp* 'so'; cf.:

Jiẽ neatẽjo, ir taĩ *mán kėlė nērimą*.	'They did not come, and that worried me.'

Additive clauses are characteristic of formal style.

Compound sentence

Sujungiamàsis sakinỹs

7.72 A compound (coordinative) sentence is composed of two or more clauses of equal syntactic status (termed conjuncts) linked by co-ordinating conjunctive words (coordinators) and by intonation, e.g.:

Bùvo vãsara, bet laukuosè žmónės niēko nedìrbo.	'It was summer, but people did not work in the fields.'
Žēmė čià derlìnga, todėl kviečiaĩ geraĩ áuga.	'The soil is fertile here, therefore wheat grows well.'

A coordinator is placed between the clauses and it expresses the semantic relationship between them. Single coordinators are used to form sentences with a closed structure and reduplicated coordinators form open structure sentences.

7.73 **Closed-structure sentences** are formed with the single coordinators *iř* 'and', *õ* 'and', *bèt* 'but', *bètgi* 'but', *ař* 'or', *arbà* 'or', *tačiaũ* 'but', *tàd* 'so, thus', *taĩ* 'so', *tiktaĩ* 'only', *vìs dėlto* 'still; however', *vis tíek* 'nevertheless', *užtaĩ/užtàt* 'therefore', *neĩ* 'nor', and also with *todėl/dėl tõ* 'therefore', *per taĩ* 'therefore'.

The constituent clauses of a structurally closed sentence can also be joined by complex conjunctions such as *o tačiaũ* 'but', *o bèt(gi)* 'but', etc., e.g.:

Tėvas bùvo labaĩ įpỹkęs, bètgi/ o bètgi nepasãkė nė̃ žõdžio.	'Father was very angry, but all the same he didn't say a word.'

In compound sentences, a conjunction is sometimes correlated with a particle or a modal word placed initially in the preceding clause: *tìk/võs... ir vẽl* lit. 'just... and again', *dár/võs... o jaũ* 'yet/just... and already', *neganà... bet dár* 'not only... but even', etc. This correlation serves to reinforce and specify the connection between the clauses, cf.:

Tìk / võs *spėjau pareĩti namõ,* ir vẽl *pradėjo lýti.*	'Hardly had I returned home, and it started raining again.'
Dár *neprasidėjo pavãsaris,* o jaũ *laukaĩ žaliúoja.*	'Spring has not come yet, but the fields are already green.'
Neganà *mán sàvo darbų̃,* bet dár *turiù svetimaĩs rū́pintis.*	'As if I didn't have enough work (lit. 'not enough work of my own'), but I have to take care of other people's work as well.'

7.74 **Open-structure sentences** are formed with the reduplicated conjunctions (see III. 9.3): *iř̃... iř̃* 'and... and', *ař̃... ař̃* 'whether... or', *arbà... arbà* 'either... or', *neĩ... neĩ* 'neither... nor', *taĩ... taĩ* 'now... now', *čià... čià* 'now... now'. The number of clauses is practically unlimited though two or three-constituent sentences are the commonest.

Ir gyvuliaĩ bùvo pašertì, ir pùsryčiai paruoštì, ir namaĩ sutvarkýti.	'(And) the animals were fed, and breakfast was ready, and the rooms were cleaned.'
Nei àš teñ buvaũ, nei galiù táu ką̃ pasakýti.	'Neither have I been there, nor can I tell you anything.'

If the clauses of an open-structure sentence share a constituent it may be placed initially in the first clause, in which case the conjunction takes the second position:

Šį́ryt ir sáulė šviesèsnė, ir paukštėliai linksmiaũ čiùlba.	'Today both (lit. 'and') the sun is brighter and the birds sing more merrily.'

7.75 In both structural types of compound sentences ("open" and "closed") the clauses are often parallel in structure and have identical word order; e.g.:

Iš rytų̃ šalẽlės saulẽlė tekėjo, o iš vakarẽlių debesẽliai ė̃jo.	'From the east the sun was rising, and from the west the clouds were coming.'

An identical predicate or subject, or any other part of the sentence can be either repeated in both clauses (1), or it may be omitted in one of the clauses (2):

(1) *Àš jùms dúosiu bandẽlę, o jū̃s mán dúokite avinẽlį.*	'I'll give you a cake, and you'll give me a lamb.'
Nei tù jõ pabársi, nei tù jõ pamókysi.	'Neither will you scold him nor will you teach him a lesson.'

(**2**) *Màno sesùtė plonaĩ kaĺba, o tù storaĩ.*	'My sister speaks in a high voice, and you in a low voice.'
Motùšė verkdamà, o Bènis šokinėdamas išvažiãvo.	'Mother left crying and Benis jumping with joy' (lit. 'Mother crying and Benis jumping with joy left').

7.76 According to the syntactic relationship between clauses, five types of coordination are distinguished: (1) copulative, (2) juxtapositive and adversative, (3) disjunctive, (4) consecutive, and (5) continuative.

Each of the types is characterized by specific coordinators. Thus, in the case of copulative coordination the conjunction *iř* 'and' and reduplicated conjunctions *iř... iř, neĩ... neĩ, taĩ... taĩ, čià... čià* are used. Juxtapositive and adversative relations are expressed by the conjunctions *õ* 'and/but', *bèt, tačiaũ, tìk(taĩ)*, and *vìs dėlto, vìs tíek, užtàt*. Disjunctive coordination is designated by the single conjunctions *ař, arbà* and reduplicated *ař... ař, arbà... arbà*. Consecutive coordination is expressed by the coordinators *tàd, taĩgi, taĩ, dėl tõ, per taĩ, todėl*, and continuative coordination by *iř, õ* and *bèt*.

The five types of compound sentences are further classified into subtypes by the additional semantic relationship between the clauses and their syntactic peculiarities.

COPULATIVE COORDINATION
Sentences with *iř*

7.77 Clauses joined by the conjunction *iř* can express either simultaneous or successive events. The temporal relationship between the clauses is primarily determined by the tense-mood form and aspect of the predicates.

Simultaneity of events is usually rendered by identical tense-mood forms of the predicates. The time of the events may coincide entirely or partly, at a given period or moment. In the former instance imperfective verbs are usually used in both clauses:

Mėnùlis šviẽčia kaip šviẽtęs, ir šuõ liūdnaĩ kiemè kaũkia.	'The moon shines as before, and the dog barks sadly in the yard.'

In the latter case, the first clause usually contains an imperfective verb, and the following clause a perfective verb:

Kar̃tą vaikaĩ válgė *miškè dúoną ir víenas trupiniùkas* nutrupėjo žẽmèn.	'Once children were eating bread in the forest, and one crumb fell to the ground.'

Successive events are usually rendered by the following means:

(1) perfective verbs in the same tense-mood form in both clauses:

Lãpai sušlãmo, *ir vė̃l vìskas* nutìlo.	'The leaves rustled (once) and everything became quiet again.'

(2) a perfective verb in the first clause and an imperfective verb in the second, both in the same or in different tense-mood forms:

Jõs výras netrùkus mìrė, *ir jì* šeimininkáuja / šeimininkãvo *šiojè sodýboje*.	'Her husband died soon, and she manages / managed this farmstead.'

In sentences denoting a succession of events one of the predicates can be a nominal or adjectival predicate:

Rẽtkarčiais prabė̃ga *kažkokià žmogystà – ir vė̃l vìskas* ramù / *visur̃* tylà.	'From time to time a man passes by running, and all is quiet again / it is silence everywhere.'

Alongside temporal relations clauses linked by *ir̃* may express causal, conditional, contrastive and other relations depending mostly on the structural properties of the clauses and on context.

CAUSAL RELATIONS

7.78 In this case the second clause denotes the consequence of what is denoted by the preceding clause.

The predicates of both clauses may be formally expressed in a variety of ways, of which the following seem to be the more common ones:

(1) One or both clauses contain nominal or adjectival predicates, or periphrastic tense forms (usually denoting state):

Tiẽ dokumeñtai bùvo riebalúoti *ir pẽlės juõs* sudrãskė.	'Those documents were greasy and mice gnawed them to shreds.'
Jìs bùvo nusisùkęs *į síeną ir àš* mačiaũ *jõ žìlą pakáušį*.	'His face was turned (lit. 'He was turned') to the wall, and I saw the grey back of his head.'

(2) One or both clauses contain a compound predicate with a modal verb:

Ežȳs susìrietė į kãmuolį, ir   'The hedgehog has rolled itself into a ball,
šuõ niẽko negãli padarýti.   and the dog can't do anything to it.'

Tù nekaltaĩ nukentėjai, ir àš   'You have suffered without being guilty
turiù atlýginti.   and I must compensate (for it).'

(3) Both predicates are simple finite verb forms usually denoting actions of unlimited duration, or repeated actions, or states:

Dabar̃ tù manę̃s nebèplaki ir   'Now you don't beat me any longer and I
àš nebeverkiù.   do not cry.'

Dùrys geraĩ neužsidãrė ir   'The door did not close tight, and cold air
pro plyšiùs ver̃tėsi į vìdų šal̃tis.   was coming through the cracks into the room.'

Such sentences are close in meaning to those with the conjunctions *taĩ, taĩgi, tàd,* denoting causal relations (see 7.103–105).

7.79 The conjunction *ir̃* may be reinforced by the adverbs *dėl tõ/todė̃l* 'therefore' and the like, which express the cause-and-consequence relationship explicitly:

Ar̃tinosi jau príetėmis, ir todė̃l   'Dusk was approaching, and therefore
Juõzas paskubėjo išeĩti.   Juozas was in a hurry to leave.'

These sentences are naturally close in meaning to compound sentences with the relative adverbs *dėl tõ/todė̃l* without *ir̃* (see 7.105). Compare also complex sentences with the conjunction *kadángi* 'because' (see 7.47).

CONDITIONAL RELATIONS

7.80 In a number of cases, the first clause may acquire the meaning of condition with respect to the subsequent clause. The predicate of the first clause is usually in initial position and carries logical stress. The predicates tend to be formally related in the following ways:

(1) The 2nd person (singular) verb form is used in the first clause and the 3rd person in the second:

Įeinì žmogùs tankumýnan, ir   'You enter (lit. 'Enter (PRES. 2. SG) (a)
kū́nas tìk eĩna pagaugaĩs.   man') the thicket and your body trembles all over.'

Móstelėsi rankelè, ir išìro   'You wave (FUT. 2. SG) your hand, and
visà tvarkà.   all order is gone (PAST) to pieces.'

(2) The future tense is used in the first or in both clauses:

Sulõs šuõ kiemè, ir pàkerta   'A dog will bark in the yard, and
Elžbiẽtai kójas.   Elizabeth's knees shake (with fright).'

Tėvas tik tar̃s žõdį, ir vìskas bùs áišku.	'Father will just say a word and everything will be clear.'

(3) The imperative mood is used in one of the clauses and the indicative in the other:

Neláidyk liežùvio – ir bùs geraĩ.	'Don't wag your tongue – and it will be all right.'

(4) The subjunctive mood is used in the first or in both clauses:

EĨgtumeis kaip prìdera, ir visì tavè ger̃btų.	'If you behaved properly everyone would respect you.'

(5) The predicate of the first clause is the impersonal verb užtèkti 'be enough' or reikė́ti/bereĩkti 'be necessary' with an infinitive often emphasized by the particles tìk 'only', dár 'yet':

Užteñka mán tik užmérkt akìs, ir tuojaũ kỹla priẽš manè vaizdaĩ.	'It is just enough for me to shut my eyes, and at once images start coming to me.'

Sentences implying condition are close in meaning to complex sentences with the conjunction jéi(gu) 'if' (see 7.53–54).

CONTRASTIVE RELATIONS

7.81 In this case the conjunction ir̃ links two clauses contrasting in meaning. One of the clauses is usually affirmative and the other is negative, or the clauses contain antonyms:

Ieškójau dukter̃s vìsą diẽną ir niẽkas neatėjo mán padė́ti.	'I was looking for my daughter all day long, and nobody came to help me.'
Kóks mãžas šitas kambarė̃lis, ir kóks platùs pasáulis!	'How small this room is, and how great the world!'

These sentences are close in meaning to sentences with the conjunctions õ, bèt, tačiaũ which bring out the contrastive meaning.

The contrastive relationship in sentences with the conjunction ir̃ may connote the additional meaning of concession, as in

Vìsą vãsarą láisčiau túos daržùs, ir niẽkas neužáugo.	'I had been watering those vegetable gardens all the summer, and nothing grew up.'

This meaning is intensified by vìs dė́lto or taĩ postposed to ir̃:

Sáulė spindė́jo grynaĩ baltà šviesà, ir vìs dė́lto nebùvo taĩp kár̃šta.	'The sun glowed white-hot, and still nevertheless it wasn't so hot.'

(Cf. complex sentences of concession with the conjunction nórs 'though', 7.58.)

RELATIONS OF PARALLELISM

7.82 In this case the predicates of both sentences are either identical or close in meaning:

Visì jà bùvo paténkinti, ir jì bùvo paténkinta.	'Everyone was pleased with her, and she was pleased.'
Àš jõs privéngiu, ir jũs pasisérgėkite!	'I avoid her, and you (should) be on guard!'

SUMMATIVE RELATIONS

7.83 The second clause introduced by *iř* is related to the preceding clause as a conclusion or a generalization over it. It often contains a generalizing pronoun (*vìskas* 'everything', *vìsas, -à* 'all', *niēkas* 'nobody, nothing', etc.):

Jì rū́pinasi tik savimì – ir vìskas.	'She takes care of herself only – and that's all.'
Sukišaũ visùs pìnigus į ū̃kį, ir niēko nematýti.	'I laid out all my money on the farm, and (there is) nothing to be seen.'

Sentences with *iř... iř*

7.84 The basic meaning and syntactic properties of sentences with the reduplicated conjunction *iř... iř* are similar to those of respective sentences with the single *iř*, but they are less commonly used and have fewer additional meanings. The conjunction emphasizes the cumulation or the parallelism of the clauses. These sentences usually denote simultaneous events, and identical tense forms are used as predicates in the coordinated clauses; cf.:

Čià ir ežerè galésime pasimáudyti, ir vaikaĩ miškè pagrybaũs.	'Here we shall be able (both) to swim in the lake, and the children will pick mushrooms in the woods.'

In the case of parallelism the predicates of both clauses are usually close in meaning, as in respective sentences with the single *iř*:

Ir dúonos tikraĩ mãža, ir viētos tikraĩ nèrà.	lit. '(And) there is really little bread, and there is really no room.'
Ir mẽs bū́sime paténkinti, ir kaimýnai džiaũgsis.	'(lit. And) we shall be both happy and the neighbours will rejoice.'

Sentences with *neĩ ... neĩ*

7.85 This conjunction is a negative counterpart of *iř... iř*. Cf.:

Ir vėjas pūtė, ir girià ūžė, ir lelijà lingãvo.	'The wind was blowing, and the woods were murmuring, and the lily was swaying.'
Nei vėjas pūtė, nei girià ūžė, nei lelijà lingãvo.	'Neither was the wind blowing, nor were the woods murmuring, nor was the lily swaying.'

The predicates of clauses conjoined by *neĩ... neĩ* can be used either with or without the negative prefix; cf.:

Nei dárbas sẽkasi/nesìseka, nei val̃gis leñda/nèlenda.	'Neither is the work going well, nor does the food go down easily.'

Sometimes, sentences expressing parallelism are used with the single *neĩ*:

Grį̃žti àš niẽkam nežadėjau, nei mán kàs bùvo liẽpęs.	'I didn't promise anyone to return, nor did anyone tell me to.'

Sentences with *taĩ ... taĩ, čià ... čià*

7.86 These sentences refer to alternating events, e.g.:

Tai bùlvės supùvo, tai rugiaĩ prapúolė.	'Now the potatoes rotted, now the rye got ruined.'
Čia màn liẽpė tylėti, čia patì pirmóji pasisãkė.	'Now she told me to keep silent, now she herself confessed (it).'

JUXTAPOSITIVE AND ADVERSATIVE COORDINATION

7.87 The most common conjunctions of juxtapositive and adversative coordination are *õ* 'and/but' and *bèt* 'but'. Less commonly, the coordinators *tačiaũ* 'however', *tìk* 'only', *vìs dėltõ* 'nevertheless', *vìs tíek* 'all the same', *užtàt* 'but, but then' are used.

Sentences with *õ*

In sentences with the conjunction *õ* a number of semantic relations between the clauses may be distinguished.

RELATIONS OF PARALLELISM

7.88 In this case a parallel is drawn between the constituents of both clauses performing the same syntactic function:

(1) the subjects:

Tėvas *bùvo kažkuř išẽjęs į* *káimą*, o mótina *dìrbo laukuosè*.	'Father was gone to the village, and mother was working in the fields.'

(2) objects (usually identical in form):

Su melagystè *netolì teeĩsi*, o su teisýbe *visuř gẽra*.	lit. 'With a lie you won't get far, and with the truth it is good everywhere.'

(3) adverbial modifiers (also identical in form as a rule):

Eĩk, sesùte, *víenu keliù*, o àš eĩsiu *kitù keliù*.	'Take, sister, one road (INSTR) and I'll take another road (INSTR).'

If the predicate is the same in both clauses it is commonly omitted in the second clause:

Senẽlis turẽjo *šuniùką*, o bobùtė *kačiùką*.	'Grandfather had a little dog, and grandmother a kitten.'
Paũkštį *plùnksnos* grãžina, o žmógų – *prõtas*.	'A bird (ACC) is adorned (ACT. PRES) by its feathers (NOM) and a man (ACC) by his intellect (NOM).'

The relation between the clauses may be similar to that in copulative coordination:

Praẽjo šveñtės, o mẽs vẽl į dárbus pasinẽrėme.	'The holidays passed, and we again got absorbed in our work.'
Papãsakojo mergáitė sàvo neláimę, o laũmės ją gúodžia.	'The girl told (them) about her misfortune, and the witches consoled her.'

Occasionally, the parallelism is drawn between syntactically different constituents (e.g. the subject and an object, the subject and an adverbial modifier, etc.):

Kìtą *užmùšti* jìs mokẽjo, o pàts *miřti* bìjo.	'He could kill another (man), but he himself is afraid to die.'
Jõs véidas *bùvo labaĩ draũgiškas*, o akysè *žýbčiojo liepsnẽlės*.	'Her face was very friendly, and in her eyes there twinkled a smile.'

CONTRASTIVE RELATIONS

7.89 In sentences with the conjunction õ expressing the contrastive relations one of the clauses is usually affirmative and the other negative. The predicates may have either the same or different stems; cf. respectively:

(1) Tù mán patinkì, o kìtos mer̃gos nepatiñka.	'I like you, and I don't like other girls.'
(2) Bùvo *tamsùs* vãkaras, o kareĩvis neturėjo kuõ žvãkės nusipir̃kti.	'It was a dark night, and/but the soldier had no money to buy a candle.'

The predicates of two clauses may be antonymous words:

Jì kaũpė *pìnigus*, o léido *výras*.	'She saved money and her husband spent it.'
Jũs lìkite *namiẽ*, o *àš* eĩsiu gìrion.	'You stay at home, and I'll go to the woods.'

In sentences with the conjunction *o* the content of one clause may be contrasted to that of the other as unexpected or contradicting it.

Ródos, visái nebùvo debesų̃, o staigà pradėjo lýti.	'It seems, there were no clouds at all, and suddenly it started to rain.'
Reĩkia pradėti pãmoką, o vaĩko nėrà.	'It is time (lit. 'It is necessary') to begin the lesson, and/but the child is not here.'
Netrùkus bùs vãkaras, o dárbas stóvi.	'It will be evening soon, but/and the work is not begun yet.'

The clauses sometimes contain paired particles or adverbs, such as *tìk/dár/võs... jaũ; tuõj... dár*, etc. which are placed initially and stress the contrast:

Dár *vištà kiaušìnio nesudėjo*, o jaũ *martì pautiẽnės panorėjo*.	lit. 'The hen has not laid an egg yet, and already the daughter-in-law wants chicken-broth.'
Tìk *išėjaũ iš namų̃*, o jaũ šaũkia grį̃žti.	'I have just left the house, and they already tell me to return.'
Tuõj *grį̃š vaikaĩ*, o dár *piẽtūs* nepradėti.	'The children will be back in no time, and I haven't started (cooking) dinner yet.'

CONCESSIVE RELATIONS

7.90 In this case sentences are also typically characterized by a contrast between a positive and a negative clause. The predicate of the first clause is often (1) a verb with the prefix *te-* or the particle *tegù/tegùl* or (2) a subjunctive or imperative mood form, or (3) the same verb repeated with negation:

(1) Tegù *manè áuksu* apìberia, o už *nemýlimo* ir sēnio neĩsiu.	'Let them shower me with gold, but (all the same) I shall not marry a man I don't love or an old man.'

(2) Atidúočiau *jám vìską* *véltui, o jìs neim̃s.* 'I would give him everything for nothing, but he won't take (anything).'

(3) Sakeĩ nesakeĩ, *o reĩkalas tùri bū́ti sutvarkýtas.* 'You may say it or not (lit. 'You said didn't say'), but the matter must be settled.'

The concessive relation may be emphasized by the complex conjunction *o vìs dė̃lto* 'and still':

Visì sėdė́jo nejudė́dami týlūs, o vìs dė̃lto *akysè bùvo matýti nèrimas.* 'All (of them) sat motionless and quiet, but still one could see anxiety in their eyes.'

CAUSAL RELATIONS

7.91 The conjunction *õ* sometimes links clauses of which the first refers to cause and the following to its consequence. These sentences are syntactically similar to sentences with the conjunction *iñ* expressing the same relation (cf. 7.78):

Čià mū́sų namaĩ, o *kókio ten šleĩvo vil̃ko nebijósim!* 'Here is our home, and we won't be scared of any bandy-legged wolf!'

Žiẽmą reĩkia veř̃pti, áusti, o tám mókslui nè valandė̃lės neliẽka. 'In winter spinning and weaving (linen) are to be done, and there is not a minute for school.'

Visì põnai, o kàs kiaũlès ganỹs. 'Everyone is a boss, but who will tend the pigs?'

RELATIONS OF EXCLUSION

7.92 In this case the clause introduced by *õ* denotes an event or entity singled out from a totality of such events or entities referred to by the first clause which often contains the plural form of the pronouns *vìsas, -à* 'all', *kìtas, -à* 'other' (cf. the explicit expression of this relation by *tìk*, see 7.99).

Visì tùri vaikų̃, o mẽs vienì. 'All people have children, and we are alone.'

Kìtos mergáitės puõšiasi, o àš ir suknẽlės neturiù. 'Other girls dress smartly, and I don't even have a dress.'

Sentences with *bèt*

Sentences with the conjunction *bèt* commonly express relations of contrast and non-correspondence, sometimes concession, exclusion and parallelism. The relation of contrast is undercurrent even if some other meaning is prevalent.

CONTRASTIVE RELATIONS

7.93 As in sentences with the conjunction õ, either (1) a positive and a negative clause or (2) clauses containing antonyms are contrasted:

(1) *Píevos ir dabař* tebèrà grãžios, *bet miškų̃ seniaĩ* nebėrà. 'The meadows are still beautiful, but the woods are long gone.'

Geraĩ *lė̃kti, bet* negeraĩ *nutū̃pti*. 'It's good to fly, but it's not good to land.'

(2) Leñgva *yrà pasakýti, bet* sunkù *padarýti*. 'It is easy to say but it is hard to do.'

Dárbo šãknys kárčios, *bet jõ vaĩsiai* sáldūs. lit. 'The roots of work are bitter but its fruits are sweet.'

(Compare the respective sentences with the conjunctions õ, *tačiaũ*; see 7.89; 98.)

7.94 The content of the second clause introduced by *bèt* frequently does not correspond to the content of the preceding clause, it is unexpected or unforeseen. One of the clauses is also often negative, the other being positive. These sentences are similar to those with õ, but the conjunction *bèt* is a more explicit means of expressing contrast.

Mė́gau skaitýti, bet pas mùs nebùvo knỹgų. 'I liked to read, but we had no books.'

(See also the examples in 7.93.)

In sentences expressing contrast, pairs of antonymous particles or adverbs (*dár... jaũ* and the like, see 7.89) are often used, e.g.:

Sáulė dár *nebùvo patekė́jusi, bet laukè* jaũ *bùvo šviesù*. 'The sun had not risen yet but it was already light outside.'

CONCESSIVE RELATIONS

7.95 Sentences with *bèt* expressing concession do not differ from respective õ sentences with regard to their syntactic properties and types of predicates (cf. 7.90), but they are more widely used. The relation of concession is superimposed upon the relation of contrast between clauses, e.g.:

Žõdžių mažaĩ tesupranta, bet gaidà jám vėria širdį̃. 'He doesn't quite understand the words, but the tune rends his heart.'

Bùvo dar žiemõs laĩkas, bet atódrėkis pranašãvo ankstývą pavãsarį. 'It was wintertime yet, but the thaw promised an early spring.'

The meaning of concession is emphasized by the units *vìs tíek* 'all the same', *vìs dẽlto* 'still', *užtàt* 'but then':

Senẽlė dár kažką́ áiškina, bet anūkẽlis vis tíek *niẽko suprа̀sti negãli.*	'Granny is still explaining something, but the little boy all the same cannot understand anything.'

RELATIONS OF EXCLUSION

7.96 These sentences are synonymous to respective sentences with *tìk(taĩ)* 'only' (see 7.99) and *õ* 'and/but' (see 7.92), but in sentences with *bèt* the contrast between the content of the clauses is more explicit, e.g.:

Visì atsìgulė, bet jì neužmiẽganti.	'Everyone has gone to bed, but she can't fall asleep.'
Svečiaĩ válgė dár ir gė́rė, bet Drūktėnis kažìn kõ lìko nósį nuléidęs.	'The guests were still eating and drinking, but Drūktėnis remained crestfallen for some reason.'

RELATIONS OF PARALLELISM

7.97 This relationship is less common in sentences with *bèt* than in those with *õ*.

The clauses connected by *bèt* often contain different forms of comparison:

Gẽra tolì *girdė́ti, bet pìkta – dár* toliaũ.	'Good words carry far, but evil words carry farther.'
Taĩp praẽjo jám pirmóji dienà, bet toliaũ dar prasčiaũ *bùvo.*	'This is how his first day passed, but later it was even worse.'

Parallelism can be reinforced by the paired particles and adverbs *ne tìk(tai)... (bet) iř̃* 'not only... (but) also', *ne víen tìk... (bet) iř̃* 'not only... (but) also', *neganà... bet dár* lit. 'not enough... but even', and the like.

Mū́sų šeimojè ne tìk tėvaĩ dìrba, bet ir vaikaĩ pàdeda.	lit. 'In our family not only the parents work, but also the children help.'
Neganà namùs prarãdom, bet dár ir sū́nų ištrėmė.	'It is not enough (that) we have lost our home, but moreover our son is exiled.'

Sentences with *tačiaũ*

7.98 With respect to meanings and syntactic properties, sentences with the conjunction *tačiaũ* 'but', are similar to those with *bèt*, but their usage is more restricted. Their most common meaning is that of non-correspondence.

Šaūkė jì ilgaĩ, tačiau niẽkas neatsìliepė.   'She shouted for a long time, but nobody ever answered.'

These sentences can also express the following related meanings:

(1) the contrastive relations:

Žẽmė, rẽgis, bùvo ta patì..., tačiau daug kàs pasìkeitė.   'The land was apparently the same, but so much was changed.'

(2) the concessive relations:

Kambarỹs bùvo tamsùs, tačiau kampè pamačiaũ kažką̃ jùdant.   'The room was dark, but I saw something moving in the corner.'

Sentences with *tìk(taĩ)*

7.99 The most characteristic relationship in these sentences is that of exclusion, a part being singled out of a whole, e.g.:

Visàs jau raidès jìs žìno, tik vienà tokià sunkì.   lit. 'He knows all the letters already, only one of them is so hard (to remember).'

Visì kaip bùvę, tik Petriùkas pasìkeitė.   lit. 'All (of them) are as before, only Petriukas (little Peter) has changed.'

Sentences with *tik* can also express the following:

(1) contrast and unexpected event:

Kótas gẽras, tik kir̃vis netìkęs.   'The helve is good, only the ax does not fit it.'

Pilnì pašaliaĩ vìsa kõ bùvo, tik nebùvo kám válgyti.   'The larder was full of good things, only there was nobody to eat all that.'

Išėjaũ į̃ kiẽmą, tik staigà šóko ant manę̃s šuõ.   'I went out into the yard, and/only suddenly a dog jumped at me.'

(2) concession:

Jaũ ir kója nebeskaũda, tik atsikélti negãlima.   'The (My) foot does not ache any longer, only I can't stand up.'

(3) condition:

Vìskas bùs geraĩ, tik nešnekė́k tiẽk daũg.   'Everything will be all right, only don't talk so much.'

Sentences with *užtaĩ/užtàt, vìs dė̃lto, vis tíek*

7.100 These coordinators are comparatively infrequent. They usually denote concession, e.g.:

Jaunìkis bùvo nusimìnęs, užtàt núotaka nèkreipė į taī nė mažiáusio dė̃mesio.	'The bridegroom was dejected, nevertheless the bride did not pay the slightest attention to it.'
Galì teñ nueĩti, vis tíek niẽko nelaimė́si.	'You can go there, all the same you won't gain anything.'
Sáulė jaũ nusiléidusi, vìs dėlto kambaryjè tvankù.	'The sun has already set, but (lit. 'all the same') it is stuffy in the room.'

DISJUNCTIVE COORDINATION

7.101 In the case of disjunctive coordination, a choice is offered between the statements expressed in the conjoined clauses. Disjunctive coordination is expressed by *ar̃/arbà* 'or', *ar̃... ar̃* 'either... or', *arbà... arbà* 'either... or'. The conjunctions *arbà* and *arbà... arbà* are used to link clauses within an affirmative sentence, while *ar̃* and correlative *ar̃... ar̃* can link clauses within both affirmative and interrogative sentences. In the latter case, the conjunction *ar̃* functionally corresponds to the interrogative particle *ar̃*.

In sentences with the reduplicated conjunctions *arbà... arbà* and *ar̃... ar̃* the disjunctive relationship is emphasized due to the repetition of the conjunction:

Arba tù, bróli, liáukis, arba àš einù šaliñ.	'Either you, brother, stop it, or I take myself off.'
Arba tō žõdžio niẽkas jõ nemókė, arba jisaĩ užmir̃šo jį̃.	'Either no one taught him that word, or he forgot it.'
Ar mēs gyvénsime kartù, ar mán išsikélti?	'Shall we live together or shall I move out?'

Sentences with the single conjunctions *arbà* and *ar̃* typically express a disjunctive relationship as well:

Gal vaĩkas pàts paklýdo, arba/ar jį̃ kas nórs suklaidìno.	'Maybe the boy himself lost his way, or somebody told him the wrong way.'
Už gìrios sugriáudė, ar gál mùms tik pasiródė.	'It thundered beyond the forest, or maybe we just imagined it.'

Sentences with the conjunctions *ar̃*, *arbà* can also express:

(1) parallelism (cf. respective sentences with the conjunction *õ* in 7.88), e.g.:

Kaimýno namaĩ net blìzga, arba štaĩ ir sõdas naujaĩ aptvértas.	'The neighbour's house (is in such perfect order that it) even shines, look, the garden has a new fence.'

(2) enumeration (as in the respective sentences with the reduplicated conjunction *taĩ... taĩ*; see 7.86):

Kar̃tais čià apsilañko gìminės, arba šiaĩp kóks praeĩvis užklýsta.	'Sometimes the relatives pay a visit here, or just a passerby drops in.'

CONSECUTIVE COORDINATION

7.102 In the case of consecutive coordination the second clause denotes the consequence or result of what is designated by the preceding clause. The coordinators are: *taĩ* 'so', *taĩgi* 'thus', *tàd* 'therefore', and also *todė̃l/dė̃l tõ* 'therefore', *užtaĩ* 'that's why'.

Sentences with *taĩ*

7.103 Sentences with *taĩ* usually express the relation of cause to its consequence.

Vaĩkas paáugo, tai tė́vas vẽdasi jį̃ namõ.	'The child has grown older, so his father is taking him home.'
Pàts šeiminiñkas... čia bùvo rẽtas svẽčias, tai nė̃ kelių̃ niẽkas netaĩsė.	'The owner himself seldom came here, so no one even repaired the roads.'

Sentences with *taĩ* can also express the conditional relations, in which case the predicate of the first clause usually has a future tense form or an imperative or subjunctive mood form; cf.:

Atvažiúosi/Atvažiúok namõ, tai pasitìksim tavè kaip brangiáusią svẽčią.	'Should you come (FUT/IMPER) home, then we shall greet you as the dearest guest.'
Bū́tum manę̃s paklaũsęs, tai dabar̃ bū́tum turtìngas.	'Had you taken my advice (SUBJ), then you would be rich now.'

The relationship of condition also holds between clauses with identical predicates, e.g.:

Šálta, tai šálta.	'If it's cold, it's cold.'
Lỹja, tai lỹja.	'If it rains, it rains.'

Sentences with *taĩgi*, *tàd*

7.104 These sentences express the meaning of consequence more explicitly than those with *taĩ* (cf. 7.103).

Bùvo piẽtų laĩkas, taigi pàkviečiau juõs priẽ stãlo.	'It was dinner time, so I invited them to the table.'

Jìs vìsas júodas, tad jõ tamsojè nè nematýti. 'He is all black, so he is invisible in the dark.'

Sentences with *todẽl, dėl tõ*

7.105 The first clause of these sentences refers to cause, and the following clause to consequence. These sentences differ from those with the above conjunctions *taĩ, taĩgi, tàd* in that they have a stronger implication of cause; e.g.:

Žẽmė teñ derlìnga, todẽl vìskas geraĩ áuga. 'The soil is fertile there, therefore everything grows well.'

Výras mažaĩ uždìrba, dėl tõ gyvẽname suñkiai. 'My husband earns little, therefore we are hard-up.'

CONTINUATIVE COORDINATION

7.106 This type of coordination holds between clauses linked by the conjunctions *iř, õ, bèt* if the second clause serves as an amplification of the entire preceding clause, or of its constituent. The second clause begins with an anaphoric thematic component which immediately follows the conjunction and can be formally expressed in the following ways:

(1) by a noun of the first clause repeated with the demonstrative pronoun *tàs, tà* 'that':

Apliñk káimą dunksójo tamsūs miškaĩ, o tuosè miškuosè bùvo daugýbė pélkių. 'Around the village there stretched dark forests, and in those forests there were numerous bogs.'

(2) by the pronouns *jìs* 'he', *jì* 'she', *tàs, tà* 'that (one)', *šìs, šì* 'this (one)' referring anaphorically to a noun in the first clause:

Sutikaũ pažį́stamą žmõgų, ir tàs/jìs manè sutìko parvèžti. 'I met an acquaintance of mine, and (that one)/he agreed to give me a lift.'

Sẽnis paprãšė Pẽtrą grąžìnti skõlą, bet jìs/šìs tik nusìjuokė. 'The old man asked Petras (Peter) to pay back the debt, but he/this (one) only laughed.'

(3) by a deverbal noun derived from the verb of the first clause, with the demonstrative pronoun *tàs, tà* 'that', *tóks, -ià* 'such':

Vaĩkas staigà nutìlo, bet tà tylà víeną minùtę tesitráukė. 'The child suddenly fell silent, but that silence lasted only a minute.'

(4) by the neuter demonstrative pronouns *taĩ* 'that', *tataĩ* 'that' (sometimes *tàs* 'that') referring to the content of the first clause:

| *Pētras ilgaĩ kalbėjosi sù manim̃*, ir taĩ/tàs *mán bùvo labaĩ malonù*. | 'Petras (Peter) talked to me for a long time, and that was a great pleasure.' |

Type (1) and (2) sentences are close in meaning to subordinate sentences with a continuative attributive clause introduced by the relative pronoun *kurìs, -ì* 'which, what', cf.:

| *Apliñk káimą dunksójo tam̃sūs miškaĩ*, kuriuosè *bùvo daugýbė pélkių*. | 'Around the village there stretched dark forests where (lit. 'in which') there were numerous bogs' (see 7.26, 2). |

Type (4) sentences correspond to complex sentences with a subordinate additive clause introduced by the relative pronoun *kàs* 'which'; cf.:

| *Pētras ilgaĩ kalbėjosi sù manim̃*, kàs *mán bùvo labaĩ malonù*. | 'Peter talked to me for a long time, which was a great pleasure' (see 7.71). |

Asyndetic sentence
Bejungtùkis sakinỹs

7.107 Clauses can be combined into a sentence asyndetically, i.e. without a conjunction. The clauses in an asyndetic sentence are linked by intonation and their semantic relationship can be indicated by a correlation between the grammatical form of predicates, and by the specific structural features of the clauses.

The clauses within an asyndetic sentence can be related in the same way as in syndetic sentences. In fact, asyndetic sentences may be close in meaning either to compound or to complex sentences. An exception is a small specific group of asyndetic sentences which have no exact counterparts among compound and complex sentences (see 7.122).

Asyndetic sentences (like syndetic sentences) can be structurally open or closed.

Open structure is mostly characteristic of asyndetic sentences corresponding to the compound sentences with copulative and juxtapositive coordination (cf. 7.77 ff., 7.86 ff.). Open-structure sentences can comprise two or more clauses of equal syntactic status; they may be parallel in syntactic structure and their sequence can be reversed, as a rule. This is especially characteristic of asyndetic copulative sentences.

Closed-structure asyndetic sentences are comprised of two clauses only, the content of one clause being dependent on the content of the other. The sequential order of the clauses is fixed and it cannot be reversed without violating the relationship between the clauses. Closed structure is characteristic of three groups of asyndetic sentences:

(1) sentences expressing temporal, conditional, concessive, contrastive and causal relations between the clauses: in this respect they correspond to non-integrated complex sentences (cf. 7.12);

(2) sentences expressing completive relations between the clauses and corresponding to integrated complex sentences (see 7.16 ff.; on sentences expressing correlative relations with the omitted conjunction *kàd* see 7.34);

(3) sentences expressing complementary relations which have no syndetic counterparts; e.g.:

Po kíek laĩko mergáitė pažiūrėjo į mótinos véidą: mótina veřkė.	'After a while the girl looked at her mother's face: her mother was crying.'

With regard to meaning, sometimes to intonation and grammatical features, closed-structure asyndetic sentences may correspond both to complex and to compound syndetic sentences with the respective additional meanings (e.g. of condition, cause, etc.); cf.:

Atẽjo laĩkas sumokė́ti – sumokė́jau.	lit. 'The time came to pay – I paid.'
Atẽjo laĩkas sumokė́ti, tai/ taigi *ir sumokė́jau.*	'The time came to pay – so I paid.' (Coordination)
Kadángi *atẽjo laĩkas sumokė́ti,* tai *ir sumokė́jau.*	'Since the time came to pay, so I paid.' (Subordination)
Atkélk vartùs – nesibélsiu.	'Open the gate – I won't knock.'
Atkélk vartùs, tai *ir nesibélsiu.*	'Open the gate, and then I won't knock.' (Coordination)
Jei *atkélsi vartùs, nesibélsiu.*	'If you open the gate I won't knock.' (Subordination).

The relations between the clauses within an asyndetic sentence are largely dependent on intonation and there is no distinct border-line between the types. The principal sphere of the use of asyndetic sentences is colloquial speech, fiction and folklore.

OPEN-STRUCTURE SENTENCES

COPULATIVE RELATIONS

7.108 These asyndetic sentences have additive force. Each clause (excepting the very last one) has a final rise which is particularly distinct in the case of syntactic parallelism.

The copulative relationship within a sentence is often reinforced (1) by a repetition of the same word or word group in all or in some of the clauses, or (2) by an adverbial modifier shared by all the clauses and placed, as a rule, in the sentence-initial position; cf.:

(1) Mán priklaũso *pušýnai*, mán priklaũso *ežeraĩ*.	'The pine-woods belong to me, the lakes belong to me.'
(2) Miẽsto pakraštyjè *jau švytė́jo langaĩ, trinksė́jo várstomos dùrys, gãtvėmis nùūžė pirmíeji troleibùsai*.	'In the suburbs there was already light in the windows, the doors were banged open, the early trolleybuses passed noisily in the streets.'

A characteristic feature of many copulative sentences is syntactic parallelism, i.e. the same word order in the clauses, identical grammatical form of the main (and often secondary) parts of the clauses, identical position of logical stress.

7.109 In sentences denoting **simultaneous** events all the predicates, or at least one predicate, are usually of the imperfective aspect; cf. respectively:

Spiẽgė *vaikaĩ*, šaũkė *móterys*, rė́kė *výrai*.	'The children were shrieking, the women were shouting, the men were bawling.'
Artė́jo *naktìs*, suspindė́jo *pìrmosios žvaĩgždės*.	'Night was falling (IMPF), the first stars appeared (PF) in the sky.'

In sentences with perfective predicates, the simultaneity may be clarified by an adverbial of time; e.g.:

Tą̃ pãčią minùtę suskam̃bo *varpaĩ*, užsìdegė *šviẽsos*, *minià* staigà nuščiùvo.	'At that moment the bells pealed, the lights went up, the crowd suddenly hushed.'

7.110 A **succession** of events is usually rendered by identical tense-mood forms of perfective verbs; e.g.:

Pasìbaigė *mišios*, *žmónės* išsiskìrstė.	'The mass was over, the congregation broke up.'

Imperfective verbs may occur in the last clause, e.g.:

Studeñtas tuõj priė́jo *prie jõs*, *abùdu daũg* kalbė́josi *ir* juõkėsi.	'The student came up to her at once, they talked a lot and laughed.'

If an imperfective verb occurs in the preceding clause, a succession of actions is necessarily indicated by a temporal adverbial:

| *Tolì káime* lójo *šuõ,* paskuĩ | 'Far away in the village a dog was |
| sužvìngo *arklỹs.* | barking, later on a horse neighed (PF).' |

In an asyndetic sentence denoting successive events, the sequence of clauses cannot be reversed.

JUXTAPOSITIVE RELATIONS

7.111 In this case the constituent clauses are usually parallel in structure and word order, tense-mood forms of the predicates being also identical, as a rule. The first clause is uttered with a final rise, and the last clause with a final fall, with a distinct pause between the clauses. Logical stress is distributed symmetrically: it falls on the juxtaposed words of both clauses, which may have identical or different syntactic functions (as a rule, there are two juxtaposed pairs, viz. the thematic and rhematic components of each clause); cf. respectively:

Tė́vas króvė prakaitúodamas,	'The father made his fortune sweating, the
sūnùs léido besijuõkdamas.	son spent (it) laughing.'
Gẽras ir žõdžio *klaũso,* pìkto *ir*	'A good man heeds a word, a bad man
lazdà *neatitaĩso.*	does not heed a stick.'

Juxtapositive sentences comprising more than two clauses are rare, though marginally possible; e.g.:

| *Galvà žmõgų vedžiója, ãkys* | 'The head leads the man, the eyes deceive, |
| *klaidìna, pìlvas gaišìna.* | the stomach wastes (his) time.' |

In most of these sentences, omission of a part of the subsequent clause(s) is common as a means of avoiding repetition:

| *Dárbas dúoną* peĩno, *tinginỹstė –* | 'Work earns bread, idleness poverty.' |
| *var̃gą.* | |

These asyndetic sentences acquire the meaning of comparison if the clauses express similarity or common properties. The comparative form of an adjective or an adverb is used in the subsequent clause:

Gamtà gražì, mergẽlė dár	'Nature is beautiful, the girl is even more
gražèsnė.	beautiful.'
Daũg var̃go su vaikaĩs, dár	'(One has) a lot of trouble with the
daugiaũ – *be vaikų̃.*	children, more trouble yet without
	children.'

If the parallelism is drawn between opposite concepts antonyms are used in both clauses, or negation with a repeated word in the second clause:

Dárbas – ne var̃gas, tinginỹstė – ne láimė.	'Work is not hardship, idleness is not happiness.'
Mùlkis dúoda, išmintìngas ìma.	'A fool gives, a clever man takes.'
Keñčia kaĺtas, keñčia nekaĺtas.	'The guilty suffers, the innocent (lit. 'not guilty') suffers too.'

CLOSED-STRUCTURE SENTENCES

Asyndetic sentences corresponding to non-integrated complex sentences

7.112 Two varieties of these sentences are distinguished with regard to clause relationship and intonation.

In sentences expressing temporal, conditional, concessive and contrastive relations, the content of the second clause is determined by the content of the preceding clause. The first clause is often uttered with a final rise, and the second with a fall and with a pause between the clauses. Each clause has one logical stress (symmetrical distribution of logical stress is uncharacteristic of these sentences). The word order in the first clause is usually inverted, the predicate preceding the subject: as a rule it is placed in the clause-initial position. The sequence of clauses is fixed and cannot be reversed.

In sentences expressing causal relations the structure of the clauses is relatively free and their sequence can be sometimes reversed, cf.:

Laukè lỹja, reĩkia pasiiñti skė̃ti.	'It is raining outside, I must take an umbrella.'
Reĩkia pasiiñti skė̃ti – laukè lỹja.	'I must take an umbrella – it is raining outside.'

The second clause usually amplifies or specifies the content of the preceding clause, which makes these sentences close in meaning to asyndetic sentences expressing complementary relations. These sentences are characterized by a specific intonation pattern: the pitch slightly falls at the end of the first clause and after an emphatic pause the second clause begins at a higher pitch which falls gradually.

TEMPORAL RELATIONS

7.113 In sentences expressing temporal relations, the same tense forms of the indicative mood are mostly used in both clauses. To express simultaneity, an imperfective verb is commonly used in the first clause, and a perfective verb in the first clause is used to express successive events; cf. respectively:

Šviẽčia *sáulė – visíems malonù dìrbti.*	'The sun shines (IMPF) – everyone enjoys working.'
Atsipū̃s *arkliaĩ – vė̃l važiúosim.*	'The horses will get rested (PF) – we'll continue our journey.'

The temporal relationship between clauses is often combined with the conditional relationship:

Išeinì *rýtą į̃ mìšką grybáuti, galì vìsą diẽną* praváikščioti.	lit. 'You go to the woods to pick mushrooms in the morning, you can spend the whole day walking there.'

CONDITIONAL RELATIONS

7.114 In this case the first clause is related to the second as condition to consequence or result:

Rū́pinsies *tik pàts savimì, niẽkas táu gyvẽnime nepadė̃s.*	'(If) you take (FUT) care only of yourself, no one will ever help (FUT) you.'

Conditional sentences are subject to a number of restrictions on the use of tense-mood verbal forms.

7.115 The relationship of condition is most prominent if **subjunctive mood forms** occur in both clauses; e.g.:

Bū́čiau žinójęs, bū́čiau *ir kójos iš namų̃* nekė́lęs.	'Had I known, I'd have stayed at home.'

If the imperative mood is used in the first clause, the second usually contains a future tense form of the indicative mood, less commonly a subjunctive mood form; e.g.:

Neveřsk *jõ dìrbti – sámanom* apaũgs.	'(If) you don't force (IMPER) him to work – he'll get overgrown (FUT) with moss.'

In generalised sentences, the present tense and imperative mood forms are also possible in the second clause:

Neprižiūrė́k *vaikų̃, paskuĩ jiẽ táu vìsą gyvẽnimą* nuõdija.	'(If) you don't look (IMPER) after the children, later they poison (PRES) all your life.'
Su juõ prasidė́k, *niẽko gẽro* neláuk.	'(Once) you get mixed up (IMPER) with him, you are (IMPER) in for trouble.'

The use of the imperative mood in the first clause is a distinctive feature of asyndetic conditional sentences (as well as syndetic compound sentences implying condition, see 7.80, 3), which is uncharacteristic of complex conditional sentences.

7.116 To express real condition, **indicative mood forms** (especially future tense) are also used in the first clause. In this case the meaning of condition carries a strong implication of temporal relationship. The condition expressed by the first clause may refer to the future, present, or past; cf. the respective use of tense forms:

(1) The future tense in the first clause:

Visų ver̃ksi – *akių* netėksi.	'(If) you bemoan (FUT) everybody, you'll lose (FUT) your eyesight.'
Paliẽsi *mygtùką pir̃štù* – skam̃ba *visì namaĩ*.	'(If) you touch (FUT) the button with your finger, the whole house rings (PRES).'
Víenas nepakélsi *dėž̃ės* – pasikviẽsk *manè*.	'(If) you can't lift (FUT) the box alone, call (IMPER) me.'

(2) The present tense in the first clause:

Neléidi *mán vèsti Verùtės, àš niẽko vèsti* nenóriu.	'(If) you don't allow (PRES) me to marry Verutė, I don't want (PRES) to marry anyone.'
Šiañdien juokíes – *rytój* ver̃ksi.	'(If) you laugh (PRES) today – you'll cry (FUT) tomorrow.'
Bijaĩ *vil̃ko* – neĩk *į̃ mìšką*.	'(If) you are afraid (PRES) of the wolf – don't go (IMPER) to the forest.'

(3) The past tense in the first clause:

Núogas gimeĩ, *núogas ir* mir̃si.	'(If) you were born (PAST) naked (= poor), naked you will die (FUT).'
Pàvogė *árklį* – pridė́k *ir bal̃ną*.	'(If) they have stolen (PAST) your horse, give (IMPER) them the saddle too.'

CONCESSIVE AND CONTRASTIVE RELATIONS

7.117 In the case of concessive relationship, the imperative mood or the 3rd person present tense form with the particles *tè*, *tegùl* 'let' or with the prefix *te-* is mainly used in the first clause (cf. (1) below). Moreover, the predicate of the first clause is often comprised of two verb forms the second of which is repeated with the negative prefix, as in (2). The second clause contains a predicate in the present or future tense form, less commonly in the imperative mood:

(1) Tegùl *mùs vė̃l* trēmia, kankìna – *láisvės* neatsižadė́sim.	'Let them deport, torment us again – we will not give up our freedom.'

(2) Nóri nenóri, reĩkia
eĩti.

'Whether you want it or not (lit. 'you want or not want'), it is necessary to go.'

Prašýk neprašýk –
sū́rio negáusi.

'You may beg or not (IMPER) you won't get any cheese.'

The first clause of a concessive sentence may begin with a relative pronoun or adverb, the predicate containing the prefix be-:

Ką̃ besakýtų kaimýnai, sàvo
dárbą àš baĩgsiu.

'Whatever my neighbours might say (SUBJ), I will finish my work.'

7.118 The second clause often expresses an unexpected result (1) or unforeseen event (2). The predicates of both clauses usually have the same tense form:

(1) Skùndėmės aukščiaũ – teisýbės
viẽton rýkščių susiláukėm.

'We complained to the authorities – instead of justice we got punished.'

(2) Iš rýto kaip visadà ateinù į
pãmoką – klãsė tuščià.

'In the morning I come to a lesson as usual – the classroom is empty.'

But not necessarily:

Nespė́jai įkópti kalvùtėn – jau riedì
pakaĩnėn.

'Hardly have you reached the top, when you start to slide (PRES) downhill.'

Some sentences with a subjunctive mood form in the second clause are close in meaning and intonation to complementary sentences:

Nebẽrà tėvẽlio, jìs tavè
pamókytų.

'Father is dead, (otherwise) he would teach you a lesson.'

Mán gaĩla kãtino, šiaĩp juõkčiausi.

'I am sorry for the cat, (otherwise) I'd laugh.'

CAUSAL RELATIONS

7.119 Cause can be referred to by the first (1) as well as by the subsequent (2) clause.

The clause expressing cause is always formally affirmative, while the other clause may be either affirmative or imperative or interrogative. Compare:

(1) Àš vélniui tarnáuju – neturiù
laĩko váikščioti.

'I serve the devil – I've no time for walking.'

Jì atvažiãvo čià lìnksmintis –
negadìnk jái núotaikos.

'She has come here to have a good time – don't spoil her pleasure.'

(2) Tą̃ pãčią akìmirką nýktelėjo
Tòmo šìrdìs: jìs prisìminė vaikùs.

'At that very moment Tom's heart gave a jump: he remembered his children.'

Nešúkauk dabar̃ kambarȳ – senẽlė miẽga.	'Don't shout in the room – granny is asleep.'
Ar̃gi ver̃ta síelotis, vìsko jùms ganà.	lit. 'Is it worthwhile grieving, you have all you need.'

The meaning of cause may be combined with that of purpose, in which case the imperative mood or future tense forms are common in both clauses:

Pardúok tą́ óbuolį mán – àš suválgysiu.	'Sell (IMPER) that apple to me – I'll eat (FUT) it.'
Mèskit ginčùs, eĩkim geriaũ užką́sti.	'Stop (IMPER) quarrelling, let's better have (IMPER) a snack.'

Asyndetic sentences corresponding to integrated sentences

In these sentences one clause amplifies, explains or specifies the content of the other clause.

COMPLETIVE RELATIONS

7.120 In these sentences one of the clauses (usually the first one) is syntactically incomplete or deficient without the other clause which is integrated into its structure as a syntactic object or subject. Two subtypes can be distinguished.

(1) The integrated clause occupies the object position after verbs of sense perception, speech and mental processes:

Taĩp áiškiai girdžiù: jiẽ válgo dúonos ir net píeno gẽria.	'I hear so clearly: they are eating bread and even drinking milk.'
Tíek kar̃tų jaũ tavè prašiaũ: neĩk vakarè iš namų̃.	'I have asked you ever so many times: don't go out in the evenings.'

The integrated object clause may occasionally take the sentence-initial position:

Mẽs nugalė́sim – àš žinaũ.	'We shall win – I know (it).'

Very close to these sentences are those in which the predicate of the first clause denotes an action aimed at obtaining information:

Pėtras dìrstelėjo į laĩkrodį – bùvo jau dvýlikta valandà.	'Petras (Peter) glanced at his watch – it was already twelve o'clock.'

(2) The second integrated clause takes the subject position:

Visíems bùvo áišku: tėvaĩ negalėjo pasirū́pinti vaikaĩs.	'It was clear to everyone: the parents couldn't take care of their children.'
Mán pasiródė – tù juokíes.	'I (DAT) thought (lit. 'It seemed to me') you were laughing.'

7.121 The first clause of an asyndetic sentence may contain a correlative dummy word (pronoun or adverb) of generalized semantics which is specified and clarified by the integrated clause:

Geriáusias bū́das atkerš̃yti bùs štaĩ kóks: àš nekalbė́siu su jaĩs.	'The best way to revenge will be this: I will not talk to them.'
Àš su támsta tik tíek sutinkù: pagrindìnė mintìs nė mán neáiški.	'I agree with you only so far: the main idea is not clear even to me.'
Taĩ visái neabejótina: táu reĩkia iš čià išvỹkti.	'There is no doubt about it (lit. 'This is quite doubtless'): you must leave this place.'

An integrated completive clause may precede the clause with a correlative word:

Tù ne eĩgeta, taĩ mẽs puĩkiai žìnome.	'You are not a beggar, we know that very well.'

Sentences of the latter kind are close in meaning to complementary sentences (see 7.122).

Asyndetic complementary sentences

7.122 This is a specific type of asyndetic sentences which has no syndetic counterpart. Both clauses can be grammatically independent and they are not subjected to any lexical or structural restrictions.

The second clause amplifies or limits the content of the preceding clause:

Taĩ bent istòrija – kitõs tokiõs dar negirdė́jau!	'That's quite a story – I never heard anything like it!'
Abìpus kẽlio mẽdžiai stovėjo tỹlūs, nė vienà šakẽlė nejudėjo.	'On both sides of the road the trees stood still, not a single twig stirred.'

The subsequent clause may convey additional information or comment; e.g.:

Pérduok linkė́jimus žmónai – mán tẽko su jà susipažìnti žiẽmą.	'Give my best regards to your wife – I had an opportunity to meet her in winter.'

Asyndetic sentences of complex structure

7.123 In an asyndetic sentence, either one or both immediate constituents can in their own turn comprise two or more asyndetically linked clauses, cf.:

Ángelas apleĩs, vélnias ateĩs – // – víenas nebū́si.	'The angel will leave, the devil will come // you won't be alone.'
Lazdà tùri dù galù: // víenas mán, kìtas táu.	'A stick has two ends: // one (is) for me, the other (is) for you.'
Júodos rañkos – baltà dúona, // báltos rañkos – juodà dúona.	lit. 'The hands (are) black – the bread (is) white, // the hands (are) white – the bread (is) black.'

An asyndetic sentence may comprise three compound constituents, each composed of two asyndetically linked clauses:

Muzikántai rė́žia – net langaĩ biřbia, // šokė́jai treñkia – net žẽmė dùnda, // seniẽji gẽria – net ãkys bą̃la...	'The band is playing – the windows are even jingling, // the dancers are stamping – the ground is even rumbling, // the old (people) drink – their eyes even grow white...'

The constituents of an asyndetic sentence can in their turn correspond to asyndetic sentences of complex structure:

Bet àš nuōlat sakýdavau: // miẽstas dìdelis, daũg jamè piktų̃ žmonių̃ gyvẽna, sáugok mán Jokū́bą!	'But I constantly repeated: // the town is large, many bad people live there, please look after Jokūbas (Jacob)!'

Mixed complex sentence

7.124 The clauses within a mixed sentence may be linked both syndetically by coordination and subordination, and asyndetically.

A mixed complex sentence is a multiple clause structure comprising at least three clauses either of equal (1) or of different (2) syntactic status. In the latter instance, a sentence contains clauses which structurally correspond either to compound, or complex, or asyndetic sentences. Compare the following examples:

(1) *Keleĩvinis traukinỹs pràlėkė pro šãlį, // valandėlę dar bùvo matýti paskutìniojo vagòno raudónas signãlas, // bet ir tàs diñgo tamsojè.*

'The passenger train rushed by, // only the red lights of the last carriage could be seen for a while, // but they soon disappeared in the dark.'

(2) *Draugaĩ susėdo po medžiù, // ir Jonas sužinójo vìską, kàs bùvo atsitìkę.*

'The friends sat down under a tree, // and Jonas (John) learned all that had happened.'

In mixed sentences, syndetic coordination and subordination and asyndetic connection may combine in a variety of ways, depending on the communicative needs. This may result in sentences of great complexity.

Below, a number of most common combinations are illustrated.

7.125 Sentences with the **principal syndetic coordination** are most commonly comprised of two constituents each in its turn corresponding either to a complex, or compound, or asyndetic sentence; e.g.:

Ką jiẽ teñ kalbėjo, ką dãrė, niẽkas nežìno, // tìk namõ grį̃žęs vaikìnas pasãkė, kad jám reĩkia išvažiúoti.

'No one knows what they had been talking about, what they had been doing, // only on (his) return home the boy announced that he had to leave.'

Žmónės seniaĩ kaĨba, kad Jõnas sugrį̃š, // bet sleñka mẽtai, o mótina jõ vìs nesuláukia.

'People keep talking that John will return, but the years pass by and his mother is still waiting for him.'

A sentence may comprise three or more coordinated constituents:

Kai sutẽmo, rengiaũsi guĨti, // bet staigà gãtvėje pasigir̃do rìksmas, // ir kažkàs ė̃mė bélstis į durìs, kuriàs buvaũ pamir̃šęs užrakìnti.

'As it grew dark, I was getting ready for bed, // but suddenly screams were heard in the street // and somebody started banging on the door which I had forgotten to lock.'

7.126 In sentences with the **principal syndetic subordination**, one or both constituents may correspond to compound or asyndetic sentences:

Niẽkaip negaliù supràsti, // iš kur̃ jìs atsibãstė ir kodėl àš turiù juõ rū́pintis.

'I can't understand // where he has turned up from and why I have to look after him.'

Jéigu im̃si giñčytis, // draũgui tikraĩ nepadėsi, bet pačiám bùs blogiaũ.

'If you start arguing, // you won't help your friend at all, but you will make things worse for yourself.'

| *Nors dienà bùvo gražì, sáulė jau aukštaĩ palypėjusi, // bet visų namų langaĩ bùvo uždarýti ir gãtvėje nesimãtė nė víeno praeĩvio.* | 'Though it was a fine day, the sun was high in the sky, // all the windows were shuttered and there was not a single passer-by in the street.' |

7.127 The **principal asyndetic connection** may join two constituents each of which may correspond to any type of composite sentences; e.g.:

| *Prašýk, bičiùli, kõ širdìs geĩdžia – // vìską padarýsiu.* | 'Ask, my friend, whatever your heart craves for – // I'll do anything for you.' |
| *Atsìminiau, kad žmõgų ùžmušiau, // šiur̃pas manè vìsą pàėmė, plaukaĩ ant galvõs atsistójo.* | 'I remembered that I had killed a man; // I was struck with terror, my hair stood on end.' |

A mixed sentence may comprise more than two asyndetically connected compound constituents (especially in a stylistically marked text):

| *Narsùs bùvo Šarū́nas, bet Šviedrỹs dár narsèsnis, // šveitrùs bùvo Šarū́no kalavìjas, bet Šviẽdrio dár šveitrèsnis; // rìstas bùvo Šarū́no žìrgas, bet Šviẽdrio dár ristèsnis.* | 'Šarūnas was courageous, but Šviedrys was even more courageous; // Šarūnas' sword shone, but Šviedrys' sword shone even brighter, // Šarūnas' steed was fast, but Šviedrys' steed was faster.' |

7.128 A mixed sentence may consist of three or more immediate constituents connected by different syntactic means. All the constituents excepting the very last one usually are connected asyndetically and the last one is linked to them by a coordinating conjunction, e.g. *ir̃* 'and' or *õ* 'and/but':

| *Põnas mìršta badù, // kùnigas – šalčiù, // o vargdiẽnis – gárdžiu válgymu.* | 'A rich man dies of hunger, // a priest (dies) of cold, // and a poor man of rich food.' |
| *Tuõ tárpu sáulė jaũ pasìslėpė už mẽdžių, // šešė́lis pàsiekė súolus, kuř sėdėjo svečiaĩ, // ir vėsõs srovė̃ pū́stelėjo iš laũko.* | 'Meanwhile the sun hid behind the trees, // the shadow reached the benches where the guests were sitting, // and a stream of cool air flowed from the fields.' |

7.129 The main constituent of a mixed sentence may subordinate two or more clauses related to different antecedents in the superordinate clause; cf.:

| *Àš vìską žinaũ, tėvai, kàs põno rū́muose dãrosi, ir sakaũ táu: nevarýk dukter̃s į̃ dvãrą.* | 'Father, I know all that goes on in the mansion, and I tell you: don't send your daughter to the manor.' |

A mixed sentence may in its turn enter as a constituent part into a more complicated sentence.

Selected bibliography

Aleksandravičius, J., *Litovskij jazyk*, Vilnius, 1988.

Amato, L.S., *La distribuzione della posposizione nel lituano antico*, Napoli, 1976.

Ambrazas, S., *Daiktavardžių darybos raida. Lietuvių kalbos veiksmažodiniai vediniai / Die Entwicklung des Systems der abgeleiteten Substantive. Deverbativa in Litauischen*, Vilnius, 1993.

Ambrazas, V. (ed.), *Dabartinės lietuvių kalbos gramatika*, Vilnius, 1994.

Ambrazas, V. (ed.), *Grammatika litovskogo jazyka*, Vilnius, 1985.

Ambrazas, V., *Lietuvių kalbos dalyvių istorinė sintaksė / Historical Syntax of the Lithuanian Participle*, Vilnius, 1979.

Ambrazas, V., Lietuvių kalbos sakinio sintaksinės ir semantinės struktūros vienetai, *Lietuvių kalbotyros klausimai*, 25, Vilnius, 1986, 4–44.

Ambrazas, V., *Sravnitelnyj sintaksis pričastij baltijskich jazykov / Vergleichende Syntax der baltischen Partizipien*, Vilnius, 1990.

Arumaa, P., *Untersuchungen zur Geschichte der litauischen Personalpronomina*, Tartu, 1933.

Augustaitis, D., Das litauische Phonationssystem, *Slavistische Beiträge*, 12, München, 1964.

Balčikonis, J. (ed.), *Jablonskio raštai*, 5 vols., Kaunas, 1933–1936.

Baldauf, L., Der Gebrauch der Pronominalform des Adjektivs im Litauischen, *Slavistische Beiträge*, 26, München, 1967.

Balkevičius, J., *Dabartinės lietuvių kalbos sintaksė*, Vilnius, 1963.

Bammesberger, A., *Abstraktbildungen in den baltischen Sprachen*, Göttingen, 1973.

Baranauskaitė, J., Čepaitienė, G., Mikulėnienė D., et. al., *Lietuvių kalba I*, edited by K. Župerka, Vilnius, 1995.

Bense, O., Das unflektierte Partizip des Präteritums auf -*us* im Litauischen, *Lietuvių kalbotyros klausimai*, 6, Vilnius, 1963, 191–212.

Buch, T., *Lithuanian Phonology in Christian Donelaitis*, Haif, 1974.

Buch, T., *Die Akzentuierung des Christian Donelaitis*, Wrocław, Warszawa, Kraków, 1961.

Būga, K., *Rinktiniai raštai*, 3 vols., ed. Z. Zinkevičius, Vilnius, 1958–1961.

Bulygina, T.V., Morfologičeskaja struktura slova v sovremennom litovskom literaturnom jazyke (v ego pis'mennoj forme), *Morfologičeskaja struktura slova v indoevropejskix jazykax*, Moskva, 1970, 7–70.

Bulygina, T. V., Opyt 'dinamičeskogo' opisanija litovskogo sprjaženija, *Problemy teorii morfologičeskix modelej*, Moskva, 1977, 238–269.

Būtėnas, P., *Lietuvių kalbos prielinksnių mokslas*, Kaunas, 1930.

Dambriūnas, L., *Lietuvių kalbos sintaksė*, Čikaga, 1963.

Dambriūnas, L., Verbal Aspects in Lithuanian, *Lingua Posnaniensis*, 7, 1958, 253–264.

Dambriūnas, L., *Lietuvių kalbos veiksmažodžių aspektai*, Boston, 1960.

Dambriūnas, L., Klimas, A., Schmalstieg, W.R., *Introduction to Modern Lithuanian*, New York, 1966.

Dini, P.U., "Le lingue baltiche fra il II e il III millennio d.C.", in Banfi, E. (ed.), *La formazione dell'Europa linguistica*, Firenze, 1993, 197–254.

Dobrovolskis, B., *Lietuvių kalba*, Kaunas, 1989.

Durys, M., *Lietuvių kalbos sintaksė*, Kaunas, 1937.

Eckert, R., *Baltistische Studien*, Berlin, 1971.

Eckert, R., Butkevičiūtė, E., Hinze, F., *Die baltischen Sprachen*, Leipzig, Berlin etc., 1994.

Endzelin, J., *Comparative Phonology and Morphology of the Baltic Languages*, the Hague, Paris, 1971.

Fraenkel, E., Der prädikative Instrumental im Slavischen und Baltischen und seine syntaktischen Grundlagen, *Archiv für slavische Philologie*, 24, 1926, 77–117.

Fraenkel, E., *Syntax der litauischen Kasus*, Kaunas, 1928.

Fraenkel, E., Litauische Beiträge, *Indogermanische Forshungen*, 45, 1927, 73–92; 46, 1928, 44–57.

Fraenkel, E., *Syntax der litauischen Postpositionen und Präpositionen*, Heidelberg, 1929.

Gargasaitė, D., Lietuvių kalbos veiksmažodžio dviskaita, *Mokslų akademijos darbai*, A ser., 2 (17), 1964, 207–217.

Gāters, A., Das bestimmte Adjektiv im Baltischen, *Zeitschrift für die vergleichende Sprachforschung auf dem Gebiete der idg. Sprachen*, 76, 1959, 136–159.

Geniušienė, E., Diatezy i zalogi v sovremennom litovskom jazyke, *Tipologija passivnyx konstrukcij. Diatezy i zalogi*, Leningrad, 1974, 203–231.

Geniušienė, E., Das Passiv des Litauischen und seine Verwendung, *Satzstruktur und Genus Verbi*, Berlin, 1976, 139–152.

Geniušienė, E., *The Typology of Reflexives*, Berlin, New York, Amsterdam, 1987.

Girdenis, A., *Fonologija*, Vilnius, 1981.

Hermann, E., *Über die Entwicklung der litauischen Konjuktionalsätze*, Jena, 1912.

Hermann, E., *Litauische Studien*, Berlin, 1926.

Heeschen, K., *Einführung in die Grundprobleme der generativen Phonologie mit besonderer Berücksichtigung der litauischen Phonologie*, Bonn, 1968.

Jablonskis, J., *Rinktiniai raštai*, edited by J. Palionis, 2 vols., Vilnius, 1957–1959.

Jakaitienė, E., *Veiksmažodžių daryba. Priesagų vediniai*, Vilnius, 1973.

Jakaitienė, E., Laigonaitė, A., Paulauskienė, A., *Lietuvių kalbos morfologija*, Vilnius, 1976.

Jašinskaitė, I., *Lietuvių kalbos ištiktukai*, Vilnius, 1975.

Jaunius, K., *Lietuvių kalbos gramatika*, Petrograd, 1916.

Jonikas, P., *Lietuvių kalba ir tauta amžių būvyje*, Chicago, 1987.

Kabelka, J., *Baltų filologijos įvadas*, Vilnius, 1982.

Kalinauskas, B., *Lietuvių kalbos žodžių junginių sintaksė*, Vilnius, 1972.

Kazlauskas, J., Lietuvių literatūrinės kalbos diferencinių elementų sistema, *Kalbotyra*, 14, 1966, 73–81.

Kazlauskas, J., *Lietuvių kalbos istorinė gramatika*, Vilnius, 1968.

Kenstowicz, M., *Lithuanian Phonology*, University of Illinois, 1972.

Kleinas, D., *Pirmoji lietuvių kalbos gramatika*, edited by J. Kruopas et al., Vilnius, 1957.

Klimas, A., *Lietuvių kalbos dalyvių vartojimas*, Vilnius, 1994.

Kniūkšta, P., *Priesagos -inis būdvardžiai*, Vilnius, 1976.

Kurschat, F., *Gramatik der litauischen Sprache*, Halle, 1876.

Labutis, V., *Žodžių junginių problemos*, Vilnius, 1976.

Labutis, V., *Lietuvių kalbos sintaksė*, 2 vols., Vilnius, 1994.

Laigonaitė, A., *Vietininkų reikšmė ir vartosena dabartinėje lietuvių kalboje*, Vilnius, 1957.

Laigonaitė, A., *Lietuvių kalbos akcentologija*, Vilnius, 1978.

Leskien, A., *Die Bildung der Nomina in Litauischen*, Leipzig, 1891.

Leskien, A., *Litauisches Lesebuch mit Grammatik und Wörterbuch*, Heidelberg, 1919.

Marvan, J., *Modern Lithuanian Declension. A Study of its Infrastructure*, Ann Arbor, 1979.

Matthews, W.K., Lithuanian Constructions with Neuter Passive Participles, *Slavonic and East European Review*, 33, 1955, 350–371.

Mažiulis, V., *Baltų ir kitų indoeuropiečių kalbų santykiai (deklinacija) / Baltisch-Indoeuropäische Sprachbeziehungen (Deklination)*, Vilnius, 1970.

Michelini, G., *Tempo (-aspetto) e modalità nelle lingue baltiche*, Parma, 1985.

Michelini, G., *Linguistica stratificazionale e morfologia del verbo con applicazione alle lingue baltiche*, Brescia, 1988.

Mielcke, Ch.G., *Anfangs-Gründe einer litauischen Sprach-Lehre*, Königsberg, 1800.

Mikalauskaitė, E., *Lietuvių kalbos fonetikos darbai*, Vilnius, 1975.

Morkūnas, K., et. al. (eds), *Lietuvių kalbos atlasas*, 3 vols., Vilnius, 1977–1994.

Musteikis, K., *Sopostavitel'naja morfologija russkogo i litovskogo jazykov*, Vilnius, 1972.

Orvydienė, E., *Učebnik litovskogo jazyka*, Vilnius, 1975.

Otrębski, J., *Gramatyka języka litowskiego*, 3 vols., Warszawa, 1958–1966.

Pakerys, A., *Lietuvių bendrinės kalbos prozodija*, Vilnius, 1983.

Pakerys, A., *Lietuvių bendrinės kalbos fonetika*, Vilnius, 1986.

Pakerys, A., *Akcentologija. I. Daiktavardis ir būdvardis*. Kaunas, 1994.

Palionis, J., *Lietuvių rašomosios kalbos istorija*, Vilnius, 1995.

Paulauskas, J., Veiksmažodžių priešdėlių funkcijos dabartinėje lietuvių literatūrinėje kalboje, *Literatūra ir kalba*, 3, 1958, 301–453.

Paulauskienė, A., *Gramatinės lietuvių kalbos veiksmažodžio kategorijos*, Vilnius, 1979.

Paulauskienė, A., *Gramatinės lietuviu kalbos vardažodžių kategorijos*, Vilnius, 1989.

Paulauskienė, A., *Lietuvių kalbos morfologija. Paskaitos lituanistams*, Vilnius, 1994.

Paulauskienė, A., Valeika, L., *Modern Lithuanian*, Vilnius, 1995.

Pederson, H., *Études Lituaniennes*, Copenhague, 1933.

Peterson, M.N., *Očerk litovskogo jazyka*, Moskva, 1955.

Pikčilingis, J., *Lietuvių kalbos stilistika*, 2 vols., Vilnius, 1971–1975.

Porżezinskij, V.K., *Vozvratnaja forma glagolov v litovskom i latyšskom jazykax*, Moskva, 1903.

Rosinas, A., *Lietuvių bendrinės kalbos įvardžių semantinė struktūra*, Vilnius, 1984.

Rosinas, A., *Baltų kalbų įvardžiai / Pronouns of the Baltic Languages*, Vilnius, 1988.

Rosinas, A., *Baltų kalbų įvardžiai: morfologijos raida*, Vilnius, 1995.

Roszko, R., *Wykładniki modalności imperceptywnej w języku polskim i litewskim*, Warszawa, 1993.

Ruhig, P., *Anfangsgründe einer litauischen Grammatik*, Königsberg, 1747.

Sabaliauskas, A., Atematiniai lietuvių kalbos veiksmažodžiai, *Kai kurie lietuvių kalbos gramatikos klausimai*, Vilnius, 1957, 77–114.

Sabaliauskas, A., *Lietuvių kalbos tyrinėjimo istorija*, 2 vols., Vilnius, 1979–1982.

Safarewicz, J., Stan badań nad aspektem czasownikowym w języku litewskiem, *Baltico-Slavica*, 3, 1938, 1–27.

Saussure, F. de, Accentuation lituanienne, *Recueil des publications scientifiques*, Heidelberg, 1922, 526–538.

Schleicher, A., *Litauische Grammatik*, Prag, 1856.

Schmalstieg, W.R., Descriptive Study of the Lithuanian Verbal System, *General Linguistics*, 3, 1958, 85–105.

Schmalstieg, W.R., *A Lithuanian Historical Syntax*, Columbus, 1987.

Schmid, W.P., *Studien zum baltischen und indogermanischen Verbum*, Wiesbaden, 1963.

Schwentner, E., *Die Wortfolge im Litauischen*, Heidelberg, 1922.

Senn, A., *Handbuch der litauischen Sprache*, 1, Heidelberg, 1966.

Sirtautas, V., *Sakinio dalys*, Kaunas, 1976.

Sirtautas, V., *Pagrindinių sakinio dalių derinimas*, Vilnius, 1978.

Sirtautas, V., Grenda, Č., *Lietuvių kalbos sintaksė*, Vilnius, 1988.

Skardžius, P., *Lietuvių kalbos žodžių daryba*, Kaunas, 1943.

Skardžius, P., Barzdukas, St., Laurinaitis, J.M., *Lietuvių kalbos vadovas*, Bielefeld, 1950.

Skardžius, P., *Lietuvių kalbos kirčiavimas*, Chicago, 1968.

Sližienė, N., Lietuvių literatūrinės kalbos sudurtinių veiksmažodžio formų struktūra, *Lietuvių kalbotyros klausimai*, 9, 1967, 63–84.

Sližienė, N., Sudurtinių neveikiamųjų veiksmažodžio formų reikšmės ir vartojimas, *Lietuvių kalbotyros klausimai*, 15, 1974, 77–89.

Sližienė, N., *Lietuvių kalbos veiksmažodžių junglumo žodynas / Dictionary of Lithuanian Verb Valence*, 1, A–M, Vilnius, 1994.

Smoczyński, W., Języki bałtyckie, in Bednarczuk, L. (ed.), *Języki indoeuropejskie*, 2, Warszawa, 1988, 817–905.

Stang, Chr. S., *Das slavische und baltische Verbum*, Oslo, 1942.

Stang, Chr. S., Die athematischen Verba im Baltischen, *Scando-Slavica*, 8, 1962, 161–170.

Stang, Chr.S., *Vergleichende Grammatik der baltischen Sprachen*, Oslo, Bergen, Tromsö, 1966.

Stepanov, J.S., *Metody i principy sovremennoj lingvistiki*, Moskva, 1975.

Stundžia, B., *Lietuvių bendrinės kalbos kirčiavimo sistema*, Vilnius, 1995.

Šukys, J., *Linksnių ir prielinksnių vartojimas*, Kaunas, 1984.

Tekorienė, D., *Bevardės giminės būdvardžiai*, Vilnius, 1990.

Tekorienė, D., *Lithuanian Basic Grammar and Conversation*, Kaunas, 1990.

Torbiörnsson, T., *Die litauischen Akzentverschiebungen und der litauische Verbalakzent*, Heidelberg, 1924.

Ul'janov, G., *Značenija glagol'nyx osnov v litovsko-slavjanskom jazyke*, 2 vols., Warszawa, 1891–1895.

Ulvydas, K., Vienaskaitos naudininko prieveiksmėjimas ir prieveiksmiai su formantais -(i)ui, -i lietuvių kalboje, *Kai kurie lietuvių kalbos gramatikos klausimai*, Vilnius, 1957, 115–169.

Ulvydas, K., Vienaskaitos kilmininko prieveiksmėjimas ir prieveiksmiai su formantais -(i)o, -(i)os dabartinėje lietuvių kalboje, *Lietuvių kalbotyros klausimai*, 7, Vilnius, 1986, 11–46.

Ulvydas, K., Vienaskaitos vietininkų prieveiksmėjimo klausimu, *Lietuvių kalbotyros klausimai*, 9, Vilnius, 1967, 6–42.

Ulvydas, K., Iš lietuvių kalbos prieveiksmių tyrinėjimų, *Lietuvių kalbotyros klausimai*, 15, Vilnius, 1974, 7–35

Ulvydas, K., et al. (eds), *Lietuvių kalbos gramatika*, 3 vols., Vilnius, 1965–1976.

Urbutis, V., *Žodžių darybos teorija*, Vilnius, 1978.

Vaitkevičiūtė, V., Lietuvių literatūrinės kalbos priebalsinių fonemų sudėtis, *Lietuvių kalbotyros klausimai*, 1, 1957, 5–66.

Valeckienė, A., Dabartinės lietuvių kalbos įvardžiuotinių būdvardžių vartojimas, *Literatūra ir kalba*, 2, Vilnius, 1957, 159–355.

Valeckienė, A., *Lietuvių kalbos morfologinė sistema. Giminės kategorija*, Vilnius, 1985.

Valeika, L., *Word Order in Lithuanian and English in Functional Sentence Perspective*, Vilnius, 1974.

Valeika, L., *Transpozicija v litovskom i anglijskom jazykax*, Vilnius, 1980.

Valiulytė, E., Priežasties prielinksnių sistema lietuvių kalboje, *Lietuvių kalbotyros klausimai*, 25, Vilnius, 1986, 97–156.

Valiulytė, E., *Vietą nusakome įvairiai*, Vilnius, 1995.

Wiedemann, O., *Handbuch der litauischen Sprache*, Strassburg, 1897.

Zinkevičius, Z., *Lietuvių kalbos įvardžiuotinių būdvardžių istorijos bruožai*, Vilnius, 1957.

Zinkevičius, Z., *Lietuvių dialektologija*, Vilnius, 1966.

Zinkevičius, Z., *Lietuvių kalbos istorinė gramatika*, 2 vols., Vilnius, 1980–1981.

Zinkevičius, Z., *Lietuvių kalbos istorija*, 6 vols., Vilnius, 1984–1994.

Zinkevičius, Z., *The History of the Lithuanian Language*, Vilnius, 1996.

Žulys, V., Bendrinės lietuvių kalbos veiksmažodžių asmens galūnės, *Kalbotyra*, 26 (1), 1975, 63–73.

Župerka, K., *Lietuvių kalbos stilistika*, Vilnius, 1983.

completive IV 7.120–121
concessive and contrastive IV 7.117–118
conditional IV 7.114–116
copulative IV 7.107–110
juxtapositive IV 7.111
of complex structure IV 7.123
temporal IV 7.113
athematic verb forms III 5.46, 87
attribute (attributive modifier) III 2.3, 5, 14; IV 2.19, 26–27, 30
attributive clauses IV 7.24–32
continuative (non – restrictive) IV 7.27
position in sentence IV 7.26, 29
restrictive IV 7.27
with noun antecedents IV 7.25–28
with pronoun antecedents IV 7.29–32
attributive participles III 5.132–140; IV 2.114; 5.23
auxiliary (copula) III 5.47, 52, 63–64, 78, 108; IV 1.4, 15, 18–19, 25; 3.71; 5.7
zero IV 1.19

basis of comparison III 6.19; IV 2.93, 121, 123, 145

case III 0.6; IV 1.6–7, 24, 26, 37–38
of adjectives III 2.2–3, 6
of nouns III 1.15, 18
of numerals III 3.1, 8–9
of participles III 5.112
of pronouns III 4.7, 14
causal clauses IV 7.44–50
causal relations
in composite sentences IV 7.33, 40, 44–50, 78–79, 91, 107, 119
causativity III 5.6–8, 15–16
causativization III 5.10
circumflex I 1.1; 6.6
clauses
additive IV 7.71, 106
attributive IV 7.24–32; 5.2
comparative III 7.11; IV 2.128; 7.65–70
completive III 5.151; 9.7; IV 7.16–23
correlative III 9.7; IV 7.33–35
gerundial *see* gerundial phrases

integrated IV 7.6, 16–35, 107
interpolated IV 4.21
link between IV.7.1
non – integrated IV 7.6, 36–71, 107
of cause IV 7.44–50
of concession IV 7.58–60
of condition IV 7.51–57
of place IV 7.63–64
of purpose III 5.48; IV 7.61–62
of time IV 7.36–43
order of IV 7.12
participial *see* participial phrases
separated by pause IV 7.4
syntactic functions IV 7.13
clitics I 6.2; III 5.13
clusters
of consonants I 4.9, 11–12
of vowels I 3.5
communicative types of sentences IV 6.1–22
comparative
of adjectives III 2.7–8, 10–12, 15–16; IV 2.118, 120–121
of adverbs III 6.16–20, 22; IV 2.139, 141, 145
comparative clauses III 7.11; IV 2.128; 7.65–70
differentiating IV 7.70
equational IV 7.65–69
comparative particles III 7.11
comparative phrases III 7.11; IV 4.8–11
word order in IV 5.29–30
comparison III 0.6
basis of III 6.19
criterion of III 8.22
in asyndetic sentences IV 7.111
in compound sentences IV 7.97
of adjectives III 2.7–16
of adverbs III 6.16–22
of numerals III 3.8
of participles III 5.139
standard of III 8.29, 32
complementary relations
in composite sentences IV 7.107, 122
complementation III 2.21; 4.4
of prepositions III 8.1, 3, 5

completive clauses III 5.151; 9.7; IV 7.16–23
    as object IV 7.21
    as subject IV 7.20
    position in sentence IV 7.22
    with subjunctive mood III 5.48
completive relations
    in composite sentences IV 7.16–23, 107, 120–121
complex sentence IV 7.2, 5–71
    compound tenses in III 5.36
    integrated IV 7.6, 16–35, 107
    non – integrated IV 7.6, 36–71, 107
    types IV 7.15
    see also clauses
composite pronouns III 4.3, 27, 37, 39
composite sentence IV 7.1–129
    asyndetic IV 7.1, 107–123
    complex IV 7.2, 5–71
    compound IV 7.2, 72–106
    mixed IV 7.124–129
    syndetic IV 7.1, 5–106
    see also semantic relations in composite sentences
compound pronouns III 4.3, 27
compound (periphrastic) tenses III 5.1, 21, 25–26, 35–40, 52, 63, 108, 153
    and simple tenses III 5.23
    conjugation III 5.109–110
    continuative III 5.21, 23, 25, 37, 108, 110
    imperfect III 5.21, 38–39, 108, 111
    perfect III 5.21, 23, 25, 35–36, 40, 108–109, 111
compound sentence IV 7.2, 72–106
    compound tenses in III 5.36
    structural parallelism IV 7.75, 88
    types IV 7.76
    see also coordination
concessive clauses IV 7.58–60
concessive relations
    in composite sentences IV 7.58–60, 81, 90, 95, 98–99, 100, 102–105, 107, 112, 117
concord *see* agreement
conditional clauses IV 7.51–57
conditional relations
    in composite sentences IV 7.51–57, 80, 99, 103, 107, 112–116

conjugation III 5.82, 97, 99, 101–106
    of compound tenses III 5.109–110
    of passive verbs III 5.111
    of the verb *būti* III 5.107
conjugations of verbs III 5.89–96
conjunctions III 9.1–7; 7.11
    and prepositions IV 9.1
    asemantic IV 7.7, 16–17, 33–34, 44, 51
    complex III 9.2; IV 7.7, 34, 43, 58, 73, 90
    coordinating III 9.3–5; IV 1.9; 2.146, 149, 151–156; 7.128
    in interrogative sentences IV 6.17
    multi – place III 9.3
    paired III 9.3; IV 7.7. 37, 47–48, 51
    reduplicated III 7.9; 9.3; IV 2.152, 154; 3.122, 7.74, 76, 101
    semantic IV 7.7, 36, 44, 51
    semantic types of III 9.5, 7
    subordinating III 9.3–4, 6–7; IV 2.151, 153–154; 4.8–11; 7.5, 7
conjuncts III 9.1
conjunctive words (conjunctives) III 5.149–150; 9.5; IV 4.13; 7.2
    see also coordinators, subordinators
connecting particles III 7.14
consonants I 4.1–14
    allophones I 4.8
    alternation II 1.22–24
    clusters I 4.9, 11–12; III 11.13
    neutralization I 4.13; II 1.22
    oppositions I 4.3
    representation in writing I 1.3–4
    soft and hard I 4.2
    syntagmatic relations I 4.9–12
continuative (non – restrictive) clauses IV 7.27
continuative tenses III 5.21, 23, 25, 37, 108, 110
contraction II 1.23; III 5.125
contrastive relations
    in composite sentences IV 7.55, 81, 89, 93–94, 98–99, 107, 112, 118
coordination IV 2.146–158; 7.2
    asyndetic IV 1.9; 2.149, 157–158
    closed and open IV 2.149

consecutive IV 2.155; 7.102–105
continuative IV 7.106
copulative IV 2.152; 7.77–86, 107
disjunctive IV 7.101, 154
in mixed composite sentences IV 7.125
juxtapositive and adversative IV 2.153; 7.87–100, 107
mixed IV 2.158
of finite verb forms IV 2.148
of prepositional phrases IV 2.147
syndetic IV 2.151–156, 158
coordinators IV 7.72–74; 87, 101–102
in compound sentences IV 7.76
copula *see* auxiliary
copulative relations IV 7.108–110
correlation
in phonology I 2.4
correlative clauses III 9.7; IV 7.33–35
correlative words
as dummy substitutes IV 7.23, 121
in subordinate clauses IV 7.11, 23, 25, 33, 36, 38, 42, 44, 61, 63, 66–67
curative verbs III 5.9

dative
interpolated IV 4.19
objective III 5.69–70, 156; IV 1.30; 2.16, 20, 24, 83–84; 3.14, 22, 29, 31–33, 35, 50, 57, 59, 62, 69, 71, 73, 80–81, 83–85, 89–91, 94–95, 97, 104, 106, 116, 130
possessive IV 2.18; 3.52–53, 72
purposive IV 2.20–21, 84, 104
subjective III 5.136, 155–156; IV 2.17, 82, 84, 116
temporal IV 2.19
with adjectives IV 2.116
with gerunds IV 4.4
with infinitive III 5.156; IV 2.84, 104, 130
with nouns IV 2.104
with prepositions III 6.12
with verbs IV 2.16–21
dativus absolutus III 5.146; IV 4.4
de Saussure's and Fortunatov's law II 2.3, 4, 8
decausativization III 5.15
declarative sentences IV 6.2

declension
of adjectives III 2.25–35
of nouns III 1.16–32
of numerals III 3.11–15
of participles III 5.115, 117, 119, 121–123, 127–128, 130
of pronouns III 4.31–37, 40, 42–43
definite formant III 5.129
definite
adjectives III 2.17–24
numerals III 3.7–8, 14
participles III 5.129–130, 136; IV 4.15
pronouns III 4.16, 42–43
degemination II 1.22
demonstrative particles III 7.7
demonstrative pronouns III 2.18–19, 23; 4.5, 18–22, 28; IV 7.11, 32
denasalization II 1.9–11
denominator
in fractions III 3.9, 15
depalatalization II 1.24
determiner III 2.18; 4.20
diacritics I 1.1–2; 6.6
differentiating pronouns III 4.26, 28
digraphs I 1.1–3
diphtongs I 3.2–3; 5.1
direct address IV 4.14–17
disjunctive relations
in composite sentences IV 7.101
dissimilation II 1.23
distinctive features I 2.2; III 0.6
of consonants I 4.14
of syllable accents I 6.8
of vowels I 3.7
dual number
athematic III 5.46
of nouns III 1.11
of numerals III 3.11
of pronouns III 4.5, 12, 40
of verbs III 5.63

elative
of adjectives III 2.14

of adverbs III 6.21

elision *see* omission

emphasis III 2.20, 23; 5.37, 44, 47, 53, 58, 143–144, 155; 6.13, 21; 7.1,8–9, 12, 15; 10.6; 11.12, 14–15; IV 1.16, 23; 2.26, 57, 100, 115, 128; 152; 3.55, 73, 93, 98, 108, 122; 4.16; 5.9–10, 21, 23–24, 29; 6.20; 7.26, 38, 63, 84, 89–90, 95, 97, 101

endings III 0.1–2; 1.16; 5.2, 21, 43, 56–57, 63; IV 1.3
- attractive II 2.3
- derivative III 1.35; 2.38–39
- strong and weak II 2.3
- verbal III 5.86–88
- vowel alternation in II 1.1–2
- zero III 5.2, 57

enumeration
- in composite sentences IV 7.86, 101

epithet III 2.20

exclamatory sentences IV 6.1, 20–22

exclusion
- in composite sentences IV 7.92, 96, 99

free variants I 2.3

functional sentence perspective IV 5.1, 3, 31

future III 5.33–34, 46, 79
- accentuation III 5.102
- and other tenses III 5.22
- compound III 5.35–37, 39–40
- conjugation III 5.102
- in subordinate clauses III 5.24
- stylistic usage III 5.26

gender III 0.6; 5.112, 116; IV 1.6, 25–27, 33, 37–38
- of adjectives III 2.2–5, 8–9, 11, 24, 26–35
- of nouns III 1.6–10, 19–30
- of numerals III 3.1, 3, 7–10, 11–14
- of pronouns III 4.2–4, 31
- *see also* neuter

generalizing pronouns III 4.26, 29; IV 7.23

genitive
- adverbialized III 6.9, 11
- and appositive nominative IV 2.108–109
- as modifier IV 2.105
- as predicative IV 1.20; 3.50, 78, 91, 109
- descriptive IV 2.92
- emphatic IV 1.23; 2.115
- in gerundial phrases IV 2.86
- intensifying IV 2.100, 115, 133
- objective III 3.4, 6, 9–10, 15; 4.28; 5.68, 151, 156; IV 1.29–30; 2.11–12, 14, 17, 21, 24, 86, 102; 3.13, 21, 28–30, 56, 59–60, 67, 83, 92–95, 118
- of comparison III 6.19; IV 2.27, 93
- of content IV 2.101, 115
- of indefinite quantity IV 2.12, 14
- of material IV 2.94
- of name IV 2.96
- of place IV 2.97
- of purpose IV 2.15, 84, 95; 5.24
- of quantity III 5.72; IV 2.15, 99
- of time IV 2.26, 98
- possessive III 4.7, 15, 17, 23, 31; 5.66; IV 2.18, 91
- subjective III 5.66, 71, 74–78, 136, 153; IV 1.22; 2.13, 34, 103; 3.100, 109
- with adjectives IV 2.115
- with adverbs IV 2.140
- with nominalizations IV 2.89
- with nouns IV 1.39; 2.91–103
- with numerals III 3.4, 6, 9–10,15; IV 2.132–134
- with prepositions III 6.12; 8.7–18, 32–33; *see also* prepositional phrases with genitive
- with pronouns IV 2.136–137
- with verbs IV 2.11–15

gerundial phrases IV 1.12, 41; 2.86; 3.101–102; 4.4

gerunds IV 1.12, 14, 41
- and active participles III 5.145
- completive III 5.151
- formation of III 5.120
- meaning and usage III 5.112, 142, 145–146; IV 2.34, 86, 113; 3.3, 74, 101–103; 4.19; 6.12
- reflexive III 5.125–126
- tense forms III 5.21
- valency IV 1.41
- with conjunctives III 5.149

government IV 1.7, 31, 36

grave I 1.1

half – participles III 5.112, 132
- formation and accentuation III 5.116

meaning and usage III 5.142–143, 145, 147, 149
reflexive III 5.125
homonymy
of endings III 0.2

idioms III 10.5; IV 2.2
illative III 1.15; IV 2.32
imperative mood III 5.41–43, 49–50; 10.3; IV 6.4
accentuation and conjugation III 5.104–105
compound forms III 5.50
in asyndetic sentences IV 7.115, 117, 119
in compound sentences IV 7.80, 90, 103
in conditional clauses IV 7.53, 56
in declarative sentences IV 6.2
in optative sentences IV 6.10
person in III 5.56
imperative sentences IV 6.4–9
imperfect tenses *see* compound tenses
imperfective verbs III 5.18, 20, 30, 35; IV 2.34; 7.37, 39, 41
impersonal sentences III 5.72, 153; IV 3.10–53, 76–85, 111–113
impersonal verbs III 5.60–62, 75; IV 2.17–18, 82; 3.3, 54–55
indefinite pronouns III 4.26–30; IV 1.23; 2.91
indicative mood III 5.42–46, 97–102
accentuation and conjugation III 5.97–102
and oblique mood III 5.51–52
in asyndetic sentences IV 7.116
in conditional clauses IV 7.53, 56
in imperative sentences IV 6.5
in optative sentences IV 6.10
infinitival phrases IV 7.19
infinitival stem III 5.79, 81, 83, 85, 101–104, 113, 118–120, 122–123
infinitive III 5.154–156; 10.8; IV 2.16–17, 21, 34, 104
as simple predicate IV 1.14; 3.3, 73, 80, 84, 95
meaning and usage III 5.155–156; IV 1.14–16, 20, 22, 29; 2.79–85, 130; 3.3, 19, 34–35, 68–71, 81–82, 96–97, 104; 4.19; 6.7, 12
negative IV 3.117
object of IV 2.84; 3.69, 71, 80, 97, 118
reflexive III 5.154

infixes III 5.80–81; 11.11, 12
inflectional stems III 1.16
inesive III 1.15
instrumental
adverbialized III 6.9, 11
as predicative IV 1.20, 35; 3.50–51, 76, 78
denoting basis of comparison IV 2.117
interpolated IV 4.19
objective IV 1.30; 2.22–24, 117; 3.15, 23, 31, 61, 65, 71, 80–81, 83, 97
of cause IV 2.28, 117; 3.36, 39
of manner IV 2.27
of place IV 2.25
of quantity IV 2.117, 141
of source IV 2.117
of time IV 2.26, 117, 142
with adjectives IV 2.117
with adverbs IV 2.141–142
with nouns IV 1.39; 2.105
with prepositions III 8.28–31, 33 *see also* prepositional phrases with instrumental
with verbs IV 2.22–28
integrated clauses IV 7.6, 16–35, 107
intensifiers III 4.43; 7.3, 13–15; IV 7.7, 34
intensifying pronouns IV 1.23
interdependence IV 1.4, 10, 21
interjections I 4.1; 5.1; III 7.12; 9.2; 10.1–9
and onomatopoeic words III 11.1
complex III 10.4
compound III 10.8
emotive III 10.1, 6
imperative III 10.1, 6; IV 6.8
in exclamatory sentences IV 6.21
interpolated IV 4.19
primary III 10. 2–8
reduplicated III 10.8–9
secondary III 10.3, 6
syntactic functions III 10.1; IV 1.14
vocative III 10.1, 7–9
with direct address IV 4.16
interpolation (parenthesis) III 5.146, 156; 8.9, 22; IV 4.18–24
functions IV 4.22

of clauses IV 4.21
of prepositional phrases IV 4.20
interrogative particles III 7.1, 10; 6.1; IV 6.13–14
interrogative pronouns III 4.5, 23–25, 28; IV 6.13, 16, 21
interrogative sentences IV 6.13–19
intonation I 2.2; III 5.49; 10.6; IV 1.3, 9, 149; 7.1, 72, 107, 112
and communicative types of sentences IV 6.1–3, 7, 10, 13–14, 19–20, 22
and functional sentence perspective IV 5.3
intransitive verbs III 5.6–11, 14–15, 19, 75–78; IV 2.14, 18, 21
intransitivization III 5.12, 14
inversion IV 5.1, 3, 23–24

juxtapositive relations
in composite sentences IV 7.111

lengthening
of vowels II 1.1, 4, 9
litotes IV 3.120
loanwords I 1.3; 3.1; 4.1, 5–6
locative
adverbialized III 6.9–10
illative IV 2.32
of manner IV 2.31
of place IV 2.18, 29, 106, 119, 143
of time IV 2.30, 119, 142
with adjectives IV 2.119
with adverbs IV 2.142–143
with nouns IV 2.106
with verbs IV 2.29–32

manner
relations of III 5.148
metatony I 2.5; II 2.8
metathesis II 1.3, 23
mixed composite sentences IV 7.124–129
modal words III 5.45, 53; 6.1; 7.5, 10
modifiers III 6.1, 24; IV 1.36–41
adverbial IV 1.36, 41; 2.84
attributive (attributes) III 2.3, 5, 14; IV 1.10, 37–40; 2.19, 26–27, 30, 148
objective IV 1.36, 41
sentence III 6.1, 28
verbal III 11.1, 15
morphonological idiomaticness II 2.8
morphonological changes II 1.1–24; III 5.82
see also alternations
mood III 0.6; 5.1, 41–54, 79
and person III 5.56
compound forms III 5.47–48, 50–52, 108–110
see also imperative mood, indicative mood, oblique mood, optative mood, subjunctive mood

necessity forms III 5.108
negation IV 3.114
double IV 3.120
intensified IV 3.121
of coordinated sentence parts IV 3.122
scope of IV 3.116, 124
negative marker IV 3.114
omission IV 3.122
position IV 3.118–119; 5.23
repeated IV 3.120
negative particles III 7.1, 3, 9–10
negative pronouns III 4.29; IV 3.123–124
negative sentences
and affirmative IV 3.114–125
neuter
adjectives III 2.2, 4–6, 11, 42; 4.21, 29
numerals III 3.8
pronouns III 2.5; 4.2–3, 28–29
neuter participles
form III 5.124
in passive constructions III 5.67–69, 72–75, 77–78
of impersonal verbs III 5.62
reflexive III 5.128
usage III 5.59, 112, 124, 150, 152–153; IV 1.14, 20, 27, 29; 3.3, 79, 110; 4.19
neutralization I 2.4
of consonants I 4.13; II 1.22
of definite adjectives III 2.19
of mood III 5.54

of syllable accent I 6.9
zero I 4.13
nomina actionis IV 2.88
nominal groups IV 2.90–114
    word order in IV 5.23–27
nominalizations IV 2.88–89, 102–103, 131
nominative
    adverbialized III 6.9
    and genitive in appositions IV 2.108–109
    and genitive of indefinite quantity IV 3.100
    as predicative IV 1.20, 33; 3.76, 78, 81, 87, 116
    interpolated IV 4.19
    objective III 5.153, 155; IV 1.29; 3.69
    of participles III 5.142, 151–152; IV 2.86
    of quantity IV 2.34–35
    of time IV 2.9, 33, 35
    subjective III 5.68–69; IV 1.4, 21–27; 2.18; 3.116
    with gerund IV 2.34
    with infinitive IV 2.34; 3.69
    with verbs IV 2.33–35, 86
non – integrated clauses IV 7.6, 36–71, 107
noun III 1.1–38; 2.3, 12
    abstract III 1.5, 13
    accentuation II 2.2–8; III 1.34–38
    case III 1.15, 18
    collective III 1.4, 13
    common III 1.1, 4–5
    common gender III 1.10
    compound III 1.35–37
    concrete III 1.4, 13–14
    consonantal stem of III 1.16, 28
    countable III 1.4, 12
    declension III 1.16–32
    derived III 1.35–38
    deverbal IV 2.88
    dual number III 1.11
    gender III 1.6–10, 19–30
    indeclinable III 1.9, 33
    inflexional stems III 1.16
    mass III 1.4, 13
    number III 1.3–5, 11–14
    proper III 1.2–3; 13–14

    use IV 1.20–22, 25–26, 29, 32, 34, 38; 2.115–119; 3.3, 81, 84, 92
    verbal reflexive III 1.21
nucleus
    of sentence IV 3.4
    of syllable I 5.1
number III 0.6; 1.11; 5.1, 63, 79, 112, 116; IV 1.6; 24–27, 33, 37–38
    and person III 5.56
    of adjectives III 2.2–3, 6, 24
    of finite verb forms III 5.79, 86; IV 1.4
    of half – participles III 5.116
    of nouns III 1.3–5, 11–14
    of numerals III 3.1, 8–9
    of pronouns III 4.5–6, 9
numeral III 2.12; 3.1–15
    accentuation III 3.11–15
    cardinal III 1.4, 14; 3.1, 3–5, 9, 11–13; IV 1.29; 2. 114, 132, 135; 3.78; 5.23
    case III 1.8–9
    collective III 3.6, 13; IV 2.132
    composite (multiword) III 3.2–4, 7–8, 11, 14–15
    compound III 3.2, 10, 14–15
    declension III 3.11–15
    definite III 3.7–8, 14
    derived III 3.2
    dual number III 3.11
    fractions III 3.9–10, 15; IV 2.134
    gender III 3.1, 3, 7–10, 11–14
    neuter III 3.8; IV 1.20; 4.19
    nominal III 3.4, 6
    number III 3.1, 8–9
    ordinal III 3.1, 7–8, 14; IV 1.20, 37; 2.114, 135; 5.23
    plural III 3.5, 12
    with prepositional phrases IV 2.135
numeral groups IV 2.132–135
numerator
    of fractions III 3.9, 15

object III 2.24; 5.136, 151, 155–156; IV 1.28–31, 41; 2.81, 83; 3.107
    direct III 5.6–8, 12; IV 1.29, 31
    expressed by completive clause IV 7.21

796 SUBJECT INDEX

in passive transformation III 5.68–70; IV 3.108
indirect III 5.12, 17, 30–32
of negated verbs IV 3.118
partitive III 5.14
promoted III 5.68–69
semantic III 5.14, 57, 153
tautological III 5.10

oblique mood III 5.41–42, 51–54, 152–153
accentuation and conjugation III 5.106
and indicative III 5.51–52
compound III 5.51–52
number in III 5.63
person in III 5.56

omission
in asyndetic sentences IV 7.111
in composite sentences IV 7.3
in compound sentences IV 7.75, 88
in coordination IV 2.147–148
of conjunctions IV 7.34
of consonants II 1.23
of auxiliary IV 1.18
of infinitive IV 2.84
of personal pronoun IV 1.22, 24
of predicate IV 3.10, 112
of preposition IV 2.55, 111
of subject IV 3.2, 108, 110

onomatopoeic words I 4.5–6; III 10.8; 11.1–15; IV 1.14, 16
and other word classes III 11.1
apophony in II 1.13
formants III 11.4–8
functions III 11.1, 15; IV 1.14
imitative III 11.3, 5, 10, 12–15
meanings III 11.14–15
paired III 11.12
verb – related III 11.2, 10

optative mood III 5.49
accentuation and conjugation III 5.105

optative particles III 7.12

optative (hortative) sentences IV 6.10–12

orthography (spelling) I 1.4

palatalization I 1.3; 4.5; II 1.24

paradigmatic relations
of vowels I 3.7
of word forms III 0.3

parallelism
relations in composite sentences IV 7.82, 85, 88, 97, 101

parenthesis *see* interpolation

participial phrases III 5.112, 149–150; IV 1.12, 35, 41; 4.2–7

participles III 5.112–153; IV 1.16; 2.86; 3.19, 102
accentuation III 5.113, 115–117, 119–123, 127–130
and voice III 5.64–67
as predicative complement IV 1.39
attributive III 5.132–140; IV 2.114; 5.23
comparison III 5.139
declension III 5.115, 117, 119, 121–123, 127–128, 130
in compound verb forms III 5.108
number III 5.63
predicative III 5.152–153; IV 3.50
semi – predicative III 5.141–151
short forms III 5.114–115, 117, 119, 125
substantivization III 5.140
tense forms III 5.21, 112
valency III 5.112
with conjunctives III 5.149–150
see also active participles, definite participles, gerunds, half – participles, neuter participles, passive participles, reflexive participles

particles III 7.1–15
accentuation III 7.2
and other word classes III 6.1; 7.1, 15; 9.2; 10.3–4, 8
as simple predicates IV 1.14
comparative III 7.11
complex III 7.3–4
compound III 7.2–4
connecting III 7.14
demonstrative III 7.7
derivation III 7.4
in general guestions IV 6.15
intensifying – emphatic III 4.43; 7.3, 13–15; IV 7.7, 34

interrogative and dubitative III 6.1; 7.1, 10; IV 6.13, 14
negative III 7.1, 3, 9, 10
optative III 7.12
paired IV 7.89
position III 7.2
specifying and limiting III 7.6
parts of speech III 0.7
passive III 5.1, 21, 64–68, 111, 147
  and active III 5.65
  compound III 5.23, 38–40, 64–65, 75
  conjugation III 5.111
  evidential III 5.77–78
  of intransitive verbs III 5.75–78
  of transitive verbs III 5.67–74
passive constructions III 4.15; IV 3.110
passive participles III 5.112; IV 4.15
  and subjunctive mood III 5.47
  future III 5.123, 138
  past III 5.38, 40, 122, 137, 139–140, 148–151
  periphrastic III 5.64
  present III 5.38, 121, 136, 140, 147, 151
  with conjunctives III 5.149
  see also definite participles, neuter participles, reflexive participles
passive transformation III 5.68–70, 76, 78; IV 3.108–110
past tense III 5.29–32, 47, 79
  accentuation III 5.100
  and other tenses III 5.22
  compound III 5.35–37, 39–40
  conjugation III 5.99
  in subordinate clauses III 5.24
past frequentative tense III 5.32, 79
  accentuation and conjugation III 5.101
  and past tense III 5.22
  compound III 5.35, 37, 39–40
  stylistic usage III 5.26
phoneme I 2.2
phonemic opposition I 2.4
phonetics I 2.1
phonology I 1.1–5.4
phonotactics (syntagmatic relations) I 2.5
  of consonants I 4.9–12
  of vowels I 3.5–6
perfect tenses *see* compound tenses
perfective verbs III 5.18–19, 30–31, 35, 40; IV 2.14; 3.56; 7.37, 39, 41, 43
person III 0.6; 4.9; 5.1, 55–62, 79, 86, 109; IV 1.4, 24
  use of personal forms III 5.58–62
personal pronouns III 4.4–5, 9–17; 5.53; 58; 7.15; IV 2.91
personal sentences
  and impersonal IV 3. 111–113
  patterns of IV 3.10–53, 76–85
place
  clauses of IV 7.63–64
pluralia tantum III 1.4–5, 14; 3.5, 10, 12; 4.29; IV 2.67
point of comparison III 2.13
polyphtongs I 3.2–3
position
  of adverbials IV 5.16, 19–20, 28
  of attributive adjectives IV 5.23
  of attributive genitive IV 5.24, 28
  of attributive instrumental IV 5.26, 28
  of comparative phrases IV 5.21
  of main sentence constituents IV 5.4–14
  of oblique object IV 5.15
  of particles IV 5.2, 22
  of predicative complement IV 5.17
  of prepositional phrases IV 5.27–28
  of standard of comparison IV 5.29
postpositions III 8.1
predicate III 5.78, 124, 126, 152–153; 11.1, 15; IV 1. 4, 10, 13–20, 24, 32–33, 36; 3.3, 9
  compound III 5.153; IV 1.15–20, 22, 25, 40; 2.79–80; 5.5, 7; 7.77–78
  concord with subject IV 1.24–27
  in impersonal sentences IV 3.3, 55, 87–88
  simple IV 1.14, 17
predicative III 2.3–6; 5.78, 156; 6.1; IV 1.18, 20, 25–26
predicative complement IV 1.33–35; 3.50–51, 78
predicative participles III 5.152–153; IV 3.50
prefix III 1.35–36, 38; 2.37–39; 5.3–4, 6, 13, 19, 43; 11.10, 12
  negative III 5.144; 7.49
prefixation III 5.10, 18
prepositions III 8.1–32; 9.2; IV 2.147

adverbial III 8.2, 16
and conjunctions III 9.1
and verbal prefixes III 8.2
complement of III 8.3, 5, 8
complex III 8.2, 7, 18
lexical meaning III 8.3, 5
primary III 8.2–4, 7
secondary (derived) III 8.2–3, 7, 16–17, 20, 30
with accusative III 8.19–27
with genitive III 8.7–18
with instrumental III 8.28–31
with various cases III 8.32–33
see also prepositional phrases

prepositional phrases III 8.1, 5, 10; IV 2.18, 23–24, 35
adverbial IV 1.32; 2.47–78, 127; 3.36, 39
adverbialized IV 2.78; 6.12, 19
as attributes IV 1.39
as predicatives IV 1.20; 3.50, 77–78, 92
as predicative complements IV 1.35
coordinated IV 2.147
denoting basis of comparison IV 2.121, 123, 145
in verbal groups IV 2.36–78
interpolated IV 4.20
objective IV 1.30; 2.36–46, 122; 3.16–18, 24–27, 30, 32–33, 62, 83
of cause IV 2.68–75; 121
of manner IV 2.78
of place IV 2.47–57, 112, 144
of purpose IV 2.76, 111
of quantity IV 2.77
of time IV 2.58–67, 112
with accusative IV 2.36–39, 48, 51–53, 55–57, 59–60, 63, 65, 67, 73, 75–78, 111–112; 3.17, 26, 30, 32
with adjectives IV 2.120–127
with adverbs IV 2.50, 54
with genitive IV 2.40–45, 48–49, 51–53, 55–56, 59, 61–64, 68–72, 74, 76–78, 111–112, 120, 125–127, 135, 144–145; 3.16, 25, 30, 62
with instrumental IV 2.46, 48, 51–52, 55, 66, 78, 111, 124; 3.18, 27, 33
with nouns IV 2.111–112
with numerals IV 2.133
with two prepositions IV 2.57, 62

present tense III 5.27–28, 46, 79
accentuation III 5.98
and other tenses III 5.22
athematic III 5.46, 87
compound III 5.35, 39–40
conjugation III 5.97
in subordinate clauses III 5.24
stylistic usage III 5.26
pronominal groups IV 2.136–138
pronouns III 2.3–4; 4.1–43; IV 2.128; 4.15
accentuation III 4.31–43
adjectival IV 2.114; 5.23
case III 4.7, 14
composite III 4.3, 27, 37, 39
compound III 4.3, 27
declension III 4.31–37, 40, 42–43
definite III 4.16, 42–43
demonstrative III 2.18–19, 23; 4.5, 18–22, 28; IV 7.11, 32
differentiating III 4.26, 28
dual III 4.5, 12, 40
gender III 4.2–4, 31
generalizing III 4.26, 29; IV 7.23
indefinite III 4.26–30; IV 1.23; 2.91
intensifying and specifying IV 1.23
interrogative and relative III 4.5, 23–25, 28; IV 6.13, 16, 21
negative III 4.29; IV 3.123–124
neuter III 2.5; 4.2–3, 28–29; IV 1.20, 22, 26, 29
number III 4.5–6, 9
personal III 4.4–5, 9–17; 5.53, 58; 7.15; IV 2.91
possessive III 4.15–16, 31, 43
reflexive III 4. 4,14; 7.15
relative IV 7.5, 8, 16, 18–19, 24–25, 27, 29
substantivized III 4.16
syntactic functions III 4.1–3, 5, 20, 26, 28–29; IV 1.20, 22–24, 29, 37; 3.79, 92
prosodic (suprasegmental) features I 2.2; 6.1–10
prosody I 2.2
purpose
clauses of III 5.48; IV 7.61–62
relations of III 5.136; IV 7.61–62, 119

questions III 7.9–10
  disjunctive IV 6.17
  embedded IV 7.18–19
  general IV 6.14–15
  negative IV 6.14, 19
  rhetorical III 7.10, 15; IV 6.19, 22
  special IV 6.16–18

reduplication
  in onomatopoeic words III 11.11
reflexiva tantum III 5.13, 57
reflexive infinitive III 5.154
reflexive marker III 5.5, 11–15, 88, 125, 127, 154
reflexive participles III 5.112, 125–128
  as predicates III 5.126
  neuter III 5.128
  non – prefixed III 5.125–126
  prefixed III 5.127
reflexive pronouns III 4.4, 14; 7.15
reflexive verbs III 5.11–17, 61–62, 67; IV 2.17, 23; 3.59
  endings III 5.88
  future tense forms III 5.102
  negative IV 3.117
  objective III 5.12, 15–16
  subjective III 5.12, 14
  subjunctive mood forms of III 5.103
  transitive III 5.12, 17
reflexivity III 5.2
reflexivization III 5.11
relative pronouns IV 7.5, 8, 16, 18–19, 24–25, 27, 29
rhematic sentences IV 5.6, 14
rheme IV 5.3, 5–6, 8–14

semantic functions IV 3.38
semantic relations in composite sentences
  causal IV 7.33, 40, 44–50, 78–79, 91, 107, 119
  complementary IV 7.107, 122
  completive IV 7.107, 120–121
  conditional IV 7.51–57, 80, 99, 103, 107, 112–116
  contrastive IV 7.55, 81, 89, 93–94, 98–99, 107, 112, 118
  copulative IV 7.108–110
  disjunctive IV 7.101
  enumaration IV 7.86, 101
  juxtapositive IV 7.111
  of concession IV 7.58–60, 81, 90, 95, 98–99, 100, 102–105, 107, 112, 117
  of exclusion IV 7.92, 96, 99
  of parallelism IV 7.82, 85, 88, 97, 101
  of purpose IV 7.61–62, 119
  summative IV 7.83
  temporal IV 7.17, 36–43, 77, 107, 109–110, 112–113
semi – predicative participles III 5.141–151
semidiphtongs I 3.2; 5.1
sentence IV 1.1
  communicative types IV 1.2
  parts IV 1.10–41
  patterns IV 1.2
  semantic structure IV 1.2, 11
  syntactic structure IV 1.2, 11
  see also composite sentence, functional sentence perspective, simple sentence
sentence modifiers III 6.1, 28
sentence patterns IV 3.4–125
  infinitival sentences IV 3.73–74
  nominal sentences IV 3.75–97
  impersonal sentences IV 3.54–74, 86–97
  personal sentences IV 3.10–53, 76–85
  verbal sentences IV 3.9–74
  omittion of constituents IV 3.105–107
  relations between IV 3.108–125
  variation of constituents IV 3.98–104
  with infinitive IV 3.19, 34–35, 68–71, 96–97
  with possessive dative IV 3.52–53, 72
shorterning
  of inflexional forms III 1.32; 2.33, 35; 4.41; 5.86, 103
  of vowels II 1.5, 7, 8
simple sentence IV 3.1–125
  declarative IV 6.2
  exclamatory III 7.15; IV 6.1, 20–22
  extended IV 4.1–24
  imperative IV 6.4–9
  indefinite – personal IV 3.2, 110
  infinitival IV 3.73

interrogative IV 6.13–19; 7.101
nominal IV 3.75
nucleus of IV 3.4
optative (hortative) IV 6.10–12
rhematic IV 5.6, 14
syntactic centre IV 3.1
types IV 3.6
volitional IV 6.3–12
see also active sentences, impersonal sentences, negative sentences, personal sentences, sentence modifiers, sentence patterns

simple tenses III 5.1, 21, 27–34
and compound tenses III 5.23
and perfect tenses III 5.36
in subordinate clauses III 5.24
see also future tense, past tense, past frequentative tense, present tense

singularia tantum III 1.4–5, 13

spelling (orthography) I 1.4

standard of comparison III 8.29, 32; IV 4.8–9

stems
acuted and non – acuted II 2.2
strong and weak II 2.2
see also verbal stems, inflectional stems

stress I 2.2; 6.1–5; III 1.34
and syllable quantity I 6.5
features of I 6.4
free I 6.1; II 2.1
position of I 6.1; II 2.1
secondary I 6.3

subject III 2.3–5, 24; 4.15; 5.124; IV 1.4, 10, 21–23; 2.82; 3.2
complex IV 1.23
concord with predicate IV 1.24–27
expressed by completive clauses IV 7.20
in passive transformation III 5.67–70
infinitive as III 5.156
of intransitive verbs III 5.7
of reflexive verbs III 5.14–17
semantic III 5.14–15, 57, 59, 63–64, 66, 71, 75, 146, 151, 156
simple IV 1.22
tautological IV 3.55

subjunctive mood III 5.41–43
accentuation and conjugation III 5.103
compound forms III 5.47–48
in asyndetic sentences IV 7.115, 118
in comparative sentences IV 7.6
in compound sentences IV 7.80, 90, 103
in conditional clauses IV 7.52, 56–57
in imperative sentences IV 6.6
in optative sentences IV 6.11

subordination IV 1.5–8, 10
adjectival IV 2.115–131
adverbial IV 2.139–145
complex IV 2.3
in composite sentences IV 7.2, 5–71
in mixed composite sentences IV 7.126
nominal IV 2.90–114
numeral IV 2.132–135
pronominal IV 2.136–138
simple IV 2.2
verbal IV 2.4–89

subordinators IV 7.5, 34, 44, 50–51, 58, 61, 63–65, 68–71
position of IV 7.10

substantiva mobilia III 1.6; IV 2.108

substantivization III 4.16; 5.140

substitution IV 1.10, 29

suffixes
accentual value II 2.7
causative III 5.6, 8; IV 2.23
comparative III 2.8, 14; 6.17
derivational III 1.35–37; 2.37–40; 3.2; 5.2–4, 8, 13, 20; 6.3, 5–8, 11, 13, 17
diminutive III 2.8
inflexional III 0.1, 3; 5.2, 43; IV 1.3
superlative III 2.9, 14; 6.17

summative relations
in composite sentences IV 7.83

superlative
adjectives IV 2.120
adverbs III 6.16–17, 21–22

supine III 5.156

suppletion III 0.4

syllable I 5.1–4

boundary I 5.2
nucleus I 5.1
stressed and unstressed I 6.1
syllable accent (tonem) I 2.2; 6.6–10
acute and circumflex I 6.6
allotones I 6.7
alternations of II 2.8
distinctive features I 6.8
neutralization I 6.9
syntactic relations IV 1.3, 10, 41; 2.1; 7.76; *see also* coordination, interdependence, subordination
syntagmatic relations (phonotactics) I 2.5
of consonants I 4.9–12
of vowels I 3.5–6

taboo III 2.24
temporal relations
in composite sentences IV 7.17, 36–43, 77, 107, 109–110, 112–113
tense III 0.6; 5.1, 21–40, 79, 112, 142, 145, 148
and aspect III 5.19–20
and mood III 5.42, 44, 51
and person III 5.56
and time III 5.23
and voice III 5.21, 65
meanings of III 5.24–25
stylistic usage III 5.26
see also compound tenses, continuative tenses, future tenses, imperfect tenses, past tense, past frequentative tense, perfect tenses, present tense, simple tenses
thematic vowels
and conjugations III 5.89
and personal endings III 5.86
and verbal stems III 5.84
in present and post tense III 5.85
theme IV 5.3, 5–6, 8–14
time
clauses of IV 7.36–43
tonem *see* syllable accent
transcription I 1.1
transitive verbs III 5.6–12, 17, 67–74; IV 2.6, 12, 16, 18, 20, 23; 3.105

transitivity III 5.2, 11
transitivization III 5.10

valency
of infinitive III 5.155
of participles IV 1.41
of verb IV 3.1–5
verb
and particles III 7.15
athematic III 5.87
auxiliary (copula) III 5.47, 52, 63–64, 78, 108
compound (periphrastic) forms III 5.108–111; IV 1.17
conjugations III 5.89–96
finite forms III 5.1, 60–62, 79–111
modal IV 1.15, 19; 2.80
morphological categories III 5.1–2, 21–78
non – finite forms III 5.1, 112–156
phasal IV 1.15; 2.80
semantic types III 5.3
suppletive forms III 5.107
valency IV 3.1–5
see also conjugation, imperfective verbs, impersonal verbs, intransitive verbs, perfective verbs, reflexive verbs, transitive verbs
verbal stems III 5.79
and thematic vowels III 5.84
infinitival III 5.85, 101–104, 113, 118–120, 122–123, 154
morphemic structure IV 5.80–81, 83
morphonological changes in III 5.82
present and past III 5.85, 89, 92–96, 120–121
verbal groups IV 2.4, 5–89
word order in IV 5.19–22
vocative III 1.15, 20; 2.6, 28; 4.7
voice III 0.6; 5.1, 64–78, 112, 142, 145, 148; IV 3.108–110
and mood III 5.51
and tense III 5.21
volitional sentences IV 6.3–12
vowels I 3.1, 3–7
alternation II 1.1–21
representation in writing I 1.2
thematic III 5.84–86, 89

word classes III 0.6
word forms IV 1.1
    abbreviation of IV 3.7
    periphrastic (analytical) III 0.5
    syntactic functions IV 1.10
    synthetic III 0.1–5
word groups IV 2.1
    adjectival IV 2.115–131
    adverbial IV 2.139–145
    and simple sentence IV 2.1
    appositive IV 2.108–110
    coordinative IV 2.1, 146–158
    interdependant IV 1.4; 2.1
    nominal IV 2.90–114
    numeral IV 2.132–135
    pronominal IV 2.136–138
    subordinative IV 2.1–145
    verbal IV 2.4–89
    see also apposition, coordination, subordination
word order IV 5.1–31
    and functional sentence perspective IV 5.3, 31
    in adjectival groups IV 5.28
    in comparative phrases IV 5.29–30
    in compound predicates IV 5.5, 7
    in interrogative sentences IV 6.13
    in nominal groups IV 5.23–27
    in rhematic sentences IV 5.6, 14
    in verbal groups IV 5.19–22
    of main sentence constituents IV 5.4–14
    structurally fixed IV 5.2
    variable IV 5.1

Lithuanian Grammar

Second editor
ARVYDAS GAIŽAUSKAS

SL 014. Baltos lankos publishers, Mėsinių 4, 2001 Vilnius, Lithuania
Printed by Vilspa printing house, Viršuliškių 80, 2056 Vilnius.

4995